Literature Links
to American History,
K–6

Recent Titles in the
Children's and Young Adult Literature Reference Series

Catherine Barr, Series Editor

Gentle Reads: Great Books to Warm Hearts and Lift Spirits, Grades 5–9
Deanna J. McDaniel

Best New Media, K–12: A Guide to Movies, Subscription Web Sites, and Educational Software and Games
Catherine Barr

Historical Fiction for Young Readers (Grades 4–8): An Introduction
John T. Gillespie

Twice Upon a Time: A Guide to Fractured, Altered, and Retold Folk and Fairy Tales
Catharine Bomhold and Terri E. Elder

Popular Series Fiction for K–6 Readers: A Reading and Selection Guide. 2nd Edition
Rebecca L. Thomas and Catherine Barr

Popular Series Fiction for Middle School and Teen Readers: A Reading and Selection Guide. 2nd Edition
Rebecca L. Thomas and Catherine Barr

Best Books for High School Readers, Grades 9–12. 2nd Edition
Catherine Barr and John T. Gillespie

Best Books for Middle School and Junior High Readers, Grades 6–9. 2nd Edition
Catherine Barr and John T. Gillespie

Green Reads: Best Environmental Resources for Youth, K–12
Lindsey Patrick Wesson

Best Books for Children: Preschool Through Grade 6. 9th Edition
Catherine Barr and John T. Gillespie

Literature Links to World History, K–12: Resources to Enhance and Entice
Lynda G. Adamson

A to Zoo: Subject Access to Children's Picture Books. 8th Edition
Carolyn W. Lima and Rebecca L. Thomas

Literature Links to American History, K–6

Resources to Enhance and Entice

Lynda G. Adamson

Children's and Young Adult Literature Reference
Catherine Barr, Series Editor

LIBRARIES UNLIMITED

AN IMPRINT OF ABC-CLIO, LLC
Santa Barbara, California • Denver, Colorado • Oxford, England

Library of Congress Cataloging-in-Publication Data

Adamson, Lynda G.
  Literature links to American history, K–6 : resources to enhance and entice / Lynda G. Adamson.
      p. cm. — (Children's and young adult literature reference)
  Includes bibliographical references and indexes.
  ISBN 978-1-59158-468-1 (acid-free paper) 1. United States—History—Juvenile literature—Bibliography. 2. United States—History—Juvenile fiction—Bibliography. 3. United States—History—CD-ROM catalogs. 4. United States—History—Juvenile films—Catalogs. I. Title.
  Z1236.A353 2010
  [E178.3]
  016.973—dc22   2010014563

ISBN: 978-1-59158-468-1

14 13 12 11 10   1 2 3 4 5

This book is also available on the World Wide Web as an eBook.
Visit www.abc-clio.com for details.

Libraries Unlimited
An Imprint of ABC-CLIO, LLC

ABC-CLIO, LLC
130 Cremona Drive, P.O. Box 1911
Santa Barbara, California 93116-1911

This book is printed on acid-free paper ∞
Manufactured in the United States of America

For Frank

CONTENTS

PREFACE

RESEARCH SHOWS THAT PEOPLE REMEMBER SOMETHING TO WHICH THEY have responded emotionally. Although they may have read many history textbooks containing information about the Underground Railroad and the difficulties slaves faced while trying to reach freedom, they may not empathize until they have heard of Henry "Box" Brown, who mailed himself to freedom in 1849 (Ellen Levine's *Henry's Freedom Box*). They will feel their bodies cramping with Henry's as he curls in a fetal position inside a box during a 27-hour journey by train and steamboat from Richmond to Philadelphia. They will comprehend more clearly that escaping slavery was a very serious decision, sometimes resulting in death, and they will return to the stories of slaves with renewed understanding. Readers will also relate to Miss Bridie, an immigrant from Ireland who arrived in 1856. Of all the items she could have chosen to bring with her to America, she brought a shovel (Leslie Connor's *Miss Bridie Chose a Shovel*). This item, carefully selected, helped her clear snow from pond ice. While skating, she met her husband. Years later, it helped her dig holes for apple trees on their farm. The practicality of this item reminds readers that immigrants cannot transport everything they own. They must leave without preferred possessions because what they do carry with them must be useful and portable. Readers' responses to these characters and the actions in which the characters participate may propel them toward other books, both fiction and nonfiction, about the quest for freedom, either from slavery or from an unfulfilled life abroad.

If a youthful reader becomes interested in a topic, a character, or a time period, and asks for books or multimedia about them, the adult consulted needs timely retrieval capabilities. I have attempted to fulfill that need. This resource connects historical fiction, historical fantasy, biography, history trade, graphic novels (including graphic biographies and graphic histories), DVDs, and compact discs for individual grade levels within specific time periods. All entries have received at least one review. The annotations avoid being qualitative, but the best books in any category win awards, and an annotation that contains awards shows that book's merits. All of the items are in print and available at press time.

The focus of this annotated bibliography is to link literature to history. Some of the books may appear in categories different from those found in library catalogs. I have specific definitions for history (must be documented), historical fiction (events must be factual but characters can be created), and biography (must be factual about a human being.) Many good biographies and history trade books are now available. For that reason, I have listed biographies about the same person by several different authors. I have not made choices as to which are best, because each has a slightly different theme and tone. Authors of biography as literature try to make their subjects come alive, and the authors, for the most part, have achieved this goal. History trade books differ from history textbooks because trade authors rely heavily on diaries, letters, documents, or other references that tell about the people who lived during the time. Thus, readers might more often respond to these books than to history textbooks that are often filled with passive voice, dull dates, and inventories of incidents. Some of the history trade books included have more illustrations than text, but they can be valuable for enticing slow or unwilling readers to look for other books about the same topic. These information books bridge the gap between books without illustrations and DVDs. The relatively new genre of the "graphic novel," a generic term that also includes graphic histories and biographies, has evolved; graphic novels also attract many reluctant readers. The multimedia category contains DVDs and compact discs.

This reference includes as many good books and DVDs published since 2000 as possible plus some highly regarded works from prior years. Adults will find the recommended titles on library shelves, in bookstores, or online. The wide range of titles will give the researcher choices if the first title selected is not readily available. My goal is for readers to have emotional responses to the people who have made history so that they, as future world citizens, can better understand themselves and the times in which they live.

INTRODUCTION

THIS RESOURCE CONTAINS TITLES IN THE CATEGORIES OF HISTORICAL fiction, historical fantasy (time travel), graphic novels, graphic history, graphic biography, biography, collective biography, history trade, DVD, and compact disc. Titles merit inclusion because they have received at least one mainstream review; annotations accompanying them are descriptive rather than evaluative.

Chapter divisions, except for the first, are chronological time periods. A chapter titled "General" comes first and includes works and topics spanning several different time periods. Although the lives of persons important in the history of the United States, such as Benjamin Franklin, George Washington, Helen Keller, and Eleanor Roosevelt, span several different chapters, I have not included them in the "General" chapter because they were part of the times in which they lived, and their actions reflect these different eras in the country's history. The remaining chapter divisions correspond as nearly as possible to periods of change in the history of America. The time frames of three chapters, however, overlap. In the late 18th, the 19th, and the early 20th centuries, three distinct groups were functioning within the area that has become the continental United States. Pioneers began traveling to the frontier, which kept moving west and displacing many Native Americans. Immigrants arrived from Asia and Europe after 1815 and moved to any area in the country where they thought they could succeed. The third group divided into factions of abolitionism, suffrage, and Anglo white male supremacy. Therefore, I have divided these general groups into three separate chapters because of their disparate concerns. Those settling the West might have a connection to the Civil War, but most often they were more anxious about encounters with Native Americans. Citizens closer to the East Coast seemed more politically attuned to slavery, women's rights, and fighting white males with voting power. Immigrants and Native Americans continue to have myriad difficulties coping with unfamiliar cultures while retaining their own traditions.

Some titles appear several in several chapters. For example, titles about Eleanor Roosevelt (1884–1962) are included in the chapters "Reconstruction, the Progressive Era, and Suffrage, 1866–1916," "World War I and the Great Depression, 1917–1941," "World War II, 1941–1945," and "The Mid-Twentieth Century, 1946–1975." The author and title of works listed in multiple chapters will appear in each chapter but reference the initial chapter of its appearance for the bibliographic data and annotation.

In each chapter, I have listed works in their specific categories of historical fiction (including historical fantasy), history trade, biography (including collective biography), graphic novels (including graphic biographies and graphic histories), DVDs, and compact discs. Each entry appears alphabetically according to the author's last name. Where there is no author, entries are alphabetized by title. I have based grade-level choices on recommended grade levels in review sources or publisher catalogs. In some cases, when the grade levels based on reading and content seemed unusually low or high, I have adjusted them after evaluating the text and the subject matter. The bibliographic information includes author, title, illustrator, translator, narrator, series, publisher or imprint, ISBN, paper imprint, paper ISBN, number of pages, and grade levels. Bibliographic information for DVDs and CDs includes number of minutes.

GENERAL

Historical Fiction and Fantasy

1. **Atwell, Debby.** *Pearl.* Walter Lorraine, 2001. 32pp. ISBN 978-0-395-88416-4. Grades K–3. The story of one family is told by an octogenarian named Pearl. Born in 1862, she remembers hearing the story of George Washington picking her grandfather, then a young boy, out of the crowd watching the Inauguration Day parade and inviting her grandfather to ride beside him. This saga spans the Civil War, women's suffrage, the transcontinental railroad, the two World Wars—with a grandson killed in the second, the Great Depression, and the Korean War. Double-spread pages cover each important event. Timeline.

2. **Drummond, Allan.** *Tin Lizzie.* Frances Foster, 2008. 32pp. ISBN 978-0-374-32000-3. Grades 1–5. Grandpa works on old cars, especially his Model T Ford. When he repairs it, he takes his grandchildren on a drive. However, as they sit in traffic, they realize that this invention was not so great because of its pollution and the country's reliance on foreign oil. They understand that they must help solve the ensuing problems. Ink-and-watercolor sketches complement the text.

3. **Gratz, Alan.** *The Brooklyn Nine: A Novel in Nine Innings.* Dial, 2009. 299pp. ISBN 978-0-8037-3224-7; Puffin, 2010, paper ISBN 978-0-14-241544-3. Grades 5–9. In nine chapters (innings), Gratz traces nine generations of a baseball-loving family in Brooklyn. Schneider family members arrive in the mid-19th century. Felix, injured in an 1845 Manhattan fire, never gets to play but loves his handsewn ball. His son Louis, fighting for the Union, saves a Confederate who talks about baseball in 1864. The family name then changes to Snider; and in 1908 Walter is upset by the racial prejudice demonstrated when the great Negro Cyclone player Joe Williams is denied a tryout. Female Kat Flint plays for the Grand Rapids Chicks during World War II and has mixed feelings when the war ends. In 1981 Michael Flint pitches a perfect Little League game, and finally in 2002, Snider Flint returns to baseball when he sees the family memorabilia. *Young Reader's Award* (Arizona) nomination and *Beehive Young Adult Book Award* (Utah) nomination.

4. **Hearne, Betsy.** *Seven Brave Women.* Illustrated by Bethanne Andersen. Trophy, 2006. Unpaged. Paper ISBN 978-0-06-079921-2. Grades K–4. Hearne tells the stories of women in her family history and their accomplishments. Her great-great-great-grandmother Elizabeth lived in the Revolutionary War; she did not fight and she raised nine children. Her great-great-grandmother lived during the War of 1812 and moved to Ohio, where her herbal medicine helped neighbors. A great-grandmother started a women's hospital in India. These seven women of peace helped shape history in their own ways. *Jane Addams Book Award, Boston Globe/Horn Book Award Honor, Horn Book Fanfare,* and *Capitol Choices Noteworthy Titles* (Washington, D.C.).

5. **Hughes, Langston.** *The Negro Speaks of Rivers.* Illustrated by E. B. Lewis. Hyperion, 2009. 32pp. ISBN 978-0-7868-1867-9. Grades 3–6. Langston Hughes's poem, written in 1919 when he was 18 years old, captures the essence of the black experience and its relationship to the rivers of the world. The Euphrates, the Nile, the Congo, and the Mississippi are all featured in this work—each with an emphasis on the necessity of life-giving water. The exquisite illustrations complement each aspect of the text. *Capitol Choices Noteworthy Titles for Children and Teens* (Washington, D.C.), *Booklist Editors Choice*, and *Coretta Scott King Award* Honor Book.

6. **McKissack, Patricia C.** *The Home-Run King.* Illustrated by Gordon C. James. (Scraps of Time) Viking, 2009. 92pp. ISBN 978-0-670-01085-1. Grades 3–6. When Gee's grandchildren find a baseball in her attic signed by Josh Gibson and Satchel Paige, she tells them a story about her baseball-loving Nashville cousins, Tank and Jimbo, who were lucky enough to have Negro League home-run king Gibson stay at their house. Illustrations augment the text. *Notable Social Studies Trade Books for Young People* and *Beverly Clear Children's Choice Book Award* (Oregon) nomination.

History

7. **Aaseng, Nathan.** *Construction: Building the Impossible.* Oliver, 1999. 144pp. ISBN 978-1-8815-0859-5. Grades 5–10. This collective biography looks at eight builders throughout history and the groundbreaking projects they constructed. Among those included are Frank Crowe and the Hoover Dam in the Nevada desert, William Lamb and the Empire State Building, and John and Washington Roebling and the Brooklyn Bridge. Photographs and drawings complement the text. Bibliography, Glossary, and Index.

8. **Aaseng, Nathan.** *You Are the General II: 1800–1899.* Oliver, 1995. 160pp. ISBN 978-1-8815-0825-0. Grades 5 up. Battles are carefully created patterns of military strategy fought to gain territory, erode an enemy army's morale, and win a broader war. The text presents eight battles and the generals who fought them. The battles are the British Army at New Orleans in 1815, the Prussian Army at Waterloo in 1815, the U.S. Army in Mexico in August 1847, the Allied Army in Crimea in September 1854, the Army of Northern Virginia at Chancellorsville in May 1863, the U.S. Army at Little Bighorn in June 1876, and the Boer Army in Natal in December 1899. Source Notes, Bibliography, and Index.

9. **Altergott, Hanna.** *Great Times in Baseball History.* (Great Teams) Raintree, 2005. 48pp. ISBN 978-1-4109-1484-2; paper ISBN 978-1-4109-1491-0. Grades 3–6. Altergott looks at the players, coaches, games, and statistics that are important to the game of baseball. Photographs of teams, team rosters, team records, player records, and other historical information add to the appeal. Chronology, Further Reading, Glossary, and Index.

10. **Ancona, George.** *Murals: Walls That Sing.* Marshall Cavendish, 2003. 48pp. ISBN 978-0-7614-5131-0. Grades 5–8. The forty murals featured in this book are "for the people" (*para el pueblo*), with themes of social justice, cultural diversity, and community. It begins with the cave paintings in Lascaux, France, and then looks at ancient Mexican frescoes and on through history to post-revolutionary Mexican murals. Photographs of murals in San Francisco, Philadelphia, Mexico, Boston, Albuquerque, Chicago, the South Bronx, and other places enhance the text.

11. **Anderson, Dale.** *The Democratic Party: America's Oldest Party.* (Snapshots in History) Compass Point, 2007. 96pp. ISBN 978-0-7565-2450-0. Grades 5–8. A history of the Democratic Party from its beginnings until contemporary times, with information about key figures, conventions, platforms, and organization. Sidebars add details about laws and other facts of interest. Maps, photographs and reproductions accompany the text. Bibliography, Glossary, Chronology, Notes, Further Reading, Web Sites, and Index.

12. **Anderson, Dale.** *The Republican Party: The Story of the Grand Old Party.* (Snapshots in History) Compass Point, 2007. 96pp. ISBN 978-0-7565-2449-4. Grades 5–8. A history of the Republican Party from its beginnings until contemporary times. It covers key figures, conventions, platforms, and organization, often using primary sources. Sidebars add information about laws and other facts of interest. Maps, photographs and reproductions accompany the text. Bibliography, Glossary, Chronology, Notes, Further Reading, Web Sites, and Index.

13. **Andryszewski, Tricia.** *Walking the Earth: The History of Human Migration.* Lerner, 2006. 80pp. ISBN 978-0-7613-3458-3. Grades 5–9. Humans have migrated across the earth in search of food, land, and peaceful life for more than 150,000 years. Readers will learn about human migrations through history—some that occurred by choice and others that were forced because of war or poverty. Hunter-gatherers left Africa more than 60,000 years ago as they began populating Eurasia. Then they eventually came to the Americas and Australia. When the general migration ended 45,000 years ago, more than five million people had created diverse populations throughout the globe. They developed appropriate tools, found good clothing materials, and established trade with each other. They sometimes brought the customs of one area to integrate or impose them into their new cultures. Photographs and reproductions augment the text. Charts, Maps, Bibliography, Further Reading, Web sites, and Index.

14. **Ansary, Mir Tamim.** *Arbor Day.* (Holiday Histories) Heinemann, 2006. 32pp. Paper ISBN 978-1-4034-8895-4. Grades 2–4. Arbor Day, the last Friday in April as designated by President Richard Nixon, celebrates trees. The text explains the history of the holiday and how people celebrate it. Illustrations highlight the text. Bibliography, Glossary, and Index.

15. **Ansary, Mir Tamim.** *Columbus Day.* (Holiday Histories) Heinemann, 2006. 32pp. ISBN 978-1-4034-8883-1; paper ISBN 978-1-4034-8896-1. Grades 2–4. Columbus Day, October 12, celebrates the discovery of America by Columbus in 1492. The text explains the history of the holiday and how people celebrate it. Illustrations augment the text. Bibliography, Glossary, and Index.

16. **Ansary, Mir Tamim.** *Election Day.* (Holiday Histories) Heinemann, 2006. 32pp. ISBN 978-1-4034-8885-5; paper ISBN 978-1-4034-8898-5. Grades 2–4. Election Day occurs on the Tuesday following the first Monday in November, the Tuesday between November 2 and 8. Federal elections in the United States occur in even-numbered years. In addition to federal elections, many states and local governments also elect their officials on this day. Illustrations enhance the text. Bibliography, Glossary, and Index.

17. **Ansary, Mir Tamim.** *Labor Day.* (Holiday Histories) Heinemann, 2006. 32pp. ISBN 978-1-4034-8888-6. Grades 2–4. Labor Day, a federal holiday, occurs on the first Monday in September. In 1882 the Central Labor Union wanted the "working man" to have a holiday, and this day was created by an Act of Congress in 1894. Illustrations highlight the text. Bibliography, Glossary, and Index.

18. **Ansary, Mir Tamim.** *Martin Luther King Jr. Day.* (Holiday Histories) Heinemann, 1998. 32pp. ISBN 978-1-57572-873-5; 2006, paper ISBN 978-1-4034-8902-9. Grades 2–4. Martin Luther King, Jr. Day occurs on the third Monday of January to honor King's birthday on January 15. Federal offices and some state governments recognize the holiday in memory of King's actions to advance civil rights in the United States. Glossary and Index.

19. **Ansary, Mir Tamim.** *Memorial Day.* (Holiday Histories) Heinemann, 2006. 32pp. ISBN 978-1-4034-8890-9; paper ISBN 978-1-4034-8903-6. Grades 2–4. Memorial Day, the last Monday in May, commemorates the men and women who have died serving in the military. Initially it honored those who died during the American Civil War, but it has expanded to include anyone who has died serving the United States. Illustrations highlight the text. Bibliography, Glossary, and Index.

20. **Ansary, Mir Tamim.** *Veterans Day.* (Holiday Histories) Heinemann, 2006. 32pp. ISBN 978-1-4034-8893-0. Grades 2–4. Veterans Day, a federal and state holiday in all states, occurs on November 11, the day that many other countries celebrate as Armistice Day or Remembrance Day. The Armistice ending World War I was signed on that date. Today, celebrations

honor military veterans of all wars. Illustrations enhance the text. Bibliography, Glossary, and Index.

21. **Armstrong, Jennifer.** *The American Story: 100 True Tales from American History.* Knopf, 2006. 358pp. ISBN 978-0-375-81256-9. Grades 1–4. Armstrong recounts one hundred true stories about Americans from the years 1565 through 2000, beginning with a story from the colony of Saint Caroline near contemporary Jacksonville, Florida. The stories cover a cross-section of people—immigrants, artists, athletes, scientists, and others. Famous people covered include Babe Ruth, Typhoid Mary, Neil Armstrong, and Maya Lin. Illustrations augment the text. Bibliography and Index.

22. **Bannatyne-Cugnet, Jo.** *Heartland: A Prairie Sampler.* Illustrated by Yvette Moore. Tundra, 2005. 37pp. Paper ISBN 978-0-8877-6722-7. Grades 3–5. This book focuses on different aspects of the North American prairie including land, agriculture, mining, wildlife, climate, and food. Realistic paintings complement the text.

23. **Barnard, Bryn.** *Outbreak! Plagues That Changed History.* Crown, 2005. 48pp. ISBN 978-0-375-82986-4. Grades 5–8. The author examines the effects of six diseases on world history—bubonic plague, smallpox, yellow fever, cholera, tuberculosis, and influenza. Humans have tried to obliterate these diseases, but nature has often stymied the attempts with drug-resistant bacteria, new diseases, and changing ecologies. Humans also become complacent after they find one solution. The text posits that poverty plays a large role in a disease's spread, but once launched, a plague does not respect either wealth or social status. Photographs and illustrations intensify the text. Bibliography, Further Reading, and Web Sites. *Voice of Youth Advocates Nonfiction Honor List.*

24. **Beller, Susan Provost.** *The History Puzzle: How We Know What We Know About the Past.* Twenty-First Century, 2006. 128pp. ISBN 978-0-7613-2877-3. Grades 5–8. Beller introduces readers to ways of thinking about history while telling the stories of events around the world from early times to the wreck of the *Edmund Fitzgerald* on the Great Lakes in 1975. Photographs and illustrations enliven the text. Further Reading, Web Sites, and Index.

25. **Bingham, Jane.** *Society and Class.* (Through Artists' Eyes) Raintree, 2006. 56pp. ISBN 978-1-4109-2237-3. Grades 4–7. Artists depict the daily lives of groups they know and observe. They have painted hunters, rulers, farmers, slaves, soldiers, and merchants. Social change has also influenced artists. In times of exciting change such as the American and French Revolutions, themes tend to be stirring, but under regimes such as communism and fascism, art can be less vibrant. Photographs and reproductions augment the text. Further Reading, Timeline, Glossary, and Index.

26. **Blackwood, Gary L.** *Enigmatic Events.* (Unsolved History) Benchmark, 2005. 72pp. ISBN 978-0-7614-1889-4. Grades 4–6. A look at a variety of mysteries that have puzzled people over time, including the death of the dinosaurs, the fate of the Lost Colony of Roanoke, the cause of the Salem Witch Trials, the disappearance of the *Mary Celeste* and the sinking of the *Maine*. Reproductions enhance the text. Bibliography, Notes, and Index.

27. **Blackwood, Gary L.** *Legends or Lies.* (Unsolved History) Benchmark, 2005. 72pp. ISBN 978-0-7614-1891-7. Grades 4–6. Atlantis, Amazons, King Arthur, Robin Hood, El Dorado, Welsh expeditions to America, and Pope Joan—these are all covered in this volume that presents both sides of the debates about these "legends." Photographs and reproductions highlight the text. Bibliography, Glossary, Notes, Further Reading, and Index.

28. **Blackwood, Gary L.** *Perplexing People.* (Unsolved History) Benchmark, 2005. 72pp. ISBN 978-0-7614-1890-0. Grades 4–6. Some people have pretended to be famous persons who have reappeared. This volume looks at several famous pretenders including people who said they were Joan of Arc, Anastasia, the French Dauphin, and Billy the Kid. Photographs and reproductions augment the text. Bibliography, Glossary, Notes, Further Reading, and Index.

29. **Bolden, Tonya.** *Tell All the Children Our Story: Memories and Mementoes of Being Young and Black in America.* Abrams, 2001. 128pp. ISBN 978-0-8109-4496-1. Grades 4–8. This book examines, in three parts, the lives of young African Americans through the centuries

and looks at the circumstances, triumphs, and struggles of children both known and unknown. Among the individuals featured are the Little Rock Nine, Ayinde Jean-Baptiste who spoke at the Million Man March in 1995 at the age of 14, and William Tucker, who was the first African American baptized in Virginia. Photographs and illustrations highlight the text. Bibliography, Notes, Further Reading, and Index. *School Library Journal Best Children's Books*.

30. **Brent, Lynnette.** *At Home: Long Ago and Today.* (Times Change) Heinemann, 2003. 32pp. ISBN 978-1-40344-531-5; paper ISBN 978-1-40344-537-7. Grades 2–4. This is a look at the changes in houses and their construction over the past one hundred years. Materials used to build them are different, and they are heated and cooled in new and evolving ways. New technology has also changed the kinds of chores involved in keeping a house in shape. Photographs enhance the text. Chronology, Bibliography, and Index.

31. **Brent, Lynnette.** *At Play: Long Ago and Today.* (Times Change) Heinemann, 2003. 32pp. ISBN 978-1-40344-532-2; paper ISBN 978-1-40344-538-4. Grades 2–4. Brent discusses the changes in leisure activities over the past hundred years. As populations moved from rural areas into urban areas, the types of games they played changed. The effects of seasons and special occasions on play are also examined. Photographs enhance the text. Chronology, Bibliography, and Index.

32. **Brent, Lynnette.** *At School: Long Ago and Today.* (Times Change) Heinemann, 2003. 32pp. ISBN 978-1-40344-533-9; paper ISBN 978-1-40344-539-1. Grades 2–4. Readers will learn about changes in the classroom over the past one hundred years—in the buildings themselves, books and lessons, recess, transportation to and from school, and activities after school. Photographs enhance the text. Chronology, Bibliography, and Index.

33. **Brent, Lynnette.** *At Work: Long Ago and Today.* (Times Change) Heinemann, 2003. 32pp. ISBN 978-1-40344-536-0; paper ISBN 978-1-40344-542-1. Grades 2–4. The author examines the changes in work over the past hundred years, looking at the types of jobs, ways of getting to work, work away from home, and working conditions. Many of these have changed dramatically as the population has shifted from rural settings to urban environments. Photographs enhance the text. Chronology, Bibliography, and Index.

34. **Burleigh, Robert.** *American Moments: Scenes from American History.* Henry Holt, 2004. 48pp. ISBN 978-0-8050-7082-8. Grades K–5. This volume examines eighteen memorable moments in American history—from 1621 to 2001—that changed life in some way: the first Thanksgiving in 1621, presenting the Declaration of Independence in 1776, Washington crossing the Delaware in 1776, Lewis and Clark reaching the Pacific in 1806, Harriet Tubman and the Underground Railroad in 1851, the assassination of Lincoln in 1865, Susan B. Anthony demanding her rights in 1873, Crazy Horse and Custer's Last Stand in 1876, immigrants arriving at Ellis Island in 1893, the Wright brothers' first flight in 1903, Houdini's escape in 1916, Georgia O'Keeffe and her art in 1929, Franklin Roosevelt's fireside chat in 1933, the flag on Iwo Jima in 1945, Rosa Parks in Montgomery in 1955, Ellington and Armstrong recording in 1961, Neil Armstrong on the moon in 1969, and September 11, 2001. Photographs and illustrations highlight the text. Notes. *Children's, Junior and Young Adult Book Award* (South Carolina) nomination.

35. **Burleigh, Robert.** *Chocolate: Riches from the Rainforest.* Abrams, 2002. 40pp. ISBN 978-0-8109-5734-3. Grades 3–6. Burleigh traces the history of chocolate from its origin as an Olmec and Maya drink and includes information about chocolate in all stages of production. Photographs highlight the text. Glossary. *Bluebonnet Award* (Texas) nomination and *Beehive Young Adult Book Award* (Utah) nomination.

36. **Byers, Ann.** *The History of U.S. Immigration: Coming to America.* (American Saga) Enslow, 2006. 128pp. ISBN 978-0-7660-2574-5. Grades 5–8. The author examines the people who first settled in America, those who arrived later, how patterns of migration have changed over the years, and the formation of the Department of Homeland Security in 2003. Byers discusses how immigrants helped America grow and develop, and how they helped define the nation until laws such as the Patriot Act began to restrict them and caused a slowing of

immigration. Photographs augment the text. Timeline, Notes, Glossary, Further Reading, Web sites, and Index.

37. **Chapman, Caroline.** *Battles and Weapons: Exploring History Through Art.* (Picture That!) Two-Can, 2007. 64pp. ISBN 978-1-58728-588-2. Grades 4 up. Readers learn about the evolution of weapons and battle strategies from ancient times to the 1950s through art reproductions. Glossary, Further Reading, Chronology, and Index.

38. **Cohan, George M.** *You're a Grand Old Flag.* Illustrated by Norman Rockwell. Atheneum, 2008. 32pp. ISBN 978-1-4169-1770-0. Grades K–3. The text of George M. Cohan's song "You're a Grand Old Flag" is paired with Norman Rockwell's pictures of families, the return of World War I soldiers, and other iconic views of a time past.

39. **Coleman, Janet Wyman.** *Secrets, Lies, Gizmos, and Spies: A History of Spies and Espionage.* Abrams, 2006. 113pp. ISBN 978-0-8109-5756-5. Grades 5–10. This overview of espionage includes information on techniques and equipment, disguises, legendary male and female spies, and the future of spies and spying. More than a history of espionage, this is a collection of anecdotes of both successful and failed spy missions along with information on fictional spies including Maxwell Smart and Austin Powers. Among the topics are codes, spy rings, double and triple agents, and traitors. Photographs embellish the text. Bibliography, Glossary, Chronology, Web Sites, and Index.

40. **Collier, Christopher, and James Lincoln Collier.** *Progressivism, the Great Depression, and the New Deal: 1901–1941.* (Drama of American History) Benchmark, 2000. 95pp. ISBN 978-0-7614-1054-6. Grades 5–8. In seven chapters covering the first four decades of the 20th century, the text describes the effect of the Great Depression on families and how people viewed their government. The results forced the government to change with Franklin D. Roosevelt's leadership through the New Deal. Bibliography and Index.

41. **Collier, Christopher, and James Lincoln Collier.** *The Rise of the Cities: 1820–1920.* (Drama of American History) Benchmark, 2001. 96pp. ISBN 978-0-7614-1051-5. Grades 5–8. In six chapters, Collier presents the growth of urban life. He notes the first American cities, the rapid movement of population toward these centers, the importance of technology, problems, and the need for reform. Bibliography and Index.

42. **Colman, Penny.** *Thanksgiving: The True Story.* Christy Ottaviano, 2008. 149pp. ISBN 978-0-8050-8229-6. Grades 5–9. Colman reports on her quest to find the first real Thanksgiving. She discovered that many groups claim it, including the Thanksgiving Mass celebrated in the Palo Duro Canyon of Texas in 1541. Others claim to be first in Florida, Maine, Virginia, and Massachusetts. Colman chooses 1621 because it was more like a contemporary Thanksgiving, although it was actually a combination of a harvest festival and a day of thanksgiving. The text also describes ways in which various ethnic groups celebrate today, as well as the foods they choose. Not everybody eats turkey, dressing, potatoes, or pumpkin pie. Photographs and reproductions enliven the text. Chronology, Notes, and Index.

43. **Colon Garcia, Aurora.** *Cinco de Mayo.* (Holiday Histories) Heinemann, 2003. 32pp. ISBN 978-1-4034-3501-9. Grades 1–3. Mexican Americans and Mexicans celebrate Cinco de Mayo (May 5) to remember the Mexican victory over the French army in Puebla, Mexico, in 1862, establishing Mexican independence. Before the war with France, the Mexicans had endured the Mexican-American war, which had not ended well for them. Colon Garcia describes the reasons behind France's attack, the important battles of Vera Cruz and Puebla, and the various traditions involved in celebrating the holiday. Illustrations and photographs highlight the text. Glossary, Chronology, Further Reading, and Index.

44. **Cook, Sally, and James Charlton.** *Hey Batta Batta Swing! The Wild Old Days of Baseball.* Illustrated by Ross MacDonald. Margaret K. McElderry, 2007. 48pp. ISBN 978-1-4169-1207-1. Grades 3–6. The text gives a glimpse of the "olden days" of baseball. It answers such questions as was baseball harder then, did players cheat, and why did the players start wearing numbers. Cartoon illustrations enhance the text.

45.   **Curlee, Lynn.** *Ballpark: The Story of America's Baseball Fields.* Atheneum, 2005. 48pp. ISBN 978-0-689-86742-2; Aladdin, 2008, paper ISBN 978-1-416-95360-9. Grades 3–6. The author examines the histories and cultural significance of America's baseball parks, the "green cathedrals" that have been an integral part of many children's lives. He looks at the change in society that led to the transformation of baseball from a minor sport into a national attraction. Among the topics covered are the Black Sox scandal, Babe Ruth in the 1920s, the Negro Leagues, the Great Depression, and the first real game at Elysian Fields in Hoboken, New Jersey. He also details the changes in the game and names some of the different fields that fans have revered in this century. Acrylic drawings complement the text. Bibliography.

46.   **Curlee, Lynn.** *Skyscraper.* Atheneum, 2007. 44pp. ISBN 978-0-689-84489-8. Grades 4– 8. A history of skyscrapers as a purely American architectural invention. After the Great Chicago fire in 1871, the first skyscrapers were built there. Tall buildings were later built in New York and around the world. Curlee discusses the engineering advances that made these buildings possible and how they affected the way people live and work. Acrylic paintings enhance the text.

47.   **Currie, Stephen.** *Escapes from Natural Disasters.* Illustrated by Stephen MacEachern. (True Stories from the Edge) Lucent, 2003. 112pp. ISBN 978-1-59018-278-9. Grades 5– 8. Among the survival stories recounted here are tales of the Johnstown Flood on May 31, 1889; the fire at Storm King Mountain in Colorado on July 3, 1994; and the Mount St. Helens eruption on May 18, 1980. Photographs and illustrations accompany the text. Bibliography, Notes, Further Reading, and Index.

48.   **Davis, Kathryn Gibbs.** *Wackiest White House Pets.* Illustrated by David Johnson. Scholastic, 2004. Unpaged. ISBN 978-0-439-44373-9. Grades 2–4. Presidential pets that have lived in the White House cover a wide range of choices and number more than four hundred. John Quincy Adams briefly had an alligator, and a 10-year-old boy sent Ronald Reagan a First Fish. Dolley Madison had a pet parrot. Lewis and Clark brought Thomas Jefferson grizzly bear cubs. Sheep grazed there in Woodrow Wilson's time, and Calvin Coolidge liked his raccoon. James Buchanan donated his gift of an elephant herd to a zoo. Teddy Roosevelt had the largest menagerie; he owned snakes, ponies, roosters, five bears, a lion, a hyena, and a zebra. Photographs and illustrations embellish the text. Bibliography.

49.   **DeCock, Luke.** *Great Teams in Hockey History.* (Great Teams) Raintree, 2005. 48pp. ISBN 978-1-4109-1486-6; paper ISBN 978-1-4109-1493-4. Grades 4–6. DeCock explores famous hockey teams, players, coaches, and games. Photographs of teams, team rosters, team records, player records, and other historical information add appeal. Further Reading, Glossary, and Index. Other titles in this series include *Great Times in College Basketball History* and *Great Times in College Football History* (both 2005).

50.   **DeGezelle, Terri.** *Ellis Island.* (First Facts) Capstone, 2003. 24pp. ISBN 978-0-7368-2292-3; 2006, paper ISBN 978-0-7368-4706-3. Grades K–2. This introduction to Ellis Island reviews its history as the first federal immigration station, the Statue of Liberty National monument, the museum, and the island's value as a symbol of the United States. Photographs, Illustrations, Maps, and Further Reading.

51.   **DeGezelle, Terri.** *The U.S. Capitol.* (First Facts) Capstone, 2003. 24pp. ISBN 978-0-7368-2294-7. Grades K–2. In eight short chapters, this volume discusses the contest for the design of the Capitol, its construction, rebuilding after the War of 1812, alterations before the Civil War, and the building's appearance today. The importance of the Capitol as a symbol of the United States becomes apparent. Photographs augment the text. Further Reading, Timeline, Glossary, Web sites, and Index.

52.   **D'Harcourt, Claire.** *Masterpieces Up Close: Western Painting from the 14th to 20th Centuries.* Chronicle, 2006. 63pp. ISBN 978-0-8118-5403-0. Grades 4–8. D'Harcourt examines more than one hundred details in each of twenty-one paintings. Among those included are the *Mona Lisa*, Michelangelo's Sistine Chapel, Rembrandt's *Night Watch*, Andy Warhol's *Marilyn*, Giotto's frescoes, and Velasquez's *Las Meninas*. Includes background on the paintings and biographical information about the artists.

53. **Dickinson, Rachel.** *Tools of Navigation: A Kid's Guide to the History and Science of Finding Your Way.* (Tools of Discovery) Nomad, 2006. 156pp. Paper ISBN 978-0-9749344-0-2. Grades 5–8. From the ancient navigators who sailed without compasses through explorers of land and sea, jungle and desert, North and South Poles, this volume examines the techniques used. In addition to information on modern aeronautical navigation and GPS technology, there are fifteen hands-on projects. Photographs, diagrams, and illustrations enhance the text. Bibliography, Glossary, Chronology, Notes, Further Reading, Web Sites, and Index.

54. **Doak, Robin.** *California 1542–1850.* (Voices from Colonial America) National Geographic, 2006. 109pp. ISBN 978-0-7922-6391-3. Grades 5–8. California became known in the 16th century when Sir Francis Drake claimed it for England, calling it New Albion. The Spanish arrived with priests and settlers to found Jesuit missions and presidios although more Indians died in those missions than were saved. Russia became a threat by establishing a fort on the coast in 1812. When Mexico became independent from Spanish rule, California was affected. But when gold fever permeated the area, California's newfound value made it the thirty-first state in 1850. Maps, Reproductions, Chronology, Further Reading, Notes, Web Sites, and Index.

55. **Downing, David.** *Democracy.* Raintree, 2007. 64pp. ISBN 978-1-4329-0233-9. Grades 5–8. The various aspects of a democracy are discussed, including representative democracy, constitutions, economic theory, voting, and the nation-state. This book also looks at Greece and Rome and how events in France and England eventually led to democracy in America. Photographs and illustrations augment the text. Glossary, Chronology, Further Reading, Web Sites, and Index.

56. **DuTemple, Lesley A.** *New York Subways.* (Great Building Feats) Lerner, 2002. 80pp. ISBN 978-0-8225-0378-1. Grades 4–7. DuTemple looks at the impact of the New York subway system on the infrastructure of the city. Topics include the financial problems of the system, its renovation, and the damage inflicted when the World Trade Center towers collapsed. Photographs and illustrations highlight the text. Bibliography, Chronology, Notes, Further Reading, Web Sites, and Index.

57. **Farman, John.** *The Short and Bloody History of Spies.* (Short and Bloody Histories) Lerner, 2002. 96pp. ISBN 978-0-8225-0845-8. Grades 5–8. This history of espionage features anecdotes about spies from around the world and through the ages. All types of people spy, including women and children. Some spies are deadly while others merely gather information. Also included is a look at gadgets and techniques. Cartoon illustrations highlight the text. Further Reading, Web Sites, and Index.

58. **Finkelman, Paul.** *The Constitution.* (American Documents) National Geographic, 2006. 48pp. ISBN 978-0-7922-7937-2. Grades 4–8. Informative two-page spreads explain the system of government before the Constitution, the realization that a Constitution was necessary, the Constitutional Convention, and the process of ratification. This volume also offers a clear explanation of the Electoral College and provides full texts of the country's first documents including the Bill of Rights and the Declaration of Independence as well as the Constitution and all its amendments.

59. **Floca, Brian.** *The Racecar Alphabet.* Richard Jackson, 2003. 40pp. ISBN 978-0-689-85091-2. Grades K–2. Using letters of the alphabet as a way to highlight a day at the races, this book looks at the cars, drivers, trucks, and spectators in auto races spanning the century between 1901 and 2001. A 1901 Ford attracts the "E" in "Eyes," and the driver's foe of a "Flat" becomes "F." Ink and watercolor illustrations augment the text.

60. **Formichelli, Linda, and W. Eric Martin.** *Tools of Timekeeping: A Kid's Guide to the History and Science of Telling Time.* (Tools of Discovery) Nomad, 2005. 137pp. Paper ISBN 978-0-9722026-7-1. Grades 5–8. Readers learn about the birth of time, how to tell time after twilight, what a clock actually is, crystals as timekeepers, and measuring time without moving. Projects include shadow clocks, sextants, and sundials. Photographs, diagrams, and illustrations highlight the text. Bibliography, Glossary, Chronology, Notes, Further Reading, Web Sites, and Index.

61. Foster, Mark. *Whale Port: A History of Tuckanucket.* Illustrated by Gerald Foster. Walter Lorraine, 2007. 64pp. ISBN 978-0-618-54722-7. Grades 4–8. This volume examines the life of a fictitious whaling village from 1683 to the present. The settlers recognize the value of whale oil and baleen (whale bone). Foster goes on to present facts about colonial life, whale blubber, maritime trades, and the difficulties of sea life, both for those at sea and those who remained on land. Index.

62. Freedman, Russell. *In Defense of Liberty: The Story of America's Bill of Rights.* Holiday House, 2003. 208pp. ISBN 978-0-8234-1585-4. Grades 5 up. This text incorporates historical background that served as a basis for the original writing of the ten amendments that compose the Bill of Rights, reviews the controversial aspects of the Bill of Rights, and discusses landmark court cases associated with them. Freedman poses questions and then proceeds to answer them with quoted and statistical information. At the end of the discussion of the Bill of Rights, Freedman outlines the Thirteenth, Fourteenth, and Fifteenth Amendments, which were added after the Civil War. Illustrations, Sources, Web Sites, List of Supreme Court Cases, and Index. *School Library Journal Best Books of the Year, American Library Association Notable Books for Children, National Council of Teachers of English Orbis Pictus Honor, Booklist Editor's Choice, Dorothy Canfield Fisher Children's Book Award* (Vermont) nomination, *Garden State Teen Book Award* (New Jersey) nomination, *Capitol Choices Noteworthy Titles* (Washington, D.C.), *Horn Book Fanfare,* and *Student Book Award* (Maine) nomination.

63. Freedman, Russell. *Who Was First? Discovering the Americas.* Clarion, 2007. 88pp. ISBN 978-0-618-66391-0. Grades 5–9. Freedman explores various theories about who actually discovered the Americas. He covers the voyages of Columbus, the belief that the the Chinese explorer Zheng may have found these shores, and that the Vikings settled in Newfoundland around 1000. Native Americans may have crossed an ice bridge from Siberia. Freedman looks at historical clues including DNA links and carbon-dated artifacts. Photographs and illustrations enhance the text. Bibliography, Notes, and Index. *Horn Book Fanfare, Booklist Editor's Choice, Voice of Youth Advocates Nonfiction Honor List, Kirkus Reviews Editor's Choice, School Library Journal Best Books for Children,* and *Bank Street College of Education Flora Stieglitz Straus Award.*

64. Giblin, James Cross. *When Plague Strikes: The Black Death, Smallpox, AIDS.* Trophy, 1997. 212pp. Paper ISBN 978-0-06-446195-5. Grades 5–9. Three major plagues have hit the world in the past thousand years: the Black Death, smallpox, and AIDS. They have killed millions and have created social, economic, and political havoc. Although each plague has helped to increase knowledge about the human body, each new one must be researched and tested for a cure. This book first tells of a plague that struck Athens in 430 B.C. Those who survived it had terrible scars or lost their eyesight or their memory. Today no one is sure what the disease might have been, although typhus, smallpox, and bubonic plague are candidates. The one sure thing is that doctors did not know how to treat it. The author then discusses the three plagues that have ravaged the world since. Source Notes, Bibliography, and Index. *American Library Association Best Books for Young Adults, Notable Children's Trade Books in the Field of Social Studies,* and *American Library Association Notable Children's Books.*

65. Giglio, Joe. *Great Teams in Pro Basketball History.* (Great Teams) Raintree, 2005. 48pp. ISBN 978-1-4109-1485-9; paper ISBN 978-1-4109-1492-7. Grades 3–6. Giglio looks at various aspects of basketball, including players, coaches, games, and statistics. Photographs of teams, team rosters, team records, player records, and other historical information add to the coverage. Chronology, Further Reading, Glossary, and Index.

66. Giglio, Joe. *Great Teams in Pro Football History.* (Great Teams) Raintree, 2005. 48pp. ISBN 978-1-4109-1488-0; paper ISBN 978-1-4109-1490-3. Grades 3–6. Giglio covers important pro football players, coaches, and games. Statistics, photographs of teams, team rosters, team records, player records, and other historical information add to the coverage. Chronology, Further Reading, Glossary, and Index.

67. Gonzales, Doreen. *A Look at the Second Amendment: To Keep and Bear Arms.* (The Constitution of the United States) Enslow, 2007. 128pp. ISBN 978-1-59845-061-3. Grades 5–

8. Gonzales reviews this amendment, why it was enacted, and the ramifications today. Photographs and illustrations highlight the text. Glossary, Chronology, Notes, Further Reading, Web Sites, and Index.

68. **Graham, Amy.** *A Look at the Eighteenth and Twenty-First Amendments: The Prohibition and Sale of Intoxicating Liquors.* (The Constitution of the United States) Enslow, 2007. 128pp. ISBN 978-1-59845-063-7. Grades 5–8. This volume examines the history of the Eighteenth Amendment and important court decisions pertaining to it. The amendment banned alcohol on January 16, 1919; this ban was rescinded by the Twenty-First Amendment on December 5, 1933. Graham debates the idea of the amendment as an individual or a collective right and provides an overview of the temperance movements in the 19th and early 20th centuries. Photographs and illustrations augment the text. Glossary, Chronology, Notes, Further Reading, Web Sites, and Index.

69. **Halls, Kelly Milner.** *Mysteries of the Mummy Kids.* Darby Creek, 2007. 72pp. ISBN 978-1-58196-059-4. Grades 4–8. This book about the practices of mummification throughout the world focuses on the mummies of children and supposes the events that might have caused their deaths. Among those included are a 7,000-year-old mummy discovered near Chile's Camarones Valley and one from Washington, D.C., that was buried during the Civil War. Interviews with scientists and mummy hunters as well as a visit to a modern embalmer offer further information about the religious and medical reasons for mummification. Photographs, maps, and reproductions reinforce the text. Bibliography, Glossary, Further Reading, Web Sites, and Index.

70. **Hamilton, Lynn.** *Memorial Day.* (American Holidays) Weigl, 2004. 24pp. ISBN 978-1-59036-105-4; paper ISBN 978-1-59036-168-9. Grades 2–4. Hamilton explains how Memorial Day honors those who fought to protect the United States and describes how the holiday is recognized.

71. **Hamilton, Lynn.** *Presidents' Day.* (American Holidays) Weigl, 2004. 24pp. ISBN 978-1-59036-108-5; paper ISBN 978-1-59036-169-6. Grades 2–4. Background information about George Washington (1732–1799) and Abraham Lincoln (1809–1865) gives readers an understanding of why a holiday honors these two men.

72. **Handyside, Chris.** *Folk.* (A History of American Music) Heinemann, 2006. 48pp. ISBN 978-1-4034-8150-4. Grades 5–9. This book explores the origins and development of folk music in America since the Civil War. It looks at social, economic, and regional influences and introduces important figures such as the Carter family, Leadbelly, Woody Guthrie, Joan Baez, and Bob Dylan. At the end, the text discusses folk rock, punk rock, and the future of folk music. Photographs and illustrations highlight the text. Glossary, Chronology, and Index.

73. **Handyside, Chris.** *Rock.* (A History of American Music) Heinemann, 2006. 48pp. ISBN 978-1-4034-8152-8. Grades 5–9. Readers will learn about the history of rock music from its beginnings in the 1950s through the 1980s. There are profiles of early artists such as Chuck Berry, Elvis Presley, Bill Haley, and B. B. King. Glossary, Chronology, and Index.

74. **Harness, Cheryl.** *The Amazing Impossible Erie Canal.* Aladdin, 1999. Unpaged. Paper ISBN 978-0-689-82584-2. Grades 2–6. This book, in two-page spreads, presents the history of the Erie Canal since its completion in 1825, when people lined the canal towpath to watch the boats float through. It discusses why the canal was built, who constructed it, the politics behind its creation, and how the locks work, as well as the reasons that people stopped using it. Bibliography.

75. **Harper, Charise Mericle.** *Flush! The Scoop on Poop Throughout the Ages.* Little, Brown, 2007. 32pp. ISBN 978-0-316-01064-1. Grades 1–5. The first toilet appeared more than ten thousand years ago, and the average person uses about twenty thousand sheets of toilet paper a year. Other interesting information in this book includes uses of urine and a description of some of the toilets of the world. It reveals that Elizabeth I rejected a mechanical toilet and that Louis XIV held meetings while sitting on a toilet shaped like a throne. Thirteen poems feature additional information about excrement disposal. Collage paintings highlight the text.

76. **Haskins, James, and Kathleen Benson.** *Africa: A Look Back.* (Drama of African-American History) Benchmark, 2006. 68pp. ISBN 978-0-7614-2148-1. Grades 5–8. In this volume, part of a history of African American roots, the authors look at slavery from 8th-century Africa through the Middle Passage in six chapters. Four chapters focus on slave narratives by Olaudah Equiano, Ayuba ben Suleiman Diallo, Mahommah Gardo Baquaqua, and Venture Smith. With complementary photographs, illustrations, documents, and maps. Glossary, Bibliography, Further Reading, and Index.

77. **Haven, Kendall.** *100 Greatest Science Discoveries of All Time.* Libraries Unlimited, 2007. 255pp. ISBN 978-1-59158-265-6. Grades 5–8. This examination of one hundred discoveries that changed science identifies each discovery, how it was made, who made it, and why it was a breakthrough. It starts with levers and buoyancy around 2650 B.C.E. and covers discoveries such as the sun-centered universe, cells, atoms, electrochemical bonding, quasars and pulsars, and the human genome. Index.

78. **Hempstead, Anne.** *The Supreme Court.* (Land of the Free) Heinemann, 2006. 32pp. ISBN 978-1-4034-7001-0; paper ISBN 978-1-4034-7008-9. Grades 4–7. Hempstead examines the history of the Supreme Court by looking at its composition, its function in the government, and its significance as an American symbol. The four chapters contain text and sidebars covering diverse peripheral information. Photographs and archival reproductions highlight the text. Glossary, Chronology, Further Reading, and Index.

79. **Hempstead, Anne.** *The U.S. Capitol.* (Land of the Free) Heinemann, 2006. 32pp. ISBN 978-1-4034-7000-3; paper ISBN 978-1-4034-7007-2. Grades 4–7. Hempstead examines the history of the United States Capitol. He looks at the inspiration behind it, its design and construction, and its significance as an American symbol. The four chapters contain text and sidebars covering diverse peripheral information. Photographs and archival reproductions highlight the text. Glossary, Chronology, Further Reading, and Index.

80. **Hempstead, Anne.** *The White House.* (Land of the Free) Heinemann, 2006. 32pp. ISBN 978-1-4034-6999-1; paper ISBN 978-1-4034-7006-5. Grades 4–7. A history of the White House, looking at its design, construction, and significance as an American symbol. Photographs and archival reproductions augment the text. Glossary, Chronology, Further Reading, and Index.

81. **Herbst, Judith.** *The History of Transportation.* (Major Inventions Through History) Twenty-First Century, 2005. 56pp. ISBN 978-0-8225-2496-0. Grades 5–8. A wide-ranging survey of transportation developments over time, from the wheel and the sail to the steam engine, the internal combustion engine, and the airplane. Photographs and illustrations augment the text. Bibliography, Glossary, Chronology, Further Reading, Web Sites, and Index.

82. **Herbst, Judith.** *The History of Weapons.* (Major Inventions Through History) Twenty-First Century, 2005. 56pp. ISBN 978-0-8225-3805-9. Grades 5–8. A history of weapons from the first gunpowder to dynamite, TNT, automatic weapons, and weapons of mass destruction. Photographs and illustrations highlight the text. Bibliography, Glossary, Chronology, Further Reading, Web Sites, and Index.

83. **Hewitt, David.** *Uncle Sam's America: A Parade Through Our Star-Spangled History.* Illustrated by Kathryn Hewitt. Simon & Schuster, 2008. 40pp. ISBN 978-1-4169-4075-3. Grades 3–6. This volume offers a patriotic view of American history with the figure of Uncle Sam guiding readers through events including the War of 1812, the frontier, immigrants arriving, the two World Wars, the civil rights movement, and the Moon landing. Illustrations complement the text.

84. **Hodgkins, Fran.** *How People Learned to Fly.* Illustrated by True Kelley. (Let's-Read-and-Find-Out Science) Collins, 2007. 33pp. Paper ISBN 978-0-06-445221-2. Grades 1–3. Hodgkins explains the scientific principles behind airplanes including gravity, thrust, and lift and explains how humans learned to master flight. Diagrams and illustrations make these complicated concepts easy to understand. There is an experiment with paper airplanes.

85.   Hopkins, Lee Bennett. *America at War.* Illustrated by Stephen Alcorn. Margaret K. McElderry, 2008. 96pp. ISBN 978-1-4169-1832-5. Grades 5–8. In eight chronological sections, fifty-four poems address conflicts involving Americans: the American Revolution, the Civil War, World Wars I and II, Korea, Vietnam, the Persian Gulf, and Iraq. Among the poets included are Sir Walter Scott, Langston Hughes, J. Patrick Lewis, Jane Yolen, Walt Whitman, Carl Sandburg, e. e. cummings, and Stephen Crane. Index.

86.   Hopkins, Lee Bennett. *Hand in Hand: An American History Through Poetry.* Illustrated by Peter Fiore. Simon & Schuster, 1994. 194pp. ISBN 978-0-671-73315-5. Grades 3–6. The history of America is presented through poems within chronologically divided sections covering the Pilgrims, the Revolution, and so forth. The poems are more notable for their subject matter than for their quality, but they give insight into the historical topics they cover.

87.   Hopkinson, Deborah. *Up Before Daybreak: Cotton and People in America.* Scholastic, 2006. 120pp. ISBN 978-0-439-63901-9. Grades 5–8. Drawing on oral histories collected by the Federal Writers Project during the 1930s and from Lowell mill workers in the 1970s and 1980s, Hopkinson tells the story of the cotton trade and how humans have been involved in its manufacture. Topics include cloth making, the cotton gin, slavery, the Great Migration, the Great Depression, and child labor. The voices of the children describe working long hours and surviving on meager diets of pork fat and flour. Photographs and illustrations highlight the text. Bibliography, Notes, Further Reading, and Index. *School Library Journal Best Books for Children, American Library Association Notable Children's Books*, and *American Library Association Best Books for Young Adults.*

88.   Hudson, Wade. *Powerful Words: More Than 200 Years of Extraordinary Writing by African Americans.* Illustrated by Sean Qualls. (Powerful Words) Scholastic, 2004. 178pp. ISBN 978-0-439-40969-8. Grades 5 up. Excerpts from letters, speeches, poetry, novels, and songs by famous African Americans are coupled with commentary on their achievements. Among the writers included are Benjamin Banneker, Dred Scott, Samuel B. Cornish, John Russwurm, Ida B. Wells Barnett, W. E. B. Du Bois, Mary McLeod Bethune, Marcus Garvey, Langston Hughes, Zora Neale Hurston, James Weldon Johnson, Thurgood Marshall, Rosa Parks, Malcolm X, Martin Luther King Jr., Toni Morrison (accepting the Nobel Prize), and Lauryn Hill (hip-hop lyrics). Topics range from slavery, discrimination, and racism to growth in the African American community. Illustrations enhance the text. Chronology, Sources, and Index. *Parents Choice Award.*

89.   Hurd, Owen. *Chicago History for Kids: Triumphs and Tragedies of the Windy City, Includes 21 Activities.* Chicago Review, 2007. Paper ISBN 978-1-55652-654-1. Grades 4–9. Using primary sources including responses from young visitors and experts, this volume looks at Chicago's history and provides twenty-one activities for children, including "constructing a model longhouse," "making a Ferris wheel," and "building a replica of Fort Dearborn." Further Reading, Glossary, Web Sites, and Index.

90.   Jackson, Ellen. *Turn of the Century.* Charlesbridge, 1998. Unpaged. ISBN 978-0-8810-6369-1; 2003, paper ISBN 978-0-8810-6370-7. Grades 3–5. Readers will learn about the lives of children in the United States and Great Britain at the beginning of each century from 1000 to 2000 C.E. Each two-page spread tells about a child living in each century, starting in Great Britain in 1000 and in the United States in 1700. Readers look into children's homes and find out about aspects of childhood such as chores, prayer, and the home. Bibliography. *Bluegrass Awards* (Kentucky), *Bluebonnet Awards* (Texas), and *Children's Informational Book Awards* (Utah).

91.   Jackson, Ellen. *The Winter Solstice.* Illustrated by Jan Davey Ellis. Millbrook, 1997. Unpaged. Paper ISBN 978-0-7613-0297-1. Grades 3–4. The winter solstice was a time of ritual and tradition for the Celts, the Romans, and the Native Americans. Its magic has had an influence throughout history and is reflected today in the celebration of Halloween and All Souls' Day. A Cherokee legend ends the presentation.

92.   Jango-Cohen, Judith. *The History of Food.* (Major Inventions Through History) Twenty-First Century, 2005. 56pp. ISBN 978-0-8225-2485-7. Grades 5–8. Canning, pasteurization, refrigeration, supermarkets, and genetically modified foods are all covered here. Before food preserving was invented, sailors ate rotten food filled with worms when they took long journeys. In the 1800s children died from drinking milk as no one knew that diseases could spread from cows to humans. Before refrigerators, large blocks of ice were delivered to homes to allow people to keep their food chilled. Photographs and illustrations highlight the text. Bibliography, Glossary, Chronology, Further Reading, Web Sites, and Index.

93. **Jedicke, Peter.** *Great Inventions of the 20th Century.* (Scientific American) Chelsea House, 2007. 72pp. ISBN 978-0-7910-9048-0. Grades 5–8. The inventions noted in the text are those that changed people's lives and that are continually being improved. For example, air conditioners once contained hazardous waste, but today the chemicals used in them are much safer for the environment. Photographs and reproductions highlight the text. Bibliography, Glossary, Further Reading, and Web Sites.

94. **Johmann, Carol A.** *Skyscrapers! Super Structures to Design and Build.* Illustrated by Michael P. Kline. Williamson, 2001. 96pp. Paper ISBN 978-1-885593-50-4. Grades 3–6. A look at the history, construction, environmental impact, and design of skyscrapers including the Empire State Building in New York, Petronas Towers in Kuala Lumpur, the Montauk Block in Chicago, and the Millennium Tower in Tokyo. The book also includes activities such as building a concrete floor with sand, cornstarch, and popsicle sticks; testing a toothpick-and-marshmallow building frame; and building an elevator. Photographs enhance the text.

95. **Johnson, Linda Carlson.** *Our National Symbols.* Millbrook, 1994. 48pp. Paper ISBN 978-1-8788-4187-2. Grades 2–4. Symbols that have achieved national significance include the Liberty Bell, the bald eagle, Uncle Sam, and the Statue of Liberty. The text discusses the importance of these and others. Chronology and Index.

96. **Johnston, Robert D.** *The Making of America: The History of the United States from 1492 to the Present.* National Geographic, 2002. 240pp. ISBN 978-0-7922-6944-1. Grades 5–8. Johnston presents each major era in the history of the United States with biographical profiles of some of the key figures and quotations from speeches. The periods are the revolutionary age (1763–1789), the new republic (1789–1848), the Civil War and Reconstruction (1848–1877), progressivism and the New Deal (1900–1941), war and social change (1941–1968), and the age of conservatism (1969–present). Among those profiled are Abigail Adams, Andrew Carnegie, Huey P. Long, Joseph McCarthy, and Sandra Day O'Connor. Bibliography, Web Sites, and Index. *School Library Journal Best Children's Books.*

97. **Jordan, Anne Devereaux, and Virginia Schomp.** *Slavery and Resistance.* (Drama of African-American History) Benchmark, 2006. 70pp. ISBN 978-0-7614-2178-8. Grades 5–8. Jordan examines in six chapters the situation of slaves during colonial America and how conditions worsened, leading to resistance. Ironically, during the Revolutionary War, when the colonists sought freedom, they needed labor to support themselves and chose to continue the practice of forced labor through slavery. Eventually the Nat Turner Rebellion revealed how horrible some slave owners' practices had become. Chapters contain relevant photographs, illustrations, documents, and maps. Glossary, Bibliography, Further Reading, and Index.

98. **Jordan, Denise M.** *Juneteenth Day.* (Holiday Histories) Heinemann, 2003. 32pp. ISBN 978-1-4034-3505-7; paper ISBN 978-1-4034-3690-0. Grades K–2. Juneteenth Day, June 19, is a holiday originating in Texas. It was on June 19 in 1865 that slaves in Texas were informed of their freedom. It is a state holiday in Texas and other states celebrating emancipation in the United States. Short chapters explain the celebration. Photographs and drawings highlight the text. Bibliography and Index.

99. **Kalman, Bobbie.** *Early Artisans.* Crabtree, 1983. 32pp. ISBN 978-0-8650-5023-5; 1981, paper ISBN 978-0-8650-5022-8. Grades 3–6. Although people had to build or make everything that they used as pioneers in the 18th and 19th centuries, many still wanted beautiful things. Artisans made silver and gold jewelry and flatware. They painted pictures and designed and wove beautiful fabric. They created artifacts for the home and decorated the ex-

teriors as well as the interiors of buildings and homes. The amount of decoration that a person had signified his or her economic class. Photographs and drawings illustrate the text. Glossary and Index.

100. **Kavin, Kim.** *Tools of Native Americans: A Kid's Guide to the History and Culture of the First Americans.* (Tools of Discovery) Nomad, 2006. 122pp. Paper ISBN 978-0-9749344-8-8. Grades 5–8. Kavin recounts the inventiveness of Native Americans throughout history with their tools, technology, and cultural achievements. As the first Americans as early as 20,000 B.C.E., they had to build appropriate shelter for the climate, find food supplies, create their religions, invent games, and fashion their jewelry. The four sections of the text address the early indigenous Americans, the regions in which Native Americans lived, recent history of Native Americans, and where to find more information. Among the regions covered are the Arctic tribes and their igloos, the Midwest tribes that discovered copper, and the Southwest tribes that grew maize and beans. Activities and illustrations augment the text. Maps, Appendix, Bibliography, Chronology, Glossary, Web Sites, and Index. *Social Studies Honor Book*.

101. **Keenan, Sheila.** *Animals in the House: A History of Pets and People.* Scholastic, 2007. 112pp. ISBN 978-0-439-69286-1. Grades 4–6. This overview of pets includes a history of pets as household residents, looks at famous pets and pet owners, and offers a history of each type of animal, giving the reasons it makes a good pet, what it was like in the wild, and how it became domesticated. It also covers superstitions about pets. Pets included are birds, rodents, lizards, fish, cats, dogs, reptiles, and others. Photographs and illustrations highlight the text. Bibliography, Web Sites, and Index.

102. **Kendall, Martha E.** *Failure Is Impossible! The History of American Women's Rights.* Lerner, 2001. 96pp. ISBN 978-0-8225-1744-3. Grades 5–8. In eight chapters, the author examines feminist ideas and women's rights in America from the Salem witch trials through the appointment of Madeleine Albright as the first female secretary of state. Women have had to fight for the right to hold jobs, vote, gain an education, own property, control their own rights of reproduction, play sports, and have equal protection under the law. Sepia illustrations enhance the text. Timeline, Selected Bibliography, Further Reading, and Index.

103. **Koscielniak, Bruce.** *About Time: A First Look at Time and the Clocks.* Houghton, 2004. Unpaged. ISBN 978-0-618-39668-9. Grades 3–5. From basic terms—day, month, year—to the development of the Western calendar and the evolution of devices for measuring time including atomic clocks, this is a thorough history. It also explains three theories of time, including that of Einstein. Illustrations enhance the text.

104. **Krensky, Stephen.** *Comic Book Century: The History of American Comic Books.* Twenty-First Century, 2007. 112pp. ISBN 978-0-8225-6654-0. Grades 5–9. Americans have read comic books for many years, and Krensky provides a history of comic books from the 1930s, when Superman and Batman became popular. He covers comics during World War II, Stan Lee's Marvel comics, and how topics have changed according to the circumstances of the times and the attitudes of readers. Illustrations enhance the text. Bibliography, Chronology, Notes, Further Reading, Web Sites, and Index. *Voice of Youth Advocates Nonfiction Honor List*.

105. **Kurlansky, Mark.** *The Story of Salt.* Illustrated by S. D. Schindler. Putnam, 2006. 48pp. ISBN 978-0-399-23998-4. Grades 4–6. This history of salt is by the author of *Salt: A World History* (2003), which is for older readers. Since salt, the only rock that humans eat, is essential for human life, finding inexpensive ways to obtain it is important. Readers will learn many facts about salt, including that Gandhi led Indians on a "salt march" to protest being forced to buy salt only from the British. Illustrations complement the text. *Dorothy Canfield Fisher Children's Book Award* (Vermont) nomination.

106. **Landau, Elaine.** *The History of Energy.* (Major Inventions Through History) Twenty-First Century, 2005. 56pp. ISBN 978-0-8225-3806-6. Grades 5–8. Landau looks at the history of energy from the earliest uses of fire and water through nuclear energy. Supposedly the ancient Persians harnessed rivers to turn waterwheels that ground grain into flour, a practice that extends into modern times with giant hydroelectric plants using water power to provide electricity to cities. In the 2nd century, the Romans burned coal, and in modern times, 90 percent of the United States coal output produces electricity. Oil was discovered in the United States in 1859, and fifty years later nearly a half-million gasoline-powered cars rolled on the country's roads. Photographs and illustrations highlight the text. Bibliography, Glossary, Chronology, Notes, Further Reading, Web Sites, and Index.

107. **Landau, Elaine.** *The History of Everyday Life.* (Major Inventions Through History) Twenty-First Century, 2005. 56pp. ISBN 978-0-8225-3808-0. Grades 5–8. The author looks at the techniques developed over time to make everyday life easier— from fireplaces to central heating, from indoor plumbing to washing machines, and so forth. The military was first to use microwave technology, but we now have microwaves in many houses. Photographs and illustrations highlight the text. Bibliography, Glossary, Chronology, Notes, Further Reading, Web Sites, and Index.

108. **Langley, Myrtle.** *Eyewitness Religion.* DK, 2005. 72pp. ISBN 978-0-7566-1087-6. Grades 4–7. Different religions or facets of religions are presented on two-page spreads illustrated with photographs, drawings, and reproductions. Among the religions and beliefs introduced in this overview are the Egyptian, Greek, Primitive, Hindu, Buddhist, Confucian, Taoist, Jainist, Sikh, Zoroastrian, Judaic, Christian, and Islamic faiths. Index.

109. **Lankford, Mary D.** *Mazes Around the World.* Illustrated by Karen Dugan. Collins, 2008. 26pp. ISBN 978-0-688-16519-2. Grades 3–4. The author looks at the history of mazes from the ancient Egyptian labyrinth that Herodotus recorded and the Minotaur's labyrinth on Crete to mazes around the world—turf mazes in the United Kingdom, maize mazes in North America, South Africa's Soekershof Mazes (hedges), and France's religious labyrinths. Notes.

110. **Lauber, Patricia.** *What You Never Knew About Beds, Bedrooms, and Pajamas.* Illustrated by John Manders. (Around the House History) Simon & Schuster, 2006. Unpaged. ISBN 978-0-689-85211-4. Grades 2–5. The history of sleeping habits, sleep attire, and bedrooms from the Stone Age to the present. In the Stone Age clans slept on the ground, as we do today on camping trips. Cartoon illustrations enliven the text.

111. **Lauber, Patricia.** *What You Never Knew About Fingers, Forks, and Chopsticks.* Simon & Schuster, 1999. Unpaged. ISBN 978-0-689-80479-3. Grades 2–5. Lauber reviews food utensils and table manners throughout history. Knives appeared during the Stone Age, table etiquette in ancient China, but fingers are still used. Illustrations enhance the text. Bibliography.

112. **Liestman, Vicki.** *Columbus Day.* Illustrated by Rick Hanson. Carolrhoda, 1991. 52pp. ISBN 978-0-8761-4444-2. Grades 1–3. Simple text tells the story of Christopher Columbus and the holiday celebrated in his name. Liestman also explains why the Europeans wanted to find new sea routes and that Columbus and his crew saw the natives as potential slaves. Although Columbus lost favor with his crew, his perseverance allowed him to find the New World.

113. **Love, Ann, and Jane Drake.** *Sweet! The Delicious Story of Candy.* Illustrated by Claudia Dávila. Tundra, 2007. 64pp. ISBN 978-0-88776-752-4. Grades 4–7. This history of candy begins in 4000 B.C. with Papua New Guinea residents cutting sugarcane for its sweet sap. It ends in contemporary times with a trip to a candy store. In between, it discusses the ingredients—bee barf, mammal secretions, aphid poop, stem sap, root pulp, bean fat—that become marshmallows, fudge, gummy worms, and chocolate-chip cookies. Visits to a jelly-bean factory, a chocolatier, and a kitchen offer other insights. Cartoon illustrations enhance the text. Chronology.

114. **McComb, Marianne.** *The Emancipation Proclamation.* (American Documents) National Geographic, 2006. 40pp. ISBN 978-0-7922-7916-7. Grades 4–8. The text reveals that the Emancipation Proclamation freed slaves in the Confederate States of America but did not end slavery in any state nor in the Confederacy. It includes background about slavery and the Civil War along with the evolution of Lincoln's thinking about this decision. Photographs and reproductions enhance the text. Bibliography, Glossary, Chronology, Further Reading, and Index.

115. Macy, Sue. *Swifter, Higher, Stronger: A Photographic History of the Summer Olympics.* National Geographic, 2008. 96pp. ISBN 978-1-4263-0290-9. Grades 5–9. A look at the history of the Olympic Games since their rebirth in the late 1800s with anecdotes about some unusual moments during the games and discussion of controversies and attitudes toward sportsmanship. Notes, Further Resources, and Index.

116. Maestro, Betsy. *The Story of Money.* Illustrated by Giulio Maestro. Clarion, 1993. 48pp. ISBN 978-0-395-56242-0; Trophy, 1995, paper ISBN 978-0-688-13304-7. Grades 3–5. Among the objects that have been used for money throughout history are tea leaves, shells, feathers, animal teeth, tobacco, blankets, barley, salt, feathers, and metal balls. When the Sumerians used metal bars of the same weight and stamped an amount on each bar, they invented the first known metal money. This book has other interesting information about money through the centuries and short chapters on American money, unusual money, and currencies of other countries. Illustrations complement the text.

117. Mark, Jan. *The Museum Book: A Guide to Strange and Wonderful Collections.* Illustrated by Richard Holland. Candlewick, 2007. 52pp. ISBN 978-0-7636-3370-7. Grades 4–6. This book looks at the word "museum" itself and at a number of famous museums throughout the world. It includes Alexandria, Egypt; the collections of Peter the Great; Oxford University's Ashmolean; and museums with Middle Ages collections. It also discusses what one might find in a museum. Photographs and illustrations highlight the text. Glossary and Index.

118. Mason, Antony. *A History of Western Art: From Prehistory to the 20th Century.* Abrams, 2007. 128pp. ISBN 978-0-8109-9421-8. Grades 5 up. An overview of Western art beginning with the Lascaux cave paintings and continuing to the present. Two-page spreads discuss different time periods or movements, contain representative work, and present aspects of the media used. Each section provides a showcase of the time period discussed. More than two hundred reproductions of sculpture, pottery, mosaics, paintings, etching, stained glass, and architecture complement the text. Index.

119. Mehling, Randi. *Great Extinctions of the Past.* (Scientific American) Chelsea House, 2007. 72pp. ISBN 978-0-7910-9049-7. Grades 5–8. The author examines mass extinctions in the history of the world, especially the dinosaurs. One of the important goals of the future is to help the environment so that mass extinctions never again occur. Photographs and reproductions highlight the text. Bibliography, Glossary, Further Reading, and Web Sites.

120. Meltzer, Milton. *The Black Americans: A History in Their Own Words 1619–1983.* Trophy, 1987. 306pp. Paper ISBN 978-0-06-446055-2. Grades 5 up. Meltzer has collected documents showing 350 years of black life in America. His subjects range from the sharecropper's struggle to the scholar Maya Angelou. Using the words of those who endured, he relates a history that stretches from 1619 to 1983. Sources and Index. *American Library Association Notable Children's Book* and *Notable Children's Trade Books in the Field of Social Studies.*

121. Mercer, Abbie. *Happy Halloween.* Powerkids, 2007. 24pp. ISBN 978-1-4042-3806-0. Grades 2–4. Mercer presents a brief history of Halloween and Halloween traditions along with recipes and crafts. Photographs and illustrations accompany the text. Glossary, Web Sites, and Index.

122. Mercer, Abbie. *Happy Thanksgiving.* Powerkids, 2007. 24pp. ISBN 978-1-4042-3807-7. Grades 2–4. Readers will learn about the history of Thanksgiving. The English settlers joined with the Wampanoags to feast after the harvest in 1621. Since that time, traditions surrounding Thanksgiving have evolved to include turkey, parades, football games, and, sometimes, working in soup kitchens to feed the less fortunate. Photographs and illustrations highlight the text. Glossary, Web Sites, and Index.

123. Michelson, Richard. *Tuttle's Red Barn: The Story of America's Oldest Family Farm.* Illustrated by Mary Azarian. Putnam, 2007. 40pp. ISBN 978-0-399-24354-7. Grades K–3. The oldest family farm in America continues to exist in Dover, New Hampshire, where the Tuttle family has lived since John Tuttle arrived from England in 1632. Through twelve generations, the Tuttles have worked the farm, experiencing relations with displaced Penacook

Indians, the Revolutionary War, the Constitution, the Underground Railroad, and the automobile. Woodcuts enhance the text. *Publishers Weekly Best Books*.

124. **Middleton, Haydn.** *Great Olympic Moments.* (Olympics) Heinemann, 2007. 32pp. ISBN 978-1-4329-0264-3. Grades 4–8. Middleton offers an overview of key events in the history of the Olympic Games. Among the sports that have generated high levels of excitement are gymnastics and soccer. Photographs accent each page. Glossary, Further Reading, Web Sites, and Index. Another volume in this series is *Modern Olympic Games* (2007).

125. **Murphy, Claire Rudolf.** *Children of Alcatraz: Growing Up on the Rock.* Walker, 2006. 64pp. ISBN 978-0-8027-9577-9. Grades 4–7. Using primary documents—anecdotes, interviews, documents, and archival and family photographs—Murphy tells the stories of children who grew up on Alcatraz Island, from the earliest Native Americans onward. They were children of soldiers, prison authorities, and lighthouse keepers. Some were there during the twenty months that Native Americans occupied the island from 1969 to 1971. Photographs highlight the text. Chronology, Further Reading, Web Sites, and Index.

126. **Nathan, Amy.** *Count on Us: American Women in the Military.* National Geographic, 2004. 96pp. ISBN 978-0-7922-6330-2. Grades 5–8. American women have been part of the Armed Forces since the Revolutionary War when Deborah Sampson, Native American Tyonajanegen, and Margaret Corbin served. Some of them had to disguise their gender to serve during the Revolutionary and Civil Wars. Today, female pilots fly Black Hawk missions. This volume looks at women who fought in the Revolutionary War, the Civil War, both World Wars, Vietnam, the Persian Gulf, and Afghanistan and Iraq. They made contributions as spies, nurses, aviators, mechanics, and more. Anecdotes enliven the text and reveal that women in the military are often pursuing the careers that please them the most although their desires sometimes are thwarted because they are women. Bibliography and Index.

127. **Nelson, Kadir.** *We Are the Ship: The Story of Negro League Baseball.* Hyperion, 2008. 96pp. ISBN 978-0-7868-0832-8. Grades 3 up. An unnamed narrator tells his grandchildren about the great players from the Negro leagues who helped break the race barrier into baseball's major leagues. They include Satchel Paige, Josh Gibson, and the man who actually succeeded in hurdling this obstacle, Jackie Robinson. Illustrations both complement and enhance the text. Bibliography, Notes, and Index. *School Library Journal Best Books for Children, Publishers Weekly Best Books, Capitol Choices Noteworthy Titles* (Washington, D.C.), and *Kirkus Reviews Editor's Choice*.

128. **Nelson, Vaunda M., and Drew Nelson.** *Juneteenth.* Illustrated by Mark Schroder. Millbrook, 2005. 48pp. ISBN 978-1-57505-876-4; First Avenue, 2006, paper ISBN 978-0-8225-5974-0. Grades 2–4. The celebration of Juneteenth began on June 19, 1865, when the slaves in Galveston, Texas, finally discovered that they were emancipated and had been so since January 1, 1863. The text highlights their joy, with a history of slavery following. Pastel illustrations complement the text.

129. *Our White House: Looking In, Looking Out.* Candlewick, 2008. 256pp. ISBN 978-0-7636-2067-7. Grades 3–8. This look at the White House includes personal accounts, letters, speeches, comics, fiction, poetry, and essays about the presidents and their families who lived there. Among the writers included are Natalie Babbitt, Jane Yolen, David Macaulay, Brian Selznick, Jon Scieszka, Steven Kellogg, Walter Dean Myers, Milton Meltzer, M. T. Anderson, Patricia MacLachlan, Russell Freedman, Jean Craighead George, Katherine Paterson, Homer Hickam, Susan Cooper, David McCullough, Barbara Kerley, and Richard Peck. Illustrations complement the text. *Publishers Weekly Best Books, Capitol Choices Noteworthy Titles* (Washington, D.C.), and *School Library Journal Best Books for Children*.

130. **Oxlade, Chris.** *Airplanes: Uncovering Technology.* (Uncovering) Firefly, 2006. 52pp. ISBN 978-1-55407-134-0. Grades 4–8. A historical overview of both civilian and military airplanes. Each spread features drawings and captioned photographs for a chronological presentation of airplanes and how they have made a difference in technology. Overlays show the inner workings of several airplanes. Index.

131. Oxlade, Chris. *Skyscrapers: Uncovering Technology.* (Uncovering) Firefly, 2006. 52pp. ISBN 978-1-55407-136-4. Grades 4–8. A historical overview of skyscrapers. Each spread features drawings and captioned photographs for a chronological presentation of skyscrapers. Among those included are the Tower of Babel, the Chrysler Building, the Petronas Tower in Kuala Lumpur, and the CCTV building planned for Beijing. Cross-section overlays reveal the inner aspects of three skyscrapers. Index.

132. Panchyk, Richard. *Archaeology for Kids.* Chicago Review, 2001. 160pp. Paper ISBN 978-1-55652-395-3. Grades 5–8. Twenty-five activities suggest ways for readers to understand the science of archaeology. They include playing a survey game, dating coins, making footprints, measuring brain capacity, building a Paleolithic fireplace, making cave art, playing a seriation game, and classifying pottery. Each of the activities gives participants a chance to observe their surroundings after they have reviewed the eight steps of archaeology, four of which are research, surveying, excavation, and preservation. Photographs and illustrations highlight the text. Bibliography, Glossary, Web Sites, and Index.

133. Pascoe, Elaine. *Fooled You! Fakes and Hoaxes Through the Years.* Henry Holt, 2005. 96pp. ISBN 978-0-8050-7528-1. Grades 4–6. The author discusses eleven notable hoaxes. P. T. Barnum exhibited a mermaid in his circus during the 19th century. Edgar Allan Poe wrote a false newspaper article about a transatlantic balloon flight. In 1917 a "fairies in the garden" photograph fooled Sir Arthur Conan Doyle. Others include an "ether" driven motor, the Piltdown Man fossil, film footage of Bigfoot, and crop circles in England. Cartoon illustrations highlight the text. Further Reading and Web Sites.

134. Peacock, Louise. *At Ellis Island: A History in Many Voices.* Illustrated by Walter Lyon Krudop. Atheneum, 2007. 44pp. ISBN 978-0-689-83026-6. Grades 2–5. Two children visit Ellis Island, one in contemporary times who has heard stories about her great-great grandmother's arrival there and has traced her family in the immigrant museum. The other, Sera, arrives in 1919 from Armenia and is almost sent back because her father arrives for her late—children are not allowed to enter the country without an adult. Sera's story is told through her letters. She writes to her mother describing the Statue of Liberty and the overwhelming baggage hall packed with foreigners. Her letters reveal that her mother was massacred. Illustrations highlight the text.

135. Peterson, Cris. *Birchbark Brigade: A Fur Trade History.* Calkins Creek, 2009. 135pp. ISBN 978-1-59078-426-6. Grades 5–9. In eleven chapters, this volume shows how important fur trading was to the European development of the American continent as beaver trappers traversed the Great Lakes area in birchbark canoes in search of a Northwest Passage. These traders met and contributed to conflicts over land and between Native Americans and hunters. When beaver hats went out of fashion in the 19th century so did the value of fur trading. Primary sources include archival illustrations and quotes from those involved. Drawings, maps, documents, and photographs enhance the text. Chronology, Notes, Bibliography, Further Reading, Places to Visit, Web Sites, and Index.

136. Pfeffer, Wendy. *The Shortest Day: Celebrating the Winter Solstice.* Illustrated by Jesse Reisch. Dutton, 2003. 40pp. ISBN 978-0-525-46968-1. Grades 2–5. A look at how humans have reacted to the sun and how they have worshiped through the centuries. Ancient Egyptian, Chinese, Inca, and European astronomers measured the sun's movements in an attempt to understand why the days became shorter during the winter. Among the winter symbols that have endured through the centuries are evergreen wreaths and tree decorations. Illustrations highlight the text. Further Reading and Web Sites.

137. Phelan, Glen. *Double Helix: The Quest to Uncover the Structure of DNA.* (Science Quest) National Geographic, 2006. 59pp. ISBN 978-0-7922-5541-3. Grades 5–8. Phelan tells the story of the discovery of DNA. Francis Crick and James Watson might not have succeeded without the work of scientists including Gregor Mendel and Rosalind Franklin. The contributions of Linus Pauling and Maurice Wilkins should also be acknowledged. Photographs and illustrations highlight the text. Glossary, Web Sites, and Index.

138. **Philip, Neil.** *The Great Circle: A History of the First Nations.* Clarion, 2006. 153pp. ISBN 978-0-618-15941-3. Grades 4–8. This history of the Native American nations from pre-Columbian times to the present offers information about land, society, religion, science, and history. Philip suggests that the major reason for the white-Native American conflict has been the differences in their world views. Native Americans see life as a sacred circle while whites view it as linear. Photographs and illustrations complement the text. Bibliography, Notes, and Index. *Booklist Editor's Choice* and *Capitol Choices Noteworthy Titles* (Washington, D.C.).

139. **Raum, Elizabeth.** *The History of the Camera.* (Inventions That Changed the World) Raintree, 2007. 32pp. ISBN 978-1-4034-9647-8; paper ISBN 978-1-4034-9653-9. Grades 2–3. Twelve chapters give a history of the camera from the earliest invention through digital cameras and medical uses today. Illustrations augment the text. Chronology, Glossary, and Index.

140. **Raum, Elizabeth.** *The History of the Car.* (Inventions That Changed the World) Raintree, 2007. 32pp. ISBN 978-1-4034-9647-8; paper ISBN 978-1-4034-9654-6. Grades 2–3. Twelve chapters give a history of the automobile from the earliest steam cars onward, looking at car sizes, types of fuel, safety measures, and the ways in which cars changed daily life, travel, and work habits. Illustrations enhance the text. Chronology, Glossary, and Index.

141. **Raum, Elizabeth.** *The History of the Computer.* (Inventions That Changed the World) Raintree, 2007. 32pp. ISBN 978-1-4034-9649-2; paper ISBN 978-1-4034-9657-7. Grades 2–3. Twelve chapters give a history of the computer from its earliest appearance through its influence on and necessity in daily life today. Illustrations highlight the text. Chronology, Glossary, and Index.

142. **Raum, Elizabeth.** *The History of the Telephone.* (Inventions That Changed the World) Raintree, 2007. 32pp. ISBN 978-1-4034-9650-8. Grades 2–3. From the earliest handset to today's cell phones, this is an overview of the evolution of technology (including telephone books, answering services, and so forth) and of the influence of this device on modern life. Illustrations highlight the text. Map, Chronology, Glossary, and Index.

143. **Reef, Catherine.** *Alone in the World: Orphans and Orphanages in America.* Clarion, 2005. 144pp. ISBN 978-0-618-35670-6. Grades 5–9. Readers will learn about the history of American orphanages since the first one opened in New Orleans in 1729. In the 18th and 19th centuries, the children who lived in these places were either poor, abandoned, or orphaned, and the orphanages had no government oversight or regulation. Children's advocates have tried to correct some of the horrible treatment that some of the children received—from indentured servitude to special schools—but the history is disturbing. Photographs and reproductions highlight the text. Bibliography, Notes, and Index.

144. **Rinard, Judith E.** *The Book of Flight: The Smithsonian National Air and Space Museum.* Firefly, 2007. 128pp. ISBN 978-1-55407-292-7; paper ISBN 978-1-55407-275-0. Grades 4–8. This guide to flight documents key milestones and profiles important men and women who are part of its history. Two-page spreads cover topics from balloons to powered flights to space exploration. Illustrations and photographs augment the text. Chronology and Glossary.

145. **Robinson, James.** *Inventions.* Kingfisher, 2006. 64pp. ISBN 978-0-7534-5973-7. Grades 3–7. Brief overviews present inventions that have served as a foundation for the modern age. Among them are surgical robots, cell phones, information technology, space travel, photography, genetic engineering, medicine, and nanotechnology. The two-page summary of computers mentions the first computer of Charles Babbage (1792–1871), shifts to the British electronic digital computer in 1943, and suggests that quantum computers will be much faster than anything imaginable today. Illustrations highlight the text. Glossary, Web Sites, and Index.

146. **Ross, Stewart.** *Conquerors and Explorers.* Stargazer, 2008. 48pp. ISBN 978-1-59604-195-0. Grades 4–6. Many illustrations complement historical information about explorers and conquerors from the Greek period through the age of space exploration. Index.

147. Rowland-Warne, L. *Costume.* DK, 2000. 63pp. ISBN 978-0-7894-5586-4. Grades 4–6. The author covers all aspects of clothes from shoes to hats. The illustrations and photographs give a good sense of dress in the 18th through 20th centuries, although references to prehistory, Roman times, and the Viking era are also included. Index.

148. Ruffin, Frances E. *St. Augustine.* (Places in American History) Gareth Stevens, 2006. 24pp. ISBN 978-0-8368-6412-0. Grades K–2. Early Spanish settlers founded St. Augustine, Florida, the first city in North America. Each double-spread covers a single topic. Maps and illustrations augment the text. Bibliography, Glossary, and Index.

149. St. George, Judith. *In the Line of Fire: Presidents' Lives at Stake.* Holiday House, 1999. 144pp. ISBN 978-0-8234-1428-4. Grades 5 up. St. George looks at the four presidential assassinations—of Lincoln, Garfield, McKinley, and Kennedy—and at the politics of the time and why the attackers decided to act. A final chapter discusses assassinations that failed, including those of Jackson, Reagan, and Ford. Bibliography and Index. *American Library Association Best Books for Young Adults.*

150. St. George, Judith. *So You Want to Be President?* Illustrated by David Small. Philomel, 2004. 52pp. ISBN 978-0-399-24317-2; 2008, paper ISBN 978-0-399-25152-8. Grades 4–8. St. George provides various basic facts of interest (such as the minimum qualifications for the position) and explains the good points of being president—a large house and personal bowling alley—and the bad points, mainly lots of homework. Anecdotes about presidents give a sense of who has lived in that big house and done all the homework. Illustrations highlight the text. *Caldecott Medal, Dorothy Canfield Fisher Children's Book Award* (Vermont) nomination, *Bluegrass Award* (Kentucky) nomination, *Young Readers Choice Awards* (Louisiana), *Garden State Teen Book Award* (New Jersey) nomination, *Buckeye Children's Book Awards* (Ohio), *Young Reader's Choice Award* (Pennsylvania) nomination, *Prairie Pasque Award* (South Dakota) nomination, *Volunteer State Book Award* (Tennessee) nomination, *Capitol Choices Noteworthy Titles* (Washington, D.C.), *School Library Journal Best Books for Children, Bulletin Blue Ribbon*, and *Bluebonnet Award* (Texas) nomination.

151. Samuels, Charlie. *America: The Making of a Nation.* Little, Brown, 2008. Unpaged. ISBN 978-0-316-03170-7. Grades 3–7. A fictional journalist looks at his collection of "memorabilia" that symbolize America to him. He has a copy of the Declaration of Independence, a flag, a Statue of Liberty, as well as items representing African Americans, Latinos, Native Americans, women, scientists, and others. The book contains flaps, pull-outs, and other devices. Watercolor illustrations complement the text.

152. Sandler, Martin W. *America Through the Lens: Photographers Who Changed the Nation.* Henry Holt, 2005. 192pp. ISBN 978-0-8050-7367-6. Grades 5 up. This volume looks at the work of twelve photographers who helped people see things in new ways and who revealed perhaps hidden aspects of American life. The photographers include Mathew B. Brady (1822–1896), Jacob Riis (1849–1914), Lewis Hine (1874–1940), Edward S. Curtis (1868–1952), James Van Der Zee (1886–1983), Dorothea Lange (1895–1965), and Margaret Bourke-White (1904–1971). Further Reading and Index.

153. Sandler, Martin W. *On the Waters of the USA: Ships and Boats in American Life.* (Transportation in America) Oxford, 2003. 64pp. ISBN 978-0-19-513227-4. Grades 5–8. Ships and boats of all kinds have moved through U.S. waters since the birch bark canoe. Sandler presents the history of American water transport and discusses vessels including canoes, clippers, schooners, sloops, whalers, flatboats, steamboats, hydrofoils, and submersibles. These have contributed to commerce and travel and have taken Americans to new areas. Photographs augment the text. Chronology, Further Reading, Web Sites, and Index.

154. Sayre, Henry. *Cave Paintings to Picasso: The Inside Scoop on 50 Art Masterpieces.* Chronicle, 2004. 93pp. ISBN 978-0-8118-3767-5. Grades 5–10. Sayre covers fifty works of art beginning with the 24,000-year-old Woman from Brassempouy to Magritte's *Son of Man* from 1964. Among the other works covered are the Bayeux Tapestry, Michelangelo's *David*, a Mogul miniature, Easter Island heads, a Moche pitcher, a Mandan hide robe, Chinese paintings, works by Picasso, and Andy Warhol's Campbell Soup Can paintings. Photographs of each piece are included with background on the artist along with its social and historical context. Chronology and Index. *Capitol Choices Noteworthy Titles* (Washington, D.C.).

155. Scandiffio, Laura. *Escapes.* Illustrated by Stephen MacEachern. (True Stories from the Edge) Annick, 2003. 170pp. ISBN 978-1-55037-823-8. Grades 5–9. Among the famous getaways reported here are that of slaves William and Ellen Craft, who pretended to be mistress and servant to escape from slavery in 1848, and the story of six Americans disguised as Canadians who escaped from Iran in 1979. Notes and Index.

156. Schroeder, Andreas. *Thieves!* (True Stories from the Edge) Annick, 2005. 164pp. ISBN 978-1-55037-932-7; paper ISBN 978-1-55037-932-7. Grades 5–9. Schroeder looks at ten crimes involving robberies, thefts, or failed heists. Dan Cooper parachuted from an airplane at night with $200,000 of extorted cash. A small group of Italians removed the *Mona Lisa* from the Louvre. Willie Sutton, well-known American bank robber, attracted many copycats who admired his technique. Others include the "Great Train Robbery," the "Purolator Caper," and the "Classiest Thief in Manhattan." Illustrations highlight the text. Bibliography and Index.

157. Shapiro, Stephen. *Battle Stations! Fortifications Through the Ages.* Illustrated by Mei Tsao and Ken Nice. Annick, 2005. 32pp. ISBN 978-1-55037-889-4; paper ISBN 978-1-55037-888-7. Grades 5–8. Early 20th-century American port defenses are among the fortifications discussed in this volume that covers everything from ancient Egypt to 18th-century Europe to the Cold War. Illustrations complement the text.

158. Sills, Leslie. *From Rags to Riches: A History of Girls' Clothing in America.* Holiday House, 2005. 48pp. ISBN 978-0-8234-1708-7; 2006, paper ISBN 978-0-8234-2048-3. Grades 3–8. Fashion has reflected society's changing views about children, and this book shows how clothes for girls have evolved since the 17th century. Photographs and illustrations highlight the text. Bibliography, Glossary, Web Sites, and Index.

159. Skurzynski, Gloria. *Sweat and Blood: A History of U.S. Labor Unions.* (People's History) Twenty-first Century, 2008. 112pp. ISBN 978-0-8225-7594-8. Grades 5 up. The concept of unions was alive in colonial times when the first strike (work stoppage) occurred in Jamestown, Virginia. John Smith denied Polish craftsmen the right to vote in 1619, and they refused to work until given that right. Two union organizations, the AFL (American Federation of Labor) and the CIO (Congress of Industrial Organizations), rose to help workers, and those against union rights often associated them with socialism or communism. Eventually the AFL and CIO united in their support of workers. Unions have changed focus somewhat, but they have been an important force in protecting workers from greedy business owners. Period photographs and prints enhance the text. Glossary, Notes, Bibliography, Further Resources, Web Sites, and Index. *Notable Social Studies Trade Books for Young People.*

160. Smith, Rich. *The Bill of Rights: Defining Our Freedoms.* (Bill of Rights) ABDO, 2008. 32pp. ISBN 978-1-59928-913-7. Grades 4–6. The author discusses the Bill of Rights and what it means, providing facts, questions, and court cases that offer an interpretation of this national document. Photographs appear on each double-spread. Glossary and Index.

161. Smith, Rich. *First Amendment: The Right of Expression.* (Bill of Rights) ABDO, 2008. 32pp. ISBN 978-1-59928-914-4. Grades 4–6. Smith discusses the First Amendment and what it means to the Constitution, with facts, questions, and court cases that interpret this amendment. Photographs appear on each double-spread. Glossary and Index.

162. Smith, Rich. *Second and Third Amendments: The Right to Security.* (Bill of Rights) ABDO, 2008. 32pp. ISBN 978-1-59928-915-1. Grades 4–6. The text discusses the Second and Third Amendments and what they mean to the Constitution. It includes facts, questions, and court cases that offer an interpretation of the two amendments. Photographs appear on each double-spread. Glossary and Index.

163. Somervill, Barbara A. *The History of the Computer.* (Our Changing World—The Timeline Library) Child's World, 2006. 32pp. ISBN 978-1-59296-437-6. Grades 3–7. Somervill looks at the history of the computer, beginning with the Chinese abacus, and progressing through slide rules, and Pascal's mechanical calculator of the 1600s. In the 20th century, ENIAC led to microcomputers and nursebots. It also reveals some of the ways in which computers have become part of our lives. Photographs and illustrations illuminate the text. Bibliography, Chronology, Glossary, and Index.

164. Somervill, Barbara A. *The History of the Library.* (Our Changing World—The Timeline Library) Child's World, 2006. 32pp. ISBN 978-1-59296-438-3. Grades 3–7. The text follows the history of the library from Ptolemy's library at Alexandria to Washington's Library of Congress to the World Wide Web. The ancient Egyptians used papyrus, but later people learned to make paper. The most important step allowing libraries to flourish was Gutenberg's invention of the printing press. Photographs and illustrations illuminate the text. Bibliography, Chronology, Glossary, and Index.

165. Somervill, Barbara A. *The History of the Motion Picture.* (Our Changing World—The Timeline Library) Child's World, 2006. 32pp. ISBN 978-1-59296-440-6. Grades 3–7. The author examines the history of the motion picture by tracing the technological developments that have made it possible. In 1420 a "magic lantern" allowed light to shine and make unusual shadows. Puppets have also been a popular method of conveying stories with movement. However, motion pictures did not show their potential until the 20th century. Photographs and illustrations enhance the text. Bibliography, Chronology, Glossary, and Index.

166. Staton, Hilarie. *The Progressive Party: The Success of a Failed Party.* (Snapshots in History) Compass Point, 2007. 96pp. ISBN 978-0-7565-2451-7. Grades 5–8. This volume presents the history of the Progressive Party, which Theodore Roosevelt founded in 1912. It covers key figures, conventions, platforms, and organization, often using primary sources. Sidebars add other facts of interest. Maps, photographs and reproductions accompany the text. Bibliography, Glossary, Chronology, Notes, Further Reading, Web Sites, and Index.

167. Steele, Philip. *Vote.* (Eyewitness) DK, 2008. 72pp. ISBN 978-0-7566-3382-0. Grades 4–8. A history of voting from ancient times to the present, discussing why people vote, voting's democratic beginnings, the first parliaments, revolution in North America and France, slaves' and women's voting aspirations, and modern struggles for a say in politics. Other chapters describe American elections and what being disenfranchised means. Chronology, Glossary, and Index.

168. Steins, Richard. *Our Elections.* Millbrook, 1994. 48pp. ISBN 978-1-56294-446-9. Grades 2–6. Steins believes that four presidential elections shaped the history of the United States: the election of 1800, when Thomas Jefferson won; the election of 1860, when Abraham Lincoln won; the election of 1920, when women began to vote; and the election of 1932, when Franklin Delano Roosevelt became president during the Great Depression. Steins explains the democratic process, campaigns and elections, the two-party system, and how a president can be elected. Chronology, Further Reading, and Index.

169. Stern, Gary M. *The Congress: America's Lawmakers.* Steck-Vaughn, 1992. 48pp. Paper ISBN 978-0-8114-5579-4. Grades 3–6. Stern gives the history of Congress; the requirements to become members of Congress; how Congress works with its committees, filibusters, and cloture rules; and some of its decisions. Among the most notable acts are the Missouri Compromise of 1820, the Civil Rights Bill of 1964, the Watergate hearings in 1973, the Bork hearings for the Supreme Court in 1987, and those for Clarence Thomas in 1991. Photographs and drawings highlight the text. Further Reading, Glossary, and Index.

170. Stewart, Mark, and Mike Kennedy. *Long Ball: The Legend and Lore of the Home Run.* Millbrook, 2006. 64pp. ISBN 978-0-7613-2779-0. Grades 4–8. During the early days of baseball, home runs were discouraged. Babe Ruth "ruined" baseball, according to Ty Cobb, when Ruth tried to hit them. This volume profiles the most famous home run hitters including Gehrig, Williams, Jackson, Sosa, and McGwire. It also chooses the ten most famous home runs in history and provides information about the hitter and the pitcher as well as the hit itself. A final chapter addresses steroid use.

171. **Sullivan, George.** *Built to Last: Building America's Amazing Bridges, Dams, Tunnels, and Skyscrapers.* Scholastic, 2005. 128pp. ISBN 978-0-439-51737-9. Grades 4–7. For more than two hundred years, Americans have built structures to improve their lives. The text looks at the construction, location, cost, and project duration of seventeen architectural and engineering feats. They include the Transcontinental Railroad, Erie Canal, Brooklyn Bridge, Empire State Building, Hoover Dam, Golden Gate Bridge, Jefferson National Expansion Memorial Arch, Cascade Tunnel, Hoosac Tunnel, Fort Peck Dam, Sears Tower, Chesapeake Bay Bridge-Tunnel, Boston's "Big Dig," and City Tunnel No. 3 in New York, scheduled to be finished in 2020. Illustrations augment the text. Bibliography and Index. *Garden State Children's Book Award* (New Jersey) nomination, *James Madison Book Award Honor Book*, *Voice of Youth Advocates Nonfiction Honor List*, and *Jefferson Cup* nomination.

172. **Sullivan, George.** *Journalists at Risk: Reporting America's Wars.* (People's History) Twenty-First Century, 2005. 128pp. ISBN 978-0-7613-2745-5. Grades 5–8. From the war with Mexico in the 1840s to the present, journalists have played a large part in America's wars. The author examines their roles, sometimes as shapers of the conflicts and sometimes as the reporters who scramble for any information available. Among the twenty-three presented are George Kendall in the Mexican War, Marguerite Higgins, Edward R. Murrow, Ernie Pyle, Walter Cronkite, and David Bloom in Iraq. Photographs augment the text. Bibliography, Further Reading, Web Sites, and Index.

173. **Swain, Ruth Freeman.** *How Sweet It Is (And Was): The History of Candy.* Holiday House, 2003. 32pp. ISBN 978-0-8234-1712-4. Grades 2–5. The author looks at popular candies and how they became connected to particular holidays—candy corn and Halloween, chocolate hearts for Valentine's Day, and so forth. Swain covers Egyptian candy, Columbus's transportation of sugar cane seedlings to the Americas, Elizabethan sweetmeats, maple sugaring, South American chocolate production, and modern Denmark, where each Dane consumes thirty-six pounds of sweets a year (Americans typically eat twenty-five pounds). Recipes for sugar paste, Vassar fudge, and belly-guts taffy are included. Cross-hatched illustrations enhance the text. Bibliography and Chronology.

174. **Swain, Ruth Freeman.** *Underwear: What We Wear Under There.* Holiday House, 2008. 32pp. ISBN 978-0-8234-1920-3. Grades 2–5. This chronological history of underwear begins with ancient breechcloths and continues to modern disposable diapers. It also includes information about future fabrics. Throughout, illustrations enhance the discussion of each noted item. Cartoon illustrations complement the text. Bibliography and Chronology.

175. **Swanson, June.** *I Pledge Allegiance.* Illustrated by Rick Hanson. First Avenue, 2002. 39pp. Paper ISBN 978-0-8761-4912-6. Grades 2–4. On the 400th birthday of Columbus's arrival in 1892, Francis Bellamy wrote the Pledge of Allegiance to the flag of the United States. In the 20th century, various minor changes occurred before it received legal sanction in 1942. The text defines the words to the pledge and discusses the controversy that often surrounds it. One year after legalization, the Supreme Court ruled that no one could make other people say the pledge against their will.

176. **Talbott, Hudson.** *River of Dreams: The Story of the Hudson River.* Putnam, 2009. 40pp. ISBN 978-0-399-24521-3. Grades 4–7. The author views the Hudson River as a place of dreams. In this volume he traces its history from the Ice Ages. The Hudson transported Native Americans and early European settlers. It played a role in the Revolutionary War and served as a waterway for both sailboats and steamships. When railroads overtook shipping in importance, the river declined in importance and became polluted. Artists and writers have celebrated the river, and recently conservationists have made major strides in restoring it to its natural state. Watercolor, ink, and colored pencil illustrations enhance the text. Notes, Further Reading, and Web Sites. *American Library Association Notable Children's Books.*

177. **Thomas, Keltie.** *How Baseball Works.* Narrated by Greg Hall. Maple Tree, 2008. 64pp. ISBN 978-1-8973-4920-5; paper ISBN 978-1-8973-4921-2. Grades 3–6. Thomas covers the game's rules, historical background, stars, stadiums, statistics, physics, strategies, and legendary stories about well-known players. Illustrations complement the text.

178. Townsend, John. *Breakouts and Blunders.* (True Crime) Raintree, 2005. 48pp. ISBN 978-1-4109-1427-9; 2006, paper ISBN 978-1-4109-1433-0. Grades 5–9. Using a scrapbook format, the author looks at successful and unsuccessful prison escapes throughout history. Illustrations and photographs augment the text. Bibliography, Glossary, Further Reading, and Index.

179. Townsend, John. *Kidnappers and Assassins.* (True Crime) Raintree, 2005. 48pp. ISBN 978-1-4109-1426-2; paper ISBN 978-1-4109-1432-3. Grades 5–9. Townsend discusses assassinations and kidnappings throughout history. Among those included as victims of kidnapping are Patty Hearst, John Paul Getty III, and Elizabeth Smart. In the assassination section are four United States presidents, Martin Luther King Jr., Malcolm X, and Robert Kennedy. Illustrations and photographs enhance the text. Bibliography, Glossary, Further Reading, and Index.

180. Turner, Ann. *Shaker Hearts.* Illustrated by Wendell Minor. David R. Godine, 2002. Unpaged. Paper ISBN 978-1-56792-231-8. Grades K–3. Using Mother Ann Lee's phrase "hands to work; hearts to God," Turner takes a poetical look at the Shaker community, one of the most successful Utopian communities in America. The verses, which describe the daily activities, almost serve as short prayers and are accompanied by illustrations revealing the life and the landscape of the Shaker people. An appendix discusses their contributions to society.

181. Vieira, Linda. *The Mighty Mississippi: The Life and Times of America's Greatest River.* Illustrated by Higgins Bond. Walker, 2005. 32pp. ISBN 978-0-8027-8943-3. Grades 2–6. With a helpful timeline, this volume tells the history of the river and events that have happened either in or on the river. These include development of Native American civilizations, European exploration, the Revolutionary War, an earthquake, the Trail of Tears, the Mormon exodus, the Civil War, the flood of 1927, and Hurricane Camille in 1969. Acrylic illustrations complement the text. Glossary.

182. Wagner, Heather Lehr. *How the President Is Elected.* (U.S. Government: How It Works) Chelsea House, 2007. 95pp. ISBN 978-0-7910-9418-1. Grades 5–8. The author examines the process of electing the president of the United States. Using the 2000 Gore vs. Bush contest as a springboard, the text provides an explanation of how the electoral college can affect the popular vote. Other topics covered include the qualifications that one needs to become a candidate for president. Photographs and illustrations highlight the text. Bibliography, Glossary, Further Reading, Web Sites, and Index.

183. Weatherford, Carole Boston. *A Negro League Scrapbook.* Boyds Mills, 2005. 48pp. ISBN 978-1-59078-091-6. Grades 3–6. In scrapbook form with verse, facts, and archival photographs, the text offers a history of the Negro Leagues beginning in 1887 and of the great players—those who received recognition for their talents and those who never did. They include Josh Gibson, Satchel Paige, James Bell, Jackie Robinson, Buck Leonard, and the three women who joined in the 1950s. Illustrations complement the text. Index.

184. Whitman, Sylvia. *Get Up and Go: The History of American Road Travel.* Lerner, 1996. 88pp. ISBN 978-0-8225-1735-1. Grades 5–9. Americans have always traveled, and Whitman looks at their history from Native Americans to the present. She covers the development of superhighways from early paths through the woods; the progression of vehicles from wagons to steam engines; and from bicycles to cars and trucks. Historic photographs augment the text. Selected Bibliography and Index.

185. Wilkinson, Philip. *Building.* Illustrated by Dave King and Geoff Dann. DK, 2000. 61pp. ISBN 978-0-7894-6026-4. Grades 4 up. Photographs and drawings give clear pictures of the various aspects of building. Topics covered in two-page spreads are structural engineering, house construction, and building materials. These include wood, earth, bricks, stone, timber frames, thatching, columns and arches, vaults, staircases, fireplaces and chimneys, doors and doorways, windows, stained glass, balconies, and building on unusual topography. Index.

186. Winner, Cherie. *Circulating Life: Blood Transfusion from Ancient Superstition to Modern Medicine.* Twenty-First Century, 2007. 112pp. ISBN 978-0-8225-6606-9. Grades 5–9. This text covers the history of our understanding of blood and circulation and looks at the advances that came with blood transfusions and blood typing. In addition, it discusses the development of artificial blood cells and "bionic" blood. Photographs and illustrations highlight the text. Bibliography, Glossary, Further Reading, Web Sites, and Index.

187. Woods, Michael. *The History of Communications.* (Major Inventions Through History) Twenty-First Century, 2005. 56pp. ISBN 978-0-8225-3807-3. Grades 5–8. Inventions such as the printing press, telephone, radio, television, and the Internet have influenced how people communicate and how information is conveyed. Photographs and illustrations highlight the text. Bibliography, Glossary, Chronology, Notes, Further Reading, Web Sites, and Index.

188. Woods, Michael, and Mary B. Woods. *The History of Medicine.* (Major Inventions Through History) Twenty-First Century, 2005. 56pp. ISBN 978-0-8225-2636-0. Grades 5–8. The author examines the history of medicine from early times through the development of anesthetics, vaccines, antibiotics, X-rays, and artificial limbs. Photographs and illustrations highlight the text. Bibliography, Glossary, Chronology, Further Reading, Web Sites, and Index.

189. Woolf, Alex. *Democracy.* (Systems of Government) World Almanac, 2006. 48pp. ISBN 978-0-8368-5883-9. Grades 4–6. The text examines the history of democracy by detailing what it is, how it works, and its problems and challenges. Photographs and illustrations augment the text. Bibliography and Index.

190. Yanuck, Debbie L. *Uncle Sam.* (First Facts) Capstone, 2003. 24pp. ISBN 978-0-7368-2295-4. Grades K–2. One of America's famous symbols is Uncle Sam, initially posed by Samuel Wilson as a representation of the American government. Uncle Sam has appeared in cartoons, on posters such as the "I Want You" campaign of World War II, and in various other forms and places. Photographs and illustrations augment the text. Further Reading, Timeline, Glossary, Web Sites, and Index.

191. Zimmerman, Karl. *Steam Boats: The Story of Lakers, Ferries, and Majestic Paddle-Wheelers.* Boyds Mills, 2007. 48pp. ISBN 978-1-5907-8434-1. Grades 4–8. Zimmerman looks at the history and mechanics of steam-powered boats from paddle boats for leisure to "workhorse" ferries and bulk carriers. Steamers also crossed the Atlantic, and the text includes details about these ships. Boxed sections provide biographical profiles and interesting features. Photographs enhance the text. Glossary, Web Sites, and Index.

Biography and Collective Biography

192. Aaseng, Nathan. *Business Builders in Broadcasting.* Oliver, 2005. 160pp. ISBN 978-1-8815-0883-0. Grades 5 up. This collective biography contains the history of American radio and television and profiles individuals including Samuel Morse, Guglielmo Marconi, and Frank Conrad as well as Ted Turner of CNN, Rupert Murdoch and his News Corporation (parent of Fox TV), Judy McGrath as head of MTV, David Sarnoff as founder of NBC, William Paley of CBS, Gerald Levin of HBO, and Catherine Hughes of the Radio One Empire. Photographs and illustrations complement the text. Bibliography, Glossary, Chronology, Notes, and Index.

193. Aaseng, Nathan. *Business Builders in Cosmetics.* Oliver, 2003. 160pp. ISBN 978-1-8815-0882-3. Grades 5–8. This collective biography looks at successful individuals in the cosmetics trade: Helena Rubinstein, Elizabeth Arden, Max Factor, David Hall McConnell (Avon), Charles Revson (Revlon), Estée Lauder, and Anita Roddick (The Body Shop). Photographs and illustrations highlight the text. Bibliography, Glossary, Chronology, Notes, and Index.

194. Aaseng, Nathan. *Business Builders in Fashion.* Oliver, 2003. 160pp. ISBN 978-1-8815-0880-9. Grades 5–8. This collective biography looks at historical highlights of clothing since medieval times and profiles individuals who have made their names in fashion in Europe and America: Charles Frederick Worth, Levi Strauss, Coco Chanel, Christian Dior, Mary Quant, Ralph Lauren, and Vera Wang. Photographs and illustrations highlight the text. Bibliography, Glossary, Chronology, Notes, and Index.

195. **Aaseng, Nathan.** *Business Builders in Oil.* Oliver, 2005. 160pp. ISBN 978-1-8815-0883-0. Grades 5 up. With an introduction to the oil industry and how it has developed, this collective biography includes information about those who have overseen this major feature of society today. Those profiled are Standard Oil founder John D. Rockefeller; Marcus Samuel of Royal Dutch/Shell; Pattillo Higgins and Andrew Mellon of Gulf; William Knox D'Arcy and Frank Phillips of Phillips Petroleum; J. Paul Getty of Getty Oil; and Robert O. Anderson of ARCO. Photographs and illustrations augment the text. Bibliography, Glossary, Chronology, Notes, and Index.

196. **Aaseng, Nathan.** *Business Builders in Real Estate.* Oliver, 2002. 160pp. ISBN 978-1-8815-0879-3. Grades 5 up. Real estate tycoons can make and lose money rapidly, and this volume profiles individuals who have probably both earned and lost millions of dollars through their real estate dealings. Those included are John Nicholson, who helped develop the capital city of Washington, D.C.; John Jacob Astor, who foresaw the growth of Manhattan; William Levitt, who founded Levittown and the movement toward suburban living; Del Webb, who created the first "active life" retirement community; Walt Disney, who orchestrated one of the biggest real estate deals of the 20th century for Disney World; Paul Reichmann, the star investor of the Olympia & York company; and the Ghermezian brothers, who have developed megamall complexes including the Mall of America. Photographs and illustrations highlight the text. Bibliography, Glossary, Chronology, Notes, and Index.

197. **Aaseng, Nathan.** *Business Builders in Sweets and Treats.* Oliver, 2005. 160pp. ISBN 978-1-8815-0884-7. Grades 5–8. Food remains an industry that continually responds to new ideas and tastes. Aaseng looks at the history of different aspects of this market and the people who have developed it. Those included are Hershey and his chocolate; Wrigley and chewing gum; Ellen Gordon's marketing skills for Tootsie Roll; recipes for Krispy Kreme donuts; Forrest Mars and his candy company; and Wally Amos of Famous Amos cookies. Photographs and illustrations highlight the text. Bibliography, Glossary, Chronology, Notes, and Index.

198. **Aaseng, Nathan.** *Business Builders in Toys and Games.* Oliver, 2003. 160pp. ISBN 978-1-8815-0881-6. Grades 5–8. People need ways to spend their leisure time other than watching television. Some companies developed games before the advent of TV, and others have flourished in recent decades. This book looks at the history of games and then gives profiles of those who have successfully created, marketed, and sold them. Those included are Milton Bradley and his board games, Hiroshi Yamauchi and Nintendo, Albert Spaulding's sporting goods, Joshua Lionel Cowen and Lionel trains, Ruth Handler's Barbie doll and Mattel Corporation, Ole Kirk Christiansen's Legos, and Gary Gygax's Dungeons and Dragons. Photographs and illustrations highlight the text. Bibliography, Glossary, Chronology, Notes, and Index.

199. **Aaseng, Nathan.** *Treacherous Traitors.* Oliver, 1997. 160pp. ISBN 978-1-8815-0838-0. Grades 5–8. This collective biography profiles twelve people in American history who have been accused of betraying the United States. It includes background about the accusations and what the people did to pass secrets to other countries. They include Benedict Arnold, John Brown, Alger Hiss, Axis Sally and Tokyo Rose, Julius and Ethel Rosenberg, the John Walker family, Edward Lee Howard, and Aldrich Ames. Photographs enliven the text. Bibliography and Index.

200. **Aaseng, Nathan.** *You Are the Explorer.* Oliver, 1999. 160pp. ISBN 978-1-8815-0855-7. Grades 4–8. The focus of this collective biography is on decisions that explorers have had to face. Those featured are Christopher Columbus, Vasco da Gama, Ferdinand Magellan, Hernán Cortés, Samuel de Champlain, Robert Scott, James Cook, and Meriwether Lewis. Each had to choose the best route to take in his travels based on what he wanted to achieve and what he knew. Some choices were disastrous while others worked. Readers can choose an option and see where it might have led. Photographs accompany the text. Bibliography, Notes, and Index.

201. Armstrong, Mabel. *Women Astronomers: Reaching for the Stars.* Stone Pine, 2008. 288pp. ISBN 978-0-9728929-5-7. Grades 5–7. Armstrong presents, in chronological order of birth, women who have made significant contributions to astronomy beginning with EnHeduanna, the chief astronomer priestess who lived around 2350 B.C.E. Others are Hypatia of Alexandria, Hildegard of Bingen, Caroline Herschel, Maria Mitchell, Williamina Stevens Fleming, Annie Jump Cannon, Henrietta Swan Leavitt, Antonia Caetano Maury, Cecilia Payne-Gaposchkin, Helen Sawyer Hogg, Margaret Burbidge, Nancy Roman, Vera Rubin, Beatrice Tinsley, Jocelyn Bell Burnell, Margaret Geller, Carolyn Shoemaker, Sally Ride, Jill Tarter, and Wendy Freedman. They had to overcome many obstacles and are role models for younger women. Photographs highlight the text. Bibliography, Glossary, and Index.

202. Atkins, Jeannine. *How High Can We Climb: The Story of Women Explorers.* Farrar, 2005. 209pp. ISBN 978-0-374-33503-8. Grades 5–8. This collective biography looks at women explorers who have overcome hardships to reach their goals. Those included are Jeanne Baret (sailed around the world disguised as a boy), Florence Baker (searched for the source of the Nile), Annie Smith Peck (mountain climber), Josephine Peary (dangerous territory of the North Pole), Arnarulunguaq (traced ancient Inuit stories), Elisabeth Casteret (spelunker), Nicole Maxwell (rain forest), Sylvia Earle (record deep sea dive), Junko Tabei (Mt. Everest), Kay Cottee (solo, nonstop voyage around the world in a 37-foot sloop), Sue Hendrickson (discovered bones of Tyrannosaurus Rex), and Ann Bancroft (Arctic explorer). Photographs and illustrations highlight the text. Bibliography, Chronology, Notes, and Index.

203. Ball, Heather. *Astonishing Women Artists.* (Women's Hall of Fame) Second Story, 2007. 120pp. Paper ISBN 978-1-897187-23-4. Grades 4–8. This collective biography examines the artistic achievements of ten women who used their understanding of art in a new way for their times. Those included are Artemisia Gentileschi (Italy, 1593–1651/1653), Elisabeth Louise Vigée Le Brun (France, 1755–1842), Emily Carr (Canada, 1871–1945), Georgia O'Keeffe (United States, 1887–1986), Louise Nevelson (Russia and United States, 1899–1988), Frida Kahlo (Mexico, 1907–1954), Elizabeth Catlett (United States, 1915–), Kenojuak Ashevak (Canadian Inuit, 1927–), Faith Ringgold (United States, 1930–), and Mary Pratt (Canada, 1935–). Bibliography. *Voice of Youth Advocates Nonfiction Honor List.*

204. Ball, Heather. *Magnificent Women in Music.* (Women's Hall of Fame) Second Story, 2005. 108pp. Paper ISBN 978-1-897187-02-9. Grades 4–8. This collective biography presents ten women who have made important contributions to music: Maria Anna "Nannerl" Mozart, Clara Schumann, Ethel Smyth, Marian Anderson, Ella Fitzgerald, Buffy Sainte-Marie, Joni Mitchell, k.d. lang, Chantal Kreviazuk, and Measha Brueggergosmanm. Anecdotes offer information about their lives and their accomplishments as well as the obstacles they had to overcome. Photographs complement the text.

205. Barber, James, and Amy Pastan. *Presidents and First Ladies.* DK, 2003. 96pp. Paper ISBN 978-0-7894-8453-6. Grades 4–8. Profiles of presidents and their wives are presented in chapters titled "The Young Republic," "Westward Expansion," "Civil War and Reconstruction," "A New Industrial Order," "Becoming a World Power," "Prosperity, Depression, and War," "Cold War America," and "America Today." Maps and Index.

206. Bausum, Ann. *Our Country's First Ladies.* National Geographic, 2007. 128pp. ISBN 978-1-4263-0006-6. Grades 4–8. The presidents who have served the United States have all had a hostess—wife, daughter, niece, sister, or friend—to help them entertain. Each of these women had a private life and interests, and often children. Dolley Madison rescued White House treasures when the British threatened Washington; Julia Grant served a meal consisting of twenty-nine courses. Lucy Hayes would not serve alcohol, and Rachel Jackson faced a bigamy charge. Lady Bird Johnson helped beautify highways, Hillary Clinton wanted to help children, and Laura Bush espoused libraries. Photographs and reproductions augment the text. Timeline, Further Reading, Web sites, Chronology, and Index.

207. Blackwood, Gary L. *Highwaymen.* (Unsolved History) Benchmark, 2005. 72pp. ISBN 978-0-7614-1017-1. Grades 5–8. Blackwood looks at eight 18th-century highwaymen in both Europe and the United States. They include Claude Duval, Mary Frith (Moll Cutpurse), William Nevison (Yorkshire Rogue), Dick Turpin (Butcher Highwayman), and John Thompson Hare. Photographs and reproductions highlight the text. Bibliography, Glossary, Notes, Further Reading, Web Sites, and Index.

208. Blackwood, Gary L. *Swindlers.* (Unsolved History) Benchmark, 2001. 72pp. ISBN 978-0-7614-1031-7. Grades 4–8. Swindlers seem to be present in all times and places, and this book looks at seven 19th-century cheats from Europe and the United States: Soapy Smith (American West con artist), Joseph "Yellow Kid" Weil (swindler), Al Capone, Billy the Kid, William Henry Ireland (Shakespeare play forger), Ellen Peck, and Fred Demara. Photographs and reproductions highlight the text. Bibliography, Glossary, Notes, Further Reading, Web Sites, and Index.

209. Bolden, Tonya. *Portraits of African-American Heroes.* Illustrated by Ansel Pitcairn. Dutton, 2004. 88pp. ISBN 978-0-525-47043-4; Puffin, 2005, paper ISBN 978-0-14-240473-7. Grades 3–5. The twenty essays in this collective biography cover Dizzy Gillespie (1917–1993), W. E. B. Du Bois (1868–1963), Gwendolyn Brooks (1917–2000), Judith Jamison (1943–), Charlayne Hunter-Gault (1942–), Matthew Henson (1866–1955), Joe Louis (1914–1981), Pauli Murray (1910–1985), Thurgood Marshall (1908–1993), Martin Luther King, Jr. (1929–1968), Paul Robeson (1898–1976), Ruth Simmons (1945–), Frederick Douglass (1818–1895), Malcolm X (1925–1965), and Ben Carson (1951–). Illustrations enhance the text. Notes and Further Reading.

210. Bolden, Tonya. *Wake Up Our Souls: A Celebration of Black American Artists.* HNA, 2004. 128pp. ISBN 978-0-81094-527-2. Grades 5 up. Among the thirty African American artists profiled here are sculptor Edmonia Lewis; painters Edward Mitchell Bannister, Norman Leis, Romare Bearden, Roy DeCarava, Betye Saar, and Augusta Savage; Faith Ringgold, with her fabric representation of the Harlem Renaissance; and photographer Gordon Parks. Bolden offers historical context about the works themselves and commentary about the social climate at the time they were created. Photographs and reproductions augment the text. Glossary, Notes, and Index. *NAPPA Gold Awards, Tayshas Reading List* (Texas), *Booklist Editor's Choice, Noteworthy Books for Children* nomination, and *Capitol Choices Noteworthy Titles* (Washington, D.C.).

211. Bowdish, Lynea. *With Courage: Seven Women Who Changed America.* Mondo, 2004. 48pp. Paper ISBN 978-1-59336-280-5. Grades 4–6. Bowdish discusses the contributions of seven women during the later half of the 20th century. Rachel Carson, a biologist, campaigned against the poisonous pesticide DDT and wrote her book *Silent Spring* about it. Katherine Graham took over the family business after her husband committed suicide and successfully ran the *Washington Post* and its subsidiaries until her death. Wilma Mankiller became leader of the Cherokee nation. Dolores Huerta helped Cesar Chavez organize farm workers in California. Maya Lin designed the Vietnam Memorial in Washington. Kathleen McGrath was the first female captain of a United States Navyship. And Condoleezza Rice became the first female African American secretary of state. Each had difficulties to overcome before contributing their talents to the country. Photographs enhance the text. Index.

212. Buckley, Susan, and Elspeth Leacock. *Journeys for Freedom: A New Look at America's Story.* Illustrated by Rodica Prato. Houghton, 2006. 48pp. ISBN 978-0-618-22323-7. Grades 4–8. Buckley examines twenty journeys—the first in 1631 and the last in 1988—taken to escape from slavery, recognition, or oppression. Pocahontas helped the settlers and went to London. Roger Williams came to the colonies to follow his faith. The Acadians were exiled from Nova Scotia. Deborah Sampson pretended to be a man in order to follow her beloved during the American Revolution. The Mormons went to Utah under the direction of Joseph Smith. The Nez Perce Indians wanted to escape the American army. The slaves on the *Amistad* rebelled against their horrendous conditions. César Chávez went to Sacramento, California, to start the first farm workers' union, and the "lost boys" of the Sudan needed to escape their plight. Illustrations augment the text. Maps, Notes, and Index.

213. Buckley, Susan, and Elspeth Leacock. *Kids Make History: A New Look at America's Story.* Illustrated by Randy Jones. Houghton, 2006. 48pp. ISBN 978-0-618-22329-9. Grades 4–8. Double-page spreads relate the stories of young Americans through history. They include Pocahontas, Sam Collier in James Towne, the Redcoats battling on Long Island in the American Revolution, Pony Express riders rushing across the country on horseback, Susie Baker celebrating her independence in 1863, Laura Ingalls working with her family on the farm, and young boys joining whaling expeditions. Some youths helped defend Pearl Harbor after the Japanese attack. In Birmingham, Alabama, Malcolm joins the nonviolent protests. In September 2001 Jukay Hsu and her peers volunteer at the Red Cross Center in New York. Illustrations augment the text. Maps, Notes, and Index.

214. Cheney, Lynne V. *A Is for Abigail: An Almanac of Amazing American Women.* Simon & Schuster, 2003. 48pp. ISBN 978-0-689-85819-2. Grades 2–4. Using the letters of the alphabet as a device, this collective biography presents brief profiles of women from the arrival of the Pilgrims to contemporary times. Some of the "letters" represent more than one woman; for instance, "E" discusses six educators. Cartoon illustrations complement the text. Notes. *Grand Canyon Reader Award* nomination.

215. Chin-Lee, Cynthia. *Amelia to Zora: Twenty-Six Women Who Changed the World.* Illustrated by Megan Halsey and Sean Addy. Charlesbridge, 2005. 32pp. ISBN 978-1-57091-522-2; 2008, paper ISBN 978-1-57091-523-9. Grades 3–7. This collective biography based on the alphabet profiles twenty-six women who helped change the world with their achievements: pilot Amelia Earhart (1897–1937); athletes Babe Didrikson Zaharias (1914–1956) and Kristi Yamaguchi (1971–); astronomer Cecilia Payne-Gaposchkin (1900–1980); activists Dolores Huerta (1930–), Nawal el Sadaawi (1931–) and Helen Keller (1880–1968); computer scientist Grace Hopper (1906–1992); artists Frida Kahlo (1907–1954), Maya Lin (1959–), Imogen Cunningham (1883–1976), and Quah Ah (1893–1949); first lady Eleanor Roosevelt (1884–1962); scientists Jane Goodall (1934–) and Rachel Carson (1907–1964); entertainers Lena Horne (1917–) and Oprah Winfrey (1954–); writers Ursula Le Guin (1929–), Chen Xiefen (1883–1923), Yoshiko Uchida (1922–1992), and Zora Neale Hurston (1891–1960); politicians Daw Aung San Suu Kyi (1945–), Patricia Schroeder (1940–), Wilma Mankiller (1945–), and Vijaya Lakshmi Pandit (1900–1990); and servant of the poor Mother Teresa (1910–1997). The text offers several paragraphs on each woman, focusing on a single accomplishment, and contains illustrations.

216. Colman, Penny. *Adventurous Women: Eight True Stories About Women Who Made a Difference.* Henry Holt, 2006. 186pp. ISBN 978-0-8050-7744-5. Grades 5–9. Women who have made a difference to society are the focus of this volume. They are Arctic explorer Louise Boyd, educator Mary McLeod Bethune, Civil War hospital ship transport nurse Katharine Wormeley, botanist Mary Gibson Henry, Hispanic landowner Juana Briones, industrial medicine physician Alice Hamilton, humanitarian Biddy Mason, and reporter Peggy Hull. Photographs enhance the text. Chronology, Notes, and Index.

217. Delano, Marfe Ferguson. *American Heroes.* National Geographic, 2005. 192pp. ISBN 978-0-7922-7208-3. Grades 5–8. This collective biography profiles fifty Americans who have made significant contributions to history: Pocahontas, William Penn, Anne Hutchinson, Benjamin Franklin, Thomas Paine, George Washington, Abigail Adams, George Mason, Lewis and Clark, Sacagawea, Tecumseh, John Chapman, Sojourner Truth, Harriet Tubman, Abraham Lincoln, Clara Barton, Mary Edwards Walker, Frederick Douglass, Elizabeth Cady Stanton, Susan B. Anthony, Sitting Bull, Chief Joseph, Andrew Carnegie, Queen Lili'uokalani, Alexander Graham Bell, George Washington Carver, the Wright brothers, Theodore Roosevelt, Jane Addams, Matthew Henson, W. E. B. Du Bois, Mary McLeod Bethune, Helen Keller, Alice Paul, Charles Lindbergh, Amelia Earhart, Franklin Delano Roosevelt, Albert Einstein, Eleanor Roosevelt, Margaret Mead, Rachel Carson, Thurgood Marshall, Rosa Parks, Jonas Salk, Jackie Robinson, John Glenn, Malcolm X, Martin Luther King, Jr., Roberto Clemente, Cesar Chavez, and Daniel K. Inouye. An introduction explains how these people were chosen. Bibliography and Index.

218. Drucker, Malka. *Portraits of Jewish American Heroes.* Illustrated by Elizabeth Rosen. Dutton, 2008. 96pp. ISBN 978-0-525-47771-6. Grades 3–6. This collective biography contains profiles of twenty Jewish inventors, educators, scientists, artists, and civil rights activists who helped others from the 18th to the 21st century. Those included are Haym Salomon (1740–1785), Levi Strauss (1829–1902), Emma Lazarus (1849–1887), Louis Dembitz Brandeis (1856–1941), Henrietta Szold (1860–1945), Rachel "Ray" Frank (1861–1948), Lillian Wald (1867–1940), Harry Houdini (Ehrich Weiss, 1874–1926), Albert Einstein (1879–1955), Golda Meir (1898–1978), Abraham Joshua Heschel (1907–1972), Henry Benjamin "Hank" Greenberg (1911–1986), Leonard Bernstein (1918–1990), Bella Savitsky Abzug (1920–1998), Ruth Bader Ginsberg (1933–), Gloria Steinem (1934–), Michael Schwerner (1939–1964) and Andrew Goodman (1943–1964), Steven Spielberg (1946–), Judith Arlene Resnik (1949–1986), and Daniel Pearl (1963–2002). The profiles tell about their work, the obstacles they overcame, and their backgrounds. Bibliography, Glossary, Chronology, Further Reading.

219. Fleming, Candace. *The Great and Only Barnum: The Tremendous, Stupendous Life of Showman P. T. Barnum.* Illustrated by Ray Fenwick. Schwartz & Wade, 2009. 160pp. ISBN 978-0-375-84197-2. Grades 4–8. Phineas Taylor Barnum (1810–1891), born poor in Connecticut, did not like farming and discovered early that people liked to be entertained. Nicknamed "Tale," he perpetrated his first hoax by purchasing a reputedly 161-year-old slave once owned by George Washington's father. He continued to mislead people with his Siamese twins, bearded ladies, and other human oddities in his museums and in his Barnum and Bailey's circus. This biography's eleven chapters reveal his strong faith and humanitarianism and contrasts these aspects with his alcoholism, abuse of family members, and corruption of young Tom Thumb. Engravings, period photographs, and advertising bills add interest. Notes, Bibliography, Web Sites, and Index. *American Library Association Notable Children's Books, American Library Association Best Books for Young Adults, Dorothy Canfield Fisher Children's Book Award* (Vermont) nomination, and *Capitol Choices Noteworthy Titles for Children and Teens* (Washington, D.C.).

220. Giff, Patricia Reilly. *Don't Tell the Girls: A Family Memoir.* Holiday House, 2005. 131pp. ISBN 978-0-8234-1813-8. Grades 4–9. With family stories and childhood photographs, Patricia Reilly Giff tells the reader about her family and gives details of her research into her Irish background that will interest young people doing genealogical studies.

221. Gourley, Robin. *Bring Me Some Apples and I'll Make You a Pie: A Story About Edna Lewis.* Clarion, 2009. 45pp. ISBN 978-0-618-15836-2. Grades K–3. African American Edna Lewis (1916–2006) became a chef and cookbook writer in New York at a time when minorities rarely rose to such heights. She grew up in Freetown, Virginia—founded by her grandfather, who was emancipated during the Civil War—and enjoyed fresh food there. She gathered berries and vegetables in spring and summer and apples and nuts in autumn, learning how to preserve them for the winter. She stressed the importance of fresh ingredients in food preparation as an adult. Watercolors enhance the text. Biographical Note and Recipes.

222. Govenar, Alan B. *Extraordinary Ordinary People: Five American Masters of Traditional Arts.* Candlewick, 2006. 85pp. ISBN 978-0-7636-2047-9. Grades 5–7. Govenar presents five traditional artists and their work. Allison "Tootie" Montana makes elaborate Mardi Gras costumes using beads and feathers in New Orleans. Dorothy Trumpold weaves rugs as her grandfather taught her in Amana, Iowa. Ralph W. Stanley builds boats on the Maine coast. Eva Castellanoz constructs delicate Mexican paper and wax coronas by folding them in Nyssa, Oregon. And Qi Shu Fang sings Chinese opera in New York City as she learned it in Beijing. Illustrations augment the text. Bibliography.

223. Harness, Cheryl. *Rabble Rousers: 20 Women Who Made a Difference.* Penguin, 2003. 64pp. ISBN 978-0-525-47035-9. Grades 2–5. Among those who spoke out against injustice and social wrongs in the United States are the women discussed here: Anne Lee (mother of the Shakers), Frances Wright (advocated education for slaves and women's rights), Emma Harl Willard (equal opportunity in education advocate), Mary Ann Shadd Cary (abolitionist activist), Elizabeth Cady Stanton (abolitionist and suffragist), Sojourner Truth (abolitionist and preacher), Dr. Mary Edwards Walker (Civil War physician who won the Medal of Honor),

Mary E. Lease (populist of Kansas), Jane Addams (social worker), Margaret Sanger (birth control advocate), Frances E. Willard (temperance activist), Ida B. Wells-Barnett (anti-lynching campaigner), Mary Harris "Mother" Jones (labor rights), Alice Paul (suffragist), Fannie Lou Hamer (civil rights), Eleanor Roosevelt (Ambassador to the United Nations and First Lady), Betty Friedan (feminist), Dolores Huerta (supporter of migrant farmworkers), and Doris Haddock (elderly supporter of campaign-finance reform). Timeline, Glossary, Bibliography, Further Reading, and Index.

224. **Harness, Cheryl.** *Remember the Ladies: 100 Great American Women.* Trophy, 2003. 64pp. Paper ISBN 978-0-06-443869-8. Grades 3–6. Harness profiles 100 notable American women beginning with Virginia Dare. The twenty double-page spreads containing watercolors give an overview of these women and their accomplishments. The back matter includes more information and a list of Web Sites on these women and the organizations important in women's lives. Bibliography, Further Reading, and Glossary.

225. **Haskins, James.** *Black Eagles: African Americans in Aviation.* Scholastic, 1997. 196pp. Paper ISBN 978-0-590-45913-6. Grades 5–8. Eugene Bullard, an African American, went to France in World War I and received high honors flying for the French. Bessie Coleman, an African American woman, received her pilot's license in France. By 1921 Hubert Fauntleroy Julian had arrived in New York City and became known as the Black Eagle. Many others gained fame for their achievements as black flyers throughout the 20th century. Dr. Mae C. Jemison was the first African American woman in space. Bibliography, Chronology, and Index. *Notable Children's Trade Books in the Field of Social Studies.*

226. **Hazell, Rebecca.** *Heroines: Great Women Through the Ages.* Abbeville, 1996. 79pp. ISBN 978-0-7892-0210-9. Grades 5–8. Profiles twelve women from ancient Greece to contemporary times. In addition to information about each woman there is background on the times in which she lived. Included are Lady Murasaki Shikibu (973?–1025?), Sacagawea (1786?–1812), Agnodice of ancient Greece, Anna Akhmatova (1888–1966), Madame Sun Yat-Sen (1893–1931), Frida Kahlo (1907–1954), Eleanor of Aquitaine (1122–1202), Joan of Arc (1412?–1431), Queen Elizabeth I (1533–1603), Harriet Tubman (1820?–1913), Marie Curie (1867–1934), and Amelia Earhart (1897–1937). Further Reading.

227. **Herron, Carolivia.** *Always an Olivia: A Remarkable Family History.* Illustrated by Jeremy Tugeau. Kar-Ben, 2007. 32pp. ISBN 978-0-8225-7049-3. Grades 1–4. In 1957, Great-Grandma Olivia tells young Carol Olivia about their ancestors, Jews forced from Spain during the Inquisition of the 1400s. They went first to Portugal and then to Venice without revealing their religion. Many years later, pirates kidnapped a woman named Sarah, and she was rescued by James, also a captive. They escaped with the help of Jews from Tripoli in Libya and went to the Georgia Sea Islands near the United States in 1805. They married and assimilated among the Geechees, the free descendants of West African slaves, with Sarah taking the name Sarah Olivia. They forgot about being Jewish although they still lit Shabbat candles. Each generation remembered Sarah by giving one child the name Olivia, meaning "peace," since Sarah's Hebrew name, Shulamit, also means "peace." Paintings recreate the various moods that fill the story. Bibliography.

228. **Hoose, Phillip.** *We Were There, Too: Young People in U.S. History.* Melanie Kroupa, 2001. 276pp. ISBN 978-0-374-38252-0. Grades 5–8. Excerpts from newspapers, diaries, and interviews tell the stories of more than seventy young people who helped shape American history. Among them are cabin boys aboard Columbus's ships, Pocahontas, Sybil Ludington outriding Paul Revere, young "newsies" who formed a union against the Hearst and Pulitzer papers, Phillis Wheatley, Bill Cody, rider of the rails Peggy Eaton, and Bill Gates. Illustrations and photographs enhance the text. Bibliography and Index. *Horn Book Fanfare.*

229. **Hudson, Wade.** *Book of Black Heroes: Scientists, Healers, and Inventors.* Just Us, 2003. 70pp. Paper ISBN 978-0-940975-97-2. Grades 5–8. This collective biography offers profiles of African American scientists, doctors, and inventors. Among those featured are Benjamin Banneker, George Washington Carver, Mae C. Jemison, Halle Tanner Johnson, Guion Bluford, Jr., Clarice Reid, and Benjamin Carson. Photographs and illustrations augment the text. Bibliography.

230. Juettner, Bonnie. *100 Native Americans Who Changed American History.* (People Who Changed American History) World Almanac, 2005. 112pp. ISBN 978-0-8368-5770-2. Grades 5–8. Capsule biographies of 100 Native Americans range from Dekanawida (ca. 1550–1600), founder of the Iroquois Confederacy, to poet and writer Sherman Alexie, giving details of their lives and their achievements. Photographs and Indexes.

231. Kimmel, Elizabeth Cody. *Ladies First: 40 Daring American Women Who Were Second to None.* National Geographic, 2006. 192pp. ISBN 978-0-7922-5393-8. Grades 4–7. This collective biography features forty American women who were "first," among them Elizabeth Blackwell, Nellie Bly, Helen Keller, Sacagawea, Harriet Quimby (first American woman to earn a pilot's license), Shirley Muldowney (first woman inductee in the Motorsports Hall of Fame), Sally Pries (first ordained female rabbi), Wilma Mankiller, Phillis Wheatley, Georgia O'Keeffe, Jane Addams, Jane Roberts (channeler), and Brenda Berkman (firefighter). Photographs and illustrations highlight the text. Bibliography, Chronology, and Index.

232. Krull, Kathleen. *Lives of Extraordinary Women: Rulers, Rebels (And What the Neighbors Thought).* Illustrated by Kathryn Hewitt. Harcourt, 2000. 95pp. ISBN 978-0-15-200807-9. Grades 5–8. Twenty of the most influential women in history appear in this collective biography with profiles relating their accomplishments and their quirks. Included are Cleopatra, Eleanor of Aquitaine, Joan of Arc, Isabella I, Elizabeth I, Nzingha, Catherine the Great, Marie Antoinette, Victoria, Harriet Tubman, Tz'u-Hsi, Gertrude Bell, Jeanette Rankin, Eleanor Roosevelt, Golda Meir, Indira Gandhi, Eva Péron, Wilma Mankiller, Aung San Suu Kyi, and Rigoberta Manchu. Illustrations enhance the text. Further Reading.

233. Krull, Kathleen. *Lives of the Artists: Masterpieces, Messes (And What the Neighbors Thought).* Illustrated by Kathryn Hewitt. Harcourt, 1995. 96pp. ISBN 978-0-15-200103-2. Grades 4–8. Vignettes, arranged chronologically, give interesting insights into artists' lives and sometimes their relationships with one another. The artists are Leonardo da Vinci (Italy, 1452–1519); Michelangelo Buonarroti (Italy, 1475–1564); Pieter Bruegel (Netherlands, 1525–1569), Sofonisba Anguissola, who served King Philip II of Spain although he was Italian (1532–1625); Rembrandt van Rijn (Holland, 1606–1669); Katsushika Hokusai (Japan, 1760–1849); Mary Cassatt (American living in France, 1845–1926); Vincent van Gogh (Holland, 1853–1890); Käthe Kollwitz (Germany, 1867–1945); Henri Matisse (France, 1869–1954); Pablo Picasso (Spain, 1881–1973); Marc Chagall (Russia, 1887–1985); Marcel Duchamp (France, 1887–1968); Georgia O'Keeffe (United States, 1887–1986); William H. Johnson (United States, 1901–1970); Salvador Dali (Spain, 1904–1989); Isamu Noguchi (United States, 1904–1988); Diego Rivera (Mexico, 1886–1957); Frida Kahlo (Mexico, 1907–1954); and Andy Warhol (United States, 1928–1987). Artistic Terms, Index of Artists, and For Further Reading and Looking. *IRA Teachers' Choices, American Bookseller Pick of the Lists,* and *New York Public Library's Books for the Teen Age.*

234. Krull, Kathleen. *Lives of the Athletes: Thrills, Spills (And What the Neighbors Thought).* Illustrated by Kathryn Hewitt. Harcourt, 1997. 96pp. ISBN 978-0-15-200806-2. Grades 4–8. In capsule biographies, Krull tells a little about the lives of some international athletes away from their sports. She includes commentary on Jim Thorpe (1888–1953), Duke Kahanamoku (1890–1968), Babe Ruth (1895–1948), Red Grange (1903–1991), Johnny Weissmuller (1903–1984), Gertrude Ederle (1906–2003), Babe Didrikson Zaharias (1911–1956), Sonja Henie (1912–1969), Jesse Owens (1913–1980), Jackie Robinson (1919–1972), Sir Edmund Hillary (1919–2008), Maurice Richard (1921–), Maureen Connolly (1934–1969), Roberto Clemente (1934–1972), Wilma Rudolph (1940–1994), Arthur Ashe (1943–1993), Pete Maravich (1947–1988), Bruce Lee (1940–1973), Pelé (1940–), and Flo Hyman (1954–1986). Selected Bibliography.

235. Krull, Kathleen. *Lives of the Musicians: Good Times, Bad Times (And What the Neighbors Thought).* Illustrated by Kathryn Hewitt. Harcourt, 1993. 96pp. ISBN 978-0-15-248010-3; 2002, paper ISBN 978-0-15-216436-2. Grades 4–8. Vignettes about musicians, arranged chronologically, give interesting insights into their lives and sometimes their relationships to one another. The musicians included are Antonio Vivaldi (Italy, 1876–1741), Johann Sebastian Bach (Germany, 1685–1750), Wolfgang Amadeus Mozart (Austria, 1756–1791), Ludwig van Beethoven (Germany, 1770–1827), Frédéric Chopin (Poland, 1810–1849), Giuseppe Verdi (Italy, 1813–1901), Clara Schumann (Germany, 1819–1896), Stephen Foster (United States, 1826–1864), Johannes Brahms (Germany, 1833–1897), Peter Ilich Tchaikovsky (Russia, 1840–1893), William Gilbert (England, 1836–1911) and Arthur Sullivan (England, 1842–1900), Erik Satie (France, 1866–1925), Scott Joplin (United States, 1868–1917), Charles Ives (United States, 1874–1954), Igor Stravinsky (Russia, 1882–1971), Nadia Boulanger (France, 1887–1979), Sergei Prokofiev (Ukraine, 1891–1953), George Gershwin (United States, 1898–1937), and Woody Guthrie (United States, 1912–1967). Musical Terms, Index of Composers, and For Further Reading and Listening. *Boston Globe-Horn Book Honor, American Library Association Notable Children's Books, Notable Children's Trade Books in the Field of Social Studies, PEN Center USA West Literary Award, IRA Teachers' Choices, New York Public Library's Books for the Teen Age*, and *Golden Kite Honor*.

236. **Krull, Kathleen.** *Lives of the Writers: Comedies, Tragedies (And What the Neighbors Thought).* Illustrated by Kathryn Hewitt. Harcourt, 1994. 96pp. ISBN 978-0-15-248009-7. Grades 4–8. Vignettes on writers, arranged chronologically, give interesting insights into their lives and sometimes their relationships to each other. Writers covered are Murasaki Shikibu (Japan, 973?–1025?), Miguel de Cervantes (Spain, 1547–1616), William Shakespeare (England, 1564–1616), Jane Austen (England, 1775–1817), Hans Christian Andersen (Denmark, 1805–1875), Edgar Allan Poe (United States, 1809–1849), Charles Dickens (England, 1812–1870), Charlotte Brontë (England, 1816–1855) and Emily Brontë (England, 1818–1848), Emily Dickinson (United States, 1830–1886), Louisa May Alcott (United States, 1832–1888), Mark Twain (United States, 1835–1910), Frances Hodgson Burnett (England, 1849–1924), Robert Louis Stevenson (Scotland, 1850–1894), Jack London (United States, 1876-1916), Carl Sandburg (United States, 1878–1967), E. B. White (United States, 1899–1985), Zora Neale Hurston (United States, 1901?–1960), Langston Hughes (United States, 1902–1967), and Isaac Bashevis Singer (Poland and United States, 1904–1991). Literary Terms, Index of Writers, and For Further Reading and Writing. *American Bookseller Pick of the Lists, National Council of Teachers of English Notable Children's Trade Books in the Language Arts*, and *International Reading Association Teachers' Choices*.

237. **Laezman, Rick.** *100 Hispanic Americans Who Changed American History.* (People Who Changed History) World Almanac, 2005. 112pp. ISBN 978-0-8368-5769-6. Grades 5–8. This volume contains capsule biographies of 100 Hispanic Americans with information about their lives and their accomplishments. Among those included are Juan Ponce de León, David Farragut, Joaquin Murieta Carlos Castaneda, Luis Alvarez, Dolores Huerta, Rita Moreno, Victor Villaseñor, Joan Baez, Geraldo Rivera, Gary Soto, Sandra Cisneros, and Gloria Estefan. Indexes.

238. **Laver, Sarah, and Rachel Hutchings.** *1000 Years of Famous People.* Kingfisher, 2002. 256pp. ISBN 978-0-7534-5540-1. Grades 4 up. This collective biography profiles more than 1,000 people who made significant achievemeents during the last millennium. They are divided into sections on world leaders, explorers, scientists, engineers and inventors, writers and reformers, stars of stage and screen, artists and architects, musicians and dancers, sports stars, and movers and shakers. Web Sites and Index.

239. **Lipsyte, Robert.** *Heroes of Baseball: The Men Who Made It America's Favorite Game.* Atheneum, 2006. 92pp. ISBN 978-0-689-86741-5. Grades 5 up. Among the baseball legends that Lipsyte identifies are "Big Al" Spaulding, Ty Cobb, Mickey Mantle, Babe Ruth, Curt Flood, Jackie Robinson, Sammy Sosa, and Mark McGuire. He looks at stories about their humanity as well as their athletic ability. The text offers many informative anecdotes about the players and is spiced with Lipsyte's opinions about them and about the game itself. Photographs highlight the text. Bibliography, Glossary, Chronology, and Index.

240. **Lucke, Deb.** *The Book of Time-Outs: A Mostly True History of the World's Biggest Troublemakers.* Simon & Schuster, 2008. 32pp. ISBN 978-1-416-92829-4. Grades 3–6. This collective biography offers profiles of fourteen people in history who also had to take "time-outs" for their behavior. They include Cleopatra, Isabella (Queen of Spain), Napoleon,

Bach, Susan B. Anthony, Babe Ruth, Louis Armstrong, Rosa Parks, and others. Illustrations complement the text.

241. **McLean, Jacqueline.** *Women with Wings.* Oliver, 2001. 160pp. ISBN 978-1-8815-0870-0. Grades 4–8. McLean profiles six female aviator pioneers and presents modern aviators in one chapter. Those who broke the gender barrier were Harriet Quimby, "America's First Woman of the Air," licensed in 1911; Bessie Coleman, an African American who showed "No Prejudice in the Sky" when she became a pilot in 1921; Amelia Earhart, "The Maverick"; Beryl Markham, the "Heroine from Africa" who tried to cross the Atlantic; Anne Morrow Lindbergh, the "Shy Pioneer"; and Jackie Cochrane who was "At the Top of the World." Glossary, Bibliography, and Index.

242. **Marcus, Leonard S.** *Pass It Down: Five Picture-Book Families Make Their Mark.* Walker, 2007. 56pp. ISBN 978-0-8027-9600-4. Grades 4 up. Leonard S. Marcus uses scrapbooks, book dummies, personal memories, final art, and model shots in this profile of five families that have multiple generations of children's book creators: Jerry Pinkney and his son Brian Pinkney, Anne and Harlow Rockwell and their daughter Lizzy, Donald Crews and Ann Jonas with their daughter Nina Crews, Walter Dean Myers and his son Christopher Myers, and Edith and Clement Hurd and their son Thacher Hurd. Their stories, stretching from the 1930s to the 1990s, reveal the connections between parent and child, artist and artist, between artist and medium, and between readers and writers. The younger generations seem to have had an easier path than their struggling parents, who were foster children, rebellious, or suffering from neglect by their own parents. Photos, Selective Bibliography, Glossary, and Index.

243. **Marzollo, Jean.** *Happy Birthday, Martin Luther King.* Illustrated by J. Brian Pinkney. Scholastic, 1993. Unpaged. ISBN 978-0-590-44065-3; 2006, paper ISBN 978-0-439-78224-1. Grades K–2. The national holiday on January 15 celebrates the birthday of Martin Luther King, Jr. (1929–1968), the man who advocated a peaceful solution to civil rights problems. The text looks at his life and comments that at his death his body was put on a farm cart and pulled slowly through Atlanta by two mules because he had done so much to help the poor.

244. **Masters, Nancy Robinson.** *Extraordinary Patriots of the United States of America: Colonial Times to Pre-Civil War.* (Extraordinary People) Children's, 2005. 288pp. ISBN 978-0-51624-404-4. Grades 5–8. This collective biography contains profiles of sixty patriotic Americans and groups, including Benjamin Rush, Casimir Pulaski, Sybil Ludington, and the Daughters of Liberty. It also covers important documents and symbols such as the Liberty Bell, the Declaration of Independence, the Purple Heart medal, and the "Star Spangled Banner." Reproductions augment the text. Further Reading, Web Sites, and Index.

245. **Morin, Isobel V.** *Women of the U.S. Congress.* Oliver, 1994. 160pp. ISBN 978-1-881508-12-0. Grades 5–7. This book looks at eleven of the women voted into Congress during the 20th century: Jeannette Rankin (1880–1973); Margaret Chase Smith (1897–1994); Helen Gahagan Douglas (1900–1980); Shirley Chisholm (b. 1924); Barbara Jordan (1936–1996); Nancy Landon Kassebaum (b. 1932); Barbara Mikulski (b. 1936); and the women elected in 1992—Dianne Feinstein, Barbara Boxer, Patty Murray, and Carol Moseley Braun. Women Who Served in the U.S. Congress, Bibliography, and Index.

246. **Morin, Isobel V.** *Women Who Reformed Politics.* Oliver, 1994. 160pp. ISBN 978-1-881508-16-8. Grades 5–8. Women who saw connections between social problems, the second-class status of women, and racial injustice worked for reforms in politics. The women profiled here are Abby Kelley Foster, crusader against slavery (1811–1887); Frances Willard, temperance fighter (1839–1898); Ida Wells-Barnett, intolerant of mob violence (1862–1931); Carrie Chapman Catt, right to vote (1859–1947); Molly Dewson, political boss (1874–1962); Pauli Murray, activist for integration (1910–1985); Fannie Lou Hamer, civil rights (1917–1977); and Gloria Steinem, women's rights (b. 1934). Major Reforms in U.S. History, Bibliography, and Index.

247. **Pile, Robert B.** *Top Entrepreneurs and Their Businesses.* (Profiles) Oliver, 1993. 159pp. ISBN 978-1-881508-04-5. Grades 4–7. In this collective biography readers will find profiles of 20th-century Americans who created their own businesses. They are Lewis Brittin, a Connecticut colonel, and his flying dream that became Northwest Airways; L. L. Bean, who hated wet feet; Walt Disney and his animation; Bruce Barton, an advertising wizard; Nathan Cummings and his Sara Lee brand; Bud Hillerich, who made baseball bats; Sam Walton and Walmart Drugs; Rose Totino and her pizza; and John Johnson, an African American who founded a publishing company and who said "don't get mad, get smart."

248. Rappaport, Doreen. *In the Promised Land: Lives of Jewish Americans.* Illustrated by Cornelius Van Wright and Ying-Hwa Hu. HarperCollins, 2005. 32pp. ISBN 978-0-688-17150-6. Grades 3–6. This collective biography profiles thirteen Jewish Americans who have made great achievements. They include Asser Levy, who gained rights for Jewish settlers in the colony of New Amsterdam, astronaut Judith Resnick, Justice Ruth Bader Ginsberg, film director Stephen Spielberg, and suffragist Ernestine Rosers. Photographs and illustrations highlight the text. Notes, Further Reading, and Web Sites.

249. Rappoport, Ken. *Profiles in Sports Courage.* Peachtree, 2006. 151pp. ISBN 978-1-56145-368-9. Grades 4–8. This volume profiles twelve outstanding athletes of the 20th century. They include Jackie Robinson, Janet Guthrie, Gail Devers, Curt Flood, Junko Tabei (the first woman to climb Everest), Jim Abbott, Muhammad Ali, Lance Armstrong, and Kerri Strug. The profiles concentrate on their specific challenges and how they overcame them to succeed. Photographs illustrate the text. Bibliography. *Voice of Youth Advocates Nonfiction Honor List.*

250. Roop, Connie, and Peter Roop. *Tales of Famous Americans.* Illustrated by Charlie Power. Scholastic, 2007. 108pp. ISBN 978-0-439-64116-6. Grades 3–6. This collective biography includes tales of the childhoods of nineteen famous Americans, plus summaries of their achievements as adults. Among those included are Pocahontas, Benjamin Franklin, Davy Crockett, Yo-Yo Ma, Mia Hamm, Jackie Robinson, George Washington, Abraham Lincoln, Sitting Bull, Harriet Tubman, Helen Keller, Susan B. Anthony, Delores Huerta, the Wright Brothers, Thomas Edison, and Martin Luther King, Jr. The four-page synopses also include a photograph related to the individual in some way. Index.

251. St. George, Judith. *So You Want to Be an Explorer?* Illustrated by David Small. Philomel, 2005. 56pp. ISBN 978-0-399-23868-0. Grades 1–4. What do explorers do anyway? This is a wide-ranging overview of exploration across the ages and covers individuals from Marco Polo and Columbus to Amelia Earhart and Yuri Gagarin. Cartoon illustrations enhance the text. Bibliography, Glossary, and Web Sites.

252. St. George, Judith. *So You Want to Be an Inventor?* Illustrated by David Small. Philomel, 2002. 53pp. ISBN 978-0-399-23593-1; Puffin, 2005, paper ISBN 978-0-14-240460-7. Grades 3–5. What does it take to be an inventor? This is a lighthearted overview that introduces inventors including Alexander Graham Bell, Charles Goodyear, and Cyrus McCormick. The author also notes that some inventions were misused, such as the cotton gin and its promotion of slavery. Illustrations complement the text. Bibliography and Notes. *Young Reader's Award* (Arizona) nomination and *Read-Aloud Book Award* (Indiana) nomination.

253. Sanderson, Ruth. *More Saints: Lives and Illuminations.* Eerdmans, 2007. ISBN 978-0-8028-5272-4. Grades 4–7. This collective biography of saints from the second millennium profiles thirty-six men and women. They include Dominic, Clare, Thomas Aquinas, Joan of Arc, Francis, Padre Pio, Teresa, Rita of Cascia, Francis Xavier, and Elizabeth Anne Seton. Pencil and oil portraits highlight the text. Glossary, Further Reading, Web Sites, and Index.

254. Schraff, Anne E. *American Heroes of Exploration and Flight.* Enslow, 1996. 112pp. ISBN 978-0-8949-0619-0. Grades 5–9. Profiles ten individuals who have contributed to exploration and flight in America, giving information about their lives, beginning with an exciting event, and a brief overview of history to show why their particular contribution was important. Those profiled include Matthew Henson (1866–1955) and Robert Peary (1856–1920), who discovered the North Pole together; Amelia Earhart (1897–1937); Jacqueline Cochran (1910–1980); Sally Ride (b. 1951); and Christa McAuliffe (d. 1986). Notes and Index.

255. Vare, Ethlie Ann. *Women Inventors and Their Discoveries.* Oliver, 1993. 160pp. ISBN 978-1-881508-06-9. Grades 4–8. Vare presents ten American women inventors and their innovations. Fannie Farmer wrote a modern cookbook using standardized measurements rather than a "pinch of this" and a "handful of that." Other inventions include Liquid Paper correction fluid, cosmetics and hair products for black women, fiber for bulletproof vests, an indigo plant capable of producing a superior dye, and the Barbie doll. These women inventors are mostly unknown, but their creations have made a mark on American society. Photographs, Bibliography, and Index.

256. Walker, Paul Robert. *Spiritual Leaders.* Facts on File, 1994. 144pp. ISBN 978-0-8160-2875-7. Grades 5 up. Religion has always been at the center of Native American life, and the individuals profiled in this collective biography are remembered for their spiritual leadership. They are Passaconaway, Son of the Bear (early 16th century); Popé, prophet of the Pueblo Revolt (late 17th century); Neolin, the Delaware prophet (mid-18th century); Handsome Lake, prophet of the Good Word (late 18th century); Tenskwatawa, the Shawnee prophet (1775–1836); Kenekuk, the Kickapoo prophet (ca. 1790–1852); Smohalla, the Washani prophet (d. 1895); John Slocum, the Shaker prophet (ca. 1840–ca. 1897); Zotom, warrior, artist, and missionary (1853–1913); Wovoka, Ghost Dance prophet (ca. 1856–1932); Black Elk, Lakota holy man (1863–1950); Mountain Wolf Woman, Winnebago visionary (1884–1960); and Ruby Modesto, desert Cahuilla medicine woman (1913–1980). Annotated Bibliography and Index.

257. Welch, Catherine. *George C. Marshall.* (History Maker Bios) Lerner, 2006. 48pp. ISBN 978-0-8225-2435-9. Grades 3–5. George C. Marshall (1880–1959) was designated a slow learner as a child, but he excelled in military school. He first served in World War I, and then as a general in World War II. After the war, he received the Nobel Peace Prize for his "Marshall Plan" that helped European countries to rebuild. He also served as chief of staff of the U.S. Army, secretary of state, and secretary of defense. The five chapters of the text give an overview of his life. Illustrations highlight the book. Bibliography, Further Reading, Glossary, Maps, Timeline, Web Sites, and Index.

258. Williams, Marcia. *Hooray for Inventors!* Candlewick, 2005. 40pp. ISBN 978-0-7636-2760-7. Grades 2–5. This collective biography profiles more than one hundred of the world's most influential inventors. Additional sidebars focus on particular inventions such as eyeglasses (1280), toothpaste tube (1892), ballpoint pens (1938), the chocolate bar (1819), and the personal computer (1977). Among the inventors mentioned are James Watt, Johannes Gutenberg, Guglielmo Marconi, John Logie Baird, Earle Dickson, Clarence Birdseye, and Antonio Meucci. Illustrations highlight the text. Index.

259. Yolen, Jane. *Sea Queens: Women Pirates Around the World.* Illustrated by Christine Joy Pratt. Charlesbridge, 2008. ISBN 978-1-58089-131-8. Grades 4–6. This collective biography of women who have taken from others includes thirteen individuals: Artemisia, Admiral-Queen, Persia (500–480 B.C.E.); Queen Teuta, Illyria, (ca. 230 B.C.E.); Alfhild, Denmark (ca. 800); Jeanne de Belleville, Brittany (ca. 1350); Grania O'Malley, Ireland (ca. 1550); Lady Killigrew, England (ca.1590); Pretty Peg and the Dutch Privateer, Holland (ca. 1600); Charlotte de Berry, England (ca. 1650); Anne Bonney and Mary Read, American colonies (ca. 1725); Rachel Wall, United States (ca. 1789); Mary Anne Talbot, England (ca. 1790); and Madame Ching, China (ca. 1800). Madame Ching wins the tile of the "most successful pirate in the world." The text tries to distinguish between the facts and legends that swirl around these women. Alfhild of Denmark kept a pet viper to deter men. Jeanne the Lioness of Brittany sold her lands, bought ships, and attacked the French to avenge the murder of her husband. And Wall was the last woman hung on Boston Common in 1789. Illustrations accompany the text. Bibliography, Web Sites, and Index.

260. Zalben, Jane Breskin. *Paths to Peace: People Who Changed the World.* Dutton, 2006. 46pp. ISBN 978-0-525-47734-1. Grades 4–8. This collective biography features sixteen peacemakers from around the world: Ralph Waldo Emerson, Mahatma Gandhi, Albert Einstein, Eleanor Roosevelt, Ralph Bunche, Mother Teresa, John F. Kennedy, Anwar El-Sadat, César Chavez, Elie Wiesel, Martin Luther King Jr., Anne Frank, Wangari Maathai, the Dalai Lama,

Aung San Suu Kyi, and Princess Diana. Illustrations enhance the text. Bibliography, Glossary, Notes, Further Reading, Web Sites, and Index.

Graphic Novels, Biographies, and Histories

261. **Hughes, Susan.** *No Girls Allowed: Tales of Daring Women Dressed as Men for Love, Freedom and Adventure.* Illustrated by Willow Dawson. Kids Can, 2008. 80pp. ISBN 978-1-55453-177-6; paper ISBN 978-1-55453-178-3. Grades 3–5. This graphic novel draws on primary documents—letters, poems, legends, and firsthand accounts—to profile seven women who have pretended to be men: Hatshepsut of Egypt, Mu Lan, the slave Ellen Craft, Viking princess Alfhild, Civil War soldier Sarah Rosetta Wakeman, British army surgeon James Barry, and sailor Esther Bandeau. Further Reading.

DVDs

262. *Bundle of Compromises.* Find the Fun, 2006. 2:30 hrs. ISBN 978-0-9714399-4-8. Grades 3–7. This DVD looks at historical, political, and social aspects of the Constitution and the protection it offers to Americans. A second section discusses the Articles of Confederation and the Constitutional Convention of 1787. A third segment discusses the convention and the plans for equal representation among the new states. The fourth part covers the Great Compromise, the ratification of the Constitution, and the Bill of Rights. Graphics, Chronologies, game shows, reenactments, and other visuals add interest.

263. *Discoveries . . . America: Pennsylvania.* Bennett-Watt, 2003. 60 mins. ISBN 978-1-932068-73-3. Grades 4 up. White settlers originally called Pennsylvania Penn's Woods. The state has played a major part in the growth and development of the United States. Philadelphia is the home of the Liberty Bell and Independence Hall; Valley Forge is nearby. Gettysburg is remembered for the famous Civil War battle. Other important sites are the Amish country, the Wharton Esherick Museum, covered bridges, and Lake Erie. Interviews with people in different positions reveal aspects of Pennsylvania's life past and present.

264. *Florida Geography, History, and Culture.* SVE & Churchill Media, 2002. 20 mins. Grades 4–9. Film footage and historical photographs reveal facts about the geography, natural resources, history, economy, government, and people of Florida. The focus is on the state government, unusual geographic features, ecology, economics, and the role of the state during the Civil War.

265. *Images of Liberty.* (Symbols of America) Film Ideas, 2002. Color. 14:39 mins. Grades 4 up. Both the Liberty Bell in Philadelphia and the Statue of Liberty in New York Harbor celebrate and honor freedom in the United States. This video discusses the history and construction of these two powerful symbols.

266. *Moving to America: Then and Now.* Educational Video, 2002. 19 mins. ISBN 978-1-58541-186-3. Grades 1–4. The people who have helped America succeed were immigrants—Native Americans of diverse cultures, the explorers, the settlers, and the pioneers. Graphics and live-action footage cover each of these groups as well as the unwilling immigrants, the slaves from Africa.

267. *Our Country's Flag.* (America's Story) Lucerne, 2002. 12 mins. ISBN 978-0-388-09410-5. Grades 4–6. Historical paintings, live-action footage, and maps enhance a discussion of America's independence. A narrator explains the evolution of flags from 1777 until today, including the addition of stars.

268. *Texas Geography, History, and Culture.* SVE & Churchill Media, 2002. 24 mins. Grades 4–9. Film footage and historical photographs reveal facts about the geography, natural resources, history, economy, government, and people of Texas. European settlement and the discovery of oil were crucial to its development. Information on historical personages Sam Houston (1793–1863) and Stephen Austin (1793–1836) add context to the state's political history.

269. *What Is Christianity?* (Understanding World Religions) Library Video, 2003. 20 mins. ISBN 978-1-4171-0579-3. Grades 4–7. This video examines the history, traditions, beliefs, spiritual sites, sacred writings, and places people worship in Christianity. A male host and a group of middle-school students, with the help of live-action scenes of places and people, clarify some abstract terms.

270. *What Is Religion?* (Understanding World Religions) Library Video, 2003. 20 mins. ISBN 978-1-4171-0583-0. Grades 4–7. This video examines the history, traditions, beliefs, spiritual sites, sacred writings, and places where people worship in various religions. A male host and a group of middle-school students, with the help of live-action scenes of places and people, clarify some abstract terms.

Compact Discs

271. Davis, Kenneth C. *Don't Know Much About History.* Narrated by Jeff Woodman. Listening Library, 2003. 19 CDs. ISBN 978-0-7366-9322-6. Grades 4–7. This informative account of American history provides useful background with humor and interesting anecdotes. It covers events through September 11, 2001, and reviews controversy and scholarship on a number of topics including the Hiss trial, slavery, the Civil War, the causes of the Great Depression, and so forth.

272. Krull, Kathleen. *Lives of Extraordinary Women: Rulers, Rebels (And What the Neighbors Thought).* Narrated by Kathryn Hewitt. Audio Bookshelf, 2001. 2 CDs; 2 hrs. ISBN 978-1-8833-3273-0. Grades 5–8. See entry 232.

273. Krull, Kathleen. *Lives of the Artists: Masterpieces, Messes (And What the Neighbors Thought).* Narrated by John C. Brown and Melissa Hughes. Audio Bookshelf, 2001. 2 CDs; 3 hrs. ISBN 978-1-883332-63-1. Grades 4–8. See entry 233.

274. Krull, Kathleen. *Lives of the Musicians: Good Times, Bad Times (And What the Neighbors Thought).* Narrated by John C. Brown and Melissa Hughes. Audio Bookshelf, 1996. 2 CDs; 2 hrs. ISBN 978-1-883332-23-5. Grades 4–8. See entry 235.

275. Krull, Kathleen. *Lives of the Writers: Comedies, Tragedies (And What the Neighbors Thought).* Narrated by John C. Brown and Melissa Hughes. Audio Bookshelf, 1996. 96pp. 3 CDs; 3 hrs. ISBN 978-1-883332-24-2. Grades 4–8. See entry 236.

276. Nelson, Kadir. *We Are the Ship: The Story of Negro League Baseball.* Narrated by Dion Graham. Brilliance, 2009. 2 CDs; 1 hr. 55 mins. ISBN 978-1-4233-7537-1. Grades 3 up. See entry 127.

NORTH AMERICA BEFORE 1600

Historical Fiction and Fantasy

277. Bruchac, Joseph. *Children of the Longhouse.* Puffin, 1998. 150pp. Paper ISBN 978-0-14-038504-5. Grades 5–8. When he hears that neighboring Mohawk adolescents are planning a raid, Ohkwa'ri, 11, tells the tribal council. However, Ohkwa'ri soon finds himself on a lacrosse team confronting Grabber, the leader of the opposing gang. With the help of his twin sister, Otsi:stia, and neighbors, Ohkwa'ri prevails. The story includes information about the Mohawks including communal sleeping, name giving, government, family relationships, and the matrilineal hierarchy.

278. Dorris, Michael. *Sees Behind Trees.* Hyperion, 1999. 96pp. Paper ISBN 978-0-7868-1357-5. Grades 4–8. In pre-Colonial America, Walnut has myopia and knows he can never see well enough to become the kind of hunter admired by his tribe. His mother suggests that he "look with his ears." Because of his ability to "see" what others cannot, the tribe chooses him to accompany the village elder, Gray Fire, on a journey to find the land of water. He fulfills this role by passing his universal and age-old tests of manhood. *School Library Journal Best Book.*

279. Lorenz, Albert, and Joy Schleh. *Journey to Cahokia: A Boy's Visit to the Great Mound City.* Abrams, 2004. Unpaged. ISBN 978-0-8109-5047-4. Grades 2–6. Around 1300 C.E., Little Hawk and his family take a fur-trading trip that lasts around two months. They leave the site of present-day Detroit and travel to Cahokia, a city located at the confluence of the Mississippi and Missouri Rivers. As big as contemporary London, Cahokia has clay buildings with thatched roofs near platform mounds. Little Hawk sees lacrosse games and a ceremony on the huge pyramid. Illustrations detail farming tools, carved containers, clothing, tattoos, and other items of the time. Note.

280. O'Dell, Scott. *Island of the Blue Dolphins.* Illustrated by Ted Lewin. Houghton, 1990. 192pp. ISBN 978-0-395-53680-3; Yearling, 1994, paper ISBN 978-0-440-43988-2. Grades 5 up. Karana is the only remaining human on her island after Aleuts kill most of the men and the others sail to the mainland. Her brother survives for a while, but a wild dog kills him. Karana learns how to live by discarding tribal taboos such as women not making weapons. Her experiences as she survives each day show that people can adapt to and work with nature. *Newbery Medal, Southern California Council on Literature for Children and Young People Awards, International Board of Books for Young People, Friends of Children and Literature Award, American Library Association Notable Books,* and *School Library Journal Best Books.*

281. O'Dell, Scott. *Zia.* Illustrated by Ted Lewin. Laurel-Leaf, 1996. 224pp. Paper ISBN 978-0-440-21956-9. Grades 4–8. Karana's niece Zia tries to rescue her in this sequel to *Island of the Blue Dolphins.* Zia and her brother sail for the island but are captured and enslaved. With the help of a captain, Karana is brought to the mainland but she cannot adjust to mission life and its rules after living alone for so many years and learning to survive by herself.

282. **Rockwood, Joyce.** *To Spoil the Sun.* Henry Holt, 2003. 192pp. ISBN 978-0-8050-7372-0. Grades 5–9. As a Cherokee of the Seven Clans during the 16th century, Rain Dove expects to pick her husband soon. But three omens disturb the clan. A snake appears in winter, a honey locust tree burns, and an ancient fire goes out. These foreshadow the arrival of smallpox. Rain Dove marries and has two children, but when the strangers arrive with smallpox, she loses both of them. Native American lives change forever.

283. **West, Tracey.** *Voyage of the Half Moon.* Silver Moon, 1993. 55pp. ISBN 978-1-881889-18-2; 1995, paper ISBN 978-1-881889-76-2. Grades 3–5. In 1609 John Hudson accompanies explorer Henry Hudson, his father, on his first trip up a river in the New World. From the deck of the *Half Moon*, he sees the life of the river, including its animals and plants. This eventful journey marks the Europeans' discovery of the Hudson River. Endpaper Maps, Historical Postscript, and Recommended Reading.

History

284. **Arnold, Caroline.** *The Ancient Cliff Dwellers of Mesa Verde.* Illustrated by Richard Hewett. Clarion, 2000. 64pp. Paper ISBN 978-0-618-05149-6. Grades 4–6. The Native Americans known today as the Anasazi migrated to southwestern Colorado in the 1st century C.E. After constructing extensive dwellings in the walls of the steep canyon cliffs, they mysteriously disappeared around 1300. Their impressive dwellings still stand in Mesa Verde National Park, Colorado.

285. **Aveni, Anthony.** *The First Americans: From the Great Migration to the Splendid Cities of the Maya.* (The First Americans) Scholastic, 2005. 125pp. ISBN 978-0-439-55144-1. Grades 4–6. Before explorers arrived in the Americas, natives had accomplished much. Among the first Americans were the Taíno; League of the Iroquois; the Ohio Moundbuilders; the Anasazi; the Kwakiutl, Tlingit, and Haida; the Timucua; and the Mississippian pyramid city of Cahokia. This volume covers the religion, food, dress, social organization, and customs of these cultures that arrived in the Americas either by boat or land bridge. Photographs, sidebars, augment the text. Maps, Chronology, Web Sites, and Index.

286. **Carter, E. J.** *The Mayflower Compact.* (Historical Documents) Heinemann, 2003. 48pp. ISBN 978-1-4034-0803-7; paper ISBN 978-1-4034-3432-6. Grades 4–6. Carter looks at the arrival of the Pilgrims in Massachusetts, their early government in Plymouth Colony, and the document known as the Mayflower Compact. A study of this document indicates who wrote it, how it was written, what the document means, how it affected those who had to live by its word, and how the document has been preserved through the centuries. Illustrations and document reproductions highlight the text. Further Reading, Glossary, and Index.

287. **Croy, Anita.** *Ancient Pueblo: Archaeology Unlocks the Secrets of America's Past.* (National Geographic Investigates) National Geographic, 2007. 64pp. ISBN 978-1-4263-0130-8. Grades 5–9. The Pueblo Native Americans (so named by the Spanish explorers) who lived from 100 C.E. to 1600 include the Hohokam, the Anasazi, and Mogollon peoples, all of whom lived in the Four Corners states of Colorado, Utah, Arizona, and New Mexico. Croy follows archaeologists' investigations and shows artifacts such as pottery, baskets, weapons, and rock carvings that give insights into daily activities such as farming and hunting and construction of canals, roads, and homes. Illustrations and photographs highlight the text. Maps, Chronology, Glossary, Bibliography, and Index.

288. **Fritz, Jean.** *Around the World in a Hundred Years: From Henry the Navigator to Magellan.* Illustrated by Anthony Bacon Venti. Puffin, 1998. 128pp. Paper ISBN 978-0-698-11638-2. Grades 4–7. In 1400 mapmakers named the space beyond the areas they had drawn "the Unknown." Later that century, explorers ventured into the Unknown searching for routes to the gold of China. The text discusses explorers beginning with Prince Henry the Navigator (1394–1460) and ending with Magellan (1480?–1521), whose ship continued around the world after he died in the Philippines. Other explorers include Bartholomew Diaz, Christopher Columbus, Vasco da Gama, Pedro Álvares Cabral, John Cabot, Amerigo Vespucci, Juan Ponce de León, and Vasco Núñez de Balboa. Notes, Bibliography, and Index.

289. Gioia, Robyn. *America's Real First Thanksgiving: St. Augustine, Florida, September 8, 1565.* Pineapple, 2007. 48pp. ISBN 978-1-56164-389-9. Grades 3–6. Gioia discusses the Spanish settlement in Florida in the 16th century, the conditions in the region at that time, and relationships between the Spanish and the Timucua Indians. She suggests that the first Thanksgiving in the Americas occurred there in 1565 with Spanish explorer Pedro Menéndez de Avilés and the Timucua near what became St. Augustine. Historical photographs augment the text. Bibliography, Glossary, Chronology, and Index.

290. Hakim, Joy. *The First Americans: Prehistory to 1600.* (History of US) Oxford, 2006. 177pp. ISBN 978-0-19-518894-3; 2007, paper ISBN 978-0-19-532715-1. Grades 5 up. This story of the Americas and their inhabitants from the earliest times until the arrival of the first Europeans is filled with photographs, prints, sidebars, boxed text, and running commentary. Hakim covers all aspects of society and all cultures in her text. Chronology of Events, More Books to Read, and Index.

291. Harrison, David L. *Cave Detectives: Unraveling the Mystery of an Ice Age Cave.* Illustrated by Biamonte Edward and Ashley Mims. Chronicle, 2007. 47pp. ISBN 978-0-8118-5006-3. Grades 4–6. In 2001 a Missouri road crew accidentally discovered a cave containing the oldest ice age fossils ever found in North America. Harrison looks at the resulting scientific exploration and how tracks and claw marks can reveal information about life hundreds of thousands of years ago. Watercolor and pencil illustrations and photographs enhance the text. Chronology and Glossary.

292. Italia, Bob. *The Lost Colony.* Checkerboard, 2001. 32pp. ISBN 978-1-57765-580-0. Grades 3–5. In twelve chapters, this volume looks at life on Roanoke Island, in contemporary North Carolina, where English colonists twice tried to establish a settlement. Topics include the early history, first explorers, the Grenville settlement, the White settlement, life in the colony, employment, food, clothing, shelter, children, and Native Americans. Reproductions augment the text. Chronology and Web Sites.

293. Lourie, Peter. *The Lost World of the Anasazi: Exploring the Mysteries of Chaco Canyon.* Boyds Mills, 2007. 48pp. Paper ISBN 978-1-59078-475-4. Grades 5–8. Lourie explores the ruins of Chaco Canyon, New Mexico, attempting to find out about the lives of the Anasazi, precursors to the Pueblo Indians, who disappeared in 1250. Topics covered include farming, pottery, and the amazing structures of several stories that they built. Photographs and illustrations augment the text. Further Reading and Index.

294. Lourie, Peter. *On the Texas Trail of Cabeza de Vaca.* Boyds Mills, 2008. ISBN 978-1-59078-492-1. Grades 5–8. Álvar Núñez Cabeza de Vaca was part of an expedition that shipwrecked near Galveston, Texas, with only four of 600 men surviving. As one of these survivors, he interacted with the native residents before traveling in Texas and Mexico for eight years and describing the flora and fauna that he saw there. He was one of the first explorers who said that the residents were people like himself rather than savages. The text covers de Vaca's probable route, with maps and illustrations showing what he most likely saw. Chronology, Further Resources, and Index.

295. Maestro, Betsy. *The Discovery of the Americas.* Illustrated by Giulio Maestro. Mulberry, 1992. Unpaged. Paper ISBN 978-0-688-11512-8. Grades K–4. Beginning with the migration of peoples into North and South America more than 20,000 years ago, this text presents theories and facts about the settlements discovered on the two continents. Cultures and explorers before Columbus include the Mayans, possibly Saint Brendan from Ireland in the 6th century, the Vikings Bjarni Herjolfsson in the 10th century and Leif Ericsson in the 11th, possibly Prince Madoc of Wales in the 12th, and the Hopewell mound builders. Explorers after

Columbus mentioned in the text are Italians John Cabot in 1497 and Amerigo Vespucci in 1499, Vasco Nuñez de Balboa from Spain in 1513, and Ferdinand Magellan from Portugal in 1519. Additional Information, Some People of the Ancient and Early Americas, The Age of Discovery, How the Americas Got Their Name, and Other Interesting Voyages.

296. Maestro, Betsy. *Exploration and Conquest: The Americas After Columbus: 1500–1620.* Illustrated by Giulio Maestro. Mulberry, 1992. Unpaged. Paper ISBN 978-0-688-15474-5. Grades K–4. Noting that Spanish discovery of the New World ignored or exploited the people who had lived there for years, the authors describe the feats and effects of explorers after Columbus. Balboa (1513) saw the Pacific. Ponce de León (1513) found Florida. Magellan began his voyage around the world in 1519, while Cortés overpowered the Aztecs. Pizarro and de Soto (1532) conquered the Incas in Peru when Cabeza de Vaca was in Texas. De Soto went to Florida in 1539, and Coronado left Mexico in search of the Seven Cities of Gold in 1540. Then European explorers arrived. John Cabot, Giovanni da Verrazano, Jacques Cartier, and John Hawkins (who began the slave trade) came. Britain's Francis Drake, Martin Frobisher, Humphrey Gilbert, John Davis, Walter Raleigh (at Roanoke), John White, and Virginia Dare added their names to history. After 1600, famous arrivals were John Smith, John Rolfe, Champlain, and Henry Hudson. Where these people arrived on shore, the indigenous cultures seemed to become less prevalent, with some actually disappearing. Additional Information, Table of Dates, Some Other Explorers, North America—1500–1620, Contacts Between Native Americans and European Explorers, Impact of the European Arrival in the Americas, Native American Contributions to the World, and European Colonies and Settlements in the New World.

297. Miller, Jake. *The Lost Colony of Roanoke: A Primary Source History.* (Primary Source Library of the Thirteen Colonies) PowerKids, 2006. 24pp. ISBN 978-1-4042-3027-9. Grades 3–5. The lost colony of Roanoke, located in present-day North Carolina, disappeared while its leaders were back in England gathering additional supplies. When they returned, the only sign they saw of the colony's existence was "CROATOAN" carved on a tree. Primary source materials include illustrations and unidentified text.

298. Miller, Lee. *Roanoke: The Mystery of the Lost Colony.* Scholastic, 2007. 112pp. ISBN 978-0-439-71266-8. Grades 4 up. In 1587 settlers arrived in the New World and founded the colony of Roanoke. They needed more supplies, and one of their leaders returned to England to secure them. When he returned in 1590, no trace of the colony remained, and nothing has ever been found. The first white child born in the colonies, Virginia Dare, disappeared along with the others. The text suggests that the fate of the colony involved several forces. The people had mistreated the Secota Indians in the area, pirates were sailing the seas, and Queen Elizabeth was not feeling as favorable about Sir Walter Raleigh, an explorer who supported the colonies. Therefore, politics may have played a major part in the colony's disappearance. Illustrations augment the text. Chronology, Notes, and Index.

299. Quigley, Mary. *Mesa Verde.* (Excavating the Past) Heinemann, 2005. 48pp. ISBN 978-1-4034-5997-8. Grades 4–6. Archaeological excavations have uncovered the home of the Mesa Verde Native Americans. Quigley explains how ancient people reached America via the land bridge from Russia and settled the North and the South. Some of them began farming in the Four Corners area of Colorado, New Mexico, Arizona, and Utah. This text covers their daily lives and current theories as to why they may have abandoned the site. Maps, Photographs and Reproductions augment the text. Glossary, Chronology, Further Reading, and Index.

300. Wulffson, Don. *Before Columbus: Early Voyages to the Americas.* Twenty-First Century, 2007. 128pp. ISBN 978-0-8225-5978-8. Grades 5–9. Wulffson asks if other civilizations arrived in the New World before Columbus and suggests that Columbus got the top billing because of the printing press, good publicity, and backing by royalty. Other groups that might have come before include the Vikings, Chinese, Irish, and Africans. The Phoenicians could have fled their Greek conquerors in 146 B.C.E., landed in New Hampshire, and built Stonehenge-shaped monuments and etched Phoenician letters on them. The Irish might have arrived first in New England as clues of Irish monks living in the country more than 1,000 years ago do exist. The "white" Mandan tribe in North Dakota could have resulted from

Prince Madoc's Welsh expedition in the 12th century. West African gold spearheads have appeared in the Olmec people's treasures. Legends, sagas, oral, and written histories along with archaeological discoveries give credibility to some of Wulffson's theories. Photographs and reproductions highlight the text. Bibliography, Notes, Further Reading, Web Sites, and Index.

301. Yolen, Jane, and Heidi Elisabet Yolen Stemple. *Roanoke: The Lost Colony: An Unsolved Mystery from History.* Illustrated by Roger Roth. Simon & Schuster, 2003. Unpaged. ISBN 978-0-689-82321-3. Grades 3–6. A young narrator looks at information about the Roanoke Colony that disappeared in 1587, never to be found. Five theories about the group's disappearance have evolved, and she discusses each of them. Illustrations complement the text. Bibliography and Web Sites.

Biography and Collective Biography

302. Adler, David A. *A Picture Book of Christopher Columbus.* Narrated by Linda Terheyden. Live Oak Media, 1992. ISBN 978-1-59112-757-4. Grades K–3. Born into a wool weaver's family in the city-state of Genoa (before Italy was founded) in 1451, Columbus (1451–1506) read of Marco Polo's travels across Asia and decided that he wanted to find China. In 1484 Columbus first attempted to get provisions for a journey to Japan, which he thought was 2,400 miles away (it is actually four times farther). Adler describes the types of people Columbus hired for the voyage and notes that the date of departure—August 3, 1492—was one day after Ferdinand and Isabella's proclamation that all unconverted Jews had to leave Spain. The pen-and-ink sketches show scenes as they might have been. The text recounts the tragedy that Columbus's arrival was for the people in the New World, who caught new diseases or were enslaved by the Spaniards, as well as the tribulations Columbus faced on his subsequent voyages. Index.

303. Aller, Susan Bivin. *Christopher Columbus.* (History Maker Bios) Lerner, 2003. 48pp. ISBN 978-0-8225-0398-9. Grades 3–5. As an explorer from Italy, Christopher Columbus (1451–1506) is best known for his discovery of America. His love for the sea and sailing therefore changed the history of a continent. Illustrations augment the text. Bibliography, Further Reading, Glossary, Maps, Timeline, Web Sites, and Index.

304. Roberts, Russell. *Pedro Menéndez de Avilés.* (Latinos in American History) Mitchell Lane, 2002. 48pp. ISBN 978-1-58415-150-0. Grades 5–9. Pedro Menéndez de Avilés (1519–1574), a Spanish seaman, came to the New World and helped to colonize Florida for his country in the new city of St. Augustine. In 1565 he had to defeat the French to assert Spain's claim to the land. Some considered him a pirate while others thought he was merely fearless in his endeavors. Illustrations enhance the text. Bibliography, Glossary, and Index.

305. Sutcliffe, Jane. *Juan Ponce de León.* (History Maker Bios) Lerner, 2005. 48pp. ISBN 978-0-8225-2944-6. Grades 3–5. Juan Ponce de León (1460?–1521), was a governor, soldier, farmer, and explorer. He first traveled with Christopher Columbus. Then he returned to the New World to search for the fountain of youth. He was unsuccessful, but he did discover Florida. The five chapters of the book give an overview of his life and exploration. Illustrations augment the text. Bibliography, Further Reading, Glossary, Maps, Timeline, Web Sites, and Index.

306. Waldman, Stuart. *We Asked for Nothing: The Remarkable Journey of Cabeza de Vaca.* Illustrated by Tom McNeely. Mikaya, 2003. 48pp. ISBN 978-1-931414-07-4. Grades 5–8. After Alvar Nuñez Cabeza de Vaca (1490?–1557) escaped the hostile natives in Florida in 1528, he shipwrecked on the coast of Texas. For the next eight years he and his three companions survived illness and hunger with the help of native tribes with which they lived during their efforts to reach Mexico's Spanish settlements. When he did reach the Spanish, Cabeza de Vaca had realized that exploiting the New World was wrong and he struggled against this effort.

The text, based on Cabeza de Vaca's journals, reveals his changes in attitude as he accepted the generosity of those who helped him survive. Paintings highlight the text. Maps.

Graphic Novels, Biographies, and Histories

307. Niz, Xavier. *The Mystery of the Roanoke Colony.*   Illustrated by Shannon Eric Denton. Graphic Library, 2006. 32pp. ISBN 978-0-7368-6494-7; paper ISBN 978-0-7368-9657-3. Grades 3–5. The Roanoke Colony—known as the "Lost Colony"—was established in North Carolina between 1585 and 1587. The first colonists went three years without supplies from England and disappeared, never to be found. They may have been assimilated into local tribes. Illustrations enhance the text. Bibliography, Glossary, Further Reading, and Index.

DVDs

308. *Colonial America 2: 1500–1776.*   (Hands-On Crafts for Kids Series 6: Back in Time) Chip Taylor Communications, 2003. 30 mins. Grades 4–6. The production begins with a narrator reading a list of materials appearing on the screen. Teachers then construct objects from Colonial America—a silver tray, a log cabin quilt, a rug, a welcome bandbox, and a wired candle holder. Each item helps explain an important aspect of the colonial culture.

309. *Dig Into History with California Jones: California Missions.*   Library Video, 2007. 23 mins. Grades 3–6. In an overview of California missions, this DVD presents mission construction, agriculture and food, games, roads and forts, and daily life. Included are Native American customs before the Spanish arrived and the destruction of groups through disease. Also included are a Spanish recipe, creating adobe bricks from mud, and the rules of games the Mission Indian children played.

310. *Hernando de Soto.*   (Famous Explorers) Film Ideas, 2003. 22 mins. ISBN 978-1-57557-366-3. Grades 5–8. Hernando de Soto (1496/1497–1542), the first European to discover the Mississippi River, also participated in Pizarro's conquest of the Inca empire. De Soto sailed Florida's west coast to Tampa Bay and explored the inland north to Alabama. Focused only on finding gold, he cruelly subjugated any natives he met and missed an opportunity to gain real wealth for Spain by establishing Spanish rule in the New World. He left a mixed legacy as illustrated through contemporary footage, maps, and period art.

311. *Native Americans: North America 1300–1700 A.D.*   (Hands-On Crafts for Kids Series 6: Back in Time) Chip Taylor Communications, 2003. 30 mins. Grades 4–6. The production begins with a narrator reading a list of materials appearing on the screen. Teachers then construct objects used by the early Native Americans. These include a wampum necklace, an owner stick, a cork painting, and a Navajo Hogan box. Each item helps explain an important aspect of the early Native American culture.

THE AMERICAN COLONIES, 1600–1774

Historical Fiction and Fantasy

312. Alsheimer, Jeanette E., and Patricia J. Friedle. *The Trouble with Tea.* Ivy House, 2002. 208pp. ISBN 978-1-57197-299-6. Grades 5–8. When Anne Wentworth breaks her leg, her friend Patience goes from her Plymouth, Massachusetts, home to Boston to see her. Patience learns about the political divide in Boston—Anne's father sympathizes with the colonists' desire not to pay taxes on tea but Anne is in love with Oliver, a young British officer and is less certain about the colonists' viewpoint. Patience becomes an unwilling witness to the tea party in the harbor.

313. Atkins, Jeannine. *Anne Hutchinson's Way.* Illustrated by Michael Dooling. Farrar, 2007. 32pp. ISBN 978-0-374-30365-5. Grades 2–5. In 1634 Anne Hutchinson and her family settle in Massachusetts after leaving England in hope of finding religious freedom. What they find is the severe world of the early Puritans, where couples are condemned for kissing in public and women considered sinful for speaking out. Hutchinson begins reading scripture and preaching in her home in opposition to the messages from the men in the pulpits. Eventually, the leaders condemn her for disturbing the peace and have her confined. Susanna, the youngest of Hutchinson's ten children, relates the story of the imbalanced treatment of women in this colony. The next year, the family reunited but in another colony. Canvas paintings enhance the text.

314. Avi. *Encounter at Easton.* Camelot, 2000. 144pp. Paper ISBN 978-0-380-73241-8. Grades 5 up. A sequel to *Night Journeys*, *Encounter at Easton* tells the story of indentured servants Elizabeth Mawes and Robert Linnly who escape from their master in 1768 and hope to find a new life in Easton, Pennsylvania. Elizabeth is wounded and Robert must make a difficult decision—who should he trust? *Charlie May Simon Book Award* (Arkansas) nomination, *Mark Twain Book* (Missouri) Award nomination, *Battle of the Books Children's Book Award* (New Mexico) nomination, and *State Reading Association for Young Readers Program* (Virginia) nomination.

315. Avi. *Night Journeys.* Avon, 2000. 160pp. Paper ISBN 978-0-380-73242-5. Grades 5 up. Twelve-year-old orphan Peter York searches for escaped bondservants so that he can claim the reward money offered by their masters. In 1768 he finds two of them near Trenton, New Jersey. While he is taking the two back to the authorities, he and the bound girl become friends. He begins to question whether one person has the right to sell another. When Peter asks his Quaker guardian, the guardian, a justice of the peace, cannot legally advise him. Peter's decision, however, pleases the Quaker. *Scott O'Dell Award for Historical Fiction.*

316. Bruchac, Joseph. *The Winter People.* Dial, 2002. ISBN 978-0-8037-2694-9; Puffin, 2004, paper ISBN 978-0-14-240229-0. Grades 5–10. In 1759 during the French and Indian War

14-year-old Saxso is one of the few Abenaki males left in his village when British soldiers attack and take his sisters and mother hostage. He sets out to track them so he can recapture his family. *Young Hoosier Book Award* (Indiana) nomination, *William Allen White Children's Book Award* (Kansas) nomination, *Student Book Award* (Maine) nomination, *School Library Journal Best Children's Books*, and *Young Adult Reading Program* (South Dakota) nomination.

317. Bulla, Clyde Robert. *A Lion to Guard Us.* Illustrated by Michele Chessare. Trophy, 1989. 118pp. Paper ISBN 978-0-06-440333-7. Grades 2–5. In 1609 Amanda, Meg, and Jemmy sail from England to meet their father in Jamestown. Although their ship is wrecked in Bermuda, they survive. During their struggle, they keep a door knocker shaped like a lion from their old home, and it gives them hope that their father still protects them. They eventually reunite with him in Jamestown. *Notable Children's Trade Books in the Field of Social Studies.*

318. Bulla, Clyde Robert. *Pocahontas and the Strangers.* Illustrated by Peter Burchard. Scholastic, 1995. 180pp. Paper ISBN 978-0-590-43481-2. Grades 2–6. Pocahontas decides to claim Captain John Smith as her prisoner, an act that saves him as she becomes the liaison between the white settlers and her tribe in 1612. The settlers then take her as a hostage, and during the time she lives with them, she meets and marries John Rolfe. After she sails to England with him and their child, she dies. Her conciliatory efforts were a key to the settlers surviving in their Virginia homes.

319. Butler, Amy. *Virginia Bound.* Clarion, 2003. 192pp. ISBN 978-0-618-24752-3. Grades 5–8. Rob Brackett, a 13-year-old beggar in London, has been looking after a young girl named Nell. But the two of them are kidnapped and sent to the new Jamestown colony in Virginia. Rob is indentured to a cruel tobacco farmer and worries about Nell's fate. He finds a friend in Mattoume, a young Pamunkey Indian girl, and he learns to trust her despite what he has been told.

320. Carbone, Elisa. *Blood on the River: James Town, 1607.* Viking, 2006. 237pp. ISBN 978-0-670-06060-3; Puffin, 2007, paper ISBN 978-0-14-240932-9. Grades 5–8. Orphan Samuel Collier, 12, travels with Captain John Smith to the New World and the colony of Jamestown in 1606, delighted to have a chance to reinvent himself. After he arrives, however, he realizes that he must carefully assess whether those who approach him are friends or foes. He details the settlers' daily food and activities while trying to adjust to this new life and learning to hunt with his Powhatan friends. *Readers Choice Award* (Virginia) nomination, *Volunteer State Book Awards* (Tennessee) nomination, *Jefferson Cup Winner*, *School Library Journal Best Books for Children*, and *Bluegrass Award* (Kentucky) nomination.

321. Clifford, Mary, and Joyce Haynes. *When the Great Canoes Came.* Firebird, 1999. 144pp. Paper ISBN 978-1-56554-646-2. Grades 5–8. The old members of the Pamunkey tribe tell the young ones about the arrival of the English settlers in Jamestown, Virginia. The promise of trinkets and English clothes lure young members of the tribe to Jamestown before the queen can even finish telling the story. Lost Owl is angry at their defection, and he must learn to cope with it. But the tribe no longer has peace after the death of Pocahontas in England, because her father no longer seems particularly interested in tribal affairs. Bibliography.

322. Cook, Peter. *You Wouldn't Want to Sail on the Mayflower: A Trip that Took Entirely Too Long.* Illustrated by Kevin Whelan. Franklin Watts, 2005. 32pp. ISBN 978-0-531-12411-6; paper ISBN 978-0-531-12391-1. Grades 3–6. Readers become the main characters in this story as they imagine themselves in various parts of the *Mayflower* on the voyage to America and in Plymouth Colony after they arrive. Illustrations, cartoons, creative dialogue, and "hints" highlight the story. Glossary, Maps, and Index.

323. Deutsch, Stacia, and Rhody Cohon. *Ben Franklin's Fame.* Illustrated by Guy Francis. (Blast to the Past) Aladdin, 2006. 119pp. Paper ISBN 978-0-689-91804-2. Grades 2–5. In a time-travel fictional biography, third-grade students Abigail, Jacob, Zack, and Bo rush to stop Benjamin Franklin from giving up his various interests.

324. Duble, Kathleen Benner. *The Sacrifice.* Margaret K. McElderry, 2005. 224pp. ISBN 978-0-689-87650-9. Grades 4–8. In 1692 authorities in Andover, Massachusetts, accuse lively 10-year-old Abigail Faulkner of being unladylike for running and hiking her skirt above her knee. Abigail's father has a mental illness and seems "possessed." Abigail and her sister Dorothy are accused of being witches and are arrested. Their mother tells them to accuse her, believing she will not be executed because she is pregnant. Abigail's courage saves the day. *William Allen White Children's Book Award* (Kansas) nomination and *Young Readers Choice Book Award* (Louisiana) nomination.

325. Edmonds, Walter. *The Matchlock Gun.* Illustrated by Paul Lantz. Putnam, 1989. 50pp. ISBN 978-0-399-21911-5; Puffin, 1998, paper ISBN 978-0-698-11680-1. Grades 3–6. Edward, 10, has to help his mother defend their home while his father is away fighting the Indians in 1757. When his mother and the other children see smoke in the distance, they know the Indians are coming. Edward's mother quickly teaches him how to fire the Spanish matchlock gun. Although the gun is twice as long as he is tall, Edward fires at the enemy and kills two men who have thrown tomahawks at his mother. The Indians burn the house, but his bravery saves their lives. *Newbery Medal.*

326. Edwards, Pamela Duncan. *Boston Tea Party.* Illustrated by Henry Cole. Putnam, 2001. 32pp. ISBN 978-0-399-23357-9. Grades 1–3. In a rhythmic cumulative tale, mice relate the events leading up to the Boston Tea Party in 1773—George III's taxes, the three ships in the Boston harbor, and the colonists in disguise heaving the tea into the water. Acrylic and pencil illustrations enhance the text. Chronology.

327. Elliott, L. M. *Give Me Liberty.* Katherine Tegen, 2006. 376pp. ISBN 978-0-06-074421-2; HarperTrophy, 2008, paper ISBN 978-0-06-074423-6. Grades 5–8. In 1774, as an indentured servant to a carriage maker in Williamsburg, Virginia, Nathaniel Dunn, 13, watches the growing divide between the patriots and the loyalists. He becomes friends with Basil, a music teacher, from whom he learns much about patriotism, philosophy, and the arts. But as his master's business loses customers, Nathaniel must support what he believes in the ensuing American Revolution.

328. Field, Rachel. *Calico Bush.* Illustrated by Allen Lewis. Simon & Schuster, 1987. ISBN 978-0-02-734610-7; Aladdin, 1998, paper ISBN 978-0-689-82285-8. Grades 4–8. In 1740 Marguerite and her grandmother arrive in the American colonies from France. Her grandmother dies soon after, and Marguerite becomes bound to a family leaving Massachusetts to go to a northern seacoast town. When they arrive, they discover that Indians think the land on which they will live is sacred, and they have burned down the house. Marguerite misses the celebration of Christmas and must use her ingenuity to solve various problems. With the help of an old Scottish woman who knows about herbs, she copes with her changed situation. *Newbery Honor.*

329. Fleischman, Sid. *The 13th Floor: A Ghost Story.* Illustrated by Peter Sís. Greenwillow, 1995. 144pp. ISBN 978-0-688-14216-2; Trophy, 2007, paper ISBN 978-0-06-134503-6. Grades 3–6. In this historical fantasy, a distress message on an answering machine calls Buddy and his sister Liz, a lawyer, to a building that has no 13th floor. Then Buddy finds himself aboard the *Laughing Mermaid*, a boat belonging to an ancestor who was a privateer, and Liz ends up in Boston in 1692, where she must save another ancestor from a witch hunter, allowing the family line to continue. Buddy recounts their adventures, which include a dead pirate, a talking fish, orphans, and mistaken identity.

330. Fritz, Jean. *Who's Saying What in Jamestown, Thomas Savage?* Illustrated by Sally Wern Comport. Putnam, 2007. 64pp. ISBN 978-0-399-24644-9. Grades 3–5. Thomas Savage, 13, comes to Virginia in 1608 and is sent to live with Native Americans and their leader Powhatan. He is to learn their language and become an interpreter. Tensions build between the Native Americans and the settlers, and Powhatan attacks a number of colonists as Thomas watches. Knowing that peace cannot exist, Thomas returns to Jamestown and becomes a landowner on the Eastern Shore. Illustrations complement the text.

331. Hermes, Patricia. *Salem Witch.* (My Side of the Story) Kingfisher, 2006. Paper ISBN 978-0-7534-5991-1. Grades 5–8. Elizabeth Putnam and her best friend George each express their views of the Salem witch trials in 1692. Elizabeth and her family believe the women are innocent; George's father vehemently believes they are guilty. When Elizabeth becomes one of the accused, George has to decide whether to support Elizabeth or his father. Readers can read Elizabeth's point of view and then flip the book over to read what George thinks.

332. **Holt, Kimberly Willis.** *Waiting for Gregory.* Illustrated by Gabriela Swiatkowska. Henry Holt, 2006. Unpaged. ISBN 978-0-8050-7388-1. Grades K–2. Iris lives in the 18th century and wants to know when her baby cousin, Gregory, will be born. The silly examples that adults give her reflect the time period, both in words and illustrations.

333. **Hurst, Carol Otis, and Rebecca Otis.** *A Killing in Plymouth Colony.* Walter Lorraine, 2003. 160pp. ISBN 978-0-618-27597-7. Grades 5–8. In 1630, 11-year-old John Bradford has a difficult relationship with his father, Plymouth Colony Governor William Bradford, after he arrives from living with a foster father in Amsterdam. His stepmother, however, loves him, and he has friends. Then his friend Sam's little sister suddenly becomes listless and stops talking—and a colonist is murdered. Are the two situations related? Glossary.

334. **Jones, Elizabeth McDavid.** *Traitor in Williamsburg: A Felicity Mystery.* American Girl, 2008. 180pp. ISBN 978-1-59369-297-1; paper ISBN 978-1-59369-296-4. Grades 3–5. In Williamsburg, Virginia, in 1776, Felicity and Elizabeth try to find out who is maligning the father of their friend Fiona. Anonymous broadsides also threaten him. Then Felicity discovers that her own father may need to be protected as well.

335. **Karr, Kathleen.** *Worlds Apart.* Marshall Cavendish, 2005. 208pp. ISBN 978-0-7614-5195-2. Grades 5–8. In 1670, 15-year-old Christopher West makes friends with a young Sewee Indian, Asha-po, in South Carolina. They learn from each other, with Asha-po teaching Christopher how to survive. Soon Christopher begins to question what his people have done to the Sewees, but the settlers continue to take for granted the Sewees' help in fighting off the Spanish. When Christopher returns from a trip inland, he sees the Sewees heading out to sea in canoes, straight into a hurricane.

336. **Kay, Verla.** *Tattered Sails.* Putnam, 2001. Unpaged. ISBN 978-0-399-23345-6. Grades K–8. With their parents, young Thomas, Edward, and Mary Jane leave the dirty, crime-ridden streets of London for the Massachusetts Bay Colony in 1635. Their ship is crowded and the voyage across the Atlantic is rough. They must cope with seasickness and bad food and water. However, they arrive in America to start a new life. Illustrations enhance the rhyming text.

337. **Keehn, Sally M.** *I Am Regina.* Puffin, 2002. 240pp. Paper ISBN 978-0-698-11920-8. Grades 4–8. In 1755, Regina is 11 years old. Allegheny Indians kidnap her and her sister after killing her father and brother. She spends eight years with them, forgets German, and speaks the Allegheny language. Within the tribe, she has both a helpful friend and a spiteful enemy. When they die of smallpox, she knows them well enough to grieve, but she and her sister still miss their mother, who sang a song they cannot forget.

338. **Kimmel, Eric A.** *Blackbeard's Last Fight.* Illustrated by Leonard Everett Fisher. Farrar, 2006. 32pp. Paper ISBN 978-0-374-30780-6. Grades 2–4. Jeremy Hobbs is a cabin boy on the ship that succeeds in capturing and executing the notorious pirate Blackbeard. Blackbeard has recently blockaded the Charleston, South Carolina, port and has plundered too many ships. In an exciting sea battle, Jeremy actually meets Blackbeard just before his death and discovers that Blackbeard's sixteen wives loved him and that he freed many Africans.

339. **Kirkpatrick, Katherine.** *Escape Across the Wide Sea.* Holiday House, 2004. 210pp. ISBN 978-0-8234-1854-1. Grades 5–8. In 1686 Daniel Bonnet, 9, and his Huguenot family escape from France on a ship they believe is bound for England. Instead they go to Africa to pick up slaves, on to Guadeloupe, and finally reach New York. Daniel, although wounded before leaving France, performs chores that take him to the ship's hold. There he meets Seynabou and learns about the slaves' conditions. Daniel's family becomes part of a group that establishes the community of New Rochelle, where Daniel's father can take up his weaving trade again. Bibliography, Glossary, and Note.

340. **Lasky, Kathryn.** *Beyond the Burning Time.* Pointe, 1996. 272pp. Paper ISBN 978-0-590-47332-3. Grades 5–9. In 1691 Mary Chase, 12, works hard with her mother on their Salem farm while her brother Caleb serves his shipbuilding apprenticeship. At the same time, the

strange actions of girls who have been visiting Tituba, Reverend Parris's slave, begin to frighten the town. A boy who works for the family accuses Mary's mother Virginia of being a witch. Mary and Caleb rescue their mother from hanging. The ending reveals that the story, in omniscient point of view, is a flashback. *American Library Association Best Books for Young Adults.*

341. **Lasky, Kathryn.** *A Journey to the New World: The Diary of Remember Patience Whipple: Mayflower/Plimoth Colony, 1620.* (Dear America) Scholastic, 1996. 173pp. ISBN 978-0-590-50214-6. Grades 5–9. When Mem is 12, she and her family sail on the *Mayflower*. She writes in her journal from October 1, 1620, until November 10, 1621, when she watches another ship come into the harbor and hopes that a girl her age will be arriving soon. She talks of the difficult times during the year as well as the Thanksgiving celebration, and dares to dream that someday their settlement will have a bakery. An epilogue gives further information about her after her diary ends.

342. **Lawson, Robert.** *Ben and Me: An Astonishing Life of Benjamin Franklin by His Good Mouse Amos.* Lilttle, Brown, 1999. 114pp. ISBN 978-0-316-52533-6; 2005, paper ISBN 978-0-316-01636-0. Grades 2–6. Amos, a mouse, describes himself as Dr. Benjamin Franklin's closest friend and adviser and the one responsible for Franklin's inventions and discoveries, especially his successes at the French court. In this biographical fiction, the mouse reveals Franklin's achievements.

343. **Lawson, Robert.** *Mr. Revere and I: Being an Account of Certain Episodes in the Career of Paul Revere, Esq., As Recently Revealed by His Horse, Scheherazade, Later Pride of His Royal Majesty's 14th Regiment of Foot.* Little, Brown, 1988. 114pp. Paper ISBN 978-0-316-51729-4. Grades 3–6. Paul Revere's horse Scheherazade tells about the life of Paul Revere from the vantage point of her shed stall, from which she can look into the kitchen. She describes the family, the silversmith trade, and the Sons of Liberty.

344. **Lenski, Lois.** *Indian Captive: The Story of Mary Jemison.* Trophy, 1995. Paper ISBN 978-0-06-446162-7. Grades 5 up. This book is based on a true story. Seneca Indians captured 12-year-old Mary Jemison in 1758 and massacred her family in retaliation for white settlers killing their own people. After two years, she felt as if she belonged to this group of Indians, who were mostly kind and courageous, and she refused to go with the English conquerors of Quebec. Lenski presents a balanced view of Native American and white settlers—none of them all bad or all good. The blond Mary, first known as "Corn Tassel," earned her name "Little-Woman-of-Great-Courage" by realizing that being with people who loved her was more important than being with people of the same race who only saw her as a pawn in a distant war. This book was first published in 1941. *Newbery Honor.*

345. **Littlesugar, Amy.** *The Spinner's Daughter.* Illustrated by Robert M. Quackenbush. Pippin, 1994. 30pp. ISBN 978-0-945912-22-4. Grades K–3. Elspeth Allen, a young Puritan living in the American colonies in the 17th century, wants to play ball with an Indian nearby, but her widowed mother tells her she has no time for games. The Indian boy makes Elspeth a cornhusk doll and she shows it to the village children. They all want one and she makes dolls for them. Disturbed by this behavior, the town elders decide she must wear a sign to show her disobedience. A judge coming through town declares that her sign should read "Child."

346. **McKissack, Patricia C.** *Look to the Hills: The Diary of Lozette Moreau, a French Slave.* (Dear America) Scholastic, 2004. 192pp. ISBN 978-0-439-21038-6. Grades 4–9. Twelve-year-old African orphaned slave Lozette Moreau escapes to the New World in 1763 with her mistress, French nobleman's daughter Mary-Louise. Mary-Louise wants to escape the marriage her brother arranged after their father's death and to keep Zettie from being sold to someone else. A friend helps them get to Spain and then to a fort in British-controlled New York state. The two become involved with people who are still fighting in the French and Indian War. Although Zettie cannot do household chores, she can read, and she helps soldiers write letters home. Additionally, she hears that the French are giving the Indians blankets infected with smallpox as a way to defeat them. As in other books in the series, Zettie records the story in her diary.

347. Murphy, Frank. *Ben Franklin and the Magic Squares.* Illustrated by Richard Walz. (Step into Reading) Random, 2001. 48pp. ISBN 978-0-375-90621-3; paper ISBN 978-0-375-80621-6. Grades 1–3. When Benjamin Franklin served as a clerk for the Pennsylvania Assembly, he created a puzzle called the magic square to keep himself from being bored. The magic square is a square grid of numbers in which all the numbers in any row—vertical, horizontal, or diagonal—add up the same. An appendix gives instructions for creating these mathematical puzzles.

348. Myers, Anna. *Spy!* Walker, 2008. 211pp. ISBN 978-0-8027-9742-1. Grades 3–7. In 1774 Jonah Hawkins, 12, loves being in class with his wonderful Connecticut teacher, Nathan Hale. Hale's wealthy brother Samuel funds Jonah's education. As the colony begins to rebel, Nathan Hale joins the Continental Army while Samuel remains a Tory businessman. When Samuel decides to return to England, Jonah does not know which man to support. An action he makes leads to Nathan Hale's discovery as a spy and his quick execution. Jonah must live with his actions and follow his convictions.

349. Platt, Richard. *Pirate Diary: The Journal of Jake Carpenter.* Illustrated by Chris Ridell. Candlewick, 2005. 64pp. Paper ISBN 978-0-7636-2865-9. Grades 3–6. Jake Carpenter, 9, joins Captain Nick at sea in 1716 to become a sailor and discovers what being a pirate entails. He keeps a journal of his observations describing whippings, food filled with maggots, death threats, limb amputation, and sea burial. Then when Jake mistakenly drops a bucket overboard, Captain Nick sets Jake's Uncle Will adrift as Jake's punishment. When pirates capture the ship, they abandon Captain Nick on an island, and he reunites with Will. Watercolor-and-ink Illustrations augment the text. Bibliography, Glossary, and Index. *Young Readers Choice Book Award* (Louisiana) nomination.

350. Richter, Conrad. *The Light in the Forest.* Illustrated by Warren Chappell. Everyman, 2005. 180pp. ISBN 978-1-4000-4426-9; Vintage, 2004, paper ISBN 978-1-4000-7788-5. Grades 5 up. True Son, 15 years old in 1765, has lived with the Cuyloga (Delaware Indians) for eleven years and thinks of himself as one of the tribe. When the settlers demand that the Cuyloga release white captives living with them, True Son has to leave. He cannot adjust to life among the settlers, whom he has learned to hate, including his biological parents.

351. Schwabach, Karen. *A Pickpocket's Tale.* Random, 2006. 225pp. ISBN 978-0-375-83379-3; Yearling, 2008, paper ISBN 978-0-375-83380-9. Grades 4–8. After being arrested for picking pockets in London in 1730, 10-year-old Molly is sent to New York City. There she is bought as an indentured servant by the Bell family, who decides she will be Jewish. What Molly does not know is that she is already Jewish. The family is kind to her even though she initially protests new habits of bathing, clothing, and food, wanting to return to the street life she knows. She then learns how to keep the house, keep kosher, and how to read. Her values eventually change so that she realizes that helping an abused slave escape is more important than her own livelihood.

352. Sewall, Martha. *The Pilgrims of Plimoth.* Aladdin, 1996. 48pp. Paper ISBN 978-0-689-80861-6. Grades 2–5. In a first-person narrative, Sewall captures the language and thoughts of the people who came from England to build new homes in America in 1620. Men, women, and children speak about their experiences on the *Mayflower* and their daily lives in the new settlement. The accompanying illustrations enhance the text. Glossary. *Boston Globe/Horn Book Award, School Library Journal Best Book, Horn Book Fanfare Honor List, International Reading Association Children's Choices,* and *Notable Children's Trade Books in the Field of Social Studies.*

353. Shaw, Janet Beeler. *Kaya's Escape! A Survival Story.* Illustrated by Bill Farnsworth and Susan McAliley. American Girl, 2002. 72pp. ISBN 978-1-58485-426-5; paper ISBN 978-1-58485-427-2. Grades 3–5. In 1764 enemy horse raiders capture Kaya and her blind sister, Speaking Rain, from their Nez Percé village. They become slaves of the enemy, but Kaka escapes in the cold winter and returns home, determined to go back for Speaking Rain. Glossary.

354. Shaw, Janet Beeler. *Meet Kaya: An American Girl.* Illustrated by Bill Farnsworth and Susan McAliley. American Girl, 2002. 70pp. ISBN 978-1-58485-424-1; paper ISBN 978-1-

58485-423-4. Grades 3–5. In 1764, Kaya, 9, lives with her Nez Percé parents and siblings, including her blind sister Speaking Rain. She wants to race her beautiful mare, Steps High, but discovers, when challenged, that such contests can be very dangerous. Notes and Glossary.

355. **Speare, Elizabeth George.** *The Sign of the Beaver.* Houghton, 1983. 144pp. ISBN 978-0-395-33890-2; Yearling, 1997, paper ISBN 978-0-440-47900-0. Grades 4–8. Matt and his father go to Maine to build a new house in 1768. When the home is ready, Matt's father leaves him alone while he returns to Massachusetts to get the rest of the family. Someone steals Matt's gun, but his worst moment comes when bees sting him so badly that he loses consciousness. An Indian boy nearby hears him screaming and comes to nurse him back to health. Matt teaches the boy to read and the boy teaches Matt how to trap, fish, and find trails. *Newbery Honor, Child Study Children's Book Committee and Bank Street College Award, Christopher Award, American Library Association Notable Children's Books, School Library Journal Best Book*, and *Scott O'Dell Award.*

356. **Speare, Elizabeth George.** *The Witch of Blackbird Pond.* Book Wholesalers, 2002. ISBN 978-0-7587-0227-2; Yearling, 1972, paper ISBN 978-0-440-49596-3. Grades 5–8. When Kit's grandfather dies in 1687, she has to leave Barbados and go to New England to live with her only relative, her deceased mother's sister. The bleak life, with no entertainment or color, depresses her, and she cannot adjust. A Quaker woman nearby, whom others in the community call a witch, helps her endure the agony. Kit is also considered a witch when she tries to teach a child to read, and they try her in court. However, when the child reads for the court, the people can no longer condemn Kit. *Newbery Medal* and *International Board of Books for Young People.*

357. **Thermes, Jennifer.** *Sam Bennett's New Shoes.* Carolrhoda, 2006. Unpaged. ISBN 978-1-57505-822-1. Grades K–2. During colonial times Sam gets new shoes, and his father hides his old ones in a wall near the chimney of their cabin. He tells Sam that this custom came from his old home and that it will keep the family safe. Sam thinks the shoes help him throughout his life, even after he has a baby and is a farmer himself. Illustrations complement the text.

358. **Tripp, Valerie.** *Meet Felicity: An American Girl.* Illustrated by Luann Roberts and Dan Andreasen. American Girl, 1991. 68pp. ISBN 978-1-56247-005-0; paper ISBN 978-1-56247-004-3. Grades 3–5. In Williamsburg, Virginia, in 1774, Felicity, 9, rises early every morning to take care of a horse owned by an alcoholic owner who beats and starves it. He will not sell the horse to her father, so Felicity helps it escape by jumping it over a fence and deliberately falling off.

359. **Wechter, Nell Wise, and Bruce Tucker.** *Teach's Light.* Univ. of North Carolina, 1999. 160pp. Paper ISBN 978-0-8078-4793-0. Grades 4–7. When Corky Calhoun and Toby Davis, two teenagers from North Carolina's Outer Banks, decide to find Teach's Light in the Little Dismal Swamp, they experience a sudden explosion and find themselves in 1681 England. There they safely float above the town and watch the orphaned Edward Teach decide to stow away on a ship crossing the Atlantic. Teach (soon to be known as Blackbeard) begins a career as a pirate in the Caribbean aboard the *Queen Anne's Revenge*. British soldiers finally behead him during a sea battle. When Corky and Toby return to the present, they have not found the light that supposedly guards some of Blackbeard's treasure, but they have learned a lot about the man who might have hidden it.

History

360. **Anderson, Dale.** *The American Colonies Declare Independence.* World Almanac, 2005. 48pp. ISBN 978-0-8368-5926-3. Grades 5–8. This look at the American colonies before they declared war on the British shows the changing ideas and expectations. Primary sources including letters, diaries, and pamphlets describe key events and reveal the treatment of

Native Americans by both the colonists and the British. Reproductions and maps enhance the text.

361. Anderson, Joan. *The First Thanksgiving Feast.* Illustrated by George Ancona. Clarion, 1989. Paper ISBN 978-0-395-51886-1. Grades K–3. This volume recreates the first harvest festival that the pilgrims celebrated after arriving in Plymouth. Photographs accompanying the text feature the living history museum of Plimoth Plantation. Recreations feature John Alden, Elizabeth Hopkins, Miles Standish, and Governor Bradford.

362. Anderson, Joan. *A Williamsburg Household.* Illustrated by George Ancona. Clarion, 1989. 48pp. Paper ISBN 978-0-395-54791-5. Grades K–3. In 1770 Williamsburg, Rippon and his parents are slaves working for different families. Although they have difficult lives, they enjoy doing errands in town because they have a chance to see each other. Photographs from the Williamsburg living history museum complement the text.

363. Appelbaum, Diana. *Giants in the Land.* Illustrated by Michael McDurdy. Houghton, 1993. Unpaged. ISBN 978-0-395-64720-2; 2000, paper ISBN 978-0-618-03305-8. Grades 1–6. Giant trees more than 250 feet tall once covered New England. These trees, branded the property of the king before the Revolutionary War, made excellent Royal Navy ship masts. Men using simple tools chopped these trees down. The text tells how they did it. *Bulletin Blue Ribbon.*

364. Arenstam, Peter, et al. *Mayflower 1620: A New Look at a Pilgrim Voyage.* Illustrated by Sisse Brimber and Cotton Coulson. National Geographic, 2003. 48pp. ISBN 978-0-7922-6142-1. Grades K–4. This volume looks at new research about the founders of Plimoth Colony and includes information about how these people traveled and their reasons for coming to the New World. They did not call themselves pilgrims, they did not leave England for religious reasons, and they did not find empty land. The photographs show reenactments of the 1620 voyage of the *Mayflower.* Maps, Chronology, Bibiliography, and Index.

365. Boraas, Tracey A. *The Salem Witch Trials.* (Let Freedom Ring) Capstone, 2004. 48pp. ISBN 978-0-7368-2464-4. Grades 4–6. In 1692 two girls succumbed to hysterical fits that led to the arrests and deaths of many women in the village of Salem, Massachusetts. Six chapters present the beginning of the scare, the spreading hunt for witches and the ensuing fear, the trials, the accusations and the hangings, and the final return to sanity. Maps, Timeline, Glossary, Further Reading, Web Sites, and Index.

366. Brower, Pauline. *Missions of the Inland Valleys: San Luis Obispo de Tolosa, San Miguel Arcángel, San Antonio de Padua, and Nuestra Señora de la Soledad.* Lerner, 1999. 80pp. Paper ISBN 978-0-8225-9833-6. Grades 4–6. In the 1700s Spain sent Roman Catholic priests to establish missions and presidios (forts) along the coast of Baja California and other areas of New Spain (present-day Southwestern United States and Mexico). Spain wanted the Indians to accept Spanish ways and become loyal subjects. In an attempt to reach Indians inland after settling the coast, Father Serra chose a site in the valley of the Coast Ranges for San Antonio de Padua, which at first faltered but then grew prosperous. Neophytes and Indians at San Luis Obispo de Tolosa, a second mission, developed durable clay tiles to replace tule reed as roofing material. Other missions were Nuestra Señora de la Soledad, so isolated that it was called the "Forgotten Mission," and San Miguel Arcángel, which gained a reputation for its frescoes painted by talented neophytes. Glossary, Chronology, and Index.

367. Brown, Gene. *Discovery and Settlement: Europe Meets the New World.* (First Person America) Twenty-First Century, 1993. 64pp. ISBN 978-0-8050-2574-3. Grades 5–8. With primary source materials and illustrations, this volume covers the discovery and settlement of America and daily life in the colonies, including the experiences of Native Americans, African Americans, and women. Bibliography and Index.

368. Bruchac, Marge. *Malian's Song.* Illustrated by William Maughan. Vermont Folklife Center, 2006. 32pp. ISBN 978-0-916718-26-8. Grades 2–4. In 1759 Malian lives happily with her Abenaki family and prepares for a wedding. But on the night before the event, Malian's father, Simôn Obomsawin, grabs her out of bed and hides her in the woods. She never sees him again. With others, she watches the British burn her village—a Mohican scout disloyal to his employers had warned them about the raid just in time. She returns to help rebuild the village and to restore a normal life with their traditional foods, clothes, ceremonies, and fishing. Illustrations complement the text. Bibliography.

369. **Chorao, Kay.** *D Is for Drums.* Abrams, 2004. Unpaged. ISBN 978-0-8109-4927-0. Grades 1–4. This alphabet book introduces Colonial Williamsburg, Virginia. Each letter illustrates an activity or name. "A" shows an apothecary shop, "D" is a drum, and "Q" represents such items as quoits, quills, and quilts. Illustrations enhance the text. Note.

370. **Cook, Peter.** *You Wouldn't Want to Be at the Boston Tea Party! Wharf Water Tea You'd Rather Not Drink.* Illustrated by David Antram. Children's Press, 2006. 32pp. Paper ISBN 978-0-531-12447-5. Grades 3–6. Readers follow the story of the Boston Tea Party through the character of a young man who is too short to join the British Army. He watches as patriots dress as Mohawk Indians to destroy the crates of British tea. Events leading up to the Tea Party are also covered. Sidebars and illustrations complement the text.

371. **Cooper, Michael L.** *Jamestown, 1607.* Holiday House, 2007. 98pp. ISBN 978-0-8234-1948-7. Grades 4–8. Cooper examines the founding of the Jamestown colony in Virginia in 1607 and how the settlers dealt with disease, winter storms, starvation, and Native American attacks. Primary sources offer background about their situation and how they survived. Period photographs, maps, and illustrations add to the text. Bibliography, Chronology, Notes, Web Sites, and Index.

372. **Davis, Kenneth C.** *Don't Know Much About the Pilgrims.* Illustrated by S. D. Schindler. HarperCollins, 2002. 45pp. ISBN 978-0-06-028609-3; 2006, paper ISBN 978-0-06-446228-0. Grades 3–5. This volume uses a question-and-answer format to give information about the Pilgrims including how and why they came to America on the *Mayflower,* how they established the colony of New Plymouth, and what happened there. It also provides information about Native Americans and how they lived and where. Illustrations enhance the text.

373. **Dell, Pamela.** *Plymouth Colony.* (Let Freedom Ring) Capstone, 2004. 48pp. ISBN 978-0-7368-2463-7. Grades 4–6. In the 1620s a group of immigrants landed in New England and established the Plymouth Colony. Six chapters present their journey, arrival, the first winter, the peace established with the American Indians, their feelings of loneliness, and the struggle to survive the experience. Illustrations augment the text. Maps, Timeline, Glossary, Further Reading, Web Sites, and Index.

374. **Doak, Robin.** *Maryland 1634–1776.* (Voices from Colonial America) National Geographic, 2007. 112pp. ISBN 978-0-7922-0144-5. Grades 5–8. Doak examines Maryland's role during the colonial period, with chapters on the Native Americans and Spaniards, the English settlers, life in the new colony, the time of troubles, tobacco, the growth of the colony, its Golden Age, and its desire for self-government. Primary source materials reveal the struggles of individuals and provide cultural data. Photographs, reproductions, augment the text. Bibliography, Chronology, Further Reading, Web Sites, and Index.

375. **Erickson, Paul.** *Daily Life in the Pilgrim Colony 1636.* Clarion, 2001. 48pp. ISBN 978-0-618-05846-4; paper ISBN 978-0-395-98841-1. Grades 3–5. In twenty-one chapters, this volume describes the daily life of the Prentiss family in New Plymouth Colony. Topics include home, family, women's work, men's work, clothing, trade, defense, cooking and eating, children's activities, government, religion, health, medicine, special occasions, celebrations, and the place of pilgrims in history. Photographs highlight the text. Chronology, Glossary, and Index.

376. **Fischer, Laura.** *Life in New Amsterdam.* (Picture the Past) Heinemann, 2003. 32pp. ISBN 978-1-4034-3798-3; paper ISBN 978-1-4034-4285-7. Grades 2–4. Life for the early colonists in New Amsterdam from 1624 to 1664 was quite different from life in New York City today. Fischer looks at the food they ate, the clothes they wore, their homes, the types of education available, the means of communication, transport, and entertainment. A comparison between life today and life then highlights the differences. Illustrations enhance the text. Maps and Timelines.

377. Fisher, Leonard Everett. *The Papermakers, the Hatters, the Potters, the Tanners.* (Colonial Craftsmen) Benchmark, 2000. 48pp. ISBN 978-0-7614-1145-1. Grades 4–6. Fisher examines the history, style, and manufacture of hats, pottery, and paper in colonial America. It also includes the history of tanning and how tanners treated animal hides during the colonial era. Illustrations enhance the text. Glossary and Index.

378. Fradin, Dennis B. *Jamestown, Virginia.* (Turning Points in U.S. History) Benchmark, 2006. 45pp. ISBN 978-0-7614-2122-1. Grades 3–6. Jamestown was not the first settlement in the New World. Fradin offers information about some of the earlier settlements, describes the difficulties facing colonists at Jamestown, and notes the legacy of Jamestown. Photographs and illustrations augment the text. Bibliography, Chronology, Web Sites, and Index.

379. Fritz, Jean. *The Lost Colony of Roanoke.* Illustrated by Hudson Talbott. Putnam, 2004. 64pp. ISBN 978-0-399-24027-0. Grades 4–6. Sir Walter Raleigh founded the colony of Roanoke, leaving fifteen people behind when he returned to England. The second expedition arrived in 1587 but found nobody left in the colony to meet them. Governor John White then returned to England to beg Elizabeth I for her help, but the war with Spain delayed his next trip west with supplies until 1590. When he arrived at Roanoke, he saw only the letters "CRO" carved in a tree. Questions remain regarding the fate of the settlers. Did they starve or were they massacred? Did they become part of the Croatan tribe? Historians have been unable to solve the mystery. Watercolor illustrations enhance the text. Notes, Bibliography, and Index.

380. George, Jean Craighead. *The First Thanksgiving.* Illustrated by Thomas Locker. Puffin, 1996. Unpaged. Paper ISBN 978-0-698-11392-3. Grades 2–5. After the Pilgrims arrived and spent a long winter with the help of Squanto and others, they celebrated their harvest with the first Thanksgiving. The text is complemented by vibrant illustrations.

381. Gillis, Jennifer Blizin. *Life in Colonial Boston.* (Picture the Past) Heinemann, 2003. 32pp. ISBN 978-1-4034-3795-2; paper ISBN 978-1-4034-4284-0. Grades 2–4. Between 1760 and 1773 life in Boston under the British caused the colonists to resent their treatment. They disliked the trade restrictions and new taxes imposed upon them. This volume looks at the food they ate, the clothes they wore, their homes, the type of education, their ability to communicate, the way they moved from one place to another, and their choices for amusement. A comparison between life today and life then highlights the differences. Illustrations enhance the text. Maps and Timelines.

382. Grace, Catherine O'Neill, and Margaret M. Bruchac. *1621: A New Look at Thanksgiving.* Illustrated by Sisse Brimber and Cotton Coulson. National Geographic, 2001. 48pp. ISBN 978-0-7922-7027-0; 2004, paper ISBN 978-0-7922-6139-1. Grades K–4. Grace looks at the actual events that took place during the first Thanksgiving in 1621. Nine chapters introduce the people of the First Light, the Hampanoag language, the Wampanoag diplomacy, the plenty of the land, the celebration, and how the holiday evolved. Photographs highlight the text. Bibliography, Chronology, and Index.

383. Hakim, Joy. *From Colonies to Country: 1735–1791.* (History of US) Oxford, 2006. 209pp. ISBN 978-0-19-518232-3; 2007, paper ISBN 978-0-19-532717-5. Grades 5 up. Full of photographs, prints, sidebars, boxed text, and running commentary, this volume tells the story of the colonies, beginning with the French and Indian War around 1755 and proceeding through the Constitutional Convention in 1787. Hakim covers all aspects of society and all cultures. The third volume in the series. Chronology of Events, More Books to Read, and Index.

384. Hakim, Joy. *Making Thirteen Colonies.* (History of US) Oxford, 2006. 179pp. ISBN 978-0-19-518895-0; 2007, paper ISBN 978-0-19-533716-8. Grades 5 up. Full of photographs, prints, sidebars, boxed text, and running commentary, this entertaining, informative story covers the colonization of the New World through the mid-18th century until the French and Indian War. Chronology of Events, More Books to Read, and Index.

385. Harkins, Susan Sales. *Jamestown: The First English Colony.* Mitchell Lane, 2006. 48pp. ISBN 978-1-58415-458-7. Grades 4–6. Harkins offers a history of the colonists' experiences trying to settle Jamestown, in Virginia. They were all naive and unaware of what they would encounter, and their lack of preparation made their task much more difficult. Illustrations enhance the text. Glossary, Chronology, and Further Reading.

386. **Harkins, Susan Sales, and William H. Harkins.** *Colonial Virginia.* Mitchell Lane, 2007. 48pp. ISBN 978-1-58415-548-5. Grades 5–9. Details bring the period to life, including the everyday roles and activities of women and children. Photographs, maps, and reproductions augment the text. Glossary, Notes, Further Reading, Web Sites, and Index.

387. **Harkins, Susan Sales, and William H. Harkins.** *Georgia: The Debtors Colony.* (Building America) Mitchell Lane, 2006. 48pp. ISBN 978-1-58415-465-5. Grades 4–7. This historical overview examines the beginnings of the colony of Georgia. The first settlers, arriving poor and debt-ridden from London, helped fulfill James Oglethorpe's dream of a better life for the unfortunate. What they did not expect was to fight off the Spanish as they tried to enter the area from Florida. Photographs, maps and reproductions enliven the text. Bibliography, Glossary, Chronology, Notes, Further Reading, Web Sites, and Index.

388. **Harness, Cheryl.** *Our Colonial Year.* Simon & Schuster, 2005. 40pp. ISBN 978-0-689-83479-0. Grades 1–4. This book looks at life in the thirteen colonies, showing one colony for each month plus one for New Year's Day. Text on the left-hand side of the double spreads is enhanced on the facing page with an illustration of children performing a typical activity.

389. **Hayward, Linda.** *The First Thanksgiving.* Illustrated by James Watling. (Step Into Reading) Random, 1990. 48pp. ISBN 978-0-679-90218-8; paper ISBN 978-0-679-80218-1. Grades 1–3. Hayward provides a summary of the events that led to the first Thanksgiving celebration when Samoset and Squanto joined the Pilgrims. The Pilgrims know the Native Americans are around them although they never know exactly where they are. Samoset and Squanto speak English and help the Pilgrims survive in the New World.

390. **Hinman, Bonnie.** *Pennsylvania: William Penn and the City of Brotherly Love.* (Building America) Mitchell Lane, 2006. 48pp. ISBN 978-1-58415-463-1. Grades 4–7. This historical overview examines the beginnings of the colony of Pennsylvania. William Penn received the land from King Charles II in repayment for a loan. Penn wanted to base his government on religious ideals, and he had to fend off the French who wanted the same area. But he prevailed and formed a government based on the tenets of Quakerism. Photographs, maps and reproductions enliven the text. Bibliography, Glossary, Chronology, Notes, Further Reading, Web Sites, and Index.

391. **Hossell, Karen.** *Delaware 1638–1776.* (Voices from Colonial America) National Geographic, 2006. 109pp. ISBN 978-0-7922-6408-8. Grades 5–8. More foreign countries claimed to own the small area known as Delaware than any of the other thirteen British colonies. Maps, illustrations, and primary sources recall Indians massacring the first European settlers, the change of the colony from Swedish to Dutch to British control, Delaware's importance in providing Pennsylvania with access to the sea, and how it became the subject of a dispute between William Penn and Maryland's Lord Baltimore. Delaware built a militia of four thousand men for the war of independence and was the first to ratify the Constitution. Maps, Reproductions, Chronology, Further Reading, Notes, Web Sites, and Index.

392. **Ichord, Loretta Frances.** *Hasty Pudding, Johnnycakes, and Other Good Stuff: Cooking in Colonial America.* Illustrated by Jan Davey Ellis. (Cooking Through Time) Millbrook, 1998. 64pp. ISBN 978-0-7613-0369-5; 1999, paper ISBN 978-0-7613-1297-0. Grades 3–5. Ichord examines food preparation in early America, with information about cooking in a fireplace, the taste of Mape Wheaten bread, how families preserved and stored food, New England clam chowder, potato cakes with rosemary, biscuits, soups, the use of corn, "soul" cooking, drinks, sugar, and desserts. Illustrations enhance the text. Bibliography and Index.

393. **Italia, Bob.** *The New York Colony.* Checkerboard, 2001. 32pp. ISBN 978-1-57765-589-3. Grades 3–5. This history of New York begins with the first explorers and looks at all aspects of the colony—life, work, food, clothing, homes, children, Native Americans, and path to statehood. Reproductions augment the text. Chronology and Web Sites.

394. Jango-Cohen, Judith. *Ben Franklin's Big Shock.* Illustrated by Kevin Lepp. (On My Own Science) Millbrook, 2006. 48pp. ISBN 978-1-57505-873-3; First Avenue paper ISBN 978-0-8225-6450-8. Grades K–2. This look at Benjamin Franklin (1706–1790) focuses on the kite experiment during which he discovered that lightning is electricity, wondering how he must have felt. Illustrations augment the text. Bibliography.

395. Jarrow, Gail. *The Printer's Trial: The Case of John Peter Zenger and the Fight for a Free Press.* Calkins Creek, 2006. 102pp. ISBN 978-1-59078-432-7. Grades 4–8. Primary sources form the basis of this account of a case involving free speech. John Peter Zenger was arrested in 1735 for seditious libel against the British royal governor. As a printer, he had published anonymous complaints against Governor William Cosby. Cosby could not squash his opposition and decided to attack Zinger instead. Jarrow presents the events leading to his trial, the influence of the trial on political publishing, and the impact on freedom of the press when Zinger was pronounced not guilty. Photographs and illustrations augment the text. Bibliography, Chronology, Notes, Further Reading, and Index.

396. Kalman, Bobbie. *Colonial Crafts.* (Historic Communities) Crabtree, 1991. 32pp. ISBN 978-0-8650-5490-5; paper ISBN 978-0-8650-5510-0. Grades 3–6. Photographs from living museums illustrate the various craftspeople and their trades as they were practiced in the 18th century. They include leather workers, cabinetmakers, coopers, wheelwrights, gunsmiths, blacksmiths, founders, silversmiths, paper makers, printers, bookbinders, milliners, wig makers, building trades, home industries, and crafts in the classroom. Glossary and Index.

397. Kalman, Bobbie. *Colonial Life.* (Historic Communities) Crabtree, 1992. 32pp. ISBN 978-0-8650-5491-2. Grades 3–6. Using photographs from a living museum, Kalman describes settlements, homes, newcomers, family, school, play, men's clothing and women's fashions, travel, taverns, work, fun, and prejudice in the lives of colonial people during the 18th century. Glossary and Index.

398. Kalman, Bobbie. *A Colonial Town: Williamsburg.* Illustrated by Antoinette DeBiasi. (Historic Communities) Crabtree, 1991. 32pp. ISBN 978-0-8650-5489-9; paper ISBN 978-0-8650-5509-4. Grades 3–6. Using photographs of the historic community, this volume looks at the beginning of the settlement and its development, the Governor's Palace, public buildings, Bruton Parish Church, the College of William and Mary, the apothecary, the windmill, the shops and their signs, and the people. Williamsburg was a thriving town, and the text shows the various levels of society, what they wore, where they worked, and how they entertained themselves. Map, Glossary, and Index.

399. Kalman, Bobbie. *Early Christmas.* Illustrated by Antoinette DeBiasi. (Early Settler Life) Crabtree, 1981. 32pp. ISBN 978-0-8650-5001-3; paper ISBN 978-0-8650-5003-7. Grades 3–6. As a celebration, Christmas has had a history based on where the settlers who celebrated it had lived before. From these various traditions, the American celebration of Christmas evolved. Kalman tells the history of Christmas in the 18th and 19th centuries, covering a wide variety of topics, from food to church celebrations, and the customs of the French, Germans, Mennonites, Scots, Dutch, Swedes, and Ukrainians. Photographs and reproductions highlight the text. Glossary and Index.

400. Kalman, Bobbie. *The Early Family Home.* (Early Settler Life) Crabtree, 1982. 32pp. ISBN 978-0-8650-5017-4. Grades 3–6. Living history photographs and drawings tell about the frontier life of families. Kalman includes information about the dwellings: the number of rooms, their size, how they were furnished, and the materials available for home construction. Glossary and Index.

401. Kalman, Bobbie. *Early Travel.* (Early Settler Life) Crabtree, 1981. 64pp. ISBN 978-0-8650-5007-5. Grades 3–6. To get from one place to another, settlers and pioneers had to walk, ride horseback, take a coach of some kind, or board a boat. This volume describes travel, where one rested along the road, and the routes available. Drawings enhance the story. Glossary and Index.

402. Kalman, Bobbie. *18th Century Clothing.* Illustrated by Antoinette DeBiasi. (Historic Communities) Crabtree, 1993. 32pp. ISBN 978-0-8650-5492-9; paper ISBN 978-0-8650-5512-

4. Grades 3–6. Photographs from the living museum in Williamsburg, Virginia, illustrate the types of clothing worn during the 18th century. Topics include making clothes from sheep's wool, carding flax for linen, and tanning leather; shoes and boots; various fashions for men and women as well as accessories such as muffs and wigs; hair and hats; underclothes; unhealthy habits for teeth and skin; children's clothing; and the attire of different social classes. Glossary and Index.

403. **Kalman, Bobbie.** *Home Crafts.* Illustrated by Antoinette DeBiasi. (Historic Communities) Crabtree, 1990. 32pp. Paper ISBN 978-0-8650-5505-6. Grades 3–6. Pioneers had to make the items they needed, producing candles, baskets, cloth, quilts, and samplers. These crafts sometimes became the center of social events, such as quilting bees. Photographs and drawings augment the text. Glossary and Index.

404. **Kalman, Bobbie.** *The Kitchen.* Illustrated by Antoinette DeBiasi. (Historic Communities) Crabtree, 1990. 96pp. ISBN 978-0-8650-5484-4; paper ISBN 978-0-8650-5504-9. Grades 3–6. Photographs and drawings show the various aspects of a pioneer kitchen where people cooked food over an open fire. The types of food, the wood and iron utensils, and the methods of preserving foods are all covered. Glossary and Index.

405. **Kalman, Bobbie, and David Schimpky.** *Old-Time Toys.* Illustrated by Antoinette DeBiasi. (Historic Communities) Crabtree, 1995. 32pp. ISBN 978-0-8650-5481-3; paper ISBN 978-0-8650-5520-9. Grades 3–6. Until the mid-1800s, adults made most children's toys in their homes. People often whittled them from wood while they sat in front of the fire in the winter. In the 19th century, toy makers made porcelain dolls, created rocking horses, and devised such toys as automated coin banks and magic lanterns. Photographs from toy museums and drawings augment the text.

406. **Kent, Deborah.** *African-Americans in the Thirteen Colonies.* (Cornerstones of Freedom) Children's, 1996. 30pp. Paper ISBN 978-0-516-20065-1. Grades 3–5. Kent looks at the slave trade, the economics behind it, and the situation of blacks in colonial times. She also discusses the ways in which Native Americans and indentured servants were able to escape their bonds. Glossary and Index.

407. **Kent, Zachary.** *Williamsburg.* (Cornerstones of Freedom) Children's, 1992. 30pp. Paper ISBN 978-0-516-44854-1. Grades 3–5. In 1699, when fire destroyed Jamestown, the capital of Virginia shifted to Middle Plantation, where the College of William and Mary had been established six years before. The town's name was changed to honor King William III of England. This volume looks at the creation of Williamsburg, from its first buildings to its renovation in the early 20th century. Index.

408. **Kostyal, K. M.** *1776: A New Look at Revolutionary Williamsburg.* Illustrated by Lori Epstein Renda. National Geographic, 2009. 48pp. ISBN 978-1-4263-0517-7. Grades 4–8. With color photographs of actors playing Williamsburg's citizens, the six chapters of this volume draw on recent archaeological discoveries to describe the lives of residents in 1776. Included are African Virginians (half the population), women, Native Americans, gentry, craftsmen, farmers, and British soldiers. Maps add context. Chronology and Notes.

409. **Laager, Hollie.** *The French and Indian War.* (Events in American History) Rourke, 2007. 48pp. ISBN 978-1-60044-131-8. Grades 4–6. Laager describes the events of the French and Indian War from Washington's surrender to the French in 1754 to the signing of the Treaty of Paris in 1763. The author covers the main causes of the war, George Washington's role as a young soldier, and the major campaigns and battles. Reproductions, maps, and illustrations accompany the text. Glossary, Chronology, Further Reading, Web Sites, and Index.

410. **Lange, Karen E.** *1607: A New Look at Jamestown.* National Geographic, 2007. 48pp. ISBN 978-1-4263-0012-7. Grades 3–6. In 1607 three ships reached the New World carrying 104 passengers, who then settled in Jamestown, next to an Indian confederacy. Within a year, about 70 of them had died—from Indian attacks, disease, and starvation. Archaeological data discovered since 1994 in a project named Jamestown Rediscovery indicate that the settlers were faced with a terrible drought while hunting, fishing, smelting iron, making glass, and refining metals. They did not surrender, as historians have thought for many years; they worked hard, but nature may have kept them from accomplishing what they had intended. Photographs, Maps, Chronology, Notes, Bibliography, Web Sites, and Index.

411. McDaniel, Melissa. *The Powhatan Indians.* Chelsea House, 1995. 80pp. ISBN 978-0-7910-2494-2. Grades 3–6. The best-known member of the Powhatan tribe is probably Pocahontas. This tribe consisted of 30 separate groups ruled by her father. Chiefs called *werowances* and priests who survived the Huskenaw initiation ruled their villages. When the British built Jamestown in their territory, the Powhatan supplied the earliest colonists with food. But as the colony expanded, fighting between the two groups broke out. Through the years, the Powhatans have tried to keep their identity, and they have official recognition in Virginia today. The text, with reproductions, photographs, and maps, tells their history. Glossary, Chronology, and Index.

412. McNeese, Tim. *Jamestown.* (Colonial Settlements in America) Chelsea House, 2007. 112pp. ISBN 978-0-7910-9335-1. Grades 5–8. McNeese examines the English settlement in Jamestown in 1607 and its struggle to survive on swampy land, without drinking water and under threat of Native American attacks. The text covers the leadership in the new settlement as well as all its hardships. Photographs, maps, and reproductions enliven the text. Bibliography, Chronology, Notes, Further Reading, Web Sites, and Index.

413. McNeese, Tim. *Plymouth.* (Colonial Settlements in America) Chelsea House, 2007. 112pp. ISBN 978-0-7910-9339-9. Grades 5–8. McNeese looks at the Pilgrims' decision to leave Plymouth, England, aboard the *Mayflower* in 1620. He details the journey, their failure to reach Virginia, their struggle in Massachusetts, and the importance of the settlement for later generations. He also includes biographical profiles of the main figures who helped found the settlement. Photographs, maps, and reproductions enliven the text. Bibliography, Chronology, Notes, Further Reading, Web Sites, and Index.

414. McNeese, Tim. *Williamsburg.* (Colonial Settlements in America) Chelsea House, 2007. 112pp. ISBN 978-0-7910-9333-7. Grades 5–8. This volume covers the colonists from nearby Jamestown who helped to found Williamsburg and their ideas for this new settlement. It also includes biographical profiles of the main figures. Photographs, maps, and reproductions enliven the text. Bibliography, Chronology, Notes, Further Reading, Web Sites, and Index.

415. Miller, Brandon Marie. *Good Women of a Well-Blessed Land: Women's Lives in Colonial America.* (People's History) Lerner, 2005. 96pp. ISBN 978-0-8225-0032-2. Grades 5 up. This social history looks at the daily lives of women in colonial America—European immigrants, Native Americans, slaves, indentured servants—in both Virginia and New England. Miller uses letters, passenger ship lists, court records, and other appropriate primary sources to tell their stories. The chronological chapters begin with the settlement in Jamestown with its few women and the importance of Native American women who farmed, built homes, tanned hides, and sewed clothing for their families. When the European women immigrants arrived, lured by a campaign that assured them a husband, they had the same duties while facing the hardships of a completely different life. Indentured servants also had to create entirely new lives for themselves, isolated from their families in a strange place. However, without women, the colonies would not have succeeded. Illustrations, Maps, Selected Bibliography, Further Reading and Websites, and Index.

416. Miller, Jake. *The Colony of Massachusetts: A Primary Source History.* (Primary Source Library of the Thirteen Colonies) PowerKids, 2006. 24pp. ISBN 978-1-4042-3028-6. Grades 3–5. Miller provides a brief history of Massachusetts from its beginnings as an English colony through its participation in the American Revolution to its joining the United States in 1788. Primary source materials are generally illustrations and text superimposed on them.

417. Owens, L. L. *Pilgrims in America.* (Events in American History) Rourke, 2007. 48pp. ISBN 978-1-60044-122-6. Grades 4–6. Owens describes the Pilgrims' arrival in America, noting who they were and giving details of their voyage on the *Mayflower,* their behavior, their new homes at Plymouth, and their first Thanksgiving. Reproductions, maps, and illustrations accompany the text. Glossary, Chronology, Further Reading, Web Sites, and Index.

418. Ransom, Candice F. *Sam Collier and the Founding of Jamestown.* Illustrated by Matthew Archambault. (On My Own History) Millbrook, 2005. 48pp. ISBN 978-1-57505-874-0; First Avenue, 2006, paper ISBN 978-0-8225-6451-5. Grades K–2. Samuel Collier (d. 1622) came to Jamestown in 1608 where he worked for John Smith. Ransom speculates about what Sam might have done during the first four months he was in Virginia. Illustrations complement the text. Bibliography.

419. Roach, Marilynne K. *In the Days of the Salem Witchcraft Trials.* Houghton, 2003. 92pp. Paper ISBN 978-0-618-39196-7. Grades 4–6. After chapters covering the law, punishment, and system of beliefs in Puritan New England around 1692, Roach looks at the individuals who were convicted of witchcraft. She shows that the culture was more diversified than is usually recognized by discussing such topics as the land, government, making a living, farming, and leisure activities. She believes the witchcraft "panic" came from personal fears that grew in a variety of ways until they permeated the entire society. Maps, Bibliography, and Index.

420. Roberts, Russell. *Life in Colonial America.* Mitchell Lane, 2007. 48pp. ISBN 978-1-58415-549-2. Grades 5–9. There was a time when the residents of colonial Virginia were starving and ate snakes and rats, chewed shoe leather, and practiced cannibalism. They—and all the other settlers—were unused to life in the New World and had to learn how to grow crops and hunt animals to sustain them through the winter. Additionally, they needed to forge relationships with the Native Americans, who could teach them new skills. They did, however, have to overcome philosophical differences with these natives whom they did not understand. Photographs, maps, and reproductions augment the text. Glossary, Notes, Further Reading, Web Sites, and Index.

421. Rosen, Daniel. *New Beginnings: Jamestown and the Virginia Colony, 1607–1699.* National Geographic, 2007. 40pp. ISBN 978-0-7922-8277-8. Grades 5–8. This history presents information in several different ways, from text boxes offering background on various settlers in Jamestown and the Virginia Colony to "Bright Ideas" that look at the discoveries that settlers made. Among the questions pondered is why a group of people would leave their homes and cross a sea to establish a new life. Reproductions augment the text. Glossary and Index.

422. San Souci, Robert D. *N. C. Wyeth's Pilgrims.* Chronicle, 1996. Unpaged. Paper ISBN 978-0-8118-1486-7. Grades 3 up. This volume uses the beautiful illustrations by N. C. Wyeth (1882–1945), completed in the 1940s, of the Pilgrims coming to America. The pictures retell the story of their arrival at New Plymouth, Massachusetts, in 1620. The facts here are less important than the illustrations.

423. Sewall, Marcia. *James Towne.* Atheneum, 2001. 40pp. ISBN 978-0-689-81814-1. Grades 3–5. A carpenter of 18 arrives in Jamestown, Virginia, in 1607 with 104 Englishmen carried on three ships that set sail December 20, 1606. Double-page spreads based on diary entries contain information about his life and that of his fellow colonists. Sewall tells readers that people cannibalized the dead during the Starving Time, and that John Smith did not originally include Pocahontas in his story about the colony. With watercolor and sepia ink illustrations. Select Bibliography, List of Characters, Glossary.

424. Sneve, Virginia Driving Hawk. *The Cherokees.* Illustrated by Ronald Himler. (First Americans) Holiday House, 1996. 32pp. ISBN 978-0-8234-1214-3. Grades 3–6. The Cherokees lived peacefully in the eastern states until President Andrew Jackson heard that their land might have gold on it. He decided that the Cherokees would walk to new land in Oklahoma. Famous Cherokee leaders include John Ross, Sequoyah, Tsali, and Wilma Mankiller. The text recounts their creation myth and their history. Notes and Index.

425. Sneve, Virginia Driving Hawk. *The Cheyennes.* Illustrated by Ronald Himler. (First Americans) Holiday House, 1996. 32pp. ISBN 978-0-8234-1250-1. Grades 3–6. Sneve covers cultural background and historical moments as she looks at the groups of men, women, and children in the Cheyenne tribe and the locations in which they lived. She includes the traits that make the Cheyenne unique from other tribes. Maps and Index.

426. Stamper, Judith Bauer. *New Friends in a New Land: A Thanksgiving Story.* Illustrated by Chet Jezierski. Steck-Vaughn, 1992. 32pp. Paper ISBN 978-0-8114-8053-6. Grades 2–5. In 1621 Damaris Hopkins and her family sailed on the *Mayflower*. Among the surprises she found in the New World was seeing three Indians trying to establish friendships with the settlers. She saw Samoset and Squanto, who spoke English, and Massasoit, who brought his tribespeople to celebrate the first Thanksgiving with Damaris and her neighbors.

427. Stefoff, Rebecca. *Cities and Towns.* (Colonial Life) Sharpe Focus, 2007. 96pp. ISBN 978-0-7656-8109-6. Grades 5–9. Stefoff offers much information about the transformation of the forts and fishing camps of the early colonial period into the cities and towns of the 17th and 18th centuries. She also addresses what life was like in these new communities. Town planners had to consider the times in which they lived. With special focus on Boston, Newport, Charleston, Philadelphia, and New York this volume also gives information on towns and cities in the French and Spanish colonies. Photographs and illustrations augment the text. Glossary, Chronology, Notes, Further Reading, Web Sites, and Index.

428. Stefoff, Rebecca. *Exploration and Settlement.* (Colonial Life) Sharpe Focus, 2007. 96pp. ISBN 978-0-7656-8108-9. Grades 5–9. Stefoff offers much information about the exploration and settlement of America, presenting various theories about who populated the Americas and including background information about events that either thwarted or encouraged European exploration in the 15th and 16th centuries. Photographs and illustrations augment the text. Glossary, Chronology, Notes, Further Reading, Web Sites, and Index.

429. Tracy, Kathleen. *Plymouth Colony: The Pilgrims Settle in New England.* (Building America) Mitchell Lane, 2006. 48pp. ISBN 978-1-58415-459-4. Grades 4–7. This historical overview examines the beginnings of the colony of Massachusetts. The one hundred and two Puritans who arrived in 1620 were on their way to Virginia but landed north of their destination and stayed there. The text continues to present the first Thanksgiving and King Philip's War. Photographs, maps and reproductions enliven the text. Bibliography, Glossary, Chronology, Notes, Further Reading, Web Sites, and Index.

430. Waters, Kate. *Samuel Eaton's Day: A Day in the Life of a Pilgrim Boy.* Illustrated by Russ Kendall. Scholastic, 1996. 40pp. Paper ISBN 978-0-590-48053-6. Grades 1–6. On July 16, 1627, Samuel Eaton, 7, is delighted to be old enough to help harvest the rye. He says he came on the *Mayflower* and his mother died during the voyage. Photographs of him at Plimoth Plantation show him getting dressed, fetching water, setting snares for game, and tying stalks of rye. He discovers that binding rye is more difficult than it looks, and he ends up with blisters. He also itches. But when his father compliments his work, he is pleased. Glossary.

431. Waters, Kate. *Sarah Morton's Day: A Day in the Life of a Pilgrim Girl.* Illustrated by Russ Kendall. Scholastic, 1993. 32pp. Paper ISBN 978-0-590-47400-9. Grades 1–6. In Plimoth Plantation in 1627 Sarah Morton's day begins at sunup when the cock crows. Sarah must build a fire, cook breakfast, feed the chickens, milk the goats, learn her letters, and memorize scripture. Sometimes she has time to play knickers (marbles) and talk to her friend. The photographs of the living history museum at Plymouth, Massachusetts, complement the text.

432. Waters, Kate. *Tapenum's Day: A Wampanoag Indian Boy in Pilgrim Times.* Illustrated by Russ Kendall. Scholastic, 1996. 390pp. Paper ISBN 978-0-590-20237-4. Grades 1–6. In 1627 while Samuel Eaton and Sarah Morton help the adults inside the Pilgrims' stockade, Tapenum, a Wampanoag boy, learns from his elders nearby. His warrior counselors refuse to initiate him, and although he at first does not understand why, he soon finds out that he needs more skill, more strength, and more wisdom. Tapenum has little interest in the Pilgrims while he tries to fulfill the requirements to earn his position as a Wampanoag brave.

433. Winters, Kay. *Colonial Voices: Hear Them Speak.* Illustrated by Larry Day. Dutton, 2008. 40pp. ISBN 978-0-525-47872-0. Grades 3–7. On December 16, 1773, colonists learn that King George will tax their tea. Ethan, a Boston printer's errand boy, must spread the news of a meeting to discuss this insult. As he delivers his message—to the baker, the school house, the tavern, the shoemaker, the blacksmith, the Native American basket maker, the milliner, and so forth—readers learn how these people feel about the issue. Ink-and-watercolor illustrations complement the text. Bibliography, Glossary, and Notes.

434. **Worth, Richard.** *Colonial America: Building Toward Independence.* (American Saga) Enslow, 2006. 128pp. ISBN 978-0-7660-2569-1. Grades 5 up. Worth looks at colonial America in the 16th and 17th centuries, discussing the settlements, agriculture, trade, slavery, society, and government. Included are brief profiles of key individuals. The author concludes that the British had lower financial reserves because they fought Spain and France, and Americans who observed Britain's trials kept America from making similar errors. Illustrations augment the text. Chronology, Notes, Further Reading, Bibliography, Glossary, Web Sites, and Index.

435. **Worth, Richard.** *New France 1534–1763.* (Voices From Colonial America) National Geographic, 2007. 64pp. ISBN 978-1-4263-0128-5. Grades 4–8. The huge French colony known as New France covered all or parts of Michigan, Minnesota, Wisconsin, Illinois, Indiana, Ohio, Pennsylvania, Vermont, Maine, and Canada. Primary source materials reveal the struggles of individuals and provide cultural data about this area. Photographs, reproductions, augment the text. Bibliography, Chronology, Further Reading, Web Sites, and Index.

436. **Yero, Judith Lloyd.** *Mayflower Compact.* National Geographic, 2006. 40pp. ISBN 978-0-7922-5891-9. Grades 4–6. Yero discusses the Pilgrims' voyage to Plymouth, Massachusetts, the establishment of their colony, and their agreement to be governed by the Mayflower Compact. These people were actually Separatists and had tried to live in Holland, but when that didn't work out they invited others, called Strangers, to join them on their journey to the New World. Sixty-six days at sea brought them to Massachusetts rather than Virginia, and there they wrote and signed the compact recognizing God, the King, and the need for laws. Nearly half of the colonists and most of the women died the first year, but their decision was the beginning of democracy in America. Photographs, maps, and historical prints highlight the text. Glossary and Index.

437. **Yolen, Jane, and Heidi Elisabet Yolen Stemple.** *The Salem Witch Trials: An Unsolved Mystery from History.* Illustrated by Roger Roth. Simon & Schuster, 2004. Unpaged. ISBN 978-0-689-84620-5. Grades 3–6. Yolen offers an overview of the witches in Salem and includes extant theories about the hysteria and some of the reactions of the townspeople. Readers are encouraged to use their own reasoning power in an attempt to understand what happened during 1692 to allow such an event to occur. The author explores the possible participation of the Parris family and their slave Tituba. Watercolor and pencil illustrations complement the text.

Biography and Collective Biography

438. **Adler, David A.** *B. Franklin, Printer.* Holiday House, 2001. 128pp. ISBN 978-0-8234-1675-2. Grades 4–8. Benjamin Franklin (1706–1790) must be considered America's true Renaissance man. With his intelligence, wit, and ingenuity, he helped to mold a nation by gathering thirteen diverse colonies into one union. He was also a printer, inventor, scientist, and writer who functioned within the confines of his time. Anecdotes, details, and quotes highlight aspects of Franklin's life along with illustrations. Bibliography, Chronology, Further Reading, Web Sites, and Index.

439. **Adler, David A.** *George Washington: An Illustrated Biography.* Holiday House, 2004. 274pp. ISBN 978-0-8234-1838-1. Grades 5–10. This biography of George Washington (1732–1799) traces his family history and his childhood before covering his teenage years as a surveyor and beginning soldier. By the time he was in his early 20s, he was already a national figure. Adler offers insight into Washington's fiery temper, his sometimes stingy ways, and his moderate views about owning slaves. Primary sources include quotes from Washington's let-

ters and biographical sketches. Maps augment the text. Bibliography, Chronology, Notes, Web Sites, and Index.

440. Adler, David A. *A Picture Book of Benjamin Franklin.* Illustrated by John and Alexandra Wallner. Holiday House, 1989. Unpaged. ISBN 978-0-8234-0792-7; 1990, paper ISBN 978-0-8234-0801-6. Grades 1–3. Benjamin was born in 1706, one of the Franklins' 17 children. An inventor even when very young, he devised swimming paddles to fit over his hands and increase his speed. And he always enjoyed writing—an endeavor that led to his success as a printer and newspaper publisher. After retirement, he invented the Franklin stove, bifocals, and the lightning rod. Additionally, he served the American colonies in England for ten years before the Revolution, and in 1776 went to France to plead support from Louis XVI. At the age 81 in 1787 Franklin was the Constitutional Convention's oldest delegate. Before his death in 1790, he recorded his dislike of slavery in his autobiography. Important Dates.

441. Adler, David A. *A Picture Book of Patrick Henry.* See entry 621.

442. Adler, David A. *President George Washington.* Illustrated by John Wallner. Holiday House, 2004. 32pp. ISBN 978-0-8234-1604-2. Grades 1–3. This biography looks at George Washington's childhood and major contributions, with an overview of the main events in his life. Watercolor illustrations reinforce the text. Bibliography, Chronology, and Further Reading.

443. Adler, David A., and Michael S. Adler. *A Picture Book of John and Abigail Adams.* Illustrated by Ronald Himler. (Picture Book Biographies) Holiday House, 2010. 32pp. ISBN 978-0-8234-2007-0. Grades K–3. A picture-book look at the lives of John Adams (1735–1826), first ambassador to Great Britain, vice president, and president, and his wife Abigail (1744–1818). Abigail was John's adviser and confidante throughout his career of public service. The text briefly covers their childhood, courtship, and marriage partnership using quotes and appropriate primary sources. Watercolor illustrations enhance the text. Chronology, Notes, Bibliography, and Web Sites.

444. Adler, David A., and Michael S. Adler. *A Picture Book of Samuel Adams.* Illustrated by Ronald Himler. Holiday House, 2005. Unpaged. ISBN 978-0-8234-1846-6. Grades 1–3. Samuel Adams (1722–1803), American patriot, spoke against unfair taxes, helped to organize the Boston Tea Party, signed the Declaration of Independence, and fought for liberty throughout his life. He later became the governor of Massachusetts as well. The text places Adams within his times. Illustrations enliven the text. Bibliography, Chronology, Notes, and Web Sites.

445. Ashby, Ruth. *The Amazing Mr. Franklin: Or, The Boy Who Read Everything.* Peachtree, 2004. 104pp. ISBN 978-1-56145-306-1. Grades 3–5. This biography of Benjamin Franklin (1706–1790) covers both his youth and adulthood, stressing his love of books and literature, his curiosity, and his statesmanship. He earned international fame as a writer, statesman, scientist, wit, and inventor of the Franklin stove, bifocals, and lightning rod. Many of his solutions to problems are still in use today. Franklin was clearly one of America's most remarkable men. Bibliography and Chronology.

446. Avi. *Finding Providence: The Story of Roger Williams.* Illustrated by James Watling. Trophy, 1997. 48pp. Paper ISBN 978-0-06-444216-9. Grades 3–4. Mary Williams tells the story of her father's trial in Massachusetts Bay Colony in 1635. Roger Williams (1603?–1683) was condemned for his beliefs about equality and left home in the middle of the night, unafraid because he spoke the language of the Narragansett Indians. They did indeed help him and gave him land for his family and his followers, which he called Providence, his way of thanking God for saving him.

447. Barretta, Gene. *Now and Ben: The Modern Inventions of Benjamin Franklin.* Henry Holt, 2006. 34pp. ISBN 978-0-8050-7917-3. Grades 2–5. Benjamin Franklin (1706–1790) had ideas that still affect us all. He either invented or investigated odometers, eyeglasses, post offices, libraries, daylight savings time, the gulf stream, and the importance of vitamin C in the diet. Watercolor cartoon illustrations enhance the text.

448. Bruns, Roger. *Thomas Jefferson.* (World Leaders Past and Present) Chelsea House, 1990. 112pp. Paper ISBN 978-0-7910-0644-3. Grades 5 up. Thomas Jefferson (1743–1826) wrote the Declaration of Independence for the colonies when he was only 33 years old, using language to make all men equal before the law. He then became, in succession, the minister to France, the secretary of state, and the president. His ideas still inspire students of political science, his diplomacy is a guide to the modern statesperson, and his name is still linked to the concept of an ideal republic. Photographs and reproductions enhance the text. Chronology, Further Reading, and Index.

449. Bulla, Clyde Robert. *Squanto, Friend of the Pilgrims.* Illustrated by Peter Burchard. Scholastic, 1990. 112pp. Paper ISBN 978-0-590-44055-4. Grades 3–6. Squanto goes to London in the early 1600s and learns about the white man's culture. He wants to return to his own people, and Captain John Smith takes him back to America in 1614. As soon as he arrives, another captain kidnaps him and takes him to Spain to sell into slavery. Because he speaks English, he gains his freedom, and in 1619 again returns home. What he finds is a tribe killed by a disease that the white settlers brought to the New World.

450. Burgan, Michael. *John Winthrop: Colonial Governor of Massachusetts.* (Signature Lives Colonial America) Compass Point, 2005. 112pp. ISBN 978-0-7565-1691-1. Grades 5–8. John Winthrop (1588–1649), the first governor of Massachusetts, came to the colonies in search of religious freedom. But he believed that Puritan beliefs should be the laws of the people. This biography discusses why he left England and the issues he met in the New World including conflicts with the Native Americans and within his community, along with war against the Pequots. Illustrations augment the text. Bibliography, Chronology, Glossary, and Index.

451. Burgan, Michael. *Roger Williams: Founder of Rhode Island.* (Signature Lives Colonial America) Compass Point, 2005. 112pp. ISBN 978-0-7565-1596-6. Grades 5–8. Roger Williams (1603–1683) founded the colony of Rhode Island for people of all religious beliefs. He felt strongly that government and religion should be separate, and he fostered that idea in his colony. He also advocated fair dealings with the Native Americans. Illustrations augment the text. Bibliography, Chronology, Glossary, and Index.

452. Chandra, Deborah, and Madeleine Comora. *George Washington's Teeth.* Illustrated by Brock Cole. Farrar, 2003. 40pp. ISBN 978-0-374-32534-3; Square Fish, 2007, paper ISBN 978-0-312-37604-8. Grades K–3. Based on diaries, historical records, and George Washington's letters, this book examines his teeth. Included is a chronology of his life coupled with reasons for the probable decay of his teeth. Dentures of gold and hippopotamus ivory replaced his real teeth, and speculation about his death includes the possibility of untreated infection on old root fragments remaining in his gums. Illustrations enhance the text. *Children's Book Award* (Georgia) nomination, *Young Hoosier Award* (Indiana) nomination, *Black-Eyed Susan Book Award* (Maryland) nomination, *Great Lakes Great Books Award* (Michigan) nomination, *Show Me State Book Award* (Missouri) nomination, *Junior Book Award* (North Carolina) nomination, *The Land Of Enchantments Children's Book Award* (New Mexico) nomination, *Young Readers Choice Book Award* (Pennsylvania) nomination, *Prairie Bud Award* (South Dakota) nomination, *Capitol Choices Noteworthy Titles* (Washington, D.C.), *School Library Journal Best Books for Children*, *Publishers Weekly Best Children's Books*, and *Bluebonnet Award* (Texas) nomination.

453. Clinton, Catherine. *Phillis's Big Test.* Illustrated by Sean Qualls. Houghton, 2008. 32pp. ISBN 978-0-618-73739-0. Grades 1–4. When Phillis Wheatley (1753–1784) was 17 years old, eighteen dignitaries—including the governor—from the Massachusetts Bay Colony asked her about the poems that she claimed to have written. They could not believe that a slave had composed them. Clinton speculates about what Wheatley might have thought during this time and discusses her education in Greek, Latin, and English and her journey on a slave ship when she was young. Mixed-media Illustrations augment the text. Bibliography.

454. Collard, Sneed B., III. *Benjamin Franklin: The Man Who Could Do Just About Anything.* (American Heroes) Benchmark, 2006. 40pp. ISBN 978-0-7614-2161-0. Grades 3–5. This biography of Benjamin Franklin (1706–1790) focuses on his humanity as well as his accomplishments as a scientist, inventor, printer, writer, statesman, and Founding Father. Anecdotes and clear descriptions help readers understand him in a different way than other biographies. Reproductions and museum images accompany the text. Glossary, Further Reading, and Index.

455. Conley, Kevin. *Benjamin Banneker: Scientist and Mathematician.* Chelsea House, 1989. 109pp. ISBN 978-1-55546-573-5. Grades 5 up. Benjamin Banneker (1731–1806), a free black man whose grandmother had been an indentured servant and grandfather a slave, taught himself astronomy with the help of books and a telescope that George Ellicott, a Quaker, loaned to him. His talents in mathematics surfaced early. When he was 21, he decided to build a clock, although he had never seen one. His clock fascinated his Maryland community, and it kept correct time for his entire life. In 1792 he helped Ellicott survey the land on which the District of Columbia now stands, and he published his first almanac, with calculations from his study of the stars. His achievements earned him the title of America's first black man of science. Chronology, Further Reading, and Index.

456. Cooper, Afua. *My Name Is Phillis Wheatley: A Story of Slavery and Freedom.* Kids Can, 2009. 152pp. ISBN 978-1-55337-812-9. Grades 5–8. Phillis Wheatley (1753–1784), born Penda Wane, was transported from Senegal where she had trained to be a *griot* in the tradition of her family when she was 12. After a horrible journey across the Atlantic, she landed in Boston and was purchased by the Wheatley family. As an experiment, they decided to see if she, a slave, could be educated. She learned to speak several languages and by the age of 19 was reading her poems to an adoring British public. Even with all these accomplishments, her family never freed her from slavery. Illustrations augment the text.

457. Fleming, Candace. *Ben Franklin's Almanac: Being a True Account of the Good Gentleman's Life.* Illustrated by Robert Parker. Simon & Schuster, 2003. 128pp. ISBN 978-0-689-83549-0. Grades 5–9. With artifacts, etchings, and quotations from the 18th century, Fleming creates a scrapbook of the life of Benjamin Franklin (1706–1790) as writer, printer, statesman, and inventor. He created the *Pennsylvania Gazette*, amended the Declaration of Independence with the phrase "We hold these truths to be self-evident," and planted America's first willow trees. He contributed to the well-being of Americans through his writing, his inventions, and his service. Bibliography, Sources, Further Reading, and Index. *American Library Association Best Books for Young Adults and Notable Children's Books, Capitol Choices Noteworthy Titles* (Washington, D.C.), *Student Book Award* (Maine) nomination, *Great Lakes Great Books Award* (Michigan) nomination, *School Library Journal Best Books for Children*, and *Publishers Weekly Best Children's Books*.

458. Fradin, Dennis B. *The Founders: The 39 Stories Behind The U.S. Constitution.* Walker, 2005. 176pp. ISBN 978-0-8027-8972-3. Grades 5–9. This collective biography profiles the thirty-nine men from twelve of the thirteen colonies who met in the summer of 1787 to create, debate, and eventually sign the United States Constitution. Among them were Rufus King, Gouverneur Morris, and the handsome Nicholas Gilman. The men came from Massachusetts, Virginia, Pennsylvania, New Jersey, Delaware, Connecticut, New Hampshire, Maryland, North Carolina, South Carolina, Georgia, and New York. Black-and-white scratchboard illustrations complement the text. Bibliography and Index.

459. Fradin, Dennis B. *Samuel Adams: The Father of American Independence.* Clarion, 1998. 182pp. ISBN 978-0-395-82510-5. Grades 5–9. Samuel Adams (1722–1803) devoted his life to American independence. Jefferson saw him as the "man of the Revolution," and others thought he was their "political father." This volume presents his youth, education, and family as well as the work he did to make independence a reality. He was complex but practical. Photographs and illustrations augment the text. Bibliography.

460. Fritz, Jean. *And Then What Happened, Paul Revere?* Illustrated by Margot Tomes. Coward, 1998. 48pp. ISBN 978-0-399-23337-1; Puffin, 1996, paper ISBN 978-0-698-11351-0. Grades 2–6. Paul Revere (1735–1818) seems scatterbrained, but Fritz shows that he actually was interested in many different things as he worked to support his large family. A silversmith by trade, he also rang the town's bells when anything occurred. On his ride, he advised John Hancock and Samuel Adams to leave Lexington, and the British actually caught Revere before becoming distracted by others arriving. Some of Revere's church bells still ring in New England steeples. Notes from the Author.

461. Fritz, Jean. *Traitor: The Case of Benedict Arnold.* Putnam, 1981. 192pp. ISBN 978-0-399-20834-8; Puffin, 1997, paper ISBN 978-0-698-11553-8. Grades 5–9. Using the metaphor of wheels that turn without going anywhere, Fritz recounts the life of Benedict Arnold (1741–1801), a boy whose alcoholic father led him to believe that wealth brought happiness and respect. Every aspect of Arnold's life seemed based on this premise. His final compromise with truth was to "sell" the new United States to the British by surrendering West Point, which he commanded by the grace of his friend George Washington. This act of treason, discovered before it was concluded, brought him exile to England and unhappiness. His name is not even carved on his tombstone. Bibliography and Index.

462. Fritz, Jean. *What's the Big Idea, Ben Franklin?* Illustrated by Margot Tomes. Putnam, 1976. 46pp. ISBN 978-0-399-23487-3; Puffin, 1996, paper ISBN 978-0-698-11372-5. Grades 2–6. Benjamin Franklin's father decided that Ben (1706–1790) would not be a Leather Apron man (following a trade) and sent him to school. When school proved to be a big expense that might lead to a poor job, his father reversed himself. Ben had other ideas, however, and even as he suffered as an apprentice to his brother, he saved money and bought books that taught him how to do things. He discovered electricity and invented the lightning rod. As Philadelphia's postmaster general, he reduced the time a letter took to reach Boston from six weeks to six days. In his later life, he lived in London for 18 years and in Paris from age 70 to 79. Additionally, he helped create the new government of the United States. Although not all of his ideas worked, enough did that he made a major contribution to American life.

463. Fritz, Jean. *Why Don't You Get a Horse, Sam Adams?* Illustrated by Trina Schart Hyman. Putnam, 1974. 48pp. ISBN 978-0-399-23401-9; Puffin, 1996, paper ISBN 978-0-698-11416-6. Grades 2–6. Samuel Adams (1722–1803) spent much of his time walking and talking with the people of Boston, trying to get them to consider claiming independence from England. John Adams finally got Sam Adams to learn to ride a horse in 1775, when he convinced Sam that riding would help the country. Because Sam Adams was so vocal about his concerns against England, he is sometimes called "The Father of Independence."

464. Fritz, Jean. *Will You Sign Here, John Hancock?* Illustrated by Trina Schart Hyman. Puffin, 1997. 47pp. Paper ISBN 978-0-698-11440-1. Grades 2–6. Although orphaned at a very young age, John Hancock (1737–1793) lived with a wealthy aunt and uncle and increased his wealth as an adult. His love of clothes and attention made him seem ostentatious. People in Boston such as Sam Adams (Patriot Party) realized that supporting John Hancock for political office would entice him to share some of his money with their cause. Hancock himself was very unhappy with the British after the Stamp Act in 1765. He owned 20 ships and saw no reason to pay the British taxes on the cargo unloaded from them, especially when the lemons were spoiled or the wine poorly corked. Thus, Hancock took part in the effort to form a new government and served as president of the Second Continental Congress, where he signed the Declaration of Independence. Notes from the Author.

465. Furbee, Mary R. *Outrageous Women of Colonial America.* Jossey-Bass, 2001. 120pp. Paper ISBN 978-0-4713-8299-7. Grades 3–6. Women from New England, the Middle Colonies, and the South are the focus of this volume. They are Anne Marbury Hutchinson (1591–1643), Queen Weetamoo (163?–1667), Margaret Brent (1601–1671), Peggy Shippen Arnold (1760–1804), Betsy Griscom Ross (1752–1836), Esther DeBerdt Reed (1746–1780), Anne Bonny (1697–17??), Eliza Lucas Pinckney (1722–1793), Anne Trotter Bailey (1743–1825), and Mary Draper Ingles (1731–1815). Furbee includes these women because they were originals who contributed to American life in unique ways. She also provides a list of other women one might consider outrageous. Further Reading and Chronology.

466. Giblin, James Cross. *The Amazing Life of Benjamin Franklin.* Illustrated by Michael Dooling. Scholastic, 2006. 48pp. Paper ISBN 978-0-439-81065-4. Grades 3–6. Benjamin Franklin (1706–1790) was first a printer and later a scientist, inventor, writer, politician, and diplomat. This biography examines his life, giving highlights of Franklin's accomplishments.

Illustrations enhance the text. *Student Book Award* (Maine) nomination, *Horn Book Fanfare*, and *Children's Book Award* (South Carolina) nomination.

467. **Giblin, James Cross.** ***The Many Rides of Paul Revere.*** Illustrated by Roland Sarkany. Scholastic, 2007. 85pp. ISBN 978-0-439-57290-3. Grades 4–8. Paul Revere (1735–1818), son of a French immigrant, made a name for himself with a single ride at midnight, but this biography indicates that he in fact made many. It also covers the rest of his life. He had a limited education but received training in his father's workshop and became a silversmith. He also served briefly in the military. As an adult, he had a large family, continued his work, and became a Revolutionary War leader. Period illustrations, artifacts, and reproductions enhance the text. Bibliography, Chronology, Notes, Web Sites, and Index. *American Library Association Notable Children's Books.*

468. **Giblin, James Cross.** ***Thomas Jefferson: A Picture Book Biography.*** Illustrated by Michael Dooling. Scholastic, 2006. 48pp. Paper ISBN 978-0-439-81067-8. Grades 3–5. Thomas Jefferson's father promised his dying friend William Randolph that he would move to his home to look after his motherless children. Then, when Thomas was 14, his father died. Thomas enjoyed the books willed to him so much that at the age of 17 he decided to go to college at William and Mary in Virginia. Two years in college and years afterward studying law led him into a practice and then to the position of writer and revisionist of the Declaration of Independence in 1776. Before that, however, he built a home called Monticello, and he married Martha Skelton in 1772. She died ten years later during the birth of their sixth child (only three lived), and Jefferson's grieving led him to agree to go to Paris as a diplomat, taking his oldest daughter. In Paris he may have met someone he loved, but he had promised his wife on her deathbed not to remarry. In his later years, he became president and then established the University of Virginia. Important Dates in Thomas Jefferson's Life, The Words of Thomas Jefferson, A Visit to Monticello, and Index. *Booklist Editors' Choice.*

469. **Gibson, Karen Bush.** ***The Life and Times of John Peter Zenger.*** (Profiles in American History) Mitchell Lane, 2006. 48pp. ISBN 978-1-58415-437-2. Grades 5–7. John Peter Zenger (1697–1746), born in Germany, came to New York in 1710. His father died at sea, and his mother raised him until New York's only printer, William Bradford, accepted Zenger as an apprentice in 1718. Zenger became Bradford's partner in 1725 but started his own printing shop the next year. In 1733 Zenger began printing America's first political party newspaper, the *New York Weekly Journal,* for the former New York attorney general, James Alexander. When Zenger criticized the governor of New York, William Cosby, in his paper, Cosby had him jailed. During Zenger's trial, his lawyer, Andrew Hamilton from Philadelphia, challenged the legality of the crimes for which Zenger was being held, and the jury declared Zenger "not guilty." They had never thought of challenging laws rather than claiming a defendant's innocence. Thus, Zenger was not guilty of "seditious libels." His trial led to the First Amendment. Photographs and reproductions augment the text. Chronology, Further Reading, Glossary, Notes, Web Sites, and Index.

470. **Gleiter, Jan, and Kathleen Thompson.** ***Pocahontas.*** Illustrated by Deborah L. Chabrian. (First Biographies) Steck-Vaughn, 1995. 32pp. Paper ISBN 978-0-8114-9350-5. Grades K–3. In this fictional biography, Pocahontas (1595?–1617) makes friends with the white men and John Smith and helps them during the "starving time." Completing the text are her marriage to John Rolfe, the birth of her son, and her voyage to England, where people called her Lady Rebecca Rolfe before she died of smallpox. Key Dates.

471. **Goodman, Joan Elizabeth.** ***Despite All Obstacles: La Salle and the Conquest of the Mississippi.*** Illustrated by Tom McNeely. (Great Explorers Books) Mikaya, 2001. 48pp. ISBN 978-1-931414-01-2. Grades 3–6. René-Robert Cavelier, Sieur de La Salle (1643–1687) discovered the Mississippi River. He claimed it for France, from its source in Canada to the Gulf. However, the French king thought it was worthless. Born in Rouen, France, La Salle became a Jesuit hoping to be assigned to a foreign place to convert its peoples. Instead, he had to teach in a French school. He decided to leave the priesthood and become an explorer. His language abilities allowed him to communicate with Indian tribes, and he found out

about the Mississippi from the Iroquois. La Salle died a poor man. Illustrations augment the text. Maps and Index.

472. Gourse, Leslie. *Pocahontas: Young Peacemaker.* (Childhood of Famous Americans) Aladdin, 1996. 192pp. Paper ISBN 978-0-689-80808-1. Grades 3–6. Pocahontas (d. 1617) grew up in the area now called Virginia, near Jamestown. There she lived in peace with her tribe until settlers arrived from England. She then became a liaison between the settlers and her father, the chief of her tribe. This fictional biography looks at her childhood with an ending chapter that discusses her marriage to John Rolfe, the changing of her name to Rebecca, and her trip to England, where she died.

473. Harkins, Susan Sales, and William H. Harkins. *The Life and Times of Patrick Henry.* (Profiles in American History) Mitchell Lane, 2006. 48pp. ISBN 978-1-58415-438-9. Grades 5–7. Patrick Henry (1736–1799) became known for the "Give me liberty or give me death" speech he made in 1775 during discussions about beginning the American Revolution. He was a radical advocate of revolution and republicanism, detesting corruption in government. He fathered seventeen children during his two marriages. Photographs and reproductions augment the text. Chronology, Further Reading, Glossary, Notes, Web Sites, and Index.

474. Harness, Cheryl. *The Adventurous Life of Myles Standish and the Amazing-But-True Survival Story of the Plymouth Colony.* (Cheryl Harness History) National Geographic, 2006. 144pp. ISBN 978-0-7922-5918-3. Grades 5–8. Myles Standish (1584?–1656) earned the name "Captaine Shrimpe" because his face turned red when he lost his temper. This volume details the history of the Pilgrims who came to Plymouth, from the reasons they left England through their first years in North America. It emphasizes the contributions of Myles Standish, the secretary of defense for the colony. When the Pilgrims arrived, Squanto spoke English and translated for them. Later Standish forced the people to construct a fortress in which to protect themselves. Illustrations enhance the text. Bibliography, Chronology, Further Reading, Web Sites, and Index.

475. Harness, Cheryl. *The Remarkable Benjamin Franklin.* National Geographic, 2005. 48pp. ISBN 978-0-7922-7882-5; 2008, paper ISBN 978-1-4263-0297-8. Grades 2–5. This biography of Benjamin Franklin (1706–1790) presents a man known for many roles, among them international diplomat, postmaster, statesman, inventor, revolutionary, and writer. It adds details not usually provided, such as the illegitimacy of Franklin's first child and the fact that others were born in a common-law relationship. Quotes and Chronology add to the illustrations of the text. Bibliography. *Young Readers Choice Book Award* (Pennsylvania) nomination.

476. Harness, Cheryl. *The Revolutionary John Adams.* National Geographic, 2003. 48pp. ISBN 978-0-7922-6970-0; 2006, paper ISBN 978-0-7922-5491-1. Grades 3–6. John Adams (1735–1826), the second president, has received less press than George Washington and Thomas Jefferson, who served before and after him. Adams attended Harvard, taught school, and became a lawyer before helping to write the Declaration of Independence. He went to France to seek help during the Revolution and was an ambassador to England. After leaving office, he served as an elder statesman, always in conflict with Jefferson. Quotes from primary sources, including some from his wife, offer additional insight into his personality. Mixed-media Illustrations augment the text. Bibliography.

477. Hinman, Bonnie. *The Life and Times of William Penn.* (Profiles in American History) Mitchell Lane, 2006. 48pp. ISBN 978-1-58415-433-4. Grades 5–7. William Penn (1644–1718), who fathered fifteen children during his two marriages, founded the Province of Pennsylvania in the English North American colony. An advocate of democracy and religious freedom, he was a Quaker who did not want war. To further the role of democracy, he signed a treaty with the Lenape Indians. Although he wanted to remain in America, financial difficulties caused him to return to England, where he died. Photographs and reproductions augment the text. Chronology, Further Reading, Glossary, Notes, Web Sites, and Index.

478. Hirschfelder, Arlene B. *Squanto, 1585?–1622.* (American Indian Biographies) Capstone, 2004. 32pp. ISBN 978-0-7368-2446-0. Grades 3–5. Squanto, a Patuxet Indian, helped the pilgrims of Plymouth establish their colony in the early 1600s. Unfortunately, he and another twenty-six Wampanoag men were kidnapped to be sold as slaves in Spain. This volume contains a traditional recipe and other pertinent information about the tribe. Illustrations enhance the text. Bibliography, Further Reading, Glossary, Web Sites, and Index.

479. **Jurmain, Suzanne.** *George Did It.*   Illustrated by Larry Day. Dutton, 2005. ISBN 978-0-525-47560-6; Puffin, 2007, paper ISBN 978-0-14-240895-7. Grades 1–3. This view of George Washington (1732–1799) shows a person who did not want to become president. Jefferson convinced him to accept, and quotes combined with memorable details describe his journey to New York, for which he had to borrow money since he was cash-poor. Illustrations complement the text. Bibliography. *Monarch Award Children's Choice Book Award* (Illinois) nomination, *Booklist Editor's Choice, School Library Journal Best Children's Books*, and *Capitol Choices Noteworthy Titles* (Washington, D.C.).

480. **Kiernan, Denise, and Joseph D'Agnese.** *Signing Their Lives Away: The Fame and Misfortune of the Men Who Signed the Declaration of Independence.*   Quirk, 2009. 255pp. ISBN 978-1-59474-330-6. Grades 5 up. Organized by state, this volume presents the daring fifty-six signers of the Declaration of Independence. Brief four- to five-page profiles emphasize unusual and memorable aspects of each person that might explain why they risked signing. Illustrations, portraits, and sidebars enhance the text. Chronology and Notes.

481. **Kjelle, Marylou Morano.** *The Life and Times of John Hancock.*   (Profiles in American History) Mitchell Lane, 2007. 48pp. ISBN 978-1-58415-443-3. Grades 5–8. John Hancock (1737–1793) was one of the signers of the Declaration of Independence. The text looks at his involvement in creating the new country of the United States and at his life. Photographs and reproductions augment the text. Chronology, Further Reading, Glossary, Notes, Web Sites, and Index.

482. **Krull, Kathleen.** *Pocahontas: Princess of the New World.*   Illustrated by David Diaz. Walker, 2007. 32pp. ISBN 978-0-8027-9554-0. Grades K–6. This biography of Pocahontas (d. 1617), daughter of the Powhatan Indian chief, covers what researchers know about her life. Named Matoaka, she helped save John Smith's life and took food to the Jamestown settlers. Later the English held her captive, she married John Rolfe, a tobacco planter, and she died in England. Cut-paper illustrations complement the text. Bibliography.

483. **Lasky, Kathryn.** *A Voice of Her Own: The Story of Phillis Wheatley, Slave Poet.*   Illustrated by Paul Lee. Candlewick, 2003. 40pp. ISBN 978-0-7636-0252-9; 2006 paper ISBN 978-0-7636-2878-9. Grades 4–6. In 1761 the Wheatley family of Boston bought a 7-year-old slave girl whom they named Phillis after the ship on which she had been transported from Africa. The family recognized her intelligence and, breaking the law about keeping slaves illiterate, they educated her. She became fluent in languages and wrote poetry. Her poem honoring the Reverend George Whitefield was read both in the colonies and in England when she was only 17. When a British company published Wheatley's verse, she became the first African American female poet in the United States. Although she had a difficult adult life in a segregated world, she is remembered for her achievements. *Emphasis on Reading* (Alabama) nomination and *Young Reader's Choice Award* (Pennsylvania) nomination.

484. **Leslie, Tonya.** *Thomas Jefferson: A Life of Patriotism.*   (Blastoff! Readers: People of Character) Children's, 2007. 24pp. ISBN 978-0-53114-715-3. Grades 1–3. The distinguishing character trait of Thomas Jefferson (1743–1826) was his love of his country. This volume looks at Jefferson's patriotism as he helped to write the Constitution of the United States and served as its president. Illustrations augment the text. Glossary, Chronology, Further Reading, and Web Sites.

485. **Lubner, Susan.** *A Horse's Tale: A Colonial Williamsburg Adventure.*   Illustrated by Margie Moore. Abrams, 2008. 32pp. ISBN 978-0-8109-9490-4. Grades K–1. Lancer, a horse in Williamsburg, Virginia, during colonial days runs loose and behaves strangely. Margaret the Milliner tells Garrick the Gardener, Lancer's owner, that Lancer looks sad. Everyone gathers to help and each says the horse needs something different—clean hooves, a nap, oats, sugar, a song, or a counterpane (blanket). Garrick appreciates the help of his friends and realizes that a friend is what Lancer needs to make him happy.

486. McDonough, Yona Zeldis. *The Life of Benjamin Franklin: An American Original.* Illustrated by Malcah Zeldis. Henry Holt, 2006. Unpaged. ISBN 978-0-8050-7856-5. Grades 2–4. This biography of Benjamin Franklin (1706–1790) recalls his childhood and his time writing as Silence Dogood and Poor Richard before looking at his political career. Some of his famous maxims and inventions also appear. Folk-art illustrations complement the text. Further Reading.

487. Mangal, Melina. *Anne Hutchinson: Religious Reformer.* (Let Freedom Ring) Capstone, 2004. 48pp. ISBN 978-0-7368-2454-5. Grades 4–6. Anne Hutchinson (1591–1643) disagreed with the religious practices in the Massachusetts Bay Colony. She espoused a "covenant of grace," thinking that faith alone was enough to achieve salvation, and she followed her beliefs instead of those widely held in the colony. She was expelled from the colony when John Winthrop became governor and went with her family to an area that later became Rhode Island. After her husband's death, she moved again, to Pelham Bay, Long Island. There she and five of her children were killed in an Indian attack in 1643. Maps, Illustrations, Further Reading, Timeline, Glossary, and Index.

488. Miller, Brandon Marie. *Benjamin Franklin, American Genius: His Life and Ideas with 21 Activities.* (Their Lives and Ideas, 21 Activities) Chicago Review, 2009. 125pp. ISBN 978-1-55652-757-9. Grades 5–8. Six chapters cover aspects of the life of Benjamin Franklin (1706–1790) with suggestions for crafts to make in emulation of his discoveries. Instructions for making paper, a leather apron, an almanac cover, and a kite show events in his youth and days as a printer. A family tree prototype, glass armonica, fancy shoe buckle, and French food celebrate his life as a statesman. His later achievements are represented in a design for a turkey seal, a barometer, and a walking stick. Illustrations enhance the text. Glossary, Further Reading, Bibliography, Web Sites, and Index.

489. Nettleton, Pamela. *Benjamin Franklin: Writer, Inventor, Statesman.* Illustrated by Jeff Yesh. (Biographies) Picture Window, 2004. 24pp. ISBN 978-1-4048-0186-8; 2006 paper ISBN 978-1-4048-0459-3. Grades K–3. Although he never served as president, Benjamin Franklin (1706–1790) remains famous for his many achievements. His legacy as a writer of the Declaration of Independence, an inventor, and a diplomat earned him a place on the hundred dollar bill. Bibliography, Glossary, Illustrations, and Index.

490. Nettleton, Pamela. *George Washington: Farmer, Soldier, President.* Illustrated by Jeff Yesh. (Biographies) Picture Window, 2004. 24pp. ISBN 978-1-4048-0184-4; 2006 paper ISBN 978-1-4048-0457-9. Grades K–3. Among the facts included in this biography of George Washington (1732–1799) are that he named his dog "Sweetlips" and his horse "Blueskin." He refused to be king of the country, but Americans named him "Father of His Country." Bibliography, Glossary, Illustrations, and Index.

491. Nettleton, Pamela. *Pocahontas: Peacemaker and Friend to the Colonists.* Illustrated by Jeff Yesh. (Biographies) Picture Window, 2004. 24pp. ISBN 978-1-4048-0187-5; 2006 paper ISBN 978-1-4048-0460-9. Grades K–3. Pocahontas (d. 1617) was one of the women the settlers encountered in the New World. The daughter of Powhatan, the chief of the Algonquin Indians in Virginia, she met the settlers after they landed at Jamestown and befriended Captain John Smith. Later she went to London. Without her, the settlers might not have survived. Bibliography, Glossary, Illustrations, and Index.

492. Nichols, Joan Kane. *A Matter of Conscience: The Trial of Anne Hutchinson.* Illustrated by Dan Krovatin. Steck-Vaughn, 1992. 101pp. Paper ISBN 978-0-8114-8073-4. Grades 5–9. Because she wanted to follow John Cotton and his teachings, Anne Hutchinson (1591–1643) left England in 1634 for the New World. On board ship, she disagreed with the preaching of Reverend Symmes. He refused to think that any layperson, much less a woman, could know what God wanted. After they landed, he accused her of being a witch. Eventually even John Cotton turned against her and in 1638 she and her husband moved to Rhode Island because the Boston Puritan community would not tolerate different beliefs. Epilogue, Afterword, and Notes.

493. Patterson, Charles. *Thomas Jefferson.* BackinPrint.com, 2000. 95pp. Paper ISBN 978-0-595-09589-6. Grades 5–9. Before becoming the third president of the United States, Thomas Jefferson (1743–1826) had participated fully in the life of the new government. This text includes a discussion of his beliefs and their influence on the Declaration of Independence. Index.

494. Pell, Ed. *John Winthrop: Governor of the Massachusetts Bay Colony.* (Let Freedom Ring) Capstone, 2004. 48pp. ISBN 978-0-7368-2455-2. Grades 4–6. John Winthrop (1588–1649) was a religious leader and governor of the Massachusetts Bay Colony. He helped pass many laws that protected Puritan beliefs. In 1638 he presided over Anne Hutchinson's trial, in which she was accused of heresy and banished from the colony. Further Reading, Timeline, Glossary, and Index.

495. Pinkney, Andrea Davis. *Dear Benjamin Banneker.* Illustrated by J. Brian Pinkney. Hyperion, 1998. Unpaged. Paper ISBN 978-0-15-201892-4. Grades K–3. A self-taught mathematician and astronomer, free black Benjamin Banneker (1731–1806) was also one of the first to speak loudly for civil rights in a 1791 letter to the secretary of state, Thomas Jefferson. Banneker's grandmother had taught him to read and write, and he studied and experimented while developing his skills as a builder and farmer. His highest goal was to calculate and publish an almanac that would be different from others. It was finally published in 1792. In it he included the cycles of the full moons and new moons, sunrise and sunset, Chesapeake Bay tide tables, and news about festivals and horse habits. He published new almanacs every year through 1797. His skills led George Washington to hire him as a surveyor for the nation's new capital in Washington, D.C. *Notable Children's Trade Books in the Field of Social Studies* and *American Bookseller Pick of the Lists.*

496. Ransom, Candice F. *Daniel Boone.* (History Maker Bios) Lerner, 2005. 48pp. ISBN 978-0-8225-2441-5. Grades 3–5. Born October 22, 1734, Daniel Boone loved hunting and playing in the woods as a child. As a young adult working as a tracker and guide, Daniel made his way west to Kentucky. He attempted several times to move his family there, only to be turned back by Indian attacks. Eventually he succeeded in blazing a new road to Kentucky and became known as the foremost contributor to the exploration and settlement of the state. Illustrations augment the text. Bibliography, Further Reading, Glossary, Maps, Timeline, Web Sites, and Index.

497. Ransom, Candice F. *George Washington.* (History Maker Bios) Lerner, 2002. 48pp. ISBN 978-0-8225-0374-3. Grades 3–5. George Washington (1732–1799) grew up in a wealthy Virginia family. When George was 11 years old, his father died and his mother remarried. Washington became an integral part of American history by serving as a general in the Revolution and accepting the position as first president of the country. The five chapters give an overview of his life. Illustrations augment the text. Bibliography, Further Reading, Glossary, Maps, Timeline, Web Sites, and Index.

498. Ransom, Candice F. *John Hancock.* (History Maker Bios) Lerner, 2004. 48pp. ISBN 978-0-8225-1547-0. Grades 3–5. John Hancock (1737–1793), a very rich man, helped to finance the Revolutionary War. Additionally, he was a philanthropist who was elected governor of Massachusetts eleven times. The five chapters discuss his life and his achievements, including his work on the Declaration of Independence and his large signature. Illustrations augment the text. Bibliography, Further Reading, Glossary, Maps, Timeline, Web Sites, and Index.

499. Rawls, James J. *Never Turn Back.* Illustrated by George Guzzi. Steck-Vaughn, 1993. 55pp. Paper ISBN 978-0-8114-8061-1. Grades 5–9. In 1749 Father Serra and a friend left Spain to become missionaries to New Spain. They established a mission in San Xavier, Baja California. But in April 1769 Father Serra left there to help the Tipais Indians in Alta California. He established San Diego de Alacalá, where he lived until his death five years later. Epilogue, Afterword, and Notes.

500. Ray, Deborah Kogan. *The Flower Hunter: William Bartram, America's First Naturalist.* Frances Foster, 2004. 40pp. ISBN 978-0-374-34589-1. Grades 2–6. One of nine children,

William Bartram (1739–1823) traveled around colonial America with his father, John Bartram, "His Majesty's Botanist for North America," collecting, identifying, and recording hundreds of species. Beginning this epistolary, first-person account of their travels, Bartram announces that he is 8 years old, known as "Billy," and that his father calls him "my little botanist." As an adult, he and his father went to Florida where they stayed ten years to study the exotic and unexpected plants they found there. He knew Benjamin Franklin and other persons instrumental in the revolution. Watercolor and gouache illustrations complement the text. Bibliography and Maps.

501. Reiter, Chris. *Thomas Jefferson.* Enslow, 2002. 48pp. ISBN 978-0-7660-5071-6. Grades 4–7. Thomas Jefferson (1743–1826), the third president of the United States, also helped to write the Declaration of Independence. The text follows his life from early childhood to death, mentioning his accomplishments and the important political points of his presidency. The design resembles Web-page format with reproductions of Web references. Archival illustrations enhance the text. Glossary, Web Sites, Further Reading, Notes, Maps, and Index.

502. Roberts, Russell. *The Life and Times of Thomas Jefferson.* (Profiles in American History) Mitchell Lane, 2007. 48pp. ISBN 978-1-58415-439-6. Grades 5–8. This biography of Thomas Jefferson (1743–1826) places him within his times. It begins with his role in the creating the government of the United States after writing the Declaration of Independence and helping to create the Constitution. Jefferson owned slaves, and his own relationship with his slave, Sally Hemings, appears in an extra portion of the text that offers isolated facts. Photographs and reproductions augment the text. Chronology, Further Reading, Glossary, Notes, Web Sites, and Index.

503. Rockwell, Anne. *Big George: How a Shy Boy Became President Washington.* Illustrated by Matt Phelan. HMH, 2009. 48pp. ISBN 978-0-15-216583-3. Grades K–3. George Washington (1732–1799) had a boyhood hero, the Roman leader Cincinnatus, from whom he learned honor. Washington was shy, awkward, fearless, and angry when people committed wrongs against others. He grieved greatly at his half-brother's death when young and rarely, if ever, spoke of it later. He disliked war but fought at Valley Forge and Yorktown because he was needed, and he became president for the same reason. Gouache and pencil illustrations highlight the text. Notes, Bibliography, and Web Sites.

504. Rushby, Pamela. *Ben Franklin: Printer, Author, Inventor, Politician.* (National Geographic History Chapters) National Geographic, 2007. 40pp. ISBN 978-1-4263-0191-9. Grades 2–4. This brief overview of the life of Benjamin Franklin (1706–1790) shows his contributions to both history and science through his many inventions and many professions. Archival photographs augment the text. Glossary, Further Reading, Web Sites, and Index.

505. Schanzer, Rosalyn. *How Ben Franklin Stole the Lightning.* HarperCollins, 2003. Unpaged. ISBN 978-0-688-16993-0. Grades 2–4. Benjamin Franklin (1706–1790) invented both practical and impractical gadgets, but his experiment of flying a kite during a rainstorm may be the best known. He was also a statesman, author, entrepreneur, musician, community leader, and activist. This biography emphasizes his inventions rather than his other roles. Dye and ink-lined illustrations embellish the text. Note. *Capitol Choices Noteworthy Titles* (Washington, D.C.), *Diamonds Book Award* (Delaware) nomination, *Monarch Award Children's Choice Book Award* (Illinois) nomination, *Garden State Nonfiction Book Award* (New Jersey) nomination, and *Sequoyah Book Award* (Oklahoma) nomination.

506. Schanzer, Rosalyn. *John Smith Escapes Again!* National Geographic, 2006. 64pp. ISBN 978-0-7922-5930-5. Grades 3–5. This biography of John Smith (1580–1631) covers his life from the age of 16 when he went from England to the Netherlands to fight Catholic Spain. He traveled around Europe before sailing on a pirate ship, was stranded on a desert island, and nearly drowned more than once. Then he came to America. Although based on his writings, this volume cannot verify whether all the tales Smith told are true. He may well have exaggerated his exciting exploits for readers. Cartoon illustrations enhance the text. Bibliography and Index.

507. Shea, Pegi Deitz. *Patience Wright: America's First Sculptor and Revolutionary Spy.* Illustrated by Bethanne Andersen. Henry Holt, 2007. Unpaged. ISBN 978-0-8050-6770-5. Grades 2–4. Patience Lovell Wright (1725–1793), born into a Quaker household in Oyster Bay, New York, became a sculptor. When her husband died, she supported her family with her wax models. She also spent time in England and, acting as a spy, sent valuable messages to the revolutionaries hidden in her creations. Illustrations augment the text. Bibliography, Chronology.

508. Sherrow, Victoria. *Benjamin Franklin.* (History Maker Bios) Lerner, 2002. 48pp. ISBN 978-0-8225-0198-5. Grades 3–5. Benjamin Franklin (1706–1790), a candle maker's son, created paddles to swim faster when he was only 12 years old. The fifteenth of seventeen children, he left home at 17. He became a printer and discovered electricity, among other interests and inventions. He also served as a statesman for the colonies and an ambassador for the country during his long and productive life. Illustrations augment the text. Bibliography, Further Reading, Glossary, Maps, Timeline, Web Sites, and Index.

509. Sherrow, Victoria. *Thomas Jefferson.* (History Maker Bios) Lerner, 2002. 48pp. ISBN 978-0-8225-0197-8; paper ISBN 978-0-8225-0382-8. Grades 3–5. Thomas Jefferson (1743–1826) was a Virginia farmer before he began his work as author of the Declaration of Independence. He was also an inventor, secretary of state, vice president, and then president for eight years. Illustrations augment the text. Bibliography, Further Reading, Glossary, Maps, Timeline, Web Sites, and Index.

510. Smalley, Carol Parenzan. *Henry Hudson.* Mitchell Lane, 2006. 32pp. ISBN 978-1-58415-479-2. Grades 1–4. This biography of Henry Hudson (d. 1611) details his life and voyages while searching unsuccessfully for a northern passage to Asia. Although his crew eventually mutinied and put him and eight others in a boat to drift, he did make discoveries in North America and interact with the Native Americans. Illustrations augment the text. Bibliography, Glossary, Chronology, and Index.

511. Somervill, Barbara A. *William Penn: Founder of Pennsylvania.* (Signature Lives Colonial America) Compass Point, 2006. 112pp. ISBN 978-0-7565-1598-0. Grades 5–9. Nine chapters discuss the important times in the life of William Penn (1644–1718) as he tried to find a place to worship without persecution. He left England and became the founder of Pennsylvania before the colonies freed themselves from the English. Illustrations augment the text. Bibliography, Chronology, Glossary, and Index.

512. Sutcliffe, Jane. *John Adams.* (History Maker Bios) Lerner, 2006. 48pp. ISBN 978-0-8225-5940-5. Grades 3–5. John Adams (1735–1826) grew up on his father's farm in the colony of Massachusetts in a town named Braintree. He expected to become a farmer, but his plans changed when the colonies decided to fight Great Britain. The five chapters discuss Adams's life and family and his role as president of the United States and as its emissary. Illustrations augment the text. Bibliography, Further Reading, Glossary, Maps, Timeline, Web Sites, and Index.

513. Thomas, Peggy. *Farmer George Plants a Nation.* Illustrated by Layne Johnson. Calkins Creek, 2008. 40pp. ISBN 978-1-59078-460-0. Grades 3–6. George Washington (1732–1799) was not only president of the United States, he was also a farmer, an inventor, and a scientist. Using primary resources such as Washington's letters and diaries, this volume reveals his ideas about making the country self-sufficient just as he tried to do for his own farm, Mount Vernon. Among his achievements were the design of a 16-sided treading barn, planting trees, breeding mules, and working with compost. Illustrations enhance the text. Chronology, bibliography, Further Reading, and Notes. *School Library Journal Best Books for Children.*

514. Todd, Anne. *George Washington: A Life of Self-Discipline.* Illustrated by Tina Walski. (Blastoff! Readers: People of Character) Bellweather, 2007. 24pp. ISBN 978-1-60014-094-5. Grades 2–4. A distinguishing character trait of George Washington (1732–1799) was his self-discipline. The text looks at his role as a leader during the American Revolution and in helping to form the government of his new country. Illustrations augment the text. Glossary, Chronology, Further Reading, and Web Sites.

515. Uglow, Loyd. *Benjamin Franklin—You Know What to Say.* Illustrated by Greg Budwine. (Another Great Achiever) Advance, 2003. 48pp. ISBN 978-1-57537-741-4. Grades 3–6. Benjamin Franklin (1706–1790) was industrious when he was young and became accomplished in many fields. He was a printer, a writer, a scientist, an inventor, the Postmaster General, an ambassador for the United States, and a representative to Congress. He was also one of the authors of the Declaration of Independence. This biography briefly covers those aspects of his life.

516. Van Vleet, Carmella. *Amazing Ben Franklin Inventions You Can Build Yourself.* Nomad, 2007. 120pp. Paper ISBN 978-0-9771294-7-8. Grades 4–8. This guide to Benjamin Franklin's inventions offers ways to create versions of them along with information about Franklin's life. Each section gives a brief explanation of why Franklin was interested in a particular process or object, followed by step-by-step instructions. Among the inventions included are a feather pen, bifocals, a lightning rod, paper currency, swim paddles, and a solar oven. Illustrations augment the text. Glossary, Further Reading, Web Sites, and Index.

517. Waxman, Laura Hamilton. *Uncommon Revolutionary: A Story About Thomas Paine.* Illustrated by Craig Orback. (Creative Minds) Carolrhoda, 2004. 64pp. ISBN 978-1-57505-180-2; paper ISBN 978-1-57505-608-1. Grades 3–5. The seven chapters of this volume reveal facts about the life of Thomas Paine (1737–1809). He was born in Britain and became a tax collector. In his late 30s, his desire for adventure drew him to the American colonies. He became convinced of the importance of democracy and he wrote articles and pamphlets in support of the revolution, especially "Common Sense." Later he went to France. Illustrations augment the text. Sources, Bibliography, and Index.

518. Welch, Catherine. *Benjamin Banneker.* (History Maker Bios) Lerner, 2008. 48pp. ISBN 978-0-8225-7167-4. Grades 3–5. This biography of Benjamin Banneker (1731–1806) covers his life from boyhood working on his family's farm through educating himself to become a surveyor and astronomer. His careful study of the stars helped him to create almanacs that instructed others about the wonders of the skies. Illustrations augment the text. Bibliography, Further Reading, Glossary, Maps, Timeline, Web Sites, and Index.

519. Welch, Catherine. *Patrick Henry.* (History Maker Bios) Lerner, 2006. 48pp. ISBN 978-0-8225-5941-2. Grades 3–5. Patrick Henry (1736–1799), a native Virginian and a lawyer, realized the power of words and he used them to spur residents of the colonies to revolt against Great Britain. The five chapters of this volume discuss his life; his spirited speeches, including the phrase "give me liberty, or give me death;" his activities during the Revolution, and his contributions after the Revolution. Illustrations augment the text. Bibliography, Further Reading, Glossary, Maps, Timeline, Web Sites, and Index.

520. Whiting, Jim. *Francisco Vasquez de Coronado.* (Latinos in American History) Mitchell Lane, 2002. 48pp. ISBN 978-1-58415-146-3. Grades 5–8. Francisco Vasquez de Coronado (1510–1554), a Spanish nobleman, searched throughout the American Southwest for the elusive Seven Cities of Gold. He made four expeditions during which he also attempted to convert and to dominate the Native Americans in the area. Eventually he was tried in Mexico City for his cruelty to the native peoples but was found innocent. However, the trial damaged his reputation, and he could no longer explore successfully. Illustrations enhance the text. Bibliography, Glossary, and Index.

521. Whiting, Jim. *Junipero José Serra.* (Latinos in American History) Mitchell Lane, 2003. 48pp. ISBN 978-1-58415-187-6. Grades 5–8. Junipero José Serra (1713–1784) was a Spanish explorer and missionary who went to Mexico and California to teach the Native Indians about Christianity. He established nine missions along the California coast in which he preached and practiced self-flagellation. He was honored with the name "Father of California." Illustrations augment the text. Glossary, Chronology, Further Reading, Web Sites, and Index.

522. Wilkie, Katherine E. *Daniel Boone: Taming The Wilds.* Illustrated by E. Harper Johnson. Chelsea House, 1990. 72pp. ISBN 978-0-7910-1407-3. Grades 2–6. Daniel Boone (1734–

1820) moved with his Quaker family from the Pennsylvania area toward Kentucky, where he formed alliances with Native Americans and helped open the territory to settlers.

523. **Yates, Elizabeth.** *Amos Fortune, Free Man.* Dutton, 1972. 181pp. ISBN 978-0-525-25570-3; Puffin, 1989, paper ISBN 978-0-14-034158-4. Grades 3–6. When an At-mun-shi tribe prince was 15 in 1725, slave traders abducted him. His owners named him Amos Fortune and taught him to read. He was finally able to buy his freedom forty-five years later. He continued his work as an expert tanner and a supportive family member, and he bought freedom for many others until he died in 1801. *Newbery Medal, William Allen White Award* (Kansas), *Herald Tribune Award*, and *Governor's Award of Distinction* (New Hampshire).

524. **Yoder, Carolyn P.** *John Adams—The Writer: A Treasury of Letters, Diaries, and Public Documents.* Calkins Creek, 2007. 144pp. ISBN 978-1-59078-247-7. Grades 5–8. This collection of the letters of John Adams (1735–1826) offer a view of him at different times during his life. The letters start when he taught grammar school at the age of 19 and continue until he is near 90. They detail his courtship of Abigail Adams, his service to the First Continental Congress, his diplomacy abroad, his presidency, and the years of his retirement. They all show his intelligence and dedication to the country and to his family. Illustrations complement the text. Chronology and Index.

Graphic Novels, Biographies, and Histories

525. **Braun, Eric.** *The Story of Jamestown.* Illustrated by Steve Erwin and Keith Williams. Graphic Library, 2005. 32pp. ISBN 978-0-7368-4967-8; paper ISBN 978-0-7368-6210-3. Grades 3–5. The Virginia colony of Jamestown was founded on May 14, 1607, the first permanent English settlement in America. Among those associated with this event are John Smith and Pocahontas, the young woman who helped the settlers survive. Illustrations augment the text. Bibliography, Glossary, Further Reading, and Index.

526. **Burgan, Michael.** *The Boston Massacre.* Illustrated by Bob Wiacek and Keith Williams. Graphic Library, 2006. 32pp. ISBN 978-0-7368-4368-3; paper ISBN 978-0-7368-9678-8. Grades 3–5. On March 5, 1770, a brawl erupted between civilians and the military. The rioting crowd charged on the British soldiers, who fired their muskets killing three civilians on the spot with two dying later. This event sparked defiance among the colonists that eventually led to the American Revolution. Illustrations depict the text. Bibliography, Glossary, Further Reading, and Index.

527. **Doeden, Matt.** *The Boston Tea Party.* Illustrated by Charles Barnett, III and Dave Hoover. Graphic Library, 2006. 32pp. ISBN 978-0-7368-4368-3; paper ISBN 978-0-7368-5243-2. Grades 3–5. The Boston Tea Party, held on Thursday, December 16, 1773, occurred because colonists were protesting British taxes and demands that they buy tea from the British East India Company. They destroyed crates of tea on the ships in the Boston Harbor. Illustrations complement the text. Bibliography, Glossary, Further Reading, and Index.

528. **Doeden, Matt.** *Samuel Adams: Patriot and Statesman.* Illustrated by Tod Smith, Wilson Keith, and Dave Hoover. (Graphic Biographies) Graphic Library, 2006. 32pp. ISBN 978-0-7368-6500-5; paper ISBN 978-0-7368-9664-1. Grades 3–5. This short graphic biography of Samuel Adams (1722–1803) reveals his life as a revolutionary politician who spoke for the "Sons of Liberty," a participant in the Boston Tea Party, a signer of the Declaration of Independence, and a governor of Massachusetts. A yellow background sets direct quotes from Adams apart from the fictional aspect of the narration. Web Sites.

529. **Englar, Mary.** *The Pilgrims and the First Thanksgiving.* Illustrated by Peter McDonnell. Graphic Library, 2006. 32pp. ISBN 978-0-7368-5492-4; paper ISBN 978-0-7368-9656-6. Grades 3–5. Squanto taught the pilgrims how to fish and grow corn and the settlers decided to celebrate after their first harvest in 1621. They invited Squanto and King Massasoit with ninety men to feast in Plymouth. Illustrations complement the text. Bibliography, Glossary, Further Reading, and Index.

530. **Espinosa, Rod.** *Benjamin Franklin.* Graphic Planet, 2007. 32pp. ISBN 978-1-60270-064-2. Grades 3–5. This fictional graphic biography presents the life of Benjamin Franklin (1706–1790) with imagined dialogue. Pictures augment the text. Chronology, Further Reading, Glossary, Web Sites, and Index.

531. **Espinosa, Rod.** *George Washington.* Graphic Planet, 2008. 32pp. ISBN 978-1-60270-067-3. Grades 3–5. This fictional graphic biography presents the life of George Washington ((1732–1799) with imagined dialogue. Pictures augment the text. Chronology, Further Reading, Glossary, Web Sites, and Index.

532. **Glaser, Jason.** *Patrick Henry: Liberty or Death.* Illustrated by Peter McDonnell. (Graphic Biographies) Capstone, 2005. 32pp. ISBN 978-0-7368-4970-8; paper ISBN 978-0-7368-9674-0. Grades 3–5. This short graphic biography of Patrick Henry (1736–1799) details his work as a patriot before and during the American Revolution. A lawyer, he is known for his statement, "Give me liberty, or give me death." A yellow background sets direct quotes from Henry apart from the fictional aspect of the narration. Web Sites.

533. **Jacobson, Ryan.** *William Penn: Founder of Pennsylvania.* Illustrated by Tim Stiles. (Graphic Biographies) Graphic Library, 2006. 32pp. ISBN 978-0-7368-6501-2; paper ISBN 978-0-7368-9665-8. Grades 3–5. This short graphic biography of William Penn (1644–1718) relates his life as a Quaker who founded the colony of Pennsylvania in 1682. As governor of the colony, he also allowed non-Quakers to settle. A yellow background sets direct quotes from Penn apart from the fictional aspect of the narration. Web Sites.

534. **Lassieur, Allison.** *The Voyage of the Mayflower.* Illustrated by Peter McDonnell. Graphic Library, 2005. 32pp. ISBN 978-0-7368-4371-3; paper ISBN 978-0-7368-6882-2. Grades 3–5. The people who sailed on the *Mayflower* wanted a better economic life and to own land. They arrived in 1620 to establish their new settlement. Illustrations complement the text. Bibliography, Glossary, Further Reading, and Index.

535. **Martin, Michael.** *The Salem Witch Trials.* Illustrated by Brian Bascle. Graphic Library, 2005. 32pp. ISBN 978-0-7368-3847-4; paper ISBN 978-0-7368-5246-3. Grades 3–5. Between February 1692 and May 1693 more than 150 people were arrested and imprisoned for witchcraft, with the courts convicting 29. Nineteen were hanged. A man who refused to say he was guilty was crushed under heavy stones. Another five died in prison. Theories as to the cause of the accusations abound. Illustrations complement the text. Bibliography, Glossary, Further Reading, and Index.

536. **Olson, Kay Melchisedech.** *Benjamin Franklin: An American Genius.* Illustrated by Gordon Purcell. Graphic Library, 2006. 32pp. ISBN 978-0-7368-4629-5; paper ISBN 978-0-7368-9666-5. Grades 3–5. This short graphic biography of Benjamin Franklin (1706–1790) depicts his life and work as a writer, inventor, scientist, statesman, and diplomat. He was one of the major forces in America during the colonial period and after the American Revolution. A yellow background sets direct quotes from Franklin apart from the fictional aspect of the narration. Web Sites.

DVDs

537. *Animated Atlas: The Early Colonies.* SVE & Churchill Media, 2003. 22 mins. Grades 4–8. Animated maps, historical footage, photographs, and icons show the development of Colonial America and how the land and location of water influenced settlements and either helped or hindered the colonists' survival. Topics include England under Elizabeth I and Roanoke Island; Jamestown, Chesapeake Bay and Early Virginia; New England; Reformation and Pilgrims and Puritans; Hudson River to New Sweden; Maryland; and Later Virginia.

538. Barretta, Gene. *Now and Ben: The Modern Inventions of Benjamin Franklin.* Spoken Arts, 2007. 12:35 mins. ISBN 978-0-8045-8055-7. Grades 2–5. Benjamin Franklin (1706–1790) had ideas that still affect us all. He either invented or investigated odometers, eyeglasses, post offices, libraries, daylight savings time, the gulf stream, and the importance of vitamin C in the diet. Watercolor cartoon illustrations enhance the text.

539. *Causes of the Revolution: 1765-1774.* (American Revolution for Students) Library Video, 2003. 23 mins. Grades 5–9. Reenactments, period paintings and illustrations, and actors portraying personages of the time give an account of the social, political, and economic conditions that influenced Americans as they became unhappy with British rule. Patriots such as Patrick Henry and Sam Adams created radical plans in response to the Stamp Act, the Coercive Acts, and others. Even though the majority wanted compromise, enough were unhappy with events and thought otherwise.

540. *Native Americans: North America 1300–1700 A.D.* (Hands-On Crafts for Kids Series 6: Back in Time) Chip Taylor Communications, 2003. 30 mins. Grades 4–6. See entry 311.

541. *Origins of Democracy: 1688–1765.* (American Revolution for Students) Library Video, 2003. 23 mins. Grades 5–9. After the American colonies developed an independent economy, they wanted to govern themselves. Reenactments, period paintings and illustrations, and actors portraying personages of the time give an account of the social, political, and economic conditions that influenced Americans.

542. *Patrick Henry: Quest for Freedom.* American Animation Studios, 2007. 34 mins. ISBN 978-0-9796681-1-1. Grades 3–6. Patrick Henry (1736–1799), best known for the phrase "give me liberty, or give me death," was one of America's founding fathers. This DVD, using an eagle, Boomer, as the host, covers Henry's childhood of "fishing and fiddling" and his encounter with Thomas Jefferson, who encouraged him to study law. Henry believed that the colonists had a right to independence, and the DVD entertainingly presents his opinions.

Compact Discs

543. Lasky, Kathryn. *A Journey to the New World: The Diary of Remember Patience Whipple: Mayflower/Plimoth Colony, 1620.* Narrated by Barbara Rosenblat and Bonnie Kelley-Young. (Dear America) Live Oak Media, 2008. 3 CDs; 3 hrs. 5 mins. ISBN 978-1-4301-0367-7. Grades 5–9. See entry 341.

544. Speare, Elizabeth George. *The Sign of the Beaver.* Narrated by Greg Schaffert. Listening Library, 2004. 3 CDs; 3 hrs. 9 mins. ISBN 978-1-4000-8497-5. Grades 4–8. See entry 355.

545. *Thomas Jefferson's America.* Greathall, 2005. 1 CD; 74 mins. ISBN 978-1-882513-86-4. Grades 5 up. This compact disc offers eleven stories in an overview of Thomas Jefferson's life from his teen years beginning in 1757 to his death on July 4, 1826. He lived near contemporary Charlottesville, Virginia, and then went to Williamsburg to William and Mary College where he studied law and revolution with Patrick Henry. He married Martha Jefferson before working with Benjamin Franklin and John Adams to write the Declaration of Independence. He went to Paris with John Adams, became president, and authorized the Louisiana Purchase. After he left office, he returned home to Monticello.

546. Tripp, Valerie. *Felicity: An American Girl.* Narrated by Carrie Hitchcock. Recorded Books, 2006. 6 CDs; 6.75 hrs. ISBN 978-1-4193-5932-3. Grades 3–6. Felicity Merriman, 9, lives in Williamsburg, Virginia, in 1774. She has heard that the colonies might try to break from England's rule because Patriots like Felicity's father do not want to pay unfair taxes on things like tea. Felicity's grandfather and her best friend Elizabeth support the king as Loyalists. Felicity has to decide what she believes and whether she is willing to lose her best friend.

THE AMERICAN REVOLUTION, 1775–1783

Historical Fiction and Fantasy

547. Anderson, Elizabeth Weiss, and Elizabeth Weiss Vollstadt. *Young Patriots: Inspiring Stories of the American Revolution.* Boyds Mills, 2004. 141pp. ISBN 978-1-59078-241-5. Grades 4–7. Fifteen young people find themselves in a number of unexpected situations during the American Revolution. Five sections focus on the years before the war, the beginning of the war, the important battles, and the years of the new nation. Among the various events featured are bells chiming for war, girls disguising themselves as boys, and friends finding themselves on different sides of the conflict. Chronology, Glossary, Web Sites, and Bibliography.

548. Avi. *The Fighting Ground.* HarperCollins, 1984. 160pp. ISBN 978-0-397-32074-5; Trophy, 1987, paper ISBN 978-0-06-440185-2. Grades 4 up. Eleven-year-old Jonathan spends a day fighting Hessians in 1778 near Trenton, New Jersey. Hessians capture him and hold him in a deserted farmhouse, where he sees a young boy hiding near his dead parents. Thinking the Hessians have killed the couple, Jonathan escapes and rejoins the group he was with earlier in the day. Then he finds out that they—not the Hessians—killed the two because the two were Tories. When Jonathan leads the same group to the Hessians, they are pleased to kill them too. *American Library Association Notable Children's Books, American Library Association Recommended Books for Reluctant Young Adult Readers, Horn Book Fanfare Honor List, New York Public Library's Books for the Teen Age,* and *Lesbian and Gay Children's/YA Award.*

549. Banim, Lisa. *Drums at Saratoga.* Illustrated by Tatyana Yuditskaya. (Stories of the States) Silver Moon, 1993. 58pp. ISBN 978-1-8818-8920-5; 1995, paper ISBN 978-1-8818-8970-0. Grades 3–5. Disgusted with the drudgery of a Canadian foundry apprenticeship, Nathaniel Phillips leaves in 1777 to fight with the British general "Gentleman Johnny" Burgoyne. He follows him to the Battle of Saratoga, where he discovers that the realities of colonial life are little different from working in the foundry. The experience gives him a more mature perspective on his own experiences. Endpaper Maps, Historical Postscript, and Recommended Reading.

550. Banim, Lisa. *A Spy in the King's Colony.* Illustrated by Tatyana Yuditskaya. (Mysteries in Time) Silver Moon, 1994. 76pp. ISBN 978-1-8818-8954-0; 1995, paper ISBN 978-1-8931-1001-4. Grades 3–5. In 1776 Emily Parker, 11, finds herself followed by someone who may be a thief. Although she does not know the person's identity, she begins to suspect almost everyone of being a spy. She is especially concerned to know if her older sister's boyfriend is a loyalist or a patriot. What she discovers is a great relief.

551. Benchley, Nathaniel. *Sam the Minuteman.* Fitzgerald, 2007. 64pp. ISBN 978-1-4242-0597-4; Trophy paper ISBN 978-0-06-444107-0. Grades 2–4. Sam's father decides that Sam can go with him to fight with the Minutemen against the British. When a friend is wounded, Sam worries about him but is ready to fight again.

552. Carlson, Drew. *Attack of the Turtle.* Illustrated by David A. Johnson. Eerdmans, 2008. 149pp. Paper ISBN 978-0-8028-5338-7. Grades 4–7. Fourteen-year-old Nate agrees to help his older cousin, David Bushnell, to build a secret weapon for the Continental Army. Although Nate is afraid of water, he crosses the Connecticut River each night to the hidden workshop. Finally they deliver the *Turtle*, Bushnell's invention designed to attach bombs to ships' hulls. It becomes the first submarine to be used in warfare.

553. Collier, Christopher, and James Lincoln Collier. *War Comes to Willy Freeman.* Yearling, 1997. 192pp. Paper ISBN 978-0-440-49504-8. Grades 4–6. Thirteen-year-old Willy, a black girl from Connecticut, watches a British soldier kill her father and returns home to find that the British have taken her mother. She disguises herself as a boy and sets out to find her. In New York City she finds work at Sam Fraunces's tavern and searches for her mother during her free time.

554. DeFelice, Cynthia. *The Ghost of Poplar Point.* Farrar, 2007. 192pp. ISBN 978-0-374-32540-4. Grades 3–7. Twelve-year-old Allie finds herself channeling the ghost of a young Seneca girl in the school pageant and reveals that Washington's troops massacred Indians in 1779 at Poplar Point. A local businessman wants the spot to build a resort. After the revelation, the town decides to protect the burial ground, and Allie is relieved to have helped the girl's ghost finally rest.

555. DeFord, Deborah H., and Harry S. Stout. *An Enemy Among Them.* Sandpiper, 1994. 203pp. Paper ISBN 978-0-395-70108-9. Grades 5–9. Margaret's brother is wounded in 1776 and when she looks after him in the hospital she also helps an enemy Hessian. Christian, the Hessian, works for Margaret's father on the family farm instead of going to prison, and as Margaret begins to fall in love with him, she finds out that he wounded her brother. Christian, however, becomes a believer in the Patriot cause, and Margaret's German American family comes to accept him.

556. Deutsch, Stacia, and Rhody Cohon. *Betsy Ross's Star.* Illustrated by Guy Francis. (Blast to the Past) Aladdin, 2006. 121pp. Paper ISBN 978-0-689-93388-5. Grades 2–5. In this time-travel biography, third-grade students Abigail, Jacob, Zack, and Bo have to decide how to preserve the memory of Betsy Ross—no one is certain whether she actually sewed the first American flag. They decide that asking her is the best way to find the right answer.

557. Deutsch, Stacia, and Rhody Cohon. *Washington's War.* Illustrated by Guy Francis. (Blast to the Past) Aladdin, 2007. 121pp. Paper ISBN 978-1-41693-390-8. Grades 2–5. Abigail, Jacob, Zack, and Bo know that George Washington must not leave Valley Forge. They travel back in time to tell him to remain there and continue to fight for the American Revolution.

558. Favole, Robert J. *Through the Wormhole.* Flywheel, 2001. 192pp. ISBN 978-1-930826-00-7. Grades 5–8. When freshman Kate's swimming coach berates her for her fear at their meets, and her friend Michael, an African American equestrian, hears slurs about being a "wannabe white," they find themselves transported to the colonial era in 1778 where they have the task of warning Lafayette about a British trap and, at the same time, saving Michael's ancestor John Banks, a free black cavalryman who serves as a Continental dragoon. During this experience, they learn to help others by using their swimming and equestrian skills and to have confidence in themselves.

559. Fleming, Candace. *A Big Cheese for the White House: The True Tale of a Tremendous Cheddar.* Illustrated by S. D. Schindler. Sunburst, 2004. 40pp. Paper ISBN 978-0-374-40627-1. Grades 1–5. In 1801 the townspeople of Cheshire, Massachusetts, decided to create a 1,235-pound cheddar cheese wheel to present to President Jefferson at his New Year's Day party because they did not like reports of him eating cheddar made in Norton, Connecticut. He declared it was the best cheese he had ever tasted. *Children's Book of the Year, Bank Street College.*

560. Fleming, Candace. *The Hatmaker's Sign: A Story by Benjamin Franklin.* Illustrated by Robert Parker. Orchard, 1998. 40pp. Paper ISBN 978-0-531-30075-6. Grades 1–5. When

Thomas Jefferson is disturbed about the number of changes suggested to the draft Declaration of Independence, Benjamin Franklin tells him a story to calm him down. The story is about a Boston hatmaker who wants a new sign for his shop. He chooses ten words and a picture of a hat. His wife deletes three words, and the reverend suggests three more. Then others want him to put words back in. In essence, everyone had a different opinion. The story is recorded in Jefferson's papers. *New York State Charlotte Award* nomination, *SCASL Book Award* (South Carolina) nomination, and *Land of Enchantment Book Award* (New Mexico) nomination.

561. Forbes, Esther. *Johnny Tremain.* Illustrated by Michael McDurdy. Houghton, 1998. 293pp. ISBN 978-0-395-90011-6; Laurel-Leaf, 1987, paper ISBN 978-0-440-94250-4. Grades 5 up. Johnny is very proud of the beautiful silver designs he has created and brags about his talents to the other apprentices. When he decides to work on Sunday to complete an order for John Hancock, he not only breaks the law against working on Sunday but he also burns his hand so severely that he is no longer able to longer work in silver. As the American Revolution begins, a friend interests him in the Whig causes of fighting against the English, and he starts to help the movement toward independence in any way that he can. This book was first published in 1943. *Newbery Medal.*

562. Fritz, Jean. *Early Thunder.* Illustrated by Lynd Ward. Puffin, 1987. 256pp. Paper ISBN 978-0-14-032259-0. Grades 5–9. In 1775 America Daniel West is 14 years old and supports the British king. But when fellow Tories throw stones into a judge's window while the man lies dying of smallpox, he becomes infuriated. He begins to change his allegiance when he sees people he respects support the rebel cause.

563. Gauch, Patricia L. *This Time, Tempe Wick?* Illustrated by Margot Tomes. Boyds Mills, 2003. 48pp. ISBN 978-1-59078-179-1. Grades 1–4. In 1781 Tempe Wick is determined to keep General Washington's mutinous soldiers from taking her horse. She hides it inside her house in Pennsylvania for more than three days. Her wits save both her house and her horse from harm.

564. Gutman, Dan. *Qwerty Stevens Stuck in Time with Benjamin Franklin.* Simon & Schuster, 2002. 192pp. ISBN 978-0-689-84553-6; 2005, paper ISBN 978-0-689-87884-8. Grades 4–8. Although Qwerty Stevens, 13, wants to retire his Anytime Anywhere Machine, he needs it one more time to help him write a paper on the American Revolution. Suddenly Benjamin Franklin is sitting on his bed. Franklin marvels at the inventions he sees in Qwerty's room and goes with him to class, where he charms Qwerty's teacher, who thinks he is an impersonator. All the while, he spouts his aphorisms. After school Qwerty and his friend Joey go with Franklin to Philadelphia on July 4, 1776, for the signing of the Declaration of Independence. There they also see John Adams and Thomas Jefferson. Unfortunately, they forgot to arrange their return to the present so they have difficulty leaving 1776. *Emphasis on Reading Award* and *Young Hoosier Award* (Indiana) nomination.

565. Harlow, Joan Hiatt. *Midnight Rider.* Margaret K. McElderry, 2005. 416pp. ISBN 978-0-689-87009-5; Aladdin, 2006, paper ISBN 978-0-689-87010-1. Grades 5–8. Orphan and indentured servant to British General Thomas Gage, 14-year-old Hannah Andrews, disguised as a boy, attends a secret meeting of the Sons of Liberty in Boston in 1775. Riding her horse, Promise, she starts passing messages to the revolutionaries. In the general's house, she overhears plans for a campaign to seize the patriots' guns and she rides miles to Salem to warn the citizens.

566. Jensen, Dorothea. *The Riddle of Penncroft Farm.* Gulliver, 2001. 180pp. Paper ISBN 978-0-15-216441-6. Grades 4–6. Lars and his parents move from Minnesota to Philadelphia to be with Lars's 90-year-old aunt, who soon dies. Lars has an unsettling experience when a family ghost from the Revolutionary War era appears and tells him about family history and the roles of his ancestors in the American Revolution. With information provided by the ghost, Lars finds his aunt's missing will and becomes her heir.

567. Keehn, Sally M. *Moon of Two Dark Horses.* Puffin, 2002. 218pp. Paper ISBN 978-0-698-11949-9. Grades 4–8. The ghost of Coshmoo, a young Indian boy killed in the Revolution-

ary War, relates how he and his friend, son of a white settler, tried to end the hostilities between their people. When the Delaware need money to survive, the differences between the
groups become more emphatic, resulting in the fighting that eventually kills Coshmoo.

568. Krensky, Stephen. *Dangerous Crossing: The Revolutionary Voyage of John and John Quincy
Adams.* Translated by Greg Harlin. Penguin, 2004. 32pp. ISBN 978-0-525-46966-7. Grades
2–4. At the age of 10 in 1778 Johnny (Quincy) Adams went with his father John on a dangerous midwinter voyage from Massachusetts to Paris on the frigate *Boston*. They wanted to
persuade the French government to support the American colonies in their revolution against
England. Johnny keeps a diary and reveals some of his father's thoughts during the storms,
seasickness, and other hardships of the voyage.

569. Krensky, Stephen. *Hanukkah at Valley Forge.* Illustrated by Greg Harlin. Dutton, 2006.
32pp. ISBN 978-0-525-47738-9. Grades 2–4. At Valley Forge in 1778, George Washington
watches a Jewish soldier from Poland light a Hanukkah candle and learns about the holiday
that commemorates an ancient conflict between the Maccabees and the Greeks over religious freedom. The two men recognize the similarity of that event and their current conflict
with the British. Watercolors enhance the text. Note.

570. Lawson, Robert. *Mr. Revere and I: Being an Account of Certain Episodes in the Career of
Paul Revere, Esq., As Recently Revealed by His Horse, Scheherazade, Later Pride of His Royal
Majesty's 14th Regiment of Foot.* See entry 343.

571. Longfellow, Henry Wadsworth. *Paul Revere's Ride.* Illustrated by Monica Vachula. Boyds
Mills, 2003. 32pp. ISBN 978-1-56397-799-2. Grades K–2. The text of Henry Wadsworth
Longfellow's poem, written in 1861, about the ride of Paul Revere (1735–1818) is accompanied by illustrations that show the British ship *Somerset* in the background and people in
windows listening to Revere's message. Revere himself was a silversmith and a spy, but his
ride was carefully planned so that he could cover much ground and tell many people. Note.

572. Longfellow, Henry Wadsworth. *Paul Revere's Ride.* Illustrated by Charles Santore.
HarperCollins, 2003. 32pp. ISBN 978-0-688-16552-9. Grades K–2. Santore's illustrations
bring Henry Wadsworth Longfellow's poem, written in 1861, about the ride of Paul Revere
(1735–1818) to life, creating a "story within a story" with the landlord of the Wayside Inn sitting in his chair. The full-page pictures draw the reader into the action. They see the Old
North Church and hear the horse's hooves on the cobblestones as Revere dashes through the
town. Note.

573. McGovern, Ann. *The Secret Soldier: The Story of Deborah Sampson.* Illustrated by Ann
Grifalconi. Scholastic, 1999. 64pp. Paper ISBN 978-0-590-43052-4. Grades 1–5. As Robert
Shurtliff, Deborah Sampson enlisted in the Continental Army to fight against the British,
who killed her fiancé. She was a bound servant to his family and forbidden to attend school
or learn a trade. This volume describes her attempts to keep her identity secret while making long, tiring marches to fight the Tories.

574. Pryor, Bonnie. *Hannah Pritchard: Pirate of the Revolution.* (Historical Fiction Adventure)
Enslow, 2008. 160pp. ISBN 978-0-7660-2851-7. Grades 5–8. After Loyalists kill her parents
and brother, 14-year-old Hannah Pritchard leaves her family farm and, disguised as a male,
joins a pirate ship that is carrying supplies for the American Revolution. She works in the
kitchen and has a number of adventures while trying to keep her gender a secret.

575. Ransom, Candice F. *Secret in the Tower.* Illustrated by Greg Call. (Time Spies) Mirrorstone, 2006. 112pp. Paper ISBN 978-0-7869-4027-1. Grades 2–4. Alex, Mattie, and Sophie
worry they will be bored at their parents' new country bed-and-breakfast. But their lives
change when they discover a secret tower room with an antique brass spyglass that has the
power to transport them back in time. The inn's first guest, a Revolutionary War reenactor,
tells them about the Battle of Yorktown. The spyglass transports them to 1781 where they
help an injured courier and must convey a message to American headquarters to keep from
being arrested themselves.

576. Reit, Seymour. *Guns for General Washington: A Story of the American Revolution.* Gulliver, 2001. 144pp. Paper ISBN 978-0-15-216435-5. Grades 4–6. In the winter of 1775, despite rough terrain and other obstacles, Colonel Henry Knox moved a large number of cannons from Fort Ticonderoga to Massachusetts to give Boston a chance to free itself from the British. The story of those who participated is re-created in this historical fiction.

577. Smith, Lane. *John, Paul, George and Ben.* Hyperion, 2006. 36pp. ISBN 978-0-7868-4893-5. Grades K–3. In this entertaining story, John Hancock, Paul Revere, George Washington, and Benjamin Franklin come into contact with Tom Jefferson. The text identifies each man with a single trait, and presents supporting references and events. John writes boldly, Paul speaks loudly to a lady in his shop, George honestly admits that he chopped down an orchard, Ben spouts platitudes at his neighbors, and Tom complains to his teacher. Illustrations augment the text. *NAPPA Gold Awards, Book Awards* (Connecticut), *Quill Awards* nomination, *New York Times Best Illustrated Books, Publishers Weekly Best Children's Books, School Library Journal Best Books for Children, Horn Book Fanfare, Bulletin Blue Ribbon, Readers' Choice Award* (Virginia) nomination, *Black-Eyed Susan Award* (Maryland) nomination, *Capitol Choices Noteworthy Titles* (Washington, D.C.), and *Bluegrass Award* (Kentucky) nomination.

578. Tripp, Valerie. *Very Funny, Elizabeth.* American Girl, 2005. 81pp. ISBN 978-1-59369-067-0; paper ISBN 978-1-59369-061-8. Grades 3–5. In 1775 Williamsburg, Felicity Merriman and her best friend Elizabeth Cole enjoy tricking Elizabeth's older sister Annabelle. Annabelle becomes engaged to Lord Harry Lacey, and the girls transfer their pranks to his sister, Miss Priscilla. When Elizabeth is told she will be sent back to London after the wedding unless she stops, the two girls cease their teasing.

579. Turner, Ann. *Katie's Trunk.* Illustrated by Ronald Himler. Aladdin, 1997. 166pp. Paper ISBN 978-0-689-81054-1. Grades K–3. Katie knows something is going on when someone yells "Tory!" at her mother, and people dump tea into Boston Harbor. Katie's father tells the family to hide in the woods if the rebels come. But when they do, Katie gets mad and runs back into the house. She hides in her mother's wedding trunk, and a rebel friend of her father finds her. He tells the other men that no one is in the room, so she realizes that rebels are not all bad.

580. Woodruff, Elvira. *George Washington's Socks.* Apple, 1993. 132pp. Paper ISBN 978-0-590-44036-3. Grades 4–6. In this historical fantasy, a rowboat on Lake Levart entices five children to step inside and head backward in time to the eve of the Battle of Trenton, when George Washington is preparing to cross the icy Delaware River. The children find themselves in the winter of 1776 struggling against Hessians and living the horrors of the war. Although they are immensely relieved when they find themselves back in the present, they have learned about the fierceness of battle firsthand.

History

581. Allen, Thomas B. *Remember Valley Forge: Patriots, Tories, and Redcoats Tell Their Stories.* (Remember) National Geographic, 2007. 61pp. ISBN 978-1-4263-0149-0. Grades 5–8. Primary sources—letters, reports, journal entries, photographs, and maps—present background on the encampment at Valley Forge during the winter of 1777–1778 from different perspectives. Among those whose thoughts are revealed are a doctor, a farmer, a soldier, and a spy. The text includes information about Washington's prior defeats at Brandywine and Germantown, the infiltration of enemy spies, and Congress's inability to get food and supplies to his army. Figures such as Lafayette, Benedict Arnold, and Molly Pitcher also appear. Period Illustrations augment the text. Glossary, Chronology, Further Reading, and Index.

582. Anderson, Dale. *The Causes of the American Revolution.* World Almanac, 2005. 48pp. ISBN 978-0-8368-5925-6. Grades 5–8. Anderson shows that the American Revolution was a revolution of ideas. He explores the causes of the war and includes information about the colonists and their desire for self-government after the British imposed new laws and restrictions on their actions. Primary sources including letters, diaries, and pamphlets provide additional details. Illustrations augment the text. Bibliography and Index.

583. Anderson, Dale. *Forming a New American Government.* World Almanac, 2005. 48pp. ISBN 978-0-8368-5932-4. Grades 5–8. Anderson offers an overview of the formation of the American government, covering the Continental Congress and the writing of the Constitution. Primary sources including letters, diaries, and pamphlets provide information. Illustrations augment the text. Bibliography and Index.

584. Anderson, Laurie Halse. *Independent Dames: The Women and Girls of the American Revolution.* Simon & Schuster, 2008. 40pp. ISBN 978-0-689-85808-6. Grades K–4. Double-page spreads offer short profiles of women who contributed to the success of America's war for independence. They include women of all occupations and all ethnic backgrounds. Illustrations complement the text.

585. Beller, Susan Provost. *Yankee Doodle and the Redcoats: Soldiering in the Revolutionary War.* Illustrated by Larry Day. (Soldiers on the Battlefront) Lerner, 2003. 96pp. ISBN 978-0-8225-6655-7. Grades 5–8. Excerpts from letters, diaries, newspapers, and other primary sources describe the everyday life of soldiers who fought on both sides in the Revolutionary War. Descriptions of the battles, in chronological order, feature male and female soldiers' comments about the weather, life in the camps, food, and equipment. They also discussed the importance of honor in their decisions to fight. Pen-and-ink drawings and reproductions augment the text. Resources, Timeline, Bibliography, and Index.

586. Blair, Margaret Whitman. *Liberty or Death: The Surprising Story of Runaway Slaves Who Sided with the British During the American Revolution.* National Geographic, 2010. 64pp. ISBN 978-1-4263-0590-0. Grades 5–8. In 1775 Virginia Governor Lord Dunmore offered slaves of patriots their freedom if they would join British forces. Between 15,000 and 20,000 took his offer and valiantly fought in the Ethiopian Regiment, a group separate from the loyalists. (Later, offered freedom from patriot owners, slaves fought in integrated units.) At the war's end, many had died, but 3,000 received transport to Nova Scotia and half of these went on Sierra Leone to a free black settlement. Those remaining in Nova Scotia were ill-treated with some being captured and returned to slavery. The text contains period photographs and documents in its five chapters. Epilogue, Chronology, Bibliography, Further Reading, Web Sites, and Index.

587. Bobrick, Benson. *Fight for Freedom: The American Revolutionary War.* Atheneum, 2004. 96pp. ISBN 978-0-689-86422-3. Grades 4–8. This overview of the American Revolution begins with the Boston Tea Party. Double-page spreads offer background on important individuals, battles, issues, documents, and events as the war progresses and ends with a new government. Photographs and illustrations augment the text. Bibliography, Glossary, Chronology, Web Sites, and Index.

588. Brenner, Barbara. *If You Were There in 1776.* Simon & Schuster, 1994. 112pp. ISBN 978-0-02-712322-7. Grades 3–6. The situation in the American colonies led the people to declare independence. Brenner looks at the lives of families around the country—on a New England farm, a southern plantation, and the frontier—to see what they talked about, believed, ate, played, created, and felt about the Revolutionary War. Photographs complement the text. Notes, Sources, and Index.

589. Cheney, Lynne V. *When Washington Crossed the Delaware: A Wintertime Story for Young Patriots.* Illustrated by Peter M. Fiore. Simon & Schuster, 2004. Unpaged. ISBN 978-0-689-87043-9. Grades 2–4. On December 25, 1776, George Washington led 2,400 men across the frozen Delaware River from Pennsylvania into New Jersey to surprise the Hessian mercenaries at Trenton. One week later, the Battle of Princeton took place. The Continental Army, spurred by the words of Tom Paine, won both battles. Cheney includes background information, including details of shoeless soldiers leaving blood stains on the ice as they returned with their prisoners of war. Illustrations enliven the text. Notes.

590. Crewe, Sabrina. *Lexington and Concord.* (Events that Shaped America) Gareth Stevens, 2004. 32pp. ISBN 978-0-8368-3398-0. Grades 4–6.   In an introduction, four chapters, and a conclusion, this volume presents the events that led to the beginning of the American Revolution at Lexington and Concord in 1775. Maps show the important immigrant groups and the routes that the Patriots and the British took. Photographs and reproductions highlight the text. Further Reading, Timeline, Glossary, Web Sites, and Index.

591. Fink, Sam. *The Declaration of Independence.*   Scholastic, 2007. 160pp. Paper ISBN 978-0-439-70315-4. Grades 4–8.   In three sections, this volume covers what happened on June 7, 1776, a discussion of the phrases in the Declaration of Independence, and then the Declaration as a complete document. Illustrations augment the different parts of the text so that a reader can ponder what the words mean. Bibliography, Glossary, Chronology, Further Reading, and Index. *School Library Journal Best Children's Books.*

592. Fleming, Thomas J. *Everybody's Revolution.*   Scholastic, 2006. 96pp. ISBN 978-0-439-63404-5. Grades 4–6.   This history emphasizes that a variety of people contributed to the success of the American Revolution—Dutch, French, Irish, African, and Indian. They were unknowns who do not appear in the history books. They include Agent 13 and Hercules Mulligan, spies for Washington. Some were teenagers like Joseph Collins who recorded the number of shots he took in each battle. Period paintings and illustrations complement the text. Glossary, Further Reading, Web Sites, and Index.

593. Fradin, Dennis B. *The Declaration of Independence.*   (Turning Points in U.S. History) Benchmark, 2006. 45pp. ISBN 978-0-7614-2129-0. Grades 3–6.   Fradin explores this document's creation, signing, and the vote to put it into effect. Photographs and illustrations augment the text. Bibliography, Chronology, Web Sites, and Index.

594. Fradin, Dennis B. *Let It Begin Here! Lexington and Concord: First Battles of the American Revolution.*   Illustrated by Larry Day. Walker, 2005. 32pp. ISBN 978-0-8027-8945-7; 2009, paper ISBN 978-0-8027-9711-7. Grades 2–5.   Fradin examines the events that led to the beginning of the American Revolution and the consequences for the leaders and the soldiers. Fradin recalls Paul Revere's ride on April 18, 1775, and the ensuing battles at Lexington and Concord the next day. He breaks the events of these two days into chronological segments to clarify the details. Watercolor illustrations enhance the text. Further Reading.

595. Freedman, Russell. *Give Me Liberty: The Story of the Declaration of Independence.*   Holiday House, 2000. 90pp. ISBN 978-0-8234-1448-2; 2002, paper ISBN 978-0-8234-1753-7. Grades 5–8.   Freedman looks at events leading up to the Revolution and their underlying reasons based on accounts in newspapers, verse, letters, and pictures. Freedman shows the risks people took and the ways in which the words of the Declaration have endured. Reproductions highlight the text. Bibliography and Index. *School Library Journal Best Books for Children* and *Capitol Choices Noteworthy Titles* (Washington, D.C.).

596. Freedman, Russell. *Washington at Valley Forge.*   Holiday House, 2008. 100pp. ISBN 978-0-8234-2069-8. Grades 3–8.   During the winter of 1777–1778, George Washington quartered his Continental Army at Valley Forge, Pennsylvania. He wanted to be near British-occupied Philadelphia in case he had a chance to retake the city. Among those who related their experiences during that winter of malnutrition, starvation, and disease were the Marquis de Lafayette, German-born General Friedrich von Steuben, and Private Joseph Plumb Martin. The army survived this difficult winter and began the spring as a toughened united group that could defeat the British and their mercenaries. Engravings, reproductions, maps, augment the text. Chronology, Notes, and Index. *Kirkus Reviews Editor's Choice* and *School Library Journal Best Books for Children.*

597. Fritz, Jean. *Shh! We're Writing the Constitution.*   Illustrated by Tomie DePaola. Putnam, 1987. 58pp. ISBN 978-0-399-21403-5; Puffin, 1998, paper ISBN 978-0-698-11624-5. Grades 4–6.   Fritz describes the writing of the Constitution and the conflicts among the delegates in Philadelphia. To get the document finished, the delegates had to compromise on various aspects and worry about resolution and ratification. Notes.

598. Graves, Kerry. *The Declaration of Independence: The Story Behind America's Founding Document.* (America in Words and Song) Chelsea Clubhouse, 2004. 32pp. ISBN 978-0-7910-7334-6. Grades 2–4. Graves recounts the circumstances that led to the Revolutionary War and the difficulties of creating the Declaration of Independence. In addition to showing the document, this volume also includes illustrations and photographs. Bibliography, Further Reading, Timeline, Glossary, Web Sites, and Index.

599. Green, Carl R. *The Revolutionary War.* Enslow, 2002. 48pp. ISBN 978-0-7660-5089-1. Grades 4–6. Six chapters cover the events of the American Revolution from the initial shot to the Treaty of Paris. With discussion of the reasons for the conflict, this volume also looks at military tactics, battles, and key individuals, drawing on historical accounts, original documents, and other pertinent sources. Photographs and illustrations augment the text. Notes, Further Reading, Web Sites, and Index.

600. Hakim, Joy. *From Colonies to Country: 1735–1791.* See entry 383.

601. Herbert, Janis. *The American Revolution for Kids: A History with 21 Activities.* Chicago Review, 2002. 139pp. Paper ISBN 978-1-55652-456-1. Grades 5–8. Brief articles cover the struggle for independence from the rebellions against George III's taxation through the Continental Congress's ratification of the Constitution. Biographical entries provide information about individuals whose names are unfamiliar—African Americans, women, and warriors on the frontier. The activities include brewing root beer, dancing the minuet, liberty tea bread, and Boston brown bread. Photographs and illustrations augment the text. Further Reading, Glossary, Web Sites, and Index.

602. Kirby, Philippa. *Glorious Days, Dreadful Days: The Battle of Bunker Hill.* Illustrated by John Edens. Steck-Vaughn, 1992. Paper ISBN 978-0-8114-8066-6. Grades 4–8. The Battle of Bunker Hill (actually Breed's Hill), which occurred in 1775, began the Revolutionary War. In that war, a group of ordinary citizens overcame the most powerful army in the world. This volume explains the causes of the battle, tells its story, and details the results. Epilogue, Afterword, and Notes.

603. Lefkowitz, Arthur S. *Bushnell's Submarine: The Best Kept Secret of the American Revolution.* Scholastic, 2006. 136pp. ISBN 978-0-4397-4352-5. Grades 5–10. David Bushnell designed and built the world's first submarine, *The Turtle.* Shaped like a barrel, it could hold one man but he could not see outside. It had no power or fresh air, and was unsuccessful in an attack on a British warship, the *HMS Eagle*, in New York's harbor on September 6, 1776. Information about the military, political, and technological background of the invention is provided. Photographs, diagrams, augment the text. Index.

604. Maestro, Betsy. *Liberty or Death: The American Revolution, 1763–1783.* Illustrated by Giulio Maestro. HarperCollins, 2005. 64pp. ISBN 978-0-688-08802-6. Grades 2–6. Maestro examines events leading to the American Revolution and the hardships, betrayals, ideals, and personalities behind the decision to fight for freedom. He covers the period from the end of the French and Indian Wars through George Washington's resignation as commander-in-chief. Among the lesser figures included are Paul Revere's fellow rider, William Dawes; John Glover, supporter of Washington during the Battle of Long Island; Haym Salomon, a financial supporter. Photographs and illustrations augment the text. Chronology and Notes.

605. Magaziner, Henry Jonas. *Our Liberty Bell.* Illustrated by John O'Brien. Holiday House, 2007. 32pp. ISBN 978-0-8234-1892-3; paper ISBN 978-0-8234-2081-0. Grades 4–6. The Liberty Bell arrived from England in 1752 with a dull ring and a body that immediately cracked. After being recast twice, it became the signal and symbol for many events in American history. It rang at the end of the French and Indian War, for the Boston Tea Party, after the battle at Lexington, to declare the signing of the Declaration of Independence, at the end of the Revolutionary War, and to announce the death of George Washington. It cracked again in 1843, but it continued to serve as a national symbol for abolitionists, suffragists, and civil rights leaders. After the Civil War ended, it toured the country to reunite a divided nation. Cartoon art enlivens the text. Glossary and Index.

606. Miller, Brandon Marie. *Growing Up in Revolution and the New Nation 1775 to 1800.* (Our America) Lerner, 2002. 59pp. ISBN 978-0-8225-0078-0. Grades 4–7. Children who lived in America from 1775 to 1800 grew up with the Revolution. Miller draws on letters, diaries, interviews, and oral histories to give a picture of their lives and what they could expect in terms of amusement and education. Accounts of actual children during the time give authenticity. Double-page spreads include one illustration, and sidebars add interesting information. Bibliography, Notes, Further Reading, and Index.

607. Minor, Wendell. *Yankee Doodle America: The Spirit of 1776 from A to Z.* Putnam, 2006. 32pp. ISBN 978-0-399-24003-4. Grades K–2. Topics included in this alphabetical look at the American Revolution include the Stamp Act, the Sons of Liberty, George Washington, Thomas Jefferson, Valley Forge, Molly Pitcher, Henry Knox, and Quakers. Paragraphs of text are accompanied by illustrations resembling hand-painted signs of the time.

608. Rappaport, Doreen, and Greg Call. *Victory or Death! Stories of the American Revolution.* Illustrated by Joan Verniero. Harpercollins, 2003. 128pp. ISBN 978-0-06-029515-8. Grades 4–8. This text looks at people and events of the American Revolution, asking such questions as what was it like crossing the Delaware River on Christmas Day 1776 in a terrible snowstorm, and did the slave James Armistead spy for Lafayette and the Americans? Other topics covered are women, Native Americans, patriots, and loyalists. Familiar and not-so-familiar names include Abigail Adams; Sybil Ludington, who rode forty miles to rally her father's militia; Francis Salvador, a Jewish nobleman living in South Carolina; Grace Growden Galloway, whose husband, a loyalist, fought with the British; and Deborah Sampson, who fought as Robert Shurtliff at the end of the war against the British. The eight short stories, arranged chronologically, begin at the Battle of Bunker Hill and are set in historical context. Illustrations augment the text. Timeline, Maps, Bibliography, Web Sites, and Index.

609. Rubel, David. *America's War of Independence: A Concise Illustrated History of the American Revolution.* Silver Moon, 1993. 48pp. Paper ISBN 978-1-881889-39-7. Grades 3–6. In this illustrated text, Rubel presents the major battles, strategies, and key personalities in clear detail. Paintings, photographs, and maps offer further clarification. Endpaper Maps.

610. St. George, Judith. *The Journey of the One and Only Declaration of Independence.* Illustrated by Will Hillenbrand. Philomel, 2005. 43pp. ISBN 978-0-399-23738-6. Grades 1–7. The Declaration of Independence has a surprisingly mobile history. Since its inception it has traveled on horseback, train, wagon, and tank. It has also been hidden at Fort Knox (during World War II). Sunlight, humidity, dirty fingers, and smoke have threatened it, but it now rests under glass in the National Archives in Washington, D.C. This lively look at an important document contains complementary humorous, colorful illustrations.

611. Sheinkin, Steve. *King George: What Was His Problem?* Illustrated by Tim Robinson. Flash Point, 2008. 192pp. ISBN 978-1-59643-319-9. Grades 5–9. This amusing approach to the causes of the Revolution catalogs the actions of King George that so incensed the colonists. Extracts from letters, unusual anecdotes, and keen characterizations enliven this account of the Revolution from the initial unrest surrounding the Stamp Act to the surrender at Yorktown. Cartoon illustrations complement the text. Notes.

612. Spencer, Eve. *A Flag for Our Country.* Illustrated by Mike Eagle. Steck-Vaughn, 1992. 32pp. Paper ISBN 978-0-8114-8051-2. Grades 2–5. In 1776 Betsy Ross continued to work making clothes in her Philadelphia shop after her husband had recently died. According to family legend, George Washington saw her through the window and asked her to make a flag for the new country. He already had a design, but she suggested five-point stars placed in a circle. No proof exists that this actually happened, but none exists that it did not happen either.

613. Trumbauer, Lisa. *George Washington and the Revolutionary War.* (Life in the Time Of) Heinemann, 2007. 32pp. ISBN 978-1-4034-9667-6; paper ISBN 978-1-4034-9675-1. Grades 3–5. Focusing on the importance of George Washington (1732–1799) to the Revolutionary War, this volume covers pivotal moments in which Washington was directly involved.

Archival photographs and illustrations augment the text. Glossary, Chronology, Further Reading, Web Sites, and Index.

614. **Yero, Judith Lloyd.** *The Declaration of Independence.* (American Documents) National Geographic, 2006. 40pp. ISBN 978-0-7922-5397-6. Grades 3–5. Yero highlights the events of the early 1770s and explains why the colonists wanted to fight for independence and how they did it. Photographs and reproductions highlight the text. Index.

Biography and Collective Biography

615. **Adler, David A.** *B. Franklin, Printer.* See entry 438.

616. **Adler, David A.** *George Washington: An Illustrated Biography.* See entry 439.

617. **Adler, David A.** *Heroes of the Revolution.* Illustrated by Donald A. Smith. Holiday House, 2003. 32pp. ISBN 978-0-8234-1471-0; 2006, paper ISBN 978-0-8234-2017-9. Grades K–4. This collective biography presents highlights of the Revolutionary War through twelve heroes who helped the colonies defeat the British. They are Ethan Allen, Crispus Attucks (former slave), Lydia Darragh (spy), Nathan Hale, Mary "Molly Pitcher" Hays (contributor to the Battle of Monmouth), Thomas Jefferson, John Paul Jones, Thomas Paine, Paul Revere, Haym Salomon (financier), Deborah Sampson, and George Washington. Illustrations augment the text. Bibliography, Chronology, and Notes.

618. **Adler, David A.** *A Picture Book of Benjamin Franklin.* See entry 440.

619. **Adler, David A.** *A Picture Book of George Washington.* Illustrated by John and Alexandra Wallner. Holiday House, 1989. Unpaged. ISBN 978-0-8234-0732-3; 1995, paper ISBN 978-0-8234-0800-9. Grades 1–3. This account of George Washington's life (1732–1799) looks at highlights of his public life. Illustrations complement the text. Important Dates.

620. **Adler, David A.** *A Picture Book of John Hancock.* Illustrated by Ronald Himler. Holiday House, 2007. Unpaged. ISBN 978-0-8234-2005-6. Grades 1–3. This biography of John Hancock (1737–1793) indicates that he was a leader who gave funds to the revolutionary cause and also risked his life and his livelihood for it. A wealthy uncle adopted Hancock after his father died, and he inherited a huge fortune at the age of 24. He was the president of the Second Continental Congress and was the first signer of the Declaration of Independence. Then he served Massachusetts as its first governor. Illustrations complement the text. Bibliography, Chronology, Notes, and Web Sites.

621. **Adler, David A.** *A Picture Book of Patrick Henry.* Illustrated by John and Alexandra Wallner. Holiday House, 1995. Unpaged. ISBN 978-0-8234-1187-0; 2001, paper ISBN 978-0-8234-1678-3. Grades 1–3. This volume looks at the life of Patrick Henry (1736–1799), who gained the support of his Virginia colleagues and led them to form a militia to fight for the colonies by declaring "Give me liberty or give me death." He also served in the Continental Congress and as Virginia's governor. Important Dates.

622. **Adler, David A.** *A Picture Book of Paul Revere.* Illustrated by John and Alexandra Wallner. Holiday House, 1995. Unpaged. ISBN 978-0-8234-1144-3; 1997, paper ISBN 978-0-8234-1294-5. Grades 1–3. Paul Revere (1735–1818) left school at 13 to work for his silversmith father and was soon praised for the sound of the bells he created. He added other trades such as cleaning and making teeth and goldsmithing to support his ever-growing family. His first wife died after giving birth to eight children; his second wife had eight more. Six of the children died young. Revere never reached Lexington (during the "ride" for which he is famous), but he served in the army in Boston until 1781. Author's Note and Important Dates.

623. **Adler, David A.** *A Picture Book of Thomas Jefferson.* Illustrated by John and Alexandra Wallner. Holiday House, 1990. Unpaged. ISBN 978-0-8234-0791-0; 1991, paper ISBN 978-0-8234-0881-8. Grades 1–3. This overview of Thomas Jefferson's life (1743–1826) emphasizes his main achievements, including his education. He invented the swivel chair and the folding ladder, wrote the Declaration of Independence, and established the University of Virginia. Some call him the "Father of Our Democracy" because he believed people should govern themselves and be free.

624. **Adler, David A.** *President George Washington.* See entry 442.

625. **Adler, David A., and Michael S. Adler.** *A Picture Book of John and Abigail Adams.* See entry 443.

626. **Adler, David A., and Michael S. Adler.** *A Picture Book of Samuel Adams.* See entry 444.

627. **Allen, Thomas B.** *George Washington, Spymaster: How the Americans Outspied the British and Won the Revolutionary War.* Illustrated by Cheryl Harness. National Geographic, 2004. 192pp. ISBN 978-0-7922-5126-2; 2007 paper ISBN 978-1-4263-0041-7. Grades 2–6. General George Washington (1732–1799) played an unexpected role in the War of Independence by deciding that his poorly supplied army was too weak to beat the British. He realized that spies, an intelligence network, and deception would be the best tools for victory. He had double agents perform covert operations under chief Benjamin Franklin, using codes, ciphers, invisible ink, and a clothesline to send secret messages. Reproductions, Sources, Notes, Annotated Bibliography, Web Sites, and Index. *American Library Association Best Books for Young Adult, Capitol Choices Noteworthy Titles* (Washington, D.C.), and *Young Reader's Choice Award* (Pennsylvania) nomination.

628. **Ashby, Ruth.** *The Amazing Mr. Franklin: Or, The Boy Who Read Everything.* See entry 445.

629. **Brimner, Larry Dane.** *Molly Pitcher.* Illustrated by Drew Rose. (Imagination) Compass Point, 2004. 32pp. ISBN 978-0-7565-0603-2. Grades K–2. Molly Pitcher (1754–1832) became a heroine of the Monmouth Court House in Freehold, New Jersey, during the American Revolution. Five chapters recall her contributions distributing water to thirsty soldiers and firing her wounded husband's cannon. One chapter offers a short introduction to her life and a recipe that she might have cooked—corn cakes. Illustrations augment the text. Maps, Further Reading, Glossary, Web Sites, and Index.

630. **Bruns, Roger.** *Thomas Jefferson.* See entry 448.

631. **Castrovilla, Selene.** *By the Sword.* Illustrated by Bill Farnsworth. Calkins Creek, 2007. 40pp. ISBN 978-1-59078-427-3. Grades 4–6. In 1776 Benjamin Tallmadge decides to sacrifice his career as a school teacher and enlist in George Washington's army after he hears about the battles at Lexington and Concord. He is shocked by the reality of war at the Battle of Long Island. When he has to retreat across the river, he realizes he has left his horse behind and returns to retrieve it. Based on Tallmadge's diaries, this volume recalls the early days of a soldier who became a valued officer. Oil on linen canvas illustrations intensify the text.

632. **Collard, Sneed B., III.** *Benjamin Franklin: The Man Who Could Do Just About Anything.* See entry 454.

633. **Conley, Kevin.** *Benjamin Banneker: Scientist and Mathematician.* See entry 455.

634. **Cooper, Michael L.** *Hero of the High Seas: John Paul Jones and the American Revolution.* National Geographic, 2006. 128pp. ISBN 978-0-7922-5547-5. Grades 4–8. John Paul Jones (1747–1792), son of a Scottish gardener, became an admiral in the navy that defeated the British during the American Revolution. He initially planned to become a Virginia aristocrat like George Washington and Thomas Jefferson, but rose in the navy instead. This biography shows him as a complex man who was a loyal captain, a superb sailor, a conceited leader, and a social climber. Additional information discusses military strategy, weaponry, and sailing. Period Illustrations augment the text. Glossary, Chronology, Further Reading, and Index.

635. **Crompton, Samuel Willard.** *Gouverneur Morris: Creating a Nation.* (America's Founding Fathers) Enslow, 2004. 128pp. ISBN 978-0-7660-2213-3. Grades 5–8. Gouveneur Morris (1752–1816) played an important role before and after the Revolution. His mother, a

Loyalist, gave the family estate to the British. A carriage accident left him with a wooden leg and this kept him out of the military; therefore, he focused on turning the colony of New York into an independent state and wrote most of the 1777 constitution for it. In the same year, he coordinated the defense for George Washington's Continental Army and the Continental Congress. He could not run for election in New York because the enemy possessed his lands so he was appointed a delegate to the Continental Congress. He is thought to have written the preamble to the Constitution, "We the People of the United States, in order to form a more perfect union . . ." Illustrations augment the text. Bibliography, Glossary, Web Sites, Timeline, and Index.

636. Fleming, Candace. *Ben Franklin's Almanac: Being a True Account of the Good Gentleman's Life.* See entry 457.

637. Fradin, Dennis B. *Samuel Adams: The Father of American Independence.* See entry 459.

638. Fradin, Dennis B. *The Signers: The 56 Stories Behind the Declaration of Independence.* Illustrated by Michael McDurdy. Walker, 2002. 164pp. ISBN 978-0-8027-8849-8; 2009, paper ISBN 978-0-8027-7726-3. Grades 4–7. This collective biography profiles each of the fifty-six men who signed the Declaration of Independence. It offers historical information about each of the colonies, and includes the history and text of the Declaration. The men came from Massachusetts, Virginia, Pennsylvania, New Jersey, Delaware, Rhode Island, Connecticut, New Hampshire, Maryland, North Carolina, South Carolina, Georgia, and New York. Black-and-white scratchboard illustrations complement the text. Bibliography and Index.

639. Fritz, Jean. *And Then What Happened, Paul Revere?* See entry 460.

640. Fritz, Jean. *The Great Little Madison.* Puffin, 1998. 169pp. Paper ISBN 978-0-698-11621-4. Grades 5–8. James Madison (1751–1836) was strongly committed to the unity of the United States, but his weak voice and small stature kept him from speaking effectively. He clashed with Patrick Henry, had a romance with and married the young widow Dolley Payne Todd, and was friends with Thomas Jefferson. He made important intellectual contributions to the beginning of the nation. Notes, Bibliography, and Index.

641. Fritz, Jean. *Traitor: The Case of Benedict Arnold.* See entry 461.

642. Fritz, Jean. *What's the Big Idea, Ben Franklin?* See entry 462.

643. Fritz, Jean. *Why Don't You Get a Horse, Sam Adams?* See entry 463.

644. Fritz, Jean. *Will You Sign Here, John Hancock?* See entry 464.

645. Giblin, James Cross. *The Amazing Life of Benjamin Franklin.* See entry 466.

646. Giblin, James Cross. *The Many Rides of Paul Revere.* See entry 467.

647. Giblin, James Cross. *Thomas Jefferson: A Picture Book Biography.* See entry 468.

648. Gillis, Jennifer Blizin. *Mercy Otis Warren: Author and Historian.* (Signature Lives) Compass Point, 2005. 112pp. ISBN 978-0-7565-0982-8. Grades 5–8. Mercy Otis Warren (1728–1814), a playwright and writer, became known as the "Conscience of the American Revolution." She refused to let gender bar her from publishing, and Jefferson said she was a genius. She was an intellectual who spoke for American independence with fervor and thoughtfulness. At the same time, she was a mother and wife. Photographs, maps, and reproductions highlight the text. Bibliography, Glossary, Chronology, Notes, Further Reading, Web Sites, and Index.

649. Harkins, Susan Sales, and William H. Harkins. *The Life and Times of Betsy Ross.* (Profiles in American History) Mitchell Lane, 2007. 48pp. ISBN 978-1-58415-446-4. Grades 5–8. Many of the stories about Betsy Ross (1752–1836) are based on conjecture. One of the few clear facts is that George Washington asked her to sew the first flag for the United States. The final chapter focuses on the legend of Betsy Ross. Photographs and reproductions augment the text. Chronology, Further Reading, Glossary, Notes, Web Sites, and Index.

650. Harkins, Susan Sales, and William H. Harkins. *The Life and Times of Patrick Henry.* See entry 473.

651. Harness, Cheryl. *The Remarkable Benjamin Franklin.* See entry 475.

652. Harness, Cheryl. *The Revolutionary John Adams.* See entry 476.

653. Kjelle, Marylou Morano. *The Life and Times of John Hancock.* See entry 481.

654. Lasky, Kathryn. *A Voice of Her Own: The Story of Phillis Wheatley, Slave Poet.* See entry 483.

655. Leslie, Tonya. *Thomas Jefferson: A Life of Patriotism.* See entry 484.

656. McNeese, Tim. *George Washington: America's Leader in War and Peace.* (Leaders of the American Revolution) Chelsea, 2006. 140pp. ISBN 978-0-7910-8619-3. Grades 4–8. This biography offers a chronological look at the life of George Washington (1732–1799) through his early years, conflicts in the wilderness as a surveyor, fighting war on the frontier, public service, and retirement. It then briefly summarizes his legacy. Photographs and illustrations augment the text. Bibliography, Chronology, Further Reading, Web Sites, and Index.

657. Miller, Brandon Marie. *George Washington for Kids: His Life and Times with 21 Activities.* Chicago Review, 2007. 130pp. ISBN 978-1-55652-655-8. Grades 5–8. Miller offers plenty of information about George Washington (1732–1799) and his youth, military service, and government work with additional details about his personality in sidebars. Notes about slaves at Mount Vernon and his religious viewpoint are also included. Among the twenty-one activities for children are a book of good manners and directions for games of quoits and whist, how to dance the minuet, making a compass and sewing a lady's cap, planting a garden, cooking Nelly's hoecake, building a weather vane, and casting a plaster life mask. Further Reading, Glossary, Web Sites, and Index.

658. Mullin, Rita T. *Thomas Jefferson: Architect of Freedom.* (Sterling Biographies) Sterling, 2007. 124pp. ISBN 978-1-4027-4750-2; paper ISBN 978-1-4027-3397-0. Grades 5–8. As the third president of the United States, Thomas Jefferson (1743–1826) was also one of the important composers of the Constitution. The text focuses on his intellect and his contributions to the young United States. Additional information includes the concept that Jefferson probably fathered children with the slave Sally Hemings. Photographs and illustrations augment the text. Bibliography, Chronology, Glossary.

659. Murphy, Frank. *Ben Franklin and the Magic Squares.* See entry 347.

660. Nettleton, Pamela. *Benjamin Franklin: Writer, Inventor, Statesman.* See entry 489.

661. Nettleton, Pamela. *George Washington: Farmer, Soldier, President.* See entry 490.

662. Patterson, Charles. *Thomas Jefferson.* See entry 493.

663. Pinkney, Andrea Davis. *Dear Benjamin Banneker.* See entry 495.

664. Powell, Walter Louis. *Benedict Arnold: Revolutionary War Hero and Traitor.* (The Library of American Lives and Times) Rosen, 2004. ISBN 978-0-8239-6627-1. Grades 5–8. Benedict Arnold (1741–1801) had to support his alcoholic father and his younger sister after his beloved mother died in 1759. Then he joined the Connecticut militia and eventually became the best general and leader in the Continental Army. In fact, without his contributions, America might have lost the Revolution. In July of 1780, he requested and received command of West Point, planning to surrender it to the British. American forces, however, intercepted British Major John André when he was carrying papers that revealed Arnold's plan. Arnold narrowly escaped capture before accepting a commission as a Brigadier General in the British Army. In 1782 Arnold went to London with his second wife, Margaret "Peggy" Shippen Arnold. His name has become synonymous with the world "traitor" for his decisions. Maps, Photographs, Reproductions, Bibliography, Chronology, Further Reading, Glossary, Web Sites, and Index.

665. Ransom, Candice F. *George Washington.* See entry 497.

666. Ransom, Candice F. *John Hancock.* See entry 498.

667. Reiter, Chris. *Thomas Jefferson.* See entry 501.

668. **Roberts, Russell.** *The Life and Times of Thomas Jefferson.* See entry 502.

669. **Rockwell, Anne.** *They Called Her Molly Pitcher.* Illustrated by Cynthia Von Buhler. Knopf, 2002. 32pp. ISBN 978-0-679-89187-1. Grades 3–5. Molly Pitcher (1754–1832) stood with her husband while he was fighting in George Washington's army. She learned how the soldiers fought, and when her husband was injured and could not shoot the cannon, she did it for him at the Battle of Monmouth in Freehold, New Jersey, in 1778. Afterward, George Washington gave her the title of "sergeant." Illustrations enhance the text. Chronology.

670. **Rushby, Pamela.** *Ben Franklin: Printer, Author, Inventor, Politician.* See entry 504.

671. **Schanzer, Rosalyn.** *George vs. George: The Revolutionary War as Seen by Both Sides.* National Geographic, 2004. 60pp. ISBN 978-0-7922-7349-3; 2007, paper ISBN 978-1-4263-0042-4. Grades 4–7. This collective biography makes comparisons between George Washington and King George III of England, two key adversaries during the American Revolution. It emphasizes that every altercation has at least two sides. The book alternates between the general and the ruler, the forms of American and British government, and the two views of taxation, with details of the Boston Tea party, the dress of their rival armies, and the battles of the Revolution. Both were good men who had the interests of their countries in mind. Watercolor illustrations complement the text. Bibliography and Index. *Capitol Choices Noteworthy Titles* (Washington, D.C.), *Young Hoosier Book Award* (Indiana) nomination, *Kirkus Starred Reviews*, *Student Book Award* (Maine) nomination, *School Library Journal Best Books of The Year*, and *Beehive Children's Book Award* (Utah) nomination.

672. **Sherrow, Victoria.** *Benjamin Franklin.* See entry 508.

673. **Sherrow, Victoria.** *Thomas Jefferson.* See entry 509.

674. **Sonneborn, Liz.** *Benedict Arnold: Hero and Traitor.* Chelsea House, 2005. 130pp. ISBN 978-0-7910-8617-9. Grades 4–8. Benedict Arnold (1741–1801), educated at West Point, betrayed his country. This biography focuses on his decision to sell military secrets to the British during the Revolutionary War and his subsequent fall from hero to traitor. Photographs and illustrations augment the text. Bibliography, Chronology, Further Reading, Web Sites, and Index.

675. **Sutcliffe, Jane.** *Abigail Adams.* (History Maker Bios) Lerner, 2006. 48pp. ISBN 978-0-8225-5942-9. Grades 3–5. Born Abigail Smith, Abigail Adams (1744–1818) was always reading the books in her father's library. She wanted to learn everything, and this made her a good match for John Adams. She lived with him in Boston, and during his time writing the Declaration of Independence, she suggested that he "remember the ladies." She then went with him to Europe and served with him as a president's wife. Five chapters discuss these and other aspects of her life. Illustrations augment the text. Bibliography, Further Reading, Glossary, Maps, Timeline, Web Sites, and Index.

676. **Sutcliffe, Jane.** *John Adams.* See entry 512.

677. **Sutcliffe, Jane.** *Paul Revere.* (History Maker Bios) Lerner, 2002. 48pp. ISBN 978-0-8225-0195-4. Grades 3–5. Paul Revere (1735–1818) began working in his father's Boston silversmith shop at the age of 13. During his life, he also worked as a dentist, coppersmith, and printer. When Great Britain's taxes started to weigh on the colonies, Revere joined those rebelling in the Boston Tea Party. When he was asked to let citizens know about the British, he did not say "The British are coming!" He said, "The Regulars are out." Revere was a valued member of his community, and the five chapters in the text acknowledge his accomplishments. Illustrations augment the text. Bibliography, Further Reading, Glossary, Maps, Timeline, Web Sites, and Index.

678. **Thomas, Peggy.** *Farmer George Plants a Nation.* See entry 513.

679. **Tieck, Sarah.** *Paul Revere.* (First Biographies) Buddy, 2006. 32pp. ISBN 978-1-59679-787-1. Grades K–3. Paul Revere (1735–1818) became a key figure at the beginning of the Revolutionary War by riding his horse to Lexington, Massachusetts, to warn the citizens that the

British soldiers were coming. Photographs and illustrations augment the text. Glossary, Chronology, and Index.

680. **Tracy, Kathleen.** *The Life and Times of Nathan Hale.* (Profiles in American History) Mitchell Lane, 2007. 48pp. ISBN 978-1-58415-447-1. Grades 5–8. Nathan Hale (1755–1776) became a teacher after graduating from Yale and then served in the Connecticut colonial regiment in 1775. In September 1776 the British arrested him for spying. The next day, after a trial, they executed him. Photographs and reproductions augment the text. Chronology, Further Reading, Glossary, Notes, Web Sites, and Index.

681. **Uglow, Loyd.** *Benjamin Franklin—You Know What to Say.* See entry 515.

682. **Wallner, Alexandra.** *Abigail Adams.* Holiday House, 2005. 32pp. Paper ISBN 978-0-8234-1942-5. Grades K–4. Abigail Adams (1744–1818), wife of the second president, was also mother of the fifth president. She spoke against slavery and for the rights of women in her letters to her husband and to others. She also managed the family farm and looked after finances during the many times her husband was away from home. Illustrations enhance the text.

683. **Wallner, Alexandra.** *Betsy Ross.* Holiday House, 1998. 32pp. Paper ISBN 978-0-8234-1355-3. Grades 2–4. Wallner presents Betsy Ross (1752–1836) and her early life. She was a Quaker who left the faith during her three marriages and her time as a businesswoman. She returned to her Quaker beliefs later in life. Ross has kept a place in history because, as a seamstress, she supposedly made the first American flag in Philadelphia, her home. Additionally, the text gives information about life in colonial America.

684. **Welch, Catherine.** *Benjamin Banneker.* See entry 518.

685. **Welch, Catherine.** *Eli Whitney.* (History Maker Bios) Lerner, 2007. 48pp. ISBN 978-0-8225-7607-5. Grades 3–5. Five chapters relate the life of Eli Whitney (1765–1825). He liked to experiment and invent things as a boy. He eventually created a cotton gin that was surprisingly unpopular because its efficiency replaced some human workers. He turned to making muskets and other items later in life. Photographs and illustrations augment the text. Bibliography, Further Reading, Glossary, Maps, Timeline, Web Sites, and Index.

686. **Welch, Catherine.** *Patrick Henry.* See entry 519.

Graphic Novels, Biographies, and Histories

687. **Burgan, Michael.** *Benedict Arnold: American Hero and Traitor.* Illustrated by Terry Beatty. (Graphic Biographies) Graphic Library, 2007. 32pp. ISBN 978-0-7368-6854-9. Grades 3–5. This short graphic biography of Benedict Arnold (1741–1801) depicts his life and work during the American Revolution and after. He attended West Point and served in the war, but afterward was accused of treason. A yellow background sets direct quotes from Arnold apart from the fictional aspect of the narration. Web Sites.

688. **Burgan, Michael.** *The Creation of the U.S. Constitution.* Illustrated by Gordon Purcell and Terry Beatty. Graphic Library, 2005. 32pp. ISBN 978-0-7368-6491-6; paper ISBN 978-0-7368-9653-5. Grades 3–5. Adopted by the Constitutional Convention in Philadelphia, Pennsylvania, on September 17, 1787, the Constitution had to be ratified by conventions in each colony. Since then it has been amended twenty-seven times with the first ten amendments called the Bill of Rights. Illustrations augment the text. Bibliography, Glossary, Further Reading, and Index.

689. **Doeden, Matt.** *George Washington: Leading a New Nation.* Illustrated by Cynthia Martin. (Graphic Biographies) Graphic Library, 2005. 32pp. ISBN 978-0-7368-4963-0; paper ISBN 978-0-7368-6195-3. Grades 3–5. This short graphic biography of George Washington (1732–1799) relates the story of his service to America as a soldier during the American Revolution, the first president of the United States, and a citizen. A yellow background sets direct quotes from Washington apart from the fictional aspect of the narration. Web Sites.

690. Doeden, Matt. *Thomas Jefferson: Great American.* Illustrated by Gordon Purcell and Terry Beatty. (Graphic Biographies) Graphic Library, 2006. 32pp. ISBN 978-0-7368-6488-7; paper ISBN 978-0-7368-6887-7. Grades 3–5. This short graphic biography of Thomas Jefferson (1743–1826) relates his life as a writer and signer of the Declaration of Independence, a Virginia lawyer and inventor, and as president of the United States. A yellow background sets direct quotes from Jefferson apart from the fictional aspect of the narration. Web Sites.

691. Doeden, Matt. *Winter at Valley Forge.* Illustrated by Ron Frenz and Charles Barnett, III. Graphic Library, 2005. 32pp. ISBN 978-0-7368-4975-3; paper ISBN 978-0-7368-6212-7. Grades 3–5. The American Continental Army was headquartered in Valley Forge, Pennsylvania, during the winter of 1777–1778. The army had to build shelters and was able to do so rapidly. Although little snow fell, the damp caused diseases to spread, and the soldiers did not have enough food. Illustrations complement the text. Bibliography, Glossary, Further Reading, and Index.

692. Espinosa, Rod. *Benjamin Franklin.* See entry 530.

693. Glaser, Jason. *Molly Pitcher: Young American Patriot.* Illustrated by Tod Smith. (Graphic Biographies) Graphic Library, 2006. 32pp. ISBN 978-0-7368-5486-3; paper ISBN 978-0-7368-6886-0. Grades 4–7. This short graphic biography of Molly Pitcher (1754–1832) relates the story of her actions during the Battle of Monmouth on June 28, 1778. She brought pitcher after pitcher of water to parched soldiers and then took over her husband's position after he was wounded. George Washington issued a warrant to her as a noncommissioned officer. A yellow background sets direct quotes from Pitcher apart from the fictional aspect of the narration. Web Sites.

694. Glaser, Jason. *Patrick Henry: Liberty or Death.* See entry 532.

695. Niz, Xavier. *Paul Revere's Ride.* Illustrated by Brian Bascle. Graphic Library, 2005. 32pp. ISBN 978-0-7368-4965-4; 2006, paper ISBN 978-0-7368-6209-7. Grades 3–5. Niz looks at Paul Revere's ride to Lexington, Massachusetts, on the night of April 18–19, 1775 to warn John Hancock and Samuel Adams that the British Army was beginning to march from Boston. Illustrations enhance the text. Bibliography, Glossary, Further Reading, and Index.

696. Olson, Nathan. *Nathan Hale: Revolutionary Spy.* Illustrated by Cynthia Martin and Brent Schoonover. (Graphic Biographies) Graphic Library, 2005. 32pp. ISBN 978-0-7368-4968-5; paper ISBN 978-0-7368-9670-2. Grades 3–5. This short graphic biography of Nathan Hale (1755–1776) relates the story of his work as a spy during the American Revolution. The British captured him, and before he was hanged, he supposedly said, "I regret that I have but one life to give to my country." A yellow background sets direct quotes from Hale apart from the fictional aspect of the narration. Web Sites.

DVDs

697. *Animated Atlas: The Revolutionary War.* SVE & Churchill Media, 1999. 20 mins. Grades 4–8. Animated maps, historical footage, photographs, and icons show the development of colonial America and how the land and location of water influenced settlements and either helped or hindered the colonists' survival. Topics extend from the end of the French and Indian War in 1763 through the victory at Yorktown in 1781 and the peace treaty in 1783.

698. *Benjamin Franklin.* (Great Americans for Children) Library Video, 2002. 23 mins. Grades K–4. As a young boy, Benjamin Franklin experimented and wrote his ideas in local newspapers under a pseudonym. Later, he also became a printer, a statesman, a scientist, an inventor, and a humanitarian. One of the founding fathers of the country, he also discovered electricity, an achievement that profoundly changed the quality of life. Reenactments and photographs underscore Franklin's contribution to America.

699. *Declaring Independence: 1774–1776.* (American Revolution for Students) Library Video, 2003. 23 mins. Grades 5–9. Reenactments, period paintings and illustrations, and actors portraying personages of the time give an account of the social, political, and economic conditions that influenced Americans in the late 18th century when some colonial leaders wanted to break from Great Britain. Among the events leading to the Revolutionary War were the battles of Lexington and Concord, Thomas Paine's pamphlet "Common Sense," unacceptable British taxes, and unfair trade laws.

700. *Patrick Henry: Quest for Freedom.* American Animation Studios, 2007. 34 mins. ISBN 978-0-9796681-1-1. Grades 3–6. See entry 542.

701. *The Revolutionary War: 1776–1783.* (American Revolution for Students) Library Video, 2003. 23 mins. Grades 5–9. Reenactments, period paintings and illustrations, and actors portraying personages of the time give an account of the social, political, and economic conditions that led Americans into the Revolutionary War. After the adoption of the Declaration of Independence, the Second Continental Congress declared its intent to found a new nation. The result could only be war with Great Britain, a powerful military force. Participants and the battles they fought show how they won at Yorktown.

702. *Revolutionary War Heroes.* (Great Americans for Children) Library Video, 2002. 23 mins. ISBN 978-1-57225-542-5. Grades K–4. In addition to key figures such as George Washington and Benjamin Franklin, many others contributed to America becoming a country. Among these men, women, and children were Nathan Hale, Sybil Ludington, Molly Pitcher, Colonel Francis Marion, John Paul Jones, and the Black Rhode Island Regiment. Reenactments and photographs introduce these brave contributors to America's freedom.

703. **St. George, Judith.** *The Journey of the One and Only Declaration of Independence.* Illustrated by Will Hillenbrand. Weston Woods, 2007. 26 mins. ISBN 978-0-439-02758-8. Grades 1–7. See entry 610.

704. **Smith, Lane.** *John, Paul, George and Ben.* Weston Woods, 2007. 10 min. ISBN 978-0-439-02752-6. Grades K–4. See entry 577.

Compact Discs

705. **Forbes, Esther.** *Johnny Tremain.* Narrated by Grace Conlin. Blackstone Audio, 2008. 7 CDs. ISBN 978-1-4332-1041-9. Grades 5 up. See entry 561.

706. **Roop, Peter, and Connie Roop.** *Buttons for General Washington.* Illustrated by Janice Lee Porter. Live Oak Media, 2007. 1 CD; 14:39 mins. ISBN 978-0-8761-4776-4. Grades 1–3. John Darragh, 14, hides encoded messages in his jacket buttons and takes them to General Washington's camp during the Revolutionary War. His Quaker family also helps to spy for the American army.

707. *Thomas Jefferson's America.* Narrated by Jim Weiss. Greathall, 2005. 1 CD; 74 mins. ISBN 978-1-882513-86-4. Grades 5 up. See entry 545.

THE EARLY UNITED STATES, 1784–1814

Historical Fiction and Fantasy

708. Anderson, Laurie Halse. *Fever 1793.* Illustrated by Lori Earley. Simon & Schuster, 2000. 256pp. ISBN 978-0-689-83858-3; Aladdin, 2002, paper ISBN 978-0-689-84891-9. Grades 5–8. In 1793 Matilda Cook, 16, faces Philadelphia's yellow fever epidemic. As people catch the disease, they become bitter toward those they suspect are infected. The city, the capital of the nation, is near collapse. Mattie's servant Eliza stays loyal to her throughout, finding medical help for Mattie's mother, looking after the household when Mattie is sent to the countryside, and assisting the Free African Society. After the epidemic, she helps Mattie reestablish the coffee house that she, her mother, and grandfather were running before the epidemic. Among personages mentioned are Drs. Benjamin Rush and Steven Girard and Master Peale, the painter, to whom Mattie's friend Nathaniel is apprenticed. During the summer and fall, more than 5,000 people—10 percent of the population—die. *Bluegrass Award* (Kentucky) nomination, *Volunteer State Award* (Tennessee) nomination, *Young Reader's Choice Award* (Pennsylvania) nomination, *Garden State Teen Book Award* (New Jersey) nomination, *Mark Twain Award* (Missouri) nomination, *Nutmeg Award* (Connecticut) nomination, *Young Reader Medal* (California) nomination, *Sunshine State Young Reader Award* (Florida) nomination, *Teen Award* (Iowa) nomination, *Maud Hart Lovelace Award* (Minnesota) nomination, *Young Readers' Award* (Nevada) nomination, *American Library Association Best Books for Young Adults*, *Children's Book Award* (Georgia) nomination, *Rebecca Caudill Award* (Illinois) nomination, *Young Hoosier Award* (Indiana) nomination, *Children's Book Award* (Massachusetts), *Great Lakes Great Books Award* (Michigan), *Charlotte Award* (New York), *Junior Book Award* (South Carolina), *Tayshas Reading List* (Texas), *Young Adult Book Award* (Utah), *Readers' Choice Award* (Virginia), Beehive Book Award (Utah), *Young Reader's Award* (Nevada), *Young Reader Medal* (California), *Young Hoosier Book Award* (Indiana), and *Golden Sower Award* (Nebraska).

709. Armstrong, Jennifer. *Thomas Jefferson: Letters from a Philadelphia Bookworm.* (Dear Mr. President) Winslow, 2001. 117pp. ISBN 978-1-890817-30-5. Grades 5–8. When Amelia Hornsby, 12, thinks she has discovered a spy, she writes to President Thomas Jefferson. Their correspondence develops over several years during which they discuss aspects of the Lewis and Clark expedition, the hot air balloon, the duel between Alexander Hamilton and Arron Burr, and the death of Jefferson's daughter. Photographs, Maps, Timelines, Bibliography.

710. Avi. *Something Upstairs: A Tale of Ghosts.* Flare, 1990. 120pp. Paper ISBN 978-0-380-70853-6. Grades 4–8. In this historical fantasy, Kenny's family moves to Providence, Rhode Island, to live in a house built in 1792. Kenny is surprised to see a figure rising out of a bloodstain on the floor of his bedroom closet. He helps the spirit of the dead slave, murdered in 1800, to uncover his killer. They must find the truth before they can escape the past.

711. **Collier, Christopher, and James Lincoln Collier.** *Jump Ship to Freedom.* Yearling, 1996. 192pp. Paper ISBN 978-0-440-44323-0. Grades 4–6. In 1787 Captain Ivers accuses Daniel Arabus, a 14-year-old slave, of stealing. Daniel is actually retrieving money that Jack, his dead father, earned to buy freedom for Daniel and his mother while substituting for Ivers during the Revolution. Ivers had promised Jack his own freedom after fighting in his place, but Ivers reneged. Then Mrs. Ivers took the notes from Daniel's mother. Ivers captures Daniel and holds him on his ship, but Daniel jumps ship during a storm. When the ship returns to shore, Daniel gets the money off the ship and establishes that his father did receive his freedom from Ivers.

712. **Davies, Jacqueline.** *Tricking the Tallyman.* Illustrated by S. D. Schindler. Knopf, 2009. 30pp. ISBN 978-0-375-83909-2. Grades 1–4. In 1790 Phineas Bump arrives in Tunbridge, Vermont. He has been away from his home for three months and his task, as one of 650 United States Marshals, is to count the population—a census. Townspeople fear higher taxes and conscription so they hide, and Mrs. Pepper claims to be Tunbridge's sole inhabitant. Then her son Boston works out that greater population means increased representation. The townspeople dress all the animals, and the count rises to 1,726. Then they realize that higher taxes and conscription are also part of the census. Bump eventually leaves with a final, accurate count of 487 inhabitants. Humorous line and wash illustrations enhance the text. Note.

713. **Glass, Andrew.** *Bewildered for Three Days: As to Why Daniel Boone Never Wore His Coonskin Cap.* Holiday House, 2000. 32pp. ISBN 978-0-8234-1446-8. Grades K–3. Daniel Boone, a Quaker boy in Pennsylvania, has a Delaware Native American companion, Tu-muk-wayatut, who teaches him how to survive in the woods when he is very young. After they part one day, braves pursue Daniel and he hides in a hollow log with a raccoon and her kits. The next morning he tells the raccoon he will never again wear one of her relatives on his head.

714. **Greeson, Janet.** *An American Army of Two.* Illustrated by Patricia Rose Mulvihill. Carolrhoda, 1992. 48pp. ISBN 978-0-8761-4664-4; First Avenue, 1991, paper ISBN 978-0-8761-4547-0. Grades K–4. When Rebecca and Abigail see British ships in the harbor near their coastal home in Massachusetts, they hide behind a tree with their fife and drum to play "Yankee Doodle." The music tricks the British into thinking that American troops await nearby, and they leave.

715. **Hopkinson, Deborah.** *John Adams Speaks for Freedom.* Illustrated by Craig Orback. (Childhood of Famous Americans) Aladdin, 2005. 32pp. Paper ISBN 978-0-689-86907-5. Grades 1–2. Although John Adams preferred to stay at home with his family, he also wanted to see the thirteen colonies freed from English rule. He knew he could help this dream become a reality and he sacrificed his desires for the greater good. He made an important speech in favor of independence, served as the United States ambassador to France (even though he did not like to travel), and became both vice president and president of the country.

716. **Ketchum, Liza.** *Where the Great Hawk Flies.* Clarion, 2005. 272pp. ISBN 978-0-618-40085-0. Grades 4–8. In 1782, 13-year-old Daniel receives a visit from his Pequot grandfather seven years after the Caughnawaga Indians who were fighting for the British destroyed his Vermont settlement. Seeing the old medicine man upsets some of the neighbors, especially the family of Hiram Combs, 11, who suffered greatly during the Caughnawaga attack. Hiram thinks that Daniel, as the child of a white father and Pequot mother, is a "dirty Injun." But Daniel slowly learns that he can benefit from having a foot in both worlds. Note.

717. **Krensky, Stephen.** *Sisters of Scituate Light.* Illustrated by Stacey Schuett. Dutton, 2008. 32pp. ISBN 978-0-525-47792-1. Grades K–5. In September of 1814 after the British have invaded Washington and burned the White House, they travel up the coast to Boston and see the Scituate Lighthouse. The lighthouse keeper, Simon, has left for the day, and his daughters—Abbie, 17, and Rebecca, 21—are keeping watch. They decide if they see British coming toward the lighthouse, Rebecca will pay "Yankee Doodle Dandy" on her flute while

Abbie drums. The British come, hear the call to battle, and think that American soldiers await them on shore. They depart. Note.

718. Lawson, Robert. *Ben and Me: An Astonishing Life of Benjamin Franklin by His Good Mouse Amos.* See entry 342.

719. McCully, Emily Arnold. *The Escape of Oney Judge: Martha Washington's Slave Finds Freedom.* Farrar, 2007. 32pp. ISBN 978-0-374-32225-0. Grades 1–5. Oney Judge, 10, belongs to Martha Washington, and when George Washington becomes president, she moves with the family to Philadelphia where she works as a seamstress. She sees for the first time that some blacks are free and that Quakers believe all blacks should be free. When Oney hears that she will be given to one of Martha Washington's relatives after her death, Oney decides that she must control her own fate. She runs away to New Hampshire and, although she marries there, she always worries that someone will take her back to slavery.

720. Minahan, John A. *Abigail's Drum.* Illustrated by Robert Quackenbush. Pippin, 1995. 64pp. ISBN 978-0-945912-25-5. Grades 2–5. Rebecca Bates, 11, and her sister Abigail are bored at the Scituate, Massachusetts, lighthouse that their father tends. As entertainment, they try to sound like the Home Guard corps when they play their fife and drum. In 1812 the British stage a supply raid and take their father captive. Rebecca and Abigail start playing their music in the lighthouse, and the echoes make them sound like a much larger group. The British think that many soldiers are advancing and they retreat.

721. Van Leeuwen, Jean. *The Amazing Air Balloon: To Soar Like a Bird.* Illustrated by Marco Ventura. Penguin, 2003. 32pp. ISBN 978-0-8037-2258-3. Grades 3–6. In Baltimore, Maryland, on June 24, 1784, Edward Warren, 13, becomes the first person in America to ascend in a hot-air balloon. Edward, an orphaned blacksmith's apprentice, watched tavern owner Peter Carnes test his experiments for months. Edward wanted to be a part of this historic event, and a day before the flight, Peter Carnes, a heavy man, decides Edward is a better choice to go up in the balloon. *Black-Eyed Susan Award* (Maryland) nomination.

722. Van Leeuwen, Jean. *Cabin on Trouble Creek.* Dial, 2004. 224pp. ISBN 978-0-8037-2548-5. Grades 4–7. In 1803 Daniel, 11, and Will, 9, stay in Trouble Creek, Ohio, to finish the log cabin and guard the land while their father returns to Pennsylvania for their mother and younger siblings. Pa plans to be gone only five or six weeks, but he does not return before winter. They must survive with only their axe and two knives plus a sack of cornmeal. They have to deal with wolves and bears and a heavy snowstorm that engulfs the settlement. Daniel feels that they are being watched, and indeed an old Indian trapper, Solomon, appears who helps them learn about poisonous and healing plants and how to set snares. They make snowshoes from branches, coats from a blanket, and use rabbit fur for hats and gloves. Based on a true story. *Great Stone Face Children's Book Award* (New Hampshire) nomination, *Black-Eyed Susan Book Award* (Maryland) nomination, *William Allen White Children's Book Award* (Kansas), *Children's Choice Award* (Iowa) nomination, *Young Hoosier Book Award* (Indiana) nomination, *Mark Twain Award* (Missouri) nomination, *Sasquatch Reading Award* (Washington) nomination, *Prairie Pasque Award* (South Dakota) nomination, *Volunteer State Book Award* (Tennessee) nomination, and *Dorothy Canfield Fisher Children's Award* (Vermont) nomination.

723. West, Tracey. *Mr. Peale's Bones.* Silver Moon, 1994. 80pp. ISBN 978-1-881889-50-2; 2000, paper ISBN 978-1-893110-14-1. Grades 4–6. In 1801, 11-year-old Will Finch and his father have the opportunity to help the artist and scientist Charles Willson Peale excavate a mammoth in upstate New York. When he later hears that Peale has mounted his "Mammoth Exhibition" in Philadelphia, Will gains a new interest in science. Endpaper Maps, Historical Postscript, and Further Reading.

724. Whelan, Gloria. *Once on This Island.* Trophy, 1996. 89pp. Paper ISBN 978-0-06-440619-2. Grades 3–6. Mary O'Shea, 12, and her brother and sister try to look after their Mackinac, Michigan, farm when their father joins the army in 1812. She is surprised to see the British flag flying over the captured fort and even more surprised that the formerly friendly Indians have banded together to support the British cause. When her father returns after three years, he is greatly relieved to find that his children have succeeded in keeping their land in order.

725. Williams, Mark London. *Trail of Bones.* Illustrated by Michael Koelsch. (Danger Boy) Candlewick, 2005. 320pp. ISBN 978-0-7636-2154-4; 2007 paper ISBN 978-0-7636-3410-0. Grades 5–8. Eli Sands and Thea, an Alexandrian scholar, time-travel to 1804 Missouri where they meet Thomas Jefferson and encounter the Lewis and Clark Expedition. Eli joins the Corps of Discovery in hope of rescuing both his friend Clyne, an intelligent dinosaur, from hostile natives, and Thea, who has been mistakenly captured as an escaped slave so that all three can return to the Fifth Dimension in 2019.

726. Wood, Frances. *Becoming Rosemary.* Delacorte, 2001. 224pp. Paper ISBN 978-0-375-89504-3. Grades 5–9. Rosemary Weston expects to continue her daily tasks in North Carolina in 1790. But a cooper and his pregnant wife arrive in town, and his wife becomes Rosemary's friend. When rumors spread about witchcraft and evil regarding her friend, Rosemary realizes she must take a stand.

History

727. Alagna, Magdalena. *The Louisiana Purchase: Expanding America's Boundaries.* (Life in the New American Nation) Rosen, 2004. 32pp. ISBN 978-0-8239-4039-4; paper ISBN 978-0-8239-4257-2. Grades 4–8. When President Thomas Jefferson decided to make the Louisiana Purchase, he was increasing the size of the United States to make it one of the world's largest countries. He thought the port of New Orleans would be especially valuable because it gave access to the Mississippi River. Among the factors weighed in this expenditure were Western expansion, the ability to keep a balance between the slave and the free states, and the legality of the purchase. But Napoleon's price of $15 million was too good for Jefferson to refuse, and the acquisition became one of the most important achievements of Jefferson's presidency. Illustrations augment the text. Bibliography, Maps, and Index.

728. Bartoletti, Susan Campbell. *The Flag Maker.* Illustrated by Claire T. Nivola. Houghton, 2004. 32pp. ISBN 978-0-618-26757-6; 2007, paper ISBN 978-0-618-80911-0. Grades 2–6. In 1812, when Caroline Pickersgill was 12 and living in Baltimore, Maryland, she helped her mother and other family members sew the large American flag that flew over Fort Henry. It took six weeks to make the flag, which measured 30 feet by 42 feet, weighed 80 pounds, and had stripes 2 feet wide and stars measuring 2 feet from point to point. The flag survived the British attack and inspired Francis Scott Key to write "The Star-Spangled Banner." Bibliography. *Diamonds Book Award* (Delaware) nomination.

729. Beyer, Mark A. *The War of 1812: The New American Nation Goes to War with England.* (Life in the New American Nation) Rosen, 2004. 32pp. ISBN 978-0-8239-4043-1; 2003, paper ISBN 978-0-8239-4261-9. Grades 4–8. In the early 19th century tensions increased between the United States and its former parent. The British violated American neutral rights and kept the Native Americans unsettled. Additionally, some Americans wanted to expand the country to the west. This volume discusses these and other aspects of the conflict that developed into the War of 1812. Reproductions augment the text. Bibliography and Index.

730. Burnett, Linda. *Pioneers: Adventure in a New Land.* Children's, 2005. 48pp. ISBN 978-0-51625-127-1; paper ISBN 978-0-51625-097-7. Grades 4–6. Pioneers had difficult lives trying to settle in a strange area. Simple chapters give background about their experiences and how they supported themselves. Photographs and reproductions enhance the text. Glossary, Further Reading, Web Sites, and Index.

731. Cheney, Lynne V. *We the People: The Story of Our Constitution.* Illustrated by Greg Harlin. Simon & Schuster, 2008. 30pp. ISBN 978-1-4169-5418-7. Grades 3–5. This volume looks at the situation in the country at the end of the Revolutionary War and shows how important the ensuing Convention was for the health of the nation. Many resolutions and arguments had to be decided before the Constitution could be written. Cheney reviews the situation as the delegates arrived in May 1787 to discuss the rules that would run the nation and ensure prosperity and freedom. Illustrations complement the text.

732. Cosson, M. J. *Yankee Whalers.* (Events in American History) Rourke, 2007. 48pp. ISBN 978-1-60044-140-0. Grades 4–6. Cosson offers a history of whaling in New England, looking at its importance for people who could not easily farm the land. Whaling struggled during the Revolutionary War, but afterward had a golden age. This volume includes a description of life on a whale ship and an explanation of why the industry declined. Reproductions, maps, and illustrations accompany the text. Glossary, Chronology, Further Reading, Web Sites, and Index.

733. Figley, Marty Rhodes. *Washington Is Burning.* Illustrated by Craig Orback. (On My Own History) Millbrook, 2005. 48pp. ISBN 978-1-57505-875-7; First Avenue, 2006, paper ISBN 978-0-8225-6050-0. Grades K–2. As the British Army advanced toward Washington, D.C., during the War of 1812, Paul Jennings, a 15-year-old slave, helped Dolley Madison save valuable items from the White House.

734. Firestone, Mary. *The Liberty Bell.* Illustrated by Matthew Skeens. (American Symbols) Picture Window, 2006. 24pp. ISBN 978-1-4048-3101-8. Grades K–4. This volume offers background on this American symbol, covering its purchase, history, value to the abolitionists, crack, and contemporary importance. It also discusses the Liberty Bell Pavilion in Philadelphia. Photographs and illustrations augment the text. Glossary, Further Reading, and Index.

735. Fradin, Dennis B. *Duel! Burr and Hamilton's Deadly War of Words.* Illustrated by Larry Day. Walker, 2008. Unpaged. ISBN 978-0-8027-9583-0. Grades 3–6. Alexander Hamilton (1757–1804) and Aaron Burr (1756–1836) had similar lives. They both had difficult childhoods, fought in the American Revolution, trained as lawyers, and worked for the federal government. They began to disagree over politics. When Burr, the third vice president of the United States, defeated Hamilton's father-in-law for a seat in the Senate and ran for president and governor of New York, Hamilton denounced him. Burr challenged Hamilton to a duel, and the two met in the early morning of July 11, 1804, on a New Jersey cliffside. Burr shot Hamilton, and Hamilton died the next day. Burr's reputation, however, was ruined. Fradin argues that both men were at fault. Illustrations augment the text. Bibliography and Further Reading. *Kirkus Reviews Editor's Choice.*

736. Gay, Kathlyn, and Martin Gay. *War of 1812.* (Voices From the Past) Twenty-First Century, 1996. 64pp. ISBN 978-0-8050-2846-1. Grades 4–6. Letters, diaries, and newspaper accounts give an overview of the causes, the battles, and the results of the War of 1812, the second war that the Americans fought against the British. Photographs, Maps, Further Reading, Notes, and Index.

737. Hakim, Joy. *The New Nation.* (History of US) Oxford, 2006. 193pp. ISBN 978-0-19-518897-4; 2007, paper ISBN 978-0-19-532718-2. Grades 5 up. Filled with photographs, prints, sidebars, boxed text, and running commentary, this lively story of the newly formed United States from 1787 to 1848 covers all aspects of society and culture. Chronology of Events, More Books to Read, and Index.

738. Hubbard-Brown, Janet. *How the Constitution Was Created.* (U.S. Government: How It Works) Chelsea House, 2007. 104pp. ISBN 978-0-7910-9420-4. Grades 5–8. The author examines the historical aspects of the Constitution and how its creators approached the tenets included in it. The book also discusses those who were disenfranchised by the Constitution—women and slaves. The final chapter examines different aspects of the Constitution that have allowed it to remain in force for more than two hundred years. Photographs and illustrations highlight the text. Bibliography, Glossary, Further Reading, Web Sites, and Index.

739. Kalman, Bobbie. *The Early Family Home.* See entry 400.

740. Kalman, Bobbie, and David Schimpky. *Old-Time Toys.* See entry 405.

741. Kendall, Martha E. *The Erie Canal.* National Geographic, 2008. 128pp. ISBN 978-1-4263-0022-6. Grades 5–8. Using anecdotes, archival images, and engravings, this volume examines the importance of the Erie Canal. At first it was called "Hawley's Folly," after Hawley wrote fourteen articles from his jail cell from 1807 to 1808 about a canal to link the Hudson River with Lake Erie via the Iroquois Great Central Trail. It then was called "Clinton's Ditch," when DeWitt Clinton began building it in 1817. In 2000 the canal became a National Heritage Corridor, and it is now considered the Eighth Wonder of the World. Maps enhance the text. Web Sites and Index.

742. Miller, Brandon Marie. *Growing Up in Revolution and the New Nation 1775 to 1800.* See entry 606.

743. Morrison, Taylor. *The Great Unknown.* Walter Lorraine, 2001. 32pp. ISBN 978-0-395-97494-0. Grades 3–5. In 1799 bones are discovered on John Masten's farm in New York State's Hudson River Valley. Uncertain what they were, people called them the "great unknown." Charles Willson Peale (1741–1827) excavated the bones from the peat bogs and assembled the body of a creature now known as a mastodon. Then Peale tried to purchase the animal and excavate another for his Philadelphia museum. Paintings augment the text. Bibliography and Glossary.

744. Murphy, Jim. *An American Plague: The True and Terrifying Story of the Yellow Fever Epidemic of 1793.* Houghton, 2003. 176pp. ISBN 978-0-395-77608-7. Grades 5–10. Concerned about the controversy surrounding President Washington's decision not to support the French in a war against Britain in 1793, the people of Philadelphia did not notice the number of dead animals in the town. They missed the beginning of the yellow fever epidemic on August 3 when a French sailor died in a local boardinghouse. By the end of the year, 10 percent of the population had died. A committee of twelve governed the city while the country's most renowned physician, Dr. Benjamin Rush, tried to help. The Free African Society, whose members were erroneously thought to be immune, contributed food, medicine, and home care. Archival Photographs, Facsimiles of Documents, Further Reading, and Index. *National Book Award* nomination, *School Library Journal Best Books of the Year, Newbery Honor Book, Robert F. Sibert Medal, American Library Association Notable Books for Children, National Council of Teachers of English Orbis Pictus Award, Boston Globe/Horn Book Award Honor, James Madison Book Award, Volunteer State Book Award* (Tennessee) nomination, *Garden State Teen Book Award* (New Jersey) nomination, *William Allen White Children's Book Award* (Kansas) nomination, *Capitol Choices Noteworthy Titles* (Washington, D.C.), *Voice of Youth Advocates Nonfiction Honor List, Bulletin Blue Ribbon,* and *Young Hoosier Book Award* nomination.

745. Pearl, Norman. *The Bald Eagle.* Illustrated by Matthew Skeens. (American Symbols) Picture Window, 2006. 24pp. ISBN 978-1-4048-2642-7. Grades K–4. This volume offers background on the bald eagle's role as an American symbol and how it gained this status, looking at its presence on coins and the Great Seal. Photographs and illustrations augment the text. Glossary, Further Reading, and Index.

746. St. Pierre, Stephanie. *Our National Anthem.* Millbrook, 1994. 48pp. Paper ISBN 978-1-878841-89-6. Grades 3–6. During the War of 1812 Francis Scott Key became stranded on a ship in Baltimore Harbor near the battle against the British. When he awoke the next morning and saw the American flag still flying, he wrote a poem. This poem became "The Star Spangled Banner," the national anthem. The text presents information about the history and significance of this song and other patriotic songs. Photographs and drawings enhance the text. Glossary and Index.

747. Schaffer, David. *The Louisiana Purchase: The Deal of the Century That Doubled the Nation.* (Wild History of the American West) Enslow, 2006. 128pp. ISBN 978-1-59845-018-7. Grades 5–9. The Louisiana Purchase from France made a huge impact on America not only because of its size but also because of the changes it brought. The purchase was discussed in songs, speeches, newspapers, diaries, and other primary sources of the time. Among the individuals who played important roles in arranging and executing the sale were Napoleon, Thomas Jefferson, and the slave leader Toussaint-L'Ouverture. Illustrations enhance the text. Bibliography, Glossary, Notes, Further Reading, and Index.

748. Schultz, Randy. *Washington Ablaze: The War of 1812.* (Events in American History) Rourke, 2007. 48pp. ISBN 978-1-60044-128-8. Grades 4–6. Schultz provides background about the events of the War of 1812 and the positions held by both sides, covering the burning of Washington, D.C., the attempt to invade Canada, and the shelling of Fort McHenry, after which Francis Scott Key wrote "The Star-Spangled Banner." Quotes from primary sources appear throughout. Photographs, maps, augment the text. Bibliography, Glossary, Chronology, Notes, Further Reading, Web Sites, and Index.

749. Sonneborn, Liz. *The Star-Spangled Banner: The Story Behind Our National Anthem.* (America in Words and Song) Chelsea Clubhouse, 2004. 32pp. ISBN 978-0-7910-7337-7. Grades 3–5. This volume recounts the circumstances that led to Francis Scott Key's writing of the "Star-Spangled Banner." His experiences in the War of 1812, when America fought the British near Baltimore, influenced him. Not until March 3, 1931, did Herbert Hoover officially sign a resolution declaring it the national anthem. Illustrations and photographs enhance the text. Bibliography, Further Reading, Timeline, Glossary, Web Sites, and Index.

750. Yero, Judith Lloyd. *The Bill of Rights.* (American Documents) National Geographic, 2006. 40pp. ISBN 978-0-7922-5891-9. Grades 3–5. The author examines each tenet in this document and places it in historical context. Photographs and reproductions highlight the text. Index.

Biography and Collective Biography

751. Adler, David A. *B. Franklin, Printer.* See entry 438.

752. Adler, David A. *George Washington: An Illustrated Biography.* See entry 439.

753. Adler, David A. *A Picture Book of Benjamin Franklin.* See entry 440.

754. Adler, David A. *A Picture Book of George Washington.* See entry 619.

755. Adler, David A. *A Picture Book of Patrick Henry.* See entry 621.

756. Adler, David A. *A Picture Book of Thomas Jefferson.* See entry 623.

757. Adler, David A. *President George Washington.* See entry 442.

758. Adler, David A., and Michael S. Adler. *A Picture Book of Samuel Adams.* See entry 444.

759. Ashby, Ruth. *The Amazing Mr. Franklin: Or, The Boy Who Read Everything.* See entry 445.

760. Bowen, Andy Russell. *A World of Knowing: A Story About Thomas Hopkins Gallaudet.* Illustrated by Elaine Wadsworth. Carolrhoda, 1995. 64pp. ISBN 978-0-8761-4871-6. Grades 3–6. Thomas Gallaudet (1787–1851) suffered from poor health for most of his life, but he became the principal of the first school for the deaf and helped develop American Sign Language. When he was young, he met Alice Cogswell, a young deaf girl with whom he began to work. Her father sent Gallaudet to Europe to study deaf education. He returned and led a new school in Hartford, Connecticut. He fell in love with one of his students, who was 11 years younger than him, and married her in 1821. She feared that their children would be deaf, but none were. American Manual Alphabet, Bibliography, and Index.

761. Brown, Don. *Dolley Madison Saves George Washington.* Houghton, 2007. Unpaged. ISBN 978-0-618-41199-3. Grades K–4. Dolley Madison (1768–1849) served as Thomas Jefferson's White House hostess when her husband was secretary of state because Jefferson was a widower. When her husband James became president, she continued for the next eight years to make people feel welcome in the White House. She redecorated the president's mansion, making sure that Gilbert Stuart's portrait of George Washington was visible. She also helped to save treasures when the British threatened Washington in 1812. Illustrations complement the text. Bibliography.

762. **Bruns, Roger.** *Thomas Jefferson.* See entry 448.

763. **Collard, Sneed B., III.** *Benjamin Franklin: The Man Who Could Do Just About Anything.* See entry 454.

764. **Conley, Kevin.** *Benjamin Banneker: Scientist and Mathematician.* See entry 455.

765. **Davies, Jacqueline.** *The Boy Who Drew Birds: A Story of John James Audubon.* Houghton, 2004. Unpaged. ISBN 978-0-618-24343-3. Grades 2–4. John James Audubon (1785–1851) came to the United States from Scotland to learn business. But at the age of 18, he roamed around his Pennsylvania home looking for birds. He wanted to know if they returned to the same nests and was the first person to band fledgling peewee flycatchers. He painted them and many other birds and became a renowned ornithological artist. Mixed-media illustrations complement the text. *Young Hoosier Book Award* (Indiana) nomination and *Capitol Choices Noteworthy Titles* (Washington, D.C.).

766. **Elish, Dan.** *James Madison.* (Presidents and Their Times) Benchmark, 2007. 96pp. ISBN 978-0-7614-2432-1. Grades 4–7. James Madison (1751–1836) was a tiny, quiet, shy man who helped to create the Constitution of the United States. He had a difficult presidency because he was unable to lead well and stubbornly stuck to his own ideas. His wife, Dolley, however, was especially adept at being a White House hostess. This text, enhanced by photographs, offers an overview of his life. Bibliography, Glossary, Chronology, Further Reading, Web Sites, and Index.

767. **Fine, Jil.** *The Transcontinental Railroad: Tracks Across America.* Children's, 2005. 48pp. ISBN 978-0-51625-128-8; paper ISBN 978-0-51625-098-4. Grades 1–2. The transcontinental railroad became the first link between the Atlantic and the Pacific Oceans when it was completed in 1869. Photographs and reproductions enhance the text. Glossary, Further Reading, Web Sites, and Index.

768. **Fleming, Candace.** *Ben Franklin's Almanac: Being a True Account of the Good Gentleman's Life.* See entry 457.

769. **Fradin, Dennis B.** *Samuel Adams: The Father of American Independence.* See entry 459.

770. **Fritz, Jean.** *And Then What Happened, Paul Revere?* See entry 460.

771. **Fritz, Jean.** *What's the Big Idea, Ben Franklin?* See entry 462.

772. **Fritz, Jean.** *Why Don't You Get a Horse, Sam Adams?* See entry 463.

773. **Fritz, Jean.** *Will You Sign Here, John Hancock?* See entry 464.

774. **Giblin, James Cross.** *The Amazing Life of Benjamin Franklin.* See entry 466.

775. **Giblin, James Cross.** *Thomas Jefferson: A Picture Book Biography.* See entry 468.

776. **Harkins, Susan Sales, and William H. Harkins.** *The Life and Times of Patrick Henry.* See entry 473.

777. **Harness, Cheryl.** *The Remarkable Benjamin Franklin.* See entry 475.

778. **Harness, Cheryl.** *The Revolutionary John Adams.* See entry 476.

779. **Harness, Cheryl.** *Thomas Jefferson.* National Geographic, 2004. 48pp. ISBN 978-0-7922-6496-5; 2007, paper ISBN 978-1-4263-0043-1. Grades 3–6. This picture-book biography discusses the life of and times in which Thomas Jefferson (1743–1826) lived. Slavery was acceptable in his society although Jefferson wrote in the Declaration of Independence that "all men are created equal." Jefferson pursued many activities as a scientist, lawyer, farmer, architect, diplomat, inventor, musician, philosopher, and third president of the United States. Watercolor, gouache, ink, and colored pencil illustrations enhance the text. Bibliography and Timeline.

780. Kjelle, Marylou Morano. *Francis Scott Key.* Mitchell Lane, 2006. 32pp. ISBN 978-1-58415-474-7. Grades 1–4. This brief biography of Francis Scott Key (1779–1843) explains why he wrote the national anthem and gives details of his childhood and adult life. Illustrations enhance the text. Bibliography, Glossary, Chronology, and Index.

781. Leslie, Tonya. *Thomas Jefferson: A Life of Patriotism.* See entry 484.

782. Melton, Buckner Will, Jr. *Aaron Burr: The Rise and Fall of an American Politician.* (The Library of American Lives and Times) PowerKids, 2004. 112pp. ISBN 978-0-8239-6626-4. Grades 5–8. Aaron Burr (1756–1836) fought a duel with Alexander Hamilton and won. This deed defines him in history, but he accomplished much more during his life. He was a lawyer, soldier, father, and politician. He believed that women should be educated and slavery abolished, both ideas ahead of the times. This volume looks at Burr's early life and his contributions to the American Revolution as well as his later life when he was indicted and acquitted of treason before moving to England. Maps, Photos, Reproductions, Bibliography, Chronology, Further Reading, Glossary, Index, Web sites.

783. Mullin, Rita T. *Thomas Jefferson: Architect of Freedom.* See entry 658.

784. Nardo, Don. *Thomas Jefferson.* (Encyclopedia of Presidents) Scholastic, 2003. 110pp. ISBN 978-0-516-22768-9. Grades 3–6. Thomas Jefferson (1743–1826) became the eighth president of the United States. While he was president, the United States both sank into depression and made the Louisiana Purchase. This volume provides information on Jefferson's life growing up in Virginia, his family, his career, his accomplishments as a scientist and inventor, and his two terms in the presidency. Further Reading, Timeline, Glossary, Historic Sites, Web Sites, and Index.

785. Nettleton, Pamela. *Benjamin Franklin: Writer, Inventor, Statesman.* See entry 489.

786. Nettleton, Pamela. *George Washington: Farmer, Soldier, President.* See entry 490.

787. Patrick, Jean L. S. *Dolley Madison.* (History Maker Bios) Lerner, 2002. 48pp. ISBN 978-0-8225-0194-7. Grades 3–5. Dolley Madison (1768–1849), wife of President James Madison, became known for her bravery when the British invaded Washington during 1814 and set the White House on fire. She rescued government papers and a portrait of George Washington. A Quaker, she did not believe in war, and she was a respected figure throughout her life. Illustrations augment the text. Bibliography, Further Reading, Glossary, Maps, Timeline, Web Sites, and Index.

788. Patterson, Charles. *Thomas Jefferson.* See entry 493.

789. Pinkney, Andrea Davis. *Dear Benjamin Banneker.* See entry 495.

790. Quackenbush, Robert. *James Madison and Dolley Madison and Their Times.* Pippin, 1992. 36pp. ISBN 978-0-945912-18-7. Grades 2–5. James and Dolley Madison were already in Washington when he was elected the fourth president of the United States in 1809. Dolley Madison loved to entertain and was hostess for Thomas Jefferson while he was president. This volume looks at their contributions to the history of the new nation.

791. Ransom, Candice F. *George Washington.* See entry 497.

792. Ransom, Candice F. *John Hancock.* See entry 498.

793. Reiter, Chris. *Thomas Jefferson.* See entry 501.

794. Roberts, Russell. *The Life and Times of Thomas Jefferson.* See entry 502.

795. Rushby, Pamela. *Ben Franklin: Printer, Author, Inventor, Politician.* See entry 504.

796. St. George, Judith. *The Duel: The Parallel Lives of Alexander Hamilton and Aaron Burr.* Viking, 2009. 97pp. ISBN 978-0-670-01124-7. Grades 5–9. Aaron Burr (1756–1836) and Alexander Hamilton (1755–1804) led very similar lives. The text traces these parallels in nine chapters that alternate between the two, looking at them as orphans, students at the same academy, college graduates, lawyers, aides to General Washington, and American Revolution heroes. But on June 11, 1804, at Weehawken, New Jersey, they parted ways when

Burr killed Hamilton in an illegal duel. He was furious with Hamilton for campaigning against him for various political positions. Afterward, Hamilton's reputation soared while Burr fell into ignominy. Illustrations add context. Bibliography and Index. *Capitol Choices Noteworthy Titles* (Washington, D.C.).

797. **Shea, Pegi Deitz.** *Noah Webster: Weaver of Words.* Illustrated by Monica Vachula. Calkins Creek, 2009. 40pp. ISBN 978-1-59078-441-9. Grades 3–7. A contemporary and friend of George Washington and Benjamin Franklin, Noah Webster (1758-1843) made many valuable contributions to American life after earning his master's degree at Yale University. He was a thinker, learner, soldier, teacher, lawyer, wordsmith, author, speaker, father and husband, and lexicographer. He thought that languages were living things and spoke several languages fluently. He espoused public education for all, helped standardize American English spellings, established copyright laws, and wrote a dictionary. Quotes form Webster's own writing tell of these achievements and others. Side bars note contemporary events, and realistic oil paintings enhance the text. Chronology Bibliography, Futher Reading, Web Sites, and Index.

798. **Sherrow, Victoria.** *Benjamin Franklin.* See entry 508.

799. **Sherrow, Victoria.** *Thomas Jefferson.* See entry 509.

800. **Sutcliffe, Jane.** *Abigail Adams.* See entry 675.

801. **Sutcliffe, Jane.** *John Adams.* See entry 512.

802. **Sutcliffe, Jane.** *Paul Revere.* See entry 677.

803. **Thomas, Peggy.** *Farmer George Plants a Nation.* See entry 513.

804. **Uglow, Loyd.** *Benjamin Franklin—You Know What to Say.* See entry 515.

805. **Weatherly, Myra.** *Dolley Madison: America's First Lady.* Morgan Reynolds, 2003. 128pp. ISBN 978-1-883846-95-4. Grades 5–8. This biography of Dolley Madison (1768–1849) traces her life from that of a young Quaker wearing plain dress to her role as hostess in the White House, wearing the beautiful and fancy clothes that she loved for Thomas Jefferson and her husband, James Madison. She showed her bravery when the British troops entered Washington by saving important historical artifacts from the White House. She was a beloved first lady, and the anecdotes included here attest to her popularity. Photographs and illustrations augment the text. Bibliography, Chronology, Notes, Web Sites, and Index.

806. **Welch, Catherine.** *Benjamin Banneker.* See entry 518.

807. **Welch, Catherine.** *Eli Whitney.* See entry 685.

808. **Welch, Catherine.** *Patrick Henry.* See entry 519.

Graphic Novels, Biographies, and Histories

809. **Chase, John.** *The Louisiana Purchase.* Pelican, 2002. 83pp. Paper ISBN 978-1-58980-084-7. Grades 5–8. Chase uses political cartoons to explore the process behind this major event in the history of the United States. He creates suspense with his characterization of important figures including Napoleon and Talleyrand.

810. **Doeden, Matt.** *George Washington: Leading a New Nation.* See entry 689.

811. **Doeden, Matt.** *Thomas Jefferson: Great American.* See entry 690.

812. **Espinosa, Rod.** *Benjamin Franklin.* See entry 530.

813. **Espinosa, Rod.** *George Washington.* See entry 531.

814. Jacobson, Ryan. *The Story of the Star-Spangled Banner.* Illustrated by Cynthia Martin and Beatty Terry. Graphic Library, 2006. 32pp. ISBN 978-0-7368-5493-1; paper ISBN 978-0-7368-6881-5. Grades 3–5. Francis Scott Key (1779–1843) watched the bombardment of American forces at Fort McHenry during the Battle of Baltimore on the night of September 13–14, 1814. After the smoke cleared, Key could still see the American flag waving, and he wrote "The Star-Spangled Banner." Illustrations complement the text. Bibliography, Glossary, Further Reading, and Index.

815. Olson, Kay Melchisedech. *Betsy Ross and the American Flag.* Illustrated by Anna Maria Cool and Sam Delarosa. Graphic Library, 2006. 32pp. ISBN 978-0-7368-4962-3; paper ISBN 978-0-7368-6201-1. Grades 3–5. The widow Betsy Ross met with George Washington and others at her Philadelphia upholstery business and they discussed the first United States flag. She showed the men that a five-pointed star could easily be created and received the commission. Illustrations enhance the text. Bibliography, Glossary, Further Reading, and Index.

816. Smalley, Roger. *Dolley Madison Saves History.* Illustrated by Anna Maria Cool and Scott Rosema. Graphic Library, 2005. 32pp. ISBN 978-0-7368-4972-2; paper ISBN 978-0-7368-9686-3. Grades 3–5. When the British were threatening to attack the White House during the War of 1812, Dolley Madison (1768–1849) decided to remove valuable objects. She gathered portraits, including one of George Washington, and books and took them away with the help of one of her slaves. Illustrations enhance the text. Bibliography, Glossary, Further Reading, and Index.

DVDs

817. *Creating a New Nation: 1783–1791.* (American Revolution for Students) Library Video, 2003. 23 mins. Grades 5–9. Reenactments, period paintings and illustrations, and actors portraying personages of the time give an account of the social, political, and economic conditions that influenced Americans after the Revolutionary War. In 1783, after the French helped the colonists to defeat the British, the thirteen separate states had to begin the work of uniting. The problems with the Articles of Confederation led to many compromises before completing the Constitution.

818. *George Washington.* (Great Americans for Children) Library Video, 2002. 23 mins. Grades K–4. George Washington (1732–1799) led the Continental Army during the Revolutionary War after working as a military scout and a farmer. In order to continue helping his country succeed, he agreed to become its first president. His decision gained him the title of "Father of Our Country." Reenactments and photographs introduce his value to America.

819. *George Washington's Teeth.* Spoken Arts, 2004. 7 mins. ISBN 978-0-8045-9695-4. Grades K–4. Brock Cole's watercolor cartoon illustrations are featured in this iconographic presentation of Deborah Chandra and Madeleine Comora's book narrated by Charles Osgood. It includes interesting, entertaining information about dentistry through history and George Washington's teeth.

820. *Patrick Henry: Quest for Freedom.* American Animation Studios, 2007. 34 mins. ISBN 978-0-9796681-1-1. Grades 3–6. See entry 542.

821. *The U.S. Constitution and the Bill of Rights.* (United States Government) Library Video, 2002. 23 mins. Grades 5–12. A female narrator on location in Washington, D.C.; historians; and words of the framers of the Constitution and Bill of Rights anchor this video that includes maps, graphics, and period art. It reveals weaknesses in the Articles of Confederation and the Constitutional Convention in Philadelphia, where competing plans had to be negotiated before the final document could be written. In addition to profiling James Madison, the video explains the importance of the Bill of Rights in assuring individual liberty and the idea of "we the people" as a philosophy for governing this new country.

822. **Venezia, Mike.** *Getting to Know the U.S. Presidents: George Washington, First President.* Getting To Know, 2007. 16 mins. Grades 1–5. With comic illustrations and humor, George Washington introduces himself and tells about his childhood and the various jobs he held before he became a soldier. He recalls his part in the French and Indian War and the Revolutionary War and he talks about his family and his life as president.

Compact Discs

823. **Anderson, Laurie Halse.** *Fever 1793.* Narrated by Emily Berg. Random, 2007. 5 CDs; 5.75 hrs. ISBN 978-0-8072-4905-2. Grades 5–8. See entry 708.

824. **Murphy, Jim.** *An American Plague: The True and Terrifying Story of the Yellow Fever Epidemic of 1793.* Narrated by Pat Bottino. Recorded Books, 2004. 4 CDs; 4 hrs. ISBN 978-1-4025-8744-3. Grades 5–9. See entry 744.

825. *Thomas Jefferson's America.* Narrated by Jim Weiss. Greathall, 2005. 1 CD; 74 mins. ISBN 978-1-882513-86-4. Grades 5 up. See entry 545.

THE SETTLING OF THE WEST, NATIVE AMERICANS, AND SEA JOURNEYS, 1775–1916

Historical Fiction and Fantasy

826. **Addy, Sharon Hart.** *Lucky Jake.* Illustrated by Wade Zahares. Houghton, 2007. Unpaged. ISBN 978-0-618-47286-4. Grades K–3. Jake and his Pa pan for gold and find a nugget. Jake is awarded part of the proceeds and, as no dogs are available as pets, he chooses a pig that he names Dog. When Dog finds kernels of corn in Pa's clothes, Jake plants them carefully. The corn in turn attracts a goat, and then Jake and his Dad start trading corn fritters for other items that they need. Illustrations complement the text.

827. **Alphin, Elaine Marie.** *Dinosaur Hunter.* HarperCollins, 2004. 48pp. Paper ISBN 978-0-06-444256-5. Grades 1–3. In 1880s Wyoming, young Ned Chapman helps his father check the fences on their ranch after a storm. He finds the skeleton of a triceratops. After a fossil hunter tries to cheat him, Ned is careful to sell his treasure to a man who will put it in a museum. Watercolor-and ink illustrations enhance the text.

828. **Antle, Nancy.** *Beautiful Land: A Story of the Oklahoma Land Rush.* Illustrated by John Gampert. Puffin, 1997. 54pp. Paper ISBN 978-0-14-036808-6. Grades 3–6. On April 22, 1889, Annie Mae's family plans a new life where they will have their own farm and not have to work for others. They participate in the race to claim land in the newly opened Oklahoma Territory. Although illegal squatters try to seize it, they reach the land claim office first and pay before anyone else gets the chance.

829. **Applegate, Katherine.** *The Buffalo Storm.* Illustrated by Jan Ormerod. Clarion, 2007. 32pp. ISBN 978-0-618-53597-2. Grades 2–4. Young Hallie and her parents join a wagon train bound for Oregon. Hallie's grandmother, who is staying behind, suggests Hallie may see buffalo on the trip. They face many problems on the trail, including bad weather, and Hallie misses her grandmother. Then one day in Wyoming she helps rescue a buffalo calf and hears what she thinks is a huge storm approaching. It is in fact the sound of a huge herd of buffalo, and Hallie feels connected to her grandmother again. Watercolor and pastel illustrations complement the text.

830. **Armstrong, Jennifer.** *Black-Eyed Susan.* Illustrated by Emily Martindale. Random, 1997. 96pp. Paper ISBN 978-0-679-88556-6. Grades 3–5. Susie, 10, and her father try to persuade her mother to enjoy the vast prairie on which they live. But her mother stays inside their sod house, dealing with the bugs that fall from the ceiling. She refuses to look outside. Susie and her father, however, decide to buy more land and commit the family to another five

years there. When an Icelandic family arrives in the area, they help Susie's mother acclimate to her situation.

831. Arrington, Frances. *Prairie Whispers.* Puffin, 2005. 176pp. Paper ISBN 978-0-14-240306-8. Grades 5–9. In South Dakota in the 1860s, 12-year-old Colleen replaces her stillborn sister with the baby of a dying woman in a nearby covered wagon. This woman wants the child to be safe from her abusive husband. The woman also gives Colleen the husband's watch and strongbox. When the man comes and demands his possessions, he also wants to know about the child. Colleen must decide whether to admit that she switched the children—her own family believes the baby is theirs. *Booklist Editor's Choice.*

832. Auch, Mary Jane. *Journey to Nowhere.* Yearling, 1999. 224pp. Paper ISBN 978-0-440-41491-9. Grades 4–7. In 1815, 11-year-old Remembrance moves with her family from Hartford, Connecticut, to the wilderness of western New York State. On the journey, Mem becomes separated from her family and after finding them once, almost loses them again. In addition to difficult terrain, they must fight bears, wolves, and mountain lions before settling into their new community.

833. Avi. *Hard Gold: The Colorado Gold Rush of 1859.* (I Witness) Hyperion, 2008. 224pp. ISBN 978-1-4231-0519-0. Grades 4–7. Early Wittcomb, 14, decides to follow his Uncle Jesse, 19, to the Pike's Peak area of the Rocky Mountains in 1858 after he gets a letter from Jesse saying he has found gold but fears it will be stolen. The local banker has demanded that Early's family sell its land to the Chicago and Western railway and threatens foreclosure. Early thinks gold will allow them to buy the farm and he signs on to a wagon train headed west. When Early finally finds Jesse he discovers that gold can change all men. Jesse has become an outlaw. Maps, diagrams, period photographs, and reproductions enhance the text. Bibliography, Glossary, and Note.

834. Avi. *Prairie School.* Trophy, 2003. 48pp. Paper ISBN 978-0-06-051318-4. Grades 2–4. In 1880, 9-year-old Noah learns how to read from his Aunt Dora as they wander around the Colorado prairie in this chapter book. He does not see any reason to read, but she continues to pressure him until he finds a new world on the printed page.

835. Avi. *The True Confessions of Charlotte Doyle.* Orchard, 1990. 215pp. ISBN 978-0-531-05893-0; Camelot, 1997, paper ISBN 978-0-380-72885-5. Grades 5–8. When Charlotte is 13 in 1832, she sails from England on the *Seahawk* to join her family in Rhode Island. She is the only passenger on board and slowly comes to understand the tensions around her. The crew is planning retaliation against the overbearing captain, and Charlotte eventually joins their side, engaging them with her willingness to take risks. The captain falsely accuses her of murder, but the old cook Zachariah rescues her before she is hanged. When she finally reaches her family, she cannot settle down in the confining role required of her, and she runs away, back to sea. *Newbery Honor, Boston Globe-Horn Book Award, Golden Kite Award,* and *Judy Lopez Memorial Award.*

836. Bader, Bonnie. *Golden Quest.* (Stories of the States) Silver Moon, 1994. 64pp. ISBN 978-1-8818-8930-4; 1995, paper ISBN 978-1-8818-8974-8. Grades 3–5. In California in 1850, there is debate over whether California should enter the Union as a free state or will allow slavery. David and Celia Taylor help their parents manage a dining hall serving gold prospectors in the hills north of San Francisco. Everyone they know is intensely involved in this discussion. Endpaper Maps, Historical Postscript, and Recommended Reading.

837. Barron, T. A. *High as a Hawk: A Brave Girl's Historic Climb.* Illustrated by Ted Lewin. Philomel, 2004. 32pp. ISBN 978-0-399-23704-1. Grades K–2. In 1905 Harriet Peters, 8, decides to climb Longs Peak in Colorado with her father to fulfill her deceased mother's dream. An old mountain-guide, Enos Mills, accompanies them. When her father becomes short of breath, Harriet decides to finish the 14,255-foot climb alone, facing blizzards and blisters without him. She becomes the youngest person ever to reach the summit. Detailed watercolors augment the text based on a true story. *Nautilus Award* Finalist.

838. Blos, Joan W. *Letters from the Corrugated Castle: Life In Gold Rush California, 1850–1852.* Atheneum, 2007. 310pp. ISBN 978-0-689-87077-4. Grades 5–9. Eldora, 13, travels to California with her adoptive aunt and uncle in the 1850s. Having been raised in Massachusetts as an orphan, she is surprised to learn that she has a mother, who lives in San Francisco and is wealthy. While Eldora waits to meet her mother, she writes letters to her cousin Sallie that describe life in the new town of San Francisco, especially the mining camps and the threat of fire. She decides to travel with her mother to San Pedro, expecting a life of luxury; however, the reality is different, and she describes it in further letters to Sallie and to her friend Luke.

839. Brenner, Barbara. *Wagon Wheels.* Illustrated by Don Bolognese. HarperCollins, 1995. 64pp. Paper ISBN 978-0-694-70001-1. Grades K–3. Ed Muldie takes his African American family west in 1878. His wife dies on the journey, leaving him looking after the three boys. He leaves 11-year-old Johnny and his brothers in Nicodemus, Kansas, while he goes ahead to find better land. Osage Indians help the townspeople survive a famine; the boys help extinguish a prairie fire; and they cope with a poisonous snake warming itself by the campfire before their father returns. *American Library Association Notable Children's Books* and *Notable Children's Trade Book in the Field of Social Studies.*

840. Brink, Carol Ryrie. *Caddie Woodlawn.* Simon & Schuster, 1973. 288pp. ISBN 978-0-02-713670-8; Aladdin, 3006, paper ISBN 978-1-416-94028-9. Grades 4–6. Eleven-year-old redhead Caddie is a tomboy who is happiest playing with the boys in her Wisconsin community in 1864. She would rather do chores outdoors than work in the kitchen. Adults discuss the Civil War, but their greater concern is the danger of Indian massacres. Caddie, however, is friendly with the Native Americans and plays a role in averting conflict. When her very proper Cousin Annabelle comes to stay, Caddie slowly comes to recognize the benefits of behaving in a more grown-up way. *Newbery Medal.*

841. Bruchac, Joseph. *Crazy Horse's Vision.* Illustrated by S. D. Nelson. Lee & Low, 2000. Unpaged. ISBN 978-1-880000-94-6; 2006, paper ISBN 978-1-58430-282-7. Grades K–5. The Lakota people call Crazy Horse (ca. 1842–1877) "Curly" on account of his hair. He shows his bravery and generosity at a young age. At the age of 14, he sees white soldiers murder Conquering Bear, and after spending three days in the hills seeking a vision, he is ready to become Tashunka Witco, or Crazy Horse. His father, however, will not grant him this name for three more years. Illustrations enhance the text. *ALA Notable Children's Book, Prairie Pasque Book Award* (South Dakota) nomination, and *Capitol Choices Noteworthy Titles* (Washington, D.C.).

842. Bruchac, Joseph. *The Journal of Jesse Smoke: A Cherokee Boy.* 206pp. ISBN 978-0-439-12197-2. Grades 5–8. In 1837 Cherokee Jesse Smoke, 16, and his family are forced to leave their Tennessee home and walk to Oklahoma on the Trail of Tears. Jesse keeps a journal detailing the daily events and the thoughts of the Cherokees. He includes the political issues of the forced removal; the spirituality of the Cherokees and their refusal as recently converted Christians to travel on Sundays; and the tribal world view. Notes.

843. Bunting, Eve. *Dandelions.* Illustrated by Greg Shed. Voyager, 2001. 48pp. Paper ISBN 978-0-15-202407-9. Grades K–5. In the spring, Zoe and her family come to Nebraska Territory from Illinois. Her mother is very lonely in the emptiness as her father tries to make a home for them. Neighbors only three hours away help, but building a new life is not easy. They plant two dandelions on the roof of the house, which mama thinks may also die of loneliness. *Notable Children's Trade Books in the Field of Social Studies.*

844. Bunting, Eve. *Train to Somewhere.* Illustrated by Ronald Himler. Clarion, 1996. 32pp. ISBN 978-0-395-71325-9; 2000, paper ISBN 978-0-618-04031-5. Grades 1–4. Marianne leaves on the Orphan Train from St. Christopher's Orphanage in 1877. Her mother left her there saying she would come get her after making a life out West. Marianne hopes to find her mother before someone adopts her. At the train's last stop, called Somewhere, her mother has not appeared, and a couple who had wanted a boy accepts her because she is the only remaining child. The woman later says that sometimes people get better than they thought they wanted.

845. Byars, Betsy C. *The Golly Sisters Go West.* HarperCollins, 1986. 58pp. ISBN 978-0-06-020884-4; Trophy, 1990, paper ISBN 978-0-06-444132-2. Grades 1–3. May-May and Rose star in four stories as they make their way to the western frontier. They first have to figure out how to make their horse move. Then they give a road show but get lost afterward. An argument precedes a nighttime scare. When they figure out how to get their horse in the act, their audiences enjoy their antics more.

846. Carlson, Laurie M. *Westward Ho! An Activity Guide to the Wild West.* Chicago Review, 1996. 149pp. Paper ISBN 978-1-55652-271-0. Grades 3–6. Chronologically organized text accompanies a large collection of relevant projects—keeping a log on the trail with Lewis and Clark, learning to pan for gold, frying bread and drying apples, songs and actions while riding on the trail, and many others. Bibliography.

847. Coerr, Eleanor. *Buffalo Bill and the Pony Express.* Illustrated by Don Bolognese. (I Can Read) Trophy, 1996. 64pp. Paper ISBN 978-0-06-444220-6. Grades K–3. The Pony Express started in 1860 with riders brave enough to face a variety of dangers as they carried mail across the country. Buffalo Bill Cody was one of the riders who survived Indians and wolves during the 18 months of the Pony Express's existence, before trains started taking the mail.

848. Coerr, Eleanor. *The Josefina Story Quilt.* Illustrated by Bruce Degen. (I Can Read) Trophy, 1989. 64pp. Paper ISBN 978-0-06-444129-2. Grades K–3. On the journey to California by wagon in 1850, Josefina, Faith's elderly pet hen, warns the family about robbers and promptly dies. Faith makes a patch celebrating Josefina's life on the quilt that tells the story of their trip.

849. Collier, James Lincoln. *Wild Boy.* Marshall Cavendish, 2002. 160pp. ISBN 978-0-7614-5126-6. Grades 5–8. Jesse, an angry 12-year-old, runs away from home after knocking out his father. He tries to live alone in the wilderness. He meets a mountain man named Larry, who teaches him how to survive and helps him understand why his mother left home several years before. Eventually, Jesse decides to return to his 19th-century prairie home and his father.

850. Couloumbis, Audrey. *Maude March on the Run: Or Trouble Is Her Middle Name.* Random, 2007. 308pp. ISBN 978-0-375-83246-8; Yearling, 2008, paper ISBN 978-0-375-83248-2. Grades 5–7. Orphans Maude, 16, and Sallie, 12, hope to settle down without being identified as outlaws in this sequel to *The Misadventures of Maude March*. Maude is accused of being a bank robber, murderer, and horse thief. She is arrested along with Black Hankie Bandit. Maude breaks out of jail, and the two begin new adventures.

851. Couloumbis, Audrey. *The Misadventures of Maude March: Or, Trouble Rides a Fast Horse.* Random, 2005. 295pp. ISBN 978-0-375-83245-1; Yearling, 2007, paper ISBN 978-0-375-83247-5. Grades 5–8. Orphans Sallie, 11, and her sister Maude, 15, escape from Reverend Peasley, a harsh taskmaster who took them in when stern Aunt Ruthie died. They take two horses and ride to Independence, Missouri. There they disguise themselves as boys while looking for their uncle. They have various adventures and become involved in a bank robbery and a murder. When posters warning about "Mad Maude" start appearing, they have to run again. Sallie especially enjoys their adventures because they resemble the dime novels she loves. *Bluebonnet Award* (Texas) nomination, *William Allen White Award* (Kansas) nomination, *Rebecca Caudill Award* (Illinois) nomination, *Children's Book Award* (Georgia) nomination, *Grand Canyon Reader Award* (Arizona) nomination, and *Sasquatch Award* (Washington) nomination.

852. Cushman, Karen. *The Ballad of Lucy Whipple.* Clarion, 1996. 210pp. ISBN 978-0-395-72806-2; Trophy, 1998, paper ISBN 978-0-06-440684-0. Grades 5–8. In Lucky Diggins, California, Lucy (California Morning) Whipple and her mother run a boardinghouse in a huge tent. Lucy wants to return to civilized New England but she has to earn the money for the journey. She writes letters to her relatives describing the horrors of the place, but after three years, during which her brother dies and her mother remarries, she grows used to the people and decides that California is her real home. *School Library Journal Best Book, Emphasis on Reading* (Alabama) nomination, *Children's Book Award* (Georgia) nomination, *Lincoln Award*

(Illinois) nomination, *William Allen White Award* (Kansas) nomination, *Children's Book Award* (Massachusetts) nomination, *Thumbs Up Award* (Michigan) nomination, *Garden State Teen Book Award* (New Jersey) nomination, *Young Readers' Award* (Nevada) nomination, *Sequoyah Book Award* (Oklahoma) nomination, *Young Reader's Choice Award* (Pennsylvania) nomination, *Junior Book Award* (South Carolina) nomination, *Volunteer State Book Award* (Tennessee) nomination, and *Notable Children's Trade Books in Social Studies.*

853. Cushman, Karen. *Rodzina.* Houghton, 2003. 215pp. ISBN 978-0-618-13351-2; Yearling, 2005, paper ISBN 978-0-440-41993-8. Grades 4–7. Polish American orphan Rodzina Clara Jadwiga Anastazya Brodski, 12, boards an Orphan Train in Chicago in March 1881. On the journey, she develops attachments to her traveling companions and hopes there will be good homes for them all. However, she soon finds herself in a series of bad situations, first as a servant in Grand Island, Nebraska, and then as a replacement wife and mother near Cheyenne, Wyoming. She eventually finds the best place for her with the distant and cold female doctor who oversees the train. *Spur Awards* nomination, *Pennsylvania Young Reader's Choice Award* nomination, *Beehive Children's Fictional Book* (Utah) Award nomination, *Dorothy Canfield Fisher Children's Book Award* (Vermont) nomination, *Charlie May Simon Children's Book Award* (Arkansas) nomination, *Wyoming Indian Paintbrush Book Award* nomination, *Garden State Children's Book Awards* (New Jersey) nomination, *Washington State Book Award, William Allen White Children's Book Award* (Kansas) nomination, *Bluegrass Award* (Kentucky) nomination, *Sequoyah Book Award* (Oklahoma) nomination, *Parents' Choice Gold Award, Booklist Editor's Choice,* and *Pacific Northwest Young Reader's Award* nomination.

854. DeFelice, Cynthia. *Bringing Ezra Back.* Farrar, 2006. 147pp. ISBN 978-0-374-39939-9. Grades 4–6. In the sequel to *Weasel* set in 1840, 12-year-old Nathan Fowler travels from his Ohio frontier farm—with peddler Owen Beckwith—to Western Pennsylvania to rescue his friend Ezra, whom the evil Weasel left alive but mute. When Nathan finds Ezra and gets him away from the owners of a freak show who have been keeping him captive, both Ezra and Beckwith help Nathan to regain some of his ability to trust.

855. DeFelice, Cynthia. *Weasel.* Aladdin, 2009. 119pp. Paper ISBN 978-0-689-83281-9. Grades 5 up. Eleven-year-old Nathan is left in charge of his sister and their cabin when his father goes hunting in 1839. His father has been gone much longer than expected when a strange man arrives at their door and shows them their dead mother's locket. With some trepidation, they follow him and find their father, wounded by an animal trap. The perpetrator is Weasel, a white Indian hunter who has become deranged. Nathan then must survive his own encounter with Weasel.

856. De Ruiz, Dana Catharine. *To Fly with the Swallows: A Story of Old California.* Illustrated by Debbe Heller. Steck-Vaughn, 1994. 53pp. Paper ISBN 978-0-8114-8074-1. Grades 5–9. In 1806, at the age of 15, Concha (María de la Concepción Arguello y Morago) lived with her family in San Francisco, where her father was commander of the Presidio, defending Spain's New World empire on the northern border of Alta California. Nikolai Petrovich Rezanov arrived from St. Petersburg, requesting supplies for his ship. He and Concha fell in love and wanted to marry. However, Rezanov was not Catholic. He left to get approval from the czar, the king of Spain, and the pope in Italy. After five years Concha received word of his death. She never married and spent her life dedicated to Saint Francis and helping those who needed her in childbirth, sickness, and death. At 60, she became California's first nun. Epilogue, Afterword, and Notes.

857. Deutsch, Stacia, and Rhody Cohon. *Sacagawea's Strength.* Illustrated by David T. Wenzel. (Blast to the Past) Aladdin, 2006. 124pp. Paper ISBN 978-1-41691-270-5. Grades 2–5. Abigail, Jacob, Zack, and Bo know that Sacagawea (ca. 1788–1812) had a dream. They are not sure what it is, but they travel back in time to find out. They discover that she, a Shoshone woman, helped Lewis and Clark map a route across the West to the Pacific.

858. Durbin, William. *Blackwater Ben.* Random, 2005. 160pp. Paper ISBN 978-0-440-42008-8. Grades 5–8. Ben, 13, drops out of 7th grade in 1898 to spend the winter with his father, who is the cook at Blackwater Logging Camp in Minnesota. Ben works in the kitchen but would prefer to be out with the loggers. Another boy, an orphan named Nevers, joins the cooking team and tells stories that give Ben some perspective, although he is still eager to find out more about his dead mother.

859. Durrant, Lynda. *The Sun, the Rain, and the Apple Seed: A Novel of Johnny Appleseed's Life.* Houghton, 2003. 208pp. ISBN 978-0-618-23487-5. Grades 5–9. In the early 1780s John Chapman, nicknamed "Johnny Appleseed," watched apples grow near his family's cabin in Longmeadow, Massachusetts. In 1799, on a visit to an apple cider press, he thought God told him to take apple seeds to settlers in Ohio, Indiana, and Illinois. He took few possessions on his journey, and planted trees to feed the pioneers for many years.

860. Edwards, David. *The Pen that Pa Built.* Illustrated by Ashley Wolff. Tricycle, 2007. Unpaged. ISBN 978-1-58246-153-3. Grades K–2. Rhyming text in the cumulative style of "The House that Jack Built" describes the process of making wool, from shearing to carding, spinning, and dyeing, and finally weaving. Woodcuts depict an 1800s farm and introduce a family of four.

861. Ellsworth, Loretta. *The Shrouding Woman.* Henry Holt, 2002. 151pp. ISBN 978-0-8050-6651-7; 2007, paper ISBN 978-0-8050-8185-5. Grades 4–8. Aunt Flo comes to live with Evie, 11, and her younger sister Mae in Crooked Creek Valley, Minnesota, after their mother dies of consumption in the mid-1800s. Mae welcomes Aunt Flo but Evie has difficulty accepting her and especially detests Flo's job of preparing bodies for burial. When Evie's father tells her that this skill is passed down through generations, Evie worries about having to do it herself. *Rebecca Caudill Young Readers Book Award* (Illinois) nomination.

862. Erdrich, Louise. *The Birchbark House.* Hyperion, 2002. 244pp. Paper ISBN 978-0-7868-1454-1. Grades 4–8. In 1847, 7-year-old Omakayas lives with her Ojibwa tribe on an island in Lake Superior. But *chimookoman* (non-Indian white) men force the tribe to move from their land. The four parts of the story cover the seasons and what happens beginning in the summer. Readers learn what Omakayas ate, where the food was grown and cooked, how they built the birchbark house, and the boredom of scraping hides. She likes the traditions of maple sugaring in the spring and winter night storytelling and interacting with her family and those in the village, especially Old Tallow, a bear-hunting woman. But after the men come, so does a French voyager who brings smallpox to the village from which Omakayas' little brother subsequently dies. Illustrations complement the text. *Hornbook Fanfare* and *Capitol Choices Noteworthy Titles* (Washington, D.C.).

863. Erdrich, Louise. *The Game of Silence.* HarperCollins, 2005. 272pp. ISBN 978-0-06-029789-3. Grades 3–7. Ojibwe Omakayas, 9, enjoys her life with her family on Lake Superior's Madeline Island. In the fall, everyone stores food for the winter and they return to their cabins. In the winter, the adults tell stories. Old Tallow is there, and Angeline, Omakayas's sister beads a coat for her boyfriend. In the spring, Omakayas has her spirit quest. In the summer, they care for starving relatives. But white men come in 1849 and change their lives by moving the entire tribe west. Scott O'Dell Award for Historical Fiction *Nene Award* (Hawaii) nomination, *Great Lakes Children's Book Award* (Michigan) nomination,*Battle of the Books Award* (Wisconsin) nomination, *Kirkus Reviews Editor's Choice, Booklist Editor's Choice,* and *Capitol Choices Noteworthy Titles* (Washington, D.C.).

864. Erdrich, Louise. *The Porcupine Year.* HarperCollins, 2008. 208pp. ISBN 978-0-06-029787-9. Grades 5–9. In this sequel, set in 1852, to *The Birchbark House* and *The Game of Silence,* 12-year-old Omakayas and her brother Pinch are separated from her Ojibwe family when they are swept down rapids during a night hunting expedition. Pinch has an encounter with a porcupine and decides to keep it as his medicine animal as they make their way back to the family campsite. The family continues to search for a new place to live—the United States government has taken away their land and created strife between the tribes. They fear a winter with nothing to eat, but finally reach a big lake where the larger tribe has set up camp. Throughout, Omakayas is making the transition to womanhood and finding challenges there too. *Capitol Choices Noteworthy Titles* (Washington, D.C.).

865. Ernst, Kathleen. *Secrets in the Hills: A Josefina Mystery.* American Girl, 2006. 183pp. Paper ISBN 978-1-59369-097-7. Grades 4–7. In the 1820s Josefina has heard there is gold and silver buried in the hills near her New Mexico home, but she never thought the stories were true. Then a stranger shows up needing medical help, and she, studying to be a *curandera*, or healer, tries to cure him. He invites her to look for the treasure with him.

866. **Fern, Tracey.** *Buffalo Music.* Clarion, 2008. 32pp. ISBN 978-0-618-72341-6. Grades K–2. This fictionalized account told from the point of view of Molly is based on the life of Mary Ann Goodnight (d. 1926), an early conservationist, who helped to save the buffalo from extinction. Molly hears huge buffalo herds when she and her husband settle in the Texas Panhandle in 1876. Hunters soon arrive and within six years there are hardly any buffalo left in their canyon. She raises two orphan calves, and cowhands bring her more, which she protects from wolves and poachers. *School Library Journal Best Books for Children.*

867. **Ferris, Jean.** *Much Ado About Grubstake.* Harcourt, 2006. 265pp. ISBN 978-0-15-205706-0. Grades 5–8. In Grubstake, Colorado, in 1888, a stranger wants to buy all the mines in town. Arley, a 16-year-old orphan who has inherited her father's mine and boarding house, is suspicious of his motives. What is so valuable in the mines? She investigates and discovers that there is osblindium in her mines. A group of eccentric characters help her rid the town of this unwelcome buyer.

868. **Figley, Marty Rhodes.** *The Schoolchildren's Blizzard.* Illustrated by Shelly O. Haas. (On My Own History) Carolrhoda, 2004. 48pp. ISBN 978-1-57505-586-2. Grades 2–5. On January 12, 1888, schoolteacher Minnie Freeman saves her students from an unexpected Nebraska blizzard. Sarah, 9, her younger sister Annie, 7, and their classmates follow her to safety. When the children left home that morning, the warm weather lulled them into thinking they were safe. But the wind and snow blow off the roof of the sod schoolhouse, and Miss Freeman must tie the sixteen children together with a long rope to guide them to shelter. Based on a true story. Watercolors enhance the text.

869. **Finley, Mary Peace.** *Soaring Eagle.* Eakin, 1998. 166pp. Paper ISBN 978-1-57168-281-9. Grades 5–8. In 1845 blond-haired, green-eyed Julio Montoya, 13, is curious about his background—he looks very different from the rest of his Mexican family. His father is killed by Apaches on a trip the two are making on the Santa Fe Trail, leaving Julio to cope alone with a snowstorm, a wolf attack, and then snowblindness. Cheyenne Indians find him, nurse him back to health, and claim him as one of their own. Still wondering about his childhood, Julio adapts to this new tribe and earns his own name, Soaring Eagle.

870. **Fleischman, Sid.** *The Ghost in the Noonday Sun.* Illustrated by Peter Sís. Trophy, 2007. 144pp. Paper ISBN 978-0-06-134502-9. Grades 4–7. On Oliver Finch's 12th birthday, while he awaits his father's return from a three-year whaling voyage, another captain kidnaps him, takes him on his ship, and tells him to find the ghost that is hoarding gold. Oliver and a sailor eventually foil the captain by hitting him on the head, making him think he is dead and seeing the ghost when he is actually looking at Oliver and his sidekick. They escape from the ship with food instead of booty, and another ship rescues them.

871. **Fleischman, Sid.** *The Giant Rat of Sumatra: or, Pirates Galore.* Illustrated by John Hendrix. Greenwillow, 2005. 208pp. ISBN 978-0-06-074238-6; Trophy, 2006, paper ISBN 978-0-06-074240-9. Grades 5–8. In 1846, 12-year-old Edmund Amos Peters, often known as "Shipwreck," finds himself involved with pirates in California during the United States' war with Mexico.

872. **Fleischman, Sid.** *Jim Ugly.* Greenwillow, 1992. 130pp. ISBN 978-0-688-10886-1; 2003, paper ISBN 978-0-06-052121-9. Grades 4–7. Jake, 12, begins his story at his father's 1894 burial in the Old West. He tries to get his father's dog, Jim Ugly, to follow him but the dog leads Jake instead. He shows Jake that his father is still alive but hiding from someone who wants to kill him. Jim Ugly helps Jake and his father escape the villains and encourages a romance between Jake's father and a lovely actress.

873. **Frederick, Heather Vogel.** *The Voyage of Patience Goodspeed.* Aladdin, 2004. 219pp. Paper ISBN 978-0-689-84869-8. Grades 4–6. Captain Goodspeed takes his children Patience, 12, and Tad, 6, on his whaling ship after their mother dies in Nantucket in 1835. Initially reluctant, Patience soon settles in and enjoys her father's lessons on navigation. When there is a mutiny and the captain and Tad are left on an island, Patience uses her new skill to rescue her father and brother. *Young Reader's Award* (Arizona) nomination, *Nutmeg Children's Book Award* (Connecticut) nomination, *Student Book Award* (Maine) nomination, and *Sequoyah Book Award* (Oklahoma) nomination.

874. **Fritz, Jean.** ***The Cabin Faced West.*** Illustrated by Feodor Rojankovsky. Coward, 1998. 124pp. ISBN 978-0-399-23223-7; Puffin, 1987, paper ISBN 978-0-698-11936-9. Grades 4–7. Ann and her family move from Gettysburg in 1784 to the wilderness frontier of Pennsylvania. She misses her friends, so her mother promises they will take time off from their work when an occasion for a party arises. One evening a stranger comes to visit, and they have a wonderful party. When the guest leaves, she is happy that she lives on Hamilton Hill. Their guest was George Washington.

875. **Fuchs, Bernie.** ***Ride Like the Wind: A Tale of the Pony Express.*** Blue Sky, 2004. 32pp. ISBN 978-0-439-26645-1. Grades K–4. Johnny Free rides his horse JennySoo for the Pony Express in Nevada in 1861. Seven Paiute warriors attack them, and an arrow knocks Johnny off JennySoo. She continues to the next station with the mail but then runs back to find Johnny. When Paiute attack again, Johnny's Paiute friend, Little Grey, rescues them.

876. **Giblin, James Cross.** ***The Boy Who Saved Cleveland: Based on a True Story.*** Illustrated by Michael Dooling. Henry Holt, 2006. 64pp. ISBN 978-0-8050-7355-3. Grades 3–4. In 1798 a malaria epidemic hits the three cabins that make up Cleveland, Ohio, at that time. Seth Doan, 10, is the only one left in his family with the strength to carry water, help the sick, and haul corn two miles uphill to be ground for the day's food. He does the same for his sick neighbors. Seth reads the Bible stories he loves in between his hauling and healing. Illustrations complement the text.

877. **Gipson, Fred.** ***Old Yeller.*** Illustrated by Carl Burger. HarperPerennial, 2001. 184pp. Paper ISBN 978-0-06-093547-4. Grades 4–8. When Travis is 14 in the 1860s, his father departs for Florida and leaves him in charge of the Texas family homestead. When an old dog arrives, his brother and mother want to keep it, calling it "Old Yeller." Although Travis does not initially want the dog, Old Yeller saves him from wild hogs. However, a wild wolf later bites Old Yeller, and Travis must kill him because he develops hydrophobia (rabies) after the bite. This book was first published in 1956. *Newbery Honor* and *American Library Association Notable Children's Books.*

878. **Gray, Dianne E.** ***Holding Up the Earth.*** Houghton, 2000. 210pp. ISBN 978-0-618-00703-5; 2006, paper ISBN 978-0-618-73747-5. Grades 5–8. Having lived in seven foster homes since her mother's death, 14-year-old Hope now visits the Nebraska farm of her new foster mother, Sarah. There she learns about previous generations of girls who lived on this land and the personal and social challenges they faced. *Mark Twain Award* (Missouri) nomination and *Student Book Award* (Maine) nomination.

879. **Gray, Dianne E.** ***Together Apart.*** Houghton, 2002. 193pp. ISBN 978-0-618-18721-8. Grades 5–9. Still grieving the death of her brothers in the deadly "School Children's Blizzard" of 1888, 14-year-old Hannah goes to work for a wealthy widow, Eliza Moore, in Prairie Hill, Nebraska. There she meets Isaac, who is also escaping demons. The two help the feminist Moore print weekly editions of the *Women's Gazette* and find a place for working women to meet. As they tell their stories in alternating chapters, they fall in love with Isaac admitting his feelings and Hannah denying hers.

880. **Greenwood, Barbara.** ***Gold Rush Fever: A Story of the Klondike, 1898.*** Illustrated by Heather Collins. Kids Can, 2001. 160pp. Paper ISBN 978-1-55074-850-5. Grades 4–7. Tim Olsen, 13, and his older brother Roy trek from Seattle to the Yukon to find their fortune during the Klondike gold rush. They face many challenges—frostbite, heavy loads, hard labor, sheer bad luck, and cabin fever. They meet dance hall girls and Mounted Police. Photographs highlight the text. Glossary and Index.

881. **Gregory, Kristiana.** ***Across the Wide and Lonesome Prairie: The Oregon Trail Diary of Hattie Campbell.*** (Dear America) Scholastic, 1997. 164pp. ISBN 978-1-59519-464-0. Grades 3–7. In 1847, after her older sisters die, 13-year-old Hattie Campbell travels with her parents and two younger brothers from Missouri to Oregon. They cross the prairies on the Oregon Trail and try to speed up after news of the Donner party reaches them. The dreadful weather, diseases, and deaths make their journey seem almost unbearable, but the births and weddings keep them going for eight months. Hattie keeps a diary of her experiences.

882. Gregory, Kristiana. *The Legend of Jimmy Spoon.* (Great Episodes) Gulliver, 2002. 164pp. Paper ISBN 978-0-15-206776-9. Grades 5–8. Bored with working in his father's store in the Mormon stronghold of Utah in 1854, Jimmy, 12, agrees to go with two Shoshoni boys to their home when they promise to give him a horse. He does not realize that they expect him to live with the tribe until he proves his manhood and earns the horse. He stays, and he eventually earns enough respect so that whether he leaves or stays becomes his own decision.

883. Gregory, Kristiana. *Seeds of Hope: The Gold Rush Diary of Susanna Fairchild, 1849.* Scholastic, 2001. 186pp. ISBN 978-0-590-51157-5. Grades 4–8. In 1849 Susanna Fairchild, 14, accompanies her mother and father on a journey to Oregon, where he plans to establish a medical practice. But her mother dies and her father loses his money on the steamship journey from New York and he decides to search for gold in California. Susanna keeps a diary of her experiences. She misses her mother, sees injustice parading as frontier justice, and observes abuse of animals. Maps and historical notes.

884. Gregory, Kristiana. *The Stowaway: A Tale of California Pirates.* Apple, 1997. 144pp. Paper ISBN 978-0-590-48823-5. Grades 4–6. In the early 1800s in Monterey, California, 11-year-old Carlito sees pirates kill his father. Determined to avenge him, Carlito stows away on the ship of the attacker, Argentinian privateer Hippolyte de Bouchard. Carlito faces many challenges and experiences many adventures but eventually returns safely home to his mother and his horse.

885. Hahn, Mary Downing. *The Gentleman Outlaw and Me—Eli: A Story of the Old West.* Clarion, 1996. 190pp. ISBN 978-0-395-73083-6; 2007, paper ISBN 978-0-618-83000-8. Grades 4–7. Eliza Yates, an orphan, disguises herself as a boy (Elijah) and heads west in search of her father. She joins up en route with a dubious young man called Calvin Featherbone, aka the Gentleman Outlaw. The two of them enjoy various escapades and risk being hanged as horse thieves.

886. Hale, Marian. *Dark Water Rising.* Henry Holt, 2006. 233pp. ISBN 978-0-8050-7585-4. Grades 5 up. In 1900, 16-year-old Seth Braeden wants to be a skilled carpenter. Then his father decides to move the family to Galveston, Texas, where he might be able to attend college. He meets and falls in love with Ella Rose and decides that moving was a good idea. However, on September 8, a horrible storm changes their lives. In one of the worst natural disasters in the nation, more than 8,000 people die and 3,600 homes are destroyed. Seth struggles to survive during the storm and worries about the safety of his loved ones. *Young Readers' Choice Award* (Louisiana) nomination and *Lone Star Reading List* (Texas).

887. Hart, Alison. *Anna's Blizzard.* Peachtree, 2005. 156pp. ISBN 978-1-56145-349-8. Grades 3–5. In 1888, 11-year-old Anna Vail and her classmates are trapped inside their Nebraska schoolhouse while a blizzard rages outside. She's not a top student but she does know how to ride her pony and herd sheep. Her expertise helps her lead her classmates out of the school and through the snow to the nearest house. This storm later becomes known as the "Schoolchildren's Blizzard" because many children who were trapped away from home died.

888. Hemphill, Helen. *The Adventurous Deeds of Deadwood Jones.* Front Street, 2008. 228pp. ISBN 978-1-59078-637-6. Grades 5–7. In April 1876, 13-year-old African American Prometheus Jones and his 11-year-old cousin Omer Shine flee Tennessee after the Dill brothers accuse them of stealing a winning raffle ticket with which Prometheus won Good Eye, a half-blind black stallion. They join a cattle drive hoping to get to Texas where Prometheus might find his father, who was sold to a Texas man before slavery ended. The drive goes north to Dakota Territory, however, and they have a series of adventures. Prometheus is a superb shot and rider and is known for his good luck.

889. Hermes, Patricia. *A Perfect Place: Joshua's Oregon Trail Diary, Book Two.* (My America) Scholastic, 2002. 108pp. ISBN 978-0-439-19999-5. Grades 3–5. In 1848, 9-year-old Joshua

McCullough (introduced in *Westward to Home*) starts a second journal recording events as his family arrives in Willamette Valley, Oregon Territory. The winter rains and floods have started and they must live in tents waiting for the ground to be ready for building. Then Joshua's grandfather drowns. Not until spring does life change for the better.

890. **Hermes, Patricia.** *Westward to Home: Joshua's Oregon Trail Diary.* (My America) Scholastic, 2002. 108pp. Paper ISBN 978-0-439-38899-3. Grades 4–7. In his March 1, 1848, diary entry, Joshua Martin McCullough, 9, shares his excitement about leaving for Oregon Territory from St. Joseph, Missouri. His father wants to take the family west because he believes President Polk's words that people should fulfill their Manifest Destiny by spreading across the country. On the trail they face dust, illness, deaths in other families, possessions lost in water, heat, hunger, and rain. Joshua proudly kills a buffalo and then overcomes his fear of water to jump in and rescue his younger sister Becky. After seven months and 2,000 miles, the family reaches its destination.

891. **Holm, Jennifer L.** *Boston Jane: An Adventure.* HarperTrophy, 2002. 273pp. Paper ISBN 978-0-064-40849-3. Grades 5 up. In 1854 Philadelphian Jennifer Peck, 16, takes a ship to the Northwest to wed her true love, William Baldt. Her time at Miss Hepplewhite's Young Ladies Academy has prepared her for neither the trip nor the rough life among the American traders and the Chinook Indians. She has to change and become Boston Jane, a fearless woman of the frontier.

892. **Holm, Jennifer L.** *Boston Jane: The Claim.* HarperCollins, 2004. 240pp. ISBN 978-0-06-029045-0. Grades 5 up. In the third and final volume of the Boston Jane trilogy, Jane Beck's Philadelphia nemesis, Sally Biddle, comes to Shoalwater Bay in 1850. Sally tries to cause trouble for Jane and, to make the situation more difficult, Jane's former fiance, William Baldt, returns to the Washington Territory to have Jane's homestead claim declared invalid. He also plans to help the governor relocate the Chinook population and tries to turn the settlers against these natives. During these trials, Jane works as a concierge at the local hotel and loves Jehu, the young sailor she met on her trip West. She also helps to find a Chinook child a safe foster home.

893. **Hopkinson, Deborah.** *Apples to Oregon.* Illustrated by Nancy Carpenter. Atheneum, 2004. Unpaged. ISBN 978-0-689-84769-1; Aladdin, 2008, paper ISBN 978-1-416-96746-0. Grades K–3. In 1847, when Papa leaves Iowa for Oregon, he takes peach, plum, and apple saplings for his new garden. His daughter, Delicious, and the seven other children must protect the saplings on the Oregon Trail. They keep them from drowning in a river, from being smashed by hailstones, from withering during a drought, and from freezing in the cold. The story is based on Henderson Luelling, who hauled hundreds of trees from Iowa to Oregon with his family in 1847 and started a nursery. *Diamond Primary Book Award* (Arkansas) nomination, *Read-Aloud Book Award* (Indiana) nomination, *Young Hoosier Book Award* (Indiana) nomination, *Young Readers Choice Book Award* (Louisiana) nomination, *Black-Eyed Susan Picture Book Award* (Maryland) nomination, *Great Lakes Children's Book Award* (Michigan) nomination, *Show Me State Book Award* (Missouri) nomination, *American Library Association Notable Children's Books*, *Children's Book Award* (North Carolina) nomination, *Picture Book Award* (South Carolina) nomination, *School Library Journal Best Books of the Year*, *Volunteer State Book Award* (Tennessee) nomination, *Publishers Weekly Best Children's Books*, and *Children's Book Award* (West Virginia) nomination.

894. **Hopkinson, Deborah.** *Cabin in the Snow.* Illustrated by Patrick Faricy. Aladdin, 2002. 80pp. Paper ISBN 978-0-689-84351-8. Grades 2–4. Just as a snowstorm begins in the 1850s, Charlie Keller, 9, and Papa set out to return home from Lawrence, Kansas, with their supplies. They see a group of pro-slavery men arguing with free-soil farmers, and Papa thinks he should stay in case the "free-soilers" need more men to protect themselves. He sends Charlie home with the team. When Charlie runs into Mr. Morgan and his daughter Flory, who need a safe place to stay, he wants to ignore them because they are pro-slave and approve of everything that Charlie's family hates. But as the blizzard starts and his mother goes into an early labor with the new baby, Charlie has to trust that having them come to their house to stay and help is the right decision.

895. **Hopkinson, Deborah.** *Into the Firestorm: A Novel of San Francisco, 1906.* Knopf, 2006. 200pp. ISBN 978-0-375-83652-7; Yearling, 2008, paper ISBN 978-0-440-42129-0. Grades 3–6. Orphaned Nicholas Dray, 11, runs away from Texas to San Francisco in 1906. He finds a job in a stationery store and when something rattles the shop on an April morning while the owner is out, Nicholas realizes he should try to save the valuables, especially his employer's dog, Shake. He also helps local rooming house boarders escape through the fires that followed the massive quake. Bibliography.

896. **Hopkinson, Deborah.** *A Packet of Seeds.* Illustrated by Bethanne Andersen. Harpercollins, 2004. 32pp. ISBN 978-0-06-009089-0. Grades 1–4. Annie's mother has been unhappy since her pioneer family left home. Annie tries to think of something to cheer her up after the birth of her sister and, with Pa and her brother Jim, she clears the earth so her Momma can plant something. Her mother remembers her sister's parting gift—packets of hollyhock, larkspur, poppy, and daisy seeds. The garden helps revive Momma's spirits. *Diamond Primary Book Award* (Arkansas) nomination and *Golden Sower Award* (Nebraska) nomination.

897. **Hopkinson, Deborah.** *Stagecoach Sal.* Illustrated by Carson Ellis. Hyperion, 2009. 40pp. ISBN 978-1-4231-1149-8. Grades 1–3. Stagecoach Sal likes to ride "shotgun" with her father when he transports passengers and mail in California during the nineteenth century. Her constant singing seems to soothe passengers and keep them from complaining. Stung by hornets one day, her father cannot take the mail, and Sal offers her service. With no passengers scheduled, her parents fear that the polite robber called Poetic Pete will take her cargo. He does arrive, but Sal puts him in shotgun and sings "Sweet Betsy from Pike" and "Polly Wally Doodle" nonstop throughout the night. When he eventually nods off, she delivers him to jail (the "hoosegow"). The story is based loosely on Delia Haskett Rawson (1861-1949), the only known woman stagecoach driver. Brown ink drawings and wash complement the text. Note.

898. **Hopkinson, Deborah, and Kimberly Bulcken Root.** *Birdie's Lighthouse.* Aladdin, 2000. 32pp. Paper ISBN 978-0-689-83529-2. Grades K–3. In the early 1800s, Birdie watches her father tend the lighthouse on their tiny and desolate island home. When he becomes sick, she is able to keep the lights burning. Her bravery keeps lost ships from wrecking. *Bulletin for the Center of Children's Books Blue Ribbon.*

899. **Hotze, Sollace.** *A Circle Unbroken.* Clarion, 1991. 202pp. Paper ISBN 978-0-395-59702-6. Grades 5–8. When she is 17, Rachel's father steals her back from the Dakota Sioux tribe that seized her when she was 10. He wants to hear nothing about her life as Kata Wi and refuses to acknowledge that her kidnapping ever occurred. She enjoys her siblings and her stepmother but remembers the kindness and love of her other family. She becomes ill and fears for her life. Her Aunt Sarah, who was also held by Indians for seven years, died after her return. Rachel decides she must go back to her Indian family. *Carl Sandburg Literary Arts Award.*

900. **Howard, Ellen.** *The Log Cabin Church.* Illustrated by Ronald Himler. Holiday House, 2002. Unpaged. ISBN 978-0-8234-1740-7. Grades K–3. On the Michigan frontier, settlers wonder if they have enough people to build a church. Young Elvirey is interested in the idea and tries to remember what a church actually is—she realizes she associates this with her mother's funeral.

901. **Howard, Ellen.** *The Log Cabin Wedding.* Illustrated by Ronald Himler. Holiday House, 2006. Unpaged. ISBN 978-0-8234-1989-0. Grades 3–4. Elvira ("Elvirey") Freshwater's grandmother and brother Bud are not well, so she suggests to her father that he ask the Widow Aiken and her sons to help with the harvest. She does not expect her father to fall in love with the widow, and she is angry when he does. She eventually realizes that the Aiken family is a good one and that it would be nice to have them in her home in the Michigan woods. The pencil drawings enhance the text.

902. **Hunt, L. J.** *The Abernathy Boys.* HarperCollins, 2004. 208pp. ISBN 978-0-06-440953-7. Grades 4–8. Bud Abernathy, 9, and his brother Temple, 5, ride their horses from Oklahoma to Santa Fe, New Mexico, and back without an adult in August 1909. They meet wolves, rattlesnakes, kindly outlaws, and scorpions. They also ride through dust storms. But they achieve their goal of exploring the "caprock" or the "Great American Desert." Illustrations complement the text. *Young Readers Choice Book Award* (Pennsylvania) nomination.

903. Kay, Verla. *Covered Wagons, Bumpy Trails.* Penguin, 2000. 32pp. ISBN 978-0-399-22928-2. Grades K–3. Four four-syllable rhymes per page tell the story of family members Mother, Father, and Baby John, as they journey by wagon from Independence, Missouri, through the Rocky and Sierra Mountains and across the desert to their new home in the Sacramento Valley of California. During the five-month journey, they endure storms and snows, the oxen lose weight, and Baby John becomes a toddler. Watercolor and gouache illustrations on marbleized paper create the landscape. Map. *Young Readers' Award* (Nevada) nomination.

904. Kay, Verla. *Gold Fever.* Illustrated by S. D. Schindler. Putnam, 1999. 32pp. ISBN 978-0-399-23027-1; Puffin, 2003, paper ISBN 978-0-14-250183-2. Grades K–3. Jasper, a farmer, hears about California's gold rush in 1849, and rushes off, leaving his family behind. On his journey he encounters grizzlies, dust storms, and vultures. At his destination, instead of riches he finds many discouraging hardships. He returns home to his farm and kisses his cow, happy to be back. Colored pencil illustrations highlight the rhyming text with details of the mining process.

905. Kay, Verla. *Iron Horses.* Illustrated by Michael McCurdy. Penguin, 1999. 32pp. ISBN 978-0-399-23119-3. Grades K–3. The men working on the Union Pacific Railroad rush to meet those working on the Central Pacific Railroad in Utah during the 1860s. The weather extremes, bunking on railroad car roofs, and hanging in baskets over rocky outcrops made life difficult and dangerous for those who brought the tracks together, forming the first transcontinental rail line. This shortened the trip across the country from six months to six days. Scratchboard and watercolor drawings on double-page drawings augment the rhyming text.

906. Kay, Verla. *The Orphan Train.* Illustrated by Ken Stark. Penguin, 2003. 32pp. ISBN 978-0-399-23613-6. Grades K–3. Orphaned in the early 1900s when their parents die from typhoid fever, Lucy, Harold, and David live on the streets until they find an orphanage that will take them. What they do not realize is that they will then be transported to the Midwest on an Orphan Train, each of them to go to a separate home, chosen by a family at one of the train stops. Although they are in different families, Harold and Lucy see each other at church. They are separated from David and wonder if they will ever see him again. Impressionistic illustrations augment the text.

907. Kelly, Jacqueline. *The Evolution of Calpurnia Tate.* Henry Holt, 2009. 340pp. ISBN 978-0-8050-8841-0. Grades 5–8. In 1899, Callie, 12, loves observing animals and keeping careful notes about what she sees; she hates needlework and cooking. As the only girl in a family of seven living fifty miles from Austin, Texas, she slowly discovers that her grandfather who generally hides in a shed called his "laboratory," is a naturalist who has actually corresponded with Charles Darwin and owns *On the Origin of the Species.* The two begin observing nature together, and when they find an unidentified vetch, they send it to the Smithsonian for classification. Throughout, Callie enjoys her brothers and tries to be obedient, her main pleasure is hypothesizing about things and experimenting to find out if she is correct. *Newbury Award* Honor Book, *American Library Association Notable Children's Books, Booklist Editors Choice, School Library Journal Best Books Of The Year, Capitol Choices Noteworthy Titles* (Washington, D.C.), *Bank Street College Of Education Book Award* winner, *Lonestar Young Adult Reading List*(Texas) nomination, *Beehive Childrens Book Award* (Utah) nomination, *American Library Association Best Books for Young Adults, Bulletin Blue Ribbon,* and *Dorothy Canfield Fisher Childrens Book Award* (Vermont) nomination.

908. Kent, Deborah. *Riding the Pony Express.* (Saddles, Stars and Stripes) Kingfisher, 2006. 149pp. ISBN 978-0-7534-6001-6. Grades 3–7. Lexie Mcdonald, 15, becomes an orphan when her father dies unexpectedly. Her brother, Callum, has been unjustly accused of theft while working for the Pony Express, and instead of going to live with her aunt in New York City, she goes in search of Callum. Dressed as a boy, she takes her favorite horse on her quest.

909. Kinsey-Warnock, Natalie. *Lumber Camp Library.* Illustrated by James Bernardin. Trophy, 2003. 96pp. Paper ISBN 978-0-06-444292-3. Grades 3–6. Ten-year-old Ruby Sawyer wants to be a teacher, but when her father dies in a logging accident she must stay home from school to look after her ten brothers and sisters. She meets a blind woman, Mrs. Graham, who has a library and loves learning. She agrees to share her books and house if Ruby and her family will help with her household chores. Illustrations augment the text. *Sunshine State Young Reader Award* (Florida) nomination, *Children's Choice Book Award* (Iowa) nomination, *William Allen White Children's Book Award* (Kansas) nomination, *Children's Book Award* (Massachusetts) nomination, *Maud Hart Lovelace Book Award* (Minnesota) nomination, *Garden State Fiction Book Award* (New Jersey) nomination, *Young Reader Award* (Nevada) nomination, *Children's Book Award* (South Carolina) nomination, and *Prairie Bud Award* (South Dakota) nomination.

910. Kirkpatrick, Katherine. *The Voyage of the Continental.* Holiday House, 2002. 297pp. ISBN 978-0-8234-1580-9. Grades 5–9. In 1866, 16-year-old orphan Emeline McCullough seeks a better life than working in the mills of Lowell, Massachusetts. Asa Mercer offers to resettle her, with other orphan daughters and Union soldier widows, in Seattle, Washington. They board the steamship *Continental* for the long voyage round the tip of South America. On arrival in Seattle, Emeline discovers that Mercer planned to sell the women to lonely settlers as brides. She recounts the intrigue and romance of this adventure in her diary.

911. Klass, Sheila S. *A Shooting Star: A Novel About Annie Oakley.* Holiday House, 1996. 192pp. ISBN 978-0-8234-1279-2. Grades 4–7. After her father dies when she is 9, Phoebe Anne Moses (Annie Oakley, 1860–1926) shoots a rabbit to feed her hungry family. Her Quaker mother does not believe females should shoot and soon the family has no money to survive. Oakley goes to a poor house and lives on a farm as an indentured servant, starving and abused. She runs away and, back home, provides for the family with her hunting skill. Oakley eventually gains fame as a sharpshooter. When she challenges and beats a champion shooter, Mr. Butler of a traveling Wild West show, he decides to marry her and feature her in his show. *Nutmeg Children's Book Award* (Connecticut) nomination.

912. Kudlinski, Kathleen. *Facing West: A Story of the Oregon Trail.* Illustrated by James Watling. Puffin, 1996. 54pp. Paper ISBN 978-0-14-036914-4. Grades 2–6. In 1845 Ben and his family begin their journey from Missouri to Oregon, a 2,000-mile trek via covered wagon. They face the same hazards as other pioneer families before them—snakes, illness, bears, rolling off cliffs, and washing down rivers—and Ben has the added problem of being asthmatic. He worries about being able to cope.

913. LaFaye, A. *Worth.* Simon & Schuster, 2004. 160pp. ISBN 978-0-689-85730-0; Aladdin, 2006, paper ISBN 978-1-416-91624-6. Grades 3–7. In the late 19th century, Nathaniel Peale, 11, breaks his leg and cannot work on his family's Nebraska farm. His father brings an orphan, John Worth, home from the Orphan Train to help, a situation that annoys Nate. Eventually the two learn to help each other when Nate finds out that John's family died in a tenement fire. *Booklist Editor's Choice, Spur Awards* nomination, *Young Reader Medal* (California) nomination, *Sunshine State Young Readers Award* (Florida) nomination, *Rebecca Caudill Young Readers Book Award* (Illinois) nomination, *Young Readers Choice Award* (Pennsylvania) nomination, *Readers Choice Award* (Virginia) nomination, *Golden Sower Award* (Nebraska) nomination, *Grand Canyon Reader Award* nomination, *Scott O'Dell Award for Historical Fiction, Children's Book Award* (Massachusetts) nomination, and *Young Readers Choice Award* (Louisiana) nomination.

914. Latham, Jean Lee. *Carry On, Mr. Bowditch.* Houghton, 2003. 256pp. ISBN 978-0-618-25081-3; paper ISBN 978-0-618-25074-5. Grades 5–9. Several years after Nathaniel Bowditch was born in 1773, his sailing captain father ran aground and lost his ship. This reversed the family's fortunes, as recounted in this fictional biography, and at the age of 12 Nat was indentured for nine years. He had desperately wanted to go to Harvard, but instead he read widely and taught himself languages (including Latin so that he could read Newton) with the help of mentors who were impressed by his enormous intelligence. His abilities helped him navigate using the moon's position. He found mistakes in charts used by sailors and dedicated himself to checking every one of the entries and publishing them in *The New American Practical Navigator* (1802). He taught others how to navigate before his death in 1838. *Newbery Medal*.

915. **Lawlor, Laurie.** *Addie Across the Prairie.* Illustrated by Gail Owens. Aladdin, 1991. 128pp. Paper ISBN 978-0-671-70147-5. Grades 3–6. Addie does not want to travel across the prairie to Dakota with her family. On the long journey, she saves herself and her brother from a rapidly spreading fire, and she acts graciously to unwelcome Indians. She shows her bravery even in uncomfortable situations.

916. **Lawlor, Laurie.** *Old Crump: The True Story of a Trip West.* Illustrated by John Winch. Holiday House, 2002. Unpaged. ISBN 978-0-8234-1608-0. Grades K–2. In 1850 a group of forty-niners tries a shortcut on a trip from Utah to California and ends up in Death Valley. Among the frightened travelers is a family that has an ox named Old Crump, and it is Old Crump who saves their lives, carrying them across the miles of desert. When the family settles in San Joaquin Valley, they treasure the ox as a valued member of the family.

917. **Lawlor, Laurie.** *The School at Crooked Creek.* Illustrated by Ronald Himler. Holiday House, 2004. 72pp. ISBN 978-0-8234-1812-1. Grades 2–5. In 1820s rural Indiana, 6-year-old Beansie reluctantly goes to school for the first time midway through the year. He and his sister Louisa, who is 9, walk to school from their one-room cabin, and on the way home are caught in a snowstorm. The ten chapters reveal his unhappiness at school, his ability to cope with his teacher and the class bullies, and his surprising resilience. Black-and-white drawings highlight the text.

918. **Leland, Dorothy Kupcha.** *Sallie Fox: The Story of a Pioneer Girl.* Tomato, 1995. 115pp. Paper ISBN 978-0-961735-76-0. Grades 4–6. Sallie Fox, 12, travels with her family from Iowa to California in the mid-1800s. She expects an exciting trip, but it becomes an ordeal and she has to spend many days without water. Many in the group die of thirst. They also have to cope with illness and avoid Indian attacks as well as each other when conflicts arise.

919. **Lendroth, Susan.** *Ocean Wide, Ocean Deep.* Illustrated by Raul Allen. Tricycle, 2008. Unpaged. ISBN 978-1-58246-232-5. Grades K–3. When her father sails to China in the 19th century, a young girl and her mother and baby brother live in a Cape Cod village. They watch the baby learn to walk and then to speak as the seasons turn. Finally the father returns. Illustrations reinforce the verse text.

920. **Levinson, Nancy Smiler.** *Snowshoe Thompson.* Illustrated by Joan Sandin. Trophy, 1996. 64pp. Paper ISBN 978-0-06-444206-0. Grades K–3. Postman Snowshoe Thompson (1827–1876) decides to make a pair of skis so that he can deliver Danny's letter to his father, who is 90 miles away, across the Sierra Nevadas. Thompson makes the trip and returns with a letter to Danny saying that his father will be home for Christmas. *Notable Children's Book in the Field of Social Studies*.

921. **Lowell, Susan.** *The Elephant Quilt: Stitch by Stitch to California!* Farrar, 2008. 40pp. ISBN 978-0-374-38223-0. Grades K–2. In 1859 young Lily Rose and her family travel to California by wagon. She laments the slow pace, but she sews all the way. On the Santa Fe Trail, on their way "to see the elephant" (something big or strange), they see buffalo, Apaches, mountains, and deserts in addition to snow on July 4. Lily Rose and her Grandma stitch the images from their journey into a quilt with an elephant hiding in the patches. Illustrations enhance the text.

922. **MacBride, Roger Lea.** *In the Land of the Big Red Apple.* Illustrated by David Gilleece. (Little House: The Rose Years) Trophy, 1995. 338pp. Paper ISBN 978-0-06-440574-4. Grades 3–6. Rose, 8, adjusts to life in the Ozarks in 1895 with her parents Almanzo and Laura Ingalls Wilder. Rose battles an ice storm, helps with the construction of the family's new farmhouse, returns to school, and celebrates their first Christmas in their new home. But she also finds that others do not have as much as she has, and she has to decide if she wants to share. The third installment in the series.

923. MacBride, Roger Lea. *Little Farm in the Ozarks.* Illustrated by David Gilleece. (Little House: The Rose Years) Trophy, 1994. 286pp. Paper ISBN 978-0-06-440510-2. Grades 3–6. In 1894, Rose's family moves from the drought of DeSmet, South Dakota, to Mansfield, Missouri. They cross the Missouri River in a dust storm, adopt a dog found on the trail, and locate a missing $100 bill in time to purchase their house. This is the second in the series about Rose and her parents, Almanzo and Laura Ingalls Wilder.

924. MacBride, Roger Lea. *Little Town in the Ozarks.* Illustrated by David Gilleece. (Little House: The Rose Years) Trophy, 1996. 338pp. Paper ISBN 978-0-06-440580-5. Grades 3–6. Rose, 10, and her family have to move to Mansfield in 1897 because they cannot keep their farm functioning during the economic slump. The noisy trains and the streets crowded with people baffle her. She has to adjust to this new experience, but she makes friends at school who show her how to enjoy life in town. The fourth volume in the series.

925. McCaughrean, Geraldine. *Stop the Train.* Harpercollins, 2003. 304pp. ISBN 978-0-06-050749-7; 2005, paper ISBN 978-0-06-050751-0. Grades 5 up. In 1893 Cissy Sissney, 10, and her family get off a train in the middle of an Oklahoma prairie with a group of other families planning to build a new town called Florence. When the townspeople refuse to sell their landholding shares to Clifford T. Rimm, owner of the Red Rock Railroad, he decides the train will not stop in their town. The press, however, works in the townspeople's favor, and he has to change his mind. Cissy's friend Kookie enjoys their new town and its inhabitants—Miss Loucien, the mail order bride with appropriately cold hands for the Swedish baker, Mr. Crew and his convincing villain roles, Honey and her earhorn, and an illiterate schoolteacher. *American Library Association Notable Children's Books, Student Book Award* (Maine) nomination, *School Library Journal Best Books for Children*, and *Publishers Weekly Best Children's Books*.

926. McGraw, Eloise Jarvis. *Moccasin Trail.* Puffin, 1986. 256pp. Paper ISBN 978-0-14-032170-8. Grades 5–9. A bear mauls Jim when he is 12, and a Crow tribe adopts him. He spends six years living with them and counting coup (the number of whites scalped), wearing his eagle feathers as a young brave. When he meets his younger siblings in a nearby settlement, they tell him that they need his signature to get the land that their father had claimed in Willamette Valley, Oregon, before dying on the trail with their mother. Jim agrees, and goes with them although they distrust each other. They eventually learn that each has talents that will help them all succeed. *Newbery Honor, Junior Literary Guild Selection*, and *Lewis Carroll Shelf Award*.

927. McGugan, Jim. *Josepha: A Prairie Boy's Story.* Illustrated by Murray Kimber. Fitzhenry & Whiteside, 2003. Unpaged. Paper ISBN 978-0-8899-5142-6. Grades 2–5. In 1900 a younger boy admiringly tells of Josepha, a kind teenager who must stay with the elementary children during school because he cannot speak English very well. Although impoverished, he carves beautiful things and protects the children. His family is inexperienced and unsuccessful at prairie farming so Josepha must leave school and go to work. But before he leaves, he gives the narrator his cherished possession, and the narrator responds by giving Josepha his own most treasured item. *Governor General's Award for Literary Merit* (illustration); *Governor General's Award for Literary Merit* (text) finalist.

928. McKissack, Patricia C. *Away West.* Illustrated by Gordon C. James. (Scraps of Time) Viking, 2006. 121pp. ISBN 978-0-670-06012-2; Puffin paper ISBN 978-0-14-240688-5. Grades 3–4. In their grandmother's attic, the Webster children learn about the life of their ancestor Everett Turner, who as a 13-year-old orphan heads west and finds himself in the all-black town of Nicodemus, Kansas. Everett can read and write, but he also develops his skills as a horse trainer and earns a spot on a wagon train.

929. MacLachlan, Patricia. *Caleb's Story.* Joanna Cotler, 2001. 128pp. ISBN 978-0-06-023605-2; Trophy, 2002, paper ISBN 978-0-06-440590-4. Grades 3–5. In 1918, after Anna moves to town for high school and bequeaths the family journal to Caleb, a stranger arrives at the farm who turns out to be John Whitting, Jacob's father and Caleb and Cassie's grandfather. Caleb and Cassie get to know John, but Jacob refuses to reconcile with him because he abandoned the family many years before. Then Caleb finds out that John cannot write, and therefore, could not let Jacob know why he left. The third installment in the Sarah Plain and Tall series. *Children's Choice Book Award* (Iowa) nomination, *Bluegrass Award* (Kentucky) nomination, *Children's Book Award* (Massachusetts) nomination, *Golden Sower Award* (Nebraska) nomination, *Garden State Teen Book Award* (New Jersey) nomination, and *Battle of the Books* (New Mexico) nomination.

930. MacLachlan, Patricia. *Grandfather's Dance.* Joanna Cotler, 2006. 84pp. ISBN 978-0-06-027560-0; HarperTrophy, 2008, paper ISBN 978-0-06-134003-1. Grades 4–6. Cassie Whiting, 9, watches her family gather for the wedding of her sister Anna. She thinks a dog would be a better companion than a husband. Then she watches her younger brother Jack adopt Grandfather's mannerisms. As Cassie remembers the wedding afterward, she recalls the smell of roses, in this last volume in the series that began with *Sarah, Plain and Tall.*

931. MacLachlan, Patricia. *Skylark.* HarperCollins, 1994. 80pp. ISBN 978-0-06-023328-0; Trophy, 1997, paper ISBN 978-0-06-440622-2. Grades 3–6. After a drought hits the region where Anna and Caleb live with their father and his new wife Sarah, Sarah takes the children to her home in Maine in this sequel to *Sarah, Plain and Tall.* The children miss their father and worry that she will stay in Maine, but when their father comes to get them after rain finally dampens the prairie, Sarah says she will make her home with them by writing her name in the dirt, a skylark that has "come to earth."

932. MacLachlan, Patricia. *Three Names.* Trophy, 1994. 32pp. Paper ISBN 978-0-06-443360-0. Grades 3–6. A little boy at the end of the 19th century goes to school on the prairie in a horse-drawn wagon. His dog, Three Names, always goes with him. In winter they travel by sleigh, and in spring they face tornadoes. The boy plays games like fox-and-geese, hide-and-seek, and marbles. Although he enjoys the summer, he looks forward to school because he can see his friends. *School Library Journal Best Book.*

933. McMullan, Kate. *My Travels with Capts. Lewis and Clark by George Shannon.* Illustrated by Adrienne Yorinks. Trophy, 2006. 272pp. Paper ISBN 978-0-06-008101-0. Grades 5–9. George Shannon, 16, travels with Lewis and Clark's Corps of Discovery from Pittsburgh to the Pacific Ocean for two years beginning July 15, 1803, and ending November 22, 1805. He records his experiences in a diary. Among the people he describes are Meriwether Lewis, William Clark, Sacagawea, trappers, soldiers, and river guides. On the journey, he becomes a man who feels comfortable in the wilderness and understands others better. Included are sketches of snakes, footprints, and other objects that enhance the text.

934. Moeri, Louise. *Save Queen of Sheba.* Puffin, 1994. 116pp. Paper ISBN 978-0-14-037148-2. Grades 5–8. After a Sioux raid on their portion of the wagon train, King David, 12, and Queen of Sheba, 6, find themselves alone. Although almost scalped himself, King David looks after Queen of Sheba as they walk along the trail. He eventually recovers and the two survive the experience and are reunited with their father.

935. Moonshower, Candie. *The Legend of Zoey.* Delacorte, 2006. 213pp. ISBN 978-0-385-73280-2; Yearling, 2007, paper ISBN 978-0-440-23924-6. Grades 4–7. In contemporary Tennessee 13-year-old Zoey Smith-Jones dislikes being Native American and having a midwife mother. When a storm hits during a school field trip, she finds herself in 1811 Missouri and meets Prudence. Prudence's mother is having a difficult pregnancy, and her preacher father is trying to convert Indians elsewhere. Prudence is also enthralled with Chief Kalopin, a Chickasaw chief who fell for a Choctaw woman. Their marriage supposedly created Lake Reelfoot when it changed the course of the Mississippi River. Zoey and Prudence survive the New Madrid, Missouri, earthquakes and the subsequent floods, and Zoey begins to come to terms with her heritage, all aspects of her experience related in her diary.

936. Moore, Billy Loran. *Little Brother Real Snake.* JuneBug, 2004. 141pp. Paper ISBN 978-1-58838-147-7. Grades 3–7. Red Squirrel has to prove himself to two members of his own tribe, an Apache, and a snake even though his own warrior father died bravely. He does not like violence and he hates snakes. His peers mimic snakes rattling when Red Squirrel appears, but he eventually overcomes his fear and proves that he is a man of the Real People.

937. Murphy, Jim. *Desperate Journey.* Scholastic, 2006. 278pp. ISBN 978-0-439-07806-1. Grades 5–8. In 1848, 12-year-old Maggie Haggerty has to take on adult responsibilities on the Erie Canal when her father goes to jail for starting a fight and her mother is sick. She must deliver a heavy barge shipment to Buffalo before the deadline in order to receive a desperately needed bonus. The mules require handling, a difficult job for her. She and her younger brother Eamon struggle with the load, and when Billy Black offers to help, she must decide if she can trust him.

938. Myers, Anna. *Hoggee.* Walker, 2004. 182pp. ISBN 978-0-8027-8926-6; 2007, paper ISBN 978-0-8027-9683-7. Grades 5–7. Fatherless Howard Gardner, 14, and his older brother Jack get jobs as hoggees on the Erie Canal around 1830. They drive the mules that pull the boats. When the canal is emptied for the winter, Howard hopes to work at a kitchen job and send money home, but this does not work and he is almost starving when Old Cyrus, mule caretaker, takes pity on him and lets him come to his home shared with a widowed daughter and three granddaughters. Howard initially does not understand what is wrong with Sara, who is so sad, but then he realizes she is a deaf mute. He quickly learns sign language and teaches it to her. Thrilled with his newfound ability, he decides to return to school.

939. Myers, Laurie. *Lewis and Clark and Me: A Dog's Tale.* Illustrated by Michael Dooling. Henry Holt, 2002. 64pp. ISBN 978-0-8050-6368-4. Grades 3–6. Seaman, Meriwether Lewis's Newfoundland dog, relates the story of the Lewis and Clark Expedition, on which he traveled from St. Louis to the Pacific Ocean. An incident in Lewis's journal follows each of his stories. Among Seaman's adventures are encounters with a squirrel, a bear, a beaver, and a buffalo. He also remembers when a Native American kidnapped them. Illustrations enhance the text. *Young Reader's Award* (Arizona) nomination, *Sunshine State Young Reader Award* (Florida) nomination, *Young Readers Choice Awards* (Louisiana), *Black-Eyed Susan* (Maryland) nomination, *Great Lakes Great Books Award* (Michigan) nomination, *Young Readers' Award* (Nevada) nomination, *Beverly Cleary Children's Choice Book Award* (Oregon) nomination, *Young Reader's Choice Award* (Pennsylvania) nomination, *Bluebonnet Award* (Texas) nomination, and *Children's Book Award* (West Virginia) nomination.

940. Nelson, S. D. *The Star People: A Lakota Story.* Abrams, 2003. 40pp. ISBN 978-0-8109-4584-5. Grades K–4. Young Wolf and his older sister, members of the Standing Rock Lakota Sioux tribe, wander away from their village following the shapes of the Cloud People. They almost walk into a raging prairie fire, but instead fall into a river. When the fire passes, their deceased grandmother, one of the Star People, guides them back home. Impressionistic illustrations enhance the text.

941. Nixon, Joan Lowery. *Caught in the Act.* (Orphan Train Adventures) Laurel-Leaf, 1996. 151pp. Paper ISBN 978-0-440-22678-9. Grades 5–8. When Mike, 11, leaves his brothers and sisters after they take the Orphan Train west, he goes to live with the Friedrichs in Missouri. The father is harsh and hostile, always willing to believe his bullying son Gunter over Mike, who he knows once stole money in New York. But Mike has a chance to prove he is innocent of Gunter's accusations before he goes to live with another family.

942. Nixon, Joan Lowery. *A Family Apart.* (Orphan Train Adventures) Laurel-Leaf, 1988. 163pp. Paper ISBN 978-0-440-22676-5. Grades 5–8. When Frances is 13 in 1860, her mother relinquishes her and her five siblings to the Children's Aid Society so they can be adopted by people in the West who have enough money to care for them. Frances cuts her hair and pretends to be a boy so she can be placed with her little brother. The family with whom they live soon discovers that she is not "Frankie," but they are pleased. She works hard and courageously when she helps her new family transport slaves along the Underground Railway. *Western Writers of America Spur Award.*

943. Nixon, Joan Lowery. *In the Face of Danger.* (Orphan Train Adventures) Laurel-Leaf, 1988. 152pp. Paper ISBN 978-0-440-22705-2. Grades 5–8. Unhappy to be separated from her family and blaming herself for all of their problems, Meg, 12, goes to Ben and Emma's house in Kansas Territory. She tries to adjust to the change, and she shows that she has learned to cope when she bravely saves the neighbors and Emma from a known killer. She suggests Ben show his marksmanship by shooting at targets she selects, and he uses all of his ammunition. The birth of Emma's baby soon after makes the effort worthwhile. *Western Writers of America Spur Award.*

944. Nixon, Joan Lowery. *A Place to Belong.* (Orphan Train Adventures) Gareth Stevens, 2000. 149pp. ISBN 978-0-8368-2641-8. Grades 5–9. Danny and Peg's foster mother dies around 1860, and Danny suggests that his foster father Alfrid invite his real mother to the West. He hopes that the two will marry. They are very different, but both find unexpected happiness in knowing each other.

945. O'Dell, Scott. *Sing Down the Moon.* Houghton, 1970. 137pp. ISBN 978-0-395-10919-9; Laurel-Leaf, 1999, paper ISBN 978-0-440-97975-3. Grades 5 up. Spanish slavers enter the Canyon de Chelly in 1864 and take Navajo girl Bright Morning and her friend south with them to sell. Soon after, the white soldiers burn the crops and force the remaining Navajos to march toward Fort Sumter. The boy she intends to marry, Tall Boy, helps Bright Morning escape from the slavers, but the soldiers retake them all. Bright Morning and Tall Boy have to endure the ignominy of the camp before they escape and return to live in the crevices of their canyon with their son. *Newbery Honor.*

946. O'Dell, Scott, and Elizabeth Hall. *Thunder Rolling in the Mountains.* Yearling, 1993. 128pp. Paper ISBN 978-0-440-40879-6. Grades 5–8. Sound of Running Feet, daughter of Chief Joseph of the Nez Perce Indians, tells about the Blue Coats (American soldiers) pursuing her people in 1877. The army forces them to leave their Oregon valley and then attacks, forcing them to fight back. She walks toward Canada with her intended husband, but another tribe, the Assiniboin, betray them. She escapes again and goes to join Sitting Bull. *Notable Children's Trade Books in the Field of Social Studies.*

947. Olson, Tod. *How to Get Rich in the California Gold Rush: An Adventurer's Guide to the Fabulous Riches Discovered in 1848.* Illustrated by Scott Allred. National Geographic, 2008. 47pp. ISBN 978-1-4263-0315-9. Grades 5–9. Thomas Hartley and two companions hope to make a fortune during the gold rush. They work hard, do well at times, and also experience disappointments. All three eventually succeed, but in different ways. In an entertaining presentation of the gold rush, Olson reveals that very few became rich panning for gold but many prospered by providing goods and services to the prospectors. Illustrations and reproductions enhance the text.

948. Olson, Tod. *How to Get Rich on a Texas Cattle Drive: In Which I Tell the Honest Truth About Rampaging Rustlers, Stampeding Steers and Other Fateful Hazards on the Wild Chisolm Trail.* Illustrated by Scott Allred and Gregory Proch. National Geographic, 2010. 48pp. ISBN 978-1-4263-0524-5. Grades 5–9. A 15-year-old cowhand travels on the Chisholm Trail through Texas, Oklahoma, and Kansas. He meets rustlers, hostile Comanches, and unhappy Kansas farmers. He copes with stampedes, bad weather, and dusty plains. Period photographs and archival prints enhance the text. Further Reading, Glossary, and Web Sites.

949. Olson, Tod. *How to Get Rich on the Oregon Trail: Adventures Among Cows, Crooks and Heroes on the Road to Fame and Fortune.* Illustrated by Scott Allred and Gregory Proch. National Geographic, 2009. 47pp. ISBN 978-1-4263-0412-5. Grades 5–9. Will Reed, 15, and his family leave Springfield, Illinois, to take the Oregon Trail in 1852. They travel for 2,000 miles while facing Indian attacks, cholera, theft, and precarious river crossings. They also worry about their wagon. Will's father is a physician and offers medical services to the emigrants. Will's enterprising brother makes money blacksmithing and running ferry services. Sidebars feature a ledger of how much they have spent and made as they have travel. Period photographs and archival prints enhance the text. Further Reading, Glossary, and Web Sites.

950. Oswald, Nancy. *Nothing Here but Stones.* Henry Holt, 2004. 224pp. ISBN 978-0-8050-7465-9. Grades 5–9. Escaping the Tsarist pogroms after her mother's death, 11-year-old Emma and her family travel from Kishinev, Russia, to Cotopaxi, Colorado, in 1882. Instead of the fruitful land they expect, they find cold, hunger, rats, and stones. They cannot speak English, and their religious practices and culture are different from those of the Jews with whom they try to form a community. After a new synagogue is dedicated, however, and a marriage is celebrated in it, the family adapts and finds the comfort and home it needs.

951. Paulsen, Gary. *Call Me Francis Tucket.* Yearling, 1996. 97pp. Paper ISBN 978-0-440-41270-0. Grades 4–8. Francis Tucket, 14, is taking a wagon train from Missouri to Oregon in 1848, Pawnee Indians kidnap him. A mountain man helps him escape and teaches him to survive. When he is on his own, he thinks he can handle anything. But he has not considered the difficulties of caring for two abandoned children, Lottie and Billy. When he tries to leave them, he realizes he has made a mistake and returns to find that their benefactor beat them for not working hard enough.

952. Paulsen, Gary. *Harris and Me: A Summer Remembered.* Harcourt, 1993. 157pp. ISBN 978-0-15-292877-3; 2007, paper ISBN 978-0-15-205880-7. Grades 5–8. The nameless 11-year-old protagonist, victim of alcoholic parents who have abused him, travels in a 1949 pickup to live on his uncle's farm. The dirty farm disgusts him, but he meets Harris, a boy who leads him into surprising adventures. They pretend to be Tarzan in the hayloft, GI Joes in the pigpen with its mire, and Gene Autry riding his horse. The protagonist learns that a real farm far from town and those associated with it can give him a sense of belonging. *Young Reader's Award* (Arizona) nomination, *American Library Association Best Books for Children*, *American Library Association Best Books for Young Adults*, *Booklist Editors Choice*, *Children's Book Awards* (Georgia) nomination, *Young Adult Book Award* (South Carolina) nomination, *Battle of the Books Award* (Wisconsin) nomination, *Teen Book Awards* (Iowa), *Rebecca Caudill Young Readers Book Awards* (Illinois), *Young Hoosier Book Award* (Indiana) nomination, and *Rosewater Award* (Indiana) nomination.

953. Paulsen, Gary. *The Legend of Bass Reeves: Being the True and Fictional Account of the Most Valiant Marshal in the West.* Wendy Lamb, 2006. 137pp. ISBN 978-0-385-74661-8; Laurel-Leaf, 2008, paper ISBN 978-0-553-49429-7. Grades 5–9. Bass Reeves, born a slave, became a respected federal marshal in Oklahoma and Texas. A runaway slave, he lived with the Creek Indians for twenty-two years until the Emancipation Proclamation freed him. He then became an Arkansas cattle rancher. As a marshal, he never drew his own gun before being provoked, arrested many fugitives, and kept peace for those in his charge. The text fictionalizes Reeves's remarkable life. *Golden Sower Award* (Nebraska) nomination and *Young Readers Choice Award* (Louisiana) nomination.

954. Paulsen, Gary. *Tucket's Ride.* Yearling, 1998. 112pp. Paper ISBN 978-0-440-41147-5. Grades 5–8. Francis Tucket and his adopted family—Lottie and Billy—head west to look for Francis's parents on the Oregon Trail during the war between the United States and Mexico. An early winter forces them to turn south and into dangerous territory. They are captured by outlaws and must rely on their loyalty to each other and their intelligence to escape.

955. Pearsall, Shelley. *Crooked River.* Knopf, 2005. 256pp. ISBN 978-0-375-82389-3; Yearling, 2007, paper ISBN 978-0-440-42101-6. Grades 5–8. In 1812 the father of 12-year-old Rebecca Carter brings a young Chippewa accused of murdering a white trapper to their Ohio settlement. He is kept chained upstairs in their home until the trial. Rebecca notices his kindness and thinks he may have been falsely accused. An inexperienced lawyer in love with Reb's sister arrives to defend Amik, saying that Amik was kind to him in the past. Rebecca sees what frontier justice can be like. *Rebecca Caudill Young Readers Book Award* (Illinois) nomination, *Student Book Award* (Maine) nomination, *Great Stone Face Book Award* (New Hampshire) nomination, and *Sequoyah Book Award* (Oklahoma) nomination.

956. Provensen, Alice. *Klondike Gold.* Simon & Schuster, 2005. 40pp. ISBN 978-0-689-84885-8. Grades 3–5. In 1896, during the Yukon gold rush, shopkeeper Bill Howell sets out from Boston for Alaska carrying a year's worth of supplies. He decides this effort is worth the possible reward. He and his friend return from the gold fields only a little richer but with continued enthusiasm. Illustrations enliven the text. *Prairie Pasque Book Award* (South Dakota) nomination and *School Library Journal Best Children's Books*.

957. Rand, Gloria. *Sailing Home: A Story of a Childhood at Sea.* North-South, 2006. 32pp. Paper ISBN 978-0-7358-2079-1. Grades 2–4. Based on a real-life journal, this is the story of the years a family—Captain Madsen, his wife, and four children—spent of their four-masted sailing ship, the *John Ena.* Between 1896 and 1910 they sailed around the world and the children lived a geography lesson. They had a governess and their father taught them astronomy, navigation, and semaphore. The oldest, Matilda, remembers a delightful life even when a terrible storm threatened to sink them. With photographs and an Afterword.

958. Randall, Alison L. *The Wheat Doll.* Illustrated by Bill Farnsworth. Peachtree, 2008. Unpaged. ISBN 978-1-56145-456-3. Grades 1–4. Mary Ann loses Betty, her cloth doll filled with wheat, during a bad storm on the Utah frontier in the 19th century. She misses carrying Betty in her apron pocket and talking to her. In the spring, she has a wonderful surprise—her doll has germinated. She digs Betty up and restores her to her former life. Oil paintings enliven the text.

959. Ransom, Candice F. *Bones in the Badlands.* Illustrated by Greg Call. (Time Spies) Mirrorstone, 2006. 111pp. Paper ISBN 978-0-7869-4028-8. Grades 2–4. In their parents' bed-and-breakfast, Alex, Mattie, and Sophie are happy to have the power to travel through time. A guest arrives who is a paleontologist on vacation from her dig in the Badlands. Their antique spyglass sends the children to 1898 Wyoming and the Bone Wars. They join dinosaur hunter Walter Granger and help him trap a thief who is trying to steal his discoveries.

960. Raymer, Dottie. *Welcome to Kaya's World 1764: Growing Up in a Native American Homeland.* Illustrated by Jodi Evert. American Girl, 2003. 64pp. ISBN 978-1-58485-722-8. Grades 3–5. Kaya, a Nez Percé girl, grows up in the middle of the 18th century in the Pacific Northwest. Illustrations complement the text.

961. Reich, Susanna. *Penelope Bailey Takes the Stage.* Marshall Cavendish, 2006. 198pp. ISBN 978-0-7614-5287-4. Grades 4–7. In 1889, 11-year-old Penny does not want to leave Berkeley to live with her Aunt Phyllis in San Francisco while her parents are doing scientific research in Hawaii. Phyllis and her very proper daughters do not interest Penny, and she becomes friends with a neighbor, Shakespearean actor Mr. Prenderwinkel; her teacher, Miss Adelaide; and Isabelle Grey. All Penny wants to do is act but Phyllis refuses to let her take a role in the school play. Penny defies her, and happily her parents return as she is getting ready to perform.

962. Roop, Peter. *The Buffalo Jump.* Illustrated by Bill Farnsworth. Northland, 1999. 32pp. Paper ISBN 978-0-8735-8731-0. Grades 1–4. Little Blaze, a Blackfoot, wants to lead the buffalo jump, but tribal leaders ask his older brother Curly Bear instead. When his brother trips after luring the herd of buffalo, Little Blaze rescues him so that the buffalo will not stampede him as they fall over the cliff.

963. Roop, Peter, and Connie Roop. *Keep the Lights Burning, Abbie.* Illustrated by Peter E. Hanson. Carolrhoda, 1985. 40pp. ISBN 978-0-8761-4275-2; 1987, paper ISBN 978-0-8761-4454-1. Grades 1–4. In 1856 Abbie Burgess has to keep the lights burning in their island lighthouse while her father is stuck on the mainland by a storm that lasts four weeks. She cleans the lamps and trims the wicks while she and her sisters look after their sick mother. She does not know if her father will return, but she realizes the importance of keeping the lights burning.

964. Rumford, James. *Don't Touch My Hat!* Knopf, 2007. 40pp. ISBN 978-0-375-83782-1. Grades K–3. Sheriff John is superstitious about his hat; he believes it helps him catch criminals in the vicinity of Sunshine in the Wild West. He will allow no one to touch it. One night he unwittingly wears one of his wife's hats and goes about keeping the law as usual. This makes him realize that he can succeed on his own. Cartoon illustrations complement the text.

965. Ryan, Pam Muñoz. *Riding Freedom.* Illustrated by Brian Selznick. Scholastic, 1999. 138pp. Paper ISBN 978-0-439-08796-4. Grades 3–6. Charley (Charlotte) Parkhurst (d. 1879) disguises herself as a boy at the age of 12 and runs away from a New Hampshire orphanage to become a coach driver. The orphanage head, Mr. Millshark, refused to let her ride because she was female. Charley gets a job as a stable hand for Mr. Ebenezer. She becomes a superb horse handler, and the best coach driver in the state. She loses her left eye and is called "One-Eyed Charley." In California, she votes as a "man" in 1868 and buys property. She holds the distinction of being the first woman to vote in the United States. *Capitol Choices Noteworthy Titles* (Washington, D.C.), *School Librarians Battle of the Books* (Alaska) nomination, *Young Reader's Award* (Arizona) nomination, *Nutmeg Children's Book Award* (Connecticut) nomination, *Sunshine State Young Reader Award* (Florida) nomination, Children's Choice Book Award (Iowa) nomination, *Young Hoosier Award* (Indiana) nomination, *Black-Eyed Susan Book Award* (Maryland) nomination, *Student Book Award* (Maine) nomination,*Battle of the Books* (New Jersey) nomination, *Battle of the Books* (New Mexico) nomination, *Children's Book Award* (South Carolina) nomination, *Junior Book Award* (South Carolina) nomination, *Beehive Young Adult Book Award* (Utah) nomination, *Charlie May Simon* (Arkansas) nomination, *Young Readers Book Awards* (California) nomination, *Rebecca Caudill Award* (Illinois) nomination, *Children's Book Award* (Massachusetts) nomination, *Student Book Award* (Maine) nomination, Readers' Choice Award (Michigan) nomination, *Maud Hart Lovelace Award* (Minnesota) nomination, *Golden Sower Award* (Nebraska) nomination,*Great Stone Face Book Award* (New Hampshire) nomination,*Garden State Children's' Book Award* (New Jersey) nomination, *Children's Book Award* (Rhode Island), *Children's Book Award* (South Carolina) nomination, *International Reading Association Teachers Choice, Bluebonnet Award* (Texas) nomination, *State Reading Association for Young Readers* (Virginia) nomination,*Sasquatch Book Awards* (Washington), and *Children's Book Award* (West Virginia) nomination.

966. Sandoz, Mari. *The Horsecatcher.* Univ. of Nebraska, 1986. 192pp. Paper ISBN 978-0-8032-9160-7. Grades 5–9. Young Elk's Cheyenne tribe expects him to be a warrior in the 1830s, but he prefers to catch and tame mustangs. The idea of killing makes him ill. One day he captures the Ghost Horse, a beautiful white horse that he wants more than anything. But he then sees Kiowa warriors on the way to invade his village, and he must free the horses he has caught and rush home to warn his people. The Kiowa reveal that he had caught and freed the Ghost Horse, and his village gives him a new name, "Horsecatcher."

967. Schultz, Jan Neubert. *Battle Cry.* Carolrhoda, 2006. 240pp. ISBN 978-1-57505-928-0. Grades 5–9. Johnny, a young settler, and Chaska, a Dakota, try to be friends in 1862. But tensions between the Dakotas, fed up with their unfair treatment, and the white newcomers make this difficult. Violence erupts and the boys are selected as interpreters for the two sides; this makes their friendship harder to maintain. However, when police arrest Chaska for a crime he did not commit, he realizes that Johnny is the only person who will help him.

968. Scillian, Devin. *Pappy's Handkerchief.* Illustrated by Chris Ellison. Sleeping Bear, 2007. 32pp. ISBN 978-1-58536-316-2. Grades 2–4. Moses, a young African American, and his family travel by wagon from their Baltimore home to Oklahoma territory where they hope to claim land in one of the Oklahoma Land Runs between 1889 and 1895. During the Run, their wagon is disabled, and his father breaks his leg. Moses continues on horseback and stakes a claim by flying his grandfather's handkerchief from a pole. Paintings augment the text.

969. Shaw, Janet Beeler. *Changes for Kirsten: A Winter Story.* Illustrated by Renee Graef and Keith Skeen. American Girl, 1990. 64pp. ISBN 978-0-937295-94-6; 1988, paper ISBN 978-0-937295-45-8. Grades 4–6. Kirsten wants to go trapping with her brother and his friend in the Minnesota woods in 1854. Although the boys do not want a young girl with them, they recognize that she knows the animals' habits best. After their house burns down, she and her brother go to visit the best trapper in the area and find him dead. He has no family, so they sell his furs and use the money to buy a new house.

970. Sneve, Virginia Driving Hawk. *Bad River Boys: A Meeting of the Lakota Sioux with Lewis and Clark.* Illustrated by Bill Farnsworth. Holiday House, 2005. 32pp. ISBN 978-0-8234-1856-5. Grades 2–5. In 1804 three Lakota boys swim out to meet a canoe arriving at their camp, expecting to meet traders. But the people in the canoe are members of Lewis and Clark's expedition. The newcomers' translator is poor and they do not understand Lakota customs; conflict seems almost certain. Illustrations complement the text.

971. Stanley, Diane. *Raising Sweetness.* Illustrated by G. Brian Karas. Putnam, 1999. Unpaged. ISBN 978-0-399-23225-1; Puffin, 2002, paper ISBN 978-0-698-11962-8. Grades K–3. After Tex, the illiterate sheriff of Possum Trot, adopts Sweetness and seven other orphans to save them from the awful Mrs. Sump, he shows he has no skill at homemaking. Sweetness learns the alphabet by listening outside the school. She then intercepts a letter from the sheriff's lost love, Miss Lucy Locket. Sweetness immediately writes her to "Kum kwik." Miss Lucy does, and Tex becomes a happy man. Illustrations augment the text. *Diamond Primary Book Awards* (Arkansas), *Hornbook Fanfare, Young Hoosier Book Awards* (Indiana) nomination, and *School Library Journal Best Books.*

972. Stanley, Diane. *Saving Sweetness.* Illustrated by G. Brian Karas. Putnam, 1996. Unpaged. ISBN 978-0-399-22645-8; Puffin, 2001, paper ISBN 978-0-698-11767-9. Grades K–3. Sweetness, the smallest orphan at Mrs. Sump's house, escapes, and the sheriff sets out to get her back from the dangerous desert. However, Sweetness seems to be coping very well. She has water when the sheriff is thirsty, she builds a fire when he is cold. And she's a match for the evil Coyote Pete. Sweetness refuses to go back to Mrs. Sump's until the sheriff tells how he will save her "fer good." *School Library Journal Best Book.*

973. Steele, William O. *The Buffalo Knife.* Harcourt, 2004. 123pp. ISBN 978-0-15-205214-0; Odyssey paper ISBN 978-0-15-205215-7. Grades 3–7. In 1782, 9-year-old Andy's uncle gives him a knife to mark the beginning of the family's flatboat journey down the Tennessee River. After whitewater rapids and Chickamauga Indian attacks, they reach the end of the journey. Andy cannot find the knife when they arrive. He feels bad about his carelessness, but his uncle arrives and tells him what happened to it. This book was first published in 1952.

974. Steele, William O. *Flaming Arrows.* Illustrated by Paul Galdone. Odyssey, 2004. 123pp. Paper ISBN 978-0-15-205213-3. Grades 3–7. When the Chickamaugas raid Cumberland in 1784, Chad, 11, and other settlers go to the nearby fort for protection. People inside accuse one boy's father of betraying them to the Indians, but that boy risks his life for those inside the fort during the ensuing battle. This book was first published in 1957.

975. Steele, William O. *Winter Danger.* Harcourt, 2004. 131pp. ISBN 978-0-15-205205-8; Odyssey paper ISBN 978-0-15-205206-5. Grades 4–8. After Caje's mother dies in the 1780s, his father takes him to his mother's sister's home for the winter. Caje, 11, worries about the family's meager food supply and decides to leave so he will not burden them further. He happens to see a bear hibernating, and he kills it and brings the carcass back to the house so they can have food for the rest of the harsh winter. This book was first published in 1954.

976. Stevens, Carla. *Trouble for Lucy.* Illustrated by Ronald Himler. Clarion, 1987. 80pp. Paper ISBN 978-0-8991-9523-0. Grades 3–6. While the family travels to Oregon from Independence, Missouri, in 1843, Lucy's mother expects a baby any day. Her father worries and tells Lilly to keep her dog away from the oxen. When the dog disappears one day, she sneaks away from the wagon train to find him. She gets lost. By the time she is found, her mother has delivered a healthy baby girl.

977. Tingle, Tim. *Crossing Bok Chitto: A Choctaw Tale of Friendship and Freedom.* Cinco Puntos, 2006. 40pp. ISBN 978-0-938317-77-7. Grades 2–4. In Mississippi in the 1800s a Choctaw girl and slave boy become friends. She knows a secret rock path just below the surface of the water of the Bok Chitto River, and when she learns that his family is in trouble, she guides them across the river to freedom. Illustrations illuminate the text. *Bluebonnet Award* (Texas) nomination, *Jane Addams Honor Book Award, Native American Youth Services Literature Award,* and *Sequoyah Book Award* (Oklahoma) nomination.

978. Tunbo, Frances G. *Stay Put, Robbie McAmis.* Illustrated by Charles Shaw. Texas Christian University, 1988. 158pp. ISBN 978-0-8756-5025-8. Grades 4 up. In 1848, Robbie, 12, becomes separated from the rest of the wagons while crossing the Big Cypress River in East Texas. With him are an infant, three younger girls, a sickly boy of 10, and Grammie, a woman who seems to live in another world. He stays put, as his uncle told him to do, and the group begins surviving on the river's shore with their few provisions and the cow. Grammie regains her senses, and she and Robbie provide a loving environment for the children as they wait for rescue. *Western Heritage Award.*

979. Turner, Ann. *Grasshopper Summer.* Aladdin, 2000. 166pp. Paper ISBN 978-0-689-83522-3. Grades 4–6. In 1874, Sam's younger brother Billy is the better student; he is also teaching an ex-slave to read, and both facts annoy Sam. Then Sam's father decides to leave Kentucky for the West, and the family travels to Dakota Territory. They have to fight their way there, and after they arrive, they have to cope with a plague of grasshoppers that destroys their first efforts at pioneering.

980. Twain, Mark, and Catherine Nichols, adapter. *The Best Fence Painter.* (Adventures of Tom Sawyer) Sterling, 2006. 32pp. Paper ISBN 978-1-4027-3288-1. Grades K–3. When Aunt Polly tells Tom Sawyer that he must whitewash her fence before he can go fishing, he decides to con his friends into helping him in the early 19th century. He convinces them that this presents a unique opportunity. The text is an adaptation of one of the episodes in Mark Twain's *Tom Sawyer.*

981. Twain, Mark, and Catherine Nichols, adapter. *A Song for Aunt Polly.* Illustrated by Amy June Bates. (Adventures of Tom Sawyer) Sterling, 2006. 32pp. Paper ISBN 978-1-4027-3287-4. Grades K–2. When Aunt Polly wants Tom to practice on the piano, he prefers to play at the swimming hole. He finagles his preference in this retold excerpt from Twain's *Tom Sawyer.*

982. Van Dusen, Chris. *The Circus Ship.* Candlewick, 2009. 40pp. ISBN 978-0-7636-3090-4. Grades K–2. In 1836 the *Royal Star* wrecks off the coast of Maine, and the fifteen circus animals aboard swim to a nearby island. They scare the townspeople until the tiger leaps through flames to save Emma Rose Abbott from a fire. When a messenger alerts the town that the circus owner, the vile Mr. Paine, is coming to claim the animals, the townspeople disguise the animals so that he cannot find them. He departs in disgust. Lively gouache illustrations enhance the rhyming text. Note. *Beehive Childrens Picture Book Award* (Utah) nomination.

983. Van Leeuwen, Jean. *Bound for Oregon.* Illustrated by James Watling. Puffin, 1996. 167pp. Paper ISBN 978-0-14-038319-5. Grades 4–6. When Mary Ellen Todd is around 13 in 1852, her father decides that the family will go west with a wagon train leaving Independence, Missouri. Although there are more than 100 wagons when they leave, by the time they reach the end of the Oregon Trail only one other family remains. The river crossings, arguments, and disease have either discouraged or destroyed the others. After they arrive, Mary Ellen writes to her grandmother, the woman who raised her for six years after her real mother died. As she recalls the hardship of the journey, she realizes that her grandmother will never be strong enough to endure the trip. That she will never see her grandmother again saddens her, but she begins to adjust to her stepmother and to their new life.

984. Van Leeuwen, Jean. *Papa and the Pioneer Quilt.* Illustrated by Rebecca Bond. Dial, 2007. 32pp. ISBN 978-0-8037-3028-1. Grades K–2. Rebecca travels with her family on a wagon train to Oregon. On the journey, she collects scraps of material to sew into a quilt that her mother has promised to make with her. Among her scraps are the handkerchief into which her grandmother cried when they left, her father's ripped shirt, a sunbonnet given to her, her brother's torn pants, and an abandoned tablecloth. In Oregon, she adds the dresses that she wore during the trip. They choose Wandering Foot as the pattern to make while living in their new cabin. Illustrations enhance the text.

985. Van Steenwyk, Elizabeth. *Prairie Christmas.* Illustrated by Ronald Himler. Eerdmans, 2006. 32pp. ISBN 978-0-8028-5280-9. Grades 1–4. On Christmas Day in rural Nebraska in 1880, 10-year-old Emma accompanies her mother across the prairie to help deliver a baby at the Van Der Meer cabin. Emma helps with the two children and cooks special Christmas porridge for breakfast. Then they decorate the tree and entertain neighbors bringing food and gifts to the family. After the baby is delivered, Emma and her mother realize they have had a memorable day. Pencil-and-watercolor enhance illuminate the text.

986. Von Ahnen, Katherine. *Heart of Naosaqua.* Illustrated by Paulette Livers Lambert. Roberts Rinehart, 1999. 114pp. Paper ISBN 978-1-57098-010-7. Grades 4–8. Naosaqua, 12, lives with her grandmother in the Mesquakie village of Saukinek, on the Mississippi River in Missouri in 1823. When soldiers come one night and burn the village and the crops, the tribe must find a new place to live. They search and eventually settle on the Iowa River. Naosaqua vows to leave her true happiness in Saukinek and to one day return. She also worries about her father's absence, but when he returns, and Gray Beaver declares his love for her, she again has peace.

987. Warren, Andrea. *Pioneer Girl: Growing Up on the Prairie.* Harpercollins, 1998. 96pp. ISBN 978-0-688-15438-7; 2000, paper ISBN 978-0-688-17151-3. Grades 3–6. Grace Mc-Cance Snyder was 3 when her family moved to a one-room sod house on the Nebraska prairie after the 1862 Homestead Act, when people could obtain 160 acres of land by building a house on it and farming it for five years. The nearest water was two miles away, but bedbugs were always nearby. Threats of rattlesnake bites or cattle charges and weather problems such as tornados, drought, or blizzards were always lurking. Snyder lived to be 100 and remembered her childhood as a "wonderful life." Illustrations and photographs highlight the text. Bibliography, Maps, and Index. *SCASL Book Award* (South Carolina) nomination, *Golden Sower Award* Nebraska) nomination, and *Young Hoosier Book Award* (Indiana) nomination.

988. Weitzman, David. *Thrashin' Time: Harvest Days in the Dakotas.* David R. Godine, 2000. 77pp. Paper ISBN 978-1-56792-110-6. Grades 4–7. In 1912, Peter, 12, has his first encounter with a new steam engine thresher. He and his father use the machine on their North Dakota farm and find that it finishes the job in much less time than their horses could do it.

989. Whelan, Gloria. *The Indian School.* Illustrated by Gabriela Dellosso. Trophy, 1997. 89pp. Paper ISBN 978-0-06-442056-3. Grades 3–6. In 1839, after the death of her parents, 11-year-old Lucy goes to live with her uncle and aunt at their Indian school in the Michigan woods. Her Aunt Emma is strict with her pupils but shows some affection for a small boy she calls Matthew rather than using his Indian name. Matthew's sister Raven refuses to answer to the Christian name given her, but she stays to watch over her brother. Raven teaches Lucy about nature as well. Lucy mourns her own losses, but she understands that the other children have had similar separations from their homes and parents.

990. Whelan, Gloria. *Next Spring an Oriole.* Illustrated by Pamela Johnson. Random, 1987. 62pp. Paper ISBN 978-0-394-89125-5. Grades 2–4. Libby, 10, travels from Virginia to Michigan with her parents in 1837. On the way, they experience problems typical to wagon trains. Her mother nurses some Potawatomi Indian children back to health after they get measles. Libby's father complains that whites treat the Indians unfairly. A member of the Indian family brings food to Libby's family during their first winter when they almost starve.

991. Whelan, Gloria. *Night of the Full Moon.* Random, 2006. 64pp. Paper ISBN 978-0-679-87276-4. Grades 3–5. In 1840, after a long Michigan winter, Libby's friend Fawn, a Potawatomi (Neshnabek) Indian, visits her. As the summer progresses, Fawn invites Libby and her family to her new brother's naming ceremony. The U.S. government's representatives warn Libby's father that Fawn's people will be removed from their land, and he passes on the threat. On the day of the naming ceremony, Libby's mother is having a baby. Libby sneaks away without permission and goes to Fawn's home. The soldiers come that day to move the Indians, and Libby is swept up with them. Fawn's family escapes so they can return Libby to her home, and her father gives them land so that they can stay in the area.

992. Wilder, Laura Ingalls. *By the Shores of Silver Lake.* Illustrated by Garth Williams. (Little House) HarperCollins, 1953. 384pp. ISBN 978-0-06-026416-1; HarperTrophy, 2007, paper ISBN 978-0-06-088541-0. Grades 3–6. In Dakota Territory, Laura's pa works on the railroad until he finds a homestead and files a claim. They all spend the winter 60 miles from civilization. In the spring of 1880, more homesteaders come and build a new town. *Newbery Medal* and *American Library Association Notable Children's Books.*

993. Wilder, Laura Ingalls. *Christmas in the Big Woods.* Illustrated by Renee Graef. (My First Little House Books) HarperCollins, 1995. 32pp. ISBN 978-0-06-024752-2; HarperTrophy,

1997, paper ISBN 978-0-06-443487-4. Grades K–1. Laura's family has Christmas with relatives, and Laura is especially happy with her new doll, which she names Charlotte. This text is adapted from *Little House in the Big Woods*.

994. Wilder, Laura Ingalls. *Dance at Grandpa's.* Illustrated by Renee Graef. (My First Little House Books) HarperTrophy, 1995. 40pp. Paper ISBN 978-0-06-443372-3. Grades K–1. The text for this adaptation comes from chapter 8 in Wilder's *Little House in the Big Woods*. Laura and her parents go to her grandparents' house for a big party. She enjoys the lovely dresses, the dancing, and the delicious food.

995. Wilder, Laura Ingalls. *Farmer Boy.* Illustrated by Garth Williams. (Little House) Harper-Collins, 1953. 384pp. ISBN 978-0-06-026425-3; HarperTrophy, 2007, paper ISBN 978-0-06-088538-0. Grades 3–6. While Laura is growing up in the West, Almanzo Wilder lives on a big farm in New York State. Although he goes to school when he can, he has much work to do. His best times are when the cobbler or the tin peddler visit or during the annual county fair. Almanzo also has a colt that his father gave him to break in when he was only 10. *American Library Association Notable Children's Books*.

996. Wilder, Laura Ingalls. *The First Four Years.* Illustrated by Garth Williams. (Little House) HarperTrophy, 2007. 160pp. Paper ISBN 978-0-06-088545-8. Grades 3–6. Laura and Almanzo Wilder begin their married life on a small prairie homestead. Each year, however, brings disasters. Storms destroy their crops, they become ill, and a fire damages their property. Although they have unpaid debts and worries, their little daughter Rose brings them much happiness. *Notable Children's Trade Books in the Field of Social Studies*.

997. Wilder, Laura Ingalls. *Going to Town.* Illustrated by Renee Graef. (My First Little House Books) HarperTrophy, 1996. 32pp. Paper ISBN 978-0-06-443452-2. Grades K–1. The text, adapted from *Little House in the Big Woods*, relates Laura's story of going to town for the first time, where all the buildings and the number of items from which her parents have to choose at the store amaze her. The family finishes the visit by eating their picnic lunch on the lakeshore.

998. Wilder, Laura Ingalls. *Little House in the Big Woods.* (Little House) HarperCollins, 2007. 256pp. ISBN 978-0-06-128980-4; HarperTrophy, 2004, paper ISBN 978-0-06-058180-0. Grades 3–6. In 1872 Laura is 5, and her family is living in the woods of Wisconsin. She loves the family togetherness of her father's stories and preparing meat, vegetables, and fruits for the long, snowy winter. When spring comes, they enjoy the maple syrup rising from the trees and celebrate it with a dance. *American Library Association Notable Children's Books, American Booksellers' Choices*, and *Lewis Carroll Shelf Award*.

999. Wilder, Laura Ingalls. *Little House on the Prairie.* (Little House) HarperCollins, 1953. ISBN 978-0-06-026445-1; HarperTrophy, 2007, paper ISBN 978-0-06-088539-7. Grades 3–6. Laura, 6, travels with her family by covered wagon to the Indian territory of Kansas. They find a spot for a log cabin, and the neighbors help them build it. The family plants the fields and plows them, hunts for food, finds and chops firewood, and feeds the cattle. A prairie fire burns too close, and they almost have an Indian uprising. Pa decides to leave when he hears that the U.S. government plans to move them. *American Library Association Notable Children's Books*.

1000. Wilder, Laura Ingalls. *Little Town on the Prairie.* Illustrated by Garth Williams. (Little House) HarperCollins, 1953. 320pp. ISBN 978-0-06-026450-5; HarperTrophy, 2003, paper ISBN 978-0-06-052242-1. Grades 3–6. After the difficult winter in town, Laura enjoys the Fourth of July celebration and her first evening social. Life is good for the family because Laura wins a teaching certificate though she is only 15. She knows she can earn money to help send Mary to college in Iowa. And Almanzo Wilder asks to walk her home from church. *Newbery Honor* and *American Library Association Notable Children's Books*.

1001. Wilder, Laura Ingalls. *The Long Winter.* Illustrated by Garth Williams. (Little House) HarperCollins, 1953. 352pp. ISBN 978-0-06-026460-4; HarperTrophy, 2004, paper ISBN 978-0-06-058185-5. Grades 3–6. When the Indians warn that the winter of 1880–1881 will be difficult, Pa moves the family into town. Blizzards cut off all supplies from the outside world, and Mary and Laura are unable to go to school. When they run out of food, Almanzo Wilder and another boy make a dangerous trip across the prairie for wheat. Not until May, when the train comes through, do the Ingalls get their Christmas presents. *Newbery Honor* and *American Library Association Notable Children's Books.*

1002. Wilder, Laura Ingalls. *On the Banks of Plum Creek.* (Little House) HarperCollins, 1953. 384pp. ISBN 978-0-06-026470-3; HarperTrophy, 2007, paper ISBN 978-0-06-088540-3. Grades 3–6. Laura, 7, and her family leave their Indian territory home and cross Kansas, Missouri, and Iowa, on their way to Minnesota, where they purchase land and move into a sod house beside Plum Creek. They eventually get a house with real windows, but grasshoppers destroy the wheat, and her father has to leave home to find work. *Newbery Honor* and *American Library Association Notable Children's Books.*

1003. Wilder, Laura Ingalls. *Summertime in the Big Woods.* Illustrated by Renee Graef. (My First Little House Books) HarperCollins, 1996. 40pp. ISBN 978-0-06-025934-1; HarperTrophy, 2000, paper ISBN 978-0-06-443497-3. Grades K–1. The text, adapted from *Little House in the Big Woods*, tells of Laura and Mary helping with chores on the farm and going to visit Mrs. Peterson, who gives them each a cookie that they share with baby Carrie. In the summer, they also look forward to visitors.

1004. Wilder, Laura Ingalls. *These Happy Golden Years.* Illustrated by Garth Williams. (Little House) HarperCollins, 1953. 416pp. ISBN 978-0-06-026480-2; HarperTrophy, 2007, paper ISBN 978-0-06-088544-1. Grades 4–7. At the age of 15, Laura Ingalls goes to teach school 12 miles from home. The students are taller than her, and she has to board with an unpleasant family. She is unhappy, but she needs the money to help her blind sister Mary go to school. Almanzo Wilder arrives every Friday and takes her home and then returns her on Sunday night. After three years, she decides to marry him. *Newbery Honor* and *American Library Association Notable Children's Books.*

1005. Wilder, Laura Ingalls. *Winter Days in the Big Woods.* Illustrated by Renee Graef. (My First Little House Books) HarperTrophy, 1995. 32pp. Paper ISBN 978-0-06-443373-0. Grades K–1. The text for this adaptation comes from Wilder's *Little House in the Big Woods*. Laura and her family have to entertain themselves during the cold winter after they have done their chores each day. Laura's father plays his fiddle, and they sing with him.

1006. Wilkes, Maria D. *Little House in Brookfield.* Trophy, 2007. 298pp. Paper ISBN 978-0-06-114821-7. Grades 3–6. Caroline, 5 years old in 1845, lives in Brookfield, Wisconsin, with her mother, grandmother, and five brothers and sisters after her father was lost at sea. She helps her mother as much as she can, and they struggle through the winter. Then in the summer, the garden grows, and the family has enough food. Best of all, she goes to school and finds that she might be able to learn rapidly along with her first best friend. This story is based on that of the mother of Laura Ingalls Wilder, author of the Little House books.

1007. Williams, Maiya. *The Hour of the Outlaw.* Amulet, 2007. 334pp. ISBN 978-0-8109-9355-6. Grades 5–8. In this sequel to *The Golden Hour* and *The Hour of the Cobra*, Xavier and Xanthe join Rowan and Nina to leave 1919 for the California gold fields of 1857. They are searching for Balthazar, the son of alleviator (time machine) inventor Archibald Weber. During their search Nina gets a job playing piano in a saloon, Xanthe works as a domestic, and Rowan searches the gold fields. Xavier becomes a bandit, the Ghost Rider, and finds Balt who has been robbing stagecoaches as the Black Rabbit. They eventually convince Balt to return to 1919.

1008. Wisler, G. Clifton. *Jericho's Journey.* Puffin, 1995. 137pp. Paper ISBN 978-0-14-037065-2. Grades 4–8. Jericho, 11, wants to move to Texas because he has heard of Davy Crockett and Sam Houston as well as his Uncle Dan's tales about the Battle of the Alamo. The journey to Texas does not meet his dreams, however, as the family—including his older brother, bossy sister, and two younger brothers—meet challenges along the way. Wisler mentions in an Afterword that some of the episodes are drawn from entries in a frontier journal.

1009. Wisniewski, David. *The Wave of the Sea-Wolf.* Clarion, 2005. Unpaged. Paper ISBN 978-0-618-56937-3. Grades 3–6. As a young girl, Kchokeen, a princess of the Tlingit tribe on the coast of Alaska, goes looking for berries. Warned by her mother to stay away from the sea, where she could be overcome by the huge wave that the tribe calls Gonakadet (the Sea Wolf), she goes inland. She falls into a huge tree, and a bear cub begins howling. She soon finds that the bear knows that Gonakadet is coming. The huge tree saves her, and when her father and brothers rescue her the following day, she becomes the tribe's warning for the arrival of Gonakadet by listening for the bear's howl. Traders come to the coast and demand more furs than the tribe can provide, so the men burn the longhouses. In this late-18th-century story, the tribe rebuilds, but the traders continue to harass them. A canoe caught in a tree when Gonakadet kills the first traders helps Kchokeen keep hope that life will return to normal.

1010. Wolf, Allan. *New Found Land: Lewis and Clark's Voyage of Discovery.* Candlewick, 2004. 512pp. ISBN 978-0-7636-2113-1; 2007, paper ISBN 978-0-7636-3288-5. Grades 5 up. Lewis's dog Seaman—or Alum (a private name)—and others tell about the Lewis and Clark Corps of Discovery in 1803 in alternating narratives. The other thirteen speakers include Sacagawea, the Field brothers, George Shannon, Thomas Jefferson, Lewis, Clark, Clark's slave York, and Hugh Hall. The poems and journal entries offer insight into the journey and the hardships of those involved. Glossary, Further Reading, and Web Sites. *American Library Association Best Books for Young Adults, Bulletin of the Center for Children's Books Recommended Titles, Read-Aloud Book Award* (Indiana) nomination, and *School Library Journal Best Books for Children.*

1011. Woodruff, Elvira. *Dear Levi: Letters from the Overland Trail.* Illustrated by Beth Peck. Random, 1998. 119pp. Paper ISBN 978-0-679-88558-0. Grades 3–6. In 1851 12-year-old Austin makes a 3,000-mile journey from Pennsylvania to Oregon and writes letters to his younger brother Levi about the trip. Austin's day starts at 4:30 in the morning, when he has to find the oxen and attach them to the wagon so the family can have breakfast and begin the day's journey by 7 a.m. They travel until noon, let the stock graze, and eat lunch. After an hour, they begin again. The letters allow the reader to experience this journey, which also has its moments of rest and entertainment.

1012. Wyss, Thelma Hatch. *Bear Dancer: The Story of a Ute Girl.* Margaret K. McElderry, 2005. 192pp. ISBN 978-1-416-94212-2. Grades 4–8. In 1860s Colorado the Cheyenne capture 15-year-old Elk Tooth Dress, sister of the Tabeguache Ute chief Ouray, and make her a slave. Ten years later, a white soldier rescues her and returns her to her people. However, she finds that the new settlers have depleted much of her tribe's population. Based on a true story, this woman later saved several white women whom the Utes captured. *Children's Book Award* (Rhode Island) nomination.

1013. Wyss, Thelma Hatch. *A Tale of Gold.* Margaret K. McElderry, 2007. 32pp. ISBN 978-1-416-94212-2. Grades 4–6. Orphaned Jamie Erickson, 14, leaves his job driving a hack in San Francisco and joins the "stampedes" heading to the Yukon gold rush in 1897. He books passage on the *Guardian* headed for Skagway, Alaska. A phony preacher named Soapy Smith steals Jamie's precious gold nugget but Jamie carries on, meeting various unusual and unsavory characters along the way including Tip, a 13-year-old girl disguised as a boy. When Jamie and Tip stake a claim at a mining settlement, an older prospector, Caribou Clyde, joins them to create a family of three.

1014. Yep, Laurence. *When the Circus Came to Town.* Illustrated by Suling Wang. Trophy, 2004. 126pp. Paper ISBN 978-0-06-440965-0. Grades 3–5. Ursula is a lively, outgoing 10-year-old until smallpox leaves scars on her face and she retreats into herself. The Chinese cook at their early 20th-century Montana stagecoach stop, Ah Sam, fails to bring her out of her misery but Ah Sam's cousins succeed when they bring their circus to town. A blizzard prevents their departure and Ursula organizes a Chinese New Year celebration in their honor. Ursula learns that appearance is not as important as character. *Young Readers Medal Program* (California) nomination, *Young Readers Choice Book Award* (Louisiana) nomination, *Children's Book Award* (Massachusetts) nomination, *Maud Hart Lovelace Book Award* (Minnesota) nomination, *Golden Sower Award* (Nebraska) nomination, *Children's Book Award* (South Carolina) nomination, and *Sasquatch Book Award* (Washington) nomination.

1015. **Yin.** *Brothers.* Illustrated by Chris K. Soentpiet. Philomel, 2006. 32pp. ISBN 978-0-399-23406-4. Grades 2–4. The year after the big fire, Ming comes from China to San Francisco to work in his brother's store. The shop is not prospering, however, and his brother Wong has gone to work on the railroads. Ming's other brother, Shek, also works in the store and leaves Ming in charge when he goes to work on a farm for extra money. Ming meets Patrick, an Irish boy, and the two become fast friends. Patrick teaches Ming some English so that Ming can advertise the store to people outside Chinatown. Photorealistic illustrations complement the text. Further Reading.

History

1016. **Alagna, Magdalena.** *The Monroe Doctrine: An End to European Colonies in America.* (Life in the New American Nation) Rosen, 2004. 32pp. ISBN 978-0-8239-4040-0; paper ISBN 978-0-8239-4258-9. Grades 4–8. President James Monroe spoke in front of Congress in 1823 and explained how the United States would treat other nations. He planned to limit European influence in the Western Hemisphere. His ideas, known as the Monroe Doctrine, became policy. Illustrations augment the text. Bibliography, Maps, and Index.

1017. **Aloian, Molly.** *Nations of the Southeast.* (Native Nations of North America) Crabtree, 2006. 32pp. ISBN 978-0-7787-0385-3; paper ISBN 978-0-7787-0477-5. Grades 3–5. Aloian looks at the history, daily life, culture, language, and customs of native peoples in the Southeast. Among those groups included are the Creek Confederacy, Seminole, Powhatan and Yuchi, Chickasaw, Choctaw, and Cherokee. Illustrations augment the text.

1018. **Aretha, David.** *The Gold Rush to California's Riches.* (Wild History of the American West) Enslow, 2006. 128pp. ISBN 978-1-59845-012-5. Grades 5–9. The California gold rush began when Marshall discovered gold in California in 1848. The possibility of instant riches attracted many adventurers to the West and began its serious development. Among the stories presented here are those of the Donner Party and Wild Bill Hickock. Archival illustrations enhance the text. Glossary, Web Sites, Further Reading, Notes, Maps, and Index.

1019. **Bial, Raymond.** *The Delaware.* (Lifeways) Benchmark, 2005. 127pp. ISBN 978-0-7614-1904-4. Grades 5–9. Bial discusses the history, social life, religious beliefs, and customs of the Delaware, one of America's native tribes. In the early 19th century, they were forced to relocate in Oklahoma, but they have kept their traditions into contemporary times. Stories from the Delawares' oral tradition are included. Photographs and illustrations enhance the text. Bibliography, Chronology, Notes, Maps, Glossary, Further Reading, Web Sites, and Index.

1020. **Bial, Raymond.** *The Menominee.* (Lifeways) Benchmark, 2006. 127pp. ISBN 978-0-7614-1903-7. Grades 5–9. Bial discusses the history, social life, religious beliefs, and customs of the Menominee, one of America's Native tribes living in Wisconsin. Stories from the Menominee oral tradition are included. Photographs and illustrations enhance the text. Bibliography, Chronology, Notes, Maps, Glossary, Further Reading, Web Sites, and Index.

1021. **Bial, Raymond.** *Nauvoo: Mormon City on the Mississippi River.* Houghton, 2006. 47pp. ISBN 978-0-618-39685-6. Grades 4–7. When members of the Church of Jesus Christ of Latter-Day Saints (Mormons) experienced violence in 1839, they left Missouri and went to Nauvoo, on the Illinois side of the Mississippi River. The Mormons prospered under the leadership of Joseph Smith and by 1846 Nauvoo was the tenth-largest city in the United States. Neighboring citizens became jealous, however, and Joseph Smith was murdered. Therefore, 14,000 Mormons had to move again in order to find a safe place to live. Photographs enhance the text. Bibliography.

1022. **Birchfield, D. L.** *The Trail of Tears.* (Landmark Events in American History) World Almanac, 2003. 48pp. ISBN 978-0-8368-5381-0. Grades 4–8. From 1838 to 1839, the United

States government forced five tribes in southeastern America—the Cherokee, Chickasaw, Choctaw, Creek, and Seminole—to leave their lands and march to Oklahoma and the Great Plains. Europeans who had arrived in the country wanted more property, and the easiest way to obtain it was to break treaties and seize it from weaker peoples. Birchfield examines the impact of this event on the country. Illustrations augment the text.

1023. Brill, Marlene Targ. *Bronco Charlie and the Pony Express.* Illustrated by Craig Orback. (On My Own History) Lerner, 2004. 48pp. ISBN 978-1-57505-587-9; paper ISBN 978-1-57505-618-0. Grades 2–4. In 1861 Julius "Bronco Charlie" Miller, 11, became the youngest rider for the Pony Express, the mail service linking the east and west coasts of the United States. Drawing on his own accounts, Brill describes Charlie's horseback adventures coping with rough and dangerous terrain, wild animals, and extreme weather. Illustrations.

1024. Britton, Tamara L. *The Alamo.* (Symbols, Landmarks, and Monuments) Checkerboard, 2003. 32pp. ISBN 978-1-59197-518-2. Grades 3–5. Britton offers background on the national monument at the Alamo memorializing the siege that took place in San Antonio, Texas, in 1836. Photographs highlight the text. Glossary, Chronology, and Index.

1025. Brodsky, Beverly. *Buffalo.* Fitzhenry & Whiteside, 2006. 32pp. ISBN 978-1-55041-587-2; paper ISBN 978-1-55041-589-6. Grades 5–8. A collection of tribal song-poems and narrative histories from the Sioux, Dakota, and other Plains Indian tribes celebrating their relationships and traditions with the buffalo. Watercolor, oil, and charcoal illustrations complement the text.

1026. Bruchac, Joseph. *Buffalo Song.* Illustrated by Bill Farnsworth. Lee & Low, 2008. Unpaged. ISBN 978-1-58430-280-3. Grades K–3. Bruchac tells the story of a Salish (Kalispel) Indian, Samuel Walking Coyote, who helped to save the buffalo from extinction with the aid of other Native Americans and some ranchers.

1027. Bruchac, Joseph. *Navajo Long Walk: The Tragic Story of a Proud People's Forced March from Their Homeland.* Illustrated by Shonto Begay. National Geographic, 2002. 47pp. ISBN 978-0-7922-7058-4. Grades 4–8. Between 1863 and 1865, United States soldiers forced thousands of Navajos to march four hundred and seventy miles from their Arizona homeland to a desolate reservation, Bosque Redondo, in New Mexico. Hundreds died on the trip, and others survived to exist in awful living conditions at their destination. The seven chapters of the text present the facts from the Navajo viewpoints. Acrylic paintings enhance the text.

1028. Calabro, Marian. *The Perilous Journey of the Donner Party.* Clarion, 1999. 192pp. ISBN 978-0-395-86610-8. Grades 5–8. Letters and diaries written by Donner Party survivors detail the experiences of the group during the winter of 1846 to 1847. Virginia Reed, 12, writes a letter to her cousin in which she tells what happened after they left Springfield, Illinois. People starved and died and some even practiced cannibalism to survive. Photographs enhance the text. Bibliography, Chronology, Further Reading, and a Roster of the Dead.

1029. Cefrey, Holly A. *The Pinckney Treaty: America Wins the Right to Travel the Mississippi River.* (Life in the New American Nation) Rosen, 2003. 32pp. ISBN 978-0-8239-4041-7. Grades 4–8. In 1795 the Pinckney Treaty, also known as the Treaty of San Lorenzo, was signed between the United States and Spain. This treaty won two concessions—the recognition of the borders of the United States at the Mississippi and the 31st parallel, and the right of Americans to ship their goods without paying fees and duties from New Orleans. These rights allowed the country to expand westward without fighting a war with Spain. Illustrations complement the text. Glossary.

1030. Cobb, Mary. *The Quilt-Block History of Pioneer Days: With Projects Kids Can Make.* Illustrated by Jan Davey Ellis. Millbrook, 1995. 64pp. Paper ISBN 978-1-56294-692-0. Grades 2–6. An album quilt was a very special quilt made for a family moving west in the pioneer days. Because many people would never see each other again, the designs and materials they used had much meaning. This volume looks at pioneer-day travels and at quilt patterns that have been popular through the years. Outlines of the patterns allow readers to copy the designs. For Further Reading and Index.

1031. Coleman, Wim, and Pat Perrin. *What Made the Wild West Wild.* (Wild History of the American West) Enslow, 2006. 128pp. ISBN 978-1-59845-016-3. Grades 4–8. The Wild West got its reputation from people, places, and events. Among the topics covered here are newspaper stories, dime novels, stage plays, Wild West shows with Buffalo Bill Cody, and Butch Cassidy and the Sundance Kid. The importance of the Native Americans, pioneers, mountain men, and the gold rush are revealed in the twenty-seven one-paragraph biographies of the most famous characters of the frontier. Illustrations, Maps, Photographs, Reproductions, Chronolgy, Further Reading, Index, Notes, and Web Sites.

1032. Coulter, Laurie. *Cowboys and Coffin Makers: One Hundred 19th-Century Jobs You Might Have Feared or Fancied.* Annick, 2007. ISBN 978-1-55451-068-9; paper ISBN 978-1-55451-067-2. Grades 3–6. This volume offers short descriptions of one hundred jobs of the 1800s. The job categories included are exploration, frontier, life and death (coffin maker), artisan, factory and mill, on-the-water, going west, traveling-here-and-there, sweet-tooth, slave labor, change-the-world, wartime, railroad, rock-hard, great-outdoors (cowboy), up-and-down, fashion, working-for-the-city, entertaining, and big-business. Cartoon illustrations augment the text. Further Reading and Index.

1033. Donlan, Leni. *Cherokee Rose: The Trail of Tears.* (American History Through Primary Sources) Raintree, 2007. 32pp. ISBN 978-1-4109-2702-6. Grades 3–6. The Cherokee were forced off their land in 1838 under the Indian Removal Act and made to walk to Oklahoma along the "Trail of Tears." This overview of their experiences includes background on the Treaty of New Acheta and other betrayals by the United States government. But the Cherokees attempted to learn about European ways through the settlers in the southeastern United States, and Sequoyah even created an alphabet that allowed the Cherokees to have a written language. Photographs and illustrations augment the text. Glossary, Further Reading, Web Sites, and Index.

1034. Elish, Dan. *The Trail of Tears: The Story of the Cherokee Removal.* (Great Journeys) Benchmark, 2001. 96pp. ISBN 978-0-7614-1228-1. Grades 5–9. The seven chapters of the text discuss the journey that thousands of Cherokees were forced to take from Georgia to Oklahoma during the winter of 1838–1839 without proper food, clothing, or shelter. This "Trail of Tears" was the result of broken treaties when whites took over their homes after they had begun to assimilate into white society. Photographs and reproductions enhance the text. Bibliography, Notes, Further Reading, and Index.

1035. Englar, Mary. *The Cherokee and Their History.* (We the People) Compass Point, 2005. 48pp. ISBN 978-0-7565-1273-6. Grades 3–5. After telling the story of the tragic removal of the Cherokee from their traditional lands in the southern Appalachian Mountains and forced march to Oklahoma, Englar offers a history of the tribe. Their story includes Sequoyah, who created a written language for them, and their struggles against white settlers. Photographs and illustrations complement the text.

1036. Englar, Mary. *The Sioux and Their History.* (We the People) Compass Point, 2005. 48pp. ISBN 978-0-7565-1275-0. Grades 3–5. During the 1800s the United States government took much of the Sioux (Dakota) traditional land through treaties or despite treaties. When gold was discovered on Sioux land in the Black Hills of South Dakota, the Sioux fought to keep the land at the Battle of Little Bighorn. But by 1881 the government had confined the Sioux to reservations. Photographs and illustrations complement the text.

1037. Faber, Harold. *Lewis and Clark: From Ocean to Ocean.* (Great Explorations) Benchmark, 2001. 80pp. ISBN 978-0-7614-1241-0. Grades 5–9. In eight chapters, this volume looks at the journey made by Lewis and Clark and the Corps of Discovery beginning in 1804. The trip was undertaken to map the west at Thomas Jefferson's behest. Faber includes background information on the major participants with a chapter dedicated to Sacagawea and firsthand accounts of events and conditions the explorers encountered. Photographs, reprints, augment the text. Bibliography, Chronology, Further Reading, Web Sites, and Index.

1038. Farrell, Nancy Warren. *The Battle of the Little Bighorn.* (In American History) Enslow, 1996. 128pp. ISBN 978-0-8949-0768-5. Grades 5–9. After providing background information about events and people prior to the Battle of Little Bighorn in June 1876, Ferrell describes the battle itself and its aftermath through the massacre at Wounded Knee in 1890. Her balanced reporting presents several sides of the conflict and introduces figures including Red Cloud, Sitting Bull, and Crazy Horse. Index.

1039. Fisher, Leonard Everett. *The Oregon Trail.* Holiday House, 1990. 64pp. ISBN 978-0-8234-0833-7. Grades 5–9. Stunning photographs of the trail, along with maps and paintings by Albert Bierstadt and A. J. Miller, highlight the story of the 300,000 people who braved terrible conditions to reach the Willamette Valley of Oregon, mainly during the 1840s and 1850s. These pioneers wanted to find jobs; claim "free" land; gain wealth in timber, fur, fish, and ore; have an adventure; convert the heathens; escape the claustrophobia of the East; or improve their health. They called the worst conditions "seeing the elephant," and some who did not want to go north to Wyoming, where a flat "bridge" over the Rocky Mountains had been located, turned south instead and suffered for this decision, like the Donners in 1846. Native Americans furious at the killing of buffalo presented another challenge. Fewer people took the journey after the Civil War began. Index.

1040. Floca, Brian. *Lightship.* Richard Jackson, 2007. Unpaged. ISBN 978-1-4169-2436-4. Grades K–2. Floca describes a lightship, a floating lighthouse, that retired in 1983. He looks at the ship in all seasons and weathers, from inside to outside. As the crew of nine works to keep the ship in shape, it waits for bad weather and the opportunity to help other ships reach harbor safely. Ink-and-watercolor illustrations enhance the text. *Booklist Editor's Choice*, *American Library Association Notable Children's Books*, and *Robert F. Sibert Honor Book*.

1041. Fradin, Dennis B. *The Alamo.* (Turning Points in U.S. History) Benchmark, 2006. 45pp. ISBN 978-0-7614-2127-6. Grades 3–6. The Battle of the Alamo (in 1836) is an important landmark in Texas history. This volume gives the background of the battle, covers the battle itself, and looks at the aftermath. It also includes information on the leaders involved. Photographs and illustrations augment the text. Bibliography, Chronology, Web Sites, and Index.

1042. Freedman, Russell. *Cowboys of the Wild West.* Clarion, 1990. 103pp. Paper ISBN 978-0-395-54800-4. Grades 5–8. The cowboy trade began in Mexico during the 16th century, when the Spanish brought the first domesticated horses and cattle to North America. *Vaqueros*, barefoot Indian cow herders, learned to work with the cattle. To keep them together, they used *la reata*, the lariat. After the Civil War, men went to Texas where the cattle roamed free and began rounding them up. They drove the herds to Kansas railroad towns for shipment to the meat-packers in Chicago. The typical cowboy was less than 30 years old—the long days and hard work tired even the strongest. Cowboys' clothes had to be rugged; hats and bandannas were useful in a variety of ways, including as tourniquets for snakebites. Movie and television stereotypes ignore the difficulty of the job and the fact that most cowboys were either black or Mexican. Bibliography.

1043. Freedman, Russell. *In the Days of the Vaqueros.* Clarion, 2001. 70pp. ISBN 978-0-395-96788-1; Sandpiper, 2008, paper ISBN 978-0-54713-365-2. Grades 5 up. After cattle and horses arrived in Spanish Mexico in 1494, the first cowboys were actually Native Americans who called themselves *vaqueros* (from *vaca*, Spanish for *cow*). When settlers came to the American West, the vaqueros taught them how to do their jobs. The seven chapters describe how the vaqueros perfected their skills and influenced the cowboys who followed them. *Charlie May Simon Book Award* (Arkansas) nomination, *Booklist Editors Choice*, and *Capitol Choices Noteworthy Titles* (Washington, D.C.).

1044. Freedman, Russell. *An Indian Winter.* Illustrated by Karl Bodmer. Holiday House, 1992. 88pp. ISBN 978-0-8234-0930-3. Grades 4–6. In 1833 Prince Alexander Philip Maximillian, a German, and Karl Bodmer, a Swiss painter, went up the Missouri River into the heart of Indian country. They spent the winter with the People of the First Man, the Mandan Indians, in contemporary North Dakota. The prince kept a detailed journal, and the artist painted everyday scenes. Freedman tells their story and that of the Indians who fed and housed them. In 1837 smallpox almost eradicated the Mandans and the Hidatsas, and when the settlers began slaughtering buffalo in the 1860s and 1870s, the tribes vanished completely. Bibliography and Index.

1045. Graves, Kerry. *Going to School in Pioneer Times.* Blue Earth, 2001. 32pp. ISBN 978-0-7368-0804-0. Grades 4–6. The five chapters of the text look at a child's new home in the West, schooling in a one-room school house, what each day in school would be like, spelling bees, and kinds of tests. It details games, activities, special events, and crafts that children would have enjoyed. Photographs, maps, and illustrations augment the text. Glossary, Web Sites, and Index.

1046. Greenwood, Barbara. *A Pioneer Sampler: The Daily Life of a Pioneer Family in 1840.* Illustrated by Heather Collins. Houghton, 1998. 240pp. Paper ISBN 978-0-395-88393-8. Grades 5–8. Greenwood introduces the Robertsons, a pioneer family on a backwoods farm in 1840. Among the chores they undertake during a year are making maple syrup, planting crops, and shearing sheep. They attend a backwoods school, visit a country store, build a house, and go to a barn dance. They cook food, churn butter, slaughter hogs, and operate a grist mill. They tell time by looking at the sun, and they have no one to tell them the next day's weather. Glossary and Index. *Notable Children's Trade Books in the Field of Social Studies.*

1047. Halpern, Monica. *Railroad Fever: The Transcontinental Railroad 1830–1870.* (Crossroads America) National Geographic, 2004. 40pp. ISBN 978-0-7922-6767-6. Grades 3–5. The transcontinental railroad changed America. During the 1830s many miles of track were laid, but not until 1862 when Abraham Lincoln signed the Pacific Railroad Act did the chance for a transcontinental railroad become reality. Six chapters examine the railroad's construction by Chinese immigrants and former slaves and its influence once it was completed. The two companies racing to meet—the Central Pacific and the Union Pacific—were in competition. The one that laid the most track made the most money. Among the topics covered here are train robbers, first-class travel in Pullman cars, and the last-class "Zulu" cars. Photographs and illustrations enhance the text. Maps, Glossary, and Index.

1048. Harness, Cheryl. *They're Off! The Story of the Pony Express.* Aladdin, 2002. 32pp. Paper ISBN 978-0-689-85121-6. Grades 2–6. Stagecoaches took three weeks to deliver mail from Missouri to California. On April 3, 1860, the Pony Express began and proved that a relay of 80 men and 500 horses could take the mail from East to West in 10 days. This volume looks at this group of men and the dangers they faced. Bibliography.

1049. Haslam, Andrew. *Living History.* Two-Can, 2001. 256pp. ISBN 978-1-58728-381-9. Grades 3–6. Each section of the text offers information about four different civilizations—the Stone Age, Ancient Egypt, Roman Empire, and the North American Indians. The background includes housing, class differences, clothing, food, art, religion, class differences, and inventions. Instructions for making items such as an Egyptian game, Roman pottery, Japanese shinto shrine, and Sioux headdress also appear. Photographs offer illustrations of the various items mentioned in the text. Glossary and Index.

1050. Higgins, Nadia. *Spanish Missions of the Old West.* Rourke, 2007. 48pp. ISBN 978-1-60044-128-8. Grades 4–6. This volume describes the role of Spanish missionaries from the colonial period in the southwestern United States to the 1830s. It details mission life and discusses why the mission era ended. Quotes from primary sources appear throughout. Photographs, maps, augment the text. Bibliography, Glossary, Chronology, Notes, Further Reading, Web Sites, and Index.

1051. Ichord, Loretta Frances. *Skillet Bread, Sourdough, and Vinegar Pie: Cooking in Pioneer Days.* Illustrated by Jan Davey Ellis. (Cooking Through Time) Millbrook, 1998. 64pp. ISBN 978-0-7613-1864-4; 1999, paper ISBN 978-0-7613-9521-8. Grades 3–5. Settlers, pioneers, cowboys, and prospectors had to either grow or find, cook, and preserve their own food. The text covers their difficulties and the complications such as bugs or sickness, and includes recipes for bacon cornbread, skillet bread, dried apple pie, sourdough starter, sourdough flapjacks, Cornish pasties, vinegar pie, and chuck wagon beans. Illustrations augment the text. Bibliography and Index.

1052. Isaacs, Sally Senzell. *The Gold Rush.* (American Adventure) Heinemann, 2003. 32pp. Paper ISBN 978-1-4034-4772-2. Grades 3–6. Isaacs looks at living and working in mining towns, how people's lives changed during this time, and what they did when they could no longer find gold. Photographs and illustrations augment the text. Glossary, Chronology, Further Reading, and Index.

1053. Isaacs, Sally Senzell. *The Lewis and Clark Expedition.* (American Adventure) Raintree, 2003. 32pp. ISBN 978-1-4034-2503-4; paper ISBN 978-1-4034-4774-6. Grades 4–6. Isaacs tells the story of the Lewis and Clark Expedition to the Pacific from its inception in 1803 until its completion in 1806. Double-page chapters give a chronological view of the journey, discussing encounters with Native Americans, natural obstacles, and other pertinent information. Maps augment the text. Glossary, Chronology, Further Reading, and Index.

1054. Josephson, Judith Pinkerton. *Growing Up in Pioneer America, 1800 to 1890.* (Our America) Lerner, 2005. 64pp. ISBN 978-0-8225-0659-1. Grades 4–6. The six chapters of the book examine the daily lives of children living between 1800 and 1890 based on primary sources including letters written by the young people and their families, diaries, epigraphs, and authentic art. Sidebars add information about specific groups of children or cultural aspects of the 19th century. Photographs, Reproductions, Notes, Glossary, and Index.

1055. Kalman, Bobbie. *A Child's Day.* Illustrated by Tammy Everts. Crabtree, 1994. 32pp. ISBN 978-0-8650-5494-3. Grades 3–6. Using living history photographs, this volume describes a child's day in 19th-century America. Included are recipes, daily chores and rituals, schools, books read, games (e.g., hoop with stick), parties (e.g., blindman's buff), Sunday and church in good clothes, visitors, a country fair, and town merchants and their goods. Glossary and Index.

1056. Kalman, Bobbie. *Early Christmas.* See entry 399.

1057. Kalman, Bobbie. *Early Pleasures and Pastimes.* Crabtree, 1983. 95pp. ISBN 978-0-8650-5025-9. Grades 3–6. Kalman explores the leisure activities of families on the American and Canadian frontiers during the 19th century. Living photographs and drawings illustrate the text. Glossary and Index.

1058. Kalman, Bobbie. *Early Schools.* Illustrated by Antoinette DeBiasi. Crabtree, 1982. 32pp. ISBN 978-0-8650-5015-0. Grades 3–6. Frontier schools usually consisted of a single room, and children had to travel long distances to get to them. This volume describes the schools, the subjects taught, and their roles in the lives of settler children. Photographs and drawings enhance the text. Glossary and Index.

1059. Kalman, Bobbie. *Early Settler Storybook.* Crabtree, 1982. 64pp. ISBN 978-0-8650-5021-1. Grades 3–6. Before families had electricity, when they lived on the frontier as pioneers, reading was a significant form of entertainment. This volume includes various stories and poems that 19th-century families read together. Drawings highlight the text. Glossary and Index.

1060. Kalman, Bobbie. *Food for the Settler.* Illustrated by Antoinette DeBiasi. (Early Settler Life) Crabtree, 1982. 96pp. ISBN 978-0-8650-5013-6; paper ISBN 978-0-8650-5012-9. Grades 3–6. Early settlers and pioneers had to grow and prepare their own food. If they drank milk, they had to milk cows. If they ate meat, they had to kill the cows. Kalman presents the various types of food that people liked and what they prepared for special occasions. Glossary and Index.

1061. Kalman, Bobbie. *Games from Long Ago.* Illustrated by Antoinette DeBiasi. (Historic Communities) Crabtree, 1982. 96pp. ISBN 978-0-8650-5482-0; paper ISBN 978-0-8650-5521-6. Grades 3–6. Kalman looks at the board games, parlor games, and other games of the 1800s. Children still play some of them today, such as duck duck goose, charades, and baseball. But few people remember some of the others, such as shinny and jackstraws. Photographs from living museums and drawings augment the text.

1062. Kalman, Bobbie. *Home Crafts.* See entry 403.

1063. Kalman, Bobbie. *The Kitchen.* See entry 404.

1064. Kalman, Bobbie. *19th Century Clothing.* Illustrated by Antoinette "Cookie DeBiasi. (Historic Communities) Crabtree, 1993. 32pp. ISBN 978-0-8650-5493-6; paper ISBN 978-0-8650-5513-1. Grades 3–6. Drawings and engravings illustrate the clothing styles worn in the 19th century. Among the items considered are pioneer clothing, working clothes, women's fashions, men's fashions, underwear, footwear, hats and hairstyles, bathing clothes, sportswear, children's clothes, and mass-produced clothing toward the end of the century. Glossary and Index.

1065. Kalman, Bobbie. *A One-Room School.* Illustrated by Antoinette DeBiasi. (Historic Communities) Crabtree, 1994. 32pp. Paper ISBN 978-0-8650-5517-9. Grades 3–6. With photographs of people acting as frontier students in the 19th century, this volume shows what school was like. Teachers were never left-handed, and the schools had only one room. Other items covered are the subjects studied, supplies, transportation to school (walking or horseback), daily routine, lunch, recess, pranks, punishment, special events like spelling bees and pageants, and games. Glossary and Index.

1066. Kalman, Bobbie. *Settler Sayings.* Illustrated by Antoinette DeBiasi. (Historic Communities) Crabtree, 1994. 32pp. ISBN 978-0-8650-5498-1; paper ISBN 978-0-8650-5518-6. Grades 3–6. Many sayings still uttered today were part of the vernacular of the early settlers. They urged each other to "show your mettle" and believed that someone was "the apple of one's eye." They also commented about a "flash in the pan." The text looks at these and other phrases that began in the mill, in the kitchen, on the farm, in battle, and in workshops. Photographs from living museums and drawings augment the text.

1067. Kalman, Bobbie. *Tools and Gadgets.* Illustrated by Antoinette DeBiasi. (Historic Communities) Crabtree, 1991. 32pp. ISBN 978-0-8650-5488-2; 1992, paper ISBN 978-0-8650-5488-2. Grades 3–6. Tools help in getting work done, and a gadget is a clever device that helps with a small job. In the pioneer days, both were extremely important. Those covered in the text are home and food gadgets, mills, metalworking tools, woodworking tools, printing shop items, medical gadgets, children's toys and gadgets, cards, hackles, wheels, and shuttles. Photographs from living museums and drawings augment the text. Glossary and Index.

1068. Kalman, Bobbie, and Tammy Everts. *Customs and Traditions.* Illustrated by Antoinette DeBiasi. (Historic Communities) Crabtree, 1994. 32pp. ISBN 978-0-8650-5494-3. Grades 3–6. After an overview of customs and traditions, including a picture of a Chinese man eating with chopsticks, the chapters cover 19th-century social life and customs. Included are community customs, Sundays for the settlers, telling and remembering stories, predicting the weather, kitchen customs, health and cleanliness, holidays, courtship and marriage, a new baby, and various other habits. Photographs and reproductions highlight the text. Glossary, Further Reading, and Index.

1069. Kalman, Bobbie, and David Schimpky. *Fort Life.* (Historic Communities) Crabtree, 1994. 32pp. ISBN 978-0-8650-5496-7. Grades 3–6. Photographs from living museums help re-create life on a fort during the early years of the colonies. The text looks at the fort garrison, life in the barracks, the officers' quarters, drilling and music, guarding the fort, food, the infirmary, and other buildings. The text takes a close look at Fort Niagara and Fort George during the War of 1812. Glossary and Index.

1070. King, David C. *Projects About the Spanish West.* (Hands-On History) Benchmark, 2006. 47pp. ISBN 978-0-7614-1982-2. Grades 3–5. King provides information about the Spanish West and projects to accompany the fictional narrative. Included in the projects are a luminaria, yarn picture, ojo de Dios (eye of God), recipes, musical instruments, and a pinata. Photographs and illustrations augment the text. Glossary, Further Reading, Web Sites, and Index.

1071. Koslow, Philip. *The Seminole Indians.* Chelsea House, 1994. 79pp. ISBN 978-0-7910-1672-5. Grades 3–7. Native Americans and African Americans trying to escape subjugation banded together and ended up in the Florida Everglades. They called themselves "Seminoles," and they are the one Native American tribe that the U.S. government never defeated. Two bloody wars, the Seminole wars, showed that the government could not fight in the swamps of Florida. Photographs and engravings enhance the text. Glossary, Chronology, and Index.

1072. Kroll, Steven. *Lewis and Clark: Explorers of the American West.* Illustrated by Richard Williams. Holiday House, 1994. 32pp. ISBN 978-0-8234-1034-7; 1996, paper ISBN 978-0-8234-1273-0. Grades 4–7. The Louisiana Purchase prompted Thomas Jefferson to ask Meriwether Lewis to lead an expedition to the West Coast. Jefferson want to find a water route to make trade and travel easier and also to learn about the Indians living there. The journey began on May 14, 1804, with the help of William Clark and others, and before it ended on September 23, 1806, it revealed much about the new country. Afterword, Important Dates, and Index.

1073. Landau, Elaine. *The Transcontinental Railroad.* (Trailblazers of the West) Children's, 2005. 48pp. ISBN 978-0-51625-128-8; paper ISBN 978-0-51625-098-4. Grades 4–6. Landau examines the building of the transcontinental railroad, the first rail link between the Atlantic and Pacific. It discusses the disagreements between the pioneers and Native Americans as well as other obstacles to this major project in the late 1860s. Photographs, maps, augment the text. Glossary, Chronology, Notes, Further Reading, and Index.

1074. Levine, Michelle, and Tonia Hogner Weavel. *The Cherokees.* (Native American Histories) Lerner, 2006. 56pp. ISBN 978-0-8225-2443-4. Grades 4–7. The Cherokee people have faced much in their history, including being driven from their homeland in the Indian Removal Act and walking the Trail of Tears to another location. This volume describes the people, their daily lives, and the food they eat. Photographs and reproductions enhance the text. Further Reading, Bibliography, Glossary, Maps, Web Sites, and Index.

1075. McDaniel, Melissa. *The Powhatan Indians.* See entry 411.

1076. Marrin, Albert. *Saving the Buffalo.* Scholastic, 2006. 128pp. ISBN 978-0-439-71854-7. Grades 4–7. From 1800 to 1900 the number of bison or North American buffalo dwindled to one thousand head. One factor in the buffalo's disappearance was the government's efforts to move the Native Americans from the American plains. Eradicating the buffalo—and its physical and spiritual importance to the Indians—was a high priority. Realizing that the buffalo would become extinct, Theodore Roosevelt and others saved it. This volume investigates the animals' importance to its habitat. Illustrations enhance the text. Glossary, Further Reading, and Index. *James Madison Honor Book* and *Voice of Youth Advocates Nonfiction Honor List.*

1077. Morrison, Taylor. *The Coast Mappers.* Houghton, 2004. 48pp. ISBN 978-0-618-25408-8. Grades 5–8. Starting in 1850, George Davidson and his colleagues worked to survey the West Coast and create accurate nautical charts. Little was known about this coastline, and ships often crashed into rocks when their captains used atlases to navigate. The team of scientists faced major difficulties including remote locations, harsh terrain, and hostile Indians. Among their tools were star maps, telescopes, chronometers, plane tables, and stadia rods. Bibliography and Glossary.

1078. Murdoch, David H. *Cowboy.* Illustrated by Geoff Brightling. DK, 2000. 72pp. ISBN 978-0-7894-5854-4. Grades 3 up. This overview of cowboys covers dress—hats, boots, chaps, and spurs, charros and vaqueros, the best horses, saddles, life on the ranch, cattle and branding, ranges, trail drives, law and order, guns and gunslingers, the South American gaucho, the Camargue Gardians of France, cowgirls, cowboys in Australia, the rodeo, and the culture of the cowboy. Index.

1079. Myers, Walter Dean. *USS Constellation: Pride of the American Navy.* Holiday House, 2004. 96pp. ISBN 978-0-8234-1816-9. Grades 5–8. The USS *Constellation*, a ship launched in 1797 as part of America's first naval fleet, had a variety of roles during its life on the sea. It patrolled and intercepted illegal African slave trade vessels, won a victory against the French frigate *Insurgente*, challenged Barbary Coast pirates, and protected the Union army during the Civil War. First-person anecdotes help present the ship's commission, service, reconstruction, retirement, and renovation, and the crews' responsibilities. It was the last all-sail warship and now resides in Baltimore Harbor. Historical drawings and photographs, Chronology, Glossary, Web Sites, and Index.

1080. Parsons-Yazzie, Evangeline. *Little Woman Warrior Who Came Home: A Story of the Navajo Long Walk.* Illustrated by Irving Toddy. Salina Bookshelf, 2005. 32pp. ISBN 978-1-89335-455-5. Grades 2–6. In 1856 United States soldiers captured Dzán'baa' and made her and other Navajos walk 450 miles from their home at Black Mesa to Fort Sumter. Those who could not keep up were shot. On arrival at Fort Sumter, they found they could not grow crops there, and the only food available consisted of rotten meat and flour infested with bugs. Dzán'baa' reached puberty during the four years there but she refused to have her coming-of-age ceremony, the kinaaldá, until she returned home. In English and Navajo.

1081. Patent, Dorothy Hinshaw. *The Buffalo and the Indians: A Shared Destiny.* Illustrated by William Munoz. Clarion, 2006. 85pp. ISBN 978-0-618-48570-3. Grades 3–7. The American Indian depended on the buffalo for well-being for centuries. This volume covers this long relationship. President Ulysses S. Grant realized that to conquer the Native Americans, the armies would have to destroy the buffalo, and the government began the task. Their success at almost eradicating the buffalo ensured white control of the tribal lands. Photographs augment the text. Web Sites and Index. *Mountains and Plains Booksellers Association Regional Book Award* and *School Library Journal Best Children's Books.*

1082. Payment, Simone. *The Pony Express: A Primary Source History of the Race to Bring Mail to the American West.* Rosen, 2005. 64pp. ISBN 978-1-4042-0181-1. Grades 5–7. Payment examines the history of the Pony Express and its new, faster way to deliver mail across the country in 1860, using primary sources to give details of its history. Photographs and illustrations augment the text. Bibliography, Glossary, Chronology, Further Reading, and Index. *Voice of Youth Advocates Nonfiction Honor List.*

1083. Raum, Elizabeth. *The California Gold Rush: An Interactive History Adventure.* (You Choose) Capstone. 2007pp. ISBN 978-1-4296-0160-3; paper ISBN 978-1-4296-1179-4. Grades 3–6. In this story, readers can choose what role they would like to play during the California gold rush. After that decision, they make other historically plausible decisions and have the opportunity to see a variety of situations from different viewpoints. Color reproductions and maps enhance the text. Bibliography.

1084. Roberts, Russell. *Texas Joins the United States.* Mitchell Lane, 2007. 48pp. ISBN 978-1-58415-550-8. Grades 5–9. In the early 1800s settlers began venturing into uninhabited areas of Texas. In the Battles of San Jacinth and the Alamo, Texas defended itself. Despite Native American raids and repeated battles with tribes including the Comanches, Texas grew rapidly until it joined the United States in the waning days of the Tyler administration in 1846. Photographs, maps, and reproductions augment the text. Glossary, Notes, Further Reading, Web Sites, and Index.

1085. Roessel, Monty. *Songs from the Loom: A Navajo Girl Learns to Weave.* Lerner, 1995. 48pp. Paper ISBN 978-0-8225-9712-4. Grades 3–6. Drawing on the stories behind the designs in Navajo rugs, the author provides a history of the tribe and looks at how it weaves its rugs today. Photographs complement the text. Word List and For Further Reading. *Society of School Librarians International Outstanding Book.*

1086. Roop, Peter, and Connie Roop. *Off the Map: The Journals of Lewis and Clark.* Illustrated by Tim Tanner. Walker, 1998. 40pp. Paper ISBN 978-0-8027-7546-7. Grades 3–6. Lewis and Clark kept journals on their journey west from May 13, 1804, to March 23, 1806. The text looks at some of the entries and the information they relate about this trip. In February 1806, Clark completed a map of the country from Missouri to the Pacific. The expedition then turned around for the long trek home. Epilogue.

1087. Roop, Peter, and Connie Roop. *River Roads West: America's First Highways.* Calkins Creek, 2007. 64pp. ISBN 978-1-59078-430-3. Grades 5–8. The authors examine the importance of rivers—the Hudson, the Ohio, the Mississippi, the Missouri, the Rio Grande, the Colorado, and the Columbia—in the history of the United States. The Erie Canal is also covered. Each chapter examines the geography of the river, the Native American civilizations that lived near the river, the impact of the European explorers on each area, and the arrival of the settlers. Maps, photographs and illustrations complement the text. Bibliography, Further Reading and Web Sites.

1088. Ruffin, Frances E. *The Alamo.* (Places In American History) Gareth Stevens, 2006. 32pp. ISBN 978-0-8368-6407-6. Grades K–3. This short history covers the Battle of the Alamo in 1836 and the fight for Texas' independence. Each double-spread covers a single topics. Maps and illustrations augment the text. Bibliography, Glossary, and Index.

1089. Sandler, Martin W. *Trapped in Ice! An Amazing True Whaling Adventure.* Scholastic, 2006. 168pp. ISBN 978-0-439-74363-1. Grades 5–8. In 1871 thirty-two whaling ships with 1,219 people aboard became trapped in icy Arctic waters but were rescued with no losses. They had left port despite Inuit warnings of an early winter. Their journals, diaries, and ships' logs describe the entire ordeal. They had to unload into rafts and go eighty miles in subzero temperatures to reach the rescue ships. Photographs, maps, and period paintings augment the text. Glossary, Further Reading, and Index.

1090. Savage, Jeff. *Gunfighters of the Wild West.* Enslow, 1995. 48pp. ISBN 978-0-8949-0600-8. Grades 3–6. In the second half of the 19th century, gunfighters were notorious in the Wild West. The text looks at the outlaws and gangs and the lawmen who eventually put them out of business. Notes, Glossary, Further Reading, and Index.

1091. Savage, Jeff. *Pony Express Riders of the Wild West.* Enslow, 1995. 48pp. ISBN 978-0-8949-0602-2. Grades 3–6. On April 3, 1860, the Pony Express began carrying mail the 2,000 miles between St. Joseph, Missouri, and Sacramento, California. Only 18 months later, the telegraph put the service out of business, but while it proceeded men showed they could ride fast enough to get the mail delivered within 10 days. The text looks at these riders, who dodged angry Native Americans and thieves. Notes, Glossary, Further Reading, and Index.

1092. Shea, Therese. *Transcontinental Railroad.* (Math for the Real World) Rosen, 2006. 32pp. ISBN 978-1-4042-3361-4; 2005, paper ISBN 978-1-4042-6075-7. Grades 4–8. This volume covers the political, economic, and social factors leading to the construction of the cross-country rail link. Among the mathematical problems associated with such a task are using ratios, proportions, and algebraic equations to determine the cost for laying each mile of line, the profits made from railroad company stock, and the number of rails that should be laid in a particular time period. Photographs and maps enhance the text. Glossary and Index.

1093. Siebert, Diane. *Rhyolite: The True Story of a Ghost Town.* Illustrated by David Frampton. Houghton, 2003. 32pp. ISBN 978-0-618-09673-2. Grades K–3. During a 1904 gold strike, the town of Rhyolite, Nevada, grew from a single gold claim to a population of 10,000. But six years later, a financial panic had overwhelmed its inhabitants and they had departed, leaving it a ghost town. Woodcuts enhance the verse text. Notes. *Western Writers of America Spur Awards* nomination and *Red Clover Award* (Vermont) nomination.

1094. Smithyman, Kathryn. *Native North American Foods and Recipes.* (Native Nations of North America) Crabtree, 2006. 32pp. ISBN 978-0-7787-0383-9; paper ISBN 978-0-7787-0475-1. Grades 3–5. The traditional foods of Native Americans are the focus of this volume, which covers how they hunted and prepared meat, such as pemmican, and looks at important staples such as corn, squash, herbs, and rice. Illustrations complement the text.

1095. Sneve, Virginia Driving Hawk. *The Cherokees.* See entry 424.

1096. Sneve, Virginia Driving Hawk. *The Cheyennes.* See entry 425.

1097. Sneve, Virginia Driving Hawk. *The Seminoles.* Illustrated by Ronald Himler. (First Americans) Holiday House, 1994. 32pp. ISBN 978-0-8234-1112-2. Grades 3–6. A group split from the Muskogee tribe in Georgia and Alabama in 1708, when the whites came, and went to Florida. The Seminoles, or "separatists," were often Spanish citizens who owned their own slaves and offered protection to slaves running away from cruel Georgian masters. Because the Seminoles fought on the British side in the Revolutionary War, Andrew Jackson raided their villages during the War of 1812 and burned them. The First Seminole War lasted until

1819. The Second Seminole War occurred when the tribe refused to go to Oklahoma at the bidding of the 1828 Indian Removal Act. Two important leaders were Osceola and Coacoochee, and they led the Seminoles into the Everglades area. Bobek, or Billy Bowlegs, steered them through the Third Seminole War in 1855 against white settlers. Also incorporated are segments on daily life and ways of celebrating special occasions in the Seminole culture. Index.

1098. Spradlin, Michael P. *Off Like the Wind! The First Ride of the Pony Express.* Illustrated by Layne Johnson. Walker, 2010. 40pp. ISBN 978-0-8027-9652-3. Grades 2–5. Three businessmen—William H. Russell, Alexander Majors, and William B. Waddell—envisioned an express service that would carry mail across the country with stations every ten to fifteen miles along the route. They made the idea work, and this volume presents the first ride, which began on April 3, 1860, with Billy Hamilton leaving St. Joseph, Missouri, and Johnny Fry riding toward him from Sacramento. Each of them arrived at the opposite end eleven days later on April 13, 1860. The riders faced challenges including bad weather, buffalo, wolves, and hostile Native Americans. The endpapers contain a map and a timeline that begins on January 27, 1860, when the idea bloomed, and ends on November 21, 1861, when the service came to an end. Oil paintings enhance the text. Notes, Bibliography, Further Reading, and Web Sites.

1099. Spradlin, Michael P. *Texas Rangers: Legendary Lawmen.* Illustrated by Roxie Munro. Walker, 2008. Unpaged. ISBN 978-0-8027-8096-6. Grades 1–4. Formed in 1823 by colonial Texas Governor Stephen Austin, the Texas Rangers' mission was to protect the colonists living in the area that would become the state of Texas. One of their leaders, John Coffee Hays, gave them Colt revolvers. They fought at the Battle of the Alamo, apprehended Bonnie and Clyde, and arrested the outlaw, John Wesley Hardin. Although some had a violent reputation, they served well for many years. Colored-ink illustrations enhance the text.

1100. Suen, Anastasia. *Trappers and Mountain Men.* (Events In American History) Rourke, 2007. 48pp. ISBN 978-1-60044-134-9. Grades 4–6. This volume explores the lives of early western trappers and mountain men, the purchase of the Louisiana Territory from the French in 1803, and the Lewis and Clark Expedition to chart the new acquisition. Quotes from primary sources appear throughout. Photographs, maps, and illustrations augment the text. Bibliography, Glossary, Chronology, Notes, Further Reading, Web Sites, and Index.

1101. Swanson, Wayne. *Why the West Was Wild.* Annick, 2004. 46pp. ISBN 978-1-55037-837-5; paper ISBN 978-1-55037-836-8. Grades 5–8. This history and collective biography introduces the wild frontier of the West from the California gold rush of 1848 through the 1890s and looks at the people who lived there. Among those included are Buffalo Bill Cody, Wild Bill Hickock, Doc Holliday, Kit Carson, and Wyatt Earp. They had to cope with gunfights, hangings, train robbers, Indian displacement, and other difficult situations. It also discusses events that influenced their lives such as the Pony Express, railroads, and homesteading. Reproductions highlight the text.

1102. Tanaka, Shelley. *Alamo: Surrounded and Outnumbered, They Chose to Make a Defiant Last Stand.* Illustrated by David Craig. (A Day that Changed America) Hyperion, 2003. 48pp. ISBN 978-0-7868-1923-2. Grades 4–8. A short history of the siege of the Alamo in Texas in 1836. American "Texians" had been moving into Mexico in the early 1830s and President Santa Anna retaliated by sending troops to San Antonio. The twelve-day siege resulted in the deaths of the Texians who challenged him. In addition to biographical information on Santa Anna, this volume also includes information about James Bowie, Davy Crockett, William Travis, Susanna Dickinson, and others. The Battle of the Alamo led to statehood for Texas in 1845 and the end of the Mexican-American War in 1848, when Mexico lost half of its area.

1103. Uschan, Michael V. *The Transcontinental Railroad.* (Landmark Events In American History) World Almanac, 2003. 48pp. ISBN 978-0-8368-5410-7. Grades 4–8. Uschan examines the construction of the Transcontinental Railroad and presents a history of railroads in the United States. He also looks at the impact of this event on the country and other transportation modes. Photographs, maps, and illustrations augment the text.

1104. Wadsworth, Ginger. *Words West: The Voices of Young Pioneers.* Houghton, 2003. 208pp. ISBN 978-0-618-23475-2. Grades 5–8. This volume draws on letters, diaries, and memoirs of young people who traveled west with their pioneer parents to give an idea of their lives and situations. They hoped to go twenty miles a day in their wagon trains on their way to Oregon or to California for gold. They had tasks to perform and helped to cook the food. Many died or had accidents on the journey. They meet hostile Native Americans and endured drastic changes in weather as they trudged over mountains or across deserts. They saw the beauty of the country unfettered by modern life. Archival photographs and reproductions enhance the text. Notes, Bibliography, Timeline, Further Reading, Chronology, and Index. *Voice of Youth Advocates Nonfiction Honor List, Spur Award* and *PEN Center USA West Literary Awards* nomination.

1105. Waldman, Stuart. *The Last River: John Wesley Powell and the Colorado River Exploring Expedition.* Illustrated by Gregory Manchess. Mikaya, 2005. 47pp. ISBN 978-1-931414-09-8. Grades 4–7. In May 1869 ten men and four rowboats—the Colorado River Exploration Expedition—set out from Green River City, Wyoming. Three months and a thousand miles later, six of the men in two remaining boats arrived in the Grand Canyon having surveyed the last uncharted river in the United States. One-armed John Wesley Powell, a geology professor, led the group. Illustrations highlight the text, which includes journal entries from some of the participants. Bibliography, Maps, Web Sites, and Index.

1106. Walker, Niki. *Native North American Wisdom and Gifts.* (Native Nations of North America) Crabtree, 2005. 32pp. ISBN 978-0-7787-0384-6; paper ISBN 978-0-7787-0476-8. Grades 3–5. Walker looks at the contributions and influence of Native Americans, including foods they introduced that we still eat today, the use of scented fishing lures, the game of lacrosse, the parka, and jojoba as a shampoo ingredient. Illustrations complement the text.

1107. Walker, Paul Robert. *Remember Little Bighorn: Indians, Soldiers, and Scouts Tell Their Stories.* National Geographic, 2006. 61pp. ISBN 978-0-7922-5521-5. Grades 5–9. Walker uses archaeological evidence and eyewitness accounts recorded by soldiers, Indians, and scouts at the Battle of Little Bighorn in 1876 to sift fact from fiction. He carefully compares the conflicting points of view of the whites and the Sioux, Cheyenne, and Arapaho fighters. Maps, diagrams, and illustrations enhance the text. Bibliography, Chronology, and Index.

1108. Walker, Paul Robert. *Remember the Alamo: Texians, Tejanos, and Mexicans Tell Their Stories.* National Geographic, 2007. 61pp. ISBN 978-1-4263-0010-3. Grades 4–8. In June 1835 Texas was still part of Mexico, but the movement to separate was afoot, and the five chapters here explain the events preceding the Battle of the Alamo, the key individuals involved, and their reasons for fighting either for or against Santa Anna. Among those connected with the Alamo are Davy Crockett, Jim Bowie, and William Travis. Walker includes primary sources from Tejanos (Mexican-born Texans), Texians (Texans not born in Mexico), slaves, and women and children. Illustrations and maps highlight the text. Chronology and Index.

1109. Wilcox, Charlotte. *The Iroquois.* (Native American Histories) Lerner, 2006. 56pp. ISBN 978-0-8225-2637-7. Grades 3–6. The Iroquois people are actually a Confederacy of Six Nations. Wilcox describes the people, their daily lives, and the food they eat. Photographs and reproductions enhance the text. Further Reading, Bibliography, Glossary, Maps, Web Sites, and Index.

1110. Wood, Leigh Hope. *The Crow Indians.* Chelsea House, 1993. 79pp. ISBN 978-0-7910-1661-9. Grades 3–6. After relating the Crow legend of creation, the text gives the history of the Crow, who have lived on the Great Plains for thousands of years. They were corn farmers more than 1,800 years ago and were well established before others came to take their lands in the 19th century. The chapters cover their way of life, including the Sun Dance, battles, and their last traditional leader, Plenty Coups. Photographs enhance the text. Glossary, Chronology, and Index.

1111. Young, Jeff C. *Bleeding Kansas and the Violent Clash over Slavery in the Heartland.* (Wild History of the American West) Enslow, 2006. 128pp. ISBN 978-1-59845-013-2. Grades 5–9. When Kansas was admitted to the United States, its residents were conflicted about whether it would be a slave state or a free state. Young looks at the debate—which in essence mirrored the problems that arose during the Civil War—using quotes from period newspapers, songs, diaries, speeches, and other primary sources. He also discusses John Brown and the Pottawatomie Massacre, the difficulty of ratifying a constitution, and the resulting free state of Kansas. Illustrations enhance the text. Maps, Glossary, Further Reading, Notes, Web Sites, and Index. Spur Awards.

1112. Young, Jeff C. *The Pony Express and Its Death-Defying Mail Carriers.* (Wild History of the American West) Enslow, 2006. 128pp. ISBN 978-1-59845-010-1. Grades 5–9. The Pony Express became the mail delivery system for a short period during the 19th century. This volume presents stories and profiles of those involved in this endeavor in the American West. Illustrations augment the text. Further Reading, Maps, Notes, Chronology, Bibliography, Web Sites, and Index.

1113. Zimmerman, Karl. *Steam Locomotives: Whistling, Steaming, Chugging Locomotives of the Past.* Boyds Mills, 2004. ISBN 978-1-5907-8165-4. Grades 4–8. Zimmerman looks at steam locomotives—how they were developed, how they were powered, and why the diesel replaced them. They range from the tiny Tom Thumb to the largest locomotive every built, Big Boy. Those who know locomotives use the Whyte Classification System to group them according to the number of wheels. Photographs enhance the text. Glossary, Notes, Web Sites, and Index.

Biography and Collective Biography

1114. Adler, David A. *A Picture Book of Davy Crockett.* Illustrated by John and Alexandra Wallner. Holiday House, 1996. Unpaged. ISBN 978-0-8234-1212-9; 1998, paper ISBN 978-0-8234-1343-0. Grades 1–3. Davy Crockett (1786–1836) lived a life that became a legend. Adler looks at the facts and fiction about a man who boasted but who was also forthright and honest. Important Dates.

1115. Adler, David A. *A Picture Book of Lewis and Clark.* Illustrated by Ronald Himler. Holiday House, 2007. Unpaged. ISBN 978-0-8234-1735-3; paper ISBN 978-0-8234-1795-7. Grades K–3. This picture-book biography introduces the lives of Meriwether Lewis (1774–1809) and William Clark (1770–1838) and tells how they formed the Corps of Discovery to cross the continent to the Pacific. The text includes the highlights of the trip from its inception in 1803. Impressionistic illustrations complement the text. Bibliography, Chronology, Further Reading, Notes, and Web Sites.

1116. Adler, David A. *A Picture Book of Sacagawea.* Illustrated by Dan Brown. Holiday House, 2005. Unpaged. ISBN 978-0-8234-1485-7; 2001, paper ISBN 978-0-8234-1665-3. Grades 1–3. After a Hidatsa war party kidnapped the Shoshone girl Sacagawea, she was sold into marriage as the second wife of Charbonneau, a white trader and trapper. He served as the translator for the Lewis and Clark Expedition, the "Corps of Discovery," to the Pacific. Sacagawea was also able to assist because of her ability to communicate with the tribes encountered along the way. She had a son named Jean Baptiste, but little is known of the end of her life. Illustrations illuminate the text. Bibliography, Chronology, and Note.

1117. Aliki. *The Story of Johnny Appleseed.* Aladdin, 1963. Paper ISBN 978-0-671-66746-7. Grades K–3. John Chapman (1774–1845), born in Massachusetts and later known as Johnny Appleseed, decided to walk west, planting apple trees. He believed in the friendliness of humans, and Indians confirmed his trust when they nursed him back to health after finding him ill. He continued to travel and plant trees until his death.

1118. Aller, Susan Bivin. *Sitting Bull.* Illustrated by Tim Parlin. (History Maker Bios) Lerner, 2004. 47pp. ISBN 978-0-8225-0700-0; paper ISBN 978-0-8225-2072-6. Grades 3–5. Sitting Bull (1831–1890), a Lakota Sioux warrior and holy man, led his people at the Battle of Little Bighorn, where he defeated General Custer. He then guided his people across the Canadian border before surrendering himself so that they would not starve. Aller discusses his life, the Lakota Sioux, his contributions to his people, and the sacrifices both they and he made when faced by the hostile United States government. Sitting Bull was murdered while under government protection. Archival photographs and illustrations augment the text. Further Reading, Timeline, Bibliography, Web Sites, and Index.

1119. Aller, Susan Bivin. *Tecumseh.* (History Maker Bios) Lerner, 2004. 48pp. ISBN 978-0-8225-0699-7. Grades 3–5. Tecumseh (1768–1813) or "Shooting Star" became a valued warrior in his Shawnee tribe. He fought against the American soldiers who tried to take his people's homeland. He was also a politician who built a tribal federation to combat the unfair government treaties that undermined the rights of the Shawnee and other Native Americans. Illustrations augment the text. Bibliography, Further Reading, Glossary, Maps, Timeline, Web Sites, and Index.

1120. Alphin, Elaine Marie. *Davy Crockett.* (History Maker Bios) Lerner, 2003. 48pp. ISBN 978-0-8225-0393-4. Grades 3–5. Davy Crockett (1786–1836) never wore a coonskin hat; he wore a broad-brimmed felt hat. He fed his family by killing game and selling it. At the same time, he showed courage and lived with honor. Illustrations augment the text. Bibliography, Further Reading, Glossary, Maps, Timeline, Web Sites, and Index.

1121. Alter, Judy. *John Barclay Armstrong: Texas Ranger.* Bright Sky, 2007. 59pp. ISBN 978-1-931721-86-8. Grades 4–7. John B. Armstrong (1850–1913) went west and joined the Texas Rangers. He led an interesting career that paralleled the life of the Rangers and of Texas itself. Photographs augment the text. Chronology and Glossary.

1122. Anderson, Paul Christopher. *George Armstrong Custer: The Indian Wars and the Battle of the Little Bighorn.* (Library of American Lives and Times) PowerKids, 2004. ISBN 978-0-8239-6631-8. Grades 4–8. George Armstrong Custer (1839–1876) is known mainly for his defeat by Native Americans at Little Big Horn in 1876. Historians admit they have difficulty separating fact from fiction and question whether Custer was a military genius or simply ambitious. Reproductions, Photographs, Maps, Bibliography, Chronology, Further Reading, Glossary, Web sites, and Index.

1123. Anderson, William. *Laura Ingalls Wilder: A Biography.* HarperCollins, 2007. 240pp. Paper ISBN 978-0-06-088552-6. Grades 4–7. Laura Ingalls Wilder (1867–1957) wrote books about her own life. In this biography, Anderson divides the chapter headings into the time periods that relate to her fiction. Wilder and her pioneer family lived in Indian territory, Plum Creek, Burr Oak, and Dakota Territory. She was a prairie girl who married and lived with her own family in Big Red Apple, on Rocky Ridge Farm, and in Gem City in the Ozarks. Her family encouraged her to write the stories that she told so vividly, and she won many awards for them. Index.

1124. Anderson, William. *Prairie Girl: The Life of Laura Ingalls Wilder.* Illustrated by Renee Graef. (Little House) Harpercollins, 2004. 80pp. ISBN 978-0-06-028973-7; Collins, 2008, paper ISBN 978-0-06-442133-1. Grades 2–5. Laura Ingalls Wilder (1867–1957) wrote the well-known Little House books about her own life growing up on the prairie in the late 1800s. Thousands of grasshoppers did eat her family's crops, and the family moved many times. Her sister Mary's fever caused Mary's blindness, Laura married Almanzo Wilder, and her daughter was Rose. Wilder, however, did not write about the two years during which her family ran a hotel in Burr Oak, Iowa. Illustrations complement the text.

1125. Anderson, William. *River Boy: The Story of Mark Twain.* Illustrated by Dan Andreasen. Harpercollins, 2003. ISBN 978-0-06-028400-8. Grades 3–5. Samuel Clemens (1835–1910) wanted to explore the land beyond his home and probably dreamed about it when he heard the steamboat whistle on the Mississippi River. After leaving school at 12 when his father died, he worked at the *Hannibal Courier*, his local newspaper in Missouri, and then he worked as a steamboat pilot and later searched for gold in Nevada Territory. He began writing, eventually penning famous novels including *The Adventures of Huckleberry Finn* and *The Adven-*

tures of Tom Sawyer, under the name of Mark Twain. Illustrations augment the text. Chronology. *Young Readers' Choice Award* (Louisiana) nomination.

1126. Armentrout, David, and Patricia Armentrout. *John Muir.* Rourke, 2001. 24pp. ISBN 978-1-58952-055-4. Grades 2–4. John Muir (1838–1914) was a naturalist who founded the Sierra Club and persuaded President Theodore Roosevelt that saving land for the country was important. Eight chapters trace his life and work. Photographs highlight the text. Bibliography, Glossary, Chronology, Web Sites, and Index.

1127. Armstrong, Jennifer A. *Audubon: Painter of Birds of the Wild Frontier.* Abrams, 2003. 40pp. ISBN 978-0-8109-4238-7. Grades 5–9. John J. Audubon (1785–1851), the son of a wealthy West Indian planter, lived in France as a young boy before coming to America to paint its wilderness between 1804 and 1812. He met Daniel Boone, slept in a sycamore tree with 9,000 swifts, and survived the New Madrid earthquake. He also observed such wonders as trumpeter swans in a battle with wolves, swallows, and 160 flocks of passenger pigeons. Watercolor illustrations, some in double-page spreads, reveal the wonder of the land and the wildlife he saw. Notes.

1128. Basel, Roberta. *Sequoyah: Inventor of Written Cherokee.* (Signature Lives) Compass Point, 2007. 112pp. ISBN 978-0-7565-1887-5. Grades 5–8. Not everyone wanted Sequoyah (1770?–1843) to create a written Cherokee language. His wife actually burned down the house to keep him from his project. But his achievement gave the Cherokee tribes pride and a basis for unification. With quotations from primary sources, photographs, and illustrations. Bibliography, Further Reading, Web Sites, and Index.

1129. Behrman, Carol H. *Andrew Jackson.* (History Maker Bios) Lerner, 2004. ISBN 978-0-8225-1543-2. Grades 3–5. Andrew Jackson (1767–1845) was called the "people's president" because he grew up on the frontier and served as a soldier. As an adult, he became a lawyer, judge, and politician. Archival photographs and illustrations augment the text. Bibliography, Chronology, Further Reading, Web Sites, and Index.

1130. Blumberg, Rhoda. *York's Adventures with Lewis and Clark: An African-American's Part in the Great Expedition.* Collins, 2007. 96pp. Paper ISBN 978-0-06-009113-2. Grades 5–8. York (1775–ca. 1815), William Clark's slave, accomplished many tasks for the Corps of Engineers while it traveled to the west coast from 1803 to 1805. He hunted for food, helped build forts, and aided in improving relations with Native Americans along the way who were interested in his skin and physique. Yet when he returned east, he was treated like a slave and did not receive the double pay and 320 acres of land awarded to other participants, nor was his name included in the official list of explorers. Portraits augment the text. Bibliography, Notes, and Index.

1131. Brenner, Barbara. *On the Frontier with Mr. Audubon.* Boyds Mills, 1997. 96pp. Paper ISBN 978-1-56397-679-7. Grades 5–9. Joseph Mason spent 18 months traveling down the Ohio and Mississippi Rivers and through the swamplands of Louisiana with John James Audubon (1785–1851). He sketched 50 of the 435 plates that Audubon later included in his book, but for which he did not give Mason credit. Mason was surprised and angered, but by the time the book was published, he had established himself as a portrait painter in Philadelphia and no longer needed Audubon's approval or acknowledgment.

1132. Brimner, Larry Dane. *Davy Crockett.* Illustrated by Donna Berger. (Tall Tales) Compass Point, 2006. 32pp. Paper ISBN 978-0-7565-0893-7. Grades K–2. Davy Crockett (1786–1836) was a frontier settler who became a congressman and the subject of tall tales. He shared adventures with animals, comets, and Congress. This volume also includes a recipe for Tennessee grits. Illustrations, Bibliography, Further Reading, Glossary, Illustrations, Web Sites, Maps, and Index.

1133. Brown, Don. *American Boy: The Adventures of Mark Twain.* Houghton, 2003. 32pp. ISBN 978-0-618-17997-8; 2006, paper ISBN 978-0-618-68950-7. Grades K–4. Samuel Clemens or Mark Twain (1835–1910) spent his childhood in Cannibal, Missouri, roaming on the banks of the Mississippi and exploring caves with his friends, activities he later included in his books. Imagery evokes the time and place of Twain, and illustrations create character. Bibliography.

1134. Bruchac, Joseph. *A Boy Called Slow: The True Story of Sitting Bull.* Illustrated by Rocco Baviera. Philomel, 1995. 32pp. ISBN 978-0-399-22692-2; Puffin, 1998, paper ISBN 978-0-698-11616-0. Grades 1–5. A young Lakota boy called "slow" became the man who defeated the Crow and earned himself the name of Tatan'ka Iyota'ke or Sitting Bull (1831–1890). Bruchac looks at the actions that earned him his name. *American Library Association Notable Books for Children.*

1135. Burleigh, Robert. *Into the Woods: John James Audubon Lives His Dream.* Illustrated by Wendell Minor. Atheneum, 2003. 40pp. ISBN 978-0-689-83040-2. Grades 2–6. This biography of John James Audubon (1785–1851) contains excerpts from his diary, his drawings, and additional illustrations that reveal his life as a young man who wanted to live in a clean outdoors environment rather than a city. Poems interact with Audubon's words to show his mission, which was in conflict with his father's wishes. Notes.

1136. Capaldi, Gina. *A Boy Named Beckoning: The True Story of Dr. Carlos Montezuma, Native American Hero.* Carolrhoda, 2008. 32pp. ISBN 978-0-8225-7644-0. Grades 2–5. The Pima Indians captured 5-year-old Yavapai boy Wassaja in 1871 and sold him to an Italian photographer. He was renamed Carlos Montezuma (1866–1923). Highly intelligent, he attended the University of Illinois and graduated at 17. He then became a doctor. Later, he returned to Arizona to search for his family, but sadly discovered that they had died. He continued to help his people as a physician. Beautiful illustrations enhance the text. Bibliography and Web Sites.

1137. Caravantes, Peggy. *An American in Texas: The Story of Sam Houston.* (Notable Americans) Morgan Reynolds, 2003. 144pp. ISBN 978-1-93179-819-8. Grades 5–8. Sam Houston (1793–1829) was the first president of the Republic of Texas and governor of the state of Texas from 1859 to 1860. His defeat of Santa Anna in a battle lasting eighteen minutes established Texas's independence from Mexico. Although a rebel as a young man, he became a teacher, a soldier, a hero, an Indian Bureau agent, a lawyer, and a governor of Tennessee before he went to Texas and became a hero. He also spent years with the Cherokee and was deeply conflicted in his relationships with Andrew Jackson and Cherokee Chief Jolly. Illustrations enhance the text. Bibliography, Chronology, Notes, Web Sites, and Index.

1138. Cavan, Seamus. *Daniel Boone and the Opening of the Ohio Country.* (World Explorers) Chelsea House, 1990. 111pp. ISBN 978-0-7910-1309-0. Grades 5 up. The story of Daniel Boone (1734–1820) is the story of the settlement along the western frontier of the American colonies and later the states. His family moved frequently, and he continued this tradition by going to Kentucky after he fought with the British in the losing battle at Monongahela. He married Rebecca in 1756 when both were young. She and ten children (later seven after Indians killed three) endured his long absences from home while exploring, until her death at 73. Boone earned and lost money enough times so that he lived both an extravagant life and a frugal one as he moved westward to St. Louis and then further west. Not until his mid-eighties did he begin to lose strength, and he died at 86. Paintings, drawings, photographs, and maps clarify the history of the times. Further Reading, Chronology, and Index.

1139. Christensen, Bonnie. *The Daring Nellie Bly: America's Star Reporter.* Random, 2003. 32pp. ISBN 978-0-375-81568-3. Grades K–2. Nelly Bly (1864–1922) had a broad career after growing up poor. She became the first woman to work at the *Pittsburgh Dispatch*, was a "stunt reporter" for the *New York World* in the late 1800s, went undercover to an insane asylum and then published a story about it, went around the world alone in seventy-two days, and served as a war correspondent during World War I. The text and illustrations tell her story. Bibliography, Chronology, and Videography.

1140. Collard, Sneed B., III. *Sacagawea: Brave Shoshone Girl.* (American Heroes) Benchmark, 2006. 40pp. ISBN 978-0-7614-2166-5. Grades 3–5. This biography of Sacagawea (ca. 1788–1812) focuses on her humanity as well as the help she provided Lewis and Clark on their mapping expedition to the Pacific. Anecdotes and clear descriptions give new insight into her life. Reproductions and museum images accompany the text. Glossary, Further Reading, and Index.

1141. Collins, David. *Mark T-W-A-I-N! A Story About Samuel Clemens.* Illustrated by Vicky Carey. Carolrhoda, 1993. 64pp. ISBN 978-0-8761-4345-2. Grades 3–6. Samuel Clemens (1835–1910) grew up in Hannibal, Missouri. He later became a newspaperman and a writer after experimenting with being a steamboat pilot, a soldier, and a gold prospector. He took his pseudonym from his experience as a steamboat pilot. Some people consider *Tom Sawyer* and *Huckleberry Finn* to be books for children; others believe they are for adults. Mark Twain was born the year that Halley's comet swept into the sky, and it came back the year he died. Books and Bibliography.

1142. Connell, Kate. *These Lands Are Ours: Tecumseh's Fight for the Old Northwest.* Illustrated by Jan Naimo Jones. Steck-Vaughn, 1992. 68pp. Paper ISBN 978-0-8114-8067-3. Grades 4–8. When white settlers and the U.S. government began to take Indian lands, one of the leaders who emerged to help his people was Tecumseh (1768–1813). He was a Shawnee warrior and orator who united a confederacy of Indians to save the Indian lands. At the Battle of Tippecanoe in 1811, the Long Knives (government soldiers) under Governor William Henry Harrison defeated the Indians. Tecumseh was furious at the setback and blamed his brother for the defeat while he had been trying to talk to other tribes. With Tecumseh's death in 1813 while fighting for the British against Harrison, the Indians lost their organizer. Epilogue, Afterword, and Notes.

1143. Crow, Joseph Medicine, and Viola Herman. *Counting Coup: Becoming a Crow Chief on the Reservation and Beyond.* National Geographic, 2006. 128pp. ISBN 978-0-7922-5391-4. Grades 5–9. Joseph Medicine Crow (1913–) began training to be a Crow warrior when he was 6 years old. He recounts the prejudices he faced at Baptist, public, and boarding schools, and his fear of whites, Sioux, and ghosts. But he succeeded and went to graduate school until leaving to fight in World War II. In Germany he completed the four war deeds expected of a Crow warrior. In 1948 he became Joseph Medicine Crow (High Bird), the tribal historian and anthropologist of his tribe. At over ninety years old, he is the last traditional chief of his people.

1144. Dennis, Yvonne Wakim J. *Sequoyah, 1770?–1843.* (American Indian Biographies) Blue Earth, 2004. 32pp. ISBN 978-0-7368-2447-7. Grades 3–5. Sequoyah invented a way to write the Cherokee language in 1821. The text includes information about the Cherokee, details of a traditional dish, and other pertinent information. Illustrations and photographs enhance the text. Maps, Bibliography, Further Reading, Glossary, Web sites, and Index.

1145. Donovan, Sandra. *Will Rogers: Cowboy, Comedian, and Commentator.* (Signature Lives) Compass Point, 2007. 112pp. ISBN 978-0-7565-2463-0. Grades 4–8. This biography of Will Rogers (1879–1935) covers his life from his childhood to his roping act and his success as a humorist. Of Cherokee heritage, he became a nationally known newspaper columnist and one of Hollywood's biggest stars. Sidebars offer quotations and explanations of related topics. Illustrations augment the text. Bibliography, Further Reading, Glossary, Maps, Timeline, Web Sites, and Index.

1146. Edwards, Judith, and Ruben Field. *The Great Expedition of Lewis and Clark: By Private Reubin Field, Member of the Corps of Discovery.* Farrar, 2003. 40pp. ISBN 978-0-374-38039-7. Grades 2–5. Private Reubin Field (ca. 1771–1822) and his brother Joseph accompanied Lewis and Clark across the country as members of the Corps of Discovery from 1803 to 1806. He recalls the hazards—grizzly bears, mountain passes, and buffalo—and the encounters with both friendly and hostile Native Americans. He knew Sacagawea, Charbonneau, and York as well as other historical figures, and records all of this in a journal. Illustrations augment the text. Bibliography.

1147. Eisenberg, Jana. *Lewis and Clark: Path to the Pacific.* Children's, 2005. 48pp. ISBN 978-0-51625-126-4; paper ISBN 978-0-51625-096-0. Grades 1–2. At the request of President Thomas Jefferson, Lewis and Clark set off in an expedition to map parts of the western United States. They met Native Americans and learned from them with the help of Saca-

gawea. The simple chapters give background about their journey. Photographs and reproductions enhance the text. Glossary, Further Reading, Web Sites, and Index.

1148. Englar, Mary. *Chief Joseph 1840–1904.* (American Indian Biographies) Capstone, 2004.
32pp. ISBN 978-0-7368-2444-6. Grades 3–5. Chief Joseph led his Nez Percé tribe of Dakota
Indians in their fight against the United States Army. General Oliver O. Howard tried to
move the tribe and other "non-treaty" Indians to a reservation in Idaho. Chief Joseph, who
had hoped to avoid violence and find freedom in Canada, finally surrendered to the Army in
1877. Chief Joseph's honorable resistance and famous words, "I will fight no more forever,"
gave him a reputation as a peacemaker and a humanitarian. Later Chief Joseph spoke in
Washington about the rights of his people. Photographs, Glossary, Maps, Illustrations, Bibliography, Further Reading, Timeline, Web sites, and Index.

1149. Engstrand, Iris Wilson. *John Sutter: Sutter's Fort and the California Gold Rush.* (Library
of American Lives and Times) PowerKids, 2004. 112pp. ISBN 978-0-8239-6630-1. Grades 4–
8. John Sutter (1803–1880) has become associated with the California gold rush. Born in
Germany, he came to America to find his fortune and spent three years trading on the Santa
Fe Trail. From there he went to Mexican California, bought 50,000 acres of land, built Sutter's Fort, and became wealthy. The discovery of gold on his land cost him his fortune while
gaining him fame. Reproductions, Photographs, Maps, Bibliography, Chronology, Further
Reading, Glossary, Web Sites, and Index.

1150. Erdrich, Liselotte. *Sacagawea.* Illustrated by Julie Buffalohead. Carolrhoda, 2003. 40pp.
ISBN 978-0-8761-4646-0. Grades 2–6. When the Shoshone girl Sacagawea was 11 years old,
members of the Hidatsa tribe kidnapped her. At age 15 she became the wife of an older
French Canadian fur trapper and gave birth to a son before she and her husband joined the
Lewis and Clark expedition in 1803. Although she was merely along for the trip because her
husband expected her to come, she saved the expedition by helping the men when they
encountered Native Americans. Illustrations complement the text. Bibliography and
Chronology.

1151. Feinstein, Stephen. *Read About Annie Oakley.* (I Like Biographies) Enslow, 2006. 24pp.
ISBN 978-0-7660-2583-7. Grades 2–4. Annie Oakley (1860–1926), her mother, and her six
siblings endured many hardships after the death of her father. She learned to shoot in order
to get food for them, and her ability eventually led her to a job as a sharpshooter in Buffalo
Bill's Wild West Show. Archival photographs and reproductions accompany the text. Chronology, Further Reading, Web Sites, and Index.

1152. Feinstein, Stephen. *Read About Geronimo.* (I Like Biographies) Enslow, 2006. 24pp. ISBN
978-0-7660-2598-1. Grades 2–4. Geronimo (1829–1909), an Apache Indian, led raids into
Mexican and American territory after both groups mistreated his people. He had reason to
be angry with their actions especially after they massacred his family. Archival photographs
and reproductions accompany the text. Chronology, Further Reading, Web Sites, and Index.

1153. Ferris, Jeri. *Native American Doctor: The Story of Susan La Flesche Picotte.* Illustrated by
Karen Ritz. Carolrhoda, 1991. 88pp. ISBN 978-0-8761-4443-5; First Avenue paper ISBN 978-
0-8761-4548-7. Grades 5–8. Susan La Flesche (1865–1915), of the Omaha tribe, went East
for her education, and after high school, received a scholarship to the Hampton Institute in
Virginia. There she met a woman doctor, and she decided that she wanted to be a doctor
herself. After medical school, she returned to help her people, despite a troublesome recur-
ring illness. She played many roles in her relationship with her people—doctor, teacher,
nurse, financial and legal adviser, translator, and fighter against alcohol. Before she died, she
helped raise money so that the Omaha people could have their own hospital. Notes, Bibliography, and Index.

1154. Fleischman, Sid. *The Trouble Begins at 8: A Life of Mark Twain in the Wild, Wild West.*
Greenwillow, 2008. 224pp. ISBN 978-0-06-134431-2. Grades 5–9. This biography of Mark
Twain (1835–1910) focuses on Twain's early days in Missouri and his adventures in the Wild
West, when he made speeches advertising that the door would open at 7 p.m. with the trou-
ble starting at 8. Twain was a steamboat pilot, journalist, prospector, and lecturer—a man

who did not mind trouble. He used his adventures as incidents in his novels *The Adventures of Tom Sawyer* and *Huckleberry Finn*. Samuel Clemens did not take the name Mark Twain until he was 30 years old. Among the comments in the biography is that Twain "did not have a gift for caution." Photographs highlight the text. Bibliography, Chronology, Notes, and Index. *Publishers Weekly Best Books, Capitol Choices Noteworthy Titles* (Washington, D.C.), and *School Library Journal Best Books for Children*.

1155. Fraser, Mary Ann. ***In Search of the Grand Canyon: Down the Colorado with John Wesley Powell.*** Henry Holt, 1997. Paper ISBN 978-0-8050-5543-6. Grades 3–6. Until May 24, 1869, when Major John Wesley Powell and nine men set out to explore the Colorado River, the area was a blank space on existing maps. The Anasazi people had once lived there, but trappers and guides had only passed by it. Powell thought it would be important as the nation grew. The text looks at each day of the exploration and tells of the rapids, whirlpools, and canyons that Powell found along the river. Photographs and drawings augment the text. Bibliography and Index.

1156. Fritz, Jean. ***Make Way for Sam Houston.*** Illustrated by Elise Primavera. Puffin, 1998. 109pp. Paper ISBN 978-0-698-11646-7. Grades 4–6. Sam Houston (1793–1863) was one of the founding fathers of Texas. He loved the limelight and dressed for every occasion as if he were playing a role on the stage. Before he got to Texas, he had been wounded in battle, elected as governor of Tennessee and to the U.S. Congress, and had left civilization to live with the Cherokees twice. He adopted an Indian name and wore a queue when he lived among the Cherokees. He had a number of nicknames such as the "Big Drunk," the "Old Dragon," the "Great Designer," and the "Hero of San Jacinto." After he went to Texas, he continued to serve his country in leadership roles. Notes, Bibliography, and Index.

1157. Furbee, Mary R. ***Outrageous Women of the American Frontier.*** Jossey-Bass, 2002. 120pp. Paper ISBN 978-0-471-38300-0. Grades 3–6. A collective biography profiling pioneer women who were influential but whom some considered too outspoken: Sacagawea (1787–18??), Gertrudis Barcelo (18??–1852), Narcissa Whitman (1808–1847), Juana Briones (1802v1889). Luzena Stanley Wilson (1821–18??), Eliza Snow (1804–1887), Bridget "Biddy" Mason (1818–1891), Charlie Parkhurst (1812–1879), Martha "Calamity Jane" Cannary (18??–1903), "Stagecoach" Mary Fields (1832–1914), Sarah Winnemucca Hopkins (1844–1891), Libbie Custer (1842–1933), Nellie Cashman (18??–1925), and Evelyn Cameron (1868–1928). Furbee includes these women because they were originals who contributed to American life in unique ways. She also lists other women one might consider outrageous. Further Reading and Chronology.

1158. Gleiter, Jan, and Kathleen Thompson. ***Kit Carson.*** Illustrated by Rick Whipple. (First Biographies) Steck-Vaughn, 1995. 32pp. Paper ISBN 978-0-8114-9352-9. Grades K–3. Kit Carson (1809–1868) and his family moved to various places with Daniel Boone's family, and Boone taught him hunting and respect for Native American ways. Carson eventually settled in Taos, New Mexico. He met and married an Arapaho woman who bore him a daughter before she died. He left his daughter in the care of others and became a guide for John Carlos Frémont's exploration between Missouri and the Rocky Mountains. Afterward, he lived with the Utes and believed that the federal government had betrayed the Indian tribes. Key Dates.

1159. Gleiter, Jan, and Kathleen Thompson. ***Sacagawea.*** Illustrated by Yoshi Miyake. (First Biographies) Steck-Vaughn, 1998. 32pp. Paper ISBN 978-0-8172-6889-3. Grades K–3. After being kidnapped from her tribe, Sacagawea (ca. 1788–1812) became Lewis and Clark's translator. Gleiter notes that Lewis and Clark did not like her husband but included him in the expedition because they needed her help. The text also suggests that the expedition would not have been successful without Sacagawea's Shoshone connections, especially with her brother, chief of the tribe. Key Dates.

1160. Green, Carl R., and William R. Sanford. ***Billy the Kid.*** (Outlaws and Lawmen of the Wild West) Enslow, 2008. 48pp. ISBN 978-0-7660-3173-9. Grades 5–6. Billy the Kid supposedly killed twenty-one men, one for each year of his life, but he probably killed only nine. He was a member of a gang known for stealing cattle and horses and having gunfights.

He always managed to escape the law. With photographs. Glossary, More Good Reading, and Index.

1161. Green, Carl R., and William R. Sanford. *Butch Cassidy.* (Outlaws and Lawmen of the Wild West) Enslow, 2008. 48pp. ISBN 978-0-7660-3175-3. Grades 5–6. Butch Cassidy (b. 1866) was an outlaw who had a gang called the Wild Bunch. Newspapers, magazines, and dime novels reported their exploits. This volume presents him, his group, and what they did. Glossary, More Good Reading, and Index.

1162. Green, Carl R., and William R. Sanford. *Jesse James.* (Outlaws and Lawmen of the Wild West) Enslow, 2008. 48pp. ISBN 978-0-7660-3172-2. Grades 5–6. Jesse James (1847–1882) and his gang held up banks, robbed trains and stagecoaches, got caught, and made escapes from the law that became famous. Some have said that James robbed from the rich to give to the poor, but others say he was a murderer who kept the money for himself. This volume tries to tell the facts. Glossary, More Good Reading, and Index.

1163. Green, Carl R., and William R. Sanford. *Wyatt Earp.* (Outlaws and Lawmen of the Wild West) Enslow, 2008. 48pp. ISBN 978-0-7660-3174-6. Grades 5–6. Wyatt Earp (1848–1929) fought against the Clanton gang in the Shootout at O.K. Corral. Earp and his brothers were trying to remove thieves from Tombstone, Arizona. Earp first became a lawman in Dodge City, Kansas. He was known for hitting people with his gun rather than shooting them. His friends included Bat Masterson and Doc Holliday. When he died, he owned mines and oil fields. Photographs, Glossary, More Good Reading, and Index.

1164. Gregson, Susan R. *James Beckwourth: Mountaineer, Scout, and Pioneer.* (Signature Lives) Compass Point, 2005. 112pp. ISBN 978-0-7565-1001-5; paper ISBN 978-0-7565-1846-2. Grades 5–8. James Beckwourth (1798–1866) was an African American slave before he became a mountain man, a Crow chief, and storyteller. The Native Americans respected him until he was forced in 1864 to assist Colonel John Chivington on a raid of Chief Black Kettle's camp. Photographs, maps, and reproductions highlight the text. Bibliography, Glossary, Chronology, Notes, Further Reading, Web Sites, and Index.

1165. Harness, Cheryl. *The Tragic Tale of Narcissa Whitman and a Faithful History of the Oregon Trail.* (Cheryl Harness History) National Geographic, 2006. 144pp. ISBN 978-0-7922-5920-6. Grades 5–8. Narcissa Whitman (1808–1847) loved reading about Christians overcoming "barbarians" when she was growing up. In 1831 a group of Native Americans arrived in St. Louis, Missouri, asking for the "White Man's Book of Heaven." She wanted to help them, and after she married Marcus Whitman in 1836, they traveled more than 2,000 miles west on the Oregon Trail, settling in Oregon and becoming missionaries. No other white woman was known to have entered that territory, and she served at Waiilatpu Mission to the Cayuse until her death in a massacre. The text includes excerpts from her journals. Line drawings enhance the text. Maps, Bibliography, Chronology, Further Reading, Web Sites, and Index.

1166. Harness, Cheryl. *The Trailblazing Life of Daniel Boone and How Early Americans Took to the Road.* National Geographic, 2007. 144pp. ISBN 978-1-4263-0146-9. Grades 4–8. This biography of Daniel Boone (1734–1820) follows his life from his childhood in Pennsylvania, through his service in the French and Indian War, his journey across the Appalachian Mountains, the War of 1812, and his final settlement of Boonesboro, Kentucky. He also traveled into Missouri as he helped to settle the frontier and battled Native Americans. A chapter looking at modes of travel ends the work. Photographs and illustrations augment the text. Bibliography, Chronology, Further Reading, and Index.

1167. Harrison, David L. *Johnny Appleseed: My Story.* Illustrated by Mike Wohnoutka. Random, 2001. 48pp. Paper ISBN 978-0-375-81247-7. Grades 1–2. In an early-reader fictional approach to Johnny Appleseed (1774–1845), the text tells of Johnny's journey to plant apple trees. He meets people who feed him, and he chops wood and tells stories about his experiences. Paintings complement the text.

1168. Haugen, Brenda. *Crazy Horse: Sioux Warrior.* (Signature Lives) Compass Point, 2005. 112pp. ISBN 978-0-7565-1001-5; paper ISBN 978-0-7565-1844-8. Grades 5–8. The Sioux people loved Crazy Horse (1842–1877) because he was generous to them and determined to protect them. He tried to save their lands from the homesteaders and helped to win the Battle of the Little Bighorn. Photographs, maps, and reproductions augment the text. Bibliography, Glossary, Chronology, Notes, Further Reading, Web Sites, and Index.

1169. Haugen, Brenda. *Geronimo: Apache Warrior.* (Signature Lives) Compass Point, 2005. 112pp. ISBN 978-0-7565-1002-2; paper ISBN 978-0-7565-1845-5. Grades 5–8. Geronimo (1829–1909) was a great warrior who fought for his people's freedom. He later refused to resettle and fled to Mexico with his supporters. The government later recaptured him and made him relocate to Fort Sill, Oklahoma. Photographs, maps, and reproductions highlight the text. Bibliography, Glossary, Chronology, Notes, Further Reading, Web Sites, and Index.

1170. Houston, Gloria. *My Great-Aunt Arizona.* Illustrated by Susan Condie Lamb. Trophy, 1997. Unpaged. Paper ISBN 978-0-06-443374-7. Grades 1–4. Great-Aunt Arizona, named for the state that her brother said was so beautiful, wanted to travel there from her home in the Blue Ridge Mountains but never did. She stayed at home, married, and taught the children who grew up there. She always encouraged those who could to go out and see the world.

1171. Jakes, John. *Susanna of the Alamo: A True Story.* Illustrated by Paul Bacon. Voyager, 1990. Unpaged. Paper ISBN 978-0-15-200595-5. Grades 2–4. Susanna Dickinson survived the massacre at the Alamo in 1836, unlike Davy Crockett, Jim Bowie, and William Barrett Travis. Mexico's General Santa Anna spared her so that she could see his power over Sam Houston's rebel Texas army. She refused to become his emissary, however, and her report that he had burned the fallen men instead of burying them inspired the Texans to defeat Santa Anna at San Jacinto.

1172. Jones, Charlotte Foltz. *Westward Ho! Eleven Explorers of the West.* Holiday House, 2005. 233pp. ISBN 978-0-8234-1586-1. Grades 5–9. This collective biography presents eleven white men who faced danger in occupied Native American lands to help open the American West in the 18th and 19th centuries. The men featured are Robert Gray (1755–1806), George Vancouver (1757–11798), Alexander Mackenzie (1764–11820), John Colter (1774 or 1775–11813), Zebulon Montgomery Pike (1779–11813), Stephen Harriman Long (1784–11864), James Bridger (1804–11881), Jedediah Strong Smith (1799–11831), Joseph Reddeford Walker (1798–11876), John C. Fremont (1813–11890), and John Wesley Powell (1834–11902). Maps, illustrations, cartoons, and portraits complement the text. Bibliography, Chronology, Notes, and Index.

1173. Jumper, Moses, and Ben Sonder. *Osceola: Patriot and Warrior.* Illustrated by Patrick Soper. Steck-Vaughn, 1992. 76pp. Paper ISBN 978-0-8114-8065-9. Grades 4–6. Osceola (1804–1838) fought to keep his Seminole people on the Florida land that the United States government had pinpointed for white settlement. The government also wanted to find the runaway slaves who had found refuge with the Seminoles and return them to their owners. In the Second Seminole War, Osceola helped some of the Seminoles flee into the Everglades, but other leaders betrayed him. Epilogue, Afterword, and Notes.

1174. Kay, Verla. *Rough, Tough Charley.* Illustrated by Adam Gustavson. Tricycle, 2007. 32pp. ISBN 978-1-58246-184-7. Grades K–3. Disguised as a man, Charley Parkhurst (1812–1879) became a stablehand and then a Wild West stagecoach driver. Because she had adopted a male identity, she was able to vote for fifty years before women in California gained this right. After Parkhurst retired from the stagecoach career, "he" joined a local lodge and settled as a respected citizen. Not until he died did doctors discover that "he" was a woman. The cryptic rhyming couplets keep the reader from knowing Charley's secret until the end. Oil illustrations enhance the text. Chronology.

1175. Kellogg, Steven. *Johnny Appleseed.* Morrow, 1988. 48pp. ISBN 978-0-688-06417-4. Grades 2–4. His mother dead within two years of his birth in Massachusetts in 1774 and his father away at war, John Chapman decided that when he was old enough to leave, he would. He took apple seeds and planted them from the Allegheny Mountains into Ohio and Indiana for the rest of his life, never settling in one place as far as anyone knows. His kindness prompted those who knew him to embellish their tales about him.

1176. Kiely Miller, Barbara. *Chief Joseph.* (Great Americans) Gareth Stevens, 2007. 24pp. ISBN 978-0-8368-8314-5; paper ISBN 978-0-8368-8321-3. Grades 2–4. Nez Percé Chief Joseph (1840–1904) grew up in the Wallowa Valley and helped his tribe flee from the United States government before he was imprisoned in Oklahoma. Then he became the spokesman for his tribe. Photographs and illustrations enhance the text. Glossary, Further Reading, Web Sites, and Index.

1177. Kiely Miller, Barbara. *John Muir.* (Great Americans) Gareth Stevens, 2007. 24pp. ISBN 978-0-8368-8318-3; paper ISBN 978-0-8368-8325-1. Grades 2–4. John Muir (838–1914) loved nature as a child living on a Wisconsin farm. He wanted to protect Yosemite's natural resources so he founded the Sierra Club. Afterward, he traveled around the world to talk and write about environmentalism. Photographs and illustrations enhance the text. Glossary, Further Reading, Web Sites, and Index.

1178. Kiely Miller, Barbara. *Sam Houston.* (Great Americans) Gareth Stevens, 2007. 24pp. ISBN 978-0-8368-8316-9; paper ISBN 978-0-8368-8323-7. Grades 2–4. Sam Houston (1793–1863) lived with the Cherokee when he was a teenager. Then he became a Tennessee representative and governor before becoming involved in the war to give Texas independence from Mexico. Photographs and illustrations enhance the text. Glossary, Further Reading, Web Sites, and Index.

1179. Klingel, Cynthia Fitterer, and Robert B. Noyed. *Chief Joseph: Chief of the Nez Percé.* (Our People) Child's World, 2002. 32pp. ISBN 978-1-56766-165-1. Grades 3–6. This brief biography of Chief Joseph, of the Nez Percé (1840–1904) offers four chapters that divide his life into his childhood, becoming a chief, the broken promises of the United States government, and his promise that, "I will fight no more forever." Photographs augment the text. Chronology, Glossary, Further Reading, and Index.

1180. Krensky, Stephen. *Davy Crockett: A Life on the Frontier.* Illustrated by Bob Dacey and Debra Bandelin. (Ready-to-Read Stories of Famous Americans) Aladdin, 2004. 48pp. Paper ISBN 978-0-689-85944-1. Grades 1–2. Although people said Davy Crockett weighed 200 pounds as a baby and leaped from his crib dancing, Krensky shows that neither was true, Crockett was fearless as a soldier and a leader. He led an unusual life because he always supported the things in which he believed. This volume provides simple accounts of many interesting incidents.

1181. Kunstler, James Howard. *Annie Oakley.* Illustrated by Fred Warter. (Rabbit Ears Storybook Classics) Simon & Schuster, 1993. 32pp. ISBN 978-1-59197-759-9. Grades K–3. Annie Oakley had a childhood of poverty and learned to shoot game as a way to put meat on her family's table. When she grew up, her fortunes changed. She formed a partnership with Frank Butler and married him. She later became a performer for Buffalo Bill Cody's Wild West Show where Sitting Bull "adopted" her into the Sioux tribe. Although she was temporarily crippled in a train crash, her later life was mainly happy and productive.

1182. Kunstler, James Howard. *Davy Crockett: The Legendary Frontiersman.* Illustrated by Steve Brodner. Spotlight, 2004. Unpaged. ISBN 978-1-59197-762-9. Grades 2–5. Beginning with Davy Crockett's 1786 birth in Tennessee and ending with the Battle of the Alamo in 1836, where he died, this volume presents many of Crockett's exploits, such as luring a bear, running for Congress, and fighting a keelboatman.

1183. Kurtz, Jane. *Johnny Appleseed.* Illustrated by Mary Haverfield. (Ready-to-Read) Simon & Schuster, 2004. 32pp. Paper ISBN 978-0-689-85958-8. Grades 1–2. John Chapman, known as Johnny Appleseed, walked along the Ohio River planting apple seeds and trading his seedlings with the settlers for food and clothes. The rhyming text addresses young readers, asking them to clap their hands for Johnny Appleseed.

1184. Lasky, Kathryn. *John Muir: America's First Environmentalist.* Illustrated by Stanley Fellows. Candlewick, 2006. 41pp. ISBN 978-0-7636-1957-2; 2008, paper ISBN 978-0-7636-3884-9. Grades 2–5. John Muir (1838–1914) loved nature and became an inventor, shepherd, farmer, writer, scholar, and explorer. He founded the Sierra Club in 1892. Muir wanted to conserve the beauty of nature and make sure that places such as Yosemite National Park existed for the enjoyment of generations to come. He walked from Wisconsin to Florida in 1867 and walked on Alaskan glaciers in 1870. Later he showed President Theodore Roosevelt the beauty of the West. Lasky draws on Muir's personal diaries for details of his life and ideas. Acrylic paintings complement the text. Bibliography and Notes.

1185. **Locker, Thomas.** *John Muir: America's Naturalist.* Fulcrum, 2003. 32pp. ISBN 978-1-55591-393-9. Grades 3–6. John Muir (1838–1914) left Scotland in the mid-1800s with his family and settled in Wisconsin. When he was young, he traveled West and devoted himself to the study of nature, especially in Yosemite, whose beauty he wanted to preserve. This volume uses quotes from Muir and full-page paintings to describe his life and interests.

1186. **Lourie, Peter.** *On the Trail of Lewis and Clark: A Journey Up the Missouri River.* Boyds Mills, 2002. 48pp. ISBN 978-1-56397-936-1; 2003, paper ISBN 978-1-59078-268-2. Grades 4–6. Peter Lourie and three friends decided to trace part of the expedition of Lewis and Clark up the Missouri River from Omaha, Nebraska, to Three Forks, Montana. Lourie compares this modern-day trip to that of Lewis and Clark using journals the expedition leaders kept. Photographs highlight the text. Bibliograpy.

1187. **Lourie, Peter.** *On the Trail of Sacagawea.* Boyds Mills, 2001. 48pp. ISBN 978-1-56397-840-1; 2004, paper ISBN 978-1-59078-266-8. Grades 4–6. Lourie and his family followed the path of the Lewis and Clark expedition, tracing the trail Sacagawea took in 1804 from Fort Mandan, North Dakota, to Fort Clatsop, Oregon. The four chapters describe their experience crossing the Continental Divide and the land that slopes toward the Pacific. They saw historic Native American lands and the traditional customs of the people as they fished and swam and traveled. Photographs enhance the text.

1188. **MacLeod, Elizabeth.** *Mark Twain: An American Star.* (Snapshots) Kids Can, 2008. 32pp. ISBN 978-1-55337-909-6. Grades 3–6. Sixteen chapters give an overview of Mark Twain's (1835–1910) life. He was born when Haley's Comet filled the sky and died when it returned. Primary and other sources chronologically relate his life as a writer of books including *Tom Sawyer* and *Huckleberry Finn*, comedian, traveler, and lecturer. Photographs and illustrations enhance the text. Further Reading and Chronology.

1189. **Macy, Sue.** *Bull's-Eye: A Photobiography of Annie Oakley.* National Geographic, 2001. 64pp. ISBN 978-0-7922-7008-9; 2006, paper ISBN 978-0-7922-5933-6. Grades 5–8. This biography of Annie Oakey (1860–1926) contains historical photographs and primary source quotes that offer her own words about her life. As Phoebe Ann Moses at the age of 8, she learned to shoot and soon killed enough game to sell to restaurants and feed her family although her Quaker mother did not want her handling a gun. She eventually met Frank Butler, also a sharpshooter, and she married him before he became her costar and manager. She joined Buffalo Will's Wild West Show and performed in the United States and Europe. Photographs and illustrations augment the text. Bibliography, Chronology, Notes, and Index. *School Library Journal Best Books for Children.*

1190. **Matthews, John.** *Pirates: Most Wanted.* Atheneum, 2007. 32pp. ISBN 978-1-4169-3934-4. Grades 1–6. Matthews relates the stories of thirteen 17th- and 18th-century pirates: Henry Morgan; William Dampier; Jean Bart; William Kidd; Thomas Tew; Henry Avery; Edward "Ned" Low; Edward Teach, also known as "Blackbeard"; Samuel Bellamy, also known as "Black Sam"; Bartholomew Roberts, also known as "Black Bart"; Charlotte de Berry; Anne Bonny; and Mary Read. Index.

1191. **Milton, Joyce.** *Sacajawea: Her True Story.* Grosset & Dunlap, 2001. 48pp. Paper ISBN 978-0-448-42539-9. Grades 1–2. When Lewis and Clark started their journey to map America, they needed a Native American who could act as an emissary for them. They chose Sacajawea, a Shoshone woman married to a French trapper, who carried her baby strapped to her back. Illustrations enhance the text.

1192. **Monroe, Judy.** *Chief Red Cloud, 1822–1909.* (American Indian Biographies) Capstone, 2004. 32pp. ISBN 978-0-7368-2445-3. Grades 3–5. Lakota leader Chief Red Cloud forced the United States government to close the Bozeman Trail, a road crossing Lakota ancestral grounds and threatening hunting. He met with President Grant in Washington to discuss the issue. The text includes information about the Lakota and details of a traditional dish and the "Sioux animal sign," a painting that warriors carried into battle. Illustrations and photographs enhance the text. Maps, Bibliography, Further Reading, Glossary, Web Sites, and Index.

1193. Morrison, Taylor. *The Buffalo Nickel.* Houghton, 2002. 32pp. ISBN 978-0-618-10855-8. Grades 3–6. James Earle Fraser, the sculptor of the buffalo nickel in 1912, grew up in the Dakota Territory where he played with Sioux children, listened to trappers telling stories, used buffalo robes for blankets, and had the town whittler for an art teacher. He watched the near extinction of the buffalo and how it affected the Plains Indians. His family moved to Chicago and there Fraser pursued his interest in art, eventually going to study in Paris and work in New York. Double-spreads depict the life of the Sioux, and smaller pictures illustrate the steps involved in making the coins—bas-relief medallion, the die, and then the coin. The back cover gives a color illustration of the buffalo on the nickel. *Bluebonnet Award (Texas) nomination.*

1194. Moses, Will. *Johnny Appleseed: The Story of a Legend.* Philomel, 2001. 32pp. ISBN 978-0-399-23153-7; Puffin, 2004, paper ISBN 978-0-14-240138-5. Grades 4–6. Although this biography of Johnny Appleseed (1774–1845) mentions his childhood, it focuses on his adult life when he planted apples and preached in Pennsylvania, the Ohio Territory, and Indiana. He also helped others do the same and had a reputation for generosity along with strange behavior. Many landscape folk-art paintings complement the text.

1195. Naden, Corinne J., and Rose Blue. *John Muir: Saving the Wilderness.* Millbrook, 1994. 48pp. Paper ISBN 978-1-56294-797-2. Grades 4–6. John Muir (1838–1914), a young immigrant from Scotland, loved to explore nature. As an adult, he realized the wilderness would disappear if someone did not save it from greedy developers. He began the Sierra Club and wrote about his explorations and the danger of losing the wilderness. Theodore Roosevelt went to visit him in Yosemite, California, and decided to establish national parks afterward. Photographs and Index.

1196. Nelson, Sharlene, and Ted Nelson. *Jedediah Smith.* Franklin Watts, 2004. 63pp. ISBN 978-0-53112-287-7. Grades 3–6. Jedediah Smith (1799–1831) explored the West after Lewis and Clark, moving through land that later became Montana, Idaho, Washington, Oregon, California, Nevada, Utah, and Wyoming. He was a hunter, fur trader, trapper, and the first white man to see many of these areas. He helped to open the West to other settlers. Maps, photographs and illustrations augment the text. Glossary, Chronology, Notes, Further Reading, and Web Sites.

1197. Nelson, Vaunda M. *Bad News for Outlaws: The Remarkable Life of Bass Reeves, Deputy U.S. Marshal.* Illustrated by R. Gregory Christie. Carolrhoda, 2009. 40pp. ISBN 978-0-8225-6764-6. Grades 3–8. In 1875 African American Bass Reeves (1838–1910) became a United States Marshal in the former Indian territory of Oklahoma. He had escaped slavery during the Civil War and learned defense skills from the Indians with whom he lived. For the next thirty-two years, he arrested or killed more than 3,000 criminals without injury to himself. His reputation for honesty and justice gained him respect from everyone, including those he hunted. Although the story is factual, it resembles a tall tale, beginning with Reeves facing killer Jim Webb and winning the contest. Textured paintings enhance the text. Notes, Glossary, Chronology, Bibliography, and Web Sites. *American Library Association Notable Children's Books, Coretta Scott King Award, The Land of Enchantment Children's Book Award* (New Mexico) nomination, *Golden Kite* Honor Book, and *Capitol Choices Noteworthy Titles for Children and Teens* (Washington, D.C.).

1198. O'Rear, Sybil J. *Charles Goodnight: Pioneer Cowman.* Eakin, 1990. 69pp. ISBN 978-0-89015-741-1. Grades 5–8. Charles Goodnight (1836–1929) lived in the Texas panhandle all his life and served his state by remaining there to fight during the Civil War. He developed the idea of the chuckwagon, and he improved the sidesaddle for women. He experimented with plants and fought against cattle diseases, trying to have laws passed protecting cattle. He loved children, and he helped the people of his state in any way he could. Glossary and Bibliography.

1199. Pinkney, Andrea Davis. *Bill Pickett: Rodeo-Ridin' Cowboy.* Illustrated by Brian Pinkney. Voyager, 1999. Unpaged. Paper ISBN 978-0-15-202103-0. Grades K–3. Bill Pickett (ca. 1860–1932) lived with his family in Texas after they became free during the Civil War. He wanted to be a cowboy, and when he saw a dog tame a bull by biting its lower lip, he thought he could do the same thing. He did, and his reputation for "bulldogging" grew. As he developed his riding abilities and his lariat skills, he became famous. He was soon the star of the 101 Ranch Wild West Show and traveled with it to Europe and South America while his family waited for him at the 101 Ranch. More about Black Cowboys and For Further Reading. *Capitol Choices Noteworthy Titles* (Washington, D.C.).

1200. Pringle, Laurence P. *American Slave, American Hero: York of the Lewis and Clark Expedition.* Illustrated by Cornelius Van Wright and Ying-Hwa Hu. Calkins Creek, 2006. 40pp. ISBN 978-1-59078-282-8. Grades 3–5. York (ca. 1775–ca. 1815) was William Clark's personal slave on the expedition west and helped to make it a success. Some thought his ability to deal with different tribes of Native Americans made him a national hero. On the journey, he was treated much better than a slave might expect. About ten years later, Clark gave York his freedom. Watercolor illustrations enhance the text.

1201. Ransom, Candice F. *Lewis and Clark.* (History Maker Bios) Lerner, 2003. 48pp. ISBN 978-0-8225-0394-1. Grades 3–5. Thomas Jefferson hired Meriwether Lewis (1774–1809) and William Clark (1770–1838) to explore the Northwest Passage in 1803, before he announced the Louisiana Purchase. The two had known each other for ten years before they spent twenty-eight months covering 7,000 miles and discovering the land's bounty and its dangers. Their mapping revealed the potential of the West. Illustrations augment the text. Bibliography, Further Reading, Glossary, Maps, Timeline, Web Sites, and Index.

1202. Rappaport, Doreen. *We Are the Many: A Picture Book of American Indians.* Illustrated by Cornelius Van Wright and Ying-Hwa Hu. HarperCollins, 2002. 28pp. ISBN 978-0-06-001139-0. Grades K–3. This collective biography contains short profiles of sixteen Native Americans: Tisquantum (Squanto), Konwatsitsienni (Molly Brant), Shunka-Ishnala (Lone Dog), Sacajawea, Asiyahola (Osceola), Susan La Flesche Picotte, Helena Conley, Ida Conley, Lyda Conley, Watha Huck (Jim Thorpe), Maria Martinez, Julian Martinez, William McCabe, Maria Tallchief, Wilma Mankiller, and Sherman Alexie. Watercolor portraits augment the text. Bibliography.

1203. Rawls, James J. *Dame Shirley and the Gold Rush.* Illustrated by John Holder. Steck-Vaughn, 1992. 55pp. Paper ISBN 978-0-8114-8062-8. Grades 3–7. Louise Amelia Knapp Smith Clappe (1819–1906) called herself Dame Shirley when she wrote letters telling the truth about the California gold rush of the early 1850s. Rumors said gold was everywhere for anyone who wanted it, but that was not the reality. Epilogue, Afterword, and Notes.

1204. Ray, Deborah Kogan. *Down the Colorado: John Wesley Powell, the One-Armed Explorer.* Frances Foster, 2007. 32pp. ISBN 978-0-374-31838-3. Grades 3–5. In 1869, John Wesley Powell (1834–1902) became a national hero when he boated down the Colorado River. This biography covers Powell's childhood and early life as well as his adult years. As a boy in Ohio, he faced taunts because his father was a staunch abolitionist and he decided to become a scientist rather than a minister as his father wished. He served in the Civil War as a Union soldier and lost an arm. He then decided to spend his life charting the unexplored areas of the nation. Watercolor and gouache illustrations enhance the text. Maps, Chronology, and Notes. *American Library Association Notable Children's Books.*

1205. Reich, Susanna. *Painting the Wild Frontier: The Art and Adventures of George Catlin.* Clarion, 2008. 176pp. ISBN 978-0-618-71470-4. Grades 5–8. This biography of George Catlin (1796–1872) includes archival prints and reproductions of Catlin's paintings with information about his travels. The text is divided into five parts—his childhood from 1796 to 1830, his frontier life from 1830 to 1837, work as a showman from 1837 to 1854, his wanderings from 1854 to 1861, and his return home from 1861 to 1872. Primary sources including letters and notes reveal his desire to paint authentic cultural rituals and individuals, although trained as a lawyer, and to support the Native Americans in their way of life. Bibliography, Chronology, Notes, Web Sites, and Index. *Kirkus Best Young Adult Books*.

1206. Roberts, Russell. *Daniel Boone.* (What's So Great About?) Mitchell Lane, 2007. 32pp. ISBN 978-1-58415-475-4. Grades 2–4. Daniel Boone, an American pioneer, was associated with the French and Indian War and the exploration of Kentucky. This volume gives an overview of his life. Illustrations augment the text. Bibliography, Glossary, Maps, and Index.

1207. Roberts, Russell. *Davy Crockett.* (What's So Great About?) Mitchell Lane, 2007. 32pp. ISBN 978-1-58415-476-1. Grades 2–4. Davy Crockett, a frontiersman and soldier who fought for Texas's independence at the Alamo, later became a congressman. This volume gives an overview of his life and achievements. Illustrations complement the text. Bibliography, Glossary, Maps, and Index.

1208. Rosa, Joseph G. *Wild Bill Hickok: Sharpshooter and U.S. Marshal of the Wild West.* (Library of American Lives and Times) PowerKids, 2004. 112pp. ISBN 978-0-8239-6632-5. Grades 4–8. James Butler "Wild Bill" Hickok (1837–1876) had careers as a sharpshooter, stagecoach driver, lawman, and showman. He was also an abolitionist, constable, Union scout, and gambler. Reproductions and photographs complement the text. Maps, Bibliography, Chronology, Further Reading, Glossary, Web Sites, and Index.

1209. Rowland, Della. *The Story of Sacajawea: Guide to Lewis and Clark.* Illustrated by Richard Leonard. Yearling, 1995. 112pp. Paper ISBN 978-0-440-40215-2. Grades 3–6. When Sacajawea (1788–1812) was 12, Minnetarees captured her from her Shoshoni Indian tribe and sold her to a French fur trader. Because of her ability to translate, she and her husband accompanied Lewis and Clark on their journey to survey the western United States when she was only 16. Highlights in the Life, For Further Study, and Index.

1210. Rumford, James. *Sequoyah: The Cherokee Man Who Gave His People Writing.* Houghton, 2004. Unpaged. ISBN 978-0-618-36947-8. Grades 1–4. The son of a Cherokee woman and a white man he never met, Sequoyah (1770?–1843) decided that the Cherokees needed a written language to strengthen their culture. He could neither speak nor read English, but he created an alphabet by scratching symbols for each word. After his cabin burned down and his work with it, he approached his task differently, creating eighty-four signs that would represent the sounds in his language. Mixed-media illustrations complement the text. Chronology and Note. *Jane Addams Book Awards*, *Black-Eyed Susan Picture Book Award* (Maryland) nomination, *Notable Social Studies Trade Books for Young People*, *Picture Book Award* (South Carolina) nomination, *Robert F. Sibert Honor Book*, *Beehive Children's Book Award* (Utah) nomination, *Horn Book Fanfare*, *School Library Journal Best Children's Books*, and *Capitol Choices Noteworthy Titles* (Washington, D.C.).

1211. Scott, Robert A. *Chief Joseph and the Nez Percés.* Facts on File, 1993. 134pp. ISBN 978-0-8160-2475-9. Grades 5 up. The American government attacked Chief Joseph's (1840–1904) Nez Percé tribe in June 1877, trying to kill the people before they could start another Sioux uprising as they marched from Oregon to a new home chosen by the government in Idaho. Women and children were slaughtered in their tipis, with soldiers saying later that they had to kill them because they were going to fight back. Chief Joseph tried to protect his people, but by October of that year, he knew they could not win. Even after this defeat, he continued to try to regain the ancestral home of his people. A description of Chief Joseph at that time by a man who later regretted the horrible treatment of the Native Americans said that he was "a splendid looking man . . . fully six feet high . . . His forehead is high, his eyes bright yet kind, his nose finely cut. . . ." Bibliography and Index.

1212. Sherman, Josepha. *Mark Twain.* (Classic Storytellers) Mitchell Lane, 2005. 48pp. ISBN 978-1-58415-374-0. Grades 4–6. This biography of Mark Twain (1835–1910), or Samuel Clemens, covers his life from birth when he came "in" with Haley's Comet until death when he went "out" with Haley's Comet. He was a steamboat pilot when very young and went on to become a writer. The text discusses social issues of the period and how Twain reacted to them. Photographs highlight the text. Chronology, Further Reading, Glossary, Notes, and Index.

1213. Spradlin, Michael P. *Daniel Boone's Great Escape.* Illustrated by Ard Hoyt. Walker, 2008. Unpaged. ISBN 978-0-8027-9581-6. Grades 2–4. This episode from the life of Daniel Boone (1734–1820) relates his experience on a snowy day in 1778. Shawnee warriors see him hunting and capture him, upset by the deaths and broken treaties suffered by their people. Boone convinces their chief, Blackfish, to let him and his men live in the Shawnee village as brothers. He will go with them in the spring to convince the settlers to surrender at Fort Boonesborough. But Boone escapes first and runs 160 miles in four days to warn the settlers at the fort that the Shawnee plan to attack. Illustrations complement the text.

1214. Stevenson, Augusta. *Sitting Bull: Dakota Boy.* Illustrated by Robert Jenney. Aladdin, 1996. 192pp. Paper ISBN 978-0-689-80628-5. Grades 4–7. While Sitting Bull (1831–1890) was still called Jumping Badger as a boy of 10, boys pretending to be his friends started calling him "Slow" so that he would begin to think that he could not win races or games. His father talked with the tribe's witch, and she told Jumping Badger to start believing in himself. She gave him a tooth to wear as a lucky charm. He began winning, and people asked him to tell them about their fates based on the tooth. By the time he was 12, he needed to earn his adult Sioux name. In a dream, he saw many buffalo sitting down as if they were wounded. His father gave him the name "Sitting Bull" because he expected him to become a great hunter. He did.

1215. Stine, Megan. *The Story of Laura Ingalls Wilder, Pioneer Girl.* Illustrated by Marcy Dunn Ramsey. Yearling, 1997. 101pp. Paper ISBN 978-0-440-40578-8. Grades 3–5. Laura Ingalls Wilder wrote her Little House books about her own life, and this biography does not reveal much more except at the end, when it tells about her marriage to Almanzo Wilder. This book is a shorter version of her life than her own series.

1216. Sutcliffe, Jane. *Chief Joseph.* Illustrated by Tim Parlin. (History Maker Bios) Lerner, 2005. 48pp. ISBN 978-0-8225-0696-6. Grades 3–5. Chief Joseph (1840–1904) led his Nez Percé tribe of Dakota Indians in their fight against the United States Army under General Oliver O. Howard. Howard tried to move the tribe and other "non-treaty" Indians to a reservation in Idaho. They finally had to surrender to the Army. Chief Joseph's honorable resistance gave him a reputation as a peacemaker and a humanitarian. Later Chief Joseph spoke in Washington about the rights of his people. Photographs, Maps, Illustrations, Further Reading, Timeline, Web Sites, and Index.

1217. Sutcliffe, Jane. *John Deere.* (History Maker Bios) Lerner, 2006. 48pp. ISBN 978-0-8225-6579-6. Grades 3–5. John Deere (1804–1886) grew up in a well-off family that sold clothing, but they never seemed to have enough money. Eventually, he went west and opened a blacksmith's shop. He watched the farmers struggling with iron plows in the sticky soil and created a plow with a steel saw blade that worked much better. The five chapters of the text recount his life and his accomplishments. Illustrations augment the text. Bibliography, Further Reading, Glossary, Maps, Timeline, Web Sites, and Index.

1218. Taylor, Gaylia. *George Crum and the Saratoga Chip.* Illustrated by Frank Morrison. Lee & Low, 2006. Unpaged. ISBN 978-1-58430-255-1. Grades 1–5. George Crum loved to cook, and his interest in cooking helped him overcome unkind remarks about his Native American and African American heritage. He became a chef at Moon's Lake House in Saratoga Springs, New York, and there he developed a way to make potatoes in the mid-1800s. He cut them in thin slices and deep-fried them so that they became the "ultimate" French fry. He eventually opened his own restaurant, Crum's Place, where he served these delicious potato chips. Illustrations complement the text.

1219. Turner, Ann. *Sitting Bull Remembers.* Illustrated by Wendell Minor. HarperCollins, 2007. Unpaged. ISBN 978-0-06-051399-3. Grades 3–6. In this biography, Sitting Bull (1831–1890) lives in captivity near the end of his life and remembers his past. He longs for the old days before the white people or Wasicu came and destroyed the Native Americans' herds and tribes. He misses his people's bravery and nobility, taken by people interested only in gold. Illustrations illuminate the text. Note.

1220. Van Steenwyk, Elizabeth. *Seneca Chief, Army General: A Story About Ely Parker.* Illustrated by Karen Ritz. Carolrhoda, 2000. 64pp. ISBN 978-1-57505-431-5. Grades 3–6. Ely Samuel Parker (1828–1895), a Seneca chief, achieved recognition in both the white and Native American worlds. Born on New York's Tonawonda Reservation, he attended mission schools and boarding schools, becoming an interpreter at the age of 15. He fought to save his reservation from a land company, and his people made him chief. He served outstandingly in the Civil War, and President Grant appointed him as the commissioner of Indian Affairs, the first Native American to have that post. Illustrations augment the text. Bibliography and Index.

1221. Venezia, Mike. *Frederic Remington.* (Getting to Know the World's Greatest Artists) Scholastic, 2002. 32pp. ISBN 978-0-516-22497-8; Children's Press, 2003, paper ISBN 978-0-516-27812-4. Grades K–5. Frederic Remington (1861–1909) knew when he was young that he wanted to be an artist. After attending school in New York and at Yale, he became a cowboy and rancher in the American West. He had many adventures in the West and traveling as a correspondent. His sculptures and paintings show the Native American as lonely and outcast. Among the most famous of his 3,000 drawings and paintings, 22 bronze sculptures, and many writings are *The Bronco Buster* and *The Cheyenne*. Illustrations augment the text.

1222. Wadsworth, Ginger. *Annie Oakley.* (History Maker Bios) Lerner, 2005. 48pp. ISBN 978-0-8225-2940-8. Grades 3–5. Annie Oakley (1860–1926) was born Phoebe Ann Moss. She helped support her family by shooting game even though her mother initially disapproved. Her talent led to Chief Sitting Bull naming her "Little Sure Shot" when she competed in shooting contests and starred with her husband, sharpshooter Frank Butler, in Buffalo Bill's Wild West show. Her story glamorized the West. Illustrations augment the text. Bibliography, Further Reading, Glossary, Maps, Timeline, Web Sites, and Index.

1223. Walker, Paul Robert. *Spiritual Leaders.* See entry 256.

1224. Waxman, Laura Hamilton. *Sequoyah.* (History Maker Bios) Lerner, 2004. 48pp. ISBN 978-0-8225-0697-3. Grades 3–5. Sequoyah is probably best known for the famous giant trees named after him and his invention of the Cherokee alphabet. With the help of just his young daughter, he created an alphabet that allowed his people to communicate in writing and record their history. In addition to being an inventor, he was a silversmith, a blacksmith, a leader, and a farmer. When his family and tribe were forced to move to Oklahoma by the U.S. government, he helped lead his people to form a peaceful and united Cherokee nation. Illustrations augment the text. Bibliography, Further Reading, Glossary, Maps, Timeline, Web Sites, and Index.

1225. Welch, Catherine. *Geronimo.* Illustrated by Tim Parlin. (History Maker Bios) Carolrhoda, 2004. 48pp. ISBN 978-0-8225-0698-0. Grades 3–5. Welch tells the story of Geronimo (1829–1909), an Apache warrior, in five chapters that cover his life, his people, his victories, and his losses. He showed enormous courage and killed in battle only when an enemy threatened his homeland. Photographs and illustrations.

1226. Wilder, Laura Ingalls. *On the Way Home: The Diary of a Trip from South Dakota to Mansfield, Missouri, in 1894.* (Little House) HarperCollins, 1962. 128pp. ISBN 978-0-06-026489-5; HarperTrophy, 1976, paper ISBN 978-0-06-440080-0. Grades 4–7. In 1894 Laura Ingalls Wilder traveled with her husband, Almanzo, and their 7-year-old daughter, Rose, from their drought-stricken farm in South Dakota to the Ozarks. She describes the towns they passed through, the rivers they crossed, and the people they met along the way. Not for 40 years would she begin to write the "Little House" books, which described her own childhood. Her journal gives a clear glimpse of the prairie while many were having difficulty surviving.

1227. Wilkie, Katherine E. *Daniel Boone: Taming the Wilds.* See entry 522.

1228. Wills, Charles M. *Annie Oakley.* (DK Biographies) Dorling Kindersley, 2007. 128pp. ISBN 978-0-7566-2986-1; paper ISBN 978-0-7566-2997-7. Grades 4–8. The thirteen chapters of this biography of Annie Oakley (1860–1926) presents her early life as a Quaker who finally got her mother to let her shoot animals to feed the family after her father's death. She later won shooting competitions and became famous while touring with Buffalo Bill's Wild

West Show. Oakley protected her privacy by giving conflicting dates in personal interviews and her own writing. Photographs and illustrations augment the text. Bibliography, Chronology, Further Reading, and Index.

1229. Wise, Bill. *Louis Sockalexis: Native American Baseball Pioneer.* Illustrated by Bill Farnsworth. Lee & Low, 2007. 31pp. ISBN 978-1-58430-269-8. Grades 2–5. Native American baseball player Louis Sockalexis (1871–1913), a Penobscot from Maine, faced terrible prejudice from both spectators and teammates. He began playing the game at the age of 12 and won an athletic scholarship to Holy Cross College. In 1897 the Cleveland Spiders signed him, and on June 16, 1897, he hit a home run off "Hoosier Thunderbolt" pitcher Amos Rusie at the Polo Grounds in a game against the New York Giants. No one had ever hit as far as he did on that day. His playing led to opportunities for other Native Americans including Charles Albert Bender and Jim Thorpe. His own career, however, was cut short by injuries and alcoholism. Some believe Sockalexis is the reason the Cleveland Spiders became the Indians. Oil paintings enhance the text.

1230. Yolen, Jane. *Johnny Appleseed: The Legend and the Truth.* Illustrated by Jim Burke. HarperCollins, 2008. Unpaged. ISBN 978-0-06-059135-9. Grades 2–4. Yolen offers an overview of Johnny Appleseed (1774–1845) and his travels. Each two-page spread covers part of the generally known story and adds "the fact," a point that gives verification of that story from primary sources. Among the revelations are his desire to go west, his love of nature, and his interaction with both Native Americans and settlers along the way. Illustrations complement the text.

1231. Zemlicka, Shannon. *Quanah Parker.* Illustrated by Tim Parlin. (History Maker Bios) Lerner, 2004. 48pp. ISBN 978-0-8225-0724-6. Grades 3–5. Quanah Parker (ca. 1848–1911) was the son of a Native American man and a white woman who tried to work with the American government to gain protection and rights for Native Americans. He became the principle chief of the Comanche Indians and was a warrior and spiritual leader. He was also a cattle rancher, judge, and a businessman. Photographs and illustrations augment the text. Bibliography, Further Reading, Glossary, Maps, Timeline, Web Sites, and Index.

Graphic Novels, Biographies, and Histories

1232. Doeden, Matt. *The Battle of the Alamo.* Illustrated by Charles Barnett, III and Phil Miller. Graphic Library, 2006. 32pp. ISBN 978-0-7368-3832-0; paper ISBN 978-0-7368-5242-5. Grades 3–5. From February 23 to March 6, 1836, the Republic of Texas and the Republic of Mexico fought at the Alamo. Antonio López de Santa Anna battled William Travis, Jim Bowie, and Davy Crockett. Texas lost, but on April 21, they attacked and defeated Santa Anna at the Battle of San Jacinto. Illustrations depict the event. Bibliography, Glossary, Further Reading, and Index.

1233. Doeden, Matt. *John Sutter and the California Gold Rush.* Illustrated by Charles Barnett, III and Ron Frenz. Graphic Library, 2005. 32pp. ISBN 978-0-7368-4369-0; paper ISBN 978-0-7368-6207-3. Grades 3–5. Gold was discovered near the mill of John Augustus Sutter (1803–1880), and he established Sutter's Fort in the area that would become Sacramento. Illustrations complement the text. Bibliography, Glossary, Further Reading, and Index.

1234. Glaser, Jason. *The Buffalo Soldiers and the American West.* Illustrated by Tod Smith and Charles Barnett, III. Graphic Library, 2005. 32pp. ISBN 978-0-7368-4966-1; paper ISBN 978-0-7368-6204-2. Grades 3–6. The first peacetime all-African American regiment in the United States Army, the "buffalo soldiers" went to the American West to fight the Native American tribes. Illustrations augment the text. Bibliography, Glossary, Further Reading, and Index.

1235. Gunderson, Jessica. *The Lewis and Clark Expedition.* Illustrated by Steve Erwin and Keith Williams. Graphic Library, 2006. 32pp. ISBN 978-0-7368-6493-0; paper ISBN 978-0-

7368-9655-9. Grades 3–5. In 1804 Meriwether Lewis (1774–1809) and William Clark (1770–1838) set out to explore the lands of the Louisiana Purchase at Thomas Jefferson's request. They charted the lands, met Native Americans with the help of Sacagawea, and reached the Pacific Coast. Illustrations enhance the text. Bibliography, Glossary, Further Reading, and Index.

1236. Gunderson, Jessica. *Sacagawea: Journey into the West.* Illustrated by Cynthia Martin and Barbara Schultz. (Graphic Biographies) Graphic Library, 2006. 32pp. ISBN 978-0-7368-6499-2; paper ISBN 978-0-7368-9663-4. Grades 3–5. This brief graphic biography of Sacagawea (ca. 1788–1812) describes her contributions to the Lewis and Clark Expedition across the United States, beginning in 1803 when she introduced them to various Native Americans along the way. Web Sites.

1237. Gunderson, Jessica. *Young Riders of the Pony Express.* Illustrated by Brian Bascle. Graphic Library, 2006. 32pp. ISBN 978-0-7368-5495-5; paper ISBN 978-0-7368-6883-9. Grades 3–5. Established to carry mail rapidly across the North American continent, the Pony Express began with a route from St. Joseph, Missouri, to Sacramento, California. The service lasted from April 1860 to October 1861, when the railroad was finished. Gunderson describes the young men who became riders for this outfit and their exploits. Illustrations complement the text. Bibliography, Glossary, Further Reading, and Index.

1238. Hudson-Goff, Elizabeth, and Dale Anderson. *The California Gold Rush.* Illustrated by Guus Floor. (Graphic Histories) Gareth Stevens, 2006. 32pp. ISBN 978-0-8368-6202-7. Grades 4–7. The California gold rush began when Marshall discovered gold there in the 19th century. The possibility of instant riches attracted many adventurers. The stories of the Donner party and Wild Bill Hickock are among the anecdotes included here. Archival illustrations enhance the text. Bibliography, Glossary, Web Sites, Further Reading, Notes, Maps, and Index.

1239. Leavitt, Amie Jane. *The Battle of the Alamo: An Interactive History Adventure.* (You Choose) Capstone, 2008. 112pp. ISBN 978-1-4296-1354-5; paper ISBN 978-1-4296-1761-1. Grades 3–5. Readers can choose whether to become a Mexican soldier or a Texan rebel during the siege of the Alamo. After that initial choice, they make other decisions that are historically plausible. Color reproductions and maps enhance the text. Bibliography.

1240. O'Hern, Kerri, and Janet Riehecky. *The Battle of the Alamo.* Illustrated by D. McHarque. (Graphic Histories) Gareth Stevens, 2006. 32pp. ISBN 978-0-8368-6201-0. Grades 3–6. This graphic history examines the circumstances surrounding the battle of the Alamo in 1836 between the Texas rebels and the Mexican army under Santa Anna. It contains glossy pages in color. Further Reading and Web Sites.

1241. Olson, Nathan. *The Building of the Transcontinental Railroad.* Illustrated by Richard Dominguez and Charles Barnett, III. Graphic Library, 2005. 32pp. ISBN 978-0-7368-6490-9; paper ISBN 978-0-7368-9652-8. Grades 3–5. The rails of the "First Continental Railroad" joined on May 10, 1869, with the "last spike" at Promontory Summit, Utah. The track covered 1,756 miles between Sacramento and Omaha. Illustrations augment the text. Bibliography, Glossary, Further Reading, and Index.

1242. Welvaert, Scott R. *The Donner Party.* Illustrated by Ron Frenz and Charles Barnett, III. Graphic Library, 2006. 32pp. ISBN 978-0-7368-5479-5; paper ISBN 978-0-7368-6874-7. Grades 3–5. In 1846 a group of about 90 formed at Little Sandy River, Wyoming, deciding to take a new route known as the "Hastings Cutoff." They went west to Fort Bridger and struck out into the unknown on August 31, crossing the Wasatch Mountains and the Great Salt Lake Desert. They rejoined the California Trail near Elko, Nevada, on September 26, three weeks later than expected. They reached the Sierra Nevada at the end of October, but snow already blocked the pass. They made a camp and slaughtered the remaining oxen for meat. In mid-December, fifteen set out for Sutter's Fort on snowshoes. Four died during a blizzard and the others resorted to cannibalism and continued the journey. Eventually two men and five women reached the western side of the mountains on January 18, 1847. Illustrations visualize their plight. Bibliography, Glossary, Further Reading, and Index.

DVDs

1243. *Animated Atlas: Expansion West and the Mexican War.* SVE & Churchill Media, 1999. 20 mins. Grades 4–8. Animated maps, historical footage, photographs, and icons show the development of colonial America and how the topography and location of water influenced settlements and either helped or hindered the colonists' survival. A review of the growth of the United States from 1789 to 1821 precedes a brief history of Mexico and Central America. Topics covered include the growth of Texas, the Texas Revolution, preparation of the war with Mexico in 1845, and the geographic results of the war in the Southwest.

1244. *California Up Close.* Discovery School, 2006. 5 DVDs; 1.4 hrs. ISBN 978-1-59380-537-1. Grades 3–5. A look at the history, culture, geography, and government of California, covering mission life, fur trading, the gold rush, earthquakes, immigration, and agriculture. It includes archival photographs, drawings, live-action footage, and reenactments.

1245. *Exploring Our Past: Comparing the Lives of Native Peoples.* Mazzarella Media, 2006. 20 mins. ISBN 978-1-934119-00-6. Grades 3–6. This DVD looks at the daily lives, cultures, and environmental circumstances of early Native American people. Reenactment footage and rare archival photographs recreate the lives of Native Americans living in America's eastern woodlands, the desert southwest, and the Great Plains. Of particular interest is the diversity of the needs and traditions of these tribes.

1246. *The Lewis and Clark Expedition: A Uniquely American Story.* Film Ideas, 2002. 46 mins. Grades 5–8. After Thomas Jefferson completed the Louisiana Purchase, he hired Lewis and Clark to explore it. This video discusses the preparations necessary for this trip and the path mapped for it. Sacagawea was among the Native Americans who helped the expedition. Art, expedition drawings, and reenactments of several events augment the videos. Part One follows the journey to the headwaters of the Missouri. In Part Two, the Corps of Discovery reaches the Pacific and returns to St. Louis two years after it left. The epilogue reports on the later lives of Lewis and Clark and other members of the Corps.

1247. *Sacagawea: St. Louis to Fort Mandan.* (Sacagawea) New Dimension Media, 2003. 15 mins. ISBN 978-1-56353-988-6. Grades 3–8. A female narrator playing the role of Sacagawea, the young kidnapped Shoshoni girl, recounts her story of being with her husband at Fort Mandan and becoming part of the Lewis and Clark Expedition. The purpose of the trip becomes clear and various individuals including Lewis, Clark, York, and the Corps of Discovery are introduced. Reenactments offer views of clothing, important locations, and equipment that the group used during their exploration.

1248. Spier, Peter. *The Star-Spangled Banner.* Weston Woods, 2004. Color. 12 mins. ISBN 978-1-55592-896-4. Grades K–5. Frances Scott Key wrote "The Star-Spangled Banner" in 1812. The scenes that stimulated Key's composition appear in pictures, and Spier explores their relationship to contemporary times. Aretha Franklin sings.

Compact Discs

1249. Couloumbis, Audrey. *The Misadventures of Maude March: Or Trouble Rides a Fast Horse.* Listening Library, 2006. 7 CDs; 8 hrs. 12 mins. ISBN 978-0-7393-3545-1. Grades 5–8. See entry 851.

1250. Cushman, Karen. *Rodzina.* Narrated by Becky Ann Baker. 4 CDs; 4 hrs. 47 mins. ISBN 978-0-8072-1576-0. Grades 4–7. See entry 853.

1251. Glass, Andrew. *Folks Call Me Appleseed John.* Narrated by Tom Stechschulte. Recorded Books, 1998. 1 cass., 0.25 hr. ISBN 978-0-7887-2260-8. Grades 1–6. When Johnny Appleseed lived in the wilderness of western Pennsylvania, his half-brother Nathaniel, 14, came to live with him in a hollow tree. Nathaniel got hungry as winter came and ate their stored food, so Johnny had to canoe to Fort Pitt for provisions. He missed the store because of ice floes on the river and had to walk back through the woods in the snow. He was worried about Nathaniel but on his return he discovered that four friendly Senecas had taught Nathaniel how to survive.

1252. Gregory, Kristiana. *Across the Wide and Lonesome Prairie: The Oregon Trail Diary of Hattie Campbell.* (Dear America) Live Oak Media, 2005. 4 CDs; 3:30 hrs. ISBN 978-1-59519-464-0. Grades 3–7. See entry 881.

1253. Hale, Marian. *Dark Water Rising.* Narrated by Stephen Hoye. Listening Library, 2007. 5 CDs; 5:19 hrs. ISBN 978-0-7393-6169-6. Grades 5 up. See entry 886.

1254. Kelly, Jacqueline. *The Evolution of Calpurnia Tate.* Narrated by Natalie Ross. Brilliance, 2009. 8 CDs; 9 hrs. 6 mins. ISBN 978-1-4418-0242-2. Grades 5–8. See entry 907.

1255. Kunstler, James Howard. *Annie Oakley.* Narrated by Keith Carradine. ISBN 978-0-88708-337-2. Grades K–3. See entry 1181.

1256. LaFaye, A. *Worth.* Narrated by Tommy Fleming. Live Oak Media, 2006. 2 CDs; 2 1/2 hrs. ISBN 978-1-59519-767-2. Grades 3–7. See entry 913.

1257. McCaughrean, Geraldine. *Stop the Train.* Full Cast Audio, 2005. 304pp. 8 CDs 7.75 hrs. ISBN 978-1-933322-42-1. Grades 5 up. See entry 925.

1258. Nelson, Vaunda M. *Bad News for Outlaws: The Remarkable Life of Bass Reeves, Deputy U.S. Marshal.* Recorded Books, 2010. 2 CDs; 50 mins. ISBN 978-1-4498-0617-0. Grades 3–8. See entry 1197.

1259. *Rainbow of the Sioux.* Tall Tales Audio, 2006. 1 CD; 57 mins. ISBN 978-1-933781-03-7. Grades K–5. In 1844 a white girl of 10 is the only survivor in a wagon train decimated by cholera. Sioux discover her on the prairie and Chief Red Sky adopts her. Kept quarantined for a month, she then begins to make friends with Singing Bird, the chief's daughter. Eventually the child, called Rainbow by the tribe, learns to ride bareback, to swim, and to hunt buffalo. Then she saves Singing Bird from a charging buffalo and cements her place in the tribe.

1260. Steele, William O. *Winter Danger.* Narrated by Richard Brewer. Listen & Live Audio, 2005. 4 CDs; 5 hrs. ISBN 978-1-59316-041-8. Grades 4–8. See entry 975.

1261. Wilder, Laura Ingalls. *By the Shores of Silver Lake.* Narrated by Cherry Jones. Harper-Children's Audio, 2004. 6 CDs; 6 hrs. ISBN 978-0-06-056501-5. Grades 3–6. See entry 992.

1262. Wilder, Laura Ingalls. *Farmer Boy.* Narrated by Cherry Jones. HarperAudio, 2004. 6 CDs; 6 hrs. ISBN 978-0-06-056506-0. Grades 3–6. See entry 995.

1263. Wilder, Laura Ingalls. *The First Four Years.* Narrated by Cherry Jones. HarperAudio, 2006. 3 CDs; 3 hrs. ISBN 978-0-06-056509-1. Grades 3–6. See entry 996.

1264. Wilder, Laura Ingalls. *Little House in the Big Woods.* Narrated by Cherry Jones. Harper-Collins, 2003. 4 CDs; 3.5 hrs. ISBN 978-0-06-054398-3. Grades 3–6. See entry 998.

1265. Wilder, Laura Ingalls. *Little House on the Prairie.* Narrated by Cherry Jones. HarperAudio, 2003. 6 CDs; 5.5hrs. ISBN 978-0-06-054399-0. Grades 3–6. See entry 999.

1266. Wilder, Laura Ingalls. *Little Town on the Prairie.* HarperChildren's Audio, 2005. 6 CDs; 6.5 hrs. ISBN 978-0-06-056505-3. Grades 3–7. See entry 1000.

1267. Wilder, Laura Ingalls. *The Long Winter.* Narrated by Cherry Jones. (Little House) 6 CDs; 9 hrs. ISBN 978-0-06-056502-2. Grades 3–6. See entry 1001.

1268. Wilder, Laura Ingalls. *On the Banks of Plum Creek.* Narrated by Cherry Jones. Harpercollins, 2003. 6 CDs; 6 hrs. ISBN 978-0-06-054400-3. Grades 3–6. See entry 1002.

1269. Wilder, Laura Ingalls. *These Happy Golden Years.* Narrated by Cherry Jones. Harper-Children's Audio, 2006. 6 CDs; 7 hrs. ISBN 978-0-06-056506-0. Grades 4–7. See entry 1004.

IMMIGRANTS, AND MULTICULTURAL HERITAGES, 1814–PRESENT

Historical Fiction and Fantasy

1270. Banks, Jacqueline Turner. *A Day for Vincent Chin and Me.* Houghton, 2001. 112pp. ISBN 978-0-618-13199-0; 2005, paper ISBN 978-0-618-54879-8. Grades 3–6. Tommy, a Japanese American sixth-grader in Kentucky, is surprised when someone sprays "KKK" on his house. His mother, survivor of a World War II Japanese internment camp, tells him to stand up for what he believes. She is planning a rally to remember Vincent Chen, who was brutally murdered in 1982. Tommy and friends build a speed bump on his street so that cars will not hurt his young deaf neighbor and Tommy realizes that he and his mother both fight for what is right.

1271. Bartone, Elisa. *Peppe the Lamplighter.* Illustrated by Ted Lewin. Lothrop, Lee & Shepard, 1993. 32pp. ISBN 978-0-688-10268-5; Mulberry, 1997, paper ISBN 978-0-688-15469-1. Grades K–3. Peppe's mother is dead and his father is sick. With eight sisters, he needs to make money. He gets a job as a lamplighter in New York's Little Italy, but his father belittles the job. When young Peppe refuses to light the lamps one night, his father comes to realize how important Peppe's job is—the lit lamps help people reach home safely, including Peppe's little sister. *Caldecott Honor.*

1272. Byars, Betsy C. *Keeper of the Doves.* Viking, 2002. 121pp. ISBN 978-0-670-03576-2; Puffin, 2004, paper ISBN 978-0-14-240063-0. Grades 5–8. Amen McGee is the youngest of four sisters in Kentucky at the end of the 19th century. She has been secretly watching the odd Polish immigrant, Mr. Tominski, a man who saved her father's life and lives in the old chapel on the family estate, as he tame his doves. Then the family pet dies and they must decide what happened and whether Mr. Tominski is involved. Twenty-six chapters, each for a letter of the alphabet, tell the story. *Charlie May Simon Book Award* (Arkansas) nomination, *William Allen White Children's Book Award* (Kansas) nomination, *Young Reader Award* (Nevada) nomination, *Charlotte Book Award* (New York) nomination, *Sequoyah Book Award* (Oklahoma) nomination, and *Dorothy Canfield Fisher Children's Book Award* (Vermont) nomination.

1273. Coerr, Eleanor. *Chang's Paper Pony.* Illustrated by Deborah Kogan Ray. (I Can Read) Trophy, 1993. 63pp. Paper ISBN 978-0-06-444163-6. Grades K–3. Around 1850 Chang and his grandfather run a hotel for the gold miners near San Francisco, California. The miners are rude to Chang, but he continues to work and study so he can have a better life away from the war in China. Chang finds gold in one of the miner's cabins, and the miner buys Chang a pony, the one thing Chang wants badly. *John and Patricia Beatty Award.*

1274. Connor, Leslie. *Miss Bridie Chose a Shovel.* Illustrated by Mary Azarian. Houghton, 2004. Unpaged. ISBN 978-0-618-30564-3. Grades K–3. When Miss Bridie leaves her Irish cottage in 1856 to travel to America, she takes a shovel with her. This proves to be a good choice. She uses it on the ship to steady herself. Once on land, she digs a garden with it and clears a path on a frozen river. It comes in handy when planting trees and coping with a flood, and eventually she buries her husband with it. Miss Bridie faces her world steadfastly and confidently. Woodcuts enhance the text. *Booklist Editor's Choice, Publishers Weekly Best Books,* and *Capitol Choices Noteworthy Titles* (Washington, D.C.).

1275. Duble, Kathleen Benner. *Hearts of Iron.* Margaret K. McElderry, 2006. 248pp. ISBN 978-1-416-90850-0. Grades 5–8. In 1820, in Mt. Riga, Connecticut, 15-year-old Lucy Pettee faces the possibility of marriage. She hesitates to commit to her friend Jesse because he wants to leave the mountain; she is happy there with all of the Northern European immigrants she knows and loves. Then her father hires Samuel Lernley from Boston to work in his store and consider Lucy as a possible wife. Lucy develops feelings for him as well and must choose between Samuel and moving to Boston or Jesse and living a less wealthy life.

1276. Durbin, William. *El Lector.* Wendy Lamb, 2006. 160pp. ISBN 978-0-385-74651-9; Yearling, 2007, paper ISBN 978-0-553-48786-2. Grades 5–8. In 1931, 13-year-old Bella Lorente lives near the cigar factory in Ybor City, Florida, with her widowed mother and four siblings. Bella's Cuban immigrant grandfather works as *el lector,* reading literature and poetry in Spanish to the workers, a job that Bella hopes to have some day. The workers become disenchanted with their conditions, and Bella's Aunt Lola is arrested for being a member of a tobacco workers' union. Then the radio replaces Bella's grandfather. Bella can no longer attend high school and must work in the factory to help support her family. But then Bella realizes that she and her grandfather can go on the radio, and they get jobs reading in Spanish to the community.

1277. Durbin, William. *Song of Sampo Lake.* Yearling, 2004. 217pp. Paper ISBN 978-0-440-22899-8. Grades 5–9. Finnish immigrant Matti Ocala, 15, works in a Minnesota iron mine in 1900. When his uncle dies tragically in a mine accident, the family members decide to demonstrate their *sisu* (strength, courage, and stubbornness) and follow their dream of homesteading on Lake Sampo. Among Matti's trials are facing a bear and rescuing his sister fallen through the ice, but Matti's father determines that building a sauna before building the cabin will help them continue their heritage. *Children's Book Award* (Rhode Island) nomination.

1278. Easton, Richard. *A Real American.* Clarion, 2002. 156pp. ISBN 978-0-618-13339-0. Grades 4–7. In 1890 Nathan McClelland, 11, is lonely. His best friend has moved away and his father is working hard to save the family farm in western Pennsylvania. Arturo Tozzi and his family move into town along with other Italian immigrants to work the mines. There is some friction between the two groups—the residents fear losing their jobs to the newcomers. But Nathan and Arturo become friends and Nathan begins to understand some of the problems that Arturo faces.

1279. Emery, Joanna. *Brothers of the Falls.* Illustrated by David Erickson. (Adventures in America) Silver Moon, 2004. 92pp. ISBN 978-1-893110-37-3. Grades 4–6. In 1847 the potato famine in Ireland persuades Thomas and James Doyle to leave for America. The ship leaves early and older brother Thomas does not board in time; 13-year-old James must sail to America alone. He gets a job at the Niagara Inn in Niagara Falls, New York, and tries to earn enough money to return to Ireland and reunite with his brother. He meets a Native American who shows him the impressive waterfalls, and he experiences other excitements that help him cope with the separation from Thomas.

1280. Giff, Patricia Reilly. *Maggie's Door.* Yearling, 2005. 160pp. Paper ISBN 978-0-440-41581-7. Grades 5–9. In this sequel to *Nory Ryan's Song* set in the 1940s, Nory and her friend Sean Red Mallon leave Ireland to escape the potato famine. The two tell their stories in alternating chapters as they try to reach Nory's sister Maggie's house in Brooklyn. They face cruelty, starvation, and filth on the way over in "coffin" ships, but they focus on the future and meeting at 416 Smith Street.

1281. Giff, Patricia Reilly. *Water Street.* Wendy Lamb, 2006. 164pp. ISBN 978-0-385-73068-6; Yearling, 2008, paper ISBN 978-0-440-41921-1. Grades 4–8. In 1875 Brooklyn, Nory (of *Nory Ryan's Song*) and Sean's 13-year-old daughter Bridget ("Bird") befriends Thomas, a lonely boy who lives upstairs. From their tenement windows, they enjoy watching men, including Bird's dad, build the Brooklyn Bridge's towers. Bird's family includes Thomas in its plans, and the two help each other in school and on the street. They have to struggle, but friendship makes it easier.

1282. Glaser, Linda. *Bridge to America: Based on a True Story.* Houghton, 2005. 208pp. ISBN 978-0-618-56301-2. Grades 3–7. In 1920, Fivel, 9, stays with his Jewish family in their Polish shtetl while his father goes to America to earn enough money for them to join him. They are very hungry, survive on watery soup, and fearful of rumored Cossack pogroms. Finally the money arrives, and they begin their journey to meet Pa in Minnesota. They arrive in New York, pass through Ellis Island, and find their father, a rag peddler, living in a house with running water, inside toilets, and electricity. At first Fivel tries to be totally American, but he eventually realizes that he can keep both worlds inside him. Note and Glossary.

1283. Haas, Jessie. *Chase.* Greenwillow, 2007. ISBN 978-0-06-112850-9. Grades 5–9. Phin Chase, a stable boy, sees a coal mine boss murdered in eastern Pennsylvania around 1875. He becomes a suspect and somehow ends up with the killer's wallet. Both the murderer and a mysterious man named Fraser pursue him on horseback through the coal mining region where the Irish immigrant Molly Maguires are at work. Phin flees first on foot and then by train. He eventually rids himself of Fraser when the man falls from the horse, and he is exonerated.

1284. Heller, Linda Peterson. *The Castle on Hester Street.* Illustrated by Boris Kulikov. Simon & Schuster, 2007. 40pp. ISBN 978-0-689-87434-5. Grades K–3. Julie's grandfather tells her about his childhood. He embellishes his journey from Russia to America, saying that a goat pulled his solid-gold wagon and that he built a castle after his arrival. Grandma corrects his humorous stories, describing the difficulties of Ellis Island and the small room that he shared with two other men. The couple emphasize that their eventual freedom from the harsh treatment of Jews in Russia was worth the hardships. Illustrations augment the text. This book was first published in 1982. *Sydney Taylor Book Award Honor Award.*

1285. Hest, Amy. *When Jessie Came Across the Sea.* Illustrated by P. J. Lynch. Candlewick, 2003. 40pp. Paper ISBN 978-0-7636-1274-0. Grades 2–6. In Eastern Europe, the local rabbi offers one ticket to America. Thirteen-year-old Jessie has to take the opportunity and migrate although it means leaving the beloved grandmother with whom she has lived since her parents died. On the ship, she meets Lou, a shoemaker, and they form a friendship. After her arrival in America, she studies English diligently and sews lace, like her grandmother. One day she meets Lou in Central Park and they renew their relationship. In three years, Jessie has become an accomplished creator of bridal gowns and has earned enough money to bring her grandmother to America. Watercolor and gouache illustrations complement the text. *ABC Children's Booksellers Choices Awards*, *Kate Greenaway Medal*, *Sequoyah Children's Award* (Oklahoma), *Young Hoosier Book Award* (Indiana), *Volunteer State Award* (Tennessee), and *Young Readers Award* (Virginia).

1286. Holm, Jennifer L. *Our Only May Amelia.* Trophy, 2001. 253pp. Paper ISBN 978-0-06-440856-1. Grades 4–7. The youngest child and only girl in a family of eight, 12-year-old May Amelia wants to have a sister in her Nasel River, Washington, home in 1899. Her Finnish father complains that she acts like a boy, and she helps save her brother Wilbert when a bear attacks him. She is delighted when her mother has a girl, but the baby dies in her sleep when May Amelia is looking after her. May Amelia's grandmother accuses her of killing the baby. May Amelia leaves home to live with her aunt and uncle in Astoria, Oregon, and gets a different perspective on life. After her grandmother dies, May Amelia returns to her family's farm. The community around her lives peacefully with the Chinook Indians, but her brother cannot date a girl of Irish descent and loggers at the nearby camp threaten their safety. But May Amelia needs to be with her family. *Bluegrass Award* (Kentucky) nomination, *Mark Twain Award* (Missouri) nomination. *Newbery Honor Book*, *The Land of Enchantment Children's*

Book Award (New Mexico) nomination, *Battle of the Books* (New Mexico) nomination, *Publishers Weekly's Best Children's Books*, *Teen Book Award* (Rhode Island) nomination, *Volunteer State Book Award* (Tennessee) nomination, *Dorothy Canfield Fisher Children's Book Award* (Vermont) nomination, and *Capitol Choices Noteworthy Titles* (Washington, DC).

1287. Hurst, Carol Otis. *Torchlight.* Houghton, 2006. 142pp. ISBN 978-0-618-27601-1. Grades 4–6. Charlotte Hodge, a fifth grader in Westfield, Massachusetts, in 1864, becomes friends with Irish Catholic immigrant Maggie Nolan. Charlotte's brother hates the Irish and her aunt disapproves of their drinking. But her uncle tries to promote Irish workers in his whip factory. Although Charlotte's other friends bully her and Maggie's family wants the two to stop being friends, the girls discover that their friendship is stronger than the bigotry in the town. Together they help to stop the mob planning to burn down the new Catholic church.

1288. Kent, Deborah. *Blackwater Creek.* (Saddles, Stars and Stripes) Kingfisher, 2005. 152pp. ISBN 978-0-7534-5885-3. Grades 4–6. In 1849 Hungarian Erika Nagy works as a rancher for Hart Lathami while her brother and father search for gold in California. Her ability to work with horses helps to pay the family's rent. When she searches for an injured horse, she finds both the horse and gold that she can claim for the family. Then they will be able to buy a farm.

1289. Krensky, Stephen. *The Iron Dragon Never Sleeps.* Illustrated by John Fuleveiler. Yearling, 1995. 85pp. Paper ISBN 978-0-440-41136-9. Grades 3–6. Winnie Tucker, 10, and her mother come to Cisco, California, in the summer of 1867, while Winnie's father works on the transcontinental railroad. Winnie becomes friends with Lee Cheng, a young Chinese tea carrier, who tells her stories about the work on the railroad—unlike those her father reports. She discovers that the Chinese workers are maltreated and that racial discrimination permeates the area. Afterword.

1290. Lee, Milly. *Landed.* Illustrated by Yangsook Choi. Frances Foster, 2006. Unpaged. ISBN 978-0-374-34314-9. Grades 3–6. Twelve-year-old Sun has sailed from China to San Francisco to live with his father, but is held at Angel Island for interrogation under the Chinese Exclusion Act of 1882. He must wait his turn and then undergo complicated questions. He has memorized many facts but the experience is grueling. Illustrations complement the text. Note.

1291. Leighton, Maxinne Rhea. *An Ellis Island Christmas.* Illustrated by Dennis Nolan. Puffin, 2005. 32pp. Paper ISBN 978-0-14-240506-2. Grades 1–4. When she is 6 years old in the early 20th century, Krysia, her mother, and her brother sail from Poland to Ellis Island to meet her father, who is already in New York. When they arrive in New York City, they all enjoy the beautiful Christmas tree, and the children are relieved that Saint Mikolaj (Saint Nicholas) can also be found in America.

1292. Levinson, Riki. *Watch the Stars Come Out.* Illustrated by Diane Goode. Puffin, 1995. Unpaged. Paper ISBN 978-0-14-055506-6. Grades K–3. A little girl listens to her grandmother tell her about another little girl and her brother who cross the ocean to America to join their parents and sister. She becomes distressed when she cannot see the stars at night over the ship and when her parents are not at Ellis Island waiting for them. She also does not know why the people wearing white jackets look at her body so carefully. But when she sees her parents at the ferry docks and looks out the window in their top floor apartment and sees the stars, she feels much better. *Children's Book Award* (Georgia) and *Best Books for Children*.

1293. Levinson, Robin K. *Miriam's Journey: Discovering a New World.* Illustrated by Drusilla Kehl. (The Gali Girls Jewish History) Gali Girls, 2005. 61pp. Paper ISBN 978-0-977367-30-6. Grades 4–5. Miriam Bloom, her two sisters, and her mother arrive at Ellis Island after leaving their Russian shtetl and fear of the Cossacks. In New York they discover that Miriam's father has died and they no longer have a sponsor to help them enter the country. A wealthy passenger on their ship with connections to the media decides to help them so that they will not have to return to Russia. Illustrations complement the text.

1294. Levitin, Sonia. *Junk Man's Daughter.* Illustrated by Guy Porfirio. (Tales of Young Americans) Sleeping Bear, 2007. Unpaged. ISBN 978-1-58536-315-5. Grades K–2. Before they immigrate in the 1930s, Papa promises Hanna and her brothers that streets in America are paved with gold. They discover instead that Papa cannot find a job. Mama remains optimistic, and Hanna's older sister notices that the street is full of bottles, paper, rubbish, and metal that can be sold. The family builds a thriving business dealing in items that others have discarded. Soon they have enough money to buy a used truck. They invest their profits and create a much larger enterprise.

1295. **Lynch, Chris.** *Gold Dust.* Trophy, 2002. 196pp. Paper ISBN 978-0-06-447201-2. Grades 5–8. In 1975 Richard Riley Moncrief, 12, son of a Midas Muffler employee, meets Napoleon Charlie Ellis, a new student from Dominica whose father is a professor. The boys become fast friends, and Richard hopes Napoleon will learn to love baseball and the Red Sox. Napoleon, however, is an excellent cricket player. At their Catholic school, racial issues destroy their friendship in subtle ways so that Napoleon decides to attend another school. *Dorothy Canfield Fisher Children's Book Award* (Vermont) nomination, *Young Reader Book Awards* (Virginia), and *Children's Book Award* (Georgia) nomination.

1296. **McDonough, Yona Zeldis.** *The Doll Shop Downstairs.* Illustrated by Heather Maione. Viking, 2009. 118pp. ISBN 978-0-670-01091-2. Grades 2–4. Anna Breittlemann, 9, lives with her two sisters above their Russian Jewish family's doll repair shop in Manhattan's Lower East Side in 1914. World War I stops the flow of doll parts from the family's German supplier, and Anna suggests that they make cloth dolls to replace the broken china ones. When the F. A. O. Schwartz toy store buyer sees their creation, Nurse Nora, the family business quickly changes. Note, Glossary, and Chronology.

1297. **Martino, Carmela A.** *Rosa Sola.* Candlewick, 2005. 256pp. ISBN 978-0-7636-2395-1. Grades 4–7. In 1966 Italian immigrant Rosa, 10, wants a sibling. Her parents announce that a child will be born, but it is stillborn. Her mother is sick, and her father is angry. As they all grieve, Rosa fears that she may have caused this tragedy. However, the friends and neighbors around help Rosa understand that none of the family can be blamed for this situation. Illustrations augment the text.

1298. **Napoli, Donna Jo.** *The King of Mulberry Street.* Wendy Lamb, 2005. 224pp. ISBN 978-0-385-74653-3; Yearling, 2007, paper ISBN 978-0-553-49416-7. Grades 5–9. In 1892, 9-year-old Beniamino, a Jew, becomes a stowaway from Naples, Italy. He believes his mother is on board the ship, but she is not. When he arrives in New York, he pretends to be Dom Napoli. He must survive with the rest of the homeless children and, with two Italian friends, begins selling sandwiches. He wants to return home as soon as he can, but after his business becomes profitable, he understands that his mother sent him there to have a better life. *American Library Association Notable Book, Dorothy Canfield Fisher Children's Book Award* (Vermont) nomination, *Sequoyah Book Award* (Oklahoma) nomination, and *Children's Book Award* (Rhode Island) nomination.

1299. **Nixon, Joan Lowery.** *Land of Dreams.* (Ellis Island) Gareth Stevens, 2001. 160pp. ISBN 978-0-8368-2810-8. Grades 5–9. In the third book of the Ellis Island series, 17-year-old Kristin Swenson reaches the colony of Great Rock Lake, Minnesota, in 1902 with her parents. There she refuses to follow the traditions of her Swedish heritage and rejects an arranged marriage. After the family's home burns and she sees how the community works together, she realizes that compromising does not mean that she has to lose her individuality. With an empathetic husband, she can also continue her support of women's right to vote and other causes important to her.

1300. **Nixon, Joan Lowery.** *Land of Hope.* (Ellis Island) Laurel-Leaf, 1993. 172pp. Paper ISBN 978-0-440-21597-4. Grades 5–9. Rebekah arrives in New York in 1902. Her family left Russia to flee the Jewish pogroms. She wants to get an education, but her family needs money, so she has to work seven days a week in a sweatshop. She hears from Rose in Chicago and Kristin in Minnesota, two girls she met on the crossing, and they tell her about their new lives. When her brother refuses an opportunity to study, Rebekah's father finally agrees to escort her to class.

1301. Nixon, Joan Lowery. *Land of Promise.* (Ellis Island) Gareth Stevens, 2001. 170pp. ISBN 978-0-8368-2812-2. Grades 5–9. Fifteen-year-old Rose arrives in Chicago from Ireland in 1902, and her brother's political connections help her get a job as a shop girl. She plans to use her salary to pay for her mother and sister to come to America. She thinks her mother will curb her father's drinking and her brother's radical activities. But her mother does not arrive in time to solve these problems. Rose joins Jane Addams's campaign to clean up Chicago and fight for world peace.

1302. Oberman, Sheldon. *The Always Prayer Shawl.* Illustrated by Ted Lewin. Boyds Mills, 1994. Unpaged. ISBN 978-1-878093-22-6; 2005, paper ISBN 978-1-59078-332-0. Grades K–3. In Russia in the late 19th century, Adam gets his eggs from chickens and his heat from wood, and he travels on a horse. But when the czar's soldiers start destroying towns nearby, Adam and his family leave Russia and Adam's grandfather, who had been his tutor. The grandfather gives Adam his own prayer shawl, which had belonged to his grandfather Adam. Although everything is different in his new home across the ocean, Adam retains two things unchanged: his name and his prayer shawl. As an old man, he promises to give his grandson Adam the prayer shawl. *National Jewish Book Award, Notable Children's Trade Books in the Field of Social Studies, Children's Booksellers Choice, International Reading Association Teachers' Choice, American Booksellers' Pick of the List, Reading Rainbow Review Book,* and *Sydney Taylor Award.*

1303. Paulsen, Gary. *The Winter Room.* Orchard, 1989. 112pp. ISBN 978-0-531-05839-8; Scholastic, 2009, paper ISBN 978-0-545-08534-2. Grades 5–8. Eleven-year-old Eldon discusses the various events of the seasons on the family's Minnesota farm at the turn of the 20th century. Although Eldon enjoys his uncle's stories in winter the best, his brother Wayne challenges them. He does not believe that anyone can cut wood the way his uncle describes. However, from a hiding place, they watch Uncle David prove that he can still perform. *Newbery Honor, American Library Association Notable Children's Books,* and *Judy Lopez Memorial Award.*

1304. Russell, Barbara Timberlake. *Maggie's Amerikay.* Farrar, 2006. 32pp. ISBN 978-0-374-34722-2. Grades 2–5. In New Orleans in 1898 Maggie McCrary has immigrated from Ireland with her parents. They work to save money for land, and then the baby gets yellow fever. Maggie's mother sews, and her father peddles goods from a pushcart, generously donating a cornet to a young African American boy named Nathan. Despite friction between Irish immigrants and African Americans, Maggie and Nathan become friends, and Nathan finds Maggie a job recording Daddy Clements's experiences as a slave and fighting in the Civil War. Soon Nathan starts playing jazz with the grownups. Paintings enhance the text.

1305. Ryan, Pam Muñoz. *Esperanza Rising.* Scholastic, 2000. 262pp. ISBN 978-0-439-12041-8; 2002, paper ISBN 978-0-439-12042-5. Grades 5–9. After bandits murder her father and her uncle decides to marry her mother, 14-year-old Esperanza and her mother escape their luxurious life in Mexico and head for California, where they work on farms during the Depression. Esperanza learns how to keep house so that she can earn money to bring her grandmother to the United States. She watches labor strikes, government sweeps of workers, and Mexicans born in the United States deported in "voluntary repatriation" without being allowed to identify themselves. But she also learns resilience. *School Librarians Battle of the Books* (Alaska) nomination, *Charlie May Simon* (Arkansas) nomination, *American Library Association Notable Books for Children, Young Readers Book Awards* (California) nomination, *Blue Spruce Young Adult Book Awards* (Colorado), *Nutmeg Children's Book Award* (Connecticut) nomination, *Capitol Choices Noteworthy Titles* (Washington, D.C.), *Sunshine State Young Reader Award* (Florida) nomination, *Children's Book Award* (Georgia) nomination, *Rebecca Caudill Award* (Illinois) nomination, *Young Hoosier Award* (Indiana) nomination, *Children's Book Award* (Massachusetts) nomination, *Maud Hart Lovelace Award* (Minnesota) nomination, *Battle of the Books* (North Carolina) nomination, *Battle of the Books* (New Jersey) nomination, *Pura Belpré Award, Junior Book Award* (South Carolina) nomination, *Prairie Pasque Award* (South Dakota) nomination, *Young Adult Book Award* (Tennessee) nomination, *Bluebonnet Award* (Texas) nomination, *Readers' Choice Award* (Virginia) nomination, and *Soaring Eagle Book Award* (Wyoming) nomination.

1306. Sanchez, Anita. *The Invasion of Sandy Bay.* Calkins Creek, 2008. 147pp. ISBN 978-1-59078-560-7. Grades 5–9. The war of 1812 is still raging in 1814. Lemuel Brooks, 12, newly arrived in the fishing village of Sandy Bay, Massachusetts, is adapting to his new life but still feels isolated. While he is out in the bay on a tiny boat learning to fish, he is captured by a British frigate. The ensuing adventure involves escapes, captures on both sides, and an eventual exchange of prisoners, and Lemuel provides valuable help to the people of Sandy Bay. Based on a true story. Bibliography.

1307. Sandin, Joan. *At Home in a New Land.* HarperCollins, 2007. 64pp. ISBN 978-0-06-058077-3. Grades K–2. Carl Erik and his family leave Sweden in the mid-19th century and must adjust to life in Minnesota. Carl Erik's responsibilities grow when his father leaves to work at a logging camp but he is determined to learn to read English and to overcome his fear of the local Ojibway Indians. The immigrant community welcomes them, and they have a happy Christmas together. Watercolor and ink illustrations augment the text.

1308. Sandin, Joan. *The Long Way to a New Land.* Fitzgerald, 2007. 64pp. ISBN 978-1-4242-0591-2; Trophy, 1986, paper ISBN 978-0-06-444100-1. Grades K–3. Carl Erik's family leaves Sweden in 1868 during a famine for the long journey to America. They sail via England and find that Carl Erik's father has a job for the winter that will help him support his family. *American Library Association Notable Children's Books, Booklist Children's Editor's Choices, Notable Children's Trade Books in the Field of Social Studies,* and *American Library Association USA Children's Books of International Interest.*

1309. Sandin, Joan. *A Long Way Westward.* Trophy, 1992. 64pp. Paper ISBN 978-0-06-444198-8. Grades K–3. In the sequel to *The Long Way to a New Land,* also in 1868, Carl Erik and his family arrive in New York and take the train to Anoka, Minnesota. The train moves so slowly that the children sometimes run along next to it. They meet all kinds of people as they journey to their new home. *American Library Association Notable Books for Children, USA Through Children's Books,* and *New York Public Library's Children's Books.*

1310. Sherman, Eileen B. *Independence Avenue.* Jewish Publication Society, 1990. 145pp. ISBN 978-0-8276-0367-7. Grades 5–8. In 1907, Elias, 14, arrives in Kansas City from Russia, alone and without work. He talks his way into a job in a department store, hoping to become a tailor, his family's trade. He meets the boss's daughter, but her aunt sees him as an immigrant and beneath Rebecca's attentions. He must learn how to cope in this new environment. He does, but he first hears of his parents' deaths in a pogrom, and his 6-year-old brother arrives to live with him.

1311. Uchida, Yoshiko. *The Best Bad Thing.* Aladdin, 1993. 136pp. Paper ISBN 978-0-689-71745-1. Grades 3–6. The second book of the trilogy beginning with *A Jar of Dreams* and ending with *The Happiest Ending* sees Rinko's mother wanting Rinko to work with Mrs. Hatta for the summer in 1936. Rinko thinks that Mrs. Hatta is slightly crazy, but when she calls Rinko outside to see the lovely spider webs floating in the air, Rinko begins to change her mind. An old man living nearby also helps the summer become the "best bad thing" when he gives Rinko a kite and calls it an extension of the sky. *American Library Association Notable Children's Book* and *School Library Journal Best Book.*

1312. Uchida, Yoshiko. *Samurai of Gold Hill.* Illustrated by Ati Forberg. Heyday, 2005. 119pp. Paper ISBN 978-1-59714-015-7. Grades 4 up. Although he wants to be a samurai, Koichi must leave Japan when he is 12 in 1869 to sail to the United States because his clan and the Shogun are defeated. In Gold Hill, California, his father and partners in the Wakamatsu colony try to start a tea and silk farm, but miners destroy their work. When Koichi sees a Maidu Indian celebrate a ritual, he realizes that it looks very much like a Japanese ritual. He knows that people are not as different as they seem.

1313. Weber, Judith Eichler. *Forbidden Friendship.* Silver Moon, 1994. 80pp. ISBN 978-1-881889-42-7; 2004, paper ISBN 978-1-893110-42-7. Grades 3–5. In North Adams, Massachusetts, Molly Bartlett finds herself in a strange predicament when she and Chen Li become friends in 1870. Molly's father owns a local shoe factory where the workers are striking. Chen's parents are among the Chinese immigrants brought into town to break the strike.

Molly has to learn about friendship as well as the realities of business and the needs of others. Endpaper Maps and Historical Postscript.

1314. Welch, Catherine. *Clouds of Terror.* Illustrated by Laurie K. Johnson. First Avenue, 1994. 48pp. Paper ISBN 978-0-8761-4639-2. Grades 2–4. Helga and Erik's family, immigrants from Sweden, face a plague of grasshoppers at their new Minnesota home during the 1870s. The grasshoppers eat everything, get into the water, and rest on top of the baby. Because there are no crops left, their father has to go away to find work. The next year, the grasshoppers hatch from eggs left the previous summer, but they fly away. *Notable Children's Trade Books in the Field of Social Studies.*

1315. Wishinsky, Frieda. *Just Call Me Joe.* Orca, 2004. 101pp. Paper ISBN 978-1-55143-249-6. Grades 2–5. Ten-year-old Joseph leaves his parents in Russia in 1909 and emigrates to New York City, where he expects life will be good for him on the Lower East Side. But other boys call him names in English that he does not understand. He replies in Yiddish. His older sister Anna, 17, works in a factory under awful conditions, and his Aunt Sophie takes in boarders. Because he speaks no English, Joseph must start school in the first grade, and although he wants friends his own age, he must resist their urgings to become a thief and a bully.

1316. Woodruff, Elvira. *The Memory Coat.* Illustrated by Michael Dooling. Scholastic, 1999. 32pp. ISBN 978-0-590-67717-2. Grades K–3. Rachel and her orphaned cousin Grisha flee from their Russian shtetl to America in the early 1900s with Rachel's family, escaping the dreaded roundups of Jews. They want to impress the inspectors at Ellis Island but an inspector notices that Grisha has a cut on his eye. Rachel decides to turn his shabby old coat, given to him by his mother, inside out to hide the doctor's chalk mark. Impressionistic oil Illustrations augment the text. Notes. *William Allen White Children's Book Award* (Kansas) nomination and *Carolyn W. Field Award* (Pennsylvania).

1317. Woodruff, Elvira. *Small Beauties: The Journey of Darcy Heart O'Hara.* Illustrated by Adam Rex. Knopf, 2006. Unpaged. ISBN 978-0-375-82686-3. Grades 1–5. In the 1840s young Irish girl Darcy Heart O'Hara has a gift for noticing small things. She collects flower petals, butterfly wings, a bead from Granny's rosary, dried blossoms of heather and buttercup, and small pebbles and takes them home in the hem of her ragged dress. Soon the potato famine ravishes her home country, and her family has to leave for America. While they are trying to adjust to their new surroundings, Darcy's small wonders remind them of their love for the old one. Illustrations enhance the text.

1318. Wright, Randall. *The Silver Penny.* Henry Holt, 2005. 208pp. ISBN 978-0-8050-7391-1. Grades 5–8. After Jeb "Deb" Corey, 11, breaks his leg, he cannot play with his cousin or his friend. His great-Grandpa "lends" him a silver penny that he says saved his life in the Revolutionary War; he also says that the penny stays with a person only as long as it is needed. The penny takes Deb on a wild journey through the early 1800s and treats him to exciting experiences that may be either magical or a dream.

1319. Yang, Belle. *Hannah Is My Name.* Candlewick, 2004. Unpaged. ISBN 978-0-7636-2223-7; 2007, paper ISBN 978-0-7636-3521-3. Grades K–3. Seven-year-old Hannah comes with her parents from Taiwan to San Francisco in the 1960s. She likes the city and enjoys learning "This Land Is My Land" and seeing Curious George in a department store. But the family constantly worries about obtaining green cards and they hide when officials come looking for papers. The coveted cards eventually arrive in the mail. Illustrations intensify the text.

1320. Yep, Laurence. *Dragon Road.* (Golden Mountain Chronicles) HarperCollins, 2008. 291pp. ISBN 978-0-06-027520-4. Grades 5 up. Calvin (Flash) Chin wants to escape his alcoholic father and earn some money in 1939, so he agrees to leave San Francisco and tour with a Chinese American basketball team, the Dragons. He and his friend Barney Young, along with four other players, travel through the West playing local teams and legends such as the Harlem Globetrotters. He is fearful of prejudice along the way and behaves with care. Eventually he returns home, happy to have played but happy to be back.

1321. Yep, Laurence. *The Dragon's Child: A Story of Angel Island.* HarperCollins, 2008. 133pp. ISBN 978-0-06-027692-8. Grades 4–8. In 1922 Gim Lew, 10, crosses the Pacific with his father and has to stay on Angel Island in San Francisco Bay until he finishes a lengthy immigration interview. This involves providing details about his home, village, and neighbors in order to prove that he is who he claims he is. He has carefully studied a book about his family and even knows the number of windows and steps in his house. To enter "The Golden Mountain," he must answer perfectly. Gim's anxiety about being left-handed and stuttering becomes apparent as he tries desperately to recall the right answers and seize his chance to stay in America. Photographs intensify the text. Bibliography. *Children's Book Award* (Rhode Island) and *Children's Book Award* (West Virginia) nomination.

1322. **Yep, Laurence.** *Dragon's Gate.* HarperCollins, 1993. 275pp. ISBN 978-0-06-022971-9; Trophy, 1995, paper ISBN 978-0-06-440489-1. Grades 5 up. In this prequel to *Dragonwings* set in 1865, Otter arrives in the Sierra Mountains from Hwangtung Province in China, and begins helping his adoptive father and uncle build the transcontinental railroad. Otter expects to see gold fields, but instead finds cleared trees and a vast cover of whiteness. His dream is to learn all he can and return to China to free it from the Manchu invaders. During the difficult work under hostile foremen, his uncle encourages him to have another dream, one in which he will be himself and do what he needs to do rather than what tradition has told him. After a strike for fewer hours and more pay, and his uncle's death, Otter decides to take his advice. *Newbery Honor, New York Public Library's Books for the Teen Age, American Booksellers Pick of the Lists, Commonwealth Club Silver Medal for Literature, John and Patricia Beatty Award*, and *American Library Association Notable Children's Book.*

1323. **Yep, Laurence.** *The Traitor: Golden Mountain Chronicles, 1885.* HarperCollins, 2003. 320pp. ISBN 978-0-06-027522-8; Trophy, 2004, paper ISBN 978-0-06-000831-4. Grades 5–8. In 1885 in Rock Springs, Wyoming, racial tensions are high but two lonely 12-year-old boys from different backgrounds become friends. Although Joseph Young considers himself American—he was born in the United States—others see him as Chinese. Michael Purdy's illegitimacy makes him an "outsider." The boys meet in a cave full of fossils that they name Star Rock. As they watch the escalation of racism in the town, Michael's intolerant mother surprises him by sheltering Joseph and his father until they can all flee the town and head for San Francisco.

1324. **Yin.** *Coolies.* Illustrated by Chris K. Soentpiet. Penguin, 2001. 40pp. ISBN 978-0-399-23227-5; Puffin, 2003, paper ISBN 978-0-14-250055-2. Grades 1–4. A grandmother tells a young boy the story of Shek and Wong, his great-great-great-grandfather and his brother, when they came to the United States from China to help build the Transcontinental Railroad in 1865. Although they are glad to have work, they must endure deafening blasts from dynamite in the Sierras, bleeding hands, and frightening avalanches during a blizzard. They participate in the worker's strike for higher pay and are denied. Then at a celebration for the joining of the eastern and western rail lines in Promontory Summit, Utah, in 1869, the "coolies" are not invited. After their four years working on the railroad, the brothers used their earnings to open a San Francisco store and bring the rest of their family to the United States. Double-page spreads reveal their adventures and the dangers they faced after saying good-bye to their mother in China. *American Library Association Notable Books for Children, Black-Eyed Susan Book Award* (Maryland) nomination, *Children's Book Award* (Rhode Island) nomination, *Beehive Children's Picture Book Award* (Utah) nomination, *SCASL Book Award* (South Carolina) nomination, *Asian Pacific American Award for Literature* nomination, *International Reading Association Children's Book Awards*, and *Children's Book Award* (Utah) nomination.

1325. **Yolen, Jane.** *Naming Liberty.* Illustrated by Jim Burke. Philomel, 2008. 32pp. ISBN 978-0-399-24250-2. Grades K–3. To escape the pogroms, Giti and her family leave Russia to join her brother Shmuel (Sammy) in the United States. They travel by cart, foot, train, and boat to reach Ellis Island. When Giti looks at the Statue of Liberty—a figure whose creation is recounted in a parallel story—Giti decides to call herself "Libby" in honor of the statue and her own new status.

History

1326. **Bial, Raymond.** *Amish Home.* Houghton, 1995. 40pp. Paper ISBN 978-0-395-72021-9. Grades 4–6. The photographs included here of contemporary Amish homes would be the same if taken when photography was in its infancy. The Germanic culture of the Amish people has stayed the same through the decades they have lived in the United States, mainly in Pennsylvania. Further Reading.

1327. **Bial, Raymond.** *Ellis Island: Coming to the Land of Liberty.* HMH, 2009. 56pp. ISBN 978-0-618-99943-9. Grades 4–8. From 1892 to 1954 Ellis Island processed more than half of the immigrants coming to America. After an arduous journey by ship, for which they had often used all their resources, these people had to endure a three- to five-hour entry process if they were healthy and a much longer one if they were not. They slept in dormitories or hospitals if detained, and they could be held for political views, criminal history, or lack of money. Of the 12 million who arrived, 2 percent were sent back home. This text elaborates on their stories and the history of the island with primary source photographs and museum images. Bibliography.

1328. **Bial, Raymond.** *Tenement: Immigrant Life on the Lower East Side.* Houghton, 2002. 48pp. ISBN 978-0-618-13849-4. Grades 5–8. Tenement life, unfamiliar to most today, was a dark and drab environment filled with people, noise, and smells. The text includes quotations, laws, personal memories, and Jacob Riis's photographs taken on the Lower East Side of New York City in the late 19th century. Their focus on small things—medicine on a dresser top, for example—shows the lives of these people coping with poverty. They often had no running water for bathing or laundering clothes, disease spread rapidly, and so many babies died that the slang term for the housing was "infant slaughterhouse." Bibliography and Web Sites.

1329. **Broida, Marian.** *Projects About Nineteen-Century European Immigrants.* (Hands-On History) Benchmark, 2006. 47pp. ISBN 978-0-7614-1980-8. Grades 3–5. Projects to help readers understand 19th-century immigrants from Europe and their cultures include a Scotch-Irish sampler, how to form a German singing group, flower trimmings for women's hats, translating messages into Morse Code as many Irish women did, dressing as a Jewish girl or British newsboy, and making Irish potato soup and German *apfel torte*. Photographs and illustrations augment the text. Glossary, Further Reading, Web Sites, and Index.

1330. **Broida, Marian.** *Projects About Nineteenth-Century Chinese Immigrants.* (Hands-On History) Benchmark, 2006. 47pp. ISBN 978-0-7614-1978-5. Grades 3–5. Projects that help readers understand 19th-century Chinese immigrants and their culture include constructing a miner's scale, an abacus, a fan, and a girl's festive crown; making Chinese-style rice and green beans; practicing the art of calligraphy; and theatrical face painting. Photographs and illustrations augment the text. Glossary, Further Reading, Web Sites, and Index.

1331. **Brooks, Philip.** *Immigration.* (20th Century Perspectives) Heinemann, 2003. 48pp. ISBN 978-1-4034-3807-2; paper ISBN 978-1-4034-4181-2. Grades 4–8. Brooks looks at many aspects of immigration, including why people left their native countries, where they usually came from in the later 19th and early 20th centuries, where they landed and lived, and the prejudices they faced. Illustrations augment the text. Bibliography, Further Reading, Glossary, Index.

1332. **Di Franco, J. Philip.** *The Italian Americans.* (Immigrant Experience) Chelsea House, 1995. 94pp. ISBN 978-0-7910-3353-1. Grades 5 up. Although this book professes to discuss only Italian Americans, it also gives a brief history of Italy through its revolutions and the Italian unification movement, *Risorgimento*, led by Guiseppe Mazzini, Giuseppe Garibaldi, and Camillo Benso di Cavour. In the19th century, however, the greed of the wealthy led to a difficult life for many southern Italians. The northern Italians emigrated first, with the southern Italians following them. The peak immigration years were 1900 to 1914, when more than 2 million Italians arrived in the United States. Not all of them remained, but by 1980, 12 million Italians had settled in the United States. Among those who influenced American life was Filippo Mazzei, a physician philosopher whom Thomas Jefferson translated and whose words closely resembled the Bill of Rights. In 1832 Lorenzo de Ponte brought opera to America. Wine growers from Italy established the Swiss Colony winery, and fruit growers began the Del Monte company. Famous Italian Americans include Fiorello La Guardia, Geraldine Ferraro, Mario Cuomo, Mother Cabrini (America's first saint), Joe DiMaggio, Mario Lanza, Frank Sinatra, Guglielmo Marconi, Enrico Fermi, Arturo Toscanini, Anne Bancroft, and Lee Iacocca. Selected References and Index.

1333. Doak, Robin. *Struggling to Become American, 1899–1940.* (Latino-American History) Chelsea House, 2007. 106pp. ISBN 978-0-8160-6443-4. Grades 5 up. Using primary sources that include significant speeches, documents, and literature, this volume shows the connection between modern America and the Latino heritage. Among the topics are United States policy regarding Puerto Rico and Cuba, immigrant racism, and repatriation of Mexicans during the Great Depression. Photographs, maps, and reproductions augment the text. Bibliography, Glossary, Chronology, Further Reading, Web Sites, and Index.

1334. Frost, Helen. *German Immigrants, 1820–1920.* Blue Earth, 2001. 32pp. ISBN 978-0-7368-0794-4. Grades 4–6. Frost looks at German immigrants' experiences and their contributions to the country. She also mentions famous German Americans. Maps, Glossary, Chronology, Further Reading, Web Sites, and Index.

1335. Goldstein, Margaret J. *Japanese in America.* (In America) Lerner, 2006. 80pp. ISBN 978-0-8225-3952-0. Grades 4–8. Goldstein explores the Japanese American experience, looking at the religious, historical, political, and cultural factors that led to immigration after Japan became open to Western influence and trade. The first Japanese came to America in the 1800s, some as "picture brides." This volume also offers information about the Japanese influence on American culture. Photographs and illustrations augment the text. Bibliography, Glossary, Chronology, Notes, Further Reading, Web Sites, and Index.

1336. Granfield, Linda. *97 Orchard Street, New York: Stories of Immigrant Life.* Tundra, 2001. 55pp. Paper ISBN 978-0-8877-6580-3. Grades 3–6. Curators of the Lower East Side Tenement Museum in New York City have recreated the apartments at 97 Orchard Street, built in 1864. This book follows four immigrant families who lived there from the end of the 19th century until 1935. Photographs and maps enhance the text.

1337. Hoobler, Dorothy, and Thomas Hoobler. *The Chinese American Family Album.* Oxford, 1998. 128pp. Paper ISBN 978-0-19-512421-7. Grades 5 up. In the 1830s Chinese sugarcane workers arrived in Hawaii and Chinese sailors entered New York City's harbor. From then to the present, the Chinese culture has enriched the experiences of all Americans. Chinese Americans have endured serious prejudice, including a law in 1924 that prohibited Chinese American citizens from bringing their wives and children into the country. The act was not repealed until 1943, when the United States and China became allies during World War II. The text, complemented by photographs, traces the history of Chinese immigrants, indicating that most have continued to live in groups or Chinatowns as they worked in laundries, restaurants, and sweatshops. Without the Chinese workers in the 19th century, the transcontinental railroad might not have been completed so rapidly. The diary entries of immigrants, tracing families as they live, work, and rest in America, enliven the text. Chinese American Timeline, Further Reading, and Index.

1338. Hoobler, Dorothy, and Thomas Hoobler. *The Italian American Family Album.* Oxford, 1998. 127pp. Paper ISBN 978-0-19-512420-0. Grades 5 up. Italian influences have been evident in American society since Christopher Columbus arrived in 1492. The text traces the lives of immigrants through diaries and photographs, especially from the 19th and early 20th centuries, that cover work, living environment, religious activities, and prejudice. Italian American Timeline, Further Reading, and Index.

1339. Hoobler, Dorothy, and Thomas Hoobler. *The Japanese American Family Album.* Oxford, 1998. 127pp. Paper ISBN 978-0-19-512423-1. Grades 5 up. Japanese American immigrants tell their stories through their own words and scrapbook pictures. The first wave of Japanese immigration occurred in the 19th century, with another in the 20th century. The text looks at treatment of Japanese Americans, including the deplorable chapter of internment during World War II. Japanese American Timeline, Further Reading, and Index.

1340. Hoobler, Dorothy, and Thomas Hoobler. *The Jewish American Family Album.* Oxford, 1998. 127pp. Paper ISBN 978-0-19-512417-0. Grades 5 up. Jewish immigrants tell their stories through their own words and scrapbook pictures. A brief history of Jewish life through the centuries precedes chapters that describe special taxes, the limit on Jewish marriages, and occupational restrictions that caused many Ashkenazi Jews to flee central Europe between 1840 and 1860. Other waves followed in the early 20th century. Chapters cover the earliest arrivals in the 16th century, new life in New York in the garment trade, going West, the neighborhoods and Yiddish theater, Jewish religious rituals, and becoming part of America. Jewish American Timeline, Further Reading, and Index.

1341. Hopkinson, Deborah. *Shutting Out the Sky: Life in the Tenements of New York 1880–1924.* Scholastic, 2003. 194pp. ISBN 978-0-439-37590-0. Grades 5–8. Hopkinson draws on oral histories and narratives to tell the experiences of five young immigrants to the Lower East Side of New York City. They came, as children or young adults, from Belarus, Italy, Lithuania, and Romania in the period between 1880 and 1919 when 17 million arrived in this country. Marcus Ravage from Romania sold chocolates on the street. Rose Cohen survived the Triangle Shirtwaist fire. Pauline Newman struggled to learn English but became one of the first female organizers for the International Ladies' Garment Workers' Union. Leonard Covello worked and studied and became a high school principle. Archival photographs highlight the text. Notes, Timeline, Further Reading, Bibliography, and Index. *National Council of Teachers of English Orbis Pictus Award* nomination, *Jane Addams Children's Book Award* nomination, *James Madison Book Award* nomination, *Booklist Editor's Choice, Emphasis on Reading Award* (Alabama) nomination, and *Garden State Teen Book Award* (New Jersey) nomination.

1342. Hossell, Karen. *Pakistani Americans.* (We Are America) Raintree, 2004. 32.pp. ISBN 978-1-4034-5023-4. Grades 3–5. Hossell looks at Pakistani Americans today and offers background on their history and customs. Chapters cover such topics as communities, festivals and celebrations, holidays, music and dancing, and food. There is an immigration chart. Photographs and illustrations augment the text. Glossary, Further Reading, and Index.

1343. Ichord, Loretta Frances. *Pasta, Fried Rice, and Matzoh Balls: Immigrant Cooking in America.* Illustrated by Jan Ellis Davey. (Cooking Through Time) Millbrook, 2005. 64pp. ISBN 978-0-7613-2913-8. Grades 3–5. Ichord presents information about the foods of groups that arrived in the United States between 1565 and 1921—among them were French, Swedish, Spanish, Portuguese, Italian, Chinese, Japanese, and Polish immigrants. Eight recipes and details of food habits and dietary laws help readers understand heritage and tradition. Photographs and illustrations augment the text. Bibliography, Notes, and Index.

1344. Kroll, Steven. *Ellis Island: Doorway to Freedom.* Holiday House, 1995. 32pp. ISBN 978-0-8234-1192-4. Grades 4–7. Until 1954 Ellis Island was a symbol of both hope and fear for immigrants arriving in New York Harbor. This volume tells the island's history from its beginning in colonial times until it became an immigrant station for the federal government. More than 16 million foreigners began their quest for American citizenship at its gates. Now a national monument, the buildings house an immigration museum. Glossary and Index.

1345. Lawlor, Veronica. *I Was Dreaming to Come to America: Memories from the Ellis Island Oral History Project.* Puffin, 1997. 40pp. Paper ISBN 978-0-14-055622-3. Grades 5 up. This collection of images and memories from children and adults who passed through Ellis Island from 1900 to 1925 gives a vibrant view of the immigrant experience. *Notable Children's Trade Books in the Field of Social Studies.*

1346. Levine, Ellen. *If Your Name Was Changed at Ellis Island.* Illustrated by Wayne Parmenter. Scholastic, 1994. 80pp. Paper ISBN 978-0-590-43829-2. Grades 3–6. Ellis Island became a center for immigrants in 1892. During the 30 years after that, more than 12 million people entered the United States through its doors. They had to answer a series of questions before they were allowed to settle in the country. This volume answers 36 questions about such topics as why immigrants left their homes, what they had to do at Ellis Island to pass inspection, where they planned to work, and whether they ever returned to their homes.

1347. Maestro, Betsy. *Coming to America: The Story of Immigration.* Illustrated by Susannah Ryan. Scholastic, 1996. Unpaged. ISBN 978-0-590-44151-3. Grades K–4. This history of immigration begins with the arrival of Native Americans thousands of years ago, coming across the Bering Strait land bridge. In more recent times, Annie Moore of Ireland, 15, was the first person to arrive at Ellis Island in New York. Maestro also discusses the harsh treatment of Indians, the forced immigration of Africans, and immigration laws. Chronology.

1348. Olson, Kay Melchisedech. *Norwegian, Swedish, and Danish Immigrants, 1820–1920.* Blue Earth, 2001. 32pp. ISBN 978-0-7368-0798-2. Grades 4–6. Olson looks at Scandinavian immigrants' experiences and their contributions to the country. She also mentions famous Scandinavian Americans. Maps, Glossary, Chronology, Further Reading, Web Sites, and Index.

1349. Peterson, Tiffany. *Greek Americans.* (We Are America) Raintree, 2004. 32.pp. ISBN 978-1-4034-5021-0. Grades 3–5. This volume explains Greek Americans' contemporary roles in society and offers background on their history and customs. Chapters cover such topics as business, work, customs and celebrations, food, and arts and entertainment. There is also an immigration chart. Photographs and illustrations augment the text. Glossary, Further Reading, and Index.

1350. Peterson, Tiffany. *Japanese Americans.* (We Are America) Raintree, 2004. 32.pp. ISBN 978-1-4034-5021-0; paper ISBN 978-1-4034-5032-6. Grades 3–5. Peterson looks at Japanese Americans' contemporary roles in society and offers background on their history and customs. Chapters cover such topics as their arrival in the United States, their treatment during World War II, arts and traditions, celebrations, food, and culture. There is also an immigration chart. Photographs and illustrations augment the text. Glossary, Further Reading, and Index.

1351. Price, Sean. *Tenement Stories: Immigrant Life, 1835–1935.* (American History Through Primary Sources) Raintree, 2007. 32pp. ISBN 978-1-4109-2412-4; paper ISBN 978-1-4109-2423-0. Grades 2–4. Primary sources—maps, newspaper clippings, and many photographs—show what it was like to live in the tenements on the Lower East Side in the 1800s. Among the topics covered are the size and condition of the apartments, laundry facilities, diseases such as cholera, leisure activities for children, and work. Glossary, Further Reading, Web Sites, and Index.

1352. Sandler, Martin W. *Island of Hope: The Story of Ellis Island and the Journey to America.* Scholastic, 2004. 144pp. ISBN 978-0-439-53082-8. Grades 3–5. Sandler offers first-person accounts of immigrants coming to Ellis Island from its opening in 1892 until the release of the last detainee in 1954. Included are a description of processing immigrants, tenement life in cities, transforming the prairie into farmland, and the role of immigrants in building railroads and working in heavy industry. Source material includes oral histories, interviews, and memoirs. Photographs augment the text. Bibliography and Index.

1353. Saxon-Ford, Stephanie. *The Czech Americans.* Chelsea House, 1998. 110pp. Paper ISBN 978-0-7910-5052-1. Grades 5 up. In the 1880s and 1890s nearly 100,000 Czechs came to America from central Europe and the regions of Bohemia and Moravia. They were skilled, literate, and able to function in many areas of society. This volume looks at their arrival, their history, what they did after they came, their religion and community, and their future. Photographs augment the text. Further Reading and Index.

1354. Stein, R. Conrad. *Ellis Island.* Children's, 1992. 32pp. Paper ISBN 978-0-516-46653-8. Grades 3–5. To many Europeans, Ellis Island was the "Isle of Tears." If immigrants did not pass the health tests, they had to return to their homes. They had all left their native countries because they hoped for a better life in America. A variety of laws have governed the acceptance of immigrants through the years, and this volume also comments about them. Index.

1355. Teichmann, Iris. *Immigration and the Law.* (Understanding Immigration) Smart Apple, 2006. 44pp. ISBN 978-1-58340-970-1. Grades 5–8. Teichmann looks at the legal aspects of immigration—from seeking asylum to becoming a citizen of the United States—and examines the control and status of immigrants and the process of seeking visas. She also offers information about illegal methods of entering the country. Photographs and reproductions reinforce the text. Glossary, Web Sites, and Index.

1356. Teichmann, Iris. *Life as an Immigrant.* (Understanding Immigration) Smart Apple, 2006. 44pp. ISBN 978-1-58340-968-8. Grades 5–8. Teichmann discusses why people decide to leave the country of their birth and move to another one. She also explores why some immigrate illegally and looks at the challenges that all immigrants face when they enter a new society. Photographs and reproductions reinforce the text. Glossary, Web Sites, and Index.

1357. Teichmann, Iris. *A Multicultural World.* (Understanding Immigration) Smart Apple, 2006. 44pp. ISBN 978-1-58340-969-5. Grades 5–8. This volume looks at the term "multiculturalism" and explains it as a convergence of many cultures. Immigration into a country has long-term ramifications because the children of those who immigrate will also stay in the country, and they will either reject or try to integrate their native cultures with those of their chosen country. Teichmann looks at various cultures and how they have influenced one another, European colonialism, and the benefits of multiculturalism. Photographs and reproductions reinforce the text. Glossary, Web Sites, and Index.

1358. Teichmann, Iris. *One Country to Another.* (Understanding Immigration) Smart Apple, 2006. 44pp. ISBN 978-1-58340-967-1. Grades 5–8. The many reasons that one might have for migrating to another area are explored in this book. It offers personal stories of immigrants and describes what life in a new country can mean. Photographs and reproductions reinforce the text. Glossary, Web Sites, and Index.

Biography and Collective Biography

1359. Argueta, Jorge. *A Movie in My Pillow/Una pelicula en mi almohada: Poems.* Illustrated by Elizabeth Gomez. Children's, 2001. 32pp. ISBN 978-0-8923-9165-3; 2007, paper ISBN 978-0-8923-9219-3. Grades 3–7. Jorge Argueta, a poet, immigrated with his family from El Salvador during the civil war there in the 1980s. His poems remember his childhood in El Salvador and in San Francisco's Mission District—his grandmother's voice, the smell of *pupusas cooking*. A bilingual collection.

1360. Chambers, Veronica. *Celia Cruz, Queen of Salsa.* Illustrated by Julie Maren. Dial, 2005. 40pp. ISBN 978-0-8037-2970-4. Grades 2–4. Celia Cruz (1925–2003) grew up in Havana, Cuba, where neighbors listened from the streets as she sang to her family. She tried to incorporate all the sounds around her when she sang, from birds to street vendors. In 1950, La Sonora Matancera, Cuba's most popular band, hired her as its lead singer. Together they created new dance music that made her famous around the world. She became a U.S. citizen after Castro took power in Cuba. Illustrations enhance the text. Notes, Discography, and Glossary of Spanish. *Capitol Choices Noteworthy Titles* (Washington, D.C.).

1361. Favor, Lesli J. *Martin Van Buren.* (Encyclopedia of Presidents) Scholastic, 2003. 110pp. ISBN 978-0-516-22770-2. Grades 3–6. Martin Van Buren (1762–1862), the eighth president of the United States was a lawyer before becoming a politician. Chapters with maps, pictures, and drawings give information about his life before becoming president and after. Further Reading, Timeline, Glossary, Web Sites, and Index.

1362. McCully, Emily Arnold. *My Heart Glow: Alice Cogswell, Thomas Gallaudet and the Birth of American Sign Language.* Hyperion, 2008. Unpaged. ISBN 978-1-4231-0028-7. Grades 2–5. In 1814 minister Thomas Gallaudet meets young Alice Cogswell, a neighbor who became a deaf mute after a bout of spotted fever at the age of 2. Alice is desperate to learn and

Gallaudet begins teaching her to read. Her physician father funds Gallaudet's trip to Europe to see if they have ways to teach the deaf. Gallaudet finds Laurent Clerc, a teacher of French Sign Language, and brings him to the United States. Together they create the American School for the Deaf in Connecticut with Alice as the first pupil. Quotations from Alice's letters to Gallaudet while he was abroad show her intense need to learn and how much she misses his help. Ink-and-watercolor Illustrations augment the text. Bibliography and Notes.

1363. **McPherson, Stephanie Sammartino.** *Levi Strauss.* (History Maker Bios) Lerner, 2007. 48pp. ISBN 978-0-8225-6581-9. Grades 3–5. Levi Strauss (1829–1902) immigrated from Germany, where Jews were not given the same rights as other citizens. Levi was attracted by stories of the gold rush, and headed west in 1853. He realized that hard-working men needed tough pants that would not tear easily, and he created jeans. Merchants waited eagerly for his product, named "Levis," to arrive in their stores because they were in great demand. The book's five chapters give an overview of Strauss's life and business success. Illustrations augment the text. Bibliography, Further Reading, Glossary, Maps, Timeline, Web Sites, and Index.

1364. **Moss, Marissa.** *Sky High: The True Story of Maggie Gee.* Illustrated by Carl Angel. Tricycle, 2009. 32pp. ISBN 978-1-58246-280-6. Grades 2–5. As a young girl in the 1930s, Maggie Gee (1912–) joined her family in spending leisure time watching airplanes take off and land at a local airstrip. She wanted to fly and World War II gave her the opportunity through the Women Airforce Service Pilots. She was one of two Chinese American women chosen to fly. She loved the training exercises and experienced fear in more serious missions. She also faced prejudice when others mistook her as a Japanese spy. This volume, based on interviews with Gee, also includes photographs. Acrylic illustrations enhance the text.

1365. **Murphy, Jim.** *Across America on an Emigrant Train.* Clarion, 1993. 150pp. ISBN 978-0-395-63390-8; 2003, paper ISBN 978-0-395-76483-1. Grades 5–8. A look at a journey the writer Robert Louis Stevenson made in 1879 when he traveled from Scotland to see the woman he loved in California. He took the cheapest transportation and wrote about it. Murphy uses Stevenson's words to tell about the construction of the transcontinental railroad and steam travel. Photographs, Drawings, Bibliography, and Index. *Orbis Pictus Award.*

1366. **Murphy, Jim.** *Pick and Shovel Poet: The Journeys of Pascal d'Angelo.* Clarion, 2000. 162pp. ISBN 978-0-395-77610-0. Grades 5–9. Pascal d'Angelo (1894–1932), who migrated to America in 1910, taught himself English from newspapers while working as an unskilled laborer. The editor of *The Nation* discovered him and published his work *Son of Italy*, in which he detailed the poverty of Italy and the hardships of immigrants. Photographs highlight the text. Bibliography, Notes, and Index.

1367. **Say, Allen.** *El Chino.* Walter Lorraine, 1993. 32pp. ISBN 978-0-395-57035-7; Sandpiper, 2008, paper ISBN 978-0-547-07680-5. Grades K–3. Bill Wong, a Chinese American, became a famous bullfighter in Spain. Say tells his story using first person to give a sense of immediacy to Wong's experiences as he won over the Spanish crowd through his exploits with the bull. *Bulletin Blue Ribbon.*

1368. **Say, Allen.** *Grandfather's Journey.* Walter Lorraine, 1993. 32pp. ISBN 978-0-395-57035-7; Sandpiper, 2008, paper ISBN 978-0-547-07680-5. Grades K–3. The narrator's grandfather leaves Japan as a young man to see America in the early 20th century. He travels around the country wearing western clothes. After he returns to Japan, he marries and brings his bride to San Francisco and raises his daughter. Then they go back to Japan to live, with the grandfather planning a return visit. But World War II destroys his hopes as well as his home and his city. The narrator carries on his grandfather's dream by living in America and raising his own daughter there. *Bulletin Blue Ribbon* and *Caldecott Medal.*

1369. **Sonder, Ben.** *The Tenement Writer: An Immigrant's Story.* (Stories of America) Steck-Vaughn, 1994. 168pp. Paper ISBN 978-0-8114-8075-8. Grades 5–9. Around 1890 Anzia Yezierska (1880?–1970) and her family arrived in New York from Poland to join her brother, renamed "Mayer." Taking the name Hattie Mayer, Anzia had to adjust to a new life in a tenement, safer than Poland but drearier. After she had worked for a long time and attended school, she began to write about the life of an immigrant who hated being poor. By the 1920s, she had become a well-known American immigrant writer. Epilogue, Afterword, and Notes.

1370. Venezia, Mike. *Igor Stravinsky.* (Getting to Know the World's Greatest Composers) Scholastic, 1996. 32pp. ISBN 978-0-516-20054-5; Children's Press, 1997, paper ISBN 978-0-516-26076-1. Grades K–5. Igor Stravinsky (1882–1971), a Russian composer, became known for his creation of new rhythmic sounds in music. He tried to recreate in his music sounds such as horses' hooves, wagon wheels on cobblestones, and church bells that he remembered from his childhood in St. Petersburg, Russia. His contributions influenced many musicians who followed him. Stravinsky moved to France in 1920 and became a U.S. citizen in 1946. Illustrations enhance the text.

1371. Wong, Li Keng. *Good Fortune: My Journey to Gold Mountain.* Peachtree, 2006. 136pp. ISBN 978-1-56145-367-2. Grades 3–7. Li Keng Wong left China with her family during the 1930s and settled in Oakland, California—"Gold Mountain." Among her trials were arriving at Angel Island and undergoing the immigration procedure, watching her father run a gambling business from the family's living room during the Depression, and observing their traditional culture in their newly transplanted lives.

1372. Yoo, Paula. *Sixteen Years in Sixteen Seconds: The Sammy Lee Story.* Lee & Low, 2005. 32pp. ISBN 978-1-58430-247-6. Grades 1–4. Sammy Lee (1920–), son of Korean immigrants, became an Olympic diving champion and later a doctor. He discovered diving when he was 12 years old, but because he was nonwhite, he could only swim in the local pool one day a week. His father wanted him to focus on medicine. However, Sammy found a coach, learned to balance his studies with his training, and achieved his two goals. He was the first Asian American to win an Olympic gold medal. After training for sixteen years, he won in a sixteen-second dive. Illustrations complement the text.

DVDs

1373. Connor, Leslie. *Miss Bridie Chose a Shovel.* Illustrated by Mary Azarian. Spoken Arts, 2005. 8 mins. ISBN 978-0-8045-8036-6. Grades K–3. See entry 1274.

Compact Discs

1374. Giff, Patricia Reilly. *Water Street.* Narrated by Coleen Marlo. Listening Library, 2006. 3 CDs; 3 hrs. 47 mins. ISBN 978-0-7393-3646-5. Grades 4–8. See entry 1281.

1375. Holm, Jennifer L. *Our Only May Amelia.* Narrated by Emmy Rossum. Listening Library, 2007. 4 CDs; 4 hrs. 38 mins. ISBN 978-0-7393-5966-2. Grades 4–7. See entry 1286.

1376. Ryan, Pam Muñoz. *Esperanza Rising.* Narrated by Trini Alvarado. Listening Library, 2007. 4 CDs; 4 hrs. 42 min. ISBN 978-0-7393-3896-4. Grades 5–9. See entry 1305.

SOCIETY, SEDITION, AND SLAVERY, 1814–1865

Historical Fiction and Fantasy

1377. Avi. *The Barn.* Camelot, 1996. 106pp. Paper ISBN 978-0-380-72562-5. Grades 3–6. In 1855, when 9-year-old Ben is at school, his sister arrives unexpectedly. She takes him home, and he discovers that his father's illness has left him unable to speak or care for himself. Their mother is dead, so the three children nurse him and work the farm. Ben gets his father to respond by asking him to blink if he agrees with him or wants something. Ben thinks that if the three children build the barn his father wanted, his father will get well. The opposite proves true, and Ben must face questions about his own intentions. *ABC Children's Booksellers' Choices*, *American Library Association Notable Children's Books*, *Booklist Editors' Choices*, and *IRA Teachers' Choices*.

1378. Avi. *The Man Who Was Poe.* Camelot, 1997. 224pp. Paper ISBN 978-0-380-73022-3. Grades 5–10. In 1848 Edmund, 11, is searching Providence, Rhode Island, for his sister, who disappeared soon after his aunt. He meets a man who helps him but who seems to think Edmund's difficulties are part of a story he is writing. When Edmund finds his mother, who has been gone for the past year, and his sister, who is sailing away in a boat, the man—Edgar Allan Poe—finally seems to understand that the situation is real. *Edgar Award* nomination.

1379. Ayres, Katherine. *North by Night: A Story of the Underground Railroad.* Random, 2000. 192pp. Paper ISBN 978-0-440-22747-2. Grades 5–9. Two suitors, Quakers Jeremiah and Jonathan, show their interest in 16-year-old Lucy. As she is deciding between them, she becomes involved in helping ten slaves escape to Canada. In 1850, the Fugitive Slave Act made helping slaves a crime, and in January 1851, Lucy writes in her diary about her concerns for the slaves. Her father has made their Ohio home a stop on the Underground Railroad, and eventually Lucy carries a newborn whose mother has died in childbirth into Canada.

1380. Blos, Joan W. *A Gathering of Days: A New England Girl's Journal, 1830–1832.* Atheneum, 1979. 144pp. ISBN 978-0-684-16340-6; Aladdin, 1990, paper ISBN 978-0-689-71419-1. Grades 4–8. Catherine keeps a journal of her eventful 14th year, during which a friend dies; another departs for the Lowell, Massachusetts, factories; her father remarries; she gives one of her deceased mother's quilts to a runaway slave hiding in the woods; and she leaves home to look after someone else's child. In 1899 she sends a letter and the journal to her great-granddaughter, who is now in her own 14th year. Her great granddaughter asks questions, and in a second letter, Catherine responds. The story reveals life in New England at that time. *Newbery Medal*.

1381. Brill, Marlene Targ. *Allen Jay and the Underground Railroad.* Illustrated by Janice Lee Porter. Carolrhoda, 1993. 47pp. ISBN 978-0-87614-776-4; First Avenue paper ISBN 978-0-

8761-4605-7. Grades 2–4. Allen Jay, 11, the oldest child in his Randolph, Ohio, Quaker family in the 1840s, begins to understand the danger of his family's role in the Underground Railroad when he helps Henry James, a runaway slave. Allen hides him and then takes him by hourse and carriage to his grandfather's family, who help Henry James continue north just ahead of the owner who is hunting him. Note.

1382. Broyles, Anne. *Priscilla and the Hollyhocks.* Illustrated by Anna Alter. Charlesbridge, 2008. 32pp. ISBN 978-1-57091-675-5. Grades 2–4. When Priscilla, a slave, is only 6, her mother is sold. Old Sylvia helps Priscilla remember her mother by making dolls from hollyhocks that Priscilla's mother planted. When Massa Basil Silkwood visits Priscilla's owner, he is interested in her but has no plans to buy slaves. After her master dies, a Cherokee buys her. She meets Silkwood again in 1838, when the government forces the Cherokees on their march known as the "Trail of Tears." Silkwood disapproves of slavery, and he buys Priscilla's freedom. Priscilla then sows the seeds of her mother's hollyhocks at the Silkwood home. This story is based on actual events.

1383. Carbone, Elisa. *Night Running: How James Escaped with the Help of His Faithful Dog.* Illustrated by E. B. Lewis. Knopf, 2008. 40pp. ISBN 978-0-375-82247-6. Grades 2–4. When young James decides to escape from Master Graham's West Virginia home in 1838, he tells his hunting dog, Zeus, to stay where he is. Zeus refuses to listen, and he later saves James when the slave catchers and their dogs attack in the woods and when the canoe in which James tries to cross the Ohio River sinks. A Quaker farmer across the river tries to drive Zeus away, but James has realized that Zeus is too important to him to let him go. Watercolors enhance the text.

1384. Carrick, Carol. *Stay Away from Simon!* Illustrated by Donald Carrick. Clarion, 1989. 64pp. Paper ISBN 978-0-8991-9849-1. Grades 2–6. In the 1800s, 11-year-old Lucy and the other children are afraid of Simon, who is older, odd, and slow to comprehend things. During a snowstorm, Lucy leaves school with her younger brother and the two get lost. Simon finds them and guides them home because he wants to share his new ability to count to ten.

1385. Clements, Bruce. *A Chapel of Thieves.* Farrar, 2002. 224pp. ISBN 978-0-374-37701-4. Grades 5–9. In 1849 Henry Desant leaves Missouri to go to Paris, where he hopes to rescue his older brother who is working as a preacher. Clayton has written that Deacon George has requested that the "true believers" show their faithfulness by giving him their material possessions. Henry realizes that Clayton's church has become a "front" for a group of pickpockets and criminals. He has an adventurous journey before arriving and convincing Clayton to return home.

1386. Dahlberg, Maurine F. *The Story of Jonas.* Farrar, 2007. 160pp. ISBN 978-0-374-37264-4. Grades 3–8. In 1859, after his mother dies, 13-year-old Jonas goes with his master's irresponsible son, Percy Hooper, on an expedition searching for gold in Kansas Territory. While on the wagon train, Jonas becomes a cook, leads the train, learns to read and count, rides on a steamboat, shops for goods in a store, and sees a city. He also meets Quincy and Miss Sky, who show him that he does not have to live in bondage. He knows that he cannot return to the plantation and must decide how to escape.

1387. De Angeli, Marguerite. *Thee, Hannah!* Herald, 2000. 96pp. Paper ISBN 978-0-836-19106-6. Grades 2–5. Unhappy with the drab clothing she must wear as a Quaker in 1850 Philadelphia, Hannah secretly wears a brightly colored sash given to her by a friend. When she gets it dirty, however, she has to buy her a new one, using the few pennies of her allowance. A runaway slave tells Hannah that if Hannah were not wearing her Quaker bonnet, she would not have known where to get help. Hannah realizes that her bonnet is a symbol and something she should wear with pride.

1388. DeFelice, Cynthia. *The Apprenticeship of Lucas Whitaker.* Farrar, 2007. 160pp. Paper ISBN 978-0-374-40014-9. Grades 5 up. After Lucas Whitaker's mother dies in 1849, he hears that he could have saved her from her fatal tuberculosis by exhuming a deceased relative, removing the heart, and burning it so that his mother could breathe the smoke. Distressed that he did not know this in time, he goes to Southwick, Connecticut, and becomes an apprentice to a local physician who is also a dentist, apothecary, undertaker, and barber. When he looks through a microscope for the first time, he learns the difference between superstition and science, and knows that he cannot blame himself for his mother's death. *School Library Journal Best Book.*

1389. Deutsch, Stacia, and Rhody Cohon. *Lincoln's Legacy.* Illustrated by David T. Wenzel. (Blast to the Past) Aladdin, 2005. 104pp. Paper ISBN 978-0-689-87024-8. Grades 2–5. Third-graders Abigail, Jacob, Zack, and Bo want to know what might have happened if Lincoln had not freed the slaves. They go back in time to 1862 and tell him not to resign before he signs the Emancipation Proclamation. They even take Lincoln to present-day Washington to show him his own memorial as a way to encourage him. Illustrations augment the text.

1390. Edwards, Pamela Duncan. *Barefoot: Escape on the Underground Railroad.* Illustrated by Henry Cole. Trophy, 1999. Unpaged. Paper ISBN 978-0-06-443519-2. Grades K–4. Escaping slave Barefoot fears both what is before and behind him as he finds himself farther away from the plantation than he has ever been. The frog croaks to show water, and a mouse leads to fruit. The heron waits to hear the heavy boots of the slave catchers, and when they come, the mosquitoes chase them away. The animals protect Barefoot and guide him to a safe house on the Underground Railroad.

1391. Ferris, Jean. *Underground.* Farrar, 2007. 176pp. ISBN 978-0-374-37243-9. Grades 5–9. Slaves Stephen and Charlotte work at Mammoth Cave and its hotel in Kentucky in 1839. Stephen finds the cave fascinating and wants to study it; Charlotte is more interested in escaping to freedom. Instead of leaving themselves, they become part of the Underground Railroad and help a runaway woman and her infant find their way to the Ohio River through the cave.

1392. Fleischner, Jennifer. *Nobody's Boy.* Missouri Historical Society, 2007. 112pp. Paper ISBN 978-1-883982-58-4. Grades 5 up. Eleven-year-old George lives in St. Louis, Missouri, and watches his mother, Lizzie Keckly (later to be Mary Todd Lincoln's seamstress and confidante), work to buy her freedom and sees a slave named Chap helping other slaves escape. George is light-skinned and able to "pass" for white. He decides to help a friend escape by posing as his white owner. Chronology, Glossary, and Further Reading.

1393. Fox, Paula. *The Slave Dancer.* Illustrated by Eros Keith. Aladdin, 2008. 192pp. Paper ISBN 978-1-4169-7139-9. Grades 5–8. In 1840, 14-year-old Jessie is captured by slavers in New Orleans and forced to serve as a fife player on a slave ship for four months. He sees African *cabocieros* sell their own people to the slavers, and he has to play to make the slaves "dance" to exercise their bodies. When the ship wrecks, he and one of the slaves survive. They wash ashore, and a black man guides them north. As an adult, Jessie cannot listen to music because of the horror of his experience. *Newbery Medal.*

1394. Fritz, Jean. *Brady.* Peter Smith, 1993. 223pp. ISBN 978-0-8446-6644-0; Puffin, 1987, paper ISBN 978-0-698-11937-6. Grades 4–7. Brady accidentally finds an Underground Railroad site in 1836 and runs home to tell his parents. They tell him he is wrong and should not make such foolish claims. When his father is injured in a fire, Brady takes slaves to another station along the Railroad without telling his father. When his father becomes aware of Brady's action, he acknowledges his approval by writing in the family Bible that Brady has done a man's job.

1395. Gayle, Sharon. *Harriet Tubman and the Freedom Train.* Aladdin, 2002. 31pp. Paper ISBN 978-0-689-85480-4. Grades 1–3. Harriet Tubman (1820?–1913), born a slave, dared to escape to freedom and then risked her life to help other slaves find freedom via the Underground Railroad. This story offers a fictional account of her actions and the people she might have encountered in her travels. Chronology.

1396. Grifalconi, Ann. *Ain't Nobody a Stranger to Me.* Illustrated by Jerry Pinkney. Hyperion, 2007. 32pp. ISBN 978-0-7868-1857-0. Grades 2–4. A little girl's grandfather speaks to everyone he meets, and she asks him why. He tells her that he was once a slave, and that a white man, Quaker James Stanton, helped him, her grandmother, and her mother escape to freedom across the Ohio River. He tells her that everyone is a friend in one's heart even if one does not know their name. He adds that when he escaped, he had apple seeds in his pocket, and the orchard on their farm grew from these seeds. Watercolors intensify the text.

1397. Hamilton, Virginia. *The House of Dies Drear.* Aladdin, 2006. 247pp. Paper ISBN 978-1-416-91405-1. Grades 5–8. African American Thomas and his family move into a house once owned by the wealthy abolitionist Dies Drear when his father takes a job teaching at an Ohio college. Drear had helped more than 40,000 slaves pass through the Underground Railroad before he and two slaves were murdered. Strange things happen around the house. Thomas and his father investigate the tunnels and secret entrances even though the hostile caretaker Pluto tries to thwart their efforts. *Edgar Allen Poe Award.*

1398. Hansen, Joyce. *I Thought My Soul Would Rise and Fly: The Diary of Patsy, a Freed Girl.* (Dear America) Scholastic, 1997. ISBN 978-0-590-84913-5. Grades 3–7. Lame and orphaned at the end of the Civil War, 12-year-old Patsy continues to work for her former master in South Carolina as a paid employee. The niece of Mrs. Davis gave her a blank journal as a joke while she was still a slave, but Patsy has learned to read and write in secret and she records her feelings during this time as she wonders what freedom means. She wants to become a teacher, and through her study with other children, she loses her stammer and keeps her goal in sight. Photographs and Note.

1399. Hart, Lenore. *The Treasure of Savage Island.* Dutton, 2005. 256pp. ISBN 978-0-525-47092-2. Grades 5–8. On an island off Virginia's Eastern Shore in the early 1800s, Molly Savage, 13, must serve the new owner of the tavern her father lost in a card game. Like others on the island, she and her family supplement their incomes with pillage that washes ashore from wrecked ships. One day Molly discovers a half-white runaway slave, Rafe, hiding in the flotsam. She wonders whether she should report him, but when news arrives of picaroons (Tory pirates active after the Revolutionary War) coming to search for treasure, the two join in an unlikely alliance to protect themselves.

1400. Hegamin, Tonya Cherie. *Most Loved in All the World.* Illustrated by Cozbi A. Cabrera. HMH, 2009. 40pp. ISBN 978-0-618-41903-6. Grades K–2. A young girl sees her mother return to their cabin at night tired and sometimes beaten but steadfastly remaining awake to sew a patch on a quilt. Eventually, the mother sends the child away to follow the Underground Railroad with the quilt as her map. The mother stays behind to help others gain freedom. However, the central patch on the quilt, representing the little girl, indicates that her mother makes her the "most loved in all the world." Note. *Beehive Childrens Picture Book Award* (Utah) nomination.

1401. Hershenhorn, Esther. *Fancy That.* Illustrated by Megan Lloyd. Holiday House, 2003. 32pp. ISBN 978-0-8234-1605-9. Grades 1–5. In 1841 Pippin Biddle tries to earn a living as a "limner," a portrait painter, and free his three orphaned sisters from the poorhouse. Unfortunately Pippin has little success as he is too frank in his work, depicting his human and animal subjects with all their faults to the fore. He returns from the road to discover that his sisters have been using their time making crafts and wreaths and have created a business that will keep the family self-sufficient. Illustrations enhance the text.

1402. Heuston, Kimberley. *The Shakeress.* Puffin, 2004. 107pp. Paper ISBN 978-0-14-240054-8. Grades 5–8. Around 1830, 13-year-old orphan Naomi Hull goes with her sister and two brothers to live with their Aunt Thankful in Portsmouth, New Hampshire. Naomi realizes they do not belong there, and she takes the children to join a Shaker community in Canterbury, New Hampshire. Although the family is welcomed there, Naomi does not feel comfortable. She wants to use her abilities as a herbalist and healer and takes a position with a large family in St. Johnsbury, Vermont. She becomes interested in the new Mormon faith, and when a wealthy man named Joseph Fairbanks falls in love with her, she must decide which life to choose.

1403. Hopkinson, Deborah. *Abe Lincoln Crosses a Creek: A Tall, Thin Tale (Introducing His Forgotten Frontier Friend).* Illustrated by John Hendrix. Schwartz & Wade, 2008. Unpaged. ISBN 978-0-375-83768-5. Grades K–3. In 1816 at the age of 7, Abe Lincoln strolls down to the rain-filled, turbulent Knob Creek with his friend Austin Gollaher. When they decide to cross it on a log, Abe falls in. Austin rescues him, and Abe says he will never forget his kindness. As a president serving in the White House, Lincoln does indeed remember his friend. Watercolor and ink illustrations complement the text.

1404. Hopkinson, Deborah. *Sweet Clara and the Freedom Quilt.* Illustrated by James Ransome. Random, 1995. 32pp. Paper ISBN 978-0-679-87472-0. Grades K–3. Eleven-year-old Clara sews a pattern in a quilt that is actually a map to help her escape via the Underground Railroad. She has worked her way out of the fields and into the Big House because she can sew. She uses this talent to her advantage as she waits to find pieces of material that will illustrate the instructions she has heard from returned runaways or slaves who have traveled. When she has the pieces together and knows the direction, she leaves.

1405. Hopkinson, Deborah. *Under the Quilt of Night.* Illustrated by James E. Ransome. Atheneum, 2002. 40pp. ISBN 978-0-689-82227-8. Grades K–2. A young slave escapes with a small group of other slaves. When they get to a town, she sees a quilt with blue center squares. She thinks the group will be safe there, and indeed the owners give them clothing, food, and shelter. The next day they leave in a wagon and eventually reach Canada and freedom. Illustrations enhance the text. *Black-Eyed Susan Picture Book Award* (Maryland) nomination, *The Land of Enchantments Children's Book Award* (New Mexico) nomination, *State Reading Association Charlotte Book Award* (New York) nomination, *Capitol Choices Noteworthy Titles* (Washington, D.C.), and *Prairie Bud Award* (South Dakota) nomination.

1406. Hostetter, Joyce Moyer. *Healing Water: A Hawaiian Story.* Calkins Creek, 2008. 218pp. ISBN 978-1-59078-514-0. Grades 5 up. When Pia contracts leprosy as a teenager in the 1860s, he is exiled to Hawaii's leprosy settlement on Molokai Island. Angry and bitter, he determines to maintain his identity by refusing to solicit help from anyone. At the same time, he watches the other villagers behave kindly toward each other. When Father Damien, a Catholic priest, comes to live with them, Pia has to change his idea of love and hope. Chronology, Glossary, Notes, and Further Resources.

1407. Hurmence, Belinda. *A Girl Called Boy.* Clarion, 2006. 180pp. Paper ISBN 978-0-618-68925-5. Grades 3–6. Boy, 11, is a black girl who shifts in time from a picnic with her family in the late 20th century to 1853. Slaves in 1853 think she is a runaway, but they take her with them because she can read, an illegal activity. After several escapes from slave owners, she reaches the stream that she crossed into 1853, but the slaves with her will not cross. When she returns to her family, she has only been gone ten minutes, but her attitude toward her slave heritage has changed forever. *Parents' Choice Award.*

1408. Hurst, Carol Otis. *Through the Lock.* Walter Lorraine, 2001. 160pp. ISBN 978-0-618-03036-1. Grades 5–8. Orphaned Etta, 11, finds an abandoned cottage along the Farmington Canal in Connecticut in the early 19th century and moves in. But then she finds that 12-year-old Walter also lives there, escaping from his alcoholic father. The two learn to coexist and become friends when they join to protect Walter from his father, who arrives, drinks profusely, and then dies. A third child joins them, and Etta tries to get her brother and sister to come too, but they are happy in their own new homes. The canal manager agrees to let them live there if they have an adult move in. They eventually make money and begin to eat well. Glossary.

1409. Johnson, D. B. *Henry Builds a Cabin.* Houghton, 2002. 32pp. ISBN 978-0-618-13201-0. Grades K–3. In this historical fantasy, Henry the Bear gives young readers a good introduction to the life of Henry David Thoreau (1817–1862). When Henry decides to build a cabin near Walden Pond from twelve trees and inexpensive used materials, his friends, among them Emerson and Alcott, have varying complaints such as "too dark" and "too small." But Henry finds the outside perfect for reading and dancing and eating. One day, when it rains, he runs inside and finds the cabin to be exactly the right size. Watercolor illustrations complement the text.

1410. Johnson, D. B. *Henry Climbs a Mountain.* Houghton, 2003. 32pp. ISBN 978-0-618-26902-0. Grades K–4. Henry, a bear modeled on Henry David Thoreau (1817–1862), refuses to pay taxes when his state supports slavery. He decides he would rather spend time in jail.

While confined, he draws pictures on the wall of a mountain path. He imagines he is walking on it and meets a slave walking north to freedom. He then equates freedom to being on top of a very high mountain.

1411. Johnson, D. B. *Henry Works.* Houghton, 2004. 32pp. ISBN 978-0-618-42003-2. Grades K–3. In the manner of Henry David Thoreau (1817–1862), Henry, a bear, helps his neighbors as he walks to work by warning them of a coming storm. He also tends to the wildflowers, builds a path across the brook, takes a letter to Emerson, helps the postmaster by giving him comfrey root for his sore foot, and relocates woodchucks. When asked what his work is, he says he is writing a book. Colored-pencil and paint illustrations complement the text. *Notable Social Studies Trade Books for Young People* and *Capitol Choices Noteworthy Titles* (Washington, D.C.).

1412. Johnson, D. B., and Linda Michelin. *Henry's Night.* Illustrated by D. B. Johnson. HMH, 2009. 32pp. ISBN 978-0-547-05663-0. Grades K–3. On his birthday, when Henry, based on Henry David Thoreau (1817–1862), has problems sleeping, he decides to search for a whippoorwill in the forest. Using his jar of fireflies for light, he discovers other creatures and plants in the forest, including tadpoles and nighthawks, that he sketches for the book's page margins. Then when fog envelops him and the forest, he builds a raft and uses the North Star to guide him home across Walden Pond—most likely in his dream. Illustrations enhance the text.

1413. Karr, Kathleen. *Mama Went to Jail for the Vote.* Illustrated by Malene Laugesen. Hyperion, 2005. 32pp. ISBN 978-0-7868-0593-8. Grades K–3. Young Susan Elizabeth wears bloomers and watches her mother march in parades before joining her in a picket line in front of the White House. She is both proud and dismayed when police arrest her mother and take her to jail for her beliefs in woman suffrage. Her mother is held for six months, but on her release she gets a pin saying "Jailed for Freedom." Illustrations enhance the text.

1414. Kay, Alan N. *On the Trail of John Brown's Body.* (Young Heroes of History) Burd Street, 2001. 175pp. Paper ISBN 978-1-57249-239-4. Grades 4–7. In 1859 Irish American David Adams steals money from his grandfather to run away from Boston to his abolitionist parents in "bleeding Kansas." Angry that he has left, David's grandfather sends David's cousin George Adams and George's father Sean after him. On the way, they become embroiled in John Brown's raid on Harper's Ferry. Convinced that Brown's group of abolitionists are so extreme that they can cause a war, David and Sean are disturbed that anyone can support them. David, however, becomes bitter when both of his parents die.

1415. Ketchum, Liza. *Newsgirl.* Viking, 2009. 327pp. ISBN 978-0-670-01119-3. Grades 4–8. In 1851, after 12-year-old Amelia Forrester arrives in San Francisco from discriminatory Boston with her family, she tries to make money selling newspapers. Amelia realizes she can sell more if she disguises herself as a boy. Her dressmaker mother and her partner also adapt by beginning to make men's clothes. Amelia befriends an orphan Patrick, and they take an unexpected flight in a hot air balloon. After crashing in Sonora, the wounded Amelia experiences life in the gold rush territory. She later convinces a newspaper editor to publish her story and returns home a heroine. *Dorothy Canfield Fisher Children's Book Award* (Vermont) nomination.

1416. Kinsey-Warnock, Natalie. *Gifts from the Sea.* Illustrated by Judy Pedersen. Knopf, 2003. 112pp. ISBN 978-0-375-82257-5; Yearling, 2005, paper ISBN 978-0-440-41970-9. Grades 5–8. Living alone with her father on Devil's Rock, a Maine lighthouse, in 1858, 12-year-old Quila McFarlane discovers a baby floating in from the sea between two mattresses that are strapped together. Quila thinks this is a gift from the sea, but in fact a ship has just sunk. They name the child Celia, and she fills the gap left in their lives by the death of Quila's mother. When an Irish woman, Margaret, appears two years later and asks about her missing niece, Quila explains about the baby. Margaret stays at the lighthouse for a few months and falls in love with Quila's father.

1417. Klass, Sheila S. *Little Women Next Door.* Holiday House, 2000. 144pp. ISBN 978-0-8234-1472-7. Grades 4–6. In 1843 Susan Wilson, 11, lives with her father and her Aunt Nell on a farm next to Fruitlands, where a group of people have come together to create a utopian community. Soon Susan meets Louisa May Alcott, and Louisa invites her to play with her, her sisters, and Will Lane, son of Charles Lane. Eventually Susan's narrow-minded widower father allows her to attend Bronson Alcott's classes, in which he employs the Socratic method as he teaches mythology, philosophy, and related topics. Among the visitors who come for conversation are Ralph Waldo Emerson and Henry David Thoreau. The Wilsons are amazed by the group's refusal to eat animal products and byproducts and by its inability to farm. The Transcendentalists make poor decisions about farm animals and become involved in heated discussions while working in the fields, forgetting their farming chores. Susan finds herself losing her stutter as Louisa encourages her to behave as she thinks a strong man might act, and when the group farm ultimately fails, all of the Wilsons have benefitted from knowing them.

1418. Krisher, Trudy. *Uncommon Faith.* Holiday House, 2003. 263pp. ISBN 978-0-8234-1791-9. Grades 5–9. A multilayered story in which ten residents of Millbrook, Massachusetts, express their views on society from the summer of 1837 to the fall of 1938. They discuss their attitudes toward slavery, religion, women's rights and other major issues of the day. Fourteen-year-old, independent-minded Faith Common, 14, is the thread that binds the narratives as women begin to assert themselves. By the end, residents have assisted on the Underground Railroad and Mount Holyoke is about to open its doors with Faith as a student. *Capitol Choices Noteworthy Titles* (Washington, D.C.).

1419. Lester, Julius. *Day of Tears: A Novel in Dialogue.* Hyperion, 2005. 177pp. ISBN 978-0-7868-0490-0; 2007, paper ISBN 978-1-4231-0409-4. Grades 5–9. It is 1859 and Pierce Butler is in trouble. His wife, Fannie Kemble, left him the year before. A British woman, she had married him unaware that he owned slaves. Now he must pay his gambling debts or go to prison. He decides to sell his slaves and on March 3 in Savannah, Georgia, holds the largest slave auction in history; 439 slaves are sold. Among the slaves he betrays are Emma and her father, Pierce's manservant and companion for his entire life. In selling Emma, the only person his daughter Sara trusts, he also betrays Sara. Sara detests slavery while her sister, Frances, sides with their father. Monologues and conversations reveal the thoughts of all the participants. *Coretta Scott King Award, Readers' Choice Award* (Virginia) nomination, *Junior Book Award* (South Carolina) nomination, *Dorothy Canfield Fisher Children's Book Award* (Vermont) nomination, *Peach Book Award for Teen Readers* (Georgia) nomination, *Volunteer State Book Award* (Tennessee) nomination, *Nene Award* (Hawaii) nomination, *American Library Association Notable Children's Books, Garden State Teen Book Award* (New Jersey) nomination, *Booklist Editor's Choice*, and *Capitol Choices Noteworthy Titles* (Washington, D.C.).

1420. Lester, Julius. *The Old African.* Illustrated by Jerry Pinkney. Dial, 2005. 80pp. ISBN 978-0-8037-2564-5. Grades 3–7. An old slave, Jaja, watches his master beat a young boy who tried to run away from the plantation. Jaja has the ability to put pictures in people's minds and ease their pain. His projection helps the young boy. He decides to use his mind to bring hope to the other slaves and to lead them back to their homeland. (In Ybo Landing, Georgia, a group of slaves supposedly walked into the water, saying that they were returning to Africa.) Illustrations enhance the text. Note.

1421. Levine, Ellen. *Henry's Freedom Box.* Illustrated by Kadir Nelson. Scholastic, 2007. 40pp. ISBN 978-0-439-77733-9. Grades 2–5. As a young slave Henry Brown (b. 1816) learned from his mother that slave children were separated from their parents, and this did indeed happen to him. As an adult, Henry married but his own family was sold away from him. He then entreated a white abolitionist to crate him in a box and mail him to Philadelphia. After twenty-seven hours of extreme discomfort, Brown arrived, a free man. Nelson's pencil, watercolor, and oils enhance the text. *American Library Association Notable Children's Books, Diamond Award* (Delaware) nomination, *Bluegrass Award* (Kentucky) nomination, *Black-Eyed Susan Award* (Maryland) nomination, *Caldecott Honor Book, Booklist Editor's Choice*, and *Bulletin Blue Ribbon*.

1422. Lyons, Mary E. *Letters from a Slave Boy: The Story of Joseph Jacobs.* Atheneum, 2007. 208pp. ISBN 978-0-689-87867-1; Simon Pulse, 2009, paper ISBN 978-0-689-87868-8. Grades

4–8. Nine-year-old slave Joseph Jacobs escapes from North Carolina to Boston in 1830. He writes letters to his mother, Harriet, about his journey there to Boston and then to New Bedford, Massachusetts, where he boards a whaling ship. He stops in New York City and then sails on toward California. Unfortunately, just before he arrives, California passes the Fugitive Slave Act, so he cannot get his freedom there as he had hoped. Gambling and his color make him a mark for others who take his money and leave him unable to buy himself freedom. His last letter tells of his planned journey to Australia and freedom, he hopes. Glossary and Further Reading.

1423. Monjo, F. N. *The Drinking Gourd: A Story of the Underground Railroad.* Illustrated by Fred Brenner. Fitzgerald, 2007. 64pp. ISBN 978-1-4242-0579-0; Trophy, 1993, paper ISBN 978-0-06-444042-4. Grades K–3. Tommy misbehaves in church and his father sends him home alone. In the barn, Tommy finds four escaped slaves who tell him they are following the "drinking gourd," or the North Star, to Canada. When Tommy's father hides them in the hay wagon and takes them to the river, Tommy realizes that his father is breaking the law. He also knows that the reward money for reporting on escaped slaves is very high. He has to adjust to the idea that some laws and some rewards are more damaging than good. *American Library Association Notable Children's Book.*

1424. Morrow, Barbara Olenyik. *A Good Night for Freedom.* Illustrated by Leonard Jenkins. Holiday House, 2004. 32pp. ISBN 978-0-8234-1709-4. Grades K–4. In 1839 Hallie discovers two runaway slaves at Levi Coffin's home. When slave catchers ask if anyone is hiding there, she has to decide whether she will follow her conscience or agree with her father that the family should not involve themselves in Coffin's affairs. She decides to mislead the slave catchers. Then she helps Susan and Margaret escape, surprised when one of the girls tells her she wants to work and earn buckets of money. Hallie wants to know what she will do with the money, and she says she will buy her "mama." Further Reading and Web Sites.

1425. Nelson, Vaunda M. *Almost to Freedom.* Illustrated by Colin Bootman. Carolrhoda, 2003. 40pp. ISBN 978-1-57505-342-4. Grades 1–4. Told from the perspective of a rag doll named Sally, this is the story of young slave Lindy and her mother escaping from their owner. At one of the Underground Railroad stops, they have to flee in the middle of the night and, sadly, Sally gets left behind. However, another child soon finds Sally and takes her to freedom. Illustrations complement the text.

1426. O'Neal, Deborah. *The Trouble with Henry: A Tale of Walden Pond.* Illustrated by S. D. Schindler. Candlewick, 2005. 40pp. ISBN 978-0-7636-1828-5. Grades K–2. Everyone in Concord, Massachusetts, except Henry David Thoreau (1817–1862) wants material things and a busy, noisy life. Thoreau goes to live at peaceful and quiet Walden Pond instead. Then a Boston firm wants to build a toothpick mill near the pond. Thoreau invites the residents to his house to see how lovely and unspoiled the pond is, convincing them that the business should not be built. Illustrations complement the text.

1427. Osborne, Mary Pope. *New York's Bravest.* Illustrated by Steve Johnson and Lou Fancher. Knopf, 2002. Unpaged. ISBN 978-0-375-82196-7; Dragonfly, 2006, paper ISBN 978-0-375-83841-5. Grades K–3. In the 1840s a New York City firefighter named Mose Humphreys was known for his bravery. This story portrays him as a legendary character who eats huge meals, has hands the size of Virginia, and is 8 feet tall. People have reported seeing him in the Dakotas, working for President Lincoln, and other places. But one night, after fighting a hotel fire, he disappeared forever. His friends claim, however, that he is always with them when they fight a fire. Illustrations enhance the text. Note. *Booklist Editor's Choice, Blue Hen Award* (Delaware) nomination, and *Picture Book Award* (Georgia) nomination.

1428. Paterson, Katherine. *Jip: His Story.* Puffin, 2005. 181pp. Paper ISBN 978-0-14-240411-9. Grades 5–9. Jip works for lazy Vermont farmers in the late 1850s. They tell him he fell out of a wagon near the house when he was a toddler, and that they have supported him ever since. But one day a stranger arrives and tells Jip that his father might be looking for him. The stranger turns out to be a slave catcher—and Jip's mother was a runaway slave. Lyddie (of the companion novel of the same name), now Jip's teacher, and her Quaker sweetheart Luke help Jip escape to Canada. This complex story presents the dark times before the Civil War. *School Library Journal Best Book* and *Capitol Choices Noteworthy Titles* (Washington, D.C).

1429. Paterson, Katherine. *Lyddie.* Lodestar, 1991. 192pp. ISBN 978-0-525-67338-5; Puffin, 2005, paper ISBN 978-0-14-240438-6. Grades 5–9. Thirteen-year-old Lyddie has to take charge of the family when her father dies because her mother seems to have lost her mind. Without economic support, the family must separate. Lyddie goes to the mills in Lowell, Massachusetts, to work in 1843. There she has to overcome the Quaker prejudices instilled by her mother and begin to assert her rights as a worker and a woman. Because she refuses to comply with the overseer's advances, she loses her job, but by that time she has enough money to save the farm. She also knows that the Quaker who is in love with her will wait until she finishes college and they can marry. *Bulletin Blue Ribbon Book, Sunshine State Young Reader Award* (Florida) nomination, *Children's Book Award* (Georgia) nomination, *Hoosier Book Award* (Indiana) nomination, *Children's Book Award* (Massachusetts) nomination, *William Allen White Award* (Kansas) nomination, *Bluegrass Award* (Kentucky) nomination, *William Allen White Award* (Kansas) nomination, *Student Book Award* (Maine) nomination, *Land of Enchantment Book Award* (New Mexico) nomination, *Young Readers' Award* (Nevada) nomination, *Sequoyah Book Award* (Oklahoma) nomination, *Young Reader's Choice Award* (Pennsylvania) nomination, *SCASL Book Award* (South Carolina) nomination, *Prairie Pasque Award* (South Dakota) nomination, *School Library Journal Best Books, Volunteer State Book Award* (Tennessee) nomination, and *Dorothy Canfield Fisher Children's Book Award* (Vermont) nomination.

1430. Pearsall, Shelley. *Trouble Don't Last.* Yearling, 2003. 160pp. Paper ISBN 978-0-440-41811-5. Grades 5–10. Eleven-year-old Samuel and 70-year-old Harrison, the slave who has looked after him since his mother was sold, try to escape to Canada on the Underground Railroad in 1859. Harrison dislikes taking orders, and Samuel does not like disguising himself as a girl. They meet a lot of people who help them on their journey from Kentucky, but many are not the kindly people one might expect. Pearsall bases her story on primary sources detailing attitudes during this time. *Booklist Editor's Choice, Nutmeg Children's Book Award* (Connecticut) nomination, *Sunshine State Young Reader Award* (Florida) nomination, *Children's Book Award* (Georgia) nomination, *Rebecca Caudill Young Readers Book Award* (Illinois) nomination, *Children's Book Award* (Massachusetts) nomination, *Mark Twain Book Award* (Missouri) nomination, *Garden State Fiction Book Award* (New Jersey) nomination, and *Children's Book Award* (West Virginia) nomination.

1431. Polacco, Patricia. *January's Sparrow.* Illustrated by author. Philomel, 2009. 96pp. ISBN 978-0-399-25077-4. Grades 4–6. Sadie Crosswhite, 8, flees with her family from Kentucky to Marshall, Michigan. Their departure is prompted by the sight of slavers beating and presumably leaving for dead her foster brother January after he tries to escape from Master Gitner. In Marshall, a town of free blacks, they hide their origin because of the Fugitive Slave Act, but Gitner's slave chasers find them four years later in 1847. The townspeople manage to hold these men off while the Crosswhites escape to Canada with January, who has survived. The double-spread pencil and marker illustrations increase the suspense. *Michigan Notable Book.*

1432. Polisar, Barry Louis. *Stolen Man: The Story of the Amistad Rebellion.* Rainbow Morning Music, 2007. 27pp. Paper ISBN 978-0-938663-50-8. Grades 3–5. Sengbe Pieh, later called Joseph Cinque, saw the *Amistad* slave rebellion. This fictional biography imagines his desire to return home, his terrible journey aboard the slave ship, the mutiny in 1839, and then his trial, when John Quincy Adams defended him before the Supreme Court. After the trial, he was given the opportunity to return home.

1433. Raven, Margot Theis. *Circle Unbroken: The Story of a Basket and Its People.* Illustrated by Earl B. Lewis. Farrar, 2004. 48pp. ISBN 978-0-374-31289-3; Square Fish, 2007, paper ISBN 978-0-312-37603-1. Grades 2–6. When the Gullahs came from West Africa to South Carolina and Georgia, they brought with them the ability to make a sweetgrass Gullah ("coil") basket. A grandmother tells her granddaughter that the child's ancestor learned how to harvest grassy reeds and weave them into baskets for rice while still in Africa. When he was captured into slavery, he found similar grasses in his new land and continued to weave the baskets along with his wife. They passed on the skill to the next generation, and the process continued down to the little girl learning to make her own basket. Illustrations complement the text. Bibliography. *Notable Social Studies Trade Books, Booklist Editor's Choice, Children's Book Award* (South Carolina) nomination, *Bluebonnet Book Award* (Texas) nomination, and *Capitol Choices Noteworthy Titles* (Washington, D.C.).

1434. Raven, Margot Theis. *Night Boat to Freedom.* Illustrated by Earl B. Lewis. Farrar, 2006. 32pp. ISBN 978-0-374-31266-4. Grades 2–6. To please his fellow slave Granny Judith, 12-year-old Christmas John risks his life many times to take runaways across the river from Kentucky to Ohio. When staying on the plantation becomes too dangerous for him, Granny Judith gives him a quilt with a red patch in it and tells him to leave. He persuades her to accompany him. Illustrations enhance the text. *Booklist Editor's Choice, Capitol Choices Noteworthy Titles* (Washington, D.C.), *Jane Addams Honor Book, Bluegrass Award* (Kentucky) nomination, and *Young Readers' Choice Award* (Louisiana) nomination.

1435. Rinaldi, Ann. *Come Juneteenth.* (Great Episodes) Harcourt, 2007. 246pp. ISBN 978-0-15-205947-7. Grades 5–9. Fourteen-year-old Luli and her Texas family do not tell their slaves that Lincoln signed the Emancipation Proclamation making them free in 1863. Sis Goose, Luli's slave, is the daughter of a white steamship captain and a black slave, and when word that she is free reaches her, the family tells her the rumors are false. When the Yankees arrive, Sis Goose and other Texas slaves learn on June 19, 1865, that they are indeed free. Luli and her family face repercussions.

1436. Rinaldi, Ann. *The Ever-After Bird: A Novel.* Harcourt, 2007. 232pp. ISBN 978-0-15-202620-2. Grades 5–9. In 1851, after a slave-owner kills her abolitionist father, 13-year-old CeCe McGill lives with her Uncle Alex, a doctor and ornithologist. He takes her on a trip to Georgia in search of the rare scarlet ibis, a bird that slaves believe can bring them freedom. With them is Earline, a free black student at Oberlin who has to pretend she is their slave once they enter the South. CeCe discovers while looking for the bird, her uncle is also giving slaves information about the Underground Railroad.

1437. Ringgold, Faith. *Aunt Harriet's Underground Railroad to the Sky.* Dragonfly, 1995. 32pp. Paper ISBN 978-0-517-88543-7. Grades K–3. In 1949, when Cassie Lightfoot and her brother Be Be fly through the sky, they meet a train full of people and Miss Harriet who tells them that every one hundred years, the railroad in the sky traces the slaves' path to freedom. Be Be hops on the train, but Cassie does not. However, Harriet Tubman guides Cassie by foot to retrace the path of the Underground Railroad. Cassie must escape from a plantation, hide in woods, traverse swamps, and learn to recognize a safe house. Eventually, she flies over Niagara Falls to Canada where she finds freedom and Be Be.

1438. Ruby, Lois. *Steal Away Home.* Aladdin, 1998. 192pp. Paper ISBN 978-0-689-82435-7. Grades 4–8. In contemporary Kansas 12-year-old Dana reluctantly strips wallpaper and finds a secret room with a skeleton and a black book inside. As she studies the black book, she pieces together the mystery of the skeleton and the life inside the house before the Civil War. The Quaker inhabitants protected a young Underground Railroad conductor who died in the house while guards were outside searching for runaway slaves.

1439. Sandburg, Carl. *Abe Lincoln Grows Up.* Illustrated by James Daugherty. Voyager, 1975. 222pp. Paper ISBN 978-0-15-602615-4. Grades 4–8. The first 27 chapters of Carl Sandburg's biography of Abraham Lincoln (1809–1865), published in 1928, concern his years of growing from a boy to a young man. As a boy, Lincoln walked four miles to school, did chores on the family farm, helped his father cut down trees, and shot wild turkeys. At 17, he split rails and became a champion "rassler" as well as an expert at skinning animals and curing hides. He saw a slave auction in New Orleans, and at 19 he set off to make his fortune. Throughout all, he read as much as he could. This book was originally published in 1956.

1440. Schwartz, Virginia Frances. *Send One Angel Down.* Holiday House, 2000. 163pp. ISBN 978-0-8234-1484-0; Fitzhenry & Whiteside, 2005, paper ISBN 978-1-55005-140-7. Grades 5–8. Abram tries to hide the horrors of being a real slave from Eliza, his light-skinned cousin who is also a daughter of the plantation owner. Eliza's slave grandmother and aunt, along with the plantation's slave nanny, work with her so that she can be a nanny if she is freed. Eventually, her father and master sells her, and she is able to realize this goal rather than having to do painful field work. *Young Adult Award* (South Carolina) nomination, *Student Book Award* (Maine) nomination, and *Children's Book Award* (Georgia) nomination.

1441. Slate, Joseph. *I Want to Be Free.* Illustrated by E. B. Lewis. Putnam, 2009. 32pp. ISBN 978-0-399-24342-4. Grades K–3. A runaway slave is caught and returned to his master, who then shackles him with a ball and chain. Throughout, the slave sings "Before I die, I want to be free." The slave again manages to break free, but the shackle remains on his ankle. Against another slave's advice, the runaway stops to help an orphan, and when the orphan touches the shackle, it mysteriously drops off his savior's ankle. An author's note bases the story on Rudyard Kipling's *Kim. Booklist Editors Choice.*

1442. Turner, Ann. *Nettie's Trip South.* Illustrated by Ronald Himler. Aladdin, 1995. 32pp. Paper ISBN 978-0-689-80117-4. Grades 1–5. When Nettie is 10 years old in the 1850s, she travels south with her journalist brother. She writes her friend to tell her how disturbed she is by what she has seen. When she watches slaves sold at auction, she vomits because she realizes that if her skin were black, she would be treated in the same way. She also realizes she would have only one name and not be identified with her real family.

1443. Wait, Lea. *Finest Kind.* Margaret K. McElderry, 2006. 246pp. ISBN 978-1-416-90952-1. Grades 4–8. Twelve-year-old Jake Webber moves with his family from Boston to a small Maine farmhouse in 1838 after his father's bank fails. His father's new logging job keeps him away from home, and Jake has to help his mother and disabled younger brother, Frankie, whom the family hides from the neighbors, fearful of rejection. Fortunately, Jake gets support from his neighbor Nabby and from the outcast Granny McPherson, a healer, and they guide him to understand that people can be the "finest kind."

1444. Wait, Lea. *Seaward Born.* Margaret K. McElderry, 2003. 156pp. ISBN 978-0-689-84719-6; Aladdin, 2004, paper ISBN 978-0-689-84860-5. Grades 4–7. Thirteen-year-old slave Michael, 13, and his friend Jim escape from Charleston, South Carolina, in 1805 and head north. Michael stows away on a ship to Boston and faces capture when a sailor finds him and wants to turn in him for a bounty. Michael continues north to Maine and changes his name to Noah Brown, but he remains afraid of the slave-hunters until he can reach Canada. Jim is caught on the journey, and although Michael/Noah is sorry, he worries more about being caught himself. *Sunshine State Young Reader Award* (Florida) nomination, *Student Book Award* (Maine) nomination, and *SCASL Book Award* (South Carolina) nomination.

1445. Wait, Lea. *Wintering Well.* Margaret K. McElderry, 2004. 186pp. ISBN 978-0-689-85646-4; Aladdin, 2006, paper ISBN 978-0-689-85647-1. Grades 5–8. In 1819 in Wiscasset, Maine, 11-year-old Cassie Ames's brother Will cuts his leg with an axe while chopping wood. He loses two-thirds of his leg. Despondent because he can no longer be a farmer with his father and brothers, he and Cassie decide to spend the winter with their sister in a nearby small town. There Will discovers other careers that are open to him, but Cassie bemoans having few choices for herself. *Volunteer State Book Award* (Tennessee) nomination, *Mark Twain Award* (Missouri) nomination, *Student Book Award* (Maine) nomination, and *Great Stone Face Book Award* (New Hampshire) nomination.

1446. Wallner, Alexandra. *An Alcott Family Christmas.* Illustrated by author. Holiday House, 1996. 32pp. ISBN 978-0-8234-1265-5. Grades K–4. When the girls in Louisa May Alcott's family are short of money to buy presents one Christmas in the mid-19th century, they prepare a Christmas feast instead. A neighbor comes to the door asking for help because his wife and baby are sick. The Alcott girls respond promptly, offering their food and deciding to entertain their parents with a play on Christmas morning.

1447. Walvoord, Linda. *Rosetta, Rosetta, Sit by Me!* Illustrated by Eric Velasquez. Marshall Cavendish, 2004. 96pp. ISBN 978-0-7614-5171-6. Grades 4–8. Nine-year-old Rosetta, the daughter of abolitionist Frederick Douglass, is the only African American child in Miss Tracy's Female Seminary in Rochester, New York, in 1848. Although the other students like her, the staff is less happy and works to keep her isolated. After two weeks, Rosetta realizes she dislikes the school, and her father begins trying to desegregate the school district. But happily for Rosetta, she is able to study with Abigail and Lydia Mott in their integrated home school. Illustrations illuminate the text. Bibliography, Chronology, and Notes.

1448. Wells, Rosemary. *Lincoln and His Boys.* Candlewick, 2009. 96pp. ISBN 978-0-7636-3723-1. Grades 3–6. Three vignettes present a picture of Abraham Lincoln (1809–1865) and his sons William Wallace Lincoln (1850–1862) and Thomas Lincoln (1853–1871). Willy, 9, describes going from Springfield, Illinois, to Chicago for clothes and politics when supporters inform his father that he will run for president. Then Willy tells about their move to Washington and how Pinkerton agents protect Lincoln from an assassination plot. He and Tad later enjoy various White House games with the Taft children. The final segment concerns Tad, who goes with his father to Richmond, Virginia, just after the South's defeat. Lincoln asks the Union army band to play "Dixie." Illustrations augment the text. Notes.

1449. Whelan, Gloria. *Friend on Freedom River.* Illustrated by Gijsbert Van Frankenhuyzen. Sleeping Bear, 2005. 48pp. ISBN 978-1-58536-222-6. Grades 2–5. In December 1850 Louis and his mother are on their own after Louis's father leaves their home on the Detroit River to work at a northern logging camp. When Louis hears a family of runaway slaves ask, "Are you a friend?" he decides to answer as his father told him. Sarah and her two children, Tyler and Lucy, tell him that slave-hunters are close behind and will grab them unless he ferries them across the icy water. He risks all their lives to reach Canada. Illustrations complement the text.

1450. Winnick, Karen. *Mr. Lincoln's Whiskers.* Boyds Mills, 1996. Unpaged. ISBN 978-1-56397-485-4; 1999, paper ISBN 978-1-56397-805-0. Grades K–3. When Grace's father brings her a picture of Abraham Lincoln (1809–1865), she thinks he looks thin. Although only 11, Grace decides to write him a letter. She sees a shadow across his face from the light outside, and she realizes he would look better with a beard. She tells him, and he answers her letter. When his train comes through Westfield, he thanks her for her advice, and she admires his new beard. *Young Reader's Award* (Virginia) nomination and *New York State Charlotte Award* nomination.

1451. Winter, Jeanette. *Follow the Drinking Gourd.* Knopf, 1988. 48pp. ISBN 978-0-394-89694-6; 1992, paper ISBN 978-0-679-81997-4. Grades K–3. Peg Leg Joe, a white sailor, teaches the Drinking Gourd song to slaves so they will know how to follow the Underground Railroad. A family follows his directions, escaping at night and watching the stars to lead them to the Ohio River. There an abolitionist waits to ferry them across to safe houses on their way to Canada.

1452. Woods, Brenda. *My Name Is Sally Little Song.* Putnam, 2006. 182pp. ISBN 978-0-399-24312-7; Puffin, 2007, paper ISBN 978-0-14-240943-5. Grades 4–7. In 1802, 12-year-old Sally and her family run away from their Georgia plantation after their master announces that he plans to sell one of them. They seek freedom from slavery and find a home with the Seminole Indians in Florida. Sally's mother died on the journey, but the Seminoles offer them safety and the chance to play, something Sally has never done. *Bluegrass Award* (Kentucky) nomination, *Nene Award* (Hawaii) nomination, *Great Stone Face Award* (New Hampshire) nomination, and *Young Readers' Choice Award* (Louisiana) nomination.

1453. Woodson, Jacqueline. *Show Way.* Illustrated by Hudson Talbott. Putnam, 2007. 48pp. ISBN 978-0-399-23749-2. Grades 2–5. Soonie's great-grandmother was sold into slavery at the age of 7. On the South Carolina plantation where Soonie lived, Big Mama told her that some people got themselves free. She taught her how to create "Show Way" quilts that were maps for slaves to follow to freedom. In the 1960s Soonie's granddaughter, Georgiana, marches for freedom, and then Georgiana's granddaughter, the author, laughs with her own daughter about a quilt with her picture embedded in it. *Booklist Editor's Choice, Hoosier Book Award* (Indiana) nomination, *Young Hoosier Award* (Indiana) nomination, *Young Readers Choice Awards* (Louisiana), *Newbery Honor, Children's Book Award* (North Carolina) nomination, *Battle of the Books* (New Mexico) nomination, *Young Readers Choice Book Award* (Pennsylvania) nomination, *SCASL Book Award* (South Carolina) nomination, *Volunteer State Book Award* (Tennessee) nomination, and *Beehive Young Adult Book Award* (Utah) nomination.

1454. Wright, Courtni C. *Journey to Freedom: A Story of the Underground Railroad.* Illustrated by Gershom Griffith. Holiday House, 1994. Unpaged. ISBN 978-0-8234-1096-5; 1997, paper ISBN 978-0-8234-1333-1. Grades K–3. This story is told from the first-person point of view of an 8-year-old runaway slave named Joshua. He, his family, and eight others are in Harriet Tubman's care while traveling the Underground Railroad. They journey by night and rest in safe houses during the day as they walk from Kentucky to Canada during the late fall, just as the snows begin.

1455. Zimmer, Tracie Vaughn. *The Floating Circus.* Bloomsbury, 2008. 198pp. ISBN 978-1-59990-185-5. Grades 4–7. Abandoned by their mother in 1852, 13-year-old Owen Burke and his younger brother Zach board an Orphan Train. But Owen hops off when he hears that Zach can be more easily adopted without him. Owen finds work on a circus boat and also a new friend, freed slave Solomon, who lets Owen clean cages and work with the elephants. The printer on board, Mr. Greene, lets him set type, and Owen makes friends with the printer's son Caleb. The boat ends up in New Orleans, but a storm and the spread of yellow fever destroys the business. Then slavers ignore the papers that declare Solomon a free man and capture him. Although Owen has the opportunity to live with Mr. Greene and Caleb in Philadelphia, he feels he must find and free Solomon.

History

1456. Bartoletti, Susan Campbell. *Kids on Strike.* Houghton, 1999. 208pp. ISBN 978-0-395-88892-6; 2003, paper ISBN 978-0-618-36923-2. Grades 5–8. Bartoletti describes American labor strikes that resulted from child labor abuses beginning in 1836. Her text is based on memoirs, oral histories, archival photographs, and newspaper reports. Among the strikes she looks at are the Lowell, Massachusetts, protest by textile factory girls (1836), newspaper deliverers in New York City (1899), young coal miners in Pennsylvania (1897, 1900, and 1902), Mother Jones's famous march from Philadelphia (1903), and the garment workers' strikes with Agnes Nestor in Chicago (1897). Photographs augment the text. Bibliography, Chronology, and Index. *School Library Journal Best Books for Children.*

1457. Bial, Raymond. *The Underground Railroad.* Houghton, 1995. 48pp. Paper ISBN 978-0-395-72915-0. Grades 4–8. Before he tells the story of the Underground Railroad, Bial gives a chronology of the antislavery movement starting in 1775. The Railroad used signal lamps in upper windows, false-bottomed wagons, and hand-dug tunnels lit with lanterns. Photographs of individuals and of memorabilia augment the verbal history of the abolitionists. Further Reading. *Notable Children's Trade Books in the Field of Social Studies.*

1458. Connell, Kate. *Tales from the Underground Railroad.* Illustrated by Debbe Heller. Steck-Vaughn, 1992. 68pp. Paper ISBN 978-0-8114-8063-5. Grades 4–7. The Underground Railroad was a major force in getting slaves away from cruel masters and on the path to freedom. It worked because many whites were willing to risk their own lives for something they knew was right. They learned to be crafty and inventive in their methods of rescuing slaves and even free blacks. The stories of William Minnis, Harriet Eglin and Charlotte Giles, and William Still appear in this book. Epilogue.

1459. Currie, Stephen. *Escapes from Slavery.* (Great Escapes) Lucent, 2004. 112pp. ISBN 978-1-59018-276-5. Grades 5–9. A number of slaves escaped to the North before the Civil War, among them Ellen and William Craft, Josiah Henson, Harriet Tubman, William Wells Brown, and Henry Brown. Ellen and William Craft left Georgia and traveled by boat and train as Ellen could pass for white. William pretended to be her slave. They arrived in Philadelphia on December 25, 1848. Josiah Henson took his wife and four children across the Ohio River to Cincinnati and on to Canada with the help of abolitionists. Harriet Tubman not only freed herself in 1849 but also helped many other slaves by returning to the South several times. Quakers helped William Wells Brown escape Missouri and settle in Ohio, where he worked on a Lake Erie steamboat. And Henry Brown mailed himself in a large wooden crate from Virginia to Philadelphia. Bibliography, Illustrations, Maps, and Index.

1460. Donlan, Leni. *Following Freedom: The Underground Railroad.* (American History Through Primary Sources) Raintree, 2007. 32pp. ISBN 978-1-4109-2418-6. Grades 2–4. Primary sources—maps, newspaper clippings, and many photographs—show the importance of the Underground Railroad to escaping slaves. Among the supports for runaways were conductors, stations, codes written in quilts, songs, and maps of the slaves' routes. Glossary, Further Reading, Web Sites, and Index.

1461. Gorrell, Gena K. *North Star to Freedom: The Story of the Underground Railroad.* Fitzhenry & Whiteside, 1996. 168pp. ISBN 978-0-7737-2988-9; 2004, paper ISBN 978-1-55005-068-4. Grades 5–8. The focus of this book, unlike other texts on the Underground Railroad, is Canada. Many of the slaves who took the railroad ended their journey in Canada with the help of abolitionists and Quakers along the way. Individual accounts from slaves who settled in Canada add new insights about this ordeal of American history. Reproductions, Bibliography, Further Reading, Notes, and Index.

1462. Hakim, Joy. *Liberty for All?* (History of US) Oxford, 2006. 213pp. ISBN 978-0-19-518234-7; 2007, paper ISBN 978-0-19-532719-9. Grades 5 up. Hakim explores the United States during the period of growth from 1848 until the beginning of the Civil War. Full of photographs, prints, sidebars, boxed text, and running commentary, this volume looks at all aspects of society and culture, including such individuals as Jedediah Smith, Emily Dickinson, John James Audubon, and Sojourner Truth. Chronology of Events, More Books to Read, and Index.

1463. Hamilton, Virginia. *Anthony Burns: The Defeat and Triumph of a Fugitive Slave.* Laurel-Leaf, 1993. 193pp. Paper ISBN 978-0-679-83997-2. Grades 5 up. When he escaped to Boston in 1854, Anthony Burns was 20. But his former owner located him and held him under the Fugitive Slave Act. Burns, however, had many abolitionist friends, and Richard Dana, a superb lawyer, decided to defend him without charge. This case inflamed Boston, and many rioted, but Burns gained freedom. His health, however, had declined, and he died at age 28. Fugitive Slave Act, Bibliography, and Index.

1464. Hamilton, Virginia. *Many Thousand Gone: African Americans from Slavery to Freedom.* Knopf, 1995. 151pp. Paper ISBN 978-0-679-87936-7. Grades 4–9. Divided into three main parts, this volume looks at slavery in America, the runaways of the 19th century, and the exodus to freedom. Among the topics and people covered are the Quaker protests, Jenny Slew, Elizabeth Freeman, the Gabriel Prosser uprising, Josiah Henson, Nat Turner, the Underground Railroad, Anthony Burns, Alexander Ross, Henry Box Brown (who mailed himself to liberty), Jackson (who escaped dressed as his wife's maid), Eliza (who inspired *Uncle Tom's Cabin* as she crossed the frozen Ohio), and the tide of freedom. Bibliography and Index.

1465. Hansen, Joyce, and Gary McGowan. *Freedom Roads: Searching for the Underground Railroad.* Illustrated by James E. Parsons. (Marcato) Cricket, 2004. 166pp. ISBN 978-0-8126-2673-5. Grades 5–9. Archaeologists and historians have sifted through corn cobs and root cellars, studied songs and quilts, and used the latest technology to find long-obscured traces of the Underground Railroad. Among the discoveries have been Florida's Fort Mose, founded by fugitive slaves in 1732. Technologies used include thermal scans that have helped find hidden closets and other secret spaces. Archaeological digs in New York and Canada reveal what might have happened at most of the "stations" on the Railroad. Most of the evidence is circumstantial, such as WPA slave narratives that are hard to document with scientific fact. The basic conclusion is that many individuals participated; there was not a single controlling organization that helped slaves to freedom. Among major court cases considered in the text are the Dred Scott decision, the Kansas-Nebraska Act, and the 1850 Fugitive Slave Law. Illustrations, Maps, Bibliography, and Index. *Capitol Choices Noteworthy Titles* (Washington, D.C.).

1466. Herda, D.J. *Furman v. Georgia: Debating the Death Penalty.* (Landmark Supreme Court Cases) Enslow, 1994. 104pp. ISBN 978-0-8949-0489-9. Grades 5–9. Herda discusses the

Supreme Court case of Furman v. Georgia that challenged the death penalty as cruel and un-usual punishment. He then presents the results of the case and its legacy. He also covers the lengthy process of getting a case to court. Photographs and reproductions augment the text. Bibliography, Notes, Further Reading, Web Sites, and Index.

1467. Hulm, David. *United States v. The Amistad: The Question of Slavery in a Free Country.* (Supreme Court Cases Through Primary Sources) Rosen, 2003. 64pp. ISBN 978-0-8239-4013-4. Grades 5–8. In an examination of the case of *United States* versus *Amistad*, the Supreme Court decided that the slaves aboard the slave ship *Amistad*, who had rebelled in 1839, had been illegally transported and were not legally slaves but free men. They were re-turned to Africa in 1842. Primary source materials provide information on other court cases on which this ruling was based, and which this ruling has affected. Bibliography and Index.

1468. Kalman, Bobbie. *Children's Clothing of the 1800s.* Illustrated by Antoinette DeBiasi. (His-toric Communities) Crabtree, 1995. 32pp. ISBN 978-0-8650-5480-6; paper ISBN 978-0-8650-5519-3. Grades 3–6. Most settler children had two outfits, and when they wore one outfit for a week, they washed it only once. Girls wore petticoats and crinolines. Boys wore skeleton suits and knickers. Photographs from living museums and drawings augment the text.

1469. Kalman, Bobbie. *19th Century Clothing.* See entry 1064.

1470. Kalman, Bobbie, and David Schimpky. *Old-Time Toys.* See entry 405.

1471. Landau, Elaine. *Fleeing to Freedom on the Underground Railroad: The Courageous Slaves, Agents, and Conductors.* Twenty-First Century, 2006. 88pp. ISBN 978-0-8225-3490-7. Grades 5 up. Primary-source questions, anecdotes, and archival images emphasize the im-portance of the Underground Railroad in helping slaves find freedom. Chapters cover the abolitionist movement, escapes, the way to freedom, and the risks involved for both run-aways and their helpers. There are spotlights on the Harriet Tubman and Levi Coffman and on the Fugitive Slave Act of 1850. Photographs and illustrations augment the text. Bibliog-raphy, Notes, Further Reading, Web Sites, and Index.

1472. Lassieur, Allison. *The Underground Railroad: An Interactive History Adventure.* Cap-stone, 2007. 112pp. ISBN 978-1-4296-0164-1. Grades 3–7. Readers can choose to be a slave, a slave catcher, or an Underground Railroad worker in this interactive book. The results of each choice are based on real-life situations and the reader will face difficult decisions. There are thirty-seven choices and sixteen endings. Illustrations and photographs enhance the text. Bibliography, Chronology, Maps, Further Reading, Glossary, Web Sites, and Index.

1473. Lester, Julius. *From Slave Ship to Freedom Road.* Illustrated by Rod Brown. Dial, 1998. 40pp. ISBN 978-0-8037-1893-7; Puffin, 1999, paper ISBN 978-0-14-056669-7. Grades 5–10. Lester presents a comprehensive study of slavery's history in America from its begin-nings through the Civil War. He recounts many of the struggles slaves faced, what they overcame, and the kinds of attempts they made to be free. Twenty-two paintings comple-ment the text and show the horror of capture, the Middle Passage, the auction block, labor and work, and the secret bonds that the slaves made within their communities and their small defiance on the plantations. *Picture Book Award* (Georgia) nomination, *Student Book Award* (Maine) nomination, and *Garden State Teen Book Awards* (New Jersey).

1474. McCully, Emily Arnold. *Manjiro.* Farrar, 2008. Unpaged. ISBN 978-0-374-34792-5. Grades 3–6. In 1841 when Manjiro, 14, and four other fishermen were swept away from Japan in a storm, they became shipwrecked on an island for six months. Because a Japanese law promised death to anyone who left the country and tried to reenter, they could not re-turn home. An American whaling ship rescued them, and Captain Whitfield took Manjiro home with him to New Bedford, Massachusetts, where he taught him to plant, cultivate, harvest, and ride a horse, illegal in Japan except for samurai. Manjiro attended school and graduated at the top of his class. Then he went to San Francisco during the California gold rush and collected $600 of gold dust in seventy days. After nine years, he returned to Japan with two of his castaways. Imprisoned for seven months, he told the officials that Americans desired to trade and that they had wonderful inventions such as railroads, wristwatches, telegraphs, and drawbridges. His stories led to the opening of Japan to the western world. Watercolors complement the text. Bibliography, Maps, and Note.

1475. McKissack, Patricia C., and Frederick McKissack. *Days of Jubilee: The End of Slavery in the United States.* Illustrated by Leo and Diane Dillon. Scholastic, 2003. 144pp. ISBN 978-0-59010-764-8. Grades 4–8. The days after the slaves were freed have been called the "Days of Jubilee." Although the Emancipation Proclamation became effective on January 1, 1863, it only ended slavery in the Confederate states. Those in the Border states were still enslaved. This volume contains letters, newspaper articles, diaries of individuals including Mary Chestnut, narratives, military orders, and other documents that recall the stages that led to the true Day of Jubilee, December, 18, 1865, the day of ratification of the Thirteenth Amendment. Archival photographs and illustrations augment the text. Bibliography, Chronology, and Index.

1476. McKissack, Patricia C., and Frederick McKissack. *Rebels Against Slavery.* Scholastic, 1996. 176pp. ISBN 978-0-590-45735-4. Grades 5–8. McKissack looks at several slave revolts and posits that each one was more intense than the previous, with all leading to the organized attempts that eventually overcame slavery. Toussaint L'Ouverture, Cato, Denmark Vesey, Gabriel Prosser, Harriet Tubman, and John Brown led the way, with others operating on the fringes. Tubman was willing to shoot any runaway who could not complete the journey to freedom. But the McKissacks think that even nonviolent resistance had its place because it helped to reach the final goal. Photographs, Chronology, and Index.

1477. Pollard, Michael. *The Nineteenth Century.* Facts on File, 1993. 78pp. ISBN 978-0-8160-2791-0. Grades 4–7. In the 19th century, towns and the cities were changing. The British went into India and Americans went West in attempts to build empires. The slave trade led to the Civil War in the United States. Other changes affected Europe, Africa, Australia, and New Zealand as steamships reshaped travel, the oil age began, and the communications revolution got underway. Illustrations augment the text. Glossary, Further Reading, and Index.

1478. Simon, Barbara Brooks. *Escape to Freedom: The Underground Railroad Adventures of Callie and William.* (I Am American) National Geographic, 2004. 40pp. Paper ISBN 978-0-7922-6551-1. Grades 4–6. Fictional characters Callie, 14, and William meet as they are making their way north on the Underground Railroad. Callie was a field worker on a plantation in Kentucky, and William had been a city slave. The people on the Railroad help them make their way to Canada. Photographs, maps, and reproductions highlight the nonfiction aspects of the text.

1479. Sonneborn, Liz. *The Mexican American War: A Primary Source History of the Expansion of the Western Lands of the United States.* Rosen, 2005. 64pp. ISBN 978-1-4042-0180-4. Grades 5–7. Sonneborn examines the Mexican American War, fought between 1846 and 1848, providing information on the conflict, the battles, and its conclusion through primary sources. Photographs and illustrations augment the text. Bibliography, Glossary, Chronology, Further Reading, and Index. *Voice of Youth Advocates Nonfiction Honor List.*

Biography and Collective Biography

1480. Adler, David A. *A Picture Book of Frederick Douglass.* Illustrated by Samuel Byrd. Holiday House, 1993. Unpaged. ISBN 978-0-8234-1002-6; 1995, paper ISBN 978-0-8234-1205-1. Grades K–4. Born around 1817, Frederick Bailey had a slave mother and an unidentified white father. He was orphaned at the age of 7 and his new female owner, evidently unaware of the law, taught him to read. When he eventually escaped via the Underground Railroad to New Bedford, Massachusetts, he took the names Johnson and then Douglass. He found a newspaper job and wrote an autobiography. But fear of capture as a runaway slave sent him to England. There, people bought his freedom, and when he returned to Massachusetts, he started his own antislavery newspaper, *The North Star.* He wrote two more books and married a white woman after the death of his first wife, "like my father," as he said. Important Dates.

1481. Adler, David A. *A Picture Book of Harriet Beecher Stowe.* Illustrated by Colin Bootman. Holiday House, 2003. Unpaged. ISBN 978-0-8234-1646-2; 2004, paper ISBN 978-0-8234-1878-7. Grades 1–3. Harriet Beecher Stowe (1811–1896), a strong opponent of slavery, wrote *Uncle Tom's Cabin*, a book that Abraham Lincoln said started the Civil War. As a child, Stowe loved to read. When her family moved from Connecticut to Cincinnati, Ohio, in 1832, she first witnessed the horrors of slavery. She became a staunch abolitionist and in 1851 started writing weekly installments for an antislavery newspaper. Many learned about slavery for the first time from her writings. Illustrations complement the text. Chronology, Further Reading, and Notes.

1482. Adler, David A. *A Picture Book of Harriet Tubman.* Illustrated by Samuel Byrd. Holiday House, 1992. Unpaged. ISBN 978-0-8234-0926-6; 1993, paper ISBN 978-0-8234-1065-1. Grades 1–3. Born in either 1820 or 1821 in Maryland, Harriet Tubman heard about Nat Turner's Rebellion in 1831 and learned that he was hanged. She later married a free man but lived with her owner before she decided to follow the Underground Railroad to Pennsylvania. There she got jobs, but she returned to the South nineteen times between 1850 and 1860 to lead more than 300 slaves to freedom. John Brown called her "General Tubman," and others called her "Moses." None of her "passengers" died on the way. She was more than 90 years old when she died in 1913. Important Dates.

1483. Adler, David A. *A Picture Book of Robert E. Lee.* Illustrated by John and Alexandra Wallner. Holiday House, 1994. Unpaged. ISBN 978-0-8234-1111-5; 1998, paper ISBN 978-0-8234-1366-9. Grades 1–3. Robert Edward Lee, son of "Light-Horse Harry" Lee and Ann Hill Carter Lee, was born in 1807, three years before his father lost the family's fortune. Robert Lee attended West Point, and soon after he began his military career, he showed his brilliance in the Mexican War. He hated war, however, because of its destruction of families. When the states disagreed about slavery, Lee sided with those who were against it, having freed all of his own slaves. But he was loyal to Virginia and did not want to fight against his family and friends, so he fought for the South in the Civil War. He preferred to attack rather than wait. At the end of the war, he realized that one more day would bring too much sacrifice, so he surrendered. Always admired and dignified, he died in 1870 after serving as president of Washington College (now Washington and Lee) in Lexington, Virginia.

1484. Adler, David A. *A Picture Book of Sojourner Truth.* Illustrated by Gershom Griffith. Holiday House, 1994. Unpaged. ISBN 978-0-8234-1072-9; 1996, paper ISBN 978-0-8234-1262-4. Grades 1–3. Sojourner Truth (1797–1883) was born a slave named Isabella and renamed herself after she became free. When accused of poisoning the leader of a religious community she had joined, she decided to leave New York and "sojourn" or visit different places and preach against the evils of slavery, for the rights of women, and about her religious views. She raised money to feed African American soldiers during the Civil War and helped care for slaves who had escaped north to freedom. Important Dates. *Notable Children's Trade Books in the Field of Social Studies.*

1485. Alexander, Sally Hobart, and Robert Alexander. *She Touched the World: Laura Bridgman, Deaf-Blind Pioneer.* Clarion, 2008. 112pp. ISBN 978-0-618-85299-4. Grades 3–6. Laura Dewey Bridgman (1829–1889) accomplished much although she was disabled, and people around the world knew about her when she was as young as 10. She had contracted scarlet fever at the age of 3 and lost her senses of sight, smell, sound, and much of her taste. Even though Helen Keller's feats overshadowed her, she and her teacher, Dr. Samuel Grindley Howe at the New England Institute for the Education of the Blind, paved the way for Keller's success. Included in the text are details of her daily schedule. Photographs and illustrations augment the text. Bibliography, Further Reading, and Web Sites. *Capitol Choices Noteworthy Titles* (Washington, D.C.).

1486. Aller, Susan Bivin. *Beyond Little Women: A Story About Louisa May Alcott.* Illustrated by Qi Z. Wang. (Creative Minds) Lerner, 2004. 64pp. ISBN 978-1-57505-602-9; paper ISBN 978-1-57505-636-4. Grades 3–5. Louisa May Alcott (1832–1888) wanted to become a famous author even as a young girl. She learned that giving was more important than receiving when her poor family gave food to an even less fortunate family, a lesson she remembered throughout her life. She began supporting her family with the proceeds from her writing and, later in her life, she became one of the most admired writers of her time with the publication of *Little Women*. Illustrations and Bibliography.

1487. Aller, Susan Bivin. *Ulysses S. Grant.* (History Maker Bios) Lerner, 2006. 48pp. ISBN 978-0-8225-2438-0. Grades 3–5. Ulysses S. Grant (1822–1885) grew up on an Ohio farm before attending West Point. He eventually led the Union army during the Civil War. The text covers his childhood, his experience as a general, and his role as president of the United States. Illustrations augment the text. Bibliography, Further Reading, Glossary, Maps, Timeline, Web Sites, and Index.

1488. Anderson, Laurie Halse. *Thank You, Sarah: The Woman Who Saved Thanksgiving.* Illustrated by Matt Faulkner. Simon & Schuster, 2003. 40pp. ISBN 978-0-689-84902-2; 2005, paper ISBN 978-0-689-85143-8. Grades 1–4. Sarah Hale (1788–1879) thought Thanksgiving was a wonderful holiday that brought families together. She added advocate to her list of accomplishments as magazine editor, teacher, feminist, widowed mother of five, and author of "Mary Had a Little Lamb." She appealed by letter to several presidents over a period of thirty-eight years, and finally Abraham Lincoln listened. He thought her idea might be a help in reuniting the Union. He declared Thanksgiving a national holiday in 1863. The illustrations augment the text. Bibliography. *Emphasis on Reading Award* (Alabama) nomination, *SCASL Book Award* (South Carolina) nomination, *Show Me Readers Award* (Missouri) nomination, *Young Hoosier Book Award* (Indiana) nomination, *Capitol Choices Noteworthy Titles* (Washington, D.C.), *Black-Eyed Susan Award* (Maryland) nomination, *Children's Book Award* (North Carolina) nomination, and *Garden State Children's Book Award* (New Jersey) nomination.

1489. Aylesworth, Jim. *Our Abe Lincoln: An Old Tune With New Lyrics.* Illustrated by author. Scholastic, 2009. 32pp. ISBN 978-0-439-92548-8. Grades K–3. During Abe Lincoln's campaign, a one-line song to the tune of "Old Gray Mare" said "Old Abe Lincoln came out of the wilderness." Aylesworth adds eleven verses in which he offers background about Lincoln's life as a boy, as president, and as an opponent of slavery. Children in the book present the song as if a stage play. Illustrations in watercolor and pen and ink depict the various scenes with a multiracial cast.

1490. Binns, Tristan Boyer. *Edgar Allan Poe: Master of Suspense.* (Great Life Stories) Franklin Watts, 2005. 127pp. ISBN 978-0-53116-751-9. Grades 5–8. Edgar Allan Poe (1809–1849) lost both his parents when he was young. He had a difficult relationship with his foster parents and exhibited erratic behaviors including melancholy and waywardness. He became a writer and created memorable characters and situations in such stories and poems as "The Pit and the Pendulum," "The Raven," and "The Cask of Amontillado." Archival photographs and illustrations augment the text. Chronology, Further Reading, Web Sites, and Index.

1491. Blumberg, Rhoda. *Shipwrecked: The True Adventures of a Japanese Boy.* Trophy, 2003. 80pp. Paper ISBN 978-0-688-17485-9. Grades 5–9. A fatherless Japanese boy, Manjiro Nakahama (1827–1898), became marooned on an island for six months in 1841. An American whaling ship captain rescued him and took him to Massachusetts where, as John Mung, he learned navigation and English. He earned some money in the gold rush and returned to Japan. He was imprisoned for several months while he told the government officials about the United States. His testimony earned him the rank of samurai and helped open Japan to the West. *Booklist Editors Choice, School Library Journal Best Books of the Year, Tennessee State Book Award* (Volunteer) nomination, *State Reading Association for Young Readers Program* (Virginia) nomination, and *Sasquatch Book Award* (Washington) nomination.

1492. Bolden, Tonya. *Maritcha: A Nineteenth-Century American Girl.* Abrams, 2004. 47pp. ISBN 978-0-8109-5045-0. Grades 4–8. Maritcha Reymond Lyons (1848–1929), born a free black girl in Manhattan, moved to Providence, Rhode Island, and sued the state to gain admission to the all-white high school, the only school in town. Archival materials, Lyons's memoir, and other primary sources tell her story and describe the destruction of the family home and business as well as the fight for public education. As an adult, Lyons spent fifty years as an educator, including a term as assistant principal of Brooklyn's Public School No. 83. Photographs and period illustrations complement the text. Bibliography and Notes. *School Library Journal Best Books for Children, Coretta Scott King Author Honor, American Library Association Notable Children's Books, Capitol Choices Noteworthy Titles* (Washington, D.C.), and *American Library Association Best Books for Young Adults.*

1493. **Brenner, Martha.** *Abe Lincoln's Hat.* Illustrated by Donald Cook. (Step Into Reading) Random, 1994. 48pp. Paper ISBN 978-0-679-84977-3. Grades 1–3. In this biography Abraham Lincoln (1809–1865) appears as a disorganized lawyer with common sense, who succeeded because people liked him. In one court case, Lincoln allowed a colt the freedom to go to its mother, showing clearly who was the rightful owner of the horse. He also defended a slave who thought he should be free in Illinois because it was a free state. Lincoln used his stovepipe hat not only to protect his head but also to protect important papers. Lincoln seems very human in this presentation.

1494. **Burleigh, Robert.** *Abraham Lincoln Comes Home.* Illustrated by Wendell Minor. Henry Holt, 2008. Unpaged. ISBN 978-0-8050-7529-8. Grades 1–4. A young boy watches Lincoln's funeral train as it passes by on its way from Washington, D.C., to Springfield, Illinois, in 1865. Although the powerful train thrills the boy, he sees his father cry for the first time. He imagines himself meeting Lincoln while mourners gather beside the track in the night and build bonfires to keep warm during their vigil. Double-page illustrations in gouache and watercolor enhance the text.

1495. **Chorlian, Meg.** *Ulysses S. Grant: Confident Leader and Hero.* (The Civil War) Cobblestone, 2005. 47pp. ISBN 978-0-8126-7906-9. Grades 4–9. Ulysses S. Grant (1822–1885) became a general during the Civil War while leading the Union forces. The biography focuses on his military career with brief profiles of other leaders with whom or against whom he fought. Maps and illustrations complement the text. Index.

1496. **Clinton, Catherine.** *When Harriet Met Sojourner.* Illustrated by Shane W. Evans. Armistad, 2007. Unpaged. ISBN 978-0-06-050425-0. Grades 3–7. As far as history has recorded, Sojourner Truth (d. 1883) and Harriet Tubman (1820?–1913) only met once. This story imagines what might have happened when they met in Boston during 1864. They contrasted in height but were similar in purpose. Illustrations intensify the text.

1497. **Cohn, Amy L., and Suzy Schmidt.** *Abraham Lincoln.* Illustrated by David A. Johnson. Scholastic, 2002. 40pp. ISBN 978-0-590-93566-1. Grades K–3. In this biography, Abraham Lincoln (1809–1865) becomes a lanky man whom everyone likes. The illustrations look at Lincoln from his childhood to his statue in the Lincoln Memorial. Cohn also shows his heroic role in American history, and his signing of the Emancipation Proclamation. Chronology. *Beehive Children's Book Award* (Utah) nomination and *Horn Book Fanfare.*

1498. **Collard, Sneed B., III.** *Abraham Lincoln: A Courageous Leader.* (American Heroes) Benchmark, 200. 40pp. ISBN 978-0-7614-2162-7. Grades 3–5. This biography of Abraham Lincoln (1809–1865) focuses on his humanity as well as his accomplishments as the sixteenth president of the United States. Anecdotes and clear descriptions help readers understand him in a way not presented in other biographies. Reproductions and museum images accompany the text. Glossary, Further Reading, and Index.

1499. **Connell, Kate.** *They Shall Be Heard: Susan B. Anthony and Elizabeth Cady Stanton.* Illustrated by Barbara Kiwak. Steck-Vaughn, 1993. 85pp. Paper ISBN 978-0-8114-8068-0. Grades 4–8. Susan B. Anthony (1820–1906) and Elizabeth Cady Stanton (1815–1902) both worked ceaselessly for women's rights. These two women met in 1851 in Seneca Falls, New York, at an antislavery meeting; they were introduced by Amanda Bloomer. Because Stanton was older, Anthony always called her Mrs. Stanton, and Stanton called her Susan. Their dedication to equality for women laid the ground for the passage in 1920 of the constitutional amendment allowing women to vote. Unfortunately, neither woman lived to see the day, but without their work it might not have existed. Epilogue, Afterword, and Notes.

1500. Corey, Shana. *You Forgot Your Skirt, Amelia Bloomer! A Very Improper Story.* Illustrated by Chesley McLaren. Scholastic, 2000. Unpaged. ISBN 978-0-439-07819-1. Grades 1–3. Amelia Jenks Bloomer (1818–1894) started a newspaper, the *Lily*, by and for women. When her friend Elizabeth Cady Stanton, brought her cousin to visit, they saw that she was not wearing a dress. Amelia decided that pantaloons would relieve American women from the heavy, tight dresses that impeded their movements. Eventually bloomers went out of style, but she opened up a new way for women to dress.

1501. Fradin, Judith Bloom, and Dennis B. Fradin. *5,000 Miles to Freedom: Ellen and William Craft's Flight from Slavery.* National Geographic, 2006. 96pp. ISBN 978-0-7922-7885-6. Grades 5–9. A light-skinned African American daughter of a master who raped her mother, Ellen Craft could pass for white. She disguised herself as a man and escaped with her husband, William, posing as her slave, by train and steamboat to Boston. Slave catchers were in pursuit, so they left for England and did not return until after the Civil War ended. They then opened a school and farm in Georgia. Photographs and maps highlight the text. Bibliography, Chronology, Notes, Further Reading, Web Sites, and Index. *American Library Association Best Books for Young Adults, Bulletin Blue Ribbon, Capitol Choices Noteworthy Titles* (Washington, D.C.), *Voice of Youth Advocates Nonfiction Honor List*, and *School Library Journal Best Books for Children.*

1502. Frazier, Joey. *Jefferson Davis: Confederate President.* Chelsea House, 2001. 80pp. ISBN 978-0-7910-6006-3. Grades 3–6. Jefferson Davis (1808–1889), born in Kentucky, was a soldier educated at West Point, a plantation owner, and a politician who became the president of the Confederate States of America. Although he lost the Civil War, he continued a full life afterward. He died in New Orleans. Illustrations enhance the text. Glossary, Chronology, Civil War Timeline, Further Reading, and Index.

1503. Freedman, Russell. *Lincoln: A Photobiography.* Clarion, 1987. 150pp. ISBN 978-0-8991-9380-9; 1989, paper ISBN 978-0-395-51848-9. Grades 5 up. Abraham Lincoln (1809–1865) had wit and good humor that attracted crowds as much as his height did. He began his career as a country lawyer, courted and married Mary Todd, and had a difficult presidency in the White House trying to oversee the Civil War. Freedman uses photographs and prints to illustrate his text about Lincoln's life. *Newbery Medal.*

1504. Frisch, Aaron. *Edgar Allan Poe.* (Voices from the Past) Creative, 2005. 48pp. ISBN 978-1-58341-344-9. Grades 3–6. One of the great American writers, Edgar Allen Poe had a number of tragedies in his life. His wife died very young, and he suffered from addictions. Yet he still wrote some of the most valued poems, short stories, and essays. Photographs and paintings augment the text.

1505. Fritz, Jean. *The Great Little Madison.* See entry 640.

1506. Fritz, Jean. *Harriet Beecher Stowe and the Beecher Preachers.* Putnam, 1994. 144pp. ISBN 978-0-399-22666-3; Puffin, 1998, paper ISBN 978-0-698-11660-3. Grades 4–8. Harriet Beecher Stowe (1811–1896) strongly opposed slavery but did not know how to stop it. Her sister-in-law encouraged her to do what she did best—write. *Uncle Tom's Cabin* was published in 1852 and Stowe became an instant celebrity. Her father was a well-known preacher but expected little from his daughters. Harriet, however, was probably the most successful of his offspring. She was known in Europe as well as the United States. People in England crowded the streets to see her. Photographs, Bibliography, and Index.

1507. Fritz, Jean. *You Want Women to Vote, Lizzie Stanton?* Illustrated by DyAnne DiSalvo-Ryan. Putnam, 1995. 88pp. ISBN 978-0-399-22786-8; Puffin, 1999, paper ISBN 978-0-698-11764-8. Grades 3–6. Elizabeth Cady's (1815–1902) father wanted her to be a boy, but she realized that women should have the same rights as men even after she married Henry Stanton and had seven children. She wore bloomers, spoke out about the right to vote at the Seneca Falls Convention in 1848, and traveled around the country expressing her opinions on equality for all, male and female, black and white. Notes, Bibliography, and Index. *American Library Association Notable Books for Children.*

1508. Gormley, Beatrice. *Maria Mitchell: The Soul of an Astronomer.* (Women of Spirit) Eerdmans, 2004. 123pp. Paper ISBN 978-0-8028-5264-9. Grades 4–8. Maria Mitchell (1818–1889) grew up in a Nantucket, Massachusetts, Quaker community that did not allow women to study mathematics. However, Mitchell's father, an amateur astronomer, decided to teach her math and what he knew about astronomy. Mitchell believed that women should refuse to follow authority if they did not agree with it—only then would they be able to accomplish what they were capable of. Mitchell was the first female professional astronomer in the United States and the first woman elected to the American Academy of Arts and Sciences. She became Vassar's professor of astronomy, and she discovered Comet Mitchell in 1847, for which she won a gold medal from King Frederick VI of Denmark. Sources, Further Reading, and Index.

1509. Gottfried, Ted. *Millard Fillmore.* (Presidents and Their Times) Benchmark, 2007. 96pp. ISBN 978-0-7614-2429-1. Grades 4–7. Millard Fillmore (1800–1874), largely self-educated, was mistreated as an apprentice to a cloth manufacturer as a young man. During the 1840s and 1850s the United States suffered many tensions including anti-immigrant sentiment, slavery, and war with Mexico. He had little success solving these problems and he is generally regarded as a rather boring president. Photographs highlight the text. Bibliography, Glossary, Chronology, Further Reading, Web Sites, and Index.

1510. Harness, Cheryl. *Young Abe Lincoln: The Frontier Days, 1809–1837.* National Geographic, 1996. Unpaged. ISBN 978-0-7922-2713-7; 2008, paper ISBN 978-1-4263-0437-8. Grades 3–6. Harness looks at the life of Abraham Lincoln (1809–1865) as a young man on the frontier of Illinois. Maps.

1511. Hausman, Gerald, and Loretta Hausman. *A Mind with Wings: The Story of Henry David Thoreau.* Shambhala, 2006. 148pp. ISBN 978-1-59030-228-6. Grades 5–8. A life of Henry David Thoreau (1817–1862), nature writer and philosopher. Each of the short chapters covers an event in Thoreau's life with dialogue coming from Thoreau's own writing. He faced several bouts of tuberculosis as he lived on Walden Pond, made innovations in the family pencil business, ran a school with his brother, and went on outdoors expeditions around the area. He helped fugitive slaves and spent a night in jail when he was arrested for failing to pay taxes that he thought the government did not deserve. He was an important and original American thinker.

1512. Henry, Joanne Landers. *Elizabeth Blackwell: Girl Doctor.* Illustrated by Robert Doremus. (Childhood of Famous Americans) Aladdin, 1996. 192pp. Paper ISBN 978-0-689-80627-8. Grades 3–6. Henry looks at the childhood of Elizabeth Blackwell (1821–1910) as she grew up in England before she and her family came to the United States. It ends with a chapter about her acceptance into medical school after many failures and having to teach two years to earn the money to pay for it.

1513. Herbert, Janis. *Abraham Lincoln for Kids: His Life and Times with 21 Activities.* Chicago Review, 2007. 154pp. ISBN 978-1-55652-656-5. Grades 5–8. This volume offers a slightly different view of Abraham Lincoln (1809–1865) and his life. It includes information about his family and a record of his accomplishments. It addresses serious concerns while adding activities that will help readers understand some of the decisions Lincoln had to make. Sidebars add other comments. Among the twenty-one activities are making a log cabin, a miniature Mississippi River flatboat, and a Sauk Indian statue; a treasure hunt; holding a debate; making a presidential beard; drawing a political cartoon; a freedom quilt collage; a time capsule; and painting a panoramic backdrop. Further Reading, Glossary, Web Sites, and Index.

1514. Jackson, Ellen. *Abe Lincoln Loved Animals.* Illustrated by Doris Ettlinger. Whitman, 2008. ISBN 978-0-8075-0123-8. Grades 2–5. This biography looks at the attachment Abraham Lincoln (1809–1865) felt for animals. He kept friends from teasing a turtle and was upset after killing a Thanksgiving turkey, vowing never to hunt again. He kept dogs, cats, rabbits, and goats, even in the White House, and he spent quiet time with them during the Civil War. When his son Tad became fond of a turkey planned for Thanksgiving dinner, Lincoln pardoned the turkey. This tradition continues today as presidents pardon one turkey each Thanksgiving. Illustrations complement the text. Bibliography.

1515. **Jakoubek, Robert E., and Heather Lehr Wagner.** *Harriet Beecher Stowe.* (American Women of Achievement) Chelsea House, 1988. 110pp. ISBN 978-1-55546-680-0. Grades 5 up. Harriet Beecher Stowe (1811–1896) grew up under the guidance of a stern religious father. She moved with her family to Cincinnati, Ohio, where she met and married the theologian Calvin Stowe. She began publishing articles after talking to both abolitionists and fugitive slaves who lived across the Ohio River in the slave state of Kentucky. When she, her husband, and five children left for Maine, she was convinced that slavery had to be abolished. Abraham Lincoln commented that her book, *Uncle Tom's Cabin*, was one of the factors leading to the Civil War. After the war, she spoke on various topics including women's rights. Photographs, engravings, and reproductions enhance the text. Chronology, Further Reading, and Index.

1516. **Jones, Lynda.** *Mrs. Lincoln's Dressmaker: The Unlikely Friendship of Elizabeth Keckley and Mary Todd Lincoln.* National Geographic, 2009. 80pp. ISBN 978-1-4263-0377-7. Grades 5–9. When Mary Todd Lincoln (1818–1882) came to Washington as the president's wife, she needed a dressmaker. Recommended to her was a former slave, Elizabeth Keckley (1818–1907). Initially, the two had difficulties, but Keckley offered Mary an ear that she needed. Alternating chapters reveal their backgrounds. Mary, a Kentucky belle, chose her husband carefully and helped him get elected, but she was unprepared for having three sons die young and her husband assassinated. Keckley had endured slavery and physical abuse but bought her freedom, ran her own business, and gained prestige through her association with a First Lady. Notes, Bibliography, and Index.

1517. **Jurmain, Suzanne.** *The Forbidden Schoolhouse: The True and Dramatic Story of Prudence Crandall and Her Students.* Houghton, 2005. 160pp. ISBN 978-0-618-47302-1. Grades 5–9. After opening a school for young white ladies in Canterbury, Connecticut, in 1830, Prudence Crandall received an admission inquiry from an African American girl. Crandall was an abolitionist, and so she agreed. The parents of the girls already in her school disapproved. Rather than refusing African American students, Crandall closed her school and reopened it with the help of her Quaker family and William Lloyd Garrison. In 1833 she opened a boarding school for African American girls but was threatened with so much violence that she closed it two years later. Bibliography, Notes, and Index. *Booklist Editor's Choice, Capitol Choices Noteworthy Titles* (Washington, D.C.), *Bulletin Blue Ribbon*, and *Children's Book Award* (Rhode Island) nomination.

1518. **Kent, Deborah.** *Elizabeth Blackwell: Physician and Health Educator.* (Spirit of America: Our People) Child's World, 2003. 32pp. ISBN 978-1-59296-002-6. Grades 3–6. Elizabeth Blackwell (1821–1910) first became a teacher but then decided she wanted to be a physician. She attended New York State's Geneva College after twenty medical schools refused to admit her. When she lost sight in one eye because of a disease, she could not be a surgeon as she wished. Instead, she opened a clinic for poor women and children and later founded the first medical school for women. Timeline, Bibliography, Glossary, Illustrations, and Index.

1519. **Kerley, Barbara.** *Walt Whitman: Words for America.* Illustrated by Brian Selznick. Scholastic, 2004. Unpaged. ISBN 978-0-439-35791-3. Grades 4–8. This biography of Walt Whitman (1819–1892) reveals the compassion for others that led him to serve as a nurse during the Civil War and to try to capture the true American in his poetry. Kerley depicts Whitman's love of words and his desire to tell everything about the "common man" and about the human spirit in his poem *Leaves of Grass*. Illustrations complement the text. Bibliography and Notes. *Bluegrass Award* (Kentucky) nomination, *American Library Association Notable Children's Books, Robert F. Sibert Honor Book, Capitol Choices Noteworthy Titles* (Washington, D.C.), *Kirkus Reviews Editor's Choice, New York Times Best Illustrated Books, Parents' Choice Silver Honors, Publishers Weekly Best Children's Books*, and *School Library Journal Best Books for Children*.

1520. **Knox, Barbara.** *Abraham Lincoln.* (First Biographies) Pebble, 2004. 24pp. ISBN 978-0-7368-2086-8. Grades 1–2. This graphic biography offers background on the life of Abraham

Lincoln (1809–1865), the man who served as president and issued the Emancipation Proclamation in 1863 during the Civil War. It includes background information important to Lincoln's life both in text and pictures.

1521. **Krass, Peter.** *Sojourner Truth: Antislavery Activist.* (Black Americans of Achievement) Chelsea House, 2004. 96pp. ISBN 978-0-7910-8165-5. Grades 5 up. As a child, Isabella (1797–1883) was sold to another slave owner and separated from her family. She won her freedom in 1827 and became a traveling preacher who took the name Sojourner Truth. Eventually renowned throughout the East Coast for her beliefs, she published the story of her life as a slave in 1850. Afterward she began lecture tours to advocate the end of slavery and the beginning of women's rights. She worked as a counselor to former slaves and started campaigns to help blacks obtain federal grants for farmland. Photographs and engravings highlight the text. Chronology, Further Reading, and Index.

1522. **Krull, Kathleen, and Paul Brewer.** *Lincoln Tells a Joke: How Laughter Saved the President (and the Country).* Illustrated by Stacy Innerst. Harcourt, 2010. 40pp. ISBN 978-0-15-206639-0. Grades K–3. Using quotations, Krull presents Abraham Lincoln (1809–1865) as a man who coped with his many sorrows and setbacks by telling jokes. He knew that the best way to combat his difficult childhood, his political loses, upheavals in his marriage, the deaths of his children, and slavery was to laugh in any way that he could, and he did. Acrylics complement the text. Notes and Bibliography.

1523. **Lange, Karen E.** *Nevermore: A Photobiography of Edgar Allan Poe.* National Geographic, 2009. 64pp. ISBN 978-1-4263-0398-2. Grades 5–8. Edgar Allan Poe (1809–1849) was only 2 years old when his mother died and his father left. He went to live with a foster family and received an education but had problems with his foster father. Instabilities led him to search for love with a wife, Virginia, who died young. He then lived in poverty, drank, and drugged himself while writing highly original prose and poetry. His creativity gained him recognition as the father of both the mystery story and the horror story. Photographs and quotes enhance the text. Chronology, Notes, Further Reading, Web Sites, and Index.

1524. **Lawrence, Jacob.** *Harriet and the Promised Land.* Aladdin, 1997. Unpaged. Paper ISBN 978-0-689-80965-1. Grades K–3. This poem about the life of Harriet Tubman (1820–1913) presents her courageous desire to help others be free.

1525. **Leslie, Tonya.** *Abraham Lincoln: A Life of Honesty.* Illustrated by Tina Walski. (Blastoff! Readers: People of Character) Bellweather, 2007. 24pp. ISBN 978-1-60014-091-4. Grades 2–4. Honesty is the distinguishing character trait of Abraham Lincoln (1809–1865), and this volume looks at his dealings with others during the Civil War. Illustrations augment the text. Glossary, Chronology, Further Reading, and Web Sites.

1526. **Locker, Thomas.** *Walking with Henry: Based on the Life and Works of Henry David Thoreau.* Fulcrum, 2002. 32pp. ISBN 978-1-55591-355-7. Grades 2–4. As Henry David Thoreau (1817–1862) walks into the wilderness, he explains his philosophy of living in harmony with nature. Locker uses Thoreau's own words to express his ideas. Illustrations enhance the text.

1527. **Lowery, Linda.** *Aunt Clara Brown: Official Pioneer.* Illustrated by Janice Lee Porter. Carolrhoda, 1999. 48pp. ISBN 978-1-57505-045-4; paper ISBN 978-1-57505-416-2. Grades 2–3. Clara Brown (1800–1885) bought her freedom and moved to Colorado. There she was successful and helped other former slaves while searching for her daughter who was sold as a child. She eventually found her child. Illustrations complement the text. *School Library Journal Best Books for Children.*

1528. **Lutz, Norma Jean.** *Frederick Douglass: Abolitionist and Author.* Chelsea House, 2001. 80pp. ISBN 978-0-7910-6003-2. Grades 3–6. Frederick Douglass (1818–1895), born into slavery, escaped and changed his life. He savored the education he was able to get from a slave owner's wife and other sources, and his perseverance helped him become a writer, an orator, and an abolitionist leader. Illustrations augment the text. Glossary, Chronology, Civil War Timeline, Further Reading, and Index.

1529. McCully, Emily Arnold. *The Bobbin Girl.* Dial, 1996. 34pp. ISBN 978-0-8037-1827-2. Grades 3–5. The life of Harriet Hanson Robinson is the basis for this story. For 15 minutes each hour between 5:30 a.m. and 7 p.m., 10-year-old Rebecca removes full bobbins from spinning frames in a Lowell, Massachusetts, textile mill and replaces them with empty ones. It is 1836, and she is happy to earn money to supplement the rent her mother receives from the girls who board at her house. And she enjoys the friendship and conversations of the older girls in the evenings. When one girl is injured in the mill and the others plan a walk-out, Rebecca's mother lets her decide whether she will join the protest and lose her job or stay inside and save it.

1530. McKissack, Patricia C., and Frederick McKissack. *Frederick Douglass: Leader Against Slavery.* Illustrated by Ned O. (Great African Americans) Enslow, 2002. 32pp. ISBN 978-0-7660-1696-5. Grades 2–4. Five chapters cover the life of Frederick Douglass (1818–1895) as he started life as a slave, was taken from his mother, escaped, and worked as an abolitionist to help free others. He also helped with the Underground Railroad and counted Harriet Tubman and Abraham Lincoln as his friends. Illustrations complement the text. Chronology, Glossary, Further Reading, Web Sites, and Index.

1531. McKissack, Patricia C., and Frederick McKissack. *Sojourner Truth: A Voice for Freedom.* (Great African Americans) Enslow, 2002. 32pp. ISBN 978-0-7660-1693-4. Grades 2–4. Sojourner Truth (1797–1883) was an American abolitionist who preached against slavery and for women's rights after she obtained her own freedom from slavery in 1827. The text looks at her early childhood, her struggles, and her extraordinary achievements. Reproductions, Glossary, and Index.

1532. McKissack, Patricia C., and Frederick McKissack. *Sojourner Truth: Ain't I a Woman.* Scholastic, 1994. 186pp. Paper ISBN 978-0-590-44691-4. Grades 5–8. Isabella (1797–1883) was born a slave in New York and was freed in 1827. Mother of five children, she sued because her son was illegally sold to someone in the South and she became one of the first black women to win a lawsuit against a white. Not until later in her life did she choose the name Sojourner Truth. She wandered from place to place speaking against slavery to anyone who would listen. Six feet tall with a resonant voice, she was a visible and vocal fighter against injustice. Although she could not read, she was a preacher who could quote the Bible word-for-word, an abolitionist, and an activist for the rights of women. Bibliography and Index. *Coretta Scott King Honor Book, American Library Association Best Books for Young Adults, American Library Association Notable Children's Books,* and *Boston Globe/Horn Book Award.*

1533. Marston, Hope Irvin. *Isaac Johnson: From Slave to Stonecutter.* Illustrated by Maria Magdalena Brown. Author House, 2003. 80pp. ISBN 978-1-4033-2754-3; paper ISBN 978-1-4033-2753-6. Grades 4–7. When Isaac Johnson was 7 years old, a sheriff came to the family farm while his father was away and took him, his mother, and brothers away and sold them into slavery. Johnson joined the Union army and when the Civil War ended, he went to Canada. There he became an accomplished stonecutter, with churches, bridges, and other structures to his credit. He wrote the story of his slave days, *Slavery Days in Old Kentucky,* to earn money for his children to attend college. Based on that book, this volume also includes conversations with his descendants. Important Dates, For Further Reading, and Index.

1534. Mattern, Joanne. *Sojourner Truth: Early Abolitionist.* (Women Who Shaped History) PowerKids, 2003. 24pp. ISBN 978-0-8239-6502-1. Grades 1–3. Sojourner Truth (1797–1883) was born a slave named Isabella. She ran away from her master in West Park, New York, who had promised her freedom in 1826, and met Isaac and Maria Van Wagener, who protected her until New York passed the State Emancipation Act in 1827. Truth then became an advocate for abolitionism and women's rights. She gave speeches throughout the north stating her views about justice for all. Photographs augment the text. Glossary, Chronology, Further Reading, Web Sites, and Index.

1535. Meltzer, Milton. *Henry David Thoreau: A Biography.* Twenty-First Century, 2007. 160pp. ISBN 978-0-8225-5893-4. Grades 5–9. Henry David Thoreau (1817–1862) was a naturalist who became known for his writings and was called the sage of Concord, Massachusetts. This text introduces Thoreau in eighteen chapters covering his early life to his college years, living on Walden Pond, refusal to pay taxes and civil disobedience, his abolitionist practices, and his relationship to John Brown at Harper's Ferry. Clearly Thoreau foreshadows some of the movements prevalent in society today as Ralph Waldo Emerson, his contemporary along with Nathaniel Hawthorne, noted in his eulogy. Ellery Channing, and Bronson Alcott participated in his funeral as well. Photographs and illustrations augment the text. Bibliography, Chronology, Notes, Further Reading, Web Sites, and Index.

1536. **Merchant, Peter.** *Sojourner Truth: Path to Glory.* Illustrated by Julia Denos. Aladdin, 2007. 47pp. Paper ISBN 978-0-689-87207-5. Grades K–2. Sojourner Truth (d. 1883), born the slave Isabella Baumfree, became a traveling preacher who advocated rights for African Americans and women. Her strong speaking persuaded many of the importance of rights for all. Illustrations enhance the text. Chronology.

1537. **Miller, William.** *Frederick Douglass: The Last Day of Slavery.* Illustrated by Cedric Lucas. Lee & Low, 1996. Unpaged. Paper ISBN 978-1-880000-42-7. Grades 1–4. Frederick Douglass faced a slave breaker when he was 17. The man apparently struck Douglass with a whip while other slaves watched in disbelief. In his autobiography, however, Douglass says that he struck the first blow and other slaves joined him in the resistance.

1538. **Mortensen, Lori.** *Harriet Tubman: Hero of the Underground Railroad.* Illustrated by Frances Moore. (Biographies) Picture Window, 2007. 24pp. ISBN 978-1-4048-3103-2. Grades K–3. As a young girl, Harriet Tubman (1820?–1913) had to work as her master chose. When she was 24, she married a free black. She herself was still not free, however, and she decided to escape, seeking help from a white woman. This woman directed her to a station on the Underground Railroad. Staying with these people and walking 130 miles on foot, she reached Philadelphia, Pennsylvania, and freedom. She wanted to help others reach freedom and risked her own by returning nineteen times to Maryland and bringing more than 300 slaves back with her. They called her "Moses." During the Civil War, she helped the wounded, spied, and became a soldier who learned about enemy tactics. In New York after the war, she established a shelter for homeless African Americans, helped educate children, and fought for suffrage. Chronology, Further Reading, Bibliography, Glossary, Web Sites, and Index.

1539. **Peltak, Jennifer.** *Edgar Allan Poe.* (Who Wrote That?) Chelsea House, 2002. 120pp. ISBN 978-0-7910-7622-4. Grades 5–8. Peltak covers the main points of the life of Edgar Allan Poe (1809–1849)—his family problems as a youth, his addictions, his marriage to a 15-year-old cousin and reaction after her death, his works, and his own mysterious death. Photographs enhance the text. Bibliography, Chronology, Further Reading, Web Sites, and Index.

1540. **Pinkney, Andrea Davis.** *Sojourner Truth's Step-Stomp Stride.* Illustrated by Brian Pinkney. Hyperion, 2009. 32pp. ISBN 978-0-7868-0767-3. Grades K–3. When Isabella (Belle) Baumfree, Sojourner Truth (1797-1883), was 9 years old, her master sold her away from her slave parents. When the new master refused to give her freedom as promised, she escaped and found her way north where she worked as a maid. Then she started speaking publicly as a feminist and as an abolitionist. In Akron, Ohio, during the 1851 Women's Rights Convention, she gave her famous "And ain't I a woman" speech to show her strength as a female. Beautiful watercolor washes showing a dry brush technique and archival portraits including one of Truth with President Lincoln enhance this biography. Notes and Bibliography.

1541. **Poolos, Jamie.** *Ralph Waldo Emerson: The Father of the American Renaissance.* (Library of American Thinkers) Rosen, 2006. 112pp. ISBN 978-1-4042-0506-2. Grades 5–8. Ralph Waldo Emerson (1803–1882) earned the name of "Father of the American Renaissance" through his nurturing of other writers and his philosophical tenets. He himself was an essayist, philosopher, poet, and the leader of the transcendentalist movement in the early 19th century, a movement he defined in his 1836 essay "Nature." He was a charismatic speaker who supported abolitionism and spoke against slavery. He said that his central doctrine was "the infinitude of the private man." Photographs and illustrations augment the text. Bibliography, Glossary, Chronology, Further Reading, Web Sites, and Index.

1542. Rabin, Staton. *Mr. Lincoln's Boys: Being the Mostly True Adventures of Abraham Lincoln's Trouble-Making Sons, Tad and Willie.* Illustrated by Bagram Ibatoulline. Viking, 2008. Unpaged. ISBN 978-0-670-06169-3. Grades 1–4. When Abraham Lincoln served in the White House, his sons Tad and Willie lived there as well. They were rambunctious and liked to play jokes. Among their exploits was tying all the bells in the house together and ringing them so that the servants did not know who had called. They interrupted their father during a meeting about the Civil War and jumped up and down on his knees. On another day, they asked for a toy soldier's pardon. Much of the information comes from family friend Julia Taft's writing. Illustrations enhance the text. Bibliography and Web Sites.

1543. Ransom, Candice F. *Clara Barton.* (History Maker Bios) Lerner, 2003. 48pp. ISBN 978-0-8225-4677-1. Grades 3–5. Clara Barton (1821–1912) showed her intelligence as a young child although she was shy. She discovered at the age of 40 that she could help by nursing the sick and wounded on Civil War battlefields. She started a school and began the American Red Cross. Illustrations augment the text. Bibliography, Further Reading, Glossary, Maps, Timeline, Web Sites, and Index.

1544. Ransom, Candice F. *Robert E. Lee.* (History Maker Bios) Lerner, 2006. 48pp. ISBN 978-0-8225-2437-3. Grades 3–5. Robert E. Lee (1807–1870), a Virginia native, was a Confederate general during the Civil War. The five chapters discuss his life as a son, soldier, and war hero. Illustrations augment the text. Bibliography, Further Reading, Glossary, Maps, Timeline, Web Sites, and Index.

1545. Rappaport, Doreen. *Abe's Honest Words: The Life of Abraham Lincoln.* Illustrated by Kadir Nelson. Hyperion, 2008. 48pp. ISBN 978-1-4231-0408-7. Grades 3–6. A free-verse life of Abraham Lincoln (1809–1865) covering his poverty, early political career, his struggle to preserve the Union, and his actions to abolish slavery after first seeing it in New Orleans. The illustrations show Lincoln at the various periods of his life. Bibliography, Notes, Chronology, and Further Reading. *Capitol Choices Noteworthy Titles* (Washington, D.C.).

1546. Rappaport, Doreen. *Escape from Slavery: Five Journeys to Freedom.* Illustrated by Charles Lilly. Trophy, 1999. 117pp. Paper ISBN 978-0-06-446169-6. Grades 4–6. Rappaport tells five stories of slaves who escaped their bondage. They are Eliza, who tried to cross a melting river of ice to save her 2-year-old daughter; Selena and Cornelia Jackson, who deceived their master with a plan for a free black settlement in Cabin Creek, Indiana; Henry Brown, who shipped himself out of slavery in a box; Jane Johnson, who faced her master in a Philadelphia courtroom; and Ellen and William Craft, who dressed as an invalid white master and slave as they traveled to the North by steamship, train, and coach. Bibliography.

1547. Raum, Elizabeth. *Julia Ward Howe.* (American Lives) Raintree, 2004. 32pp. ISBN 978-1-4034-4995-5; paper ISBN 978-1-4034-5708-0. Grades 2–4. Julia Ward Howe (1819–1910) spent her childhood in New England and wrote poetry before she married her doctor husband. Her poems were later published, as was a song she wrote in honor of her country, *The Battle Hymn of the Republic.* She became a proponent of peace and won honors for her willingness to support peace and women's suffrage. Illustrations complement the text. Glossary, Further Reading, and Index.

1548. Rockwell, Anne. *Only Passing Through: The Story of Sojourner Truth.* Knopf, 2000. Unpaged. ISBN 978-0-679-89186-4; Dragonfly, 2002, paper ISBN 978-0-440-41766-8. Grades 4–8. Sojourner Truth (d. 1883) was born into slavery in New York and named Isabella. At the age of 9, her master sold her away from her parents. She later became one of the great abolitionists as a free black. She renamed herself Sojourner and traveled around telling people what slave life was. Six feet tall, she was an imposing figure, and her message moved many. Acrylic paintings enhance the text.

1549. Roop, Peter, and Connie Roop. *Sojourner Truth.* Scholastic, 2003. 128pp. Paper ISBN 978-0-439-26323-8. Grades 3–5. Based on primary resources including letters, newpaper articles, photographs, and other information, this volume covers the life of Sojourner Truth (1797–1883), the slave who freed herself and her children and then spent her life as an abolitionist and advocate of women's rights. She was illiterate, and dictated her autobiography to a friend. Others wrote down her speeches against slavery, for women, and for social reforms. In 1981 she was inducted into the National Women's Hall of Fame. Bibliography, Chronology, Further Reading, Web Sites, and Index.

1550. Russell, Sharman Apt. *Frederick Douglass: Abolitionist Editor.* Chelsea House, 2004. 96pp. ISBN 978-0-7910-8157-0. Grades 5 up. Frederick Douglass (1818–1895) escaped slavery and became an orator, writer, and leader in the antislavery movement in the early 19th century. His newspaper, the *North Star,* helped others learn what was happening in the abolitionist movement. Black-and-white illustrations enhance the text. Bibliography, Chronology, and Index.

1551. St. George, Judith. *Stand Tall, Abe Lincoln.* Illustrated by Matt Faulkner. Philomel, 2005. Unpaged. ISBN 978-0-399-24174-1. Grades 1–4. Abraham Lincoln (1809–1865) showed early that he cared about fairness and was aware of the feelings of other people. His family, especially his mother and stepmother, helped Lincoln feel that he could accomplish much in his life, and he proved them correct. Humorous illustrations add humanity to this account of Lincoln's early life. Bibliography.

1552. Sandburg, Carl. *Abe Lincoln Grows Up.* See entry 1439.

1553. Sandler, Martin W. *Lincoln Through the Lens: How Photography Revealed and Shaped an Extraordinary Life.* Walker, 2008. 97pp. ISBN 978-0-8027-9666-0. Grades 5 up. This biography of Abraham Lincoln (1809–1865) offers photographs of him and his family throughout his life. It also contains images of other politicians, Civil War generals loyal to both sides, the battlefield, and the site of the Gettysburg address. Sandler discusses Mathew Brady, Lincoln's primary photographer. There is a picture of Lincoln's second inauguration with several of his conspirators in the background, including John Wilkes Booth. The accompanying text meshes well with the images presented. Notes.

1554. Sapp, Richard. *Ulysses S. Grant and the Road to Appomattox.* (In the Footsteps of American Heroes) World Almanac, 2005. 64pp. ISBN 978-0-8368-6431-1; paper ISBN 978-0-8368-6433-5. Grades 5–8. This biography of Ulysses S. Grant (1822–1885) presents his life and accomplishments. He grew up in Point Pleasant, Ohio, before attending West Point and preparing himself to become the important Union military leader in the Civil War. His battles led him to Appomattox courthouse to accept Robert E. Lee's surrender of the Confederate forces. Then he was elected president. The final chapter covers the troubles of Grant's presidency and his reputation. Photographs and illustrations augment the text. Chronology and Web Sites.

1555. Schott, Jane A. *Abraham Lincoln.* (History Maker Bios) Lerner, 2002. 48pp. ISBN 978-0-8225-0196-1. Grades 3–5. Abraham Lincoln (1809–1865) grew up in Illinois, earning the nicknames "Honest Abe" and "the Rail-Splitter." He eventually was elected to public office. When he decided to run for president, he won; however, the argument over slavery that led to the Civil War coincided with his term in office. His Emancipation Proclamation in 1863 freed the slaves. But John Wilkes Booth assassinated him before the war ended, and he could not oversee the reconstruction effort. Illustrations augment the text. Bibliography, Further Reading, Glossary, Maps, Timeline, Web Sites, and Index.

1556. Schroeder, Alan. *Minty: A Story of Young Harriet Tubman.* Illustrated by Jerry Pinkney. Dial, 1996. 40pp. ISBN 978-0-8037-1888-3; Puffin, 2000, paper ISBN 978-0-14-056196-8. Grades K–3. Minty (Araminta) was too clumsy to work in the house and Mistress Brodas sent her to work in the fields. Although the field hands warned her to avoid any confrontations, she still found herself in trouble. The overseer whipped her and threatened to sell her "downstream." Knowing she would probably not change, her father taught her how to cope outdoors and how to navigate. These skills helped her survive when she attempted to escape and when she later became the Harriet Tubman who led the Underground Railroad.

1557. Silverthorne, Elizabeth. *Louisa May Alcott.* Chelsea House, 2002. 119pp. ISBN 978-0-7910-6721-5. Grades 4–7. Louisa May Alcott (1832–1888) became famous for *Little Women,* a story that paralleled her own family's life. This same family also influenced the rest of her writing, as did the social forces of the time, including the Civil War. Archival photographs enhance the text. Bibliography and Index.

1558. Slade, Suzanne. *Frederick Douglass: Writer, Speaker, and Opponent of Slavery.* Illustrated by Robert McGuire. (Biographies) Picture Window, 2007. 24pp. ISBN 978-1-4048-3102-5. Grades K–3. Frederick Bailey (1818–1895) was born a slave in Tuckahoe, Maryland. His grandmother raised him until his owner made him work when he was 7. At the age of 8, he went to the Auld family in Baltimore, where Mrs. Auld broke the law by teaching him to read. Douglass asked neighborhood boys to teach him writing, and he read anything he could find. His research showed him that many people disapproved of slavery. He eventually escaped by boat and train to New York City in 1838 and married Anna Murray, the Baltimore woman who had helped him. He moved further north to New Bedford, Massachusetts, and changed his name to Douglass. He began speaking against slavery, and his powerful delivery made him an asset for the abolitionists. He wrote a book about his life in 1845 and started a newspaper in 1847, the *North Star*. After the Civil War, he went to Washington and became the U.S. Marshal for the city, continuing to work until he died. Chronology, Further Reading, Bibliography, Glossary, Web Sites, and Index.

1559. Slade, Suzanne. *Sojourner Truth: Preacher for Freedom and Equality.* Illustrated by Natascha Alex Blanks. (Biographies) Picture Window, 2008. 24pp. ISBN 978-1-4048-3726-3. Grades K–3. Isabella was born in New York in 1797 to slaves who spoke Dutch. The family's owner sold all but her younger brother Peter when she was 9, and her new owners, Mr. and Mrs. Neely, spoke English. Her parents were too old to sell, so the former owner's surviving family gave them land on which to grow crops until they died. Sojourner was then sold two more times before marrying Tom, another slave, when she was 18. They had five children whom she took with her into the fields while she worked. In 1827, when she was 29, a New York law freed the slaves in the state. Isabella later became a preacher. She was nearly 6 feet tall, and many people came to hear her speak against slavery. In 1843 she changed her name to Sojourner Truth. She wrote her life story in 1850, and after the Civil War she continued to fight for rights of women and freed slaves. At the time of her death, she lived in Battle Creek, Michigan. Chronology, Further Reading, Bibliography, Glossary, Web Sites, and Index.

1560. Stearns, Dan. *Harriet Tubman and the Underground Railroad.* (In the Footsteps of American Heroes) World Almanac, 2006. 64pp. ISBN 978-0-8368-6428-1; 2005, paper ISBN 978-0-8368-6433-5. Grades 5–8. This examination of Harriet Tubman (1820?–1913) focuses on her involvement in the Underground Railroad during the Civil War. She risked her own life to rescue runaway slaves and escort them to safety. For this work she was known as "Moses." She also worked as a nurse and a spy. The text also contains information about the Fugitive Slave Act and John Brown. Illustrations complement the text. Notes.

1561. Stone, Tanya Lee. *Elizabeth Leads the Way: Elizabeth Cady Stanton and the Right to Vote.* Illustrated by Rebecca Gibbon. Henry Holt, 2008. Unpaged. ISBN 978-0-8050-7903-6. Grades 1–4. Elizabeth Cady Stanton (1815–1902) began championing women's rights as soon as she graduated from college. This book covers key events in her life—when she refused to take her abolitionist husband's name and when she founded the women's rights movement at Seneca Falls, New York, in 1848. Her tireless work led to women achieving the right to vote. Illustrations complement the text.

1562. Sullivan, George. *Abraham Lincoln.* (In Their Own Words) Scholastic, 2000. 128pp. Paper ISBN 978-0-439-09554-9. Grades 3–6. In this biography of Abraham Lincoln (1809–1865), Sullivan uses speeches and letters to present Lincoln's life and choices. Illustrations augment the text. Chronology, Further Resources, Bibliography, and Index.

1563. Swain, Gwenyth. *Dred and Harriet Scott: A Family's Struggle for Freedom.* Borealis, 2004. 102pp. Paper ISBN 978-0-87351-483-5. Grades 5–9. When the United States Supreme Court decided in "Dred Scott v. Sandford" that Dred Scott could not have his freedom, abolitionists became furious, and the situation led to the Civil War. Dred Scott had lived on the Blow family's Virginia plantation before he traveled with his new owner, a military doctor, to Alabama, Missouri, Illinois and the area that would eventually become Minnesota. He met his wife Harriet at Fort Snelling, near St. Paul, Minnesota, and they traveled with their master to Florida and to Missouri, settling in St. Louis. Both Dred and Harriet were hired out for wages, and at that time they began collecting information to use in their suit for freedom, submitted in 1846. After moving through the local and state courts, their case reached the Supreme Court in 1857. The Scotts wanted their children, Elisa and Lizzie, to live as free citizens, and they refused to settle for less. Scott's owner returned him to the Blow family in Missouri, who could free him, and on May 26, 1857, he and his family received their freedom. Photographs, Reproductions, Bibliography, Chronology, Glossary, Notes, Web Sites, and Index.

1564. Swain, Gwenyth. *The Road to Seneca Falls: A Story About Elizabeth Cady Stanton.* Illustrated by Mary O'Keefe Young. Carolrhoda, 1995. 64pp. ISBN 978-0-87614-947-8. Grades 3–6. Elizabeth Cady Stanton (1815–1902) heard her father say many times that he wished she had been a boy. He was especially distressed after the death of her older brother. Elizabeth decided to be like a boy and studied Greek, Latin, and other rigorous subjects. She eventually started going to her father's law office. When Elizabeth heard a widow's distress when her son would not let her live in her own house, she discovered the discrimination against women in the laws. She devoted her life to changing those laws. After she met Lucretia Mott, she and her husband, Henry, became spokespersons for women and slaves. Bibliography and Index.

1565. Taylor, Kimberly Hayes. *Black Abolitionists and Freedom Fighters.* Oliver, 1996. 160pp. ISBN 978-1-881508-30-4. Grades 5 up. Taylor looks at eight African American leaders of the abolitionist and freedom fighter movements: Richard Allen (1760–1831), Sojourner Truth (1797?–1883), Nat Turner (1800–1831), Henry Highland Garnet (1815–1882), Frederick Douglass (1818–1895), Harriet Ross Tubman (1820–1913), Booker T. Washington (1856–1915), and Mary Church Terrell (1863–1954). An additional chapter presents capsules of information on additional individuals of note. Bibliography and Index.

1566. Trump, Fred. *Lincoln's Little Girl: A True Story.* Illustrated by Kit Wray. Boyds Mills, 2000. 184pp. Paper ISBN 978-1-56397-852-4. Grades 5–8. When Grace Bedell (b. 1848 or 1849) was 11 in 1860, she wrote Abraham Lincoln a letter. She suggested that he grow whiskers because they would increase his chances of becoming president. This book goes on to document Bedell's later life— her husband's service in the Civil War, homesteading in Kansas, fighting grasshopper plagues, tornadoes, prairie fires, and other disasters.

1567. Turner, Glennette Tilley. *An Apple for Harriet Tubman.* Illustrated by Susan Keeter. Whitman, 2006. 32pp. ISBN 978-0-8075-0395-9. Grades 1–4. When Harriet Tubman (1820?–1913) was 7 years old, she had the responsibility of looking after the baby of an unpleasant white woman, who whipped her. Later she ate an apple from a man's orchard, and he lashed her. The scars from these beatings lasted Tubman's entire life. When Tubman was able to purchase her own home in upstate New York, she planted many apple trees and shared the fruit with her neighbors. Paintings intensify the text.

1568. Waxman, Laura Hamilton. *Sojourner Truth.* (History Maker Bios) Lerner, 2008. 48pp. ISBN 978-0-8225-7172-8. Grades 3–5. Waxman presents the life of Sojourner Truth (d. 1883) and her work as an abolitionist. The five chapters cover her life in New York as a slave, her freedom, her new name and life, how she helped others, and how she continued to fight for rights. Illustrations augment the text. Bibliography, Further Reading, Glossary, Maps, Timeline, Web Sites, and Index.

1569. Weatherford, Carole Boston. *Moses: When Harriet Tubman Led Her People to Freedom.* Illustrated by Kadir Nelson. Hyperion, 2006. 42pp. ISBN 978-0-7868-5175-1. Grades 2–5. Harriet Tubman (1820?–1913) follows the voice of God when she learns she is about to be sold from a Maryland plantation to one further south. She escapes and then returns many times, risking her own freedom, to help others. Her selfless work as a conductor on the Underground Railroad earns her the name "Moses," because she takes these desperate slaves to the "promised land." Luminous illustrations accompany the text. *Horn Book Fanfare, Caldecott Honor, School Library Journal Best Books for Children, Bulletin Blue Ribbon,* and *Capitol Choices Noteworthy Titles* (Washington, D.C.).

1570. Weidt, Maryann N. *Harriet Tubman.* (History Maker Bios) Lerner, 2003. 48pp. ISBN 978-0-8225-4676-4. Grades 3–5. Harriet Tubman (1820?–1913), born as Harriet Ross near Bucktown, Maryland, was a slave along with her family of ten siblings. Eventually she escaped north, but she wanted to rescue others from slavery and worked on the Underground Railroad, earning the name "Moses." The five chapters of the text recount her childhood, escape, dangerous returns to the South, war hero status, and her life after the war. Illustrations augment the text. Bibliography, Further Reading, Glossary, Maps, Timeline, Web Sites, and Index.

1571. Welch, Catherine, and Tim Parlin. *Frederick Douglass.* (History Maker Bios) Lerner, 2002. 48pp. ISBN 978-0-8225-4672-6. Grades 3–5. Frederick Douglass (1818–1895), son of a white man and an African American woman, was a runaway slave who became an abolitionist, a suffragist, a writer, a public speaker, an acquaintance of John Brown, and an adviser to Abraham Lincoln. His master's wife had taught to read and write even though it was illegal, and he used this ability to start a newspaper and speak to others about the ills of slavery. Illustrations augment the text. Bibliography, Further Reading, Glossary, Maps, Timeline, Web Sites, and Index.

1572. Whiting, Jim. *Edgar Allan Poe.* Mitchell Lane, 2005. 48pp. ISBN 978-1-58415-373-3. Grades 5–8. This brief biography looks at the life and work of Edgar Allan Poe (1809–1849), including his depression, alcohol dependency, and loss of loved ones. Photographs and illustrations complement the text.

1573. Williams, Jean Kinney. *Bridget "Biddy" Mason: From Slave to Businesswoman.* (Signature Lives) Compass Point, 2005. 112pp. ISBN 978-0-7565-1001-5; paper ISBN 978-0-7565-1843-1. Grades 5–8. Bridget "Biddy" Mason (1818–1891), lived in Georgia, Mississippi, and Utah Territory, on the trail of Mormons, before her owner moved her to California. There she sued for her freedom and was declared "free forever." Then she began to work as a nurse. Photographs and illustrations augment the text. Bibliography, Further Reading, Web Sites, and Index.

1574. Winters, Kay. *Abe Lincoln: The Boy Who Loved Books.* Illustrated by Nancy Carpenter. Simon & Schuster, 2003. Unpaged. ISBN 978-0-689-82554-5; Aladdin, 2006, paper ISBN 978-1-416-91268-2. Grades K–2. This illustrated biography of Abraham Lincoln (1809–1865) focuses on his childhood love of reading. Even though he was unable to attend school formally, once he learned to read, he devoured everything he could find. Books were expensive and not readily available, especially when his family had to move to a camp with no wall on one side. Illustrations enhance the text. *Picture Book Award* (Georgia) nomination and *Keystone to Reading Book Award* (Pennsylvania) nomination.

Graphic Novels, Biographies, and Histories

1575. Burgan, Michael. *Nat Turner's Slave Rebellion.* Illustrated by Richard Dominquez and Bob Wiacek. Graphic Library, 2006. 32pp. ISBN 978-0-7368-5490-0; paper ISBN 978-0-7368-6879-2. Grades 3–5. Educated illegally in the home of one of his masters, Nat Turner (1800?–1831) knew the horrors of slavery. In 1831 he decided to organize a rebellion against the slave owners. Planned for July 4, it was delayed to August 21 because of illness and ongoing debate. The rebels traveled from house to house freeing slaves and killing any white people they saw. By the time a militia reached them, they had killed fifty-five people. Turner was not caught until October 30 and was tried, convicted, and hung on November 11. Illustrations augment the text. Bibliography, Glossary, Further Reading, and Index.

1576. Dunn, Joe. *Abraham Lincoln.* Illustrated by Rod Espinosa. Graphic Planet, 2007. 32pp. ISBN 978-1-60270-064-2. Grades 3–5. This fictional graphic biography presents the life of Abraham Lincoln (1809–1865) with created dialogue. Pictures augment the text. Chronology, Further Reading, Glossary, Web Sites, and Index.

1577. Glaser, Jason. *John Brown's Raid on Harper's Ferry.* Illustrated by Al Milgrom, Bill Anderson, and Charles Barnett. Graphic Library, 2005. 32pp. ISBN 978-0-7368-4369-0; paper ISBN 978-0-7368-9679-5. Grades 3–5. Abolitionist John Brown (1800–1859) thought an armed insurrection would end slavery. In 1859 he led a raid on the federal armory at Harpers Ferry, Virginia (now West Virginia), and seized the federal arsenal. Seven people died and ten more were injured. He wanted to arm slaves with the weapons, but within thirty-six yours, his men had either fled or been captured or killed. Federal forces captured Brown, tried him for treason, and executed him by hanging in Charles Town, Virginia. Illustrations enhance the text. Bibliography, Glossary, Further Reading, and Index.

1578. Lassieur, Allison. *Clara Barton: Angel of the Battlefield.* (Graphic Biographies) Graphic Library, 2005. 32pp. ISBN 978-0-7368-4632-5; paper ISBN 978-0-7368-9669-6. Grades 3–5. This short graphic biography of Clara Barton (1821–1912) reveals the story of a woman who wanted to help people. She became a nurse during the Civil War, tending to wounded soldiers. A yellow background sets direct quotes from Barton apart from the fictional aspect of the narration. Web Sites.

1579. Lemke, Donald B. *The Brave Escape of Ellen and Wiliam Craft.* Illustrated by Phil Miller and Charles Barnett, III. Graphic Library, 2005. 32pp. ISBN 978-0-7368-4973-9; paper ISBN 978-0-7368-6203-5. Grades 3–5. Slaves Ellen and William Craft married in 1846. Ellen, daughter of a slave and her white master, was light-skinned enough to disguise herself as a white man. She pretended that her husband, William, was her servant. In 1848 they boarded a train in Macon for Savannah and continued by steamship to Philadelphia. They told others that they were getting medical attention for Ellen in Philadelphia and arrived there on December 25, 1848. Illustrations enhance the text. Bibliography, Glossary, Further Reading, and Index.

1580. Martin, Michael. *Harriet Tubman and the Underground Railroad.* Illustrated by Dave Hoover and Bill Anderson. Graphic Library, 2005. 32pp. ISBN 978-0-7368-3829-0; paper ISBN 978-0-7368-9345-6. Grades 3–5. After escaping from slavery in Maryland, Harriet Tubman returned nearly three hundred times to rescue other slaves and take them to Underground Railroad stops on their way to freedom. People called her "Moses" for taking others to the "promised land." Illustrations augment the text. Bibliography, Glossary, Further Reading, and Index.

1581. Robbins, Trina. *Elizabeth Blackwell: America's First Woman Doctor.* (Graphic Biographies) Graphic Library, 2005. 32pp. ISBN 978-0-7368-6497-8; paper ISBN 978-0-7368-9660-3. Grades 3–5. This short graphic biography of Elizabeth Blackwell (1821–1910) relates the story of a woman who wanted to be a doctor. Refused entry to all but one medical school, she achieved her goal and then opened a school for women. A yellow background sets direct quotes from Blackwell apart from the fictional aspect of the narration. Web Sites.

DVDs

1582. *Abraham Lincoln.* (Great Americans for Children) Library Video, 2002. 23 mins. Grades K–4. Born in rural Kentucky, Abraham Lincoln rose to the position of president of the United States and led the country during the dark times of the Civil War. He determined to maintain the union of North and South throughout the conflict and to speak against slavery. Without his efforts, the country might not exist, and slavery might not have ended.

1583. *Abraham Lincoln: Traditional Values.* Bestrom Agency, 2005. 47 mins. Grades K–5. Gerald Bestrom, an Abraham Lincoln re-enactor, offers a one-man show dressed as Lincoln in a black suit and a stovepipe hat. He talks about books Abe read, and the difficulty in getting them, how children were expected to recite, and the clothing he wore as a child—buckskin pants and a coonskin cap. Then he recites the Gettysburg Address after having his audience sing "America the Beautiful."

1584. *Civil War: American Against American.* 3 DVDs, 35 mins. ea. Grades 4–7. Using original music, music of the period, and reenactments, this three-part DVD chronicles the lives of children from 1850 to 1865. The first volume, 1850 to 1860 contrasts black children in the South with white children in the North and South. The second volume discusses the preparations for the war and the first Battle of Bull Run. The final volume covers the rest of the war and its continued effect on people today. Among the individuals presented are James Thomas, a former slave who became a wealthy man, and the Grimke sisters, who were important abolitionist leaders.

1585. *Harriet Tubman.* (Great Americans for Children) Library Video, 2003. 23 mins. ISBN 978-1-57225-545-6. Grades K–4. Harriet Tubman (1820?–1913) escaped from slavery and then risked recapture—or her life—by returning to help hundreds of others reach freedom. She was an important conductor on the Underground Railroad.

1586. *Henry Builds a Cabin.* Weston Woods, 2004. 7:16 mins. ISBN 978-1-55592-890-2. Grades K–3. James Naughton narrates the text of this picture book in an iconographic production. Limited animation shows moving arms and butterflies. The DVD includes footage of the exterior and interior of Thoreau's cabin and pictures of Walden Pond.

1587. *Heroes of Freedom: Harriet Tubman and Rosa Parks.* Mazzarella Media, 2008. 22 mins. ISBN 978-1-934119-57-0. Grades 3–8. This DVD begins by describing Harriet Tubman's life as a slave, what she had to do and how she was punished and separated from her family. Other chapters highlight her Underground Railroad work and her escape to freedom during the Civil War. She died in 1913, the same year that Rosa Parks was born. This second section of the program looks at life for African Americans at the time, the rise of the civil rights movement, and Parks's part in the defiance of Jim Crow laws. It reveals that twelve years before Rosa Parks was arrested, she had an incident with the same bus driver. Other topics presented are the Ku Klux Klan, school desegregation, the NAACP, and the Civil Rights Act of 1964. The DVD uses live action, shot at restoration villages.

1588. *Safe Harbor: A Story of the Underground Railroad.* Main Street Media, 2003. 56 mins. Grades 5 up. This DVD looks at the contributions of the Great Lakes region to the Underground Railroad and the many individuals of all races, on farms and in towns, who risked their lives to help escaped slaves reach freedom. These slaves had instructions for following "the drinking gourd" and "wading in the water," directions embedded in spirituals. When they traveled through Pennsylvania, they were led to Lake Erie, the crossing place into Canada. Harry T. Burleigh's song, transcribed after hearing his former slave grandfather sing it, serves as a fitting backdrop to the story.

Compact Discs

1589. Adler, David A. *A Picture Book of Harriet Tubman.* Narrated by Gail Nelson. Live Oak Media, 2005. 1 CD; 14:40 mins. ISBN 978-1-59519-385-8. Grades 1–3. See entry 1482.

1590. Avi. *The Man Who Was Poe.* Narrated by George Guidall. Recorded Books, 1997. 5 CDs; 5.25 hrs. ISBN 978-0-7887-0202-0. Grades 5–10. See entry 1378.

1591. Brill, Marlene Targ. *Allen Jay and the Underground Railroad.* Live Oak Media, 2007. 1 CD; 19:28 mins. ISBN 978-1-59519-949-2. Grades 2–4. See entry 1381.

1592. Eickhoff, Diane. *Frontier Freedom Fighter: The Story of Clarina Nichols.* Narrated by Diane Eickhoff. Quindaro, 2006. 75 mins. ISBN 978-0-9764434-7-6. Grades 5 up. Clarina Nichols (1810–1885), one of America's first female newspaper editors, crossed the American West speaking in favor of rights for women, abolition, and temperance before these subjects interested many people. Eickhoff portrays this woman who overcame difficulties of three small children and an irrational first husband to help others. Her second marriage to editor

George Nichols was happy but also difficult because she had to relocate, work, and fight illness.

1593. Freedman, Russell. *Lincoln: A Photobiography.* Narrated by Robert Petkoff. Listening Library, 2008. 2 CDs; 2 1/2 hrs. ISBN 978-0-7393-7255-5. Grades 5 up. See entry 1503.

1594. Lester, Julius. *Day of Tears: A Novel in Dialogue.* Recorded Books, 2006. 3 CDs; 3 hrs. ISBN 978-1-4193-6811-0. Grades 5–9. See entry 1419.

1595. *New Manchester Girl.* Narrated by Cathy Kaemmerlen. Tattling Tales, 2003. 45mins. ISBN 978-0-9714236-1-9. Grades 5–11. When Gen. William Tecumseh Sherman pillaged the South during the Civil War, he also destroyed the mills. The daughter of Walter Washington Stewart, Scynthia worked in a textile mill in New Manchester, Georgia, until the Confederate Army commandeered it to make goods. She and her family were taken to Louisville, Kentucky, as prisoners of war. Eventually they all were reunited and returned home to survive on strawberries for the rest of the year. This true story, told by actress Cathy Kaemmerlen, took place from 1851 to 1867.

THE CIVIL WAR, 1861–1865

Historical Fiction and Fantasy

1596. Alphin, Elaine Marie. *Ghost Soldier.* Henry Holt, 2001. 216pp. ISBN 978-0-8050-6158-1. Grades 5–7. Alexander, 13, goes with his father to North Carolina while his father is trying to decide if he will remarry and move there. When the new lady friend and her two children go with them to a Civil War reenactment, Alexander meets Richeson Francis Chamblee, the ghost of a Confederate soldier ghost who wants help finding his family and learning what happened to his sister after Sherman's march through the area. Alex's gift of communing with spirits is something his father, a computer programmer, could never understand so Alex tries to help Richeson by going to a museum to investigate. During the process, Richeson helps him understand that his mother left of her own will and that his father needs to start a new life.

1597. Avi. *Iron Thunder: The Battle Between the Monitor and the Merrimac.* (I Witness) Hyperion, 2007. 205pp. ISBN 978-1-4231-0446-9. Grades 4–8. In 1862, after his father is killed in a Civil War battle, 13-year-old Tom Carroll must get a job to support the family. He finds one at the Brooklyn Navy Yard working on "Ericsson's Folly," the ironclad destined to become the *Monitor.* Northern "Copperheads" who sympathize with the Rebels are particularly interested in its development and Tom's job makes him a target of their attention. Eventually Tom moves on board the *Monitor* to protect it. When the ship joins the Union blockade fleet and fights the *Merrimac,* Tom feels proud of his contribution. Archival photographs enhance the text. Glossary and Note.

1598. Beatty, Patricia. *Turn Homeward, Hannalee.* Beech Tree, 1999. 208pp. Paper ISBN 978-0-688-16676-2. Grades 5–9. In 1864 the Yankees accuse Hannalee and her brother of treason (because they were helping the Confederacy by making cloth) and transport them from Georgia to Indiana to work in textile mills there. Hannalee disguises herself as a boy and escapes. She finds her brother and uses her mill wages to pay for train tickets to Nashville. On their long journey home, they go through a horrible battle, but a peddler helps them survive. Their older brother returns, unlike their father, but missing one arm. The family survives the war, but barely.

1599. Blackwood, Gary L. *Second Sight.* Speak, 2007. 268pp. Paper ISBN 978-0-14-240747-9. Grades 5–8. In 1864 Joseph Ehrlich and his father, Nicholas, perform their mind-reading act in Washington, D.C., and begin to draw larger and larger crowds. Joseph enjoys meeting the famous John Wilkes Booth. Joseph forms a close bond with an orphan named Cassandra, who really does have second sight. She is increasingly disturbed about her dreams and visions concerning President Lincoln, including his murder. She tells Joseph, and he plans how to prevent this terrible thing from happening. *Dorothy Canfield Fisher Children's Book Award* (Vermont) nomination.

1600. Borden, Louise W. *A. Lincoln and Me.* Illustrated by Ted Lewin. Scholastic, 2001. 32pp. Paper ISBN 978-0-590-45715-6. Grades 4–8. Ben shares his birthday, February 12th, with Abraham Lincoln and discovers he has similar physical traits as well. Tall, gangly, and uncoordinated, the boy feels a kinship with Lincoln. Ben's friends call him "Butterfingers" or "Butterfeet," and Ben knows that Lincoln's friends also nicknamed him "gorilla" or "baboon." Ben admires Lincoln for becoming president and passing the Emancipation Proclamation, and he hopes that he also shares some of the traits that led to Lincoln's success and that he will excel at something as he becomes older. *Florida Reading Association Children's Book Award* nomination, *SCASL Book Award* (South Carolina) nomination; *Nevada Young Readers Award* nomination.

1601. Bruchac, Joseph. *March Toward the Thunder.* Dial, 2008. 304pp. ISBN 978-0-8037-3188-2. Grades 5–9. Fifteen-year-old Louis Nollette, an Abenaki Indian from Canada, decides to join New York's Irish Brigade in 1864 to fight for the Union in the Civil War. He sees the reality of battle from the hospitals and their doctors, called "sawbones" for a good reason, and he notes that experienced soldiers would not go into battle without their names pinned to their uniforms. His friend, Artis, a Mohawk, and he trade insults that other soldiers do not understand, and they face prejudice as well. Among the figures he encounters are Clara Barton, Walt Whitman, President Lincoln, and General Grant. Maps and Bibliography.

1602. Crisp, Marty. *Private Captain: A Story of Gettysburg.* Puffin, 2002. 293pp. Paper ISBN 978-0-698-11969-7. Grades 5–8. Twelve-year-old Ben travels with his dog Captain, a Jersey cow, and his unwelcome younger cousin Danny, 11, to Gettysburg to find his older brother Reuben. Ben's father has died, and Ben sneaked away from home during the night to ask Reuben to come home and take care of the family store. Ben finds himself in the middle of the Battle of Gettysburg. He does what he can to help, tending to the wounded and trying to remove dead animals from the field. He has a chance meeting with Mathew Brady before he sends Captain to find Reuben. Captain succeeds.

1603. Denslow, Sharon Phillips. *All Their Names Were Courage: A Novel of the Civil War.* Tom Green County Historical, 2003. 135pp. ISBN 978-0-06-623810-4. Grades 2–6. In 1862 William Burd, a soldier, exchanges letters with his 11-year-old sister Sallie, as she also writes to Confederate and Union generals about their horses. She wants to write a book that will be illustrated by her friend Isaac. She receives responses from Lee and Grant. Lee talks about his horse Traveler. Stonewall Jackson has Little Sorrel. By the time the book is almost finished the war ends and William returns home.

1604. Donahue, John. *An Island Far from Home.* Carolrhoda, 1997. 179pp. Paper ISBN 978-1-57505-076-8. Grades 4–7. During the present time, a boy and his grandfather find a button in an attic trunk emblazoned with an "A." The grandfather knows no one whose name begins with "A." The next chapter shifts to Tilton, Massachusetts, in 1864, when Joshua Loring is 12. Joshua hopes to join the army to fight against the enemy who killed his father. His Uncle Robert, a civilian lawyer and a wartime deputy commander of a fort called George's Island, tries to convince him that war is terrible. Uncle Robert gets Joshua to write to John, a young rebel soldier imprisoned on George's Island. Joshua quickly understands that John is very much like him. *Notable Children's Trade Books in the Field of Social Studies, IRA Children's Book Award*, and *Society of School Librarians Outstanding Book*.

1605. Durrant, Lynda. *Imperfections.* Clarion, 2008. ISBN 978-0-547-00357-3. Grades 5–10. Rosemary Elizabeth's mother takes 14-year-old Rosemary, her younger brother Isaac, and her baby sister Anne, to the Shaker community of Pleasant Hill, Kentucky, and leaves them. Rosemary is delighted to escape her father's abuse and the fear of the Civil War in this protected group. The Shakers believe they have Heaven on earth if they live in perfect order. Rosemary, as Sister Bess, sleeps on her back with her hands folded across her chest, walks with her right foot first, and takes everything with her right hand. Isaac accepts all the rules in his anxiety, but Rosemary balks at some strictures, making artistic rather than perfect brooms and arguing to allow kittens in the barns. As she continues to display her own imperfections, she begins to realize that everyone there is merely trying to hide aspects of themselves that they want to deny. She decides to make peace with the village and prepare herself for life outside it.

1606. Durrant, Lynda. *My Last Skirt: The Story of Jennie Hodgers, Union Soldier.* Clarion, 2006. 199pp. ISBN 978-0-618-57490-2. Grades 5–8. While still in Ireland, Jennie Hodgers decided to disguise herself as a man to earn a higher salary, and when she immigrates to the United States after her father's death, she keeps the disguise and takes the name Albert Cashier. In this role, she becomes a Union soldier in the 95th Illinois Infantry. She fights in the South, has sexual feelings toward fellow soldier Frank Moore, and feels lonely. She does not reveal her true gender for fifty years, and she becomes the first woman to get a Civil War veteran's pension. Bibliography and Web Sites.

1607. Fireside, Bryna J. *Private Joel and the Sewell Mountain Seder.* Illustrated by Shawn Costello. Kar-Ben, 2008. 48pp. ISBN 978-0-8225-7240-4; paper ISBN 978-0-8225-9050-7. Grades 2–4. In 1862 homesick J. A. Joel camps in West Virginia's Sewell Mountains. With permission from his commander, he decides to organize a Passover seder for the twenty-one Jewish soldiers serving with him in Ohio's 23rd Regiment. As Passover celebrates freedom, he includes three freed African American members of the regiment. Cider replaces wine, carrot tops become parsley, and a brick symbolizes charoset. Illustrations enhance the text.

1608. Fleischman, Paul. *Bull Run.* Illustrated by David Frampton. Trophy, 1995. 104pp. Paper ISBN 978-0-06-440588-1. Grades 5 up. Told from many points of view, this is the story of the early Civil War and the thoughts of participants—from North and South—in the First Battle of Bull Run in 1861. Their views of the war as they start and finish the battle are very different. A photographer tells of capturing the expressions of men not expecting to be alive the next evening; another character thinks of a depressed woman who has considered suicide. Other characters are slaves, soldiers, and citizens from North and South who seem to be mere observers until the battle begins. *Scott O'Dell Award, American Library Association Notable Children's Books, American Library Association Best Books for Young Adults, Horn Book Fanfare Book, School Library Journal Best Books, Notable Children's Trade Books in the Field of Social Studies, Booklist Books for Young Editors' Choices, IRA Teachers' Choices, Publishers Weekly Year's Best Books,* and *New York Public Library Books for the Teen Age.*

1609. Fletcher, Susan. *Dadblamed Union Army Cow.* Illustrated by Kimberly Bulcken Root. Candlewick, 2007. 32pp. ISBN 978-0-7636-2263-3. Grades 2–5. A faithful cow accompanies a Union soldier and other Indiana Volunteers into Civil War battles. It accompanies its master to the recruiting station, rides on the train, lives in the campsites, and marches to battle. Eventually the "dadblamed" cow helps the unnamed soldier back to health after he is hit by a musket ball. Presumably such a cow did accompany the Fifty-Ninth Regiment of Indiana Volunteers. The watercolor illustrations enhance the text.

1610. Friedman, Robin. *The Silent Witness: A True Story of the Civil War.* Illustrated by Claire A. Nivola. Houghton, 2005. 32pp. ISBN 978-0-618-44230-0; 2008, paper ISBN 978-0-54701-436-4. Grades K–4. At the beginning of the Civil War, Lula McLean, 4, her rag doll, and her family relocate to Appomattox Court House, Virginia, after General Beauregard commandeers the family's home at Bull Run. Other events that affect the family are the Union blockade of southern ports and Sherman's march through the South. Then on April 9, 1865, General Lee surrenders to General Grant in their home. Watercolor and goauche illustrations enhance the text.

1611. Gauch, Patricia L. *Thunder at Gettysburg.* Illustrated by Stephen Gammell. Boyds Mills, 2003. 46pp. ISBN 978-1-59078-180-7; paper ISBN 978-1-59078-186-9. Grades 2–5. On July 1, 1863, Tillie takes a chair to her attic window so she can watch the battle on Seminary Ridge in Gettysburg. By late afternoon, she finds herself in the middle of the fighting as she tries to escape. She stops to carry pails of water to wounded soldiers. After the battle ends, she is relieved to know that the Union has won and that her family is safe.

1612. *Grace's Letter to Lincoln.* (Chapters) Hyperion, 1998. 64pp. Paper ISBN 978-0-7868-1296-7. Grades K–3. The rest of Grace Bedell's New York state family works to elect Abraham Lincoln as part of the Wide-Awake movement, but Grace has to stay home and do chores.

She wants to help, and she soon realizes that she can write a letter to Lincoln and suggest that he grow whiskers because they would make him more popular and help him win more votes. He accepts her idea and changes his appearance accordingly. When his victory train passes through her town after the election, Lincoln acknowledges Grace and her good advice.

1613. Hahn, Mary Downing. *Hear the Wind Blow: A Novel of the Civil War.* Clarion, 2003. 208pp. ISBN 978-0-618-18190-2. Grades 5–9. Haswell Magruder, 13, and his sister, 7, leave their dead mother and burned home in Shenandoah, Virginia, toward the end of the Civil War and head for their grandparents' home. Haswell leaves his sister with the grandparents, and sets out to find his older brother Avery, a Confederate soldier. He thought war would be filled with glory, but on his journey, he discovers that it is not at all what he envisaged.

1614. Hansen, Joyce. *Which Way Freedom?* Camelot, 1992. 120pp. Paper ISBN 978-0-380-71408-7. Grades 5–9. After hearing that they will be sold, Obi and Easter escape from the plantation where they are slaves in 1861. Confederate soldiers stop them, but Obi escapes to the South Carolina coastal islands. There he joins Union troops and meets a "colored Yankee" who begins teaching him to read. At the end of the war, Obi is wounded but alive, and he starts searching for Easter and the little boy she wanted to save on the plantation.

1615. Harness, Cheryl. *Ghosts of the Civil War.* Aladdin, 2004. 48pp. Paper ISBN 978-0-689-86992-1. Grades 3–5. While visiting a Civil War reenactment Lindsey is whisked back in time by the ghost of President Lincoln's older son, Willie. She experiences the Civil War from both sides and witnesses the Lincoln-Douglas debates, major battles, and the assassination of President Lincoln, at which time he is reunited with Willie and Lindsey returns to her parents. Maps and illustrations complement the text. Bibliography, Glossary, Chronology, and Index.

1616. Hart, Alison. *Gabriel's Horses.* (Racing to Freedom) Peachtree, 2007. 161pp. ISBN 978-1-56145-398-6. Grades 5–8. In Kentucky during the Civil War, 12-year-old slave Gabriel has dreams of becoming a jockey like his father. But his father, head trainer of thoroughbreds on the plantation, leaves to fight for the Union, and a new horse trainer arrives, one who is cruel to the horses. Then the Confederates follow, wanting to steal the horses to use in battle. Gabriel has to decide how to keep the horses from dying needlessly.

1617. Hart, Alison. *Gabriel's Triumph.* (Racing to Freedom) Peachtree, 2007. 164pp. ISBN 978-1-56145-410-5. Grades 5–8. In 1864, Gabriel Alexander, 13, is newly freed by his owner, Mr. Giles, for saving eight thoroughbred racers from Rebel soldiers. Mr. Giles decides to enter his best horse in the Saratoga Chase race in New York. He chooses Gabriel to ride. Gabriel's excitement is muted when he experiences vehement racism and segregation in a place where he expected to have complete freedom. He does, however, win the race.

1618. High, Linda Oatman. *The Cemetery Keepers of Gettysburg.* Illustrated by Laura Francesca Filippucci. Walker, 2007. 32pp. ISBN 978-0-8027-8094-2. Grades 2–5. Fred Thorn, 7, has a happy life as the son of Gettysburg cemetery caretakers until the Civil War starts. Fred's mother is pregnant, and his father has left to fight for the Union. They have to cope first with the three-day battle between the Union and Confederate armies. They leave their home on Cemetery Hill and stay in a nearby farmhouse with wounded soldiers. Then they return home and have to bury many soldiers at the battle's end. Several months later Abraham Lincoln arrives and honors the dead with his famous address. Illustrations illuminate the text.

1619. Hopkinson, Deborah. *Billy and the Rebel.* Illustrated by Brian Floca. Atheneum, 2005. 48pp. ISBN 978-0-689-83964-1; Aladdin, 2006, paper ISBN 978-0-689-83396-0. Grades 1–4. Billy Bayly and his mother help a young Confederate soldier who has deserted. He arrives at their Gettysburg farm in 1863 and is reluctant to talk—he doesn't want them to know that he is a southerner. He silently helps them when marauders demand food and he rescues Billy from a tricky situation. Watercolors enhance the text. Map and Note.

1620. Hopkinson, Deborah. *From Slave to Soldier: Based on a True Civil War Story.* Illustrated by Brian Floca. Aladdin, 2007. 48pp. ISBN 978-0-689-83965-8; 2007, paper ISBN 978-0-689-

83966-5. Grades K–3. When the Union army comes by the farm where Johnny is a slave and asks if he wants to join them, he quickly says "yes." He begins driving an army mule team, and his ability to do this well earns him his own uniform and the hope of being free at the end of the Civil War. Illustrations enhance the text.

1621. Hughes, Pat. *Seeing the Elephant: A Story of the Civil War.* Illustrated by Ken Stark. Farrar, 2007. 32pp. ISBN 978-0-374-38024-3. Grades 2–4. Ten-year-old Izzie wants to fight the Confederates like his older brothers. Then his Aunt Bell, a nurse, takes him to a hospital in Washington, D.C., and introduces him to a captured Confederate soldier. He realizes that war is not what he thought. He writes his brother that he did not "see the elephant" but that he realized he was an ugly beast. Realistic paintings complement the text.

1622. Hunt, Irene. *Across Five Aprils.* Pearson Prentice Hall, 2000. 190pp. ISBN 978-0-13-437499-4; Berkley, 2002, paper ISBN 978-0-425-18278-9. Grades 5–8. Jethro turns 9 in 1861, and his life changes. This story traces the activities of his Illinois family through the four years of the Civil War, during which brothers fight on opposite sides. Jethro assumes the male responsibilities of the household when his father has a heart attack, and he learns about Abraham Lincoln and Robert E. Lee, both greatly respected by some and greatly reviled by others. When one of his brothers deserts, Jethro writes to Lincoln requesting amnesty. On Lincoln's death, the family mourns along with the nation. *Newbery Honor* and *Society of Midland Authors Book Award*.

1623. Ives, David. *Scrib: Some Characters, Adventures, Letters and Conversations from the Year 1863.* HarperCollins, 2005. 208pp. ISBN 978-0-06-059841-9. Grades 5–9. In 1863, 16-year-old Billy Christmas or "Scrib" becomes an amanuensis, writing letters for illiterate westerners who want to let their families back home know what they are doing or to communicate with the government. His spelling is questionable and some of what he says is more pun than pleasantry. He and his horse Gabe deliver these missives until he is threatened and has to stop his work. He is almost killed, almost jailed as a criminal, and delivers a letter to a Paiute Indian from President Lincoln. When he solves the mystery of his nemesis, he is able to resume work.

1624. Johnson, Nancy. *A Sweet-Sounding Place: A Civil War Story of the Black 54th Regiment.* Down East, 2008. 160pp. Paper ISBN 978-0-8927-2770-4. Grades 4–7. Moses Morning's mother dies as soon as he is born, and he is taken to Boston where his Uncle Daniel and his Aunt Ruth raise him as a free black. When he is 16, he joins the newly formed 54th Massachusetts Regiment with other black volunteers. In the South, he hopes to find information about his parents, but instead he finds others who need to be freed. He helps three boys, a girl, and a black Indian who rescued him after an alligator attack in the Okefenokee Swamp. Although he does not find his parents, he finds other rewards. Illustrations reinforce the text. Glossary and Notes.

1625. Karr, Kathleen. *Exiled: Memoirs of a Camel.* Marshall Cavendish, 2006. 240pp. Paper ISBN 978-0-7614-5291-1. Grades 5–8. Ali, a camel, finds himself transported from Egypt to serve in the United States Camel Corps in Texas before and during the Civil War. He describes missing his mother and his love of the sand dunes of home. Divided into three parts, the novel tells the story of this short-lived military unit and of Ali's life. After being trained for a failed artillery experiment, the camels form a caravan and carry supplies across the desert to help the army build a new road. Eventually Ali wins Fatinah as his mate and the two escape with their son into the Mojave Desert.

1626. Keehn, Sally M. *Anna Sunday.* Philomel, 2002. 266pp. ISBN 978-0-399-23875-8. Grades 4–8. In 1863, 12-year-old Anna, disguised as a boy, and her younger brother Jed leave their Pennsylvania home with their horse, Samson. They have heard that their father has been badly wounded in Virginia. They cross rebel lines to take him herbal medicines and foods that Anna thinks will restore him to health. When they find their father, they discover that a Confederate widow, Mrs. McDowell, has been caring for him, and they have to revise their attitudes and realize that people are never all bad or all good.

1627. Kent, Deborah. *Chance of a Lifetime.* (Saddles, Stars and Stripes) Kingfisher, 2006. 172pp. ISBN 978-0-7534-6001-6. Grades 3–7. While Jacquetta May Logan is visiting relatives during the Civil War, Union soldiers take over the family plantation and turn it into a hospital. Her parents have to leave. Jacquetta finds herself alone in enemy territory with only her beloved horse, a bay named Chance. A slave girl and boy, Peace and Witness, help her devise a plan to rescue her parents' Morgan horses from the plantation and take them across the Mississippi River to safety. When she meets a kind Union soldier, she has to start rethinking her attitudes toward both slavery and the Union.

1628. Klein, Lisa. *Two Girls of Gettysburg.* Bloomsbury, 2008. 393pp. ISBN 978-1-59990-105-3; 2010, paper ISBN 978-1-59990-383-5. Grades 4–6. In 1860 Rosanna's parents send her from Richmond to Gettysburg to be with her cousin and good friend Lizzie, 15. They want to separate Rosanna from John, a beau they find undesirable. Soon after her arrival, the Civil War begins, and when Lizzie's father and brother join the Union, Lizzie must run the family butcher shop instead of attending the Ladies' Seminary with Rosanna. Rosanna returns home where she reunites with and marries John. He joins the Confederates and when he is wounded Rosanna goes to help him and discovers she wants to become a nurse. Alternating chapters reveal the two lives along with important background information and insights about wartime. *Notable Social Studies Trade Books for Young People.*

1629. McGowen, Tom. *Jesse Bowman: A Union Boy's War Story.* (Historical Fiction Adventure) Enslow, 2008. 160pp. ISBN 978-0-7660-2929-3. Grades 5–8. Jesse Bowman, 17, joins the Chicago Zouave regiment of the Union army. He has only a romantic idea of war, but after he enlists he soon discovers how awful war is—from the daily boredom and hardship of a soldier's life to the horror of battle. Additionally, he is shocked when his commander seems to condone the soldiers' actions when they ransack Athens, Georgia.

1630. McMullan, Margaret. *How I Found the Strong: A Civil War Story.* Houghton, 2004. 144pp. ISBN 978-0-618-35008-7; Laurel Leaf, 2006, paper ISBN 978-0-553-49492-1. Grades 5–8. Frank Russell (Shanks), 10, of Mississippi wants to enlist in the Confederate army in the spring of 1861 to fight alongside his father and brother Henry. However, he has to stay home with his mother, grandparents, and the family slave, Buck. As their needs grow, Shanks begins to see Buck as much like himself, with the same hopes and dreams, strengths and weaknesses. When the war comes closer and Buck visits a battlefield, he sees a pile of arms and legs, socks and shoes still covering severed limbs. He changes his mind about a lot. Henry dies of pneumonia, and his father returns home missing an arm. Shanks convinces him to help Buck escape to the north. They are then caught in a terrible battle near Strong River, and Shanks saves his father's life. *Dorothy Canfield Fisher Children's Book Award* (Vermont), *Young Hoosier Book Award* (Indiana) nomination, and *Sequoyah Book Award* (Florida) nomination.

1631. Nixon, Joan Lowery. *A Dangerous Promise.* (Orphan Train Adventures) Laurel-Leaf, 1999. 146pp. Paper ISBN 978-0-440-21965-1. Grades 5–8. In 1861, Mike Kelly and his friend Todd practice to become army drummers. They run away to join the Kansas Infantry and fight for the Union. In a Missouri battle, Mike is left for dead and Todd is killed. Mike watches a thief steal Todd's watch. Mike is rescued by someone he met on the orphan train to the Midwest. Because Mike had promised to return Todd's watch to his sister, he spends much time behind Confederate lines looking for the thief.

1632. Nixon, Joan Lowery. *Keeping Secrets.* (Orphan Train Adventures) Laurel-Leaf, 1996. 163pp. Paper ISBN 978-0-440-21992-7. Grades 5–8. When she is 11 in 1863, Peg Kelly thinks her mother should treat her like the young woman she almost is. Peg meets and helps a woman escaping from the Confederates, Violet Hennessey. Violet needs Peg to pretend to be her daughter so she can safely deliver secrets to the Union army. Peg agrees, and their efforts help the army win, but not quickly enough to save Peg's brother from the Confederates.

1633. Noble, Trinka Hakes. *The Last Brother: A Civil War Tale.* Illustrated by Robert Papp. (Tales of Young Americans) Sleeping Bear, 2006. 48pp. ISBN 978-1-58536-253-0. Grades 3–

5. Eleven-year-old Gabe, a bugler in the Union army, is trying to learn the sixty different battle calls. He is also watching out for his brother Davy, a 16-year-old foot soldier. Two of Gabe's
brothers have already died. When Gabe meets Orlee, a Confederate bugler, on the day before the Battle of Gettysburg, they like each other and want to become friends. But they
have to decide whether country or friendship is more important. The illustrations complement the text. *Independent Publisher Book Award Honor* and *Young Readers Choice Award*
(Louisiana).

1634. Osborne, Mary Pope. *Civil War on Sunday.*   Illustrated by Sal Murdocca. (Magic Tree
House) Random, 2000. 96pp. ISBN 978-0-679-99067-3; paper ISBN 978-0-679-89067-6.
Grades 2–5. Jack and Annie journey back to the Civil War where they save the life of their
own great-great-great-grandfather. They meet Clara Barton and work with her to help
wounded soldiers. *Children's Book Award* (Colorado) nomination.

1635. Paulsen, Gary. *Soldier's Heart: Being the Story of the Enlistment and Due Service of the Boy*
Charley Goddard in the First Minnesota Volunteers.   Delacorte, 1998. 106pp. ISBN 978-0-
385-32498-4; Laurel-Leaf, 2000, paper ISBN 978-0-440-22838-7. Grades 5–8. Charley Goddard, 16, enthusiastically signs up to fight with the Minnesota Volunteers in the Civil War;
he expects the war to end quickly. He trains, endures camp life, and fights in four battles, beginning in First Manassas and ending in Gettysburg. He is wounded and returns home,
where his body mends but not his heart. He suffers a "soldier's heart," a condition later identified in World War I as "shell shock" and currently called "post-traumatic stress disorder."
Sunshine State Young Reader Award (Florida) nomination, *Lincoln Award* (Illinois) nomination,
Hoosier Book Award (Indiana) nomination, *Black-Eyed Susan Book Award* (Maryland) nomination, *Golden Sower Award* (Nebraska) nomination, *Sequoyah Book Award* (Oklahoma) nomination, *Tayshas Reading List* (Texas) nomination, *Young Adult Book Award* (Utah) nomination,
Evergreen Young Adult Award (Washington) nomination, *Battle of the Books Award* (Wisconsin)
nomination, and *Indian Paintbrush* (Wyoming) nomination.

1636. Philbrick, Rodman. *The Mostly True Adventures of Homer P. Figg.*   Blue Sky, 2009. 224pp.
ISBN 978-0-439-66818-7. Grades 5–8. Furious that his Uncle Squinton Leach sold his un-
derage brother, Harold, 17, into the Union army in place of a rich man's son, 12-year-old
Homer leaves Pine Swamp, Maine, in 1863 and heads south to save Harold. Along the way,
Homer stretches truth as he becomes involved in the Underground Railroad, plays "pig boy"
in a traveling medicine show, and is robbed. He reaches Gettysburg only to discover that
Harold likes his job. Homer fights for the Union, but unintentionally wounds Harold, end-
ing his army career. Notes and Glossary. *American Library Association Notable Children's Books,*
Newbery Honor Book, Bluegrass Book Award (Kentucky) nomination, *Dorothy Canfield Fisher*
Children's Book Award (Vermont) nomination, and *Capitol Choices Noteworthy Titles for Children*
and Teens (Washington, D.C.).

1637. Pinkney, Andrea Davis. *Abraham Lincoln: Letters from a Young Slave Girl.*   (Dear Mr.
President) Winslow, 2001. 136pp. ISBN 978-1-890817-60-2. Grades 5–7. In the early 1860s,
13-year-old slave Lettie Tucker is taught how to read by the daughter of the South Carolina
plantation owner. With Katherine's encouragement, Lettie begins a correspondence with
President Lincoln in which Lettie describes her own life and her family's circumstances.
She asks the president to consider freeing the slaves. Lincoln tells her about his own life in
the White House with his two sons and his wife, how the war is progressing, and his own
change of mind in regard to slavery. The correspondence eventually leads to Lincoln signing the Emancipation Proclamation. Then Lettie writes him about her family's new life in
Philadelphia. Illustrations and prints, reproductions, and other items give a sense of the time.

1638. Polacco, Patricia. *Pink and Say.*   Philomel, 1994. Unpaged. ISBN 978-0-399-22671-7.
Grades 4 up. African American Pinkus (Pink) Aylee saves white Sheldon (Say), 15, after he
has been shot in the leg for deserting his unit of the Union army. Pink takes him home to
his mother, a slave still living on the plantation after everyone else has left. While they are
healing, marauders come and murder Pink's mother, the woman who has made Say feel like
he belonged to her. The two boys, almost immediately captured, end up at the Confederate

Andersonville prison camp, where Say survives; Pink is most likely hung hours after they arrive. *Jefferson Cup Award*.

1639. Porter, Connie. *Happy Birthday, Addy! A Springtime Story.* Illustrated by Bradford Brown. American Girl, 1994. 60pp. ISBN 978-1-56247-082-1; paper ISBN 978-1-56247-081-4. Grades 3–5. Addy and her family move to a boardinghouse in Philadelphia where she meets a friend, M'dear. Because Addy, like many others who grew up in slavery, does not know her birthday, her friend suggests she claim one day as her own. A Peek into the Past.

1640. Porter, Connie. *Meet Addy: An American Girl.* Illustrated by Melodye Rosales and Dahl Taylor. American Girl, 1994. 60pp. ISBN 978-1-56247-076-0. Grades 3–5. In the summer of 1864, Addy's parents decide to escape from the plantation where they are slaves. Before they can leave, the master sells some of the family. Addy, disguised as a boy, makes her way to Philadelphia. On one part of the journey, she almost enters a camp of Confederate soldiers. She arrives safely, and after the war, the family reunites in the city.

1641. Rappaport, Doreen. *Freedom Ship.* Illustrated by Curtis James. Hyperion, 2006. 32pp. ISBN 978-0-7868-0645-4. Grades 3–6. On May 13, 1862, Robert Smalls, 23, a black wheel man on a Confederate steamship, the *Planter*, reportedly joined eight other members of the ship's slave crew to seize the vessel and take it to the Union army so that five women and three children could gain their freedom. This is based on a true story. Smalls later participated in several naval battles and served in the United States House of Representatives for five terms. Chalk-pastel drawings enhance the text. Bibliography, Further Reading, and Web Sites.

1642. Reeder, Carolyn. *Across the Lines.* Illustrated by Robin Moore. Camelot, 1998. 224pp. Paper ISBN 978-0-380-73073-5. Grades 4–7. Twelve-year-old Edward is surprised when his young slave, Simon, runs away when the Union army arrives. Edward's family flees to Petersburg, and the constant shell bombardment frays Edward's nerves. Simon finds that being free and serving in the army can also be lonely. The boys provide alternating perspectives of the same conflict.

1643. Reeder, Carolyn. *Shades of Gray.* Simon & Schuster, 1989. 171pp. ISBN 978-0-02-775811-5; Aladdin, 1999, paper ISBN 978-0-689-82696-2. Grades 5–7. During the Civil War Jed's sisters die of typhoid, Yankees kill his father and brother, and his mother dies of grief. At the age of 12, he must go to his mother's sister's home. There he has to adjust to the rural life of Virginia and to an uncle who refuses to fight for the South or the North. Jed must overcome his own prejudices and ignore the neighbors' jeers as he begins to understand the strength that his uncle shows in standing by his own convictions. *Scott O'Dell Award, Child Study Children's Book Award, Jefferson Cup Award, American Library Association Notable Children's Books, Nutmeg Children's Book Award* (Connecticut) nomination, *Sunshine State Young Reader Award* (Florida) nomination, *Children's Book Award* (Georgia) nomination, *Rebecca Caudill Award* (Illinois) nomination, *Young Hoosier Award* (Indiana) nomination, *Children's Choice Award* (Iowa) nomination, *Bluegrass Award* (Kentucky) nomination, *Children's Book Award* (Maryland) nomination, *Black-Eyed Susan* (Maryland) nomination, *Maud Hart Lovelace Award* (Minnesota) nomination, *Garden State Teen Book Award* (New Jersey) nomination, *Land of Enchantment Book Award* (New Mexico) nomination, *Sequoyah Book Award* (Oklahoma) nomination, *Young Reader's Choice Award* (Pennsylvania) nomination, *SCASL Book Award* (South Carolina) nomination, and *Bluebonnet Award* (Texas) nomination.

1644. Rinaldi, Ann. *Girl in Blue.* Scholastic, 2004. 320pp. Paper ISBN 978-0-439-67646-5. Grades 5–8. Seeking to control her own life, 16-year-old Sara Louisa Wheelock leaves her Michigan home and an unwanted arranged marriage to fight in the Civil War. Disguised as a man, Neddy Compton, she becomes a soldier in Virginia and then a spy for the Union army while working as a maid in the house of Confederate supporter Rose O'Neal Greenhow in Washington, D.C. *Young Hoosier Book Awards* (Indiana) nomination and *Junior Book Award* (South Carolina) nomination.

1645. Rinaldi, Ann. *Juliet's Moon.* Harcourt, 2008. 256pp. ISBN 978-0-15-206170-8. Grades 5 up. By 1863, Juliet Bradshaw, 12, has already seen a lot. Then Union soldiers imprison her for aiding Quantrill's Raiders, an anti-Union group to which her brother belongs. The prison collapses, killing several women, and Juliet escapes. She has to fend for herself and get help from her brother, Seth, to get through the trauma of the Civil War.

1646. Rinaldi, Ann. *The Last Silk Dress.* Laurel-Leaf, 1999. 350pp. Paper ISBN 978-0-440-22861-5. Grades 5 up. Fourteen-year-old Susan wants to do something meaningful to support the Confederacy during the Civil War. Her mother, however, worries that Susan's older brother's scandalous reputation will hurt Susan, so she makes her stay home. When the Yankees approach Richmond, Susan and her friend convince their mothers to let them collect silk dresses to make a balloon that will help spy on the Yankees. In the meantime, Susan meets her brother, who is banished from the house, and he tells her family secrets. When she almost faces treason for her actions and falls in love with a Yankee, she knows she must hurt someone she loves.

1647. Spain, Susan Rosson. *The Deep Cut.* Marshall Cavendish, 2006. 217pp. ISBN 978-0-7614-5316-1. Grades 5–8. Lonzo Rosson, 13, tries to help his Culpeper, Virginia, family during the Civil War, but he does not believe in killing. His shopkeeper father considers him "slow," and Lonzo is always trying to gain his approval. After Lonzo's two uncles and cousins join the Confederate Army, Lonzo goes to help his widowed Aunt Mariah run her inn and farm. The Union army establishes quarters in the inn, allowing Lonzo to observe them personally and to realize that both good and bad soldiers fight on both sides. When Lonzo discovers his aunt's plans to poison biscuits for a Yankee after her sons die, he stops her. He realizes that his grandparents will be the first to eat them, not the soldier. This act finally gains Lonzo's father's approval.

1648. Steele, William O. *The Perilous Road.* Harcourt, 2004. 156pp. ISBN 978-0-15-205203-4; Odyssey paper ISBN 978-0-15-205204-1. Grades 4–8. When Union troops take the food that Chris's family stored for the winter, the 11-year-old boy decides he will support the Rebels. But his brother joins the Union army in 1863 without telling Chris. Before Chris realizes, he almost gets his brother killed by telling the Rebels that a federal wagon train has moved into the region. *Newbery Honor* and *Jane Addams Book Award*.

1649. Weber, Elka. *The Yankee at the Seder.* Illustrated by Adam Gustavson. Tricycle, 2009. 40pp. ISBN 978-1-58246-256-1. Grades 2–5. Ten-year-old Jacob is sitting on his southern front steps eating matzoh in 1865 when a Yankee Jew, Myer Levy, sees him and asks if he may join him. Surprised, Jacob rushes inside and reports to his mother. She reminds him of the Passover commitment to hospitality and Levy is invited to join the family seder. An ensuing discussion examines, through the traditional Four Questions, the need to end slavery and have freedom for all. *Sydney Taylor Book Award Honor Book* and *Bulletin Blue Ribbon*.

1650. Wilson, John. *Battle Scars.* Kids Can, 2005. 168pp. ISBN 978-1-55337-702-3; 2004, paper ISBN 978-1-55337-703-0. Grades 5–8. Cousins Walt, from Canada, and Nate, from South Carolina, fight on the opposite sides of the Civil War. Nate's father's former slave, Sunday, who uses sign language because he has no tongue, enlists in the Union army. The three meet in Richmond where Walt is imprisoned while Nate is a guard. The two use Sunday as a messenger to help the northern prisoners escape. The story is told in the form of a flashback as Nate considers joining Walt and Sunday in Canada after Lee surrenders.

1651. Winnick, Karen. *Lucy's Cave: A Story of Vicksburg, 1863.* Calkins Creek, 2008. 32pp. ISBN 978-1-59078-194-4. Grades K–3. Eleven-year-old Lucy McRae and her family move into a cave for the 47-day seige of the town of Vicksburg. They live on cornmeal, sweet-potato coffee, and other non-perishables. Liddy, the Reverend's daughter, begins to annoy Lucy by visiting her pony constantly. But Liddy can draw silhouettes on the walls, and Lucy changes her mind. Oil illustrations complement the text.

1652. Wisler, G. Clifton. *Mr. Lincoln's Drummer.* Puffin, 1997. 131pp. Paper ISBN 978-0-14-038542-7. Grades 4–8. Willie Johnston, 10 years old when the war starts in 1861, plays the drum for a captain seeking recruits. He makes enough money to help his family, and when his father joins, Willie decides to go with the Vermont group as the drummer boy. He is transferred to be a nurse, and his bravery wins him the Congressional Medal of Honor in 1863. The real Willie Johnston was the seventh soldier to receive that honor.

1653. Wisler, G. Clifton. *Red Cap.* Puffin, 1994. 176pp. Paper ISBN 978-0-14-036936-6. Grades 4–8. Ransom J. Powell, 13 and 4 feet tall, runs away from his home in Frostburg, Maryland, in 1862 to fight with the Union army in the Civil War. He becomes the drummer boy. Two years later, the Confederates capture him and take him to Camp Sumter, a prison in Andersonville, Georgia. He refuses to renounce his loyalty to the Union, a move that would release him from the stockade, and he again has the job of drummer boy, this time for the camp. This position and the kindness of a guard help him survive this terrible ordeal.

History

1654. Allen, Thomas B. *Harriet Tubman, Secret Agent: How She and Other African-Americans Helped Win the Civil War.* National Geographic, 2006. 191pp. ISBN 978-0-7922-7889-4. Grades 5–8. Drawing on primary sources—military and intelligence archives, diaries, and memoirs from ex-slaves—this volume offers a biography of Harriet Tubman (1820?–1913), an American spy who risked her life for freedom. She helped the Union troops by having ex-slaves who worked in the South pass information to her. She was also a secret agent, a military leader who conducted a raid along the Combahee River, and an abolitionist. Illustrations, maps, and reproductions highlight the text. Chronology, Notes, Further Reading, Web Sites, and Index.

1655. Allen, Thomas B., and Roger MacBride Allen. *Mr. Lincoln's High-Tech War: How the North Used the Telegraph, Railroads, Surveillance Balloons, Iron-Clads, High-Powered Weapons and More to Win the Civil War.* National Geographic, 2009. 144pp. ISBN 978-1-4263-0379-1. Grades 5 up. In twelve chapters and three situation reports, this volume shows the Civil War as both the last "ancient" war and the first modern one. Although as a boy Lincoln used tools like those of his great-great-great-great-grandfather, he was the first president to claim his own patent. He developed a device that lifted boats to keep their bottoms from scraping across rocks. He understood that new ways to fight might help the Union. When a balloonist, Thaddeus Lowe, espoused spying on the enemy from a balloon and telegraphing the findings, Lincoln commanded General Scott to use try this strategy. Railroads transported soldiers and supplies, and submarines and ironclads were new weapons. Mass-produced repeating rifles and other armaments offered an advantage when they replaced slow-loading guns. Appropriate period drawings and photographs along with sidebars and maps enhance the text. Bibliography, Further Resources, Web Sites, and Index. *Capitol Choices Noteworthy Titles* (Washington, D.C.) and *American Library Association Notable Children's Books*.

1656. Anderson, Dale B. *The Civil War at Sea.* (World Almanac Library of the Civil War) World Almanac, 2004. 48pp. ISBN 978-0-8368-5585-2. Grades 4–6. The North and the South fought at sea during the Civil War. This volume explores the blockades and how they were beaten, new fighting techniques and strategies, privateers and raiders, the daily life on these ships, and the way in which the ships were able to win in battle. Maps, Photos, Reproductions, Chronology, Further Reading, Glossary, Web Sites, and Index. *Capitol Choices Noteworthy Titles* (Washington, D.C.).

1657. Anderson, Dale B. *The Civil War in the East (1861–July 1863).* (World Almanac Library of the Civil War) World Almanac, 2004. ISBN 978-0-8368-5582-1. Grades 4–6. The war was fought mainly in the eastern United States. This volume examines the sites along the states from Pennsylvania south that found themselves in the heat of battle. It also includes interesting anecdotes and information about the war. Maps, Photos, Reproductions, Chronology, Further Reading, Glossary, Web Sites, and Index.

1658. **Anderson, Dale B.** *The Civil War in the West.* (World Almanac Library of the Civil War) World Almanac, 2004. 48pp. ISBN 978-0-8368-5583-8. Grades 4–6. The battles fought in the western region of the United States differed from those fought in the East. Some took place in the far West and the Southwest. Eventually the Union moved south along the Mississippi, and took control of the river and the area west of it. Maps, Photos, Reproductions, Chronology, Further Reading, Glossary, Web Sites, and Index.

1659. **Anderson, Dale B.** *The Home Fronts in the Civil War.* (World Almanac Library of the Civil War) World Almanac, 2004. 48pp. ISBN 978-0-8368-5587-6. Grades 4–6. Seven chapters cover different aspects of life in the North and the South during the Civil War. Discussions also center on African Americans in the war, the difficulty of creating a new nation, Lincoln's role as president, and the aftermath. Among the concerns for citizens were politics and the issue of slavery. Photographs and reproductions highlight the text. Maps, Timeline, Glossary, Further Reading, Web Sites, and Index.

1660. **Arnold, James R., and Roberta Wiener.** *On to Richmond: The Civil War in the East, 1861–1862.* Lerner, 2001. 72pp. ISBN 978-0-8225-2313-0. Grades 5–8. Arnold examines several battles of the Civil War including the First Battle of Bull Run, the Battle of Antietam, and the clash between the *Monitor* and the *Virginia* before presenting the effects of the war on both Confederate and Union soldiers. Photographs and reproductions highlight the text. Bibliography, Glossary, Chronology, and Index.

1661. **Arnold, James R., and Roberta Wiener.** *This Unhappy Country: The Turn of the Civil War, 1863.* Lerner, 2002. 72pp. ISBN 978-0-8225-2316-1. Grades 5–8. Arnold examines events in 1863, the year in which Stonewall Jackson died, the battle of Vicksburg took place, and the Battle of Gettysburg, the turning point, shocked everyone. The text also comments about the effects of the war on both the Confederate and Union soldiers. Photographs and reproductions highlight the text. Bibliography, Glossary, Chronology, and Index.

1662. **Bolotin, Norman.** *The Civil War A to Z: A Young Readers' Guide to Over 100 People, Places, and Points of Importance.* Dutton, 2002. 148pp. ISBN 978-0-525-46268-2. Grades 4–8. Bolotin includes more than one hundred entries about important people, places, and events during the Civil War, arranged alphabetically. Each entry averages two paragraphs with more space devoted to the most important topics. Photographs and illustrations augment the text. Glossary, Chronology, Notes, Further Reading, and Index.

1663. **Chang, Ina.** *A Separate Battle: Women and the Civil War.* Puffin, 1996. 103pp. Paper ISBN 978-0-14-038106-1. Grades 5–8. Through primary source materials including letters and diaries, Chang shows the women who rolled bandages, nursed the injured, fought disguised as men, and tried to protect their homes. Some of the well-known figures she presents are Clara Barton, Harriet Tubman, and Belle Boyd. Maps, photographs, and reproductions complement the text. Bibliography and Index.

1664. **Damon, Duane.** *Growing Up in the Civil War: 1861–1865.* (Our America) Lerner, 2005. 64pp. ISBN 978-0-8225-0656-0. Grades 4–7. In six chapters, this book examines the daily lives of children living between 1860 and 1865 based on primary sources including letters written by young people and their families, diaries, epigraphs, and authentic art. Sidebars add information about specific groups of children or cultural aspects of the Civil War. Photographs, Reproductions, Notes, Glossary, and Index.

1665. **Flanagan, Alice K.** *Women of the Union.* (We the People) Compass Point, 2006. 48pp. ISBN 978-0-7565-2035-9; paper ISBN 978-0-7565-2047-2. Grades 4–6. This collective biography offers profiles of women who helped the Union succeed during the Civil War. It covers a wide variety of occupations, from writers and nurses to soldiers and spies. Maps, photographs, and reproductions illustrate the text. Glossary, Chronology, Further Reading, Web Sites, and Index.

1666. **Gillis, Jennifer Blizin.** *The Confederate Soldier.* (We the People) Compass Point, 2006. 48pp. ISBN 978-0-7565-2025-0; paper ISBN 978-0-7565-2037-3. Grades 4–6. This volume offers background on what life was like for the Confederate soldiers during the Civil War. It covers their clothes, living quarters, weapons, and food along with other topics. Maps, photographs, and reproductions illustrate the text. Glossary, Chronology, Further Reading, Web Sites, and Index.

1667. Graves, Kerry. *Going to School During the Civil War: The Confederacy.* Blue Earth, 2001. 32pp. ISBN 978-0-7368-0802-6. Grades 4–6. This volume looks at a child's life in the Confederacy during the Civil War—schooling on plantations and in boarding schools, secret slave schools, and southern life in general. It details games, activities, special events, and crafts that children would have enjoyed. Photographs, maps, and illustrations augment the text. Glossary, Web Sites, and Index.

1668. Graves, Kerry. *Going to School During the Civil War: The Union.* Blue Earth, 2001. 32pp. ISBN 978-0-7368-0801-9. Grades 4–6. Five chapters look at a child's life in the North during the Civil War, the education available, and the focus on preserving the Union. The book details games, activities, special events, and crafts that children would have enjoyed. Photographs, maps, and illustrations augment the text. Glossary, Web Sites, and Index.

1669. Hakim, Joy. *War Terrible War: 1855–1865.* (History of US) Oxford, 2006. 161pp. ISBN 978-0-19-518899-8; 2007, paper ISBN 978-0-19-532720-5. Grades 5 up. Filled with photographs, prints, sidebars, boxed text, and running commentary, this story of the Civil War years shows the war's horror. Hakim covers all aspects of society and all cultures. Chronology of Events, More Books to Read, and Index.

1670. Hale, Sarah Elder. *Young Heroes of the North and South.* (The Civil War) Cobblestone, 2005. ISBN 978-0-8126-7901-4. Grades 4–9. Children participated in the Civil War both at home and on the battlefield. They wrote letters to soldiers in the field, took care of homes and farms, tried to raise money for food and supplies, and entertained troops when they could. They also helped to nurse soldiers, served as spies, and marched as drummer boys. Some became soldiers themselves. Illustrations augment the text. Glossary and Index.

1671. Lalicki, Tom. *Grierson's Raid: A Daring Cavalry Strike Through the Heart of the Confederacy.* Farrar, 2004. 200pp. ISBN 978-0-374-32787-3. Grades 3–6. In 1863 Benjamin Grierson, a Union colonel, led several successful raids from LaGrange, Tennessee, to Baton Rouge, Louisiana. He damaged a Confederate rail line, disrupted communication, and destroyed enemy supply lines. These encroachments kept the Confederates from being ready for the battle at Vicksburg, a major defeat for them. This volume describes the daily action and provides background information on the participants. Photographs, reproductions, and maps enhance the text. Bibliography, Glossary, and Index.

1672. Lewis, J. Patrick. *The Brothers' War: Civil War Voices in Verse.* National Geographic, 2007. 31pp. ISBN 978-1-4263-0036-3. Grades 5–9. Eleven poems, each paired with an appropriate archival photograph, reveal the pain, confusion, fear, and horror of the Civil War. Among the images portrayed in words are a slave with a scarred back, an armless veteran, and a young soldier waiting for battle. Map, Chronology, and Notes.

1673. Lincoln, Abraham. *The Gettysburg Address.* Illustrated by Michael McCurdy. Houghton, 1995. Unpaged. ISBN 978-0-395-69824-2; 1998, paper ISBN 978-0-395-88397-6. Grades K up. McCurdy has carefully illustrated the words of the Gettysburg Address so that they are accessible to all readers. By showing only a few words per page, he underlines the brevity and power of the speech. *Notable Children's Trade Books in the Field of Social Studies.*

1674. McPherson, James M. *Fields of Fury: The American Civil War.* Atheneum, 2002. 96pp. ISBN 978-0-689-84833-9. Grades 5–8. McPherson looks at the events and the effects of the Civil War, during which 620,000 soldiers—2 percent of the population—died. (Two percent of the contemporary population would be 5.5 million.) He offers information about individual battles, leaders, the Emancipation Proclamation, life at home, prisoner of war treatment, African American soldiers, and the effects of Reconstruction. The two-page chapters contain several paragraphs on each topic with photographs and prints. Bibliography, Glossary, Web Sites, and Index. *Garden State Nonfiction Book Award* (New Jersey) nomination, and *Beehive Children's Book Award* (Utah) nomination.

1675. Murphy, Jim. *A Savage Thunder: Antietam and the Bloody Road to Freedom.* Margaret K. McElderry, 2009. 103pp. ISBN 978-0-689-87633-2. Grades 4–8. The battle at Antietam in Sharpsburg, Maryland, on September 15, 1862, was the bloodiest day in American history, with 22,717 casualties. The twelve chapters plus preface trace that day through firsthand accounts and newspaper reports. Murphy posits that before this battle the war focused on preserving the Union, but after General Robert E. Lee and his Confederate Army faced the skittish General George McClelland and his army of the Potomac, the war shifted to a battle over slavery. Lincoln signed the Emancipation Proclamation at the end of the battle. Period photographs and maps augment the text. Notes, Bibliography, and Index.

1676. O'Brian, Patrick. *Duel of the Ironclads: The Monitor vs. the Virginia.* Walker, 2007. Paper ISBN 978-0-8027-9562-5. Grades 2–6. O'Brian offers background information on the Civil War battleships *Monitor* and *Virginia* (the Union called this ship the *Merrimack*), including their construction, the battles in which they fought, and their impact on the Civil War. The *Merrimack* was originally a sailing ship. In 1861, when it was defeated in a battle, the Union partially burned and sank it rather than let the Confederates have it. However, the Confederates raised it and rebuilt it as an ironclad vessel renamed the *Virginia*. The Union's *Monitor* engaged the *Virginia* in Hampton Roads in the first battle between two ironclad ships. Watercolor and gouache illustrations and maps complement the text.

1677. Read, Thomas Buchanan. *Sheridan's Ride.* Illustrated by Nancy Winslow Parker. Kessenger, 2007. 31pp. ISBN 978-0-548-52293-6; paper ISBN 978-0-548-50957-9. Grades 3–6. On the morning of October 19, 1864, Major General Philip H. Sheridan, commander of the Union army of the Shenandoah, was preparing to destroy the Confederates' food supply. But General Early of the Confederate Army of the Valley was planning a surprise attack at Cedar Creek, Virginia. When Sheridan heard artillery fire at eight in the morning, he started riding south toward his men and stopped them from retreating. He rallied his troops and formed a battle line to attack the Confederate army. At four o'clock that afternoon, they drove the Confederates off the field. Many were killed and wounded, but the Confederate army left the Shenandoah Valley for the rest of the war. This poem commemorates that feat. Military and Historical Notes.

1678. Rebman, Renee C. *The Union Soldier.* (We the People) Compass Point, 2006. 48pp. ISBN 978-0-7565-2030-4; paper ISBN 978-0-7565-2042-7. Grades 4–6. This volume offers background on what life was like for the Union soldiers during the Civil War. It covers their clothes, living quarters, weapons, and food along with other topics. Maps, photographs, and reproductions illustrate the text. Glossary, Chronology, Further Reading, Web Sites, and Index.

1679. Richards, Kenneth. *The Gettysburg Address.* Children's, 1993. 31pp. Paper ISBN 978-0-516-46654-5. Grades 3–5. Richards describes the battle at Gettysburg, Pennsylvania, between the Confederate and Union armies on July 3–5, 1863. In the autumn after this battle, at which the North lost 23,000 men and the South 28,000, Abraham Lincoln took the train to Gettysburg to deliver a speech at a cemetery dedication. Although very short in comparison to the other speech made that day, the address remains a strong statement about the importance of adhering to one's beliefs in freedom. Index.

1680. Schomp, Virginia. *The Civil War.* Benchmark, 2003. 95pp. ISBN 978-0-7614-1660-9. Grades 5–8. Using letters from soldiers, women, and African Americans, Schomp describes the Civil War. She looks at fighting for the Confederacy, support for the Union, black troops, women on the front, and the aftermath. Also covered are race relations and other pertinent social history. Photographs highlight the text. Bibliography, Glossary, Chronology, Notes, Further Reading, and Index.

1681. Sheinkin, Steve. *Two Miserable Presidents: Everything Your Textbooks Didn't Tell You About the American Civil War.* Illustrated by Tim Robinson. Flash Point, 2008. 192pp. ISBN 978-1-59643-320-5. Grades 5–9. This view of the Civil War offers extracts from letters, unusual anecdotes, and characterizations that enliven the presentation. It covers all aspects of the time leading up to the Civil War and the conflict itself, with profiles of key figures. Cartoon illustrations complement the text. Notes.

1682. Silvey, Anita. *I'll Pass for Your Comrade: Women Soldiers in the Civil War.* Clarion, 2008. 115pp. ISBN 978-0-618-57491-9. Grades 5–9. Many women disguised as men took part in the Civil War, among them Loreta Janeta Velazquez (Lt. Harry T. Buford) at the Battle of Bull Run, Canadian Sarah Emma Edmonds who joined the Michigan Volunteers, and Jennie Hodgers who fought in the Illinois infantry and pretended to be a man until her death in 1911. These women wanted to be near lovers, to escape harsh home conditions, to earn money, or to have adventure and excitement. Primary sources present women who contributed to war at such battles as Bull Run and Antietam, with details of how they kept their disguises in the field and while wounded in hospitals or imprisoned. Period photography and archival reproductions and documents augment the text. Bibliography, Notes, Further Reading, and Index. *Notable Social Studies Trade Books for Young People.*

1683. Somervill, Barbara A. *Women of the Confederacy.* (We the People) Compass Point, 2006. 48pp. ISBN 978-0-7565-2033-5; paper ISBN 978-0-7565-2045-8. Grades 4–6. This collective biography offers profiles of women who helped the Confederacy during the Civil War. Although they did not prevail, they kept the war going for four years. The text covers a wide variety of occupations, from writers and nurses to soldiers and spies. Maps, photographs, and reproductions illustrate the text. Glossary, Chronology, Further Reading, Web Sites, and Index.

1684. Swanson, James L. *Chasing Lincoln's Killer.* Scholastic, 2009. 208pp. ISBN 978-0-439-90354-7. Grades 5 up. On April 14, 1865, John Wilkes Booth (1938–1865) assassinated Abraham Lincoln (1809–1865). The fourteen chapters and epilogue detail the twelve days that followed, during which Booth tried to escape those hunting him. Booth had originally planned to kidnap Lincoln, but when that plot failed, he began preparations to kill the president, the vice president, and the secretary of state simultaneously. This plot went awry and only Lincoln died; Booth's sidekicks failed with Seward. Period photographs enhance the text. No end notes. *American Library Association Best Books for Young Adults, Young Readers Choice Book Award* (Pennsylvania) nomination, and *Junior Book Award* (South Carolina) nomination.

1685. Tanaka, Shelley. *Gettysburg: The Legendary Battle and the Address That Inspired a Nation.* Illustrated by David Craig. (A Day that Changed America) Hyperion, 2003. 48pp. ISBN 978-0-7868-1922-5. Grades 4–8. This short history of the Battle of Gettysburg includes the commemorative address that President Abraham Lincoln made on November 18, 1863. Lincoln took a train to Gettysburg on that day, and at a ceremony to dedicate the battlefield, Edward Everett delivered a very long speech. He then asked Lincoln if he would like to add a "few remarks." The resultant words redefined the Civil War and the office of the presidency while inspiring the Union. This volume looks at the geography of the town and area around it, analyzes the key fights during each day of the battle, and highlights both the personalities involved and artifacts resulting from the fray. Maps, Photos, Further Reading, Glossary, Web Sites, and Index.

1686. Trumbauer, Lisa. *Abraham Lincoln and the Civil War.* (Life in the Time Of) Heinemann, 2007. 32pp. ISBN 978-1-4034-9668-3; paper ISBN 978-1-4034-9676-8. Grades 3–5. The relationship of Abraham Lincoln (1809–1865) to the Civil War is the focus of this text. Lincoln wrote the Emancipation Proclamation, won reelection, and then was assassinated, all seminal moments of the Civil War. Archival photographs and illustrations augment the text. Glossary, Chronology, Further Reading, Web Sites, and Index.

1687. Warren, Andrea. *Under Siege! Three Children at the Civil War Battle for Vicksburg.* Farrar, 2009. 166pp. ISBN 978-0-374-31255-8. Grades 5–8. The Union army attempted to take Vicksburg, Mississippi, from December 1862 until the town surrendered on July 4, 1863. One of the tactics was a 47-day siege. This volume presents the points of view of three eyewitnesses—a businessman's daughter, 10-year-old Lucy McRae; the Episcopalian minister's son, Willie Lord, 11; and Fred, the 12-year-old son of Ulysses S. Grant. Lucy's family survived in a cave where they hid to escape shelling. Fred's account is unusual because he accompanied his father to the battle, and although he contracted malaria and typhoid fever and was shot in the leg, he enjoyed himself immensely. Period photographs, quotes, maps, and paintings enhance the text. Bibliography, Further Reading, Endnotes, Web Sites, and Index.

Biography and Collective Biography

1688. Adler, David A. *A Picture Book of Robert E. Lee.* See entry 1483.

1689. Aller, Susan Bivin. *Ulysses S. Grant.* See entry 1487.

1690. Armstrong, Jennifer. *Photo by Brady: A Picture of the Civil War.* Atheneum, 2005. 160pp. ISBN 978-0-689-85785-0. Grades 5–9. Mathew B. Brady (1822–1896) realized that photography deserved a place in the Civil War. He hired a group of field photographers from New York City and Washington to travel with the troops in Virginia and record images that still appear in books and movies about the Civil War today. By the 1840s he had photographed and created a catalog of America's most distinguished citizens. Lincoln credited him with helping him become president. Photographs highlight the text. Other information in the text includes details from soldiers' letters and diaries. Bibliography, Notes, and Index. *School Library Journal Best Children's Books* and *Capitol Choices Noteworthy Titles* (Washington, D.C.).

1691. Chorlian, Meg. *Ulysses S. Grant: Confident Leader and Hero.* See entry 1495.

1692. Clinton, Catherine. *Hold the Flag High.* Illustrated by Shane W. Evans. Amistad, 2005. 32pp. ISBN 978-0-06-050428-1. Grades 2–5. After the 1863 Civil War battle of Morris Island, South Carolina, Sergeant William H. Carney preserved the flag and became the first African American to earn the Congressional Medal of Honor. He flew the flag at Fort Wagner during the bloody charge of the 54th Massachusetts regiment and, although wounded, carried it safely in the Union retreat that followed. Photographs and illustrations augment the text. Chronology, Further Reading, and Web Sites.

1693. Denenberg, Barry. *Lincoln Shot: A President's Life Remembered.* Feiwel & Friends, 2008. 40pp. ISBN 978-0-312-37013-8. Grades 5 up. This biography of Abraham Lincoln (1809–1865) resembles a 19th-century newspaper, both in size and appearance, with period typography, advertisements from 1866, pen-and-ink drawings, and archival photography. It presumes to be a commemorative issue published one year after Lincoln's death and covers the actual event, the hunt for the men involved, and the swift justice. It then offers a detailed account of Lincoln's life and background on the Civil War. Bibliography available on a Web site. *School Library Journal Best Books for Children.*

1694. Donlan, Leni. *Mathew Brady: Photographing the Civil War.* (American History Through Primary Sources) Raintree, 2007. 32pp. ISBN 978-1-4109-2699-9. Grades 3–6. Mathew B. Brady (1822–1896) realized that photography deserved a place in the Civil War. He hired a group of field photographers from New York City and Washington to travel with the troops in Virginia and record the images that still appear in books and movies about the Civil War today. By the 1840s he had photographed and created a catalog of America's most distinguished citizens. Lincoln credited Brady with helping him become president. Photographs highlight the text. The text also includes details from soldiers' letters and diaries. Bibliography, Notes, and Index.

1695. Dubowski, Cathy East. *Clara Barton: I Want to Help!* Bearport, 2005. 32pp. ISBN 978-1-59716-075-9. Grades 2–4. Clara Barton (1821–1912), a shy child, overcame her fear to become a teacher and then a nurse during the Civil War, braving cannon fire on the battlefields to help the wounded. She later established the American Red Cross. Photographs and reproductions illuminate the text. Bibliography, Glossary, Chronology, Further Reading, Web Sites, and Index.

1696. Ford, Carin T. *Daring Women of the Civil War.* (The Civil War Library) Enslow, 2004. 48pp. ISBN 978-0-7660-2250-8. Grades 4–6. Women helped fight the Civil War on both sides. They had to do "men's work" around the home, they held office jobs, worked in factories, served as nurses, disguised themselves as soldiers, or spied on the enemy. Among the women presented are author Louisa May Alcott; Sarah Rosetta Wakeman, who disguised herself as a man to fight as an army private; runaway slave Susie King Taylor who worked as a nurse; and Confederate spy Rose O'Neal Greenhow. Maps, Notes, Timeline, Web Sites, Glossary, and Index.

1697. Fritz, Jean. *Stonewall.* Illustrated by Stephen Gammell. Puffin, 1997. 160pp. Paper ISBN 978-0-698-11552-1. Grades 3–8. Tom Jackson (1824–1863) saw his mother working in menial jobs because his father had frittered away the family money before he died. After her death, when Tom was 7, he decided to make something of his life. His rules for life were to tell the truth, not to break promises, and to do what he planned. After living with an uncle, Tom's break came when he had a chance to go to West Point even though he was not well educated. He graduated, became a hero in the Mexican War, taught at Virginia Military Institute, and fought for the South in the Civil War, where he earned the name "Stonewall." Strong religious convictions and strict rules governed his life. He died of pneumonia after one of his soldiers accidentally shot him in the arm. Bibliography.

1698. Furbee, Mary R. *Outrageous Women of Civil War Times.* Jossey-Bass, 2002. 124pp. Paper ISBN 978-0-471-22926-1. Grades 3–6. Furbee presents twelve women who were outrageous around the time of the Civil War. They were reformers and writers, saviors and leaders, soldiers and spies, and first ladies: Louisa May Alcott (1832–1888), Amelia Bloomer (1818–1894), Susan B. Anthony (1820–1906), Sojourner Truth (1797–1883), Clara Barton (1821–1912), Dorothea Dix (1802–1887), Harriet Tubman (1820?–1913, Belle Boyd (1844–1900), Pauline Cushman (1833–1893), Loreta Janeta Velázquez (1842–?), Mary Todd Lincoln (1818–1882), and Varina Howell Davis (1826–1906). Furbee includes these women because they were originals who contributed to American life in unique ways. She also lists other women one might consider outrageous. Further Reading and Chronology.

1699. Giblin, James Cross. *Good Brother, Bad Brother: The Story of Edwin Booth and John Wilkes Booth.* Clarion, 2005. 256pp. ISBN 978-0-618-09642-8. Grades 5–9. The Booth brothers, John Wilkes (1838–1865) and Edwin (1833–1893), supported opposing sides during the Civil War. This biography reviews their family, friends, careers, and political ideologies. Edwin became an actor, the best classical actor of his time, after touring with his actor father to keep him from drinking too much. John Wilkes was a cheerful child who proved to be the opposite when he concocted the plot to assassinate Lincoln. Photographs highlight the text. Bibliography, Further Reading, and Index. *Taysha's High School Reading List* (Texas), *Beehive Children's Book Award* (Utah) nomination, *Boston Globe/Horn Book Award Honor, School Library Journal Best Children's Books,* and *Dorothy Canfield Fisher Children's Book Award* (Vermont) nomination.

1700. Hale, Ed. *Abraham Lincoln: Defender of the Union.* (The Civil War) Cobblestone, 2005. ISBN 978-0-8126-7902-1. Grades 4–9. A young boy who grew up in a one-room log cabin became the president of the United States during one of its most difficult periods. Abraham Lincoln had the courage to pass the Emancipation Proclamation to free the slaves, and then he gave one of the most remembered speeches in the country's history at Gettysburg. This volume is divided into thirteen sections that cover Lincoln's childhood, courtship of Mary Todd, family life, political life, the Lincoln-Douglas debates, and so forth. Illustrations, photographs, and maps enhance the text.

1701. Hale, Ed. *Gettysburg: Bold Battle in the North.* (The Civil War) Cobblestone, 2005. 47pp. ISBN 978-0-8126-7903-8. Grades 4–9. When Robert E. Lee took his troops into Union territory, he hoped to change the war for the Confederates. The three-day battle, however, was horrible for both sides, leaving thousands of soldiers dead. This volume presents an account of the battle and the strategies of its leaders. Illustrations augment the text. Chronology, Glossary, and Index.

1702. **Hale, Sarah Elder.** *Robert E. Lee: Duty and Honor.* (The Civil War) Cobblestone, 2005. 47pp. ISBN 978-0-8126-7905-2. Grades 4–9. During the Civil War, Robert Edward Lee (1807–1870) had to decide whether to support the country for which he had served in the military for thirty years or his home state of Virginia. Offered command of the Union army by Lincoln, he chose instead to stay with Virginia. This biography focuses on his military career with brief profiles of other leaders with whom or against whom he fought. Maps and illustrations complement the text. Index.

1703. **Halfmann, Janet.** *Seven Miles to Freedom: The Robert Smalls Story.* Illustrated by Duane Smith. Lee & Low, 2008. 40pp. ISBN 978-1-60060-232-0. Grades 1–5. While working on the docks as a young slave in Beaufort, South Carolina, Robert Smalls learned how to sail a ship. After becoming a husband and father, Smalls got his family aboard the *Planter,* a Confederate ship, and using his knowledge of Confederate whistle signals, cruised out of port while the crew was ashore having parties. Oil illustrations complement the text. Bibliography and Note.

1704. **Holzer, Harold.** *The President Is Shot! The Assassination of Abraham Lincoln.* Boyds Mills, 2004. 184pp. ISBN 978-1-56397-985-9. Grades 5–9. Holzer offers a balanced look at Abraham Lincoln (1809–1865) to show why John Wilkes Booth wanted to shoot him. Booth, a southerner, supported slavery. He achieved fame by assassinating Lincoln on April 14, 1865, but he also sacrificed his name. The text begins five days before Lincoln's death, recounting Lincoln's actions and the attitudes of those around him. Bibliography and Index.

1705. **Kennedy, Robert F., Jr.** *Joshua Chamberlain and the American Civil War.* Illustrated by Nikita Andreev. (Robert F. Kennedy Jr.'s American Heroes) Hyperion, 2007. 38pp. ISBN 978-1-4231-0771-2. Grades 3–6. This biography offers an overview of the life of Joshua Lawrence Chamberlain (1828–1914), a Civil War Union general from Maine. In 1862 Chamberlain left both his position as a professor at Bowdoin College and his family to fight for the North. He had prepared himself for battle by reading military histories and manuals, but after the reality of the battles at Antietam and Fredericksburg, he was ready to command himself. He led defenses at Little Round Top and Big Round Top at Gettysburg and in twenty-two other battles. Ink and watercolor illustrations complement the text. Bibliography.

1706. **Leslie, Tonya.** *Abraham Lincoln: A Life of Honesty.* See entry 1525.

1707. **Pflueger, Lynda.** *Stonewall Jackson: Confederate General.* Enslow, 1997. 128pp. ISBN 978-0-89490-781-4. Grades 5–8. Stonewall Jackson (1824–1863) led Confederate troops who followed him faithfully because he planned carefully and was fearless in battle. This biography looks at his impact on American history as it examines his life. Factboxes and maps augment the text. Notes, Glossary, Further Reading, and Index.

1708. **Pittman, Rickey.** *Jim Limber Davis: A Black Orphan in the Confederate White House.* Illustrated by Judith Hierstein. Pelican, 2007. Unpaged. ISBN 978-1-58980-435-7. Grades 2–4. Jefferson Davis adopted a free black orphan boy, Jim, and after the Union army arrested Davis, northerners took the boy North. They showed the scars on his back and said Davis had mistreated him. However, Jim's uncle had scarred his back before Davis adopted him.

1709. **Ransom, Candice F.** *Clara Barton.* See entry 1543.

1710. **Ransom, Candice F.** *Robert E. Lee.* See entry 1544.

1711. **Rappaport, Doreen, and Joan C. Verniero.** *United No More! Stories of the Civil War.* Illustrated by Rick Reeves. HarperCollins, 2006. 132pp. ISBN 978-0-06-050599-8. Grades 4–7. Primary sources reveal the lives of seven participants in the Civil War from both the North and the South. The fictionalized characters include two soldiers, Massachusetts 54th Colored Infantry volunteer William H. Carney and naval commander David Farragut, who stormed Mobile Bay. Women are Julia Ward Howe, who wrote "The Battle Hymn of the Republic"; a woman who refused to respect Union troops in New Orleans, Eugenia Phillips; and the leader of a Richmond food riot, Mary Jackson. The last two "portraits" reveal Lincoln's second inaugural and Lee's surrender at Appomattox. Illustrations augment the text. Further Reading, Bibliography, Chronology, Web Sites, and Index.

1712. **Sapp, Richard.** *Ulysses S. Grant and the Road to Appomattox.* See entry 1554.

1713. **Schott, Jane A.** *Abraham Lincoln.* See entry 1555.

1714. **Waryncia, Lou.** *Stonewall Jackson: Spirit of the South.* (The Civil War) Cobblestone, 2005. 47pp. ISBN 978-0-8126-7907-6. Grades 4–9. As a young man in the United States-Mexican War, Thomas "Stonewall" Jackson (1824–1863) was promoted three times. His commander realized he could be a great leader. During the Civil War, he became a general and Confederate hero as he led campaigns at Manasssas, in the Shenandoah Valley, and at Chancellorsville. This volume reviews his days at West Point and his teaching experience at Virginia Military Institute as well. Illustrations, photographs, and maps enhance the text.

Graphic Novels, Biographies, and Histories

1715. **Abnett, Dan.** *The Battle of Gettysburg: Spilled Blood on Sacred Ground.* Illustrated by Dheeraj Verma. (Graphic Battles of the Civil War) Rosen, 2006. 48pp. ISBN 978-1-4042-0777-6. Grades 4–9. This graphic history presents the three days of the Battle of Gettysburg, July 1–4, 1863. The panels present both the Confederate and Union sides of the war, with their leaders speaking in present tense to add immediacy to the action. Glossary, Maps, Further Reading, Web Sites, and Index.

1716. **Burgan, Michael.** *The Battle of Gettysburg.* Illustrated by Steve Erwin. Graphic Library, 2006. 32pp. ISBN 978-0-7368-5491-7; paper ISBN 978-0-7368-6880-8. Grades 3–5. On July 1, 1863, the Union and Confederate armies under George G. Meade and Robert E. Lee, respectively, met in Gettysburg, Pennsylvania. The ensuing battle lasted three days and led to nearly 47,000 casualties, with the Union claiming victory and the Confederates stopped from advancing further north. Illustrations depict the event. Bibliography, Glossary, Further Reading, and Index.

1717. **Hama, Larry, and Scott Moore.** *The Battle of Antietam: "The Bloodiest Day of Battle."* (Graphic Battles of the Civil War) Rosen, 2006. 48pp. ISBN 978-1-4042-0775-2. Grades 4–9. On September 17, 1862, a battle near Antietam Creek in Sharpsburg, Maryland, between the Union and Confederate soldiers became the bloodiest day of the war. The six chapters describe the leaders involved, their strategies, and the results of combat. Photographs augment the text. Glossary, Further Reading, Web Sites, and Index.

1718. **Hama, Larry, and Scott Moore.** *The Battle of First Bull Run: The Civil War Begins.* (Graphic Battles of the Civil War) Rosen, 2006. 48pp. ISBN 978-1-4042-0776-9. Grades 4–9. On July 21, 1861, the battle known as the First Battle of Bull Run or the First Battle of Manassas, as the Confederates called it, was the first major land conflict of the Civil War. The six chapters describe Union Brigadier General Irvin McDowell's advance against the two brigadier generals of the Confederates, Joseph E. Johnston and P. G. T. Beauregard. The book also details the battle and the aftermath, when the Union forces had to retreat to Washington, D.C. Photographs augment the text. Glossary, Further Reading, Web Sites, and Index.

1719. **Hama, Larry, and Scott Moore.** *The Battle of Shiloh: Surprise Attack!* (Graphic Battles of the Civil War) Rosen, 2006. 48pp. ISBN 978-1-4042-0779-0. Grades 4–9. On April 6 and 7, 1862, the battle of Shiloh, or the Battle of Pittsburg Landing, was fought in southwestern Tennessee. The six chapters describe the Confederates under Generals P. G. T. Beauregard and Albert Sidney Johnston surprising the Union army under Major General Ulysses S. Grant. The southern forces came exceeding close to defeating Grant. The six chapters detail the leaders, the battle, and the aftermath. Photographs augment the text. Glossary, Further Reading, Web Sites, and Index.

1720. **Olson, Kay Melchisedech.** *The Assassination of Abraham Lincoln.* Illustrated by Otha Zackariah Edward Lohse. Graphic Library, 2006. 32pp. ISBN 978-0-7368-3831-3; paper ISBN

978-0-7368-5241-8. Grades 3–5. This graphic history covers the assassination of Abraham Lincoln on April 14, 1865. Bibliography, Glossary, Further Reading, and Index.

DVDs

1721. *Abraham Lincoln.* (Great Americans for Children) Library Video, 2002. 23 mins. Grades K–4. See entry 1582.

1722. Borden, Louise W. *A. Lincoln and Me.* Illustrated by Ted Lewin. Nutmeg, 2005. 32pp. 9 mins. ISBN 978-0-9771510-3-5. Grades 4–8. See entry 1600.

Compact Discs

1723. Hunt, Irene. *Across Five Aprils.* Narrated by Terry Bregy. Audio Bookshelf, 2002. 5 CDs; 6 hrs. ISBN 978-1-8833-3275-4. Grades 5–8. See entry 1622.

1724. Philbrick, Rodman. *The Mostly True Adventures of Homer P. Figg.* Listening Library, 2009. 4 CDs; 4 hrs. ISBN 978-0-7393-7232-6. Grades 5–8. See entry 1636.

1725. Porter, Connie. *Addy.* Narrated by Cynthia Adams. Recorded Books, 2006. 6 CDs; 6 hrs. ISBN 978-1-4193-5917-0. Grades 3–6. Addy, 9, sees her father and brother sold to another plantation during the Civil War. She and her mother decide to risk escaping to freedom in the North. To get away, they must leave Addy's baby sister in the slave quarters. Once in Philadelphia, they try to get money to bring the family together. Addy realizes that freedom costs in many unexpected ways.

1726. Seguin, Marilyn Weymouth. *Knothole in the Closet: A Story About Belle Boyd, a Confederate Spy.* Narrated by Kate Fleming. In Audio, 2003. 1 CD, 24 mins. ISBN 978-1-58472-276-2. Grades 3 up. Belle Boyd, 19, lived in Fort Royal, Virginia, at the beginning of the Civil War. She became a Confederate courier, relaying information to General Stonewall Jackson after spying on the Yankees. Unlike many other women of her time, she exhibited independence. Although she endured hardships in her job, she helped the Confederates intelligently. Her information helped them win a major victory on May 23, 1862, driving the Union army out of Fort Royal.

1727. Steele, William O. *The Perilous Road.* Narrated by Ramon De Ocampo. Listen & Live Audio, 2005. 4 CDs; 5 hrs. ISBN 978-1-59316-040-1. Grades 4–8. See entry 1648.

1728. Swanson, James L. *Chasing Lincoln's Killer.* Narrated by Will Paton. Scholastic, 2009. 4 CDs; 3 hrs., 58 mins. ISBN 978-0-545-11943-6. Grades 5 up. See entry 1684.

RECONSTRUCTION, THE PROGRESSIVE ERA, AND SUFFRAGE, 1866–1916

Historical Fiction and Fantasy

1729. Ackerman, Karen. *Bean's Big Day.* Illustrated by Paul Mombourquette. Kids Can, 2004. 32pp. ISBN 978-1-55337-444-2. Grades K–2. In the early 20th century, the inhabitants of Bean, Pennsylvania, are excited to hear that one of them will be in a moving picture, playing a singing cowboy. Eight-year-old Cricket describes the reaction to the news and how everyone dresses up to meet the man from the movies. The visitor chooses the least likely candidate—Slip, the livery boy—leaving many disappointed citizens.

1730. Andreasen, Dan. *The Giant of Seville: A "Tall" Tale Based on a True Story.* Abrams, 2007. 32pp. ISBN 978-0-8109-0988-5. Grades K–3. Martin Van Buren Bates (b. 1845), a retired circus performer and Confederate soldier, decides to settle in Seville, Ohio. Unfortunately, nothing fits him there because he is 7 feet 11 inches tall, and his wife is as tall as he is. He has to stick his feet out the window to sleep and adjust in many other ways. Illustrations enhance the text. Note.

1731. Angell, Judie. *One-Way to Ansonia.* BackinPrint.com, 2001. 183pp. Paper ISBN 978-0-595-15830-0. Grades 5–8. After escaping from Russian pogroms, Rose, 11, and her siblings arrive at Ellis Island in 1893 to meet their father and his new wife. Rose surprises her family when she decides to attend night school after her long workdays, but she realizes she must work hard to escape the poverty of New York tenement life.

1732. Armstrong, Jennifer. *Magnus at the Fire.* Illustrated by Owen Smith. Simon & Schuster, 2005. 32pp. ISBN 978-0-689-83922-1. Grades 1–4. Enjoying his job as a fire horse, Magnus does not want to retire when the Broadway Fire House gets a motorized fire engine. He and the rest of the team, Billy and Sparks, dislike the pasture enclosing them, and when the fire bell rings, Magnus leaps across the fence to the fire. On the way to the fire, the fire truck breaks down, and Magnus becomes famous for taking over his old job. Oil illustrations complement the text.

1733. Armstrong, Jennifer. *Theodore Roosevelt: Letters from a Young Coal Miner.* (Dear Mr. President) Winslow, 2001. 118pp. ISBN 978-1-890817-27-5. Grades 4–7. Young Polish coal miner Frank Kovacs, 13, takes part in the Anthracite Coal Strike of 1902 in western Pennsylvania and he begins corresponding with President Theodore Roosevelt about the strike. He describes the difficult lives of the miners and their families, and Roosevelt tells him about his own family. Photographs, timeline, bibliography, index.

1734. **Avi.** *The Seer of Shadows.* HarperCollins, 2008. 208pp. ISBN 978-0-06-000015-8. Grades 4–6. Horace Carpentine, 14, is a photographer's apprentice in New York City in 1872. The photographer plans to hoodwink a woman who wants him to catch the image of her deceased daughter. Horace is unhappy with this twist in his work; he is skeptical of anything other-worldly. Then he discovers, however, that he himself has the ability to summon up spirits but cannot control their coming or going. He finds out that this family mistreated their adopted daughter and caused her death. He must try to put the ghost to rest and save lives in the process. *School Library Journal Best Books for Children.*

1735. **Baker, Sharon Reiss.** *A Nickel, a Trolley, a Treasure House.* Illustrated by Beth Peck. Viking, 2007. 32pp. ISBN 978-0-670-05982-9. Grades 2–5. When Lionel is 9 years old in the early 1900s, he lives with his Jewish family on Ludlow Street in a New York City tenement. His siblings sell chestnuts, shine shoes, and make deliveries to help the family, but all he likes to do is draw. He sketches on any piece of paper he can find, and he keeps his drawings hidden between cardboard. His teacher sees them and says she will take him to the Metropolitan Museum of Art. Lionel worries about his nickel for the streetcar. She pays, however, and the beauty of the building stuns him along with all of the wonderful pictures inside.

1736. **Bedard, Michael.** *Emily.* Illustrated by Barbara Cooney. Doubleday, 1992. 36pp. ISBN 978-0-385-30697-3; Dragonfly, 2002, paper ISBN 978-0-440-41740-8. Grades K–3. A little girl moves to Amherst, Massachusetts, in the 1880s and finds she lives on the same street as an odd woman who does not have visitors and whom the neighbors call "The Myth." When the girl's mother goes to play the piano for the lady, the girl goes with her and meets Emily Dickinson. They exchange unusual gifts.

1737. **Blegvad, Lenore.** *Kitty and Mr. Kipling: Neighbors in Vermont.* Illustrated by Erik Blegvad. Margaret K. McElderry, 2005. 144pp. ISBN 978-0-689-87363-8. Grades 3–6. When Rudyard Kipling moves in next door to Kitty and her family in Dummerston, Vermont, in 1892, he and Kitty becomes friends and he shares stories from his work in progress, *The Jungle Book.* Unfortunately Mrs. Kipling's brother, Beatty Balestier, also lives in town and relations between him and the Kiplings, never good, deteriorate further. Eventually the Kiplings returns to England and Kitty loses her friend. Bibliography. Illustrations enhance the text.

1738. **Boling, Katharine.** *January 1905.* Harcourt, 2004. 170pp. ISBN 978-0-15-205119-8; 2006, paper ISBN 978-0-15205-121-1. Grades 5–9. Pauline and Arlene, 11-year-old twins, are at odds with each other. Pauline works in the local cotton mill although she would prefer to stay home like her sister. But Arlene, who has a deformed foot, longs to work at the mill where she could earn money instead of doing housework and cooking. When Pauline injures her own foot, she finds out that being unable to walk properly is more debilitating than she ever imagined. Arlene replaces Pauline at the mill and learns about the conditions there. Eventually, they realize that each can be the other's best friend.

1739. **Bradby, Marie.** *More than Anything Else.* Illustrated by Chris K. Soentpiet. Orchard, 1995. Unpaged. ISBN 978-0-531-09464-8. Grades K–3. When Booker T. Washington (1856–1915) hears a black man read aloud, he hopes he can learn too. His mother gets him an alphabet book, but he can't understand anything until the man he heard read shows him how. He reads every evening after a long day in the salt works. *School Library Journal Starred Review.*

1740. **Bradley, Kimberly Brubaker.** *The President's Daughter.* Yearling, 2006. 176pp. Paper ISBN 978-0-440-41995-2. Grades 5–7. Ethel Roosevelt moves into the White House in 1901 at the age of 10 when her father, Theodore, becomes president. She attends boarding school during the week and feels insecure there. On weekends she rides on horseback through Rock Creek Park with her father. When her older, more courageous sister Alice comes home, Ethel hopes to learn how to make her father proud of her. Alice dares her to climb under a table at dinner in the East Room, and this gives her confidence that she can succeed. *Children's Book Award* (Rhode Island) nomination and *Sunshine State Young Reader Award* (Florida) nomination.

1741. Brown, Don. *The Notorious Izzy Fink.* Roaring Brook, 2006. 160pp. ISBN 978-1-59643-139-3. Grades 4–8. On the Lower East Side of New York City in the 1890s, half-Irish and half-Russian Jewish Sam Glodsky hopes to rise from poverty by selling newspapers, picking up lumps of coal, and avoiding his arch rival, Izzy. Sam meets a health inspector who is looking for a cholera victim who may have escaped from a quarantined ship in the harbor. Then notorious gangster and animal lover Monk Eastman hires Sam and Izzy to rescue a prized carrier pigeon from the diseased ship. On board, Izzy breaks the bird's wing and gets Sam locked in the cage. Sam's father, roused from the two-year depression that has afflicted him since the death of Sam's mother, rescues him.

1742. Brown, Elizabeth Ferguson. *Coal Country Christmas.* Illustrated by Harvey Stevenson. Boyds Mills, 2003. 32pp. ISBN 978-1-59078-020-6. Grades K–4. In the mid-1800s a little girl arrives at her grandmother's house in Pennsylvania coal country for Christmas. She notes that many men are dead from lung disease and coal gas in this loving town, including her grandfather, whose chair sits empty. Illustrations complement the text.

1743. Bruchac, Joseph. *Jim Thorpe: Original All-American.* Dial, 2006. 277pp. ISBN 978-0-8037-3118-9. Grades 5 up. A Sac and Fox Indian called Wa-Tho-Huk (Bright Path), Jim Thorpe (1887–1953), recognized today as one of the greatest athletes who ever lived, attended Haskell and Carlisle Indian boarding schools. There he demonstrated his abilities at football, baseball, and track. At the 1912 Olympics he won two gold medals, which he lost when a rumor emerged that he had previously played professionally. At college, he trained with "Pop" Warner, an extraordinary coach who not only controlled Thorpe but also the proceeds from the games in which he played. He lived his adult life in poverty. His medals were restored thirty years after he died.

1744. Buckey, Sarah Masters. *The Stolen Sapphire: A Samantha Mystery.* Illustrated by Jean-Paul Tibbles. American Girl, 2006. 181pp. Paper ISBN 978-1-59369-099-1. Grades 2–4. When Samantha and her adopted sister Nellie sail for Europe with their parents in the early 1900s, an archaeologist named Fitzwilliam Wharton is also on the ship. He is carrying the legendary Blue Star sapphire to a London museum. When the jewel disappears, Samantha helps find the thief, thereby removing suspicion from her French tutor. At the same time, Nellie faces discrimination as an Irish girl.

1745. Carvell, Marlene. *Sweetgrass Basket.* Dutton, 2005. 160pp. ISBN 978-0-525-47547-7. Grades 4–9. In the early 20th century, two Mohawk sisters—Mattie and Sarah—attend Pennsylvania's Carlisle Indian Boarding School because their widowed father thinks they will have a better life. They tell their stories in alternating free-verse chapters. The vicious school director falsely accuses Mattie of theft and beats her in public. Sarah is also mistreated. A few of the adults help them, but the girls struggle to survive in hostile atmosphere. *Jane Addams Book Awards.*

1746. Cheng, Andrea. *Anna the Bookbinder.* Illustrated by Ted Rand. Walker, 2003. 32pp. ISBN 978-0-8027-8831-3. Grades K–4. Anna has watched her father work in their bindery for years; she loves the smell of paper, the glue, and the leather. When Anna's father must stop work in the early 1900s because her mother is having a baby, Anna decides to jump in and finish an important order. She restitches the leather-bound books perfectly. Watercolor illustrations complement the text.

1747. Clark, Clara Gillow. *Hattie on Her Way.* Candlewick, 2005. 208pp. ISBN 978-0-7636-2286-2. Grades 5–9. In 1883, 11-year-old Hattie Belle Basket goes to live with her grandmother in Kingston, New York, while her father works as a logger. She is still grieving over her mother's death, but she tries to learn how to act properly in Kingston's genteel society. But where is her grandfather and why are there rumors about her mother's death? Over the months she forges a relationship with her grandmother and learns about the mental illness that plagued both her grandfather and her mother.

1748. Coleman, Evelyn. *Shadows on Society Hill: An Addy Mystery.* American Girl, 2007. 181pp. ISBN 978-1-59369-163-9; paper ISBN 978-1-59369-162-2. Grades 4–7. Eleven-year-old African American Addy looks forward to living in Philadelphia's Society Hill in 1866, but soon discovers that the family's new home with her father's new boss, architect Albert Radisson, has secrets. One of them connects directly to the North Carolina plantation from which she escaped in 1864. Radisson's father was an abolitionist, but his mother was not. When his fiancée Elizabeth arrives, she accepts Addy at first but then accuses her of stealing a lost necklace.

1749. **Conrad, Pam.** *My Daniel.* HarperCollins, 1991. 137pp. Paper ISBN 978-0-06-440309-2. Grades 5 up. Ellie's grandmother Julia tells her about being 12 years old in the early 1900s and finding dinosaur bones on their Nebraska farm with her brother Daniel. Their father hoped the bones would bring enough money to save the farm. Ellie hears the story as they visit the Natural History Museum in New York, where the dinosaurs are on display. After Julia and Daniel made their find, lightning struck Daniel, and Julia's life changed. Looking at the bones in the museum brings back memories. *Notable Children's Trade Books in the Field of Social Studies, American Library Association Best Books for Young Adults, Booklist Children's Editor's Choice, IRA Teachers' Choices, Silver Spur Award for Best Juvenile Fiction, New York Public Library Children's Books,* and *New York Public Library's Books for the Teen Age.*

1750. **Cooney, Barbara.** *Hattie and the Wild Waves: A Story from Brooklyn.* Puffin, 1993. Unpaged. Paper ISBN 978-0-14-054192-9. Grades K–3. In the 19th century, Hattie walks on the beach at Far Rockaway near Brooklyn and wonders what the waves say to each other. She likes to paint them in the winter and in the summer as the years pass. Her sister marries, her brother becomes a businessman, and her mother wonders what will become of Hattie. Hattie expects the waves to tell her, and they tell her to draw. In this story, Cooney honors her mother's stories as the child of immigrants. *Lupine Award.*

1751. **Cooney, Barbara.** *Island Boy.* Puffin, 1988. 32pp. Paper ISBN 978-0-14-050756-0. Grades K–3. In the 19th century, Matthais goes with his family to live on Tibbetts Island off the coast of New England. He becomes a ship's captain and travels all over the world, but he always returns to the island. He raises his family, and his own grandson Matthais lives with him when he is old. *School Library Journal Best Book.*

1752. **Cotten, Cynthia.** *Abbie in Stitches.* Farrar, 2006. Unpaged. ISBN 978-0-374-30004-3. Grades 2–3. Abbie has to go with her sister Sarah to Mrs. Brown's house every Wednesday to learn how to embroider on a sampler. Throughout, Abbie had rather be reading. Then she graduates to creating her own pattern and chooses one that at first surprises everyone, but they eventually understand. She finally has a book of her own. Illustrations complement the text.

1753. **Crisp, Marty.** *Titanicat.* Illustrated by Robert Papp. Sleeping Bear, 2008. 32pp. ISBN 978-1-585-36355-1. Grades 1–4. Jim Mulholland is delighted with his new job as a cabin boy on the *Titanic.* One of his responsibilities is to care for the ship's cat—she has recently had a litter of kittens. He sees her taking the litter ashore before the ship leaves, and he rushes after her with the last kittens that she cannot carry. As he stands ashore, he watches the ship leave dock. After the ship sinks, Jim thanks the mother cat for saving him. Illustrations complement the text. Bibliography and Note.

1754. **Crisp, Marty.** *White Star: A Dog on the Titanic.* Holiday House, 2004. 150pp. ISBN 978-0-8234-1598-4; Scholastic, 2006, paper ISBN 978-0-439-71265-1. Grades 5–8. On the maiden voyage of the *Titanic,* 12-year-old Sam Harris volunteers to help with the dogs in the kennel. He and Star, an Irish setter belonging to J. Bruce Ismay, the ship's owner, quickly bond. He can play with Star and avoid thinking about his return to America—after six years with his grandmother in England he will reunite with his mother and meet his stepfather. When the ship begins sinking, Sam does not want to leave the dog, and the two jump overboard. Photographs and illustrations augment the text. Chronology, Further Reading, and Notes.

1755. **Deutsch, Stacia, and Rhody Cohon.** *Bell's Breakthrough.* Illustrated by David T. Wenzel. (Blast to the Past) Aladdin, 2005. 105pp. Paper ISBN 978-0-689-87026-2. Grades 2–5. In this time travel fictional biography, third-grade students Abigail, Jacob, Zack, and Bo, meet Alexander Graham Bell (1847–1922) before he finishes inventing the telephone. They know its value to society and they convince him not to abandon his efforts. The third volume in the series.

1756. Doyle, Bill. *Swindled: The 1906 Journal of Fitz Morgan.* (Crime Through Time) Little, Brown, 2006. 139pp. Paper ISBN 978-0-316-05736-3. Grades 4–8. In 1906, Fitz, 14, and his new friend Justine Pinkerton try to find out the source of cyanide poisonings on a Continental Express train bound from New York City to San Francisco. They discover connections to a counterfeit ring during their sleuthing.

1757. Drummond, Allan. *Liberty!* Farrar, 2006. 40pp. Paper ISBN 978-0-374-44397-9. Grades K–3. On October 28, 1886, Frédéric Auguste Bartholdi plans to unveil his sculpture, the Statue of Liberty, in New York Harbor. A young boy is to relay the "go" signal to Bartholdi, who will dramatically release a tricolor veil to expose the Lady of Liberty's face. The boy describes the scene—the people, the rain, the boatload of suffragists irritated that Liberty could be a woman when they did not have the right to vote. And then a young girl in the crowd sneezes; the boy offers her his handkerchief, inadvertently giving Bartholdi the signal. Illustrations complement the text.

1758. Esbaum, Jill. *To the Big Top.* Illustrated by David Gordon. Farrar, 2008. 32pp. ISBN 978-0-374-39934-4. Grades 2–5. In the early 1900s Benny and Sam hear the circus train whistle in their small town of Willow Grove. They help to set up the tent and are given two free tickets for the performance. Sam loses his ticket when they are playing with the monkeys and realizes that one of the monkeys has taken it. He offers his candy apple in exchange. Illustrations complement the text.

1759. Fleischman, Sid. *The Midnight Horse.* Illustrated by Peter Sís. Torch, 2004. 144pp. Paper ISBN 978-0-06-072216-6. Grades 4–8. Touch, an orphan, goes to live with his great-uncle in New Hampshire in the 1870s. He sees a thief and saves his inheritance as well as Miss Sally's. With magic tricks and other events, he and the village unseat the unsavory Judge Wigglesworth, which helps him avoid the orphanage. *Edgar Allen Poe Award* and *School Library Journal Best Book*.

1760. Gaffney, Timothy R. *Wee and the Wright Brothers.* Illustrated by Bernadette Prons. Henry Holt, 2004. 40pp. ISBN 978-0-8050-7172-6. Grades K–2. In 1903 Wee, a journalist mouse who writes and publishes *Mouse News*, lives with his family in Wilbur and Orville Wright's Dayton, Ohio, bicycle shop. His ability to escape the Wright traps has stymied the inventors for some time, and they never catch Wee. In hopes of reporting their exciting flight to his readers, Wee hides in the crate in which they pack their Flyer to take to Kitty Hawk, North Carolina. In Kitty Hawk, Wee actually rides the Flyer for its first flight.

1761. Garland, Sherry. *The Buffalo Soldier.* Illustrated by Ronald Himler. Pelican, 2006. 32pp. ISBN 978-1-58980-391-6. Grades 3–6. A freed slave heads west to join the Tenth Cavalry, an all-black regiment the Cheyenne call "Buffalo Soldiers" because of their strength and curly hair. He works protecting new settlements. He is lonely and misses his family back home, but the benefits of the regular salary and the chance to learn outweigh these disadvantages. (This cavalry lasted from 1866 to 1953. The soldiers served on the western frontier, helped in the Spanish-American War in 1898, and fought in Korea. Finally in 1953, they integrated into the main army.) Illustrations enhance the text.

1762. Gerstein, Mordicai. *Sparrow Jack.* Farrar, 2003. 32pp. ISBN 978-0-374-37139-5. Grades K–2. When John Bardsley immigrated from England to Philadelphia in 1868, he found a city covered with inchworms. No one knew how to get rid of the worms; none of the local birds would eat them. Bardsley returned to England where he gathered a thousand sparrows and brought them back. When he let them fly around Philadelphia, they ate the inchworms. Bardsley knew sparrows loved inchworms because he had fed a hungry baby sparrow when he was young, and the sparrow had gobbled the treat. Bardsley became known as "Sparrow Jack." Light cross-hatched illustrations augment the text.

1763. Glass, Andrew. *The Wondrous Whirligig: The Wright Brothers' First Flying Machine.* Holiday House, 2003. 32pp. ISBN 978-0-8234-1717-9. Grades K–4. When Orville (1871–1948) and Wilbur (1867–1912) Wright's father brought home a whirligig one day, the two boys became interested in things that fly. They started experimenting as they enjoyed watching this "Big Bat" or flying propeller with their sister Kate and their mother. Illustrations augment the text.

1764. Greenwood, Barbara. *Factory Girl.* Kids Can, 2007. 136pp. ISBN 978-1-55337-648-4; paper ISBN 978-1-55337-649-1. Grades 3–5. In 1912, 12-year-old Emily Watson works twelve hours a day in the Acme Garment Factory for four dollars a week. Although she is under age, her family desperately needs the money because her absent father has stopped sending funds. She refuses to protest the sweatshop's rats, filth, noise, and horrible bosses until a fire breaks out that injures her and kills her best friend. Then, encouraged by social reformers, Jane Addams, and union activists, she speaks to reporters about the dreadful conditions. Lewis Hine's archival photographs augment the text. Chronology, Glossary, and Index. *Voice of Youth Advocates Nonfiction Honor List.*

1765. Gregory, Kristiana. *Earthquake at Dawn.* (Great Episodes) Gulliver, 2003. 192pp. Paper ISBN 978-0-15-204681-1. Grades 5–8. In 1906 Daisy, 15, and Edith Irvine, a photographer, plan a journey around the world. On the day of their departure, a devastating earthquake shakes San Francisco. Instead of traveling, they help others construct tents and rescue people during the aftershocks. When they return to Edith's home, they have both real and mental photographs of the severe damage suffered throughout the city. *American Library Association Best Books for Young Adults, Notable Children's Trade Books in the Field of Social Studies,* and *New York Public Library's Books for the Teen Age.*

1766. Griffin, Peni. *Switching Well.* Puffin, 1994. 218pp. Paper ISBN 978-0-14-036910-6. Grades 5–8. Two 12-year-old girls—Ada and Amber—wish they lived in another time and a haunted well gives them the opportunity. Ada moves from 1891 to 1991 and is shocked by the busy life of San Antonio, where she is almost accosted by a child molester. Amber, on the other hand, goes from 1991 to 1891 and is distressed by the prejudice and lack of opportunity for women. She is disturbed that the deaf are considered no different than the retarded and that Christians have more rights than Jews. An African American girl helps them return to their times after an unexpected inheritance.

1767. Gross, Virginia T. *The Day It Rained Forever: The Story of the Johnstown Flood.* Illustrated by Ronald Himler. (Once Upon America) Puffin, 1993. 52pp. Paper ISBN 978-0-14-034567-4. Grades 3–6. Tina's mother saves herself and a newborn baby, but Tina's uncle and his fiancée drown in the Johnstown, Pennsylvania, flood of 1887. Tina's brother is very bitter toward the greedy men who neglected a weak dam. When the flood recedes, somewhere between 2,000 and 7,000 people are dead, and no one claims the baby. Because Tina's mother had lost a baby only two months before, they decide to raise the child.

1768. Gutman, Dan. *Race for the Sky: The Kitty Hawk Diaries of Johnny Moore.* Simon & Schuster, 2003. 192pp. ISBN 978-0-689-84554-3. Grades 4–7. Johnny Moore, 14, of Nags Head, North Carolina, witnesses the experiments that Wilbur and Orville Wright perform at Kitty Hawk. On January 1, 1900, he starts writing in his diary about the new century. At first he considers the Wright brothers to be "dingbatters." Other topics he covers are baseball, the assassination of President McKinley and the beginning of Teddy Roosevelt's presidency. Eventually Johnny becomes impressed by the Wright brothers and includes a lot of information about the plane in his diaries. He even takes a ride in their plane after the famous flight. *Volunteer State Book Award* (Tennessee) nomination and *Junior Book Award* (South Carolina) nomination.

1769. Hall, Donald. *Lucy's Christmas.* Illustrated by Michael McCurdy. David R. Godine, 2007. Unpaged. Paper ISBN 978-1-56792-342-1. Grades K–2. In a New England town at the turn of the century, Lucy makes Christmas presents during the autum—a clothespin doll and a pen-wiper for her friends and family. She tells about the summer wagon with wheels and the winter one, a sleigh. When a new stove arrives, this is a major event for the family. *American Bookseller Pick of the Lists* and *Parents' Choice Awards.*

1770. Hall, Donald. *Lucy's Summer.* Illustrated by Michael McCurdy. David R. Godine, 2008. 40pp. Paper ISBN 978-1-56792-348-3. Grades K–3. In 1910, when Lucy is 7 years old, her mother opens a millinery shop in the front parlor of their New Hampshire home. She sells hats that she designed and accepts old hats for remodeling. When the hat trade is slack in the summer, Lucy, her mother, and her sister can food for the winter. While they work, a photographer arrives; they celebrate July 4th; an organ grinder and his monkey visit; gypsies barter picture frames for hat decorations; and Lucy goes with her mother to Boston to buy new materials for winter hats. *American Bookseller Pick of the Lists* and *Parents' Choice Awards*.

1771. Hamilton, Virginia. *The Bells of Christmas.* Illustrated by Lambert Davis. Harcourt, 1997. 64pp. Paper ISBN 978-0-15-201550-3. Grades 4–6. In 1890, 12-year-old Jason Bell and his family look forward to celebrating Christmas at their Springfield, Ohio, home near the National Road. Relatives will visit and they will go to church together. Jason is especially happy this year because his uncle has made a mechanical wooden leg for his father. *Coretta Scott King Honor Book* and *American Library Association Notable Children's Book*.

1772. High, Linda Oatman. *City of Snow: The Great Blizzard of 1888.* Illustrated by Laura Francesca Filippucci. Walker, 2004. Unpaged. ISBN 978-0-8027-8910-5. Grades 1–3. A young girl and her family prepare for and experience the "Great White Hurricane" that hit New York City in 1888. In this verse story, they brave the storm to walk to P. T. Barnum's circus in Madison Square Garden. Walking home, they think they are battling a frightening wild animal. They get home safely, but other people have problems moving around the city and finding provisions. Illustrations complement the text.

1773. High, Linda Oatman. *Tenth Avenue Cowboy.* Illustrated by Bill Farnsworth. Eerdmans, 2008. Unpaged. ISBN 978-0-8028-5330-1. Grades K–3. In 1910 Ben and his family move to New York City from their western ranch. He misses the cowboys and the prairies as he wanders around the city. Then he hears about the Tenth Avenue Cowboys, men who ride horses beside the train tracks to warn children playing or people crossing that the train is coming. Allowed to ride with one of the cowboys, he finally feels welcome in New York. Illustrations complement the text. Glossary and Note.

1774. Hopkinson, Deborah. *Girl Wonder: A Baseball Story in Nine Innings.* Illustrated by Terry Widener. Atheneum, 2006. 34pp. Paper ISBN 978-1-4169-1393-1. Grades 1–3. Alta Weiss from Ohio pitches with a semi-pro all-male team in 1907. When she is 17, she hears of a team called the Vermilion Independents and asks to play. She is a superb pitcher, and the coach finally agrees to let her try out for the team. She then becomes the first woman to play on a men's semi-pro team. Weiss goes on to be a physician but still plays from time to time. Illustrations enhance the text. Notes and Timeline. *Children's Book Award* (North Carolina) nomination.

1775. Howard, Elizabeth Fitzgerald. *Chita's Christmas Tree.* Illustrated by Floyd Cooper. Aladdin, 2007. 32pp. Paper ISBN 978-1-4169-6156-7. Grades K–3. On a Saturday before Christmas in Baltimore at the turn of the 20th century, Chita and her father go to the nearby woods to look for a tree that they want Santa to bring on Christmas. Chita's father carves her name on the selected tree, but Chita worries that Santa will not find it. She is relieved on Christmas to see that Santa got it right. *American Library Association Notable Children's Book*.

1776. Howard, Elizabeth Fitzgerald. *Virgie Goes to School with Us Boys.* Simon & Schuster, 2000. Unpaged. ISBN 978-0-689-80076-4; Aladdin, 2005, paper ISBN 978-0-689-87793-3. Grades 1–4. Virgie, the youngest in a family of boys, wants to learn to read and write like her brothers. They leave every Monday morning for Jonesborough, Tennessee, where they board at the Quaker school for freed slaves for the rest of the week. This involves a seven-mile walk carrying their clothes and books. It takes a summer, but Virgie eventually persuades her parents to let her go too. Watercolor illustrations illuminate the text. *Coretta Scott King Illustrator Honor Book*.

1777. Howard, Ellen. *Edith Herself.* Illustrated by Ronald Himler. Aladdin, 2007. 137pp. Paper ISBN 978-1-4169-6454-4. Grades 5–7. Edith's mother dies around 1890, and Edith has to move in with her sister and her strict Christian husband John as well as his sour-smelling mother. Edith has blackouts, later diagnosed as epilepsy, and her sister wants her to stay home from school in case she has a seizure in front of the other children. But Edith wants to go to school, and John supports her desire. *School Library Journal Best Book, Children's Book Award* (Georgia) nomination and *SCASL Book Award* (South Carolina) nomination.

1778. Hughes, Pat. *The Breaker Boys.* Farrar, 2004. 247pp. ISBN 978-0-374-30956-5. Grades 5–9. In 1897, after being expelled from boarding school, motherless Nate comes home. His father is occupied with his new wife, the former governess, and his colliery business. Nate is lonely. Riding his bicycle he meets several "breaker boys"—immigrants who work in the mines—and becomes friends with Johnny. Nate does not talk about Johnny with his father, and he does not tell Johnny that his father owns the mine. Then there is a strike and Nate is caught in between, infuriating both sides. He sees the awful conditions the mineworkers suffer but also remains loyal to his father.

1779. Hurst, Carol Otis. *Terrible Storm.* Illustrated by S. D. Schindler. Greenwillow, 2007. 32pp. ISBN 978-0-06-009001-2. Grades K–3. Grandpa Otis (Walt) and Grandpa Clark (Fred) remember the great March blizzard of 1888, the "Great White Hurricane," which paralyzed much of the East Coast of the United States. Walt, an extrovert, tells his tale of being caught alone in his barn. After the snow stopped, he anxiously dug himself out so he could join his friends in the pub. Introvert Fred, on the other hand, got caught in the town's tavern and was relieved to escape to the quiet of his home after he dug himself out. The two dug past each other on the road, each delighted to escape their refuges during the snow. Ink and watercolor Illustrations augment the text.

1780. Hurwitz, Johanna. *Dear Emma.* HarperCollins, 2002. 150pp. ISBN 978-006-829840-1. Grades 5–7. Twelve-year-old Hadassa "Dossi" Rabinowitz is back in New York after spending a summer with a Vermont farm family—in *Faraway Summer* (1998). She finds that much has changed in her absence and she writes to her new friend Emma Meade about the living conditions in the tenement where she and her older sister Ruthi share a room. Dossi also provides information about the Jewish traditions of her family. When Ruthi marries widower Meyer Reisman, a pharmacist, she quits her job at the Triangle Shirtwaist Factory. Many of the neighbors are quarantined for diphtheria, and then Ruthi's friend Rosa and other women die in the horrible factory fire. When Ruthi's baby is born, both she and Dossi escape their problems in enjoyment of the baby.

1781. Hurwitz, Johanna. *The Unsigned Valentine: And Other Events in the Life of Emma Meade.* Illustrated by Mary Azarian. HarperCollins, 2006. 176pp. ISBN 978-0-06-056053-9. Grades 5–9. Sixteen-year-old Emma confides to her diary in 1911 that she wants to become the farmer wife of Cole Berry some day. But her parents say she is too young for courting. During the year, her brother marries and her mother becomes pregnant, so Emma leaves school to take on more of the work on their Vermont farm. During a February choir practice, Emma receives an unsigned Valentine and guesses it comes from Cole. He later rescues her after she falls into a river during a flood.

1782. Johnson, Angela. *I Dream of Trains.* Illustrated by Loren Long. Simon & Schuster, 2003. 32pp. ISBN 978-0-689-82609-2. Grades K–3. In 1900 a young African American son of a sharecropper thinks engineer Casey Jones (1863–1900) is wonderful. He wants to travel with him and his engineer, Sim Webb, on their train, but Casey dies in a crash. The boy's father helps the boy feel purpose in his life after the accident by letting him know that dreams can still come true. Illustrations augment the text.

1783. Kerby, Mona. *Owney, the Mail-Pouch Dog.* Farrar, 2008. Unpaged. ISBN 978-0-374-35685-9. Grades 1–4. In 1888, a stray dog called Owney wanders into the post office in Albany, New York, and falls asleep. He then helps deliver mail, riding in the mail wagons. He takes trains and guards the mail, collecting depot tags as souvenirs. He goes across the country making friends everywhere. eventually became a semi-official mascot in the United States Postal Service. He is featured in newspapers, and when he is 8 years old, he gets to go around the world on a steamship. Today, he is preserved in the Smithsonian. Watercolor illustrations complement the text.

1784. Kimmel, Eric A. *Stormy's Hat: Just Right for a Railroad Man.* Illustrated by Andrea U'Ren. Farrar, 2008. Unpaged. ISBN 978-0-374-37262-0. Grades K–3. Railroad engineer George

"Stormy" Kromer wants the perfect hat. It should not blow off, shade his eyes too much, or be too hot. His wife, Ida, wants to help him, but he only asks his friends. She finally sews one for him that works exactly as he wants. Although fictional, this story recalls how the engineer's cap was created in the early 1900s. Paintings recreate the midwestern setting's multicultural characters, country scenes, and cityscapes.

1785. Kimpton, Diana. *Edison's Fantastic Phonograph.* Illustrated by M. P. Robertson. Frances Lincoln, 2004. 32pp. Paper ISBN 978-1-84507-262-9. Grades 1–3. When Thomas Edison (1847–1931) invented the phonograph, the world had no way to play recorded sounds. Edison's daughter Dot (nicknamed for a Morse Code symbol) tells about her father recording sound for the first time. He promised to surprise her, and he did.

1786. Kittredge, Frances. *Neeluk: An Eskimo Boy in the Days of the Whaling Ships.* Alaska Northwest, 2001. 88pp. Paper ISBN 978-0-8824-0546-9. Grades 3–5. In a series of vignettes set in the late 1800s, Inupiat Eskimo Neeluk trades his cap for a puppy, spears his first fish, and waits for a trading ship to arrive. Neeluck gets new boots, his friend's father goes bear hunting, and the men of his tribe go whale hunting, and the walrus hunters have a catch. Illustrations augment the text. Glossary and Further Reading.

1787. Knight, Joan. *Charlotte in New York.* Illustrated by Melissa Sweet. Chronicle, 2006. 52pp. ISBN 978-0-8118-5005-6. Grades 3–7. In 1894 Charlotte Gidden travels with her family from Giverny, France, to New York, where her father's paintings will be featured at an exhibition. They sail from Le Havre on the *Champagne* and they leave the heat of New York for an artist's colony in New Hampshire. She meets artists Childe Hassam and William Merrit Chase and records her impressions in a journal-sketchbook. She sends a packet of candy, "Good and Plenty," to Monsieur Monet in Giverny because he asked for a souvenir. Illustrations complement the text.

1788. Kudlinski, Kathleen. *Earthquake! A Story of Old San Francisco.* Illustrated by Ronald Himler. Puffin, 1995. 64pp. Paper ISBN 978-0-14-036390-6. Grades 2–6. When terrified dogs and horses awaken him on April 18, 1906, Phillip tries to calm them. Almost immediately, however, an earthquake topples him, and aftershocks follow. Soon exploding gas lines start fires, and the wind blows the fires over the city. Phillip and the animals escape, but others still need help.

1789. Kurtz, Jane. *Bicycle Madness.* Illustrated by Beth Peck. Henry Holt, 2003. 128pp. ISBN 978-0-8050-6981-5. Grades 4–6. Lillie, 12, reluctantly moves to the other side of town after her mother's death in 1893. But she discovers she has an interesting new neighbor, Frances Elizabeth Willard (1839–1898), who is a labor and women's rights activist. Miss Frances wants to learn to ride the newfangled bicycle and, although he is not happy about this friendship, Lillie's father agrees to let her see Miss Frances. Lillie learns about social injustice and voting rights for women while preparing for a spelling bee. Illustrations complement the text. Note.

1790. Lalicki, Tom. *Danger in the Dark: A Houdini and Nate Mystery.* Illustrated by Carlyn Cerniglia. Farrar, 2006. 186pp. ISBN 978-0-374-31680-8. Grades 5–8. In 1911, Nathaniel, 13, and the magician Houdini join forces to expose a phony spiritual adviser who is attempting to relieve Nathaniel's great-aunt Alice of her fortune. The man, Mr. Trane, comes to visit his aunt after Nate has gone to bed, and he hears their voices in the family parlor. When Nate meets Houdini at the hatter's where Aunt Alice has him working, they become friends, and Nate and his mother describe Mr. Trane and his late-night séances. They concoct a way to reveal his deceit.

1791. Lalicki, Tom. *Shots at Sea: A Houdini and Nate Mystery.* Illustrated by Carlyn Cerniglia. Farrar, 2007. 203pp. ISBN 978-0-374-31679-2. Grades 4–8. Nate Makeworthy Fuller IV, 13, boards the *Lusitania* in 1911 with his mother and Great Aunt Alice. Also on the ship are Harry Houdini and Teddy Roosevelt. Nate and Houdini team up to save Roosevelt from an assassin.

1792. Lawlor, Laurie. *He Will Go Fearless.* Simon & Schuster, 2006. 210pp. ISBN 978-0-689-86579-4. Grades 5–8. Billy, 15, goes west from his Missouri home after the Civil War to find his father in Virginia City, Montana Territory. He is advised to get a job handling oxen on a freight wagon train. This life is very rugged, but he soon learns how to handle the animals. Frenchy, an older teamster, helps him. Billy must deal with a number of challenges on the way and does not quite reach his intended destination.

1793. Lee, Milly. *Earthquake.* Illustrated by Yangsook Choi. Farrar, 2006. 32pp. Paper ISBN 978-0-374-41946-2. Grades K–3. In April 1906 a young girl and her family leave their damaged Chinatown home in San Francisco after the earthquake and find shelter in the tent city erected in Golden Gate Park. They take food and clothing along with the portraits of their ancestors and the statute of the Goddess of Mercy, Kwan Yin. They experience an aftershock, but they eventually reach safety. Illustrations enhance the text.

1794. Lenski, Lois. *Strawberry Girl.* HarperCollins, 1945. 193pp. ISBN 978-0-397-30109-6; Trophy, 1995, paper ISBN 978-0-06-440585-0. Grades 5 up. Two families in Florida during the early 1900s, the Slaters and the Boyers, have to adjust to each other's ways. The Boyers strive to succeed through work and education, while the Slater family's father seems to thrive on destroying their efforts. When the Slater mother and children become ill while the father is away, Mrs. Boyer comes to nurse them back to health. Her kindness and the influence of an itinerant preacher help Mr. Slater realize the value of being a good neighbor and an honest employee. *American Library Association Notable Children's Books* and *Newbery Medal*.

1795. Lerangis, Peter. *Smiler's Bones.* Scholastic, 2005. 160pp. ISBN 978-0-439-34485-2; 2007, paper ISBN 978-0-439-34488-3. Grades 5–9. In 1897 Robert Peary brings Minik, a young Eskimo boy to New York from Greenland "in the interest of science" and displays him and five other Eskimos at the American Museum of Natural History. The others return home or become sick and die, including Minik's father. Minik remains alone. Perhaps the worst is seeing his father's bones on display in the museum while he is stranded in New York for twelve years. Bibliography and Notes.

1796. Levinson, Nancy Smiler. *Clara and the Bookwagon.* Illustrated by Carolyn Croll. Trophy, 1991. 64pp. Paper ISBN 978-0-06-444134-6. Grades 1–3. In 1905 Clara lives on the family farm and wants a book. When they pass the general store's "book station," her father tells her they can't afford to buy a book. Later the first traveling bookwagon comes to the farm and the librarian persuades her father to let her borrow a book and begin learning to read. He agrees because the books are free.

1797. Lieurance, Suzanne. *The Locket: Surviving the Triangle Shirtwaist Fire.* Enslow, 2008. 160pp. ISBN 978-0-7660-2928-6. Grades 4–6. In 1911, Russian-Jewish immigrant Galena, 11, and her older sister Anya leave their one-room tenement six days a week to walk to the Triangle Shirtwaist Factory. Every morning, Galena asks to see the family pictures in Anya's locket before they part to work on different floors. Galena becomes disturbed with Anya's growing interest in Dmitri, a young man working at a unionized factory. She worries that Anya might get in trouble. Then fire breaks out in their factory, and Anya dies along with 145 other immigrants. Galena must identify her by the locket. Afterward, Galena decides to join Dmitri at a union meeting and begin to protest the awful factory conditions.

1798. Littlefield, Holly. *Fire at the Triangle Factory.* Illustrated by Mary O'Keefe Young. Carolrhoda, 1996. 48pp. ISBN 978-0-8761-4868-6; 1995, paper ISBN 978-0-87614-970-6. Grades K–3. On March 25, 1911, while 14-year-olds Minnie and Tessa are working in the Triangle Shirtwaist factory in New York City, the building catches fire. Minnie helps Tessa out of the room, and Tessa finds water to pour on Minnie's dress when flames shoot out of the hemline. All other exits are blocked and they climb on the roof. Someone on the next building gets a ladder for them to crawl across and they escape. After the fire, Minnie's Jewish father realizes that Tessa, an Italian Catholic, is a true friend and he helps her home because she has a sprained ankle. Afterword.

1799. Long, Loren, and Phil Bildner. *Game 1: Three Kids, a Mystery, and a Magic Baseball.* Illustrated by Loren Long. (Barnstormers) Simon & Schuster, 2007. 133pp. ISBN 978-1-4169-1863-9. Grades 3–6. In the late 1800s three children—Griffith, Ruby, and Graham—help a traveling baseball team that needs $10,000. Their late father's baseball has strange powers that work in their favor and help them answer several questions before they leave Cincinnati on their way to Louisville.

1800. **Long, Loren, and Phil Bildner.** *Game 2: The River City.* Illustrated by Loren Long. (Barnstormers) Simon & Schuster, 2007. 208pp. ISBN 978-1-4169-1864-6. Grades 3–6. After her father dies, Ruby, her brothers Griffith and Graham, 7, and her mother barnstorm with the Travelin' Nine, a baseball team of Rough Riders touring the country in 1899 to raise money. A mysterious letter from their uncle tells them that the Chancellor must not learn of the baselll their father gave them. When they all hold it at the same time, former Kentucky Derby winner horses appear on the baseball field, and they help the team win the game. No one, other than the team and the children, can see them.

1801. **Long, Loren, and Phil Bildner.** *Game 3: The Windy City.* Illustrated by Loren Long. (Barnstormers) Simon & Schuster, 2008. 208pp. ISBN 978-1-416-91865-3. Grades 3–6. In 1899 Griffith, Ruby, and Graham take a trip to Chicago while trying to raise money with the Travelin' Nine. They know that the Chancellor who wants to steal their money is close behind. But things get confusing when they realize that their Uncle Owen is missing. Fireballs, burning bats, and a huge cow that kicks end up on the field during the baseball game. Illustrations complement the text.

1802. **McClintock, Barbara.** *Adèle and Simon in America.* Frances Foster, 2008. Unpaged. ISBN 978-0-374-39924-5. Grades K–3. Adèle and Simon travel on the *Lusitania* to visit their Aunt Cécile in New York City. She takes them by train to Boston, San Francisco, Washington, D.C., and back to New York. In each place, Simon loses something. But Aunt Cécile has prepared ahead by labeling each item he owns with his name and her address. When they get back to New York City, all of Simon's things have already arrived from points around the country. Watercolor and ink illustrations complement the text. *Publishers Weekly Best Books.*

1803. **McCully, Emily Arnold.** *The Ballot Box Battle.* Dragonfly, 1998. Unpaged. Paper ISBN 978-0-679-89312-7. Grades 2–4. In the summer of 1880 in Tenafly, New Jersey, Cordelia enjoys riding Mrs. Stanton's horse and listening to stories about her childhood when her family's main concern was not that Elizabeth Cady could speak Greek but that she was not a boy. When Cordelia goes with Mrs. Stanton to the ballot box where she attempts to vote, she sees Mrs. Stanton's courage in facing the taunts of the men, and Cordelia becomes brave herself.

1804. **McKissack, Patricia C.** *Ma Dear's Aprons.* Illustrated by Floyd Cooper. Atheneum, 1997. 32pp. ISBN 978-0-689-81051-0; Aladdin, 2000, paper ISBN 978-0-689-83262-8. Grades K–2. In the early 20th century, Ma Dear and David clean clothes for white folks using their rub board. They also make and sell pies using their own fruit and run errands with their horse and buggy. Throughout their hard week, David always knows the day because Ma Dear wears a special apron except on Sunday. That day, they can enjoy their love for each other.

1805. **MacLachlan, Patricia.** *More Perfect than the Moon.* Joanna Cotler, 2004. 96pp. ISBN 978-0-06-027559-4; 2005 paper ISBN 978-0-06-075179-1. Grades 3–5. Cassie Witting, 8, discovers that her mother, Sarah, is expecting a child. Cassie would prefer a pet lamb named Beatrice. Then she worries that her mother will die, as Caleb's mother did when he was born. But her grandfather assures her that Sarah will be okay. Her older half-sister Anna works in town with Dr. Sam and plans to marry Justin. While writing about it in the journal that belonged to her half-brother, Caleb, now working on the farm, Cassie comes to understand that Sarah will continue to love her even with a second child, a lovely boy who might be "more perfect than the moon." This volume is the fourth in the saga that began with *Sarah, Plain and Tall. Charlie May Simon Children's Book Award* (Arkansas) nomination.

1806. **McMullan, Margaret.** *When I Crossed No-Bob.* Houghton, 2007. 224pp. ISBN 978-0-618-71715-6. Grades 4–8. Addy O'Donnell, 12, finds herself abandoned in Mississippi ten years after the Civil War. Her newly married teacher, Frank Russell, gives her a home. She observes racism and the rise of the Ku Klux Klan. She sees a black school burn and a child murdered before discovering that her own father is the perpetrator. He appears several days later to reclaim her. When she returns to her home of No-Bob, she sees his true nature and must decide what to do with the rest of her own life. *School Library Journal Best Books for Children.*

1807. Martin, Jacqueline Briggs. *On Sand Island.* Illustrated by David Johnson. Houghton, 2003. Unpaged. ISBN 978-0-618-23151-5. Grades 1–3. In 1916, Carl, 10, wants to build himself a boat on Lake Superior's Sand Island. By bartering work for materials including nails, paint, and help, Carl slowly builds his boat so that he can sail around the island. Illustrations embellish the text. *Publishers Weekly Best Children's Books* and *Capitol Choices Noteworthy Titles* (Washington, D.C.).

1808. Miller, Sarah. *Miss Spitfire: Reaching Helen Keller.* Atheneum, 2007. 208pp. ISBN 978-1-416-92542-2. Grades 5–9. When she is 21, Annie Sullivan (1866–1936) travels from Massachusetts to Alabama to work with 6-year-old Helen Keller, who has been blind and deaf since the age of 2. This novel, based on Sullivan's letters, shows how she taught words to a child who could only feel sensations. Passages detail the difficulty and the physical altercations between the two as they struggle to teach and to learn. Sullivan is an enormously intelligent woman wanting love and to belong, just like Helen. She believes that words are miracles, and she works to show that. Photographs highlight the text. Bibliography, Notes, and Chronology. *Booklist Editor's Choice.*

1809. Nelson, Theresa. *Devil Storm.* BackinPrint.com, 2000. 214pp. Paper ISBN 978-0-595-14413-6. Grades 5–8. Walter, 13, and his sister befriend old Tom in 1900, even though their father has told them not to talk to the man, who says he is the son of pirate Jean LaFitte. They like his stories, and in return they give him food. When a hurricane hits their Texas town while Walter's father is away on business, old Tom rushes to help the family escape.

1810. Paterson, Katherine. *Bread and Roses, Too.* Clarion, 2006. 275pp. ISBN 978-0-618-65479-6; Sandpiper, 2008, paper ISBN 978-0-54707-651-5. Grades 5–8. In 1912 a textile mill strike in Lawrence, Massachusetts, becomes known as the Bread and Roses Strike. Rosa Serutti meets Jake Beale, who is sleeping in a trash pile, when she is outside looking for shoes she hid. They become friends, and Rosa discovers that Jake works in the same mill as her mother and sister. Jake is trying to support himself and his alcoholic father. During the strike, the children are shipped to other places including Barre, Vermont, in case violence occurs. Jake's father dies and Rosa sneaks him away with her; they become a "family" at the home of the Gerbatis in Barre. *Booklist Editor's Choice, Emphasis on Reading* (Alabama) nomination, *Dorothy Canfield Fisher Children's Book Award* (Vermont), and *Great Stone Face Award* (New Hampshire) nomination.

1811. Paterson, Katherine. *Preacher's Boy.* Trophy, 2001. 168pp. ISBN 978-0-395-83897-6; 2001, paper ISBN 978-0-06-447233-3. Grades 5–8. The son of a rural Vermont preacher, 10-year-old Robbie Hewitt is tired of worrying about being good and decides to become an "apeist" on Decoration Day in May 1899. Whatever short time he has on earth, he will be happier doing what he pleases rather than what pleases God. When his mentally disabled brother becomes endangered, Robbie nearly chokes another boy in anger, and he almost causes a man to be executed because of his own kidnapping scheme. Robbie reassesses his decision by January 1, 1900. *Booklist Editor's Choice, Bluegrass Awards* (Kentucky), *Young Readers Choice Awards Master List* (Pennsylvania), and *Children's Book Award* (South Carolina) nomination.

1812. Peck, Richard. *Fair Weather.* Penguin, 2001. 160pp. ISBN 978-0-8037-2516-4; Puffin, 2003, paper ISBN 978-0-14-250034-7. Grades 5–8. In 1893, 13-year-old Rosie Beckett attends the World's Columbian Exposition Fair in Chicago (World's Fair). Her Aunt Euterpe, a wealthy Chicago widow, invites Rosie's mother and the three children to the event. Rosie's mother stays home, and Rosie, Lottie, and Buster take the train alone. Among the wonders of the fair are Buffalo Bill Cody, Susan B. Anthony, Scott Joplin, Lillian Russell, the first Ferris wheel, electric lights, and hamburgers. The practical children and their delightful, honest grandfather contrast with the socially aware conversation of Aunt Euterpe's would-be friends. *Capitol Choices Noteworthy Titles* (Washington, D.C.), *American Library Association Best Books for Young Adults, Grand Canyon Reader Award* (Arizona) nomination, *School Library Journal Best Books of the Year, New York Times Notable Books of the Year, Young Reader's Choice Award* nomination, *Charlie May Simon Children's Book Award* (Arkansas) nomination, *Children's Book Award (Colorado) nomination*, Rebecca Caudill Young Reader's Book Award *(Illinois) nomination*, Mark Twain Award *(Missouri) nomination*, Pacific Northwest Young Reader's Award *nomination*, Heartland Award *(Kansas) nomination*, William Allen White Children's Book Award *(Kansas) nomination*, Judy Lopez Memorial Award *nomination*, *Black-Eyed Susan Book Award* (Maryland) nomination, *Children's Book Award* (Massachusetts) nomination, *Golden Sower Award* (Nebraska) nomination, *Great Stone Face Children's Book Award* (New Hampshire) nomination, *Sequoyah Book Award* (Oklahoma) nomination, *SCASL Book Award* (South Carolina) nomination, *Bluebonnet Award* (Texas) nomination, *Children's Choice Award* (Iowa) nomination, *Great Lakes Book Awards*, *Publishers Weekly Best Children's Books*, *Voice of Youth Advocates Perfect Ten List*, and *ABC Children's Booksellers Choices Awards*.

1813. **Peck, Richard.** ***Here Lies the Librarian.*** Dial, 2006. 145pp. ISBN 978-0-8037-3080-9; Puffin, 2007, paper ISBN 978-0-14-240908-4. Grades 5–8. Parentless Eleanor "Peewee" McGrath, a 14-year-old tomboy who loves automobiles and idolizes her big brother Jake, lives in Hazelrigg Settlement in Hendricks County, Indiana, in 1914. One day Irene Ridpath and three of her female library student friends arrive in town in their Stoddard-Dayton, needing repair. They returned to reopen the town's library, closed since the death of the former librarian, Electra Dietz. Peewee realizes that she can be an independent female herself and goes on to win the ten-mile stock car race. *Children's Book Award* (Georgia) nomination, *Parents Choice Award*, *Land of Enchantment Book Award* (New Mexico) nomination, and *Charlie May Simon Children's Book Award* (Arkansas) nomination.

1814. **Peck, Richard.** ***The Teacher's Funeral: A Comedy in Three Parts.*** Dial, 2003. 190pp. ISBN 978-0-8037-2736-6; Puffin, 2006, paper ISBN 978-0-14-240507-9. Grades 5–8. In August 1904 when Miss Myrt Arbuckle dies, 15-year-old Russell is happy. He expects the board to reject hiring a new teacher for the six students in the Hominy Ridge School in backwoods Indiana. But they do—Russell's annoying older sister Tansy—thereby destroying his hopes of going to work with the new threshing machines. To get rid of Tansy, he and the others set a fire in the privy and hide a puff adder in her desk drawer. But she prevails, and Russell grows up in unexpected ways. *The Land of Enchantment Children's Book Award* (New Mexico) nomination, *Charlie May Simon* (Arkansas) nomination, *Hoosier Book Award* (Indiana) nomination, *Young Hoosier Award* (Indiana) nomination, *Young Readers Choice Award* (Louisiana) nomination, *Pacific Northwest Young Reader's Choice Book Award* nomination, *Readers' Choice Award* (Virginia) nomination, *Bluegrass Award* (Kentucky) nomination, *Great Stone Face Book Award* (New Hampshire) nomination, *Dorothy Canfield Fisher Children's Book Award* (Vermont) nomination, *American Library Association Best Books for Young Adults*, *American Library Association Notable Children's Books*, *Christopher Book Award*, and *Kirkus Reviews Editor's Choice*.

1815. **Pfitsch, Patricia Curtis.** ***Riding the Flume.*** Aladdin, 2004. 232pp. Paper ISBN 978-0-689-86692-0. Grades 5–8. In 1894, at a time of friction between loggers and conservationists, 15-year-old Francie finds a note hidden in a giant sequoia tree. It was written by her sister before she died. The note implies danger and gives various clues. To investigate further, Francie has to risk her life riding a log flume down the long water shoot to St. Joseph. There she discovers that the largest sequoia tree ever seen in the Sierra Nevada mountains, the Boole Tree, was willed to her sister. Francie proves herself, and helps her family overcome its grief. *Mark Twain Book Award* (Missouri) nomination, *Volunteer State Book Award* (Tennessee) nomination, and *State Reading Association for Young Readers Program* (Virginia) nomination.

1816. **Porter, Connie.** ***Addy Saves the Day: A Summer Story.*** Illustrated by Bradford Brown. American Girl, 1994. 60pp. Paper ISBN 978-1-56247-083-8. Grades 3–5. In Philadelphia, after the Civil War ends, people are trying to reunite with their families. Addy works at the church fair beside her conceited friend Harriet to raise money for those hurt by the war. The money raised at the fair is stolen and Addy helps to catch the thief. A Peek into the Past.

1817. **Porter, Tracey.** ***Billy Creekmore: A Novel.*** Joanna Cotler, 2007. 320pp. ISBN 978-0-06-077570-4; 2009, paper ISBN 978-0-06-077572-8. Grades 4–7. In 1905, 10-year-old Billy Creekmore is rescued from the Guardian Angels Home for Boys by an uncle who takes him to West Virginia. Billy looks forward to living in a family, but instead he has to work in the mines and gets in trouble for supporting a union. His uncle is killed in a riot and Billy runs away to join a traveling circus. Billy has gifts that draw others toward him.

1818. Rigsby, Annelle, and Edwina Raffa. *Race to Kitty Hawk.* (Adventures in America) Silver Moon, 2003. 84pp. ISBN 978-1-893110-33-5. Grades 4–6. In 1903 Tess Raney, a 12-year-old traveling with her older sister on the Orphan Train, meets Miss Harriet in Dayton, Ohio, and she adopts them. Their neighbor is Bishop Wright, father of Orville and Wilbur. Tess is fascinated with the idea of flying and becomes interested in the Wright family. She soon discovers that one of Miss Harriet's boarders, who pretends to be disinterested in the Wrights' plan, is actually planning to stop the Wright brothers from being the first to fly. She works to counteract his plan.

1819. Rinaldi, Ann. *Brooklyn Rose.* Harcourt, 2005. 222pp. ISBN 978-0-15-205117-4; 2006, paper ISBN 978-0-15-205538-7. Grades 5–8. In 1900, 15-year-old Rose Brampton leaves St. Helena Island, South Carolina, for Brooklyn with her new wealthy silk importer husband Rene Dumarest, a man she only recently met. In her journal, she records her new circumstances. As mistress of a large Victorian estate, she must make decisions for her household and establish her independence. She barely knows her husband, however, and must adjust to him as well as to her new life. Bibliography.

1820. Riskind, Mary. *Apple Is My Sign.* Peter Smith, 1999. 146pp. ISBN 978-0-8446-7004-1; Houghton, 1993, paper ISBN 978-0-395-65747-8. Grades 5–9. Ten-year-old Harry bravely travels by train to Philadelphia in 1899 to attend a school for the deaf. Worried about being accepted by the other students, he soon finds a place for himself when he plays football and makes clever drawings. He thrives in an environment that accepts him as he is, and he carries his newfound confidence home with him. *American Library Association Notable Children's Books.*

1821. Robinet, Harriette Gillem. *Children of the Fire.* Aladdin, 2001. 144pp. Paper ISBN 978-0-689-83968-9. Grades 4–6. Hallelujah, an 11-year-old orphan whose mother escaped from slavery on the Underground Railroad, lives with a Chicago couple who promise her that she can go watch the next fire. This next fire is the worst, earning the name of the Chicago Fire of 1871. She works to save people, including a wealthy white girl. The two go on to help others and begin a friendship. *Friends of American Writers Juvenile Book Merit Award* and *Notable Children's Trade Books in the Field of Social Studies.*

1822. Robinet, Harriette Gillem. *Missing from Haymarket Square.* Aladdin, 2003. 160pp. Paper ISBN 978-0-689-85490-3. Grades 4–6. African American Dinah and her two friends try to free Dinah's father, who was imprisoned for participating in Chicago's Haymarket Riot in 1886 when protesting in favor of an eight-hour working day. Dinah's mother has lost an arm in the factory machines, and she and Dinah live with two other families in one room. Dinah and her friend Olive work twelve-hour days and earn such low wages that they have to steal to pay for food and rent.

1823. Rosen, Michael J. *A Drive in the Country.* Illustrated by Marc Burckhardt. Candlewick, 2007. 32pp. ISBN 978-0-7636-2140-7. Grades K–3. In the early 20th century, a family of five takes a ride on a Sunday afternoon with no destination in mind. They merely want to enjoy the beauty of the countryside and the farm stands, and to play games in the car. Illustrations illuminate the text.

1824. Rubright, Lynn. *Mama's Window.* Lee & Low, 2005. 92pp. ISBN 978-1-58430-160-8; paper ISBN 978-1-60060-335-8. Grades 4–6. In the early 20th century, 11-year-old Sugar (James Earle) goes to live with his Uncle Free in the Mississippi swamp to fulfill his dying mother's request. He is afraid of the animals in the swamp but enjoys watching the new community church being built. His mother had saved money for a stained-glass window, and when Sugar discovers that her funds have been used for bricks, he is devastated. But an anonymous donor (Uncle Free) alleviates his anguish, and the window shines in the new building.

1825. Schlitz, Laura Amy. *A Drowned Maiden's Hair: A Melodrama.* Candlewick, 2006. 389pp. ISBN 978-0-7636-2930-4; 2008, paper ISBN 978-0-7636-3812-2. Grades 4–8. In 1909 Miss

Hyacinth and her sisters adopt orphaned Maud Flynn, 11, and treat her well but keep her hidden. Maud learns she must help them stage elaborate séances for the bereaved, playing the role of a drowned maiden. *Horn Book Fanfare, Bulletin Blue Ribbons, Dorothy Canfield Fisher Children's Book Award* (Vermont), and *Great Stone Face Award* (New Hampshire) nomination.

1826. **Schulz, Walter A.** *Will and Orv.* Illustrated by Janet Schulz. First Avenue, 1992. 46pp. Paper ISBN 978-0-8761-4568-5. Grades 1–3. On December 17, 1903, Wilbur and Orville Wright made history when they flew an aircraft powered by an engine. Schutz presents this day from the point of view of young Johnny Moore of Nag's Head, North Carolina, one of the five people who witnessed the first flight.

1827. **Sebestyen, Ouida.** *Words by Heart.* Yearling, 1997. 144pp. Paper ISBN 978-0-440-41346-2. Grades 4–8. Lena Sills, 12 years old in 1910, is the daughter of the only black family in town. She wins a memorization contest and refuses the first prize of a bow tie (a white boy was expected to be champion). The family arrives home to find a big butcher knife stabbed through the bread on their table. Because Lena has only been concerned with making her father proud, she has been unaware of the prejudice surrounding her. *International Children's Book Awards* and *American Book Award*.

1828. **Selznick, Brian.** *The Houdini Box.* Atheneum, 2008. 56pp. ISBN 978-1-416-96878-8; Aladdin, 2001, paper ISBN 978-0-689-84451-5. Grades 2–4. The feats of Harry Houdini enthrall Victor, and he tries to recreate them in his home by locking himself in a trunk, holding his breath underwater, and trying to walk through walls. He happens to meet Houdini, and when Houdini invites Victor to his house, Victor expects to learn some of the magician's secrets.

1829. **Shea, George.** *First Flight: The Story of Tom Tate and the Wright Brothers.* Illustrated by Don Bolognese. Fitzgerald, 2007. 46pp. ISBN 978-1-4242-0608-7; Trophy, 1997, paper ISBN 978-0-06-444215-2. Grades 1–3. Tom Tate met Orville and Wilbur Wright in Kitty Hawk, North Carolina, in 1900 when he was 12. He saw them when they came each year, and they let him try to fly the glider once when there was not enough wind to support an adult. The dialogue recreates the excitement that flying engendered in Tom.

1830. **Smucker, Anna Egan.** *Golden Delicious: A Cinderella Apple Story.* Whitman, 2008. Unpaged. ISBN 978-0-8075-2987-4. Grades 1–4. In 1914 Farmer Anderson Mullins sends three golden apples from a single apple tree to the Stark Nurseries in Missouri. The brothers taste the apples and find them delicious. They rush to West Virginia to obtain twigs to graft onto their own apple trees to produce the Golden Delicious apple, a fruit that would become famous around the world. Pastel illustrations complement the text. Note.

1831. **Spedden, Daisy Corning Stone.** *Polar the Titanic Bear.* Little, Brown, 2001. 64pp. Paper ISBN 978-0-316-80909-2. Grades 2 up. The story of Polar, a toy bear belonging to a little boy who survives the *Titanic* sinking in 1912, reveals the life of a wealthy family that traveled to different homes and different parts of the world. Polar belongs to 6-year-old Douglas, and Douglas leaves Polar behind on the lifeboat when he is rescued. A sailor finds Polar and reunites him with his master. Accompanying the text and illustrations are photographs of the family in places throughout the world, some of them including Polar, a Steiff toy. (The author and her son were on the *Titanic*, and this story was the mother's Christmas gift to her son the year after the sinking.)

1832. **Stevens, Carla.** *Anna, Grandpa, and the Big Storm.* Illustrated by Margot Tomes. Puffin, 1998. 64pp. Paper ISBN 978-0-14-130083-2. Grades 1–4. When Anna is 7 years old in 1888, she and her grandfather get caught on an elevated train in New York City during a blizzard. Her grandfather's kindness to everyone on the train helps them return safely to their homes.

1833. **Stevens, Carla.** *Lily and Miss Liberty.* Illustrated by Deborah Kogan Ray. Little Apple, 1993. 80pp. Paper ISBN 978-0-590-44920-5. Grades 3–5. In New York in 1885, Lily, 8, waits for the statue to arrive on a French ship. The city is raising money for a pedestal. Because this statue will greet immigrants seeking freedom in the United States, Lily wants to help. She and her friend decide to make crowns, and they give the money they earn to the cause.

1834. Tavares, Matt. *Mudball.* Candlewick, 2005. 32pp. ISBN 978-0-7636-2387-6. Grades 1–5. In 1903 the Minneapolis Millers are playing in the rain and the field is full of mud puddles. In the ninth inning, with two outs and the bases loaded, Little Andy Oyler, the shortest player in his league, hits a ball that disappears into the mud. All four runners cross the plate before the ball is found. Andy hit the shortest home run in history. Pencil and watercolor illustrations complement the text.

1835. Taylor, Mildred. *The Well: David's Story.* Puffin, 1998. 92pp. Paper ISBN 978-0-14-038642-4. Grades 4–6. In the early 1900s, 10-year-old African American David Logan (later the father in *Roll of Thunder, Hear My Cry* and other books) and his brother Hammer are living on a farm with the only working well in a long Mississippi drought. They allow neighbors—black and white—to share their water until the white Simms brothers pick a fight with Hammer. Hammer does not back down and the Simms retaliate by poisoning the Logans' well. *American Library Association Notable Books for Children, Charlie May Simon* (Arkansas) nomination, *Nutmeg Children's Book Award* (Connecticut) nomination, *Children's Book Award* (Georgia) nomination, *Rebecca Caudill Award* (Illinois) nomination, *Children's Choice Award* (Iowa) nomination, *William Allen White Award* (Kansas) nomination, *Student Book Award* (Maine) nomination, *Garden State Teen Book Award* (New Jersey) nomination, *Young Reader's Choice Award* (Pennsylvania) nomination, *Volunteer State Book Award* (Tennessee) nomination, *Bluebonnet Award* (Texas) nomination, and *Young Adult Book Award* (Utah) nomination.

1836. Tripp, Valerie. *Changes for Samantha: A Winter Story.* Illustrated by Luann Roberts and Dan Andreasen. American Girl, 1990. 72pp. ISBN 978-0-937295-95-3; 1988, paper ISBN 978-0-937295-47-2. Grades 3–5. In 1904, when wealthy Samantha goes to New York City to live with her aunt and uncle, she waits to hear from her servant friend Nellie, recently orphaned and planning to come to the city to live with her own uncle. She eventually finds Nellie abandoned in an orphanage. Samantha convinces Nellie to run away so she will not have to go West on the Orphan Train. Samantha's aunt takes in Nellie and her sisters.

1837. Tripp, Valerie. *Nellie's Promise.* Illustrated by Dan Andreasen and Susan McAliley. American Girl, 2004. 85pp. ISBN 978-1-58485-893-5; paper ISBN 978-1-58485-890-4. Grades 3–5. Orphaned Nellie and her two younger sisters hope in 1906 that Samantha Parrington and her wealthy New York City family will adopt them. Nellie's Uncle Mike finds her and wants her to go to work in a factory instead. Nellie has to devise a way to keep the girls together as her dying mother requested. Illustrations augment the text.

1838. Wallace, Barbara Brooks. *Peppermints in the Parlor.* Aladdin, 2005. 208pp. Paper ISBN 978-0-689-87417-8. Grades 4–6. In the late 19th century, 11-year-old orphan Emily Luccock looks forward to living at Sugar Hill Hall in San Francisco, a place she remembers fondly. But when she arrives, life is different. The house is quiet and seems evil. She wonders where her Uncle Twice has gone and why Aunt Twice is a prisoner in her own home. She slowly uncovers the truth as she works to help people she loves. *Indian Paintbrush Book Award* (Wyoming) nomination.

1839. Wallace, Barbara Brooks. *The Perils of Peppermints.* Simon & Schuster, 2003. 272pp. ISBN 978-0-689-85043-1; Aladdin, 2005, paper ISBN 978-0-689-85045-5. Grades 4–6. In the sequel to *Peppermints in the Parlor,* orphan Emily Luccock is sent to an awful boarding school, Mrs. Spilking's Select Academy for Young Ladies in New York City, when her Aunt and Uncle Twice sell Sugar Hill Hall and leave for India. Emily is told she has lost her fortune and she must become a servant.

1840. Wenberg, Michael. *Elizabeth's Song.* Illustrated by Cornelius Van Wright. Beyond Words, 2002. 29pp. ISBN 978-1-58270-069-4. Grades K–3. In 1903 in Chapel Hill, North Carolina, 10-year-old Elizabeth "Libba" Cotten plays her brother's guitar left-handed and upside down. When he leaves for the North, she works odd jobs to buy her own guitar. She spends hours writing a song for her brother that she titles "Freight Train." The term "cotton-picking" came from Libba's unusual method of playing guitar. Illustrations and Epilogue. *Bluegrass Award* (Kentucky) nomination.

1841. Wetterer, Margaret K. *Kate Shelley and the Midnight Express.* Illustrated by Karen Ritz. Carolrhoda, 1990. 48pp. ISBN 978-0-8761-4425-1; First Avenue, 1991, paper ISBN 978-0-8761-4541-8. Grades K–3. When Kate Shelley is 15 in 1881, a violent storm destroys the bridge over Honey Creek, near her home. She rushes out and crosses the rickety bridge to get to the train station so that the midnight express train can be stopped before many lose their lives. Her railroad friends reward her bravery by letting her out in front of her house every time she rides the train.

1842. Wetterer, Margaret K. *The Snow Walker.* Illustrated by Mary O'Keefe Young. Carolrhoda, 1996. 48pp. ISBN 978-0-8761-4891-4; paper ISBN 978-0-8761-4959-1. Grades K–3. Milton Daub, 12, awakens in 1888 to see snow everywhere around his home in the Bronx. He and his father make a pair of snowshoes from barrel hoops and old roller skates so that he can go out to buy milk for his family. Soon he buys supplies for everyone in the neighborhood, and they declare him a hero. *American Bookseller Pick of the List.*

1843. Whelan, Gloria. *Hannah.* Illustrated by Leslie Bowman. Random, 1993. 64pp. Paper ISBN 978-0-679-82698-9. Grades 3–5. In the fall of 1887, Hannah, 9, attends school at the urging of her father and the new teacher, Miss Robbin, when the teacher comes to live with the family in Michigan. Hannah's mother opposes the idea because Hannah is blind. But Hannah learns to count with an acorn abacus, and other students help her win contest money so she can purchase a Braille writing machine.

1844. White, Linda Arms. *I Could Do That! Esther Morris Gets Women the Vote.* Illustrated by Nancy Carpenter. Farrar, 2005. 32pp. ISBN 978-0-374-33527-4. Grades 2–4. In 1869, Esther Morris (1814–1902) led Wyoming to become the first state in which women could vote. She was a wife, mother, pioneer, hat maker, and activist who infuriated the judge so much that he quit; she took his job and became the first woman in the United States to hold public office. Her attitude of "I can do that" helped her overcome much and persuade others that they could also be successful. Illustrations complement the text. Bibliography, Glossary, Chronology, Notes, Further Reading, Web Sites, and Index. *Booklist Editor's Choice* and *Capitol Choices Noteworthy Titles* (Washington, D.C.).

1845. Wilson, Diane Lee. *Firehorse.* Margaret K. McElderry, 2006. 325pp. ISBN 978-1-4169-1551-5. Grades 5–8. Rachel Selby, 15, moves to Boston in 1872 when her father takes a newspaper job there. She is furious because she had to sell her horse, Peaches. Soon she finds Governor's Girl, a famous and badly burned firehorse. Rachel gets permission to care for Governor's Girl in a stable behind her house, and during the convalescence, Rachel realizes she wants to become a veterinarian. Her parents disapprove, as does society in general. Her father believes women belong in the home. At the same time, fires begin to erupt in Boston, and the firehorses fall ill with distemper. As horses haul the city's fire engines, the situation is dire; the Great Boston Fire threatens the entire city. Eventually others begin to support Rachel's dream, and her goal seems a possibility.

1846. Winthrop, Elizabeth. *Counting on Grace.* Wendy Lamb, 2006. 232pp. ISBN 978-0-385-74644-1; Yearling, 2007, paper ISBN 978-0-553-48783-1. Grades 5–8. In 1910, Grace, 12, and her best friend Arthur have to leave school to work in the mill. Grace tries to help her mother, the fastest worker on the loom, but doffing is for right-handed people, and Grace is left-handed. The only time she feels worthy is on Sundays when she and Arthur have special lessons with their teacher. They decide to write a letter to the Child Labor Board about underage children in the Pownal, Vermont, mill. A few weeks later, Lewis Hines shows up with his camera to collect evidence. Grace begins to feel as if she has helped when she sees her pictures, and life changes in the textile mills. Photographs enhance the text. *Dorothy Canfield Fisher Children's Book Award* (Vermont) nomination, *Jane Addams Honor Book Award*, *Book Award* (Massachusetts) nomination, and *Capitol Choices Noteworthy Titles* (Washington, D.C.).

1847. Wright, Betty Ren. *The Blizzard.* Illustrated by Ronald Himler. Holiday House, 2003. 32pp. ISBN 978-0-8234-1656-1; 2005, paper ISBN 978-0-8234-1981-4. Grades K–4. Billy is disappointed when his cousins can't attend his birthday party in the early 20th century because of a blizzard. Mr. Carter comes to the one-room schoolhouse to tell Billy's teacher, Miss Bailey, that taking the children home is too dangerous. Miss Bailey decides to take them to the nearest house, which happens to be Billy's. He ends up having a better day than he expected because his teacher and classmates stay overnight until the storm ends. Illustrations enhance the text.

1848. Yep, Laurence. *The Earth Dragon Awakes: The San Francisco Earthquake of 1906.* Harper-Collins, 2006. 117pp. ISBN 978-0-06-027524-2; HarperTrophy, 2007, paper ISBN 978-0-06-000846-8. Grades 3–7. In 1906 Henry Travis, 8, son of a prominent banker, and his 9-year-old friend Chin, 9, son of Henry's family's "houseboy" share a love for "penny dreadful" novels in which heroes do wonderful things. Then on April 17, 1906, both witness real heroism during the San Francisco earthquake and fire. Chin and his father survive the collapse of their Chinatown tenement, and Henry's family escape the destruction of their expensive Nob Hill home. The time, date, and location heading each chapter allow readers to follow the sequence of events. When it is all over, Henry and Chin are no longer interested in their fictional heroes.

1849. Yolen, Jane. *My Uncle Emily.* Illustrated by Nancy Carpenter. Philomel, 2009. 32pp. ISBN 978-0-399-24005-8. Grades K–4. Emily Dickinson, who lives next door, gives her 6-year-old nephew Gil a dead bee and a poem about it to take to his class. His teacher reads the poem but no one understands it. A larger boy named Jonathan insults Gil's "Uncle Emily" and Gil sprains his ankle while defending her. He does not want to tell her what happened. But Emily Dickinson gives him a second poem, "Tell all the truth/ but tell it slant," that allows him to finally explain the situation. The pen and ink drawings with pastel colors reveal the time during which the two were best friends.

History

1850. Anderson, Wayne. *Plessy v. Ferguson: Legalizing Segregation.* (Supreme Court Cases Through Primary Sources) Rosen, 2003. 64pp. ISBN 978-0-8239-4011-0. Grades 5–8. After hearing this case, the Supreme Court decided that segregation was legal as long as public facilities for blacks were equal to those for whites. It upheld the Louisiana law allowing racial segregation in public facilities because those for blacks were equal to those for whites in that state. Primary source materials examine the state of race relations as they existed at the time of the trial in 1892—when Plessy, one-eighth black, was considered black and had to sit in the "Colored" section—and other court cases this ruling affected. Bibliography and Index.

1851. Ballard, Robert D. *Finding the Titanic.* Illustrated by Ken Marschall. Scholastic, 1993. 64pp. Paper ISBN 978-0-590-47230-2. Grades 1–4. Dr. Robert Ballard became fascinated with the story of the *Titanic.* When the tether of the tiny submarine *Alvin* was extended to 13,000 feet, Ballard realized he could reach the wreck, which lay two and one-half miles under the sea. In July 1986 he finally saw the ship that had last been above the water on April 14, 1912. On that night, only 705 of the 1,500 people aboard the magnificent ship reached the safety of a rescue vessel, the *Carpathia.* Ballard returned to the *Titanic* eight times, going inside and reliving the scene based on what he had read or heard from survivors of the doomed voyage. Further Reading, Glossary, and *Titanic* Timeline. *American Library Association Best Books for Young Adults, School Library Journal Best Books of the Year,* and *Horn Book Fanfare.*

1852. Bartoletti, Susan Campbell. *Growing Up in Coal Country.* Illustrated by Claire T. Nivola. Houghton, 1996. 112pp. ISBN 978-0-395-77847-0; 1999, paper ISBN 978-0-395-97914-3. Grades 2–6. Bartoletti looks at the life in the mining towns of Pennsylvania in the early 20th century, in particular at the plight of the children who suffered poverty and difficult working conditions. Oral history, archival documents, and black-and-white photographs add interest. Bibliography and Index.

1853. **Bauer, Marion Dane.** *The Statue of Liberty.*   Illustrated by John Wallace. (Wonders of America) Simon & Schuster, 2007. 32pp. ISBN 978-1-4169-3480-6; Aladdin paper ISBN 978-1-4169-3479-0. Grades K–2. Bauer presents a brief history of the Statue of Liberty, linking it to the school children who worked hard to raise money for the statue's pedestal. Illustrations augment the text.

1854. **Blackwood, Gary L.** *The Great Race: The Amazing Round-the-World Auto Race of 1908.* Abrams, 2008. 144pp. ISBN 978-0-8109-9489-8. Grades 5–9. In 1908 the *New York Times* and the French paper *Le Matin* sponsored a round-the-world race in which six cars competed. They crossed America, Siberia, and then Europe before ending in Paris. Cars were not dependable in those days and racers needed a crew able to display ingenuity when dealing with mechanical malfunctions. Cars had several gas tanks, got no more than eight miles per gallon, and could go as fast as fifty miles per hour. Among the problems were broken crankshafts, twisted axles, and blown pistons. Illustrations enhance the text. Bibliography, Notes, and Web Sites.

1855. **Burgan, Michael.** *The Haymarket Square Tragedy.*   (We the People) Compass Point, 2005. 48pp. ISBN 978-0-7565-1265-1; paper ISBN 978-0-7565-1728-1. Grades 4–6. On Tuesday May 4, 1886, an altercation took place between striking workers and police in Chicago. When police tried to disperse the crowd, a bomb was thrown at them. The bomb and the resulting gunfire resulted in the deaths of seven police officers and a number of civilians. Eight anarchists were tried for murder with four being put to death and a fifth committing suicide while in prison. Photographs and reproductions accompany the text. Glossary, Chronology, Further Reading, Web Sites, and Index.

1856. **Caper, William.** *Nightmare on the Titanic.*   (Code Red) Bearport, 2007. 32pp. ISBN 978-1-59716-362-0. Grades 3–6. Caper examines the sinking of the "unsinkable" vessel, drawing on primary sources from those who were present. He includes background information and describes how people reacted to the event. Brief profiles of individuals who were involved also appear. Photographs, maps, and reproductions highlight the text. Glossary, Further Reading, Web Sites, and Index.

1857. **Carlson, Laurie M.** *Queen of Inventions: How the Sewing Machine Changed the World.* Millbrook, 2003. 32pp. ISBN 978-0-7613-2706-6. Grades 3–5. In 1850 Isaac Merritt Singer (1811–1875) transformed the history of sewing with his invention of a practical "stitching machine." Before, sewing clothes and hemming sheets and towels was laborious and time-consuming. Singer realized, when looking at a spring on his son's popgun, how a sewing machine might be made affordable. Photographs and illustrations of the time highlight the text. Bibliography, Further Reading, and Web Sites.

1858. **Clee, Paul.** *Before Hollywood: From Shadow Play to the Silver Screen.*   Clarion, 2005. 192pp. ISBN 978-0-618-44533-2. Grades 5–9. Clee looks at cinematography beginning with Leonardo da Vinci's description of the camera obscura in 1500 through movies of the 20th century. He includes background on the magic lantern, Étienne-Jules Marey and the first true films, Thomas Edison and the American movie machine, dioramas, cycloramas, stereopticons, and the stories that movies tell. Photographs and illustrations augment the text. Bibliography, Chronology, Notes, Further Reading, Web Sites, and Index.

1859. **Crewe, Sabrina, and Adam Schaefer.** *The Triangle Shirtwaist Factory Fire.*   (Events that Shaped America) Gareth Stevens, 2004. 32pp. ISBN 978-0-8368-3402-4. Grades 4–6. In 1911 a fire broke out in the Triangle Shirtwaist factory, killing 146. Many of the young immigrant women working there could not escape because the exits were locked from outside. Their working conditions—long hours, little pay, dismal lighting, and poor treatment—were highlighted by this disaster, igniting the labor movement. Reproductions of newspaper articles, archival photographs, and a diagram of the factory provide additional information. Bibliography, Maps, and Index.

1860. Crosbie, Duncan. *Titanic: The Ship of Dreams.* Illustrated by Bob Moulder, Peter Kent, and Tim Hutchinson. Orchard, 2007. Unpaged. ISBN 978-0-439-89995-6. Grades 4–6. Pop-up spreads, pull tabs, booklets, and illustrations offer a detailed tour of the *Titanic* before it sank. Sidebars provide additional information.

1861. Curlee, Lynn. *Brooklyn Bridge.* Atheneum, 2001. 40pp. ISBN 978-0-689-83183-6. Grades 3–6. Curlee describes the need for, the planning, the 16-year construction period, and the history of New York City's Brooklyn Bridge, called the eighth wonder of the world. John August Roebling designed it. He died after his first surveying trip, but his son Washington took over the project. When Washington was incapacitated, his wife Emily helped propel the project to completion. On May 24, 1883, President Chester A. Arthur presided over the celebration to open the bridge. Illustrations, including cross-sections of the bridge, enhance the text. Specifications, Timeline, Bibliography. *Garden State Nonfiction Book Award* (New Jersey) nomination, *Robert F. Sibert Honor Book*, and *Capitol Choices Noteworthy Titles* (Washington, D.C.).

1862. Curlee, Lynn. *Liberty.* Aladdin, 2003. 41pp. Paper ISBN 978-0-689-85683-9. Grades 3–8. Curlee tells the story of the design and creation of the famous French gift to the United States. Designed by Frédéric Auguste Bartholdi (1834–1904), the Statue of Liberty was shipped with funds raised mainly by Joseph Pulitzer. Curlee explains the difficulties that plagued her construction. Illustrations complement the text. Chronology. *Student Book Award* (Maine) nomination, *Capitol Choices Noteworthy Titles* (Washington, D.C.), and *Children's Book Awards* (Rhode Island).

1863. Dolan, Edward F. *The Spanish-American War.* Millbrook, 2001. 112pp. ISBN 978-0-7613-1453-0. Grades 5–8. When the *Maine* exploded off the coast of Cuba on February 15, 1898, 260 American soldiers and sailors were killed. President William McKinley became impatient with revolutionary activities in Spain and Cuba, and the newspapers of the time stirred up talk of impending war. The resulting conflict established the United States as a world power. Among those who fought in this short war were Theodore Roosevelt and William Shafter. Dolan recounts the battles at sea and on land and reveals the successful and the unsuccessful strategies of this engagement. Illustrations augment the text. Maps, Bibliography, and Index.

1864. Donnelly, Judy. *Titanic: Lost and Found.* Illustrated by Keith Kohler. (Step Into Reading) Random, 1987. 47pp. Paper ISBN 978-0-394-88669-5. Grades 1–3. The *Titanic* sank in 1912. A 1987 expedition led by Robert Ballard discovered its remains. This simple volume for younger readers offers an introduction to the "biggest ship the world has ever seen" that supposedly could not sink with dramatic watercolor renditions that show its interior and cross-sections. Clear information about Ballard's amazing recovery of the wreck reveals the wonder of modern underwater technology.

1865. Dooling, Michael. *The Great Horseless Carriage Race.* Holiday House, 2002. Unpaged. ISBN 978-0-8234-1640-0. Grades 2–4. Six cars compete in a fifty-two-mile race in the winter of 1895. Many other vehicles never made it to the starting line, plagued with mechanical problems. The competitors faced icy conditions. Frank Duryea was the first across the finish line, with an average speed of seven miles per hour. Illustrations augment the text.

1866. Fandel, Jennifer. *The Statue of Liberty.* Illustrated by Tyler Crogg. (What in the World?) Creative Education, 2005. 48pp. ISBN 978-1-58341-377-7. Grades 3–5. This volume provides background about the building of the Statue of Liberty in France, its shipment to America, and its reassembly on a pedestal in New York Harbor. Much negotiation was necessary to arrange financing for this huge metal sculpture that Frédéric Auguste Bartholdi created. Photographs and art highlight the text. Chronology and Index.

1867. Ferrell, Claudine L. *Reconstruction.* (Greenwood Guides to Historic Events) Greenwood, 2003. 220pp. ISBN 978-0-313-32062-0. Grades 5 up. This volume draws on speeches, proclamations, letters, and diary entries to give readers an understanding of the process of the Reconstruction that occurred after the Civil War. Photographs augment the text. Bibliography and Index.

1868. Flanagan, Timothy. *Reconstruction: A Primary Source History of the Struggle to Unite the North and South After the Civil War.* Rosen, 2005. 64pp. ISBN 978-1-4042-0177-4. Grades 5–7. Using primary sources, Flanagan offers details about Reconstruction from its beginnings. Photographs and illustrations augment the text. Bibliography, Glossary, Chronology, Further Reading, and Index. *Voice of Youth Advocates Nonfiction Honor List.*

1869. Freedman, Russell. *Kids at Work: Lewis Hine and the Crusade Against Child Labor.* Illustrated by Lewis Hine. Clarion, 1994. 104pp. ISBN 978-0-395-58703-4; 1998, paper ISBN 978-0-395-79726-6. Grades 5 up. Lewis Wickes Hine (1874–1940) photographed thousands of working children before World War I. In 1911 more than 2 million American children under the age of 16 were part of the workforce, many working twelve or more hours a day, six days a week, in hazardous conditions for pitiful wages. Hine risked his life to get his photographs—no employer wanted images of their underage employees. Hine learned photography to offer his students an after-school activity. He became a master photographer when he spent time at Ellis Island, making images of the immigrants and giving them the grace and dignity they deserved. His work led the National Child Labor Committee to fight for, and gain, stronger laws against child labor. Hine, however, died in poverty, unable to get funding for his projects and finally having to sell all that he owned. Declaration of Dependence, Child Labor Then and Now, Bibliography, and Index. *Orbis Pictus Honor Book* and *Jane Addams Children's Book Award.*

1870. Greene, Jacqueline Dembar. *The Triangle Shirtwaist Fire.* (Code Red) Bearport, 2007. 32pp. ISBN 978-1-59716-359-0. Grades 3–6. Greene examines the fire at the Triangle Shirtwaist Factory in New York City on March 25, 1911, that killed 146 people, most of them young women. She describes how the fire started, why the workers could not leave the building, and how the fire was finally controlled. Additional brief profiles of people who affected the situation are also included. Photographs, maps, and reproductions highlight the text. Glossary, Further Reading, Web Sites, and Index.

1871. Greene, Janice. *Our Century: 1900–1910.* Gareth Stevens, 1993. 64pp. ISBN 978-0-8368-1032-5. Grades 3–10. Written as if a newspaper; this book's short articles give an overview of the decade. Included are statistics, daily life in America, the Boxer Rebellion in China, Boers and British fighting in South Africa, Russia and Japan at war, Russia's workers and peasants revolting, McKinley assassinated, San Francisco's earthquake and fire, Admiral Peary at the North Pole, Henry Ford, Marie Curie, Ivan Pavlov, Albert Einstein, Sigmund Freud, the first World Series, Christy Mathewson, Ty Cobb, Jack Johnson, Jack London, Upton Sinclair, Rudyard Kipling, Isadora Duncan, Pablo Picasso, the Wright brothers, Helen Keller, J. P. Morgan, and Typhoid Mary. Glossary, Books for Further Reading, Places to Write or Visit, and Index.

1872. Greene, Meg. *Into the Land of Freedom: African Americans in Reconstruction.* (People's History) Lerner, 2004. ISBN 978-0-8225-4690-0. Grades 5–8. After the Civil War ended, freed African Americans had to make new lives for themselves. They searched for lost family members, began their own churches and schools, found a way to support themselves, and exercised their right to vote. Courts, however, worked to curb their rights through a number of laws, mainly the Fourteenth and Fifteenth Amendments and the Civil Rights Act of 1875. This volume includes slave narratives and other available primary sources. Photographs and illustrations augment the text. Bibliography, Further Reading, Maps, Web Sites, and Index.

1873. Hakim, Joy. *An Age of Extremes: 1880–1917.* (History of US) Oxford, 2006. 215pp. ISBN 978-0-19-518901-8; 2007, paper ISBN 978-0-19-532722-9. Grades 5 up. With many photographs, prints, sidebars, boxed text, and running commentary, this volume covers the history of the United States at the beginning of the twentieth century up to 1917, providing background on all aspects of society. Chronology of Events, More Books to Read, and Index.

1874. Hale, Ed. *Rebuilding a Nation: Picking Up the Pieces.* (The Civil War) Cobblestone, 2005. 47pp. ISBN 978-0-8126-7909-1. Grades 4–9. After the Civil War ended in 1865, reuniting the country was a difficult task. Among the problems that evolved over the next few years were the impeachment trial of Andrew Johnson, based on his disagreement with Congress about

Reconstruction; the three constitutional amendments that were enacted; and African American men getting the vote. Among individuals important in this period was Booker T. Washington, who was able to get an education once he was free. Illustrations augment the text. Chronology, Glossary, and Index.

1875. Hochain, Serge. *Building Liberty: A Statue Is Born.* National Geographic, 2004. 48pp. ISBN 978-0-7922-6765-2. Grades 3–6. The design, building, shipping to the United States, and reassembling of the Statue of Liberty are presented through the point of view of four fictional boys. France gave the statue in 1885 as a gift for the 100th anniversary of the United States, and it has come to symbolize freedom to many people. Using a comic-book style, Hochain introduces Leo, a young apprentice who meets sculptor Frédéric Auguste Bartholdi and engineer Gustave Eiffel; Francois, a crew member on the steamship *Isere*, who sees the component parts of the statue loaded and transported across the Atlantic; Benjamin, a newsboy for *The World*, who helps collect money to build a pedestal for the statue; and Angus Donegal, who works on constructing the statue's iron skeleton and copper exterior after its arrival. Includes sketches from Bartholdi's papers.

1876. Hossell, Karen. *Kitty Hawk: Flight of the Wright Brothers.* (20th Century Perspectives) Heinemann, 2002. 48pp. Paper ISBN 978-1-4034-0714-6. Grades 4–8. This volume not only details the achievements of the Wright brothers and their success at Kitty Hawk but also includes a brief history of previous efforts and subsequent successes. Illustrations augment the text. Bibliography, Further Reading, Glossary, Index.

1877. Hudson, David L., Jr. *The Fourteenth Amendment: Equal Protection Under the Law.* Enslow, 2002. 128pp. ISBN 978-0-7660-1904-1. Grades 5–8. This volume details the history and provisions of the Fourteenth Amendment. Its "due process" and "equal protection" clauses have been the basis for many important legal decisions, including ones dealing with abortion, discrimination, and physician-assisted suicide. With complementary photographs, the text includes a copy of the Constitution and a list of the amendments. Notes, Further Reading, Web Sites, and Index.

1878. Josephson, Judith Pinkerton. *Growing Up in a New Century: 1890–1914.* (Our America) Lerner, 2002. 64pp. ISBN 978-0-8225-0657-7. Grades 5–8. The six chapters offer an overview of life for a child at the turn of the 20th century in the United States. Topics include play, work, and education. Examples include a girl growing up on a southern plantation and Kermit, the son of Teddy Roosevelt. Photographs augment the text. Bibliography, Notes, Further Reading, Web Sites, and Index.

1879. Kalman, Bobbie. *Children's Clothing of the 1800s.* See entry 1468.

1880. Kalman, Bobbie. *Early City Life.* Illustrated by Antoinette "Cookie DeBiasi. (Early Settler Life) Crabtree, 1983. 32pp. ISBN 978-0-8650-5029-7. Grades 3–6. Cities and towns grew in the 19th century, especially in the latter half. Kalman describes the urban lifestyle at the time, including buildings, schools, homes, and stores. Glossary and Index.

1881. Kalman, Bobbie. *19th Century Clothing.* See entry 1064.

1882. Karwoski, Gail Langer. *Quake! Disaster in San Francisco, 1906.* Illustrated by Robert Papp. Peachtree, 2004. 153pp. ISBN 978-1-56145-310-8; 2006, paper ISBN 978-1-56145-369-6. Grades 4–6. In 1906, 13-year-old Jacob Kaufman lives in a San Francisco boarding house with his father and younger sister. While he is outside with his dog, a major earthquake cracks the streets and downs buildings. He rescues San, a Chinese boy, and the two of them begin to search for their families, for food, and for somewhere to stay. They meet many strangers who help them, even though some show prejudice toward San, something that Jacob has already experienced as a Jew. *Sunshine State Young Reader's Award* (Florida) nomination and *Children's Book Award* (Massachusetts) nomination.

1883. Laughlin, Rosemary. *The Pullman Strike of 1890.* (American Workers) Morgan Reynolds, 2006. 144pp. ISBN 978-1-931798-89-1. Grades 5–9. Laughlin describes the causes, major figures, and events of the labor-management conflict that closed down railroads across the

Midwest. Photographs and illustrations augment the text. Bibliography, Chronology, Web Sites, and Index.

1884. Leathers, Daniel. *The Johnstown Flood, 1889.* Mitchell Lane, 2008. 32pp. ISBN 978-1-58415-570-6. Grades 3–6. Five chapters describe one of the worst floods in the history of the United States, starting with a dramatic rescue story and then looking at the causes, how the South Fork Dam broke, what happened to the town when the flood hit, and how the nation helped the stricken residents. Chronology, Bibliography, Further Reading, Web Sites, Glossary, and Index.

1885. Liberatore, Karen. *Our Century: 1910–1920.* Gareth Stevens, 1993. 64pp. ISBN 978-0-8368-1033-2. Grades 3 up. Written as if a newspaper, this book's short articles give an overview of the decade. Included are statistics, daily life in America, the Titanic sinking, Archduke Ferdinand's murder, World War I, Nicholas I of Russia's overthrow, Bolsheviks, the flu epidemic, suffragettes, Prohibition, Pancho Villa's border town raids, the first assembly line, Panama Canal progress, the Black Sox baseball scandal, Woodrow Wilson, Vladimir Lenin, Louis B. Brandeis, Eugene Debs, Margaret Sanger, D. W. Griffith, Mary Pickford, and Charlie Chaplin. Glossary, Books for Further Reading, Places to Write or Visit, and Index.

1886. McHugh, Janet. *The Great Chicago Fire.* (Code Red) Bearport, 2007. 32pp. ISBN 978-1-59716-360-6. Grades 3–6. In 1871 a raging fire spread through Chicago, killing many people, destroying property, and leaving thousands homeless. Illustrations enhance the text. Bibliography, Further Reading, Glossary, Web Sites, and Index.

1887. McKendry, Joe. *Beneath the Streets of Boston: Buiding America's First Subway.* David R. Godine, 2005. Unpaged. ISBN 978-1-56792-284-4. Grades 3–6. The subway tunnels under Boston were built seven years before those in New York. This volume covers the planning and construction of the Boston system, which took place from 1895 to 1916. The subways were needed to replace the terrible congestion of private carriages, electric trolleys, and horse-drawn cabs. Photographs, maps, cross-sections, and illustrations augment the text.

1888. Maestro, Betsy. *The Story of the Statue of Liberty.* Illustrated by Giulio Maestro. Mulberry, 1989. 40pp. Paper ISBN 978-0-688-08746-3. Grades K–4. The building of the Statue of Liberty began in 1871 after Frédéric Auguste Bartholdi visited New York and saw Bedloe's Island in the harbor. This was the perfect setting for a statue that he would create for the French government to present as a gift to the United States on the occasion of its birthday. He completed it in 1884, and money raised by a New York newspaper funded the completion of the base so that it could be mounted when it arrived from France in 1885. Information About the Statue of Liberty.

1889. Molony, Senan. *Titanic: A Primary Source History.* (In Their Own Words) Gareth Stevens, 2006. 48pp. ISBN 978-0-8368-5980-5. Grades 5–8. Using primary sources from newspapers, government documents, letters, poems, telegrams, speeches, radio broadcasts, songs, and contemporary interviews, this volume covers the sinking of the *Titanic* in 1912. Photographs, maps, and illustrations enhance the text. Glossary, Chronology, and Index.

1890. Murphy, Jim. *Blizzard: The Storm That Changed America.* Scholastic, 2006. 136pp. Paper ISBN 978-0-590-67310-5. Grades 5–9. On March 10, 1888, families were having picnics outside. Not long afterward a blizzard hit New York City, crippling it for four days and extending from Delaware to Maine and as far west as the Mississippi River. New York City had 21 inches of snow, and Troy, New York, had 55. Food became scarce, trains stopped, power lines snapped, and nearly 200 ships were lost at sea. More than 800 people died in New York City. This volume recalls the event in eight chapters. Illustrations augment the text. Bibliography and Index. *Robert F. Sibert Honor Book, Bluegrass Award* (Kentucky) nomination, *Student Book Award* (Maine) nomination, *Young Reader's Choice Award* (Pennsylvania) nomination, *Young Adult Book Awards* (Tennessee), *Dorothy Canfield Fisher Children's Book Award* (Vermont) nomination, *Horn Book Fanfare, School Library Journal Best Books for Children, Bulletin Blue Ribbon,* and *Capitol Choices Noteworthy Titles* (Washington, D.C.).

1891. Murphy, Jim. *The Great Fire.* Scholastic, 1995. 144pp. ISBN 978-0-590-47267-8; 2006 paper ISBN 978-0-439-20307-4. Grades 5 up. One of the major disasters in American history was the Great Fire of 1871, when Chicago became a wasteland. The damage was so widespread that few believed the city would recover. It began when a small fire broke out in O'Leary's barn on a Sunday evening but no one was particularly concerned. However, the city's wooden sidewalks burned when a steady wind fueled the flames. This volume includes personal accounts of survivors and facts about the devastation and the rebuilding effort. Bibliography and Sources and Index. *Bulletin Blue Ribbon Book, American Library Association Notable Children's Books, American Library Association Best Books for Young Adults, Newbery Honor Book, Orbis Pictus Award, Booklist Editors' Choices, Horn Book Fanfare Books, American Library Association Quick Picks for Reluctant Young Adult Readers, Notable Children's Trade Books in the Field of Social Studies, School Library Journal Best Books of the Year, and Boston Globe-Horn Book Honor.*

1892. Nelson, Scott Reynolds. *Ain't Nothing But a Man: My Quest to Find the Real John Henry.* National Geographic, 2007. 64pp. ISBN 978-1-4263-0000-4. Grades 5–8. Nelson examined many variants of the song "John Henry," researched post-Civil War railway projects, prison records, census data, and visited a number of sites to try to learn about the real John Henry. He concludes that John Henry may have been a convict who died from lung disease and was buried with other imprisoned African Americans—or may have been a composite character created from many heroic individuals. The book includes a map of the Chesapeake & Ohio Railroad in 1873 and suggests ways in which readers can learn to be an historian. Photographs and illustrations enhance the text. Bibliography, Further Reading, Notes, and Index. *Publishers Weekly Best Books.*

1893. Norworth, Jack. *Take Me Out to the Ballgame.* Illustrated by Jim Burke. Little, Brown, 2006. 32pp. ISBN 978-0-316-75819-2. Grades 1–2. Norworth's well-known song is set in the context of a 1908 game between the New York Giants and the Chicago Cubs. Katie roots for the Giants and their pitcher, Christy Mathewson, and has a competition with her boyfriend. With illustrations, many historical tidbits, and an introduction by Pete Hamill.

1894. Rappaport, Doreen. *Free at Last! Stories and Songs of Emancipation.* Illustrated by Shane Evans. Candlewick, 2003. 64pp. ISBN 978-0-7636-1440-9; 2006, paper ISBN 978-0-7636-3147-5. Grades 3–8. First-person accounts, songs, poetry, memoirs, letters, and court testimony reveal the indignities and loss of rights suffered by freed African Americans in the South from Emancipation in 1863 to the 1954 Supreme Court decision declaring segregation illegal. These describe the experiences of leaders and everyday citizens who suffered through Ku Klux Klan raids, lynchings, and beatings but found strength to cope through the love of family and community. Among the better-known figures included are Booker T. Washington, Ida B. Wells, artists of the Harlem Renaissance, Jackie Robinson, and Thurgood Marshall. Illustrations, Chronology, Bibliography, Notes, and Index.

1895. Rappaport, Doreen. *Lady Liberty: A Biography.* Candlewick, 2008. Unpaged. ISBN 978-0-7636-2530-6. Grades 3–8. Many people helped to build the Statue of Liberty both in France and the United States, some involved in the construction and others in raising funds. Rappaport begins with the design and construction steps taken in France and proceeds to preparations for the Atlantic journey, the arrival in New York, and the celebration for the 1886 unveiling. Poems in free verse present the views of the designer, Frédéric Auguste Bartholdi; of Emma Lazarus, the poet who wrote the words etched on the base; of Joseph Pulitzer, a major fund raiser in the United State; and of Florence de Forest, who sold roosters to help the cause. Watercolor and ink and pencil illustrations along with a fold-out of the statue enhance the text. Bibliography and Chronology. *Capitol Choices Noteworthy Titles* (Washington, D.C.).

1896. Rossi, Ann, and Rosen Daniel. *Bright Ideas: The Age of Invention in America 1870–1910.* National Geographic, 2005. 40pp. ISBN 978-0-7922-8276-1. Grades 5–7. Several important discoveries were made during this period, changing everyday life. Rossi looks at the creative process and at the inventions and the persons who made them—Thomas Edison, the Wright brothers, Henry Ford, and lesser-known individuals such as Jan Matzeliger, Granville T. Woods, Lewis Latimer, Amanda Theodosia Jones, and Margaret Knight. Reproductions and illustrations augment the text. Glossary and Index.

1897. Santella, Andrew. *Roosevelt's Rough Riders.* (We the People) Compass Point, 2005. 48pp. ISBN 978-0-7565-1268-2; paper ISBN 978-0-7565-1732-8. Grades 4–6. Primary documents offer valuable information about Theodore Roosevelt's formation of the Rough Riders at the beginning of the Spanish-American War. This group of volunteer soldiers saw action in 1898 when they ended up fighting on foot as infantry. Photographs and reproductions accompany the text. Glossary, Chronology, Further Reading, Web Sites, and Index.

1898. Shea, Pegi Deitz. *Liberty Rising: The Story of the Statue of Liberty.* Illustrated by Wade Zahares. Henry Holt, 2005. 44pp. ISBN 978-0-8050-7220-4. Grades 2–4. To visualize the completed statue, designer Frédéric Auguste Bartholdi (1834–1904) had a four-foot model built that helped him decide the process of construction. When the statue was finally completed in France, 214 train cars took it to Rouen and the ship on which it was transported to New York. After its arrival in 1885, it was reassembled and dedicated on October 28, 1886. This volume follows the steps involved to create Liberty, the tallest structure in the world at the time. Illustrations complement the text.

1899. Sonneborn, Liz. *The Pledge of Allegiance: The Story Behind Our Patriotic Promise.* (America in Words and Song) Chelsea Clubhouse, 2004. 32pp. ISBN 978-0-7910-7336-0. Grades 3–5. Sonneborn details the circumstances that led Francis Bellamy to write the Pledge of Allegiance. It was first recited to students on Columbus Day in 1892. An examination of each phrase and the controversy surrounding it gives insight into its intended meaning. Illustrations and photographs enhance the text. Bibliography, Further Reading, Timeline, Glossary, Web Sites, and Index.

1900. Stroud, Bettye, and Virginia Schomp. *The Reconstruction Era.* (Drama of African-American History) Benchmark, 2006. 70pp. ISBN 978-0-7614-2181-8. Grades 5–8. Stroud examines the problems freed slaves encountered during the Reconstruction era. The Freedman's Bureau, established to help them, found that southern landowners tried to thwart its plans. This volume includes commentary by figures such as W. E. B. Du Bois and Frederick Douglass. Chapters contain complementary photographs, illustrations, documents, and maps. Glossary, Bibliography, Further Reading, and Index.

1901. Temple, Bob. *The Titanic: An Interactive History Adventure.* (You Choose) Capstone, 2007. 2007pp. ISBN 978-1-4296-0163-4; paper ISBN 978-1-4296-1182-4. Grades 3–6. Readers can choose what role they would like to play during the sinking of the *Titanic*. Will they be saved or will they die? Other historically plausible decisions follow. Color reproductions and maps enhance the text. Bibliography.

1902. Warren, Andrea. *We Rode the Orphan Trains.* Harcourt, 2001. 144pp. ISBN 978-0-618-11712-3; Sandpiper, 2004, paper ISBN 978-0-618-43235-6. Grades 4–8. To help children living in orphanages and foster homes, a young New York minister named Charles Loring Brace established the Children's Aid Society. He began helping children find families, and between 1854 and 1929 more than 200,000 children from the eastern United States rode trains west to unite with families who wanted children. Among the children featured in the text are Betty, whose new family lived in a lovely hotel; Nettie Evans and her twin, who had to be rescued from their abusive first family; and brothers Howard and Fred, who lived with different families but kept in touch. Some had exciting lives and others had to cope with difficult families until they became adults. The question remains as to whether the children would have been better off left in orphanages or if their new lives were an improvement. Bibliography and Index. *Bluegrass Award* (Kentucky) nomination and *Reader's Choice Awards* (Virginia) nomination.

1903. Weitzman, David. *A Subway for New York.* Farrar, 2005. 40pp. ISBN 978-0-374-37284-2. Grades 4–7. Weitzman details the construction of New York City's first subterranean train system. In 1904 the city was congested with carriages, pedestrians, and other traffic that made a new way to travel around town necessary. This volume describes the building of tracks, the electrical system, and the design of passenger stations. Illustrations include side views and cutaways with human figures providing scale. Bibliography.

1904. Whitelaw, Nancy. *The Homestead Steel Strike of 1892.* Morgan Reynolds, 2006. 176pp. ISBN 978-1-931798-88-4. Grades 5–9. In 1892 the Homestead Steel workers staged a strike against Andrew Carnegie and Henry C. Frick, two of the most powerful businessmen in America. Carnegie, born in Scotland, was a self-made man; Frick was his partner. They monopolized the steel industry and refused to improve working conditions or salaries for their employees. The two wanted to destroy the Amalgamated Association of Iron and Steel Workers at their Homestead, Pennsylvania, factory, and while Carnegie was vacationing in Scotland, Frick hired Pinkerton Agency men to break the strike. Men died, and the union broke. However, Frick faced personal tragedy, and Carnegie sold the company to J. P. Morgan. Reproductions and drawings augment the text. Bibliography, Chronology, Web Sites, and Index.

1905. Whiting, Jim. *The Sinking of the Titanic.* (Monumental Milestones) Mitchell Lane, 2006. 48pp. ISBN 978-1-58415-472-3. Grades 5–8. Whiting offers a history of the *Titanic* from its design and construction to its sinking in 1912. He includes new findings that question whether the sinking was due to the ship's design or to human errors. This volume names some of the passengers and details their fates. Photographs, sidebars, and illustrations augment the text. Glossary, Chronology, and Index.

1906. Whitman, Sylvia. *This Land Is Your Land: The American Conservation Movement.* Lerner, 1994. 88pp. ISBN 978-0-8225-1729-0. Grades 5–9. Yellowstone National Park was founded in 1872. Theodore Roosevelt later met John Muir, who persuaded Roosevelt to place a priority on the nation's natural resources. Among others mentioned as having important roles in saving the environment and conserving land are Rachel Carson and the Sierra Club. Photographs augment the text. Bibliography and Index.

1907. Wilson, Kate. *Earthquake! San Francisco, 1906.* Illustrated by Richard Courtney. Steck-Vaughn, 1993. 62pp. Paper ISBN 978-0-8114-8056-7. Grades 5–9. After an earthquake struck San Francisco in 1906, fires began to destroy many buildings. The quake had broken water pipes throughout the city, and firefighters were helpless. George Lowe reported for the *San Francisco Chronicle*, and Helen Dare (on vacation) reported for the *Los Angeles Examiner.* They realized they must get the news to the outside world, so they took the ferry across the bay to Oakland, where they could send their stories. Others also moved rapidly to overcome the devastation. One of these was General Funston, a man who had mapped Death Valley. He organized a militia for rebuilding; others collected mail in all forms (such as writing on sleeve cuffs) and sent it to worried relatives. Epilogue, Afterword, and Notes.

Biography and Collective Biography

1908. Adler, David A. *A Picture Book of George Washington Carver.* Illustrated by Dan Brown. Holiday House, 2000. Unpaged. ISBN 978-0-8234-1429-1; paper ISBN 978-0-8234-1633-2. Grades 1–3. George Washington Carver (1864?–1943) was born into slavery before raiders kidnapped him and his mother and took them to Arkansas. His mother was never found, and Mr. Carver, the man who owned them, brought him back to the farm and raised him and his brother. This biography describes his life, his education, and his accomplishments as a scientific researcher in the field of agriculture, especially peanuts. Illustrations complement the text. Notes.

1909. Adler, David A. *A Picture Book of Harriet Tubman.* See entry 1482.

1910. Adler, David A. *A Picture Book of Helen Keller.* Illustrated by John and Alexandra Wallner. Holiday House, 1990. Unpaged. ISBN 978-0-8234-0818-4; 1992, paper ISBN 978-0-8234-0950-1. Grades 1–3. Left blind and deaf from an illness when she was one-and-a-half years old, Helen Keller (1880–1968) was fortunate to have parents who could find a teacher for her. Anne Mansfield Sullivan dedicated her life to Keller and gave her words with which to communicate. Keller published several books and received the Presidential Medal of Freedom. Important Dates.

1911. Adler, David A. *A Picture Book of Sojourner Truth.* See entry 1484.

1912. Adler, David A. *A Picture Book of Thomas Alva Edison.* Illustrated by John and Alexandra Wallner. Holiday House, 1996. Unpaged. ISBN 978-0-8234-1246-4; 1999, paper ISBN 978-0-8234-1414-7. Grades 1–3. Adler provides background on Thomas Alva Edison (1847–1931) and his dedication to his experiments and his inventions. Important Dates.

1913. Aliki. *A Weed Is a Flower: The Life of George Washington Carver.* Aladdin, 1988. Paper ISBN 978-0-671-66490-9. Grades K–3. Born the son of slaves in 1860 and soon separated from his parents by death and deviousness, George Washington Carver asked questions about almost everything in the homes of those who raised him. Neighbors called him the "Plant Doctor" when he was very young and asked his advice because his own garden grew so beautifully. Although unable to save enough money for college until he was 30, he finally went, and decided not to be an artist but to be an agriculturist. He taught and researched at Tuskegee, finding more than 100 things that could be made from sweet potatoes and dispelling the idea that peanuts were only "monkey food." He worked until he died at 80.

1914. Aller, Susan Bivin. *George Eastman.* (History Maker Bios) Lerner, 2004. 48pp. ISBN 978-0-8225-0200-5. Grades 3–5. George Eastman (1854–1932) first worked in a bank and spent his evenings making film. He eventually established a company that he called Kodak. His employees loved him, and his inventions made photography possible for the average person. The five chapters of the text give an overview of his life and accomplishments. Illustrations augment the text. Bibliography, Further Reading, Glossary, Maps, Timeline, Web Sites, and Index.

1915. Aller, Susan Bivin. *Juliette Low.* (History Maker Bios) Lerner, 2007. 48pp. ISBN 978-0-8225-6580-2. Grades 3–5. Juliette Gordon Low (1860–1927), called "Daisy," grew up in Savannah, Georgia, where she attended private school. After she married, she lived in England and Scotland. When her husband died, she wanted to be useful to others. She met the founder of the Boy Scouts and Girl Guides, Sir Robert Baden-Powell, and realized she could offer this organization for girls in the United States. She started the first American Girl Guide groups in 1912 back in Savannah, becoming the first president. Eventually the group became known as the Girl Scouts. The book's five chapters present her life and her accomplishments. Illustrations augment the text. Bibliography, Further Reading, Glossary, Maps, Timeline, Web Sites, and Index.

1916. Aller, Susan Bivin. *Madam C. J. Walker.* (History Maker Bios) Lerner, 2007. 48pp. ISBN 978-0-8225-6582-6. Grades 3–5. Madam C. J. Walker (1867–1919) was born a free black after the Civil War. As she grew up, she saw that African American women suffered hair loss due to poor diet and lack of time to groom themselves properly. She became educated and realized that an effective hair treatment would help her people. She created a hair-care and cosmetics business that made her the most successful African American in the country while helping others. The book's five chapters give an overview of her life. Illustrations augment the text. Bibliography, Further Reading, Glossary, Maps, Timeline, Web Sites, and Index.

1917. Aller, Susan Bivin. *Ulysses S. Grant.* See entry 1487.

1918. Allport, Alan. *Theodore Roosevelt.* (Great American Presidents) Facts on File, 2003. 100pp. ISBN 978-0-7910-7606-4. Grades 5–7. Theodore Roosevelt (1858–1919) was the governor of New York before becoming vice president of the United States under William McKinley. He then became the twenty-sixth president. During his life, he accomplished much, including fighting during the Spanish-American War. The six chapters discuss his childhood, his upbringing and family, events that influenced his ideas, the issues of his presidency, and his accomplishments. Photographs enhance the text. Timeline, Appendix, and Index.

1919. Berger, Melvin, and Gilder Berger. *Can You Fly High, Wright Brothers?* (Science Super-Giants) Scholastic, 2007. 48pp. Paper ISBN 978-0-439-83378-3. Grades 3–4. This brief biography of the Wright brothers, Orville (1871–1948) and Wilbur (1867–1912), reveals their intense desire to create a flying machine. They also became involved in several adventures when they became adults. This volume includes a few experiments, such as blowing on a long strip of paper to see how air currents cause it to rise. Illustrations augment the text. Chronology and Index.

1920. Berger, Melvin, and Gilder Berger. *Did You Invent the Phone Alone, Alexander Graham Bell?* (Science SuperGiants) Scholastic, 2007. 48pp. Paper ISBN 978-0-439-83381-3. Grades 3–4. This brief biography of Alexander Graham Bell (1847–1922) shows that Bell was very interested in sound and spent his life working on it. He invented the telephone and then improved it during his lifetime. Activities include the process of feeling the vibrations in one's throat when speaking. Photographs and illustrations enhance the text. Chronology and Index.

1921. Berry, S. L. *Emily Dickinson.* Illustrated by Stermer Dugald. (Voices from the Past) Creative, 1994. 45pp. ISBN 978-0-8868-2609-3. Grades 5 up. Emily Dickinson (1830–1886) lived in Amherst, Massachusetts, and rarely left her home. Her innovative poetry about the world around her is still appreciated today. Bibliography and Index.

1922. Bolden, Tonya. *George Washington Carver.* Abrams, 2008. 41.pp. ISBN 978-0-8109-9366-2. Grades 4–8. Born into slavery and cruelly separated from his mother, George Washington Carver (1864?–1943) was raised by German American farmers in the Ozark Mountains of Missouri. He was the first African American to attend Iowa State College and hesitated to leave the Midwest for Tuskegee Institute. Influenced by his former master's desire not to waste things, Carver devoted his scientific research to finding ways to use common products including vegetables for fuel. He garnered the nicknames "Wizard of the Goober and the Yam" and "Wizard of Tuskegee." His work with peanuts is well known, but he contributed much to science with his thoughtful inquiries. Photographs and reproductions of Carver's own paintings enhance the text. Bibliography and Notes.

1923. Bolden, Tonya. *Maritcha: A Nineteenth-Century American Girl.* See entry 1492.

1924. Borden, Louise, and Mary Kay Kroeger. *Fly High! The Story of Bessie Coleman.* Illustrated by Teresa Flavin. Simon & Schuster, 2001. 40pp. ISBN 978-0-689-82457-9; Aladdin, 2004, paper ISBN 978-0-689-86462-9. Grades K–4. Bessie Coleman (1892–1926) had to leave the school that she loved to pick cotton as a girl, but she decided that she would achieve something in her life and moved to Chicago in 1915. There she heard from veterans who had fought during World War I that women in France could be pilots. Determined to become the first African American woman to fly, she worked and saved to go to France and earn her pilot's license in 1921. She performed as a stunt pilot, a job that she loved. She told young African Americans wherever she went that they could do what they wanted. Coleman never regretted her career choice. She died in a plane crash. Gouache paintings highlight the rhythmic text delineating Coleman's life and the era in which she lived. *Pennsylvania Young Reader's Choice Award* nomination and *Bluebonnet Award* (Texas) nomination.

1925. Borden, Louise, and Trish Marx. *Touching the Sky: The Flying Adventures of Wilbur and Orville Wright.* Illustrated by Peter Fiore. Margaret K. McElderry, 2003. 64pp. ISBN 978-0-689-84876-6. Grades 3–6. In 1909, six years after their first flight at Kitty Hawk, Wilbur (1867–1912) and Orville (1871–1948) were well-known personalities. Wilbur piloted a flying machine over the heads of New Yorkers while Orville entertained onlookers in Germany and France. Back in Dayton, they continued their experiments. Chronology and Maps. Illustrations augment the text.

1926. Bowdish, Lynea. *George Washington Carver.* (Rookie Biographies) Scholastic, 2004. 32pp. ISBN 978-0-516-23610-0; paper ISBN 978-0-516-24644-4. Grades K–2. George Washington Carver (1864?–1943) overcame his life of poverty to make important discoveries in agriculture. This volume looks at his achievements without spending much time on his personal trials. Illustrations augment the text.

1927. Braun, Eric. *Bessie Coleman.* Pebble, 2005. 24pp. ISBN 978-0-7368-4229-7. Grades K–2. This biography of Bessie Coleman (1892–1926) offers an overview of her life and her achievement as the first African American woman to earn a pilot's license. Photographs highlight the text. Glossary, Further Reading, Web Sites, and Index.

1928. Brighton, Catherine. *Keep Your Eye on the Kid: The Early Years of Buster Keaton.* Flash Point, 2008. Unpaged. ISBN 978-1-59643-158-4. Grades 3–5. Buster Keaton (1895–1966) joined his father on the vaudeville stage when he was only 4 years old. He earned his nickname when Houdini commented after he fell down the steps that he had a "buster." On stage with his father, he was not allowed to smile and his father would whisper "face" to him as a reminder. He became fascinated with films, but his father did not want him to become involved. Keaton ran away to New York and met Fatty Arbuckle, a movie maker. At Arbuckle's studio he learned the art and became one of silent movies' famous stars. Illustrations complement the text. Bibliography. *Kirkus Reviews Editor's Choice.*

1929. Brown, Don. *Bright Path: Young Jim Thorpe.* Roaring Brook, 2006. 40pp. ISBN 978-1-59643-041-9; Square Fish, 2008, paper ISBN 978-0-312-37748-9. Grades 2–4. Jim Thorpe (1887–1953), a Native American Olympic athlete from Oklahoma, had the tribal name of "Bright Path." Rather aimless as a boy, Thorpe impulsively cleared a high jump with more room to spare than anyone else on his Indian school's track team. At the Olympics, he won the Pentathlon and the decathlon. Watercolor illustrations reinforce the text. Bibliography and Notes.

1930. Brown, Don. *Ruth Law Thrills a Nation.* Houghton, 1993. Unpaged. ISBN 978-0-395-66404-9; 1995, paper ISBN 978-0-395-73517-6. Grades K–2. In 1916 Ruth Law set out to fly from Chicago to New York City in one day. Although she did not succeed—the tailwinds did not propel her as she had hoped, and she had to stop for fuel—she broke the record with a nonstop flight of 590 miles.

1931. Brown, Don. *Teedie: The Story of Young Teddy Roosevelt.* HMH, 2009. 32pp. ISBN 978-0-618-17999-2. Grades 1–4. A wealthy young, New York City boy, Theodore Roosevelt (1858–1919) was frail, undersized, and asthmatic. His father encouraged him to build both his body and his mind by exercising vigorously and reading everything that interested him. After he attended Harvard, he became a solider, a writer, the youngest president of the United States, and a naturalist who established national parks. Ink cross-hatching and watercolors complement the text. Note. *Capitol Choices Noteworthy Titles for Children and Teens* (Washington, D.C.).

1932. Brown, Don. *A Voice from the Wilderness: The Story of Anna Howard Shaw.* Houghton, 2001. 32pp. ISBN 978-0-618-08362-6. Grades 1–3. Anna Howard Shaw (1847–1919) immigrated to America, lived in Massachusetts, and traveled to the Michigan frontier with her mother and siblings while her father and brothers stayed in the East. She became a schoolteacher and later earned a degree in theology. She preached about a woman's right to vote but did not live to see women's suffrage enacted.

1933. Brown, Fern G. *Daisy and the Girl Scouts: The Story of Juliette Gordon Low.* Illustrated by Marie De John. Whitman, 2005. 111pp. Paper ISBN 978-0-8075-1441-2. Grades 3–6. Juliette Gordon Low (1860–1927), known as "Daisy," founded the American Girl Scouts. Her wealthy background allowed her the luxury of travel, and she met Lord Baden-Powell, founder of the Boy Scouts, in England. This encounter gave her the idea of establishing the Girl Scouts in the United States. This volume looks at her life as well as the organization of the group. Chronology and Index.

1934. Bryant, Jen. *A River of Words: The Story of William Carlos Williams.* Illustrated by Melissa Sweet. Eerdmans, 2008. Unpaged. ISBN 978-0-8028-5302-8. Grades 3–6. This biography of William Carlos Williams (1883–1963) reveals his love of nature as a child; perhaps this association affected the rhythms in his poetry. While a physician as an adult, he grabbed time whenever he could to write a few lines. Also included are a few of his short poems. Mixed-media collages enhance the text. Chronology and Further Reading. *Kirkus Reviews Editor's Choice, Capitol Choices Noteworthy Titles* (Washington, D.C.), and *School Library Journal Best Books for Children.*

1935. Bundles, A'leila, and Perry Bundles. *Madam C. J. Walker: Entrepreneur.* Chelsea House, 2008. 112pp. ISBN 978-1-60413-072-0. Grades 5–8. The daughter of former slaves, Madam C. J. Walker (1867–1919) became America's first black female millionaire. She was widowed at 20 and worked as a laundress for 20 years afterward. In 1905 she invented a hair-care product for black women and sold it door-to-door. When it became successful, she started her own company. With her money, she made contributions to black schools, orphanages, and civil rights organizations. She campaigned for the rights of black war veterans and for federal anti-lynching legislation while insisting that blacks had to defend themselves. Photographs enhance the text. Chronology, Further Reading, and Index.

1936. Butcher, Nancy. *It Can't Be Done, Nellie Bly! A Reporter's Race Around the World.* Illustrated by Jen L. Singh. Peachtree, 2003. 136pp. ISBN 978-1-56145-289-7. Grades 3–7. Nellie Bly (1864–1922) accomplished many unusual things for a woman of her time. One of them was a 22,000-mile trip around the world in 1888. She took one dress and a satchel; she added a monkey in Singapore. Her goal was to circle the world in fewer than eighty days, and she traveled from London to France to Italy, Egypt, Yemen, Sri Lanka, Malaysia, Singapore, China, Japan, and San Francisco before returning to Hoboken, New Jersey, in seventy-seven days. Bibliography and Notes.

1937. Carlson, Laurie M. *Thomas Edison for Kids: His Life and Ideas, 21 Activities.* Chicago Review, 2006. Paper ISBN 978-1-55652-584-1. Grades 5–9. This brief biography covers the life and inventions of Thomas Edison (1847–1931). Slightly deaf, he was thought to be a slow learner as a child, but he was always investigating and after his teens he seems to have been a workaholic. The activities provided use simple materials and sometimes require the help of an adult. Photographs and illustrations augment the text. Further Reading, Glossary, Web Sites, and Index.

1938. Carney, Mary Lou. *Dr. Welch and the Great Grape Story.* Illustrated by Sherry Meidell. Boyds Mills, 2005. 32pp. ISBN 978-1-59078-039-8. Grades 1–3. Thomas Bramwell Welch, a dentist and amateur inventor, wanted to create a non-alcoholic drink that everyone could enjoy and that alcoholics could use for Communion. He and his son worked with grapes, and he invented grape juice. Watercolors enhance the text.

1939. Carson, Mary Kay. *Alexander Graham Bell: Giving Voice to the World.* (Sterling Biographies) Sterling, 2007. 124pp. ISBN 978-1-4027-4951-3; paper ISBN 978-1-4027-3230-0. Grades 5–8. Carson covers the life of Alexander Graham Bell (1847–1922) and the reasons for his fame. After a summary of his life and the contributions he made, the text includes information about his early family life and education. It examines him in relationship to the times in which he lived. Photographs enhance the text. Bibliography, Chonology, Glossary, and Index.

1940. Chorlian, Meg. *Ulysses S. Grant: Confident Leader and Hero.* See entry 1495.

1941. Cline-Ransome, Lesa. *Helen Keller: The World in Her Heart.* HarperCollins, 2008. Unpaged. ISBN 978-0-06-057074-3. Grades K–4. This look at Helen Keller (1880–1968) as a child just as she meets Annie Sullivan draws on Keller's own autobiography. It reveals Keller's reactions to external stimuli: anger when a stranger arrived and started drawing pictures in her palm all day long; frustration at the smell of vanilla cake and the feeling of bumps on the road when she cannot see the cake nor know where she is going. The fictional biography imagines what Keller was thinking as she finally made the connection to "water" and began learning the different flowers by relating their smells and shapes to their names. Illustrations complement the text.

1942. Cline-Ransome, Lesa. *Major Taylor, Champion Cyclist.* Illustrated by James E. Ransome. Simon & Schuster, 2003. 40pp. ISBN 978-0-689-83159-1. Grades 2–4. When Marshall Taylor was 13 years old in 1891, he was hired at a famous Indiana bicycle shop, Hay and Willits, for his ability to ride a bike forward, backward, or perched on the handlebars. He wore a military uniform at first, earning the name "Major." Taylor worked to become a speed cyclist, turned professional at 18, and won the 1899 World Championship title three years later. Although a superb rider, he had to combat racism; white racers would deliberately hem him in to stop him from breaking out of the pack. He was allowed to ride in the United States only because he had joined the League of American Wheelmen before they voted to exclude African Americans. In France he was more accepted, and his victory over the French bicycle champion Edmond Jacquelin was admired. But Taylor died as a forgotten competitor at the age of 53. Paintings enhance the text. *Emphasis on Reading Award* (Alabama) nomination, *Young Hoosier Book Award* (Indiana) nomination, *Golden Sower Award* (Nebraska) nomination, and *Capitol Choices Noteworthy Titles* (Washington, D.C.).

1943. Collins, Mary. *Airborne: A Photobiography of Wilbur and Orville Wright.* National Geographic, 2003. 64pp. ISBN 978-0-7922-6957-1. Grades 5 up. Although the Wright brothers, Wilbur (1867–1912) and Orville (1871–1948), never graduated from high school, they became the first to construct a practical airplane that solved the problems of powered flight and led to the famous flight on December 17, 1903, at Kitty Hawk. The book includes sixty duo-tone archival photographs of the two brothers at work as they perfected their invention to become the world's first aeronautical engineers. Photographs range from a mundane picture of Wilbur cooking in the hangar in 1902 to a delightful image of French farmers with ox-drawn carts watching Wilbur fly above. The text includes definitions of terms and diagrams to illustrate technical explanations. Photographs, Bibliography, Chronology, Illustrations, and Index. *Booklist Editor's Choice.*

1944. Cooney, Barbara. *Eleanor.* Viking, 1996. Unpaged. ISBN 978-0-670-86159-0; Puffin, 1999, paper ISBN 978-0-14-055583-7. Grades 1–3. Cooney begins the story of Eleanor Roosevelt's life (1884–1962) by noting her mother's disappointment with her. She gives an overview of her life in boarding school and her achievements, emphasizing Roosevelt's ability to overcome difficulties. *School Library Journal Best Book* and *Capitol Choices Noteworthy Titles* (Washington, D.C.).

1945. Cooper, Floyd. *Coming Home: From the Life of Langston Hughes.* Philomel, 1994. Unpaged. ISBN 978-0-399-22682-3. Grades K–4. Cooper takes information about the childhood of Langston Hughes (1902–1967) and tells it as if it were fiction. He notes that Hughes lived with his grandparents and aunt and uncle rather than his parents because his father left for Mexico. Cooper also discusses Hughes's early interest in writing and some of the poems he wrote while in school. The last page is a short summary of Hughes's lifetime achievements to show that Hughes finally discovered that "home" was within himself. Bibliography.

1946. Covert, Ralph, and Riley G. Mills. *Sawdust and Spangles: The Amazing Life of W.C. Coup.* Illustrated by Giselle Potter. Abrams, 2007. 40pp. ISBN 978-0-8109-9351-8. Grades K–3. As a young boy, William Cameron Coup (1837–1895) became enthralled with the circus. He ran away to join one, joined forces with P. T. Barnum, and became a major innovator. He also created the New York Aquarium. Illustrations enhance the text.

1947. Crowe, Ellie. *Surfer of the Century: The Life of Duke Kahanamoku.* Illustrated by Richard Waldrep. Lee & Low, 2007. Unpaged. ISBN 978-1-58430-276-6. Grades 3–6. Duke Kahanamoku (1890–1968), a Hawaiian, started training for the 1912 Olympics after a coach saw his natural swimming ability. In August 1911 he shattered records, but the Amateur Athlete Union refused to believe his times. He finally earned the right to enter the Olympics and won both a silver and a gold, and became friends with Jim Thorpe. He also competed in three more Olympic Games—in 1920, 1924, and 1932. He was an expert surfer known for a two-mile ride on an enormous wave, and popularized surfing around the world. Throughout his life and career, he ably handled the racial discrimination that he encountered. Illustrations enhance the text. Maps, Bibliography, Chronology, and Notes.

1948. Cummins, Julia. *Women Daredevils: Thrills, Chills, and Frills.* Illustrated by Cheryl Harness. Dutton, 2008. 48pp. ISBN 978-0-525-47948-2. Grades 3–5. This collective biography presents profiles of fourteen stunt performers who were active from 1880 to 1929. These performers— ranging in age from 15 to 63—went over the Niagara Falls in barrels, rode bareback, shot out of cannons, tamed tigers, rode on airplane wings, and other stunts. They were Zazel, Annie Edson Taylor, Mademoiselle d'Zizi, Gertrude Breton, Isabelle Butler, the La Rague Sisters, May Wirth, Georgia "Tiny" Broadwick, Mabel Stark, Gladys Roy, Gladys Ingle, Mabel Cody, and Sonora Webster Carver. Photographs and illustrations augment the text. Chronology and Notes.

1949. Delano, Marfe Ferguson. *Helen's Eyes: A Photobiography of Annie Sullivan, Helen Keller's Teacher.* National Geographic, 2008. 64pp. ISBN 978-1-4263-0209-1. Grades 5–8. When

Annie Sullivan (1866–1936) started working with Helen Keller (1880–1968), she realized that if she succeeded, this would be the most important aspect of her life. Daughter of poor Irish immigrants, she too had vision loss. After her mother died, her abusive father abandoned her (at the age of 8) and her brother; they went to the poor house. She did not go to school until she was 14, but left six years later as valedictorian. Her next hurdle was dealing with Keller, and again she succeeded. Primary source quotes reveal not only Sullivan's life but what was happening at the time around the world. Photographs highlight the text. Notes. *School Library Journal Best Books for Children.*

1950. Dixon-Engel, Tara, and Mike Jackson. *The Wright Brothers: First in Flight.* (Sterling Biographies) Sterling, 2007. 124pp. ISBN 978-1-4027-4954-4; paper ISBN 978-1-4027-3231-7. Grades 5–8. This volume looks at the lives of the Wright Brothers, Orville (1871–1948) and Wilbur (1867–1912) and their historic flight. After a summary of their lives and contributions, the text includes information about their childhood and education. It examines them in relationship to the times in which they lived. Photographs enhance the text. Bibliography, Chronology, Glossary, and Index.

1951. Doeden, Matt. *George Washington Carver.* (History Maker Bios) Lerner, 2007. 48pp. ISBN 978-0-8225-7605-1. Grades 3–5. In five chapters, this volume relates the life of George Washington Carver (1864?–1943) and describes his ability as a plant doctor. He searched for information as both a student and teacher and found many uses for the simple peanut. During his life he helped others to increase their agricultural production. Photographs and illustrations augment the text. Bibliography, Further Reading, Glossary, Maps, Timeline, Web Sites, and Index.

1952. Donlan, Leni. *Mathew Brady: Photographing the Civil War.* See entry 1694.

1953. Dooling, Michael. *Young Thomas Edison.* Holiday House, 2005. 40pp. ISBN 978-0-8234-1868-8. Grades 1–3. Thomas Edison (1847–1931) became interested in science very early and was studious and hard working as a child although he attended school for only three months. When a teacher accused him of being inattentive, probably because he had hearing difficulty, his mother homeschooled him. He started his first laboratory in his family's cellar when he was only 9 years old. Among his inventions were the phonograph, the kinetoscope for movies, and the incandescent light bulb. Paintings highlight the text. Further Resources. *Black-Eyed Susan Award* (Maryland) nomination.

1954. Dray, Philip. *Yours for Justice, Ida B. Wells: The Daring Life of a Crusading Journalist.* Illustrated by Stephen Alcorn. Peachtree, 2008. Unpaged. ISBN 978-1-56145-417-4. Grades 1–5. African American Ida B. Wells-Barnett (1862–1931) was born a slave but became a respected teacher and newspaper journalist known for her crusade against lynching, "execution outside the law." By the age of 16, she had become a teacher and used her salary to support her siblings. Ink and watercolor illustrations complement the text. Bibliography, Chronology, and Further Reading.

1955. Dubowski, Cathy East. *Clara Barton: I Want to Help!* See entry 1695.

1956. Dwyer, Christopher. *Robert Peary and the Quest for the North Pole.* (World Explorers) Chelsea House, 1992. 110pp. ISBN 978-0-7910-1316-8. Grades 5 up. Many people competed with Robert Peary (1856–1920) to become the first to reach the North Pole, among them Frederick Albert Cook, Elisha Kent Kane, Charles Francis Hall, Edward Parry, Fridtjof Nansen, and Adolphus Greely. They risked starvation, frostbite, scurvy, and various other maladies to reach their goal. Peary sacrificed 23 years of his life, his health, his money, some of his toes, and probably his sanity before he claimed the North Pole as his discovery in 1909. Photographs and reproductions enhance the text. Chronology, Further Reading, and Index.

1957. Edwards, Pamela Duncan. *The Wright Brothers.* Illustrated by Henry Cole. Hyperion, 2003. 32pp. ISBN 978-0-7868-2682-7. Grades K–3. The process leading to the Wright Brothers' first flight in 1903 is described in rhyming, cumulative text. Included are references to the bicycle shop, their printing press, their interest in flying, and their achievements. A quartet of mice add humor. The endpapers display a timeline. Illustrations highlight the tale.

1958. El Nabli, Dina. *Eleanor Roosevelt: First Lady of the World.* Trophy. 48pp. ISBN 978-0-06-057614-1; paper ISBN 978-0-06-057613-4. Grades 4–8. Primary sources including interviews with experts make up this biography of Eleanor Roosevelt (1884–1962). It covers the significant events in Roosevelt's life, her accomplishments, and personal anecdotes. She had an unhappy childhood with an alcoholic father who died while she was still young and a cold, distant grandmother. She became emotionally estranged from her husband but supported social issues while First Lady and afterward. Illustrations and photographs illuminate the text.

1959. Elish, Dan. *Theodore Roosevelt.* (Presidents and Their Times) Benchmark, 2007. 96pp. ISBN 978-0-7614-2429-1. Grades 4–7. Theodore Roosevelt (1858–1919) was a man of action. His dynamism allowed him to accomplish much to protect the environment; he was also determined to stop corruption. Elish looks at the successes and failures of his life along with his personal tragedies. Photographs augment the text. Bibliography, Glossary, Chronology, Further Reading, Web Sites, and Index.

1960. Feinberg, Barbara Silberdick. *Eleanor Roosevelt: A Very Special First Lady.* Millbrook, 2003. 48pp. ISBN 978-0-7613-2623-6. Grades 3–5. This biography of Eleanor Roosevelt (1884–1962) covers her childhood and adolescence, her marriage and her family, her White House years, her political leanings, and her humanitarian work. Photographs enhance highlight the text. Bibliography, Chronology, Further Reading, Web Sites, and Index.

1961. Fitzgerald, Dawn. *Vinnie and Abraham.* Charlesbridge, 2007. Unpaged. ISBN 978-1-57091-658-8. Grades 2–4. Vinnie Ream (1847–1914) defied the conventions of Civil War Washington, D.C., and became one of the United States Postal Service's first female employees. While doing this, she was also modeling clay. By the time she was 18, she was meeting daily with President Lincoln to sculpt his head. After he was assassinated, Congress commissioned her—the first woman to receive a government commission—to sculpt a marble statue of the late president. It continues to reside in the Capitol rotunda today. Other important figures she sculpted included Ulysses S. Grant, Robert E. Lee, and Sequoyah. Photographs and illustrations complement the text. Further Resources.

1962. Fleischman, Sid. *Escape! The Story of the Great Houdini.* Greenwillow, 2006. 210pp. ISBN 978-0-06-085094-4. Grades 4–8. Ehrich Weisz (1874–1926) took the name Harry Houdini after moving to the United States from Hungary and aspiring to become a well-known magician and escapologist. He became, perhaps, the most successful one in the world. He was also a stunt performer, film producer, actor, and spiritualist investigator. Fleischman adds insight by revealing his own experiences as an amateur magician and friend of the late Houdini's wife although he never reveals Houdini's secrets. Photographs enhance the text. Bibliography, Notes, and Index. *Boston Globe/Horn Book Awards Honor Book, Dorothy Canfield Fisher Children's Book Award* (Vermont) nomination, *Sydney Taylor Book Award* nomination, *Publishers Weekly Best Children's Books, School Library Journal Best Books for Children, American Library Association Notable Children's Books, Capitol Choices Noteworthy Titles* (Washington, D.C.), *Publishers Weekly Best Books,* and *American Library Association Best Books for Young Adults.*

1963. Fradin, Dennis B., and Judith Bloom. *Fight On! Mary Church Terrell's Battle for Integration.* Houghton, 2003. 192pp. ISBN 978-0-618-13349-9. Grades 5–9. Mary "Mollie" Church Terrell (1863–1954), daughter of an ex-slave, was the best-educated African American woman of her time when she graduated from Oberlin College in 1884. She was a founder of the National Association for the Advancement of Colored People (NAACP) and the first African American member of the Board of Education in Washington, D.C. She also worked with Susan B. Anthony to win the vote for women. When she was 89 years old, the case she had started by documenting refusals to serve her in Washington, D.C., restaurants reached the Supreme Court, which ruled to integrate the restaurants. Among her friends were Frederick Douglass, Susan B. Anthony, Paul Laurence Dunbar, and Ida B. Wells. Her husband was a judge, and she was a teacher. Photographs, Notes, Bibliography, and Index. *American Library Association Best Books for Young Adults.*

1964. Fradin, Dennis B., and Judith Bloom Fradin. *Ida B. Wells: Mother of the Civil Rights Movement.* Clarion, 2001. 178pp. ISBN 978-0-395-89898-7. Grades 5 up. Ida B. Wells-Barnett (1862–1931), born into slavery, had to raise her orphaned siblings. She taught school, became a probation officer, and then started writing for newspapers. She reported the horrors around her and became a strong activist against the heinous practice of lynching. She knew Susan B. Anthony, Frederick Douglass, and Harriet Tubman. She was outspoken, sometimes risking her life, and prefigured some of the militant African Americans who succeeded her. Photographs and illustrations augment the text. Bibliography and Index. *School Library Journal Best Books for Children* and *Capitol Choices Noteworthy Titles* (Washington, D.C.).

1965. Fradin, Dennis B., and Judith Bloom Fradin. *Jane Addams: Champion of Democracy.* Clarion, 2006. 216pp. ISBN 978-0-618-50436-7. Grades 3–8. Jane Addams (1860–1935) worked on behalf of the poor and those without political advocates. She established one of the first settlement houses, Hull House, and fought as a suffragist, civil rights activist, and pacifist. Photographs highlight the text. Bibliography, Notes, and Index.

1966. Frazier, Joey. *Jefferson Davis: Confederate President.* See entry 1502.

1967. Freedman, Russell. *Eleanor Roosevelt: A Life of Discovery.* Clarion, 1993. 198pp. ISBN 978-0-8991-9862-0; 1997, paper ISBN 978-0-395-84520-2. Grades 5 up. "If anyone were to ask me what I want out of life I would say—the opportunity to do something useful, for in no other way, I am convinced, can true happiness be attained." Eleanor Roosevelt (1884–1962), who considered herself an "ugly duckling," showed her values with that statement. As a young girl, she was very serious and reserved. She had to change when she began to travel extensively and to go where her wheelchair-bound husband could not. After his death, she was an American delegate to the United Nations, and Harry Truman called her the "First Lady of the World." Photographs, Books About and By Eleanor Roosevelt, and Index. *Newbery Honor* and *Bulletin Blue Ribbon.*

1968. Freedman, Russell. *Franklin Delano Roosevelt.* Clarion, 1990. 200pp. ISBN 978-0-8991-9379-3; 1992, paper ISBN 978-0-395-62978-9. Grades 5–8. Born in 1882 to a wealthy family, Franklin Delano Roosevelt (1882–1945) became a philatelist, naturalist, and photographer before he entered Harvard. His father's death while he was a freshman freed his mother to come to Boston and live near him. At Harvard, Roosevelt was happiest working on the university newspaper, *Crimson.* After graduation, he married Eleanor Roosevelt. He became the secretary of the navy during World War I, and his idea to mine the North Sea to stop German U-boats proved successful. The Battle of Verdun and the 500,000 who died there horrified him, and he wanted to join the army, but the war ended too soon. Eleanor found out by 1920 that he had been unfaithful, and they began an emotional estrangement that probably lasted throughout their marriage. But in 1921, when polio struck Franklin, their lives changed. Eleanor encouraged and supported his continued public life, although his mother did not. His illness helped him understand the difficulties of people who found themselves in situations through no fault of their own. Roosevelt became president in 1932 during the height of the Depression, and his New Deal program, including the Works Progress Administration, helped save the country. The first part of his term is known as the "Hundred Days." During his fourth term, and near the end of World War II, his strength waned, and he died in 1945 at Warm Springs, Georgia. Places to Visit, FDR Photo Album, Books About FDR, and Index. *Bulletin Blue Ribbon.*

1969. Freedman, Russell. *The Wright Brothers: How They Invented the Airplane.* Holiday House, 1994. 129pp. Paper ISBN 978-0-8234-1082-8. Grades 4–8. The Wright brothers, Wilbur (1867–1912) and Orville (1871–1948), were extraordinarily close. Their first flight in 1903, which lasted for one minute and 36 seconds, caused Amos Root to say, ". . . like [Columbus] . . . these two brothers have probably not even a faint glimpse of what their discovery is going to bring to the children of men." Their repeatedly longer flights attracted attention from other experimenters. By 1905 they could stay in the air more than 30 minutes. In 1908, although the French were suspicious of their plane and considered themselves the aviation leaders, Wilbur went to France to help. He awed them with his plane's grace and reported to Orville that Blériot was ecstatic. (Blériot himself flew across the English Channel in 1909.) Orville seemed to lose interest in aviation with Wilbur's death from typhoid. Now wealthy, he spent his time tinkering with all types of mechanical things, including the toys of his nieces and nephews. When *Apollo 11* landed on the moon, Neil Armstrong carried a piece of the cotton wing from the 1903 flight that started it all. Places to Visit, For Further Reading, and Index. *Booklist Starred Review, Bulletin Blue Ribbon, Horn Book Fanfare Honor List, Kirkus Pointer Review, Notable Children's Trade Books in the Field of Social Studies*, and *School Library Journal Best Book*.

1970. Freedman, Suzanne. *Louis Brandeis: The People's Justice.* Enslow, 1996. 104pp. ISBN 978-0-8949-0678-7. Grades 5–8. Louis Brandeis (1856–1941) was the first Jew to serve on the Supreme Court. Woodrow Wilson nominated him in 1916. Brandeis was also the first progressive justice, a social reformer. The text looks at his life and his contributions to the court. Bibliography, Glossary, Notes, and Index.

1971. Fritz, Jean. *Bully for You, Teddy Roosevelt.* Illustrated by Mike Wimmer. Putnam, 1997. 128pp. Paper ISBN 978-0-698-11609-2. Grades 5–8. Theodore Roosevelt (1858–1919) described things he especially liked as "Bully!" Among the activities he pursued were studying birds, shooting lions, roping steers, writing books, and exploring South American rivers. He fought corruption and worked for peace, winning the Nobel Peace Prize. He met with John Muir, saw the beauty of America, and used his presidential power to preserve it. Notes, Bibliography, and Index.

1972. Fritz, Jean. *Harriet Beecher Stowe and the Beecher Preachers.* See entry 1506.

1973. Fritz, Jean. *You Want Women to Vote, Lizzie Stanton?* See entry 1507.

1974. Garmon, Anita. *Alexander Graham Bell Invents.* (National Geographic History Chapters) National Geographic, 2007. 40pp. ISBN 978-1-4263-0189-6. Grades 2–4. This brief overview of the life of Alexander Graham Bell (1847–1922) offers highlights of his contributions to science and history. Archival photographs and illustrations augment the text. Glossary, Further Reading, Web Sites, and Index.

1975. Gayle, Sharon. *Teddy Roosevelt: The People's President.* Aladdin, 2004. 32pp. Paper ISBN 978-0-689-85825-3. Grades 1–4. As a child, Theodore Roosevelt (1858–1919) was weak and sickly. He overcame these disabilities to become a robust outdoors man, Rough Rider leader, and the twenty-sixth president of the United States. This biography focuses on his bravery and compassion. He was also the inspiration for the "Teddy Bear." Chronology. Illustrations complement the text.

1976. Gerstein, Mordicai. *What Charlie Heard.* Farrar, 2002. 40pp. ISBN 978-0-374-38292-6. Grades 3–5. Composer Charles Ives (1874–1954) sought to express everyday sounds in his music. However, many people simply heard his compositions as noise and he did not receive much approval during his life. His father was a small-town bandleader, and the music he played was a large influence on Ives. Illustrations of sounds in different colored typeface enhance the text. *Children's Book Award* (Georgia) nomination, *Horn Book Fanfare* and *Red Clover Book Award* (Vermont) nomination.

1977. Gleiter, Jan, and Kathleen Thompson. *Booker T. Washington.* Illustrated by Rick Whipple. (First Biographies) Steck-Vaughn, 1995. 32pp. Paper ISBN 978-0-8114-9353-6. Grades K–3. When Booker T. Washington (1856–1915) moved to West Virginia with his family, he realized the importance of reading. In 1871 he met a mine owner's wife, and she hired him to work in her home. She taught him the importance of thoroughness, and when his interviewer at Hampton Institute asked him to clean a room before she accepted him, he cleaned it perfectly. He went to Tuskegee Institute in 1881 and was its president when he died. Key Dates.

1978. Gormley, Beatrice. *Maria Mitchell: The Soul of an Astronomer.* See entry 1508.

1979. Graham, Amy. *Thomas Edison: Wizard of Light and Sound.* (Inventors Who Changed the World) Enslow, 2007. 128pp. ISBN 978-1-59845-052-1. Grades 5–8. Thomas Alva Edison (1847–1931) made great advancements in science during his life, but he had many failures before he achieved success. Graham examines his life and relates these various stage. Links to Web pages may entice readers to look for further resources about his experiments and decisions. Photographs and illustrations supplement the text. Glossary, Notes, Further Reading, Web Sites, and Index.

1980. Greenfield, Eloise. *Mary McLeod Bethune.* Illustrated by Jerry Pinkney. Trophy, 1994. 34pp. Paper ISBN 978-0-06-446168-9. Grades 1–5. Because she wanted to learn to read so badly, Mary McLeod (1875–1955) walked five miles to and from school as a young girl. Her siblings stayed on the farm working, and she taught them what she learned when she returned home. She continued her schooling with scholarships. When she was denied the chance to serve as a missionary in Africa, she started her own college in Florida and served as its president. She also started a hospital for blacks. Her work led Franklin D. Roosevelt to ask her to head the National Youth Administration during the Depression to help young blacks get jobs. Her work and care helped many throughout her life.

1981. Grimes, Nikki. *Talkin' About Bessie: The Story of Aviator Elizabeth Coleman.* Illustrated by E. B. Lewis. Scholastic, 2002. 48pp. ISBN 978-0-439-35243-7. Grades 3–8. Jim Crow laws and segregation kept Elizabeth "Bessie" Coleman (1892–1926) from doing many things. However, she decided to become the first African American female pilot when the Wright brothers first flew their plane when she was 11. Grimes tells the story in short monologues offered by the people sitting in a Chicago room mourning Bessie at her death. Each describes, in lyrical words, a different aspect of Bessie's life and achievements. Among the twenty at the wake are Bessie's mother, sister, a flight instructor, a young fan, and a news reporter. Impressionistic double-spread watercolors highlight the text. *American Library Association Notable Children's Books, Capitol Choices Noteworthy Titles* (Washington, D.C.), *Booklist Editor's Choice, Young Readers' Choice Award* (Louisiana) nomination, *Coretta Scott King Author Honor, Coretta Scott King Illustrator Award, Horn Book Fanfare,* and *Prairie Pasque Award* (South Dakota) nomination.

1982. Harness, Cheryl. *The Groundbreaking, Chance-Taking Life of George Washington Carver and Science and Invention.* National Geographic, 2008. 144pp. ISBN 978-1-4263-0196-4. Grades 4–8. In five chapters this biography covers the life of George Washington Carver (1864?–1943) from his birth through his contributions to agriculture, education, and the lives of Americans. It refers to the politics, scientific discoveries, births, deaths, and cultural trends during Carver's life. He faced continual hardships, with racism affecting his career choices. Harness mentions debates as to whether he was a great scientist or an important public thinker whose concerns about science helped him understand the world better. Photographs and illustrations augment the text. Bibliography, Further Reading, and Index.

1983. Harness, Cheryl. *The Remarkable Rough-Riding Life of Theodore Roosevelt.* National Geographic, 2007. 144pp. ISBN 978-1-4263-0008-0. Grades 5–8. This biography offers information about the childhood years and early accomplishments of Theodore Roosevelt (1858–1919) who became the twenty-sixth president of the United States. Quotes and Chronology add to the illustrations of the text. Bibliography.

1984. Harrah, Madge. *Blind Boone: Piano Prodigy.* (Trailblazers) Lerner, 2005. 112pp. ISBN 978-1-57505-057-7. Grades 5–9. The son of a runaway slave, John William "Blind" Boone (1864–1927) lost his sight when he was only six months old from an infection. In Missouri he earned money playing a tin whistle and a harmonicaon street corners and in trains. He could reproduce sounds after hearing them only once, and after music training at the Missouri School for the Blind in St. Louis, he became a concert pianist and composer. Interested in all styles from ragtime to classical music, he performed in churches and concert halls around the world. Harrah uses interviews, archival materials, and period photographs to describe the life of a talented man who was denied entry into many places that once welcomed him after Jim Crow laws spread across the country. Chronology, Notes, Bibliography, Web Sites, Disography, and Index. *Land of Enchantment Award* (New Mexico) nomination.

1985. Harris, Lois V. *Mary Cassatt: Impressionist Painter.* Pelican, 2007. 32pp. ISBN 978-1-58980-452-4. Grades 2–4. As a child, Mary Cassatt (1844–1926) lived with her family in Paris. When they returned to Philadelphia, Cassatt realized she needed to live in Paris where she could be an artist on her own terms. She went back and painted in the impressionist style. She loved the work of Edgar Degas and was a good friend of his. This short biography offers tidbits of her life with illustrations and reproductions.

1986. Hill, Lee Sullivan. *The Flyer Flew! The Invention of the Airplane.* Illustrated by Craig Or-back. (On My Own Science) Millbrook, 2006. 48pp. ISBN 978-1-57505-758-3; First Avenue paper ISBN 978-1-57505-855-9. Grades K–3. This volume follows the process of the Wright brothers, Wilbur and Orville, as they invented and flew the first airplane in 1903. They first opened a bicycle shop and then began experiments with gliders after reading the research of Otto Lilienthal, a German who died in a crash. Although not formally trained, they understood the physics necessary to finally get a machine off the ground. Watercolors enhance the text. Bibliography and Glossary.

1987. Hopkinson, Deborah. *Fannie in the Kitchen: The Whole Story from Soup to Nuts of How Fannie Farmer Invented Recipes with Precise Measurements.* Illustrated by Nancy Car-penter. Atheneum, 2001. 40pp. ISBN 978-0-689-81965-0; Aladdin, 2004, paper ISBN 978-0-689-86997-6. Grades K–3. Although unhappy that her mother has hired an assistant for their kitchen because she herself likes to cook, Marcia Shaw soon realizes that Fannie Farmer (1857–1915) has special culinary gifts. Fannie teaches Marcia and the *Fannie Farmer Cookbook* comes into being. Collage illustrations enhance the text. Biographical sketch of Fannie Farmer.

1988. Hopkinson, Deborah. *Home on the Range: John A. Lomax and His Cowboy Songs.* Illustrated by S. D. Schindler. Putnam, 2009. 40pp. ISBN 978-0-399-23996-0. Grades K–2. As a boy, John Avery Lomax (1867–1948) liked working on his family's Texas farm and listening to the cowboys sing. He wanted to collect their songs for posterity, but was discouraged from doing this at the University of Texas. Later, as a musicology professor, he returned to the range with a bulky Ediphone into which he asked cowboys to sing. Many balked, but Lomax eventually documented such tunes as "Home on the Range," "Poor Lonesome Cowboy," "Sweet Betsy from Pike," and "Git Along, Little Doggies." Pen and wash pastel illustrations enhance the text. End notes.

1989. Hopkinson, Deborah. *Susan B. Anthony: Fighter for Women's Rights.* Illustrated by Amy Bates. Aladdin, 2005. 32pp. Paper ISBN 978-0-689-86909-9. Grades 2–5. Susan B. Anthony (1820–1906) was an advocate for women's rights. A Quaker, she got an education and then taught at a boarding school until she returned home to Rochester, New York, where she helped slaves escape via the Underground Railroad. She then spent much of her time working for suffrage along with her friend Elizabeth Cady Stanton. Chronology.

1990. Hubbard, Crystal. *The Last Black King of the Kentucky Derby: The Story of Jimmy Winkfield.* Illustrated by Robert McGuire. Lee & Low, 2008. Unpaged. ISBN 978-1-58430-274-2. Grades 2–4. Jimmy Winkfield (1882–1974), known as "Wink," wanted to become a jockey and worked hard to become the best. The son of sharecroppers, he started with a job as a stable hand. Then he became an exercise rider and finally a jockey. In the late 1800s and early 1900s he won prestigious races, but racism eventually forced him off the track. In 1902 he was the last African American to win the Kentucky Derby, his second win in that race. He then raced in Europe and spent the last years of his life living on a horse farm in France. Oil paintings complement the text.

1991. Jakoubek, Robert E., and Heather Lehr Wagner. *Harriet Beecher Stowe.* See entry 1515.

1992. Johnson, Dolores. *Onward: A Photobiography of African-American Polar Explorer Matthew Henson.* National Geographic, 2005. 64pp. ISBN 978-0-7922-7914-3; 2007, paper ISBN 978-1-4263-0268-8. Grades 5–8. Matthew Alexander Henson (1866–1955), son of African American sharecroppers, shared a dream with the wealthy Robert E. Peary—to conquer the North Pole. Henson's physical stamina and ability to speak Inuit allowed him to develop relationships with the Arctic peoples on whom they would depend to reach their goals. He also mastered driving a dog sled, leading a team over the layers of ice covering the Arctic Ocean. Henson probably arrived at the North Pole before Peary, but he was not recognized for this achievement; he was considered Peary's servant. He, however, is the only person to whom the National Geographic Society awarded its Hubbard Medal posthumously. Photographs enhance the text. Bibliography, Chronology, Web Sites, and Index. *Booklist Ed-*

itor's Choice, Jefferson Cup nomination, and *Children's Book Awards* (Rhode Island) nomination.

1993. Keating, Frank. *Theodore.* Illustrated by Mike Wimmer. Simon & Schuster, 2006. Unpaged. ISBN 978-0-689-86532-9. Grades 2–6. This first-person picture-book biography of Theodore Roosevelt (1858–1919) explores his childhood, youth, experiences around the world, and life as the youngest president of the United States. By the time he was 15 he had hunted jackals, climbed Egypt's Great Pyramid, and looked inside a volcano. He began keeping a diary when he was 10 years old and wrote thiry-five books during his life. Among his other occupations were rancher, soldier, father, and governor of New York while suffering from poor eyesight and asthma. Paintings illustrate the text. *Keystone to Reading Book Award* nomination, and *Book Award* (Oklahoma) finalist.

1994. Keating, Frank. *Will Rogers: An American Legend.* Illustrated by Mike Wimmer. Harcourt, 2002. 32pp. ISBN 978-0-15-202405-5. Grades 2–4. Will Rogers (1879–1935) of Oklahoma became known for his humorist monologues and essays. This volume includes some of his entertaining comments such as "no man is great if he thinks he is" and "I never met a man I didn't like" without actually discussing his life. Realistic oil paintings illustrate the text. *Emphasis on Reading* (Alabama) nomination, *Spur Award*, and *Book Award* (Oklahoma) nomination.

1995. Keller, Kristin Thoennes. *Carrie Chapman Catt: A Voice for Women.* (Signature Lives) Compass Point, 2005. 112pp. ISBN 978-0-7565-0991-0. Grades 5–8. Carrie Chapman Catt (1859–1947), a leader in the women's movement and a close colleague of Susan B. Anthony, served as president of the National American Woman Suffrage Association (NAWSA) twice—from 1900 to 1904 and from 1915 to 1920. She made hundreds of speeches and was influential in the adoption of the Nineteenth Amendment to the U.S. Constitution in 1920. She then formed the League of Women Voters. Photographs, maps, and reproductions complement the text. Bibliography, Glossary, Chronology, Notes, Further Reading, Web Sites, and Index.

1996. Kelso, Richard. *Building a Dream: Mary Bethune's School.* Illustrated by Debbe Heller. Steck-Vaughn, 1994. 46pp. Paper ISBN 978-0-8114-8057-4. Grades 3–6. In 1904 Mrs. Mary McLeod Bethune (1875–1955) arrived in Daytona Beach, Florida. She dreamed of building a school for girls, and although she only had $1.50 and was black, she persevered. In 1907 she opened Faith Hall with money donated by a man who believed in her. Epilogue, Afterword, and Notes.

1997. Kent, Deborah. *Elizabeth Blackwell: Physician and Health Educator.* See entry 1518.

1998. Kent, Deborah. *Hellen Keller: Author and Advocate for the Disabled.* (Spirit of America: Our People) Child's World, 2003. 32pp. ISBN 978-1-59296-005-7. Grades 3–6. This look at Helen Keller (1880–1968) presents her childhood and the onset of her disability, her education with Annie Sullivan, her motivation to become a thinker, and her scholarly achievements. Photographs enhance the text. Bibliography, Glossary, Timeline, Further Reading, and Index.

1999. Kerley, Barbara. *The Extraordinary Mark Twain (According to Susy).* Illustrated by Edwin Fotherinham. Scholastic, 2010. 48pp. ISBN 978-0-545-12508-6. Grades 3–6. In 1885–1886, Susy Clemens (1872–1896), the daughter of Mark Twain (1835–1910), wrote a 130-page biography of her father to show that he was more than a mere humorist. She included family anecdotes and revealed his smoking habit, love for cats and family, pool playing, characteristic impatience, and jokes. She noted that he had both "fine" and "not-so-fine" qualities. Smaller folded pages enclosed between Kerley's picture-book pages contain quotes from the biography in a font resembling handwriting and including Susy's misspellings. Susy also commented that her mother sometimes removed unseemly passages from her father's manuscripts. Digitally enhanced photographs enhance the text with one showing a cross-section of their home and Twain going about his daily activities inside. Chronology, Notes, and Guidelines for Biography Writing.

2000. Kerley, Barbara. *What to Do About Alice?* Illustrated by Edwin Fotheringham. Scholastic, 2008. 32pp. ISBN 978-0-439-92231-9. Grades 2–4. Alice Lee Roosevelt Longworth (1884–1980), daughter of Theodore Roosevelt, was unconventional from a young age. She had a pet snake, joined an all-boys club, played poker, and slid down the White House stairs on a sled. She read widely in her father's library and become one of his trusted advisers. *Kirkus Reviews Editor's Choice, Boston Globe/Horn Book Award Honor, School Library Journal Best Books for Children, Capitol Choices Noteworthy Titles* (Washington, D.C.), and *Publishers Weekly Best Books.*

2001. Kimmel, Elizabeth Cody. *Dinosaur Bone War: Cope and Marsh's Fossil Feud.* Random, 2007. 192pp. ISBN 978-0-375-91349-5. Grades 4–7. Edward Drinker Cope and Othniel Marsh were fast friends until Marsh tried to take over Cope's archaeological dig. They then became bitter rivals, each seeking to find the best dinosaur bones. Their competition and arguments in scientific journals contributed greatly to the establishment of the field of paleontology. However they also destroyed valuable specimens during their quarrels. Photographs and illustrations augment the text. Bibliography and Index.

2002. Kimmel, Eric A. *A Horn for Louis.* Illustrated by James Bernardin. Random, 2005. 96pp. ISBN 978-0-375-83252-9; 2006, paper ISBN 978-0-375-84005-0. Grades 2–4. At the age of 7, Louis Armstrong (1901–1971) slept with his mother and sister on a quilt and worked part-time to help his mother pay rent. One day his old tin horn was smashed, and for Hanukkah his employers, the Karnofskys, give him an old cornet. His mother has told him always to pay his own way, so he does not accept the horn but Mr. Karnofsky works out a payment plan so that Louis can enjoy playing his music. Illustrations reinforce the text. Glossary.

2003. Klingel, Cynthia Fitterer, and Robert B. Noyed. *Susan B. Anthony: Reformer.* (Our People) Child's World, 2002. 32pp. ISBN 978-1-56766-171-2. Grades 3–6. This brief biography of Susan B. Anthony (1820–1906) focuses on her commitment to women's suffrage. Photographs augment the text. Chronology, Glossary, Further Reading, and Index.

2004. Knudsen, Shannon. *Nellie Bly.* (History Maker Bios) Lerner, 2005. 48pp. ISBN 978-0-8225-2943-9. Grades 3–5. Elizabeth Jane Cochran (1864–1922) was a wealthy Pennsylvania resident until her father died. She then began helping to support the family and landed a job writing newspaper articles. Using a pen name, Nellie Bly, she wrote funny and sometimes serious stories, but her tale of traveling around the world in seventy-two days made her famous. Illustrations augment the text. Bibliography, Further Reading, Glossary, Maps, Timeline, Web Sites, and Index.

2005. Kraft, Betsy Harvey. *Theodore Roosevelt: Champion of the American Spirit.* Houghton, 2003. 192pp. ISBN 978-0-618-14264-4. Grades 5–8. Theodore Roosevelt (1858–1919) became the twenty-sixth president of the United States after a varied career. He led the Rough Riders to victory in the Spanish-American War in 1898, served as governor of New York, and was a police commissioner in New York City as well as a devoted father, writer, historian, cowboy, conservationist, and Nobel Peace Prize winner. The text draws on Roosevelt's journals and letters, newspaper articles, and his autobiography, along with memoirs of his family and friends. Notes, Chronology, Bibliography, Web Site, and Index. *American Library Association Notable Books for Children, Capitol Choices Noteworthy Titles* (Washington, D.C.), and *Garden State Teen Book Award* (New Jersey) nomination.

2006. Krass, Peter. *Sojourner Truth: Antislavery Activist.* See entry 1521.

2007. Krensky, Stephen. *A Man for All Seasons: The Life of George Washington Carver.* Illustrated by Wil Clay. HarperCollins, 2008. 32pp. ISBN 978-0-06-027885-4. Grades K–4. George Washington Carver (1864?–1943), a slave and an orphan, was raised after the Civil War by the couple who had owned him and his brother. They hired a tutor for the intelligent George as he was barred from the nearby white school, and at the age of 12, he left to gain more knowledge. He had a life of recognition coupled with setbacks. Asked to lead Tuskegee's agricultural institute, he had to scavenge for supplies. He was always curious and able to overcome obstacles and had numerous inventions to his credit. Illustrations illuminate the text. Chronology.

2008. Krull, Kathleen. *Houdini: World's Greatest Mystery Man and Escape King.* Illustrated by Eric Velasquez. Walker, 2007. 32pp. Paper ISBN 978-0-8027-9646-2. Grades 2–4. In this biography of Harry Houdini (1874–1926) Krull offers poems about his feats from the point of view of children in an audience, showing reactions to his amazing shows. She also includes information about his life and his character. He was fierce about being right and developing his talent while wanting to make his money honestly. Oil paintings illustrate the text. Bibliography.

2009. Krull, Kathleen. *The Road to Oz: Twists, Turns, Bumps, and Triumphs in the Life of L. Frank Baum.* Illustrated by Kevin Hawkes. Borzoi, 2008. Unpaged. ISBN 978-0-375-93216-8. Grades 1–4. L. Frank Baum (1856–1919), born into a wealthy family, had a number of different jobs before he wrote and published his best-selling *The Wizard of Oz.* He was an actor, a salesman, a journalist, a shopkeeper, and a window-dresser who arranged hardware like a tin man. He had no sense of business and even with the success of his book, he had to declare bankruptcy eleven years later. Illustrations enhance the text. Bibliography.

2010. Krull, Kathleen. *A Woman for President: The Story of Victoria Woodhull.* Illustrated by Jane Dyer. Walker, 2004. 32pp. ISBN 978-0-8027-8908-2; 2006, paper ISBN 978-0-8027-9615-8. Grades 3–5. Victoria Woodhull (1838–1927) was a feminist, spiritualist, and activist. Although American women could not vote in 1872, she ran for president of the United States. She had been the first woman to have a seat on the New York Stock Exchange, to own a newspaper, and to speak before Congress. She began supporting her family as a child preacher at the age of 8. She married, divorced, and moved to New York. There she met Cornelius Vanderbilt, received financial advice from the spirit world, and became a millionaire. The Equal Rights Party, an organization that she founded and funded, nominated her for president. Bibliography. *Emphasis on Reading Award* (Alabama) nomination.

2011. Lakin, Patricia. *Helen Keller and the Big Storm.* Illustrated by Diana Magnuson. (Ready-to-Read Childhood of Famous Americans) Aladdin, 2002. 32pp. Paper ISBN 978-0-689-84104-0. Grades 1–2. When her teacher, Annie Sullivan, rescued Helen Keller from the tree where she was sheltering in a storm, Helen learned important lessons about the power of natural forces and of friendship.

2012. Landau, Elaine. *Annie Oakley: Wild West Sharpshooter.* (Best of the West) Enslow, 2004. 48pp. ISBN 978-0-7660-2205-8. Grades 3–6. Phoebe Ann Moses (1860–1926) shot game after her father's death to feed her family after suffering in a foster home. She became such a sharp shooter that she won the heart of Frank Butler and a place in Buffalo Bill's Wild West show as Annie Oakley. She was a feminist who shared her wealth with others. Landau includes anecdotes about Oakley's performances to give insight into her character and spirit. Reading list, Timeline, Web Sites, Glossary, and Index.

2013. Langley, Wanda. *Women of the Wind: Early Women Navigators.* Morgan Reynolds, 2006. 160pp. ISBN 978-1-931798-81-5. Grades 4–9. This collective biography presents profiles of nine women who were involved in the early days of flight. They include Harriet Quimby, Bessie Coleman, Anne Morrow Lindbergh, Amelia Earhart, Katherine Stinson, Ruth Law, Ruth Nichols, Louise Thaden, and Jacqueline Cochrane. The chapters cover their lives and achievements along with the obstacles that almost thwarted their goals. Photographs highlight the text. Bibliography, Chronology, Notes, Web Sites, and Index.

2014. Lasky, Kathryn. *Vision of Beauty: The Story of Sarah Breedlove Walker.* Illustrated by Nneka Bennett. Candlewick, 2000. Unpaged. ISBN 978-0-7636-0253-6; 2006, paper ISBN 978-0-7636-1834-6. Grades 2–4. Madam C. J. Walker (1867–1919) was born in poverty as Sarah Breedlove Walker, the daughter of former slaves. She became an orphan at the age of 7, and was married and widowed by the age of 20. She developed hair and beauty products for African American women and became a successful businesswoman who operated her own manufacturing company. Illustrations enhance the text. *Children's Book Award* (South Carolina) nomination.

2015. Lawler, Mary. *Marcus Garvey: Black Nationalist Leader.* (Black Americans of Achievement) Chelsea House, 2004. 112pp. ISBN 978-0-7910-8159-4. Grades 5 up. Marcus Garvey

(1887–1940) believed in the Back to Africa movement—for blacks to return to Africa and establish a central homeland. He began his fight for black rights in 1914 and tried to heighten racial pride and improve economics and education. People called him "Black Moses" for his efforts, but a failed business venture hampered him. Photographs enhance the text. Chronology, Further Reading, and Index.

2016. **Lawlor, Laurie.** *Helen Keller: Rebellious Spirit.* Holiday House, 2001. 168pp. ISBN 978-0-8234-1588-5. Grades 4–8. The fifteen chapters of this biography cover the life of Helen Keller (1880–1968), known for her triumph over deafness and blindness to become a writer. She had strong religious, political, and social beliefs that show she was more than just a woman who achieved something with the help of her teacher, Annie Sullivan. Photographs and illustrations complement the text. Chronology, Notes, Further Reading, and Index. *School Library Journal Best Books for Children* and *Capitol Choices Noteworthy Titles* (Washington, D.C.).

2017. **Leavitt, Amie Jane.** *Elizabeth Blackwell.* (What's So Great About?) Mitchell Lane, 2008. 32pp. ISBN 978-1-58415-579-9. Grades 2–4. Elizabeth Blackwell (1821–1910) was the first American woman to attend a medical school and become a doctor. Because of her difficulty in being accepted at a medical school, she established one so that more women could have the opportunity to become physicians. The text gives an overview of her life. Illustrations augment the text. Bibliography, Chronology, Glossary, Further Reading, Web Sites, and Index.

2018. **Leavitt, Amie Jane.** *Helen Keller.* (What's So Great About?) Mitchell Lane, 2008. 32pp. ISBN 978-1-58415-583-6. Grades 2–4. Helen Keller (1880–1968), with the help of her teacher Annie Sullivan, learned to communicate with others even though she was deaf and blind. She attended college and then became a lecturer, writer, and advocate for the disabled. This volume gives an overview of her life. Illustrations augment the text. Bibliography, Chronology, Glossary, Further Reading, Web Sites, and Index.

2019. **Levin, Pamela.** *Susan B. Anthony: Fighter for Women's Rights.* Chelsea House, 1993. 79pp. ISBN 978-0-7910-1762-3. Grades 3–5. Susan B. (Susan Brownell) Anthony (1820–1906) was a crusader for a variety of causes in the 19th century, including women's family and voting rights. Without her tireless efforts, much of the gains that women claim today would not have happened. Bibliography and Index.

2020. **Lindbergh, Reeve.** *Nobody Owns the Sky: The Story of "Brave Bessie" Coleman.* Illustrated by Pamela Paparone. Candlewick, 1998. Unpaged. Paper ISBN 978-0-7636-0361-8. Grades K–4. Bessie Coleman (1892–1926) faces many problems but dreams of flying from the time she sees airplanes in Texas cotton fields. She could not afford to stay in college so she went to France in the 1920s to learn how to fly, becoming the first African American woman to earn a pilot's license. When she returned to America, she took barnstorming trips across the country and spoke about flying. She realized her dream before she died in a Jacksonville, Florida air show. *Young Readers Award* (Nevada).

2021. **Lutz, Norma Jean.** *Frederick Douglass: Abolitionist and Author.* See entry 1528.

2022. **McCully, Emily Arnold.** *Marvelous Mattie: How Margaret E. Knight Became an Inventor.* Farrar, 2006. 32pp. ISBN 978-0-374-34810-6. Grades K–3. When she was 12, Margaret E. Knight (1838–1914) used the tools in the toolbox that her father gave her to design a metal guard that stopped shuttles from shooting off textile looms and injuring the workers. She recorded her ideas in a notebook titled "My Inventions." Among them were a foot warmer, snow sleds, a bat-shaped kite, and a machine to make paper bags. A machine-shop worker stole her paper bag idea, and she had to go to court to show that the invention was hers. She established the Eastern Paper Bag Company and continued to invent things for the rest of her life, obtaining twenty-two patents and creating ninety original inventions. Pen and ink illustrations enhance the text. *Bluebonnet Awards* (Texas) nomination, *Children's Book Award* (North Carolina) nomination, *Young Readers Choice Award* (Pennsylvania) nomination, *Horn Book Fanfare*, and *Diamonds Award* (Delaware) nomination.

2023. MacKinnon, Christy. *Silent Observer.* Gallaudet University, 1993. 42pp. ISBN 978-1-56368-022-9; Harcourt, 2001, paper ISBN 978-0-15-314376-2. Grades 2–4. Christy MacKinnon (1889–1981) became deaf when she was 2 years old as a result of whooping cough. She went to a special school in Halifax, Nova Scotia, and then received a scholarship to study at the Boston Museum of Fine Arts. She continued drawing and painting throughout her life, working both as a teacher and as a commercial artist. The text and complementary illustrations tell about her childhood of horse-drawn sleighs crossing frozen lakes, farming and family life, and attending a one-room school.

2024. McKissack, Patricia C., and Frederick McKissack. *Booker T. Washington: Leader and Educator.* Illustrated by Michael Bryant. (Great African Americans) Enslow, 2001. 32pp. ISBN 978-0-7660-1679-8. Grades K–3. Booker T. Washington (1856–1915) was born a slave. After he gained his freedom, he was determined to get an education and he walked many miles to college in Hampton, Virginia. This volume looks at his childhood, his education, and his career at Tuskegee Institute, where he became the principal. He was determined to achieve, and he tried to help other African Americans make choices that would benefit their own lives. Photographs, Glossary, and Index.

2025. McKissack, Patricia C., and Frederick McKissack. *Carter G. Woodson: The Father of Black History.* Illustrated by Ned O. (Great African Americans) Enslow, 2001. 32pp. ISBN 978-0-7660-1698-9. Grades 2–4. The father of Carter G. Woodson (1875–1950) believed it was never too late to achieve things in life. Woodson took this advice to heart. He could not attend high school until he was 18, but he then graduated in 18 months. He went on to college and eventually received a Ph.D. from Harvard. He taught in Washington, D.C., and began to collect works written by African Americans because none of the existing history books included them. He celebrated contributions by African Americans one week of the year, the beginning of today's expanded Black History Month. Words to Know and Index.

2026. McKissack, Patricia C., and Frederick McKissack. *Frederick Douglass: Leader Against Slavery.* See entry 1530.

2027. McKissack, Patricia C., and Frederick McKissack. *George Washington Carver: The Peanut Scientist.* Illustrated by Edward Ostendorf. (Great African Americans) Enslow, 2002. 32pp. ISBN 978-0-7660-1700-9. Grades 2–4. George Washington Carver (1864?–1943) became a scientist who promoted the idea of crop rotation and found many uses for peanuts. Many initially thought his ideas were foolish. Black-and-white photographs and drawings enhance the text. Glossary and Index.

2028. McKissack, Patricia C., and Frederick McKissack. *Ida B. Wells-Barnett: A Voice Against Violence.* Illustrated by Edward Ostendorf. (Great African Americans) Enslow, 2001. 32pp. ISBN 978-0-7660-1677-4. Grades 2–4. Ida B. Wells-Barnett (1862–1931), a black woman journalist, campaigned for the civil rights of women and other minorities. She was also a founder of the National Association for the Advancement of Colored People in 1909. Black-and-white photographs and drawings enhance the text. Glossary and Index.

2029. McKissack, Patricia C., and Frederick McKissack. *Madam C. J. Walker: Self-Made Millionaire.* Illustrated by Michael Bryant. (Great African Americans) Enslow, 2001. 32pp. ISBN 978-0-7660-1682-8. Grades 2–4. The daughter of slaves, Sarah Breedlove (1867–1919) proved that she was free. She did something that no other American woman had done: start a business and become a millionaire. She created hair products to improve her own hair and, when they worked, she sold them to others. She built a factory in Indiana and hired people to help her run her business properly. After only one year, she had 950 salespeople. She continued to work and to support other blacks by encouraging them to start their own businesses. Words to Know and Index.

2030. McKissack, Patricia C., and Frederick McKissack. *Mary Church Terrell: Leader for Equality.* (Great African Americans) Enslow, 2001. 32pp. ISBN 978-0-7660-1697-2. Grades 2–4. Five chapters cover the life of Mary Church Terrell (1863–1954), who was one of the first African American women to earn a college degree. She was born free and was wealthy, but she faced problems of exclusion as did other African Americans. She became a strong fighter for civil rights and joined the NAACP. Illustrations complement the text. Glossary, Chronology, Further Reading, Web Sites, and Index.

2031. **McKissack, Patricia C., and Frederick McKissack.** *Mary McLeod Bethune: A Great Teacher.* Illustrated by Ned O. (Great African Americans) Enslow, 2001. 32pp. ISBN 978-0-7660-1680-4. Grades 2–4. McKissack introduces Mary McLeod Bethune (1875–1955) by focusing on her childhood, her education, and her leadership role in the U.S. government. With only $1.50, she opened a school for black girls in Florida in 1904. Her determination led to the expansion of her school into an accredited four-year college. Photographs highlight the text. Glossary and Index.

2032. **McKissack, Patricia C., and Frederick McKissack.** *Paul Robeson: A Voice to Remember.* Illustrated by Ned O. (Great African Americans) Enslow, 2001. 32pp. ISBN 978-0-7660-1674-3. Grades 2–4. Paul Robeson (1898–1976), a baritone, also became an actor. He performed in Eugene O'Neill's plays and in *Show Boat*. His dismay at the treatment of African Americans caused him to support leftist ideals, and he suffered for his beliefs. The text looks at his childhood, his education, and his career as actor and singer. Photographs, Glossary, and Index.

2033. **McKissack, Patricia C., and Frederick McKissack.** *Sojourner Truth: A Voice for Freedom.* See entry 1531.

2034. **McKissack, Patricia C., and Frederick McKissack.** *Sojourner Truth: Ain't I a Woman.* See entry 1532.

2035. **MacLeod, Elizabeth.** *Alexander Graham Bell: An Inventive Life.* (Snapshots) Kids Can, 1999. 32pp. ISBN 978-1-55074-456-9; paper ISBN 978-1-55074-458-3. Grades 3–6. Alexander Graham Bell (1847–1922) liked to experiment, and began his investigations as a child in Edinburgh, Scotland. The thirteen chapters describe his move to Canada, where he experimented with sound until he invented the telephone. He became especially interested in helping deaf people, and worked with the hearing-impaired in Boston, including Helen Keller. Photographs enhance the text. Chronology and Index.

2036. **MacLeod, Elizabeth.** *George Washington Carver: An Innovative Life.* (Snapshots) Kids Can, 2007. 32pp. ISBN 978-1-55337-906-5; paper ISBN 978-1-55337-907-2. Grades 3–6. Born a slave, George Washington Carver (1864?–1943) overcame prejudice and being an orphan to be a successful botanist. The spreads contain illustrations and comments from Carver about plants. He was also a painter, inventor, singer, and a believer in equal rights. Photographs and illustrations augment the text. Maps, Chronology, and Index.

2037. **MacLeod, Elizabeth.** *Harry Houdini: A Magical Life.* (Snapshots: Images of People and Places in History) Kids can, 2005. 32pp. ISBN 978-1-55337-769-6; paper ISBN 978-1-55337-770-2. Grades 3–7. Harry Houdini (1874–1936) claimed to have the ability to escape from anything—from an airless coffin to chains while submerged in a river. Two-page chapters trace his birth into poverty in Budapest, Hungary, to performing acrobatics at the age of 9 to earn money for the family, through his maturity where he experienced enormous success. Photographs and illustrations augment the text. Chronology, Web Sites, and Index.

2038. **MacLeod, Elizabeth.** *Helen Keller: A Determined Life.* (Snapshots: Images of People and Places in History) Kids Can, 2004. 32pp. ISBN 978-1-55337-508-1; paper ISBN 978-1-55337-509-8. Grades 3–7. With the help of her teacher, Annie Sullivan, Helen Keller (1880–1968) overcame her blindness and deafness to become a scholar and speaker. This scrapbook-style biography uses double-spreads with text and photographs. Additional information about Braille and a look at Keller's handwriting enhance the presentation. Chronology and Index.

2039. **MacLeod, Elizabeth.** *The Wright Brothers: A Flying Start.* (Snapshots: Images of People and Places in History) Kids Can, 2002. 32pp. ISBN 978-1-55074-933-5; paper ISBN 978-1-55074-935-9. Grades 3–7. Wilbur Wright (1867–1912) and Orville Wright (1871–1948) created a flying machine, an invention with an impact on all our lives. Double-page spreads using a scrapbook format cover various aspects of their lives. Chronology, Web Sites, and Index.

2040. McPherson, Stephanie Sammartino. *Alexander Graham Bell.* (History Maker Bios) Lerner, 2007. 48pp. ISBN 978-0-8225-7606-8. Grades 3–5. Alexander Graham Bell (1847–1922) invented a wheat husker and a talking machine when he was 15 years old. His mother, a musician, began to lose her hearing, and he was concerned about the deaf. He taught deaf children to talk while living in Boston. Eventually he created the telephone. Among other interests were metal detectors and hydrofoils. Illustrations augment the text. Bibliography, Further Reading, Glossary, Maps, Timeline, Web Sites, and Index.

2041. McPherson, Stephanie Sammartino. *Susan B. Anthony.* (History Maker Bios) Lerner, 2006. 48pp. ISBN 978-0-8225-5938-2. Grades 3–5. A Quaker, Susan B. Anthony (1820–1906) did not believe in war. She was an independent woman with a strong voice who fought for women's rights and the abolition of slavery. She was arrested for voting in the 1872 presidential election, started a newspaper for women, and was a friend of Sojourner Truth. Her work led to women getting the vote. The text's five chapters give an overview of her life and achievements. Illustrations augment the text. Bibliography, Further Reading, Glossary, Maps, Timeline, Web Sites, and Index.

2042. Macy, Sue. *Bylines: A Photobiography of Nellie Bly.* (Photobiographies) National Geographic, 2009. 64pp. ISBN 978-1-4263-0513-9. Grades 4–7. Elizabeth Jane Cochran (1864–1922), known as Nellie Bly, saw her widowed mother marry an alcoholic and decided she would never depend on a man to support her. She established a career as a journalist who risked her reputation to report abuse. She had herself admitted to the Lunatic Asylum on New York's Blackwell Island and wrote about the mistreatment she experienced there. She championed women factory workers and decried the Mexican government's censorship. Then she circled the world in seventy-two days to beat Jules Verne's fictionalized Phineas Fogg's eighty days. Quotes, artifacts, and period photographs augment the text. Notes, Chronology, Further Reading, Bibliography, Web Sites, and Index.

2043. Mannis, Celeste Davidson. *Julia Morgan Built a Castle.* Illustrated by Miles Hyman. Viking, 2006. 40pp. ISBN 978-0-670-05964-5. Grades 1–5. Julia Morgan (1872–1957) became an architect when women rarely entered that field. She was the only woman to graduate in engineering from Berkeley in 1895 and the first in architecture from the École des Beaux-Arts in Paris. She continued her career in California, where she spent twenty years as the architect of Hearst Castle. Full-bleed paintings illustrate the text. Bibliography and Note.

2044. Mara, Wil. *Thomas Alva Edison.* (Rookie Biographies) Scholastic, 2004. 31pp. ISBN 978-0-516-21843-4; paper ISBN 978-0-516-25822-5. Grades K–2. Thomas Alva Edison (1847–1931) invented the light bulb. This simple biography looks at scientists and what they do, with a few comments about his personal life. Photographs, Illustrations, and Index.

2045. Marston, Hope Irvin. *Isaac Johnson: From Slave to Stonecutter.* See entry 1533.

2046. Mattern, Joanne. *Sojourner Truth: Early Abolitionist.* See entry 1534.

2047. Matthews, Tom L. *Always Inventing: A Photobiography of Alexander Graham Bell.* National Geographic, 2006. 64pp. Paper ISBN 978-0-7922-5932-9. Grades 4–7. Primary sources—including photographs and quotations from Alexander Graham Bell (1847–1922)—reveal details of his childhood in Scotland, his work with the deaf, and his invention of the telephone. This biography also offers background about his family. Photographs and illustrations augment the text. Bibliography, Chronology, and Index. *School Library Journal Best Books for Children*.

2048. Micklos, John. *Alexander Graham Bell: Inventor of the Telephone.* HarperCollins, 2006. 48pp. ISBN 978-0-06-057619-6; Trophy paper ISBN 978-0-06-057618-9. Grades 3–5. This biography of Alexander Graham Bell (1847–1922) reveals his accomplishments and includes anecdotes about his personal life. It also includes an interview with an "expert." Period photographs appear on each page as the text recounts Bell's lifelong work with the deaf while developing the telephone and other sound-related devices. A chronology offers information about society and history at the time Bell was working.

2049. Miller, Robert H. *Buffalo Soldiers: The Story of Emanuel Stance.* Illustrated by Michael Bryant. Just Us, 2004. Unpaged. Paper ISBN 978-0-940975-69-9. Grades 1–4. After the Civil War ended, Congress voted to add four all-black infantry units to the army. These units went west to protect white settlers from Indian raids, and their effectiveness earned the respect of the Indians they defeated. Named buffalo soldiers because their hair resembled buffalo's hair, they were awarded several Medals of Honor, with the first going to Emanuel Stance, who was 19 years old. His story is told here.

2050. Mitchell, Barbara. *We'll Race You, Henry! A Story About Henry Ford.* Illustrated by Kathy Haubrich. (Creative Minds Biographies) Carolrhoda, 1986. 56pp. ISBN 978-0-8761-4291-2. Grades 3–6. People twice wanted to put money in Henry Ford's cars, but Ford (1863–1947) refused to start production until he thought the car was ready. Not until he had built racing prototypes, and one that lasted through a hard race, did he think that cars with his name should be sold. Another man then offered to put money into the business, and on June 13, 1903, Ford Motor Company started and is still functioning today. The text looks at the influences that caused Ford to want to develop horseless carriages, including his early interest in mechanical things such as springs and gears and cogs. *Outstanding Science Trade Book for Children.*

2051. Mitchell, Barbara. *The Wizard of Sound: A Story About Thomas Edison.* Illustrated by Hetty Mitchell. Carolrhoda, 1992. 56pp. ISBN 978-0-8761-4445-9. Grades 3–6. Thomas Alva Edison (1847–1931) was a sickly child who became a shy and inept student. The focus of this volume is on Edison's favorite invention, the phonograph. Other inventions are listed in the back of the book. Bibliography.

2052. Moore, Heidi. *Ida B. Wells-Barnett.* (American Lives) Raintree, 2004. 32pp. ISBN 978-1-4034-4997-9; paper ISBN 978-1-4034-5706-6. Grades 2–4. Ida B. Wells-Barnett (1862–1931), born into slavery, became an important voice against lynching and other racist horrors through her own newspaper. In two-page chapters, this volume covers her parents' deaths from yellow fever, her teaching to support her siblings, her journalism career, her life in Chicago, working for suffragists, and her crusade against lynching. Illustrations augment the text. Glossary, Further Reading, and Index.

2053. Mortensen, Lori. *Thomas Edison: Inventor, Scientist, and Genius.* Illustrated by Jeffrey Thompson. (Biographies) Picture Window, 2007. 24pp. ISBN 978-1-4048-3105-6. Grades K–3. Thomas Edison (1847–1931) accumulated 1,093 patents for his inventions. As a young boy, however, he had hearing problems, and his teachers thought he was dumb. His mother decided to teach him at home and he read everything he could find. He had luck meeting a wealthy man who taught him to use the telegraph. He experimented and was successful with many of his ideas, but not everything he considered worked. He founded the Edison Portland Cement company but expensive concrete did not appeal. He tried repeatedly to mine iron ore but did not succeed in constructing a machine to extract iron from unusable ore. He used all of his savings on this failure. But his successes such as the light bulb, the phonograph, and the motion picture camera changed lives around the world. Chronology, Further Reading, Bibliography, Glossary, Web Sites, and Index.

2054. Moss, Marissa. *Brave Harriet: The First Woman to Fly the English Channel.* Illustrated by C. F. Payne. Silver Whistle, 2001. 32pp. ISBN 978-0-15-202380-5. Grades 2–4. In 1912, Harriet Quimby (1875–1912) became the first woman to fly solo across the English Channel. Quimby was a newspaper reporter when she saw her first airplane. She began flying lessons that very day, becoming the first American woman to earn a pilot's license. Her flight across the Channel on April 16, 1912, went almost unnoticed because the *Titanic* had just sunk. She died later the same year when her plane crashed in Massachusetts. *Young Hoosier Award* (Indiana) nomination and *Young Reader Award* (Virginia) nomination.

2055. Nichols, Catherine. *Madam C. J. Walker.* Children's, 2005. 24pp. ISBN 978-0-51624-941-4; paper ISBN 978-0-51625-096-0. Grades 1–2. Madam C. J. Walker (1867–1919), born in Delta, Louisiana, created hair-care products for African American women. She marketed them effectively and became a millionaire. The simple text describes her accomplishments. Photographs enhance the text. Glossary, Further Reading, Web Sites, and Index.

2056. Old, Wendie C. *To Fly: The Story of the Wright Brothers.* Illustrated by Robert Andrew Parker. Clarion, 2002. 48pp. ISBN 978-0-618-13347-5. Grades 3–5. Brief chapters begin with the Wright brothers' childhoods and their fascination with flying, from toy helicopters to kites. Their interest led them to discover how to develop the first machine–powered aircraft. Watercolor illustrations complement the text. Chronology, Notes, Further Reading. *Boston Globe/Horn Book Award Honor, Bulletin Blue Ribbon,* and *Capitol Choices Noteworthy Titles* (Washington, D.C.).

2057. Orr, Tamra. *The Life and Times of Susan B. Anthony.* (Profiles in American History) Mitchell Lane, 2007. 48pp. ISBN 978-1-58415-445-7. Grades 5–8. Susan B. Anthony (1820–1906) was arrested in 1872 for voting illegally. Anthony started her activist career in the temperance movement and then became a spokesperson for women's rights. A Susan B. Anthony dollar coin was minted in her memory. Photographs and reproductions augment the text. Chronology, Further Reading, Glossary, Notes, Web Sites, and Index.

2058. O'Sullivan, Robyn. *The Wright Brothers Fly.* (National Geographic History Chapters) National Geographic, 2007. 40pp. ISBN 978-1-4263-0188-9. Grades 2–4. A brief overview of the lives of the Wright brothers, Orville (1871–1948) and Wilbur (1867–1912) and their contributions to history and science with their flying machine. Archival photographs and illustrations augment the text. Glossary, Further Reading, Web Sites, and Index.

2059. Parker, Steve. *The Wright Brothers and Aviation.* Chelsea House, 1995. 32pp. ISBN 978-0-7910-3013-4. Grades 3–7. Parker presents the early years of the Wright brothers, Wilbur and Orville, and the gliding skills learned from their early experiments with bicycles. They taught themselves about machines and mechanics and made a small combustion engine. Although they were not the first to attempt powered flight, they were the first to succeed, overcoming the three basic problems of flight: designing wings that lift the craft, figuring out how to control it in the air, and building a power plant to propel it. The final chapter looks at aviation after the Wrights made their flight on December 17, 1903. The World in the Wrights' Time, Glossary, and Index.

2060. Pasachoff, Naomi. *Alexander Graham Bell: Making Connections.* Oxford, 1996. 140pp. ISBN 978-0-19-509908-9. Grades 5–9. This volume looks at Alexander Graham Bell (1847–1922) and his contributions as an educator and inventor more than at his personal life. Clear explanations of his experiments and the scientific principles behind them enliven the text and clarify his work, especially as a teacher of the deaf. Photographs and reproductions highlight the text. Further Reading and Index.

2061. Poolos, Jamie. *Ralph Waldo Emerson: The Father of the American Renaissance.* See entry 1541.

2062. Porter, A. P. *Jump at de Sun: The Story of Zora Neale Hurston.* First Avenue, 1992. 95pp. Paper ISBN 978-0-8761-4546-3. Grades 4–6. This biography presents the life of Zora Neale Hurston (1891–1960) as a story befitting the novelist, playwright, essayist, and folklorist she was. It traces her life from childhood in Florida. Her mother died and her father remarried, to a woman who rejected Zora. Then Zora went to school and on to college where she excelled as a folklorist. She lived in Harlem with other members of the Harlem Renaissance, and later in life returned to Florida. Photographs highlight the text. Bibliography, Notes, and Index.

2063. Ransom, Candice F. *Clara Barton.* See entry 1543.

2064. Rappaport, Doreen. *Eleanor, Quiet No More.* Illustrated by Gary Kelley. Hyperion, 2009. 48pp. ISBN 978-0-7868-5141-6. Grades 2–5. After her mother, who unflatteringly called her "Granny," and her adored father both died, Eleanor Roosevelt (1884–1962) lived with a grandmother who supported her materially but not emotionally. Only when Eleanor went to study in London and travel in Europe was she able to begin being herself. Quotes from Eleanor's writings are sprinkled throughout the text, which shows her maturing from adolescence to wife of Franklin Delano Roosevelt to mother to First Lady and then to United Nations ambassador. Throughout, she championed the rights of those less privileged and ignored those who disapproved of her candid ideas. Subdued pastels complement the text. Chronology, Notes, Bibliography, Further Reading, and Web Sites. *Capitol Choices Noteworthy Titles for Children and Teens* (Washington, D.C.).

2065. Raum, Elizabeth. *Alice Paul.* (American Lives) Raintree, 2004. 32pp. ISBN 978-1-4034-4996-2; paper ISBN 978-1-4034-5703-5. Grades 2–4. Alice Paul (1885–1977) became an important force for women's rights as Mrs. Pankhurst's assistant in England. She marched there and came to Washington for a big parade. Then she met with President Wilson. She was arrested for her support for equal rights, but her efforts helped women everywhere. Illustrations complement the text. Glossary, Further Reading, and Index.

2066. Raum, Elizabeth. *Jane Addams.* (American Lives) Raintree, 2004. 32pp. ISBN 978-1-4034-4992-4; paper ISBN 978-1-4034-5707-3. Grades 2–4. Jane Addams (1860–1935) grew up feeling unattractive, but she was intelligent and able to recognize what she could do to help others. She saw the awful conditions suffered by immigrants and women, and she established Hull House in Chicago. She spoke about the needs of women and children and for world peace. Her work earned her the Nobel Peace Prize. Illustrations complement the text. Glossary, Further Reading, and Index.

2067. Raum, Elizabeth. *Julia Ward Howe.* See entry 1547.

2068. Ray, Deborah Kogan. *Dinosaur Mountain: Digging into the Jurassic Age.* Frances Foster, 2010. 40pp. ISBN 978-0-374-31789-8. Grades 3–6. People began to search earnestly for dinosaurs in 1877 after bones were discovered in Colorado. Andrew Carnegie hired Earl Douglass (1862–1931), a fossil expert at the Carnegie Museum of Natural History in Pittsburgh, to find something important. Douglass liked working in the field as a "bone hunter." He believed dinosaurs had lived in the Uinta Basin of northeastern Utah and in 1908 he found a large bone there. A year later he discovered bones from a *Brontosaurus* (*Apatosaurus*), one of the largest animals ever. He dug ten different species of Jurassic dinosaurs before he closed the quarry in 1924. Huge lettering covers the title page, with pictures of dinosaurs on the endpages and colorful paintings. Glossary, Maps, Bibliography, and Note.

2069. Rockwell, Anne. *Only Passing Through: The Story of Sojourner Truth.* See entry 1548.

2070. Roop, Peter, and Connie Roop. *Sojourner Truth.* See entry 1549.

2071. Ruffin, Frances E. *Frederick Douglass: Rising Up from Slavery.* (Sterling Biographies) Sterling, 2007. 124pp. ISBN 978-1-4027-5799-0; paper ISBN 978-1-4027-4118-0. Grades 5–8. Frederick Douglass (1818–1895), a slave who escaped to freedom, became a spokesman against slavery and for rights for all people. He also edited a newspaper and wrote about his beliefs. Both African Americans and whites condemned Douglass for marrying a white woman after his first wife died, but he refused to be chastened. Photographs, documents, and illustrations augment the text. Bibliography, Glossary, Chronology, and Index.

2072. Russell, Sharman Apt. *Frederick Douglass: Abolitionist Editor.* See entry 1550.

2073. Sapp, Richard. *Ulysses S. Grant and the Road to Appomattox.* See entry 1554.

2074. Schmidt, Gary D. *Robert Frost.* Illustrated by Henri Sorensen. Sterling, 1994. 48pp. ISBN 978-0-8069-0633-1; 2008, paper ISBN 978-1-4027-5475-3. Grades 3 up. After an introductory biographical sketch of Frost (1874–1963), the editor arranges some of his more famous poems thematically by season. Index.

2075. Schroeder, Alan. *Booker T. Washington: Educator and Racial Spokesman.* Chelsea House, 2005. 150pp. ISBN 978-0-7910-8253-9. Grades 5 up. Booker T. Washington (1856–1915) was born a slave on a Virginia farm and got his freedom when the Civil War ended. He then went to work in the salt furnaces and coal mines of West Virginia. At 16, he walked 200 miles to enroll at Virginia's Hampton Institute. He became a teacher, and in 1881 he went to Tuskegee, Alabama, where he was the first teacher in a school that became one of the largest and best-endowed of the black institutions. He worked for a better life for blacks and wanted them to accept white society in their attempts to raise themselves economically. Photographs enhance the text. Chronology, Further Reading, and Index.

2076. Schroeder, Alan. *Minty: A Story of Young Harriet Tubman.* See entry 1556.

2077. Sheldon, David. *Barnum Brown: Dinosaur Hunter.* Walker, 2006. 32pp. ISBN 978-0-8027-9602-8. Grades 1–3. Barnum Brown (1873–1963), named after P. T. Barnum of circus fame, was interested in collecting fossils around his family's Kansas farm at a young age. As an adult, he became a paleontologist at the American Museum of Natural History in New York, in charge of adding a dinosaur to the museum's collection. He often had to compete with other fossil hunters for finds, but he seemed to have an ability to look in the right spot. His most important discovery was a Tyrannosaurus rex. Illustrations enhance the text. Further Reading and Web Sites.

2078. Silverthorne, Elizabeth. *Louisa May Alcott.* See entry 1557.

2079. Slade, Suzanne. *Booker T. Washington: Teacher, Speaker, and Leader.* Illustrated by Siri Weber Feeney. (Biographies) Picture Window, 2008. 24pp. ISBN 978-1-4048-3977-9. Grades K–3. Born into slavery in Virginia, Booker T. Washington (1856–1915) worked with his siblings. In 1865 the Civil War ended and his family, now free, walked 200 miles to West Virginia. He worked in a salt furnace and studied the alphabet at night. Soon he was able to attend school, and at 16, he went to Hampton Normal and Agricultural Institute in Virginia where he worked to pay his tuition. In 1875, when he graduated, he became a teacher. In 1881 he became the principal of the Tuskegee Normal School for Teachers in Alabama. Through the years, he helped the school and its students excel. By 1895 he had become a spokesman for African Americans across the country, and in 1901 he wrote *Up from Slavery* about his life. Chronology, Further Reading, Bibliography, Glossary, Web Sites, and Index.

2080. Slade, Suzanne. *Frederick Douglass: Writer, Speaker, and Opponent of Slavery.* See entry 1558.

2081. Slade, Suzanne. *Sojourner Truth: Preacher for Freedom and Equality.* See entry 1559.

2082. Slade, Suzanne. *Susan B. Anthony: Fighter for Freedom and Equality.* Illustrated by Craig Orback. (Biographies) Picture Window, 2007. 24pp. ISBN 978-1-4048-3104-9. Grades K–3. Susan Brownell Anthony (1820–1906) was the second of eight children in a Massachusetts Quaker family. She learned to read and write and later taught at a boarding school. She later lived in Rochester, New York, and campaigned for abolition and suffrage. She was arrested for trying to vote in 1872. When she died in 1906 only four states allowed women to vote. However, in 1920, the Nineteenth Amendment gave women this right. Chronology, Further Reading, Bibliography, Glossary, Web Sites, and Index.

2083. Stafford, Mark. *W. E. B. Du Bois: Scholar and Activist.* (Black Americans of Achievement) Chelsea House, 2004. 127pp. ISBN 978-0-7910-8158-7. Grades 5 up. W. E. B. Du Bois (1868–1963) had degrees from Fisk and Harvard and studied at the University of Berlin in Germany. At the age of 26, as a college professor, he began publishing a series of sociological studies on black life. In *The Souls of Black Folk,* he attacked Booker T. Washington's position that blacks should wait until their economic status rose before they began to seek equality. He co-founded the National Association for the Advancement of Colored People (NAACP). In 1961 he went to live in Africa because of his dissatisfaction with American society. Photographs enhance the text. Chronology, Further Reading, and Index.

2084. Stearns, Dan. *Harriet Tubman and the Underground Railroad.* See entry 1560.

2085. Steig, William. *When Everybody Wore a Hat.* Joanna Cotler, 2003. 40pp. ISBN 978-0-06-009700-4; 2005, paper ISBN 978-0-06-009702-8. Grades 1–4. William Steig, the author of many picture books, was 8 years old in the Bronx in 1916. Life was different. Horses pulled fire engines, television did not exist, and movies cost a nickel. Everyone wore a hat. Boys ignored girls, and children went to the library for books. Steig remembers how his immigrant mother reacted to news from her home, the beginning of World War I, and that he wanted to be both an artist and a seaman. He did not go to sea, but he delighted many with his art throughout his life. Watercolor and ink illustrations enhance the text. *Publishers Weekly Best Children's Books* and *New York Times Notable Books of the Year*.

2086. **Stone, Tanya Lee.** *Elizabeth Leads the Way: Elizabeth Cady Stanton and the Right to Vote.* See entry 1561.

2087. **Streissguth, Thomas.** *Rocket Man: The Story of Robert Goddard.* Carolrhoda, 1995. 86pp. ISBN 978-0-8761-4863-1. Grades 5–8. From a young age Robert Goddard (1882–1945) was interested in science and especially with the idea of space travel. He suffered from tuberculosis, but he did not let his poor health keep him from making major advancements in science while working as a professor. The text looks at his many achievements. Notes, Glossary, Bibliography, and Index.

2088. **Sullivan, George.** *Helen Keller.* (In Their Own Words) Scholastic, 2000. 128pp. Paper ISBN 978-0-439-09555-6. Grades 3–6. This biography uses excerpts from the autobiography of Helen Keller (1880–1968) to describe her life with Annie Sullivan and her education. Photographs and illustrations augment the text. Bibliography, Chronology, Further Reading, and Index.

2089. **Sullivan, George.** *Helen Keller: Her Life in Pictures.* Scholastic, 2007. 80pp. ISBN 978-0-439-91815-2. Grades 3–6. In this biography of Helen Keller (1880–1968) with references to Annie Sullivan (1866–1936), the author uses images and Keller's own writings to relate her life, her choices, and her accomplishments. Illustrations enhance the text. Chronology, Further Resources, Bibliography, and Index.

2090. **Sutcliffe, Jane.** *George S. Patton, Jr.* (History Maker Bios) Lerner, 2006. 48pp. ISBN 978-0-8225-2436-6. Grades 3–5. George S. Patton, Jr. (1885–1945) knew as a child that he wanted to lead men into battle as a military commander. A great general, he never lost a battle. He was the first to use automobiles in battle and he used tanks in both world wars. As a soldier, he designed a new type of blade and gained the name "Master of the Sword." Illustrations augment the text. Bibliography, Further Reading, Glossary, Maps, Timeline, Web Sites, and Index.

2091. **Sutcliffe, Jane.** *John Deere.* See entry 1217.

2092. **Sutcliffe, Jane.** *Milton Hershey.* (History Maker Bios) Lerner, 2004. 48pp. ISBN 978-0-8225-0247-0. Grades 3–5. Milton Hershey (1857–1945) established a chocolate business that continues today. The five chapters of the text discuss his failures and then his success at creating the right recipe for his candy. He built a factory in a Pennsylvania cornfield that survived the Great Depression. Illustrations augment the text. Bibliography, Further Reading, Glossary, Maps, Timeline, Web Sites, and Index.

2093. **Swain, Gwenyth.** *The Road to Seneca Falls: A Story About Elizabeth Cady Stanton.* See entry 1564.

2094. **Swain, Gwenyth.** *Theodore Roosevelt.* (History Maker Bios) Lerner, 2004. 48pp. ISBN 978-0-8225-1548-7. Grades 3–5. As a child, Theodore Roosevelt (1858–1919), who grew up in a wealthy New York family, suffered from asthma. The five chapters of this book discuss his young life, his time in college and as a cowboy, his enjoyment of the outdoors, and his tenure as president. He wanted to preserve the land, and his legacy includes national parks and other reserves. Illustrations augment the text. Bibliography, Further Reading, Glossary, Maps, Timeline, Web Sites, and Index.

2095. **Tieck, Sarah.** *Wright Brothers.* (First Biographies) Buddy, 2006. 32pp. ISBN 978-1-59679-790-1. Grades K–3. Without the Wright brothers, Orville (1871–1948) and Wilbur (1867–1912), discovering how to control their motorized aircraft, airplane travel would most likely have been delayed until later in the century. They were the first of many experimenters to understand that they had to control pitch, yaw, and roll movements in their heavier-than-air machine. Their flight was a stunning achievement. Photographs and illustrations augment the text. Glossary, Chronology, and Index.

2096. Towle, Wendy. *The Real McCoy: The Life of an African-American Inventor.* Illustrated by Wil Clay. Scholastic, 1995. Unpaged. Paper ISBN 978-0-590-48102-1. Grades 2–5. After studying engineering in Scotland, Canadian-born African American Elijah McCoy (1844–1929) patented more than 50 inventions. From his name came the expression "the real McCoy," because people knew that the automatic oil cup he invented for locomotives and heavy machinery was much better than the imitations.

2097. Trollinger, Patsi B. *Perfect Timing: How Isaac Murphy Became One of the World's Greatest Jockeys.* Illustrated by Jerome Lagarrique. Viking, 2006. 32pp. ISBN 978-0-670-06083-2. Grades 2–5. Isaac Murphy (1861–1896), 12-year-old grandson of slaves, got the chance to ride a racehorse in Lexington, Kentucky, in 1873. After that first opportunity, he kept on riding and became one of the most successful jockeys in history. Some of his records have never been broken. He and his horse won the Kentucky Derby three times. If Murphy had tried to race either twenty years earlier or twenty years later, he would have been excluded. African Americans were kept out of the sport as slaves, and whites later denied them equal rights. Trying to keep his weight down, Murphy died of an eating disorder at 35. Illustrations augment the text.

2098. Turner, Glennette Tilley. *An Apple for Harriet Tubman.* See entry 1567.

2099. Venezia, Mike. *Horace Pippin.* (Getting to Know the World's Greatest Artists) Scholastic, 2007. 32pp. ISBN 978-0-531-18527-8; Children's Press, 2008, paper ISBN 978-0-531-14758-0. Grades K–5. Horace Pippin (1888–1946) began art as therapy for an arm injured in World War I. He is an important American primitive painter whose works are exhibited around the world. Illustrations accompany the text.

2100. Venezia, Mike. *James McNeill Whistler.* (Getting to Know the World's Greatest Artists) Scholastic, 2003. 32pp. ISBN 978-0-516-22578-4; Children's Press, 2004, paper ISBN 978-0-516-26978-8. Grades K–5. James McNeill Whistler (1834–1903) lived in Europe most of his life. He believed in "art for art's sake" and liked the idea of the painting and its color more than the subject or the style of the painting. His most famous painting is *The Artist's Mother.* Illustrations enhance the text.

2101. Venezia, Mike. *John Philip Sousa.* (Getting to Know the World's Greatest Composers) Scholastic, 1998. 32pp. ISBN 978-0-516-20761-2; Children's Press, 1999, paper ISBN 978-0-516-26401-1. Grades K–5. John Philip Sousa (1854–1932) grew up in Washington, D.C., and heard many military bands as a boy during the Civil War. When he was only 11 years old, he led a band of seven adult men that became very popular. Later he wrote famous marches that bands still play in parades. One of the most famous is the "Washington Post March." Illustrations augment the text.

2102. Venezia, Mike. *Mary Cassatt.* (Getting to Know the World's Greatest Artists) Scholastic, 1990. 32pp. ISBN 978-0-516-02278-9; Children's Press, 1991, paper ISBN 978-0-516-42278-7. Grades K–5. Mary Cassatt (1844–1926) was an American impressionist painter who lived much of her life in France. She is especially known for the figures of mothers and children incorporated in her paintings. Illustrations supplement the text.

2103. Venezia, Mike. *Winslow Homer.* (Getting to Know the World's Greatest Artists) Scholastic, 2004. 32pp. ISBN 978-0-516-22579-1; Children's Press paper ISBN 978-0-516-26979-5. Grades K–5. Winslow Homer (1836–1910) was an engraver who became a painter. He had a rustic, naturalistic style because of his love of landscape and seascape. This contrasted with artists of his time who continued to paint in the mannered classical style. He illustrated scenes from the Civil War and then began using watercolors along with oil paint. Among his paintings are "Banks Fisherman," "Eight Bells," "Gulf Stream," "Rum Cay," "Mending the Nets," and "Searchlight, Harbor Entrance, Santiago de Cuba." Illustrations enhance the text.

2104. Viegas, Jennifer. *William James: American Philosopher, Psychologist, and Theologian.* (Library of American Thinkers) Rosen, 2006. 112pp. ISBN 978-1-4042-0505-5. Grades 5–8. This profile of William James (1842–1910) offers information about his early life, his education, and his impact on his disciplines. It also looks at other thinkers who influenced

James's ideas and theories as well as how his contemporaries reacted to his writings such as *The Principles of Psychology* (1890) and *The Varieties of Religious Experience* (1902). He is often considered the "father" of American psychology. Photographs and illustrations augment the text. Bibliography, Glossary, Chronology, Further Reading, Web Sites, and Index.

2105. Wadsworth, Ginger. *Camping with the President.* Illustrated by Karen Dugan. Calkins Creek, 2009. 32pp. ISBN 978-1-59078-497-6. Grades 3–5. In 1903 Theodore Roosevelt (1858–1919) went west to meet John Muir (1838–1914) and camped with him for four days at Bridal Veil Falls in Yosemite. They climbed Glacier Peak and rode horses through the giant sequoias. Wadsworth describes the visit, the reporters who tried to document it, and Roosevelt's later conservation efforts. Quotes from Roosevelt and watercolors enhance the text. Notes, Bibliography, and Further Reading.

2106. Wadsworth, Ginger. *The Wright Brothers.* (History Maker Bios) Lerner, 2004. 48pp. ISBN 978-0-8225-0199-2. Grades 3–5. As children, Wilbur Wright (1867–1912) and Orville Wright (1871–1948) played together and enjoyed building things. When their father gave them a toy helicopter, they examined it and played with it. After working in the printing business, they opened a bicycle shop, and there they began to design a plane that would fly, a feat they eventually accomplished. The five chapters of the text give an overview of their lives and interests. Illustrations augment the text. Bibliography, Further Reading, Glossary, Maps, Timeline, Web Sites, and Index.

2107. Waxman, Laura Hamilton. *W. K. Kellogg.* (History Maker Bios) Lerner, 2006. 48pp. ISBN 978-0-8225-6578-9. Grades 3–5. Willie Keith Kellogg (1860–1951) grew up in Battle Creek, Michigan, where he helped his family with their vegetable-growing business and broom factory. His family valued work over education, and he soon learned how to run a business. The five chapters of the text give an overview of his life and his invention of corn flakes. He developed more cereals and established an empire. Illustrations augment the text. Bibliography, Further Reading, Glossary, Maps, Timeline, Web Sites, and Index.

2108. Waxman, Laura Hamilton. *Woodrow Wilson.* (History Maker Bios) Lerner, 2006. 48pp. ISBN 978-0-8225-6053-1. Grades 3–5. Called "Tommy," Woodrow Wilson (1856–1924) grew up in Virginia and Georgia during the Civil War. He loved books and studying with his father, eventually attending Princeton. He rejected the idea of becoming a minister and opted instead for being a good leader. First a professor, he was later elected president of the United States. He helped to form the League of Nations in hope of keeping peace after World War I. The five chapters of the book discuss these aspects of Wilson's life. Illustrations augment the text. Bibliography, Further Reading, Glossary, Maps, Timeline, Web Sites, and Index.

2109. Weidt, Maryann N. *Harriet Tubman.* See entry 1570.

2110. Weidt, Maryann N. *Matthew Henson.* (History Maker Bios) Lerner, 2002. 48pp. ISBN 978-0-8225-0397-2; paper ISBN 978-0-8225-1565-4. Grades 3–5. Although never a slave, Matthew Henson (1866–1955) worked hard as a sharecropper in Maryland. The five chapters in this volume relate his experiences as an explorer and explain that he most likely reached the North Pole in 1909 before Robert Peary, the man with whom he was traveling. Peary's frostbitten feet meant that Eskimos had to transport him to the Pole on a sled. Illustrations augment the text. Bibliography, Further Reading, Glossary, Maps, Timeline, Web Sites, and Index.

2111. Weitzman, David. *The Mountain Man and the President.* Illustrated by Charles Shaw. Steck-Vaughn, 1992. 40pp. Paper ISBN 978-0-8114-8064-2. Grades 4–6. John Muir (1838–1914) loved the California woods and mountains and wanted to save their beauty for everyone. President Teddy Roosevelt (1858–1919) read Muir's articles and arranged to walk with him in the Sierra Mountains in 1903. Impressed by the beauty of the land Muir showed him, Roosevelt—himself a naturalist trained at Harvard—created five new national parks and 16 national monuments. Afterword and Notes.

2112. Welch, Catherine. *Frederick Douglass.* See entry 1571.

2113. Wilds, Mary. *A Forgotten Champion: The Story of Major Taylor, Fastest Bicycle Racer in the World.* Avisson, 2002. 87pp. Paper ISBN 978-1-888105-52-0. Grades 5–8. Major Taylor (1878–1932), an African American from Indianapolis, discovered bicycling as a child. He became a racer, winning a gold medal at the age of 14. He was the first African American to win both national and world championships and to set an official world record in his sport. Although people ostracized him at home, he was adored abroad. When he died in 1932, few remembered his exploits. Illustrations complement the text.

2114. Williams, Brian. *Bell and the Science of the Telephone.* Barron's, 2006. 32pp. ISBN 978-0-7641-5972-5; 2007, paper ISBN 978-0-7641-3488-3. Grades K–3. This biography of Alexander Graham Bell (1847–1922) focuses on his invention of the telephone. The twelve brief chapters look at Bell's childhood, the science behind sound waves, and other aspects of the telephone's creation. Among the things that helped him were the Morse code and a tuning fork. Photographs and illustrations augment the text. Glossary, Web Sites, and Index.

2115. Williams, Jean Kinney. *Bridget "Biddy" Mason: From Slave to Businesswoman.* See entry 1573.

2116. Winter, Jeanette. *My Name Is Georgia.* Silver Whistle, 1998. Unpaged. ISBN 978-0-15-201649-4; Voyager, 2003, paper ISBN 978-0-15-204597-5. Grades 1–4. From the time she was a young girl, Georgia O'Keeffe (1887–1986) seemed to view the world in her own way. She drew pictures and was determined to ignore society's mores. Born in Wisconsin, she went to school in Chicago and New York. Finally she bought a home in New Mexico where she could look out over the desert as she painted. Illustrations complement the text. *Children's Book Award* (South Carolina) nomination.

2117. Woodside, Martin. *Thomas A. Edison: The Man Who Lit Up the World.* (Sterling Biographies) Sterling, 2007. 124pp. ISBN 978-1-4027-4955-1; paper ISBN 978-1-4027-3229-4. Grades 5–8. Woodside looks at the life of Thomas Alva Edison (1847–1931) as he struggled to succeed after trying "one more time" after "one more time." Following a summary of his life and the contributions he made, the author includes information about his early family life and education and places him in relationship to the times in which he lived. Photographs enhance the text. Bibliography, Chronology, Glossary, and Index.

2118. Yolen, Jane. *My Brothers' Flying Machine: Wilbur, Orville, and Me.* Illustrated by Jim Burke. Liltle, Brown, 2003. 32pp. ISBN 978-0-316-97159-1. Grades 1–4. Katherine Wright, the younger sister of Orville and Wilbur, encouraged them throughout their many inventions. She watched them play with a toy flying machine as children. Although Katherine was 29 in 1903 she seems childlike in her memories of their experiments through the years. While Will and Orv worked, she kept the store so they had economic support. Illustrations augment the text. Notes. *Parents Choice Award* and *Book Award* (Massachusetts).

2119. Zemlicka, Shannon. *Thomas Edison.* (History Maker Bios) Lerner, 2003. 48pp. ISBN 978-0-8225-0239-9. Grades 3–5. Nicknamed "Al" for Alva, his middle name, Thomas Edison (1847–1931) was curious about many things as a child. Four chapters cover his childhood, his beginnings as an inventor, the chance for success, his discovery of electricity, and his depiction in movies and music. Photographs and illustrations augment the text. Bibliography, Further Reading, Glossary, Maps, Timeline, Web Sites, and Index.

2120. Zuehlke, Jeffrey Bivin. *Henry Ford.* (History Maker Bios) Lerner, 2007. 48pp. ISBN 978-0-8225-6582-2. Grades 3–5. Henry Ford (1863–1947), a natural mechanic, began tinkering with machines when he was a boy. As he grew older, he read about scientific experiments in magazines and newspapers. He was fascinated when he heard about the gas engine and soon mastered repairing it. He founded the Ford Motor company in 1903 and began manufacturing the Model T automobile. Eventually he developed the assembly line, a new way to produce affordable automobiles of quality. Illustrations augment the text. Bibliography, Further Reading, Glossary, Maps, Timeline, Web Sites, and Index.

Graphic Novels, Biographies, and Histories

2121. Braun, Eric, and Cynthia Martin. *Booker T. Washington: Great American Educator.* Graphic Library, 2005. 32pp. ISBN 978-0-7368-4630-1. Grades 3–5. This short graphic biography of Booker T. Washington (1856–1915) depicts his life and his efforts to promote education for African Americans. A yellow background sets direct quotes from Washington apart from the fictional aspect of the narration. Web Sites.

2122. Doeden, Matt. *The Sinking of the Titanic.* Illustrated by Charles Barnett, III. Graphic Library, 2005. 32pp. ISBN 978-0-7368-3834-4; paper ISBN 978-0-7368-5247-0. Grades 3–5. When the *Titanic* sank on April 14, 1912, the *Carpathia* was ten miles away. The ship rushed to rescue survivors. Women and children got first place in the *Titanic's* lifeboats, so many more men died. Illustrations augment the text. Bibliography, Glossary, Further Reading, and Index.

2123. Gunderson, Jessica. *The Triangle Shirtwaist Factory Fire.* Illustrated by Phil Miller and Charles Barnett, III. Graphic Library, 2006. 32pp. ISBN 978-0-7368-6878-5; paper ISBN 978-0-7368-6872-3. Grades 3–5. On March 25, 1911, the Triangle Shirtwaist Factory caught fire, the largest industrial disaster in New York City's history. Employees could not get out of the building because the doors were locked, and 146 garment workers died from the fire or from jumping out windows. Illustrations depict the event. Bibliography, Glossary, Further Reading, and Index.

2124. Hoena, B. A. *Matthew Henson: Arctic Adventurer.* Illustrated by Phil Miller and Charles Barnett, III. (Graphic Biographies) Graphic Library, 2005. 32pp. ISBN 978-0-7368-4634-9; paper ISBN 978-0-7368-9671-9. Grades 4–7. This short graphic biography of Matthew Henson (1866–1955) tells the story of the African American explorer who reached the North Pole in 1909, most likely before Robert Peary although he never received the credit. A yellow background sets direct quotes from Henson apart from the fictional aspect of the narration. Web Sites.

2125. Lutes, Jason. *Houdini: The Handcuff King.* Narrated by Nick Bertozzi. Hyperion, 2007. 96pp. ISBN 978-0-7868-3902-5; 2008, paper ISBN 978-0-7868-3903-2. Grades 5–8. This graphic biography focuses on Harry Houdini's life, specifically on May 1, 1908, when he jumped into the freezing river in Boston while handcuffed. Houdini (1874–1926) was a master of public promotion for his craft, but he also wanted to do the best he could at his tricks. He was committed to science and to disproving spiritualism. He experienced anti-Semitism. Houdini was devoted to his wife, Bess, and this volume posits that Bess may have contributed to his tricks—in the case of the river handcuffs, she might have passed the key or a lock pick to him in a kiss. Bibliography. *Bulletin Blue Ribbon.*

2126. Miller, Connie Colwell. *Elizabeth Cady Stanton: Women's Rights Pioneer.* Illustrated by Cynthia Martin. Graphic Library, 2005. 32pp. ISBN 978-0-7368-4630-1; 2006, paper ISBN 978-0-7368-6194-6. Grades 3–5. This short graphic biography of Elizabeth Cady Stanton (1815–1902) depicts her life and work as a suffragist. Throughout her life, she was dedicated to getting women the right to vote. A yellow background sets direct quotes from Stanton apart from the fictional aspect of the narration. Web sites.

2127. Miller, Connie Colwell. *Mother Jones: Labor Leader.* Illustrated by Steve Erwin and Charles Barnett, III. (Graphic Biographies) Graphic Library, 2006. 32pp. ISBN 978-0-7368-5487-0; paper ISBN 978-0-7368-9662-7. Grades 3–5. This short graphic biography of Mother Jones (1843?–1930) describes her work supporting labor organizations in the United States. She organized and led strikes around the country, fighting against child labor and grim conditions for mineworkers. A yellow background sets direct quotes from Jones apart from the fictional aspect of the narration. Web Sites.

2128. Niz, Xavier. *The Story of the Statue of Liberty.* Illustrated by Cynthia Martin and Brent Schoonover. Graphic Library, 2006. 32pp. ISBN 978-0-7368-5494-8; paper ISBN 978-0-7368-6882-2. Grades 3–5. Designed by Frédéric Auguste Bartholdi and built in France, the Statue of Liberty arrived in the United States in 1885. Contributions from all over the country funded the completion of its base. Bibliography, Glossary, Further Reading, and Index.

2129. Olson, Nathan. *George Washington Carver: Ingenious Inventor.* Illustrated by Keith Tucker. (Graphic Biographies) Graphic Library, 2006. 32pp. ISBN 978-0-7368-5484-9; paper ISBN 978-0-7368-6884-6. Grades 3–5. This short graphic biography of George Washington Carver (1864?–1943) relates his childhood of poverty and how he overcame it to make scientific discoveries about agriculture and the peanut that have helped many people. A yellow background sets direct quotes from Carver apart from the fictional aspect of the narration. Web Sites.

2130. Olson, Nathan. *Theodore Roosevelt: Bear of a President.* Illustrated by Cynthia Martin and Mark G. Heike. (Graphic Biographies) Graphic Library, 2007. 32pp. ISBN 978-0-7368-6849-5; paper ISBN 978-0-7368-7901-9. Grades 3–5. This short graphic biography of Theodore Roosevelt (1858–1919) explores his life as a soldier in the Spanish American War, president of the United States, and preserver and creator of national parks. A yellow background sets direct quotes from Roosevelt apart from the fictional aspect of the narration. Web Sites.

2131. Welvaert, Scott R. *Helen Keller: Courageous Advocate.* Illustrated by Cynthia Martin and Keith Tucker. (Graphic Biographies) Graphic Library, 2005. 32pp. ISBN 978-0-7368-4964-7; paper ISBN 978-0-7368-6196-0. Grades 3–5. This short graphic biography of Helen Keller (1880–1968) relates the story of her life from the time of her illness as a young child when she was stricken blind and deaf through her lessons from Annie Sullivan to her life as an educated woman sharing her world views. A yellow background sets direct quotes from Keller apart from the fictional aspect of the narration. Web Sites.

DVDs

2132. *Americana: 1900's to Present Day.* (Hands-On Crafts for Kids Series 6: Back in Time) Chip Taylor Communications, 2003. 30 mins. Grades 4–6. The production begins with a narrator reading a list of materials appearing on the screen. Teachers then construct objects from 20th-century America—a Star Travel game, an art deco bulletin board, a teddy bear, an Old Glory fresco, and a Delta airplane. Each item helps explain an important aspect of American culture.

2133. *The Grange Fair: An American Tradition.* (Minutes of History) Inecom, 2008. 86 mins. Grades 5 up. The Centre County (Pennsylvania) Grange Fair was founded in 1874 and is the oldest one in the country. Families spend nine nights camping in tents and RVs on the fair site. Competitions at the fair involve cooking and canning, animal husbandry, and decorative arts. The DVD reveals the anguish of loss, sometimes to a younger sibling, and the glory of winning.

2134. *Mary Cassatt: American Impressionist.* (Artists' Specials) Devine, 2001. 55 mins. Grades 5–9. Mary Cassatt (1844–1926) lives an orderly life in Paris as an impressionist painter and close friend of Edgar Degas. When her brother and his wife arrive with their three unruly children, she realizes they can be her models. Her niece Katherine intends to marry, but after being exposed to Cassatt's way of living and ideas she changes her mind. *American Library Association Notable Children's Video Award, Platinum Award, Oppenheim Toy Portfolio, Kids First! Coalition of Quality Children's Media, Emmy Award,* and *Parents' Choice Gold Award.*

2135. *Susan B. Anthony.* (Great Americans for Children) Library Video, 2003. 23 mins. ISBN 978-1-57225-535-7. Grades K–4. As late as the early 1900s, women were not allowed to vote in the United States. Susan B. Anthony (1820–1906) thought this was wrong. She first worked to free slaves as an abolitionist and then, after the Civil War, she became a suffragist, seeking more rights for women. Stills and reenactments reveal her contribution to American history.

2136. **White, Linda Arms.** *I Could Do That! Esther Morris Gets Women the Vote.* Illustrated by Nancy Carpenter. Weston Woods, 2006. 17 mins. ISBN 978-0-439-90569-5. Grades 2–4. See entry 1844.

2137. *Winslow Homer: An American Original.* (Artists' Specials) Devine, 2000. 49 mins. ISBN 978-1-894449-63-2. Grades 5–9. In 1874 Winslow Homer (1836–1910) finds the aftermath of the Civil War discouraging and retires to his remote Houghton Farm, leaving his post at *Harpers' Weekly.* There he meets two teenagers, also distressed by the conflict, and they become his models. *American Library Association Notable Children's Video Award* and *Kids First! Coalition of Quality Children's Media.*

Compact Discs

2138. **Adler, David A.** *A Picture Book of Harriet Tubman.* Narrated by Gail Nelson. Live Oak Media, 2005. 1 CD; 14:40 mins. ISBN 978-1-59519-385-8. Grades 1–3. See entry 1482.

2139. **Bruchac, Joseph.** *Jim Thorpe: Original All-American.* Listening Library, 2007. 5 CDs; 6:26 hrs. ISBN 978-0-7393-6229-7. Grades 5 up. A Sac and Fox Indian called Wa-Tho-Huk (Bright Path), Jim Thorpe (1887–1953), recognized today as one of the greatest athletes who ever lived, attended Haskell and Carlisle Indian boarding schools. There he demonstrated his abilities at football, baseball, and track. At the 1912 Olympics he won two gold medals, which he lost when a rumor emerged that he had previously played professionally. At college, he trained with "Pop" Warner, an extraordinary coach who not only controlled Thorpe but also the proceeds from the games in which he played. He lived his adult life in poverty. His medals were restored thirty years after he died.

2140. **Fleischman, Sid.** *Escape! The Story of the Great Houdini.* Audio Bookshelf, 2007. 3 CDs; 3 hrs. 20 min. ISBN 978-0-9761932-5-8. Grades 4–8. See entry 1962.

2141. **Hurwitz, Johanna.** *Dear Emma.* Narrated by Barbara McCulloh. Recorded Books, 2003. 3 CDs; 3 hrs. ISBN 978-1-402-54130-8. Grades 5–7. See entry 1780.

2142. **Long, Loren, and Phil Bildner.** *Game 1: Three Kids, a Mystery, and a Magic Baseball.* (Barnstormers) Simon & Schuster, 2007. 1 CD; 75 mins. ISBN 978-0-7435-6111-2. Grades 3–6. See entry 1799.

2143. **Long, Loren, and Phil Bildner.** *Game 3: The Windy City.* (Barnstormers) Simon & Schuster, 2008. 2 CDs; ca. 2 hrs. ISBN 978-0-7435-7083-1. Grades 3–6. See entry 1801.

2144. **MacLachlan, Patricia.** *More Perfect than the Moon.* Narrated by Glenn Close. (HarperTrophy) HarperCollins, 2004. 1 hr. 15 mins. ISBN 978-0-06-073592-0. Grades 3–5. See entry 1805.

2145. **Murphy, Jim.** *Blizzard: The Storm That Changed America.* Narrated by Taylor Mali. Audio Bookshelf, 2003. 2 CDs; 2.5 hrs. ISBN 978-1-883332-91-4. Grades 5–9. See entry 1890.

2146. **Murphy, Jim.** *The Great Fire.* Narrated by Taylor Mali. Audio Bookshelf, 2003. 2 CDs; 2.5 hrs. ISBN 978-1-883332-92-1. Grades 5 up. See entry 1891.

2147. **Paterson, Katherine.** *Bread and Roses, Too.* Listening Library, 2006. 6 CDs; 6 hrs. 50 mins. ISBN 978-0-7393-3107-1. Grades 5–8. See entry 1810.

2148. **Peck, Richard.** *Fair Weather.* Listening Library, 2001. 3 CDs; 3 hrs. ISBN 978-0-307-24632-5. Grades 5–8. See entry 1812.

2149. **Peck, Richard.** *Here Lies the Librarian.* Narrated by Lara Everly. Listening Library, 2006. 4 CDs; 3 hrs., 41 min. ISBN 978-0-3072-8406-8. Grades 5–8. See entry 1813.

2150. **Peck, Richard.** *The Teacher's Funeral: A Comedy in Three Parts.*   Narrated by Dylan Baker. Listening Library, 2007. 4 CDs; 4 hrs. 42 mins. ISBN 978-0-7393-3898-8. Grades 5–8. See entry 1814.

2151. **Rinaldi, Ann.** *Brooklyn Rose.*   Narrated by Kate Forbes. Recorded Books, 2005. 3 CDs; 3.5 hrs. ISBN 978-1-4193-3852-6. Grades 5–8. See entry 1819.

2152. **Schlitz, Laura Amy.** *A Drowned Maiden's Hair: A Melodrama.*   Recorded Books, 2007. 8 CDs; 9 hrs. ISBN 978-1-4281-6306-5. Grades 4–8. See entry 1825.

2153. **Wallace, Barbara Brooks.** *Peppermints in the Parlor.*   Narrated by Angela Lansbury. Random, 2004. 3 CDs; 5 hrs. 7 mins. ISBN 978-0-8072-8784-2. Grades 4–6. See entry 1838.

2154. **Wallace, Barbara Brooks.** *The Perils of Peppermints.*   Narrated by Suzanne Toren. Recorded Books, 2003. 4 CDs; 6 hrs. ISBN 978-1-4193-1809-2. Grades 4–6. See entry 1839.

WORLD WAR I AND THE
GREAT DEPRESSION, 1917–1941

Historical Fiction and Fantasy

2155. Abraham, Susan Gonzales, and Denise Gonzales Abraham. *Cecilia's Year.* Cinco Puntos, 2004. 216pp. ISBN 978-0-9383178-7-6; 2007, paper ISBN 978-1-9336930-2-6. Grades 5–8. In New Mexico in the 1930s, 14-year-old Cecilia Gonzales wants to continue her education and become a teacher, but her mother has traditional ideas about women's roles. She wants her to become a housewife and live on a farm. Episodic chapters each cover one month.

2156. Adler, David A. *Don't Talk To Me About the War.* Viking, 2008. 176pp. ISBN 978-0-670-06307-9. Grades 5–8. Tommy, 14 in 1940, lives in the Bronx and is only interested in radio and the Brooklyn Dodgers. His friend Beth tries to tell him about the war abroad, but he has adopted his father's belief that America should stay out of the war. When he and Beth meet Sarah, a young Jew who has fled from Germany with her family, he begins to understand the danger of isolationism.

2157. Armstrong, William O. *Sounder.* HarperCollins, 1969. 207pp. ISBN 978-0-06-020143-2; Perennial, 2001, paper ISBN 978-0-06-093548-1. Grades 5 up. During the Depression, a black boy's father steals a ham to feed his starving family. For this he is sent to jail. The boy has to work to support his family, but while his father is away he learns to read and finds support in his beloved dog Sounder. Sounder is the only character in the story to have a name, and he waits faithfully for his master's return just as Argus, the dog of Odysseus, waited. When the father returns, Sounder dies peacefully. *Newbery Medal, Lewis Carroll Shelf Award, American Library Association Notable Children's Books, Horn Book Fanfare Honor List, School Library Journal Best Children's Books, New York Times Outstanding Children's Book,* and *Publishers Weekly Select Children's Books.*

2158. Avi. *Silent Movie.* Atheneum, 2003. 48pp. ISBN 978-0-689-84145-3. Grades K–2. A Swedish family arrives to America in 1909 but get separated at the dock. Separately, they figure out how to get around, go to work, and locate friends from Sweden to help them in their new life. A movie director discovers young Gustav and chooses him to star in a silent movie. He earns an enormous sum and his father sees him on the screen, allowing the family to reunite. Black-and-white glossy illustrations presented in a movie "still" format highlight the text.

2159. Ayres, Katherine. *Macaroni Boy.* Yearling, 2004. 182pp. Paper ISBN 978-0-440-41884-9. Grades 5–8. In 1933 Mike Costa is in sixth-grade in Pittsburgh, where his family owns a food warehouse. The school bully, Andy Simms, calls him "macaroni boy." Mike's job is to set rat traps in the basement. He finds he's catching fewer rats and those he does catch seem to be sick. Mike investigates and his sleuthing leads him directly to Andy Simms. *Nutmeg*

Children's Book Award (Connecticut) nomination, *Children's Book Award* (Georgia) nomination, *Young Hoosier Award* (Indiana) nomination, *William Allen White Award* (Kansas) nomination, and *Children's Book Award* (West Virginia) nomination.

2160. Barrows, Annie. *The Magic Half.*   Bloomsbury, 2008. 224pp. ISBN 978-1-59990-132-9. Grades 3–6. Eleven-year-old Miri Gill, sandwiched between two sets of twins, often feels left out. Her family moves to an old Victorian house where she looks through the lens of an old eyeglass and finds herself transported to 1935, where she meets abused orphan Molly. Can Miri bring Molly into the present day?

2161. Beccia, Carlyn. *Who Put the B in the Ballyhoo? The Most Amazing, Bizarre, and Celebrated Circus Performers.*   Houghton, 2007. 32pp. ISBN 978-0-618-71718-7. Grades K–5. This rhyming alphabet book relies on posters of circus performers in the early 1900s, featuring Annie Oakley, Houdini, the bearded Lady Esau, and the "Wild Men of Borneo." Facts about popular circus acts and personalities of the past are interspersed among the posters.

2162. Bildner, Phil. *The Hallelujah Flight.*   Illustrated by John Jolyfield. Putnam, 2010. 32pp. ISBN 978-0-399-24789-7. Grades K–3. James Banning (1899–1933) wanted to be the first African American to complete a transcontinental flight. His copilot, Thomas Allen, describes their departure from Los Angeles on October 9, 1932, in an old biplane, an OXX6 Eagle Rock. They raised money for fuel and food by allowing people to write their names on the wings. On their cross-country trip they had to cope with whites who refused them food and restroom privileges and with a violent storm in Pennsylvania. But they saw the beautiful Grand Canyon, and after they landed in Long Island, New York, Harlem welcomed the "Flying Hoboes" as heroes. Colorful acrylics illustrations complement the text.

2163. Bildner, Phil. *Shoeless Joe and Black Betsy.*   Illustrated by C. F. Payne. Simon & Schuster, 2002. 40pp. ISBN 978-0-689-82913-0; Aladdin, 2006, paper ISBN 978-0-689-87437-6. Grades K–5. Shoeless Joe Jackson goes into a hitting slump just before he begins playing baseball in the minor leagues. His friend Charlie Ferguson makes Shoeless Joe a special bat that Shoeless Joe names Black Betsy. Shoeless Joe sleeps with the bat and wraps it in cotton, and by caring for the bat he helps himself. Shoeless Joe gained a reputation as one of baseball's greatest hitters. Mixed media illustrations enhance the text. Synopsis of career. *Bluebonnet Award* (Texas), *Show Me Readers Award* (Missouri) nomination, and *Young Hoosier Book Award* (Indiana) nomination.

2164. Blume, Lesley M. M. *Tennyson.*   Knopf, 2008. 228pp. ISBN 978-0-375-84703-5. Grades 5–8. After their poet mother Sadie disappears, their father leaves 11-year-old Tennyson and her younger sister with batty Aunt Henrietta and Uncle Twig in Aigredoux, in Depression-era Louisiana. Their father goes off to search for Sadie. Tennyson begins having strange dreams about a peacock that sounds like a human in this old house full of southern history. She "sees" the family's ruin during the Civil War and writes about them in stories that she sends to her mother's favorite literary magazine. The stories get published, and her mother writes to say that she will not return. At the same time, the magazine's editor comes to see Tennyson, thinking he has discovered a great writer.

2165. Brown, Don. *The Train Jumper.*   Deborah Brodie, 2007. 122pp. ISBN 978-1-59643-218-5. Grades 4–8. In 1934 Edward "Collie" Collier's father has died, and his older brother Bill is spending too much money on alcohol. Then Bill attacks their mother before running off to join the Civilian Conservation Corps. Collie should stay and help his mother through her anguish, but he also wants to get his brother back. He sets out, jumping on trains and living like a hobo as he crosses the country to Colorado. Collie's experiences show a side of the Depression that was familiar to many. Although he finds Little Bill, the facts are not what he expects.

2166. Bryant, Jennifer. *The Trial.*   Knopf, 2004. 169pp. ISBN 978-0-375-92752-2; Yearling, 2005, paper ISBN 978-0-440-41986-0. Grades 5–9. In 1935, 12-year-old Katie Leigh Flynn, living in Flemington, New Jersey, writes poems to describe the trial of Bruno Hauptmann for kidnapping and murdering Charles Lindbergh's baby son. A parallel story involves one of Katie's friends who is unjustly accused of vandalism. *Isinglass Teen Read Award* nomination.

2167. Bunting, Eve. *Pop's Bridge.* Harcourt, 2006. 32pp. ISBN 978-0-15-204773-3. Grades K–3. Robert's iron worker father is helping to build San Francisco's Golden Gate Bridge in 1937. Even though the father of his best friend, Charlie Shu, works on the bridge as a painter, Robert is sure his father's job is more important. When several of the workers die in a serious accident, Robert realizes that the bridge belongs to everyone who is working on it. *Parents Choice Award* and *Black-Eyed Susan Award* (Maryland) nomination.

2168. Campbell, Bebe Moore. *Stompin' at the Savoy.* Illustrated by Richard Yarde. Philomel, 2006. 32pp. ISBN 978-0-399-24197-0. Grades K–4. Five-year-old Mindy is nervous about her forthcoming jazz dance recital until she hears a magical talking drum outside her window. Suddenly she is inside the Savoy Ballroom in Harlem during the 1920s. Her great-aunts are suddenly youthful aunts and Mindy finds herself entered in a dance context. She then begins moving her "happy feet" with all of the others, transported by the music. When she finds herself back in her room, she is ready for her recital. Gouache and pastel illustrations enhance the text.

2169. Celenza, Anna Harwell. *Gershwin's Rhaposody in Blue.* Charlesbridge, 2006. 32pp. ISBN 978-1-57091-556-7. Grades K–4. In 1924 George Gershwin, a pianist of 26, gets a request to compose a new concerto that exemplifies American music. He has only five weeks in which to accomplish this. As he searches for inspiration, he realizes that the music must be like the people it will represent, a melting pot of harmonies, sounds, and rhythms. Illustrations enhance the text and there is an accompanying CD recording of the piece. *Sydney Taylor Notable Book Award.*

2170. Choldenko, Gennifer. *Al Capone Shines My Shoes.* Dial, 2009. 274pp. ISBN 978-0-8037-3460-9. Grades 5–8. In 1935, 12-year-old baseball fanatic Moose Flanagan, protagonist of *Al Capone Does My Shirts*, discovers that he owes Alcatraz prisoner #85, "Scarface," a favor. Scarface has helped Moose's autistic sister, Natalie, gain entrance to a special needs school in San Francisco. Surprised by the note in his pillow saying "it's your turn," Moose thinks that a yellow rose for Capone's visiting wife is all that is needed. But when Natalie arrives with a bar stretcher in her luggage that will help convicts escape, Moose realizes that more is at stake than his honor and potentially his father's guard job. He must make decisions to protect all involved. *Indies Choice Book Awards* finalist.

2171. Cohen, Miriam. *Mimmy and Sophie All Around the Town.* Illustrated by Thomas F. Yezerski. Farrar, 2004. 80pp. ISBN 978-0-374-34989-9. Grades 2–4. In Brooklyn, New York, during the Depression, Mimmy tries to protect her little sister Sophie from the children in the neighborhood even though Sophie herself can be a pest. Six short stories tell of various escapades. The girls get front-row seats at the cinema, but Sophie gets lost going to the bathroom. They love to play in the mud but feel guilty when their mother has to spend time scrubbing their clothes. They hunt for treasure in a vacant lot, pretend that Kool-Aid is wine, and talk back to their Rice Krispies at breakfast. Black-and-white drawings enhance the text. *School Library Journal Best Children's Books.*

2172. Collier, James Lincoln. *The Dreadful Revenge of Ernest Gallen.* Bloomsbury, 2008. 232pp. ISBN 978-1-59990-220-3. Grades 5–7. In the 1930s, 12-year-old Gene is visited by a vengeful ghost that tells him that his father and grandfather were part of a terrible crime in a town called Magnolia when he was a baby. Soon after, the father of Gene's friend Sonny dies at a construction site, and the father of another friend, Sam, is injured in a traffic accident. Voices had also haunted these men. Gene, Sonny, and Sam investigate.

2173. Collier, Kristi. *Throwing Stones.* Henry Holt, 2006. 204pp. ISBN 978-0-8050-7614-1. Grades 5–9. In 1923, 14-year-old Andy Soaring, of Pierre, Indiana, makes the high school basketball team but almost immediately breaks his arm and his collarbone. He decides to report on his team's games for the local newspaper. During the previous five years, he watched his parents grieve over the loss of Andy's brother Pete, and Andy wants to become the star basketball player that Pete was. Bennie Esposito, a new freshman and superb basketball player, becomes his friend even though Bennie steals the girl Andy secretly loves. During the year without basketball, Andy learns while writing that the crops are not doing well, his parents' marriage involves a secret, and the farm's mortgage note is due. Eventually, all the ends come together.

2174. Curtis, Christopher Paul. *Bud, Not Buddy.*   Narrated by James Avery. Delacorte, 1999. 245pp. ISBN 978-0-385-32306-2; Yearling, 2002, paper ISBN 978-0-440-41328-8. Grades 4–7.   Motherless Bud Caldwell, 10, runs away his Michigan foster home in 1929 to find his father. He believes his father is a legendary jazz musician. On his journey, he faces some danger but also receives a lot of kindness—in the Hooverville squatter camp, in the library, in the food line, and along the road. Finally, a man takes him to Grand Rapids, Michigan, where Herman E. Calloway and his jazz band are playing. But this man is old and crotchety. The band members accept Bud and teach him to play an instrument; Miss Thomas makes him feel like part of a family. And he is able to prove his family relationship with Mr. Calloway through his treasured rocks. *Newbery Medal, School Librarians Battle of the Books* (Alaska) nomination, *Young Reader's Award* (Arizona) nomination, *American Library Association Best Books for Young Adults, Coretta Scott King Book Award, Libraries' Blue Hen Award* (Delaware) nomination, *Sunshine State Young Reader Award* (Florida) nomination, *Nene Award* (Hawaii) nomination, *Rebecca Caudill Award* (Illinois) nomination, *Bluegrass Award* (Kentucky) nomination, *Young Readers Choice Award* (Louisiana) nomination, *Battle of the Books* (North Carolina) nomination, *Juvenile Fiction State Book Award* (North Dakota) nomination, *The Land of Enchantment Children's Book Award* (New Mexico) nomination, *Buckeye Children's Book Awards* (Ohio), *Young Readers Choice Book Award* (Pennsylvania) nomination, *Volunteer State Book Award* (Tennessee) nomination, *Bluebonnet Award* (Texas) nomination, *Dorothy Canfield Fisher Children's Book Award* (Vermont) nomination, Children's Book Award (West Virginia) nomination, *Capitol Choices Noteworthy Titles* (Washington, D.C.), and *School Library Journal Best Books for Children.*

2175. Decker, Timothy. *The Letter Home.*   Front Street, 2005. 32pp. ISBN 978-1-9324255-0-5. Grades 5 up.   In the trenches of France in World War I, a medic writes his son a letter carefully describing what he sees and hears. Waiting for battle is boring, but when conflict comes he is very busy. Some nights, he says, are filled with fireworks. He did not want to write until he knew he would be home soon. Finally he gets news that the war has ended, on November 11, 1918. Pen-and-ink illustrations augment the text.

2176. Denenberg, Barry. *Mirror, Mirror on the Wall: The Diary of Bess Brennan.*   (Dear America) Scholastic, 2002. 144pp. ISBN 978-0-439-19446-4. Grades 4–8.   Twelve-year-old Bess lost her sight in a sledding accident and her twin sister Elin keeps a diary for her, in which Bess describes her life at Perkins School for the Blind in Watertown, Massachusetts, in 1932. Bess returns home at weekends and tells Elin about navigating the campus with the help of another student, learning to read Braille, and trying to use her senses of smell and hearing more acutely. Although she has a cruel housemother and a timid roommate, Bess survives. Photographs highlight the text. Notes.

2177. Deutsch, Stacia, and Rhody Cohon. *Disney's Dream.*   Illustrated by David T. Wenzel. (Blast to the Past) Aladdin, 2005. 112pp. Paper ISBN 978-0-689-87025-5. Grades 2–5.   Third-graders Abigail, Jacob, Zack, and Bo travel back to 1928 to meet Walt Disney (1901–1966). They discover that he is neither famous nor wealthy and is thinking about giving up his attempt to make the first animated movie with sound.

2178. De Young, C. Coco. *A Letter to Mrs. Roosevelt.*   112pp. ISBN 978-0-440-41529-9. Grades 3–7.   In 1933, when she is 11 years old and living with her family in Johnstown, Pennsylvania, Margo Bandini discovers that her father cannot make payments on their home. The Sheriff Sale sign goes up in the yard because the family has had to pay for Margo's younger brother Charlie's emergency leg surgery. In a letter assigned to her class, Margo writes to the president's wife, Eleanor Roosevelt, to ask her help. She encloses her father's World War I victory medal. Mrs. Roosevelt gets the letter because Margo's teacher knows her personally, and Mrs. Roosevelt saves the family by getting Margo's father enrolled in a New Deal plan to help those suffering during the Great Depression. Although seemingly unbelievable, the story is based on the experience of the author's grandfather. *Student Book Award* (Maine) nomination, *Sunshine State Young Reader's Book Award* (Florida) nomination, *Children's Book*

Award (Maryland) nomination, *Maud Hart Lovelace Award* (Minnesota) nomination, *Rebecca Caudill Young Reader's Book Award* (Illinois) nomination, *Sasquatch Reading Award* (Washington) nomination, *SCASL Book Award* (South Carolina) nomination, *Volunteer State Book Award* (Tennessee) nomination, *Diamond Award* (Delaware) nomination, and *Children's Book Award* (Massachusetts) nomination.

2179. Dowell, Frances O'Roark. *Dovey Coe.* Atheneum, 2000. 181pp. ISBN 978-0-689-83174-4; Aladdin, 2001, paper ISBN 978-0-689-84667-0. Grades 4–7. In 1928, 12-year-old Dovey Coe of Indian Creek, North Carolina, is outspoken about her dislike of wealthy Parnell Caraway and her discomfort when he starts courting her sister Caroline. Parnell is murdered and Dovey is accused of and tried for the crime. In order to save herself, she investigates Parnell's death further and discovers that her deaf brother, Amos, killed him to keep him from further terrorizing their sister. *School Librarians Battle of the Books* (Alaska) nomination, *Young Reader's Award* (Arizona) nomination, *American Library Association Association Notable Books for Children*, *Bulletin of the Center for Children's Books*, *Children's Picture Book Award* (Georgia) nomination, *Children's Choice Book Award* (Iowa) nomination, *Rebecca Caudill Award* (Illinois) nomination, *Bluegrass Award* (Kentucky) nomination, *Student Book Award* (Maine) nomination, *Battle of the Books* (North Carolina) nomination, *Children's Book Award* (Rhode Island), *Capitol Choices Noteworthy Titles* (Washington, D.C.), *School Library Journal Best Books for Children*, and *Children's Book Award* (West Virginia) nomination.

2180. Dudley, David L. *The Bicycle Man.* Clarion, 2005. 249pp. ISBN 978-0-618-54233-8. Grades 5–8. Carrisa, 12, lives in Georgia in 1927 with her widowed mother, who does laundry for the whites. One day, they decide to help a drifter named Bailey, who rides a shiny bicycle. He will work for a little bit of food and a place to stay. Bailey teaches Carissa to ride his bicycle, tells her about the places he has visited, and helps her face truths about her family. At the same time, she helps him accept a secret from his past and decide whether he can stay or needs to leave.

2181. Ernst, Kathleen. *Midnight in Lonesome Hollow: A Kit Mystery.* Illustrated by Jean-Paul Tibbles. American Girl, 2007. 181pp. Paper ISBN 978-1-59369-160-8. Grades 3–6. Kit goes to stay with her Aunt Millie in Kentucky's Appalachian mountains during the summer of 1934. A researcher looking for information about the area's folklore comes to town, and Kit enjoys helping her. But who is sabotaging the researcher's efforts?

2182. Franklin, Kristine L. *Grape Thief.* Candlewick, 2003. 304pp. ISBN 978-0-7636-1325-9. Grades 5–9. In 1925, 12-year-old Croatian American Cuss wants to stay in school, but the difficult financial situation in Roslyn, Washington, may force him to begin working to help his family. He is called "Cuss" because he can swear in fourteen languages. His brothers become involved in a murder and must flee the town, leaving Cuss to choose between difficult options.

2183. Friedrich, Elizabeth. *Leah's Pony.* Illustrated by Michael Garland. Boyds Mills, 1996. 32pp. ISBN 978-1-56397-189-1; 1999, paper ISBN 978-1-56397-828-9. Grades 1–4. During the Great Depression of the 1930s, Leah and her family live in the midwestern Dust Bowl, where drought and grasshoppers are killing the crops. When her family's farm is to be auctioned off, she decides to sell her beloved pony in hopes of getting enough money to buy her father's tractor for him. Her bid of one dollar stands at the auction, and inspires others to bid ridiculously low prices and then returning the items to the family. The next day, Leah finds her pony back in the barn.

2184. Fuqua, Jonathon Scott. *Darby.* Candlewick, 2002. 256pp. ISBN 978-0-7636-1417-1; 2006, paper ISBN 978-0-7636-2290-9. Grades 4–7. In 1926 wealthy white 9-year-old Darby Carmichael makes friends Evette Robinson, an African American girl who lives in the tenant house on Darby's family's property in Marlboro, South Carolina. Evette likes to write, and she inspires Darby; together they write for the *Bennettsville Times*. Eventually Darby, with Evette's editing, begins to write thoughtful pieces. Then Darby becomes upset when no one does anything about a black sharecropper's son being beaten to death for stealing a chicken. Darby writes a story about civil rights that ignites the KKK.

2185. Gonzalez, Lucia. *The Storyteller's Candle.*   Illustrated by Lulu Delacre. Children's, 2008. 32pp. ISBN 978-0-8923-9222-3. Grades K–4.   In 1929 Hildamar, a Puerto Rican who has been in the country only a few months, and her cousin Santiago want to go to the library in Manhattan's El Barrio. Titi Maria tells them that no one at the library speaks Spanish. But librarian Pura Belpré visits their school class and speaks Spanish. She invites them all to the library and has a Three Kings celebration for them on January 6, 1930, with sweets, music, and a Puerto Rican story. Oil-and-collage illustrations enliven the text.

2186. Gutman, Dan. *Babe Ruth and the Ice Cream Mess.*   (Childhood of Famous Americans) Aladdin, 2004. 31pp. Paper ISBN 978-0-689-85529-0. Grades K–2.   As a 7-year-old George "Babe" Ruth (1895–1948) loses the only baseball in the neighborhood by hitting it through someone's window. He then grabs a dollar off the bar of his family's tavern and runs to buy everyone a rare ice-cream treat. He is accused of stealing the dollar. Photographs complement the text. Chronology.

2187. Gutman, Dan. *Shoeless Joe and Me: A Baseball Card Adventure.*   Trophy, 2003. 144pp. Paper ISBN 978-0-06-447259-3. Grades 4–7.   A baseball card propels 13-year-old Joe Stoshack back to the time of Shoeless Joe Jackson (1888–1951), who tries to prevent some of the players from "fixing" the World Series. Shoeless Joe is wrongly accused, and Stosh wants to make things right in 1919. He spends the night with Jackson and his wife, overhears crooks plotting the fix, and meets long-dead personalities who died during the flu epidemic. *Battle of the Books* (New Jersey) nomination.

2188. Hale, Marian. *The Truth About Sparrows.*   Henry Holt, 2004. 256pp. ISBN 978-0-8050-7584-7; Square Fish, 2007, paper ISBN 978-0-312-37133-3. Grades 5–9.   Twelve-year-old Sadie Winn and her family leave Missouri in 1933 because her father cannot make money farming. They go to the gulf coast of Texas near the Arkansas Pass Seawall, where her father, with his polio-withered leg, begins fishing. They live on a houseboat, and Sadie works in a cannery cleaning shrimp. She misses her best friend, but she learns that others are even less fortunate than she. *Booklist Editor's Choice, Young Reader's Award* (Arizona) nomination, *Children's Book Award* (Georgia) nomination, *Young Hoosier Book Award* (Indiana) nomination, *Young Readers Choice Book Award* (Louisiana) nomination, *Mark Twain Book Award* (Missouri) nomination, *Golden Sower Award* (Nebraska) nomination, and *Prairie Pasque Book Award* (South Dakota) nomination.

2189. Hall, Bruce Edward. *Henry and the Kite Dragon.*   Illustrated by William Low. Penguin, 2004. 32pp. ISBN 978-0-399-23727-0. Grades K–4.   Henry Chu helps his friend Grandfather Chin make beautiful kites in New York City in the 1920s. When Tony Guglione and his friends from Little Italy throw rocks at the one with the butterfly chasing a pigeon, Henry becomes distressed. Finally, Henry and his friends from Chinatown retaliate. Then they discover that Tony and his friends raise homing pigeons, and the kites frighten the birds. The two groups compromise by deciding to fly the kites in the morning so that the birds can fly in the afternoon. This story is based on a real event. Illustrations enhance the text. *Jane Addams Children's Book Award* nomination, *Children's Book Award* (North Carolina) nomination, and *Show Me Readers Award* nomination.

2190. Harlow, Joan Hiatt. *Blown Away.*   Margaret K. McElderry, 2007. 258pp. ISBN 978-1-4169-0781-7. Grades 4–8.   Jake, 13, lives in the Florida key of Matacume in 1935. He becomes friends with Mara, a new girl in town who babysits for his sister Star while he works for a fishing guide. Star contracts encephalitis about the same time as a hurricane is forecast. The Labor Day storm, a "Storm of the Century," destroys their homes, and the family struggles to help Star overcome her illness.

2191. Harlow, Joan Hiatt. *Joshua's Song.*   Aladdin, 2003. 192pp. Paper ISBN 978-0-689-85542-9. Grades 5–8.   Thirteen-year-old Joshua Harper faces challenges. His father died in the 1918 influenza pandemic. Joshua's voice has begun to change and he has to stop singing in the Boston Boys' Choir. He gets a job as a newsboy, and his mother takes in boarders. When a tanker of molasses explodes in Boston's North End, twenty-one people die. Joshua helps the survivors, and his "voice" returns. *Nutmeg Children's Book Award* (Connecticut) nomination, *William Allen White Children's Book Awards* (Kansas), *Battle of the Books Children's Book*

Award (New Mexico) nomination, *Young Reader Award* (Nevada) nomination, and *Children's Book Award* (Rhode Island) nomination.

2192. Harper, Jo. *Finding Daddy: A Story of the Great Depression.* Illustrated by Ron Mazellan. Turtle, 2005. 42pp. ISBN 978-1-8905-1531-7. Grades K–4. After a neighbor makes fun of Bonnie's father for being out of work during the Depression, he leaves Bonnie and her mother to look for work. Bonnie loves to sing with him at home but gets nervous when she sings in public. When she hears that her father might be at the nearby port, she takes a chance and skips school. On the way, she stops at a restaurant and sings for pennies. This small success tells her she might have a way to earn money for the family herself. When he comes home, she wants to sing "Happy Days Are Here Again."

2193. Harris, Carol Flynn. *A Place for Joey.* Boyds Mills, 2001. 90pp. ISBN 978-1-56397-108-2; 2004, paper ISBN 978-1-59078-284-2. Grades 4–8. In 1919 Joey Calabro's Italian immigrant family wants to move to the country and buy a farm. But 12-year-old Joey is determined to stay in Boston and starts looking for a job. On the day of the Great Molasses Flood he saves the life of the Irish policeman who has tried to stop him from skipping school. Joey realizes that he can go with his family and one day return to Boston as a policeman.

2194. Hathaway, Barbara. *Missy Violet and Me.* Houghton, 2004. 100pp. ISBN 978-0-618-37163-1; 2008, paper ISBN 978-0-618-80919-6. Grades 3–6. Eleven-year-old Viney works with Missy Violet, the local midwife, "catchin' babies" during the 1930s in the rural South. The fact that babies do not arrive in big black bags surprises Viney. In short episodic chapters Viney learns about healing herbs, dealing with the old, and coping with adventurous characters. Illustrations augment the text. *Coretta Scott King Award.*

2195. Henson, Heather. *Angel Coming.* Illustrated by Susan Gaber. Atheneum, 2005. 40pp. ISBN 978-0-689-85531-3. Grades K–3. A young girl and her pregnant mother prepare for the new baby's arrival and the girl watches for the angel on horseback she believes will arrive with the baby in a saddlebag. Leaving the house one day to go up the mountain, the girl returns to finds a tall lady there and her mother holding the baby. An author's note explains that the Frontier Nursing Service to help in childbirth began in 1925. Illustrations complement the text.

2196. Henson, Heather. *That Book Woman.* Illustrated by David Small. Atheneum, 2008. Unpaged. ISBN 978-1-4169-0812-8. Grades 2–5. In the 1930s, the Book Woman rides her horse high into the Appalachian mountains to bring books to the family. Although Cal's sister, Lark, loves to read, he cannot be bothered. Then the Book Woman arrives in the middle of a snowstorm, and her bravery impresses Cal so much that he thinks that reading must be an important thing to do. He gets Lark to teach him. The Book Woman was part of a WPA program founded to take books to remote areas during the Depression. Ink, watercolor, and pastel illustrations embellish the text.

2197. Hesse, Karen. *Out of the Dust.* Scholastic, 1997. 227pp. ISBN 978-0-590-36080-7. Grades 5–9. In a series of poems, 15-year-old Billie Jo describes the hardships of life on their Oklahoma wheat farm during the Dust Bowl years. Her father refuses to plant anything other than wheat, and the winds and dust destroy crop after crop. Billie Jo gets some solace from playing the piano, but her mother dies after mistaking a bucket of kerosene for water and her adolescent sister has terribly burned hands. She tries to escape but realizes that what she already has is better than nothing. *Newbery Medal, Charlie May Simon Book Awards* (Arkansas), *William Allen White Children's Book Awards* (Kansas), *Bluegrass Awards* (Kentucky), *Student Book Award* (Maine) nomination, *Readers Choice Awards* (Michigan), *Mark Twain Book Awards* (Missouri), *Great Stone Face Book Awards* (New Hampshire), *Garden State Children's Book Award* (New Jersey), *Buckeye Children's Book Awards* (Ohio), *Young Readers Choice Books* (Pennsylvania), *Scott O'Dell Award for Historical Fiction, Volunteer State Book Awards* (Tennessee), *State Reading Association for Young Readers* (Virginia), *Dorothy Canfield Fisher Children's Book Awards* (Vermont), *Golden Archer Book Awards* (Wisconsin), *Capitol Choices Noteworthy Titles* (Washington, D.C.), and *Battle of the Books Award* (Wisconsin) nomination.

2198. Hesse, Karen. *Spuds.* Illustrated by Wendy Watson. Scholastic, 2008. Unpaged. ISBN 978-0-439-87993-4. Grades 1–4. Three siblings—Jack (the narrator and the middle child), Maybelle, and young Eddie—head for Mr. Kenney's fields as dark falls. They have waited for their mother to leave for her night job, and they plan to gather potatoes left after the harvest. When they get home, they discover they have collected mostly stones, and their angry mother makes them return to Mr. Kenney. Mr. Kenney says he's pleased to have the stones removed from his field and he allows them to keep the few potatoes for their Depression-era table. Illustrations enhance the text.

2199. **Hesse, Karen. *Witness.*** Scholastic, 2001. 176pp. ISBN 978-0-439-27199-8; 2003, paper ISBN 978-0-439-27200-1. Grades 5–9. In a series of free verse poems, Hesse looks at the reactions of eleven people in a small Vermont town in 1924 to an incursion by the Ku Klux Klan. Among the characters are two children new to the town, 12-year-old African American Leonora Sutter and 6-year-old Jewish Esther Hirsh. *School Library Journal Best Books for Children.*

2200. **Heyes, Eileen. *O'Dwyer and Grady Starring in Acting Innocent.*** Aladdin, 2003. 128pp. Paper ISBN 978-0-689-84920-6. Grades 4–6. In 1932 New York City child actor Billy O'Dwyer is making a new movie with Roscoe "Chubby" Muldoon when he learns that police have arrested Chubby for murdering actress Amelia St. Augustine. He and his co-star, Virginia Grady, team up to find the real murderer and clear Chubby. They must function in a world of Depression, Prohibition, and the advent of the "talkies."

2201. **Hoberman, Mary Ann. *Strawberry Hill.*** Illustrated by Wendy Anderson Halperin. Little, Brown, 2009. 230pp. ISBN 978-0-316-04136-2; 2010, paper ISBN 978-0-316-04135-5. Grades 3–5. Allie Sherman, 10, moves with her Jewish parents from New Haven to Stamford, Connecticut, during the Great Depression. Although unhappy about the change, Allie delights in her new address, 12 Strawberry Hill, and looks forward to strawberries. There are none, but she finds possible friends in wealthy, Catholic Martha next door and overweight, sad Mimi across the street. Martha's friend, Cynthia, makes an anti-Semitic comment to Allie, and Allie wonders if she can be friends with someone who condones Cynthia's behavior. Mimi, however, needs Allie's academic help and her support. Thus Allie learns during fourth grade that all people are complex, and one must make choices. Drawings enhance the story. *Sydney Taylor Book Award* Notable Book.

2202. **Hopkinson, Deborah. *Sky Boys: How They Built the Empire State Building.*** Illustrated by James E. Ransome. Schwartz & Wade, 2006. 32pp. ISBN 978-0-375-83610-7. Grades K–4. A young boy and his unemployed father watch the construction of the Empire State Building during the year and forty-five days that it takes, beginning in 1931. The free verse text complements oil paintings that show the growth of the building and the dizzying downward views. *Boston Globe/Horn Book Award Honor.*

2203. **Horvath, Polly. *The Happy Yellow Car.*** Sunburst, 2004. 150pp. Paper ISBN 978-0-374-42879-2. Grades 4–7. In 1930s Missouri, Betty Grunt, 12, does not have the dollar she needs for flowers so she can be crowned Pork-Fry Queen of her sixth-grade class. A story that grandma hid money leads Betty and her brothers on a big search. When her father comes home with a yellow car, actually purchased with money Mrs. Grunt had saved for Betty's college fund, everyone wonders how he will pay for gas. The family's antics and positive attitudes reveal that people can be happy even without money.

2204. **Houston, Gloria. *The Year of the Perfect Christmas Tree.*** Illustrated by Barbara Cooney. Dial, 1988. 32pp. ISBN 978-0-8037-0299-8; Puffin, 1996, paper ISBN 978-0-14-055877-7. Grades K–3. Ruthie's father leaves Appalachia for World War I in the spring of 1918, but before he goes he and Ruthie pick out a Christmas tree. When he has not returned by Christmas Eve, Ruthie and her mother cut the tree down and take it to the church for the pageant. Ruthie has a part as an angel, but the best aspect of the evening is that her father arrives just before the celebration begins. *Picture Book Awards* (Georgia) nomination, *Children's Book Awards* (North Carolina) nomination, *Children's Book Awards* (South Carolina) nomination, and *Bluebonnet Awards* (Texas) nomination.

2205. **Hurst, Carol Otis. *You Come to Yokum.*** Illustrated by Kay Life. Walter Lorraine, 2005. 144pp. ISBN 978-0-618-55122-4. Grades 3–6. Twelve-year-old Frank Carlyle and his family live on a Massachusetts farm until 1920 when Frank's father decides to move them to

Yokum, a vacation lodge that he plans to manage. Frank's suffragist mother drives the family car to Washington, D.C., and chains herself to the White House fence. Back at the lodge, she tries—despite her husband's disapproval—to recruit the farm women of the area to suffragism. At the same time, the family strives to make visits to Yokum enjoyable for guests in the face of many challenges.

2206. **Jackson, Alison.** *Rainmaker.* Boyds Mills, 2005. 176pp. ISBN 978-1-59078-309-2. Grades 5–9. In 1939, 13-year-old Pidge hopes Miss Millie Boze, the famous elderly rainmaker brought from Oxford, Mississippi, to Frostfree, Florida, can stop the drought so that her family will not lose its orange farm. The town pays Miss Millie a lot and is upset when all she does is sit on a quilt, read the paper, and eat strawberries. Miss Millie explains that she does not make rain—it just seems to follow her. But Pidge needs more than rain. She also wants her brother Jack to stay out of trouble; she needs to understand why her mother died; and she hopes her father won't marry the pretty church organist. After Miss Millie leaves, the rain starts, and Pidge has to confront her strong emotions.

2207. **Kennedy, Fran.** *The Pickle Patch Bathtub.* Tricycle, 2004. 32pp. ISBN 978-1-58246-112-0. Grades 1–5. In 1925 Donna and her siblings have outgrown the washtub but the family cannot afford to pay Sears, Roebuck the $10.75 required to deliver a bathtub. They decide to grow cucumbers from seeds for the local pickle factory. They earn all but 10 cents of what they need, and one of the children contributes his Christmas dime. The tub arrives and they install it. Illustrations complement the text.

2208. **Kinsey-Warnock, Natalie.** *A Doctor Like Papa.* HarperCollins, 2002. 80pp. ISBN 978-0-06-029319-2. Grades 2–4. Eleven-year-old Margaret has always wanted to be a doctor, but when the influenza epidemic comes to Vermont in 1918 she has to reconsider. The profession is much more serious than she realized. She has watched her father work, and she uses her knowledge to save her brother, herself, and another young girl. At the same time she worries about her Uncle Owen, who has been declared missing in France. *Beverly Cleary Children's Choice Book Award* (Oregon) nomination.

2209. **Kinsey-Warnock, Natalie.** *The Night the Bells Rang.* Illustrated by Leslie W. Bowman. Puffin, 2000. 64pp. Paper ISBN 978-0-14-130986-6. Grades 4 up. In 1918 Vermont, Mason tries to avoid Aden, a big boy who knocks him down and fills his hat with snow. But Aden also helps Mason retrieve a drawing that he made for his father. Mason therefore has mixed feelings when Aden enlists. His feelings change to sadness when he hears that Aden has died. As the bells ring to signal the end of the war, Mason knows that his attitude has changed toward Aden and toward others who have annoyed him, including his younger brother.

2210. **Kirk, Daniel.** *Breakfast at the Liberty Diner.* Hyperion, 1997. 23pp. ISBN 978-0-7868-0303-3. Grades K–3. One morning in 1939, Bobby Potter, his mother, and his baby brother George go to the Liberty Diner, which is located in a railcar. They plan to meet Uncle Angelo, who works at Lucky's 24-Hour Garage, and Bobby is especially excited because he has not left home since contracting polio. After their food and drinks are served, President Franklin Delano Roosevelt arrives. Roosevelt sees Bobby's leg brace and realized he also is a polio victim. He inspires Bobby to think he can overcome his physical disabilities as well. *Young Reader's Award* (Arizona) nomination.

2211. **Koch, Ed, and Pat Koch Thaler.** *Eddie: Harold's Little Brother.* Illustrated by M. Sarah Klise. Putnam, 2004. 32pp. ISBN 978-0-399-24310-3. Grades K–3. Eddie aspires to be an accomplished athlete like his brother Harold. But he lacks the requisite skills, and it takes Harold's insight to convince Eddie of his real talent—talking. This story is based on the childhood of the authors, former New York City mayor Ed Koch and his sister.

2212. **Koch, Ed, and Pat Koch Thaler.** *Eddie's Little Sister Makes a Splash.* Illustrated by James Warhola. Putnam, 2007. 32pp. ISBN 978-0-399-24310-3. Grades K–3. In the 1930s, 5-year-old Patty, her older brother Eddie, and their parents head to a nearby lake for two weeks. Patty wants to play with her brother, but he seems impatient with her. When she hears voices nearby, Patty ventures to the lake alone and loses her footing. Eddie is able to rescue her before anything happens. Watercolor illustrations evoke the childhood fun of an earlier time.

2213. Koller, Jackie French. *Nothing to Fear.* Gulliver, 1993. 279pp. Paper ISBN 978-0-15-257582-3. Grades 5–7. Danny worries about his pregnant mother and his father, who left their Manhattan home in 1932 to seek work. When his mother goes to the hospital in a coma, Danny finds a letter saying that his father died on the rails four months earlier. Another victim of the Depression, whom they have nursed back to health, helps them in turn, and Danny's mother decides she will marry him. *IRA Young Adults' Choices.*

2214. Kroeger, Mary Kay, and Louise Borden. *Paperboy.* Illustrated by Ted Lewin. Clarion, 1996. 34pp. ISBN 978-0-395-64482-9; 2001, paper ISBN 978-0-618-11142-8. Grades K–3. Willie Brinkman likes delivering the Cincinnati, Ohio, *Times-Star* newspaper in 1927 and is pleased to bring home his pay for his family. He wants to be the first to shout that Jack Dempsey has beat Gene Tunney in the upcoming fight, but when Dempsey loses, Willie must adjust.

2215. LaFaye, A. *The Strength of Saints.* Aladdin, 2007. 183pp. Paper ISBN 978-1-4169-5869-7. Grades 5–8. In 1936, 14-year-old Nissa Bergen needs support from her independent mother, Heirah; her father, Ivar; her stepmother, and others in Harper, Louisiana, when she stands against racial prejudice. She creates two separate but equal libraries in the same space for African Americans and whites, and when a new cannery comes to town, she checks out books from a bookmobile in front of the cannery to everyone, regardless of color. Her actions start a riot that she has to quell. *Volunteer State Book Award* (Tennessee) nomination.

2216. LaFaye, A. *The Year of the Sawdust Man.* Milkweed, 2008. 220pp. Paper ISBN 978-1-57131-679-0. Grades 5–8. In Harper, Louisiana, in 1934, 11-year-old Nissa comes home one day to find her mother, Heirah, is gone. Heirah, normally high-spirited even in the face of small-town life, was despondent after losing three babies. Nissa's father, Ivar, begins to date another woman and Nissa has trouble coping. Her mother eventually returns for a while to reconnect with Nissa and helps her accept her father's planned remarriage.

2217. Lawrence, Iain. *The Séance.* Delacorte, 2008. 272pp. ISBN 978-0-385-73375-5. Grades 5–8. Scooter King, 13, helps with his mother's séances in New York in the mid-1920s. Houdini arrives, trying to expose false mediums. Houdini himself uses some of the same tricks known to Scooter's mother making his own magic. Murder ensues and Scooter and Houdini investigate.

2218. Levine, Gail Carson. *Dave at Night.* Trophy, 2001. 281pp. Paper ISBN 978-0-06-440747-2. Grades 5–9. In 1926, 11-year-old Dave has to go to the Hebrew Home for Boys in Harlem after his father dies and his mother no longer wants him. There he loses all his possessions including a lovely carving of Noah's Ark that his father made for him. He wants to run away, but he will not go without his ark. He sneaks out one night and meets Solly, a "fortune teller" who takes him to a rent party where he encounters the wealthy Irma Lee. Her mother holds salons for the artists, musicians, and writers of the Harlem Renaissance. There Dave discovers a world of wonder that helps him cope with the realities of his life. *Nutmeg Children's Book Award* (Connecticut) nomination, *Rebecca Caudill Award* (Illinois) nomination, *Mark Twain Award* (Missouri) nomination, *Great Stone Face Book Award* (New Hampshire) nomination, *Young Readers Choice Book Award* (Pennsylvania) nomination, *Publishers Weekly's Best Books, SCASL Book Award* (South Carolina) nomination, *Volunteer State Book Award* (Tennessee) nomination, *Young Reader Book Award* (Virginia) nomination, *Dorothy Canfield Fisher Children's Book Award* (Vermont) nomination, *Capitol Choices Noteworthy Titles* (Washington, D.C.), *School Library Journal Best Books for Children*, and *Sasquatch Book Awards* (Washington).

2219. Levine, Kristin. *The Best Bad Luck I Ever Had.* Putnam, 2009. 266pp. ISBN 978-0-399-25090-3; Puffin, 2010, paper ISBN 978-0-14-241648-8. Grades 5–9. In 1917 the new postmaster in Moundville, Alabama, is African American. This surprises 12-year-old Dit enough, but he was also expecting that Mr. Walker to bring a son. He shows up, however, with a daughter, Emma, also 12, who likes books and the piano. Dit wants a companion with whom he can fish and climb. Emma agrees to learn these things and Dit considers reading books. Her family's conversations make him see the Civil War's results differently and persuade him that the South's prejudices should change. The two young people work together to save an African American barber from hanging after he shot the racist sheriff in self-defense. *American Library Association Best Books for Young Adults* and *State Reading Association for Young Readers Program* (Virginia) nomination.

2220. Lied, Kate. *Potato: A Tale from the Great Depression.* Illustrated by Lisa Campbell Ernst. National Geographic, 2002. Unpaged. Paper ISBN 978-0-7922-6946-5. Grades 5–8. When the author was 8, she wrote this story about her grandparents, Agnes and Clarence, during the Depression. Clarence first lost his job and then they lost their home. They found work in Idaho picking potatoes for a farmer who allowed them to gather for themselves at the end of the workday. The potatoes they gleaned in two weeks then saw them through until Clarence found another job. Watercolor illustrations enhance the text. *Horn Book Fanfare* and *Boston Globe/Horn Book Award Honor.*

2221. Lowry, Lois. *The Silent Boy.* Laurel Leaf, 2005. 208pp. Paper ISBN 978-0-440-41980-8. Grades 5–8. In the early 20th century 13-year-old Katy Thatcher's physician father hires Peggy Stoltz to work for them. Katy gets to know Peggy's brother Jacob, also 13, a boy who doesn't speak but only makes sounds. Katy discovers that he is gentle and kind. Katy does not mention the word "autistic," but Jacob mimics noises, refuses to look people in the eye, and communicates well with animals. Peggy and Jacob have a sister Nellie, who has an unwanted child. This child is found dead and Jacob is blamed, spending the rest of his life in the town's asylum. As an elderly doctor, Katy Thatcher reminisces about these events and the sympathy and understanding she felt for Jacob. *Bluegrass Award* (Kentucky) nomination, *Young Reader's Choice Award* (Pennsylvania) nomination, *Charlie May Simon Children's Book Award* (Arkansas) nomination, and *Indian Paintbrush Award* (Wyoming) nomination.

2222. Lyon, George Ella. *Borrowed Children.* Univ. of Kentucky, 1999. 154pp. Paper ISBN 978-0-8131-0972-5. Grades 5–9. Amanda, 12, the oldest in a Kentucky family suffering during the Depression, quits school to help her mother recover from a difficult childbirth. As a reward for all her work, she gets a vacation with her grandparents in Memphis. Although the Memphis family members have few financial worries, Mandy observes her alcoholic aunt's unhappy marriage and appreciates her own home, sparse as it is. *Golden Kite Award* and *School Library Journal Best Books.*

2223. Mackall, Dandi Daley. *Rudy Rides the Rails: A Depression Era Story.* Illustrated by Chris Ellison. Sleeping Bear, 2007. Unpaged. ISBN 978-1-58536-286-8. Grades 3–6. In 1932, 13-year-old Rudy is standing in a bread line with his father in Akron, Ohio, when his father tells him he has to look after himself. Rudy rides the rails to find work. Stopping to do little jobs, he makes his way to California. But it has no more to offer him than other places. However, he does learn that hoboes and many others help each other in any way they can. When he returns home, he paints the symbol for "kindness here" on his porch.

2224. McKissack, Patricia C. *The All-I'll-Ever-Want Christmas Doll.* Illustrated by Jerry Pinkney. Schwartz & Wade, 2007. 40pp. ISBN 978-0-375-83759-3. Grades K–3. During the Great Depression, African American Laura Nell Person, the middle of three sisters, sees a Baby Betty doll advertised in a newspaper. She asks Santy [sic] Claus to bring it to her. To the sisters' surprise, he does, but he brings it to all three girls. They fight over the doll and Laura wins but soon discovers that a doll is not as much fun as her sisters, and she invites them to a Baby Betty tea party. Watercolor illustrations complement the text. *American Library Association Notable Children's Books.*

2225. McKissack, Patricia C. *A Song for Harlem: Scraps of Time, 1928.* Illustrated by Gordon C. James. Viking, 2007. 96pp. ISBN 978-0-670-06209-6; 2008, paper ISBN 978-0-14-241238-1. Grades 1–4. Gee tells her three grandchildren about their great-great aunt, Lilly Belle. In 1928, when Lilly Belle was 12, she won a writing contest to study with Zora Neale Hurston in Harlem at the Dark Tower, A'Lelia Walker's famous salon. Lilly Belle left Smyrna, Tennessee, and went to stay with her Aunt Odessa during the class. One of her classmates plagiarizes a story in the magazine *Crisis* and Lilly Belle does not know how to handle the situation. She talks with Alice, the culprit, and after hearing about all the trouble the girl has at home, the two become friends. Notes.

2226. Matthews, Kezi. *Flying Lessons.* Cricket, 2002. 162pp. ISBN 978-0-8126-2671-1. Grades 5–8. In 1937, 13-year-old LaMarr is living with her aunt and uncle, waiting to hear about her mother, who was last seen taking off with a stunt pilot in a plane that then disappeared over the ocean. LaMarr wants to believe that her mother has gone to Hollywood and that she will call any day. A motley crowd of characters surrounds her as she comes to terms with reality when the Hindenburg explodes and Amelia Earhart disappears.

2227. Meltzer, Milton. *Tough Times.* Clarion, 2007. 168pp. ISBN 978-0-618-87445-3. Grades 5–8. In Worcester, Massachusetts, in 1932 Joey Singer struggles to earn money. He has a milk route; his father washes windows. Then his girlfriend's father, a journalist, reports on the awful conditions in the surrounding mill towns and loses his job. Joey and his father—along with his classmate Hank and Hank's father—go to Washington, D.C., to join in the Bonus March, during which veterans of World War I demand the bonuses they were promised in 1924. Instead of money, Herbert Hoover sends federal troops with tanks, machine guns, tear gas, and cavalry. The event traumatizes Joey, and he ends up riding the rails as a hobo. Note.

2228. Michelson, Richard. *Happy Feet: The Savoy Ballroom Lindy Hoppers and Me.* Illustrated by E. B. Lewis. Gulliver, 2005. 32pp. ISBN 978-0-15-205057-3. Grades K–4. In the mid-1930s Happy Feet, a boy who loves music and dance, sits with his father in Pop's Shoeshine Shop in Harlem and hears the story of his birth on March 12, 1926, the night that the Savoy Ballroom opened across the street. Happy Feet's father and mother danced there until his mother needed to go home for Happy Feet's birth. Watercolor illustrations reinforce the text.

2229. Miller, William. *Joe Louis, My Champion.* Illustrated by Rodney S. Pate. Lee & Low, 2003. Unpaged. ISBN 978-1-58430-161-5. Grades K–4. In 1937 African American Sammy hears a radio broadcast of one of the fights of Joe Louis (1914–1981) and is inspired. Sammy takes boxing lessons from a friend. When he is discouraged, his family helps him to understand that he does not have to be as great as Louis. If he works hard, he can overcome racial prejudice and be a champion in whatever field he chooses. Oil paintings enhance the text.

2230. Miller, William. *Rent Party Jazz.* Illustrated by Charlotte Riley Webb. Lee & Low, 2001. 32pp. ISBN 978-1-58430-025-0; 2008, paper ISBN 978-1-600-60344-0. Grades 1–4. When Sonny Comeaux's mother loses her job during the Depression, Sonny wants to quit school and go to work. His mother refuses to allow him to stop learning. Sonny meets Smiling' Jack, a jazz musician who is visiting New Orleans from Mississippi, and the man tells him how to have a "rent party." Sonny has the party, and the man plays for him. They get enough money to pay their rent without Sonny working. Acrylic illustrations enhance the text.

2231. Miller, William. *Richard Wright and the Library Card.* Illustrated by Gregory R. Christie. Lee & Low, 1997. 32pp. ISBN 978-1-880000-57-1; 1999, paper ISBN 978-1-880000-88-5. Grades K–4. Richard Wright, 17, lives in Memphis, Tennessee, during the 1920s and cannot borrow books from the segregated library because he is African American. Wright circumvents the problem by convincing his white co-worker, Jim Falk, to lend him his library card. Then Wright pretends to be borrowing books for Falk and reads these books secretly at night. Wright reads about whites who have also suffered—Charles Dickens, Leo Tolstoy, and Stephen Crane. Impressionistic illustrations augment the text. *Emphasis on Reading Award* and *Young Reader's Choice Award* (Pennsylvania) nomination.

2232. Mitchell, Margaree King. *Uncle Jed's Barbershop.* Illustrated by James Ransome. Simon & Schuster, 1993. 34pp. ISBN 978-0-671-76969-7; Aladdin, 1998, paper ISBN 978-0-689-81913-1. Grades 3–6. The only black barber in his county of the segregated South during the 1920s, 5-year-old Sarah Jean's Uncle Jed has to travel around to cut people's hair. He wants to open his own barbershop and is saving money for it. When Sarah Jean needs an emergency operation, he gives his money to the doctor. When the Depression comes, he loses his money in a bank failure. Finally he opens his shop when he is 79 years old; the adult Sarah Jean gets to twirl around in his new barber's chair. *Coretta Scott King Honor Book.*

2233. Muse, Daphne. *The Entrance Place of Wonders: Poems of the Harlem Renaissance.* Illustrated by Charlotte Riley Webb. Abrams, 2006. 32pp. ISBN 978-0-8109-5997-2. Grades 2–6. Harlem Renaissance poets such as Langston Hughes, Countee Cullen, Claude McKay, James Weldon Johnson, Effie Lee Newsome, Dorothy Vena Johnson, and Gladys May Caseley-Hayford composed the twenty poems included here. Among the topics are the difficulties of city life, the attempt to escape problems in the city, what it means to be black, and racism. Colorful illustrations enhance the text.

2234. Noble, Trinka Hakes. *The Orange Shoes.* Illustrated by Doris Ettlinger. Sleeping Bear, 2007. 40pp. ISBN 978-1-585-36277-6. Grades 1–4. During the Depression, Delly Porter's one-room school is having a shoebox social to raise money for art supplies. Delly has no shoes to wear so she can show them under a curtain when her box is displayed as a hint to who decorated the box. Her father needs tires, but he buys her orange shoes. Mean girls at school scuff them during recess. She then paints flowers on them and on her shoebox. At the social, someone special buys her box—her father.

2235. Nuzum, K. A. *A Small White Scar.* Joanna Cotler, 2006. 180pp. ISBN 978-0-06-075639-0. Grades 5–8. In Colorado in 1940, 15-year-old Will Bennon decides to become a cowboy and leaves home to escape the burden of caring for his mentally retarded twin brother, Denny. Since their mother's death seven years before, Will has been Denny's caregiver. Denny, however, follows him when he leaves. As they follow the rodeo circuit, with Will finally doing the riding he has always desired, he begins to understand how important Denny is to him. *Dorothy Canfield Fisher Award* (Vermont), *Great Stone Face Award* (New Hampshire), and *Booklist Editor's Choice.*

2236. O'Connor, Sandra Day. *Chico: A True Story from the Childhood of the First Woman Supreme Court Justice.* Illustrated by Dan Andreasen. Dutton, 2005. 32pp. ISBN 978-0-525-47452-4. Grades K–3. One day in the 1930s, 6-year-old Sandra encounters a rattlesnake while riding her horse Chico on the family ranch. Chico jumps and almost throws her off his back. He then takes her home. Sandra still wants to see the newborn calf she was on her way to visit, and when her father offers to take her, she decides that the snake will be gone and agrees. Illustrations enhance the text.

2237. Oneal, Zibby. *A Long Way to Go.* Illustrated by Michael Dooling. Puffin, 1992. 64pp. Paper ISBN 978-0-14-032950-6. Grades 2–6. In 1917, 10-year-old Lila does not understand why she can't vote when her brother can—she is smarter than he is. She sees her grandmother go to jail after picketing for women's suffrage in Washington, and Lila begins to notice how laws prohibit women from doing many things. She disagrees with the laws and tells her father he should not oppose letting women vote.

2238. Peck, Richard. *A Long Way from Chicago: A Novel in Stories.* Dial, 1998. 148pp. ISBN 978-0-8037-2290-3; Puffin, 2004, paper ISBN 978-0-14-240110-1. Grades 4–8. From 1929 when Joey is 9 years old until 1935, he and his younger sister Mary take a train from Chicago each summer to spend a week with their Grandma Dowdel in a small Illinois town. Her behavior—helping herself illegally to boats and fish, which she then cooks for hungry drifters, for example—constantly amazes them. She refuses to follow rules that hurt others—bank foreclosures, Prohibition, and other silly decisions. Joey remembers her antics as his troop train passes through the town in 1942. *Capitol Choices Noteworthy Titles* (Washington, D.C.), *School Librarians' Battle of the Books* (Alaska) nomination, *Young Reader's Award* (Arizona) nomination, *American Library Association Best Books for Young Adults, Nutmeg Children's Book Award* (Connecticut) nomination, *Sunshine State Young Reader Award* (Florida) nomination, *Nene Award* (Hawaii) nomination, *Children's Choice Book Award* (Iowa) nomination, *Young Hoosier Award* (Indiana) nomination, *William Allen White Award* (Kansas) nomination, *Bluegrass Award* (Kentucky) nomination, *Black-Eyed Susan Book Award* (Maryland) nomination, *Student Book Award* (Maine) nomination, *Mark Twain Award* (Missouri) nomination, *National Book Awards, Newbery Honor Book, Flicker Tales* (North Dakota) nomination, *Battle of the Books* (New Jersey) nomination, *Battle of the Books* (New Mexico) nomination, *Sequoyah Book Award* (Oklahoma) nomination, *Young Readers Choice Book Award* (Pennsylvania) nomination, *Pacific Northwest Young Reader's Choice Book Award* nomination. *Children's Book Award* (Rhode Island), *Children's Book Award* (South Carolina) nomination, *Junior Book Award* (South Carolina) nomination, *Volunteer State Book Award* (Tennessee) nomination, *Beehive Young Adult Book Award* (Utah) nomination, *Dorothy Canfield Fisher Children's Book Award* (Vermont) nomination, *Battle of the Books Award* (Wisconsin) nomination, *Golden Archer Books Award* (Wisconsin) nomination, and *Hornbook Fanfare.*

2239. Peck, Richard. *A Year Down Yonder.*   Dial, 2000. 130pp. ISBN 978-0-8037-2518-8; Puffin, 2002, paper ISBN 978-0-14-230070-1. Grades 5–8. In 1937, 15-year-old Mary Alice reluctantly leaves Chicago to live with her grandmother in rural Illinois. Her grandmother is eccentric, opinionated, and difficult to confront. But Mary Alice recognizes that she is kind and generous in unexpected ways. *Nene Award* (Hawaii) nomination, *Newbery Honor Book*, *Dorothy Canfield Fisher Children's Book Award* (Vermont) nomination, *Rebecca Caudill Award* (Illinois) nomination, *Bluegrass Award* (Kentucky) nomination, *Student Book Award* (Maine) nomination, *Flicker Tales* (North Dakota) nomination, *Buckeye Children's Book Awards* (Ohio), *Volunteer State Book Award* (Tennessee) nomination, *Battle of the Books Award* (Wisconsin) nomination, *School Library Journal Best Books for Children*, and *Capitol Choices Noteworthy Titles* (Washington, D.C.).

2240. Peterson, Jeanne Whitehouse. *Don't Forget Winona.*   Illustrated by Kimberly Bulcken Root. Joanna Cotler, 2004. ISBN 978-0-06-027197-8. Grades K–3. Sarah and her family travel west from Oklahoma in 1937 along Route 66. Her little sister Winona worries about being left behind each time the family stops, and she yells "Don't forget me!" Although the family faces hardships, their concern for each other helps them survive the Dust Bowl and face their new lives picking oranges in the winter and strawberries in spring. Illustrations complement the text.

2241. Polacco, Patricia. *John Philip Duck.*   Philomel, 2004. 40pp. ISBN 978-0-399-24262-5. Grades K–2. During the Depression, Edward stays at the Peabody Hotel in Memphis with his Dad during the week. His father is working there, away from their farm. Edward's father allows him to keep his duck in the hotel even though this is against the rules. Edward teaches the duck to march to John Philip Sousa music. Eventually, the hotel manager, strict Mr. Schutt, discovers the duck. But when he sees the duck's talent, he asks Edward to train a group of ducks as marching tourist attractions. Edward becomes the hotel's official "Duckmaster," a position that the real Edward Pembroke held for fifty years. *Diamond Primary Book Award* (Arkansas) nomination, *Young Hoosier Book Award* (Indiana) nomination, *Show Me State Book Award* (Missouri) nomination, and *Volunteer State Book Award* (Tennessee) nomination.

2242. Ray, Delia. *Ghost Girl: A Blue Ridge Mountain Story.*   Clarion, 2003. 224pp. ISBN 978-0-618-33377-6. Grades 5–9. Called "ghost girl" because she has white-blonde hair and blue eyes, April, 11, looks forward to attending the new school that President and Mrs. Hoover have built in Madison County, Virginia, during the Depression. However, April's mother continues to mourn the death of April's young brother Riley and refuses to let her go. Finally her grandmother and the teacher, Miss Vest, convince her mother. Then April reveals that she thinks she caused Riley's accidental death while they were learning to waltz, and the family becomes estranged. April goes to live with Miss Vest for two years and learns to read using a Sears, Roebuck catalog.

2243. Reeder, Carolyn. *Grandpa's Mountain.*   Simon & Schuster, 1991. 171pp. ISBN 978-0-02-775811-5. Grades 4–6. Carrie, 11, has always enjoyed her summers with her grandparents in Virginia's Blue Ridge Mountains. But this summer during the Depression is different because the government is trying to take Grandpa's land for a national park. He fights to save it and is disappointed that so many of the neighbors gladly take the money rather than keep their land. When he fails, Carrie realizes that he has done the best he can.

2244. Reeder, Carolyn. *Moonshiner's Son.*   Aladdin, 2003. 171pp. Paper ISBN 978-0-689-85550-4. Grades 3–7. Because 12-year-old Tom wants to please his father, he tries to make the best whiskey he can even though it is illegal in 1919. A new preacher arrives and speaks out against liquor. The police arrest Tom's father. At the same time Tom sees bad behaviors caused by drunkenness. He slowly realizes that his wood carvings, which he can sell to the townsfolk, will fulfill his creative urges. His father, remorseful at having beaten his son, stops running the still.

2245. Ringgold, Faith. *Tar Beach.*   Crown, 1991. 32pp. ISBN 978-0-517-58030-1; Dragonfly, 1996, paper ISBN 978-0-517-88544-4. Grades K–3. In 1939, 8-year-old Cassie dreams of flying above New York City's George Washington Bridge. When she flies, Cassie realizes she can go anywhere and have anything she wants. In her fantasy flights over Brooklyn and Tar Beach, she also imagines that she is helping others. *Caldecott Honor; Children's Book Video and Software Award* (California), *Coretta Scott King Award, New York Times Best Illustrated Book of the Year, Parents' Choice Award, American Library Association Notable Children's Books*, and *School Library Journal Best Book*.

2246. Ryan, Pam Muñoz. *Amelia and Eleanor Go for a Ride.* Illustrated by Brian Selznick. Scholastic, 1999. 40pp. Paper ISBN 978-0-590-96075-5. Grades 1–5. On an evening in April 1933, dressed in evening gowns, Amelia Earhart and Eleanor Roosevelt disappear from a White House dinner, take an Eastern Air Transport plane, and fly to Baltimore. Then Eleanor, who has also studied for a pilot's license, treats Amelia to a ride in her fast new car. The two women delight in their moment of independence and fun away from the public eye. *Book Sense Book of the Year* nomination, *American Library Association Notable Books for Children, Black-Eyed Susan Book Award* (Maryland) nomination, *Washington Children's Choice Picture Book* nomination, *SCASL Book Award* (South Carolina) nomination, *Young Hoosier Book Award* (Indiana) nomination, *Land of Enchantment Book Award* (New Mexico) nomination, *Young Readers Award* (Nevada) nomination, *Young Readers' Choice Award* (Louisiana) nomination, *ABC Children's Booksellers Choices Award, Capitol Choices Noteworthy Titles* (Washington, D.C.), and *Readers' Choice Award* (Virginia) nomination.

2247. Schroeder, Alan. *Satchmo's Blues.* Illustrated by Floyd Cooper. Yearling, 1999. Unpaged. Paper ISBN 978-0-440-41472-8. Grades 1–4. Louis Armstrong works in any job he can find to earn the five dollars needed to buy a cornet in a pawn shop window. In Armstrong's archival autobiography, he says he bought the horn; he did not get one for free at the Colored Waif's Home for Boys in New Orleans as some people said. This fictional story traces Armstrong's quest to make music as a young boy.

2248. Schwabach, Karen. *The Hope Chest.* Random, 2008. 288pp. ISBN 978-0-375-84095-1. Grades 4–6. In 1920, 11-year-old Violet Mayhew discovers that her parents have not been giving her letters written to her by her older sister Chloe. Their parents disowned Chloe because she wanted both an education and a career and spent her dowry money on a Model T. Violet runs away to New York City to find her, meeting an African American orphan girl named Myrtle, who agrees to help her find Chloe. They go to Washington, D.C., and on to Tennessee, where Chloe is working on the Susan B. Anthony Amendment. They join her fight for women's suffrage although the women face both sexism and racism with Jim Crow laws, Prohibition, and men shell-shocked from World War I. Historical notes and Chronology.

2249. Stauffacher, Sue. *Bessie Smith and the Night Riders.* Illustrated by John Holyfield. Putnam, 2006. 32pp. ISBN 978-0-399-24237-3. Grades 2–4. One July night in 1927 Ku Klux Klan members disrupt Bessie Smith's show in Concord, North Carolina. They try to collapse the tent in which she is singing her blues songs. Emmerane, a young fan listening from outside, reports that Bessie uses her 6-foot-tall frame to threaten the Night Riders, calling them "sissies." They leave without torching the tent. Illustrations enhance the text.

2250. Sternberg, Libby. *The Case Against My Brother.* Bancroft, 2007. 224pp. ISBN 978-1-8908-6251-0. Grades 5–8. In 1922, while the Ku Klux Klan is working to make Catholic schools illegal in Portland, Oregon, 15-year-old Carl Matuski and his older brother Adam move there to live with their Uncle Pete after their mother dies. Adam starts dating a lovely, wealthy girl, and the family accuses him of stealing jewelry. When Carl starts investigating the situation, knowing that Adam is innocent, he uncovers the anti-Catholic, anti-Polish sentiment that is rife in this bigoted town.

2251. Stuchner, Joan Betty. *Josephine's Dream.* Illustrated by Chantelle Walther. Silver Leaf, 2008. Unpaged. ISBN 978-1-934393-04-8. Grades K–2. Josephine Baker (1906–1975) could not achieve her dreams in America before civil rights improved, so she went to France after spending an impoverished childhood in St. Louis. She was a dancer who wanted to see her name in lights. The French appreciated her talents, and she remained there, working in the Resistance during World War II. Afterward, she adopted twelve children who lived with her on a country estate in France. Illustrations embellish the text.

2252. Tate, Eleanora E. *Celeste's Harlem Renaissance: A Novel.* Little, Brown, 2007. 279pp. ISBN 978-0-316-52394-3; 2009, paper ISBN 978-0-316-11362-5. Grades 4–7. Celeste Lassiter Massey, 13, leaves Raleigh, North Carolina, in 1921 for Harlem and her glamorous Aunt Valentina. She discovers, however, that her aunt is not a famous singer and dancer but is in fact barely supporting herself. Celeste scrubs theater floors to earn money, but she does get to meet many of the figures of the vibrant Harlem Renaissance in a local café. Soon Celeste has to return to North Carolina to care for her Aunt Society who has had a stroke. Her experiences have made Celeste stronger, and she is well on her way to her target of becoming a doctor.

2253. Taylor, Mildred. *The Friendship.* Illustrated by Max Ginsburg. Dial, 1987. 56pp. ISBN 978-0-8037-0417-6; Puffin, 1998, paper ISBN 978-0-14-038964-7. Grades 2–6. In 1933, 9-year-old Cassie and her brothers go to the Wallace store for medicine for a neighbor even though their parents have warned them never to go there. The storekeeper once gave an old black man, Tom Bee, permission to call him by his first name because Old Tom saved his life. However, on this day onlookers shocked by Tom Bee's familiarity goad the storekeeper into action and he shoots Tom Bee in the leg. The children witness this despicable act. *Boston Globe—Horn Book Award, Coretta Scott King Award,* and *American Library Association Notable Children's Books.*

2254. Taylor, Mildred. *Roll of Thunder, Hear My Cry.* Illustrated by Jerry Pinkney. Phyllis Fogelman, 2000. 210pp. ISBN 978-0-8037-2647-5; Puffin, 2004, paper ISBN 978-0-14-240112-5. Grades 5 up. In 1933, 9-year-old Cassie Logan lives in Mississippi and goes to the school for black children, which only has old books. Her family owns land but is struggling to keep it. They face hostility from the neighboring Harlans and from the Wallaces, racists who run the local store and lead the "night riders." Mrs. Logan loses her job teaching, and the cooperative that they start leads to increased harassment. The strong love the family members have for each other helps them survive the continuing crises. *Newbery Medal* and *George C. Stone Center for Children's Books Recognition of Merit Award.*

2255. Taylor, Mildred. *Song of the Trees.* Illustrated by Max Ginsburg. Dial, 1975. 64pp. ISBN 978-0-8037-5452-2; Puffin, 2003, paper ISBN 978-0-14-250075-0. Grades 2–5. Cassie Logan, 8 years old in 1932, loves to listen to the old pines and other trees outside her window talk to each other, even though her family says she is only hearing the wind. Her father has gone to Louisiana to earn money to pay the mortgage on their land. While he is away, Mr. Anderson comes and tries to cheat Cassie's grandmother out of their trees. Mr. Logan returns and threatens the man but cannot save the trees that Anderson has already cut.

2256. Tocher, Timothy. *Bill Pennant, Babe Ruth, and Me.* Cricket, 2009. 184pp. ISBN 978-0-8126-2755-8. Grades 5–9. In 1920, 16-year-old Hank Cobb finds himself training the New York Giants' newest mascot—a Mexican wildcat named Bill Pennant. The wildcat is difficult to train and so Hank stays in New York at the field that the team shares with the Yankees while the team tours. The Yankee manager asks Hank to befriend the team's newest player— Babe Ruth.

2257. Tocher, Timothy. *Chief Sunrise, John McGraw, and Me.* Cricket, 2004. 160pp. ISBN 978-0-8126-2711-4. Grades 5–8. Hank Cobb, 15, leaves his alcoholic and abusive minor league baseball-playing father in 1919. He meets Chief Sunrise, 19, a Seminole on his way to New York to convince the Giants to give him a tryout. The two travel north, working in various jobs including playing for a girls' team. They must cope with prejudice against the Chief. They arrive in New York and the Chief wins a starting position while Hank is hired as a gofer. Hank finds out that the Chief's name is Charlie Burns and that he is actually part African American. Charlie must pretend to be Native American or he will be kicked off the team.

2258. Tripp, Valerie. *Changes for Kit: A Winter Story, 1934.* Illustrated by Walter Rane and Susan McAliley. American Girl, 2001. 70pp. ISBN 978-1-58485-027-4; paper ISBN 978-1-58485-026-7. Grades 3–5. In 1934 Kit's uncle comes to Cincinnati to live in her family's boardinghouse. He inspires her to write letters to the local newspaper asking people to support children sheltered in the soup kitchen by giving them food and clothes.

2259. Tripp, Valerie. *Happy Birthday Kit! A Spingtime Story, 1934.* Illustrated by Walter Rane and Susan McAliley. American Girl, 2001. 70pp. ISBN 978-1-58485-023-6; paper ISBN 978-1-58485-022-9. Grades 3–5. In 1934 Cincinnati, Kit understands that she will not have a birthday party—her father is out of work and money is tight. However, Aunt Millie comes to visit from Kentucky, and her thrifty ways and good ideas help Kit have a wonderful birthday. Illustrations complement the text.

2260. Tripp, Valerie. *Kit Saves the Day: A Summer Story, 1934.* Illustrated by Walter Rane and Susan McAliley. American Girl, 2001. 68pp. ISBN 978-1-58485-025-0; paper ISBN 978-1-58485-024-3. Grades 3–5. Bored with doing chores, Kit meets Will, a hobo who is helping in the family garden in exchange for food, and decides to jump on a freight train with him. Her decision quickly lands her in trouble. Illustrations complement the text.

2261. Turner, Ann. *Dust for Dinner.* Illustrated by Robert Barrett. (I Can Read) Fitzgerald, 2007. 64pp. ISBN 978-1-4242-0580-6; Trophy, 1997, paper ISBN 978-0-06-444225-1. Grades K–3. In the 1930s Jake's family survives three years of dust and drought before his father decides that they will go to California. He finally gets a job as a watchman, and the family has a home again.

2262. Van Steenwyk, Elizabeth. *First Dog Fala.* Illustrated by Michael G. Montgomery. Peachtree, 2008. Unpaged. ISBN 978-1-56145-411-2. Grades 1–5. Fala, Franklin Roosevelt's black Scottish terrier, lived with him in the White House for five years. He chased butterflies in the yard, escaped into the streets of Washington, and was a close companion to Roosevelt during World War II. Although Fala lived several years after Roosevelt died in 1945, this volume focuses on his life with Roosevelt and offers a view of the war. Oil-on-canvas illustrations complement the text.

2263. Waldman, Neil. *Say-Hey and the Babe: Two Mostly True Baseball Stories.* Holiday House, 2006. 32pp. ISBN 978-0-8234-1857-2. Grades 4–6. Babe Ruth has the entire Yankee team autograph a baseball that he then gives to a young girl who was hit by one of his balls. The ball is later lost, but in 1951 Peter, a stickball fan watching Say-Hey Willie Mays play, goes after a Spauldeen that Mays hit over seven sewers. What Peter retrieves under the sewer grate is the ball lost in 1927.

2264. Weatherford, Carole Boston. *Dear Mr. Rosenwald.* Illustrated by R. Gregory Christie. Scholastic, 2006. 32pp. ISBN 978-0-439-49522-6. Grades 2–5. In the early 1920s Julius Rosenwald, president of Sears, Roebuck, has offered a challenge grant for a school that will serve the children of sharecroppers and other poor families. Ten-year-old Ovella helps her community raise money. The land, lumber, and labor are either free or cheaply purchased and the supplies are donated from white schools. Within a year students in Ovella's community are studying in non-drafty buildings. Gouache and colored pencil illustrations augment the text. *Golden Kite Honors.*

2265. Wells, Rosemary. *Wingwalker.* Illustrated by Brian Selznick. Hyperion, 2002. 80pp. ISBN 978-0-7868-0397-2. Grades 4–7. Reuben, 7, wins an airplane ride with a stunt flyer at the 1933 Oklahoma Air Race, and he hates it. Reuben's father loses his job as a dance instructor when the dust storms hit, and he responds to an advertisement for a carnival wing walker in Minnesota. They move from Ambler, Oklahoma, to the carnival, which has a tattooed lady and a fire eater. The carnival's fat man helps Reuben overcome his fears about his father dancing on the wings of an airplane. Illustrations augment the text. *Bluebonnet Award* (Texas), *Book Award* (Oklahoma) nomination, and *Sequoyah Book Award* (Florida) nomination.

2266. Wells, Rosemary, and Tom Wells. *The House in the Mail.* Illustrated by Dan Andreasen. Viking, 2002. 32pp. ISBN 978-0-670-03545-8; Puffin, 2004, paper ISBN 978-0-14-240061-6. Grades 2–5. In 1927, 12-year-old Emily Cartwright's family orders a ready-to-assemble house from a Sears, Roebuck catalog. She keeps a scrapbook of the progress as the Kentucky family digs a hole, lays a foundation, meets the train carrying the house parts, raises the roof, and finally moves inside. For the first time they have indoor plumbing, electricity, and a bathtub. They also have a Hoosier cabinet and a "modern" icebox.

2267. Whitmore, Arvella. *The Bread Winner.*   Houghton, 2004. 138pp. Paper ISBN 978-0-618-49479-8. Grades 4–6. Sarah, 12 in 1932, goes with her parents to live in town after they sell their farm. She looks forward to a different life, but her father cannot find a job. He even goes to California in search of work. Sarah decides to sell a few loaves of bread made with an award-winning family recipe as a way to help the family. People want more than a few loaves of her bread, and her business grows until the family decides to start a bakery in their small town.

2268. Wickham, Martha. *Mysterious Journey: Amelia Earhart's Last Flight.*   Illustrated by David Lund. (Smithsonian Odyssey) Soundprints, 1997. 32pp. ISBN 978-1-56899-407-9; paper ISBN 978-1-56899-408-6. Grades 2–5. When Lucy, Tomas, Emma, and Kevin visit the National Air and Space Museum in Washington, they stop at the Amelia Earhart exhibit. They are transported to 1937 and join Earhart and her navigator, Fred Noonan, on the last part of the journey from which she did not return. They know from the map that she is very close to the end of her journey before they are whisked back to the present.

2269. Winter, Jonah. *Steel Town.*   Illustrated by Terry Widener. Atheneum, 2008. Unpaged. ISBN 978-1-4169-4081-4. Grades 2–4. In the mid-1930s steel towns—especially Pittsburgh, Pennsylvania—spewed smoke that colored the sky gray. Winter describes a day in such a town and the constant hard work, filling the furnaces with coal and producing steel at the end of the day. Illustrations complement the text. *Kirkus Reviews Editor's Choice.*

2270. Winthrop, Elizabeth. *Franklin Delano Roosevelt: Letters from a Mill Town Girl.*   (Dear Mr. President) Winslow, 2001. 128pp. ISBN 978-1-890817-61-9. Grades 4–7. The daughter of Italian immigrants, 12-year-old Emma Bartoletti quizzes her Aunt Dora about the Depression. Frustrated with all the questions, Aunt Dora suggests that Emma write President Roosevelt and ask him why no one has any money. Emma tells Roosevelt about her own family's life as textile mill workers suffering food shortages. Roosevelt explains in return that the federal government is trying to help everyone by establishing new programs including the National Recovery Act and Works Progress Administration. Their correspondence lasts until 1937, during which time the economy in the nation actually improves.

2271. Wyatt, Leslie J. *Poor Is Just a Starting Place.*   Holiday House, 2005. 196pp. ISBN 978-0-8234-1884-8. Grades 5–8. Artie Wilson, 12, wants to escape the drudgery of plowing, planting, and milking on her family's poor Kentucky farm during the Great Depression. She wants to get an education and she wants a better relationship than she sees between her often-pregnant mother, who has tuberculosis, and her often-angry father.

2272. Yee, Paul. *A Song for Ba.*   Illustrated by Jan Peng Wang. Groundwood, 2004. 32pp. ISBN 978-0-8889-9492-9. Grades 2–5. Wei Lim lives with his grandfather and father, Ba, a Chinese opera troupe singer who specializes in playing generals and leaders. Wei Lim's father does not want Wei Lim to become a singer, believing there is little future in this career in Canada. Wei Lim's grandfather, who sang women's roles, teaches him the movements, melodies, and techniques necessary for those parts. After his grandfather returns to China, Wei Lim's father needs to learn a new role in which he must be female. Wei Lim coaches him, using what he has learned. Oils on textured canvas illustrations complement the text.

2273. Yolen, Jane. *Letting Swift River Go.*   Illustrated by Barbara Cooney. Litlte, Brown, 1995. 32pp. Paper ISBN 978-0-316-96860-7. Grades K–3. In the 1930s Sally Jane's hometown is flooded with the creation of the Quabbin Reservoir in Massachusetts to collect water for Boston's residents. Before the village is submerged, the residents remove graves and prepare to live elsewhere. Sally Jane decides she will remember the pleasures of the past and look toward the future.

2274. Young, Judy. *The Lucky Star.*   Illustrated by Chris Ellison. Sleeping Bear, 2008. 40pp. ISBN 978-1-58536-348-3. Grades K–3. In 1933, 9-year-old Ruth's father is working away from home with the Civilian Conservation Corps. Her town cannot afford a teacher so her school is closed. She worries about her future and that of her younger sister Janie. Their mother says they have enough and tries to cheer them. Then Ruth realizes she can help by teaching the younger children. They have no paper and pencils but she can use the flour left on the table from making biscuits as a blackboard. Pastel illustrations enhance the text.

History

2275. Appelt, Kathi, and Jeanne Cannella Schmitzer. *Down Cut Shin Creek: The Packhorse Librarians of Kentucky.* HarperCollins, 2001. 64pp. ISBN 978-0-06-029135-8. Grades 5–8. During the Great Depression, the Works Progress Administration's packhorse libraries brought reading materials to people in the isolated areas of Kentucky. The men and women who rode these horses woke before dawn and traveled dangerous mountain trails to reach remote homes and one-room schoolhouses. Archival photographs highlight the text. Bibliography.

2276. Banting, Erinn. *Empire State Building.* Weigl, 2007. 32pp. ISBN 978-1-59036-721-6; paper ISBN 978-1-59036-722-3. Grades 5–9. At the time of its completion in 1931, the Empire State Building was the tallest building in the world. Banting examines the technology that made it possible to build the structure, and its significance at the time. Photographs highlight the text. Glossary, Further Reading, Web Sites, and Index.

2277. Beller, Susan Provost. *The Doughboys Over There: Soldiering in World War I.* (Soldiers on the Battlefront) Lerner, 2003. 112pp. ISBN 978-0-8225-6295-5. Grades 5–8. Beller examines the events leading up to the war, the principal battles, the horrors that the troops faced, and the major leaders involved. Fact boxes cover such topics as poison gas. Black and white photographs highlight the text. Bibliography, Chronology, Further Reading, Web Sites, and Index.

2278. Blair, Margaret Whitman. *The Roaring Twenty: The First Cross-Country Air Race for Women.* National Geographic, 2006. 128pp. ISBN 978-0-7922-5389-1. Grades 5–8. The first cross-country air race for women took place in 1929, and the aviators who participated tried to fly from Santa Monica, California, to Cleveland, Ohio. From the beginning of the nine-day race, mechanical failures, bad weather, and sabotage were rampant. One of the favored participants, Marvel Crosson, died as a result of engine failure. Another contestant collided with a spectator's car. Among the women who flew were Amelia Earhart, "Pancho" Barnes, and Louise Thaden. Fourteen of the original twenty finished the race. They formed an organization called the Ninety-Nines with Amelia Earhart serving as the first president. Maps and photographs enhance the text. Bibliography, Notes, and Index. *Voice of Youth Advocates Nonfiction Honor List.*

2279. Bodden, Valerie. *Mount Rushmore.* (Modern Wonders of the World) Creative Education, 2006. 32pp. ISBN 978-1-58341-440-8. Grades 3–6. The monument at Mount Rushmore in South Dakota was built between 1927 and 1941 and honors four presidents—George Washington, Thomas Jefferson, Theodore Roosevelt, and Abraham Lincoln. Bodden examines why these men were chosen and the design of the 60-foot-tall carvings. Photographs enhance the text. Glossary and Index.

2280. Brown, Harriet. *Welcome to Kit's World, 1934: Growing Up During America's Great Depression.* Illustrated by Walter Rane, Jamie Young, and Philip Hood. American Girl, 2002. 60pp. ISBN 978-1-58485-359-6. Grades 3–6. Photographs, illustrations, and anecdotes (both true and fiction) recall life in the United States during the Great Depression. Double-page spreads focus on topics including the 1930s, outdoor fun, fashion, and other aspects of Kit Kittredge's life during this period.

2281. Cooper, Michael L. *Dust to Eat: Drought and Depression in the 1930's.* Clarion, 2004. 81pp. ISBN 978-0-618-15449-4. Grades 5–8. The seven chapters of this volume look at the Great Depression and the Dust Bowl of the late 1930s, when drought drove farmers and their families from the Great Plains down Route 66 to California searching for work. Primary sources—including letters and interviews as well as eyewitness reports from individuals including John Steinbeck and Woody Guthrie—describe the times. Children died in the fields from malnutrition and disease, lived in the harsh conditions of migrant camps, and struggled to survive. Black-and-white photographs augment the text. Bibliography, Further Reading, and Index. *Young Hoosier Book Award* (Indiana) nomination, *William Allen White Children's Book Award* (Kansas) nomination, *Great Lakes Children's Book Award* (Michigan) nomination, *No-*

table Social Studies Trade Books for Young People, *VOYA Nonfiction Honor List*, and *Capitol Choices Noteworthy Titles* (Washington, D.C.).

2282. Costantino, Maria. *Fashions of a Decade: The 1930s.* Chelsea House, 2007. 64pp. ISBN 978-0-8160-6719-0. Grades 5 up. Chapters in this book look at dancing in the Depression, Hollywood, art deco, new materials such as rayon, halter necks and bias cuts, Schiaparelli and the surrealists, health and fitness, and the sweaters and trousers that appeared in *Vogue* magazine toward the end of the decade. Glossary, Reading List, Time Chart, and Index.

2283. Davis, Barbara J. *The Teapot Dome Scandal: Corruption Rocks 1920s America.* (Snapshots in History) Compass Point, 2007. 96pp. ISBN 978-0-7565-3336-6. Grades 5–8. In the 1920s political appointees and personal friends of President Warren G. Harding used their positions of power to solicit bribes from large oil companies in return for western oil leases. The secretary of the interior, Albert Fall, said he needed to protect national security, but congressional investigations led to the appointment of the government's first special prosecutor. Government secrecy, abuse of power, and cronyism threatened the success of the president. Photographs highlight the text. Bibliography, Glossary, Notes, Further Reading, Web Sites, and Index.

2284. DeGezelle, Terri. *Franklin D. Roosevelt and the Great Depression.* (Life in the Time Of) Heinemann, 2007. 32pp. ISBN 978-1-4034-9670-6; paper ISBN 978-1-4329-0597-2. Grades 3–5. The relationship of Franklin Delano Roosevelt (1882–1945) to the Depression and how it changed life for others is this volume's focus. It looks at life in the United States during the 1920s before the stock market crash in 1929, the Depression, the New Deal, World War II, and Roosevelt's death along with the end of the war. Archival photographs and illustrations augment the text. Glossary, Chronology, Further Reading, Web Sites, and Index.

2285. Doak, Robin. *Black Tuesday: Prelude to the Great Depression.* (Snapshots in History) Compass Point, 2007. 96pp. ISBN 978-0-7565-3327-4. Grades 5–8. On October 29, 1929, a day known as Black Tuesday, the stock market crashed. This has been attributed to a lack of regulation during a time of misguided economic optimism. Photographs highlight the text. Bibliography, Glossary, Notes, Further Reading, Web Sites, and Index.

2286. Downing, David. *The Great Depression.* (20th Century Perspectives) Heinemann, 2001. 48pp. ISBN 978-1-57572-435-5; paper ISBN 978-1-58810-374-1. Grades 5–8. The Great Depression began with the precipitous fall of the stock market in October 1929. Many jobs were lost and the weather conditions that created the Dust Bowl in the Midwest exacerbated the problem. Downing examines the causes and effects of this dismal period in American history. Illustrations augment the text. Bibliography, Further Reading, Glossary, Index.

2287. Dowswell, Paul. *Weapons and Technology of World War I.* (20th Century Perspectives) Heinemann, 2002. 48pp. ISBN 978-1-58810-662-9; paper ISBN 978-1-58810-922-4. Grades 5–8. New technologies introduced new weapons during World War I. Among these were more-effective machine guns; the "Big Bertha" howitzer; gas grenades containing chlorine, phosgene, or mustard gas; improved communication via radio and telephone; tanks known as "the Chariots of God;" and planes. This volume discusses these improvements and their uses. Illustrations augment the text. Bibliography, Further Reading, Glossary, Index.

2288. Dubowski, Cathy East, and Mark Dubowski. *A Horse Named Seabiscuit.* Illustrated by Mark Rowe. (All Aboard Reading) Penguin, 2003. 48pp. Paper ISBN 978-0-448-43342-4. Grades 2–4. Seabiscuit was a runt who looked funny and slept strange hours before trainer Tom Smith decided to take a chance on him. Then he became a champion. He set sixteen track records and won more money than any previous horse. During the Depression his winning invigorated a cheerless populace, and people wanted information about his every move. They read newspapers and magazines and listened to radio shows to find out the latest about him. The one race that remained elusive for him was the Santa Anita Handicap in California, but before he was retired he managed to win that race as well.

2289. Fandel, Jennifer. *Golden Gate Bridge.* Creative Education, 2006. 32pp. ISBN 978-1-58341-437-8. Grades 3–5. The Golden Gate Bridge spanning San Francisco Bay was constructed in the 1930s and remains a recognizable landmark. This volume looks at its design and construction, as well as its current use and maintenance. Maps and illustrations augment the text. Glossary and Index.

2290. Feigenbaum, Aaron. *The Hindenburg Disaster.* (Code Red) Bearport, 2007. 32pp. ISBN 978-1-59716-361-3. Grades 3–6. In 1937 the hydrogen-powered airship *Hindenburg* caught fire, crashed, and killed the thirty-six people aboard. Photographs show the tragedy as it unfolds. Bibliography, Further Reading, Glossary, Web Sites, and Index.

2291. Finkelstein, Norman H. *Three Across: The Great Transatlantic Air Race of 1927.* Calkins Creek, 2008. 134pp. ISBN 978-1-59078-462-4. Grades 5–8. Finkelstein looks at the rise of aviation from its beginning at Kitty Hawk to the 1927 Orteig Prize, awarded to the first person to fly nonstop across the Atlantic. The first three flights to accomplish this feat were the *Spirit of St. Louis* with Charles Lindbergh piloting, the *Columbia* piloted by Clarence Chamberlain, and the *America* with the Arctic explorer Richard E. Byrd. Photographs highlight the text. Bibliography, Notes, and Index.

2292. Freedman, Russell. *Children of the Great Depression.* Clarion, 2005. 120pp. ISBN 978-0-618-44630-8. Grades 5–8. Primary sources including diaries, letters, memoirs, and other firsthand accounts reveal the lives of children who suffered economic and social changes during the Depression. One child tells her teacher that her sister gets to eat that day. Other anecdotes describe Hoovervilles, soup kitchens, dust storms, and kids at work and on trains. Photographs by Dorothea Lange, Russell Lee, Arthur Rothstein, Ben Shahn and Walker Evans reveal the disconsolate faces of children with little hope—children of sharecroppers, factory workers, and migrant farm laborers. Bibliography, Notes, and Index. *Booklist Editor's Choice* and *Beehive Children's Book Award* (Utah) nomination.

2293. Freedman, Russell. *Kids at Work: Lewis Hine and the Crusade Against Child Labor.* See entry 1869.

2294. Grant, R. G. *Armistice 1918.* (World Wars) Raintree, 2001. 64pp. ISBN 978-0-7398-2753-6. Grades 5–9. Primary source documents and firsthand accounts detail the negotiations for peace at the end of World War I. Grant reviews the trench warfare, the main battles, and other aspects of the conflict before the terms of the Treaty of Versailles were reached and the League of Nations was formed. Illustrations and photographs enhance the text. Maps, Chronology, Bibliography, and Glossary.

2295. Halpern, Monica. *Moving North: African Americans and the Great Migration 1915–1930.* (Crossroads America) National Geographic, 2004. 40pp. ISBN 978-0-7922-8278-5. Grades 4–6. During the first half of the 20th century, many African Americans migrated from southern states to the North. One of the main questions is why people leave the familiar for the unknown, and Halpern tries to answer this, giving reasons as to why the North seemed attractive and what cities the migrants chose. The text covers the period generally from the Harlem Renaissance through the Great Depression. Among the figures mentioned and quoted are Langston Hughes, Richard Wright, James Weldon Johnson and W. E. B. Du Bois. Photographs and Jacob Lawrence's paintings complement the text. Glossary and Index.

2296. Herald, Jacqueline. *Fashions of a Decade: The 1920s.* Chelsea House, 2007. 64pp. ISBN 978-0-8160-6718-3. Grades 5 up. The 1920s reflected the Jazz Age when Prohibition was the law. It was also the beginning of "talkie" movies that flouted social conventions. The eight chapters of the text cover various aspects of the 1920s in relation to clothing. Photographs and illustrations augment the text. Glossary, Chronology, Further Reading, Index.

2297. Hill, Laban Carrick. *Harlem Stomp! A Cultural History of the Harlem Renaissance.* Illustrated by Christopher Myers. Megan Tingley, 2004. 160pp. ISBN 978-0-316-81411-9. Grades 5–9. Hill offers a survey of the Harlem Renaissance, emphasizing the artists who flourished during the time of the great migration from the South. He also includes background about racism, the desire for equal rights, the role of churches, traditional funeral rites, rent parties, and other pertinent topics. Among those featured are Langston Hughes and his poetry, Paul Robeson and his operatic voice, and James VanDerZee and his photography. Illustrations enhance the text. Index. *Publishers Weekly Best Children's Books, School Library Journal Best Books for Children*, and *Capitol Choices Noteworthy Titles* (Washington, D.C.).

2298. Lawrence, Jacob. *The Great Migration: An American Story.* Trophy, 1995. Unpaged. Paper ISBN 978-0-06-443428-7. Grades 3–6. Around the time of World War I, African Americans began leaving their homes in the rural South and moving to the North. This sequence of paintings illustrates this "Great Migration." The accompanying text tells about the movement of a people who wanted to improve their lives with better opportunities. *Notable Children's Trade Books in the Field of Social Studies, American Library Association Notable Children's Books, Booklist Editors' Choices, IRA Teachers' Choices, Carter G. Woodson Outstanding Merit Book,* and *New York Public Library's Books for the Teen Age.*

2299. Liberatore, Karen. *Our Century: 1910–1920.* See entry 1885.

2300. McCarthy, Meghan. *Aliens Are Coming! The True Account of the 1938 War of the Worlds Radio Broadcast.* Knopf, 2006. 32pp. ISBN 978-0-375-83518-6. Grades 2–4. On October 30, 1938, a Halloween radio prank made much of the United States believe that the Martians had invaded. Orson Welles broadcast a radio show starting with a bulletin, "Aliens Are Coming!" H. G. Wells's "War of the Worlds" followed, and people believed that aliens had landed in New Jersey. The exaggerated illustrations enhance the text and make readers wonder if listeners could be duped again. Bibliography, Notes, and Web Sites. *School Library Journal Best Children's Books.*

2301. McCarthy, Meghan. *Seabiscuit: The Wonder Horse.* Simon & Schuster, 2008. Unpaged. ISBN 978-1-4169-3360-1. Grades K–2. Grandson of famous racehorse Man o' War, Seabiscuit lost almost all his races until Charles Howard, an automobile tycoon, bought him. With his new trainer, "Silent Tom" Smith, and his new rider, John "Red" Pollard, Seabiscuit started winning. His races were broadcast on the radio during the Depression, and his wins gave everyone hope and happiness. In one of his last races, he competed against War Admiral, a very successful horse. Seabiscuit's regular jockey could not ride that day, but he passed all his knowledge on to the substitute jockey and Seabiscuit won the race. Bibliography and Notes.

2302. McKerley, Jennifer Guess. *Man O' War: Best Racehorse Ever.* Illustrated by Terry Widener. Random, 2005. 47pp. ISBN 978-0-375-83164-5. Grades 1–3. Man O' War, Seabiscuit's grandfather, had a mind of his own. He was difficult to saddle and fidgeted. But even so, in 1999 he was called the "Greatest Horse of the Century" because of the many races he won and the winners he sired. Illustrations enhance the text.

2303. McKissack, Patricia C., and Frederick McKissack. *Black Diamond: The Story of the Negro Baseball Leagues.* Scholastic, 1998. 184pp. Paper ISBN 978-0-590-68213-8. Grades 4–9. Because African Americans were not allowed to play in white baseball leagues for nearly a century, they formed leagues of their own. Many participants were superb players—Cool Papa Bell, Josh Gibson, and Satchel Paige, to name just a few. The text covers the leagues' history from the beginning of baseball through the first African Americans to play in the major leagues: Jackie Robinson, Willie Mays, and Hank Aaron. Player Profiles, Hall of Fame, Timeline, Bibliography, and Index. *Coretta Scott King Honor* and *Notable Children's Trade Books in the Field of Social Studies.*

2304. Mann, Elizabeth. *Empire State Building: When New York Reached for the Skies.* Illustrated by Alan Witschonke. (Wonders of the World) Mikaya, 2003. 48pp. ISBN 978-1-931414-06-7; 2006, paper ISBN 978-1-931414-08-1. Grades 4–8. Construction of the Empire State Building began in 1929 and was completed in 1931. It was then the tallest building in the world. Mann looks at the design, engineering, and financial aspects of raising this 86-floor structure. Lewis Hine's photographs and Alan Witschonke's paintings and diagrams enhance the text. Glossary and Bibliography. *National Council of Teachers of English Orbis Pictus Honor Book, Bluebonnet Award* (Texas) nomination, *Voice of Youth Advocates Nonfiction Honor List,* and *Garden State Children's Book Awards* (New Jersey) nomination.

2305. Marrin, Albert. *Years of Dust: The Story of the Dust Bowl.* Dutton, 2009. 128pp. ISBN 978-0-525-42077-4. Grades 5–9. In nine chapters, this volume chronicles America's "worst environmental disaster," the Dust Bowl that the Great Plains became during the 1930s. Farmers, ranchers, and hunters who came to the area introduced non-native plants, killed animals including buffalo and prairie dogs, and started cattle-grazing that destroyed the natural habitat. A huge 1,000-mile-wide dust storm on "Black Friday" in 1935 led to a mass movement of farm families to the west, hoping to find work as migrant workers. Marrin includes first-person accounts and information on aid available through New Deal programs and also looks at possible future dust bowls. Period photographs, illustrations, and maps enhance the text. Glossary, Chronology, Notes, Bibliography, Further Resources, and Index. *Booklist Editors Choice, American Library Association Notable Children's Books*, and *School Library Journal Best Books of the Year.*

2306. Miller, Debbie. *The Great Serum Race: Blazing the Iditarod Trail.* Illustrated by Jon Van Zyle. Walker, 2006. 32pp. Paper ISBN 978-0-8027-7723-2. Grades 2–4. In 1925 sled dogs delivered antitoxin serum to victims of diphtheria in Nome, Alaska. Perhaps the best known of the dogs is the Siberian Husky named Togo. The Iditarod Sled Dog Race is held every year to commemorate the legendary effort. Paintings of teams and their mushers complement the text. Bibliography. *Garden State Nonfiction Book Award* (New Jersey) nomination, *State Reading Association Charlotte Book Award* (New York) nomination, and *Young Readers Choice Book Award* (Pennsylvania) nomination.

2307. Myers, Walter Dean. *The Harlem Hellfighters: When Pride Met Courage.* Illustrated by William Miles. Amistad, 2006. 150pp. ISBN 978-0-06-001136-9. Grades 5–8. During World War I, fighters in the 369th Infantry Regiment were African American men known as the Harlem Hell Fighters. Drawing on primary sources, Myers explores the origin of the regiment and its combat on French soil, with the French treating them as equals. Photographs enhance the text. Bibliography.

2308. Nobleman, Marc Tyler. *The Hindenburg.* (We the People) Compass Point, 2005. 48pp. ISBN 978-0-7565-1266-8; paper ISBN 978-0-7565-1729-8. Grades 4–6. The rigid airship *Hindenburg* was trying to land when it exploded on a New Jersey airfield in May 6, 1937. Thirty-five of the ninety-seven people on board died, and the tragedy signaled the end of trans-Atlantic passenger airship service. Photographs and reproductions accompany the text. Glossary, Chronology, Further Reading, Web Sites, and Index.

2309. Norrell, Robert J. *We Want Jobs! A Story of the Great Depression.* Illustrated by Jan Naimo Jones. Steck-Vaughn, 1992. 40pp. Paper ISBN 978-0-8114-8069-7. Grades 4–8. John Waskowitz, a Pennsylvania steelworker, lost his job in 1929 like millions of others during the Great Depression. His family was among many that suffered as jobs disappeared. It was not until 1933 that work started to become more available. Epilogue, Afterword, and Notes.

2310. Olson, Steven P. *The Trial of John T. Scopes: A Primary Source Account.* (Great Trials of the 20th Century) Rosen, 2003. 64pp. ISBN 978-0-8239-3974-9. Grades 5–8. Using photographs, original transcripts, political cartoons, and direct quotes from the participants, Olson examines the Scopes trial, which took place in July 1925. A high school teacher, John Scopes, was charged with illegally teaching the theory of evolution. The arguments covered evolution versus creationism, separation of church and state, and the extent of government power. The lawyers representing the defendant and the prosecution were two of the best of their time, Clarence Darrow and William Jennings Bryan, and they attracted enormous attention from the press. Bibliography, Illustrations, and Index.

2311. O'Neal, Claire. *The Influenza Pandemic of 1918.* Mitchell Lane, 2008. 32pp. ISBN 978-1-58415-569-0. Grades 3–6. On March 11, 1918, Albert Mitchell started cooking for the soldiers at Fort Riley, Kansas. The base was unprepared for all the soldiers who had arrived for training before going to the front lines in Europe. The base had no heat, hot water, or toilets. Spanish flu broke out among the men, and then those who had it and survived spread it abroad. No one had heard of this disease before it infested Fort Riley. Approximately 20 million to 100 million people died of the flu throughout the world before June 1920. Chronology, Bibliography, Further Reading, Web Sites, Glossary, and Index.

2312. Owen, Marna. *Our Century: 1930–1940.* Gareth Stevens, 1993. 64pp. ISBN 978-0-8368-1035-6. Grades 3–10. Written as if a newspaper, this book's short articles give an overview of the decade. Included are statistics, daily life in America, the Spanish king's abdication and civil war in Spain, General Franco, Edward VIII of Britain abdicating, the Nazis' rise, Stalin and Hitler, Hoover, Roosevelt, the end of Prohibition, the Scottsboro case, the Empire State Building, Boulder Dam, New York's World Fair, Babe Didrikson, Lou Gehrig, Joe Louis, Eugene O'Neill, Jane Addams, Huey Long, and Amelia Earhart. Glossary, Books for Further Reading, Places to Write or Visit, and Index.

2313. Rappaport, Doreen. *Free at Last! Stories and Songs of Emancipation.* See entry 1894.

2314. Rau, Dana Meachen. *The Harlem Renaissance.* (We the People) Compass Point, 2005. 48pp. ISBN 978-0-7565-1264-4; paper ISBN 978-0-7565-1727-4. Grades 4–6. The Harlem Renaissance established African Americans as major contributors to the arts. Among the names associated with the period are Langston Hughes, Zora Neale Hurston, and Claude McKay. Primary sources offer valuable information. Photographs and reproductions accompany the text. Glossary, Chronology, Further Reading, Web Sites, and Index.

2315. Roensch, Greg. *The Lindbergh Baby Kidnapping Trial: A Primary Source Account.* (Great Trials of the 20th Century) Rosen, 2003. 64pp. ISBN 978-0-8239-3971-8. Grades 5–8. Roensch uses primary sources—photographs, political cartoons, copies of original transcripts, and quotes from those involved—to retell the story of the Lindbergh baby kidnapping and the trial of Bruno Hauptmann. Charles Lindbergh gained international fame as an early aviator. In 1932 his son, Charles Lindbergh, Jr., was kidnapped and murdered. Hauptmann was accused of the crime and tried and convicted in what was considered the "Crime of the Century." Bibliography and Index.

2316. Ross, Stuart. *Leaders of World War I.* (World Wars) Raintree, 2003. 64pp. ISBN 978-0-7398-5481-5. Grades 5–9. Primary source documents and firsthand accounts detail the characters and actions of World War I leaders. The text includes sections on generals and politicians, emperors, Allied commanders, and commanders of the Central Powers. Among those presented are Woodrow Wilson, Nicholas II, and Leon Trotsky. Illustrations and photographs enhance the text. Chronology, Bibliography, Glossary, and Index.

2317. Sandler, Martin W. *The Dust Bowl Through the Lens: How Photography Revealed and Helped Remedy a National Disaster.* Walker, 2009. 96pp. ISBN 978-0-8027-9547-2. Grades 5–9. This photo-essay chronicles—in forty-four double-page spreads—the causes, hardships, and aftermath of the drought and dust storms that hit the prairies in the 1930s. Notes, Bibliography, Further Reading, Map, and Index.

2318. Saunders, Nicholas. *World War I: A Primary Source History.* (In Their Own Words) Gareth Stevens, 2005. 48pp. ISBN 978-0-8368-5982-9. Grades 5–8. Among the topics covered in this overview of World War I using primary sources are the circumstances that led to the war, international leaders at the time, how it affected the rest of the century, the memorials to the dead, the depiction of the war in art, and the artifacts from that war that are still being discovered today. Maps, photographs and illustrations complement the text. Glossary, Chronology, and Index.

2319. Schaefer, Adam. *Harlem Renaissance.* (20th Century Perspectives) Heinemann, 2003. 48pp. ISBN 978-1-4034-0150-2; paper ISBN 978-1-4034-3858-4. Grades 4–8. Schaefer looks at the African American writers, intellectuals, musicians, and artists who made up the Harlem Renaissance, and at the experiences and hopes that they voiced. Illustrations augment the text. Bibliography, Further Reading, Glossary, Index.

2320. Schultz, Stanley. *The Great Depression: A Primary Source History.* (In Their Own Words) Gareth Stevens, 2006. 48pp. ISBN 978-0-8368-5978-2. Grades 5–8. Using primary sources—newspapers, government documents, letters, poems, telegrams, speeches, radio broadcasts, songs, and contemporary interviews—this volume looks at the impact of the Great Depression. Photographs, maps, and illustrations enhance the text. Glossary, Chronology, and Index.

2321. Sorensen, Lita. *The Scottsboro Boys Trial: A Primary Source Account.* (Great Trials of the 20th Century) Rosen, 2004. 64pp. ISBN 978-0-8239-3975-6. Grades 5–8. After two white women riding a freight train during the Depression were raped, black teenagers were arrested for the crime. During the trial the women were shown to be prostitutes, and there was doubt about the "quality" of the sperm during the exam. Years later, the nine were finally freed or pardoned after being falsely accused. Court transcripts reveal the many trials and re-trials of the boys, the verdicts, and the impact on civil rights and American culture. Photographs and illustrations augment the text. Bibliography, Glossary, Chronology, Web Sites, and Index.

2322. **Standiford, Natalie.** *The Bravest Dog Ever: The True Story of Balto.* Illustrated by Donald Cook. Random, 1989. 47pp. Paper ISBN 978-0-394-89695-3. Grades 1–3. In 1925 two children lay sick in Nome, Alaska. They needed serum to save their lives. A train rushed from Anchorage, Alaska, but a blizzard stopped it 700 miles away. A dog sled relay was set up. Balto was the lead dog on the next-to-last team. When they got to the last stop, no one was there, and his team had to continue. They reached Nome in five and a half days instead of the anticipated 15, after traveling 20 hours nonstop. The team driver gave all the credit to Balto. He said he could not see in the blizzard, and only Balto could have got them back to Nome.

2323. **Yuan, Margaret Speaker B.** *The Royal Gorge Bridge.* (Building World Landmarks) Blackbirch, 2003. 48pp. ISBN 978-1-56711-352-5. Grades 5–8. The Royal Gorge Bridge was built in Colorado in 1929. An amazing engineering accomplishment, it was the highest suspension bridge in the world and one of the safest—no one died during its rapid construction. Photographs and illustrations augment the text. Chronology, Further Reading, Glossary, Web Sites, and Index.

Biography and Collective Biography

2324. **Adler, David A.** *America's Champion Swimmer: Gertrude Ederle.* Illustrated by Terry Widener. Harcourt, 2000. ISBN 978-0-15-201969-3; Voyager, 2005, paper ISBN 978-0-15-205251-5. Grades K–4. When Gertrude "Trudy" Ederle (1905–2003) was 7 years old, she nearly drowned in a pond and her father decided she must learn to swim. She discovered that swimming was her passion. At 15 she started winning medals and breaking records. At 16 she swam from Lower Manhattan to Sandy Hook, New Jersey. When she was 17 she won three medals at the 1924 Olympics in Paris. By 1927 she had set twenty-nine U.S. and world records. A woman had never crossed the English Channel's twenty-one miles from England to France, and she decided to attempt that. She failed the first time, but was determined to succeed and tried again. After fourteen hours in the cold water, she reached the opposite shore, setting a world record. *American Library Association Notable Children's Books, Capitol Choices Noteworthy Titles* (Washington, D.C.), *Bluegrass Award* (Kentucky) nomination, *Black-Eyed Susan Award* (Maryland) nomination, *Show Me Award* (Missouri) nomination, *Garden State Children's Book Award* (New Jersey) nomination, *Young Reader's Choice Award* (Pennsylvania) nomination, *School Library Journal Best Books for Children, Bulletin Blue Ribbon,* and *Red Clover Picture Book Award* (Vermont) nomination.

2325. **Adler, David A.** *Joe Louis: America's Fighter.* Illustrated by Terry Widener. Gulliver, 2005. Unpaged. ISBN 978-0-15-216480-5. Grades 1–4. Joe Louis (1914–1981), the grandson of slaves, was a successful boxer from the start. He turned professional in 1934 and became a champion with unprecedented support of whites when he fought Germany's Max Schmeling in 1936. Although he lost the first match, they met again in 1938, and Louis became the new world champion, symbolically defeating the Nazis. Later Schmeling saved children from the Nazis, and he and Louis became friends. Acrylics intensify the text. Bibliography. *Emphasis on Reading Children's Choice* (Alabama) nomination.

2326. **Adler, David A.** *A Picture Book of Dwight David Eisenhower.* Holiday House, 2002. 32pp. ISBN 978-0-8234-0702-5; 2004, paper ISBN 978-0-8234-0830-5. Grades 1–3. This biography of Dwight David Eisenhower (1890–1969) introduces him as a war hero after World War II when he paraded through New York City in 1945. He grew up in Kansas before attending

West Point. He loved sports and, in addition to his heroism in World War II, he fought in World War I, married, and had a family. He also served the United States as its thirty-fourth president. Photographs enhance the text. Bibliography, Chronology, Notes, and Web Sites.

2327. Adler, David A. *A Picture Book of Eleanor Roosevelt.* Illustrated by Robert Casilla. Holiday House, 1991. Unpaged. ISBN 978-0-8234-0856-6; 1995, paper ISBN 978-0-8234-1157-3. Grades 1–3. Born to wealthy parents in 1884, Eleanor Roosevelt seemed destined for a life of happiness, but both her parents died before she was 10, and she had to live with her stern grandmother. As a young woman, she married a distant cousin, Franklin Delano Roosevelt. The most famous man in her family at that time was her uncle, President Theodore Roosevelt. When her husband became president during the Depression, she spoke publicly for women's rights and the rights of Indians, the homeless, young people, and minorities. She even severed her relationship with the Daughters of the American Revolution when the group refused to let the African American singer Marian Anderson perform in Constitution Hall. Roosevelt arranged for Anderson to sing at the Lincoln Memorial instead. President Truman called her "First Lady of the World." Important Dates. *Notable Children's Trade Books in the Field of Social Studies.*

2328. Adler, David A. *A Picture Book of George Washington Carver.* See entry 1908.

2329. Adler, David A. *A Picture Book of Helen Keller.* See entry 1910.

2330. Adler, David A. *A Picture Book of Thomas Alva Edison.* See entry 1912.

2331. Adler, David A. *Satchel Paige: Don't Look Back.* Illustrated by Terry Widener. Harcourt, 2007. 32pp. ISBN 978-0-15-205585-1. Grades K–3. One of the best African American baseball players, Satchel Paige (1906–1982) starred in the Negro Baseball Leagues before he was hired in 1947, at the age of 42, to play for the Brooklyn Dodgers with Jackie Robinson. The seventh of eleven children, he went to reform school for petty theft, but became known for his pitching ability. He called his pitches by names including "trouble ball" and "whimsey-dipsey-do." He became the first African American to pitch in a World Series game. Illustrations complement the text. Chronology and Notes.

2332. Aliki. *A Weed Is a Flower: The Life of George Washington Carver.* See entry 1913.

2333. Aller, Susan Bivin. *George Eastman.* See entry 1914.

2334. Aller, Susan Bivin. *Juliette Low.* See entry 1915.

2335. Allport, Alan. *Franklin Delano Roosevelt.* (Great American Presidents) Facts on File, 2003. 100pp. ISBN 978-0-7910-7598-2. Grades 5–7. Allport presents the life of Franklin Delano Roosevelt (1882–1945), the thirty-second president of the United States, who was reelected to office three times. Six chapters examine his childhood, his maturation, events that affected him, his accomplishments, his death, and his legacy. Photographs enhance the text. Timeline, Appendix, and Index.

2336. Alphin, Elaine Marie. *Dwight D. Eisenhower.* (History Maker Bios) Lerner, 2004. 48pp. ISBN 978-0-8225-1544-9. Grades 3–5. Dwight D. Eisenhower (1890–1969) grew up in Kansas before becoming an important member of the military. He rose to the rank of general and commanded the armies of nineteen countries in the Allied effort to win World War II. Then he was elected president of the United States. During his tenure, he approved the Interstate Highway system and created NASA. He also oversaw the peaceful end to the Korean War. Illustrations augment the text. Bibliography, Further Reading, Glossary, Maps, Timeline, Web Sites, and Index.

2337. Anderson, William. *Prairie Girl: The Life of Laura Ingalls Wilder.* See entry 1124.

2338. Appel, Martin. *Joe DiMaggio.* Chelsea House, 1990. 64pp. ISBN 978-0-7910-1164-5. Grades 5–9. In addition to information about DiMaggio, son of an Italian immigrant, Appel presents a brief history of baseball on the West Coast. DiMaggio's fame began in 1933, when he had a 61-game hitting streak for his San Francisco team. In 1936 DiMaggio left for New York and the Yankees, the team of Babe Ruth and Lou Gehrig. His record there astounded baseball fans, and he played consistently until injuries sidelined him. Appel includes photographs of DiMaggio with his family and his ex-wife Marilyn Monroe. Statistics, Chronology, Further Reading, and Index.

2339. Barasch, Lynne. *Knockin' on Wood: Starring Peg Leg Bates.* Lee & Low, 2004. Unpaged. ISBN 978-1-58430-170-7. Grades 1–3. Born a sharecropper's son, African American "Peg Leg" Bates lost his leg in a factory accident when he was 12 years old. He was determined to dance, got a wooden leg, and was soon performing for audiences. He even appeared on the Ed Sullivan television show. Illustrations enhance the text. *Children's, Junior and Young Adult Book Award* (South Carolina) nomination, *Black-Eyed Susan Award* (Maryland) nomination, and *Children's Book Award* (Florida) nomination.

2340. Barbour, Karen. *Mr. Williams.* Henry Holt, 2005. 32pp. ISBN 978-0-8050-6773-6. Grades K–3. J. W. Williams (1929–) describes what his life was like as a young boy growing up in the small town of Arcadia, Louisiana, in the 1930s. Children he knew worked in the fields in the summer, and they walked five miles to school in the winter. He avoided white people because they would hurt him. But his family enjoyed working together, eating good food, and listening to older people tell traditional folktales. Gouache-and-ink illustrations complement the text. *School Library Journal Best Children's Books* and *Young Readers Choice Book Award* (Louisiana) nomination.

2341. Bardhan-Quallen, Sudipta. *Franklin Delano Roosevelt: A National Hero.* (Sterling Biographies) Sterling, 2007. 124pp. ISBN 978-1-4027-4747-2; paper ISBN 978-1-4027-3545-5. Grades 5–8. This volume looks at the life of Franklin Delano Roosevelt (1882–1945) as he led the United States during the Great Depression and World War II. After a summary of his life and the contributions he made, the text includes information about his early family life and education. It examines him in relationship to the times in which he lived. Photographs enhance the text. Bibliography, Glossary, and Index.

2342. Barton, Chris. *The Day-Glo Brothers: The True Story of Bob and Joe Switzer's Bright Ideas and Brand-New Colors.* Charlesbridge, 2009. 48pp. ISBN 978-1-57091-673-1. Grades 4–6. Paints that glow in both daylight and fluorescent light were invented in 1933 by brothers Joe and Bob Switzer. Joe was looking to brighten up his magic act while Bob hoped to earn enough to pay the medical bills he incurred in an industrial accident. Their discovery helped airplanes land safely on World War II carriers and marketers embellish advertisements. Cartoon-style illustrations adding day-glo colors to the final pages enhance the text. Notes. *American Library Association Notable Children's Books, The Land of Enchantments Children's Book Award* (New Mexico), and *Robert F. Sibert Informational Book Award* Honor Book.

2343. Bass, Hester. *The Secret World of Walter Anderson.* Illustrated by E. B. Lewis. Candlewick, 2009. 48pp. ISBN 978-0-7636-3583-1. Grades 2–5. Mississippi-born Walter Inglis Anderson (1903–1965) painted lovely renditions of the Gulf Coast. He kept a room secret from his wife and children and after his death, his wife opened the door to find a lovely mural of another coastal scene. The watercolor illustrations present his life as do reproductions of several of his paintings. (Hurricane Katrina destroyed the family's personal collection; most of his other works are displayed in an Ocean Springs, Louisiana, museum.) Note.

2344. Berne, Emma Carlson. *Laura Ingalls Wilder.* (Essential Lives) ABDO, 2007. 112pp. ISBN 978-1-59928-843-7. Grades 5–8. This biography of Laura Ingalls Wilder (1867–1957) covers events leading to publication of the *Little House in the Big Woods*. It then details the effects of the Great Depression on Wilder and how her daughter Rose helped her edit and submit her books for publication. Wilder left much out of her books that she thought would be too distressing for readers, such as the family subsisting on turnips through a particularly difficult winter. Photographs and reproductions enhance the text. Chronology, Further Reading, Glossary, Notes, Web Sites, and Index.

2345. Berry, S. L. *Langston Hughes.* (Voices from the Past) Creative, 1994. 44pp. ISBN 978-0-8868-2616-1. Grades 5 up. This biography of Langston Hughes (1902–1967) shows a versatile poet who spent his career writing about the experiences of African Americans in their dialects. He went to Columbia, lived in Harlem, and flirted with socialism. Bibliography and Index.

2346. Bolden, Tonya. *George Washington Carver.* See entry 1922.

2347. Braun, Eric. *Bessie Coleman.* See entry 1927.

2348. Brown, Don. *Bright Path: Young Jim Thorpe.* See entry 1929.

2349. Brown, Don. *Mack Made Movies.* Roaring Brook, 2003. 32pp. ISBN 978-0-7613-1538-4; 2005, paper ISBN 978-1-59643-091-4. Grades 2–5. Mack Sennett (1880–1960) made movies with slapstick clowns including the Keystone Kops, Charlie Chaplin, Fatty Arbuckle, Mabel Normand, and Ben Turpin. He created the Keystone Kops, filmed the first "pie-in-the-face" skit, and introduced Charlie Chaplin to the movie-going public. He began as a vaudeville actor in 1900 when he played a "horse's rear end" and ended his career as the "King of Comedy." Illustrations enhance the text. Note and Bibliography. *ALA Notable Books for Children*, *James Madison Book Award* nomination, and *Bluebonnet Award* (Texas) nomination.

2350. Brown, Fern G. *Daisy and the Girl Scouts: The Story of Juliette Gordon Low.* See entry 1933.

2351. Bruchac, Joseph. *Jim Thorpe's Bright Path.* Illustrated by S. D. Nelson. Lee & Low, 2004. Unpaged. ISBN 978-1-58430-166-0. Grades 1–4. This biography of "Wa-tho-huck" ("Bright Path") or Jim Thorpe (1887–1953) focuses on his childhood and how his education prepared him for international fame and Olympic gold medals. As he changed boarding schools, he found sports much more interesting than academics, and he overcame his distress at the deaths of his parents and his twin brother. He did well at Carlisle Indian School. In 1999 Thorpe was recognized by the United States Congress as the "Athlete of the Century." Chronology and Notes. *Spur Awards* finalist, *Children's Book Award* (North Carolina) nomination, *Black-Eyed Susan Award* (Maryland) nomination, and *Children's Book Awards* (Rhode Island) nomination.

2352. Bryant, Jen. *Georgia's Bones.* Illustrated by Bethanne Andersen. Eerdmans, 2005. 32pp. ISBN 978-0-8028-5217-5. Grades K–3. Georgia O'Keeffe (1887–1986) was intrigued by shapes and spaces. In the desert and elsewhere, she would collect bones to draw in her paintings. This volume looks briefly at her life and her love of the natural—not only bones but also feathers, flowers, windows and doors, and holes. Reproductions enhance the text.

2353. Burleigh, Robert. *Stealing Home: The Jackie Robinson Story.* Illustrated by Mike Wimmer. Simon & Schuster, 2007. Unpaged. ISBN 978-0-689-86276-2. Grades 1–4. This biography of Jackie Robinson (1919–1972) emphasizes the difficulty of "stealing home," which Robinson managed to do in a 1955 World Series game. Burleigh also looks at Robinson's experience as a star of multiple sports at UCLA, playing as the first African American in major league baseball, his family, and other important aspects of his life. Photographs and illustrations augment the text.

2354. Casil, Amy Sterling. *John Dewey: The Founder of American Liberalism.* (Library of American Thinkers) Rosen, 2006. 112pp. ISBN 978-1-4042-0508-6. Grades 5–8. John Dewey (1859–1952)—American philosopher, psychologist, and educator—thought that schools and civil society needed attention and that everyone should have full voting rights. He wanted all to know about and understand the policies for which they were voting, and believed that communication in a society was of utmost importance. He also helped to found functional psychology, which emphasized a person's response to his or her environment, and supported the progressive movement in U.S. schooling during the first half of the 20th century. Photographs and illustrations augment the text. Bibliography, Glossary, Chronology, Further Reading, Web Sites, and Index.

2355. Cline-Ransome, Lesa. *Satchel Paige.* Illustrated by James E. Ransome. Simon & Schuster, 2000. Unpaged. ISBN 978-0-689-81151-7; Aladdin, 2003, paper ISBN 978-0-689-8568-15. Grades 2–4. Leroy "Satchel" Paige (1906–1982) experienced many hardships in his effort to become the first African American to pitch in a Major League World Series. He was the king of the Negro League before being allowed to play in the majors, and he was the first African American Baseball Hall of Fame inductee. Oil illustrations enhance the text. *Student Book Award* (Maine), *Children's Book Award* (South Carolina) nomination, and *Capitol Choices Noteworthy Titles* (Washington, D.C.).

2356. Collins, David. *To the Point: A Story About E. B. White.* Illustrated by Amy Johnson. Carolrhoda, 1989. 56pp. ISBN 978-0-8761-4345-2. Grades 3–6. The youngest of several children, E. B. White (1899–1985) spent his teenage years alone. When he was 12, *St. Nicholas* magazine published his first story. He filled many days with writing but never became serious about it—or anything—until, while attending Cornell, he began to feel guilty that he was too small to join the army and fight in World War I. He learned from his professor, William Strunk, Jr., to be precise and witty but also serious when necessary. He never forgot this advice—not during his work at the *New Yorker* and *Harper's* nor while he wrote *Stuart Little*, *Charlotte's Web*, and *The Trumpet of the Swan*. In his later years, he edited Strunk's book *The Elements of Style*, and it became a publication by Strunk and White.

2357. Cooney, Barbara. *Eleanor.* See entry 1944.

2358. Cooper, Ilene. *Jack: The Early Years of John F. Kennedy.* Dutton, 2003. 168pp. ISBN 978-0-525-46923-0. Grades 5–9. The biography presents the childhood and youth of John Fitzgerald Kennedy (1917–1963), thirty-fifth president of the United States. As a child he was ill a lot, enjoyed intense sibling rivalry, played jokes, dreamed, faced prejudice against him as an Irish Catholic, and received mixed messages about achievement from his parents. They expected his older brother, Joe, to become president, but Joe died too young to achieve that. Jack maintained his identity at home and at Choate where he attended school. Photographs highlight the text. Bibliography, Notes, and Index. *Student Book Award* (Maine) nomination and *Capitol Choices Noteworthy Titles* (Washington, D.C.).

2359. Crowe, Ellie. *Surfer of the Century: The Life of Duke Kahanamoku.* See entry 1947.

2360. Cummins, Julia. *Women Daredevils: Thrills, Chills, and Frills.* See entry 1948.

2361. Darby, Jean. *Dwight D. Eisenhower: A Man Called Ike.* Lerner, 2004. 112pp. ISBN 978-0-8225-0813-7. Grades 5 up. Complemented with photographs, this text on the life of Dwight David Eisenhower (1890–1969) covers the main aspects of his youth in Abilene, Kansas, and his attendance at West Point. He excelled in his military career, rising to commander of the Allied forces in Europe. He came back to the United States after the war as a hero and was elected president. He endured heartaches but rose to his responsibilities. Appendix, Glossary, Further Reading, and Index.

2362. Deitch, Kenneth M., and JoAnne B. Weisman. *Dwight D. Eisenhower: Man of Many Hats.* Illustrated by Jay Connolly. History Compass, 1990. 48pp. ISBN 978-1-878668-02-8. Grades 5 up. Although the illustrations are interesting and representative of Dwight David Eisenhower's life (1890–1969), the text is more difficult than the pictures imply. Among the hats that Eisenhower wore throughout his life are high school sports enthusiast, West Point cadet, general in the army, recipient of honorary degrees, president, and golfer. No table of contents or index.

2363. DePaola, Tomie. *Christmas Remembered.* Putnam, 2006. 86pp. ISBN 978-0-399-24622-7. Grades 3 up. Tomie dePaola recalls fifteen different Christmases spanning six decades. He remembers Christmas when he was 11 years old and received art supplies, in high school and his father winning the family's first television set, at college, as a novice at a Vermont priory. He also celebrated in San Francisco, New York City, Santa Fe, and New Hampshire.

2364. Doeden, Matt. *George Washington Carver.* See entry 1951.

2365. Donovan, Sandra. *Marcus Garvey.* Raintree, 2003. 64pp. ISBN 978-0-7398-6870-6; paper ISBN 978-1-4109-0038-8. Grades 4–6. Marcus Garvey (1887–1940) educated himself and worked to end discrimination against Africans throughout the world. He also tried to help black Africans regain control of their countries from colonial powers, and to promote pride among all black people. He began the Back to Africa movement. The text covers his childhood, the people who helped him, and his achievements. Further Reading, Chronology, Glossary, and Index.

2366. Donovan, Sandra. *Mary McLeod Bethune.* (African-American Biographies) Raintree, 2003. 64pp. ISBN 978-0-7398-6868-3; paper ISBN 978-1-4109-0039-5. Grades 4–6. African American educator Mary McLeod Bethune (1875–1955) founded the Bethune-Cookman

College and helped Franklin D. Roosevelt improve opportunities for her people as a civil rights activist. This volume highlights her childhood and her achievements. Bibliography and Index.

2367. Donovan, Sandra. *Will Rogers: Cowboy, Comedian, and Commentator.* See entry 1145.

2368. Dray, Philip. *Yours for Justice, Ida B. Wells: The Daring Life of a Crusading Journalist.* See entry 1954.

2369. Duggleby, John. *Artist in Overalls: The Life of Grant Wood.* Chronicle, 1996. 57pp. ISBN 978-0-8118-1242-9. Grades 4–7. One of the best-known American paintings is Grant Wood's *American Gothic.* This volume looks at Grant Wood's life (1891–1942). He grew up in Iowa a shy but stubborn boy. He was educated in Minneapolis, Chicago, and Paris, and returned to Iowa, where he taught high school to support himself. He saw irony in the discrepancy between the romantic ideals and realistic situations in American life, and he translated these concepts into his paintings. Included are reproductions of his paintings. *Capitol Choices Noteworthy Titles* (Washington, D.C.).

2370. Dunlap, Julie. *Birds in the Bushes: A Story About Margaret Morse Nice.* Illustrated by Ralph L. Ramstad. (Creative Minds) Carolrhoda, 1996. 63pp. ISBN 978-1-57505-006-5. Grades 4–6. Margaret Morse Nice (1883–1974) attended Mount Holyoke College and majored in languages. She returned to school for a master's degree in psychology. One day, on a walk with her daughters, she realized that she wanted to study nature and birds. She began to do research on birds and their habits, including the ways in which males establish territories by fighting with other males. Scientists at first saw her research as the work of a mere housewife, but the integrity of the results propelled her into a position as one of the world's best ornithologists. Bibliography and Index.

2371. El Nabli, Dina. *Eleanor Roosevelt: First Lady of the World.* See entry 1958.

2372. Farris, Christine King. *My Brother Martin: A Sister Remembers Growing Up with the Rev. Dr. Martin Luther King Jr.* Illustrated by Chris Soentpiet. Simon & Schuster, 2003. Unpaged. ISBN 978-0-689-84387-7; Aladdin, 2005, paper ISBN 978-0-689-84388-4. Grades K–3. Martin Luther King, Jr. (1929–1968) had an older sister Christine, who reports that when their mother told him that the parents of white boys across the street had forbidden them to play with Martin because he was black, Martin replied that he would change the world. She also shows that he and his siblings were mischievous and that they had a close family while learning to stand up for justice and equality. Watercolor illustrations enhance the text. *Young Reader's Award* (Arizona) nomination, *William Allen White Award* (Kansas) nomination, *Show Me State Book Award* (Missouri) nomination, *Keystone to Reading Book Award* (Pennsylvania) nomination, *Young Readers Choice Book Award* (Pennsylvania) nomination, *SCASL Book Award* (South Carolina) nomination, and *Volunteer State Book Award* (Tennessee) nomination.

2373. Feinberg, Barbara Silberdick. *Eleanor Roosevelt: A Very Special First Lady.* See entry 1960.

2374. Feinstein, Stephen. *Read About Amelia Earhart.* (I Like Biographies) Enslow, 2006. 24pp. ISBN 978-0-7660-2582-0. Grades 2–4. Amelia Earhart (1898–1937) saw a barnstormer as a young girl in Kansas and then cared for wounded pilots in Canada during World War I. These events inspired her to become a pilot and she set records before disappearing in 1937. Archival photographs and reproductions accompany the texts. Chronology, Further Reading, Web Sites, and Index.

2375. Ferris, Jeri. *What I Had Was Singing: The Story of Marian Anderson.* First Avenue, 1994. 96pp. Paper ISBN 978-0-8761-4634-7. Grades 4–7. African American Marian Anderson (1897–1993) was one of the 20th century's greatest singers. Although she was appreciated in Europe, she had to overcome prejudice against her race in her own country. In 1955 she finally became the first African American to sing at the Metropolitan Opera House. This book looks at her life and what she achieved. Legacy, Bibliography, and Index. *Notable Children's Trade Books in the Field of Social Studies* and *Carter G. Woodson Award.*

2376. Fleming, Candace. *Our Eleanor: A Scrapbook Look at Eleanor Roosevelt's Remarkable Life.* Atheneum, 2005. 176pp. ISBN 978-0-689-86544-2. Grades 5–9. With photographs and other memorabilia reminiscent of a scrap book, this biography looks at the life of Eleanor Roosevelt (1884–1962). It presents her roles as mother, wife, newspaper columnist, civil rights supporter, champion of the underprivileged, and United Nations delegate. Bibliography, Notes, and Index. *Society of Midland Authors Award Honor, School Library Journal Best Children's Books, Voice of Youth Advocates Nonfiction Honor List,* and *Jefferson Cup Honor Book.*

2377. Fradin, Dennis B., and Judith Bloom. *Fight On! Mary Church Terrell's Battle for Integration.* See entry 1963.

2378. Fradin, Dennis B., and Judith Bloom Fradin. *Ida B. Wells: Mother of the Civil Rights Movement.* See entry 1964.

2379. Freedman, Russell. *Babe Didrikson Zaharias: The Making of a Champion.* Clarion, 1999. 192pp. ISBN 978-0-395-63367-0. Grades 5 up. Mildred "Babe" Didrikson Zacharias (1911–1956) rose to fame as an All-American basketball player, an Olympic gold medalist in track and field, a champion golfer, tennis player, baseball player, diver, and bowler. In 1950 she received the accolade of Woman Athlete of the Half Century. She was born into a poor Texas family and realized that sports could help her earn recognition and money. She participated in the 1932 Olympics on the track and field team and won two gold medals. She married wrestler George Zacharias, and Betty Dodd, a fellow golfer, lived with them. Zacharias started the Ladies Professional Golf Association and won more than eighty titles. She showed that hard work and a little bit of self-promotion could be profitable. Photographs highlight the text. Bibliography and Index. *American Library Association Best Books for Young Adults, Tashas High School Reading List* (Texas), *Capitol Choices Noteworthy Titles* (Washington, D.C.), *School Library Journal Best Books for Children, Bulletin Blue Ribbon,* and *Dorothy Canfield Fisher Children's Book Awards* (Vermont).

2380. Freedman, Russell. *Eleanor Roosevelt: A Life of Discovery.* See entry 1967.

2381. Freedman, Russell. *Franklin Delano Roosevelt.* See entry 1968.

2382. Freedman, Russell. *The Voice that Challenged a Nation: Marian Anderson and the Struggle for Equal Rights.* Clarion, 2004. 114pp. ISBN 978-0-618-15976-5. Grades 5–8. Marian Anderson (1897–1993) grew up in Philadelphia singing in church choirs. She applied to a music conservatory as a teenager but was told that the school would not take "colored." She and her accompanist faced Jim Crow laws in the United States, but in Europe she performed for royalty and received the highest accolades from musicians who recognized excellence. Arturo Toscanini declared her voice to be "heard once in a hundred years." She sang most of her repertoire in its native language. In 1939 the Daughters of the American Revolution refused to allow Anderson to sing in their concert hall. Eleanor Roosevelt arranged for her to sing on the steps of the Lincoln Memorial on Easter Sunday, and 75,000 fans came to listen. Although Anderson did not see herself as an activist, she did what was needed to help her people. Photographs highlight the text about this talented woman and her devotion to her craft. Bibliography, Chronology, Discography, Notes, Web Sites, and Index. *Newbery Honor, Robert F. Sibert Medal, Horn Book Fanfare, School Library Journal Best Books for Children, American Library Association Best Books for Young Adults, American Library Association Notable Children's, Bulletin Blue Ribbon, Orbis Pictus Honor, Capitol Choices Noteworthy Titles* (Washington, D.C.), *Kirkus Reviews Editor's Choice, Dorothy Canfield Fisher Children's Book Award* (Vermont), *Flicker Tales* (North Dakota) nomination, *Parents Choice Award, James Madison Honor Book, Jefferson Cup Honor Book,* and *Charlie May Simon Children's Book Award* (Arkansas) nomination.

2383. Freedman, Suzanne. *Louis Brandeis: The People's Justice.* See entry 1970.

2384. Gentry, Tony, and Heather Lehr Wagner. *Jesse Owens: Champion Athlete.* (Black Americans of Achievement) Chelsea House, 2005. 116pp. ISBN 978-0-7910-8252-2. Grades 5 up. Gentry first recounts Owens's experience at the 1936 Olympics in Berlin, when Hitler spurned him as non-Aryan while the crowds loved his fluid running style. Then Gentry turns to Owens's childhood in the South and in Cleveland, where he met his future wife and the Irish coach who encouraged him. After breaking track records, Owens (1913–1980) met

Olympic gold medal winner Charlie Paddock and decided he wanted to become an Olympian himself. In Berlin, Owens became good friends with his chief competitor in the long jump, Luz Long. The two seemed to bring out the best in each other as they exchanged jump after jump before Owens finally won the gold and Long the silver. Photographs, Chronology, Further Reading, and Index.

2385. Gerstein, Mordicai. *What Charlie Heard.* See entry 1976.

2386. Gherman, Beverly. *Norman Rockwell: Storyteller with a Brush.* Atheneum, 2000. 57pp. ISBN 978-0-689-82001-4. Grades 4–8. Norman Rockwell (1894–1978) painted both traditional and contemporary subjects. This biography examines his life and his works in ten chapters. During his career, he painted many covers for *The Saturday Evening Post,* and toward the end he painted some subjects that seemed controversial to his viewers. Reproductions of his work augment the text. Bibliography, Chronology, Notes, Web Sites, and Index. *Student Book Award* (Maine) nomination.

2387. Giblin, James Cross. *Charles A. Lindbergh: A Human Hero.* Clarion, 1997. 212pp. ISBN 978-0-395-63389-2. Grades 5–10. Charles Augustus Lindbergh (1902–1974) became known internationally after he made a 33-hour solo flight across the Atlantic in 1927. He also gained the sympathy of the world after his child was kidnapped and murdered. He was an adventurer, environmentalist, family man, and anti-Semite. The text also reveals his contentious relationship with journalists who followed him everywhere, never allowing him privacy. Quotes from Lindbergh himself as well as others give veracity to the text. Photographs complement the text. Bibliography and Index.

2388. Greenfield, Eloise. *Mary McLeod Bethune.* See entry 1980.

2389. Halasa, Malu. *Elijah Muhammad: Religious Leader.* (Black Americans of Achievement) Chelsea House, 1990. 110pp. ISBN 978-1-55546-602-2. Grades 5 up. As a young boy, Elijah Poole (1897–1975) was forbidden to go into the woods on the way home from school. One day he did so, however. He saw a man from his church lynched by a group of white men, and he never forgot the horror. He moved to the North, where he had to go on relief during the Depression before he could find a job to support his family. He was interested in Marcus Garvey's Black Nationalism and Ali's Moorish Temple of America. But when he heard Fard talk about his Nation of Islam, Elijah in turn eloquently proclaimed the values of Islam to the black community. He became Elijah Muhammad, the founder of the Black Muslims. Chronology, Further Reading, and Index.

2390. Harness, Cheryl. *The Groundbreaking, Chance-Taking Life of George Washington Carver and Science and Invention.* See entry 1982.

2391. Hart, Philip S. *Up in the Air: The Story of Bessie Coleman.* (Trailblazers) Carolrhoda, 1996. 80pp. Paper ISBN 978-0-8761-4978-2. Grades 4–6. Growing up in the South in the early 1900s Bessie Coleman (1892–1926) had to stay at home to watch her sister while her mother worked, but she planned to make something of her life. In 1920 she became the first African American woman to fly an airplane, and built a career as a barnstorming pilot in the 1920s. She did not live long enough to open a school for black aviators, but she became an inspiration to many who followed her into new and risky occupations. Notes, Bibliography, and Index.

2392. Haugen, Brenda. *Douglas MacArthur: America's General.* (Signature Lives Modern America) Compass Point, 2005. 112pp. ISBN 978-0-7565-0994-1; paper ISBN 978-0-7565-1855-4. Grades 5–8. Born into a military family, Douglas MacArthur (1880–1964) carried on the family tradition and became a general in the United States Army. He rose in command during World War II and Korea after which he became the Army chief of staff. Most of the information here concerns his career and his popularity with the American people. Photographs highlight the text. Bibliography and Index.

2393. Haugen, Brenda. *Franklin Delano Roosevelt: The New Deal President.* (Signature Lives) Compass Point, 2006. 112pp. ISBN 978-0-7565-1586-7. Grades 5–8. This biography of Franklin Delano Roosevelt (1882–1945) covers his childhood, personal life, period as governor, and his presidency. He came to the presidency during the Depression, and he continued in the job during World War II. A number of his policies still have a major influence in the country, and excerpts from some of his and Churchill's speeches are included. Photographs and illustrations augment the text. Bibliography, Glossary, Chronology, Notes, Further Reading, and Index.

2394. Haugen, Brenda. *Langston Hughes: The Voice of Harlem.* (Signature Lives) Compass Point, 2005. 112pp. ISBN 978-0-7565-0993-4; paper ISBN 978-0-7565-1860-8. Grades 4–8. Langston Hughes (1902–1967), African American writer, published in several genres including poetry, short stories, and essays. The text looks at his childhood and his work as well as his travels and his value as a member of the Harlem Renaissance. Photographs enhance the text. Index.

2395. Healy, Nick. *Paul Robeson.* (African-American Biographies) Raintree, 2003. 64pp. ISBN 978-0-7398-6874-4; paper ISBN 978-1-4109-0040-1. Grades 4–6. African American Paul Robeson (1898–1976) attended college, where he excelled at athletics, and then began an acting and singing career as a bass-baritone. He was also multilingual and became active in civil rights. This volume highlights his childhood and his achievements and honors, including the Spingarn Medal and the Stalin Peace Prize. Bibliography and Index.

2396. Hopkinson, Deborah. *Sweet Land of Liberty.* Illustrated by Leonard Jenkins. Peachtree, 2007. 32pp. ISBN 978-1-56145-395-5. Grades 1–5. When Oscar L. Chapman (1896–1978) was a poor young white boy in rural Virginia, his teacher asked him to select a picture for the school. He chose Abraham Lincoln and the bigoted school board expelled him. Later, in 1939, he was the assistant secretary of the interior and had a chance to find a place for Marian Anderson to sing in Washington, D.C., when the Daughters of the American Revolution banned her from their hall. He lobbied Franklin D. Roosevelt, and the ensuing concert at the Lincoln Memorial drew more than 75,000 people, a major moment in the civil rights movement.

2397. Hubbard, Crystal. *Catching the Moon: The Story of a Young Girl's Baseball Dream.* Illustrated by Randy Duburke. Lee & Low, 2005. 32pp. ISBN 978-1-58430-243-8. Grades K–2. Marcenia Lyle Alberga (1921–1996) loves to play baseball in the 1930s, but her parents think she acts too much like a tomboy. Then the St. Louis Cardinals manager, Gabby Street, opens a baseball day camp. Marcenia's determination and skill overcome his objections and he accepts her in the program, even giving her the baseball shoes she needs. An afterword indicates that she was the first female roster member of a professional Negro League. She played as Toni Stone.

2398. Jones, Victoria Garrett. *Marian Anderson: A Voice Uplifted.* (Sterling Biographies) Sterling, 2007. 124pp. ISBN 978-1-4027-5802-7; paper ISBN 978-1-4027-4239-2. Grades 5–8. This biography of Marian Anderson (1897–1993) contains anecdotes about her stable childhood and her struggles as a young adult to develop her amazing contralto voice. She became an inspiration for civil rights activists, known and celebrated throughout the world but banned from singing at Washington, D.C.'s Constitution Hall. Eleanor Roosevelt arranged for her concert near the Lincoln Memorial and invited her to the White House, an unheard-of event during segregation. Photographs, documents, and illustrations augment the text. Bibliography, Glossary, Chronology, and Index.

2399. Keating, Frank. *Will Rogers: An American Legend.* See entry 1994.

2400. Keller, Emily. *Margaret Bourke-White: A Photographer's Life.* Lerner, 1996. 127pp. ISBN 978-0-8225-4916-1. Grades 5 up. Margaret Bourke-White (1904–1971) helped to develop the photo-essay style of *Life* magazine's news reporting. Her photographs of industrial scenes and machinery, people coping during the Depression, World War II battlefields, and a variety of other subjects helped people see these things in a different way. Her work retains its timeless quality. Photographs, Sources, Bibliography, and Index.

2401. Kent, Deborah. *Dorothy Day: Friend to the Forgotten.* Eerdmans, 2004. 146pp. Paper ISBN 978-0-8028-5265-6. Grades 5–9. Dorothy Day (1897–1980) was known throughout the world as the leader of the Catholic Worker movement. She was a journalist who thought that community service and social justice defined what it means to be human. She helped publish a newspaper, reached out to all in need, gave solace to the indigent, and guided those who wanted to pursue a life of contemplation. She went to jail many times in the 1950s for protesting against nuclear weapons. Photographs and Index.

2402. Kent, Deborah. *Hellen Keller: Author and Advocate for the Disabled.* See entry 1998.

2403. Kerby, Mona. *Amelia Earhart: Courage in the Sky.* Illustrated by Eileen McKeating. (Women of Our Time) Puffin, 1996. 57pp. Paper ISBN 978-0-14-034263-5. Grades 3–6. Amelia Earhart (1898–1937) was the first woman to pilot a plane across the Atlantic. Kerby presents her life and how she became interested in flight. Her plane disappeared while flying over the Pacific. Bibliography and Index.

2404. Kittredge, Mary. *Barbara McClintock.* Chelsea House, 1991. 103pp. ISBN 978-1-55546-666-4. Grades 5 up. As a young woman working for a male scientist studying genes in maize (corn), Barbara McClintock (1902–1992) realized he was looking in the wrong places for the differences among the ten genes. She looked in the right place, made the scientist furious, and McClintock lost her job. But she had begun to establish her name in the study of cytogenetics. She worked mainly at the labs of the Carnegie Institution in Cold Spring Harbor, New York, researching maize. She cross-pollinated various kinds of corn to see what happened to the offspring. Her major discovery—that genetic material moved from place to place on chromosomes—occurred 30 years before scientists realized she was right. They refused to acknowledge her research at the time; they were more interested in the discovery of DNA. She won the Nobel Prize in 1983 for her work, and other awards and prizes followed but none of them changed her methods or her appreciation of life. She said her work had given her much pleasure through the years. Photographs enhance the text. Chronology, Further Reading, and Index.

2405. Kliment, Bud. *Count Basie.* Chelsea House, 1992. 127pp. ISBN 978-0-7910-1118-8. Grades 5 up. Count Basie (1904–1984) was a drummer who switched to playing the piano. He toured in vaudeville acts to sharpen his timing and to learn a variety of styles. In 1935 he formed his own group, backing vocalists including Billie Holiday. Photographs and reproductions enhance the text. Chronology, Further Reading, and Index.

2406. Krensky, Stephen. *A Man for All Seasons: The Life of George Washington Carver.* See entry 2007.

2407. Krull, Kathleen. *The Boy on Fairfield Street: How Ted Geisel Grew Up to Become Dr. Seuss.* Illustrated by Steve Johnson and Lou Fancher. Random, 2004. 43pp. ISBN 978-0-375-82298-8. Grades K–4. Ted Geisel (1904–1991) took the name "Dr. Seuss" when he began to write children's picture books. He loved books and animals because his mother read to him and his father worked in a zoo in Springfield, Massachusetts, where Geisel grew up. He doodled all the time and tended to break enough rules in the one art class he took that his teachers—in school, at Dartmouth, and at Oxford—did not think he would achieve much in his life. He moved to New York City when he was 22 and began the career that shaped his life and gave children delightful books to read. Full-page oil-on-gessoed-paper paintings illustrate the text. *Bluebonnet Award* (Texas) nomination, *Children's Book Award* (North Carolina) nomination, *Charlotte Award* (New York) nomination, *Capitol Choices Noteworthy Titles* (Washington, D.C.), *Beehive Children's Informational Book Award* (Utah) nomination, *Young Hoosier Book Award* (Indiana) nomination, and *Garden State Children's Book Award* (New Jersey) nomination.

2408. Krull, Kathleen. *The Boy Who Invented TV: The Story of Philo Farnsworth.* Knopf, 2009. 40pp. ISBN 978-0-375-84561-1. Grades 2–5. When Philo Farnsworth (1906–1971) was only 3, he drew schema of trains and was fascinated by phonographs and telephones. Eleven years later, as he plowed potato rows on the family farm, he began to imagine transmitting pictures via airwaves. Then when he was 21 in 1927, he invented the first television. His wife, Pem, was the first person ever televised. But few identify Farnsworth as inventor of the television because, as Krull comments in a note, RCA (Radio Corporation of America) skillfully wrestled the patent from him and he got neither royalties nor credit for his amazing contribution to civilization. Mixed-media illustrations enhance the text. *Outstanding Science Trade Books for*

Students, Beehive Children's Book Award (Utah), and *School Library Journal Best Books of the Year.*

2409. Krull, Kathleen. *Harvesting Hope: The Story of Cesar Chavez.* Illustrated by Yuyi Morales. Harcourt, 2003. 48pp. ISBN 978-0-15-201437-7. Grades 2–6. César Chávez (1927–1993) had a difficult childhood working as a migrant with his family in California and wanted to change the system. He believed in nonviolent protests and he organized a historic one when he was 38. Eventually, working conditions were improved. The text attempts to give a sense of his complexity—both his experiences and his feelings. Acrylic illustrations. *School Library Journal Best Books for Children* and *Capitol Choices Noteworthy Titles* (Washington, D.C.).

2410. Lakin, Patricia. *Amelia Earhart: More Than a Flier.* Illustrated by Alan and Lea Daniel. (Ready-to-Read Childhood of Famous Americans) Aladdin, 2003. 48pp. Paper ISBN 978-0-689-85575-7. Grades 1–2. Amelia Earhart was the first woman to fly across the Atlantic Ocean alone. Her plane disappeared when she tried to become the first woman to fly around the world. From the time she was a child, Earhart loved adventure. She was willing to risk danger to pursue her dreams.

2411. Langley, Wanda. *Women of the Wind: Early Women Navigators.* See entry 2013.

2412. Lassieur, Allison. *Eleanor Roosevelt: Activist for Social Change.* (Great Life Stories) Franklin Watts, 2006. 111pp. ISBN 978-0-531-13871-7; 2007, paper ISBN 978-0-53117-846-1. Grades 5–8. Eleanor Roosevelt (1884–1962) worked hard all her life. At first she wanted to be loved, and then after she became a wife and mother, she worked to overcome her fear of public speaking to campaign for her husband. She began promoting equal rights for all humans. During Roosevelt's administration and after his death, she spoke for all, and then became U.S. ambassador to the United Nations. Photographs accompany the text. Chronology, Further Reading, Web Sites, and Index.

2413. Lauber, Patricia. *Lost Star: The Story of Amelia Earhart.* Scholastic, 1989. 106pp. Paper ISBN 978-0-590-41159-2. Grades 5–8. In 1937 Amelia Earhart (1897–1937) attempted to fly around the world at the equator. Her plane was lost, and no one has ever found a trace of it. Earhart's mother was the first woman to reach Pikes Peak and made bloomers for Amelia and her sister like those introduced by Amelia Jenks Bloomer. While alcoholism was destroying her father, Amelia became interested in airplanes and eventually flying. She married a publicist, George Putnam, who supported her interests. She was the first woman to fly across the Atlantic and the first person to cross the Pacific. People speculate that Earhart might have crashed in the Pacific islands controlled by the Japanese, where no one was allowed to search. For Further Reading and Index.

2414. Lawler, Mary. *Marcus Garvey: Black Nationalist Leader.* See entry 2015.

2415. Lawlor, Laurie. *Helen Keller: Rebellious Spirit.* See entry 2016.

2416. Leavitt, Amie Jane. *Amelia Earhart.* (What's So Great About?) Mitchell Lane, 2008. 32pp. ISBN 978-1-58415-576-8. Grades 2–4. Amelia Earhart (1898–1937) became the first woman to fly alone across the Atlantic Ocean. Then she tried to fly around the world and was lost at sea. This volume gives an overview of her life. Illustrations augment the text. Bibliography, Chronology, Glossary, Further Reading, Web Sites, and Index.

2417. Leavitt, Amie Jane. *Helen Keller.* See entry 2018.

2418. Lyons, Mary E. *Catching the Fire: Philip Simmons, Blacksmith.* (African-American Artists and Artisans) Houghton, 1997. 47pp. ISBN 978-0-395-72033-2. Grades 3–6. Philip Simmons (1912–), an African American artist and great-grandson of slaves, has achieved renown for his ornamental wrought-iron work. He grew up in Charleston, South Carolina, where an older craftsman trained him. The text quotes Simmons throughout as it gives a brief overview of his life with a wife who died young and children who had to live with relatives as he concentrated on his craft to support them. Photographs of Simmons's work augment the text. *Children's Book Award* (South Carolina) nomination and *Capitol Choices Noteworthy Titles* (Washington, D.C.).

2419. McCarthy, Meghan. *Strong Man: The Story of Charles Atlas.* Knopf, 2007. 40pp. ISBN 978-0-375-82940-6. Grades K–3. Bullies picked on Angelo Siciliano after he arrived at Ellis Island as a young boy. But then he reinvented himself as Charles Atlas (1893–1972), growing from a 98-pound weakling into "The World's Most Perfectly Developed Man." He developed the Dynamic Tension fitness program and sold it to young men around the world who felt ungainly and weak. He was a sideshow strongman and body builder who helped others. Illustrations complement the text. Bibliography and Notes. *Booklist Editor's Choice.*

2420. McDonough, Yona Zeldis. *Hammerin' Hank: The Life of Hank Greenberg.* Walker, 2006. 32pp. ISBN 978-0-8027-8997-6. Grades K–3. Henry Benjamin Greenberg (1911–1986) wanted to become a baseball player in the 1930s. He refused to let prejudice stop him, and he became America's first Jewish baseball star. Although his Orthodox parents expected him to go to college, he wanted only to play. He joined the Detroit Tigers, and during the 1934 season he had to decide whether to play or observe the High Holy Days. He split the difference by playing on Rosh Hashanah and going to synagogue on Yom Kippur. Eventually he was elected to the Baseball Hall of Fame. Gouache illustrations enhance the text. Statistics, Bibliography, Chronology, and Glossary.

2421. MacKinnon, Christy. *Silent Observer.* See entry 2023.

2422. McKissack, Patricia C., and Frederick McKissack. *Carter G. Woodson: The Father of Black History.* See entry 2025.

2423. McKissack, Patricia C., and Frederick McKissack. *George Washington Carver: The Peanut Scientist.* See entry 2027.

2424. McKissack, Patricia C., and Frederick McKissack. *Ida B. Wells-Barnett: A Voice Against Violence.* See entry 2028.

2425. McKissack, Patricia C., and Frederick McKissack. *Jesse Owens: Olympic Star.* (Great African Americans) Enslow, 2001. 32pp. ISBN 978-0-7660-1681-1. Grades 2–4. Jesse Owens (1913–1980) broke several world records when he ran for Ohio State University. At the 1936 Olympics, held in Berlin during Hitler's regime, he won four gold medals and became an Olympic legend. Index.

2426. McKissack, Patricia C., and Frederick McKissack. *Langston Hughes: Great American Poet.* Illustrated by Michael David Biegel. (Great African Americans) Enslow, 2002. 32pp. ISBN 978-0-7660-1695-8. Grades 2–4. Langston Hughes (1902–1967) lived with his father only briefly because his father moved to Mexico where he could practice law. When Hughes and his mother went to join him, an earthquake frightened his mother back to Kansas. Hughes lived mainly with his grandmother before he attended college in New York. He decided, against his father's will, to become a writer. He wrote drama, poetry, essays, and newspaper articles during his career, and he traveled widely. Some have called him "Harlem's Poet" because he wrote so well about his own people. Words to Know and Index.

2427. McKissack, Patricia C., and Frederick McKissack. *Louis Armstrong: Jazz Musician.* Illustrated by Edward Ostendorf. (Great African Americans) Enslow, 2001. 32pp. ISBN 978-0-7660-1675-0. Grades 2–4. Born in New Orleans, Louisiana, Louis Armstrong (1901–1971) became a jazz trumpeter known as "Satchmo." His skill with the trumpet increased interest in this instrument for solo performance. Black-and-white photographs and drawings enhance the text. Glossary and Index.

2428. McKissack, Patricia C., and Frederick McKissack. *Marian Anderson: A Great Singer.* Illustrated by Edward Ostendorf. (Great African Americans) Enslow, 2001. 32pp. ISBN 978-0-7660-1676-7. Grades 2–4. African American singer Marian Anderson (1897–1993) struggled against prejudice to become one of the great opera performers of the century. Black-and-white photographs and drawings enhance the text. Glossary and Index.

2429. McKissack, Patricia C., and Frederick McKissack. *Mary Church Terrell: Leader for Equality.* See entry 2030.

2430. McKissack, Patricia C., and Frederick McKissack. *Mary McLeod Bethune: A Great Teacher.* See entry 2031.

2431. McKissack, Patricia C., and Frederick McKissack. *Paul Robeson: A Voice to Remember.* See entry 2032.

2432. McKissack, Patricia C., and Frederick McKissack. *Ralph J. Bunche: Peacemaker.* (Great African Americans) Enslow, 2002. 32pp. ISBN 978-0-7660-1701-6. Grades 2–4. Ralph Bunche (1904–1971) worked to help his fellow African Americans have a better life. But he was also interested in the lives of other races. In 1950 he received the Nobel Prize for his work on the United Nations Palestine Commission. Photographs and illustrations augment the text. Glossary and Index.

2433. MacLeod, Elizabeth. *George Washington Carver: An Innovative Life.* See entry 2036.

2434. MacLeod, Elizabeth. *Helen Keller: A Determined Life.* See entry 2038.

2435. Mannis, Celeste Davidson. *Julia Morgan Built a Castle.* See entry 2043.

2436. Mara, Wil. *Franklin D. Roosevelt.* (Rookie Biographies) Scholastic, 2004. 31pp. ISBN 978-0-516-21844-1; Children's paper ISBN 978-0-516-25823-2. Grades K–2. Franklin D. Roosevelt (1882–1945), the cousin of the twenty-sixth president, Theodore Roosevelt, became the thirty-second president. After he contracted polio and needed a wheel chair, he led the country with the help of his wife, Eleanor Roosevelt. Photographs, Illustrations, and Index.

2437. Mayo, Gretchen Will. *Frank Lloyd Wright.* (Trailblazers of the Modern World) World Almanac, 2004. ISBN 978-0-8368-5101-4. Grades 5–8. Frank Lloyd Wright (1867–1959) had his own style of architecture, fitting the building to the setting in which it would live. His work made him America's best-known architect, and the places he designed—especially the Robie House in Chicago; Fallingwater in Bear Run, Pennsylvania; the Johnson Wax Building in Racine, Wisconsin; and the Solomon R. Guggenheim Museum in New York—are destinations for all interested in innovative architecture. Photos, Chronology, Further Reading, Glossary, Index, Web Sites.

2438. Meltzer, Milton. *Dorothea Lange: Life Through the Camera.* Illustrated by Donna Diamond. Syracuse University, 2000. 64pp. Paper ISBN 978-0-8156-0622-2. Grades 2–6. Childhood polio left Dorothea Lange (1895–1965) with a limp. She disliked school and avoided it as much as possible while a teenager. She lived with her grandparents after her parents divorced. When she was 17, she knew she wanted to be a photographer, although she had never taken a picture. She had seen poor people in the street, and she wanted to record their lives. While working, she traveled across the country and took photographs of the hungry and homeless during the Great Depression. Those photographs give insight into a difficult time in history. *Booklist Editor's Choice.*

2439. Micklos, John. *Unsolved: What Really Happened to Amelia Earhart?* Enslow, 2007. 144pp. ISBN 978-0-7660-2365-9. Grades 4–8. After becoming the first woman to fly across the United States and the first woman to fly solo across the Atlantic Ocean, Amelia Earhart (1897–1937) wanted to fly around the earth at the equator. Instead of being known for her "firsts," she is more famous for disappearing in the Pacific Ocean during the most dangerous portion of her trip. The text discusses the many theories that circulate about her disappearance, including one that Japanese captured her and her co-pilot. Maps, photographs, and illustrations enhance the text. Chronology, Notes, Further Reading, Glossary, Web Sites, and Index.

2440. Miller, Norma, and Alan B. Govenar. *Stompin' at the Savoy: The Story of Norma Miller.* Illustrated by Martin French. Candlewick, 2006. 54pp. ISBN 978-0-7636-2244-2. Grades 4–8. Conversations with Norma Miller (1919–) form the basis of this biography. She recalls her long life as a teacher, choreographer, and dancer as she continues to do each. Born after her father died, she remembers her mother's struggle to keep the family together in their Harlem home on 140th Street near the Savoy Ballroom. She would dance outside for pennies. By the age of 12 she was dancing inside, and at 15 she went to Europe to become a professional Lindy Hopper. She worked with Duke Wellington, Ethel Waters, and the Marx Brothers and performed around the world and in movies and on television. Ink and wash illustrations enhance the text. *Bulletin Blue Ribbon.*

2441. Mitchell, Barbara. *We'll Race You, Henry! A Story About Henry Ford.* See entry 2050.

2442. Mohr, Nicholasa. *All for the Better: A Story of El Barrio.* Illustrated by Rudy Gutierrez. Steck-Vaughn, 1992. Paper ISBN 978-0-8114-8060-4. Grades 2–5. Evelina Lopez Antonetty came alone from Puerto Rico to New York and the Bronx at the age of 11 during the Depression. She adjusted to English and to a new school and then convinced her proud neighbors to accept food stamps from the federal government. She eventually formed the United Bronx Parents Group to help the Hispanic community.

2443. Mortensen, Lori. *Thomas Edison: Inventor, Scientist, and Genius.* See entry 2053.

2444. Moss, Marissa. *Mighty Jackie: The Strike Out Queen.* Illustrated by C. F. Payne. Simon & Schuster, 2004. Unpaged. ISBN 978-0-689-86329-5. Grades K–3. In 1931, when she was 17 years old, Jackie Mitchell (1914–1987), a pitcher for the Chattanooga Lookouts, struck out both Babe Ruth and Lou Gehrig in an exhibition game. Her father and Dazzy Vance, a Brooklyn Dodger, taught her how to play. Illustrations complement the text. Bibliography. *Readers Choice Award* (Virginia) nomination, *Children's, Junior and Young Adult Book Award* (South Carolina) nomination, *Monarch Award* nomination, *Black-Eyed Susan Award* (Maryland) nomination, *Volunteer State Book Award* (Tennessee) nomination, *Diamonds Award* (Delaware) nomination, *Children's Choice Picture Book Award* (Washington) nomination, *Capitol Choices Noteworthy Titles* (Washington, D.C.), and *Young Readers' Choice Award* (Louisiana) nomination.

2445. Myers, Walter Dean. *Ida B. Wells: Let the Truth Be Told.* Amistad, 2008. 38pp. ISBN 978-0-06-027705-5. Grades 3–6. This biography of Ida B. Wells-Barnett (1862–1931) presents an incredibly accomplished African American woman who became an educator, writer, journalist, activist, suffragette, and voice against lynching long before the civil rights movement. She raised her siblings after her parents died from yellow fever. After she took a seat in the ladies' coach of a train and was forced from her seat, she sued the railroad. She then became a businesswoman who protested injustice. As a writer, she told the world after the lynching of businessmen friends. She never stopped speaking for people who were denied rights that were legally theirs. Illustrations complement the text. Chronology.

2446. Niven, Penelope. *Carl Sandburg: Adventures of a Poet.* Illustrated by Mark Nadel. Harcourt, 2003. 32pp. ISBN 978-0-15-204686-6. Grades 1–4. This biography examines the life of Carl Sandburg (1878–1967), a journalist, poet, and historian who won Pulitzer Prizes for both his poetry and his history. Anecdotes about his life, examples of his writing, and photographs and illustrations complete the text.

2447. Nobleman, Marc Tyler. *Boys of Steel: The Creators of Superman.* Illustrated by Ross MacDonald. Borzoi, 2008. Unpaged. ISBN 978-0-375-83802-6. Grades 4–6. This biography relates the story of Jerry Siegel (1914–1996) and Joe Shuster (1914–1992), who met as young men in Cleveland. They both felt they were misfits, and both loved science fiction and pulp magazines. In 1934 they created a superhero, and four years later they convinced a publisher to publish their story about a Man of Steel in a comic book format: Action Comics # 1. Unfortunately, they sold all the rights to Superman for a very small sum. Illustrations complement the text. Bibliography. *Capitol Choices Noteworthy Titles* (Washington, D.C.).

2448. Panchyk, Richard. *Franklin Delano Roosevelt for Kids: His Life and Times with 21 Activities.* Chicago Review, 2007. 148pp. ISBN 978-1-55652-657-2. Grades 4–8. Panchyk offers plenty of information about Franklin Delano Roosevelt (1882–1945) and his youth and work as president during the Great Depression and World War II, with additional information about his personality in sidebars. Among the twenty-one activities for children are how to stage a radio show, give a fireside chat, start a stamp collection, go bird watching, decode a Navy signal flag message, play charades, and participate in a political debate. Further Reading, Glossary, Web Sites, and Index.

2449. Parker, Robert Andrew. *Piano Starts Here: The Young Art Tatum.* Schwartz & Wade, 2007. Unpaged. ISBN 978-0-375-83965-8. Grades K–4. Born almost blind, Art Tatum (1910–1956) taught himself to play the piano and became a renowned jazz pianist, performing around the world. This biography looks at him as a young boy playing for his parents to dance, at church where he loved the smells of furniture polish and flowers, and in clubs beginning when he was 16 in 1926. The illustrations show Tatum engrossed in his work, probably indulging in his legendary improvisations. Watercolor and scratched-ink lines complement the text.

2450. Petrick, Neila S. *Katherine Stinson Otero: High Flyer.* Illustrated by Daggi Wallace. Pelican, 2006. 32pp. ISBN 978-1-58980-368-8. Grades K–3.   Katherine Stinson Otero (1891–1977) was the fourth licensed female aviator in the United States. Her mother refused to let anyone stop her daughters from flying, and she opened a school in which they could teach. Otero traveled around the world and performed for the Chinese emperor in 1917. She was denied permission to fly in Europe during World War I so she flew exhibitions in the United States and earned more than two million dollars for the war effort before driving an ambulance for the Red Cross. Pastel illustrations enhance the text.

2451. Pflueger, Lynda. *Amelia Earhart: Legend of Flight.* (Historical American Biographies) Enslow, 2003. 128pp. ISBN 978-0-7660-1976-8. Grades 5–9.   Amelia Earhart (1898–1937) was the first woman passenger to fly across the Atlantic Ocean, and four years later she became the first female pilot to accomplish the feat. This biography traces her life from her early years, through her first flight, her establishment of the Ninety-Nines organization for women pilots, and her preparations for the flight in which she disappeared. Photographs augment the text. Glossary, Chronology, Notes, Further Reading, Web Sites, and Index.

2452. Pinkney, Andrea Davis. *Duke Ellington: The Piano Prince and His Orchestra.* Hyperion, 1998. 32pp. ISBN 978-0-7868-0178-7; 2007, paper ISBN 978-0-7868-1420-6. Grades K–2.   This biography of Duke Ellington (1899–1974) offers an overview of his musical career from playing ragtime in pool halls to his concert at Carnegie Hall in 1943. The text has a rhythm that sounds like Ellington's own music. He disliked the music that he heard at a young age because of its boring, steady rhythm and changed this to something that brought joy to both performers and audience. Illustrations enhance the text. Notes. *Caldecott Honor, Coretta Scott King Book Awards, Young Hoosier Award* (Indiana) nomination, *Children's Book Award* (North Carolina) nomination, *Garden State Teen Book Award* (New Jersey) nomination, *Children's Book Award* (Rhode Island), *SCASL Book Award* (South Carolina) nomination, *Capitol Choices Noteworthy Titles* (Washington, D.C.), and *School Library Journal Best Books of the Year.*

2453. Plourde, Lynn. *Margaret Chase Smith: A Woman for President.* Illustrated by David McPhail. Charlesbridge, 2008. Unpaged. ISBN 978-1-58089-234-6; paper ISBN 978-1-58089-235-3. Grades 3–5.   In 1964 Margaret Chase Smith (1897–1995) became the first woman from a major political party to run for president of the United States. She served in the Senate representing Maine, taking her husband's seat after his death. She remained there for thirty-two years. In 1950 she spoke against McCarthyism, one of the few serving in the Senate to have the nerve to oppose the powerful senator. Photographs illuminate the text. Chronology, Further Reading, Web Sites, and Index.

2454. Porter, A. P. *Jump at de Sun: The Story of Zora Neale Hurston.* See entry 2062.

2455. Rappaport, Doreen. *Eleanor, Quiet No More.* See entry 2064.

2456. Raum, Elizabeth. *Alice Paul.* See entry 2065.

2457. Ray, Deborah Kogan. *Wanda Gág: The Girl Who Lived to Draw.* Viking, 2008. Unpaged. ISBN 978-0-670-06292-8. Grades 2–4.   Wanda Gág (1893–1946) grew up in Minnesota with her immigrant parents and siblings listening to German fairy tales. Her artist father's dying wish was that she should attend school. Using quotes from diaries, this biography describes how she continued to educate herself and other family members while working to feed the family. Not until two of her younger sisters had finished school was she able to attend. Then in 1928, at a gallery show in New York, a publisher saw her work and offered her a contract for *Millions of Cats.* Often called the first modern picture book, her work remains in print. Illustrations complement the text. Bibliography and Notes. *Kirkus Reviews Editor's Choice.*

2458. Rhynes, Martha E. *I, Too, Sing America: The Story of Langston Hughes.* (World Writers) Morgan Reynolds, 2002. 144pp. ISBN 978-1-883846-89-3. Grades 5–9. Langston Hughes (1902–1967), perhaps the most celebrated African American poet, had a difficult childhood but overcame it to help others and to become a poet, essayist, and fiction writer who celebrated being an African American. The ten chapters look at his influence during the Harlem Renaissance, the people he knew, and his activism. Photographs augment the text. Bibliography, Glossary, Chronology, Further Reading, Web Sites, and Index.

2459. Roberson, Elizabeth Whitley. *Tiny Broadwick: The First Lady of Parachuting.* Pelican, 2001. 112pp. Paper ISBN 978-1-56554-780-3. Grades 4–8. Georgia "Tiny" Thompson Brown Broadwick (1893–1978) came from a poor family and defied her North Carolina neighbors by joining a hot-air balloon act, and then, as a teen, becoming the first woman to parachute. She had many successful jumps, but she also experienced some terrifying "near" misses. She was forgotten until the 1960s when aviation groups began honoring her, a 4-foot 11-inch female parachutist. The five chapters cover her leaving home, on the road with Charles Broadwick, in the air with Glenn Martin, and becoming the first lady of parachuting. Bibliography and Index.

2460. Rodriguez, Rachel. *Through Georgia's Eyes.* Illustrated by Julie Paschkis. Henry Holt, 2006. 2006pp. ISBN 978-0-8050-7740-7. Grades K–3. That Georgia O'Keeffe became an artist was unusual as it was mainly men who had that opportunity during her early life. O'Keeffe exhibited her independence in both her career and lifestyle. After living, marrying, and working in New York, she moved to New Mexico and lived alone in an isolated area, surrounded by sky and desert vistas. The illustrations offer a sense of O'Keeffe's own art.

2461. Rubin, Susan Goldman. *Edward Hopper: Painter of Light and Shadow.* Abrams, 2007. 48pp. ISBN 978-0-8109-9347-1. Grades 5–10. Edward Hopper (1882–1967) struggled for recognition as an artist when critics and viewers were uninterested in realism, still enjoying Impressionists. Among the images in his pictures are lighthouses, boats, and buildings. He effectively used dark and shadow to create the idea of some of his subjects being alone and isolated from society. Every page contains a reproduction of one of his pieces, among them *Night Hawks*, *Ground Swell*, and *New York Movie*. Bibliography, Further Reading, and Notes. *Voice of Youth Advocates Nonfiction Honor List.*

2462. St. George, Judith. *Make Your Mark, Franklin Roosevelt.* Illustrated by Spencer Britt. Philomel, 2007. Unpaged. ISBN 978-0-399-24175-8. Grades 2–5. Franklin Delano Roosevelt (1882–1945) grew up wealthy but had a strong sense of social and civic responsibility that was encouraged by a governess and headmaster. His mother, however, called him "Baby," kept his hair in long curls, and clothed him in dresses He decided to follow his fifth cousin, Teddy Roosevelt, into politics. Caricatures complement the text. Bibliography.

2463. Sakany, Lois. *Joe DiMaggio.* (Baseball Hall of Famers) Rosen, 2003. 112pp. ISBN 978-0-8239-3779-0. Grades 4–6. Joe DiMaggio (1914–1999) was one of baseball's great players. This volume traces his life and career with emphasis on his playing years. It ends with a picture of the Hall of Fame plaque and several pages of statistics.

2464. Schmidt, Gary D. *Robert Frost.* See entry 2074.

2465. Schroeder, Alan. *Josephine Baker: Entertainer.* Chelsea House, 2006. 127pp. ISBN 978-0-7910-9212-5. Grades 5 up. Josephine Baker (1906–1975) tried to escape poverty in St. Louis, Missouri, by entertaining her friends and visiting the city's black vaudeville houses. At 13, when she made her debut, she decided to base her comedy on an ill-fitting costume. In 1925 she sailed to France, and the French loved both her beauty and her dancing. During World War II the French Resistance recruited her as a secret agent. After the war she turned her estate in southern France into a tourist resort. She was one of the first civil rights crusaders and she adopted 12 children from different nations to show that people of different backgrounds can live in peace. Photographs complement the text. Chronology, Further Reading, and Index.

2466. Schuman, Michael A. *Eleanor Roosevelt: First Lady and Humanitarian.* BackinPrint.com, 2000. 128pp. Paper ISBN 978-0-595-00741-7. Grades 5–9. Among the titles used to describe Eleanor Roosevelt (1884–1962) are First Lady, journalist, activist, and delegate to the United Nations. Her concern for others showed in her attempts to help people of all races and economic levels although she had a wealthy and privileged background. She was an early advocate of women's rights, child labor laws, the eight-hour workday, and equality for African Americans. Chronology, Notes, and Index.

2467. Shaughnessy, Dan. *The Legend of the Curse of the Bambino.* Illustrated by C. F. Payne. Paula Wiseman, 2005. 32pp. ISBN 978-0-689-87235-8. Grades 2–5. One of baseball's greatest legends ended in 2004 after eighty-six years. Babe Ruth (1895–1948) played for the Boston Red Sox until he was sold to the New York Yankees after the 1919 season. From then until 2004—eighty-six years—the Red Sox suffered many last-minute defeats and failed to win a World Series. Many saw this as a curse that finally came to an end.

2468. Sloate, Susan. *Amelia Earhart: Challenging the Skies.* Fawcett, 1995. 118pp. Paper ISBN 978-0-449-90396-4. Grades 5–8. Amelia Earhart (1898–1937) disappeared during an attempt to fly around the world. Sloate considers the idea that the Japanese took her prisoner and that she might have lived a quiet life with another identity somewhere else. Although this idea is interesting, there is no evidence to support it. Earhart is presented as a woman exuding feminism and compassion while breaking records in a field considered to be reserved for men. Bibliography.

2469. Smith, Charles R., Jr. *Black Jack: The Ballad of Jack Johnson.* Neal Porter. 40pp. ISBN 978-1-59643-473-8. Grades 2–6. Black Jack, born Arthur John Johnson (1878–1946) in Galveston, Texas, was bullied as a child, and his mother, a former slave, told him to stand up for himself. He did, and discovered that he could fight. He worked at numerous jobs—dockworker, carriage painter, shop sweeper, horse trainer, baker, and porter—and along the way he was always boxing. His initial challenges to white heavyweight champions were rebuffed—they did not want to fight a black man. But eventually, they each fought him and lost. Vibrant color illustrations enhance the text. Bibliography.

2470. Stafford, Mark. *W. E. B. Du Bois: Scholar and Activist.* See entry 2083.

2471. Stone, Tanya Lee. *Sandy's Circus: A Story About Alexander Calder.* Illustrated by Boris Kulikov. Viking, 2008. Unpaged. ISBN 978-0-670-06268-3. Grades 2–4. Alexander "Sandy" Calder (1898–1976), the son of artists, became an engineer who loved art. Hired to draw pictures of the Ringling Brothers and Barnum and Bailey Circus, he started making his own kinetic circuses from wire, cork, buttons, yarns, and string. These pleased audiences from New York to Paris. Mixed-media collages enhance the text. Bibliography. *Kirkus Reviews Editor's Choice* and *School Library Journal Best Books for Children.*

2472. Streissguth, Thomas. *Rocket Man: The Story of Robert Goddard.* See entry 2087.

2473. Streissguth, Thomas. *Say It with Music: A Story About Irving Berlin.* Illustrated by Jennifer Hagerman. (Creative Minds) Carolrhoda, 1994. 64pp. ISBN 978-0-8761-4810-5. Grades 3–6. Irving Berlin (1888–1989), born Israel Baline, came to the United States with his family at the age of 5. He had to sell newspapers on the corner to help his family survive, and sometimes he would sing and receive tips. His singing led to an unexpected career as a songwriter. He wrote "God Bless America" and "White Christmas" as well as many other songs during his long life. Afterword and Bibliography.

2474. Sullivan, George. *Berenice Abbott, Photographer: An Independent Vision.* Clarion, 2006. 170pp. ISBN 978-0-618-44026-9. Grades 5–9. Berenice Abbott (1898–1991) grew up in Ohio, moved to Greenwich Village in 1918, and then went on to Paris. There she decided to become a photographer. Upon her return to New York, she got funding from the Federal Art Project for her own idea, Changing New York. She photographed the streets and buildings of the city as the building boom began and skyscrapers replaced older structures in many neighborhoods. Photographs highlight the text.

2475. Sullivan, George. *Helen Keller.* See entry 2088.

2476. Sullivan, George. *Helen Keller: Her Life in Pictures.* See entry 2089.

2477. Sutcliffe, Jane. *Amelia Earhart.* (History Maker Bios) Lerner, 2003. 48pp. ISBN 978-0-8225-0396-5. Grades 3–5. As a girl growing up in Kansas, Amelia Earhart (1898–1937) wore bloomers and played outside, unlike other girls she knew. As an adult working as a nurse's aide, she saw a stunt pilot and, although she had been uninterested in the Wright brothers and their plane, this time she became intrigued. She developed a desire to set records and this led to her attempt to fly around the world and her disappearance in 1937. The book's five chapters give an overview of her life. Illustrations augment the text. Bibliography, Further Reading, Glossary, Maps, Timeline, Web Sites, and Index.

2478. Sutcliffe, Jane. *George S. Patton, Jr.* See entry 2090.

2479. Sutcliffe, Jane. *Milton Hershey.* See entry 2092.

2480. Tanaka, Shelley. *Amelia Earhart: The Legend of the Lost Aviator.* Illustrated by David Craig. Abrams, 2008. 48pp. ISBN 978-0-8109-7095-3. Grades 3–6. Amelia Earhart (11898–1937) was 11 years old when she saw her first plane. As a college student volunteering as a nurse's aide in World War I, she decided to become a pilot. She became the first woman passenger on a transatlantic flight and then began to set her own records. Earhart represented herself well in the media through her own writing and speaking. Tanaka reveals the fragility of airplanes of the 1930s and the difficulties of navigation. Illustrations enhance the text. Bibliography, Notes, Web Sites, and Index.

2481. Tanenhaus, Sam. *Louis Armstrong: Musician.* (Black Americans of Achievement) Chelsea House, 1988. 127pp. ISBN 978-1-55546-571-1. Grades 5 up. Louis Armstrong (1901–1971) revolutionized jazz and helped establish it as one of the nation's most popular African American art forms. His father deserted the family, and his mother raised him until he was sent to reform school at 13. There he learned to play the cornet. He continued perfecting his art as he watched others play in the New Orleans entertainment areas. He went to Chicago and then New York before he became America's official goodwill ambassador in 1960. Photographs complement the text. Chronology, Further Reading, and Index.

2482. Taylor-Butler, Christine. *Thurgood Marshall.* (Rookie) Children's, 2006. 31pp. ISBN 978-0-51625-015-1; paper ISBN 978-0-51627-099-9. Grades 1–2. The first African American Supreme Court justice, Thurgood Marshall (1908–1993) was seen as an advocate of rights for all. This volume looks at his achievements from his early life in Baltimore through his education and his seat on the Supreme Court. Photographs enhance the text. Glossary.

2483. Towle, Wendy. *The Real McCoy: The Life of an African-American Inventor.* See entry 2096.

2484. Venezia, Mike. *Dorothea Lange.* (Getting to Know the World's Greatest Artists) Scholastic, 2000. 32pp. ISBN 978-0-516-22026-0; Children's Press, 2001, paper ISBN 978-0-516-27171-2. Grades K–5. Dorothea Lange (1895–1965) had polio as a child and always limped. She learned photography in New York City and opened a portrait studio in San Francisco. During the Depression she became an influential American documentary photographer and photojournalist when she photographed people who suffered terribly from both the Depression and from the Dust Bowl. Her work for the Farm Security Administration (FSA) was a major influence on the development of documentary photography.

2485. Venezia, Mike. *Duke Ellington.* (Getting to Know the World's Greatest Composers) Scholastic, 1995. 32pp. ISBN 978-0-516-04540-5; Children's Press, 1996, paper ISBN 978-0-516-44540-3. Grades K–5. Duke (Edward Kennedy) Ellington (1899–1974), born in Washington, D.C., played the piano, led orchestras, and composed music for fifty years, performing for presidents, queens, and the common people. He composed such important works as "Rockin' in Rhythm," "Satin Doll," "New Orleans," "A Drum Is a Women," "Take the 'A' Train," "Happy-Go-Lucky Local," "The Mooche," and "Crescendo in Blue." Illustrations and photographs enhance the text.

2486. Venezia, Mike. *Edward Hopper.* (Getting to Know the World's Greatest Artists) Scholastic, 1990. 32pp. ISBN 978-0-516-02277-2; Children's Press paper ISBN 978-0-516-42277-0. Grades K–5. Edward Hopper (1882–1967) studied art in New York with Robert Henri, one of the fathers of American realism. When he visited Europe, he liked Rembrandt's painting of *The Night Watch*. His best paintings are simple and somewhat sad as the people in them often look lonely. He painted lighthouses, places in New England, buildings in cities, and deserted streets. Among his works are *Early Sunday Morning, Gas*, and *New York Movie*.

2487. Venezia, Mike. *George Gershwin.* (Getting to Know the World's Greatest Composers) Scholastic, 1994. 32pp. ISBN 978-0-516-04536-8; Children's Press, 1995, paper ISBN 978-0-516-44536-6. Grades K–5. George Gershwin (1898–1937), born in New York City, was one of the first composers to mix popular music with symphonic music. He learned to play the piano as a young boy and he got a job in Tin Pan Alley, playing songs for performers who might want to use them in their acts. (Before radio, the only way to hear a song was if someone played it in person.) When he played *Rhapsody in Blue* for the first time in 1924 on live radio, the public approved. He followed it with *An American in Paris* and *Porgy and Bess*, his favorite work.

2488. Venezia, Mike. *Georgia O'Keeffe.* (Getting to Know the World's Greatest Artists) Scholastic, 1993. 32pp. ISBN 978-0-516-02297-0; Children's Press, 1994, paper ISBN 978-0-516-42297-8. Grades K–5. Georgia O'Keeffe (1887–1986) is known for her paintings of flowers in the colors of the Southwest American desert around Taos, New Mexico, a place she loved. Illustrations augment the text.

2489. Venezia, Mike. *Grandma Moses.* (Getting to Know the World's Greatest Artists) Scholastic, 2003. 32pp. ISBN 978-0-516-22027-7; Children's Press, 2004, paper ISBN 978-0-516-27913-8. Grades K–5. Anna Mary Moses (1860–1961), known as Grandma Moses, began painting when she was almost 70 years old. She liked to depict the rural life that she knew, and her painting *The Old Checkered Inn in Summer* became the image for a national advertising campaign. She painted many works in her primitive style, and she sold many before her death. Illustrations augment the text.

2490. Venezia, Mike. *Grant Wood.* (Getting to Know the World's Greatest Artists) Scholastic, 1995. 32pp. ISBN 978-0-516-02284-0; Children's Press, 1996, paper ISBN 978-0-516-42284-8. Grades K–5. Grant Wood (1892–1942) was born in Iowa and studied painting in Europe where he fell in love with French Impressionism. When he visited Munich he admired early Dutch paintings. Back in Iowa, he began using the Regionalist style and chose to paint everyday subjects including workers in the Midwest. His best-known painting is *American Gothic*. Illustrations augment the text.

2491. Venezia, Mike. *Horace Pippin.* See entry 2099.

2492. Venezia, Mike. *Jackson Pollock.* (Getting to Know the World's Greatest Artists) Scholastic, 1994. 32pp. ISBN 978-0-516-02298-7; Children's Press paper ISBN 978-0-516-42298-5. Grades K–5. Jackson Pollock (1912–1956) was an American artist who splashed paint over his canvases to create nonrepresentational scenes. One of his paintings, *Blue Poles*, sold to the Australian government for $2 million, the highest price paid for a modern painting. Illustrations augment the text.

2493. Venezia, Mike. *John Philip Sousa.* See entry 2101.

2494. Venezia, Mike. *Leonard Bernstein.* (Getting to Know the World's Greatest Composers) Scholastic, 1997. 32pp. ISBN 978-0-516-20492-5; Children's Press, 1998, paper ISBN 978-0-516-26244-4. Grades K–5. Leonard Bernstein (1918–1990), born in Lawrence, Massachusetts, was both an accomplished pianist and composer. After he became the maestro for the New York Symphony Orchestra, he began teaching children and adults the wonders of music. A member of a Jewish family, he thought music should be part of the worship of God. Among the famous works he composed are *West Side Story, Candide*, and *Chichester Psalms*.

2495. Venezia, Mike. *Mary Cassatt.* See entry 2102.

2496. Venezia, Mike. *Norman Rockwell.* (Getting to Know the World's Greatest Artists) Scholastic, 2000. 32pp. ISBN 978-0-516-21594-5; Children's Press, 2001, paper ISBN 978-0-516-27173-6. Grades K–5. Norman Rockwell (1894–1978) became famous for his illustrations of everyday life for *The Saturday Evening Post*. He produced more than 4,000 original works; one of the best known is *Rosie the Riveter*. Illustrations augment the text.

2497. Vernon, Roland. *Introducing Gershwin.* Chelsea House, 2000. 32pp. ISBN 978-0-7910-6040-7. Grades 3–6. George Gershwin (1898–1937), son of a Jewish immigrant, made many musical innovations with his compositions. Double-page spreads show various phases of his career, with sidebars discussing the times he lived in, including Prohibition and the Great Depression. Photographs and reproductions highlight the text. Time Chart, Glossary, and Index.

2498. Viola, Kevin. *Lou Gehrig.* (Sports Heroes and Legends) Lerner, 2004. 106pp. ISBN 978-0-8225-1794-8. Grades 4–6. Lou Gehrig (1903–1941) shyly said goodbye to his fiends at Yankee Stadium after he was diagnosed with amyotrophic lateral sclerosis (ALS), now known as "Lou Gehrig's Disease." The son of German immigrants, he helped his family out of poverty using his baseball ability. He played in many games and broke many records. This biography offers information about his background and his playing career. Photographs highlight the text. Bibliography, Glossary, Web Sites, and Index.

2499. Walker, Alice. *Langston Hughes: American Poet.* Illustrated by Catherine Deeter. Amistad, 2006. 48pp. Paper ISBN 978-0-06-079889-5. Grades 3–6. This volume focuses mainly on the childhood and early adult life of Langston Hughes (1902–1967). Anecdotes reveal his distant relationship with his father and his grandmother's care for him as he matured and gained fame as the most important African American writer of his time.

2500. Wallner, Alexandra. *Grandma Moses.* Holiday House, 2004. 32pp. ISBN 978-0-8234-1538-0. Grades K–3. Anna Mary Robertson, known as Grandma Moses (1860–1961), began painting when she was 67 years old after she had raised her family, helped run a farm, and her husband had died. During her earlier years, she had stored the images of her childhood landscape and was ready to use them as subject matter. Not until she turned 80 did people begin to appreciate her paintings. Illustrations augment the text. Bibliography and Notes.

2501. Warren, Andrea. *Orphan Train Rider: One Boy's True Story.* Houghton, 1996. 80pp. Paper ISBN 978-0-395-91362-8. Grades 4–8. Alternating chapters contain information about the Orphan Train and relate the actual experiences of Lee Nailling, who rode the train west in 1926. He was rejected several times before he eventually found a good home. His emotional turmoil reflects that of the many children who took the Orphan Train to a new life, which for some did not fulfill their hopes. Bibliography and Index. *Boston-Globe Horn Book Award* and *School Library Journal Best Book*.

2502. Waxman, Laura Hamilton. *Franklin D. Roosevelt.* (History Maker Bios) Lerner, 2004. 48pp. ISBN 978-0-8225-1545-6. Grades 3–5. Franklin Delano Roosevelt (1882–1945) made history by being the first U.S. president to be elected to four terms. Roosevelt led America through some of the most difficult times it ever faced: the Great Depression and World War II. Illustrations augment the text. Bibliography, Further Reading, Glossary, Maps, Timeline, Web Sites, and Index.

2503. Waxman, Laura Hamilton. *W. K. Kellogg.* See entry 2107.

2504. Waxman, Laura Hamilton. *Woodrow Wilson.* See entry 2108.

2505. Weatherford, Carole Boston. *Before John Was a Jazz Giant: A Song of John Coltrane.* Illustrated by Sean Qualls. Henry Holt, 2008. 24pp. ISBN 978-0-8050-7994-4. Grades K–4. Growing up in the South in the 1930s, John Coltrane (1926–1967) heard music all around him. He transformed the sounds—from pots, ukeleles, trains, birdsong, horns, radios, phonographs, and so forth—to create his own special songs. Mixed-media full-bleed spreads enhance the text.

2506. Weatherford, Carole Boston. *I, Matthew Henson: Polar Explorer.* Illustrated by Eric Velasquez. Walker, 2008. Unpaged. ISBN 978-0-8027-9688-3. Grades 2–5. In first-person poems, Matthew Alexander Henson (1866–1955) describes the prejudice and erroneous perceptions that he endured while a cabin boy, stock boy, and then explorer with Robert Peary. It took Peary a long time to trust Henson. He took him to Greenland because Henson had visited the Inuit and learned their language. Eventually, Peary realized that he could not have reached the North Pole without Henson's help. Full-bleed spreads of soft pastels on textured paper enhance the text. *Kirkus Reviews Editor's Choice.*

2507. **Weatherford, Carole Boston.** *Jesse Owens: Fastest Man Alive.* Illustrated by Eric Valesquez. Walker, 2006. 32pp. ISBN 978-0-8027-9550-2. Grades 1–5. Jesse Owens (1913–1980), an African American track and field athlete, won four gold medals at the 1936 Olympic Games in Berlin, Germany, where Hitler disdained him as a member of an inferior race. He became aware of his delight in running as a child, and he attributed his success to the encouragement of his junior-high track coach. While at Ohio State University, he won eight individual NCAA championships. He never received a college scholarship, always paying for his schooling with part-time jobs. Pastel illustrations augment the prose poetry of the text.

2508. **Weidt, Maryann N.** *Matthew Henson.* See entry 2110.

2509. **Weidt, Maryann N.** *Oh, the Places He Went: A Story About Dr. Seuss.* Illustrated by Kerry Maguire. Carolrhoda, 1994. 64pp. ISBN 978-0-8761-4823-5. Grades 2–6. Theodor Seuss Geisel (1904–1994) lived three blocks from the library and six blocks from the zoo as he was growing up in Springfield, Massachusetts. At first discouraged by his lack of success with his animal drawings, he wrote and illustrated 48 books during his life. They sold more than 200 million copies. An award for aspiring illustrators has been established in his name and carries a large cash prize. Afterword and Bibliography.

2510. **Wells, Rosemary.** *Mary on Horseback: Three Mountain Stories.* Illustrated by Peter McCarty. Dial, 1999. 1999pp. ISBN 978-0-670-88923-5; Puffin, 2000, paper ISBN 978-0-14-130815-9. Grades 3–6. Mary Breckinridge (1881–1965), founder of the Frontier Nursing Service, became the first nurse to offer medical care to isolated residents in the Appalachian Mountains. Another nurse, 18-year-old Miss Ireland, came from Scotland to help her and started to dispense treasured diphtheria serum to the children. A child, distraught about her mother's death, refused to talk until she learned from Mary that helping others was its own reward and that Mary's husband as well as her own children had died. A boy, John, who nearly faints when he sees a needle and a syringe, thanks Mary for saving his logger father's leg and their livelihood. *Young Hoosier Book Awards* (Indiana) nomination, *Bluegrass Awards* (Kentucky) nomination, *Student Book Award* (Maine) nomination, *Notable Social Studies Trade Books, Children's Book Awards* (Rhode Island) nomination, *Children's Book Award* (South Carolina) nomination, *International Reading Association, Bluebonnet Awards* (Texas), and *Capitol Choices Noteworthy Titles* (Washington, D.C.).

2511. **Wilkerson, J. L.** *Sad-Face Clown: Emmett Kelly.* (The Great Heartlanders) Acorn, 2004. 118pp. Paper ISBN 978-0-966447-09-5. Grades 5–8. The twenty-one chapters of this biography look at the life of circus clown Emmett Kelly (1898–1979). He grew up in Kansas and wanted to be an artist. As he could not find work in his field, he invented a clown, Weary Willie, who displayed both sadness and joy. Kelly then performed with the Ringling Brothers and Barnum and Bailey Circus, becoming known throughout the western world. He also appeared in movies, television, theater, and nightclubs. Photographs and illustrations augment the text. Glossary.

2512. **Wing, Natasha.** *An Eye for Color: The Story of Josef Albers.* Henry Holt, 2009. 40pp. ISBN 978-0-8050-8072-8. Grades 3–6. As a child in Europe, Josef Albers (1888–1976) watched his handyman father lovingly paint houses. In 1933 Albers immigrated to the United States and moved to North Carolina to head Black Mountain College. After traveling to Mexico, where he seemed to rediscover color, he became a color theorist who painted only rectangles. These rectangles changed according to their colors and those of the ones near them. Albers realized that juxtaposition of different colors altered both the viewer's concept of distance and emotion. Gouache illustrations, some with directions for viewing, show how his experiments worked. Note. *American Library Association Notable Children's Books* and *Red Clover Book Award* (Vermont) nomination.

2513. **Winget, Mary.** *Eleanor Roosevelt.* (History Maker Bios) Lerner, 2003. 48pp. ISBN 978-0-8225-4675-7; paper ISBN 978-0-8225-4801-0. Grades 3–5. Eleanor Roosevelt (1884–1962), wife of President Franklin Delano Roosevelt, grew up a shy girl who learned to speak in public when her husband needed her to campaign for him. She then promoted the issues that she found important including civil rights, women's rights, and unemployment. She wrote a newspaper column and became the U.S. ambassador to the United Nations. Illustrations augment the text. Bibliography, Further Reading, Glossary, Maps, Timeline, Web Sites, and Index.

2514. Winter, Jeanette. *My Name Is Georgia.* See entry 2116.

2515. Winter, Jonah. *Beisbol: Latino Baseball Pioneers and Legends.* Narrated by Bruce Markusen Rodriguez. Lee & Low, 2001. 32pp. ISBN 978-1-58430-012-0; paper ISBN 978-1-58430-234-6. Grades 3–8. This collective biography profiles fourteen extraordinary Latino baseball players from Cuba, Puerto Rico, and the Dominican Republic. Designed like a baseball card collection, the profiles contain a photograph of each player, important statistics, and anecdotes. Among those included are Martin Dihigo, Dolf Luque, Cristobal Torriente, Tetelo Vargas, José Mendez, Perucho Cepeda, Minnie Minos, Juan Marichal, Luis Tiant Sr., and Roberto Clemente.

2516. Zuehlke, Jeffrey Bivin. *Henry Ford.* See entry 2120.

Graphic Novels, Biographies, and Histories

2517. Anderson, Jameson. *Amelia Earhart: Legendary Aviator.* Illustrated by Rod Whigham and Charles Barnett, III. (Graphic Biographies) Graphic Library, 2006. 32pp. ISBN 978-0-7368-6496-1; paper ISBN 978-0-7368-9659-7. Grades 3–5. This short graphic biography of Amelia Earhart (1898–1937) depicts her life and work as an aviator who wanted to set records. On one of these attempts, her plane disappeared. A yellow background sets direct quotes from Earhart apart from the fictional aspect of the narration. Web Sites. Glossary, Further Resources, Bibliography, and Index.

2518. Boeden, Matt. *The Hindenburg Disaster.* Illustrated by Keith Williams and Charles Barnett, III. Graphic Library, 2006. 32pp. ISBN 978-0-7368-5481-8; paper ISBN 978-0-7368-6876-1. Grades 3–5. On May 6, 1937, the German rigid airship *Hindenburg* was attempting to dock at Lakehurst Naval Air Station in Manchester, New Jersey. It caught fire and disintegrated within one minute. Of the ninety-seven people on board, thirty-five died, as did one on the ground. Newsreel coverage and a radio eyewitness report gave the disaster wide coverage. Illustrations depict the event. Bibliography, Glossary, Further Reading, and Index.

2519. Glaser, Jason. *Jackie Robinson: Baseball's Great Pioneer.* Illustrated by Bob Lentz. (Graphic Biographies) Graphic Library, 2005. 32pp. ISBN 978-0-7368-4633-2. Grades 3–5. This short graphic biography of Jackie Robinson (1919–1972) relates the story of his life as a player in the Negro Leagues and then as the first African American to break into the major leagues. His greatness led to his initiation into the Baseball Hall of Fame. A yellow background sets direct quotes from Robinson apart from other aspects of the narration. Web Sites.

2520. Hoena, B. A. *Matthew Henson: Arctic Adventurer.* See entry 2124.

2521. Miller, Connie Colwell. *Mother Jones: Labor Leader.* See entry 2127.

2522. O'Hern, Kerri. *Louis Armstrong.* Illustrated by Gini Holland and Alex Campbell. (Graphic Biographies) World Almanac, 2005. 32pp. ISBN 978-0-8368-6194-5; paper ISBN 978-0-8368-7885-1. Grades 3–5. This graphic biography presents Louis Armstrong (1901–1971), an important figure in American music who shifted jazz from an ensemble performance to a solo with his trumpet virtuosity. It includes background information important to Armstrong's life both in text and pictures.

2523. O'Hern, Kerri, and Lucia Raatma. *Jackie Robinson.* Illustrated by Alex Campbell and Anthony Spay. (Graphic Biographies) World Almanac, 2007. 32pp. ISBN 978-0-8368-7882-0; paper ISBN 978-0-8368-7889-9. Grades 3–5. This graphic biography presents Jackie Robinson (1919–1972), an important figure in American baseball because he integrated the major league teams. It includes important background information both in text and pictures.

2524. Olson, Nathan. *George Washington Carver: Ingenious Inventor.* See entry 2129.

2525. Phelan, Matt. *The Storm in the Barn.* Candlewick, 2009. 201pp. ISBN 978-0-7636-3618-0. Grades 5–8. In 1937 Kansas, 11-year-old Jack Clark has not seen rain in four years. He feels useless much of the time and he is bullied by older boys. His sister Dorothy suffers from "dust pneumonia" and fantasizes through another Dorothy from Kansas in *The Wizard of Oz*. The store owner, Ernie, entertains Jack by telling stories of another Jack who has accomplished amazing feats by fighting the West and Northeast Winds and Blizzards. Words and pale sepia watercolors tell this Jack's story as he investigates an unusual light in an abandoned barn and comes upon a threatening figure with a face that rains and a bag that flashes lightning. Jack confronts this Storm King, gets it to release the much-needed rain, and gains an honored place in his community. *Booklist Editor's Choice, Capitol Choices Noteworthy Titles* (Washington, D.C.), *American Library Association Notable Children's Books, Young Adult Library Services Association (YALSA) Great Graphic Novels for Teens, Hornbook Fanfare List,* and *Scott O'Dell Award for Historical Fiction* winner.

2526. Robbins, Trina. *Bessie Coleman: Daring Stunt Pilot.* (Graphic Biographies) Graphic Library, 2007. 32pp. ISBN 978-0-7368-6851-8; paper ISBN 978-0-7368-7903-3. Grades 3–5. This short graphic biography of Bessie Coleman (1892–1926) depicts her life and work as the first African American to earn a pilot's license. She went to France and became a stunt pilot on her return. A yellow background sets direct quotes from Coleman apart from the fictional aspect of the narration. Web Sites.

2527. Taylor, Sarah Stewart. *Amelia Earhart: This Broad Ocean.* Hyperion, 2010. 96pp. ISBN 978-1-4231-1337-9. Grades 4–8. In June 1928 (only a year after Charles Lindbergh's flight to Paris), Amelia Earhart (1897–1937) arrived in Trepassey, Newfoundland, to become the first woman passenger to cross the Atlantic by plane. Interested in meeting her is Grace Goodland, a young girl who wants to be a reporter. Both pictures and words tell about Earhart's goals and some of her earlier aspirations. When Earhart lands in Europe, she telegraphs Grace so that Grace, also wanting an unconventional career, can have her first major news story. Notes.

2528. Vollmar, Rob. *The Castaways.* Illustrated by Pablo G. Callejo. ComicsLit, 2007. Unpaged. ISBN 978-1-56163-492-7. Grades 5 up. In this graphic novel set in 1932, 13-year-old Tucker Freeman hops on a train with only 15 cents to his name after his aunt makes him leave to find a job. He meets a black tramp, Elijah, who shows him both the danger and intrigue of a hobo's life. Tucker discovers there are worse things than being homeless and poor and Elijah helps him find his inner abilities.

2529. Welvaert, Scott R. *Helen Keller: Courageous Advocate.* See entry 2131.

DVDs

2530. *Americana: 1900's to Present Day.* (Hands-On Crafts for Kids Series 6: Back in Time) Chip Taylor Communications, 2003. 30 mins. Grades 4–6. See entry 2132.

2531. *Animated Atlas: Overview of World War One.* SVE & Churchill Media, 2002. 30 mins. Grades 4–8. Animated maps, historical footage, photographs, and icons offer an overview of World War I with a discussion of Europe and its geography in 1910. The rest of the presentation looks at the roles of allies and enemies after Archduke Ferdinand's assassination in 1914 and America's entering the war in 1917.

2532. *Dropping In on Grant Wood.* Crystal, 2005. 19 mins. ISBN 978-1-56290-357-2. Grades 3–6. This animated program about Grant Wood (1891–1942) shows how his style evolved from his interests in life and his heroes. His most famous painting is an American icon, *American Gothic*.

2533. *Dropping In on Romare Bearden*. Crystal, 2007. 19 mins. ISBN 978-1-56290-541-5. Grades 1–4. In this animated program, Romare Bearden (1911–1988) explains his collages of solid and patterned papers. Puffer the penguin asks Bearden about his life from his birth in North Carolina, and Bearden explains the important influences in his art. He had his first show in 1944. Six of Bearden's collages show his use of different materials to achieve his artistic effects.

2534. *Eleanor Roosevelt*. (Great Americans for Children) Library Video, 2003. 23 mins. ISBN 978-1-57225-543-2. Grades K–4. Although Eleanor Roosevelt (1884–1962) was extremely wealthy, she decided to work for those less fortunate and supported human rights, overcoming poverty, and world peace. Archival footage and photographs help to reveal her life and how she changed from a very shy girl into a strong woman who spoke her mind. She redefined the role of First Lady during the Depression and World War II. After her husband died, she helped create the Universal Declaration of Human Rights. Some said she was "Eleanor Everywhere," but she wanted to help those in need.

2535. Harper, Jo. *Finding Daddy: A Story of the Great Depression*. Nutmeg, 2006. 17 mins. ISBN 978-1-933938-16-5. Grades K–4. See entry 2192.

Compact Discs

2536. Choldenko, Gennifer. *Al Capone Shines My Shoes*. Listening Library, 2009. 7 CDs; 7 hrs. 52 min. ISBN 978-0-7393-8004-8. Grades 5–8. See entry 2170.

2537. Curtis, Christopher Paul. *Bud, Not Buddy*. Narrated by James Avery. Listening Library, 2006. 5 CDs; 5 hrs. 15 min. ISBN 978-0-7393-3179-8. Grades 4–7. See entry 2174.

2538. Hesse, Karen. *Out of the Dust*. Narrated by Marika Washburn. Listening Library, 2006. 2 CDs; 2 hrs. 10 mins. ISBN 978-0-307-28403-7. Grades 5–9. See entry 2197.

2539. Levine, Gail Carson. *Dave at Night*. Narrated by Johnny Heller. Recorded Books, 2000. 6 CDs; 6.25 hrs. ISBN 978-0-7887-6161-4. Grades 5–9. See entry 2218.

2540. Levine, Kristin. *The Best Bad Luck I Ever Had*. Narrated by Kirby Heyborne. Listening Library, 2010. 6 CDs; 6 hrs. ISBN 978-0-307-71056-7. Grades 5–9. See entry 2219.

2541. Lowry, Lois. *The Silent Boy*. Narrated by Karen Allen. Random, 2004. 4 CDs 3hrs. 57 mins. ISBN 978-0-8072-1766-5. Grades 5–8. See entry 2221.

2542. Peck, Richard. *A Long Way from Chicago: A Novel in Stories*. Narrated by Ron McLarty. Listening Library, 2005. 4 CDs; 4.25hrs. ISBN 978-0-307-24320-1. Grades 4–8. See entry 2238.

2543. Peck, Richard. *A Year Down Yonder*. Narrated by Lois Smith. Listening Library, 2004. 3 CDs. ISBN 978-1-4000-8496-8. Grades 5–8. See entry 2239.

2544. Taylor, Mildred. *Roll of Thunder, Hear My Cry*. Narrated by Lynne Thigpen. Listening Library, 2005. 6 CDs; 7 hrs.26 mins. ISBN 978-0-307-28172-2. Grades 5 up. See entry 2254.

WORLD WAR II, 1941–1945

Historical Fiction and Fantasy

2545. Adler, David A. *Mama Played Baseball.* Illustrated by Chris O'Leary. Gulliver, 2003. 32pp. ISBN 978-0-15-202196-2. Grades K–3. During World War II, while Amy's father is overseas, her mother gets a job in the newly established women's professional baseball team. Amy thinks it is a strange job, but she becomes proud of her, especially when her father comes home unexpectedly wearing his uniform.

2546. Avi. *Don't You Know There's a War On?* Trophy, 2003. 208pp. Paper ISBN 978-0-380-81544-9. Grades 4–7. While his father is fighting overseas in 1943, 11-year-old Howie Crispers finds out that the principal plans to fire his favorite teacher, Miss Gossim. Howie's friend Denny wonders if the principal is a Nazi spy. Howie asks his teacher and she tells him she has broken the rules by marrying a pilot and getting pregnant. Howie and Denny circulate a petition to save her job, and she stays until the end of the year. Each chapter begins with newspaper headlines from the front, and there are details of life at that time in Brooklyn, New York.

2547. Avi. *Who Was That Masked Man, Anyway?* HarperCollins, 1994. 142pp. Paper ISBN 978-0-380-72113-9. Grades 4–8. During World War II, 11-year-old Frankie prefers listening to the radio to doing his homework. When his brother returns home wounded, the war becomes more real to Frankie. Then his teacher's boyfriend is killed abroad. Drawing on expertise gleaned from his favorite radio shows, Frankie plots to get his brother and his teacher together. They do meet, but not as Frankie has imagined.

2548. Banim, Lisa. *American Dreams.* Illustrated by Tatyana Yuditskaya. (Stories of the States) Silver Moon, 1993. 58pp. ISBN 978-1-8818-8934-2; 1995, paper ISBN 978-1-8818-8969-7. Grades 3–5. Jeannie Bosold and Amy Mochida, a Japanese American, enjoy going to the movies and discussing their favorite movie stars. Then the government takes Amy and her family away from their home in southern California after the bombing of Pearl Harbor in 1941. Jeannie does not understand why children must suffer on account of adult problems. Endpaper Maps, Historical Postscript, and Recommended Reading.

2549. Borden, Louise. *Across The Blue Pacific: A World War II Story.* Illustrated by Robert Andrew Parker. Houghton, 2006. 48pp. ISBN 978-0-618-33922-8. Grades 2–5. As a woman Molly remembers her fourth-grade teacher's assignment that the students write letters to soldiers fighting in World War II. She chose her neighbor, Ted Walker, who was serving on the *Albacore*, a submarine in the Pacific, and wrote him to weekly from her midwestern hometown. She also remembers the telegram that arrived and how his family and friends reacted to the distressing news of his death. The free-verse stanzas and illustrations convey the times.

2550. Bruchac, Joseph. *Code Talker: A Novel About the Navajo Marines of World War II.* Dial, 2005. 231pp. ISBN 978-0-8037-2921-6; Penguin, 2006, paper ISBN 978-0-14-240596-3. Grades 5 up. At the age of 6 Navajo Kii Yazhi was sent to a mission school in Gallup, New Mexico, where he was no longer allowed to wear his hair long, speak his language, or use his name. He was renamed Ned Begay. As a grandfather, Ned Begay tells his story to his grandchildren. He became a code expert during World War II when the United States government realized that only Navajos speak their difficult language well. Ned and his fellow Navajos communicated information that no other country could decode, and their services were invaluable.

2551. Buchanan, Jane A. *Goodbye, Charley.* Farrar, 2004. 176pp. ISBN 978-0-374-35020-8. Grades 5–8. When Celie is 12 years old in 1943, her father brings home Charley, a rhesus monkey. Charley takes Celie's mind off the war, giving her something else on which to focus. She worries about the bombs and submarines that lurk off the shore near her Massachusetts home and about her big brother, who is looking forward to a chance to fight abroad. Her little brother is not interested in her, and her best friend has left town. Then Celie's mother starts working, and irritating Joey Bentley moves in next door with his unpleasant grandmother. But the worse aspect of the summer is Celie's inability to handle Charley. Joey turns out to be a valuable ally. At the summer's end, Celie realizes that a wild animal needs to be in the zoo, and that a friend whose father has been killed in the war has worse problems than she.

2552. Buckey, Sarah Masters. *The Light in the Cellar: A Molly Mystery.* Illustrated by Jean-Paul Tibbles. American Girl, 2007. 165pp. Paper ISBN 978-1-59369-158-5. Grades 3–6. Molly and her British friend Emily volunteer at Oak Knoll Hospital as magazine delivery girls during World War II. When rationed sugar and flour are stolen from the hospital and sold on the black market, they try to find the culprit. They need these ingredients to make cookies for soldiers who will be arriving at the train station.

2553. Burg, Ann E. *Rebekkah's Journey: A WWII Refugee Story.* Illustrated by Joel Iskowitz. (Tales of Young Americans) Sleeping Bear, 2006. Unpaged. ISBN 978-1-58536-275-2. Grades 3–5. In 1944, Rebekkah, 7, and her Jewish mother escape the Nazis in Italy and come to a vacant army base in Oswego, New York, planning to build a new life. They were two of the 1,000 European displaced persons that President Roosevelt invited.

2554. Chaconas, Dori. *Pennies in a Jar.* Illustrated by Ted Lewin. Peachtree, 2007. 32pp. ISBN 978-1-56145-422-8. Grades 1–3. A boy's father leaves to fight in World War II and, although his father tells him to be brave, the boy remains full of fears. He is afraid of the horses pulling wagons through the streets, the ragman, the milkman, and other things. When he sees a photographer walk by with a pony named Freedom, he decides he must conquer his fears. He takes 50 cents that he has been saving for his father's present and gets up in the pony's saddle for a picture. Then he sends it to his father as his gift. Photorealistic watercolors enhance the text.

2555. Chaikin, Miriam. *Friends Forever.* Illustrated by Richard Egielski. Iuniverse, 2001. 120pp. Paper ISBN 978-0-59519-879-5. Grades 3–6. Molly overhears rumblings in her Brooklyn neighborhood about problems Jews are having in Europe, especially in Poland, where her mother's family lives. She focuses her worries on getting into advanced math in seventh grade and decides to help herself do well on tests by writing formulas on her palm. However, she feels guilty for cheating. After her graduation from sixth grade, she gets a boyfriend and prepares to enjoy the summer.

2556. Cooper, Floyd. *Willie and the All-Stars.* Philomel, 2008. Unpaged. ISBN 978-0-399-23340-1. Grades 1–4. In 1942, 10-year-old Willie dreams of playing major league baseball at nearby Wrigley Field like Joe DiMaggio or Dizzy Dean. He hears men discussing players he does not know, such as Cool Papa Bell, Josh Gibson, and Satchel Paige. They tell him when he talks about playing in the majors that there is one major problem—he is the wrong color. But when the Negro League plays the Major League All-Stars, Willie has a chance to see African Americans play and win, and he understands that they are superb players too. At the end of the game, when two of the opposing players shake hands, he has hope for the unification of black and white. Illustrations enhance the text. Note.

2557. Davies, Jacqueline. *Where the Ground Meets the Sky.* Marshall Cavendish, 2004. 224pp. Paper ISBN 978-0-7614-5187-7. Grades 5–9. In 1944, 12-year-old Hazel has to leave her happy life in New Jersey for somewhere in New Mexico called the "Hill." Her physicist father has a secret job, the Big Mystery. His inability to share his work exacerbates Hazel's mother's mental illness. Hazel observes yellow stars that signify the death of a serviceman in the family (and a cat's death from radiation). Eventually they return to New Jersey, all changed.

2558. Fleming, Candace. *Boxes for Katje.* Illustrated by Stacey Dressen-McQueen. Farrar, 2003. 40pp. ISBN 978-0-374-30922-0. Grades K–4. Not much remains of Katje's town of Olst, Holland at the end of World War II. She wears patched clothes and has no milk, sugar, shoes, or soap. Then Rosie, a young American girl from Mayfield, Indiana, sends her a care package through the Children's Aid Society. It contains soap, socks, and chocolate. Katje sends a "thank you" letter and shares her treasures with people in the town. Soon many more packages arrive and Katje shares those as well. Two years later the town sends something back to America—beautiful tulip bulbs to brighten the spring. The story is based on the author's mother's own experiences. *Capitol Choices Noteworthy Titles* (Washington, D.C.), *Publishers Weekly Best Children's Books, William Allen White Award* (Kansas) nomination, *Show Me Award* (Missouri) nomination, *Children's Book Award* (Rhode Island) nomination, *Prairie Bud Award* (South Dakota) nomination, *Young Reader Medal* (California) nomination, *Black-Eyed Susan Award* (Maryland) nomination, *Diamond Primary Book Award* (Arkansas) nomination, *Young Reader Award* (Virginia) nomination, *Volunteer State Book Award* (Tennessee) nomination, *Young Hoosier Award* (Indiana) nomination, *Picture Book Award* (South Carolina) nomination, *Young Reader Medal* (California) Winners, *Great Lakes Book Awards, Reading Association Children's Book Award* (Florida), *Children's Choice Picture Book* (Washington nomination), *Red Clover Award* (Vermont) nomination, and *Golden Sower Award* (Nebraska) nomination.

2559. Giff, Patricia Reilly. *Lily's Crossing.* Doubleday, 1997. 180pp. ISBN 978-0-385-32142-6; Yearling, 1999, paper ISBN 978-0-440-41453-7. Grades 5–8. Lily looks forward to summer at the family home in Far Rockaway in 1944 until she learns her best friend won't be there. The only playmate around is Albert, a Hungarian boy who left Europe to escape World War II. When Lily hears that her father is going to Europe as an engineer, she worries that he will not return. Lily dislikes Albert at first, but soon realizes he has his own fears, and the two become friends. *Charlie May Simon Book Awards* (Arkansas) nomination, *Blue Spruce* (Colorado) nomination, *William Allen White Children's Book Awards* (Kansas) nomination, *Bluegrass Awards* (Kentucky) nomination, *Readers Choice Awards* (Michigan) nomination, *Mark Twain Book Awards* (Missouri) nomination, *Golden Sower Awards* (Nebraska) nomination, *Great Stone Face Book Awards* (New Hampshire) nomination, *Garden State Children's Book Awards* (New Jersey) nomination, *The Land of Enchantment Children's Book Awards* (New Mexico) nomination, *Sequoyah Book Awards* (Oklahoma) nomination, *Young Readers Choice Awards* (Pennsylvania) nomination, *Children's Book Award* (South Carolina) nomination, *Dorothy Canfield Fisher Children's Book Awards* (Vermont) nomination, *Golden Archer Book Awards* (Wisconsin) nomination, *Capitol Choices Noteworthy Titles* (Washington, D.C.), *Boston-Globe/Horn Book Award*, and *Newbery Honor.*

2560. Giff, Patricia Reilly. *Willow Run.* Wendy Lamb, 2005. 149pp. ISBN 978-0-385-73067-9. Grades 4–7. Eleven-year-old Meggie Dillon moves to Willow Run, Michigan, from Rockaway, New York, in 1944. Her father will be building B-24 bombers. They live in makeshift housing, and although Meggie was secretly glad to leave her quirky German American grandfather behind, she discovers that she misses him. She also worries about her brother Eddie, fighting in Europe, and when the family receives news that he is missing after the invasion of Normandy, she tries to make everyone feel better. *Booklist Editor's Choice.*

2561. Graff, Nancy Price. *Taking Wing.* Clarion, 2005. 224pp. ISBN 978-0-618-53591-0. Grades 4–8. In 1942, 13-year-old Gus becomes the caretaker for a nest of seven orphaned duck eggs while staying on his grandparents' Vermont farm. His father is serving in the Army Air Corps and his mother is coping with tuberculosis. Louise, a poor Quebeçois girl, helps Gus with the ducklings and they become friends despite prejudice against her family in the community. Gus learns about many things during this period. *Booklist Editor's Choice, Student Book Award* (Maine) nomination, and *Dorothy Canfield Fisher Children's Book Award* (Vermont) nomination.

2562. **Griffis, Molly Levite.** *The Feester Filibuster.* Eakin, 2002. 236pp. Paper ISBN 978-1-57168-694-6. Grades 4–8. In this sequel to *The Rachel Resistance,* John Alan discovers that his Apache, Oklahoma, fifth-grade classmate Rachel thinks he is spying for the Japanese after the bombing of Pearl Harbor in December of 1941 and wants him deported. Until that time, he has had no use for the war. Surprised by her accusations, he simultaneously is trying to hide the news that his mother is leaving their family. *Volunteer State Book Award* (Tennessee) nomination.

2563. **Griffis, Molly Levite.** *The Rachel Resistance.* Eakin, 2001. 232pp. Paper ISBN 978-1-57168-553-7. Grades 4–8. Fifth-grader Rachel Dalton and her friend Paul spread the news that their small town in Oklahoma is the home of spies and traitors after the Japanese bomb Pearl Harbor. But John Alan Feester thinks that Pearl Harbor makes no difference in Oklahoma because ships cannot possibly invade the state. When the war begins to affect some of the town's families, he begins to understand their patriotism.

2564. **Gutman, Dan.** *Satch and Me: A Baseball Card Adventure.* Amistad, 2009. 192pp. Paper ISBN 978-0-06-059493-0. Grades 3–6. Joe Stosh, 13, can travel through time thanks to his magic baseball cards. To solve a question about whether Satchel Paige actually pitched the fastest ball on record, Joe transports his coach and a radar gun back to 1942. (Satch's team had no baseball cards and Joe has to substitute a postcard that he locates on eBay.) Joe and Flip arrive in Spartanburg, South Carolina, a few days before the Negro League World Series. They meet with Paige and travel with him to the big game in Pittsburgh. On the way, they witness the awful racial discrimination that he had to endure everyday.

2565. **Gwaltney, Doris.** *Homefront.* Simon & Schuster, 2006. 310pp. ISBN 978-0-689-86842-9. Grades 5–9. Twelve-year-old Margaret Ann Motley, 12, only wants a room of her own in Wight County, Virginia. But suddenly her Aunt Mary Lee and Cousin Courtney arrive from England, fleeing World War II. Everybody seems to prefer Courtney, including Margaret Ann's boyfriend. Then the Japanese bomb Pearl Harbor. Not until Margaret Ann's brother enlists in the navy do Margaret and Courney form a bond.

2566. **Hahn, Mary Downing.** *Stepping on the Cracks.* Clarion, 1991. 216pp. ISBN 978-0-395-58507-8; 2009, paper ISBN 978-0-547-07660-7. Grades 5–8. In 1944 Elizabeth and her friend Margaret spend time riding bicycles and trying to avoid Gordy, a bully who annoys them in College Hill, Maryland. When they follow him through the woods, they find out he is protecting a brother who has run away from the army. Their abusive father will beat him if he returns home. The girls hear the brother coughing and decide that they must help. When Margaret's family receives word of the death of her brother, who had been fighting abroad, they have to cope with the ethical problems of helping a deserter. *Bulletin Blue Ribbon, Joan G. Sugarman Children's Book Award, American Library Association Notable Children's Books, School Library Journal Best Book, Sunshine State Young Reader Award* (Florida) nomination, *Children's Choice Book Awards* (Iowa) nomination, *Rebecca Caudill Award* (Illinois) nomination, *Young Hoosier Award* (Indiana) nomination, *William Allen White Children's Book Awards* (Kansas) nomination, *Black-Eyed Susan Award* (Maryland) nomination, *Student Book Awards* (Maine) nomination, *Maud Hart Lovelace Book Awards* (Minnesota) nomination, *Children's Book Awards* (North Carolina) nomination, *Young Readers Choice Award* (Pennsylvania) nomination, *Children's Book Awards* (Rhode Island) nomination, *Junior Book Award* (South Carolina) nomination, *Bluebonnet Awards* (Texas) nomination, *Children's Book Award* (Utah) nomination, *Dorothy Canfield Fisher Children's Book Awards* (Vermont) nomination, and *Scott O'Dell Award.*

2567. **Herman, Charlotte.** *My Chocolate Year.* Illustrated by LeUyen Pham. Simon & Schuster, 2008. 176pp. ISBN 978-1-4169-3341-0. Grades 3–6. During the summer of 1945 in Chicago, Dorrie looks forward to the fifth-grade dessert making contest. Her teacher, Mrs. Fitzgerald, has added a new ingredient this year—the contest will also be a fundraiser for children in post-World War II Europe. Dorrie and her friends try a variety of recipes, many with unforeseen results. At the same time Dorrie's family discovers that everyone in their Jewish Polish family has perished apart from 16-year-old Cousin Victor. The family works to reunite with him. Illustrations reinforce the text.

2568. Hesse, Karen. *Aleutian Sparrow.* Illustrated by Evon Zerbetz. Margaret K. McElderry, 2003. 160pp. ISBN 978-0-689-86189-5; Aladdin, 2005, paper ISBN 978-1-416-90327-7. Grades 5–10. After the Japanese bomb Pearl Harbor, Vera and her Aleutian family have to relocate under orders of the United States government. They move to resettlement centers in the Southwest, supposedly for their own good. During the three years they stay there, many of them die because they are far from the sea in an alien forest climate. When the survivors return home in April 1945, they find their villages destroyed. *Capitol Choices Noteworthy Titles* (Washington, D.C.).

2569. Hest, Amy. *Love You, Soldier.* Candlewick, 2000. 48pp. ISBN 978-0-7636-0943-6. Grades 3–5. Katie, 7, stays with her mother and her mother's friend Louise in New York City while her father and Louise's husband fight in World War II. Over the next two years, Katie exchanges letters with her father and gets Louise to the hospital in the snow when she goes into labor while Katie's mother is away. After the war ends, Katie's father does not return, and Katie resents her mother's growing interest in Louise's brother Sam. An elderly neighbor advises her that love is risky but worth the effort, and Katie slowly adjusts to the idea of moving to Texas.

2570. Johnson, Angela. *Wind Flyers.* Illustrated by Loren Long. Simon & Schuster, 2007. Unpaged. ISBN 978-0-689-84879-7. Grades 2–4. A young boy tells of his great-great-uncle's love of flying and how he became a Tuskegee Airman, a fighter in the 332nd fighter group during World War II. As a young boy, the uncle loved to "catch" air by jumping from haylofts; he then became a "flying barnstormer." In World War II his fighter group never lost a bomber to enemy fire. The boy's uncle continued to fly when he came home from the war, becoming a crop duster. Acrylics highlight the text. *Picture Book Award* (Georgia) nomination.

2571. Klages, Ellen. *The Green Glass Sea.* Viking, 2006. 321pp. ISBN 978-0-670-06134-1; Puffin, 2008, paper ISBN 978-0-14-241149-0. Grades 5–8. In 1943 Dewey Kerrigan, 11, takes the train to Los Alamos, New Mexico, to live with her father. On the train she tries to design a radio, and a fellow passenger, Dick Feynman, offers to help her. At Los Alamos Dewey discovers that her dad is working on a top-secret government program and that discarded "science" things often show up in the dump. She likes to work on her inventions and raid the dump, interests that her classmates do not share. When her father has to go to Washington, she moves in with Suze, and although they initially dislike each other, they form a bond that lasts after Robert Oppenheimer tells Dewey that her father has been killed in a car accident. *Student Book Awards* (Maine) nomination, *Horn Book Fanfare, Scott O'Dell Award, Bluegrass Award* (Kentucky) nomination, *Nene Award* (Hawaii) nomination, and *Isinglass Award* (New Hampshire) nomination.

2572. Kochenderfer, Lee. *The Victory Garden.* Yearling, 2003. 166pp. Paper ISBN 978-0-440-41703-3. Grades 4–6. Teresa, 11, wants to contribute to the war effort during World War II so she organizes her friends to look after Mr. Burt's victory garden when he has an accident. Although Mr. Burt and her own father were competing to grow the best tomato, Teresa and her friends weed, water, pick, and sell his vegetables. Teresa has to work hard herself to keep her friends motivated and she sees the activity as a diversion from thinking about her brother Jeff in the Air Corps and about Billy Riggs, who keeps pestering her. *Sunshine State Young Reader Award* (Florida) nomination, *Young Hoosier Award* (Indiana) nomination, and *William Allen White Award* (Kansas) nomination.

2573. Kudlinski, Kathleen. *Pearl Harbor Is Burning! A Story of World War II.* Illustrated by Ronald Himler. Puffin, 1993. 54pp. Paper ISBN 978-0-14-034509-4. Grades 2–6. Lonely and isolated from his friends while living in Hawaii in 1941, Frank, 10, meets a Japanese American boy named Kenji. As they play in Frank's tree house one morning, they see planes bombing the harbor below and Kenji realizes they are Japanese. During this time, the families have to learn how to deal with their conflicting emotions of loyalty toward friends and patriotism.

2574. Lee, Milly. *Nim and the War Effort.* Illustrated by Yangsook Choi. Sunburst, 2002. Unpaged. Paper ISBN 978-0-374-45506-4. Grades 2–5. During World War II, Nim wants to win the competition to see who can collect the most for the newspaper drive. She wants to defeat Garland Stephenson, the boy who says that a Chinese person better not win and steals papers so that others cannot get them. Nim finds a hoard of newspapers in the Nob Hill area and persuades the police to help her get them to her school. At home, however, she faces punishment for breaking the family's rules by leaving her neighborhood. Illustrations complement the text. *Young Readers Book Awards* (California) nomination, *Children's Picture Book Award* (Georgia) nomination, *Bluegrass Award* (Kentucky) nomination, *Notable Social Studies Trade Books for Young People*, and *Capitol Choices Noteworthy Titles* (Washington, D.C.).

2575. Lee-Tai, Amy. *A Place Where Sunflowers Grow: Sabaku Ni Saita Himawari.* Illustrated by Felicia Hoshino. Children's, 2006. 31pp. ISBN 978-0-8923-9215-5. Grades 1–3. During World War II, Japanese American Mari and her family are interned at the Topaz Relocation Center in Utah. She enrolls in an art class, makes a friend, plants sunflowers, and waits for them to grow. Since everything around her seems gray, she paints colorful pictures that help her feel better. And then the sunflower seeds sprout, showing her that her father was right when he said that in spring, the flowers bloom again. He also lets her know that peace comes after war. Illustrations reinforce the text. Note.

2576. Lisle, Janet Taylor. *The Art of Keeping Cool.* Aladdin, 2002. 207pp. Paper ISBN 978-0-689-83788-3. Grades 5–8. In Rhode Island in 1942, 13-year-olds Robert and his cousin Elliot uncover some family secrets while becoming involved with a German artist, Abel Hoffman, who is living in a shack near the beach and is suspected by townspeople of spying. Robert begins to understand why his father left his parents' home as a teenager and did not return and why Elliot never opposes his grandfather. *Dorothy Canfield Fisher Children's Book Awards* (Vermont), *Sunshine State Young Readers Awards* (Florida), *Rebecca Caudill Young Readers Book Awards* (Illinois), *Student Book Award* (Maine) nomination, and *Young Reader Book Awards* (Virginia).

2577. Lowry, Lois. *Crow Call.* Scholastic, 2009. 32pp. ISBN 978-0-545-03035-9. Grades K–4. Delighted that her father has returned from fighting World War II in 1945, Lizzie, 8, accompanies him on a November morning to a nearby Pennsylvania farm to hunt crows that eat the crops. Her father has bought her a huge plaid hunting shirt and several servings of cherry pie for breakfast. Then he gives her the "crow call" whistle that will gather crows into a tree so that they can be shot. But, to Lizzie's relief, her father never raises his gun, and they continue their quiet day of reconnection after his long absence. Watercolor and gouache illustrations enhance the text. *American Library Association Notable Children's Books* and *Georgia Children's Book Award* nomination.

2578. Lurie, April. *Dancing in the Streets of Brooklyn.* Yearling, 2004. 194pp. Paper ISBN 978-0-440-41825-2. Grades 5–8. In Brooklyn's Norwegian community in 1944, 13-year-old Judy Strand finds out that her real father is an alcoholic who abandoned the family in Norway. Her mother emigrated and met "Pa," who adopted her. Judy does not know how to react and wants to hide the truth from others. She distances herself from her boyfriend because his father often drinks too much. But she also observes others suffering and becomes more understanding.

2579. McDonough, Yona Zeldis. *The Doll with the Yellow Star: An American Original.* Illustrated by Kimberly Bulcken Root. Henry Holt, 2005. 96pp. ISBN 978-0-8050-6337-0. Grades 3–5. Nine-year-old Claudine, a young Jewish girl living in France in World War II, sees her friends wearing yellow stars and decides to sew a star on the inside of her favorite doll's cape. Then she can decide if she wants Violette's star to show. Claudine goes to live with relatives in America, and Violette disappears in a shipboard fire. After the war ends, her father joins her in New York and they return to France. Claudine's mother has died and they no longer want to live there so they go back to New York, where Claudine grows up and Violette amazingly reappears. *Children's Choice Book Award* (Iowa) nomination.

2580. Manley, Joan B. *She Flew No Flags.* Houghton, 1995. 269pp. ISBN 978-0-395-71130-9. Grades 4–8. In 1944, 10-year-old Janet and her family return to the United States after living in India for seven years. The ship travels through enemy waters with no lights or radio contact, zigzagging to avoid torpedoes. It has no name and flies no flag so that the enemy will not attack it. She and her brothers explore the ship, and she wonders about the other people aboard. When she arrives in America, it is not what she expects, and she has to adjust not only to wartime but also to her new country.

2581. Mazer, Harry. *A Boy at War: A Novel of Pearl Harbor.* Simon & Schuster, 2001. ISBN 978-0-689-84161-3; Aladdin, 2002, paper ISBN 978-1-416-81460-6. Grades 5–9. Adam Pelko, recently arrived in Honolulu with his family, meets Davi Mori, son of a Japanese couple. Adam's military father implies that he cannot be friends with Davi, but when the Japanese bomb Pearl Harbor on December 7, 1941, Adam and Davi are fishing there. They are nearly killed, but Adam is more concerned about his father, serving on the USS *Arizona*. Eventually his father is declared missing in action, and the family has to return to the mainland. *Emphasis on Reading Children's Choice* (Alabama) nomination, *Young Reader's Award* (Arizona) nomination, *Nene Reading List* (Hawaii) nomination, *Teen Award* (Iowa) nomination, *Young Hoosier Book Awards* (Indiana) nomination, *Maud Hart Lovelace Book Award* (Minnesota) nomination, *Great Stone Face Book Award* (New Hampshire) nomination, *Children's Book Award* (South Carolina) nomination, *Tayshas High School Reading List* (Texas) nomination, and *Golden Archer Book Award* (Wisconsin) nomination.

2582. Mazer, Harry. *Heroes Don't Run: A Novel of the Pacific War.* Simon & Schuster, 2005. 113pp. ISBN 978-0-689-85534-4; Aladdin, 2007, paper ISBN 978-1-416-93394-6. Grades 5–9. In the third part of Adam Pelko's story, following *A Boy at War* (2001) and *A Boy No More* (2004), 17-year-old Adam lies about his age so that he can join the Marines in 1944. He endures boot camp and then goes to battle, ending up fighting the Japanese on Okinawa. There he is wounded and watches some of his friends die.

2583. Mercer, Peggy. *There Come a Soldier.* Illustrated by Ron Mazellan. Handprint, 2007. Unpaged. ISBN 978-1-59354-192-7. Grades 2–5. Papa leaves his rural Georgia home to become a paratrooper in World War II. He drops from the airplane to fight in the Ardennes Forest and thinks of his family in their sharecropper's shack as he finds a barn in which to shelter. Paintings complement the text.

2584. Mochizuki, Ken. *Baseball Saved Us.* Illustrated by Dom Lee. Lee & Low, 1993. Unpaged. ISBN 978-1-8800-0001-4; 1995, paper ISBN 978-1-8800-0019-9. Grades 3–6. Shorty and his family are sent to an internment camp because they are Japanese. When the young people start acting insolently toward the adults, his father realizes that they need baseball. The adults create a field, and soon people of all ages are playing. Shorty gets better at the game, and when he leaves the camp and people call him "Jap," he gets angry and proves he can play baseball as well as anyone. *Parents' Choice Award*.

2585. Noguchi, Rick, and Deneen Jenks. *Flowers from Mariko.* Illustrated by Michelle Reiko Kumata. Lee & Low, 2001. 32pp. ISBN 978-1-58430-032-8. Grades K–3. Mariko and her Japanese family are finally freed from their internment camp after World War II. They have to live in a temporary trailer park, and her gardener father has no work. But she decides to plant a tiny garden, and it helps him recover his hope for a new life.

2586. Paterson, John, and Katherine Paterson. *Blueberries for the Queen.* Illustrated by Susan Jeffers. HarperCollins, 2004. 32pp. ISBN 978-0-06-623942-2. Grades K–3. In 1942 Queen Wilhelmina of the Netherlands has fled the Nazis and is living in Lee, Massachusetts, with her daughter and granddaughters, close to William's family. At night, William imagines he is a brave knight winning battles, but in the morning he is back to normal. He decides he will be brave enough to take the queen a basket of blueberries he has picked himself. Surprisingly, the lady who answers the door, Princess Juliana, invites him inside to meet the queen, and he discovers that she is a kind grandmother with sturdy shoes and a black cat. The story is loosely based on an experience John Paterson had as a young man in Massachusetts during World War II. *Capitol Choices Noteworthy Titles* (Washington, D.C.), *Diamond Primary Book Award* (Arkansas) nomination, and *Golden Sower Award* (Nebraska) nomination.

2587. Paulsen, Gary. *The Cookcamp.*   Scholastic, 2003. 116pp. Paper ISBN 978-0-439-52357-8. Grades 5–8. In 1944 a 5-year-old unnamed protagonist's mother comes home with a man whom she identifies as his uncle and makes sounds on the couch with the man that bother him. His mother then sends him to stay with his grandmother in Minnesota. She cooks for a group of men building a road into Canada. The huge men frighten the boy at first, but then they invite him to sit in their trucks and tractors with them, and he begins to feel comfortable in their company. He regrets having to leave. *School Library Journal Best Book.*

2588. Paulsen, Gary. *The Quilt.*   Wendy Lamb, 2004. 83pp. ISBN 978-0-385-72950-5; Yearling, 2005, paper ISBN 978-0-440-22936-0. Grades 3–7. An unnamed 6-year-old boy goes to live with his grandmother, Alida, in her rural Minnesota Norwegian community during World War II while his father fights in Europe and his mother works in Chicago. He goes with his grandmother to visit his pregnant cousin Kristina, who delivers a son, and soon after hears that her husband has been killed in the war. The women gather to make a quilt and remember the deceased with each patch sewn into the design.

2589. Peck, Richard. *On the Wings of Heroes.*   Dial, 2007. 148pp. ISBN 978-0-8037-3081-6. Grades 4–8. Before World War II, Davy Bowman has two heroes—his older brother Bill who is an Army Air Force cadet and his father who owns the local service station. Then Bill has to go to Germany to fly B-17 missions, and the family waits for news. Davy meanwhile attends school and he and his friend Scooter collect rubber, metal, newspapers, and milkweed fluff for the war effort. They experience rationing of coffee and sugar and see the sacrifices that everyone in their Illinois town makes.

2590. Rinaldi, Ann. *Keep Smiling Through.*   Harcourt, 2005. 208pp. Paper ISBN 978-0-15-205399-4. Grades 4–7. Kay, a 5th-grader in 1943, is dealing with an unpleasant stepmother and a penurious father. She struggles with understanding who is on what side during the war. A German neighbor is kind and helpful, while her own grandfather's comments let her know that he sympathizes with the Germans. Ann has to learn that nationality does not automatically reveal one's political or moral direction and that she is not guilty for the death of her stepmother's baby.

2591. Rodman, Mary Ann. *Jimmy's Stars.*   Farrar, 2008. 272pp. ISBN 978-0-374-33703-2. Grades 5–8. In 1943, Ellie, 11, says goodbye to her beloved older brother Jimmy as he leaves to fight in World War II. He tells her that he will be back by Christmas, and if he is late, to leave the tree standing until he returns. The family hangs out a blue service star for him, and the Pittsburgh community outwardly appears normal. The family does not hear from Jimmy after D-Day, and when news of his death arrives, Ellie prays that it is a mistake and then gets angry at Jimmy for not keeping his part of their bargain.

2592. Salisbury, Graham. *House of the Red Fish.*   Wendy Lamb, 2006. 291pp. ISBN 978-0-385-73121-8; Laurel-Leaf, 2008, paper ISBN 978-0-440-23838-6. Grades 5–8. In this sequel to *Under the Blood-Red Sun*, Tomi Nakaji, 14, worries about his Japanese American grandfather and father when they are arrested after the bombing of Pearl Harbor. When they are interned, Tomi decides to raise his father's fishing boat, which the army sank. His friends, including the haole (white) Billy, help him. All of them must cooperate to plan what tools to use—pontoons, air compressors, rope, and muscle—to accomplish their goal. At the same time, Tomi must deal with his nemesis, the bully Keet Wilson, who was once his friend.

2593. Salisbury, Graham. *Under The Blood-Red Sun.*   Random, 2005. 246pp. Paper ISBN 978-0-553-49487-7. Grades 5–8. When Tomi Nakaji is in 8th grade in Hawaii, the Japanese bomb Pearl Harbor. As the son and grandson of Japanese immigrant workers who have been proud of their heritage but who are interned as a result of the bombing, Tomi becomes an enemy himself. He, his sister, and his mother live through the trauma of the times with the help of others who know that they are not guilty for decisions made by others who happen to be of the same heritage. *Scott O'Dell Award.*

2594. Say, Allen. *Music for Alice.* Houghton, 2004. 32pp. ISBN 978-0-618-31118-7. Grades 3 up. Alice Sumida, a Japanese American woman who loves to dance, marries Mark soon after World War II begins. Then they have to leave their home but are allowed to grow food instead of being interned in a camp. They learn to use their difficult situation to their advantage by turning rocks and wastelands into beets, and then after the war, into flowers. Alice and her husband work hard to establish the largest gladiola bulb farm in the United States in the latter half of the twentieth century. The sepia-toned illustrations enhance the text.

2595. Schubert, Leda. *Ballet of the Elephants.* Illustrated by Robert Andrew Parker. Roaring Brook, 2006. 34pp. ISBN 978-1-59643-075-4. Grades K–3. In 1942 in St. Petersburg, Florida, expatriate Russian choreographer George Balanchine created a dance for the elephants in John Ringling North's circus. He used the music of his good friend Igor Stravinsky, an expatriate Russian composer. They practiced with an Indian elephant, Modoc, performing a *pas de deux* with Vera Zorina, a ballet and Broadway star. All the elephants wore pink tutus. Illustrations enhance the text. Bibliography, Note, and Web Sites. *Bluebonnet Book Award* (Texas) nomination.

2596. Smith, Icy. *Mei Ling in China City.* Illustrated by Gayle Garner Roski. East West Discovery, 2008. Unpaged. ISBN 978-0-9701654-8-0. Grades 3–5. In 1942 Mei Ling Lee describes her life in the China City section of Los Angeles and her efforts to raise money for the United China Relief fund. Her Japanese friend has to leave for Manzanar when her family is interned and their friendship continues by letter. Illustrations and black-and-white photographs augment the text.

2597. Tavares, Matt. *Oliver's Game.* Candlewick, 2004. 32pp. ISBN 978-0-7636-1852-0. Grades 1–5. Oliver Hall loves baseball. He helps his Grandpa Hall in his baseball memorabilia store near Wrigley Field, and listens to his baseball stories. When Oliver finds an old Cubs uniform in his grandpa's closet, grandpa tells Oliver the best story of all, how he almost joined the Chicago Cubs baseball team. He was invited to try out for the team in 1941 when the manager saw him play street stickball, but World War II intervened and he was wounded in service. Oliver gets to wear grandpa's jersey while they sit on their rooftop seats across from the field during games. Illustrations enhance the text. *Young Hoosier Award* (Indiana) nomination and *Parents' Choice Award* nomination.

2598. Taylor, Theodore. *The Cay.* Random, 1989. 138pp. ISBN 978-0-385-07906-8; Laurel-Leaf, 2003, paper ISBN 978-0-440-22912-4. Grades 4–8. In 1942, Phillip, 11, sails with his mother from Curaçao to the United States. The Germans sink their ship and an old black man named Timothy saves Phillip and a cat. On the raft, Phillip finds that he is blind from a head injury sustained during the ship's explosion. On the island where they wash up, Timothy teaches Phillip how to be independent in spite of his disability so that Phillip can survive if Timothy dies. *Jane Addams Book Award.*

2599. Taylor, Theodore. *Timothy of the Cay.* Harcourt, 2007. 160pp. Paper ISBN 978-0-15-206320-7. Grades 4–8. Phillip has survived his ship being sunk by Nazis because he ended up on a tiny Caribbean island with a man called Timothy. Phillip was blinded in the shipwreck but Timothy carefully taught him survival skills before he died. One day a ship sees the smoke from Phillip's fire and rescues him. Twelve-year-old Phillip tells the story of Timothy's life, beginning in 1884 as a young cabin boy, and his own story as he hopes to regain his sight. After he is healed, his parents take him back to the cay and Timothy's grave. *American Library Association Best Books for Young Adults, Notable Children's Trade Books in the Field of Social Studies,* and *New York Public Library's Books for the Teen Age.*

2600. Thesman, Jean. *Molly Donnelly.* Houghton, 1993. 186pp. ISBN 978-0-395-64348-8. Grades 5–9. On December 7, 1941, the Japanese bomb Pearl Harbor and life begins to change for Molly Donnelly in Seattle, Washington. The blackouts begin that night. Her best friend Emily Tanaka and her family are taken away to an internment camp. Her brother and father put in longer shifts for Boeing Aircraft, and her mother begins working. During the war, two of her cousins die, she has her first date, and she becomes interested in a young soldier. What she realizes as she looks around is that getting a college education is the only way she can escape the limited choices for women.

2601. Tripp, Valerie. *Brave Emily.* Illustrated by Nick Backes. (American Girl) American Girl, 2006. Paper ISBN 978-1-59369-210-0. Grades 2–4. Eight-year-old Emily Bennett is sent from England to America for her own safety during World War II and stays with Molly's family. Although homesick and experiencing problems at school, she tries to make the best of her situation. Molly helps Emily and shows her how brave she is when Emily makes a mistake and must rely on Molly for help.

2602. Tripp, Valerie. *Changes for Molly: A Winter Story.* Illustrated by Nick Backes. American Girl, 1990. 67pp. ISBN 978-0-937295-96-0; 1988, paper ISBN 978-0-937295-49-6. Grades 3–5. Molly is 10 years old in 1944 and wants to be Miss Victory in her dance recital. She worries about her hair and other things but her main concern is whether her father will return safely from the war. On the day of the recital, Molly becomes ill. She stays at home, depressed, but her father appears unexpectedly and her earlier problems disappear.

2603. Uchida, Yoshiko. *The Bracelet.* Illustrated by Joanna Yardley. Philomel, 1993. 32pp. ISBN 978-0-399-22503-1; Puffin, 1996, paper ISBN 978-0-698-11390-9. Grades K–3. When 7-year-old Emi leaves her home for the internment camp in 1942, she takes with her a bracelet with a heart charm from her best friend Laurie. When she arrives at the camp, she loses the bracelet. Her mother tells her that she can carry Laurie in her heart just as she does her father, who has been interned elsewhere.

2604. Uchida, Yoshiko. *Journey to Topaz.* Illustrated by Donald Carrick. Heyday, 2005. 144pp. Paper ISBN 978-1-890771-91-1. Grades 4 up. Yuki Sakane, 11, born in America as a Nisei and therefore a citizen, looks forward to Christmas in 1941, but the Japanese bomb Pearl Harbor. The FBI comes and takes her father away, and then they take her, her mother, and her brother to Topaz, Utah, to an internment camp. She makes new friends but faces hardships such as dust storms and a tragedy that disturbs everyone. Eventually the family reunites, but their lives have been altered permanently. *American Library Association Notable Children's Book.*

2605. Weston, Elise. *The Coastwatcher.* Peachtree, 2006. 132pp. ISBN 978-1-56145-350-4. Grades 4–8. In 1943, Hugh, 11, and his family spend the summer on the South Carolina coast, trying to avoid both the war and the polio epidemic. Hugh spends a lot of time looking at the Atlantic through his binoculars. Then he thinks he sees a periscope in the water. His family discourage this as fantasy, but he decides to show that he is correct. He is sure that Germans are living in an abandoned house nearby when he sees German cigarettes and an unreadable map. What he uncovers is a plot to destroy the Charleston Naval Base. *Agatha Awards* nomination, *Great Stone Face Book Award* (New Hampshire), *Children's Book Award* (Rhode Island) nomination, and *Volunteer State Book Award* (Tennessee) nomination.

2606. White, Ruth. *Way Down Deep.* Farrar, 2007. 197pp. ISBN 978-0-374-38251-3. Grades 4–7. In 1944 a red-haired toddler appears on the courtroom steps of Way Down Deep, West Virginia. Miss Arbutus Ward, the local boardinghouse proprietor, claims her and for the next several years, Ruby June is loved by everyone in this town full of eccentric characters. Then a family turns up who offers a connection to Ruby June's past. *Booklist Editor's Choice.*

2607. Woodson, Jacqueline. *Coming On Home Soon.* Illustrated by Earl B. Lewis. Putnam, 2004. Unpaged. ISBN 978-0-399-23748-5. Grades K–3. During World War II, Ada Ruth's mama goes to Chicago to clean railroad cars leaving Ada Ruth and her grandmother in their rural home. Ada Ruth misses walking in the snow with her and waits for the mail to arrive with either news or money. Watercolors illustrate the text. *Booklist Editor's Choice, Caldecott Honor Book, Young Reader's Award* (Arizona) nomination, *Young Reader Medal* (California) nomination, *Monarch Award Children's Choice* (Illinois) nomination, *Young Hoosier Award* (Indiana) nomination, *Young Readers Choice Awards* (Louisiana), *Capitol Choices Noteworthy Titles* (Washington, D.C.), *Bulletin Blue Ribbon*, and *Picture Book Award* (South Carolina) nomination.

2608. Yep, Laurence. *Hiroshima: A Novella.* Apple, 1996. 56pp. Paper ISBN 978-0-590-20833-8. Grades 3–6. This story begins with details about the *Enola Gay* and its cargo—an atomic bomb. It continues with the situation in Hiroshima on August 6, 1945, when the plane drops its atomic bomb. Sachi, a young girl of 12, survives but her sister dies. Because of her terrible scars, Sachi stays inside for three years, but eventually she comes to the United States for free treatment. Afterword and Sources. *Booklist Editors' Choices* and *Notable Children's Trade Books in the Field of Social Studies.*

History

2609. Aaseng, Nathan. *Navajo Code Talkers.* Walker, 2002. 114pp. Paper ISBN 978-0-8027-7627-3. Grades 5–9. In World War II, Navajo Marines devised and used a code that they based on their native language. This volume recounts their story and adds information on Indian culture, Indian lore, the reservations, and the treatment of Indians in the military. The text includes details about the code creation as well as how the messages were sent. Photographs, Bibliography, and Index.

2610. Allen, Thomas B. *Remember Pearl Harbor: American and Japanese Survivors Tell Their Stories.* (Remember) National Geographic, 2001. 57pp. ISBN 978-0-7922-6690-7. Grades 5–9. Japanese and American men and woman offer eyewitness accounts of the bombing of Pearl Harbor. The text starts in Kyushu, Japan, where Japanese pilots and submarine crews trained for the attack. It then relates the responses of survivors at Pearl Harbor from the cockpit of a plane, the deck of a ship, and the shore. A final chapter tells how Japanese Americans were unjustly interned in the United States after the bombing. Photographs augment the text. Bibliography and Index. *Prairie Pasque Book Award* (South Dakota) nomination.

2611. Baker, Patricia. *Fashions of a Decade: The 1940s.* Chelsea House, 2007. 64pp. ISBN 978-0-8160-6720-6. Grades 5 up. World War II brought more conservative fashions with fewer frilly collars and trim. Photographs and illustrations enhance the text. Glossary, Further Reading, Chronology, and Index.

2612. Beller, Susan Provost. *Battling in the Pacific: Soldiering in World War II.* (Soldiers on the Battlefront) Lerner, 2003. 96pp. ISBN 978-0-8225-6381-5. Grades 5–8. Beller examines the events leading up to the war, the principal battles, and the major leaders involved. She describes the horrors that the Allied troops faced. Factboxes cover extraneous but important information about such topics as Tokyo Rose. Black and white photographs highlight the text. Bibliography, Chronology, Further Reading, Web Sites, and Index.

2613. Bolden, Tonya. *Take-Off: American All-Girl Bands During World War II.* Knopf, 2007. 76pp. ISBN 978-0-375-82797-6. Grades 5–8. During World War II, female jazz bands began performing as male band members left for the front. This volume contains newspaper and magazine articles, posters, and other documents relating the history of these groups. They had to show that they were good, and they had to overcome the stigma against women performing particular kinds of music, including jazz. Photographs highlight the text. Bibliography, Further Resources, Notes, and Index.

2614. Chorlton, Windsor. *Weapons and Technology of World War II.* (20th Century Perspectives) Heinemann, 2002. 48pp. ISBN 978-1-58810-663-6; paper ISBN 978-1-58810-923-1. Grades 5–8. World War II brought some radically new weapons such as the long-range rocket and the atomic bomb. Otherwise, the military often used the same weapons as those used in World War I but with major improvements, especially in aircraft and tanks. The text discusses weapons including radar, code, and propaganda, their uses, and the effects of their use. Illustrations augment the text. Bibliography, Further Reading, Glossary, Index.

2615. Colman, Penny. *Rosie the Riveter: Women Working on the Home Front in World War II.* Crown, 1998. 120pp. Paper ISBN 978-0-517-88567-3. Grades 5–8. Colman explores the importance of women and their work during World War II. Chapters include getting ready for the war and the opportunities for women, the concern during the war that led women to try all kinds of jobs, the final years of the war, and the loss of these jobs to the men when they returned from the war. What women did not lose was the knowledge that they could do well in the workplace. Photographs, Chronology, Bibliography, and Index. *Bulletin Blue Ribbon Book*, *American Library Association Notable Books for Children*, and *American Library Association Best Books for Young Adults.*

2616. Cooper, Michael L. *Remembering Manzanar: Life in a Japanese Relocation Camp.* Houghton, 2002. 68pp. ISBN 978-0-618-06778-7. Grades 5–8. Diaries, memoirs, journals, school newspaper essays, and oral histories tell the stories of Japanese Americans forced to live at Manzanar, the first internment camp in World War II. There were ten different camps for Japanese Americans. Many were American citizens who had to leave their jobs, their friends, and their homes to live in one-room partitions in barracks and eat in mess halls. They tried to live as normally as possible—going to school, playing baseball, attending Saturday night dances, and publishing newspapers. Photographs (some by Ansel Adams and Dorothea Lange), Notes, Web Sites, and Index. Carter G. Woodson Book Award.

2617. Gorman, Jacqueline Laks. *Pearl Harbor: A Primary Source History.* (In Their Own Words) Gareth Stevens, 2009. 48pp. ISBN 978-1-4339-0047-1. Grades 5–8. In seven chapters based on primary sources, the text examines the events that led to the Japanese bombing of Pearl Harbor on December 7, 1941. It discusses the opening and expansion of Japan, the beginnings of World War II in Europe with Hitler's invasion, the shift from conflict to outright war in 1939, the bombing and the later part of World War II after the Americans entered, Pearl Harbor in culture, the context of Pearl Harbor in history, and the major figures in Pearl Harbor. Period photographs enhance the text. Glossary and Index.

2618. Gourley, Catherine. *War, Women, and the News: How Female Journalists Won the Battle to Cover World War II.* Atheneum, 2007. 198pp. ISBN 978-0-689-87752-0. Grades 5–9. Gourley looks at the history of women journalists, focusing on those who won the right to cover World War II. Among those working in the 1920s and 1930s were Dorothea Lange and Martha Gelhorn. And among those working during World War II were photographer Dickey Chapelle and reporters Margaret Bourke-White, Helen Kirkpatrick, and Dorothy Thompson. Publishers and editors initially thought women were too fragile for the grimness of war and should only cover "soft" news. Photographs highlight the text. Bibliography, Notes, and Index.

2619. Hakim, Joy. *War, Peace, and All That Jazz: 1918–1945.* (History of US) Oxford, 2006. 220pp. ISBN 978-0-19-530738-2; 2007, paper ISBN 978-0-19-532723-6. Grades 5 up. Filled with photographs, prints, sidebars, boxed text, and running commentary, this account of the United States from 1918 through World War II covers all aspects of society. Chronology of Events, More Books to Read, and Index.

2620. Hynson, Colin. *World War II: A Primary Source History.* (In Their Own Words) Gareth Stevens, 2005. 48pp. ISBN 978-0-8368-5983-6. Grades 5–8. Among the topics covered in this overview of World War II using primary sources are the circumstances that led to the war, international leaders at the time, how the war affected the rest of the century, the memorials to the dead, the depiction of the war in art, and the artifacts from that war that are still being discovered today. Maps, photographs and illustrations complement the text. Glossary, Chronology, and Index.

2621. Jones, Steven L. *The Red Tails: World War II's Tuskegee Airmen.* Perfection Learning, 2001. 64pp. ISBN 978-0-7569-0251-3; 2002, paper ISBN 978-0-7891-5487-3. Grades 4–8. The Tuskegee Airmen were the first African American pilots in the United States armed forces. Jones looks at their training, their many successful missions, their problems with segregation and prejudice, and their almost spotless military record. They fought with courage and dignity even though they did not receive the respect they deserved when they came home. Photographs enhance the text. Glossary.

2622. Josephson, Judith Pinkerton. *Growing Up in World War II: 1941–1945.* (Our America) Lerner, 2002. 64pp. ISBN 978-0-8225-0660-7. Grades 5–8. Six chapters offer an overview of life for a child during World War II. The topics include play, work, educational activities, and the struggles that are inherent during war. Photographs augment the text. Bibliography, Notes, Further Reading, Web Sites, and Index.

2623. Levy, Pat. *The Home Front in World War II.* (World Wars) Raintree, 2003. 64pp. ISBN 978-0-7398-6065-6. Grades 5–8. Primary source documents and firsthand accounts detail life at home for citizens in both Axis and Allied countries during World War II. Many worked in factories and farms, and many became displaced by bombing. Soldiers returned home needing unexpected care. The war changed each country in some way. Illustrations and photographs enhance the text. Maps, Chronology, Bibliography, and Glossary.

2624. Nathan, Amy. *Yankee Doodle Gals: Women Pilots of World War II.* National Geographic, 2001. 89pp. ISBN 978-0-7922-8216-7. Grades 5–8. With firsthand accounts and photographs, this volume presents the story of the first women who piloted planes for the United States. Called the Women Airforce Service Pilots (WASPs), they helped train anti-aircraft troops, delivered planes to air bases, and tested repaired planes. More than one thousand women flew fighters and bombers during World War II between 1942 and 1944, and thirty-eight lost their lives. The country did not recognize their contributions until 1977. Photographs, maps, and illustrations enhance the text. Notes, Further Reading, and Index.

2625. Nobleman, Marc Tyler. *The Sinking of the USS Indianapolis.* (We the People) Compass Point, 2006. 48pp. ISBN 978-0-7565-2031-1. Grades 4–7. Soon after the *Indianapolis* delivered component parts for the atomic bomb intended to end World War II, the Japanese attacked the ship and sank it. The ship was moving into position for its next mission when enemy torpedoes hit on July 30, 1945. For three days before rescuers arrived the surviving men battled dehydration, exposure to the sun, and sharks attacks. This sinking was the greatest loss for the United States Navy, with only 317 of 1,199 crew members surviving. Maps, Photographs, Reproductions, Chronology, Further Reading, Glossary, Web Sites, and Index.

2626. Santella, Andrew. *Navajo Code Talkers.* (We the People) Compass Point, 2004. 48pp. ISBN 978-0-7565-0611-7. Grades 4–6. During the Battle of Iwo Jima, six Navajo code talkers worked constantly, sending more than eight hundred messages without any mistakes. Based on the Navajo language, the code they used was so successful that no enemy could break it, and not until 1969 did the military acknowledge its existence. Since that time, Presidents Reagan, Clinton, and G. W. H. Bush have honored these men who helped the United States win the war. Archival war photographs highlight the text. Maps, Further Reading, Chronology, Glossary, Web sites, and Index.

2627. Schomp, Virginia. *World War II.* Benchmark, 2003. 96pp. ISBN 978-0-7614-1662-3; 2009, paper ISBN 978-0-7614-3619-5. Grades 5–8. Using letters from individuals of different races in different branches of the military, this volume describes World War II from various perspectives: going to war; the services on land, sea, and air; the "Jim Crow" army; women in uniform; and the progress from D-Day to victory. Also covered are race relations and other pertinent social history. Photographs highlight the text. Bibliography, Glossary, Chronology, Notes, Further Reading, and Index.

2628. Tames, Richard. *Pearl Harbor: The US Enters World War II.* (Point of Impact) Heinemann, 2006. 32pp. ISBN 978-1-4034-9142-8; paper ISBN 978-1-4034-9149-7. Grades 5–8. In two-page chapters, Tames offers an account of the Japanese attack on Pearl Harbor, the aftermath of the attack, and the historical impact. He also notes the debates surrounding the attack and whether it was a wise decision. Photographs and reproductions intensify the text. Glossary, Chronology, Further Reading, and Index.

2629. Tanaka, Shelley. *D-Day: They Fought to Free Europe from Hitler's Tyranny.* Illustrated by David Craig. (A Day that Changed America) Hyperion, 2004. 48pp. ISBN 978-0-7868-1881-5. Grades 4–7. Four soldiers who survived the Allied landing on the beaches of Normandy on June 6, 1944, give their accounts of the battle. A paratrooper, a P-47 pilot, a combat medic, and a landing craft crew member each offer a different perspective of the day that may have changed America's destiny. Maps, Photos, Further Reading, Glossary, Web Sites, and Index.

2630. Taylor, Theodore. *Air Raid—Pearl Harbor! The Story of December 7, 1941.* Gulliver, 2001. 179pp. Paper ISBN 978-0-15-216421-8. Grades 5–8. This look at the Japanese raid on Pearl

Harbor examines what was happening throughout the world at the time and the sequence of events that led to the bombing. Taylor lists key figures. Bibliography.

2631. Tracy, Kathleen. *Top Secret: The Story of the Manhattan Project.* (Monumental Milestones) Mitchell Lane, 2005. 48pp. ISBN 978-1-58415-399-3. Grades 5–8. Tracy looks at the Manhattan Project, which began when the Japanese attacked Pearl Harbor. Scientists worked tirelessly to create a bomb that could end the war. And creating the bomb before any other country could do so became the ultimate goal. Photographs accompany the text. Glossary, Chronology, Notes, Further Reading, Web Sites, and Index.

2632. Tunnell, Michael O., and George W. Chilcoat. *The Children of Topaz: The Story of a Japanese-American Internment Camp Based on a Classroom Diary.* Holiday House, 1996. 74pp. ISBN 978-0-8234-1239-6. Grades 4–7. A third-grade teacher in the Topaz, Utah, internment camp recorded her students' thoughts about their situation in 1943. The authors use this diary as a basis for a discussion of the internment of Japanese Americans after the bombing of Pearl Harbor. For Further Reading and Index.

2633. Whiting, Jim. *The Story of the Attack on Pearl Harbor.* (Monumental Milestones) Mitchell Lane, 2005. 48pp. ISBN 978-1-58415-397-9. Grades 5–8. Whiting looks at the attack on Pearl Harbor, presenting a detailed description of how it happened and why it led the United States to enter World War II. He also includes background information about Matthew Perry's initial visit to Tokyo in 1854 and the five most important moments of the Battle of Midway, when the tide turned in the Pacific. Photographs and illustrations augment the text. Glossary, Chronology, Further Reading, Notes, Web Sites, and Index.

2634. Whitman, Sylvia. *Uncle Sam Wants You! Military Men and Women of World War II.* Lerner, 1993. 80pp. ISBN 978-0-8225-1728-3. Grades 5–9. Both men and women made major contributions during World War II. Whitman looks at the draft, boot camp, stateside duty, and combat in Europe and the Pacific. He uses eyewitness accounts to describe battlefield conditions and examines the role of African Americans and women during the war. Both groups had to cope with prejudice, while all participants dealt with homesickness and periods of fear. Photographs, Bibliography, and Index. *New York Public Library's Books for the Teen Age.*

Biography and Collective Biography

2635. Adler, David A. *A Picture Book of Dwight David Eisenhower.* See entry 2326.

2636. Adler, David A. *A Picture Book of Eleanor Roosevelt.* See entry 2327.

2637. Adler, David A. *A Picture Book of Helen Keller.* See entry 1910.

2638. Adler, David A. *A Picture Book of Jackie Robinson.* Illustrated by Robert Casilla. Holiday House, 1994. Unpaged. ISBN 978-0-8234-112-1; 1997, paper ISBN 978-0-8234-1304-1. Grades 1–3. Jack Roosevelt Robinson (1919–1972), youngest of five children, was born in Georgia. His father left home for Florida when Jackie was six months old and never returned. The family had to leave their sharecropping home and moved to California. Jackie starred in sports throughout school and college, becoming the first four-letter winner at the University of California at Los Angeles. His army career ended after World War II because he was mistreated. He played baseball for a Negro League team, and soon the president of the Brooklyn Dodgers hired him to be the first black player in modern major league baseball. In spite of fierce opposition from players and fans, Robinson became Rookie of the Year in 1947 and Most Valuable Player in 1949. He retired in 1956, and in 1962 was the first African American inducted into the Baseball Hall of Fame. Author's Note and Important Dates.

2639. Allport, Alan. *Franklin Delano Roosevelt.* See entry 2335.

2640. Alphin, Elaine Marie. *Dwight D. Eisenhower.* See entry 2336.

2641. Bardhan-Quallen, Sudipta. *Franklin Delano Roosevelt: A National Hero.* See entry 2341.

2642. Bass, Hester. *The Secret World of Walter Anderson.* See entry 2343.

2643. Bruning, John R., Jr. *Elusive Glory: African-American Heroes of World War II.* Avisson, 2001. 135pp. Paper ISBN 978-1-8881-0548-3. Grades 5–8. Bruning looks at fifteen African American men who served in the ground forces or air corps during World War II. Seven of these men were awarded the Medal of Honor in 1997. Six were Tuskegee airmen, including Ben Davis, Jr., a Tuskegee Red Tails combat pilot who became a general. Bruning also discusses racism in the armed forces and how these men fought for a country that would not accept them as full members of society when they returned home. Photographs enhance the text.

2644. Cooney, Barbara. *Eleanor.* See entry 1944.

2645. Darby, Jean. *Dwight D. Eisenhower: A Man Called Ike.* See entry 2361.

2646. Deitch, Kenneth M., and JoAnne B. Weisman. *Dwight D. Eisenhower: Man of Many Hats.* See entry 2362.

2647. DePaola, Tomie. *I'm Still Scared.* Putnam, 2006. 83pp. ISBN 978-0-399-24502-2; Puffin, 2007, paper ISBN 978-0-14-240826-1. Grades 2–4. In the second installment of his autobiography, Tomie dePaola reacts to the bombing of Pearl Harbor on December 7, 1941. He hears what people say at home, at church, and at school, where there are special assemblies to discuss air raids. When Tomie does not hear what he needs to know at school, he asks at home. There he can begin to overcome his fears about the war. Black-and-white sketches highlight the text.

2648. DePaola, Tomie. *Things Will Never Be the Same.* Putnam, 2003. 80pp. ISBN 978-0-399-23982-3; Puffin, 2004, paper ISBN 978-0-14-240155-2. Grades 2–5. Tomie dePaola receives a diary for Christmas in 1940, and for the next year records his activities. In January, he loves sledding on his new Junior Flexible Flyer in his Connecticut hometown. He gets car sick on the way to Nana Fall-River's for Easter, and he plays a pirate in a dance recital. In the second grade, he gets a real art teacher and learns that artists do not copy. On December 7, he hears about the bombing of Pearl Harbor and he knows his world has changed. Illustrations enhance the text.

2649. DePaola, Tomie. *Why? The War Years.* (26 Fairmont Avenue) Putnam, 2007. 87pp. ISBN 978-0-399-24692-0. Grades 2–4. In this segment of his autobiography, Tomie dePaola covers 1942 from New Year's Day until April 20. He hears about rationing and hoarding, peeks from behind the family's blackout curtains, and realizes he will no longer be able to chew Fleer bubblegum. At the same time, he has a hard time with his second-grade penmanship, wants to make the school Valentine mailbox, and visits a meatpacking warehouse. On April 20, the family receives news that Tomie's cousin Blackie has died in the war, shot out of a European sky. He wonders "why." Illustrations complement the text.

2650. Donovan, Sandra. *Mary McLeod Bethune.* See entry 2366.

2651. El Nabli, Dina. *Eleanor Roosevelt: First Lady of the World.* See entry 1958.

2652. Feinberg, Barbara Silberdick. *Eleanor Roosevelt: A Very Special First Lady.* See entry 1960.

2653. Fleischman, John. *Black and White Airmen: Their True History.* Houghton, 2007. 160pp. ISBN 978-0-618-56297-8. Grades 4–8. Not until 1997 did John Leahr and Herb Heilbrun become friends. They met at a Tuskegee Airmen reunion and did not remember knowing each other. A picture of their third-grade class in Cincinnati, Ohio, shows them standing side by side, but they did not speak to each other because one was black and the other was white. They worked in the same factory before the war, and they also flew several missions together during World War II. The text includes information about airplanes and about racism. Photographs highlight the text. Further Reading, Web Sites, and Index.

2654. Fleming, Candace. *Our Eleanor: A Scrapbook Look at Eleanor Roosevelt's Remarkable Life.* See entry 2376.

2655. Freedman, Russell. *Eleanor Roosevelt: A Life of Discovery.* See entry 1967.

2656. Freedman, Russell. *Franklin Delano Roosevelt.* See entry 1968.

2657. Freedman, Russell. *The Voice that Challenged a Nation: Marian Anderson and the Struggle for Equal Rights.* See entry 2382.

2658. Gentry, Tony, and Heather Lehr Wagner. *Jesse Owens: Champion Athlete.* See entry 2384.

2659. Gherman, Beverly. *Norman Rockwell: Storyteller with a Brush.* See entry 2386.

2660. Greenfield, Eloise. *Mary McLeod Bethune.* See entry 1980.

2661. Haugen, Brenda. *Douglas MacArthur: America's General.* See entry 2392.

2662. Haugen, Brenda. *Franklin Delano Roosevelt: The New Deal President.* See entry 2393.

2663. Healy, Nick. *Paul Robeson.* See entry 2395.

2664. Jones, Victoria Garrett. *Eleanor Roosevelt: A Courageous Spirit.* (Sterling Biographies) Sterling, 2007. 124pp. ISBN 978-1-4027-4746-5; paper ISBN 978-1-4027-3371-0. Grades 5–8. This volume looks at the life of Eleanor Roosevelt (1884–1962) as the wife of the president of the United States. After a summary of his life and the contributions she made, it includes information about her early family life and education and examines her in relationship to the times in which she lived and her need to support her husband after he contracted polio. Although she was basically shy and hated public speaking, she became a strong-willed person who said what she believed and campaigned for her husband when he was unable. Photographs enhance the text. Bibliography, Glossary, and Index.

2665. Josephson, Judith Pinkerton. *Louis Armstrong.* (History Maker Bios) Lerner, 2008. 48pp. ISBN 978-0-8225-7169-8. Grades 3–5. In five chapters this biography looks at the life of Louis Armstrong (1901–1971) and his career as a jazz musician. Illustrations augment the text. Bibliography, Further Reading, Glossary, Maps, Timeline, Web Sites, and Index.

2666. Kaye, Judith. *The Life of Benjamin Spock.* (Pioneers in Health and Medicine) Twenty-First Century, 1993. 80pp. ISBN 978-0-8050-2301-5. Grades 4–7. Benjamin Spock (1903–1998) told parents to trust themselves. He first published *Baby and Child Care* in 1946, and it changed the way parents raised American children, for good or for bad. In his later life he involved himself in larger issues, such as nuclear disarmament and world peace. He even went to jail for his beliefs. For Further Reading and Index.

2667. Keller, Emily. *Margaret Bourke-White: A Photographer's Life.* See entry 2400.

2668. Kent, Deborah. *Dorothy Day: Friend to the Forgotten.* See entry 2401.

2669. Kent, Deborah. *Hellen Keller: Author and Advocate for the Disabled.* See entry 1998.

2670. Kittredge, Mary. *Barbara McClintock.* See entry 2404.

2671. Kliment, Bud. *Count Basie.* See entry 2405.

2672. Lassieur, Allison. *Eleanor Roosevelt: Activist for Social Change.* See entry 2412.

2673. McKissack, Patricia C., and Frederick McKissack. *Langston Hughes: Great American Poet.* See entry 2426.

2674. McKissack, Patricia C., and Frederick McKissack. *Louis Armstrong: Jazz Musician.* See entry 2427.

2675. McKissack, Patricia C., and Frederick McKissack. *Marian Anderson: A Great Singer.* See entry 2428.

2676. McKissack, Patricia C., and Frederick McKissack. *Ralph J. Bunche: Peacemaker.* See entry 2432.

2677. Macleod, Elizabeth. *Eleanor Roosevelt: An Inspiring Life.* (Snapshots: Images of People and Places in History) Kids can, 2006. 32pp. ISBN 978-1-55337-778-8; paper ISBN 978-1-55337-811-2. Grades 3–7. Eleanor Roosevelt (1884–1962) was known as a poor little rich girl because her parents died when she was young and her grandmother called her "Granny" because she though Eleanor looked old. Eleanor was able to attend school in England where she gained confidence. She returned to the United States and met her second cousin, Franklin Delano Roosevelt, who asked to marry her. She helped him win political office, and when he contracted polio, she spoke for him around the country. She fought for civil rights and world peace. Illustrations augment the text. Chronology, Web Sites, and Index.

2678. McPherson, Stephanie Sammartino. *Albert Einstein.* (History Maker Bios) Lerner, 2004. 48pp. ISBN 978-0-8225-0350-7. Grades 3–5. Albert Einstein (1879–1955) was expelled from school as a youngster but loved his high school. In college, he thought his professors were not teaching the most important aspects of science. He wanted to become a professor, but educational politics prohibited his appointment. While working elsewhere, he wrote theories on space, gravity, matter, time, and energy. Eventually he won the Nobel Prize for the work that became known as the theory of relativity. Illustrations augment the text. Bibliography, Further Reading, Glossary, Maps, Timeline, Web Sites, and Index.

2679. Mayo, Gretchen Will. *Frank Lloyd Wright.* See entry 2437.

2680. Meltzer, Milton. *Albert Einstein: A Biography.* Holiday House, 2008. 32pp. ISBN 978-0-8234-1966-1. Grades 3–6. Meltzer covers not only Albert Einstein's (1879–1955) background and achievements but also his beliefs and personality. He points out that Einstein attended only the college classes in which he had interest and that as an older man he espoused peace. Additionally, Meltzer explains Einstein's theory of relativity in terms readers can understand. Photographs augment the text. Chronology and Bibliography.

2681. Nelson, Marilyn. *Sweethearts of Rhythm: The Story of the Greatest All-Girl Swing Band in the World.* Illustrated by Jerry Pinkney. Dial, 2009. 80pp. ISBN 978-0-8037-3187-5. Grades 4–10. From 1937 to 1946 an interracial (one wore blackface in order to play) group of women toured in an African American swing jazz band. They played local venues, the Cotton Club, the Apollo, and overseas in USO concerts after World War II's end. The twenty poems of the text each take the point-of-view of an instrument left in a New Orleans pawnshop. Each tells about the style and talent of the woman who played it, revealing their diversity and ability to delight an audience with such pieces as "Chattanooga Choo-Choo" and "Lady, Be Good." They also give a sense of the times with mentions of victory gardens, Rosie the Riveter, and the segregation under Jim Crow laws. Color pencil, collage, and watercolor depict the times. Notes, Bibliography, and Chronology. *Booklist Editors Choice, Capitol Choices Noteworthy Titles for Children and Teens* (Washington, D.C.), and *American Library Association Notable Children's Books.*

2682. Nelson, S. D. *Quiet Hero: The Ira Hayes Story.* Lee & Low, 2006. Unpaged. ISBN 978-1-58430-263-6. Grades 1–4. Ira Hayes (1923–1955), a Pima Indian, was one of the six soldiers who helped raise the United States flag on Iwo Jima during World War II. A shy and silent boy, he attended a government-run boarding school for Indians before joining the marines. When he returned home, people who had seen him in Joe Rosenthal's famous photograph treated him like a hero. He believed that only those who died were real heroes. Photographs enhance the text. Note.

2683. Nicholson, Dorinda Makanaonalani Stagner. *Pearl Harbor Child: A Child's View of Pearl Harbor—from Attack to Peace.* Woodson House, 2005. 64pp. Paper ISBN 978-0-931503-02-3. Grades 4–8. Nicholson was in first grade in Pearl Harbor when the Japanese bombs fell in 1941. She remembers that the noise of the planes kept her from hearing the incendiary bullets that hit her family's house. She tells of the evacuation afterward, the increase in military personnel, blackouts, and rationing. Her mother would rub pieces of newspaper together to soften them enough to become effective toilet paper. Photographs.

2684. O'Connor, Jim. *Jackie Robinson and the Story of All-Black Baseball.* Random, 1989. 48pp. ISBN 978-0-394-82456-7. Grades 2–4. Jackie Robinson (1919–1972), the first African American baseball player in the modern major leagues, joined the Brooklyn Dodgers in 1947. His abilities showed the strength of the all-black baseball teams that existed before the major leagues integrated.

2685. O'Sullivan, Robyn. *Jackie Robinson Plays Ball.* (National Geographic History Chapters) National Geographic, 2007. 40pp. ISBN 978-1-4263-0190-2. Grades 2–4. This brief overview of the life of Jackie Robinson (1919–1972) offers highlights of his contributions to the sport and character of baseball by breaking the racial barrier. Archival photographs and illustrations augment the text. Glossary, Further Reading, Web Sites, and Index.

2686. **Parker, Robert Andrew.** *Piano Starts Here: The Young Art Tatum.* See entry 2449.

2687. **Pinkney, Andrea Davis.** *Duke Ellington: The Piano Prince and His Orchestra.* See entry 2452.

2688. **Porter, A. P.** *Jump at de Sun: The Story of Zora Neale Hurston.* See entry 2062.

2689. **Rappaport, Doreen.** *Eleanor, Quiet No More.* See entry 2064.

2690. **St. George, Judith.** *Make Your Mark, Franklin Roosevelt.* See entry 2462.

2691. **Schroeder, Alan.** *Satchmo's Blues.* See entry 2247.

2692. **Schuman, Michael A.** *Eleanor Roosevelt: First Lady and Humanitarian.* See entry 2466.

2693. **Slade, Suzanne.** *Albert Einstein: Scientist and Genius.* Illustrated by Robert McGuire. (Biographies) Picture Window, 2008. 24pp. ISBN 978-1-4048-3730-0. Grades K–3. Albert Einstein (1879–1955), born in Ulm, Germany, was shy and quiet. When he was 5 years old, he was intrigued by the compass his father gave him and wondered what made it point north. At 12, he received a geometry book that he studied on his own. He attended college and worked in a patent office before marrying Mileva Maric in 1903. In 1905 he wrote four important papers that changed the concept of space and time. His new discovery involved a formula, $E=mc^2$. In 1914 he began teaching at a Berlin university, and in 1919 he divorced and remarried. In 1921 he received the Nobel Prize for Physics, and in 1933 he moved to the United States to continue his research. During World War II he worked on the atomic bomb but never thought anyone would use it. That the United States bombed Japan greatly upset him. Chronology, Further Reading, Bibliography, Glossary, Web Sites, and Index.

2694. **Stone, Tanya Lee.** *Sandy's Circus: A Story About Alexander Calder.* See entry 2471.

2695. **Streissguth, Thomas.** *Rocket Man: The Story of Robert Goddard.* See entry 2087.

2696. **Streissguth, Thomas.** *Say It with Music: A Story About Irving Berlin.* See entry 2473.

2697. **Sullivan, George.** *Helen Keller.* See entry 2088.

2698. **Sutcliffe, Jane.** *George S. Patton, Jr.* See entry 2090.

2699. **Tanenhaus, Sam.** *Louis Armstrong: Musician.* See entry 2481.

2700. **Taylor-Butler, Christine.** *Thurgood Marshall.* See entry 2482.

2701. **Venezia, Mike.** *Dorothea Lange.* See entry 2484.

2702. **Venezia, Mike.** *Duke Ellington.* See entry 2485.

2703. **Venezia, Mike.** *Edward Hopper.* See entry 2486.

2704. **Venezia, Mike.** *Grandma Moses.* See entry 2489.

2705. **Venezia, Mike.** *Jackson Pollock.* See entry 2492.

2706. **Venezia, Mike.** *Jacob Lawrence.* (Getting to Know the World's Greatest Artists) Scholastic, 1999. 32pp. ISBN 978-0-516-21012-4; Children's Press, 2000, paper ISBN 978-0-516-26533-9. Grades K–5. Jacob Lawrence (1917–2000) used bright colors in his work after he became famous at the young age of 24 for his *Migration of the Negro*, a series of 60 paintings with realistic and abstract styles. He studied art in Harlem and portrayed the poverty, health, and racism he saw facing African Americans. Illustrations enhance the text.

2707. **Venezia, Mike.** *Norman Rockwell.* See entry 2496.

2708. **Waxman, Laura Hamilton.** *Franklin D. Roosevelt.* See entry 2502.

2709. **Weidt, Maryann N.** *Oh, the Places He Went: A Story About Dr. Seuss.* See entry 2509.

2710. Welch, Catherine. *Margaret Bourke-White.* Illustrated by Jennifer Hagerman. Carolrhoda, 1997. 56pp. ISBN 978-0-8761-4890-7. Grades 2–4. Margaret Bourke-White (1904–1971) became interested in photography at a young age and began to make money at it after the death of her father. She was able to capture the artistic side of steel mills and skyscrapers as well as recording the reality of life and war. She worked as a photojournalist for *Life* magazine in World War II and the Korean War. She also exposed working conditions in India and the tragedy of the Great Depression. None of her photographs is included, but illustrations augment the text.

2711. Winget, Mary. *Eleanor Roosevelt.* See entry 2513.

2712. Wooten, Sara McIntosh. *Robert Frost: The Life of America's Poet.* (People to Know Today) Enslow, 2006. 128pp. ISBN 978-0-7660-2627-8. Grades 5–8. Robert Frost (1874–1963) described the life and nature around him in his poetry. He battled depression and poverty after suffering an abusive, alcoholic father during his childhood. He received four Pulitzer Prizes for his work. Photographs enhance the text. Chronology, Further Reading, Notes, Web sites, and Index.

Graphic Novels, Biographies, and Histories

2713. Abnett, Dan. *The Battle of Midway: The Destruction of the Japanese Fleet.* Illustrated by Richard Elson. (Graphic Battles of World War II) Rosen, 2007. 48pp. ISBN 978-1-4042-0783-7. Grades 4–9. Abnett looks at the Battle of Midway, which took place in the North Pacific from June 4 to 7, 1942. Introductory background precedes a description of the battle, the strategies of both the United States and Japan, and the ultimate American victory.

2714. Abnett, Dan, and Larry Hama. *The Battle of Guadalcanal: Land and Sea Warfare in the South Pacific.* Illustrated by Anthony Williams. (Graphic Battles of World War II) Rosen, 2007. 48pp. ISBN 978-1-4042-0784-4. Grades 4–9. Many consider the Battle of Guadalcanal, which lasted six months on both land and sea, to be the turning point of World War II. Abnett gives background about the Japanese and why the war began before presenting the leaders, the battle itself, and the results. The drawings complement the text in this graphic history. Maps, Bibliography, Glossary, Further Reading, Web Sites, and Index.

2715. Cain, Bill. *The Battle of the Bulge: Turning Back Hitler's Final Push.* Illustrated by Dheeraj Verma. (Graphic Battles of World War II) Rosen, 2007. 48pp. ISBN 978-1-4042-0782-0. Grades 4–9. Cain presents details of the Battle of the Bulge, which took place in Ardennes, France, from December 16, 1944, to January 25, 1945. It offers background on the war as well as commentary on the major commanders involved. Photographs and illustrations augment the text.

2716. Hama, Larry. *The Battle of Iwo Jima: Guerrilla Warfare in the Pacific.* Illustrated by Anthony Williams. (Graphic Battles of World War II) Rosen, 2007. 48pp. ISBN 978-1-4042-0781-3. Grades 4–9. Hama begins with background about the Japanese and why World War II began, then focuses on the arrival of three Japanese botany students as the battle at Iwo Jima is about to begin and reveals that the Japanese generals had spent some time in the United States. Information that humanizes the war augments the drawings and text in this graphic history. Maps, Bibliography, Glossary, Further Reading, Web Sites, and Index.

2717. Murray, Doug. *D-Day: The Liberation of Europe Begins.* Illustrated by Anthony Williams. (Graphic Battles of World War II) Rosen, 2007. 48pp. ISBN 978-1-4042-0786-8. Grades 4–9. This account of D-Day, on June 6, 1944, presents details of the event. It offers background on the war as well as information on the major commanders involved. Photographs and illustrations augment the text. Bibliography, Glossary, Web Sites, and Index.

2718. O'Hern, Kerri. *Louis Armstrong.* See entry 2522.

2719. Sutcliffe, Jane. *The Attack on Pearl Harbor.* Illustrated by Bob Lentz. Graphic Library, 2006. 32pp. ISBN 978-0-7368-5477-1; paper ISBN 978-0-7368-6872-3. Grades 3–5. On December 7, 1941, the Japanese bombed the Pearl Harbor naval base in a surprise strike. Illustrations visualize the event. The Japanese sank four United States Navy battleships and damaged four more. The attack sank three cruisers, three destroyers, and one minelayer, destroyed 188 aircraft, and killed 2,402. Another 1,282 were wounded. Illustrations depict the event. Bibliography, Glossary, Further Reading, and Index.

DVDs

2720. Brickell, Beth. *Mr. Christmas.* Channel Sources, 2007. 1.5 hrs. ISBN 978-0-9773287-0-3. Grades K–6. Joel, a father who does not receive his Christmas bonus in 1941 because his boss worries about the war that has just begun, cannot afford to buy his 5-year-old daughter Carol Lee the bicycle that she wants from Santa Claus. When he walks home on Christmas Eve, a dog follows him. The next morning his daughter is delighted with her gift because a dog was her second choice. She calls him "Mr. Christmas."

2721. *Franklin D. Roosevelt.* (20th Century Presidents) Landmark Media, 2006. 19 mins. Grades 4 up. A child gives an overview of the life of Franklin Delano Roosevelt (1882–1945), who assumed the presidency in the middle of the Great Depression and served during the years of World War II. The programs that he started helped the American people regain their confidence and start producing. He gave speeches on the radio each week that he called "fireside chats" and made the comment that "The only thing we have to fear is fear itself."

2722. *Silent Wings: The American Glider Pilots of WWII.* (Minutes of History) Inecom, 2006. 1:53 hrs. Grades 5 up. Pilots of unpowered and unarmed gliders played an important part in World War II. This documentary uses archival footage and interviews to describe glider participation in Sicily, D-Day, the invasions of France and Holland, the Battle of the Bulge, and Germany. The men usually flew at night and carried men and weapons behind the enemy lines. Hal Holbrook narrates and the commentators include Walter Cronkite and Andy Rooney.

Compact Discs

2723. Bruchac, Joseph. *Code Talker: A Novel About the Navajo Marines of World War II.* Narrated by Derrick Henry. Recorded Books, 2006. 5 CDs; 6 hrs. ISBN 978-1-4281-6571-7. Grades 5 up. See entry 2550.

2724. Giff, Patricia Reilly. *Willow Run.* Narrated by Staci Snell. Listening Library, 2005. 3 CDs; 3:20 hrs. ISBN 978-0-307-28299-6. Grades 4–7. See entry 2560.

2725. Kadohata, Cynthia. *Weedflower.* Narrated by Kimberly Farr. Listening Library, 2006. 5 CDs; 6.19 hrs. ISBN 978-0-3072-8413-6. Grades 5–8. Sumiko, 12, and her family are relocated to an internment camp on a Mojave Indian reservation in Arizona. The government has already removed her grandfather and uncle. Sumiko tries to become friends with Frank, a Mojave boy who resents their presence and the fact that the newcomers have been given electricity, a luxury his people have not enjoyed. At the same time, she plants a garden and holds on to her dream of owning a flower shop someday. *Booklist Editor's Choice, Bluebonnet Award* (Texas) nomination, *Dorothy Canfield Fisher Children's Book Award* (Vermont) nomination, and *Jane Addams Book Award.*

2726. **Klages, Ellen.** *The Green Glass Sea.*   Recorded Books, 2007. 7 CDs; 7.5 hrs. ISBN 978-1-4281-4639-6. Grades 5–8. See entry 2571.

2727. **Salisbury, Graham.** *House of the Red Fish.*   Recorded Books, 2006. 6 cass; 6:39 hrs. ISBN 978-1-4281-2238-3. Grades 5–8. See entry 2592.

2728. **Tripp, Valerie.** *Molly: An American Girl.*   Narrated by Katherine Kellgren. Recorded Books, 2007. 6 CDs; 7 hrs. ISBN 978-1-4281-3432-4. Grades 3–5. In 1944 Molly McIntire is living with her family in Illinois. Her father, an Army doctor, has been sent to London, and while he is gone her two close friends help her cope with his absence. Other Molly stories included here are "Meet Molly," "Molly Learns a Lesson," "Molly's Surprise," "Happy Birthday, Molly," "Molly Saves the Day," and "Changes for Molly."

THE MID-TWENTIETH CENTURY, 1946–1975

Historical Fiction and Fantasy

2729. Armistead, John. *The Return of Gabriel.* Illustrated by Fran Gregory. Milkweed, 2002. 218pp. Paper ISBN 978-1-57131-638-7. Grades 5–9. In 1964, 13-year-old Cooper Grant has two best friends—Jubal Harris and "Squirrel" Kogan—and a secret club called the Scorpions. Freedom workers arrive in Tupelo, Mississippi, trying to register black voters, but Cooper's father tells him to attend a Ku Klux Klan meeting rather than help. As tension rises, Cooper worries about his friends, especially after the Klan burns a cross in front of Squirrel's home. His friends question his loyalty when they see him go to the Klan meeting, but Cooper's actions prevent the Klan from bombing a church.

2730. Auch, Mary Jane. *One-Handed Catch.* Henry Holt, 2006. 248pp. ISBN 978-0-8050-7900-5. Grades 5–8. In 1946, Norman, 12, has to learn to live without the hand he lost in the meat grinder at his father's butcher shop. He wants to play baseball and to draw pictures. His mother urges him to work at overcoming his disability rather than seeking sympathy. He figures out how to field, throw, and bat and then learns how to excel in other areas of his life.

2731. Barasch, Lynne. *Ask Albert Einstein.* Farrar, 2005. 32pp. ISBN 978-0-374-30435-5. Grades 2–5. In 1952, 7-year-old April writes to Dr. Einstein at Princeton's Institute for Advanced Study, asking for his help on her 15-year-old sister Annabel's math problem. She sends him a copy of the problem, and in his response, he offers Annabel a clue that will help her find the answer. Illustrations augment the text.

2732. Beaty, Andrea. *Cicada Summer.* Amulet, 2008. 176pp. ISBN 978-0-8109-9472-0. Grades 4–7. In Olena, Illinois, in the 1950s, 12-year-old Lily has retreated into silence since the accident that killed her brother Pete two years before. Many people assume she is brain-damaged. Then the general store owner's niece, Tinny Bridges, arrives in town and sees Lily reading. She decides to expose Lily's secret. But Tinny has her own problems and vulnerabilities, and the two girls must face challenges and threats together.

2733. Bildner, Phil. *The Greatest Game Ever Played: A Football Story.* Illustrated by Zachary Pullen. Putnam, 2006. 40pp. ISBN 978-0-399-24171-0. Grades K–3. Sam and Pop love the New York Giants, but the baseball team moves to California and Sam misses spending afternoons with his father. He then discovers a football team with the same name, and when Sam is laid off his boss gives him tickets to the New York Giants' championship game against the Baltimore Colts in 1958. Pop agrees to accompany him and the two enjoy the historic game even though the Giants lose.

2734. Bildner, Phil. *The Shot Heard 'Round the World.* Illustrated by C. F. Payne. Simon & Schuster, 2005. 32pp. ISBN 978-0-689-86273-1. Grades 2–5. In 1951 the Dodgers play the Giants in a final, third tie-breaker to decide who will face the Yankees in the World Series. A young fan describes the progress of the Dodgers during that season and how the Brooklyn neighborhood in which they played became completely involved in the game. But Bobby Thompson's home run for the Giants keeps the Dodgers out of the game for yet another year. Illustrations complement the text.

2735. Birtha, Becky. *Grandmama's Pride.* Illustrated by Colin Bootman. Whitman, 2005. 32pp. ISBN 978-0-8075-3028-3. Grades 1–4. When 6-year-old Sarah visits her grandmother in the South in 1956, she and her sister and mother sit in the back of the bus because her mother says those are the best seats. Her mother packs a lunch so they can eat it while other passengers go to a restaurant. At the train station, their grandmother waits for them in a room without seats. The next summer, when they come, things are different. What she does not know is that the Supreme Court has passed a law desegregating the buses, schools, and public places. Illustrations augment the text. Note. *Diamond Primary Book Award* (Arkansas) nomination, *Picture Book Award* (Georgia) nomination, and *Show Me State Book Award* (Missouri) nomination.

2736. Blume, Lesley M. M. *Cornelia and the Audacious Escapades of the Somerset Sisters.* Knopf, 2006. 264pp. ISBN 978-0-375-83523-0. Grades 4–6. Cornelia, 11, lives a lonely life in Greenwich Village where servants look after her. She prefers words to music, unlike her concert pianist mother who is always away. Then an elderly woman named Virginia Somerset moves in next door. She tells Cornelia stories about the travels she and her sisters took after World War II. They met Picasso, rescued a starving Indian orphan, and had other fantastic adventures. But hearing the stories allows Cornelia to gain more confidence in herself.

2737. Blume, Lesley M. M. *The Rising Star of Rusty Nail.* Knopf, 2007. 270pp. ISBN 978-0-375-93524-4. Grades 4–6. McCarthyism is rampant in Rusty Nail, Minnesota, in 1953 when Russian Olga Malenkov arrives. Although she is married to a lawyer and is a famous musician, there are many who suspect she is a spy. Ten-year-old Franny Hansen, already a talented piano player, wants to persuade Olga to take her as a student.

2738. Brimner, Larry Dane. *Birmingham Sunday.* Calkins Creek, 2010. 32pp. ISBN 978-1-59078-613-0. Grades 5–8. On September 15, 1963, four nicely dressed girls went to their church. They were Addie May Collins, 14; Denise McNair, 11; Carole Robertson, 14; and Cynthia Wesley, 14. When dynamite exploded the thirty-inch-thick stone and brick walls of their Sixteenth Street Baptist Church, the four died. On the same day, a policeman and a white boy killed two African American males in the streets. Using primary sources and materials such as FBI reports and court records with period photographs, the text relates their story against the backdrop of racial hatred in which they lived. Pictures of the Ku Klux Klan with fully costumed children, sit-ins, the origin of the NAACP, and the dynamiting of Rev. Fred L. Shuttlesworth's home because he espoused school integration and racial equality augment the text. Further Reading and Notes.

2739. Bruchac, Joseph. *Hidden Roots.* Scholastic, 2004. 136pp. Paper ISBN 978-0-439-35359-5. Grades 5–9. In his French Canadian community in New York State in 1954, Howard (Sonny), 11, and his mother cannot predict his father Jake's abusive rages. They seem to happen after long days working at the paper mill and when Uncle Louis visits. Eventually Sonny makes friends with the new school librarian, and she helps him gather strength to confront his mother and uncle about a family secret that seems to be consuming his father. His father is an Abenaki Indian who began concealing his identity when the Vermont Eugenics Project became law in 1931 and allowed the state to sterilize Native Americans. *Dorothy Canfield Fisher Children's Book Award* (Vermont) nomination.

2740. Bryant, Jen. *Kaleidoscope Eyes.* Knopf, 2009. 2640pp. ISBN 978-0-375-84048-7. Grades 5–8. Lyza Bradley, 13, lives with her father, a professor, and a hippie sister in Willowbank, New Jersey, in 1968. Her beloved grandfather dies suddenly, and in his attic she finds an envelope with her name on it. Inside are maps to a treasure buried by Captain William Kidd. Lyza enlists the help of her best friends, African American Malcolm and tiny white Carolann. Their search, depicted in a series of poems, takes place against a background of Vietnam deaths and Lyza's mother's two-year absence.

2741. Bryant, Jennifer. *Call Me Marianne.* Illustrated by David Johnson. Eerdmans, 2006. 32pp. ISBN 978-0-8028-5242-7. Grades 2–4. A little boy is riding a bus to the Brooklyn zoo when a woman dressed in black and wearing a tri-cornered hat gets on. At the zoo she tells Jonathan she is a poet. He enjoys listening to her descriptions of the animals and she tells him about writing poetry. The story closes with a one-page biography of Marianne Moore (1887–1972). Illustrations enhance the text.

2742. Burg, Shana. *A Thousand Never Evers.* Delacorte, 2008. 320pp. ISBN 978-0-385-73470-7. Grades 4–8. In 1963 Addie Ann Pickett starts junior high in a segregated school in Kucka-choo, Mississippi. She hears about the church bombing in Birmingham, Alabama, and en-counters racism closer to her when the Klan chases her brother. Then she discovers the awful circumstances surrounding her father's death. Her uncle, falsely accused of destroying a gar-den, has to have the NAACP defend him until Addie Ann can reveal the real culprit.

2743. Cheng, Andrea. *Eclipse.* Front Street, 2006. 129pp. ISBN 978-1-9324252-1-5. Grades 4–7. In the summer of 1952, 8-year-old Peti is disgruntled. His Hungarian relatives—includ-ing the bullying 12-year-old Gabor—are using his room. And he worries about this grandfather, who's still behind the Iron Curtain. When Peti's librarian takes him to Rankin House, a stop on the Underground Railroad, he begins to appreciate his own family more.

2744. Coleman, Evelyn. *Freedom Train.* Margaret K. McElderry, 2008. 160pp. ISBN 978-0-689-84716-5. Grades 3–6. In 1947, Clyde Thompson, 12 years old and the shortest boy in sev-enth grade, becomes friends with African American William after William rescues him from a bully. Clyde looks forward to his brother Joseph's arrival on the Freedom Train, on which he is a guard. The train is touring the country with copies of the Gettysburg Address, the Constitution, and the Bill of Rights. Clyde discovers that his brother also has an African American friend, and although he has never known whites and African Americans to be friends, he thinks it makes sense. When racial tensions erupt in Atlanta, Clyde stands up for his new belief.

2745. Corbett, Sue. *12 Again.* Dutton, 2002. 227pp. ISBN 978-0-525-46899-8; Puffin, 2007, paper ISBN 978-0-14-240729-5. Grades 5–8. In 1972 reporter Bernadette McBride is working at her deceased mother's house, away from the interruptions of her family, when she helps her-self to a drink and wishes she were young again. The next morning, her 40th birthday, she awakes to find she is 12 years old again. Her laptop does not work, and her mother is alive. Her youth, however, is not what she remembered—she needs help from Patrick, her 12-year-old son, to survive the middle school they are both attending. He does not know who she is so their meeting is odd. She realizes she needs to return to her life and needs help from both her mother and her son to succeed. *Young Readers Medal Program Winners* (California), *Children's Choice Book Award* (Iowa) nomination, and *Bluegrass Book Award* (Kentucky) nom-ination.

2746. Cormier, Robert. *Tunes for Bears to Dance To.* Laurel-Leaf, 1994. 101pp. Paper ISBN 978-0-440-21903-3. Grades 5 up. Henry, 11, works for a grocer in the new town that he and his parents moved to after World War II. They left their previous home to forget the pain of his brother's accidental death the previous year. The grocer, a man with evil intent, tries to get Henry to ruin a carving created by a Holocaust survivor.

2747. Couloumbis, Audrey. *Summer's End.* Speak, 2007. 184pp. Paper ISBN 978-0-14-240783-7. Grades 5–9. In 1965 on the day before she is 13, Grace watches her brother Collin burn his draft card at a sit-in. Her furious stepfather, a Korean War veteran, makes him leave home despite the fact that his wife supports Collin's action. While Collin heads for Canada, Grace retreats to her grandmother's farm and spends time with her cousins. A tragedy finally brings the family together.

2748. Crum, Shutta. *Spitting Image.* Clarion, 2003. 218pp. ISBN 978-0-618-23477-6. Grades 5–8. It's the summer of 1967 in Baylor, Kentucky, and 12-year-old Jessie Bovey has lots to do. She wants to control her temper and to keep out of the way of her grandmother. She wants to know who her father is. And she wants to help her friend Robert, son of an alcoholic father, get enough money to buy glasses. Jessie agrees to introduces Miss Woodruff, the VISTA volunteer from the President's War on Poverty, to the community but this does not go as well as she expects. *Bluegrass Award* (Kentucky) nomination and *Junior Book Award* (South Carolina) nomination.

2749. Curtis, Christopher Paul. *The Watsons Go to Birmingham—1963.* Yearling, 1997. 210pp. Paper ISBN 978-0-440-41412-4. Grades 5–8. Kenny, 10, narrates this story. He and his African American family live in Flint, Michigan, and when his older brother Byron needs more discipline, his parents decide to take him to his grandmother in Birmingham, Alabama. Their trip south gets them to Birmingham before a bomb explodes in a church. Kenny thinks his sister may be one of the four children killed. The importance of the civil rights movement is brought home to him. *Bulletin Blue Ribbon Book, Bank Street College's Children's Book Award, Newbery Honor Book, Coretta Scott King Honor Book, American Library Association Notable Children's Books, American Library Association Best Book for Young Adults,* and *Horn Book Fanfare.*

2750. Cushman, Karen. *The Loud Silence of Francine Green.* Clarion, 2006. 225pp. ISBN 978-0-618-50455-8. Grades 5–9. Francine, 13, attends a Catholic school for girls in Los Angeles in 1949. She becomes friends with Sophie Bowman, who constantly questions authority and invites punishment by the nuns. Her actions lead Francine to question her own values. Eventually Sophie paints "There is no free speech here" on the gymnasium's floor and gets expelled. *Parents Choice Award.*

2751. Deutsch, Stacia, and Rhody Cohon. *King's Courage.* Illustrated by David T. Wenzel. (Blast to the Past) Aladdin, 2005. 105pp. Paper ISBN 978-1-4169-1269-9. Grades 2–5. Third-grade students Abigail, Jacob, Zack, and Bo travel back to 1965 to encourage Martin Luther King, Jr. (1929–1968) not to give up his goals. Illustrations complement the text.

2752. DiCamillo, Kate. *Great Joy.* Illustrated by Bagram Ibatoulline. Candlewick, 2007. 32pp. ISBN 978-0-7636-2920-5. Grades K–2. In the 1940s Frances sees an organ grinder with a sad-eyed monkey outside their apartment window. She asks her mother where they go at night, and her mother busily hems Frances's costume for the Christmas pageant rather than responding. Frances continues to watch them and comes to understand that they have no home. On the way to church, she invites them to the pageant. They arrive while she is searching for a forgotten line; she quickly remembers it and shouts "Great Joy!" Illustrations augment the text.

2753. Dowell, Frances O'Roark. *Shooting the Moon.* Atheneum, 2008. 176pp. ISBN 978-1-4169-2690-0. Grades 5–8. Jamie Dexter, 12, and her brother TJ are Army brats, children of a colonel. But neither of their parents is happy to hear that TJ has enlisted during the Vietnam War. TJ, a photographer, sends Jamie, who wishes she could enlist too, rolls of film to develop. At first he sends pictures of the moon, but when she sees the pictures of the horrors of war, her views change. At the same time her father becomes more disenchanted with Army life. *Kirkus Reviews Editor's Choice* and *Boston Globe/Horn Book Award Honor.*

2754. Downing, Wick. *The Trials of Kate Hope.* Houghton, 2008. 336pp. ISBN 978-0-618-89133-7. Grades 5–9. At the young age of 14, Kate Hope takes advantage of an old Colorado territorial loophole and obtains a license to practice law with her grandfather. It is 1973 and her grandfather came out of retirement after Kate's father and brother died in a car accident. Grandfather is old and frail and Kate takes over his case involving a dog that has been impounded for allegedly vicious behavior.

2755. Dunagan, Ted. *A Yellow Watermelon.* John F. Blair, 2007. 256pp. ISBN 978-1-58838-197-2. Grades 5–9. In Alabama in 1948, 12-year-old Ted makes friends with cotton field worker Poudlum Robinson and escaped convict Jake, both African American. Ted decides to get a job in the field so he can work with Jake, and he figures out a way to rob the boss, Old Man Cliff Creel. Ted plans to get Jake to California and to pay off the Robinsons' back property taxes. Ted likes the idea of being a modern-day Robin Hood.

2756. Dylan, Bob. *Forever Young.* Illustrated by Paul Rogers. Atheneum, 2008. Unpaged. ISBN 978-1-4169-5808-6. Grades K–4. Bob Dylan recorded "Forever Young" in 1974. This picture book looks at the song from the perspective of a boy living Dylan's life through the period of the 1960s when Dylan began to grow into an adult. It shows a boy who takes the guitar a busker hands to him outside of Gerde's Folk City, and then at the end, the boy passes it to a younger girl. But during his time with the guitar, he sings for Joan Baez, takes Highway 61 in a Volkswagen Beetle, and marches carrying anti-war signs along with Martin Luther King, Jr., and others.

2757. Elster, Jean Alicia. *Just Call Me Joe Joe.* Illustrated by Nicole Tagdell. (Joe Joe in the City) Judson, 2001. 32pp. ISBN 978-0-8170-1398-1. Grades 2–5. Joe Joe, 10, an African American, faces a shopowner who thinks that he belongs to a gang that has just vandalized his store. Joe Joe has just read a book about the brave men like James "Cool Papa" Bell who played in the Negro Baseball Leagues, and he knows he must be brave and convince him that he took no part in the destruction. Illustrations augment the text.

2758. Enderle, Dotti. *Man in the Moon.* Illustrated by Kristina Swarner. Delacorte, 2008. 152pp. ISBN 978-0-385-73566-7. Grades 4–6. In July 1961 Mr. Lunas appears on Janine's Texas farm, and her unemployed father recognizes him as the man who saved his life in World War II. Janine is bored with life. Her chronically ill brother Ricky wants to build a go-cart but does not have the strength. Mr. Lunas, who seems to change shape with the moon, helps the family overcome its malaise and guides Ricky toward his goal. During the process Janine learns about herself and how to improve her family's outlook on life.

2759. English, Karen B. *Francie.* Farrar, 1999. 202pp. ISBN 978-0-374-32456-8; Sunburst, 2002, paper ISBN 978-0-374-42459-6. Grades 5–8. African American Francie, 12, lives in racially prejudiced Noble, Alabama, in the early 1950s helping her mother in the homes of white women. Her brother Prez and her cousin Perry pick cotton after school, and her father works in Chicago as a Pullman porter. Francie wants to join him—he has told her she can take piano lessons. Francie is an excellent student at Miss Beach's Boarding House for Colored and her teacher lends her books. Then Francie starts helping Jesse Pruit, 16, learn to read. When the sheriff blames Jesse of murdering a white man, Francie decides to help him and compromises her family's safety. *American Library Association Notable Children's Books, Sunshine State Young Reader Award* (Florida) *Young Hoosier Award* (Indiana) nomination, *Coretta Scott King Author Honor Book, Judy Lopez Memorial Award* nomination, and *Capitol Choices Noteworthy Titles* (Washington, D.C.).

2760. Evans, Freddi Williams. *A Bus of Our Own.* Illustrated by Shawn Costello. Whitman, 2003. 32pp. Paper ISBN 978-0-8075-0971-5. Grades K–4. In the late 1940s Mable Jean walks five miles to school each day while white children yell at her from their bus. Mable Jean wonders why African American children do not have a bus. Her community of Mississippi sharecroppers decides to organize transportation for their children, and they all work extra hours picking cotton, washing clothes, and cleaning houses to earn the money to buy two old buses from which they create one working vehicle.

2761. Faulkner, Matt. *A Taste of Colored Water.* Simon & Schuster, 2008. Unpaged. ISBN 978-1-4169-1629-1. Grades 1–5. In the 1960s, white children Jelly and LuLu think their friend's tales of visiting the city and seeing "water bubblers" labeled "Colored," are exciting and they speculate about possible flavors. Then the two accompany Jelly's father to town and arrive in the middle of a civil rights march. They find a fountain labeled "Colored" and start to drink from it only to find themselves in big trouble. Watercolor illustrations complement the text.

2762. Fredericks, Anthony D. *The Tsunami Quilt: Grandfather's Story.* Illustrated by Tammy Yee. (Tales of Young Americans) Sleeping Bear, 2007. Unpaged. ISBN 978-1-58536-313-1. Grades 1–4. Each spring Kimo and his grandfather placed a lei on a monument at Hawaii's Laupahoehoe Point. After his grandfather's death Kimo learns that they were honoring those who died during a tsunami in 1946. Kimo visits the place with his own father and goes to see the memorial quilt in the Pacific Tsunami Museum in Hilo. Illustrations enhance the text. Notes.

2763. Fritz, Jean. *Homesick: My Own Story.* Illustrated by Margot Tomes. Putnam, 1982. 160pp. ISBN 978-0-399-20933-8; Puffin, 2007, paper ISBN 978-0-14-240761-5. Grades 3–7. Born in China, Jean Fritz did not come to America until she was 10. During the last two years that she and her parents were in Hankow, China, the conflict between Chiang Kai-shek (Sun Yat-sen's successor) and Mao Tse-tung was beginning. The autobiographical story must be cat-alogued as fiction because Fritz admits that she told her story as a storyteller rather than as an autobiographer. Therefore, the reader learns about a child who meets adult problems such as the death of another child, the divorce of a friend's parents, and a war in which her servant friends are being hurt by enemies and by families turned Communist. Background of Chinese History, 1913–1927.

2764. Fuqua, Jonathon Scott. *The Willoughby Spit Wonder.* Candlewick, 2004. 160pp. ISBN 978-0-7636-1776-9. Grades 5–8. In 1953 Carter lives on Willoughby Spit Beach in Norfolk, Virginia, during the Cold War, the Korean War, and McCarthyism. He admires the comic book hero Prince Namor, whose mother is from Atlantis, and who can breathe underwater. Carter decides that his mother is also from Atlantis. At the same time, Carter worries about his ill father who seems to have lost the will to live. Carter wants to show his father that anything is possible, and during a hurricane he runs into the crashing waves. His ability to tread water saves him, and Carter finally realizes that his father has been struggling to stay alive for as long as he has.

2765. Geisert, Bonnie. *Lessons.* Walter Lorraine, 2005. 192pp. ISBN 978-0-618-47899-6. Grades 4–6. In South Dakota in 1954, 10-year-old Rachel is delighted when her brother Matthew is born. But her father will not hold the baby very long, is often angry, and gets drunk one day. Finally her mother explains that he is grieving for a son who died before Rachel was born. The child had not been baptized and the Lutheran minister refused him a Christian burial. This haunts Rachel's father until their current minister assures him that the baby will not be damned because he died before he was christened.

2766. Greenberg, David T. *A Tugging String.* Dutton, 2008. 167pp. ISBN 978-0-525-47967-3. Grades 5–9. In 1965, 12-year-old David Duvy Greenberg worries about his father and about his baseball game. His father, Jack Greenberg is a lawyer who works for Martin Luther King, Jr., and the civil rights movement. Duvy is afraid the Klan will attack his father. Duvy also sees the effects of the Jim Crow laws on the Miltons, an African American couple he knows. Duvy asks his father questions and decides his life is not as safe after he has the answers. Based on the author's own life. Notes.

2767. Gutman, Dan. *Mickey and Me: A Baseball Card Adventure.* HarperCollins, 2003. 160pp. ISBN 978-0-06-029247-8; 2004, paper ISBN 978-0-06-447258-6. Grades 5–8. Joe Stoshack wants to save Mickey Mantle from an injury that will end his baseball career, but his friend Samantha switches his baseball cards, and he arrives seven years too early. He finds himself in Milwaukee in 1944 on D-Day (June 6), and meets an all-female professional baseball team and their star player, Mickey Maguire. These women have to wear skirts that do not protect them from painful bruises, and they can be fined for not wearing lipstick during games. But they play so well that Joe is shocked. He also recognizes their courage while waiting for news about their loved ones fighting in the war.

2768. Hamilton, Kersten R. *Firefighters to the Rescue.* Illustrated by Rich Davis. Viking, 2005. 32pp. ISBN 978-0-670-03503-8. Grades K–2. This look at firefighting in the 1950s includes men in fire hats and yellow slickers who roar through the streets to a house fire in their fire engine. When they are not fighting fires, they stay in the station house cleaning and cook-ing and joking with each other. However, when they get to the fire, they make a courageous rescue.

2769. Hamilton, Virginia. *Drylongso.* Illustrated by Jerry Pinkney. Harcourt, 1997. 56pp. Paper ISBN 978-0-15-201587-9. Grades 3–5. In 1975, west of the Mississippi, Lindy's family is trying to cope with prolonged drought and a dust storm when Drylongso arrives. Only a boy, Drylongso helps the family find water with his dowsing rod and has seed for them to plant in the spring. After the garden begins growing, Drylongso leaves Lindy's family. They prepare for the next drought season, expected in the1990s.

2770. Harrar, George. *The Wonder Kid.*   Illustrated by Anthony Winiarski. Houghton, 2006. 245pp. ISBN 978-0-618-56317-3. Grades 4–7.   During the summer of 1954 Jesse James MacLean, 11, stays inside because his mother is worried that he will contract polio. Jesse draws, reads comic books, and makes up games. He also enjoys a wonderful relationship with his grandfather. But after Gramps dies, and despite Jesse's mother's vigilance, Jesse gets the disease. He loses the use of his legs, and the family is quarantined. Jesse creates a comic strip about a Wonder Kid, a boy with polio who has special powers, and it is published in the newspaper. Note.

2771. Harrington, Janice N. *Going North.*   Illustrated by Jerome Lagarrigue. Melanie Kroupa, 2004. Unpaged. ISBN 978-0-374-32681-4. Grades 2–4.   In 1964 Jessie and her family leave Alabama for Nebraska. Poetic language describes her journey north buying fuel at "Negro stations" and shopping at "Negro stores" in the Jim Crow South. She does not want to leave her home and peeling sweet potatoes with "Big Mama," but as they get closer to Lincoln, she seems to feel the freedom of new opportunities. *Booklist Editor's Choice, Notable Social Studies Trade Books for Young People, Red Clover Book Award* (Vermont) nomination, *Bulletin Blue Ribbon,* and *Capitol Choices Noteworthy Titles* (Washington, D.C.).

2772. Hassett, Ann. *The Finest Christmas Tree.*   Illustrated by John Hassett. Walter Lorraine, 2005. 32pp. ISBN 978-0-618-50901-0. Grades K–2.   In the New England mountains in the late 1950s, Farmer Tuttle runs a Christmas tree farm. He has no money to buy his wife a new Christmas hat because suddenly everyone is buying artificial trees. On the day before Christmas, however, he gets a letter from a man who says he will send a crew to cut Farmer Tuttle's finest tree. From a distance, Farmer Tuttle watches tiny figures, sees a partial view of reindeer, and a figure in a red plaid suit. Left behind in payment is a Christmas hat for Mrs. Tuttle. Each year, the tradition recurs. Illustrations enhance the text.

2773. Herrera, Juan Felipe. *Downtown Boy.*   Scholastic, 2005. 293pp. ISBN 978-0-439-64489-1. Grades 5–8.   Ten-year-old Juanito Paloma is tired of moving constantly around 1950s California with his parents who are migrant workers. Sometimes he stays with relatives in San Francisco's Mission District and his mother tells him to behave properly. His father has bad diabetes and is often away seeking cures in Mexico. Juanito's father returns from an absence and the family moves to San Diego, where Juanito hopes to find friends and stability. A novel written in verse with Spanish words sprinkled throughout. *Tomas Rivera Mexican-American Children's Book Award.*

2774. Hill, Kirkpatrick. *The Year of Miss Agnes.*   Margaret K. McElderry, 2000. 115pp. ISBN 978-0-689-82933-8; Aladdin, 2002, paper ISBN 978-0-689-85124-7. Grades 3–6.   Fred (Frederika), 10, waits for her new teacher in her Athapascan village in Alaska in 1948 although she expects this teacher won't stay long. None of the others has. Miss Agnes Sutterfield arrives and teaches differently. Miss Agnes loves opera, displays the children's artwork, and reads them Greek myths and *Robin Hood.* She also has them write their own books about village activities such as tanning moose hides, fishing, curing the catch, and winter trapping. She teaches them how to make mathematical calculations so they will not be cheated when selling their animal pelts. And Miss Agnes learns sign language so that Fred's sister Bokko, 12, can attend school for the first time. At the end of the year, Fred expects Miss Agnes to leave, but she is surprised. *Charlie May Simon* (Arkansas) nomination, *Young Readers Book Awards* (California) nomination, *Nutmeg Children's Book Award* (Connecticut) nomination, *Capitol Choices Noteworthy Titles* (Washington, D.C.), *Sunshine State Young Reader Award* (Florida) nomination, *Children's Book Award* (Georgia) nomination, *Rebecca Caudill Award* (Illinois) nomination, *Young Hoosier Book Award* (Indiana) nomination, *Bluegrass Award* (Kentucky) nomination, *Young Readers Choice Award* (Louisiana) nomination, *Student Book Award* (Maine) nomination, *Children's Book Award* (Maryland) nomination, *Maud Hart Lovelace Award* (Minnesota) nomination, *Flicker Tales* (North Dakota) nomination, *Golden Sower Award* (Nebraska) nomination, *Battle of the Books* (New Mexico) nomination, *Children's Book Award* (Rhode Island), *Children's Book Award* (South Carolina) nomination, *Volunteer State Book Award* (Tennessee) nomination, *Bluebonnet Award* (Texas) nomination, *Young Reader Book Award* (Virginia) nomination, *Dorothy Canfield Fisher Children's Book Award* (Vermont) nomination, *Sasquatch Book Awards* (Washington), and *Children's Book Award* (West Virginia) nomination.

2775. Holm, Jennifer L. *Penny from Heaven.* Random, 2006. 274pp. ISBN 978-0-375-83687-9; Yearling, 2007, paper ISBN 978-0-375-83689-3. Grades 3–7. In 1953, 11-year-old Penny Falucci lives with her mother and grandparents, estranged from her deceased father's Italian family. Over the summer, her mother starts dating the milkman, Penny's arm gets caught in the washing machine, and they all worry about the polio virus. Secrets about her father begin to surface in the general tension. Penny discovers that, as an Italian American, he had been restricted during World War II, and this had had disastrous results.

2776. Johnson, Angela. *A Sweet Smell of Roses.* Illustrated by Eric Valesquez. Simon & Schuster, 2004. Unpaged. ISBN 978-0-689-83252-9; Aladdin, 2007, paper ISBN 978-1-416-95361-6. Grades 1–5. Two young African American girls, Minnie and her sister, hear about a freedom march and walk downtown to see it, smelling flowers along the way. Illustrations capture the time as the girls listen to Martin Luther King Jr.'s powerful words. *Capitol Choices Noteworthy Titles* (Washington, D.C.).

2777. Johnston, Julie. *Hero of Lesser Causes.* Tundra, 2003. 192pp. Paper ISBN 978-0-8877-6649-7. Grades 5–8. Keely Connor, 12, loves to imagine that she is a knight riding a steed instead of a breadwagon horse. Her brother is paralyzed by polio in 1946 and she spends the next year trying to interest him in living. He nearly dies before he realizes the value of his life.

2778. Judge, Lita. *One Thousand Tracings: Healing the Wounds of World War II.* Hyperion, 2007. Unpaged. ISBN 978-1-4231-0008-9. Grades 2–5. At the age of 6, a young girl was delighted when her father returned from World War II to their farm in the Midwest. Soon after, her mother received a letter from a German friend, Dr. Kramer, telling them that the war left them with nothing. The family sent him food and clothing and he responded that others now needed their help. Many Germans sent tracings of their feet so that the Hamerstroms could find shoes among their friends for needy German children. The relief effort helped more than three thousand people. Collage and watercolor illustrations enhance the text. Note. *American Library Association Notable Children's Books, International Reading Association Children's and Young Adult Book Award, William Allen White Children's Book Award* (Kansas) nomination, *Children's Book Award* (North Carolina) nomination, *Jane Addams Children's Honor Book, Show Me State Book Award* (Missouri), *Michigan Notable Books, Diamonds Award* (Delaware) nomination, and *Prairie Pasque Book Award* (South Dakota) nomination.

2779. Kadohata, Cynthia. *Cracker! The Best Dog in Vietnam.* Atheneum, 2007. 260pp. ISBN 978-1-416-90637-7; Aladdin, 2008, paper ISBN 978-1-416-90638-4. Grades 4–8. Rick Hanski, 17, enrolls in the army and goes to Vietnam, expecting to see the world and avoid a routine job. He becomes a member of the scout-dog team with his partner, Cracker. Cracker, Magnificent Dawn of Venus von Braun, was trained as a show dog but then broke a leg. Willie, her owner, volunteers her to the cause in Vietnam. Cracker and Rick become extremely close as they train to track the enemy, detect booby traps and mines, and rescue POWs. At the war's end, Willie realizes that he can never mean the same to Cracker as Rick does, and he gives her to Rick.

2780. Kadohata, Cynthia. *Kira-Kira.* Atheneum, 2004. 256pp. ISBN 978-0-689-85639-6; Aladdin, 2006, paper ISBN 978-0-689-85640-2. Grades 5–8. Katie "Kira-Kira" Takeshima, 10, adores her older sister Lynn, who knows everything and takes care of her and her little brother Sam in the late 1950s while their parents work long hours in rural Georgia. Because no one would buy from their grocery store in Iowa, they moved south to work in the poultry industry. Fourteen-year-old Lynn falls ill and Katie has to look after her. It becomes clear that Lynn will die, and Katie goes through the stages of grief during Lynn's illness and death. *Newbery Medal, Booklist Editor's Choice*, and *Capitol Choices Noteworthy Titles* (Washington, D.C.).

2781. Kinsey-Warnock, Natalie. *The Canada Geese Quilt.* Illustrated by Leslie W. Bowman. Puffin, 2000. 64pp. Paper ISBN 978-0-14-130462-5. Grades 4 up. When Ariel is 10 in 1946, she and her grandmother work on a quilt for the new baby. Her grandmother has a stroke and begins to act in ways that Ariel cannot understand. Ariel refuses to talk to her for a while but eventually overcomes her feelings and helps finish the Canada geese quilt before the baby arrives. What makes her happiest is the quilt her grandmother secretly made for her. *American Library Association Notable Children's Book*.

2782. Klages, Ellen. ***White Sands, Red Menace.*** Viking, 2008. 337pp. ISBN 978-0-670-06235-5. Grades 5–9. In the sequel to *The Green Glass Sea*, after 13-year-old Dewey's father dies in a traffic accident, she moves in with her friend Suze and the rest of the Gordon family in the New Mexico town of Alamogordo in 1946. Suze's father is working hard on building a rocket and fights with his wife, who wants peace and is still upset about the bombing of Hiroshima. Dewey, who wants to be an engineer, enjoys a close relationship with Mrs. Gordon until her birth mother arrives. Her mother left the family when Dewey was only 2 years old. Suze herself has to deal with her increasingly estranged parents while wanting to be an artist.

2783. Kroll, Virginia. ***Especially Heroes.*** Illustrated by Tim Ladwig. Eerdmans, 2003. Unpaged. ISBN 978-0-8028-5221-2. Grades 3–5. The narrator remembers being in fourth grade in 1962 when the nuns spoke of "martyrs"—people who would give their lives for others. She wondered if she would ever want to sacrifice her life for anyone or for any idea. The same evening, six white racists attack the house and car of the beloved family next door, and she sees her father and their friends retaliate with violence toward the racists in order to protect the older African American woman. She thinks they are heroes or even martyrs. Illustrations complement the text.

2784. Kwasney, Michelle D. ***Itch.*** Henry Holt, 2008. 256pp. ISBN 978-0-8050-8083-4. Grades 5–8. In 1968 Delores "Itch" Colchester and her grandmother move from Florida to an Ohio trailer park after her grandfather dies. While trying not to keep in touch with her friends in Florida, she makes friends in her sixth-grade class. One of them, Wendy, has bruises and welts that she hides. Itch has to decide how to handle the knowledge that Wendy's mother is physically abusing her.

2785. Lamstein, Sarah. ***Hunger Moon.*** Front Street, 2004. 112pp. ISBN 978-1-932425-05-5. Grades 5–8. In 1953 Chicago, 12-year-old Ruth Tepper has a lot to cope with. She looks after her three brothers, including retarded Eddy. Her parents own a bookstore but argue constantly because it is not providing enough to support the family. Ruthie is a "star reader" at school, but her parents do not offer her any encouragement or praise. All Ruthie's mother provides is perfectly baked cakes, and they have no lasting value.

2786. Lawrence, Iain. ***Gemini Summer.*** Delacorte, 2006. 261pp. ISBN 978-0-385-73089-1; Yearling, 2008, paper ISBN 978-0-440-41935-8. Grades 5–8. In 1965, 8-year-old Danny River has been overwhelmed by grief since his big brother Beau died. Beau fell into a hole that their father, a World War II veteran, dug in the yard, fearing for their lives during the Vietnam War. A stray dog arrives in Hog's Hollow and adopts Danny. Danny believes Beau has returned as a dog, and names the dog "Rocket" in memory of Beau's desire to be an astronaut. Danny decides that he and Rocket will go to Cape Canaveral to see a Gemini mission. He reaches his destination, and Gus Grissom returns him home in a T-38 fighter plane.

2787. Lemna, Don. ***When the Sergeant Came Marching Home.*** Holiday House, 2008. 224pp. ISBN 978-0-8234-2083-4; paper ISBN 978-0-8234-2211-1. Grades 3–7. When Dad returns from World War II in 1946, 10-year-old Donald is happy. But then his father decides to move the family to an isolated farm in Montana without electricity or plumbing. Donald is surrounded by chickens and pigs and attends a one-room school with forty-three students. Although he initially thinks about running away, he slowly learns the rhythms of farm life and enjoys fun with friends he makes at school.

2788. Leonetti, Mike. ***In the Pocket: Johnny Unitas and Me.*** Chronicle, 2008. Unpaged. ISBN 978-0-8118-5661-4. Grades 3–6. In 1958 Billy wants to play quarterback for the Baltimore Colts like his hero, Johnny Unitas. But his coach says that he must be a receiver until he grows. Billy is especially excited when his father gets them tickets to see the National Football League championship between the Colts and the Giants in New York. They take the train to the game and watch the score change between the teams until the Colts finally win. Acrylic paintings complement the text.

2789. **Leonetti, Mike.** *Swinging for the Fences: Hank Aaron and Me.* Chronicle, 2008. Unpaged. ISBN 978-0-8118-5662-1. Grades 1–3. Little Leaguer Mark is fascinated by Hank Aaron's pursuit of Babe Ruth's record. Mark's coach suggests that Mark just try to get on base, but Mark continues to swing as hard as he can and misses the ball completely. When he meets Aaron at a ballpark, Aaron advises him to be a team player. Illustrations complement the text.

2790. **Levine, Ellen.** *Catch a Tiger by the Toe.* Viking, 2005. 208pp. ISBN 978-0-670-88461-2. Grades 5–9. In the Bronx in 1953, 12-year-old Jamie Morse's life changes after her father is exposed as a member of the Communist Party. He is fired, and Jamie loses her position on the school newspaper. The turmoil stirred by the McCarthy hearings undermines her community. Teachers are fired and books are removed from the library. When Jamie sees her father defy McCarthy himself, she is proud that he stands up for what he believes.

2791. **Lorbiecki, Marybeth.** *Jackie's Bat.* Illustrated by J. Brian Pinkney. Simon & Schuster, 2006. 40pp. ISBN 978-0-689-84102-6. Grades K–3. When he is batboy for the Brooklyn Dodgers in 1947, Joey's father tells him to help all the players but one, the new man on the roster— Jackie Robinson. Joey tries to do what his father has told him, but Robinson's skill and gentlemanly behavior make helping him more important than obeying his father. Eventually, both Joey and his father admit that Robinson deserves "his place in history." Illustrations enhance the text.

2792. **Lord, Bette Bao.** *In the Year of the Boar and Jackie Robinson.* Illustrated by Marc Simont. HarperCollins, 1984. 176pp. ISBN 978-0-06-024004-2; Trophy, 1986, paper ISBN 978-0-06-440175-3. Grades 3–7. Young Bandit Wong, soon to be known as Shirley Temple Wong, arrives in Brooklyn from China in 1947 full of optimism. However, she faces more challenges than she expected. Not until she shows ability at stickball playing with her classmates does she gain friends and start to feel comfortable. She also becomes a loyal fan of the Brooklyn Dodgers. *American Library Association Notable Children's Books, School Library Journal Best Book, Notable Children's Trade Books in the Field of Social Studies, New York Public Library's Children's Books,* and *Jefferson Cup Award.*

2793. **Love, D. Anne.** *Semiprecious.* Margaret K. McElderry, 2006. 293pp. ISBN 978-0-689-85638-9. Grades 5–9. In the early 1960s, 13-year-old Garnet and her older sister Opal reluctantly accompany their mother Melanie from Texas to Oklahoma. There the girls stay with Aunt Julia, whom they have never met before, while their mother heads for Nashville to become a star. Her aunt and her aunt's friends help Garnet overcome her disappointment in her mother and her dislike of her father's absences on the oil rig where he works.

2794. **Luddy, Karon.** *Spelldown: The Big-Time Dreams of a Small-Town Word Whiz.* Simon & Schuster, 2007. 224pp. ISBN 978-1-416-91610-9; Aladdin, 2008, paper ISBN 978-1-416-95452-1. Grades 5–8. Thirteen-year-old Karlene lives in boring Red Clover, South Carolina, in 1968. She hopes that winning spelling bees will help her escape, but she has problems reaching the final round. Her Latin teacher, Mrs. Harrison, agrees to help her and they develop a close relationship. Meanwhile, Karlene's alcoholic father has problems sticking to the Twelve Step Plan and Karlene becomes interested in Billy Ray. But she succeeds in winning the Shirley County Spelldown and the state spelldown, earning a place at the national in Washington, D.C.

2795. **Lyon, George Ella.** *Sonny's House of Spies.* Richard Jackson, 2004. 304pp. ISBN 978-0-689-85168-1. Grades 5–8. Sonny, 13, lives in Mozier, Alabama, in the 1950s. He is determined to find out why his father left the family seven years before. Working over the summer at his "Uncle" Marty's donut shop, Sonny finds a letter from his father and learns that his father is a homosexual. As Sonny struggles to understand this—and his father's relationship with Marty, Sonny also comes to recognize the racism that their African American maid, Mamby, faces. *Bluegrass Award* (Kentucky) nomination and *Volunteer State Book Award* (Tennessee) nomination.

2796. McCord, Patricia. *Pictures in the Dark.* Bloomsbury, 2004. ISBN 978-1-58234-848-3. Grades 4–7. In 1950s Spokane, Washington, 12-year-old Sarah and Carlie, 15, struggle to cope with their mentally ill mother. Their father has a floor-cleaning business and is out of the house often when their mother goes into rages, verbally and physically abusing them. She deprives them of food and will not allow them to use the bathroom. The two resilient sisters tell no one about her behavior and try to entertain themselves by drawing pictures in the dark of their attic bedroom. Not until their mother gets a job and Josephine comes to look after them do they realize that their family is not normal. When Carlie runs away after being beaten, Sarah decides to tell her father about her mother's behavior.

2797. McDowell, Marilyn Taylor. *Carolina Harmony.* Delacorte, 2009. 323pp. ISBN 978-0-385-73590-2; Yearling, 2010, paper ISBN 978-0-440-42285-3. Grades 4–8. In the 1960s, after Carolina's parents and brother die in an accident, she moves into Auntie Shen's Blue Ridge Mountain home. They work and grieve together until Auntie Shen has a stroke. Then the social service workers place Carolina in a foster home. She runs away from two of them before she finds a place she can tolerate, Harmony Farm. There, three people—Lucas, Mr. Ray, and Miss Latah—help her feel loved. They hear about the Civil Rights Act and the Vietnam War, but those problems seem far away.

2798. McKissack, Patricia C. *Abby Takes a Stand.* Illustrated by Gordon C. James. (Scraps of Time) Viking, 2005. 112pp. ISBN 978-0-670-06011-5; Puffin, 2006, paper ISBN 978-0-14-240687-8. Grades 4–8. Maggie Rae and her cousins enjoy looking at artifacts in their grandmother's attic and wonder why she has kept a 1960 menu from the Monkey Bar restaurant in Nashville, Tennessee. Grandmother Abby tells them that she was 10 that year and was turned away from the new restaurant because she was African American. When people she knew staged a sit-in, she distributed flyers against segregation. Illustrations augment the text. *Black-Eyed Susan Book Award* (Maryland) nomination and *Children's Book Award* (South Carolina) nomination.

2799. McKissack, Patricia C. *A Friendship for Today.* Scholastic, 2007. 172pp. ISBN 978-0-439-66098-3. Grades 3–7. It is 1954 and 10-year-old Rosemary must attend a desegregated school for the first time in Kirkland, Missouri. She makes friends with Grace Hamilton, a student others call "white trash," and Rosemary realizes that all races have prejudices. Her teacher, a shopkeeper, her mother, and a cat give her support, and she watches her best friend J.J. try to walk again after having polio. All of the adversity seems to give her more strength. McKissack bases the story on her own experiences.

2800. McKissack, Patricia C. *Goin' Someplace Special.* Illustrated by Jerry Pinkney. Atheneum, 2001. 40pp. ISBN 978-0-689-81885-1; Aladdin, 2009, paper ISBN 978-1-416-92735-8. Grades K–3. Young 'Tricia Ann wants to go "someplace special" by herself in 1950s Nashville. On her journey she encounters "For Whites Only" signs and she has to find courage to continue toward the public library where "All Are Welcome." *Diamond Primary Book Award* (Arkansas) nomination, *Young Readers Medal Program* (California) nomination, *Children's Book Award* (Colorado) nomination, *Coretta Scott King Book Award*, *Picture Book Award* (Georgia) nomination, *Monarch Award Children's Choice Book Award* (Illinois) nomination, *Young Readers Choice Book Award* (Louisiana), *Show Me State Book Award* (Missouri) nomination, *Young Readers Choice Awards* (Pennsylvania) master list, *Children's Book Award* (South Carolina) nomination, *Prairie Pasque Book Award* (South Dakota) nomination, and *Bluebonnet Award* (Texas).

2801. McNamara, Margaret. *Martin Luther King Jr. Day.* Illustrated by Mike Gordon. Aladdin, 2007. 32pp. Paper ISBN 978-1-416-93494-3. Grades K–1. A first-grade class visiting a museum learns about Dr. Martin Luther King, Jr., and his contribution to American history. There they also learn about his "I Have a Dream" speech. Illustrations augment the text.

2802. Madden, Kerry. *Gentle's Holler.* (Maggie Valley) Viking, 2007. 278pp. ISBN 978-0-670-05998-0; Puffin paper ISBN 978-0-14-240751-6. Grades 5–8. Twelve-year-old Livy Two Weems wants to see the world beyond North Carolina, but her family's plight limits her opportunities. In this novel set in 1963, her mother is pregnant yet again and her father is unemployed after a severe car accident. Livy Two wants to write songs, and as she looks after her sweet but nearly blind little sister Gentle, she decides to try to transform the family dachshund into a Seeing Eye dog and keep the family on the farm rather than moving to the awful house of their grandmother.

2803. Madden, Kerry. *Jessie's Mountain.*   Viking, 2008. 256pp. ISBN 978-0-670-06154-9. Grades 5–9. In this sequel to *Louisiana's Song,* set in 1963, Livy Two (Olivia) Weems, 12, decides to run away to Nashville to try to sell some of her songs and ease the family's financial difficulties. As she leaves, her 10-year-old sister Jitters decides to go with her. They are unsuccessful and return home disappointed. Then Livy Two reads her mother's diary, given to her by her Grandma Horace, and discovers some unexpected facts. At the same time Livy Two gets another idea—to open a music hall. This scheme keeps the family from having to move to Grandma Horace's home.

2804. Madden, Kerry. *Louisiana's Song.*   Viking, 2007. 278pp. ISBN 978-0-670-06153-2. Grades 5–8. In the sequel to *Gentle's Holler* set in Appalachia in 1963, Livy Two Weems still wants to become a songwriter. Her father's brain damage means he can't support the family and she and her nine brothers and sisters will have to support themselves. Grandma Horace, however, plans for everyone to come live with her. At the same time, the school system wants to send Gentle to a school for the blind and Louisiana, 11, to an art school. Livy Two merely wants the family to stay together. Throughout, Livy Two writes song lyrics that appear in the text.

2805. Marcum, Lance. *The Cottonmouth Club.*   Farrar, 2005. 336pp. ISBN 978-0-374-31562-7. Grades 5–9. In 1963, 12-year-old Mitch Valentine dreads spending the summer with his Pipkin, Louisiana, grandfather, but his Air Force father is busy elsewhere. Mitch is shocked to live without air conditioning and television, and he also faces an angry bull, burns himself on a rope swing, and has an accident involving an Army convoy. Eventually he begins to enjoy his five male cousins and their sister Skeeter, although he never overcomes his dread of snakes. *Young Readers Choice Book Award* (Louisiana) nomination and *The Land of Enchantments Children's Book Award* (New Mexico) nomination.

2806. Marino, Nan. *Neil Armstrong Is My Uncle: And Other Lies Muscle Man McGinty Told Me.*   Roaring Brook, 2009. 154pp. ISBN 978-1-59643-499-8. Grades 3–6. In Massapequa Park on Long Island in 1969, 10-year-old Tamara is furious with the new foster kid across the street, Douglas McGinty, who has replaced her best friend, Kebsie Grobser, overnight. Trying to gain friends, Douglas, whom Tamara calls "Muscle Man" because he claims to be training for the 1972 Olympics, also announces that Neil Armstrong is his uncle and that he has sung on Broadway. No one else joins Tamara in ridiculing him, and she slowly begins to realize that external factors such as the Vietnam War and the moon walk affect everyone. *Golden Kite* Honor Book and *Dorothy Canfield Fisher Children's Book Award* (Vermont) nomination.

2807. Martin, Ann M. *A Corner of the Universe.*   Scholastic, 2002. 189pp. ISBN 978-0-439-38880-1; 2004, paper ISBN 978-0-439-38881-8. Grades 5–8. In 1960, while Hattie waits to become 12, she plans to spend a quiet summer reading, doing small errands, and continuing to avoid her grandmother. Her autistic uncle, of whom she was unaware, returns home to his parents after spending half his life at an institutional school. Although Adam seems to be a burden to her parents and grandparents, his rapid speech and free association—plus use of dialogue from "I Love Lucy"—intrigue Hattie. Adam falls in love with someone at the boarding house, and when rejected, commits suicide. The family, with Hattie's help, has to accept how quickly things can change. *Charlie May Simon* (Arkansas) nomination, *Young Reader's Award* (Arizona) nomination, *Blue Spruce Young Adult Book Awards* (Colorado), *Nene Award* (Hawaii) nomination, *Teen Award* (Iowa) nomination, *William Allen White Award* (Kansas) nomination, *Bluegrass Award* (Kentucky) nomination, *Newbery Honor, Flicker Tales* (North Dakota) nomination, *Garden State Teen Book Award* (New Jersey) nomination, *Battle of the Books* (New Mexico) nomination, *Volunteer State Book Award* (Tennessee) nomination, *Dorothy Canfield Fisher Children's Book Award* (Vermont) nomination, *Horn Book Fanfare,* and *Soaring Eagle Book Award* (Wyoming) nomination.

2808. Martin, Ann M. *Here Today.*   Scholastic, 2004. 2004pp. ISBN 978-0-439-57944-5; paper ISBN 978-0-439-57945-2. Grades 4–8. In 1963 after John F. Kennedy's assassination, Ellie Dingman's mother, Doris Day Dingman, decides she will try her fortune in New York. She leaves her family, only to return once. Eleven-year-old Ellie (named after Eleanor Roosevelt) becomes the surrogate mother of her younger siblings Albert (after Albert Einstein) and Marie (after Marie Curie). When Ellie visits her mother in New York, she discovers that she only works in a department store. *Booklist Editor's Choice, Children's Book Award* (Georgia) nomination, *Young Hoosier Book Award* (Indiana) nomination, *Bluegrass Book Award* (Kentucky) nomination, *Garden State Fiction Book Award* (New Jersey) nomination, *Volunteer State Book Award* (Tennessee) nomination, *Dorothy Canfield Fisher Children's Book Award* (Vermont) nomination, and *Capitol Choices Noteworthy Titles* (Washington, D.C.).

2809. Martin, Ann M. *On Christmas Eve.* Scholastic, 2006. 149pp. ISBN 978-0-439-74588-8; 2007, paper ISBN 978-0-439-74589-5. Grades 3–5. In 1958 Tess, 8, still believes in Santa Claus. And she tries to stay awake to see him because she has an important request. The father of her best friend, Sarah, has cancer, and Tess wants Santa to use his special magic, help him get well, and let him spend Christmas at home instead of in the hospital. She has a snow globe as a special gift for Santa. After midnight Tess does observe miracles but not necessarily the ones she requests.

2810. Mathews, Ellie. *The Linden Tree.* Milkweed, 2007. 169pp. Paper ISBN 978-1-571316-74-5. Grades 3–6. In the spring of 1948 when Katy Sue Hanson is 9 years old, meningitis kills her mother. She is buried under a linden tree on the family property in Iowa. Katy's older sister tries to look after the family and cook until their mother's sister, Aunt Katherine, moves in and takes over. The children all have difficulty adjusting, especially when they discover that their aunt and their father are romantically interested in each other.

2811. Michelson, Richard. *Across the Alley.* Illustrated by Earl B. Lewis. Putnam, 2006. 32pp. ISBN 978-0-399-23970-0. Grades K–3. Jewish Abe's grandfather wants him to play the violin while African American Willie's father wants him to be a great baseball pitcher. The boys talk across the alley from their windows at night and learn that Willie is interested in the violin and that baseball delights Abe. When the truth comes out, Willie gets to play the violin in temple, and he is so good that the audience forgets that he is black. Abe plays well in the baseball game later that afternoon. The best part is they can be friends in the daytime after their triumphs, regardless of their racial differences. Watercolor illustrations intensify the text.

2812. Mochizuki, Ken. *Heroes.* Illustrated by Dom Lee. Lee & Low, 1997. Unpaged. Paper ISBN 978-1-8800-0050-2. Grades 3–6. Japanese American Donnie hates to play war games in the 1960s—his friends always want him to be the enemy because he looks like "them." When he tells his friends that his father and uncle both served in the United States Army, they refuse to believe it. Donnie continues to suffer until his father and uncle realize they must help him.

2813. Moranville, Sharelle Byars. *Over the River.* Henry Holt, 2002. 228pp. ISBN 978-0-8050-7049-1. Grades 5–9. In 1947, 11-year-old Willa Mae's life is upended when her father—who has been away in the war for five years—comes to retrieve her from her grandparents' house, where she has lived since her mother died. The family has secrets that she does not understand, especially why her father waited two years after the war to show up and why the unknown Baby Clark lies buried in the cemetery. Her father takes her to Oklahoma, where he gets a job wiring houses for electricity. He teaches her how to do this too and he tries to help her understand that people who have disagreements with each other can still love her. *Children's Choice Book Award* (Iowa) nomination and *Young Readers Choice Book Award* (Louisiana) nomination.

2814. Moses, Shelia P. *The Baptism.* Margaret K. McElderry, 2007. 130pp. ISBN 978-1-4169-0671-1. Grades 4–6. In 1940s Occoneechee Neck, North Carolina, 12-year-old twins Leon and Luke Curry are told to stay out of trouble—their baptisms are one week away. But Leon's not convinced that he wants to give up sinning as it's so much fun. At the same time he sees injustice and racism all around him. His father was killed by a white man who was never charged, and his stepfather is stealing his mother's savings. Finally, his older brother, who was saved the year before, remains "Joe Nasty," as mean as ever.

2815. Moses, Shelia P. *The Legend of Buddy Bush.* Margaret K. McElderry, 2004. 224pp. ISBN 978-0-689-85839-0; Simon Pulse, 2005, paper ISBN 978-1-416-90716-9. Grades 5–9. Pattie Mae Sheals, 12, dreams of escaping Rich Square, North Carolina, in 1947. She wants to move to Harlem, where she will not have to put up with "post slaves stuff, " as her Uncle Buddy calls having to move off the sidewalk when a white person walks by. Police arrest Uncle Buddy for allegedly attempting to rape a white woman (he acknowledged her attractiveness), and a doctor diagnoses her grandfather with terminal brain cancer. Before Uncle Buddy goes on trial, the Klan nearly kills him, but the family helps him escape. After these problems, Pattie Mae has a chance to go north.

2816. Moses, Shelia P. *The Return of Buddy Bush.* Margaret K. McElderry, 2005. 149pp. ISBN 978-0-689-87431-4; Simon Pulse, 2008, paper ISBN 978-1-4169-3925-2. Grades 5–9. In this sequel to *The Legend of Buddy Bush*, 12-year-old Pattie Mae Sheals goes to visit her sister in Harlem after her grandfather dies and her Uncle Buddy disappears after being wrongfully accused of raping a white woman. Harlem in 1947 in no way resembles her home town of Rich Square, North Carolina. The African Americans in Harlem speak, dress, and act differently. When Pattie Mae meets Richard Wright by chance, she realizes that her own life has unlimited possibilities. She finds Buddy and gets him to return home by telling him that his mother is ill. But he has to spend time in the State Correction Center to protect himself before he is acquitted in a trial. Buddy then leaves North Carolina.

2817. Moses, Shelia P. *Sallie Gal and the Wall-a-Kee Man.* Illustrated by Niki Daly. Scholastic, 2007. 152pp. ISBN 978-0-439-90890-0. Grades 3–5. In North Carolina, 8-year-old Sallie Gal wants to wear ribbons in her hair like her cousin Wild Cat. But her father is fighting in Vietnam and her mother has no money for ribbons. Sallie Gal tries selling lemonade but attracts few customers and breaks her mother's glass pitcher. Then Wall-a-Kee Man, who carries a traveling store in his station wagon, gives her some ribbons. She hides them so her mother won't make her return them, but then she feels guilty.

2818. Murphy, Pat. *The Wild Girls.* Viking, 2007. 288pp. ISBN 978-0-670-06226-3. Grades 5–9. Eleven-year-old Joan tells about her experiences after moving from Connecticut to northern California in 1972. She meets Sarah, a girl who calls herself Fox, while walking in the woods one day. They become best friends despite their disparate backgrounds. Joan's conventional mother is trying to deal with an unhappy husband. Fox lives with her father, a science fiction writer, and pretends that her mother who left many years before turned into a fox. The girls are accepted into Berkeley's summer writing program. There they both gain confidence through exploring their problems in their writing and listening to their unusual instructor, Verla Volante.

2819. Myers, Walter Dean. *Patrol: An American Soldier in Vietnam.* Illustrated by Ann Grifalconi. Trophy, 2005. 40pp. Paper ISBN 978-0-06-073159-5. Grades 4–8. While awaiting combat in Vietnam's forests, a young soldier feels terribly afraid and wonders who the enemy might be. When the soldier finally encounters his enemy, he sees that the enemy is his age. Neither fires. Collage illustrations augment the text. *Young Reader Medal* (California) nomination, *Student Book Award* (Maine) nomination, *Great Lakes Great Books Award* (Michigan) nomination, *Dorothy Canfield Fisher Children's Book Award* (Vermont) nomination, *Capitol Choices Noteworthy Titles* (Washington, D.C.), *Booklist Editors' Choice, American Library Association Best Books for Young Adults, Bulletin Blue Ribbon, Peach Award* (Georgia) nomination, and *Children's Book Award* (West Virginia) nomination.

2820. Nelson, Vaunda M. *Mayfield Crossing.* Illustrated by Leonard Jenkins. Puffin, 2002. 96pp. Paper ISBN 978-0-698-11930-7. Grades 3–7. In 1960 Meg looks forward to going to the new school that has a larger baseball field. She and her friends arrive only to find no one wants them there because they are black. When Meg and her friends challenge the others to a baseball game, one of the Parkview students refuses to continue the hostility and joins their team so they will have enough players.

2821. Park, Linda Sue. *Keeping Score.* Clarion, 2008. 208pp. ISBN 978-0-618-92799-9. Grades 4–6. In 1951, 9-year-old Maggie likes to listen to the Brooklyn Dodgers games on the radio at the fire station. Jim, a new recruit, teaches her how to keep score and convinces her of the value of the Giants' Willy Mays. Soon Jim is drafted and sent to Korea, and Maggie writes to him. When he returns home in trauma, Maggie decides to help him recover. She persists, and by the time she is 13, Jim shows a very slight improvement.

2822. Paterson, Katherine. *Jacob Have I Loved.* Crowell, 1980. 244pp. ISBN 978-0-690-04078-4; Trophy, 1990, paper ISBN 978-0-06-447059-9. Grades 5 up. Louise (Wheeze) grows up on a Chesapeake Bay island in the early 1940s thinking that everyone loves her younger twin Caroline more than her. Wheeze learns about crabbing and being a waterman from her father, while Caroline sings and wins money to go to school on the mainland. Not until Wheeze leaves the island herself does she understand that everyone has always thought she was strong but that Caroline needed help. *Newbery Medal, American Book Award for Children's Literature Nominee, American Library Association Notable Children's Books, American Library Association Best Books for Young Adults, Horn Book Fanfare Honor List, School Library Journal Best Book, Booklist Children's Editors' Choices, New York Times Outstanding Books*, and *New York Public Library's Children's Books.*

2823. Peck, Richard. *A Season of Gifts.* Dial, 2009. 164pp. ISBN 978-0-8037-3082-3; Puffin, 2010, paper ISBN 978-0-14-241729-4. Grades 5–8. Twelve-year-old Bob Barnhardt, his sisters, mother, and Methodist-minister father move in next door to Mrs. Dowdel in 1958. Bob first meets this 90-year-old after local bullies have stripped him of his clothes, taped his mouth shut, and hung him in her privy. She refuses to tell about this while during the months that follow, she helps 6-year-old Ruth Ann restore her belief in Santa Claus and connives with Mrs. Barnhardt to stop Phyllis from sneaking out with a ne'er-do-well Elvis look-alike. Then she subtly leads people to the almost-empty Methodist Church by asking Mr. Barnhardt to conduct a funeral service for the remains of a Kickapoo princess mysteriously discovered in her yard. During the season before Christmas, Bob watches a nonbeliever offer just the right gift to each person he knows. *Indies Choice Book Awards* finalist and *Booklist Editors Choice.*

2824. Pérez, L. King. *Remember as You Pass Me By.* Milkweed, 2007. 224pp. ISBN 978-1-57131-677-6; paper ISBN 978-1-57131-678-3. Grades 5–8. Silvy, 12, is unhappy that she is discouraged from spending time with her best friend, African American Mabelee. The ruling in *Brown v. Board of Education* brings turmoil to her hometown of Hughes Springs, Texas, and Silvy's family considers leaving the state.

2825. Perkins, Lynne Rae. *All Alone in the Universe.* Trophy, 2001. 140pp. Paper ISBN 978-0-380-73302-6. Grades 5–8. In the 1970s, 13-year-old Debbie is especially bewildered when her friend since third grade, Maureen, leaves her to be best friends with Glenna Faiber. Debbie notices that Glenna must have some quality that she could not see that was attractive to Maureen. A teacher helps Debbie realize that Maureen made the choice to leave, that Glenna did not come between the two. Then Debbie begins to realize that other girls can be friends as well. *Young Hoosier Book Awards* (Indiana) nomination, *Bulletin Blue Ribbon*, and *Horn Book Fanfare.*

2826. Pinkney, Andrea Davis. *Boycott Blues: How Rosa Parks Inspired a Nation.* Illustrated by J. Brian Pinkney. Amistad, 2008. Unpaged. ISBN 978-0-06-082118-0. Grades 3–6. Rhythmic text with a blues cadence and double-page, ink-on-board spreads tell the story of the bus boycott that began in Montgomery, Alabama, in December 1955 with Rosa Parks's refusal to relinquish her bus seat to a white man and continued to Martin Luther King, Jr.'s speech calling for a boycott. Defeating the Jim Crow laws took thirteen months for the more than 40,000 protesters who participated daily in the nonviolent march against the bus company. Notes and Further Resources.

2827. Pinkney, Andrea Davis. *Sit-In: How Four Friends Stood Up by Sitting Down.* Illustrated by Brian Pinkney. Little, Brown, 2010. 40pp. ISBN 978-0-316-07016-4. Grades 2–5. In 1960 four African American college students decided to take seats at the Greensboro, North Carolina, Woolworth's whites-only lunch counter. This "sit-in" led to others across the country as people asked to be treated like human beings. The free-verse text employing food metaphors is complemented by double-spread watercolors adorned with quotes from Martin Luther King, Jr. Chronology and Bibliography.

2828. Pinkwater, Daniel. *The Neddiad: How Neddie Took the Train, Went to Hollywood, and Saved Civilization.* Houghton, 2007. 307pp. ISBN 978-0-618-59444-3. Grades 5–9. During the 1940s Nedworth Wentworthstein and his family travels from Chicago to Los Angeles on the Super Chief train. On the journey Neddie is given a turtle carved from a meteorite; this artifact has special powers and is much sought after by individuals including the evil Sandor Eucalpytus. The denouement of this funny, exciting story includes aliens and a live woolly mammoth.

2829. Ransom, Candice F. *Finding Day's Bottom.* Carolrhoda, 2006. 168pp. ISBN 978-1-57505-933-4. Grades 4–6. After Jane-Ery's father dies in a sawmill accident in the 1950s, her grandfather comes down from his Virginia mountaintop to live with her and her mother. Jane-Ery, 11, misses her father and his songs and pet names for her. Grandpap tries to help her by taking her to pick blackberries and explaining why he talks to bees. He also teaches her to weave baskets from pine needles and tells her about Day's Bottom, a mysterious, happy place.

2830. Ray, Delia. *Singing Hands.* Clarion, 2006. 248pp. ISBN 978-0-618-65762-9. Grades 5–9. In Birmingham, Alabama, in 1848, 12-year-old Gussie Davis likes to sing out loud in her father's deaf church. Her deaf parents cannot hear her and she assumes no one else can; however, a hearing visitor tells them what she is doing. Then she becomes even more rebellious—skipping Sunday School, using collection money to buy a soda, and stealing a love letter from one of their boarders. Gussie's father punishes her by refusing to let her visit her favorite aunt in Texas. She has to work on his missionary efforts supporting the use of sign language at the Alabama School for the Deaf.

2831. Reynolds, Aaron. *Back of the Bus.* Illustrated by Floyd Cooper. Philomel, 2010. 32pp. ISBN 978-0-399-25091-0. Grades 1–4. On December 1, 1955, in Montgomery, Alabama, a little boy watches Mrs. Parks from his seat on the back of the bus. He sees her refuse to leave her seat in the front. Then the bus stops and waits for a policeman to arrive. The boy is frightened to see Mrs. Parks sitting in that seat "like a turnip pile." Although he fears that the situation will not turn out well, he sees her determination and a similar expression on his mother's face. When he looks at his marble with its shining tiger eye, he feels better. Soft pictures in oil enhance the text.

2832. Rubel, Nicole. *It's Hot and Cold in Miami.* Farrar, 2006. 202pp. ISBN 978-0-374-33611-0. Grades 3–5. In 1964, 5th-grader Rachel Ringwood feels invisible next to her perfect twin sister Rebecca. Rachel has a very active imagination and and seems to be a magnet for the wrong kind of attention. Her sister finally recognizes her artistic talent when Rachel wins a contest.

2833. Rylant, Cynthia. *When I Was Young in the Mountains.* Illustrated by Diane Goode. Dutton, 1982. 32pp. ISBN 978-0-525-42525-0; Puffin, 1985, paper ISBN 978-0-14-054875-4. Grades K–3. The narrator recalls the times in the mountains during the mid-20th century when grandfather came home covered with coal dust from the mines, as well as the rituals of school and church. A photograph of four children with a long, dead black snake draped around their necks also brings many memories. Although they have no modern conveniences, their lives are full and happy. *American Library Association Notable Children's Books.*

2834. St. Anthony, Jane. *The Summer Sherman Loved Me.* Farrar, 2006. 144pp. ISBN 978-0-374-37289-7. Grades 5–8. Margaret, 12, wonders what she should have said when the boy next door, Sherman, said "I love you." He then pretends to be dead from a bicycle accident. This frightens her and it is not until the end of the summer that he apologizes for upsetting her. By then, she has begun to work through her feelings about Sherman and decides that she cares about him. Set in the early 1960s. *Student Book Award* (Maine) nomination.

2835. Schmidt, Gary D. *The Wednesday Wars.* Clarion, 2007. 264pp. ISBN 978-0-618-72483-3. Grades 5–9. In Long Island in 1967, Presbyterian Holling Hoodhood remains in Mrs. Baker's 7th-grade English class while his classmates go to catechism or Hebrew school. With her, he reads William Shakespeare's plays and learns that some of the wisdom in those plays applies to his daily life. *Booklist Editor's Choice, Newbery Honor Book, American Library Association Notable Children's Books, Kirkus Reviews Critics Choice*, and *Publishers Weekly Best Books*.

2836. Schwartz, Amy. *Annabelle Swift, Kindergartner.* Orchard, 1991. 32pp. Paper ISBN 978-0-531-07027-7. Grades K–2. On her first day in kindergarten in 1950s California, Annabelle asks a lot of questions as her sister Lucy has told her to do. She only confuses her teacher. But delighted to be chosen milk monitor, she is especially happy when she counts the money properly. She and Lucy are loyal to each other, and Lucy gives her much advice.

2837. Schwartz, Ellen. *Stealing Home.* Tundra, 2006. 160pp. Paper ISBN 978-0-8877-6765-4. Grades 4–6. Ten-year-old Joey, an orphan of mixed race is having a bewildering time in the late 1940s. He goes to live in Brooklyn with Jewish relatives he has never heard of before. Although his Aunt Frieda and cousin Bobbie make him welcome, his grandfather is hostile. Joey must adapt to new social perspectives and learn to love the Brooklyn Dodgers. Note.

2838. Shelton, Paula Young. *Child of the Civil Rights Movement.* Illustrated by Raul Colón. 48pp. ISBN 978-0-375-84314-3. Grades K–3. Daughter of civil rights activist Andrew Young, Shelton draws on her own and her family's memories of the time after her parents took the family from New York back to Atlanta, Georgia, where Jim Crow laws were thriving. She overheard conversations between her parents, the Kings, Ralph Abernathy, Dorothy Cotton, and others as they tried to end racial inequality. She herself staged a protest by crying loudly after a restaurant owner refused to seat her family. She culminates her story, told in free verse, with the march from Selma to Montgomery when she was 4 years old. Brief biographies of each leader complete the backmatter.

2839. Sherlock, Patti. *Letters from Wolfie.* Viking, 2004. 228pp. ISBN 978-0-670-03694-3; Puffin, 2007, paper ISBN 978-0-14-240358-7. Grades 5–8. When 13-year-old Mark donates his dog Wolfie to the army during the Vietnam War, he does not realize what the dog will have to do. He learns about the role that German shepherds play through letters from his brother Danny. Mark wants Wolfie back and begins to protest. His father believes in sacrificing everything for one's country while Mark's mother is sympathetic. *Young Reader Medal* (California) nomination, *Lone Star Reading List* (Texas), and *Teen Book Award* (Rhode Island) nomination.

2840. Smalls, Irene. *Don't Say Ain't.* Illustrated by Colin Bootman. Charlesbridge, 2003. 32pp. ISBN 978-1-57091-381-5; 2004, paper ISBN 978-1-57091-382-2. Grades K–4. In 1957 when young Dana gets the highest grade on a city test and the advanced integrated school accepts her, she does not want to leave her African American friends. She feels uncomfortable at her new school and has to learn correct grammar. Realistic oil paintings enhance the text.

2841. Smiley, Jane. *The Georges and the Jewels.* Knopf, 2009. 240pp. ISBN 978-0-375-86227-4; Yearling, 2010, paper ISBN 978-0-375-86228-1. Grades 5–8. In California during the 1960s, 12-year-old Abby works with the horses, named either Jewel or George according to their sex, on her family's stud farm. Her older brother Danny, 16, has already escaped her father's tyrannical, evangelical opinions. Abby has difficulty believing that the horses should not be handled individually. When she has difficulty staying on Ornery George's back, she decides to try her own tactics. She becomes attached to an orphaned horse, and begins to realize that horses, like people, respond to kindness in ways neither her father nor the Big Four female clique at school has ever imagined.

2842. Smith, D. *The Boys of San Joaquin.* Atheneum, 2005. 231pp. ISBN 978-0-689-87606-6; Aladdin, 2006, paper ISBN 978-1-4169-1619-2. Grades 5–8. In Orange Grove City, California, in 1951, Italian Irish Paolo, 12, his younger brother Georgie, and his deaf cousin Billy try to solve the mystery of why their dog Rufus has a half-eaten $20 bill. They discover that it belongs to the local Catholic Church, and during the process of investigating, they make new friends.

2843. Smith, D. *It Was September When We Ran Away the First Time.* Atheneum, 2008. 230pp. ISBN 978-1-4169-3809-5. Grades 5–8. In 1951 Paolo O'Neill lives with his Italian Irish family in San Joaquin, California. Billy, Paolo's deaf cousin and best friend, begins holding hands with a Chinese girl named Veronica. Their relationship provokes residents who are experiencing prejudices and suspicions. The O'Neills' tree house is burned down and insults are sprayed on the garage. Who's doing this? It could be the racist Jensen brothers or the biology teacher with a ham radio.

2844. Smith, D. J., and James D. Smith. *Probably the World's Best Story About a Dog and the Girl Who Loved Me.* Atheneum, 2006. 234pp. ISBN 978-1-4169-0542-4. Grades 5–8. In Orange Grove, California, in 1951, 12-year-old Paolo O'Neil, his 6-year-old brother Georgie, and their 9-year-old deaf cousin Billy try to find their missing dog Rufus. Their only clue is a ransom note. Paolo and the others investigate.

2845. Smothers, Ethel Footman. *Down in the Piney Woods.* Eerdmans, 2003. 151pp. Paper ISBN 978-0-8028-5248-9. Grades 5–9. Annie Rye, 10, loves her Georgia summers with her grandfather in the 1950s. She is surprised by having to share her experiences of the "rolling store" and going possum hunting with half-sisters. She also has to adjust to a little white girl who visits and to finding rattlesnakes in the house that have to be smoked out.

2846. Smucker, Anna Egan. *No Star Nights.* Illustrated by Steve Johnson. Knopf, 1989. 48pp. ISBN 978-0-679-86724-1; 1994 paper ISBN 978-0-679-86724-1. Grades K–2. When the narrator was a child living in the coal mine area of Pennsylvania, she remembers the red fires lighting the skies and her father sleeping through the day after working the night shift. She loved going to baseball games with her father in Pittsburgh. She recalls her school and her Catholic teachers with their habit collars white in the smoky air, holidays, and playing games with other children in the streets. *International Reading Association Children's Book Award* and *American Library Association Notable Children's Book.*

2847. Strickland, Brad. *The House Where Nobody Lived.* (John Bellairs Mystery) Dial, 2006. 173pp. ISBN 978-0-8037-3148-6. Grades 4–7. In the 1950s, Lewis Barnavelt, 12, and Rose Rita, his best friend, think they see ghostly warriors outside Hawaii House, an old house in their hometown of New Zebedee, Michigan. Lewis's Uncle Jonathan tells him that a retired sea captain built the house for his wife, a Hawaiian princess, and all of the people living in it died in their sleep. Several years later, David and his family move into the house, and Lewis realizes he must help David get rid of the evil spirits still in the house. With Uncle Jonathan, a sorcerer, and Mrs. Zimmermann, a pleasant witch, they encounter the supernatural inhabitants of the house, including an angry Hawaiian goddess.

2848. Sullivan, Jacqueline Levering. *Annie's War.* Eerdmans, 2007. 183pp. ISBN 978-0-8028-5325-7. Grades 4–6. Annie, 10, lives in Walla Walla, Washington, with her difficult grandmother in 1946 and has a lot to cope with. She holds imaginary conversations with President Truman that help her deal with that fact that her pilot father is missing in action and her Uncle Billy (a hardened war veteran) is prejudiced against the new African American tenant. Her father eventually returns, blind and amnesiac.

2849. Talbert, Marc. *The Purple Heart.* Luniverse, 2000. 135pp. Paper ISBN 978-0-595-09771-5. Grades 4–8. Delighted that his father is returning early from Vietnam in 1967, Luke finds reality a disappointment. His father is disinterested in everything around him. The Purple Heart his father received fascinates Luke, but his father dismisses it as something one gets for being wounded—nothing special. Although his father needs much time to recover from the horrors of the war, he eventually learns to love his family again.

2850. Taylor, Debbie B. *Sweet Music in Harlem.* Illustrated by Frank Morrison. Lee & Low, 2004. 32pp. ISBN 978-1-58430-165-3. Grades K–3. Uncle Click, a Harlem jazz musician, forgets his hat when he goes to get his photograph taken. He sends his nephew, C. J., to look for it. C. J. runs from the barbershop to the diner to the jazz club. Instead of the hat, however, C. J. finds other things that Uncle Click has left. Other well-known jazzmen want to be in the picture too and they follow C. J. back to his uncle. After the picture is taken, Uncle Click gives C. J. a new clarinet as an early birthday present, and C. J. finds the hat in the box. In 1958 Art Kane took a picture of 57 jazz musicians on brownstone steps in Harlem. *Young Readers' Choice Award* (Louisiana) nomination.

2851. Taylor, Mildred. *The Gold Cadillac.* Illustrated by Michael Hays. Dial, 1987. 48pp. ISBN 978-0-8037-0342-1; Puffin, 1998, paper ISBN 978-0-14-038963-0. Grades 2–6. After 'lois's father buys a new 1950 gold Cadillac, he decides to drive it from Ohio to Mississippi to visit the family. Friends warn 'lois's father that he should avoid appearing in the South in such a grand car—the police will stop him because they don't expect a black person to own one. 'lois and her family cannot stay in motels or eat in restaurants along the way, and for the first time she experiences the difficulties of being black in the South. Her father decides that the car is not worth the hassle. *Christopher Award.*

2852. Testa, Maria. *Almost Forever.* Candlewick, 2003. 80pp. ISBN 978-0-7636-1996-1; 2007, paper ISBN 978-0-7636-3366-0. Grades 2–6. A young girl of 6 misses her physician father during the year he serves in Vietnam. She watches new of the war on television, reads his daily letters home, and becomes fearful when the letters stop. Poems describe her days and her worries. He comes home in February 1969. Illustrations augment the text.

2853. Uchida, Yoshiko. *Journey Home.* Illustrated by Charles Robinson. Aladdin, 1992. 144pp. Paper ISBN 978-0-689-71641-6. Grades 5–9. In the sequel to *Journey to Topaz,* Yuki and her mother return from the internment camp to Berkeley, California, after World War II. They and the neighbors have to work together to restart their lives. They learn the meaning of forgiveness and acceptance when neighbors whose son was killed in Japan help them rebuild their firebombed store and invite them to celebrate Thanksgiving.

2854. Uhlberg, Myron. *Dad, Jackie, and Me.* Illustrated by Colin Bootman. Peachtree, 2005. 32pp. ISBN 978-1-56145-329-0. Grades 2–5. In 1947 a young Dodger fan and his deaf father go to a Giants versus Dodgers game at Ebbets Field after Jackie Robinson has become the first baseman on the team. Through the season, his father's attempt to yell Robinson's name as "AH-GHEE" embarrasses the boy, but in the last game, Robinson throws a ball straight to his father, and he catches it barehanded. By that time, the boy has learned to respect his father's achievements and his lack of prejudice. Watercolors illustrate the text.

2855. Uhlberg, Myron. *The Printer.* Illustrated by Henri Sorensen. Peachtree, 2003. 32pp. ISBN 978-1-56145-221-7. Grades 2–5. In 1940 a young boy's deaf father saves many fellow workers from a fire at a big New York daily newspaper. He has a job there because the deaf cannot hear the noisy print machines pounding all day. When he discovers the fire, he uses sign language to warn the others, and they escape. Illustrations enhance the text.

2856. Von Ahnen, Katherine. *Charlie Young Bear.* Illustrated by Paulette Livers Lambert. Roberts Rinehart, 1994. 42pp. Paper ISBN 978-1-57098-001-5. Grades 2–4. In 1955 the U.S. government finally pays the Mesquakie Indians for their land in Iowa. The money is being distributed in various ways. Charlie Young Bear wants a bicycle more than anything but his family's share will go to his mother's new stove. He decides to appeal to the Great Spirit. When every child in the tribe gets a new red bicycle, Charlie goes to his private place to thank the Great Spirit for his own wonderful bicycle.

2857. Waldman, Neil. *Say-Hey and the Babe: Two Mostly True Baseball Stories.* See entry 2263.

2858. Waters, Zack C. *Blood Moon Rider.* Pineapple, 2006. 126pp. ISBN 978-1-56164-350-9. Grades 5–8. Harley Wallace's father died in the Pacific during World War II and his stepmother abandons him, so at the age of 14 he goes to live in Florida with his grandfather, a man he has never met. Soon after his arrival there, someone murders his grandfather's cowman and best friend. This marks the beginning of an adventure involving danger, espionage, and German U-boats.

2859. Weatherford, Carole Boston. *Freedom on the Menu: The Greensboro Sit-Ins.* Illustrated by Jerome Lagarrigue. Dial, 2004. Unpaged. ISBN 978-0-8037-2860-8; Puffin, 2007, paper ISBN 978-0-14-240894-0. Grades K–4. Connie, 8, and her mother often stop in the Woolworth's in Greensboro, North Carolina, for a drink, but as African Americans they cannot sit at the lunch counter. After Martin Luther King, Jr., speaks at a local college, Connie's brother is one of four black students who decide to make a nonviolent protest and sit down at the counter on February 1, 1960. By July 25th that year lunch counters throughout the South have become open to all customers. Illustrations embellish the text. *Children's Book Award* (North Carolina) nomination, *Capitol Choices Noteworthy Titles* (Washington, D.C.), and *Young Readers Choice Award* (Pennsylvania) nomination.

2860. White, Alana J. *Come Next Spring.* BackinPrint.com, 2002. 170pp. Paper ISBN 978-0-595-22698-6. Grades 4–8. In 1949 in the Tennessee mountains, 12-year-old Salina dislikes a number of changes—the proposal to put a new highway through farmland, the new girl called Scooter, the growing distance between Salina and her former best friend.

2861. White, Ruth. *Belle Prater's Boy.* Farrar, 1996. 176pp. ISBN 978-0-374-30668-7; Yearling, 1998, paper ISBN 978-0-440-41372-1. Grades 5–9. During the 1950s, Beauty (Gypsy Arbutus Leemaster) has lovely golden curls, while her cousin Woodrow is cross-eyed and ill-dressed. Otherwise, they have things in common, such as one missing parent and deep pain. When Woodrow's mother, Belle Prater, deserts him, and his alcoholic father cannot look after him, he comes to live with his grandparents next door to Gypsy in Coal Station, Virginia, on the best street in town. Meanwhile, Gypsy has had to come to terms with the knowledge that her father committed suicide. Woodrow and Gypsy enjoy each other's jokes and stories as they cope with situations neither wants to admit. *Boston-Globe/Horn Book Award*, *School Library Journal Best Book*, *Newbery Honor*, and *Capitol Choices Noteworthy Titles* (Washington, D.C.).

2862. White, Ruth. *Little Audrey.* Farrar, 2008. 160pp. ISBN 978-0-374-34580-8. Grades 4–7. Eleven-year-old Audrey is known as "Skeleton Girl" because she lost weight while fighting scarlet fever. Her companions challenge her to feats such as climbing the water tower, but Audrey's eyesight was compromised by the fever. Audrey worries about her family. Her father drinks away his money on payday; her mother is mourning the death of the baby, Betty Gail; and her three sisters are incredibly irritating. But at least Audrey has a friend, a classmate named Virgil, who has the sense to keep her off the water tower.

2863. White, Ruth. *The Search for Belle Prater.* Farrar, 2005. 176pp. ISBN 978-0-374-30853-7; Yearling, 2007, paper ISBN 978-0-440-42164-1. Grades 5–9. In 1955 Woodrow Prater and his cousin Gypsy meet Cassie Caulborne, the new girl in their Coal Station, Virginia, 7th-grade class. Woodrow's mother disappeared a year before, and when Woodrow gets a call on his birthday he is convinced it's from his mother. The three of them set out to find her. Cassie has second sight, and this helps them in their quest.

2864. Whittenberg, Allison. *Sweet Thang: A Novel.* Delacorte, 2006. 149pp. ISBN 978-0-385-73292-5; Yearling, 2007, paper ISBN 978-0-440-42086-6. Grades 5–8. In Philadelphia in 1975, Charmaine Upshaw, 14, wants justice for all but seems to get none herself at home or at school. She has to share a room with her brother Leo and cope with her 6-year-old cousin Tracy John, who has just moved in. And light-skinned Dinah Coverdale gets all the interesting guys. As Charmaine reluctantly babysits for Tracy John, she begins to understand his troubles since the death of his mother and to become more self-confident.

2865. Williams-Garcia, Rita. *One Crazy Summer.* Amistad, 2010. 218pp. ISBN 978-0-06-076088-5. Grades 5–8. In 1968, African American Delphine, 11, and her two younger sisters leave their father and Big Ma in Brooklyn to visit their mother Cecile, who abandoned them seven years before, in Oakland, California. Instead of Disneyland, they find an unwelcoming women who sends them to the Black Panthers' People's Center for breakfast and to a Chinese restaurant for dinner. They stay for the Panthers' summer camp, learning about a different attitude toward life. They also learn that their mother is a poet, known to her friends as Sister "Nzila."

2866. Woods, Brenda. *The Red Rose Box.* Putnam, 2002. 144pp. ISBN 978-0-399-23702-7; Aladdin, 2003, paper ISBN 978-0-14-250151-1. Grades 5–8. In 1953, 10-year-old Leah Hopper, her little sister Ruth, and their mother travel from their Sulphur, Louisiana, home to Los Angeles. Their train tickets arrived from Aunt Olivia in a red rosewood box for Leah's birthday. Leah is shocked by the lack of Jim Crow restrictions and impressed with Aunt Olivia and her husband's beautiful home. At the same time, she misses the familiarity of her own home. Later the girls visit without their mother, and while they are in Los Angeles, a hurricane hits their home and kills their parents. The girls have to adjust to permanent changes in their life.

2867. Woods, Ron. *The Hero.* Yearling, 2003. 192pp. Paper ISBN 978-0-440-22978-0. Grades 5–9. In 1957, 14-year-old Jamie West and his older cousin Jerry ask weakling neighbor Dennis Leeper to join them on their maiden journey by raft down the fast-flowing Payette River near their Idaho home. The current sweeps them away and Dennis drowns. At the funeral Jamie lies and says Dennis died trying to save him. *Young Reader Award* (Nevada) nomination.

2868. Woodson, Jacqueline. *Feathers.* Putnam, 2007. 118pp. ISBN 978-0-399-23989-2. Grades 4–7. A white student called "The Jesus Boy" because of his longish hair joins her sixth-grade class in 1971, and he and Frannie become friends. Frannie has recently been interested in hope and is questioning the world around her and her own faith. She thinks about her older, deaf brother's social problems and her mother's continuing difficult pregnancies. She watches her new friend face harassment from the boys even as her religious friend Samantha suspects he may indeed be the savior.

2869. Woodworth, Chris. *Georgie's Moon.* Farrar, 2006. 176pp. ISBN 978-0-374-33306-5. Grades 5–8. In 1970 Georgie Collins is attending 7th grade in Glendale, Indiana, while her father is in Vietnam with the United States Air Force. Classmates who are against the war think her father should not be fighting there, and she tries to control her anger. Georgie looks at the sky each night because her father said he would send her his love via the moon. But Georgie is trying to deal with her father's death, a reality she cannot yet admit. *Children's Book Award* (Georgia) nomination.

2870. Ylvisaker, Anne. *Little Klein.* Candlewick, 2007. 186pp. ISBN 978-0-7636-3359-2. Grades 3–6. "Little Klein" lives with his three older brothers—Matthew, Mark, and Luke, called the "Bigs"—in a small midwestern town in the 1940s. He's short and looks more like 4 years old than 7, so he is often overlooked and rarely heard because of his small voice. He can whistle, however, and he attracts dogs. A stray that he names LeRoy becomes his constant companion and the two have adventures that eventually earn "Little Klein" his real name, "Harold."

History

2871. Anderson, Michael. *The Civil Rights Movement.* (20th Century Perspectives) Heinemann, 2003. 48pp. Paper ISBN 978-1-4034-4179-9. Grades 5–8. Anderson covers the groups involved in the civil rights movement, including the NAACP and the Southern Christian Leadership Council. He also presents some of the main figures in the fight for equal rights. Illustrations augment the text. Bibliography, Further Reading, Glossary, Index.

2872. Anderson, Wayne. *Brown versus Board of Education: The Case Against School Segregation.* (Supreme Court Cases Through Primary Sources) Rosen, 2003. 64pp. ISBN 978-0-8239-3974-9. Grades 5–8. After considering the case of *Brown v. Board of Education*, the Supreme Court decided that segregation was unlawful. Twenty-one states could no longer have separate schools for African Americans and whites. This decision changed race relations in the United States. Primary source materials examine the background of race relations, the status quo in education before the ruling, and other court cases affected by this ruling. Bibliography and Index.

2873. Baker, Patricia. *Fashions of a Decade: The 1940s.* See entry 2611.

2874. Baker, Patricia. *Fashions of a Decade: The 1950s.* Chelsea House, 2006. 64pp. ISBN 978-0-8160-6721-3. Grades 5 up. In the 1950s people were concerned with the Cold War, the Cuban Revolution, and women themselves. Women experimented with the new fabric of rayon while businessmen chose gray flannel suits. Hollywood began to influence clothing with delineations between "girl next door" personalities and sirens. Photographs and illustrations enhance the text. Glossary, Further Reading, Chronology, and Index.

2875. Bertholf, Bret. *The Long Gone Lonesome History of Country Music.* Little, Brown, 2007. 56pp. ISBN 978-0-316-52393-6. Grades 4–6. Bertholf looks at the legends of country music and the musical styles that influenced it. He also explores the instruments that are popular with these musicians, early recordings, television, cowboys, definitions, and other entertaining tidbits about this industry.

2876. Britton, Tamara L. *The Vietnam Veterans Memorial.* (Symbols, Landmarks, and Monuments) Checkerboard, 2004. 32pp. ISBN 978-1-59197-523-6. Grades 3–5. Britton offers background on the memorial located in Washington, D.C., and discusses the controversy around the memorial's design. Despite initial criticism, the wall—with its carefully carved names—has become a highly reverential spot. Photographs highlight the text. Glossary, Chronology, and Index.

2877. Brooks, Philip. *The McCarthy Hearings.* (20th Century Perspectives) Heinemann, 2003. 48pp. ISBN 978-1-4034-3808-9; paper ISBN 978-1-4034-4178-2. Grades 4–8. Brooks explores various aspects of the McCarthy Hearings led by Senator Joseph McCarthy after he reported having a list of members of the Communist Party and of a spy ring who worked in the State Department. The hearings began in 1954, and little happened to substantiate his accusations. Illustrations augment the text. Bibliography, Further Reading, Glossary, Index.

2878. Brown, Gene. *The Nation in Turmoil: Civil Rights and the Vietnam War, 1960–1973.* (First Person America) Twenty-First Century, 1993. 64pp. ISBN 978-0-8050-2588-0. Grades 5–8. At the beginning of the 1960s, America had a new, young president, John F. Kennedy, who gave idealistic college students the Peace Corps. Integration began to be a reality. Kennedy's assassination in 1963 changed the mood of the country and subsequent events, including the assassinations of Robert Kennedy and Martin Luther King, Jr. changed the nation again. Riots over both the Vietnam War and civil rights shook the cities. In the early 1970s social changes—for women and homosexuals—gained momentum while the Arab nations imposed an oil embargo. Then Richard Nixon compromised the presidency by lying to the country and resigned in 1972. Photographs enhance the text. Timeline, For Further Reading, and Index.

2879. Carter, E. J. *The Cuban Missile Crisis.* (20th Century Perspectives) Heinemann, 2003. 48pp. ISBN 978-1-4034-3806-5; paper ISBN 978-1-4034-4180-5. Grades 4–8. Carter covers the causes of the Cuban Missile Crisis, its issues, aftermath, and consequences. This event took the world to the brink of nuclear war. Among the topics discussed are the Bay of Pigs disaster and John F. Kennedy's secret missile-swapping agreement with Khrushchev. Illustrations augment the text. Bibliography, Further Reading, Glossary, Index.

2880. Chaikin, Andrew L. *Mission Control, This Is Apollo: The Story of the First Voyages to the Moon.* Illustrated by Alan Bean and Victoria Kohl. Viking, 2009. 114pp. ISBN 978-0-670-01156-8. Grades 5–8. Chaikin looks at twelve of the seventeen Apollo program endeavors, from *Apollo 1*'s fatal cockpit fire until the last, *Apollo 17*. Alan Bean, the fourth astronaut to walk on the moon, illustrates these missions with his paintings; NASA photographs and diagrams are also included. Bean's comments add interesting details about each mission's purpose and about food, bathroom procedures, space sickness, and television inside the space "home." The integration of picture and print offers an accessible and memorable overview of the space program after Sputnik. Chronology, Bibliography, Further Reading, Films, and Web Sites. *Hornbook Fanfare List, Booklist Editors Choice,* and *Capitol Choices Noteworthy Titles for Children and Teens* (Washington, D.C.).

2881. Chin, Steven A. *When Justice Failed: The Fred Korematsu Story.* Illustrated by David Tamura. Steck-Vaughn, 1992. 105pp. Paper ISBN 978-0-8114-8076-5. Grades 5–9. In 1967 Karen Korematsu listened to her friend give a report about a man who challenged the U.S. government's decision to intern Americans of Japanese descent. What she heard was the story of her father, Fred Korematsu, who decided that the edict was unfair. The American Civil Liberties Union represented Korematsu and took his case to the Supreme Court, where it failed. In 1982, it was discovered that at least two studies of Japanese Americans before the war had concluded that they were not a threat to U.S. security. Because this information was not initially revealed to the courts, a new review reversed the earlier decision. Afterword and Notes.

2882. Connikie, Yvonne. *Fashions of a Decade: The 1960s.* Chelsea House, 2007. 64pp. ISBN 978-0-8160-6722-0. Grades 5 up. In the 1960s the youth culture became important and a new generation of designers sprang up to fulfill the expectations of this new clientele. Styles were freer and ranged from cocktail dresses and beehive hairdos to Beatnik garb, mods and minis, a psychedelic explosion, and flower power. Glossary, Reading List, Time Chart, and Index.

2883. Cook, Michelle. *Our Children Can Soar: A Celebration of Rosa, Barack, and the Pioneers of Change.* Illustrated by Cozbi A. Cabrera, et al. Bloomsbury, 2009. 32pp. ISBN 978-1-59990-418-4. Grades K–5. Almost a cumulative tale, the text reiterates what people such as Rosa Parks and Martin Luther King, Jr., contributed so that Barack Obama could become president. It traces history from freed slaves to Hattie McDaniel's victory in the movie *Gone with the Wind*, Ruby Bridges' integrating of schools, the Olympian Jesse Owens, and Supreme Court Justice Thurgood Marshall. Different eminent African American illustrators such as the Dillions, A. G. Ford, Pat Cummins, James Ransome, and E. B. Lewis created the illustrations. Biographical Sketches. *Young Readers Choice Book Award* (Pennsylvania) nomination.

2884. Crewe, Sabrina, and Dale Anderson. *The First Moon Landing.* (Events that Shaped America) Gareth Stevens, 2004. 32pp. ISBN 978-0-8368-3397-3. Grades 4–6. The Apollo space program of the United States, successfully landed the first humans on the moon in 1969, fulfilling a challenge set by President John F. Kennedy. The four main chapters of the text introduce the space program, the *Apollo 11* mission, the value of moon science, and what happened after Apollo. Most interesting is that reaching the moon was achieved at a time when color television was not widespread. Photographs and drawings highlight the text. Further Reading, Chronology, Glossary, Activities, Web Sites, and Index.

2885. Donnelly, Karen J. *Cruzan v. Missouri: The Right to Die.* (Supreme Court Cases Through Primary Sources) Rosen, 2003. 64pp. ISBN 978-0-8239-4014-1. Grades 5–8. In an examination of the case of *Cruzan v. Missouri* in 1990, the Supreme Court decided that the family of Nancy Cruzan had not provided "clear and convincing evidence" that Nancy Cruzan did not want her life artificially preserved. Cruzan was left permanently unconscious—in a "persistent vegetative state"—after an automobile accident in 1983. Her family wanted to have her feeding tube removed. The family later presented the evidence required in Missouri courts and won the case. Primary source materials offer background information and details of other court cases this ruling has affected. Bibliography and Index.

2886. Dowswell, Paul. *The United Nations.* (20th Century Perspectives) Heinemann, 2002. 48pp. ISBN 978-1-4034-0152-6; 2003, paper ISBN 978-1-4034-4622-0. Grades 5–8. The United Nations, founded in 1945 to replace the League of Nations, aims to stimulate international cooperation in the areas of security, law, social progress, economic development, and human rights. Its strengths and weaknesses become apparent as it discusses international peace but has little means to stop war. Individual organizations within the UN, such as the World Health Organization, are effective around the world. Illustrations augment the text. Bibliography, Further Reading, Glossary, Index.

2887. Dyer, Alan. *Mission to the Moon.* Simon & Schuster, 2009. 80pp. ISBN 978-1-4169-7935-7. Grades 5–8. Celebrating the 40th anniversary of the moon landing, the text examines the moon from several perspectives but focuses on the space race. It covers the selection of astronauts for the Apollo missions beginning with 11 and includes more than 200 photographs from NASA's archives. It also contains cross-sections and diagrams of rockets, space suits, and equipment important for landing a man on the moon. DVD, Glossary, and Index.

2888. Edelman, Rob. *The Vietnam War.* (People at the Center Of) Blackbirch, 2003. 48pp. ISBN 978-1-56711-771-4. Grades 5–8. Edelman discusses fourteen individuals who were closely associated with the Vietnam War, among them Lyndon Johnson, Ho Chi Minh, Abbie Hoffman, and John McCain. The profiles include information showing how each person influenced events during the war.

2889. **Floca, Brian.** *Moonshot: The Flight of Apollo 11.* Atheneum, 2009. 48pp. ISBN 978-1-416-95046-2. Grades 2–5. In 1969 three astronauts—Buzz Aldrin, Michel Collins, and Neil Armstrong—left on *Apollo 11* for the moon. This picture book, with its line-and-wash illustrations depicting the momentous journey from lift-off to splash-down, offers a clear, succinct recounting of the event. Endpapers include a chronology, diagrams, and a brief history of NASA's moon program. The accessible approach offers a simple introduction for young readers. *American Library Association Notable Children's Books, Bulletin Blue Ribbon, Hornbook Fanfare List, American Library Association Best Books for Young Adults, Booklist Editors Choice, School Library Journal Best Books of the Year, Bank Street College of Education Book Award Winner, NAPPA Gold Awards* winner, *Robert F. Sibert Informational Book Award* honor book, *Indies Choice Book Awards* nomination, and *Capitol Choices Noteworthy Titles for Children and Teens* (Washington, D.C.).

2890. **Freedman, Russell.** *Freedom Walkers: The Story of the Montgomery Bus Boycott.* Holiday House, 2006. 114pp. ISBN 978-0-8234-2031-5. Grades 4–6. Freedman offers an overview of the 381-day resistance known as the Montgomery Bus Boycott, which followed Rosa Parks's arrest on December 1, 1955. He describes efforts to organize the boycott and the actions people took—rising early to take neighbors to work so they would not have to use the bus. The bus system could not function without the revenue. Protestors risked their jobs and their lives by participating but they won the right for everyone to have a seat on the bus. Photographs, maps, and illustrations intensify the text. Bibliography, Notes, and Index. *Young Hoosier Award* (Indiana) nomination, *Children's Book Award* (Rhode Island), *Horn Book Fanfare,* and *School Library Journal Best Books of the Year.*

2891. **Good, Diane L.** *Brown v. Board of Education: A Civil Rights Milestone.* (Cornerstones of Freedom) Children's, 2004. 48pp. ISBN 978-0-516-24225-5; 2007 paper ISBN 978-0-516-24225-5. Grades 4–6. This volume presents the history of segregation in the United States and the cases that tested the law of "separate but equal" treatment. The NAACP and its Legal Defense Fund lawyers combined five different cases into one that became *Brown v. Board of Education,* which was tried in 1954. Photographs, Chronology, Further Reading, Glossary, Web Sites, and Index.

2892. **Gordon, Olivia.** *Cold Case File: Murder in the Mountains.* (Crime Solvers) Bearport, 2007. 32pp. ISBN 978-1-59716-547-1. Grades 3–6. Readers learn about police procedures, witness interviews, forensic evidence, and so forth as they follow the investigations into the murder of Michele Wallace in Colorado in 1974. Sidebars add facts. Photographs and illustrations augment the text. Glossary, Further Reading, Web Sites, and Index.

2893. **Hakim, Joy.** *All the People: Since 1945.* (History of US) Oxford, 2006. 208pp. ISBN 978-0-19-530737-5; 2007, paper ISBN 978-0-19-532724-3. Grades 5 up. With many photographs, prints, sidebars, boxed text, and running commentary, this is the story of the United States after World War II, covering all aspects of society. Chronology of Events, More Books to Read, and Index.

2894. **Hampton, Wilborn.** *Kennedy Assassinated! The World Mourns: A Reporter's Story.* Candlewick, 1997. 96pp. ISBN 978-1-56402-811-2. Grades 5–8. When the author was a cub reporter assigned to the White House in 1963, he found himself in the center of the tragedy of President John F. Kennedy's assassination. He was alone at the news desk when the call came on November 22 saying that three shots had been fired at the president's motorcade in Dallas. The call set off intense activity, but he tried to remain impartial. At the hospital, he tied up a line so that his news service would have access to it at all times. Finally, when he saw Jackie Kennedy putting her own wedding ring on her dead husband's finger and Kennedy pronounced dead, he broke into tears. Photographs augment the text. Index. *Student Book Award* (Maine) nomination, *Bulletin for the Center of Children's Books Blue Ribbon,* and *Bluebonnet Award* (Texas).

2895. **Herald, Jacqueline.** *Fashions of a Decade: The 1970s.* Chelsea House, 2006. 64pp. ISBN 978-0-8160-6723-7. Grades 5 up. Among the fashions of the 1970s were platform shoes, bell-bottom pants, hot pants, and miniskirts. People also wore afghans and cheesecloth fabrics, making the time one of the most diverse in fashion choices. Photographs and illustrations augment the text. Glossary, Chronology, Further Reading, Index.

2896. Hill, Prescott. *Our Century: 1970–1980.* Gareth Stevens, 1993. 64pp. ISBN 978-0-8368-1039-4. Grades 3 up. Written as if a newspaper, this book's short articles give an overview of the decade. Included are statistics, daily life in America, Vietnam, Arabs and Israelis at war, Chile's Allende overthrow, bombs in Beirut, the Guyana mass suicide, the Sandinistas taking control, the Islamic overthrow of the Shah of Iran, the Attica prison revolt, Jimmy Carter, the first test tube baby, Arab terrorists, Hank Aaron, O. J. Simpson, Billie Jean King, Muhammad Ali, Golda Meir, George Wallace, and Barbara Jordan. Glossary, Books for Further Reading, Places to Write or Visit, and Index.

2897. Hilliard, Richard. *Ham the Astrochimp.* Boyds Mills, 2007. 32pp. ISBN 978-1-59078-459-4. Grades 2–4. On January 31, 1961, during the final testing phase of the Mercury space program, a 3-year-old chimpanzee called Ham became the first intelligent being to orbit the Earth. Scientists wanted to learn what might affect humans in such a situation. The text discusses the path that Ham took from equatorial Africa to NASA to space, exile at the National Zoo, and his last two years in a North Carolina zoo. Acrylic paintings highlight the text.

2898. Ingram, Scott. *Tsunami! The 1946 Hilo Wave of Terror.* (X-Treme Disasters That Changed America) Bearport, 2005. 32pp. ISBN 978-1-59716-010-0. Grades 3–5. In 1946 an earthquake off the coast of Alaska caused a tsunami that hit Hilo, Hawaii. There was no way to warn residents and more than 150 people died. A second tsunami hit in 1960, but by then a warning system was functioning. Photographs enhance the text. Bibliography, Glossary, Further Reading, Web Sites, and Index.

2899. Kelso, Richard. *Days of Courage: The Little Rock Story.* Illustrated by Mel Williges. Steck-Vaughn, 1992. 88pp. Paper ISBN 978-0-8114-8070-3. Grades 4–7. When Elizabeth Eckford was 15 in 1957, she was one of nine black students chosen to integrate Little Rock High School in Arkansas. She and the other eight faced danger from hostile white adults who were determined that their children would not attend school with blacks. The governor of the state, Orval Faubus, was no help because he supported the white parents, defying a Supreme Court order for immediate integration. President Eisenhower had to intervene so that these young people could go to school. Epilogue, Afterword, and Notes.

2900. Kelso, Richard. *Walking for Freedom: The Montgomery Bus Boycott.* Illustrated by Michael Newton. Steck-Vaughn, 1992. 52pp. Paper ISBN 978-0-8114-8058-1. Grades 4–7. In 1949 Mrs. Robinson, who usually drove her car, rode a Montgomery, Alabama, bus and inadvertently sat in the whites-only section. The driver's hostile and rude treatment toward her led her to suggest a bus boycott to the Woman's Political Council. They waited six years until the time was right to put the plan into effect. When Rosa Parks refused to rise from her seat for a white man in 1955, the boycott began. It lasted until November 1956, when Montgomery officials changed their laws. Epilogue, Afterword, and Notes.

2901. Koestler-Grack, Rachel A. *Going to School During the Civil Rights Movement.* (Going to School in History) Blue Earth, 2001. 32pp. ISBN 978-0-7368-0799-9. Grades 4–6. The five chapters of this book look at a child's life in the South during the civil rights movement. Schools were segregated, and African Americans received limited education. The students themselves became activists in some cases, struggling to get the things they needed. They worked for school integration, and when it became law, they gained access to better educational resources. The book details games, activities, special events, and crafts that children would have enjoyed. Photographs, maps, and illustrations augment the text. Glossary, Web Sites, and Index.

2902. LeBoutillier, Nate. *The Story of the Chicago Bears.* (NFL Today) Creative, 2009. 48pp. ISBN 978-1-58341-750-8. Grades 5–8. The text examines the history of the Chicago Bears football team with entertaining anecdotes about the players and games. Names of legendary team members such as Gale Saylers, Dick Butkus, and Walter Payton will appeal to football fans. Photographs enhance the text. Index.

2903. Low, William. *Old Penn Station.* Henry Holt, 2007. Unpaged. ISBN 978-0-8050-7925-8. Grades 3–6. A pictorial celebration of the original Pennsylvania Railroad Station in downtown Manhattan, this volume looks at the history of the building from its construction and opening in 1910 through its destruction in the 1960s. It was demolished to build a smaller, subterranean station that exists today underneath Madison Square Garden. Low laments the demise of a historical building that should have been preserved. Full-bleed illustrations enhance the text. *Kirkus Reviews Editor's Choice.*

2904. McKissack, Patricia C., and Frederick McKissack. *Black Diamond: The Story of the Negro Baseball Leagues.* See entry 2303.

2905. Morrison, Toni. *Remember: The Journey to School Integration.* Houghton, 2004. 78pp. ISBN 978-0-618-39740-2. Grades 5 up. This collection of photographs and text recalls the events that took place during school desegregation. The pictures clearly reveal the emotions of the children involved and demonstrate what "separate but equal" meant. *Coretta Scott King Award, Parents Choice Award, Diamonds Award* (Delaware) nomination, and *Bulletin Blue Ribbon.*

2906. Myers, Walter Dean. *A Place Called Heartbreak: A Story of Vietnam.* Illustrated by Frederick Porter. Steck-Vaughn, 1993. 71pp. Paper ISBN 978-0-8114-8077-2. Grades 5–9. Major Fred Cherry was shot down on a routine mission near Hanoi in North Vietnam in 1965. He was the 43rd American and the first black to be captured. He was beaten and abused for 92 days straight and then hospitalized. He lived in solitary confinement for almost a year before being imprisoned with other Americans who had devised a means of communicating by tapping on the walls. Cherry was a prisoner for seven and a half years before the war ended and he was finally free. Epilogue, Afterword, and Notes.

2907. Partridge, Elizabeth. *Marching for Freedom: Walk Together, Children, and Don't You Grow Weary.* Viking, 2009. 72pp. ISBN 978-0-670-01189-6. Grades 5–9. Although Lyndon Johnson signed the Civil Rights Act outlawing segregation in school and work in 1964, black voters in Alabama were still deterred by illegal poll taxes and literacy tests that few could pass. This collection of songs and photographs with background from personal interviews presents some of the children who used Martin Luther King, Jr.'s nonviolent, but not passive, techniques to achieve the Voting Rights Act of August 6, 1965. Their parents would lose their jobs if seen protesting, so among those who became their surrogates were Joanne Blackmon, 10, her sister Lynda, and Charles Mauldin. The racist Sheriff Clark and his deputies arrested them and many other children for holding placards and complaining. The main march was the 55-day walk from Selma to Montgomery in March 1965, led by Dr. King, and detested by Governor George Wallace. The group gained national attention, especially when police beat innocent citizens with clubs. Period photographs effectively offer information impossible to convey in words. Notes, Bibliography, Further Resources, Web Sites, and Index. *American Library Association Best Books for Young Adults, American Library Association Notable Children's Books, Booklist Editors Choice,* and *Capitol Choices Noteworthy Titles* (Washington, D.C.).

2908. Payment, Simone. *Roe v. Wade: The Right to Choose.* (Supreme Court Cases Through Primary Sources) Rosen, 2003. 64pp. ISBN 978-0-8239-4012-7. Grades 5–8. In an examination of the case of *Roe v. Wade,* the Supreme Court decided that women had a right to chose whether to have an abortion. Jane Roe challenged a Texas statute saying that she could not have an abortion unless her life was threatened. This ruling was the first time that the court recognized a woman's constitutional right to privacy. Primary source materials examine the case and other court cases this ruling has affected. Bibliography and Index.

2909. Pinkney, Jerry. *God Bless the Child.* Harpercollins, 2004. 32pp. ISBN 978-0-06-028797-9. Grades K–5. In the early 1930s, the Great Migration of African Americans from the rural South to the urban, industrial North reached a climax. The people no longer wanted to pick cotton and moved to the cities where they hoped for a better life. A compact disc with Billie Holiday singing "God Bless the Child" accompanies the text. Notes. *Coretta Scott King Illustrator Honor.*

2910. Rappaport, Doreen. *Nobody Gonna Turn Me 'Round: Stories and Songs of the Civil Rights Movement.* Illustrated by Shane W. Evans. Candlewick, 2006. 63pp. ISBN 978-0-7636-1927-5; 2008, paper ISBN 978-0-7636-3892-4. Grades 4–8. With first-person accounts, songs, poems, letters, and court testimony, this volume recalls the brave actions of those fighting for civil rights during the 1960s. Among the figures included are Rosa Parks, Fannie Lou Hamer, and Martin Luther King, Jr. Also featured is Mose Wright, an African American who testified in the Emmett Till case, most likely the first time he had spoken against a white man. The illustrations depict the freedom rides, sit-ins, and jail sentences that protestors faced. Bibliography, Notes, Further Reading, and Index. *Parents' Choice Silver Honors.*

2911. Rappaport, Doreen. *The School Is Not White: A True Story of the Civil Rights Movement.* Illustrated by Curtis James. Hyperion, 2005. 32pp. ISBN 978-0-7868-1838-9. Grades 2–5. In 1965, when the schools in Drew, Mississippi, were desegregated, Mae Bertha and Matthew Carter decided to enroll their seven children in formerly all-white schools because they had better resources and better buildings. They faced enormous hostility but the family's love helped support them during this difficult time. An appendix details how education helped the Carter children. Bibliography. *Young Readers Choice Book Award* (Louisiana) nomination.

2912. Santella, Andrew. *The Korean War.* (We the People) Compass Point, 2006. 48pp. ISBN 978-0-7565-2027-4. Grades 4–7. Seven chapters cover the start of the war, its progress, and its conclusion. On June 25, 1950, North Korean troops entered South Korea. The United States responded by sending troops to help the South Koreans. Other help came from members of the United Nations in the form of combat units, food, medical teams, and supplies. The war lasted for more than three years, with both military and civilian lives lost. Photographs enhance the text. Glossary, Bibliography, Chronology, Further Reading, Web Sites, and Index.

2913. Scher, Linda. *The Texas City Disaster.* (Code Red) Bearport, 2007. 32pp. ISBN 978-1-59716-363-7. Grades 3–6. Scher examines the events that occurred in 1947 when fertilizer in the hold of a ship caught fire and exploded in Texas City, Texas. A chain reaction began that led to 550 deaths. The fire might have been prevented if the fertilizer bags had had warning labels printed on them. There are brief profiles of key figures. Photographs, maps, and reproductions highlight the text. Glossary, Further Reading, Web Sites, and Index.

2914. Shange, Ntozake. *We Troubled the Waters.* Illustrated by Rod Brown. Amistad, 2009. 32pp. ISBN 978-0-06-133735-2. Grades 4 up. Poems, complemented by appropriate acrylics on the facing page that express emotions impossible to capture in words, reflect the troubles and burdens of those without civil rights. Among those who questioned society's treatment of them are a cleaning woman, a worker, children walking to school, victims of lynching, Martin Luther King, Jr., Rosa Parks, and Malcolm X.

2915. Shore, Diane Z., and Jessica Alexander. *This Is the Dream.* Illustrated by James Ransome. Amistad, 2006. 40pp. ISBN 978-0-06-055519-1. Grades K–6. This extended rhythmic poem recreates the events of the civil rights movement. It is accompanied by descriptive photographs, paintings, and collages of the era's segregated lunch counters, schools, and buses. Among the individuals featured are Dr. Martin Luther King Jr., Walter White, Thurgood Marshall, and Ella Baker. Notes. *Red Clover Award* (Vermont) nomination and *Black-Eyed Susan Award* (Maryland) nomination.

2916. Sonneborn, Liz. *Miranda v. Arizona: The Rights of the Accused.* (Supreme Court Cases Through Primary Sources) Rosen, 2003. 64pp. ISBN 978-0-8239-4010-3. Grades 5–8. In an examination of the case of *Miranda v. Arizona*, the Supreme Court ruled that persons detained by the police have the "right to remain silent." Police arrested Ernesto Miranda, a poor Mexican immigrant, for rape and kidnapping in 1963. They questioned him for two hours, and he signed a confession. Convicted and sentenced to sixty years in jail, he had never been told that he could remain silent and had the right not to incriminate himself. He also had a right to counsel. He appealed. Primary source materials present background information and details of other court cases this ruling has affected. Bibliography and Index.

2917. Stamper, Judith Bauer. *Save the Everglades.* Illustrated by Allen Davis. Steck-Vaughn, 1992. 58pp. Paper ISBN 978-0-8114-8059-8. Grades 5–9. This is the story of the protests against plans to build a huge airport near Miami, Florida, which would have destroyed much of the wetlands of the Big Cypress Swamp near the Everglades. Joe Browder and Marjory Douglas fought together to keep the wetlands. Disagreement in Washington led President Nixon to send an emissary to the area. Julie Nixon, his daughter, realized that the destruction of this area would be a loss for the nation and supported the Browder and Douglas position. Epilogue, Afterword, and Notes.

2918. Steins, Richard. *The Postwar Years: The Cold War and the Atomic Age.* Twenty-First Century, 1993. 64pp. ISBN 978-0-8050-2587-3. Grades 5–8. Television became a part of American life during the 1950s. At the same time Joseph McCarthy was conducting a campaign of terror against Communist sympathizers. There was a war in Korea and civil rights unrest domestically. Among the individuals noted here are Lillian Hellman, the Rosenbergs, Elvis Presley, Dr. Spock, and Martin Luther King, Jr. Photographs enhance the text. Timeline, For Further Reading, and Index.

2919. Supples, Kevin. *Speaking Out: The Civil Rights Movement 1950–1964.* (Crossroads America) National Geographic, 2005. 40pp. ISBN 978-0-7922-8279-2. Grades 4–6. Supples explores topics topics that offer an introduction to the civil rights movement—the Great Migration, the Jim Crow laws, the beginning of the NAACP, Thurgood Marshall, *Brown v. Board of Education*, the Little Rock Nine, and the differences between the philosophies of Martin Luther King, Jr., and Malcolm X. Sidebars include quotations from figures in the movement. Glossary and Index.

2920. Taylor, David. *The Cold War.* (20th Century Perspectives) Heinemann, 2001. 48pp. ISBN 978-1-57572-434-8; 2002, paper ISBN 978-1-58810-373-4. Grades 5–8. The Cold War, between East and West, developed after World War II. Taylor explains some of the major tensions of the period until 1989 when the Berlin Wall fell. The rivalry involved military coalitions, ideology, espionage, and psychology. Both groups spent huge amounts of money on a space race and keeping their defenses updated with the best technology. Illustrations augment the text. Bibliography, Further Reading, Glossary, Index.

2921. Thimmesh, Catherine. *Team Moon: How 400,000 People Landed Apollo 11 on the Moon.* Houghton, 2006. 80pp. ISBN 978-0-618-50757-3. Grades 5 up. Thimmesh looks at all the people who were instrumental in the success of *Apollo 11*, which landed the first man on the moon on July 20, 1969. Using a conversational tone, she introduces computer scientists, seamstresses who sewed space suits, and some of the 400,000 others from different fields who tested, checked, retested, and checked their work again. Photographs augment the text. Bibliography, Glossary, Notes, and Index. *Bluebonnet Award* (Texas) nomination, *Robert F. Sibert Medal, Golden Kite Honor Book, Orbis Pictus Award Honor Book, American Library Association Notable Children's Books,* and *Best Books for Young Adults, Capitol Choices Noteworthy Titles* (Washington, D.C.), and *Beehive Award* (Utah) nomination.

2922. Tracy, Kathleen. *The Watergate Scandal.* (Monumental Milestones) Mitchell Lane, 2006. 48pp. ISBN 978-1-58415-470-9. Grades 5–8. A look at the events surrounding the Watergate scandal, which erupted after a break-in on June 17, 1972, and led to President Richard Nixon's impeachment and resignation on August 9, 1974. Photographs, sidebars, and illustrations augment the text. Glossary, Chronology, and Index.

2923. Vogt, Gregory. *Disasters in Space Exploration.* Twenty-First Century, 2003. 79pp. ISBN 978-0-7613-2895-7. Grades 5–8. Vogt discusses the tragedies and near-disasters of space exploration from its early days to the present. He includes problems aboard *Apollo 13* and the Russian space station *Mir*; and the loss of the *Columbia* shuttle in February 2003. Vogt explains the circumstances of each event and the lessons designers and engineers learned from it. Photographs augment the text. Glossary, Further Reading, Web Sites, and Index.

2924. Walker, Paul Robert. *Remember Little Rock: The Time, the People, the Stories.* National Geographic, 2009. 64pp. ISBN 978-1-4263-0402-6. Grades 5–8. Nine students who became known as the "Little Rock Nine" integrated Central High School in Little Rock, Arkansas, in 1957. They faced a hostile place where Jim Crow was the law and a governor, Orval Faubus, who used the National Guard to keep them off school property. Primary source quotes and archival photographs chronicle this story that lasted nine months until the first African American graduated. Chronology, Bibliography, and Notes.

2925. Weatherford, Carole Boston. *Birmingham, 1963.* Word Song, 2007. 40pp. ISBN 978-1-59078-440-2. Grades 4–8. In free verse an unidentified narrator recalls the day she turned 10, when at 10:22 in the morning Jesus's face blew out of the only stained glass window left standing in Birmingham's Sixteenth Street Baptist Church. Racists had bombed the church, killing four young African American girls nearby. The case was not closed, nor the perpetrators brought to justice, for thirty-nine years. Further Reading and Web Sites. *Kirkus Reviews Editor's Choice.*

2926. Willoughby, Douglas. *The Vietnam War.* (20th Century Perspectives) Heinemann, 2001. 48pp. ISBN 978-1-57572-439-3; paper ISBN 978-1-58810-378-9. Grades 5–9. The American military involvement inside Vietnam began with a conflict in 1959 and ended on April 30, 1975, when the last American troops left the country. After more than 15 years of hostilities, the North Vietnamese were victorious and the Americans suffered a major political defeat. This volume examines the causes of the war, the role of the United States in the war, and the aftermath. Illustrations augment the text. Bibliography, Further Reading, Glossary, Index.

Biography and Collective Biography

2927. Aaseng, Nathan. *Business Builders in Computers.* Oliver, 2000. 160pp. ISBN 978-1-8815-0857-1. Grades 5 up. This collective biography offers a history of the computer industry and those who have been involved in its success. It contains information on Thomas Watson Jr. (IBM); An Wang (Wang Laboratories); Seymour Cray (Cray Research); Robert Noyce and Gordon Moore (Intel); Bill Gates (Microsoft); Steve Jobs (Apple Computer); and Steve Case (America Online). Photographs and illustrations augment the text. Bibliography, Glossary, Chronology, Notes, and Index.

2928. Aaseng, Nathan. *Business Builders in Fast Foods.* Oliver, 2001. 160pp. ISBN 978-1-8815-0858-8. Grades 5 up. Aaseng gives an overview of how fast food restaurants began and profiles key figures: Fred Harvey (Harvey Houses); Walter Anderson and Billy Ingram (White Castle); J. F. McCullough and Harry Axene (Dairy Queen); the McDonald brothers and Ray Kroc (McDonald's); Harland Sanders (Kentucky Fried Chicken); and Tom Monaghan (Domino's Pizza). Photographs and illustrations augment the text. Bibliography, Glossary, Chronology, Notes, and Index.

2929. Adler, David A. *Campy: The Story of Roy Campanella.* Illustrated by Gordon C. James. Viking, 2007. Unpaged. ISBN 978-0-670-06041-2. Grades 2–4. The first African American catcher in the major leagues, Roy Campanella (1921–1993) joined the Brooklyn Dodgers in 1948, one year after Jackie Robinson. He won the National League's "Most Valuable Player" trophy three times, but in 1958 he was paralyzed in an accident. The biography shows his loving spirit and desire to live his life as well as he could without complaint. Oil paintings highlight the text.

2930. Adler, David A. *Dr. Martin Luther King, Jr.* Illustrated by Colin Bootman. Holiday House, 2001. 48pp. ISBN 978-0-8234-1572-4; 2003, paper ISBN 978-0-8234-1803-9. Grades 1–3. Martin Luther King, Jr. (1929–1968) courageously stood up for civil rights and nonviolent protest. Adler looks at King's early life and family influence along with his importance during the Montgomery bus boycott and many marches. He also covers King's 1963 "I Have a Dream" speech in Washington, D.C. Bibliography, Chronology, and Further Reading.

2931. Adler, David A. *A Picture Book of Dwight David Eisenhower.* See entry 2326.

2932. Adler, David A. *A Picture Book of Eleanor Roosevelt.* See entry 2327.

2933. Adler, David A. *A Picture Book of Jackie Robinson.* See entry 2638.

2934. Adler, David A. *A Picture Book of John F. Kennedy.* Illustrated by Robert F. Casilla. Holiday House, 1992. Unpaged. ISBN 978-0-8234-0884-9; paper ISBN 978-0-8234-0976-1. Grades 1–3. One of nine children of a wealthy Catholic family, John Kennedy (1917–1963) had various illnesses as a youngster but enjoyed athletics and disliked studying until his third year at Harvard. Before he became president of the United States, he wrote two books about the state of the world and his service in World War II. As president, he was concerned about civil rights, the arts, the space program, and establishing the Peace Corps. Important Dates.

2935. Adler, David A. *A Picture Book of Martin Luther King, Jr.* Illustrated by Robert Casilla. Holiday House, 1989. Unpaged. ISBN 978-0-8234-0770-5; 1990, paper ISBN 978-0-8234-0847-4. Grades 1–3. In Atlanta, Georgia, on January 15, 1929, Martin Luther King, Jr. began his journey through a segregated world. His intelligence led him to Morehouse College and Boston University on his way to preach in Montgomery, Alabama, where Rosa Parks had been arrested for sitting in the whites-only section of a bus. King's peaceful marches for freedom there and in Atlanta culminated in 1963 with the March on Washington, where he gave his "I Have a Dream" speech. In 1964 he won the Nobel Peace Prize. James Earl Ray assassinated him in 1968. Important Dates. *Notable Children's Trade Books in the Field of Social Studies.*

2936. Adler, David A. *A Picture Book of Rosa Parks.* Illustrated by Robert Casilla. Holiday House, 1993. Unpaged. ISBN 978-0-8234-1041-5; 1995, paper ISBN 978-0-8234-1177-1. Grades 1–3. In 1955 Rosa Parks (1913–2005) confronted a bus driver, refusing to move to the back of the bus. Twelve years before, she would not reenter a bus in the back after paying at the front door—and the bus driver was the same one. Her silent clash is considered by many the beginning of the civil rights movement. Parks is often called the "Mother of the Civil Rights Movement" and she continued to fight discrimination for many years. Illustrations, including one of the Ku Klux Klan, enhance the text. Author's Notes.

2937. Adler, David A. *A Picture Book of Thurgood Marshall.* Illustrated by Robert Casilla. Holiday House, 1997. Unpaged. ISBN 978-0-8234-1308-9; 1999, paper ISBN 978-0-8234-1506-9. Grades 1–3. Thurgood Marshall (1908–1993) became a justice of the Supreme Court after helping to establish the civil rights movement. This volume introduces his life and his accomplishments. Important Dates.

2938. Aldrin, Buzz. *Reaching for the Moon.* Illustrated by Wendell Minor. HarperCollins, 2005. 40pp. ISBN 978-0-06-055445-3; 2008, paper ISBN 978-0-06-055447-7. Grades K–5. Buzz Aldrin was the second man to step on the moon. As a boy, he loved to collect rocks, an interest that he thinks helped him choose specific rocks from the face of the moon. After he attended college at West Point, he took flight training and was admitted into the space program. Aldrin also mentions that his father took him in an airplane painted like an eagle when he was 2 and that his mother's maiden name was "Moon." Photographs highlight the text. Chronology. *Children's, Junior and Young Adult Book Award* (South Carolina) nomination, *Young Readers Choice Award* (Louisiana) nomination, and *Publishers Weekly Best Children's Books.*

2939. Alphin, Elaine Marie. *Dwight D. Eisenhower.* See entry 2336.

2940. Appel, Martin. *Joe DiMaggio.* See entry 2338.

2941. Appelt, Kathi. *Miss Lady Bird's Wildflowers: How a First Lady Changed America.* Illustrated by Joy Fisher Hein. HarperCollins, 2005. 40pp. ISBN 978-0-06-001107-9. Grades K–3. Lady Bird Johnson (1912–2007), the wife of President Lyndon Johnson, fell in love with the beauty of flowers when she was growing up in Piney Woods, Texas. As First Lady, she worked to add beauty and she had flowers planted, some in formal gardens and others in wildflower plantings under the Highway Beautification Act. Illustrations enhance the text. Bibliography, Notes, and Web Sites.

2942. Apte, Sunita. *César Chavez: We Can Do It!* Bearport, 2005. 32pp. ISBN 978-1-59716-073-5. Grades 3–4. This brief biography of César Chavez (1927–1993) covers his childhood in Arizona and move to California during the Great Depression. During this time he saw enough discrimination against workers that he eventually organized the National Farm Workers Association in 1962. Photographs enhance the text.

2943. Aronson, Billy. *Richard M. Nixon.* (Presidents and Their Times) Benchmark, 2007. 96pp. ISBN 978-0-7614-2428-4. Grades 4–7. Richard M. Nixon (1913–1994), the thirty-seventh president, was the only president to resign from office. His strict father and Quaker mother had a strong influence on him. He served in Congress before being elected vice president. John F. Kennedy defeated him when he first ran for president, but he later succeeded in 1968. Nixon was ruthless with his enemies—as his involvement in the Watergate scandal illustrates—but he also invested more money in social programs than most other presidents. The text offers an overview of his life. Photographs highlight the text. Bibliography, Glossary, Chronology, Further Reading, Web Sites, and Index.

2944. Ashby, Ruth. *Rosa Parks: Freedom Rider.* Sterling, 2008. 128pp. ISBN 978-1-4027-5804-1; paper ISBN 978-1-4027-4865-3. Grades 5–8. The name Rosa Parks (1913–2005) is synonymous with civil rights. Her decision to take a seat on a Montgomery, Alabama, bus started a boycott that damaged the local bus company financially. Others, heartened by her action, also became willing to stand up for what they believed. Photographs, documents, and illustrations augment the text. Bibliography, Glossary, Chronology, and Index.

2945. Bass, Hester. *The Secret World of Walter Anderson.* See entry 2343.

2946. Bausum, Ann. *Freedom Riders: John Lewis and Jim Zwerg on the Front Lines of the Civil Rights Movement.* National Geographic, 2006. 79pp. ISBN 978-0-7922-4173-7. Grades 5–9. Bausum tells the stories of two young civil rights workers of the 1960s. Jim Zwerg, a white Wisconsin native, became involved while on an exchange visit to Nashville. John Lewis was a black seminarian and student leader of the nonviolence movement. They ended up in jail together. The chapters compare and contrast their families, childhoods, teenage years, and their involvement in the events leading to the rides. Zwerg felt he got more attention because he was white. With forewords by each man. Photographs highlight the text. Bibliography, Chronology, Notes, Further Reading, and Index. *Booklist Editor's Choice, Robert F. Sibert Honor Book, Bulletin Blue Ribbon,* and *Capitol Choices Noteworthy Titles* (Washington, D.C.).

2947. Berry, S. L. *Langston Hughes.* See entry 2345.

2948. Bertrand, Diane Gonzales, and Anthony Accardo. *Ricardo's Race / La Carrera de Ricardo.* Pinata, 2007. 32pp. ISBN 978-1-55885-481-9. Grades 2–4. When he was young Ricardo Romo helped in his father's family business, a small grocery store, in San Antonio. He enjoyed running, became a member of the track team, and won an athletic scholarship to the University of Texas, even though a counselor recommended that he attend a technical school. He went on to earn a Ph.D. in history at UCLA before returning to his hometown to become the president of the University of Texas at San Antonio. Illustrations reinforce the text.

2949. Biebuyck, Valerie. *Electra to the Rescue: Saving a Steamship and the Story of Shelburne Museum.* David R. Godine, 2008. 47pp. ISBN 978-1-56792-308-7. Grades 2–5. Wealthy Electra Havemeyer Webb (1888–1960) started collecting American folk art when she was 19 years old. She liked toys, wooden Indians, glass pieces, tools, a lighthouse, and the steamship *Ticonderoga*. She created the Shelburne (Vermont) Museum and displayed her collection there in rooms recreated from the past. She also decided to dock the steamship outside the museum. Photographs enliven the text. Glossary and Further Resources.

2950. Billus, Kathleen. *Judy Johnson.* (Baseball Hall of Famers of the Negro League) Rosen, 2001. 112pp. ISBN 978-0-8239-3476-8. Grades 4–7. Judy Johnson (1900–1989) broke into the Negro Leagues as a third baseman before professional baseball integrated in 1947. He had to deal with prejudice and the difficulties shared by all African American players at that time. He became an outstanding coach, manager, and scout. Today he is part of the Baseball Hall of Fame. Photographs and illustrations augment the text. Glossary, Chronology, Further Reading, Web Sites, and Index.

2951. Blue, Rose, and Corinne J. Naden. *Barbara Jordan.* Chelsea House, 1992. 110pp. ISBN 978-0-7910-1131-7. Grades 5 up. Barbara Jordan (1936–1996), born in one of the poorest black neighborhoods in Texas, became the South's first black U.S. congresswoman. She established a law firm in Houston before she started campaigning for state office. In Congress she helped investigate Watergate, and in 1976 she gave the keynote address at the Democratic National Convention. She retired to become a professor and to cope with a neurological disease that confined her to a wheelchair, but she continued to show her intelligence and compassion. Photographs enhance the text. Chronology, Further Reading, and Index.

2952. Bohannon, Lisa Frederiksen. *Woman's Work: The Story of Betty Friedan.* Morgan Reynolds, 2004. 144pp. ISBN 978-1-931798-41-9. Grades 5–10. Betty Friedan (1921–2006) wrote the book that helped jump-start the women's revolution—*The Feminine Mystique.* An intelligent Jewish woman who dropped out of graduate school to marry and raise a family, Friedan was dissatisfied with her life and wondered what other women were thinking. She sent a survey to her classmates at Vassar and discovered that many felt the same way. She then wrote her book and founded the National Organization for Women. Photographs highlight the text. Bibliography, Chronology, Notes, Web Sites, and Index.

2953. Bolden, Tonya. *M.L.K.: The Journey of a King.* Abrams, 2007. 128pp. ISBN 978-0-8109-5476-2. Grades 4–8. This photo-filled biography of Martin Luther King, Jr. (1929–1968) examines his life in three chapters introduced with quotes: "How Could I Love a Race of People Who Hated Me?," "I Hope Thousands Will Join Me," and "I've Got to March." The text focuses on King's dream of equality for all and his adoption of Gandhi's policy of nonviolence. Photographs intensify the text. Notes and Further Reading. *Voice of Youth Advocates Nonfiction Honor List.*

2954. Borden, Louise. *The Journey that Saved Curious George: The True Wartime Escape of Margret and H. A. Rey.* Illustrated by Allan Drummond. Houghton, 2005. 80pp. ISBN 978-0-618-33924-2. Grades 3–7. This biography of Margret and H. A. Rey, creators of *Curious George,* presents their lives in two parts. The first covers their childhoods in Germany. Then they married and lived in Rio de Janeiro, Brazil, and Paris, France. In 1940, as German Jews, they were almost unable to escape from France, but a complicated route finally got them to Rio. They went from there to New York. With them they had several illustrated manuscripts, and after they reached New York they published their first book featuring Curious George. Photographs highlight the text. Bibliography. *William Allen White Children's Book Award* (Kansas) nomination, *Student Book Award* (Maine) nomination, and *Children's Book Award* (North Carolina) nomination.

2955. Braun, Eric. *Wilma Rudolph.* Pebble, 2005. 24pp. ISBN 978-0-7368-4234-1. Grades K–2. This biography of Wilma Rudolph (1940–1994) offers an overview of her life and her achievement as the first African American woman to win three gold medals at the Olympics. It also covers her bout with polio at a young age and her efforts to overcome her disability. Photographs highlight the text. Glossary, Further Reading, Web Sites, and Index.

2956. Bridges, Ruby, and Margo Lundell. *Through My Eyes.* Scholastic, 1999. 63pp. ISBN 978-0-590-18923-1. Grades 5–8. At the age of 6, Ruby Bridges was one of the first African American children to attend an all-white school in 1960. The text contains commentary from Bridges as an adult, news reports, and her personal memories. Her mother and United States marshals escorted her to the school, and she met her supportive white teacher alone in the classroom. She thought the shouting and barricades meant it was Mardi Gras. When a little white boy refuses to play with her because she is a "nigger," she realizes that everything that happened could be blamed on the color of her skin. Photographs highlight the text. *Rebecca Caudill Award* (Illinois) nomination, *Young Hoosier Award* (Indiana) nomination, *Mark Twain Award* (Missouri) nomination, *Golden Sower Award* (Nebraska) nomination, *Young Readers Choice Book Award* (Pennsylvania) nomination, *Children's Book Award* (Rhode Island), *SCASL Book Award* (South Carolina) nomination, *Bluebonnet Award* (Texas) nomination, *Dorothy Canfield Fisher Children's Book Award* (Vermont) nomination, *Capitol Choices Noteworthy Titles* (Washington, D.C.), *School Library Journal Best Books for Children, Bulletin Blue Ribbon,* and *Sasquatch Book Awards* (Washington).

2957. Brown, Jonatha. *César Chávez.* (Trailblazers of the Modern World) World Almanac, 2004. 48pp. ISBN 978-0-8368-5097-0. Grades 5 up. Mexican American César Chávez (1927–1993) became a labor leader and founded the United Farm Workers of America union to foster better wages and working conditions for migrants and other farm workers. As a young boy in Yuma, Arizona, Chavez disliked school because he attended more than thirty of them. He left school after eighth grade to become a farm worker because his father had been wounded and did not want Chavez's mother to work in the fields. He served in the Navy during World War II then returned to the United States and married. He started working as a union organizer for the Community Services Organization, a Latino civil rights group. He tried to get Mexican Americans to register and vote, and he became the national director of the organization in the late 1950s. Then he cofounded the National Farm Workers Association with Dolores Huerta, later to become the UFW. Photographs, Chronology, Further Reading, Glossary, Web Sites, and Index.

2958. Bryant, Jen. *Georgia's Bones.* See entry 2352.

2959. Christensen, Bonnie. *Woody Guthrie: Poet of the People.* Knopf, 2001. 32pp. ISBN 978-0-375-81113-5. Grades 3–5. Woody Guthrie (1912–1967) faced many difficulties in his childhood—his sister died, his father lost his job, and his mother had a nervous disorder. Woody, however, loved music, and as a teenager he traveled around and listened to what people were doing and singing. He believed people needed labor unions and to work together for change. He wrote more than one thousand songs based on his experiences and beliefs. Like his mother, he, too, died of Huntington's disease. Illustrations augment the text. Chronology. *Horn Book Fanfare, Boston Globe/Horn Book Award Honor,* and *Capitol Choices Noteworthy Titles* (Washington, D.C.).

2960. Cline-Ransome, Lesa. *Satchel Paige.* See entry 2355.

2961. Cohen, Charles D. *The Seuss, the Whole Seuss and Nothing but the Seuss: A Visual Biography of Theodor Seuss Geisel.* Random, 2004. 400pp. ISBN 978-0-375-82248-3. Grades 3 up. Theodore Geisel (1904–1991) created many favorites for children. This biography focuses on his illustrations in posters, books, and newspapers. Many illustrations of his work enhance the text. Bibliography, Notes, and Index. *Publishers Weekly Best Children's Books.*

2962. Cole, Michael D. *John Glenn: Astronaut and Senator.* Enslow, 2000. 104pp. ISBN 978-0-7660-1532-6. Grades 5–8. In February 1962 John Glenn (b. 1921) rocketed into space to become the first American to orbit Earth in a space capsule. The text chronicles Glenn's family background, influences on his life, and his military career as a pilot and astronaut. He eventually became a U.S. senator from Ohio. Notes, Glossary, Further Reading, and Index.

2963. Coles, Robert. *The Story of Ruby Bridges.* Illustrated by George Ford. Scholastic, 2004. Unpaged. Paper ISBN 978-0-439-59844-6. Grades 1–3. Ruby Bridges, born in 1953, was selected to be the first black child in her elementary school in 1960. For almost a year, she had to be protected from angry crowds of white people as she walked to school. One day her teacher, watching from the window, saw her stop and talk to the group. When she entered the empty classroom, she told her teacher that she had not stopped to talk, but to pray, as she did every day. *Notable Children's Trade Books in the Field of Social Studies* and *Children's, Junior, and Young Adult Book Award* (South Carolina) winner.

2964. Collard, Sneed B., III. *Rosa Parks: The Courage to Make a Difference.* (American Heroes) Benchmark, 2006. 40pp. ISBN 978-0-7614-2163-4. Grades 3–5. This biography of African American Rosa Parks (1913–2005) focuses on her humanity as well as her refusal to give up her seat on a Montgomery, Alabama, bus in 1955. Anecdotes and clear descriptions give additional insight. Reproductions and museum images accompany the text. Glossary, Further Reading, and Index.

2965. Collins, David. *To the Point: A Story About E. B. White.* See entry 2356.

2966. Collins, David R. *Farmworker's Friend: The Story of Cesar Chavez.* Carolrhoda, 1996. 80pp. ISBN 978-0-8761-4982-9; First Avenue paper ISBN 978-1-57505-031-7. Grades 4–7. Cesar Chavez (1927–1993) was himself part of a migrant worker family. Distressed by the pay and working conditions of these migrants, he became an activist seeking to make life better for others. He helped to build a union for farm workers and continued to fight for their rights throughout his life. Important Dates.

2967. Cooney, Barbara. *Eleanor.* See entry 1944.

2968. Crews, Donald. *Bigmama's.* Greenwillow, 1991. 32pp. ISBN 978-0-688-09950-3; Mulberry, 1998, paper ISBN 978-0-688-15842-2. Grades K–3. A memoir celebrating summers spent with the author's grandmother, Bigmama. Crews describes the train trip south and key aspects of his summer environment—the stars at night, the outhouse, the kerosene lamps, and the well, which he contrasts to the city skyline of his adult life. *American Library Association Notable Children's Books.*

2969. Cunningham, Kevin. *J. Edgar Hoover: Controversial FBI Director.* (Signature Lives) Compass Point, 2005. 112pp. ISBN 978-0-7565-0997-2. Grades 5–8. J. Edgar (John Edgar) Hoover (1895–1972) was director of the Federal Bureau of Investigation for a number of years. This profile covers his childhood and his career, offering little information about his adult personal life. Hoover manipulated public opinion, illegally investigated citizens, and kept confidential files on them. He zealously pursued war protesters and civil rights supporters. Photographs and illustrations augment the text. Bibliography, Further Reading, Web Sites, and Index.

2970. Darby, Jean. *Dwight D. Eisenhower: A Man Called Ike.* See entry 2361.

2971. Darby, Jean. *Martin Luther King, Jr.* Lerner, 2005. 144pp. ISBN 978-0-8225-2471-7. Grades 5–9. This fictional biography is almost a history of the civil rights movement. It covers Martin Luther King, Jr.'s life from his birth in 1929 until his assassination in 1968. Using examples to emphasize the situation, Darby shows segregation in the South, how Gandhi influenced King, Rosa Parks's confrontation in Montgomery, the bus boycott, the Woolworth's lunch counter sit-in in 1960, James Meredith's enrollment in the University of Mississippi, and the "I Have a Dream" speech at the 1963 March on Washington. Darby also recounts the events in Memphis leading up to the moment when James Earl Ray shot King. Glossary, Further Reading, Index.

2972. Dean, Tanya. *Theodor Geisel.* Chelsea House, 2002. 112pp. ISBN 978-0-7910-6724-6. Grades 4–7. Theodor Geisel, the real name of author Dr. Seuss, became famous for his children's books. His first career was in advertising. Twenty-seven publishers rejected his first book. The times in which he lived, including World War II, greatly affected his work. Color photographs enhance the text. Bibliography and Index.

2973. Deitch, Kenneth M., and JoAnne B. Weisman. *Dwight D. Eisenhower: Man of Many Hats.* See entry 2362.

2974. Delano, Marfe Ferguson. *Genius: A Photobiography of Albert Einstein.* National Geographic, 2005. 64pp. ISBN 978-0-7922-9544-0; 2008, paper ISBN 978-1-426-30294-7. Grades 5–9. This biography of Albert Einstein (1879–1955) recounts his life from a childhood of privilege in Austria to his role in World War II as the originator of the theory of relativity necessary to create the atomic bomb. Einstein was a pacifist. He also believed in justice and personal freedom, causing him to speak out against both Hitler and Joseph McCarthy. This volume summarizes some of his scientific theories. Illustrations augment the text. Bibliography, Chronology, Notes, Web Sites, and Index. *Capitol Choices Noteworthy Titles* (Washington, D.C.).

2975. Denenberg, Barry. *All Shook Up: The Life and Death of Elvis Presley.* Scholastic, 2003. 288pp. Paper ISBN 978-0-439-52811-5. Grades 5–9. Elvis Presley (1935–1977) burst into the public eye in 1958. This profile looks at his hard and penurious life in two parts, the first covering the years until 1958 and the second from 1959 until his death. His manager, Colonel Tom Parker, was not a good influence and Presley seemed to be flirting with disaster throughout his years of fame. Photographs highlight the text. Bibliography, Videography, Chronology, Discography, Filmography, and Index.

2976. De Ruiz, Dana Catharine, and Richard Larios. *La Causa: The Migrant Farmworkers' Story.* Illustrated by Rudy Gutierrez. Steck-Vaughn, 1992. 92pp. Paper ISBN 978-0-8114-8071-0. Grades 5–9. As a young boy in 1940, Cesar Chavez (1927–1993) watched his father, who had left his home to find work, faithfully fulfill a contract but remain unpaid. Dolores Huerta watched workers, desperate to help their families survive, struggle to pay their rent. The two met and began fighting against the inequity between workers and owners in the fields of California. Their efforts, including a nonviolent strike, finally led to the formation of the United Farm Workers in 1966. This was only the beginning of their work to preserve dignity and hope. Epilogue, Afterword, and Notes.

2977. Donovan, Sandra. *Fannie Lou Hamer.* (African-American Biographies) Raintree, 2003. 64pp. ISBN 978-0-7398-7030-3; paper ISBN 978-1-4109-0316-7. Grades 4–6. Fannie Lou Hamer (1917–1977) was the last of twenty children born in her sharecropper father's family in Mississippi. She failed in an attempt to vote when she was 45 years old and she began her career as a civil rights activist. Her work helped achieve this important goal. Illustrations augment the text. Glossary, Chronology, Further Reading, and Index.

2978. Donovan, Sandra. *Mary McLeod Bethune.* See entry 2366.

2979. Donovan, Sandra. *Rosa Parks.* (African-American Biographies) Raintree, 2003. 64pp. ISBN 978-0-7398-7032-7; paper ISBN 978-1-4109-0320-4. Grades 4–6. Rosa Parks (1913–2005) rode home on the bus on December 1, 1955, in Montgomery, Alabama. Although Jim Crow laws demanded that she give her seat to a white person, she refused and her action started a bus boycott. She has been called the "Mother of the Modern-Day Civil Rights Movement." Illustrations augment the text. Bibliography, Further Reading, Glossary, Maps, Timeline, Web Sites, and Index.

2980. Dubowski, Cathy East. *Rosa Parks: Don't Give In.* Bearport, 2005. 32pp. ISBN 978-1-59716-078-0. Grades 2–4. The refusal by Rosa Parks (1913–2005) to give up her seat to a white woman on a crowded Montgomery, Alabama, bus in 1955 helped start the civil rights movement with the ensuing Montgomery bus boycott. Photographs and reproductions illuminate the text. Bibliography, Glossary, Chronology, Further Reading, Web Sites, and Index.

2981. Dunlap, Julie. *Birds in the Bushes: A Story About Margaret Morse Nice.* See entry 2370.

2982. Ehrlich, Amy. *Rachel: The Story of Rachel Carson.* Illustrated by Wendell Minor. Silver Whistle, 2003. 32pp. ISBN 978-0-15-216227-6; Voyager, 2008, paper ISBN 978-0-15-206324-5. Grades K–3. Rachel Carson (1907–1964) grew to love nature through spending time with her biologist mother. She also loved to write and at college she discovered that she could write about the environment. Her research persuaded her that humans were poisoning the earth with pesticides, and she began the environmental movement with her controversial book *Silent Spring.* Illustrations complement the text. Bibliography.

2983. El Nabli, Dina. *Eleanor Roosevelt: First Lady of the World.* See entry 1958.

2984. Englar, Mary. *Le Ly Hayslip.* (Asian-American Biographies) Raintree, 2005. 64pp. ISBN 978-1-4109-1055-4. Grades 5–8. Le Ly Hayslip, born in Vietnam in 1949, founded the Mother's Love Clinic there and then immigrated to America in 1970. This volume recounts her childhood and her struggles to raise her children. Her father believed that she should protect the land of her ancestors so she started the East Meets West Foundation to encourage healing between American and Vietnamese after the Vietnam War. Photographs highlight the text. Glossary, Further Reading, and Index.

2985. Farris, Christine King. *March On! The Day My Brother Martin Changed the World.* Scholastic, 2008. Unpaged. ISBN 978-0-545-03537-8. Grades 1–4. Martin Luther King Jr.'s sister Christine describes the civil rights work that culminated at the foot of the Lincoln Memorial on August 28, 1963, when King gave his "I Have a Dream" speech. She watched the event at home on television, but she had seen him working on his speech and knew that he stayed up late the night before to polish it. Many leaders joined King and supported his nonviolent approach to civil rights. Illustrations complement the text.

2986. Feinberg, Barbara Silberdick. *Eleanor Roosevelt: A Very Special First Lady.* See entry 1960.

2987. Fiorelli, June Estep. *Fannie Lou Hamer: A Voice for Freedom.* Avisson, 2005. 117pp. Paper ISBN 978-1-888105-62-9. Grades 5 up. At the age of 44 in 1962 Fannie Lou Hamer was denied the right to register and vote. She became a civil rights activist at that time. The twentieth child of Mississippi sharecroppers, she and her family were beaten and suffered many indignities, and when she was denied her rights, she protested. Photographs accompany the text. Bibliography, Notes, and Index.

2988. Fleming, Alice. *Martin Luther King, Jr.: A Dream of Hope.* (Sterling Biographies) Sterling, 2008. 128pp. ISBN 978-1-4027-5803-4; paper ISBN 978-1-4027-4439-6. Grades 5–8. This biography of Martin Luther King, Jr. (1929–1968) offers background on King's accomplishments during the civil rights movement. Also included are profiles of key contemporaries. Photographs, documents, and illustrations augment the text. Bibliography, Glossary, Chronology, and Index.

2989. Fleming, Candace. *Our Eleanor: A Scrapbook Look at Eleanor Roosevelt's Remarkable Life.* See entry 2376.

2990. Fletcher, Ralph. *Marshfield Dreams: When I Was a Kid.* Henry Holt, 2005. 192pp. ISBN 978-0-8050-7246-2. Grades 5–8. Ralph Fletcher remembers growing up in the 1950s and 1960s in Marshfield, Vermont. He had friends, liked his siblings (all eight of them), and enjoyed playing wandering through the woods. His mother compared mushrooms with strangers—some were trustworthy while others could hurt. He adds that his great-grandmother would bury the kids' old teeth in the garden.

2991. Ford, Carin T. *Jackie Robinson: Hero of Baseball.* (Heroes of American History) Enslow, 2006. 32pp. ISBN 978-0-7660-2600-1. Grades 2–4. Jackie Robinson (1919–1972) became the first African American player in the major baseball leagues when he debuted with the Brooklyn Dodgers. He earlier served in the army. He played on six World Series teams, and the Baseball Hall of Fame inducted him in 1962. He also participated in the civil rights movement and wrote a syndicated newspaper column for several years. Photographs augment the text. Bibliography, Glossary, Chronology, and Index.

2992. Frampton, David. *Mr. Ferlinghetti's Poem.* Eerdmans, 2006. 32pp. ISBN 978-0-8028-5290-8. Grades K–3. In his poem "Fortune," Lawrence Ferlinghetti recalls the pleasure of a hot summer day in Brooklyn when the firemen turn their hoses on the children. Illustrations enhance the text.

2993. Freedman, Russell. *Eleanor Roosevelt: A Life of Discovery.* See entry 1967.

2994. Gentry, Tony, and Heather Lehr Wagner. *Jesse Owens: Champion Athlete.* See entry 2384.

2995. George-Warren, Holly. *Shake, Rattle and Roll: The Founders of Rock and Roll.* Illustrated by Laura Levine. Houghton, 2001. 32pp. ISBN 978-0-618-05540-1; 2004, paper ISBN 978-0-618-43229-5. Grades 4–8. This collective biography looks at the contributions of fourteen musicians who helped create rock and roll, changing popular music. It includes details about their childhoods, their careers, their greatest hits, and any personal traits that made them distinctive. Included are LaVern Baker, Wanda Jackson, Bo Diddley, Jerry Lee Lewis, Little Richard, Elvis Presley, Carl Perkins, Fats Domino, Chuck Berry, the Everly Brothers, Buddy Holly, Ritchie Valens, and James Brown.

2996. Gerstein, Mordicai. *The Man Who Walked Between the Towers.* Roaring Brook, 2003. 40pp. ISBN 978-0-7613-1791-3; Square Fish, 2007, paper ISBN 978-0-312-36878-4. Grades K–4. In 1974 French aerialist Philippe Petit walked across a tightrope set up between the two towers of the World Trade Center in New York City. To entertain further, he also danced and performed tricks while on the rope. To secure the rope between the towers, he and companions dressed as construction workers and went to the top of the towers. His partner shot a line with a bow and arrow from the top of the opposite tower, and Petit secured it. The next day, he walked the 140 feet between the towers. He was arrested afterward, and his sentence was to perform for children in a nearby park. Illustrations enhance the text. *Boston Globe/Horn Book Award Honor, School Library Journal Best Books for Children, Publishers Weekly Best Children's Books, Caldecott Medal, Bulletin Blue Ribbon,* and *Horn Book Fanfare.*

2997. Gerstein, Mordicai. *What Charlie Heard.* See entry 1976.

2998. Gherman, Beverly. *Norman Rockwell: Storyteller with a Brush.* See entry 2386.

2999. Gillis, Jennifer Blizin. *Dolores Huerta.* (American Lives) Raintree, 2005. 32pp. ISBN 978-1-4034-6980-9. Grades 3–6. Dolores Huerta (1930–) has spent much of her life fighting for the rights of poverty-stricken farm workers. Gillis presents Huerta's life and character. Born in New Mexico, she spent most of her life in California, where her mother ran a hotel. Although she first became a teacher, she remembered farm workers she had met and decided she needed to work to improve their living and working conditions. She helped to create the National Farm Workers Association (NFWA). Photographs and illustrations augment the text. Glossary, Chronology, Further Reading, and Index.

3000. Giovanni, Nikki. *Rosa.* Illustrated by Bryan Collier. Henry Holt, 2005. Unpaged. ISBN 978-0-8050-7106-1; Square Fish, 2007, paper ISBN 978-0-312-37602-4. Grades 3–5. In 1955 Rosa Parks (1913–2005) refused to give her seat to a white woman on a Montgomery, Alabama, bus. After years of eating at separate lunch counters and attending separate schools, Parks was tired. Her friend Jo Ann Robinson, president of the Women's Political Council, was pleased with Parks' decision and the group made posters asking people to boycott the buses. They did, and the bus system suffered terribly. Martin Luther King Jr. came to speak on behalf of the action. Watercolor and collage illustrations complement the text. *Caldecott Medal Honor, Coretta Scott King Award, Parents Choice Award, SIBA Book Award, Children's, Junior and Young Adult Book Award* (South Carolina) nomination, *Keystone to Reading Book Award* nomination, *Capitol Choices Noteworthy Titles* (Washington, D.C.), *Black-Eyed Susan Award* (Maryland) nomination, and *Diamonds Award* (Delaware) nomination.

3001. Goble, Paul. *Hau Kola: Hello Friend.* Illustrated by Gerry Perrin. (Meet the Author) Richard C. Owen, 1994. 32pp. ISBN 978-1-8784-5044-9. Grades 2–5. As a child in England, Goble liked the outdoors. During World War II he collected bullet shells and pieces of German bombs that fell close to his house. Because he loved everything to do with Indians, he moved to the United States and has been making paintings about Indian legends and history throughout his adult life. He uses the Lakota words "Hau Kola," meaning "Hello, Friend," as the title of his book.

3002. Golenbock, Peter. *Hank Aaron: Brave in Every Way.* Illustrated by Paul Lee. Gulliver, 2001. Unpaged. ISBN 978-0-15-202093-4; Voyager, 2005, paper ISBN 978-0-15-205250-8. Grades 2–4. This biography of Hank Aaron (1934–) emphasizes his quest to break Babe Ruth's home run record. When Aaron was 13, Jackie Robinson integrated the Major Leagues. Then when Aaron was 16, someone saw him play baseball and recruited him for the team. Aaron's mother wanted him to attend college, but his father encouraged his baseball, and Aaron decided to join the Milwaukee Braves in 1954. As he got closer to Ruth's record of 714 homers, people started writing hate letters to Aaron. When this was publicized, others wrote letters of support. In 1974 he broke the record by hitting number 715. Acrylic drawings enhance the text. *Emphasis on Reading Children's Choice* (Alabama) and *Capitol Choices Noteworthy Titles* (Washington, D.C.).

3003. Golenbock, Peter. *Teammates.* Illustrated by Paul Bacon. Gulliver, 1990. Unpaged. ISBN 978-0-15-200603-7; Voyager, 1992, paper ISBN 978-0-15-284286-4. Grades K–6. Branch Rickey of the Brooklyn Dodgers decided to hire the best player for his team, regardless of color, at a time when baseball teams were segregated. He chose Jackie Robinson after Robinson promised to try not to fight back when taunted by racist fans. One person who stood by Robinson was his teammate Pee Wee Reese. *Children's Choice Picture Book Award* (Virginia), *Sequoyah Children's Awards* (Oklahoma), *Young Readers Choice* (Pennsylvania), *Volunteer State Book Awards* (Tennessee), and *Children's Choice Picture Book Awards* (Washington).

3004. Green, Michelle Y. *A Strong Right Arm: The Story of Mamie "Peanut" Johnson.* Dial, 2002. 111pp. ISBN 978-0-8037-2661-1; Puffin, 2004, paper ISBN 978-0-14-240072-2. Grades 4–7. Mamie "Peanut" Johnson wanted to be a professional baseball player. She threw a hard curveball and, after being refused by the all-white and all-male Police Athletic League, she became one of only three women ever to play in the professional Negro Leagues. She pitched for the Indianapolis Clowns from 1953 to 1955, dealing not only with racism but also with sexism. She fulfilled her desire after Jackie Robinson broke the color barrier in the major leagues. Photographs highlight the text. Bibliography, Notes, Further Reading, and Web Sites. *Children's Choice Book Award* (Iowa) nomination, *Rebecca Caudill Young Readers Book Award* (Illinois) nomination, *Young Hoosier Book Award* (Indiana) nomination, *Bluegrass Book Award* (Kentucky) nomination, *Children's Book Award* (Massachusetts) nomination, *Great Stone Face Book Award* (New Hampshire) nomination, *Children's Book Award* (Rhode Island) nomination, *Volunteer State Book Award* (Tennessee) nomination, *Bluebonnet Book Award* (Texas) nomination, *State Reading Association for Young Readers Program* (Virginia) nomination, *Capitol Choices Noteworthy Titles* (Washington, D.C.), and *Dorothy Canfield Fisher Children's Book Award* (Vermont) nomination.

3005. Greenberg, Jan, and Sandra Jordan. *Action Jackson.* Illustrated by Robert Andrew Parker. Roaring Brook, 2002. 32pp. ISBN 978-0-7613-1682-4; Square Fish, 2007, paper ISBN 978-0-312-36751-0. Grades 1–5. For two months in 1950 Jackson Pollock worked on a painting, "Lavender Mist," that he later called "Number 1, 1950." This volume follows Jackson's daily routine, names his pets, and reveals that music, nature, and other artists influenced his work. He was nicknamed "Action Jackson" for his kinetic style of swooping and leaping while he trailed paint across a canvas lying on the floor. Although Jackson drank and became depressed, he worked well otherwise. His controversial splattered abstract paintings were unique and innovative for his time, and today they hang in art galleries around the world. Included is a photograph of the finished work. Biography, Bibliography, Notes, and Sources. *Publishers Weekly Best Children's Books, School Library Journal Best Books of the Year, Robert F. Sibert Honor Book, American Library Association Notable Books for Children, New York Times Notable Books of the Year, Booklist Editor's Choice, Red Clover Award* (Vermont) nomination, *Bulletin Blue Ribbon*, and *Capitol Choices Noteworthy Titles* (Washington, D.C.).

3006. Greenfield, Eloise. *Rosa Parks.* Illustrated by Eric Marlow. Trophy, 1995. 34pp. Paper ISBN 978-0-06-442025-9. Grades 1–5. Aware of injustice almost since her birth in 1913, but never actively planning to counter it, Rosa Parks (d. 2005), tired after a long day's work bending over a sewing machine, refused to move from her seat in the black section of a Montgomery, Alabama, bus for a white man. She had paid the same fare as he. Her action got her arrested and fired from her job, but it began the bus boycott, led by Dr. Martin Luther King, that lasted long enough for the Supreme Court to rule that the bus company was unconstitutional in its actions. She has been called "Mother of the Civil Rights Movement." *Notable Children's Trade Books in the Field of Social Studies* and *Carter G. Woodson Award*.

3007. Guzmán, Lila, and Rick Guzmán. *César Chávez: Fighting for Fairness.* (Famous Latinos) Enslow, 2006. 32pp. ISBN 978-0-7660-2370-3. Grades 3–4. César Chávez (1927–1993), son of migrant workers, wanted to help those around him who suffered the same discrimination and mistreatment as his own family. He campaigned for a nonviolent solution to labor problems and established the United Farm Workers union. Photographs augment the text. Glossary, Chronology, Further Reading, Web Sites, and Index.

3008. Halasa, Malu. *Elijah Muhammad: Religious Leader.* See entry 2389.

3009. Hamilton, Sue L. *The Killing of a Candidate: Robert F. Kennedy.* (Days of Tragedy) ABDO, 1989. 32pp. ISBN 978-0-939179-57-2. Grades 4–6. In 1968 Robert F. Kennedy (b. 1925) was assassinated after winning the California primary for the Democratic presidential nomination. This volume looks at his life and his close relationship with his older brother John. It also reviews the life of Sirhan Sirhan, the man who killed him. Photographs and Sources.

3010. Hampton, Wilborn. *Elvis Presley: Up Close.* (Up Close) Viking, 2007. 208pp. ISBN 978-0-670-06166-2. Grades 5–9. This biography of Elvis Presley (1935–1977) covers his life from the time he was a poor boy living in a Tupelo, Mississippi, neighborhood called Shake Rag. He was given a guitar as a gift, and this instrument and his exposure to gospel music helped him develop his personal style of rock-'n'-roll. He was a library assistant, appeared on the Grand Ole Opry, and had a great a success on television on the Ed Sullivan show. The biography also touches on his drug use, the personal problems he faced, and his early death. Photographs augment the text. Bibliography, Notes, and Index.

3011. Haskins, James. *Delivering Justice: W. W. Law and the Fight for Civil Rights.* Illustrated by Benny Andrews. Candlewick, 2005. 32pp. ISBN 978-0-7636-2592-4. Grades 2–4. A biography of Westley Wallace Law (1923–2002), who advocated nonviolence in his struggle to gain equal rights for African Americans. As a young mailman he tried to unite blacks and whites along his Savannah, Georgia, route. As a college graduate, he began helping blacks pass the test to vote. The Savannah school system would not hire him because he was a member of the NAACP. It was probably due to his efforts that Savannah declared all of its citizens equal three years before the federal Civil Rights Act was passed. Oil and collage illustrations augment the text. *Jane Addams Award* and *Book Awards* (Connecticut) nomination.

3012. Haskins, James, and Kathleen Benson. *John Lewis in the Lead: A Story of the Civil Rights Movement.* Lee & Low, 2006. 40pp. ISBN 978-1-58430-250-6. Grades 3–5. After growing up in the segregated South, John Lewis (b. 1940) became one of the "Big Six" civil rights leaders during the 1960s. In 1963 he was elected chairman of the Student Nonviolent Coordinating Committee. He participated in the Freedom Rides; the march from Selma to Montgomery, Alabama, in 1964; and the March on Washington, where he was the youngest speaker at the age of 23. He later became a congressman from Georgia. Chronology.

3013. Haugen, Brenda. *Henry B. Gonzalez: Congressman of the People.* (Signature Lives Modern America) Compass Point, 2005. 112pp. ISBN 978-0-7565-0996-5. Grades 5–8. Henry B. Gonzalez (1916–2000), a Texas Democratic congressman, championed the poor and those facing discrimination during his thirty-seven years in the United States House of Representatives, beginning in 1961. A child of refugees from the Mexican Revolution, he faced segregation and discrimination himself as he attended college and law school before becoming a member of the Texas Senate for five years. Illustrations augment the text. Bibliography, Glossary, Maps, and Index.

3014. Haugen, Brenda. *Langston Hughes: The Voice of Harlem.* See entry 2394.

3015. Healy, Nick. *Paul Robeson.* See entry 2395.

3016. Heiligman, Deborah. *High Hopes: A Photobiography of John F. Kennedy.* National Geographic, 2003. 64pp. ISBN 978-0-7922-6141-4. Grades 4–7. John F. Kennedy (1917–1963) became the 35th president of the United States. With many photographs, this volume tells the story of his life. He was a wealthy but sickly child who went on to study at Harvard and become a hero in World War II. When his older brother died, he became a politician. During his thousand-day presidency, he faced the Bay of Pigs invasion, the Cuban missile crisis, and other challenges. He also established the Peace Corps. In 1963 he was assassinated in Dallas, Texas. Bibliography, Further Sources, Timeline, Web Sites, and Index. *Keystone to Reading Book Award* nomination.

3017. Hilliard, Richard. *Godspeed, John Glenn.* Boyds Mills, 2006. 32pp. ISBN 978-1-5907-8384-9. Grades 1–4. This biography of John Glenn (1921–) focuses on his descent to Earth in his Project Mercury capsule *Friendship* 7 in 1962 and the scary loss of communication between the capsule and ground control. Hilliard also summarizes some of the key events in Glenn's life. Acrylic paintings enhance the text.

3018. Hodge, Marie. *John F. Kennedy: Voice of Hope.* (Sterling Biographies) Sterling, 2007. 124pp. ISBN 978-1-4027-4749-6; paper ISBN 978-1-4027-3232-4. Grades 5–8. As the thirty-fifth president of the United States, John Fitzgerald Kennedy (1917–1963) was the youngest man to hold that office. This volume briefly examines why his time in office was called "Camelot." He presided over changes in racial relations and overcame a confrontation with the Soviet Union. His assassination in 1963 caused great mourning, and those alive on that day still remember it. Photographs and illustrations augment the text. Bibliography, Chronology, Glossary.

3019. Hoose, Phillip. *Claudette Colvin: Twice Toward Justice.* Farrar, 2009. 133pp. ISBN 978-0-374-31322-7. Grades 5–9. In two parts, Hoose presents the story of Claudette Colvin (b. 1939) through many of her own words and the landmark court case in which she was one of four plaintiffs. In March 1955, nine months prior to the famous incident when Rosa Parks refused to leave her seat on a Montgomery, Alabama, bus, Colvin, 15, had refused to rise and been subsequently jailed for her inaction. Colvin, however, was unwed, pregnant, and emotional so civil rights leaders decided not to broadcast her actions. However, in 1956, she did participate in the case (*Browder* v. *Gale*) that declared Montgomery's segregated bus system unconstitutional. Also appearing in the text are important leaders including Martin Luther King, Jr. and Ralph Abernathy. Archival photographs and reproductions of period newspapers and documents complement the text. Epilogue, Notes, Bibliography, and Index. *Booklist Editors Choice, Newbery Medal* Honor Book, *National Book Awards* winner, *Bulletin Blue Ribbon, Hornbook Fanfare List, Capitol Choices Noteworthy Titles* (Washington, D.C.), *American Library Association Notable Children's Books, Robert F. Sibert Informational Book Award* Honor Book, *School Library Journal Best Books of the Year, American Library Association Best Books for Young Adults*, and *Dorothy Canfield Fisher Children's Book Award* (Vermont) nomination.

3020. Issa, Kai Jackson. *Howard Thurman's Great Hope.* Illustrated by Arthur L. Dawson. Lee & Low, 2008. Unpaged. ISBN 978-1-60060-249-8. Grades 2–5. This picture-book biography of theologian and civil rights activist Howard Thurman (1900–1981) focuses on his youth. He lived with his grandmother and sisters while his widowed mother cleaned houses, and as the school in his Florida town stopped at seventh grade, he did not expect to continue his education afterward. The principal, however, agreed to tutor him for an extra year so that he could take an entrance exam for a high school 100 miles away. He made a perfect score, attended the high school, then Morehouse College, and finally, was one of only a few African Americans to attend the Rochester Theological Seminary. Illustrations complement the text. Note.

3021. Jakoubek, Robert E., and Heather Lehr Wagner. *Martin Luther King, Jr.* (Black Americans of Achievement) Chelsea House, 2004. 143pp. ISBN 978-0-7910-8161-7; Checkmark, 2008, paper ISBN 978-1-6041-3328-8. Grades 5 up. Martin Luther King, Jr. (1929–1968) grew up in the South, where he attended Atlanta's Morehead College and then went to Crozer Seminary and Boston University for advanced theological degrees. He returned to the South in 1954 to begin his pastorate in Montgomery, Alabama, and his fight for civil rights. The text tells of his important affiliations and his philosophy of nonviolence. Photographs enhance the text. Chronology, Further Reading, and Index.

3022. Jones, Veda Boyd. *John F. Kennedy.* Children's, 2006. 31pp. ISBN 978-0-51625-038-0; paper ISBN 978-0-51629-797-2. Grades 1–2. This short biography of John F. Kennedy (1917–1963) covers his achievements. He served in the Navy during World War II, became a United States senator, and then led the country as its president. The text also includes some information about his two children, his wife, and his assassination. Photographs and illustrations complement the text. Glossary.

3023. Josephson, Judith Pinkerton. *Louis Armstrong.* See entry 2665.

3024. Kaye, Judith. *The Life of Benjamin Spock.* See entry 2666.

3025. Kehret, Peg. *Small Steps: The Year I Got Polio.* Whitman, 2006. 179pp. ISBN 978-0-8075-7459-1. Grades 4–6. In 1949 Kehret was one of the 42,000 polio cases in the United States, the only person to contract it in her small town. She tells about the diagnosis and treatment, but more importantly, the frustration and the pain. She talks about the totally unexpected onset of the disease and the immediate paralysis accompanying it. Kehret tells what it was like to give up the dreams of youth and live in an artificial environment. *Capitol Choices Noteworthy Titles* (Washington, D.C.).

3026. Keller, Emily. *Margaret Bourke-White: A Photographer's Life.* See entry 2400.

3027. Kent, Deborah. *Dorothy Day: Friend to the Forgotten.* See entry 2401.

3028. Kent, Deborah. *Hellen Keller: Author and Advocate for the Disabled.* See entry 1998.

3029. Kinsey-Warnock, Natalie. *From Dawn Till Dusk.* Illustrated by Mary Azarian. Houghton, 2006. Unpaged. Paper ISBN 978-0-618-73750-5. Grades K–3. Kinney-Warnock recalls her days as a child on a Vermont farm enjoying her siblings and the changing seasons. She describes the work, often complicated by mud, snow, and weeds, of picking up loose stones in the fields in the spring and the rewards of maple sugar and snow in the fall and winter. Woodcuts enhance the text. *Red Clover Book Award* (Vermont) nomination.

3030. Kittredge, Mary. *Barbara McClintock.* See entry 2404.

3031. Kliment, Bud. *Count Basie.* See entry 2405.

3032. Koestler-Grack, Rachel A. *The Story of Helen Keller.* (Breakthrough Biographies) Facts on File, 2003. 32pp. ISBN 978-0-7910-7315-5. Grades 2–4. Helen Keller (1880–1968) became ill in her first year of life and was left deaf and blind. Her dedicated teacher, Annie Sullivan, taught her to "see" with her hands so that eventually Keller could write and lecture. The text also provides information about sign language and Braille with further information about viewing the Braille alphabet on a Web site. Photographs augment the text. Timeline, Further Reading, Glossary, Web Sites, and Index.

3033. Kristy, Davida. *George Balanchine: American Ballet Master.* Lerner, 1996. 128pp. ISBN 978-0-8225-4951-2. Grades 5 up. Gyorgy Balanchivadze (1904–1983) did not want to be a dancer, and ran away when his mother enrolled him in ballet school. However, he returned and discovered that the rigorous training gave him ideas about new movements and new stories to tell through dance. Later he traveled throughout Europe and met an American who believed Americans would like ballet. He changed his Russian name to George Balanchine and created popular dances for Broadway, film, and the circus before forming his own ballet company. This volume looks at his life and accomplishments. Sources, Bibliography, and Index.

3034. Krull, Kathleen. *Albert Einstein.* Illustrated by Boris Kulikov. (Giants of Science) Viking, 2009. 141pp. ISBN 978-0-670-06332-1. Grades 5–8. Referring to his "bedhead," Krull draws readers into an accessible account of the personality, appearance, and achievements of Albert Einstein (1879–1955). The titles of her thirteen chapters introduce him as a dropout, someone who explodes experiments in the lab, an office clerk refused academic employment, a researcher, a junior professor, a famous personality, a migrant to America to escape the Nazis, the subject of an FBI investigation, and a man with a great legacy. Not a stellar student, Einstein nevertheless tried to answer his own questions about the universe. Simultaneously, he continued to think and solidify his ideas so that during 1905, his "miracle year," he developed his theories of special relativity (E=mc²) and general relativity. Always placing science before his family relationships, his ideas changed science's concepts of "matter, motion, time, space, and energy." Pen and ink sketches augment the text. Bibliography, Notes, and Index. *Outstanding Science Trade Books for Students.*

3035. Krull, Kathleen. *Wilma Unlimited: How Wilma Rudolph Became the World's Fastest Woman.* Illustrated by David Diaz. Harcourt, 1996. Unpaged. ISBN 978-0-15-201267-0; Voyager, 2000, paper ISBN 978-0-15-202098-9. Grades K–5. Wilma Rudolph (1940–1994) came into the world at a disadvantage. She weighed "just over four pounds" at birth; she was black and lived in the South; and she was poor. And then polio crippled her. But with her strong mother, nineteen older sisters and brothers, deep faith, and amazing inner strength, she recovered. She trained as a sprinter and won three Olympic gold medals. *American Bookseller Pick of the Lists, Bulletin Blue Ribbon,* and *Capitol Choices Noteworthy Titles* (Washington, D.C.).

3036. Landau, Elaine. *Rachel Carson and the Environmental Movement.* (Cornerstones of Freedom) Childrens, 2004. 48pp. ISBN 978-0-516-24232-3. Grades 4–6. Rachel Carson (1907–1964), an author and marine biologist, realized that the pesticides being used were harming the environment. In 1962, she wrote *Silent Spring.* Her book helped people become aware of how easily the environment could be destroyed, and corporations who did not want to change their produces condemned her findings. Photographs enhance the text. Chronology, Further Reading, Glossary, Web Sites, and Index.

3037. Lassieur, Allison. *Eleanor Roosevelt: Activist for Social Change.* See entry 2412.

3038. Lawlor, Laurie. *Helen Keller: Rebellious Spirit.* See entry 2016.

3039. Leavitt, Amie Jane. *Helen Keller.* See entry 2018.

3040. Leslie, Tonya. *Martin Luther King, Jr.: A Life of Fairness.* (Blastoff! Readers: People of Character) Children's, 2007. 24pp. ISBN 978-0-53114-712-2. Grades 1–3. The distinguishing character trait of Martin Luther King, Jr. (1929–1968) was fairness. The text looks at King's fairness as he tried to keep the civil rights movement from being violent. Illustrations augment the text. Glossary, Chronology, Further Reading, and Web Sites.

3041. Leslie, Tonya. *Rosa Parks: A Life of Courage.* Illustrated by Tina Walski. (Blastoff! Readers: People of Character) Bellweather, 2007. 24pp. ISBN 978-1-60014-088-4. Grades 2–4. The distinguishing character trait of Rosa Parks (1913–2005) was courage. This volume looks at her decision to keep her seat on the Montgomery, Alabama, bus in 1955 when she risked being jailed. Illustrations augment the text. Glossary, Chronology, Further Reading, and Web Sites.

3042. MacKinnon, Christy. *Silent Observer.* See entry 2023.

3043. McKissack, Patricia C., and Frederick McKissack. *Jesse Owens: Olympic Star.* See entry 2425.

3044. McKissack, Patricia C., and Frederick McKissack. *Langston Hughes: Great American Poet.* See entry 2426.

3045. McKissack, Patricia C., and Frederick McKissack. *Louis Armstrong: Jazz Musician.* See entry 2427.

3046. McKissack, Patricia C., and Frederick McKissack. *Martin Luther King, Jr.: Man of Peace.* (Great African Americans) Enslow, 2001. 32pp. ISBN 978-0-7660-1678-1. Grades 2–4. Martin Luther King, Jr. (1929–1968) wanted to help his people have a better life. The text uses photographs and illustrations to augment the information about his determination. The racism he faced is not the center of his story. Glossary and Index.

3047. McKissack, Patricia C., and Frederick McKissack. *Mary Church Terrell: Leader for Equality.* See entry 2030.

3048. McKissack, Patricia C., and Frederick McKissack. *Mary McLeod Bethune: A Great Teacher.* See entry 2031.

3049. McKissack, Patricia C., and Frederick McKissack. *Paul Robeson: A Voice to Remember.* See entry 2032.

3050. McKissack, Patricia C., and Frederick McKissack. *Ralph J. Bunche: Peacemaker.* See entry 2432.

3051. MacLeod, Elizabeth. *Albert Einstein: A Life of Genius.* (Snapshots) Kids Can, 2003. 32pp. ISBN 978-1-55337-396-4; paper ISBN 978-1-55337-397-1. Grades 4–7. Albert Einstein (1879–1955), a poor student, became a brilliant scientist who formed theories of light, gravity, and time that changed concepts of the universe. The text gives an overview of his early thinking, physics before his discoveries, his best year for creating, his role as a professor, his concept of the theory of relativity, his fame, his departure from Germany, his role in the creation of the atom bomb that ended World War II, and physics since his death. Photographs highlight the text. Maps, Chronology, and Index.

3052. MacLeod, Elizabeth. *Helen Keller: A Determined Life.* See entry 2038.

3053. McPherson, Stephanie Sammartino. *Albert Einstein.* See entry 2678.

3054. Marlin, John. *Mickey Mantle.* (Sports Heroes and Legends) Lerner, 2004. 106pp. ISBN 978-0-8225-1796-2. Grades 4–6. When he was 21, Mickey Mantle (1931–1995) hit a long-distance ball of 563 feet (including the bounce and the roll) now called the "Washington Wallop," his first "tape-measure" home run (a hit measured to see if it is the longest home run recorded to that date). Mantle came from an impoverished background to be a successful player with the New York Yankees. This biography offers information about his background and his playing career. Photographs highlight the text. Bibliography, Glossary, Web Sites, and Index.

3055. Marx, Christy B. *Grace Hopper: The First Woman to Program the First Computer in the United States.* (Women Hall of Famers in Mathematics and Science) Rosen, 2003. 112pp. ISBN 978-0-8239-3877-3. Grades 4–8. Grace Hopper (1906–1992) earned a Ph.D. in mathematics from Yale and spent her career in the United States Navy. She was a major figure on the team creating and standardizing the COBOL computer program. Her first Navy assignment was at Harvard working with Mark I, the first real computer. When the computer stopped, she discovered a dead moth inside, removed it, and announced that she had "debugged" the computer. Hopper retired in 1986 with full military honors on board the USS *Constitution*. Photos, Bibliography, Chronology, Further Reading, Glossary, Index, and Web Sites.

3056. Mattern, Joanne. *Coretta Scott King: Civil Rights Activist.* (Women Who Shaped History) PowerKids, 2003. 24pp. ISBN 978-0-8239-6504-5. Grades 1–3. Coretta Scott King (1927–2006), wife of Martin Luther King Jr., became an activist for civil rights herself. This brief biography reveals that she also struggled for world peace. Photographs highlight the text. Glossary, Chronology, Further Reading, Web Sites, and Index.

3057. Mayo, Gretchen Will. *Frank Lloyd Wright.* See entry 2437.

3058. Medearis, Angela Shelf. *Dare to Dream: Coretta Scott King and the Civil Rights Movement.* Illustrated by Anna Rich. Puffin, 1999. 42pp. Paper ISBN 978-0-14-130202-7. Grades 3–4. Coretta Scott King (b. 1927) wanted to be an opera singer. She earned a scholarship to the Boston Conservatory of Music, but before she finished she met Martin Luther King, Jr. He wanted a wife who would help him in his ministry, and she agreed to put aside her career. She continued to support his work for equal rights after his assassination.Selected Bibliography, Further Reading, and Index.

3059. Meltzer, Milton. *Albert Einstein: A Biography.* See entry 2680.

3060. Michelson, Richard. *As Good as Anybody: Martin Luther King Jr. and Abraham Joshua Heschel's Amazing March Toward Freedom.* Illustrated by Raul Colón. Borzoi, 2008. Unpaged. ISBN 978-0-375-83335-9. Grades 2–5. Polish rabbi Abraham Joshua Heschel (1907–1972) was a friend of Martin Luther King Jr. (1929–1968). They both believed nonviolence was the best way to end discrimination. Herschel grew up in Poland. He escaped the Nazis but lost many family members during the Holocaust. Illustrations show King and Heschel marching with arms around each other during the 1965 march to Montgomery. Colored pencil and watercolor illustrations enhance the text.

3061. Miller, Debra A. *Dolores Huerta: Labor Leader.* (20th Century's Most Influential Hispanics) Lucent, 2007. 104pp. ISBN 978-1-59018-971-9. Grades 5 up. Dolores Huerta (1930–) was a teacher who decided that the plight of migrant workers was more important. Quotations testify to her effectiveness. Photographs and reproductions enhance the text. Chronology, Notes, Further Reading, Web Sites, and Index.

3062. Miller, Norma, and Alan B. Govenar. *Stompin' at the Savoy: The Story of Norma Miller.* See entry 2440.

3063. Moore, Heidi. *Luisa Moreno.* (American Lives) Raintree, 2005. 32pp. ISBN 978-1-4034-6978-6; paper ISBN 978-1-4034-6985-4. Grades 3–6. Luisa Moreno (d. 1992) spent an affluent childhood in Guatemala and came to the United States in her 20s. Distressed by working conditions in factories, she began to crusade for workers' rights. She created a union for garment workers and then became a leader of the AFL. The text discusses her accomplishments and the difficulties she faced. Photographs and illustrations augment the text. Glossary, Chronology, Further Reading, and Index.

3064. Myers, Walter Dean. *I've Seen the Promised Land: The Life of Dr. Martin Luther King, Jr.* Illustrated by Leonard Jenkins. HarperCollins, 2004. Unpaged. ISBN 978-0-06-027703-1. Grades 1–4. Dr. Martin Luther King, Jr. (1929–1968) led African Americans in their quest for equality by advocating nonviolent social justice. Some of the highlights of his career were leading the 1955 bus boycott in Montgomery, Alabama, after Rosa Park's arrest; giving his "I Have a Dream" speech at the 1963 march on Washington; and his 1968 support of the sanitation workers in Memphis, Tennessee, where he was assassinated.

3065. Myers, Walter Dean. *Malcolm X: By Any Means Necessary.* Scholastic, 1994. 210pp. Paper ISBN 978-0-590-48109-0. Grades 5 up. Malcolm Little's father died during the Depression, and his mother slowly went insane trying to feed her children and keep shelter over their heads. After she was committed to an asylum, Malcolm resented having to live in a foster home. He left for Boston and New York, where he was eventually arrested for theft and imprisoned for ten years. After he was released, he began working with the Nation of Islam and Elijah Muhammad. Malcolm (1925–1965) took the last name "X" and spoke out against racial discrimination. When the two men split because Malcolm refused to curb his comments, Malcolm went on a pilgrimage to Mecca. On his return he established his own group, but he was soon assassinated as he prepared to give a public speech. Chronology, Bibliography, and Index. *Coretta Scott King Honor Book, American Library Association Best Books for Young Adults, American Library Association Notable Children's Books, Capitol Choices Noteworthy Titles* (Washington, D.C.), *School Library Journal Best Books for Children*, and *Horn Book Fanfare Books*.

3066. Myers, Walter Dean. *Young Martin's Promise.* Illustrated by Barbara Higgins Bond. Steck-Vaughn, 1992. 32pp. Paper ISBN 978-0-8114-8050-5. Grades 2–5. Martin Luther King Jr. (1929–1968) did not understand why he could no longer play with his white friends after they started elementary school. His parents were also restricted from doing certain things. This background led to his strong support of civil rights as an adult and shows why the nation now celebrates a holiday in his honor.

3067. O'Connor, Jim. *Jackie Robinson and the Story of All-Black Baseball.* See entry 2684.

3068. Orgill, Roxanne. *Footwork: The Story of Fred and Adele Astaire.* Illustrated by Stephane Jorisch. Candlewick, 2007. 48pp. ISBN 978-0-7636-2121-6. Grades 1–4. In 1905, 5-year-old Fred Astaire and his sister Adele, 7, went to New York with their mother to attend dancing school. After a year, their teacher entered them in a show. They then traveled around the country dancing until they finally got to Broadway. After being successful in both New York and London, Adele quit and married an English nobleman. Fred continued dancing and performed in movies. Orgill offers background about their childhood and early career, noting that Fred's role was to show off Adele. Ink, watercolor, and gouache illustrations complement the text.

3069. O'Sullivan, Robyn. *Jackie Robinson Plays Ball.* See entry 2685.

3070. Parker, Robert Andrew. *Piano Starts Here: The Young Art Tatum.* See entry 2449.

3071. Parks, Rosa, and James Haskins. *I Am Rosa Parks.* Illustrated by Wil Clay. Puffin, 1999. 48pp. Paper ISBN 978-0-14-130710-7. Grades K–3. Rosa Parks, the woman who refused to give up her seat on an Alabama bus one day in 1955, tells her story from childhood. Her decision led to the Montgomery bus boycott and led to the Supreme Court ruling that Montgomery buses could not segregate passengers.

3072. Parks, Rosa, and James Haskins. *Rosa Parks: My Story.* Illustrated by Wil Clay. Dial, 1992. 48pp. ISBN 978-0-8037-0673-6; Puffin, 1999, paper ISBN 978-0-14-130120-4. Grades 4–6. Rosa Parks (1913–2005) said about her decision not to give up her bus seat, "The only tired I was, was tired of giving in." Her action started the Montgomery bus boycott in 1955, which lasted more than a year and led to a federal injunction against segregation on buses. She was always proud of her heritage and her family and believed that all races were equal. She was an activist before sitting on the bus, and afterward she became a speaker for civil rights. Her husband encouraged her to complete her education and register to vote. She has earned the title "Mother to a Movement." Chronology and Index.

3073. Paulsen, Gary. *How Angel Peterson Got His Name: And Other Outrageous Tales of Extreme Sports.* Random, 2004. 111pp. Paper ISBN 978-0-440-22935-3. Grades 5–9. With humor and nostalgia Paulsen (b. 1939) recalls being 13 years old and the risks he and his friends would take: bicycle jumping, peeing on electric fences, shooting waterfalls in a barrel, riding skies tied to the back of a moving car, and wrestling with bears. *American Library Association Best Books for Young Adults, Peach Teen Readers Choice Book Award* (Georgia) nomination, *William Allen White Children's Book Award* (Kansas) nomination, *Bluegrass Book Award* (Kentucky) nomination, *Mark Twain Book Award* (Missouri) nomination, *Garden State Nonfiction Book Award and Teen Award* (New Jersey) nominations, *Junior Book Award* (South Carolina) nomination, *Young Adult Reading Program* (South Dakota) nomination, *Children's Book Award* (Utah) Winner, *Golden Archer Book Award* (Wisconsin) nomination, and *Dorothy Canfield Fisher Children's Book Award* (Vermont) nomination.

3074. Peet, Bill. *Bill Peet: An Autobiography.* Houghton, 1989. 190pp. ISBN 978-0-395-50932-6; 1994, paper ISBN 978-0-395-68982-0. Grades 3–6. Bill Peet (1915–2002) describes life in 20th-century America, including the Depression, when he tried to get work as an artist. He had enormous success working for Disney Studios and helped to create the animation for *Dumbo, Fantasia, Cinderella, Song of the South, Peter Pan, Alice in Wonderland, The Sword in the Stone,* and *101 Dalmatians.* His humorous illustrations interact with the text. *Caldecott Honor Book.*

3075. Pinkney, Andrea Davis. *Duke Ellington: The Piano Prince and His Orchestra.* See entry 2452.

3076. Pinkney, Andrea Davis. *Ella Fitzgerald: The Tale of a Vocal Virtuosa.* Illustrated by Brian Pinkney. Hyperion, 2002. 32pp. ISBN 978-0-7868-0568-6; Disney, 2007, paper ISBN 978-0-7868-1416-9. Grades K–4. Scat Cat Monroe, a cat dressed in a zoot suit, tells how Ella Fitzgerald went from "small-town girl to the First Lady of Song." The text, divided into four "tracks," explains that Fitzgerald performed on street corners as a child in Yonkers. Then in 1934 she sang in a talent contest at the Apollo Theatre because she was too nervous to dance as planned. This gave her her start. She sang in all venues and among all races, including performing at Carnegie Hall with Dizzy Gillespie. Bibliography, Videography, and Selected Discography. *American Library Association Notable Children's Books, Capitol Choices Noteworthy Titles* (Washington, D.C.), and *Garden State Children's Book Award* (New Jersey) nomination.

3077. Plourde, Lynn. *Margaret Chase Smith: A Woman for President.* See entry 2453.

3078. Polacco, Patricia. *Firetalking.* Richard C. Owen, 1994. 32pp. ISBN 978-1-878450-55-5. Grades 2–5. This look at the influences on Patricia Polacco's life gives insights into how she chooses her stories and why she incorporates certain figures in her drawings. The title comes from her Ukrainian grandmother's name for telling stories by her California fire that were always true but may not have happened. As a child, Polacco and her brother lived with their Irish father in Michigan during the summer; the rest of the year they lived with their mother in Oakland, California. Polacco married an Italian Jewish immigrant from Poland. The accessible text and photographs introduce Polacco's family, her coping with a learning disability well enough to achieve a doctorate in art history, and her work conditions at home where she has at least one rocking chair in every room.

3079. Porter, A. P. *Jump at de Sun: The Story of Zora Neale Hurston.* See entry 2062.

3080. Randall, Tina. *Luis Walter Alvarez.* (Hispanic-Americans) Raintree, 2005. 64pp. ISBN 978-1-4109-1295-4; paper ISBN 978-1-4109-2136-9. Grades 4–8. Luis W. Alvarez (1911–1988), a physicist, worked at the Radiation Laboratory at the University of California for most of his career. During World War II he helped with three important radar systems. His research, mainly in optics and cosmic rays, led him to discover the "East-West effect," and in later life he focused on nuclear physics. In 1968, he won the Nobel Prize in Physics. Photographs illustrate the text. Glossary, Chronology, Further Reading, and Index.

3081. Ransom, Candice F. *Maria von Trapp: Beyond the Sound of Music.* (Trailblazers) Carolrhoda, 2002. 112pp. ISBN 978-1-57505-444-5. Grades 4–6. This biography of Maria Augusta von Trapp, the Austrian singer who escaped during World War II, draws on her own writings. It details her life in Austria, on which the *The Sound of Music* is based. It also covers her migration to America, where she initially toured and then settled in Vermont to run a music camp and later manage a ski lodge. Photographs highlight the text. Bibliography, Chronology, Notes, and Index.

3082. Rappaport, Doreen. *Eleanor, Quiet No More.* See entry 2064.

3083. Rappaport, Doreen. *Martin's Big Words: The Life of Dr. Martin Luther King, Jr.* Illustrated by Bryan Collier. Hyperion, 2001. 32pp. ISBN 978-0-7868-0714-7; 2007, paper ISBN

978-1-4231-0635-7. Grades K–4. Using some of Martin Luther King, Jr.'s (1929–1968) own words, this is a brief account of his life. The quotations capture his character, the value of the civil rights movement, and his policy of nonviolence. Cut-paper, photographs and watercolor illustrations enhance the text. *Coretta Scott King Book Awards, Monarch Award Children's Choice Book Award* (Illinois) nomination, *Great Lakes Great Books Award* (Michigan) Winner, *Charlotte Book Award* (New York) nomination, *Children's Book Award* (South Carolina) nomination, *Capitol Choices Noteworthy Titles* (Washington, D.C.), *Caldecott Honor, Bulletin Blue Ribbon*. and *Prairie Bud Award* (South Dakota) nomination.

3084. **Rembert, Winfred, Charles Baker, and Rosalie F. Baker.** *Don't Hold Me Back: My Life and Art.* Cricket, 2003. 40pp. ISBN 978-0-8126-2703-9. Grades 5–9. Winfred Rembert, the son of Georgia sharecroppers, faced many challenges to become an artist. He vividly remembers the civil rights movement. He found his own talent when he was in jail, watching a fellow inmate create designs in leather. His paintings on leather decorate the pages of his story.

3085. **Robinson, Sharon.** *Promises to Keep: How Jackie Robinson Changed America.* Scholastic, 2004. 64pp. ISBN 978-0-439-42592-6. Grades 4–7. The daughter of Jackie Robinson (1919–1972) remembers Robinson as a father and friend, and looks at his roles as the first African American player in major league baseball and as a civil rights activist. She says he always encouraged his children to do the best they could regardless of the circumstances. Photographs enhance the text. *American Library Association Best Books for Young Adults, Student Book Award* (Maine) nomination, *Capitol Choices Noteworthy Titles* (Washington, D.C.), *Diamond Award* (Delaware) nomination, *Young Hoosier Award* (Indiana) nomination, *Children's Book Award* (South Carolina) nomination, *Garden State Children's Book Award* (New Jersey) nomination, and *Garden State Teen Book Award* (New Jersey) nomination.

3086. **Rochelle, Belinda.** *Witnesses to Freedom: Young People Who Fought for Civil Rights.* Puffin, 1997. 97pp. Paper ISBN 978-0-14-038432-1. Grades 5–8. Adults are not the only individuals to fight for civil rights. Rochelle tells the stories of several children who defied Jim Crow laws in the 1950s and 1960s. Claudette Colvin, 15, refused to give her bus seat to a white passenger. Elizabeth Eckford faced a crowd spitting on her and calling her names as she tried to enter Little Rock High School in Arkansas. Sheyann Webb, 9, marched in Selma, Alabama, to protest racism. Others profiled are Barbara Johns, Spottswood Thomas Bolling, Jr., Rosa Parks, Harvey Gantt, Dianne Nash, and Raymond Greene. Sources, Further Reading for Children, and Index.

3087. **Rubin, Susan Goldman.** *Andy Warhol: Pop Art Painter.* Abrams, 2006. 48pp. ISBN 978-0-8109-5477-9. Grades 5–9. In this biography of Andy Warhol (1928–1987), Rubin looks at the artist's life starting with his Pittsburgh childhood. She focuses on his art rather than his film career or adult life. She shows the connections between his inspirations and his art, including quotes from his nephew, James Warhol, and others who knew Warhol personally. Rubin also places Warhol in the context of the history of art. Reproductions augment the text. Glossary, Notes, and Index.

3088. **Rubin, Susan Goldman.** *Andy Warhol's Colors.* Chronicle, 2007. Unpaged. ISBN 978-0-8118-5721-5. Grades K–2. Rhyming text presents figures from Andy Warhol's paintings on each board-book double-spread. Colors appear in capital letters. Reproductions enhance the text.

3089. **Rubin, Susan Goldman.** *Whaam! The Art and Life of Roy Lichtenstein.* Abrams, 2008. 47pp. ISBN 978-0-8109-9492-8. Grades 4–8. Roy Lichtenstein (1923–1997) liked comic books, and even as he spent his early career as an expressionist he was secretly making paintings from comic books and advertising. This biography shows that both fine art and comic-book art inspired him—everything from Henri Matisse's *The Red Studio* to shoe advertisements. He carefully applied Benday dots to canvas in primary colors to create his works. Almost all of his major works are shown, and there is a brief overview of his life. Glossary, Notes, Further Reading, and Index.

3090. **Sakany, Lois.** *Joe DiMaggio.* See entry 2463.

3091. Santella, Andrew. *Jackie Robinson Breaks the Color Line.* Children's, 1996. 30pp. Paper ISBN 978-0-516-26031-0. Grades 3–5. Santella recalls the situation when Jackie Robinson (1919–1972) began to play Major League baseball for the Brooklyn Dodgers and what it meant at the time. Robinson's strength of character and behavior became an example to all. Glossary and Index.

3092. Schmidt, Gary D. *Robert Frost.* See entry 2074.

3093. Schmidt, Julie. *Satchel Paige.* (Baseball Hall of Famers of the Negro League) Rosen, 2001. 112pp. ISBN 978-0-8239-3478-2. Grades 4–7. Leroy "Satchel" Paige (1906–1982) did not break into the major leagues until his 40s. He was the 1948 Rookie of the Year. Paige was the first African American to be inducted into the Baseball Hall of Fame. In addition to information about Paige, this volume provides background on the Negro League teams. Photographs and illustrations augment the text. Glossary, Chronology, Further Reading, Web Sites, and Index.

3094. Schroeder, Alan. *Josephine Baker: Entertainer.* See entry 2465.

3095. Schroeder, Alan. *Satchmo's Blues.* See entry 2247.

3096. Schuman, Michael A. *Eleanor Roosevelt: First Lady and Humanitarian.* See entry 2466.

3097. Scieszka, Jon. *Knucklehead: Tall Tales and Mostly True Stories of Growing Up Scieszka.* Viking, 2008. 106pp. ISBN 978-0-670-01106-3; paper ISBN 978-0-670-01138-4. Grades 3–7. As a young boy growing up with his five brothers, Jon Scieszka (1954–) enjoyed a Catholic education, comic books, summers on the lake, babysitting, television, and family jokes. Chapters include scrapbook snapshots and comic-book reproductions. The boys must use proper anatomical terms (their mother was a nurse), wear hand-me-down Halloween costumes, and charging admission to neighborhood children who wanted to watch the youngest brother eat a cigarette butt. Entertaining, the book offers an insight into the live of a vibrant family during the 1950s and 1960s. *Capitol Choices Noteworthy Titles* (Washington, D.C.).

3098. Shange, Ntozake. *Coretta Scott.* Illustrated by Kadir Nelson. Amistad, 2009. 32pp. ISBN 978-0-06-125364-5. Grades 4–8. Although the title purports to tell the story of Martin Luther King, Jr.'s wife, Coretta Scott (1927–2006), it speaks less of her than it does of her husband. However, some details of her childhood growing up in a racist society are included. The lovely oil paintings compensate for the less-than-thorough free-verse text. Biographical sketch.

3099. Shange, Ntozake. *Ellington Was Not a Street.* Illustrated by Kadir Nelson. Simon & Schuster, 2004. Unpaged. ISBN 978-0-689-82884-3. Grades 3–8. Ntozake Shange recalls her childhood home and the group of musicians, scholars, and civil rights advocates—including Duke Ellington, W. E. B. DuBois, Ray Barretto, "Sonny Til" Tilghman, Kwame Nkrumah, Dizzy Gillespie, and Paul Robeson—who gathered there. They could go few other places because they were African American, and America was segregated. As a small girl, she observed them and heard their discussions. The book's text is Shange's poem, written in 1983, "Moon Indigo." Kadir Nelson's strong Illustrations augment the text. *Coretta Scott King Award, American Library Association Notable Books for Children,* and *Capitol Choices Noteworthy Titles* (Washington, D.C.).

3100. Slade, Suzanne. *Albert Einstein: Scientist and Genius.* See entry 2693.

3101. Stafford, Mark. *W. E. B. Du Bois: Scholar and Activist.* See entry 2083.

3102. Stone, Tanya Lee. *Almost Astronauts: 13 Women Who Dared to Dream.* Candlewick, 2009. 133pp. ISBN 978-0-7636-3611-1; paper ISBN 978-0-7636-4502-1. Grades 5–8. NASA established its space program in 1958. In 1960, the astronauts' physician wondered if women could survive the extensive testing that men underwent to be accepted in the program. Jerrie Cobb accepted the challenge and passed them all. Twenty-four other women tried, and twelve succeeded. But politics, gender, a directive from Vice President Lyndon B. Johnson, and other factors combined to keep members of the "Mercury 13" from accompanying John Glenn and Scott Carpenter, even though Cobb, for one, had flown more hours as a pilot than either man. Not until 1978, when Sally Ride was admitted to the program, were women allowed to become astronauts. She finally flew in 1983. Since then, women have risen to top positions as NASA astronauts. Clearly discrimination unfairly kept them from achieving these heights earlier. Photographs augment the text. Notes, Bibliography, Further Reading, Web Sites, and Index. *Boston Globe-Horn Book Awards* Honor Book and *Robert F. Sibert Informational Book Award* winner, *American Library Association Notable Children's Books*, *American Library Association Best Books for Young Adults*, *Bank Street College of Education Book Award* winner, *Outstanding Science Trade Books for Students*, and *Beehive Childrens Book Award* (Utah).

3103. **Stone, Tanya Lee.** *Sandy's Circus: A Story About Alexander Calder.* See entry 2471.

3104. **Streissguth, Thomas.** *Say It with Music: A Story About Irving Berlin.* See entry 2473.

3105. **Sullivan, George.** *Helen Keller.* See entry 2088.

3106. **Sullivan, George.** *Helen Keller: Her Life in Pictures.* See entry 2089.

3107. **Sutcliffe, Jane.** *John F. Kennedy.* (History Maker Bios) Lerner, 2004. 48pp. ISBN 978-0-8225-1546-3. Grades 3–5. John F. Kennedy was the youngest man and the first Roman Catholic ever elected president. He was a best-selling author by age 24 and was stranded on a deserted island while in the Navy. As president, he created the Peace Corps, ended the Cuban Missile Crisis, supported the civil rights movement, and started the process to put a man on the moon. Illustrations augment the text. Bibliography, Further Reading, Glossary, Maps, Timeline, Web Sites, and Index.

3108. **Tallchief, Maria, and Rosemary Wells.** *Tallchief: America's Prima Ballerina.* Viking, 1999. 28pp. ISBN 978-0-670-88756-9; Puffin, 2001, paper ISBN 978-0-14-230018-3. Grades 3–5. Osage Maria Tallchief grew up on a reservation in Oklahoma and developed a love of dance. She and her parents moved to Los Angeles, where Maria took lessons from the best teachers. She was then ready to dance with the Ballet Russes de Monte Carlo, the top dance company in the world. This biography ends as she leaves for New York at the age of 17. Pastel illustrations enhance the text.

3109. **Tanenhaus, Sam.** *Louis Armstrong: Musician.* See entry 2481.

3110. **Taylor-Butler, Christine.** *Thurgood Marshall.* See entry 2482.

3111. **Thomas, Pamela Duncan.** *The Bus Ride that Changed History: The Story of Rosa Parks.* Illustrated by Danny Shanahan. Houghton, 2005. 32pp. ISBN 978-0-618-44911-8. Grades K–3. This cumulative chant honors Rosa Parks (1913–2005) and her refusal to give up her seat on a Montgomery, Alabama, bus in 1955. The photographs enhance the text. Chronology and Notes.

3112. **Tillage, Leon Walter.** *Leon's Story.* Illustrated by Susan L. Roth. Farrar, 1997. 107pp. ISBN 978-0-374-34379-8; Sunburst, 2000, paper ISBN 978-0-374-44330-6. Grades 4 up. Leon Walter Tillage (1936–), son of a sharecropper in Fuquay-Varina, North Carolina, grew up in the Jim Crow south. At home, he enjoyed his religious family's support. He attended inferior schools, had to enter the bus from the back, use segregated doors, and worry about the Ku Klux Klan. A carful of drunken white teenagers killed his father but were never arraigned. In the 1950s, he joined the civil rights movement. Later, as a custodian in a Baltimore school, he began telling his story in assembly as part of the curriculum. This volume comes from his presentation. Collage illustrations enhance the text. *Children's Book Award* (Georgia) nomination, *Rebecca Caudill Award* (Illinois) nomination, *William Allen White Award* (Kansas) nomination, *Student Book Award* (Maine) nomination, *Battle of the Books* (New Mexico), *Young Readers Choice Awards* (Pennsylvania), *Volunteer State Book Awards* (Tennessee), *Capitol Choices Noteworthy Titles* (Washington, D.C.), *Boston Globe/Horn Book Award Honor*, and *Lonestar Reading List* (Texas).

3113. **Todd, Anne.** *John F. Kennedy: A Life of Citizenship.* (Blastoff! Readers: People of Character) Children's, 2007. 24pp. ISBN 978-0-53114-709-2. Grades 1–3. The distinguishing character trait of John F. Kennedy (1917–1963) was citizenship. This volume looks at

Kennedy's service to the United States as both a Navy officer and president. Illustrations augment the text. Glossary, Chronology, Further Reading, and Web Sites.

3114. Venezia, Mike. *Andy Warhol.* (Getting to Know the World's Greatest Artists) Scholastic, 1996. 32pp. ISBN 978-0-516-20053-8; Children's Press, 1997, paper ISBN 978-0-516-26075-4. Grades K–5. Andy Warhol (1928–1987) was an American painter with an extravagant personality who helped develop Pop Art and made art fun. He painted unexpected subjects, as in *Campbell's Soup Can* (1968), and celebrities including Marilyn Monroe, Troy Donahue, and Elizabeth Taylor. Illustrations enhance the text.

3115. Venezia, Mike. *Dorothea Lange.* See entry 2484.

3116. Venezia, Mike. *Duke Ellington.* See entry 2485.

3117. Venezia, Mike. *Edward Hopper.* See entry 2486.

3118. Venezia, Mike. *Faith Ringgold.* (Getting to Know the World's Greatest Artists) Scholastic, 2007. 32pp. ISBN 978-0-531-18526-1; Children's Press, 2008, paper ISBN 978-0-531-14757-3. Grades K–5. Faith Ringgold (1930–), a "woman of color," has been influenced by Harlem, where she has lived for much of her life. She loved working with textiles as a child and has used many pieces of fabric in her work. She is a professor of art and has exhibited in many galleries around the world. Among her many awards are a Guggenheim Foundation Award and a Caldecott Honor and a Coretta Scott King Award for her book *Tar Beach*. She has also published *Aunt Harriet's Underground Railroad in the Sky*, *The Invisible Quilt*, and *Cassie's Word Quilt*. Illustrations complement the text.

3119. Venezia, Mike. *Georgia O'Keeffe.* See entry 2488.

3120. Venezia, Mike. *Grandma Moses.* See entry 2489.

3121. Venezia, Mike. *Jackson Pollock.* See entry 2492.

3122. Venezia, Mike. *Jacob Lawrence.* See entry 2706.

3123. Venezia, Mike. *Norman Rockwell.* See entry 2496.

3124. Venezia, Mike. *Roy Lichtenstein.* (Getting to Know the World's Greatest Artists) Scholastic, 2001. 32pp. ISBN 978-0-516-22030-7; Children's Press, 2002, paper ISBN 978-0-516-25963-5. Grades K–5. Roy Lichtenstein (1923–1997) was a leader in the Pop Art movement, often portraying cowboys and Native Americans. Many of his later paintings look like comic book pictures. Illustrations augment the text.

3125. Wadsworth, Ginger. *Rachel Carson: Voice for the Earth.* Lerner, 1992. 128pp. ISBN 978-0-8225-4907-9. Grades 5–9. Portrayed as sensitive and passionate in this biography, Rachel Carson (1907–1964) grew up loving nature. She became a biologist whose literary success allowed her to leave her government job and devote her energy to research and observing how humans were destroying the planet. These findings propelled her to voice her concerns and become a leader of the environmental and conservation movement. Selections from her work pepper the text along with good black-and-white photographs. Bibliography and Index.

3126. Walker, Paul Robert. *Pride of Puerto Rico: The Life of Roberto Clemente.* Odyssey, 1991. 157pp. Paper ISBN 978-0-15-263420-9. Grades 4–8. Puerto Rican Baseball Hall of Famer Roberto Clemente (1934–1972) was a right fielder for the Pittsburgh Pirates before he died in a plane crash while trying to help earthquake victims in Nicaragua. Bibliography and Roberto Clemente's Career Record.

3127. Wallner, Alexandra. *Grandma Moses.* See entry 2500.

3128. Warhola, James. *Uncle Andy's: A Faabbbulous Visit with Andy Warhol.* Puffin, 2005. 32pp. ISBN 978-0-399-23869-7; 2005, paper ISBN 978-0-14-240347-1. Grades K–3. As a young boy, James Warhola loved visiting his Uncle Andy in New York and seeing his artwork. James's own father, a junkman, also had lots of treasures, but Uncle Andy's rooms were filled with pictures of Coca Cola cans, crumpled cars, wigs, and cats. James decides to become an artist himself, and he begins to collect unusual objects. Illustrations enhance the text. *Capitol Choices Noteworthy Titles* (Washington, D.C.).

3129. Waxman, Laura Hamilton. *Coretta Scott King.* (History Maker Bios) Lerner, 2008. 48pp. ISBN 978-0-8225-7168-1. Grades 3–5. Many consider Coretta Scott King (1927–2006) to be the "First Lady of the U.S. civil rights movement." She was an asset to her husband, Martin Luther King Jr., in his leadership of the fight for African American equal rights in the 1950s and 1960s. She continued her work after he was assassinated, espousing freedom, equality, and peace. Photographs and illustrations augment the text. Bibliography, Further Reading, Glossary, Maps, Timeline, Web Sites, and Index.

3130. Waxman, Laura Hamilton. *Jimmy Carter.* (History Maker Bios) Lerner, 2006. 48pp. ISBN 978-0-8225-5939-9. Grades 3–5. Jimmy Carter (1924–), known as "Hotshot," attended the Naval Academy and became a businessman after he left the navy. Georgia elected him as its governor, and then he became president of the United States. In his role as a former president, he has served the country as a peacemaker and an advocate for the poor. Illustrations augment the text. Bibliography, Further Reading, Glossary, Maps, Timeline, Web Sites, and Index.

3131. Weidt, Maryann N. *Oh, the Places He Went: A Story About Dr. Seuss.* See entry 2509.

3132. Weidt, Maryann N. *Rosa Parks.* (History Maker Bios) Lerner, 2003. 48pp. ISBN 978-0-8225-4673-3. Grades 3–5. Rosa Parks (1913–2005) had a difficult childhood and worked hard as an adult. When she was riding home on the bus in her town of Montgomery, Alabama, in 1955 Jim Crow laws demanded that she give her seat to a white person. When she refused, her action started a bus boycott, and became an important milestone in the civil rights movement. Illustrations augment the text. Bibliography, Further Reading, Glossary, Maps, Timeline, Web Sites, and Index.

3133. Weinstein, Howard. *Mickey Mantle.* (Baseball Hall of Famers) Rosen, 2003. 112pp. ISBN 978-0-8239-3779-0. Grades 4–6. Mickey Mantle (1931–1995) was a Major League baseball player known for his strong hitting ability for the New York Yankees. His father, a worker in the Oklahoma mines, always wanted a better life for his son, and Mantle fulfilled these dreams when he became the star center fielder on the team. He won twelve pennants and seven championships in his first fourteen seasons, hitting more home runs than any switch-hitter in history. Photographs highlight the text.

3134. Welch, Catherine. *Margaret Bourke-White.* See entry 2710.

3135. Whitehead, Kathy. *Art from Her Heart: Folk Artist Clementine Hunter.* Illustrated by Shane W. Evans. Putnam, 2008. Unpaged. ISBN 978-0-399-24219-9. Grades K–3. Clementine Hunter (1886?–1988), a self-taught artist, started painting on scraps and gourds when she was 50. She recorded life on the plantation around her on old shades, glass bottles, or old boards—she had no canvas. Her work was exhibited at a major museum, the first such exhibition by an African American artist. Because she was African American, she was not allowed to attend but a friend took her inside after dark. Mixed-media illustrations complement the text. Bibliography.

3136. Wilkerson, J. L. *Sad-Face Clown: Emmett Kelly.* See entry 2511.

3137. Winget, Mary. *Eleanor Roosevelt.* See entry 2513.

3138. Winget, Mary. *Martin Luther King, Jr.* (History Maker Bios) Lerner, 2003. 48pp. ISBN 978-0-8225-4674-0. Grades 3–5. Martin Luther King, Jr. (1929–1968) grew up in the South before heading to Boston to earn a Ph.D. in theology. His ability to speak clearly and eloquently placed him in a leadership position during the civil rights movement. Then he used the phrase "I have a dream" in his speech at the Lincoln Memorial. He went to Memphis, Tennessee, twice to support the garbage strike, and the second time, on April 4, 1968, he was assassinated. His desire for a peaceful resolution to segregation earned him a place in history with a holiday bearing his name. Illustrations augment the text. Bibliography, Further Reading, Glossary, Maps, Timeline, Web Sites, and Index.

3139. Winter, Jeanette. *My Name Is Georgia.* See entry 2116.

3140. Winter, Jonah. *Beisbol: Latino Baseball Pioneers and Legends.* See entry 2515.

3141. Winter, Jonah. *Dizzy.* Illustrated by Sean Qualls. Arthur A. Levine, 2006. 32pp. ISBN 978-0-439-50737-0. Grades 3–8. As a child in South Carolina, Dizzy Gillespie (1917–1993) received a trumpet from his teacher. This changed his life—he was able to translate the anger and hurt of his father's abusiveness into music. He went to New York City and mimicked its sounds on his trumpet. And he turned his notes and rhythms into thrilling jazz and bebop. Illustrations intensify the text. *School Library Journal Best Books for Children, Horn Book Fanfare, Bulletin Blue Ribbons, Booklist Editor's Choice, American Library Association Notable Children's Books*, and *Capitol Choices Noteworthy Titles* (Washington, D.C.).

3142. Winter, Jonah. *Muhammad Ali: Champion of the World.* Illustrated by Francois Roca. Schwartz & Wade, 2008. ISBN 978-0-375-83622-0. Grades 2–5. Winter looks at the men who paved the way for Muhammad Ali (1942–)—Jack Johnson, the first black American heavyweight champion of the world, and Joe Louis and Sonny Liston. This lively profile with matching text looks at Ali's life.

3143. Winter, Jonah. *Roberto Clemente: Pride of the Pittsburgh Pirates.* Illustrated by Raul Colón. Anne Schwartz, 2005. 40pp. ISBN 978-0-689-85643-3; Aladdin, 2008, paper ISBN 978-1-416-95082-0. Grades 2–4. Winter chronicles the life of Puerto Rican baseball player Roberto Clemente (1934–1972), a star of the Pittsburgh Pirates in 1971 and 1972 who had failed to gain widespread recognition. He died in 1972 in a plane crash, on the way to take aid to earthquake victims in Central America. Mixed media Illustrations augment the text.

3144. Winter, Jonah. *You Never Heard of Sandy Koufax?!* Illustrated by André Carrilho. Schwartz & Wade, 2009. 40pp. ISBN 978-0-375-83738-8. Grades K–4. Before the Dodgers moved to Los Angeles from New York in 1957, Sandy Koufax (1935–) warmed the bench and walked hitters. Then in 1961, he transformed into the Dodgers' star left-handed pitcher, winning games and leading statistics. He kept this status until 1966, when he inexplicably quit playing. An "old-timer," using dialect and vernacular, recalls Koufax's glory but notes discrimination against him as one of the first Jewish players. Koufax, in fact, refused to pitch when the beginning game of the 1965 World Series conflicted with Yom Kippur, a High Holy Day. Illustrations in graphite colored with red, gold, and Dodger blue enhance the text. Glossary. *Sydney Taylor Book Award* Honor Book, *Flicker Tale Children's Book Award* (North Dakota) nomination, *American Library Association Notable Children's Books, Booklist Editors Choice, Beehive Children's Book Award* (Utah) nomination, *Young Readers Choice Book Award* (Pennsylvania) nomination, and *Capitol Choices Noteworthy Titles* (Washington, D.C.).

3145. Wishinsky, Frieda. *What's the Matter with Albert? A Story of Albert Einstein.* Illustrated by Jacques Lamontagne. Maple Tree, 2002. Unpaged. ISBN 978-1-894379-31-1; 2004, paper ISBN 978-1-897066-15-7. Grades 2–4. In 1954 Billy has an assignment for his Princeton Elementary School newspaper—to interview Albert Einstein, "the smartest man in the world." During the interview, Einstein tells him that he had an unpromising childhood but came to love mathematics. Dr. Einstein gets sick and cannot have visitors so Billy has to research additional information. The text distinguishes between Einstein's writings and the information from secondary sources. Illustrations complement the text. Chronology.

3146. Wooten, Sara McIntosh. *Robert Frost: The Life of America's Poet.* See entry 2712.

3147. Wukovits, John F. *Jackie Robinson and the Integration of Baseball.* (Lucent Library of Black History) Lucent, 2006. 104pp. ISBN 978-1-59018-913-9. Grades 5–8. This biography of Jackie Robinson (1919–1972) makes clear his important achievement in breaking through baseball's history of racial exclusion. Robinson served in the military and played baseball in the Negro Leagues before signing with the Brooklyn Dodgers as the first African American to play in the major leagues. He remained calm and kind in the face of continuing discrimination. Photographs highlight the text. Index.

3148. Zemlicka, Shannon. *Neil Armstrong.* (History Maker Bios) Lerner, 2003. 48pp. ISBN 978-0-8225-0395-8; paper ISBN 978-0-8225-1563-0. Grades 3–5. From the moment Neil Armstrong left the ground on his first plane ride, he knew he wanted to fly. After becoming a pilot and joining the navy, Armstrong applied to become an astronaut. Following years of training, he was chosen to lead the United States' historic first mission to land on the moon.

Illustrations augment the text. Bibliography, Further Reading, Glossary, Maps, Timeline, Web Sites, and Index.

Graphic Novels, Biographies, and Histories

3149. Adamson, Thomas K. *The First Moon Landing.* Illustrated by Gordon Purcell and Terry Beatty. Graphic Library, 2006. 32pp. ISBN 978-0-7368-6492-3; paper ISBN 978-0-7368-9654-2. Grades 3–5. On July 20, 1969, astronauts Neil Alden Armstrong and Edwin Eugene "Buzz" Aldrin, Jr., became the first two humans to land on the moon. While they walked, Michael Collins orbited above them. Illustrations augment the text. Bibliography, Glossary, Further Reading, and Index.

3150. Braun, Eric. *César Chávez: Fighting for Farmworkers.* Illustrated by Harry Roland. Graphic Library, 2005. 32pp. ISBN 978-0-7368-4630-1; 2006, paper ISBN 978-0-7368-6191-5. Grades 3–5. This short graphic biography of César Chávez (1927–1993) depicts his life and his efforts to promote fair working conditions for farm laborers. A yellow background sets direct quotes from Chávez apart from the fictional aspect of the narration. Web Sites.

3151. Fandel, Jennifer. *Martin Luther King, Jr.: Great Civil Rights Leader.* Illustrated by Brian Bascle. (Graphic Biographies) Graphic Library, 2006. 32pp. ISBN 978-0-7368-6498-5; paper ISBN 978-0-7368-9661-0. Grades 3–5. This short graphic biography of Martin Luther King, Jr. (1929–1968) describes his life as a minister who supported nonviolent civil rights action. His leadership in Montgomery during the bus boycott and his March on Washington helped gain civil rights for African Americans. A yellow background sets direct quotes from King apart from the fictional aspect of the narration. Web Sites.

3152. Glaser, Jason. *Jackie Robinson: Baseball's Great Pioneer.* See entry 2519.

3153. Hudson-Goff, Elizabeth, and Dale Anderson. *The First Moon Landing.* Illustrated by Guus Floor, Floor Campbell, and Anthony Spay. World Almanac, 2006. Unpaged. ISBN 978-0-8368-6203-4; 2005, paper ISBN 978-0-8368-6255-3. Grades 3–6. This graphic history describes the first moon landing and gives key background information.

3154. Lemke, Donald B. *The Apollo 13 Mission.* Illustrated by Keith Tucker. (Graphic History) Capstone, 2006. 32pp. ISBN 978-0-7368-5476-4; paper ISBN 978-0-7368-6871-6. Grades 3–5. On the third manned lunar-landing mission of Project Apollo, *Apollo 13*, an electrical fault in the oxygen tank caused an explosion on April 13, 1970, after two days in space. The three astronauts used the Lunar Module as their space "lifeboat" while the Service Module remained functional on internal batteries. Since that module had only enough electricity for reentry, the flight was cut short. It was a "successful failure." Illustrations augment the event. Bibliography, Glossary, Further Reading, and Index.

3155. Miller, Connie Colwell. *Rosa Parks and the Montgomery Bus Boycott.* Illustrated by Dan Kalal and Charles P. Henry. (Graphic Biographies) Graphic Library, 2006. 32pp. ISBN 978-0-7368-6495-4; paper ISBN 978-0-7368-9658-0. Grades 3–5. This short graphic biography of Rosa Parks (1913–2005) relates the story of her decision not to sit at the back of the bus in Montgomery, Alabama, an action that started a bus boycott and invigorated the civil rights movement. A yellow background sets direct quotes from Parks apart from the fictional aspect of the narration. Web Sites.

3156. O'Hern, Kerri. *Louis Armstrong.* See entry 2522.

3157. O'Hern, Kerri, and Lucia Raatma. *Jackie Robinson.* See entry 2523.

3158. O'Hern, Kerri, and Frank Walsh. *The Montgomery Bus Boycott.* Illustrated by D. McHargue. World Almanac, 2006. Unpaged. ISBN 978-0-8368-6205-8; paper ISBN 978-0-8368-6257-7. Grades 3–6. This graphic history describes the residents of Montgomery, Alabama, as they banded together to protest against segregation on public buses in 1955. It gives background information important to the situation both in text and images.

3159. Olson, Nathan. *John F. Kennedy: American Visonary.* Illustrated by Brian Bascle. (Graphic Biographies) Graphic Library, 2007. 32pp. ISBN 978-0-7368-6852-5; paper ISBN 978-0-7368-7904-0. Grades 3–5. This short graphic biography of John F. Kennedy (1917–1963) describes his experiences as a naval officer in World War I, a senator, and then as the youngest president of the United States before his assassination. A yellow background sets direct quotes from Kennedy apart from the fictional aspect of the narration. Web Sites.

3160. Shone, Rob. *Muhammed Ali: The Life of a Boxing Hero.* Illustrated by Nik Spender. (Graphic Biographies) Rosen, 2006. 48pp. ISBN 978-1-4042-0856-8; paper ISBN 978-1-4042-0919-0. Grades 3–5. This graphic biography profiles Muhammad Ali (1942–), once known as Cassius Clay, a man who rose to become heavyweight boxing champion of the world. It includes background information important to Ali's life in text and pictures.

3161. Shone, Rob. *Rosa Parks: The Life of a Civil Rights Heroine.* Illustrated by Nik Spender. (Graphic Biographies) Rosen, 2006. 48pp. ISBN 978-1-4042-0864-3; paper ISBN 978-1-4042-0927-5. Grades 3–8. This graphic biography offers background on the life of Rosa Parks (1913–2005), a woman who risked her safety to sit down on a Montgomery, Alabama, bus in 1955.

3162. Vining, James. *First in Space.* Oni, 2007. Unpaged. Paper ISBN 978-1-932664-64-5. Grades 4–6. After narrowing the field from monkeys to chimpanzees, NASA decided that a chimp named Ham should be first in space. Ham returned alive, and his point of view prevails in this graphic novel. He is not particularly happy to be chosen, with some of his dreams suggesting that animal testing is painful.

DVDs

3163. *Americana: 1900's to Present Day.* (Hands-On Crafts for Kids Series 6: Back in Time) Chip Taylor Communications, 2003. 30 mins. Grades 4–6. See entry 2132.

3164. *Dropping In on Andy Warhol.* Crystal, 2005. 19 mins. ISBN 978-1-56290-432-6. Grades 3–6. This animated program about Andy Warhol (1928–1987) offers information about his life and career with large images of his artwork. Puffer the penguin asks Warhol about his work, and Warhol describes the different media that he has used to create his pieces.

3165. *Dropping In on Romare Bearden.* Crystal, 2007. 19 mins. ISBN 978-1-56290-541-5. Grades 1–4. See entry 2533.

3166. *Ellington Was Not a Street.* Narrated by Phylicia Rashad. Weston Woods, 2005. Unpaged. 12 mins. ISBN 978-0-439-77582-3. Grades 3–8. Ntozake Shange recalls her childhood home and the group of musicians, scholars, and civil rights advocates—including Duke Ellington, W. E. B. DuBois, Ray Barretto, "Sonny Til" Tilghman, Kwame Nkrumah, Dizzy Gillespie, and Paul Robeson—who gathered there. They could go few other places because they were African American, and America was segregated. As a small girl, she observed them and heard their discussions. The book's text is Shange's poem, written in 1983, "Moon Indigo." Kadir Nelson's strong illustrations augment the presentation. *Coretta Scott King Award, American Library Association Notable Books for Children,* and *Capitol Choices Noteworthy Titles* (Washington, D.C.).

3167. *Heroes of Freedom: Harriet Tubman and Rosa Parks.* Mazzarella Media, 2008. 22 mins. ISBN 978-1-934119-57-0. Grades 3–8. See entry 1587.

3168. *John F. Kennedy.* (20th Century Presidents) Landmark Media, 2006. 22 mins. Grades 4 up. A child gives an overview of the life of John F. Kennedy (1917–1963), the youngest man elected to the presidency. He also served in the Navy and in the Senate. He had barely 1,000 days as president before he was assassinated in Dallas, Texas.

3169. *Martin Luther King, Jr.* (Great Americans for Children) Library Video, 2002. 23 mins. ISBN 978-1-4171-0276-1. Grades K–4. Dr. Martin Luther King Jr. fought peacefully for equal rights and opportunities for blacks at a time when violence seemed the only option. He was a minister in Alabama before becoming a leader in the civil rights movement. His efforts led to *Brown* vs. *Board of Education*, the Montgomery bus boycott, and the March on Washington, at which he gave his famous "I Have a Dream" speech.

3170. **Pinkney, Andrea Davis.** *Ella Fitzgerald: The Tale of a Vocal Virtuosa.* Narrated by Billy Dee Williams. Weston Woods, 2003. 34 mins. ISBN 978-0-439-79931-7. Grades K–4. See entry 3076.

3171. *Walt: The Man Behind the Myth.* Narrated by Dick Van Dyke. Disney Educational, 2002. Color. 84:11 mins. ISBN 978-0-7888-3961-0. Grades 4 up. Dick Van Dyke narrates the life story of Walt Disney with archival footage from home movies and interviews with family, former employees, and friends. Disney made technical breakthroughs with Technicolor, animation, mixing music and sound effects in cartoons, and the multiplane camera that gives animation added depth of field.

Compact Discs

3172. *Alabama Moon.* Narrated by Nick Landrum. Recorded Books, 2007. 8 CDs; 8:45 hrs. ISBN 978-1-4281-3392-1. Grades 5–8. See entry 3202.

3173. **Aldrin, Buzz.** *Reaching for the Moon.* Narrated by Buzz Aldrin. Live Oak Media, 2005. 1 CD. ISBN 978-1-59519-582-1. Grades K–5. See entry 2938.

3174. **Auch, Mary Jane.** *One-Handed Catch.* Full Cast Audio, 2008. 6 CDs; 5.75 hrs. ISBN 978-1-934180-16-7. Grades 5–8. See entry 2730.

3175. **Burg, Shana.** *A Thousand Never Evers.* Narrated by Kenya Brome. Listening Library, 2008. 7 CDs. ISBN 978-0-7393-6740-7. Grades 4–8. See entry 2742.

3176. **Cushman, Karen.** *The Loud Silence of Francine Green.* Listening library, 2006. 225pp. 5 CDs; 5 hrs. 36 mins. ISBN 978-0-618-50455-8. Grades 5–9. See entry 2750.

3177. **Gerstein, Mordicai.** *The Man Who Walked Between the Towers.* Live Oak Media, 2005. 1 CD; 15 mins. ISBN 978-1-59519-425-1. Grades K–4. See entry 2996.

3178. **Greenberg, Jan, and Sandra Jordan.** *Action Jackson.* Narrated by Ed Harris. Live Oak Media, 2005. 23 mins. ISBN 978-1-59112-964-6. Grades 1–6. See entry 3005.

3179. **Holm, Jennifer L.** *Penny from Heaven.* Listening Library, 2006. 5 CDs; 5 hrs. 36 mins. ISBN 978-0-7393-3111-8. Grades 3–7. See entry 2775.

3180. **Kadohata, Cynthia.** *Kira-Kira.* Narrated by Elaina Erika Davis. Listening Library, 2005. 4 CDs; 4:30 hrs. ISBN 978-0-307-28186-9. Grades 5–8. See entry 2780.

3181. **Madden, Kerry.** *Gentle's Holler.* (Maggie Valley) Recorded Books, 2007. 4 CDs; 5.75 hrs. ISBN 978-1-4193-7128-8. Grades 5–8. See entry 2802.

3182. **Martin, Ann M.** *On Christmas Eve.* Listening Library, 2006. 2 CDs. ISBN 978-0-7393-3776-9. Grades 3–5. See entry 2809.

3183. **Moses, Shelia P.** *The Return of Buddy Bush.* Recorded Books, 2006. 3 CDs; 2.75 hrs. ISBN 978-1-4193-5319-2. Grades 5–9. See entry 2816.

3184. **Peck, Richard.** *A Season of Gifts.* Listening Library, 2009. 3 CDs; 3 hrs. 50 min. ISBN 978-0-7393-8546-3. Grades 5–8. See entry 2823.

3185. **Pinkwater, Daniel.** *The Neddiad: How Neddie Took the Train, Went to Hollywood, and Saved Civilization.* Recorded Books, 2007. 4 CDs; 4:30 hrs. ISBN 978-1-4281-4869-7. Grades 5–9. See entry 2828.

3186. **Schmidt, Gary D.** *The Wednesday Wars.* Narrated by Joel Johnstone. Scholastic, 2007. 6 CDs; 7 hrs. 28 mins. ISBN 978-0-439-92501-3. Grades 5–8. See entry 2835.

3187. **Scieszka, Jon.** *Knucklehead: Tale Tales and Mostly True Stories About Growing Up Scieszka.* Brilliance, 2009. 2 CDs; 1 hr. 59 mins. ISBN 978-1-4233-9974-2. Grades 3–7. See entry 3097.

3188. **Stone, Tanya Lee.** *Almost Astronauts: 13 Women Who Dared to Dream.* Brilliance, 2009. 3 CDs; 3 hrs. 42 mins. ISBN 978-1-4418-2501-8. Grades 5–8. See entry 3102.

3189. **White, Ruth.** *Belle Prater's Boy.* Listening Library, 2005. 3 CDs. ISBN 978-0-307-20655-8. Grades 5–9. See entry 2861.

SINCE 1975

Historical Fiction and Fantasy

3190. Adler, David A. *The Number on My Grandfather's Arm.* Uri, 1987. 28pp. ISBN 978-0-8074-0328-0. Grades 2–4. A young girl asks her grandfather about the number tattooed across his forearm. He tells her his story of World War II, not in graphic detail, but so she can understand that he had a terrible time and almost lost his life while in Auschwitz. *Sydney Taylor Award.*

3191. Antle, Nancy. *Lost in the War.* Illustrated by Stephen Marchesi. Puffin, 2000. Paper ISBN 978-0-14-130836-4. Grades 5–8. Lisa Grey, 12, lives with her mother, who still has post-traumatic nightmares resulting from her days as a nurse in the Vietnam War. Lisa's parents met in Vietnam, and her father died there. Her mother agrees to talk to her class about the war, but Lisa resents having to worry about her. Then in 1982 when they go to Washington, D.C., to the dedication of the Vietnam Veterans Memorial they find Lisa's father's name on "the Wall" and start to cope better.

3192. Cooper, Susan. *Victory.* Margaret K. McElderry, 2006. 195pp. ISBN 978-1-4169-1477-8; Aladdin, 2007, paper ISBN 978-1-4169-1478-5. Grades 5–8. Molly, a homesick British girl living in America because of her stepfather's job, finds herself connecting with Sam, 11, a boy serving in the British Royal Navy in 1803 aboard HMS *Victory.* Molly dreams about Sam, his ship, and the brutality of the Napoleonic Wars. When Molly returns to England for a visit, she goes to see the *Victory,* and realizes she must try to improve life for both herself and Sam. *Booklist Editor's Choice.*

3193. Day, Karen. *No Cream Puffs.* Wendy Lamb, 2008. 208pp. ISBN 978-0-375-83775-3. Grades 5–9. In 1980 Michigan 12-year-old Madison prefers baseball to makeup and stylish clothes. Her brother David recognizes her pitching ability and finds a boys team that will let her play. With her superb hitting and pitching, the team goes on to the championship and causes a media storm in southern Michigan. Madison is disappointed when she's told she plays like a boy, and she regrets that she has jeopardized her relationship with her best friend.

3194. Ellsworth, Loretta. *In Search of Mockingbird.* Henry holt, 2007. 181pp. ISBN 978-0-8050-7236-5. Grades 5–9. When Erin becomes 16 in 1986, her father gives her the diary that her mother kept when she was 16. This diary, a few photographs, and her mother's favorite copy of *To Kill a Mockingbird* are the only items that link Erin to her mother, who died when Erin was three days old. She learns that her mother, who—like Erin—wanted to be a writer, sought advice from Harper Lee, the author of *To Kill a Mockingbird.* Unhappy with her father's decision to remarry, Erin runs away, heading by bus from Minnesota to Alabama in hopes of meeting Harper Lee, and learns much about herself along the way.

3195. Flood, Pansie Hart. *Secret Holes.* Illustrated by Felicia Marshall. Carolrhoda, 2003. 122pp. ISBN 978-0-8761-4923-2. Grades 3–6. In this sequel to *Sylvia and Miz Lula Maye*, Sylvia, 10, learns more about her family. When Miz Lula Maye begins pulling documents out of other places, Sylvia begins to wonder if more family mysteries might be in "secret holes." Then she discovers her own identity, a surprising truth. And she also discovers that the family never needs to worry about money again.

3196. Flood, Pansie Hart. *Sometimey Friend.* Illustrated by Felicia Marshall. Carolrhoda, 2005. 128pp. ISBN 978-1-57505-866-5. Grades 3–6. After the aunt who raised her returns to Florida in 1979, Sylvia, an 11-year-old African American girl, moves in with Miz Lula Maye, her great-grandmother. She goes to a new school, where the children tease her for living with a "witch." Sylvia is embarrassed and then annoyed with herself for feeling that way. When fall carnival arrives, Miz Lula Maye suggests that they both dress alike—as angels!

3197. Flood, Pansie Hart. *Sylvia and Miz Lula Maye.* Illustrated by Felicia Marshall. Carolrhoda, 2002. 113pp. ISBN 978-0-8761-4204-2. Grades 3–6. Sylvia, 10, dislikes the dusty road down which she and her mother live in Wakefield, South Carolina, after they move there in 1978. But nearby is Miz Lula Maye, who is almost one hundred years old. She teaches Sylvia to cook and takes her to church while Sylvia's mother works in the pepper fields all day. Soon a stranger appears who happens to be Miz Lula Maye's long-lost grandson. He turns out to be Sylvia's father, who did not know she existed as her mother had never told him after he left to fight in Vietnam. When he returned from Vietnam, he was disoriented and could locate neither his sweetheart nor his grandmother. Sylvia's mother clearly does not love him, and now Sylvia knows that Miz Lula Maye is actually her great-grandmother and her best friend.

3198. Fritz, Jean. *Homesick: My Own Story.* See entry 2763.

3199. Going, K. L. *The Liberation of Gabriel King.* Putnam, 2005. 192pp. ISBN 978-0-399-23991-5; Puffin, 2007, paper ISBN 978-0-14-240766-0. Grades 4–7. In 1976 Georgia, Gabriel King is a white boy plagued by fears. He's so intimidated by two 6th-grade bullies that he would prefer to stay in 4th grade rather than graduating to 5th and sharing a cafeteria with them. His friend Frita, an African American used to facing prejudice, wants Gabe to move up with her and decides to help him overcome his fears. Between them, they accomplish much over the summer. *Golden Sower Award* (Nebraska) nomination, *SCASL Book Award* (South Carolina) nomination, *Keystone to Reading Book Award* nomination, *Black-Eyed Susan Book Award* (Maryland) nomination, *Capitol Choices Noteworthy Titles* (Washington, D.C.), *Children's Book Award* (Massachusetts) nomination, *Great Stone Face Book Award* (New Hampshire) nomination, and *Beehive Young Adult Book Award* (Utah) nomination.

3200. Hartfield, Claire. *Me and Uncle Romie: A Story Inspired by the Life and Art of Romare Bearden.* Dial, 2002. Unpaged. ISBN 978-0-8037-2520-1. Grades K–3. James leaves North Carolina to visit his uncle, collage artist Romare Bearden (1911–1988) in Harlem. His uncle seems very busy at first and James decides he's not much fun. James spends most of his time with his Aunt Nanette. But on James's birthday, his aunt has to leave and Uncle Romie spends time with him. James discovers that his uncle can have fun and even knows about baseball.

3201. Kerley, Barbara. *Greetings from Planet Earth.* Scholastic, 2007. 246pp. ISBN 978-0-439-80203-1. Grades 4–7. In 1977, 12-year-old Theo is assigned a science project for which he must write a one-minute statement telling someone in space about Earth. As he ponders this, he also wonders why his father has not yet returned from Vietnam and why his mother keeps secrets. He receives a birthday card from his father in Vietnam and recognizes his grandmother's handwriting, but he knows he must never ask questions about his father at home. He talks to his grandmother, looks at his mother's hidden letters, and does research in the library in his attempt to find the answers he needs for both projects.

3202. Key, Watt. *Alabama Moon.* Farrar, 2006. 294pp. ISBN 978-0-374-30184-2; Square Fish, 2008, paper ISBN 978-0-312-38428-9. Grades 5–8. Ten-year-old Moon and his Vietnam veteran father have been living in the Alabama forest by themselves, surviving on what they can hunt and gather and avoiding society. When his father dies in 1980, Moon is turned over to the local boys' home, Moon cannot stand the confinement and runs away with two other boys, Kit and Hal. They live in the woods until Kit needs medical attention. Then Moon is again alone and beginning to question his father's lifestyle. After a stint in jail where he especially likes the food, Moon finds a home with an uncle he never knew existed. He looks forward to a new life.

3203. Lasky, Kathryn. _The Night Journey._ Illustrated by Trina. S. Hynam. Viking, 2005. 152pp. ISBN 978-0-670-05963-8; Puffin paper ISBN 978-0-14-240322-8. Grades 5–9. Not until she is 13 does Rache hear the story of Jewish pogroms and her grandmother's escape from Russia with her family in 1900. Her grandmother hid under chicken crates, paraded as a Purim player, and crossed the border with her cookies. The cookies held the family's gold. _National Jewish Awards, American Library Association Notable Children's Books, Association of Jewish Libraries Award,_ and _Sydney Taylor Book Award._

3204. Marsden, Carolyn, and Virginia Shin-Mui Loh. _The Jade Dragon._ Candlewick, 2006. 169pp. ISBN 978-0-7636-3012-6; 2008, paper ISBN 978-0-7636-4061-3. Grades 3–4. In 1983, 7-year-old Ginny Liao welcomes another Chinese girl in her class, but Stephanie was adopted from China and wants to be Caucasian like her parents. The two eventually become friends with Ginny giving Stephanie a valuable jade dragon.

3205. Pollet, Alison. _Nobody Was Here: 7th Grade in the Life of Me, Penelope._ Orchard, 2004. 224pp. ISBN 978-0-439-58394-7; Scholastic, 2005, paper ISBN 978-0-439-58395-4. Grades 5–8. Penelope Schwartzbaum, 12, is having problems at home and at her new school in 1981. She is worried about her mother's relationship with a client, and she is confused by the social rules imposed by the "in crowd" and by the attitudes of her old friends. Then she meets a new girl called Cass with whom she has more in common.

3206. Salisbury, Graham. _Night of the Howling Dogs._ Wendy Lamb, 2006. 191pp. ISBN 978-0-385-73122-5. Grades 5–8. Dylan, the senior patrol leader of his Hilo, Hawaii, scout troop looks forward to camping on the south flank of a volcano, in 1975. When Louie announces he is joining the group, Dylan's enthusiasm wanes—he and Louie have an unpleasant history. During the night an earthquake hits, followed by a tsunami. Dylan and Louie must work together to rescue the other boys and the injured scout master. Based on a true story. _Lone Star Reading List_ (Texas).

3207. Stead, Rebecca. _When You Reach Me._ Wendy Lamb, 2009. 199pp. ISBN 978-0-385-73742-5. Grades 5–8. Living in Manhattan in 1979, 12-year-old Miranda is a latchkey kid with a single mom law-school dropout who wants to win the $20,000 Pyramid Show on television. While Miranda is walking home from school one day with Sal, someone hits him in the face. After the incident, Sal refuses to be her friend. Then the unthreatening attacker, Marcus, argues with Miranda at school about the logic in L'Engle's _A Wrinkle in Time,_ Miranda's favorite book. Other puzzles in Miranda's life are the origin of the neighborhood vagrant, "The Laughing Man," and a note that she receives, saying "I am coming to save your life and my own." Over the next few months, Miranda tries to solving the unsettling mystery and reunite with Sal. _Newbery Medal, NAPPA Gold Awards_ winner, _Land of Enchantments Book Award_ (New Mexico), _Indies Choice Book Awards, American Library Association Best Books for Young Adults, American Library Association Notable Children's Books, Booklist Editors Choice, Young Readers Choice Book Award_ (Pennsylvania) nomination, _Lonestar Young Adult Reading List_ (Texas) nomination, _Dorothy Canfield Fisher Children's Book Award_ (Vermont) nomination, and _Capitol Choices Noteworthy Titles for Children and Teens_ (Washington, D.C.).

3208. Vaupel, Robin. _My Contract with Henry._ Holiday House, 2003. 244pp. ISBN 978-0-8234-1701-8. Grades 5–9. Rachel, 13, new to her school and eighth-grade class, has to join three others—Beth Gardner, Stuart Garfield, and the nerdy Hollis—for a school project on Henry David Thoreau. They decide to recreate Walden, building a cabin, cooking simple meals, eating from the forest, observing wildlife, and writing about it. Even after they have finished the assignment, they continue the experiment that has changed them and touched others in their school and community.

3209. Waldron, Kathleen Cook. *Roundup at the Palace.*   Illustrated by Alan and Lea Daniel. (Northern Lights Books for Children) Red Deer, 2006. 32pp. ISBN 978-0-88995-319-2. Grades K–3. In the 1990s Zack and his Dad take their bull, Buster, to the National Western Stock Show in Denver. The weather changes and the snowfall becomes a blizzard. They have to drive through central Denver. Buster bursts out of the truck and through the front doors of the Brown Palace Hotel where he confronts Alice, daughter of the hotel gift shop owner. Illustrations augment the text. Note.

History

3210. Beech, Linda Ward. *The Exxon Valdez's Deadly Oil Spill.*   (Code Red) Bearport, 2007. 32pp. ISBN 978-1-59716-366-8. Grades 3–4. In March 1989 the *Exxon Valdez*, under Captain Joseph Hazelwood, ran aground and spilled millions of gallons of oil into Prince William Sound in Alaska, harming wildlife and the environment. It was the worst oil spill disaster in the United States. The cleanup involved more than 10,000 volunteers and workers, among them animal rescuers. The disaster enraged environmental groups and led to new government regulations for oil tankers. Illustrations enhance the text. Bibliography, Further Reading, Glossary, Web Sites, and Index.

3211. Britton, Tamara L. *Air Force One.*   (Symbols, Landmarks, and Monuments) Checkerboard, 2004. 32pp. ISBN 978-1-59197-520-5. Grades 3–5. This volume looks at Air Force One, the airplane used by the president of the United States. The name remains the same even though the planes change. Photographs highlight the text. Glossary, Chronology, and Index.

3212. Caper, William. *The Challenger Space Shuttle Explosion.*   (Code Red) Bearport, 2007. 32pp. ISBN 978-1-59716-367-5. Grades 3–4. On January 28, 1986, the space shuttle *Challenger* lifted off but exploded 73 seconds later, killing all those on board. It was one of NASA's worst disasters. One of the seven victims was Sharon Christa McAuliffe, the first school teacher chosen for the space program. An accompanying brief history of the space program emphasizes the horror of this event. Photographs augment the text. Bibliography, Further Reading, Glossary, Web Sites, and Index.

3213. Carnegy, Vicky. *Fashions of a Decade: The 1980s.*   Chelsea House, 2007. 64pp. ISBN 978-0-8160-6724-4. Grades 5 up. In the 1980s fashions ranged from designer suits to ripped jeans. Interest in crinolines also returned. Princess Diana's sense of fashion alerted women to elegance and understated clothing. Photographs and illustrations enhance the text. Glossary, Further Reading, Chronology, and Index.

3214. Cook, Michelle. *Our Children Can Soar: A Celebration of Rosa, Barack, and the Pioneers of Change.*   See entry 2883.

3215. Feigenbaum, Aaron. *Emergency at Three Mile Island.*   (Code Red) Bearport, 2007. 32pp. ISBN 978-1-59716-364-4. Grades 3–6. The malfunction of the nuclear reactor at Three Mile Island in 1979 is the focus of this volume, which describes what happened and how people reacted. There are brief profiles of key individuals. Photographs, maps, and reproductions complement the text. Glossary, Further Reading, Web Sites, and Index.

3216. Foran, Jill. *Martin Luther King Jr. Day.*   (American Holidays) Weigl, 2004. 24pp. ISBN 978-1-59036-107-8; 2000, paper ISBN 978-1-59036-167-2. Grades 2–4. Foran offers information about Martin Luther King, Jr. (1929–1968) to explain why a holiday honors him. Trivia tidbits and photographs give background on his life and legacy.

3217. Greene, Jacqueline Dembar. *The 2001 World Trade Center Attack.*   (Code Red) Bearport, 2007. 32pp. ISBN 978-1-59716-365-1. Grades 3–4. On September 11, 2001, two planes crashed into the towers of the World Trade Center in New York City. This volume includes information about those who died, the firefighters of Ladder Company 6 in New York, and another rescue team led by chief Pitch. Photographs augment the text. Bibliography, Further Reading, Glossary, Web Sites, and Index.

3218. Hossell, Karen. *The Persian Gulf War.* (20th Century Perspectives) Heinemann, 2003. 48pp. ISBN 978-1-4034-1143-3; paper ISBN 978-1-4034-4178-2. Grades 4–8. The text covers the war that began on August 2, 1990, and ended on February 28, 1991. A coalition force of thirty-five nations fought Iraq after it invaded Kuwait. The fighting was confined to Iraq, Kuwait, and areas of Saudi Arabia. Also examined are the issues, the causes, and the effects of this war. Illustrations augment the text. Bibliography, Further Reading, Glossary, Index.

3219. Kalman, Maira. *Fireboat: The Heroic Adventures of the John J. Harvey.* Penguin, 2002. 32pp. ISBN 978-0-399-23953-3; 2005, paper ISBN 978-0-14-240362-4. Grades K–4. The *John J. Harvey*, a New York City fireboat, was launched in 1931, the year of the Empire State Building, the George Washington Bridge, Babe Ruth's 611th home run, and the introduction of Snickers. The boat was retired in 1995, but on September 11, 2001, it came into service again to help firemen at the World Trade Center. Pictures of New York City and expressionistic illustrations of the horrible fire highlight the text. *SCASL Book Award* (South Carolina) nomination, *Volunteer State Book Award* (Tennessee) nomination, *Children's Choice Picture Book* (Washington) nomination, *Publishers Weekly Best Children's Books, School Library Journal Best Books of the Year, American Library Association Notable Books for Children, New York City Book Awards, Boston Globe/Horn Book Awards, ABC Children's Booksellers Choices Awards, Georgia Children's Picture StoryBook Award* nomination, *Red Clover Award* (Vermont) nomination, *Young Reader's Choice Award* (Pennsylvania), *Emphasis on Reading Award* (Alabama) nomination, *Horn Book Fanfare, Bulletin Blue Ribbon,* and *Capitol Choices Noteworthy Titles* (Washington, D.C.).

3220. Leathers, Daniel. *Tornado Outbreak, 1985.* (Natural Disasters) Mitchell Lane, 2008. 32pp. ISBN 978-1-58415-570-6. Grades 3–6. On May 31, 1985, unexpected tornadoes hit Ohio and Pennsylvania causing death and destruction. The unprepared residents had to seek support from other areas to help them rebuild and to recover from the devastation of these awful storms. Chronology, Bibliography, Further Reading, Web Sites, Glossary, and Index.

3221. Levy, Pat, and Sean Sheehan. *From Compact Discs to the Gulf War: The Mid 1980s to the Early 1990s.* (Modern Eras Uncovered) Raintree, 2005. 56pp. ISBN 978-1-4109-1790-4. Grades 5–9. This volume covers the decade from the mid-1980s to the mid-1990s, looking at topics including international politics, fashion, and pop culture. Photographs and illustrations augment the text. Glossary, Chronology, and Index.

3222. Levy, Pat, and Sean Sheehan. *From Punk Rock to Perestroika: The Mid 1970s to the Early 1980s.* (Modern Eras Uncovered) Raintree, 2005. 56pp. ISBN 978-1-4109-1789-8. Grades 5–9. This volume looks at the decade from the mid-1970s to the mid-1980s, covering topics from international politics to fashion and pop culture. It links economic recession and unemployment to the rebellious punk rock that attracted young people. Photographs and illustrations augment the text. Glossary, Chronology, and Index.

3223. McCarthy, Meghan. *City Hawk: The Story of Pale Male.* Paula Wiseman, 2007. Unpaged. ISBN 978-1-4169-3359-5. Grades K–3. In 1991 a red-tailed hawk made its home on a building in New York City. Residents watching the bird in its nest near Central Park named it "Pale Male" because of its lightly colored feathers. Pale Male took a mate (Lola) and the pair settled in, eventually producing eggs that hatched and young ones they taught to fly. Bibliography.

3224. Macdonald, Fiona. *The First "Test-Tube" Baby.* (Days that Changed the World) Gareth Stevens, 2004. 48pp. ISBN 978-0-8368-5567-8; 2003, paper ISBN 978-0-8368-5574-6. Grades 5–8. The six chapters give background information about the search for a way to overcome infertility. Topics discussed include DNA, egg collecting, fertilization, implants, ethics, and the danger of genetic engineering. Photographs enhance the text. Chronology, Further Reading, Glossary, Web sites, and Index.

3225. Margaret, Amy. *Gerald R. Ford Library and Museum.* (Presidential Libraries) PowerKids, 2003. 24pp. ISBN 978-0-8239-6270-9. Grades 3–6. The Gerald R. Ford Library is located in

Ann Arbor, Michigan, and the Museum in Grand Rapids, Michigan. This volume describes what each building holds—the documents, materials, and exhibits relating to Ford, his family, and his presidency. Illustrations and photographs augment the text.

3226. Margaret, Amy. *Jimmy Carter Library and Museum.* (Presidential Libraries) PowerKids, 2004. 24pp. ISBN 978-0-8239-6271-6. Grades 3–6. The Jimmy Carter (1924–) Library and Museum in Atlanta, Georgia, opened in 1986. It houses documents, materials, and exhibits that concern him and his family. Ten double-page chapters offer information. Illustrations and photographs augment the text.

3227. Margaret, Amy. *John F. Kennedy Library and Museum.* (Presidential Libraries) PowerKids, 2004. 24pp. ISBN 978-0-8239-6269-3. Grades 3–6. The John F. Kennedy Library and Museum in Boston, Massachusetts, opened in 1979. It houses documents, materials, and exhibits relating to the president and his family. Ten double-page chapters describe the collection. Illustrations and photographs augment the text.

3228. Margaret, Amy. *Ronald Reagan Presidential Library.* (Presidential Libraries) PowerKids, 2004. 24pp. ISBN 978-0-8239-6272-3. Grades 3–6. The Ronald Reagan Library and Museum opened in 1991 in Simi Valley, California,. It houses the documents, materials, and exhibits that concern him, his family, and his presidency. Illustrations and photographs augment the text.

3229. Parker, Toni Trent. *Sienna's Scrapbook: Our African American Heritage Trip.* Illustrated by Janell Genovese. Chronicle, 2005. 61pp. ISBN 978-0-8118-4300-3. Grades 3–6. Sienna is not looking forward to visiting African American historical sights on the family trip from Hartford, Connecticut, to North Carolina. But she soon finds that history is more interesting than she expected. Along the way they stop at the *Amistad*, the Apollo Theater, the homes of Louis Armstrong and Frederick Douglass, the National Air and Space Museum, the Great Blacks in Wax Museum, Mendenhall Plantation in Jamestown, and the Woolworth's Civil Rights Museum. She keeps a scrapbook with the historical facts attached to each place. Photographs and illustrations augment the text. Web Sites and Notes.

3230. Petersen, Christine. *The Iran-Contra Scandal.* (Cornerstones of Freedom) Children's, 2004. 48pp. ISBN 978-0-516-24228-6. Grades 4–6. The political scandal known as the Iran-Contra Affair became public in 1987. Members of the executive branch during the Reagan administration sold weapons to Iran and illegally used the profits to continue funding anti-Sandinista rebels, the Contras, in Nicaragua. These officials destroyed or withheld many documents from investigators after the arms sales became public in November 1986. President Ronald Reagan announced that the sales had occurred, but one week later, he admitted the transfer of weapons to Iran while denying that they were part of a hostage exchange. Not all of the participants were prosecuted, and much has still not been revealed about this affair. Photographs highlight the text. Chronology, Further Reading, Glossary, Web sites, and Index.

3231. Roessel, Monty. *Songs from the Loom: A Navajo Girl Learns to Weave.* See entry 1085.

3232. Schulman, Janet. *Pale Male: Citizen Hawk of New York City.* Illustrated by Meilo So. Borzoi, 2008. Unpaged. ISBN 978-0-375-84558-1. Grades 3–6. A red-tailed hawk chose a mate and built a nest on a New York City window ledge near Central Park in 1991. The residents did not like the mess the birds created and removed the nest, but animal protection agencies and bird watchers protested. Pale Male, as fans called the hawk, was allowed to return and he eventually produced twenty-three chicks. Watercolor and pencil illustrations add details. *School Library Journal Best Books for Children* and *Capitol Choices Noteworthy Titles* (Washington, D.C.).

3233. Suter, Joanne. *Our Century: 1980–1990.* Gareth Stevens, 1993. 64pp. ISBN 978-0-8368-1040-0. Grades 3–10. Written as if a newspaper column, this book's short articles give an overview of the decade. Included are statistics, daily life in America, technology, American hostages in Iran, civil war in Lebanon, Contra forces in Nicaragua, assassins killing Indira Gandhi, the battle against apartheid, Philippine unrest, U.S. forces in Panama, Eastern Europe falling, AIDS, Ronald Reagan, John Lennon, the *Challenger* explosion, George Bush,

Mount St. Helens, Magic Johnson, Larry Bird, Steven Spielberg, George Lucas, Mikhail Gorbachev, Jesse Jackson, and Margaret Thatcher. Glossary, Books for Further Reading, Places to Write or Visit, and Index.

3234. Vogt, Gregory. *Disasters in Space Exploration.* See entry 2923.

Biography and Collective Biography

3235. Aaseng, Nathan. *Business Builders in Computers.* See entry 2927.

3236. Adler, David A. *A Picture Book of Thurgood Marshall.* See entry 2937.

3237. Alagna, Magdalena. *Mae Jemison: The First African American Woman in Space.* (Women Hall of Famers in Mathematics and Science) Rosen, 2003. ISBN 978-0-8239-3878-0. Grades 4–8. Mae Jemison (1956–) was the youngest of three children. Her uncle introduced her to science, and she became interested in archaeology, anthropology, and astronomy while still very young. She earned degrees in chemical engineering and Afro-American studies from Stanford University before attending medical school at Cornell. She practiced medicine in Cambodia and in West Africa. She was working in Los Angeles when she was accepted at NASA, and she became the first African American woman to travel into space in 1992. Photographs highlight the text. Bibliography and Index.

3238. Appelt, Kathi. *Miss Lady Bird's Wildflowers: How a First Lady Changed America.* See entry 2941.

3239. Blue, Rose, and Corinne J. Naden. *Barbara Jordan.* See entry 2951.

3240. Braun, Eric. *Mae Jemison.* Pebble, 2005. 24pp. ISBN 978-0-7368-4231-0. Grades K–2. This biography of Mae Jamison (1956–) offers an overview of her life and her achievements as the first African American woman astronaut. It also explores her other interests and contributions. Photographs highlight the text. Glossary, Further Reading, Web Sites, and Index.

3241. Braun, Eric. *Wilma Rudolph.* See entry 2955.

3242. Bryant, Jen. *Georgia's Bones.* See entry 2352.

3243. Deans, Karen. *Playing to Win: The Story of Althea Gibson.* Illustrated by Elbrite Brown. Holiday House, 2007. Unpaged. ISBN 978-0-8234-1926-5. Grades K–3. Althea Gibson (1927–2003), an African American tennis player who won many important tournaments, helped to break racial barriers. Her parents were South Carolina sharecroppers who sent her to live with an aunt in Harlem because they could not afford to feed her. There, adults urged Gibson toward sports as a way to use her intense energy. As an adult, she won the French Open, Wimbledon, and the US Open tournaments. Collage figures enhance the text. Bibliography, Chronology, Further Reading, Web Sites.

3244. Denenberg, Barry. *All Shook Up: The Life and Death of Elvis Presley.* See entry 2975.

3245. Englar, Mary. *I. M. Pei.* (Asian-American) Raintree, 2003. 64pp. ISBN 978-1-4109-1056-1; 2005, paper ISBN 978-1-4109-1129-2. Grades 5–8. I. M. Pei (1917–), a Chinese American architect, lived in China as a child and immigrated to the United States in 1935. Among the buildings he designed are the East Wing of the National Gallery in Washington, D.C., and the pyramid at the Louvre in Paris. Photographs highlight the text. Glossary, Further Reading, and Index.

3246. George-Warren, Holly, and Laura Levine. *Honky-Tonk Heroes and Hillbilly Angels: The Pioneers of Country and Western Music.* Houghton, 2006. 32pp. ISBN 978-0-618-19100-0. Grades 3–5. This collective biography, a companion to *Shake, Rattle, and Roll*, profiles fourteen stars who changed the face of country music: the Carter Family, Johnny Cash, Hank Williams, Kitty Wells, Buck Owens, Jimmie Rogers, Roy Acuff, Gene Autry, Bill Monroe,

George Jones, Patsy Cline, and Loretta Lynn. Each profile contains an overview of the performer's career, some song titles, and how that person influenced a musician who followed. Personal problems such as Hank Williams's drug use and George Jones's alcohol problem are mentioned but are not the focus. Illustrations augment the text.

3247. Golenbock, Peter. *Hank Aaron: Brave in Every Way.* See entry 3002.

3248. Guidici, Cynthia. *Adriana Ocampo.* (Hispanic-Americans) Raintree, 2005. 64pp. Paper ISBN 978-1-4109-1305-0. Grades 4–8. Adriana Ocampo, a planetary geologist, spent her childhood in South America. She immigrated to California where she studied science, leading to work at NASA's Jet Propulsion Laboratory. Photographs illustrate the text. Glossary, Chronology, Further Reading, and Index.

3249. Haugen, Brenda. *Henry B. Gonzalez: Congressman of the People.* See entry 3013.

3250. Issa, Kai Jackson. *Howard Thurman's Great Hope.* See entry 3020.

3251. Iverson, Teresa. *Ellen Ochoa.* (Hispanic-Americans) Raintree, 2005. 64pp. ISBN 978-1-4109-1299-2; paper ISBN 978-1-4109-1307-4. Grades 4–8. This biography of Ellen Ochoa, the first Latina to become an astronaut, looks at her childhood in California, education, and career with NASA. It covers both professional and private aspects of her life. Photographs illustrate the text. Glossary, Chronology, Further Reading, and Index.

3252. Kaye, Judith. *The Life of Benjamin Spock.* See entry 2666.

3253. Krull, Kathleen. *Albert Einstein.* See entry 3034.

3254. Latham, Donna. *Ellen Ochoa: Reach for the Stars!* Bearport, 2005. 32pp. ISBN 978-1-59716-076-6. Grades 2–4. Ellen Ochoa (1958–), an excellent student who also played the flute, studied to be an engineer. She then became an astronaut and the first Latina to travel in outer space. She is also an inventor. Photographs and reproductions illuminate the text. Bibliography, Glossary, Chronology, Further Reading, Web Sites, and Index.

3255. Lowery, Linda. *Wilma Mankiller.* Illustrated by Janice Lee Porter. Carolrhoda, 1996. 56pp. ISBN 978-0-8761-4880-8. Grades K–3. When 11-year-old Wilma Mankiller (1945–2010) moved with her family to San Francisco, she knew she would return to the Oklahoma hills and her heritage. She became the chief of the Cherokee in 1985. Important Dates.

3256. Marlin, John. *Mickey Mantle.* See entry 3054.

3257. Mattern, Joanne. *Coretta Scott King: Civil Rights Activist.* See entry 3056.

3258. Naden, Corinne J., and Rose Blue. *Mae Jemison: Out of This World.* Millbrook, 2002. 48pp. ISBN 978-0-7613-2570-3. Grades 2–5. This biography of Mae Jamison (1956–) profiles the first African American woman to travel into space. She has been a doctor, Peace Corps worker, NASA employee, astronaut, college professor, and public lecturer. Photographs and illustrations augment the text. Bibliography, Further Reading, Web Sites, and Index.

3259. Parr, Ann. *Gordon Parks: No Excuses.* Illustrated by Gordon Parks. Pelican, 2006. 32pp. ISBN 978-1-58980-411-1. Grades 3–6. Gordon Parks became a successful photographer for *Life* magazine, but to reach this goal, he had to overcome poverty in Kansas. His mother encouraged him and told him he could do anything that a white boy could do. Featured photographs reveal Parks's unusual use of light and shadow.

3260. Peet, Bill. *Bill Peet: An Autobiography.* See entry 3074.

3261. Pinkney, Andrea Davis. *Alvin Ailey.* Illustrated by Brian Pinkney. Hyperion, 1995. Unpaged. Paper ISBN 978-0-7868-1077-2. Grades K–3. After Alvin Ailey and his mother moved to San Francisco, Ailey saw Katherine Dunham's dance troupe from outside the stage door. He knew then that he wanted to dance. After many lessons, he and his friends danced *Blues Suite* on March 30, 1958, in New York. The reviews hailed this performance, and the theater asked the group to return. From that time, his troupe has been a major presenter of African American dances and dancers.

3262. Plourde, Lynn. *Margaret Chase Smith: A Woman for President.* See entry 2453.

3263. Polacco, Patricia. *Firetalking.* See entry 3078.

3264. Ride, Sally, and Susan Okie. *To Space and Back.* Lothrop, Lee & Shepard, 1986. 96pp. ISBN 978-0-688-06159-3. Grades 5–9. With lots of photographs and interesting details, Ride describes her journey on the space shuttle. Glossary.

3265. Rubin, Susan Goldman. *Andy Warhol: Pop Art Painter.* See entry 3087.

3266. Rubin, Susan Goldman. *Andy Warhol's Colors.* See entry 3088.

3267. Say, Allen. *El Chino.* See entry 1367.

3268. Sloate, Susan. *Ray Charles: Young Musician.* Illustrated by Meryl Henderson. (Childhood of Famous Americans) Aladdin, 2007. 203pp. Paper ISBN 978-1-416-91437-2. Grades 3–6. Ray Charles (1930–2004) became blind when he was 5 years old, the same year that his brother died tragically. This volume explores Charles's early life and how he became a musician. Bibliography.

3269. Smith, Charles R., Jr. *Twelve Rounds to Glory: The Story of Muhammad Ali.* Illustrated by Bryan Collier. Candlewick, 2007. 80pp. ISBN 978-0-7636-1692-2. Grades 5 up. Twelve rhyming poems recreate the life of Muhammad Ali (1942–), one of America's great boxers and winner of an Olympic gold medal in 1960. Topics covered include his fights with Sonny Liston and Joe Frazier, his lighting of the Olympic torch at the 1996 Atlanta games, and his battle with Parkinson's disease. Watercolor and collage illustrations complement the text. Chronology.

3270. Stauffacher, Sue. *Nothing but Trouble: The Story of Althea Gibson.* Illustrated by Greg Couch. Knopf, 2007. 40pp. ISBN 978-0-375-83408-0. Grades 1–4. In 1957, Althea Gibson (1927–2003) was the first African American to win a tennis title at Wimbledon. One of her neighbors in Harlem, Buddy Walker, saw her playing street tennis with a wooden paddle and recognized her ability. He gave her her first racket with strings. She went on to play at the Harlem River Tennis Courts and then, with the support of Juan Sorrel and the advice of professional coaches, at the Cosmopolitan Tennis Club. Illustrations enhance the text.

3271. Streissguth, Thomas. *Say It with Music: A Story About Irving Berlin.* See entry 2473.

3272. Taylor-Butler, Christine. *Thurgood Marshall.* See entry 2482.

3273. Turner, Pamela S. *A Life in the Wild: George Schaller's Struggle to Save the Last Great Beasts.* Melanie Kroupa, 2008. 103pp. ISBN 978-0-374-34578-5. Grades 4–8. George B. Schaller (1933–), a conservationist, has studied wildlife around the world—counting animals, observing them, and photographing them in their habitats. He has looked at animals from Central Africa's mountain gorillas to Tibet's snow leopards. This volume examines six of his studies in detail—a gorilla forest in the Belgian Congo (1959–1960), a tiger clan in central India (1963–1965), lions in Tanzania (1966–1969), the snow leopard in the Himalayas of Pakistan and Nepal (1969–1975), pandas in central China (1980–1985), and asses and antelopes on the Tibetan Plateau of western China (1985 to the present). Photographs and illustrations enhance the text. Bibliography, Further Reading, Web Sites, and Index.

3274. Venezia, Mike. *Andy Warhol.* See entry 3114.

3275. Venezia, Mike. *Faith Ringgold.* See entry 3118.

3276. Venezia, Mike. *Georgia O'Keeffe.* See entry 2488.

3277. Venezia, Mike. *Roy Lichtenstein.* See entry 3124.

3278. Wade, Mary Dodson. *Joan Lowery Nixon: Masterful Mystery Writer.* (Authors Teens Love) Enslow, 2004. 128pp. ISBN 978-0-7660-2194-5. Grades 5–9. Award-winning author of more than 140 books, Joan Lowery Nixon wrote about able heroines who could solve their own problems. This biography draws on personal interviews to present her life and work. Photographs accompany the text. Glossary, Chronology, Notes, Further Reading, Web Sites, and Index.

3279. Waxman, Laura Hamilton. *Colin Powell.* (History Maker Bios) Lerner, 2006. 48pp. ISBN 978-0-8225-2433-5. Grades 2–5. Colin Powell (1937–) grew up in the Bronx before he began a career in which he distinguished himself as a military leader. He rose to be the chairman of the Joint Chiefs of Staff and secretary of state during the George W. Bush administration. Waxman discusses the effects of discrimination and segregation on him and includes information on the civil rights movement, protests during the Vietnam War, and the conflicts in Iraq. Photographs enhance the text. Bibliography, Further Reading, Timeline, Web Sites, and Index.

3280. Waxman, Laura Hamilton. *Coretta Scott King.* See entry 3129.

3281. Waxman, Laura Hamilton. *Jimmy Carter.* See entry 3130.

3282. Weidt, Maryann N. *Oh, the Places He Went: A Story About Dr. Seuss.* See entry 2509.

3283. Winter, Jeanette. *My Name Is Georgia.* See entry 2116.

3284. Wukovits, John F. *Ellen Ochoa: First Female Hispanic Astronaut.* (20th Century's Most Influential Hispanics) Lucent, 2007. 104pp. ISBN 978-1-59018-976-4. Grades 5 up. Ellen Ochoa became the first Latina astronaut. Quotations about her work at NASA and her family reveal her accomplishments. Photographs and reproductions enhance the text. Chronology, Notes, Further Reading, Web Sites, and Index.

3285. Young, Jeff C. *César Chávez.* (American Workers) Morgan Reynolds, 2007. 160pp. ISBN 978-1-59935-036-3. Grades 5–8. César Chávez (1927–1993) led migrant workers in their fight against unfair labor practices and formed the National Farm Workers Association. Gandhi inspired Chavez to focus on nonviolent methods to achieve his goals. Quotes clarify his ideals and his tactics of hunger strikes, protest marches, and boycotts across the nation. Photographs highlight the text. Bibliography, Chronology, Notes, Web Sites, and Index.

Graphic Novels, Biographies, and Histories

3286. Adamson, Heather. *The Challenger Explosion.* Illustrated by Brian Bascle. Graphic Library, 2006. 32pp. ISBN 978-0-7368-5478-8; paper ISBN 978-0-7368-6873-0. Grades 3–5. On January 28, 1986, an external tank containing liquid hydrogen and oxygen along with two solid rocket boosters broke apart seventy-three seconds into the flight of the space shuttle *Challenger.* The spacecraft disintegrated at 11:30 EST with seven crew members on board. An O-ring failure caused the mishap. Among those on board was Christa McAuliffe, a science teacher. Illustrations depict the event. Bibliography, Glossary, Further Reading, and Index.

3287. Engfer, Lee. *Wilma Rudolph: Olympic Track Star.* Illustrated by Cynthia Martin and Anne Timmons. (Graphic Biographies) Graphic Library, 2006. 32pp. ISBN 978-0-7368-5489-4; paper ISBN 978-0-7368-6888-4. Grades 3–5. This short graphic biography of Wilma Rudolph (1940–1994) reveals her accomplishments as the first woman from the United States to win three gold medals in a single Olympics, a feat she achieved in Rome in 1960. She fought polio and scarlet fever as a child but overcame both her poverty and her disabilities to be a success. A yellow background sets direct quotes from Rudolph apart from the fictional aspect of the narration. Web Sites.

3288. Shone, Rob. *Muhammed Ali: The Life of a Boxing Hero.* See entry 3160.

3289. Siegel, Siena Cherson. *To Dance: A Ballerina's Graphic Novel.* Illustrated by Mark Siegel. Richard Jackson, 2006. Unpaged. ISBN 978-0-689-86747-7; Aladdin paper ISBN 978-1-416-92687-0. Grades 4–8. Siena Cherson Siegel was 6 years old when she began to dream of dancing. She left Puerto Rico and went to Boston before finally realizing her dream of performing with the New York City Ballet. She actually left ballet when she reached college, but returned to it because she realized "I still need to dance." She details her private life, including the dissolution of her parents' marriage, and her respect for ballet master George

Balanchine. She also discusses the foot pains and leg injuries that sideline all those who want to dance. *Publishers Weekly Best Children's Books*, *School Library Journal Best Books for Children*, *Robert F. Sibert Honor Book*, and *American Library Association Notable Children's Books*.

DVDs

3290. *César Chávez.* (Great Americans for Children) Library Video, 2002. 23 mins. Grades K–4. Impoverished as a Hispanic American and migrant farmer, César Chávez (1927–1993) overcame his situation to help organize a successful union for America's farm workers. He used boycotts of produce and nonviolent strikes and protests to help the laborers get better pay and working conditions. His efforts as a labor leader changed the basic relationship between farm owners and workers.

3291. *Christa McAuliffe: Reach for the Stars.* Traipsing Thru Films, 2005. 75 mins. Grades 5 up. Interviews with family members, friends, NASA personnel, and colleagues, plus footage from McAuliffe's many public appearances before her launch date on the *Challenger* shuttle offer insight into her personality and her life. She clearly had an enthusiasm for life and for education, and the explosion on January 28, 1986, was a loss for many.

Compact Discs

3292. Going, K. L. *The Liberation of Gabriel King.* Listening Library, 2005. 3 CDs; 3hr, 3 mins. ISBN 978-0-3072-4553-3. Grades 4–7. See entry 3199.

3293. Kalman, Maira. *Fireboat: The Heroic Adventures of the John J. Harvey.* Narrated by Judd Hirsch. Live Oak Media, 2004. 15 mins. ISBN 978-1-59112-988-2. Grades K–4. See entry 3219.

AUTHOR INDEX

Reference is to entry number.

Aaseng, Nathan, 7, 8, 192–200, 2609, 2927, 2928
Abnett, Dan, 1715, 2713, 2714
Abraham, Denise Gonzales, 2155
Abraham, Susan Gonzales, 2155
Accardo, Anthony, 2948
Ackerman, Karen, 1729
Adamson, Heather, 3286
Adamson, Thomas K., 3149
Addy, Sharon Hart, 826
Adler, David A., 302, 438–440, 442–444, 617, 619–623, 1114–1116, 1480–1484, 1908, 1910, 1912, 2156, 2324–2327, 2331, 2545, 2638, 2929, 2930, 2934–2937, 3190
Adler, Michael S., 443, 444
Alagna, Magdalena, 727, 1016, 3237
Aldrin, Buzz, 2938
Alexander, Jessica, 2915
Alexander, Robert, 1485
Alexander, Sally Hobart, 1485
Aliki, 1117, 1913
Allen, Roger MacBride, 1655
Allen, Thomas B., 581, 627, 1654, 1655, 2610
Aller, Susan Bivin, 303, 1118, 1119, 1486, 1487, 1914–1916
Allport, Alan, 1918, 2335
Aloian, Molly, 1017
Alphin, Elaine Marie, 827, 1120, 1596, 2336
Alsheimer, Jeanette E., 312
Alter, Judy, 1121
Altergott, Hanna, 9
Ancona, George, 10
Anderson, Dale, 11, 12, 360, 582, 583, 1238, 2884, 3153
Anderson, Dale B., 1656–1659
Anderson, Elizabeth Weiss, 547
Anderson, Jameson, 2517
Anderson, Joan, 361, 362
Anderson, Laurie Halse, 584, 708, 1488
Anderson, Michael, 2871
Anderson, Paul Christopher, 1122
Anderson, Wayne, 1850, 2872
Anderson, William, 1123–1125

Andreasen, Dan, 1730
Andryszewski, Tricia, 13
Angell, Judie, 1731
Ansary, Mir Tamim, 14–20
Antle, Nancy, 828, 3191
Appel, Martin, 2338
Appelbaum, Diana, 363
Appelt, Kathi, 2275, 2941
Applegate, Katherine, 829
Apte, Sunita, 2942
Arenstam, Peter, 364
Aretha, David, 1018
Argueta, Jorge, 1359
Armentrout, David, 1126
Armentrout, Patricia, 1126
Armistead, John, 2729
Armstrong, Jennifer, 21, 709, 830, 1690, 1732, 1733
Armstrong, Jennifer A., 1127
Armstrong, Mabel, 201
Armstrong, William O., 2157
Arnold, Caroline, 284
Arnold, James R., 1660, 1661
Aronson, Billy, 2943
Arrington, Frances, 831
Ashby, Ruth, 445, 2944
Atkins, Jeannine, 202, 313
Atwell, Debby, 1
Auch, Mary Jane, 832, 2730
Aveni, Anthony, 285
Avi, 314, 315, 446, 548, 710, 833–835, 1377, 1378, 1597, 1734, 2158, 2546, 2547
Aylesworth, Jim, 1489
Ayres, Katherine, 1379, 2159

Bader, Bonnie, 836
Baker, Charles, 3084
Baker, Patricia, 2611, 2874
Baker, Rosalie F., 3084
Baker, Sharon Reiss, 1735
Ball, Heather, 203, 204
Ballard, Robert D., 1851
Banim, Lisa, 549, 550, 2548
Banks, Jacqueline Turner, 1270
Bannatyne-Cugnet, Jo, 22
Banting, Erinn, 2276

Barasch, Lynne, 2339, 2731
Barber, James, 205
Barbour, Karen, 2340
Bardhan-Quallen, Sudipta, 2341
Barnard, Bryn, 23
Barretta, Gene, 447, 538
Barron, T. A., 837
Barrows, Annie, 2160
Bartoletti, Susan Campbell, 728, 1456, 1852
Barton, Chris, 2342
Bartone, Elisa, 1271
Basel, Roberta, 1128
Bass, Hester, 2343
Bauer, Marion Dane, 1853
Bausum, Ann, 206, 2946
Beatty, Patricia, 1598
Beaty, Andrea, 2732
Beccia, Carlyn, 2161
Bedard, Michael, 1736
Beech, Linda Ward, 3210
Behrman, Carol H., 1129
Beller, Susan Provost, 24, 585, 2277, 2612
Benchley, Nathaniel, 551
Benson, Kathleen, 76, 3012
Berger, Gilder, 1919, 1920
Berger, Melvin, 1919, 1920
Berne, Emma Carlson, 2344
Berry, S. L., 1921, 2345
Bertholf, Bret, 2875
Bertrand, Diane Gonzales, 2948
Beyer, Mark A., 729
Bial, Raymond, 1019–1021, 1326–1328, 1457
Biebuyck, Valerie, 2949
Bildner, Phil, 1799–1801, 2162, 2163, 2733, 2734
Billus, Kathleen, 2950
Bingham, Jane, 25
Binns, Tristan Boyer, 1490
Birchfield, D. L., 1022
Birtha, Becky, 2735
Blackwood, Gary L., 26–28, 207, 208, 1599, 1854
Blair, Margaret Whitman, 586, 2278
Blegvad, Lenore, 1737
Bloom, Judith, 1963

TITLE INDEX

Reference is to entry number.

SUBJECT INDEX

Reference is to entry number.

ABOUT THE AUTHOR

LYNDA G. ADAMSON is Professor Emeritus of Literature, Prince George's Community College, where she has taught American, Children's, and Comparative Literature courses. She has published 12 reference works. Her many books include *Thematic Guide to the American Novel* (2002), *Notable Women in American History* (1999), and *Recreating the Past: A Guide to American and World Historical Fiction for Children and Young Adults* (1994).